PSYCHOLOGY

Ninth Edition

PSYCHOLOGY
Concepts & Connections
Brief Version

SPENCER A. RATHUS
THE COLLEGE OF NEW JERSEY

WADSWORTH
CENGAGE Learning™

Australia • Brazil • Japan • Korea • Mexico • Singapore • Spain • United Kingdom • United States

**Psychology: Concepts and Connections,
Brief Edition, Ninth Edition**
Spencer A. Rathus

Acquisitions Editor: Tim Matray

Developmental Editors: Shannon LeMay-Finn,
Nicolas Albert

Assistant Editor: Paige Leeds

Editorial Assistant: Lauren Moody

Media Editor: Mary Noel

Marketing Manager: Jessica Egbert

Marketing Communications Manager:
Laura Localio

Content Project Manager: Rita Jaramillo

Design Director: Rob Hugel

Art Director: Pam Galbreath

Print Buyer: Karen Hunt

Rights Acquisitions Specialist: Don Schlotman

Production Service: Aaron Downey, Matrix
Productions

Text Designer: Delgado and Company

Photo Researcher: Kim Adams Fox,
Roaring Lion Images

Text Researcher: Pablo D'Stair

Cover Designer: Denise Davidson

Cover Image: © Nikada/Vetta/Getty Images

Compositor: Integra

Library of Congress Control Number: 2011931080

International Edition:
ISBN-13: 978-1-133-04984-5
ISBN-10: 1-133-04984-2

Cengage Learning International Offices

Asia
www.cengageasia.com
tel: (65) 6410 1200

Australia/New Zealand
www.cengage.com.au
tel: (61) 3 9685 4111

Brazil
www.cengage.com.br
tel: (55) 11 3665 9900

India
www.cengage.co.in
tel: (91) 11 4364 1111

Latin America
www.cengage.com.mx
tel: (52) 55 1500 6000

UK/Europe/Middle East/Africa
www.cengage.co.uk
tel: (44) 0 1264 332 424

**Represented in Canada by
Nelson Education, Ltd.**
www.nelson.com
tel. (416) 752 9100 / (800) 668 0671

Cengage Learning is a leading provider of customized learning solutions with office
locations around the globe, including Singapore, the United Kingdom, Australia, Mexico,
Brazil, and Japan. Locate your local office at: **www.cengage.com/global**

For product information and free companion resources: **www.cengage
.com/international**
Visit your local office: **www.cengage.com/global**
Visit our corporate website: **www.cengage.com**

Printed in Canada
1 2 3 4 5 6 7 15 14 13 12 11

To Lois

In Profile: About the Author

© Spencer Rathus

Numerous personal experiences enter into Spencer Rathus's textbooks. He was the first member of his family to go to college and found college textbooks to be cold and intimidating. When his opportunity arrived to write college textbooks, he wanted them to be different—warm and encouraging, especially to students who were also the first generation in their families to be entering college.

Rathus's first professional experience was teaching high school English. Part of the task of the high school teacher is to motivate students. Through this experience he learned the importance of humor and personal stories, which later became part of his textbook approach. Rathus wrote poetry and novels while he was an English teacher—and some of the poetry was published in poetry journals. The novels never saw the light of day—which Rathus admits has saved him from a great deal of embarrassment.

Rathus earned his Ph.D. in psychology and then entered clinical practice and teaching. He has published research articles in journals such as *Behavior Therapy, Journal of Clinical Psychology, Behaviour Research and Therapy, Journal of Behavior Therapy and Experimental Psychiatry, Adolescence*, and *Criminology*. His research interests lie in the areas of human growth and development, psychological disorders, methods of therapy, and psychological assessment.

Rathus has since poured his energies into writing textbooks in introductory psychology, developmental psychology, the psychology of adjustment, human sexuality, and abnormal psychology. He has taught at Northeastern University, St. John's University, New York University, and The College of New Jersey. His professional activities include service on the American Psychological Association Task Force on Diversity Issues at the Precollege and Undergraduate Levels of Education in Psychology, and on the Advisory Panel, American Psychological Association, Board of Educational Affairs (BEA) Task Force on Undergraduate Psychology Major Competencies.

Rathus is proud of his family. His wife, Lois Fichner-Rathus, is a successful textbook author and a professor of art history at The College of New Jersey. His daughter Allyn graduated from New York University's M.A. program in educational theatre and is a teacher in New York City. His daughter Jordan is enrolled in an M.F.A. program, with specialization in video art. Rathus's youngest daughter, Taylor, is a musical theatre major at NYU, has performed professionally, and can dance the pants off of both her parents. Rathus's eldest daughter, Jill, is a psychologist and teaches at C. W. Post College of Long Island University.

Brief Contents

Chapter 1   What Is Psychology?   *2*

Chapter 2   Biology and Psychology   *38*

Chapter 3   Sensation and Perception   *78*

Chapter 4   Consciousness   *118*

Chapter 5   Learning   *152*

Chapter 6   Memory: Remembrance of Things Past—and Future   *182*

Chapter 7   Thinking, Language, and Intelligence   *218*

Chapter 8   Motivation and Emotion   *258*

Chapter 9   The Voyage Through the Life Span   *296*

Chapter 10   Personality: Theory and Measurement   *338*

Chapter 11   Stress, Health, and Coping   *368*

Chapter 12   Psychological Disorders   *398*

Chapter 13   Methods of Therapy   *432*

Chapter 14   Social Psychology   *466*

Appendix A   Statistics   *500*

Appendix B   Answer Keys to Self-Assessments and Active Reviews   *511*

References   *517*

Glossary   *567*

Name Index   *583*

Subject Index   *591*

Credits   *607*

Contents

Chapter 1 — What Is Psychology? 2

© age fotostock/SuperStock

Psychology as a Science 4

What Psychologists Do: Something for Everyone? 5
- Fields of Psychology: From the Clinic to the Colosseum 6

Where Psychology Comes From: A History 8
- Structuralism: The Elements of Experience 9
- Functionalism: Making Psychology a Habit 9
- Behaviorism: Practicing Psychology in Public 10
- Gestalt Psychology: Making Psychology Whole 10
- Psychoanalysis: Digging Beneath the Surface 11
- CONCEPT REVIEW 1.1: Historic Schools of Psychology 12

How Today's Psychologists View Behavior and Mental Processes 13
- The Evolutionary and Biological Perspectives: It's Only Natural 14
- The Cognitive Perspective: Keeping Psychology "in Mind" 14
- The Humanistic–Existential Perspective: The Search for Meaning 15
- The Psychodynamic Perspective: Still Digging 15
- Perspectives on Learning: From the Behavioral to the Cognitive 15
- The Sociocultural Perspective: How Do You Complete the Sentence "I Am..."? 16

Gender, Ethnicity, and Psychology: Real People in the Real World 17
- Women in Psychology: Opening the Floodgates 17
- Ethnicity and Psychology 18

Critical Thinking: Sorting Truth from Fiction 19
- Principles of Critical Thinking 20
- LIFE CONNECTIONS: Thinking Critically About Psychological Advice on the Internet: Are There Any Quick Fixes? 21

How Psychologists Study Behavior and Mental Processes 22
- The Scientific Method: Putting Ideas to the Test 22
- Video Connections—Facial Analysis—The Scientific Method in Action 23
- Samples and Populations: Hitting the Target Population 23
- Methods of Observation: The Better to See You With 24
- SELF-ASSESSMENT: DARE YOU SAY WHAT YOU THINK? THE SOCIAL-DESIRABILITY SCALE 25
- Correlation: On How Things Go Together—Or Not 29
- The Experimental Method: Trying Things Out 29
- CONCEPT REVIEW 1.2: Research Methods 32

Ethical Issues in Psychological Research and Practice 33
- Research with Humans 33
- Research with Animals 35

Chapter 2 — Biology and Psychology 38

© Colin Anderson/Getty Images

Evolution and Evolutionary Psychology: "Survivor" Is More Than Just a TV Show 39
- A CLOSER LOOK: CHARLES DARWIN 40
- Doing What Comes Naturally 41
- Evolutionary Psychology 42

Heredity: The Nature of Nature 43
- Genetics and Behavioral Genetics 43
- Genes and Chromosomes: The Building Blocks of Heredity 43
- Kinship Studies: Is the Behavior of Relatives Related? 45
- A CLOSER LOOK: ARE YOU A HUMAN OR A MOUSE? SOME FASCINATING FACTS ABOUT GENES 46
- Genetic–Environmental Correlation: The Interaction of Nature and Nurture 48
- The Epigenetic Framework 48

The Nervous System: On Being Wired 49
- Neurons: Into the Fabulous Forest 49
- The Neural Impulse: Let Us "Sing the Body Electric" 50

Video Connections—The Action Potential 52
- Neurotransmitters: The Chemical Keys to Communication 53
- The Parts of the Nervous System 56

The Brain: The Star of the Human Nervous System 59
- Seeing the Brain Through the Eyes of the Psychologist 59
- A Voyage Through the Brain: Revealing the Central Processing Unit 60
- The Cerebral Cortex: The "Bark" That Reasons 63

A CLOSER LOOK: MIRROR, MIRROR, IN THE BRAIN: WHO'S THE FAIREST IMITATOR OF THEM ALL? 66

- Left Brain, Right Brain? 67
- Handedness: Is Being Right-Handed Right? 68
- Split-Brain Experiments: How Many Brains Do You Have? 68

The Endocrine System: Chemicals in the Bloodstream 70

CONCEPT REVIEW 2.1: The Endocrine System 70
- The Hypothalamus: Master of the Master Gland 71
- The Pituitary Gland: The Pea-Sized Governor 71
- The Pineal Gland 71
- The Thyroid Gland: The Body's Accelerator 71
- The Adrenal Glands: Coping with Stress 71
- The Testes and the Ovaries 72

LIFE CONNECTIONS: Coping with PMS 74

Chapter 3 Sensation and Perception 78

© Chung Sung-Jun/Getty Images

Sensation and Perception: Your Tickets of Admission to the World Outside 80
- Absolute Threshold: So, Is It There or Not? 80
- Subliminal Stimulation 81
- Difference Threshold: Is It the Same, or Is It Different? 81
- Signal-Detection Theory: Is Being Bright Enough? 82
- Feature Detectors in the Brain: Firing on Cue 82
- Sensory Adaptation: Where Did It Go? 83

Vision: Letting the Sun Shine In 83
- Light: How Dazzling? 83
- The Eye: The Better to See You With 84
- Color Vision: Creating an Inner World of Color 87
- Theories of Color Vision: How Colorful? 89
- Color-Blindness 91

Visual Perception: How Perceptive? 91
- Perceptual Organization: Getting It Together 92
- Perception of Motion: Life on the Move 94
- Depth Perception: How Far Is Far? 95

CONCEPT REVIEW 3.1: Monocular Cues for Depth Perception 97

- Perceptual Constancies: Keeping the World a Stable Place 97

Video Connections—The Ames Room 97
- Visual Illusions: Is Seeing Believing? 98

Hearing: Making Sense of Sound 100
- Pitch and Loudness 100
- The Ear: The Better to Hear You With 101
- Locating Sounds: Up, Down, and Around 101

A CLOSER LOOK: IPODS ON CAMPUS: THE SOUNDS OF OBLIVION? 102
- Perception of Loudness and Pitch 102
- Deafness: Navigating a World of Silence 103

The Chemical Senses: Smell and Taste 104
- Smell: Sampling Molecules in the Air 104
- Taste: Yes, You've Got Taste 105

A CLOSER LOOK: ADVANCES IN SCIENCE? THE CASE OF THE AROMATIC T-SHIRTS 106

The Skin Senses (Yes, It Does) 106
- Touch and Pressure: Making Contact 106
- Temperature: Sometimes Everything Is Relative 107
- Pain 107

LIFE CONNECTIONS: Pain, Pain, Go Away—Don't Come Again Another Day 110

Kinesthesis and the Vestibular Sense 110
- Kinesthesis: How Moving? 110
- The Vestibular Sense: How Upright? 111

Extrasensory Perception: Is There Perception Without Sensation? 112
CONCEPT REVIEW 3.2: The Senses 113

Chapter 4 Consciousness 118

© Colin Anderson/Brand X Images/Getty Images

The Many Meanings of Consciousness 119
- Consciousness as Awareness 119
- Conscious, Preconscious, Unconscious, and Nonconscious 120
- Consciousness as Personal Unity: The Sense of Self 121
- Consciousness as the Waking State 121

Sleep and Dreams: Other Worlds Within? 121
- Biological and Circadian Rhythms 121
- The Stages of Sleep: How Do We Sleep? 122
- The Functions of Sleep: Why Do We Sleep? 124
- Dreams: What Is the "Stuff" of Dreams? 125
- Sleep Disorders 127
SELF-ASSESSMENT: ARE YOU GETTING YOUR Z'S? 128
LIFE CONNECTIONS: Strategies for Coping with Insomnia 129

Altering Consciousness Through Hypnosis, Meditation, and Biofeedback 131
- Hypnosis: On Being Entranced 131

- Meditation: On Letting the World Fade Away 134
- Biofeedback: On Getting in Touch with the Untouchable 134

Altering Consciousness Through Drugs 135
- Substance Abuse and Dependence: Crossing the Line 136
- Causal Factors in Substance Abuse and Dependence 138
- Depressants 138
SELF-ASSESSMENT: DO YOU HAVE A PROBLEM WITH ALCOHOL? 140
- Stimulants 142
A CLOSER LOOK: DEPENDENCE ON COCAINE? DENIAL AT WORK 144
Video Connections—Why Is Nicotine So Addictive? 145
- Hallucinogenics 146
A CLOSER LOOK: ON THE EDGE WITH ECSTASY 146
LIFE CONNECTIONS: Is Marijuana Harmful? Should It Be Available as a Medicine? 148
CONCEPT REVIEW 4.1: Psychoactive Drugs and Their Effects 149

Chapter 5 Learning 152

© Corbis Photography/Veer

Learning: Experience and Change 153

Classical Conditioning: Learning What Is Linked to What 154
- Stimuli and Responses in Classical Conditioning 155
- Taste Aversion: Are All Stimuli Created Equal? 156
- Extinction and Spontaneous Recovery 157
- Generalization and Discrimination 159
- Higher Order Conditioning 159
Video Connections—Little Albert 160
- Preparedness and the Conditioning of Fear 160

A CLOSER LOOK: WHO WAS "LITTLE ALBERT"? 160
Video Connections—Conditioning of Fear 161
- Applications of Classical Conditioning 161

Operant Conditioning: Learning What Does What to What 163
- Edward L. Thorndike and the Law of Effect 163
- B. F. Skinner and Reinforcement 163
- Methods of Operant Conditioning 164
- Types of Reinforcers 165
- Extinction and Spontaneous Recovery in Operant Conditioning 166

- Reinforcers Versus Rewards and Punishments 167

LIFE CONNECTIONS: Why Do Many Psychologists Disapprove of Punishment? 168

- Discriminative Stimuli: Do You Step on the Accelerator When the Light Is Green or Red? 168

A CLOSER LOOK: ROBO RATS? USING OPERANT CONDITIONING TO TEACH RATS HOW TO SEARCH FOR SURVIVORS OF DISASTERS 169

- Schedules of Reinforcement: How Often? Under What Conditions? 170
- Shaping 171
- Applications of Operant Conditioning 172

Cognitive Factors in Learning 173
- Latent Learning: Forming Cognitive Maps 173
- Observational Learning: Monkey See, Monkey May *Choose* to Do? 174

A CLOSER LOOK: CONTINGENCY THEORY 174

Video Connections—Mirror Neurons 175

- Media Violence and Aggression 175

LIFE CONNECTIONS: Teaching Children *Not* to Imitate Media Violence 177

CONCEPT REVIEW 5.1: Kinds of Learning 178

Chapter 6 Memory: Remembrance of Things Past—And Future 182

© J. Price/Getty Images

Kinds of Memory: Pressing the "Rewind" and "Fast-Forward" Buttons 184

SELF-ASSESSMENT: FIVE CHALLENGES TO YOUR MEMORY 184

- Explicit Memory: When Memory Is Out in the Open 185
- Implicit Memory: When Remembering Is Doing 185
- Retrospective Memory Versus Prospective Memory 186

A CLOSER LOOK: WILL YOU REMEMBER YOUR PSYCHOLOGY GRADE IN 2062? 187

CONCEPT REVIEW 6.1: The Relationships Among the Various Kinds of Memories 188

Processes of Memory: Processing Information in Our Most Personal Computers 189
- Encoding: The Memory's "Transformer" 189
- Storage: The Memory's "Save" Function 190
- Retrieval: The Memory's "Find" Function 190

Stages of Memory: Making *Sense* of the *Short* and the *Long* of It 191
- Sensory Memory: Flashes on the Mental Monitor 191

- Short-Term Memory: Keeping Things "in Mind" 193
- Long-Term Memory: Your Memory's "Hard Drive" 196

A CLOSER LOOK: CAN WE TRUST EYEWITNESS TESTIMONY? 199

Video Connections—Reconstructive Memory 200

Forgetting: Will You Remember How We Forget? 204
- Memory Tasks Used in Measuring Forgetting 205
- Interference Theory 206
- Repression: Ejecting the Unwanted from Consciousness 207
- Infantile Amnesia: Why Can't Johnny Remember? 207

A CLOSER LOOK: DO PEOPLE REALLY RECOVER REPRESSED MEMORIES OF CHILDHOOD SEXUAL ABUSE? 208

- Anterograde and Retrograde Amnesia 209

LIFE CONNECTIONS: Using the Psychology of Memory to Enhance Your Memory 210

The Biology of Memory: The Brain as a Living Time Machine 212
- Neural Activity and Memory: "Better Living Through Chemistry" 212
- Brain Structures and Memory 214

Chapter 7

Thinking, Language, and Intelligence 218

© Tetra Images/Getty Images

Thinking: Reasoning about Reasoning 220
- Concepts: Building Blocks of Thinking 220
- Problem Solving: Getting from Here to There 222

SELF-ASSESSMENT: PUZZLES, PROBLEMS, AND JUST PLAIN FUN 223

Video Connections—Problem Solving 225
- Judgment and Decision Making 228

Language: Of Signs, Grammar, and Many Things 230
- Going Ape Over Language? 231
- What Is Language? 232
- Language and Cognition: Do We Need Words to Think? 232
- Language and Culture 233
- Language Development: The 2-Year Explosion 234
- Nature and Nurture in Language Development: Why Houseplants Don't Talk 235

A CLOSER LOOK: "MOTHERESE"—OF "YUMMY YUMMY" AND "KITTY CATS" 236

Intelligence: The Most Controversial Concept in Psychology? 237
- Theories of Intelligence 238

A CLOSER LOOK: EMOTIONAL INTELLIGENCE AND SOCIAL INTELLIGENCE 241

- Creativity and Intelligence 242

CONCEPT REVIEW 7.1: Theories of Intelligence 242

SELF-ASSESSMENT: THE REMOTE ASSOCIATES TEST 243

- The Measurement of Intelligence 244
- Differences in Intellectual Functioning 247
- Nature and Nurture in Intelligence: Where Does Intelligence Come From? 250

LIFE CONNECTIONS: Enhancing Intellectual Functioning 251

Chapter 8

Motivation and Emotion 258

© Dugald Bremner Studio/National Geographic/Getty Images

The Psychology of Motivation: The Whys of Why 260

Theories of Motivation: Which Why Is Which? 261
- The Evolutionary Perspective: The Fish, the Spiders, and the Bees 261
- Drive-Reductionism and Homeostasis: "Steady, Steady…" 261
- The Search for Stimulation: Is Downtime a Downer? 262

SELF-ASSESSMENT: THE SENSATION-SEEKING SCALE 263

- Humanistic Theory: "I've Got to Be Me"? 263

Hunger: Do You Go by "Tummy-Time"? 265
- Biological Influences on Hunger 265
- Psychological Influences on Hunger 266
- Being Overweight: A Serious and Pervasive Problem 266

Video Connections—Childhood Obesity 267

LIFE CONNECTIONS: The Skinny on Weight Control 268

- Eating Disorders: Is It True That "You Can Never Be Too Rich or Too Thin"? 268

Video Connections—Anorexia Nervosa 270

SELF-ASSESSMENT: EATING DISORDERS QUIZ 273

Sexual Motivation and Sexual Orientation: Pressing the Start Button and Finding Direction 273
- Hormones and Sexual Motivation: Adding Fuel to the Fire 274
- Sexual Response and Sexual Behavior 274

A CLOSER LOOK: IS THE HUMAN SEX DRIVE AFFECTED BY PHEROMONES? 275

- Sexual Orientation: Which Way Is Love? 277

Aggression 280
- Biology, Chemistry, and Aggression 280
- Psychological Aspects of Aggression 281
- Situational Factors and Aggression 282

Achievement Motivation: "Just Do It"? 283
- What Flavor Is Your Achievement Motivation? 283

Emotion: Adding Color to Life 284
- The Expression of Emotions: The Smile Seen Round the World? 285
- "Is Evvvvrybody Happy?" An Excursion into Positive Psychology 286

- The Facial-Feedback Hypothesis: Does Smiling Make You Happy? 287

  LIFE CONNECTIONS: "Come On! Get Happy!" A Possible or Impossible Dream? 287

- Theories of Emotion: "*How* Do You Feel?" 288

  A CLOSER LOOK: JUST WHAT DO LIE DETECTORS DETECT? 292

Chapter 9   The Voyage Through the Life Span   296

How Psychologists Study Human Development 297
- Longitudinal Studies 298
- Cross-Sectional Studies 298

Prenatal Development: The Beginning of Our Life Story 299
- Environmental Influences on Prenatal Development 300

Video Connections—Prenatal Assessment 301
- Genetic Counseling and Prenatal Testing 301

Childhood: On the Edge of Reason? 301
- Neonates: In the New World 302
- Physical Development: The Drama Continues 302
- Cognitive Development: On the Edge of Reason 304

Video Connections—The Visual Cliff 305

A CLOSER LOOK: IS DEVELOPMENT CONTINUOUS OR DISCONTINUOUS? 305

Video Connections—Piaget's Sensorimotor Stage 307
- Social and Emotional Development 311

LIFE CONNECTIONS: Day Care: Blessing, Headache, or Both 316

Adolescence: "Neither Fish nor Fowl"? 317
- Physical Development: Fanning the Flames 317
- Cognitive Development: The Age of Reason? 318

Video Connections—Piaget's Formal Operational Stage: Hypothetical Propositions 320

- Social and Emotional Development: Storm and Stress, Smooth Sailing, or Both? 320

A CLOSER LOOK: ARE THERE GENDER DIFFERENCES IN MORAL DEVELOPMENT? 320

Emerging Adulthood: A New Stage of Development? 323

Early Adulthood: Becoming Established 324
- Physical Development 324
- Cognitive Development 324
- Social and Emotional Development 325

Middle Adulthood: The "Sandwich Generation"? 325
- Physical Development 326
- Cognitive Development 326
- Social and Emotional Development 326

Late Adulthood: Of Wisdom, Decline, and Compensation 328
- Physical Development 328
- Cognitive Development 329

A CLOSER LOOK: AGING, GENDER, AND ETHNICITY 330

SELF-ASSESSMENT: HOW LONG WILL YOU LIVE? THE LIFE-EXPECTANCY SCALE 330
- Social and Emotional Development 331

On Death and Dying: The Final Chapter 332
- "Lying Down to Pleasant Dreams…" 333

Chapter 10   Personality: Theory and Measurement   338

The Psychodynamic Perspective: Excavating the Iceberg 340
- Sigmund Freud's Theory of Psychosexual Development 340
- Neo-Freudians 343
- Evaluation of the Psychodynamic Perspective 345

The Trait Perspective: The Five-Dimensional Universe 346
- From Hippocrates to the Present 346
- Hans Eysenck's Trait Theory: A Two-Dimensional View 347
- The "Big Five": The Five-Factor Model 347

Video Connections—Personality Theories and Measurement 348

A CLOSER LOOK: VIRTUOUS TRAITS—POSITIVE PSYCHOLOGY AND TRAIT THEORY 348

- Biology and Traits 349
- Evaluation of the Trait Perspective 350

Learning-Theory Perspectives: All the Things You Do 350
- Behaviorism: On Being Easy in One's Harness? 351
- Social-Cognitive Theory: Is Determinism a Two-Way Street? 351
- Evaluation of the Learning Perspective 352

SELF-ASSESSMENT: WILL YOU BE A HIT OR A MISS? THE EXPECTANCY FOR SUCCESS SCALE 353

A CLOSER LOOK: BIOLOGY, SOCIAL COGNITION, AND GENDER-TYPING 354

The Humanistic–Existential Perspective: How Becoming? 356
- Abraham Maslow and the Challenge of Self-Actualization 356
- Carl Rogers's Self Theory 356

SELF-ASSESSMENT: DO YOU STRIVE TO BE ALL THAT YOU CAN BE? 357

LIFE CONNECTIONS: Enhancing Self-Esteem 358
- Evaluation of the Humanistic–Existential Perspective 359

The Sociocultural Perspective: Personality in Context 360
- Individualism versus Collectivism: Who Am I (in This Cultural Setting)? 360
- Acculturation, Adjustment, and Self-Esteem: Just How Much Acculturation Is Enough? 361
- Evaluation of the Sociocultural Perspective 361

CONCEPT REVIEW 10.1: Perspectives on Personality 362

Measurement of Personality 362
- Objective Tests 364
- Projective Tests 365

© Blend Images Photography/Veer

Chapter 11 Stress, Health, and Coping 368

Stress: What It Is, Where It Comes From 370
- Daily Hassles: The Stress of Everyday Life 370
- Life Changes: Variety May Be the Spice of Life, But Does Too Much Spice Leave a Bad Taste? 371

SELF-ASSESSMENT: GOING THROUGH CHANGES—HOW STRESSFUL IS YOUR LIFE? 372
- Hassles, Life Changes, and Health Problems 373
- How Are Daily Hassles and Life Changes Connected with Health Problems? 373
- Conflict: Darned If You Do, Darned If You Don't 374
- Irrational Beliefs: Ten Doorways to Distress 375

A CLOSER LOOK: STRESS IN AMERICA 375
- The Type A Behavior Pattern: Burning Out from Within? 377

SELF-ASSESSMENT: ARE YOU TYPE A OR TYPE B? 377

Psychological Moderators of Stress 378
- Self-Efficacy Expectations: "The Little Engine That Could" 378
- Psychological Hardiness: Tough Enough? 379
- Sense of Humor: "A Merry Heart Doeth Good Like a Medicine" 379
- Predictability and Control: "If I Can Stop the Roller Coaster, I Don't Want to Get Off" 379

SELF-ASSESSMENT: THE LOCUS OF CONTROL SCALE 380
- Social Support: On Being in It Together 381

Stress and the Body: The War Within 382
- The General Adaptation Syndrome 382

A CLOSER LOOK: "FIGHT OR FLIGHT" OR "TEND AND BEFRIEND"? DO MEN AND WOMEN RESPOND DIFFERENTLY TO STRESS? 384

Video Connections—Health and Stress 385
- Effects of Stress on the Immune System 385

LIFE CONNECTIONS: Preventing and Coping with Stress 386

Psychology and Health 388

- Headaches: When Stress Presses and Pounds 388

CONCEPT REVIEW 11.1: Factors in Heart Disease and Cancer 389

- Coronary Heart Disease: Taking Stress to Heart 390

LIFE CONNECTIONS: Preventing and Coping with Headaches 391

LIFE CONNECTIONS: Reducing the Risk of CHD Through Behavior Modification 393

- Cancer: Swerving Off Course 393

LIFE CONNECTIONS: Preventing and Coping with Cancer 395

Chapter 12   Psychological Disorders 398

© Katrina Wittkamp/Taxi/Getty Images

What Are Psychological Disorders? 399

- Perspectives on Psychological Disorders 401
- Classifying Psychological Disorders 402
- Prevalence of Psychological Disorders 403

Anxiety Disorders: Real Life "Fear Factors" 404

- Types of Anxiety Disorders 404
- Origins of Anxiety Disorders 408

Dissociative Disorders: Splitting Consciousness 410

- Types of Dissociative Disorders 410
- Origins of Dissociative Disorders 410

Somatoform Disorders: When the Body Expresses Stress 411

- Types of Somatoform Disorders 411
- Origins of Somatoform Disorders 412

Mood Disorders: Up, Down, and Around 412

- Types of Mood Disorders 412

SELF-ASSESSMENT: ARE YOU DEPRESSED? 413

A CLOSER LOOK: THE CASE OF WOMEN AND DEPRESSION 414

- Origins of Mood Disorders 414
- Suicide 415

LIFE CONNECTIONS: Preventing Suicide 418

Schizophrenia: When Thinking Runs Astray 418

- Symptoms of Schizophrenia 419

A CLOSER LOOK: WHEN THE "FATTY ACID" PLACES SODA OFF LIMITS 420

- Types of Schizophrenia 420
- Origins of Schizophrenia 421

Video Connections—Schizophrenia 421

A CLOSER LOOK: SHOULD WE BAN THE INSANITY PLEA? 424

Personality Disorders: Making Oneself or Others Miserable 425

- Types of Personality Disorders 425
- Origins of Personality Disorders 426

CONCEPT REVIEW 12.1: Psychological Disorders 428

Chapter 13   Methods of Therapy 432

© David Buffington/Photographer's Choice/Getty Images

What Is Psychotherapy? 434

Video Connections—Virtual Reality Therapy 434

- The History of Therapies 435

Psychodynamic Therapies: Digging Deep Within 436

- Traditional Psychoanalysis: "Where Id Was, There Shall Ego Be" 436
- Modern Psychodynamic Approaches 439

Humanistic Therapies: Strengthening the Self 439

- Client-Centered Therapy: Removing Roadblocks to Self-Actualization 439
- Gestalt Therapy: Getting It Together 441

Behavior Therapy: Adjustment Is What You Do 442

- Fear-Reduction Methods 442
- Aversive Conditioning 443
- Operant-Conditioning Procedures 443

SELF-ASSESSMENT: DO YOU SPEAK YOUR MIND OR DO YOU WIMP OUT? THE ASSERTIVENESS SCHEDULE 445

- Self-Control Methods 446

A CLOSER LOOK: EYE-MOVEMENT DESENSITIZATION AND REPROCESSING 447

Cognitive Therapies: Adjustment Is What You Think (and Do) 447
- Aaron Beck's Cognitive Therapy: Correcting Cognitive Errors 447
- Albert Ellis's Rational-Emotive Behavior Therapy: Overcoming "Musts" and "Shoulds" 449
- Cognitive-Behavior Therapy 449

Group Therapies: On Being in It Together 450
- Couple Therapy 451
- Family Therapy 451
- Self-Help and Support Groups 452

Does Psychotherapy Work? 452
- Problems in Conducting Research on Psychotherapy 453
- Analyses of the Effectiveness of Psychotherapy 453
- Evidence-Based Practices 454
- Ethnicity and Psychotherapy 455

Biological Therapies 456
- Drug Therapy: In Search of the Magic Pill? 456
- Electroconvulsive Therapy 457
- Psychosurgery 458
- Does Biological Therapy Work? 458

A CLOSER LOOK: CONTEMPORARY PSYCHOSURGERY FOR TREATMENT-RESISTANT OBSESSIVE–COMPULSIVE DISORDER AND DEPRESSION 459

LIFE CONNECTIONS: Alleviating Depression: Getting Out of the Dumps 460

CONCEPT REVIEW 13.1: Methods of Therapy 462

© Steve Raymer/Corbis

Chapter 14 Social Psychology 466

Attitudes: "The Good, the Bad, and the Ugly" 468
- The A–B Problem: Do We Act in Accord with Our Beliefs? 468
- Origins of Attitudes 469
- Changing Attitudes Through Persuasion: How Persuasive? 470
- Changing Attitudes and Behavior by Means of Cognitive Dissonance: "I Think, Therefore I Am…Consistent"? 472

A CLOSER LOOK: THE FOOT-IN-THE-DOOR TECHNIQUE 473

Prejudice: A Particularly Troublesome Attitude 474
Video Connections—Stereotype Threat 475
- Discrimination 475
- Sources of Prejudice 475

LIFE CONNECTIONS: Combating Prejudice 476

Interpersonal Attraction: On Liking and Loving 477
- Physical Appearance: How Important Is Looking Good? 477
- The Attraction-Similarity Hypothesis: Do "Opposites Attract" or Do "Birds of a Feather Flock Together"? 478

A CLOSER LOOK: WHEN IT COMES TO SEX, RED MAY MEAN "GO" 479
- Other Factors in Attraction: Reciprocity and the Nearness of You? 480
- Love: The Emotion That Launched a Thousand Ships? 480

SELF-ASSESSMENT: THE TRIANGULAR LOVE SCALE 482

Social Perception: Looking Out, Looking Within 483
- Primacy and Recency Effects: The Importance of First Impressions 483
- Attribution Theory: You're Free to Choose, but I'm Caught in the Middle? 484

A CLOSER LOOK: WHO ARE THE SUICIDE TERRORISTS? A CASE OF THE FUNDAMENTAL ATTRIBUTION ERROR? 485

Social Influence: Are You an Individual or One of the Crowd? 486
- Obedience to Authority: Does Might Make Right? 486
- Conformity: Do Many Make Right? 490

Group Behavior: Is a Camel a Horse Made by a Committee? 492
- Social Facilitation: Monkey See, Monkey Do Faster? 492
- Group Decision Making 492
- Polarization and the "Risky Shift" 493
- Groupthink: When Smart People Think as One, Bad Decisions May Follow 494
- Mob Behavior and Deindividuation: The "Beast with Many Heads" 495
- Altruism and the Bystander Effect: Some Watch While Others Die 495

Appendix A # Statistics 500

Descriptive Statistics 502
- Measures of Central Tendency 503
- Measures of Variability 504

The Normal Curve 506

Inferential Statistics 507
- Statistically Significant Differences 508

Appendix B # Answer Keys to Self-Assessments and Active Reviews 511

References 517

Glossary 567

Name Index 583

Subject Index 591

Credits 607

| Features

A CLOSER LOOK

- Charles Darwin 40
- Are You a Human or a Mouse? Some Fascinating Facts about Genes 46
- Mirror, Mirror, in the Brain: Who's the Fairest Imitator of Them All? 66
- iPods on Campus: The Sounds of Oblivion? 102
- Advances in Science? The Case of the Aromatic T-Shirts 106
- Dependence on Cocaine? Denial at Work 144
- On the Edge with Ecstasy 146
- Who Was "Little Albert"? 160
- Robo Rats? Using Operant Conditioning to Teach Rats How to Search for Survivors of Disasters 169
- Contingency Theory 174
- Will You Remember Your Psychology Grade in 2062? 187
- Can We Trust Eyewitness Testimony? 199
- Do People Really Recover Repressed Memories of Childhood Sexual Abuse? 208
- "Motherese"—Of "Yummy Yummy" and "Kitty Cats" 236
- Emotional Intelligence and Social Intelligence 241
- Is the Human Sex Drive Affected by Pheromones? 275
- Just What Do Lie Detectors Detect? 292
- Is Development Continuous or Discontinuous? 305
- Are There Gender Differences in Moral Development? 320
- Aging, Gender, and Ethnicity 330
- Virtuous Traits—Positive Psychology and Trait Theory 348
- Biology, Social Cognition, and Gender-Typing 354
- Stress in America 375

- "Fight or Flight" or "Tend and Befriend"? Do Men and Women Respond Differently to Stress? 384
- The Case of Women and Depression 414
- When the "Fatty Acid" Places Soda Off Limits 420
- Should We Ban the Insanity Plea? 424
- Eye-Movement Desensitization and Reprocessing 447
- Contemporary Psychosurgery for Treatment-Resistant Obsessive–Compulsive Disorder and Depression 459
- The Foot-in-the-Door Technique 473
- When It Comes to Sex, Red May Mean "Go" 479
- Who Are the Suicide Terrorists? A Case of the Fundamental Attribution Error? 485

CONCEPT REVIEW

- Historic Schools of Psychology 12
- Research Methods 32
- The Endocrine System 70
- Monocular Cues for Depth Perception 97
- The Senses 113
- Psychoactive Drugs and Their Effects 149
- Kinds of Learning 178
- The Relationships among the Various Kinds of Memories 188
- Theories of Intelligence 242
- Perspectives on Personality 362
- Factors in Heart Disease and Cancer 389
- Psychological Disorders 428
- Methods of Therapy 462

SELF-ASSESSMENT

- Dare You Say What You Think? The Social-Desirability Scale 25
- Are You Getting Your Z's? 128

- Do You Have a Problem with Alcohol? *140*
- Five Challenges to Your Memory *184*
- Puzzles, Problems, and Just Plain Fun *223*
- The Remote Associates Test *243*
- The Sensation-Seeking Scale *263*
- Eating Disorders Quiz *273*
- How Long Will You Live? The Life-Expectancy Scale *330*
- Will You Be a Hit or a Miss? The Expectancy for Success Scale *353*
- Do You Strive to Be All That You Can Be? *357*
- Going Through Changes: How Stressful Is Your Life? *372*
- Are You Type A or Type B? *377*
- The Locus of Control Scale *380*
- Are You Depressed? *413*
- Do You Speak Your Mind or Do You Wimp Out? The Assertiveness Schedule *445*
- The Triangular Love Scale *482*

LIFE CONNECTIONS

- Thinking Critically about Psychological Advice on the Internet: Are There Any Quick Fixes? *21*
- Coping with PMS *74*
- Pain, Pain, Go Away—Don't Come Again Another Day *110*
- Strategies for Coping with Insomnia *129*
- Is Marijuana Harmful? Should It Be Available as a Medicine? *148*
- Why Do Many Psychologists Disapprove of Punishment? *168*
- Teaching Children *Not* to Imitate Media Violence *177*
- Using the Psychology of Memory to Enhance Your Memory *210*
- Enhancing Intellectual Functioning *251*
- The Skinny on Weight Control *268*

- "Come On! Get Happy!" A Possible or Impossible Dream? *287*
- Day Care: Blessing, Headache, or Both? *316*
- Enhancing Self-Esteem *358*
- Preventing and Coping with Stress *386*
- Preventing and Coping with Headaches *391*
- Reducing the Risk of CHD Through Behavior Modification *393*
- Preventing and Coping with Cancer *395*
- Preventing Suicide *418*
- Alleviating Depression: Getting Out of the Dumps *460*
- Combating Prejudice *476*

VIDEO CONNECTIONS

- Facial Analysis—The Scientific Method in Action *23*
- The Action Potential *52*
- The Ames Room *97*
- Why Is Nicotine So Addictive? *145*
- Little Albert *160*
- Conditioning of Fear *161*
- Mirror Neurons *175*
- Reconstructive Memory *200*
- Problem Solving *225*
- Childhood Obesity *267*
- Anorexia Nervosa *270*
- Prenatal Assessment *301*
- The Visual Cliff *305*
- Piaget's Sensorimotor Stage *307*
- Piaget's Formal Operational Stage: Hypothetical Propositions *320*
- Personality Theories and Measurement *348*
- Health and Stress *385*
- Schizophrenia *421*
- Virtual Reality Therapy *434*
- Stereotype Threat *475*

Preface

PSYCHOLOGY: CONCEPTS & CONNECTIONS, BRIEF VERSION, 9E

My favorite psychology professor told the class, "You probably judge how well you did in the course by your grade. I judge how well *I* did in the course in terms of how many additional psychology courses you take."

Now, it's my turn. Users of this textbook will judge what they have obtained from it in various ways. I will consider myself to have been successful if it inspires students to take additional courses in psychology.

I had several goals in writing this introductory textbook: They include painting psychology as the rigorous science it is, teaching students how to think critically, and introducing students to the various fields of psychology and the concepts they investigate. But it was also essential to me to inspire students with the subject matter. Thus, I have tried to use a warm, engaging writing style, including humor and personal anecdotes. I also believed it is important to show students how psychology connects with important issues in their own lives. Psychology is not just "out there." Its many concepts provide information and ideas that all students can apply for their own benefit and that of those whom they care about.

A final goal in this "brief edition" was to be succinct. The text is intended for the one-semester introductory psychology course, and it is organized into fourteen chapters so that professors can teach about one chapter per week. Although there is adequate text to give psychology the coverage it deserves and to provide ample pedagogical devices, there is little "fluff." We watched our word count so that busy students can also attend to other matters, and busy professors can readily see what the text expects of students.

PSYCHOLOGY: CONCEPTS AND CONNECTIONS, BRIEF VERSION—MORE THAN JUST A TITLE

All academic disciplines have their own concepts, and psychology is no exception. One of the key tasks of any introductory course is to acquaint students with the basic concepts of the discipline. Students of introductory psychology are probably not surprised that concepts such as *intelligence, personality, stress, mental illness* (which we refer to as *psychological disorders*), and *psychotherapy* are important to the discipline. They may be surprised to learn that psychologists debate whether some familiar concepts, such as *psychoanalysis*, have a place—other than a historical place—in psychology as a science. Students are unlikely to be surprised that the concepts of *personality* and *learning* and *memory* are found in psychology, but they may find that these concepts—as defined and used by psychologists—are not quite what they thought they were. Students may also be somewhat surprised that the very concept they had of the field of psychology—of what psychology *is*—probably makes up less than half of what they will find in this textbook.

All this is very good. Psychology consists of things that are familiar and things that are new. One of the purposes of this course is to set the record straight, to show students what does and what does not belong within the science of psychology.

THINKING CRITICALLY— IN LIFE AND IN THE CLASSROOM

Another goal of this course is to show that psychologists, like other scientists, are skeptical and open-minded. They thrive on debate. They do not even necessarily agree on the definitions of the topics they discuss. For example, there is no one definition of *psychology* that all psychologists agree on. When we approach the topic of learning, we will similarly see that experts in that field disagree about how to define *learning*. Later, we will see that psychologists disagree as to what *intelligence* is and as to whether there is one kind of general intelligence or there are several "intelligences." As if this were not enough, we will see that there is also major controversy over the origins of intelligence.

Again, all of this is very good. Scientific debate should not be confused with pointless argument. Honest debate helps psychologists—and students—come ever closer to the truth. Students will, of course, memorize standard definitions; however, it is just as important that they come away from this course with an understanding of the true scientific nature of psychology and of the controversies within psychology.

Critical thinking is the key to understanding these controversies—and also the key to productive citizenship. I believe too many individuals blindly follow the demands of the media and authority figures, and it is my goal to help students hone their critical thinking skills so that they can evaluate the arguments they hear in the media and from authority figures. In fact, I have incorporated numerous Critical Thinking exercises throughout the text to encourage students to think critically about the content of the text and the real-life situations they encounter every day. The Learning Connections sections in every chapter contain a Critical Thinking item. Here is a sampling:

- From Chapter 1, "What Is Psychology?": Do you believe that the richness and complexity of human behavior can be explained as the summation of so many instances of learning? Explain.
- From Chapter 2, "Biology and Psychology": Do you believe that this textbook, and other textbooks, should present the theory of evolution? Why or why not?
- From Chapter 7, "Thinking, Language, and Intelligence": Do the talents of dancers, gymnasts, artists, and musicians strike you as kinds of intelligences? Why or why not?
- From Chapter 12, "Psychological Disorders": When does a psychological problem become a "psychological disorder"? Is the border clearly defined?
- From Chapter 14, "Social Psychology": Critical thinkers do not overgeneralize. Most people would probably agree that it is good for children to be obedient. But is it always good for children—and for adults—to be obedient? How do you define the limits?

Come into this course as you will. Leave this course as a skeptic. Believe nothing about psychology until you have had an opportunity to see and evaluate the evidence—for yourself.

MAKING LIFE CONNECTIONS

One of the wonderful things about psychology is how the topics in the field relate to your daily life. These connections are found throughout the text.

Given that the first chapter is about psychology as a science, the Life Connections section focuses on "Thinking Critically About Psychological Advice on the Internet: Are There Any Quick Fixes?" It teaches students how they can learn to sort out truth from fiction when they are surfing the Internet.

Chapter 3 is about "Sensation and Perception"—how people make sense (excuse the pun) of the world in which they dwell. The Life Connections section in that chapter—"Pain, Pain, Go Away—Don't Come Again Another Day"—is about what we can do to alleviate pain. After reading this section, you may go to the psychology cabinet as well as the medicine cabinet for relief.

In Chapter 8 we will learn that two out of three Americans are overweight, and half of these are obese. The chapter explores why we eat, and why the majority of us overeat. One of the chapter's Life Connections sections, "The Skinny on Weight Control," offers concrete advice as to how we can avoid overeating and putting on the pounds.

MAKING LEARNING CONNECTIONS

My emphasis on making connections is also reflected in the book's pedagogical package. The book's pedagogy is designed to help students understand the concepts presented so they *take away* more of that knowledge from the book. *Psychology: Concepts and Connections, Brief Version* fully integrates the PQ4R method in every chapter to help students learn and retain the subject matter.

PQ4R—A Complete Pedagogical Package

PQ4R is the acronym for Preview, Question, Read, Reflect, Review, and Recite, a method that is related to the work of educational psychologist Francis P. Robinson. PQ4R is more than the standard built-in study guide. It goes well beyond a few pages of questions and exercises that are found at the ends of the chapters of many textbooks. It is an integral part of every chapter. It begins and ends each chapter, and it accompanies the student page by page.

Students do not passively soak up the subject matter as sponges soak up water. The PQ4R method stimulates students to *actively* engage the subject matter. It encourages students to become *proactive* rather than *reactive*.

Chapter Previews Previewing the material helps shape students' expectations. It enables them to create mental templates, or "advance organizers," into which they categorize the subject matter. Each chapter of *Psychology: Concepts and Connections, Brief Version* previews the subject matter with

- an outline of **Major Topics**,
- a list of **Features**,
- and a **Truth or Fiction?** section.

The *Truth or Fiction?* items stimulate students to delve into the subject matter by challenging folklore and common sense (which, too often, is common nonsense).

Following is a sampling of *Truth or Fiction?* items from various chapters:

- Fear can give you indigestion.
- A single brain cell can send out hundreds of messages each second—and manage to catch some rest in between.
- It may be easier for you to recall the name of your first-grade teacher than the name of someone you just met at a party.
- If you study with the stereo on, you would probably do better to take the test with the stereo on.
- A man shot the president of the United States in front of millions of television witnesses, yet he was found not guilty by a court of law.
- In the Middle Ages, innocent people were drowned to prove that they were not possessed by the Devil.
- It is abnormal to feel anxious.
- Opposites attract.
- Seeing is believing.

Question Devising questions about the subject matter, before reading it in detail, is another feature of the PQ4R method.

Writing questions gives students goals: They attend class or read the text *so they can answer the questions.* Questions are placed in all primary sections of the text to help students use the PQ4R method most effectively. The questions are numbered, and they are repeated, along with their numbers, in the summaries at the end of each chapter. When students see a question, they can read the following material to answer that question. If they wish, they can also write the questions and answers in their notebooks, as recommended by Robinson.

Read *Reading* is the first R in the PQ4R method. Although students will have to read for themselves, they are not alone while they are doing it. The text helps them by providing

- **previews** that help students organize the material and stimulate them by challenging common knowledge and folklore;
- presentation of the subject matter in clear, stimulating prose;
- a **running glossary** that defines key terms in the margin of the text, near where the terms appear in the text; and
- development of **concepts** in an orderly fashion so that new concepts build on previously presented ones.

I have also chosen to use a personal writing style. It speaks directly to students and employs humor and personal anecdotes designed to motivate and stimulate them.

Review The second R in PQ4R stands for *Review.* Regular reviews of the subject matter help students learn. Therefore, Reviews are incorporated into Learning Connections sections that follow all major sections in the text.

Learning Connections contain three types of items that foster active learning, retention, and critical thinking. The *Active Review* is the first type of item. It is called an Active Review because it is presented in a fill-in-the-blank format that asks students to *produce,* not simply *recognize,* the answer. The fill-in blanks are numbered, and the answers are provided in Appendix B. For example, the *Active Review* on "The Endocrine System" in the chapter on "Biology and Psychology" reads as follows:

ACTIVE REVIEW (22) The _____ secretes hormones that regulate the pituitary gland. (23) The pituitary hormone _____ regulates maternal behavior in lower animals and stimulates production of milk in women. (24) The thyroid hormone _____ affects the metabolism. (25) Epinephrine is secreted by the adrenal _____ and is involved in emotional arousal.

Because reviewing the subject matter is so important and because of the value of visual cues in learning, *Concept Reviews* are also found throughout the text. Concept Reviews are presented in dynamic layouts that readily communicate the key concepts and the relationships among concepts. Here is a sampling of the Concept Reviews:

- Chapter 1: Historic Schools of Psychology
- Chapter 2: The Endocrine System

- Chapter 6: The Relationships among the Various Kinds of Memories
- Chapter 10: Perspectives on Personality
- Chapter 12: Psychological Disorders

Reflect Students learn more effectively when they *Reflect* (the third R in PQ4R) on, or relate to, what they are learning. Psychologists who study learning and memory refer to reflection on subject matter as *elaborative rehearsal.* One way for students to reflect on a subject is to *relate* it to things they already know about, whether it be academic material or events in their own lives. Reflecting on, or relating to, the material makes it meaningful and easier to remember. It also makes it more likely that students will be able to *apply* the information to their own lives. Through effective reflection, students can embed material firmly in their memory so that rote repetition is unnecessary.

Because reflecting on the material is intertwined with relating to it, the second kind of item in each Learning Connections section is termed *Reflect and Relate.* Here is the Reflect and Relate item from Chapter 2's Learning Connections section on the endocrine system:

REFLECT AND RELATE Have you heard that adolescents are "hormonal" or affected by "glands"? If so, which glands would they be?

The following *Reflect and Relate* item is found in Chapter 7, "Thinking, Language, and Intelligence":

REFLECT AND RELATE Have you ever known someone to claim that a pet could "speak" or "understand" English or another language? Did the pet really speak? Did the pet understand language? What was the nature of the evidence?

Recite The PQ4R method recommends that students *Recite* the answers to the questions aloud. Reciting answers aloud helps students remember them by means of repetition, by stimulating students to produce concepts and ideas they have learned, and by associating them with spoken words and gestures.

Recite sections are found at the end of each chapter. They help students summarize the material, but they are active summaries. For this reason, the sections are termed "**Recite—An Active Summary.**" They are written in question-and-answer format. To provide a sense of closure, the active summaries repeat the questions found within the chapters, and they are numbered. The answers are concise but include most of the key terms found in the text.

Students can also access interactive versions of the Learning Connections), and the PQ4R method of studying, as well as flashcards, quizzing, and videos at Psychology CourseMate.

FEATURES

Psychology: Concepts and Connections, Brief Version includes a number of features that are intended to motivate students, enhance learning, and foster critical thinking. These include emphasis on the evolutionary perspective, emphasis on diversity, A Closer Look features, and Self-Assessments.

Emphasis on the Evolutionary Perspective

Psychology today recognizes the influence of evolution not only on physical traits but also on behavior and mental processes. *Psychology: Concepts and Connections* addresses the impact of the evolutionary perspective throughout the text. The evolutionary perspective receives the full emphasis it deserves in the current edition, while still providing thorough coverage of other traditional and contemporary perspectives. Following are examples of coverage of evolution:

- Chapter 2: Begins with the section "Evolution and Evolutionary Psychology: 'Survivor' Is More Than Just a TV Show."
- Chapter 3: The evolutionary perspective on how pain and the location of taste buds are adaptive and promote survival.
- Chapter 5: Discussion of the evolutionary value of taste aversions and the likelihood that we may be "biologically prepared" to develop fears of certain objects and situations, such as fears of snakes and heights.
- Chapter 8: Discussion of evolution and instinct, stimulus motives, aggression, and universal recognition of facial expressions.
- Chapter 11: Discussion of gender differences in response to threats—such as the (predominantly male?) tendency for "fight or flight" compared with the (predominantly female?) tendency to "tend and befriend."
- Chapter 14: Discussion of the evolutionary benefits of altruism and self-sacrifice.

Emphasis on Diversity

Although the profession of psychology focuses mainly on the individual's behavior and mental processes, we often cannot understand people's behavior and mental processes without reference to their diversity—their ethnic background, gender, socioeconomic status, age, and other factors. When we consider perspectives other than our own, it's important that we understand the role of a culture's beliefs, values, and attitudes in behavior and mental processes. Acknowledging and studying why people from diverse cultures behave and think in different ways enrich the science of psychology.

You will find reference to human diversity integrated within the main body of the text. For example, a feature in Chapter 12, "Psychological Disorders," discusses possible reasons for the greater incidence of depression among women than men.

A Closer Look Features

A Closer Look boxes pursue certain topics in greater depth. These features tend to focus on themes such as research, diversity, and real-life applications. Chapter 2's "A Closer Look: Are You a Human or a Mouse? Some Fascinating Facts About Genes" points out that human's genetic codes overlap a surprising amount with organisms such as chimpanzees (our closest living relatives) and mice. A number of these boxes underscore the indispensability of human diversity within the field of psychology. For example, Chapter 9's "A Closer Look: Aging, Gender, and Ethnicity" discusses why women tend to outlive men and why people from some ethnic groups outlive people from other ethnic groups.

Self-Assessments

Self-Assessments are another way in which the text connects with students. The Self-Assessments stimulate student interest by helping them satisfy their curiosity about themselves and enhance the relevance of the text to their lives. Following is a sampling of the Self-Assessments found in the text:

- Chapter 4: "Are You Getting Your Z's?" and "Do You Have a Problem with Alcohol?"
- Chapter 7: "The Remote Associates Test" (a self-test of creativity)
- Chapter 8: "The Sensation-Seeking Scale" and the "Eating Disorders Quiz"
- Chapter 10: "Do You Strive to Be All That You Can Be?" (a self-test of whether one is a self-actualizer)
- Chapter 11: "The Locus of Control Scale"
- Chapter 13: "Do You Speak Your Mind or Do You Wimp Out? The Assertiveness Schedule"

A MAJOR REVISION

Psychology: Concepts and Connections, Brief Version is quite new—a major revision. Every topic has been updated. There are hundreds of new references. Following is a sampling of what is new in each chapter:

Chapter 1: What Is Psychology?

Chapter 1 has a new chapter-opening vignette, new coverage on forensic psychologists, new coverage on the role of women in psychology, and a new Life Connections feature: "Thinking Critically about Psychological Advice on the Internet: Are There Any Quick Fixes?"

Chapter 2: Biology and Psychology

This chapter has been thoroughly updated and revised and contains expanded coverage of evolutionary psychology and a new chapter-opening vignette. There is a new A Closer Look on mirror neurons: "Mirror, Mirror, in the Brain: Who's the Fairest Imitator of Them All?"

Chapter 3: Sensation and Perception

This chapter includes updates throughout, a new chapter-opening vignette, new coverage of subliminal stimulation, and a new A Closer Look on "iPods on Campus: The Sounds of Oblivion?"

Chapter 4: Consciousness

This chapter has been thoroughly updated and revised and includes a new chapter-opening vignette and new features: a Self-Assessment titled "Do You Have a Problem with Alcohol?" and A Closer Look: "Dependence on Cocaine? Denial at Work"

Chapter 5: Learning

This chapter includes a new chapter-opening vignette, new coverage of biological preparedness and the conditioning of fear, new coverage of mirror neurons and observational learning, and has been updated throughout.

Chapter 6: Memory: Remembrance of Things Past—and Future

This chapter has been thoroughly updated and includes two new A Closer Look features: "Will You Remember Your Psychology Grade in 2062?" and "Do People Really Recover Repressed Memories of Childhood Sexual Abuse?"

Chapter 7: Thinking, Language, and Intelligence

This chapter has been updated throughout and includes a new chapter-opening vignette, expanded coverage of the genetic aspects of intellectual functioning, and two new A Closer Look features on "Emotional Intelligence and Social Intelligence" and "'Motherese'—Of 'Yummy Yummy' and 'Kitty Cats.'" We have also added a new Life Connections feature, "Enhancing Intellectual Functioning."

Chapter 8: Motivation and Emotion

This chapter has been updated and has a new chapter-opening vignette. It includes two new features: a Self-Assessment, the "Eating Disorders Quiz," and an A Closer Look, "Just What Do Lie Detectors Detect?"

Chapter 9: The Voyage Through the Life Span

This chapter (Chapter 3 in the previous edition) has been thoroughly revised and includes a new chapter-opening vignette, a new section on research methods in developmental psychology, a new A Closer Look, "Are There Gender Differences in Moral Development?" and revised and expanded coverage of early adulthood, middle adulthood, and late adulthood.

Chapter 10: Personality: Theory and Measurement

This chapter includes a new chapter-opening vignette, updating throughout, expanded coverage of the five-factor ("Big Five") model of personality, a new Self-Assessment, "Will You Be a Hit or a Miss? The Expectancy for Success Scale," new coverage of the reliability and validity of personality tests, and a new Life Connections feature on "Enhancing Self-Esteem."

Chapter 11: Stress, Health, and Coping

This chapter includes a revised chapter-opening vignette on the tsunami that struck Japan in 2011. In addition to generally updated coverage, there is new coverage of the ongoing study of "Stress in America" by the American Psychological Association and new coverage of problem-focused coping versus emotion-focused coping.

Chapter 12: Psychological Disorders

Chapter 12 includes coverage of new research throughout, such as updated research on the biological correlates of various disorders, including genetics, evolution, biochemistry, and physiology. There is a new chapter-opening vignette. There is a new section on perspective/models of psychological disorders. There is also new discussion of the reliability and validity of psychiatric diagnoses. There are several new case studies—for example, on panic disorder, generalized anxiety disorder, obsessive–compulsive disorder, bipolar disorder, and paranoid schizophrenia. There is a new Self-Assessment, "Are You Depressed?" and a new A Closer Look, "When the 'Fatty Acid' Places Soda Off Limits."

Chapter 13: Methods of Therapy

This chapter includes new research throughout on the uses and effectiveness of psychotherapy and of psychotherapy versus biological therapies. There is expanded coverage of cognitive–behavior therapy, and new coverage of the behavior-therapy method of flooding, of self-help and support groups, and of evidence-based practices. The chapter has new A Closer Look feature on "Contemporary Psychosurgery for Treatment-Resistant Obsessive–Compulsive Disorder and Depression."

Chapter 14: Social Psychology

Chapter 14 is updated throughout, as in reporting the results of recent research on obedience to authority. The chapter-opening vignette is also updated. There is a new major section on prejudice, including the effect of names on prejudice and automatic prejudice. There is a new A Closer Look in the section on Interpersonal Attraction": "When It Comes to Sex, Red May Mean 'Go.'" The section on groupthink is completely revised, focusing on the group decision to invade Iraq and similar decisions. There is also a new A Closer Look box on "The Foot-in-the-Door Technique."

ANCILLARIES

For the Instructor

Test Bank
By Deborah Schwiesow, Creighton University. For each chapter of the text, the Test Bank offers over 100 multiple-choice questions, 10 completion questions, 10 true/false questions, and 5 essay questions, along with answer keys with references to main text page numbers, learning objectives, difficulty level, and type of question. The Test Bank also includes a midterm and final exam, which each consists of 50 multiple-choice questions.

Instructor's Resource Manual
By Kelly Henry, Western Missouri State University. Thoroughly revised, this manual contains teaching tips, a sample syllabus, activities for the first day of class, and a substantially increased number of website listings (with brief descriptions). Each chapter contains learning objectives, detailed lecture outlines, and a major section called "Ideas for Instruction," which includes lecture topics, classroom activities, and journal entry prompts.

PowerLecture with Examview This one-stop lecture and class preparation tool contains ready-to-use PowerPoint® slides that allows you to assemble, edit, publish, and present custom lectures for your course. PowerLecture lets you bring together text-specific lecture outlines and art from Rathus's text along with videos or your own materials, culminating in a powerful, personalized media-enhanced presentation. The DVD also includes the ExamView® assessment and tutorial system, which guides you step-by-step through the process of creating tests.

WebTutor™ on WebCT™ and Blackboard Jumpstart your course with customizable, rich, text-specific content within your Course Management System.

Psychology CourseMate Cengage Learning's Psychology CourseMate brings course concepts to life with interactive learning, study, and exam preparation tools that support the printed textbook. Go to **www.cengagebrain.com**.

Psychology CourseMate includes

- an interactive eBook;
- interactive teaching and learning tools, including
  - quizzes,
  - flashcards,
  - videos,
  - and more; plus
- the Engagement Tracker, a first-of-its-kind tool that monitors student engagement in the course.

For the Student

Psychology CourseMate Make the most of your study time by accessing everything you need to succeed in one place. Read your textbook, take notes, review flashcards, watch videos, and take practice quizzes—online with CourseMate. Go to **www.cengagebrain.com**.

Psychology CourseMate includes

- an interactive eBook, with highlighting, note-taking, and search capabilities;
- interactive learning tools, including
  - quizzes,
  - flashcards,
  - videos,
- and more!

ACKNOWLEDGMENTS

Writers of novels and poems may secrete themselves in their studies and complete their work in solitude. Not so the textbook author. Writing a textbook is a partnership—a partnership between the author and peers who review the manuscript at every step of the way to make sure it is accurate and covers the topics it should be covering. My partners for the current edition of *Psychology: Concepts and Connections* included

Melanie M. Arpaio, Sussex County Community College

James R. Bean, Lockhaven University

Belinda Blevins-Knabe, University of Arkansas–Little Rock

Stephen Buggie, University of New Mexico

Marilyn Douglass, Bowling Green State University—Firelands

Paul A. Franco, South Suburban College

Laura Gaudet, Chadron State College

Chris Goode, Georgia State University

Melinda Green, Cornell College

Dr. Julie Guay McIntyre, Russell Sage College

Mark Hager, Menlo College

Claudine Harris, Los Angeles Mission College

Norman E. Kinney, Southeast Missouri State University

Nancy J. Melucci, Long Beach City College

Neelam Rattan, San Jose State University

Melissa Ryan, Minnesota School of Business/Globe University

Nick Schmitt, Heartland Community College

Kathy Sexton-Radek, Elmhurst College

Staci Simmelink-Johnson, Walla Walla Community College

Michael A. Vandehey, Midwestern State University

Sally Vyain, Ivy Tech Community College

Stephen P. Weinert, Cuyamaca College

David Yells, Utah Valley University

Nancy A. Zook, Purchase College

In addition to the reviewers for the current edition, I would like to extend my continued gratitude to the reviewers of previous editions who have helped shaped my book over the years:

Carrie Canales, Los Angeles City College; Judy Coleman, Dabney S. Lancaster Community College; Mary Ellen Dello Stritto, Ball State University; June S. Fessenden, Glendale Community College; Maria Fitzpatrick, Chaffey College; Krista Forrest, University of Nebraska–Kearney; Rebecca Fraser-Thill, Bates College; Daniel Houlihan, Minnesota State University–Mankato; Mark D. Kelland, Lansing Community College; Christopher Mruk, Bowling Green State University Firelands College; Katherine Neidhardt, Cuesta College; Ralph G. Pifer, Sauk Valley Community College; Patrick W. Prindle, New Mexico Junior College; Sadie Oates, Pitt Community College; Don Smith, Everett Community College; Gary Springer, Texas State University; Christian D. Amundsen, North Lake College; Beth Arrigo, Central Piedmont Community College; Jeffrey Bartel, Kansas State University; David E. Baskind, Delta College; Julia A. Bishop, Maple Woods Community College; Susan R. Burns, Kansas State University; Saundra K. Ciccarelli, Gulf Coast Community College; Mary Webber Coplen, Hutchinson Community College; Joseph Culkin, Queensborough Community College–The City University of New York; Teddi S. Deka, Missouri Western State College; Susan R. Edwards, Mott Community College; B. J. Hart, Glendale Community College; Mark Kelland, Lansing Community College; Gloria J. Lawrence, Wayne State College; Vicki Lucey, Las Positas College; Laura Madson, New Mexico State University; Joseph Manganello, Gloucester County College; Horace Marchant, Westfield State College; Marnie Moist, St. Francis University; Alinde J. Moore, Ashland University; Russell Ohta, Phoenix College; Brian J. Oppy, California State University–Chico; Debra Parish, Tomball College–North Harris Montgomery Community College District; Michelle L. Pilati, Rio Hondo College; Laura Reichel, Front Range Community College; Theresa Rufrano-Ruffner, Indiana University of Pennsylvania; H. R. Schiffman, Rutgers University; Debra Schwiesow, Creighton University; Carolyn E. Tasa, Erie Community College; Sheralee Tershner, Western New England College; Rhonda G. Trollinger, Guilford Technical Community College; Karen M. Wolford, State University of New York College at Oswego.

Finally, I would like to thank the fine group of publishing professionals at Wadsworth/Cengage. They handled editorial duties and details too numerous to mention, which somehow took a printed manuscript and transformed it into the colorful book you are now holding in your hands.

They include new friends and old friends, a glorious combination: Sean Wakely, President, who one time in Boston refused to let me leave a room until I signed a contract (he won, but he also had two additional burly editors with him at the time); Jon-David Hague, Jaime Perkins, and Tim Matray, a trio of psychology editors who have all, in one way or another, had a hand in bringing this 9th edition to fruition; Shannon LeMay-Finn, the finest of developmental editors, who saw clearly what needed to be done in this new edition and shaped me into doing it—in no uncertain terms; Nic Albert, the in-house development editor; Paige Leeds, for her work on the instructor and student supplements; Mary Noel, for handling the media products that accompany this book; Lauren Moody, the editorial assistant; Jessica Egbert and Anna Andersen in marketing; Rita Jaramillo, the content project manager who kept everyone on track; Vernon Boes, the art director, for managing yet another great design and cover; and project manager Aaron Downey of Matrix Productions for managing all the production details with grace under pressure.

—*Spence Rathus*

PSYCHOLOGY

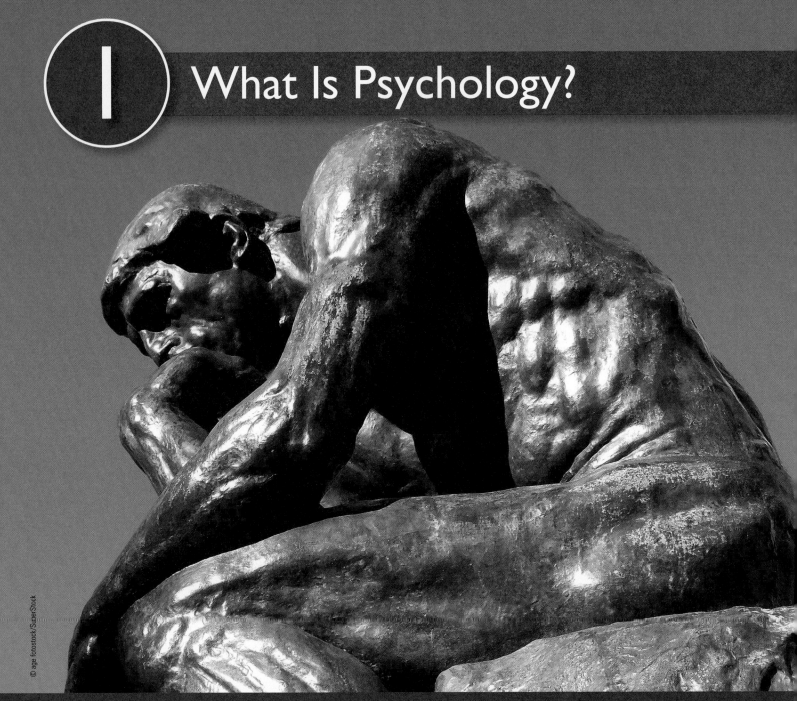

1 What Is Psychology?

MAJOR TOPICS

Psychology as a Science *4*

What Psychologists Do: Something for Everyone? *5*

Where Psychology Comes From: A History *8*

How Today's Psychologists View Behavior and Mental Processes *13*

Gender, Ethnicity, and Psychology: Real People in the Real World *17*

Critical Thinking: Sorting Truth from Fiction *19*

How Psychologists Study Behavior and Mental Processes *22*

Ethical Issues in Psychological Research and Practice *33*

FEATURES

Concept Review 1.1: Historic Schools of Psychology *12*

Life Connections: Thinking Critically About Psychological Advice on the Internet: Are There Any Quick Fixes? *21*

Self-Assessment: Dare You Say What You Think? The Social-Desirability Scale *25*

Concept Review 1.2: Research Methods *32*

T F Psychologists attempt to control people's behavior and mental processes.

page 4

T F More than 2,000 years ago, Aristotle wrote a book on psychology with contents similar to the book you are now holding.

page 8

T F The ancient Greek philosopher Socrates suggested a research method that is still used in psychology.

page 8

T F As psychologist Wilhelm Wundt lay on his deathbed, his main concern was to analyze the experience of dying.

page 9

T F Men receive the majority of doctoral degrees in psychology.

page 17

T F Even though she had worked to complete all the degree requirements, the first female president of the American Psychological Association turned down the doctoral degree that was offered to her.

page 17

T F People who claim they have been abducted by aliens are lying.

page 19

T F You could survey millions of voters and still not accurately predict the outcome of a presidential election.

page 23

T F In many experiments, neither the participants nor the researchers know who is receiving the real treatment and who is not.

page 32

Are these items truth or fiction? We will be revisiting them throughout the chapter.

There is a riot of dogs in my home, including Nadine, the Chihuahua queen who rules the roost, and Jackson, the toy poodle who now and then protests that fact. I have trained them well. For example, they bark madly when someone comes to the door, but after I pretty much ineffectively reprimand them for 5 minutes, they quiet down. Then I usually add a biscuit as a reward.

Jackson is subtle. One day I spotted him and Nadine chewing bones on the living room sofa. Humans sometimes think that the grass is always greener on the other side of the fence, and Jackson always seems to think that the other dog's bone looks tastier. He got up from the sofa and sniffed his way toward Nadine's bone, but having 4 pounds and 5 years of ferocity on him, Nadine growled protectively and Jackson deferred. After a few additional attempted approaches, Jackson apparently tried a stratagem based on another fact of dog life: The bone that is getting away is more attractive than the bone one possesses. Accordingly, Jackson nosed his own bone toward the edge of the sofa. The movement of the other bone shook Nadine out of her bone-chew trance, and she eyed it closely. Now the bone fell off the edge of the world—the sofa—and Nadine, after a chew-pause, got up to investigate. Jackson, who had been observing, snatched Nadine's bone and leapt with it to the nearby chair before she was even aware of the crime.

Jackson was long in chew-bliss before Nadine, deciding against the jump to the floor, turned around to return to her bone. Seeing the bone was gone, she looked Jackson's way.

Perhaps I should have let the drama play out, but I'm a psychologist, not a canine EMT. So I conducted a mini-experiment. I restored everything to as it had been. I took Nadine's bone from Jackson with only a minor protest (I outweighed him considerably) and gave it back to her. She very quickly became reabsorbed in its delights. I picked up Jackson's bone from the floor, the one he perceived to be of lesser value, and restored it to him on the sofa. Did Jackson now resign himself to the bone he'd been given?

Not by a long shot. Jackson paused for a while, then once again nosed his bone toward the edge of the sofa. Attentive to Jackson's movement, Nadine darted over to his bone before it fell, snatched it, and leapt to another chair, safe with her prize. She stole it right from under his nose. Or did she?

If I were not a psychologist, I might just have enjoyed the family pets, checked the status of my friends on Facebook, and picked up on my ruminations from before the incident—namely, whether I should go out and get a double-shot espresso skim-latte. But being a psychologist, I was faced with countless questions about Jackson and Nadine:

- When I gave them a biscuit after the fracas by the door, was I rewarding them for quieting down or for barking, or for doing both, in sequence? Which was more important—my behavior toward them or the biscuit? And what role do rewards serve? Do they work for both dogs and humans? Are rewards a mechanical way of changing behavior? Do they let dogs and people know when we are pleased with their behavior? Or is a biscuit sometimes just a biscuit?

- Was Jackson, weighing about 5 pounds and not a year old, with ridiculous ears that flopped over inside out, really capable

Queen Nadine   **Jackson**

of planning to distract Nadine so that he could retrieve her bone? Or was he, like the infant in the high chair who repeatedly drops food onto the floor with a giggle, more interested in observing the effects of pushing the bone onto the floor? Was his capture of Nadine's bone just a coincidence? And, after all, how can one know what a dog "thinks," if it thinks at all? Yet thinking, in humans, is a key topic in psychology—how we reflect on the past and the future, how we make plans, and how we regulate our behavior to achieve them.

- What were these quarreling animals anyhow? They were the same species as wolves, *Canis lupus,* yet they had been selectively bred for physical traits and for temperament over some 15,000 years to yield the silly results in my home. What were the origins of their possessive behavior? Of the warning growl? And what of our own history? Where do we humans come from? What of our own "Do not trespass" warnings? What of our willingness to share our last crumb with the less fortunate? We will see that our own history begins in Africa and that we can now trace our probable ancestry back more than 4 million years.

- What about the dogs' leaping ability, their visual–motor coordination when they saw a bone and went after it? They weren't born leaping or running or with sensorimotor coordination. How did these skills develop? Were they inborn, or did they require practice? How do humans "learn" to sit up or walk or talk? Which developments are shaped by the environment, and which are sort of built in, involving mainly the unfolding of our genetic heritage with nourishment and time?

- What about the animals' smell and taste preferences? Dog food smelled awful to me, yet they apparently liked it well enough—even though they would be happy to get the very occasional table treat. And did they prefer the treat because it smelled or tasted better or simply because it was novel? And what of our own preferences in smell and taste—a hot dog on the griddle, a chunk of chocolate, a sip of wine? (And why do both dogs and humans like some novelty?)

These questions are the province of psychology. **Question 1: What is psychology?**

● PSYCHOLOGY AS A SCIENCE

Psychology is the scientific study of behavior and mental processes. Topics of interest to psychologists include the nervous system, sensation and perception, learning and memory, intelligence, language, thought, growth and development, personality, stress and health, psychological disorders, ways of treating those disorders, sexual behavior, and the behavior of people in social settings such as groups and organizations.

Sciences have certain goals. **Question 2: What are the goals of psychology?** Psychology, like other sciences, seeks to describe, explain, predict, and control the events it studies. **Truth or Fiction Revisited:** Psychology thus seeks to describe, explain, predict, and control behavior and mental processes. Note that the goal of *controlling* behavior and mental processes doesn't mean that psychologists seek ways to make people do

Psychology The science that studies behavior and mental processes.

their bidding, like puppets on strings. Rather, psychologists seek to understand the factors that influence behavior and apply this knowledge for the public good—for example, to help individuals cope with problems such as anxiety and depression.

When possible, descriptive terms and concepts are interwoven into **theories.** Theories are formulations of apparent relationships among observed events. They allow us to derive explanations and predictions. Many psychological theories combine statements about behavior (such as eating or aggression), mental processes (such as attitudes and mental images), and biological processes. For instance, many of our responses to drugs such as alcohol and marijuana can be measured as overt behavior, and they are presumed to reflect the actions of these drugs and of our (mental) expectations about their effects.

A satisfactory psychological theory allows us to predict behavior. For instance, a theory of hunger should allow us to predict when people will or will not eat. If our observations cannot be adequately explained by, or predicted from, a given theory, we should consider revising or replacing it.

The remainder of this chapter presents an overview of psychology as a science. You will see that psychologists have diverse interests and fields of specialization. We discuss the history of psychology and the major perspectives from which today's psychologists view behavior. Finally, we consider the research methods psychologists use to study behavior and mental processes.

LearningConnections • PSYCHOLOGY AS A SCIENCE

ACTIVE REVIEW (1) Psychology is defined as the study of _____ and mental processes. (2) Psychology seeks to describe, explain, _____, and control behavior. (3) Behavior is explained through psychological _____, which are sets of statements that involve assumptions about behavior.

REFLECT AND RELATE How would you have defined psychology before you began this course?

CRITICAL THINKING What is the difference between the way scientists view the world and the way laypeople view the world?

 Go to Psychology CourseMate at **www.cengagebrain.com** for an interactive version of these questions.

● WHAT PSYCHOLOGISTS DO: SOMETHING FOR EVERYONE?

Psychologists share a keen interest in behavior, but in other ways, they may differ markedly. **Question 3: Just what do psychologists do?** Psychologists engage in research, practice, and teaching. Some researchers engage primarily in basic, or pure, research. **Pure research** is undertaken because the researcher is interested in the research topic. Pure research has no immediate application to personal or social problems and has therefore been characterized as research for its own sake. Others engage in **applied research**, which is designed to find solutions to specific personal or social problems. Although pure research is sparked by curiosity and the desire to know and understand, not by the desire to find a specific solution, today's pure research frequently enhances tomorrow's way of life. Pure research on learning and motivation in pigeons, rats, and monkeys done early in the 20th century has found applications in today's school systems. It has shown, for example, that learning often takes time, requires repetition, and profits from "booster shots" (that is, repetition even after the learning goal has been reached). Pure research into the workings of the nervous system has enhanced knowledge of disorders such as epilepsy, Parkinson's disease, and Alzheimer's disease.

Many psychologists do not conduct research. Instead, they *practice* psychology by applying psychological knowledge to help individuals change their behavior so that they can meet their own goals more effectively. However, many practitioners are involved in research into the effectiveness of various methods of therapy. They may also teach students who are learning to engage in clinical practice by discussing students' clinical experiences with them. Still other psychologists engage primarily in teaching. They share psychological knowledge in classrooms, seminars, and workshops. Psychologists may also engage in all three: research, practice, and teaching.

Theory A formulation of relationships underlying observed events.

Pure research Research conducted without concern for immediate applications.

Applied research Research conducted in an effort to find solutions to particular problems.

Fields of Psychology: From the Clinic to the Colosseum

Psychologists are found in a number of specialties. Although some psychologists wear more than one hat, most carry out their functions in one of the following fields.

Clinical psychologists help people with psychological disorders adjust to the demands of life. People's problems may range from anxiety and depression to sexual dysfunctions to loss of goals. Clinical psychologists evaluate these problems through interviews and psychological tests. They help their clients resolve their problems and change self-defeating behavior. Clinical psychologists are the largest subgroup of psychologists, comprising 54.8% of doctoral-level psychologists (American Psychological Association [APA], 2009a). The proportion of clinical psychologists is growing, as shown by the fact that they make up 62% of psychologists with new doctoral degrees (American Psychological Association, 2009a; see Table 1.1 ■). Doctoral-level psychologists typically have Ph.D. (doctor of philosophy) or Psy.D. (doctor of psychology) degrees. The Ph.D. generally requires somewhat more study of research methods and a doctoral dissertation that involves original research. The Psy.D. is generally more applied—requiring somewhat more supervised clinical experience and a dissertation that may be a review of the research literature in a given area of practice.

Counseling psychologists, like clinical psychologists, use interviews and tests to define their clients' problems. For example, clients may have trouble making academic or vocational decisions. They may experience marital or family conflict, have physical disabilities, or have adjustment problems such as those encountered by people who lose

TABLE 1.1 ■ New Doctorates in Psychology (Median Age = 32)

Demographic Factors	
Women	78.1%
Men	21.7%
Asian American/Pacific Islander	4.8%
African American	5.6%
Latin American	6.3%
Native American	<1.0%
European American	76.4%
Type of Degree	
Ph.D.	52.9%
Psy.D.	47.1%
Work Setting	
Academia	20.2%
Hospitals	19.6%
Other Human Service	16.0%
Independent Practice	13.7%
Business/Government	13.5%
Schools/Educational	7.8%
Managed Care	7.3%
Other	1.9%
Primary Work Activity	
Health Service	69.5%
Education	13.7%
Research	10.2%
Administration	4.1%
Other	3.5%
Selected Subfields	
Clinical Psychology	62.0%
Counseling Psychology	11.1%
School Psychology	9.5%
Clinical Child Psychology	6.4%
Other	10.7%

Source: Adapted from American Psychological Association (2009a). *Doctoral Psychology Workforce Fast Facts.* Health Service Provider Subfields. Center for Workforce Studies. http://research.apa.org/fastfacts-09.pdf. © Copyright 2009 APA Center for Workforce Studies. Washington, DC.

their jobs because of a recession. They help clients clarify their goals and draw upon their strengths and resources to take action on their problems. They counsel and do psychotherapy with individuals, couples and families, and organizations such as businesses, hospitals, and schools.

School psychologists are employed by school systems to identify and assist students who have problems that interfere with learning. Such problems range from social and family problems to emotional disturbances and learning disorders. They help schools make decisions about the placement of students in special classes.

Educational psychologists, like school psychologists, attempt to facilitate learning, but they usually focus on course planning and instructional methods for a school system rather than on individual children. Educational psychologists research issues such as how learning is affected by psychological factors such as motivation and intelligence, sociocultural factors such as poverty and acculturation, and teachers.

Developmental psychologists study the changes—physical, cognitive, social, and personality—that occur throughout the life span. They attempt to sort out the influences of heredity and the environment on development. Developmental psychologists conduct research on issues such as the effects of maternal use of drugs on an embryo, the outcomes of various patterns of child rearing, children's concepts of space and time, conflicts during adolescence, and problems of adjustment among older people.

Developmental Psychology Developmental psychologists study the changes that occur throughout the life span. They attempt to sort out the influences of heredity and the environment. Their concerns range from the effects of day care on infants to the adjustment issues of older people.

Personality psychologists focus on goals such as identifying and measuring human traits; determining influences on human thought processes, feelings, and behavior; and explaining psychological disorders. They are particularly concerned with issues such as anxiety, aggression, and gender roles.

Social psychologists are primarily concerned with the nature and causes of individuals' thoughts, feelings, and behavior in social situations. Whereas personality psychologists tend to look within the person for explanations of behavior, social psychologists tend to focus on interpersonal influences.

Environmental psychologists study the ways that people and the environment—the natural environment and the human-made environment—influence one another. For example, we know that extremes of temperature and loud noises interfere with learning in school. Some generations ago, people seemed to be at the mercy of the environment, but in recent years, we have gained the capacity to do significant harm to the environment. As a result, environmental psychologists study ways to encourage people to recycle and to preserve bastions of wilderness. We have learned that initial resistance to recycling, for example, usually gives way to cooperation as people come to accept it as the norm.

Psychologists in all specialties may conduct experiments. However, those called *experimental psychologists* specialize in basic processes such as the nervous system, sensation and perception, learning and memory, thought, motivation, and emotion. For example, experimental psychologists have studied what areas of the brain are involved in processing math problems or listening to music.

Industrial psychology and organizational psychology are related fields. *Industrial psychologists* focus on the relationships between people and work. *Organizational psychologists* study the behavior of people in organizations such as businesses. *Human factors psychologists* make technical systems such as automobile dashboards and computer keyboards more user-friendly. *Consumer psychologists* study the behavior of shoppers in an effort to predict and influence their behavior. They advise store managers how to lay out the aisles of a supermarket in ways that boost impulse buying, how to arrange window displays to attract customers, and how to make newspaper ads and TV commercials more persuasive.

Health psychologists study the effects of stress on health problems such as headaches, cardiovascular disease, and cancer. Health psychologists also guide clients toward healthier behavior patterns, such as exercising, quitting smoking, and making better food choices.

Javier Bardem in the Film *No Country for Old Men* Why are people so fascinated by crime, and by psychopaths such as the one played by Bardem? Forensic psychologists and personality psychologists investigate the personalities of criminals and also bring psychological expertise to hostage negotiations, threat assessment, the decision to use deadly force, and the interrogation of offenders and witnesses to crime.

Introspection Deliberate looking into one's own cognitive processes to examine one's thoughts and feelings and to gain self-knowledge.

Structuralism The school of psychology that argues the mind consists of three basic elements—sensations, feelings, and images—that combine to form experience.

Crime is popular—on TV shows and in films, if not in your neighborhood. Many *forensic psychologists* work with criminal justice agencies to apply psychological expertise to activities such as hostage negotiations, police assessment of threats, decision making as to the use of deadly force, and the interrogation of witnesses and offenders (Crighton & Towl, 2010). Since September 11, 2001, forensic psychologists have also turned their attention to the study of terrorism—trying to understand who terrorists are and how law enforcement agencies can prevent terrorist acts (DeAngelis, 2009; Horgan, 2009). They also engage in personality assessment of law enforcement agents and offenders and study deviant social groups such as sex offenders and gang members.

Sport psychologists help people improve their performance in sports. They help athletes concentrate on their performance and not on the crowd, use cognitive strategies such as positive visualization (imagining themselves making the right moves), and avoid choking under pressure (Jackson & Beauchamp, 2010; Wylleman, et al., 2009).

LearningConnections • WHAT PSYCHOLOGISTS DO: SOMETHING FOR EVERYONE?

ACTIVE REVIEW (4) Some psychologists engage in basic, or _____, research, which has no immediate applications. (5) Clinical psychologists help people resolve problems through _____. (6) _____ psychologists assist students with problems that interfere with learning. (7) _____ psychologists study the changes that occur throughout the life span. (8) _____ psychologists study the nature and causes of our thoughts, feelings, and behavior in social situations. (9) _____ psychologists conduct research into basic psychological processes, such as sensation and perception, learning and memory, and motivation and emotion.

REFLECT AND RELATE Think of a friend who either has experienced a problem or is experiencing one now. Would you advise him or her to see a psychologist? Why or why not?

CRITICAL THINKING What unites all the various fields of psychology?

 Go to Psychology CourseMate at **www.cengagebrain.com** for an interactive version of these questions.

WHERE PSYCHOLOGY COMES FROM: A HISTORY

Aristotle Aristotle argued that science could rationally treat only information that was gathered by the senses. He numbered the so-called five senses of vision, hearing, smell, taste, and touch. He pointed out that people differ from other living things in their capacity for rational thought. He explained how the imagination and dreams contained images based on experience. He outlined laws of *associationism* that have lain at the heart of learning theory for more than 2,000 years. Aristotle also declared that people are motivated to seek pleasure and avoid pain. This view remains as current today as it was in ancient Greece.

The ancient Greek philosopher Socrates advised "Know thyself." Psychology, which is in large part the endeavor to know ourselves, is as old as history and as modern as today. Knowledge of the history of psychology allows us to appreciate its theoretical conflicts, its place among the sciences, the evolution of its methods, and its social and political roles.

Question 4: Who were some of the ancient contributors to psychology? One of them is the ancient Greek philosopher Aristotle (384–322 BCE). **Truth or Fiction Revisited:** It is true that more than 2,000 years ago, Aristotle wrote a book on psychology with contents similar to the book you are now holding. In fact, the outline for this textbook could have been written by Aristotle. One of Aristotle's works, *Peri Psyches*, translates as "About the Psyche." Like this book, *Peri Psyches* begins with a history of psychological thought and historical perspectives on the nature of the mind and behavior. Aristotle argued first that human behavior, like the movements of the stars and the seas, is subject to rules and laws. Then he delved into his subject matter topic by topic: personality, sensation and perception, thought, intelligence, needs and motives, feelings and emotion, and memory. This book presents these topics in a different order, but each topic is here.

Other ancient Greek philosophers also contributed to psychology. Around 400 BCE, Democritus suggested that we could think of behavior in terms of a body and a mind. (Contemporary psychologists still talk about the interaction of biological and mental processes.) He pointed out that our behavior is influenced by external stimulation. Democritus was one of the first to raise the question of whether there is free will or choice. Putting it another way, where do the influences of others end and our "real selves" begin?

Truth or Fiction Revisited: It is true that Socrates suggested a research method that is still used in psychology. It is based on his advice to "Know thyself," which has remained a motto of psychology ever since. Socrates claimed that we could not attain reliable self-knowledge through our senses because the senses do not mirror reality exactly. Because the senses provide imperfect knowledge, Socrates suggested that we should rely on processes such as rational thought and **introspection**—careful examination of one's own thoughts and emotions—to gain self-knowledge. He also pointed out that people are social creatures who influence one another.

Had we room enough and time, we could trace psychology's roots to thinkers farther back in time than the ancient Greeks, and we could trace its development through the great thinkers of the Renaissance. As it is, we must move on to the development of psychology as a laboratory science during the second half of the 19th century. Some historians set the marker date at 1860. It was then that Gustav Theodor Fechner (1801–1887) published his landmark book *Elements of Psychophysics,* which showed how physical events (such as lights and sounds) are related to psychological sensation and perception. Fechner also showed how we can scientifically measure the effect of these events. Most historians set the debut of modern psychology as a laboratory science in the year 1879, when Wilhelm Wundt established the first psychological laboratory in Leipzig, Germany.

Structuralism: The Elements of Experience

The German psychologist Wilhelm Wundt (1832–1920) saw the mind as a natural event that could be studied scientifically, like light, heat, and the flow of blood. Wundt used introspection to try to discover the basic elements of experience. When presented with various sights and sounds, he and his colleagues tried to look inward as objectively as possible to describe their sensations and feelings.

Wundt and his students founded the school of psychology called *structuralism.* **Question 5: What is structuralism?** Structuralism attempted to break conscious experience down into *objective* sensations, such as sight or taste, and *subjective* feelings, such as emotional responses, and mental images like memories or dreams. Structuralists believed that the mind functions by combining objective and subjective elements of experience.

Truth or Fiction Revisited: In keeping with his theory of structuralism, Wundt became preoccupied with trying to analyze the experience of dying during a serious illness. He kept an extensive diary of his conscious experiences, breaking them down into objective sensations such as what he was seeing and smelling and into subjective feelings such as his depressive emotional responses, his will to live, and his memories of childhood and recent events, even his dreams. However, he recovered and went on to live a long life.

Functionalism: Making Psychology a Habit

Toward the end of the 19th century, psychologist William James (1842–1910) became a major figure in the development of psychology in the United States. He focused on the relation between conscious experience and behavior. He argued, for example, that the stream of consciousness is fluid and continuous. Introspection convinced him that experience cannot be broken down into objective sensations and subjective feelings as the structuralists maintained.

James was a founder of the school of **functionalism. Question 6: What is functionalism?** The school of functionalism focused on behavior in addition to the mind or consciousness. Functionalists looked at how our experience helps us function more adaptively in our environments—for example, how habits help us cope with common situations. (When eating with a spoon, we do not create an individual plan to bring each morsel of food to our mouths.) They also turned to the laboratory for direct observations as a way to supplement introspection. Structuralists tended to ask, "What are the pieces that make up thinking and experience?" In contrast, functionalists tended to ask, "How do behavior and mental processes help people adapt to the requirements of their lives?"

James was also influenced by Charles Darwin's (1809–1882) theory of evolution. Earlier in the 19th century, the British naturalist Darwin had argued that organisms with adaptive features—that is, the "fittest"—survive and reproduce. Functionalists adapted Darwin's theory and proposed that adaptive behavior patterns are learned and maintained. Maladaptive behavior patterns tend to drop out, and only the fittest behavior patterns survive. These adaptive actions tend to be repeated and become habits. James wrote that "habit is the enormous flywheel of society." Habit keeps the engine of civilization running.

Wilhelm Wundt German psychologist Wilhelm Wundt did poorly in school at first—his mind would wander—and he had to repeat a grade. Eventually, he attended medical school because he wanted to earn a good living. He did not like working with patients, however, and dedicated himself to philosophy and psychology.

"I wished, by treating Psychology like a natural science, to help her become one."

WILLIAM JAMES

William James James, brother of novelist Henry James, has been called the first true American psychologist. He came from a wealthy family, and his home was visited regularly by the likes of Ralph Waldo Emerson, Henry David Thoreau, Nathaniel Hawthorne, Alfred Lord Tennyson, and John Stuart Mill. He made his career teaching at Harvard and described his views in the first modern psychology textbook. James was also fascinated by religious experience and occult phenomena such as extrasensory perception.

Functionalism The school of psychology that emphasizes the uses or functions of the mind and behavior rather than just the elements of experience.

John B. Watson Perhaps his most renowned experiment was with "Little Albert," an infant who was conditioned by Watson and his student, Rosalie Rayner, to develop a fear of furry white animals (see Chapter 5). Watson later resigned his position at Johns Hopkins University and moved to New York, where he worked as a psychologist for the J. Walter Thompson advertising agency. He grew wealthy through successful ad campaigns for products such as Camel cigarettes, Johnson & Johnson Baby Powder, and Maxwell House Coffee. In his ad campaign for Maxwell House, he introduced the idea of the "coffee break."

Habits include such deceptively simple acts as how we lift a spoon or turn a door-knob. At first, these acts require our full attention. If you're in doubt, stand by with paper towels and watch a baby's first efforts at eating oatmeal by himself. Through repetition, the movements that make up self-feeding become automatic, or habitual. The multiple acts involved in learning to drive a car also become routine through repetition, so we can focus on other matters such as joking with a passenger and switching radio channels. (Many state legislatures have concluded, however, that it is too dangerous for drivers to use handheld phones.) This idea of learning by repetition is also basic to the behavioral tradition in psychology.

Behaviorism: Practicing Psychology in Public

Imagine you have placed a hungry rat in a maze. It meanders down a pathway that ends in a T. It can then turn left or right. If you consistently reward the rat with food for turning right at this point, it will learn to turn right when it arrives there, at least when it is hungry. But what does the rat *think* when it is learning to turn right? "Hmm, last time I was in this situation and turned to the right, I was given some Purina Rat Chow. Think I'll try that again"?

Does it seem absurd to try to place yourself in the "mind" of a rat? So it seemed to John Broadus Watson (1878–1958), the founder of American behaviorism. Watson was asked to consider the contents of a rat's "mind" as one of the requirements for his doctoral degree, which he received from the University of Chicago in 1903—a demand that dumbfounded him. Functionalism was the dominant view of psychology at the University of Chicago, and functionalists were concerned with the stream of consciousness as well as observable behavior. But Watson (1913) believed that if psychology was to be a natural science, like physics or chemistry, it must limit itself to observable, measurable events—that is, to behavior alone—hence the term *behaviorism*.

Question 7: What is behaviorism? Behaviorism is the school of psychology that focuses on the learning and effects of observable behavior. "Observable" does not only mean visible to the eye—as in activities such as pressing a lever, turning left or right, eating and mating, and dilation of the pupils of the eyes—but also includes behaviors that are observable by means of specialized instruments, such as heart rate, blood pressure, and emission of brain waves. Note that these behaviors are *public*. They can be measured by simple observation or by laboratory instruments, and different observers would agree about their existence and features. Given their focus on behavior, it should come as no surprise that behaviorists define psychology as the scientific study of *behavior*, not of *behavior and mental processes*.

Another major contributor to behaviorism was Harvard University psychologist B. F. Skinner (1904–1990). He believed that organisms learn to behave in certain ways because they have been **reinforced** for doing so—that is, their behavior has a positive outcome. He demonstrated that laboratory animals can be trained to carry out behaviors through strategic use of reinforcers such as food. He trained rats to turn in circles, climb ladders, and push toys across the floor. Because Skinner demonstrated that remarkable combinations of behaviors could be taught by means of reinforcement, many psychologists adopted the view that, in principle, one could explain complex human behavior in terms of thousands of instances of learning through reinforcement.

The Power of Reinforcement In the photo on the left, we see a feathered friend that has learned to drop shapes into their proper places through reinforcement. In the photo on the right, a raccoon shoots a basket. Behaviorists teach animals complex behaviors such as shooting baskets by first reinforcing approximations to the goal (or target behavior). As time progresses, closer approximations are demanded before reinforcement is given.

Gestalt Psychology: Making Psychology Whole

In the 1920s, another school of psychology—Gestalt psychology—was prominent in Germany. In the 1930s, the three founders of the school—Max Wertheimer (1880–1943),

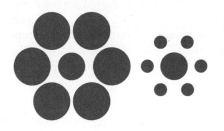

A. Are the dots in the center of the configurations the same size? Why not take a ruler and measure them?

B. Is the second symbol in each line the letter B or the number 13?

C. Which one of the gray squares is brighter?

Figure 1.1 ■ The Importance of Context Gestalt psychologists have shown that our perceptions depend not only on our sensory impressions but also on the context of our impressions. You will interpret a man running toward you very differently depending on whether you are on a deserted street at night or at a track in the morning.

Kurt Koffka (1886–1941), and Wolfgang Köhler (1887–1967)—left Europe to escape the Nazi threat. They carried on their work in the United States, giving further impetus to the growing American ascendance in psychology.

Question 8: What is Gestalt psychology? Gestalt psychologists focused on perception and on how perception influences thinking and problem solving. The German word *gestalt* translates roughly to "pattern" or "organized whole." In contrast to behaviorists, Gestalt psychologists argued that we cannot hope to understand human nature by focusing only on overt behavior. In contrast to structuralists, they claimed that we cannot explain human perceptions, emotions, or thought processes in terms of basic units. Perceptions are *more* than the sums of their parts: Gestalt psychologists saw our perceptions as wholes that give meaning to parts, as we see in Figure 1.1 ■.

Gestalt psychologists illustrated how we tend to perceive separate pieces of information as integrated wholes depending on the contexts in which they occur. In part A of Figure 1.1 the dots in the centers of the configurations are the same size, yet we may perceive them as being of different sizes because of what surrounds them. The second symbol in each line in part B is identical, but in the top row we may perceive it as a B and in the bottom row as the number 13. The symbol has not changed, but the context in which it appears has. The inner squares in part C are equally bright, but they do not appear so because of their contrasting backgrounds. There are many examples of this in literature and everyday life. In *The Prince and the Pauper,* Mark Twain dressed a peasant boy as a prince, and the kingdom bowed to him. Do clothes sometimes make the man or woman? Try wearing cutoffs for a job interview!

Gestalt psychologists believed that learning could be active and purposeful, not merely responsive and mechanical as in Watson's and Skinner's experiments. They demonstrated that much learning, especially in problem solving, is accomplished by **insight**, not by mechanical repetition, as we see in the following classic experiment that took place early in the last century.

Have you ever pondered a problem for quite a while and then, suddenly, seen the solution? Did the solution seem to come out of nowhere? In a "flash"? Wolfgang Köhler was marooned during World War I on one of the Canary Islands, where the Prussian Academy of Science kept a colony of apes, and his research while there gave him, well, insight into the process of learning by insight. Consider Köhler's research with chimpanzees, as shown in Figure 1.2 ■. At first the chimp is unsuccessful in reaching bananas suspended from the ceiling. Then it suddenly stacks the boxes and climbs up to reach the bananas. It seems the chimp has experienced a sudden reorganization of the mental elements of the problem—that is, it has had a "flash of insight." Köhler's findings suggest that we often manipulate the elements of problems until we group them in such a way that we believe we will be able to reach a goal. The manipulations may take quite some time as mental trial and error proceeds. Once the proper grouping has been found, however, we seem to perceive it all at once as a clear pattern, or whole.

Psychoanalysis: Digging Beneath the Surface

Psychoanalysis, the school of psychology founded by Sigmund Freud (1856–1939), differs from the other schools in both background and approach. Freud's theory has

Behaviorism The school of psychology that defines psychology as the study of observable behavior and studies relationships between stimuli and responses.

Reinforcement A stimulus that follows a response and increases the frequency of the response.

Gestalt psychology The school of psychology that emphasizes the tendency to organize perceptions into wholes and to integrate separate stimuli into meaningful patterns.

Insight In Gestalt psychology, the sudden reorganization of perceptions, allowing the sudden solution of a problem.

School/Major Proponent(s)	Key Concepts	Current Status

Structuralism
Wilhelm Wundt

Wilhelm Wundt
© Archives of the History of American Psychology, The Center for the History of Psychology—The University of Akron

The mind can be studied scientifically by using introspection to discover the basic elements of experience. Conscious experience can be broken down into objective sensations such as sight or taste and subjective feelings such as emotional responses, will, and mental images like memories or dreams.

We do not encounter structuralists today, but cognitive and experimental psychologists study related topics such as sensation and perception, emotion, memory, and states of consciousness (including dreams).

Functionalism
William James

William James
© Archives of the History of American Psychology, The Center for the History of Psychology—The University of Akron

There is a relationship between consciousness and behavior. Consciousness flows streamlike. Experience cannot be broken down into objective sensations and subjective feelings. Functionalists focused on how experience helps us function more adaptively in our environments.

We do not have pure functionalists today, but functionalism preceded behaviorism in its interest in how habits are formed by experience and help us adapt. Behavior is seen as evolving: Adaptive behavior is maintained, whereas maladaptive behavior tends to drop out.

Behaviorism
John B. Watson, B. F. Skinner

John B. Watson
© Archives of the History of American Psychology, The Center for the History of Psychology—The University of Akron

B. F. Skinner
© Christopher Johnson/Stock Boston, Inc.

Psychology must limit itself to observable, measurable events—to behavior, not mental processes. Organisms learn to behave in certain ways because of the effects of their behavior.

Some "pure" behaviorists remain, but behaviorism more generally has contributed to experimental psychology, the psychology of learning, and methods of therapy (behavior therapy). Although many contemporary psychologists argue that it is desirable to study consciousness and mental processes, the behaviorist influence has encouraged them to base many of their conclusions on measurable behaviors.

Gestalt Psychology
Max Wertheimer, Kurt Koffka, Wolfgang Köhler

A. Are the dots in the center of the configurations the same size? Why not take a ruler and measure them?

Gestalt psychologists focused on perception, thinking, and problem solving. Whereas structuralists tried to isolate basic elements of experience, Gestalt psychologists focused on the tendency to see perceptions as wholes that give meaning to parts.

Gestalt principles continue to be studied in the field of sensation and perception. Other Gestalt ideas, such as those involving thinking and problem solving, continue to be studied by cognitive psychologists and experimental psychologists. Gestalt therapy—which aims to help people integrate conflicting parts of their personalities—remains in use.

Psychoanalysis
Sigmund Freud, Carl Jung, Alfred Adler, Karen Horney, Erik Erikson

Sigmund Freud
© Bettmann/Corbis

Karen Horney
© Bettmann/Corbis

Erik Erikson
© UPI/Bettmann/Corbis

Visible behavior and conscious thinking are influenced by unconscious ideas and conflicts. People are motivated to gratify primitive sexual and aggressive impulses, even if they are unaware of their true motives. Unconscious processes are more influential than conscious thought in determining human behavior.

Psychoanalytic thinking remains quite alive in the popular culture. Among psychologists, many discount psychoanalysis altogether because many of its concepts cannot be studied by scientific means. Modern psychoanalytic therapists tend to place more emphasis on the roles of conscious motives, conscious thinking, and decision making.

Figure 1.2 ■ Some Insight into Insight
At first, the chimpanzee cannot reach the bananas hanging from the ceiling. After some time has passed, it has an apparent "flash of insight" and piles the boxes on top of one another to reach the fruit.

invaded popular culture, and you may be familiar with a number of its concepts. For example, perhaps a friend has tried to "interpret" a slip of the tongue you made or has asked what you thought might be the meaning of an especially vivid dream.

Question 9: What is psychoanalysis? Psychoanalysis is the name given to the theory of personality and to the method of therapy originated by Sigmund Freud. As a theory of personality, psychoanalysis was based on the idea that much of our lives are governed by unconscious ideas and impulses that have their origins in childhood conflicts. As a method of psychotherapy, psychoanalysis aims to help patients gain insight into their conflicts and to find socially acceptable ways of expressing wishes and gratifying needs. We'll discuss psychoanalysis in more depth in Chapter 10.

LearningConnections • WHERE PSYCHOLOGY COMES FROM: A HISTORY

ACTIVE REVIEW The Greek philosopher (10) _____ was among the first to argue that human behavior is subject to rules and laws. (11) _____ founded the school of structuralism. (12) William James founded the school of _____, which dealt with behavior as well as conscious experience. (13) _____ founded the school of behaviorism. (14) _____ psychologists saw our perceptions as wholes that give meaning to parts. (15) _____ founded the school of psychoanalysis.

REFLECT AND RELATE Psychologist William James visited Helen Keller as a child and brought her an ostrich feather. If

you had been Helen Keller, would you have appreciated this gift? Explain.

CRITICAL THINKING Do you believe that the richness and complexity of human behavior can be explained as the summation of so many instances of learning? Explain.

 Go to Psychology CourseMate at **www.cengagebrain.com** for an interactive version of these questions.

● HOW TODAY'S PSYCHOLOGISTS VIEW BEHAVIOR AND MENTAL PROCESSES

Today we no longer find psychologists who describe themselves as structuralists or functionalists. And although the school of Gestalt psychology gave birth to current research approaches in perception and problem solving, few would consider themselves Gestalt psychologists. On the other hand, we do find Gestalt therapists who focus on helping clients integrate conflicting parts of their personality (making themselves "whole"). The numbers of orthodox behaviorists and psychoanalysts have been declining (Robins et al., 1999). Many contemporary psychologists in the behaviorist tradition look on themselves as *social-cognitive theorists,* and many psychoanalysts consider themselves *neoanalysts* rather than traditional Freudians.

The history of psychological thought has taken many turns, and contemporary psychologists differ in their approaches. Today, there are several broad, influential

Psychoanalysis The school of psychology that asserts that much of our behavior and mental processes is governed by unconscious ideas and impulses that have their origins in childhood conflicts

perspectives in psychology: the evolutionary, biological, cognitive, humanistic–existential, psychodynamic, learning, and sociocultural perspectives. Each emphasizes different topics of investigation. Each approaches topics in its own ways.

The Evolutionary and Biological Perspectives: It's Only Natural

Psychologists are interested in the roles of evolution and heredity in behavior and mental processes such as psychological disorders, criminal behavior, and thinking. Generally speaking, our heredity provides a broad range of behavioral and mental possibilities. Environmental factors interact with inherited factors to determine specific behavior and mental processes. **Question 10: What is the evolutionary perspective?**

The **evolutionary perspective** focuses on the evolution of behavior and mental processes as created in the cauldron of natural selection. Charles Darwin argued that in the age-old struggle for existence, only the fittest (most adaptive) organisms manage to reach maturity and reproduce. For example, fish that swim faster or people who are naturally immune to certain diseases are more likely to survive and transmit their genes to future generations. Individuals die, but species tend to evolve in adaptive directions. Evolutionary psychologists suggest that much human social behavior, such as aggressive behavior and mate selection, has a hereditary basis. People may be influenced by social rules, cultural factors, and even personal choice, but evolutionary psychologists believe that inherited tendencies sort of whisper in people's ears and tend to move them in certain directions.

When we ask the question "What evolves?" the answer is biological processes and structures. These processes and structures may give rise to ideas and behaviors, but it is not believed that ideas and behavior exist in the absence of biological substance. Psychologists assume that thoughts, fantasies, and dreams—and the inborn, or **instinctive**, behavior patterns of various species—are made possible by the nervous system and especially by the brain. **Question 11: What is the biological perspective?**

Psychologists with a **biological perspective** seek the links between the electrical and chemical activity of the brain, the chemical activity of hormones, and heredity, on the one hand, and behavior and mental processes, on the other. They use techniques such as computerized axial tomography (CAT) scans and functional magnetic resonance imaging (fMRI) that show which parts of the brain are involved in such activities as language, mathematical problem solving, and music (Goghari & MacDonald, 2009; Henseler et al., 2009). For example, fMRI can show how the blood flow in the brain changes as we are thinking. We have learned how natural chemical substances in the brain are involved in the formation of memories. Experiments have shown that in some animals, electrical stimulation of parts of the brain prompts the expression of "prewired," or inborn, sexual and aggressive behaviors.

Biological psychologists are also concerned with the influences of the endocrine system on behavior and mental processes. The endocrine system consists of glands that secrete hormones and release them into the bloodstream. In people, for instance, the hormone prolactin stimulates production of milk. But in many species, such as rats, prolactin also gives rise to maternal behavior (Numan & Stolzenberg, 2009). In many animals, sex hormones determine whether mating behavior will follow stereotypical masculine or feminine behavior patterns. In humans, sex hormones regulate the menstrual cycle and are also connected with feelings of psychological well-being.

The biological perspective tends to focus on events that occur below the level of consciousness. The cognitive perspective, on the other hand, is the essence of consciousness. **Question 12: What is the cognitive perspective?**

The Cognitive Perspective: Keeping Psychology "in Mind"

Psychologists with a **cognitive perspective** venture into the realm of mental processes to understand human nature. They investigate the ways we perceive and mentally represent the world, how we learn, remember the past, plan for the future, solve problems, form judgments, make decisions, and use language. Cognitive psychologists, in short, study those things we refer to as the *mind*.

The cognitive tradition has roots in Socrates' advice to "Know thyself" and in his suggested method of introspection. We also find cognitive psychology's roots in

Evolutionary perspective The view that our behavior and mental processes have been shaped, at least in part, by natural selection as our ancestors strived to meet prehistoric and historic challenges.

Instinctive An inborn pattern of behavior that is triggered by a particular stimulus.

Biological perspective The approach to psychology that seeks to understand the nature of the links between biological processes and structures such as the functioning of the brain, the endocrine system, and heredity, on the one hand, and behavior and mental processes, on the other.

Cognitive perspective The approach to psychology that focuses on the nature of consciousness and on mental processes such as sensation and perception, memory, problem solving, decision making, judgment, language, and intelligence.

structuralism, functionalism, and Gestalt psychology, each of which, in its own way, addressed issues that are of interest to cognitive psychologists. In general, cognitive science has experienced a rapid expansion in the past couple of decades and continues to attract interest and inspire research.

The Humanistic–Existential Perspective: The Search for Meaning

The humanistic–existential perspective is cognitive in flavor, yet it emphasizes the role of subjective (personal) experience. **Question 13: What is the humanistic–existential perspective?** Let's consider each of the parts of this perspective: *humanism* and *existentialism*. **Humanism** stresses the human capacity for self-fulfillment and the central roles of consciousness, self-awareness, and decision making. Humanistic psychology considers personal, or subjective, experience to be the most important event in psychology. Humanists believe that self-awareness, experience, and choice permit us, to a large extent, to "invent ourselves" and our ways of relating to the world as we progress through life. **Existentialism** views people as free to choose and be responsible for choosing ethical conduct. Humanistic–existential psychologists stress the importance of subjective experience and assert that people have the freedom to make choices. Consciousness—our sense of being in the world—is seen as the force that unifies our personalities. Grounded in the work of Carl Rogers (1951) and Abraham Maslow (1970), the humanistic perspective continues to find many contemporary adherents (Elkins, 2009).

The Psychodynamic Perspective: Still Digging

In the 1940s and 1950s, psychodynamic theory dominated the practice of psychotherapy and was influential in scientific psychology and the arts. Most psychotherapists were psychodynamically oriented. Many renowned artists and writers consulted psychodynamic therapists as a way to liberate the expression of their unconscious ideas. Today Freud's influence continues to be felt, although it no longer dominates methods of psychotherapy.

Question 14: What is the role of psychoanalysis today? Contemporary psychologists who follow theories derived from Freud are likely to call themselves *neoanalysts*. Famous neoanalysts such as Karen Horney (1885–1952) and Erik Erikson (1902–1994) focused less on unconscious processes and more on conscious choice and self-direction.

We should also note that many Freudian ideas are retained in some form by the population at large. For example, we occasionally have ideas or desires that seem unusual for us. We may even say that it sometimes seems as if an unconscious idea or impulse is trying to get the better of us. Followers of Freud tend to attribute dreams and unusual ideas or desires to unconscious processes, and dreams are commonly viewed this way in popular culture.

Perspectives on Learning: From the Behavioral to the Cognitive

Many contemporary psychologists study the effects of experience on behavior. Learning, to them, is the essential factor in describing, explaining, predicting, and controlling behavior. The term *learning* has different meanings to psychologists of different persuasions, however. Some students of learning find roles for consciousness and insight. Others do not. This distinction is found today among those who adhere to the behavioral and social-cognitive perspectives. **Question 15: What are the two major perspectives on learning?**

For the founder of American behaviorism, John B. Watson, behaviorism was an approach to life as well as a broad guideline for psychological research. Not only did Watson despair of measuring consciousness and mental processes in the laboratory, but he also applied behavioral analysis to virtually all situations in his daily life. He viewed people as doing things because of their learning histories, their situations, and rewards rather than because of conscious choice.

Humanism The philosophy and school of psychology that asserts that people are conscious, self-aware, and capable of free choice, self-fulfillment, and ethical behavior.

Existentialism The view that people are free and responsible for their own behavior.

Like Watson, contemporary behaviorists emphasize environmental influences and the learning of habits through repetition and reinforcement. Modern **social-cognitive theorists** (once termed *social-learning theorists*), in contrast, suggest that people can modify or even create their environments. They also grant **cognition** a key role. They note that people engage in intentional learning by observing others. Since the 1960s, social-cognitive theorists have gained influence in the areas of personality development, psychological disorders, and psychotherapy.

The Sociocultural Perspective: How Do You Complete the Sentence "I Am . . ."?

© David Buffington/Getty Images

The profession of psychology focuses mainly on the individual and is committed to the dignity of the individual. However, many psychologists believe we cannot understand people's behavior and mental processes without reference to their diversity (Alarcón et al., 2009). Studying perspectives other than their own helps psychologists understand the role of a culture's beliefs, values, and attitudes in behavior and mental processes. It helps them perceive why people from diverse cultures behave and think in different ways and how the science of psychology is enriched by addressing those differences (Denmark, 1998; Le et al., 2009).

Question 16: What is the sociocultural perspective? The **sociocultural perspective** addresses many of the ways that people differ from one another. It studies the influences of ethnicity, gender, culture, and socioeconomic status on behavior and mental processes (Sanchez et al., 2009; Vodosek, 2009). For example, what is often seen as healthful, self-assertive, outspoken behavior by most U.S. women may be interpreted as brazen behavior in Latin American or Asian American communities.

ETHNICITY One kind of diversity involves people's ethnicity. Members of an **ethnic group** are united by their cultural heritage, race, language, and common history. The experiences of various ethnic groups in the United States highlight the impact of social, political, and economic factors on human behavior and development (Phinney & Ong, 2007).

The probing of human diversity enables students to appreciate the cultural heritages and historical problems of ethnic groups. This textbook considers many psychological issues related to ethnicity, such as the representation of ethnic minority groups in psychological research studies, substance abuse among adolescents from various ethnic minority groups, bilingualism, and ethnic differences in intelligence test scores. We also look into the prevalence of suicide among members of different ethnic groups, ethnic differences in vulnerability to physical problems and disorders ranging from obesity to cancer, multicultural issues in the practice of psychotherapy, and prejudice.

GENDER Gender refers to the culturally defined concepts of *masculinity* and *femininity*. Gender is not fully defined by anatomical sex. It involves a complex web of cultural expectations and social roles that affect people's self-concepts and hopes and dreams as well as their behavior. How can sciences such as psychology and medicine hope to promote the welfare of the individual if they accept traditional gender roles that limit opportunities for women? Although the times are changing, throughout the last century, most research was conducted on men and by men. For such reasons, more information has been obtained on the health of men, and so-called masculine behavior has frequently been seen as the norm (Dart et al., 2006).

Just as members of ethnic minority groups have experienced prejudice, so too have gays and lesbians. Even much of the scientific research on gender roles and gender differences assumes that the behavior and attitudes of heterosexuals represent the norm (Lee & Crawford, 2007).

Our discussion of the sociocultural perspective naturally leads us to reflect—in the following section—on the roles of women and people from various racial and ethnic backgrounds in psychology.

Social-cognitive theory A school of psychology in the behaviorist tradition that includes cognitive factors in the explanation and prediction of behavior; formerly termed social-learning theory.

Cognition The use of mental processes to perceive and mentally represent the world, think, and engage in problem solving and decision making.

Sociocultural perspective The view that focuses on the roles of ethnicity, gender, culture, and socioeconomic status in behavior and mental processes.

Ethnic group A group characterized by common features such as cultural heritage, history, race, and language.

Gender The culturally defined concepts of masculinity and femininity.

ACTIVE REVIEW (16) _____ psychologists note that only the fittest organisms reach maturity and reproduce, thereby transmitting their genes to future generations and causing species to evolve in adaptive directions. (17) _____ psychologists study the ways that we perceive and mentally represent the world. (18) Humanistic–_____ psychologists stress the importance of self-awareness and people's freedom to make choices. (19) _____ cognitive theorists are in the behaviorist tradition but also find roles for intentional learning and note that people can create or modify their environments.

REFLECT AND RELATE Which contemporary perspective on human behavior has the most personal appeal to you? Why?

CRITICAL THINKING Many psychologists argue that Freud's views have not been supported by research evidence and are thus of no more than historical interest and should not be emphasized in psychology textbooks. Some psychologists would even exclude Freud from a scientific textbook. What do you think?

 Go to Psychology CourseMate at **www.cengagebrain.com** for an interactive version of these questions.

GENDER, ETHNICITY, AND PSYCHOLOGY: REAL PEOPLE IN THE REAL WORLD

It's all about access. **Question 17: How have access to education and the field of psychology historically influenced the participation of women and people from various ethnic and racial backgrounds?** Until the 20th century, women and people of color were systematically excluded from most institutions of higher learning. Thus, it is not surprising that the overwhelming majority of psychologists in the 1800s and early 1900s were European and European American males. Nevertheless, a few pioneering women and individuals from various racial and ethnic backgrounds were able to open the door to an education and to the field of psychology.

© Archives of the History of American Psychology, The Center for the History of Psychology—The University of Akron

Mary Whiton Calkins At a time when men dominated the discipline of psychology, Calkins was one of the pioneers who fought the male-centered bias and encouraged psychology to incorporate the values of the "new woman" (D. Rogers, 2009). She pioneered research in memory at Wellesley College, where she founded a psychology laboratory in 1891. She introduced the method of paired associates, discovered the primacy and recency effects, and engaged in research into the role of the frequency of repetition in the vividness of memories.

Women in Psychology: Opening the Floodgates

Although American women have attended college only since 1833, when Oberlin College opened its doors to women, most American college students today are in fact women. **Truth or Fiction Revisited:** Women now receive the majority of undergraduate degrees in psychology and, as shown previously in Table 1.1 (refer to page 6), some 78% of the doctoral degrees (American Psychological Association, 2009a).

Mary Whiton Calkins (1863–1930), the first female president of the American Psychological Association, "just said no." She had completed all the requirements for the Ph.D., but she believed that accepting the degree would endorse prejudice against women. So she turned it down. Calkins studied psychology at Harvard University. However, she had to attend Harvard as a "guest student" because Harvard was not yet admitting women. It did not matter that William James considered Calkins to be his brightest student. When she completed her degree requirements, Harvard would not award her the degree because of her gender. Instead, Harvard offered to grant her a doctorate from its sister school, Radcliffe. She declined the offer. **Truth or Fiction Revisited:** It is therefore true that the woman who became the first female president of the American Psychological Association turned down the doctoral degree that had been offered to her.

Christine Ladd-Franklin (1847–1930), like Calkins, was born during an era in American history when women were expected to remain in the home and were excluded from careers in science. She nevertheless pursued a career in psychology, taught at Johns Hopkins and Columbia Universities, and formulated a theory of color vision.

Margaret Floy Washburn (1871–1939) was the first woman to receive a Ph.D. in psychology. Washburn wrote *The Animal Mind*, a work containing many ideas that

Kenneth Bancroft Clark and Mamie Phipps Clark Kenneth and Mamie Clark are among the best-known African American psychologists. Kenneth earned his bachelor's degree from Howard University, where he met and married Mamie Phipps. Although Mamie was the daughter of a physician, she had attended a segregated school in her hometown in Arkansas and was compelled to use public facilities labeled for "coloreds only." The couple earned their doctorates in psychology at Columbia University, where Kenneth was the first African American to do so.

Which Dolls Did They Prefer, and Why? In one study by Kenneth Clark and Mamie Phipps Clark, African American children were shown white and brown dolls and asked to "Give me the pretty doll" or "Give me the doll that looks bad." Most children's choices showed that they preferred the white dolls over the brown ones. Studies like these convinced the Supreme Court that "separate but equal" schools were not in fact equal at all.

would later become part of behaviorism. Helen Bradford Thompson (1874–1947) was the first psychologist to study psychological gender differences. Her 1903 book *The Mental Traits of Sex* analyzed the performance of 25 women and 25 men on tests of intellect, emotional response, and sensation and perception. Thompson was ahead of her time in her conclusion that gender differences in these areas appeared to be strongly influenced by the social environment from infancy through adulthood.

In more recent years, Mary Salter Ainsworth (1913–1999) revolutionized our understanding of attachment between parents and children by means of her cross-cultural studies and her innovation of the Strange Situation method (see Chapter 9). Elizabeth Loftus (e.g., Laney & Loftus, 2009) has shown that our memories are not snapshots of the past. Instead, they often consist of something old (what actually happened), something new (that is, influenced by more recent events), something borrowed (for example, further shaped by our biases and prejudices), and something blue (altered by tinges of color or emotion).

Susan Nolen-Hoeksema (e.g., Nolen-Hoeksema & Hilt, 2009) is contributing to our understanding of the ways in which self-destructive ruminating (that is, going back and forth repeatedly over the same issues) prevents us from making decisions and heightens feelings of depression (see Chapter 12). The number of women making such contributions today is truly countless.

Ethnicity and Psychology

Like women, individuals from certain ethnic and racial groups have struggled for recognition in psychology. Back in 1901, Gilbert Haven Jones was the first African American to receive a Ph.D. in psychology, but he had to do so in Germany. J. Henry Alston engaged in research on perception of heat and cold and was the first African American psychologist to be published in a major psychology journal (the year was 1920).

In the 1940s, Kenneth Bancroft Clark (1914–2005) and Mamie Phipps Clark (1917–1983) conducted research that showed the negative effects of school segregation on African American children. The Clarks concluded that the children had swallowed the larger society's prejudiced views that favored European Americans. Clark's research was cited by the Supreme Court in 1954 when it overturned the "separate but equal" schools doctrine that had allowed inequalities in school services for various ethnic groups.

Today African Americans continue to have a powerful impact on the profession of psychology. For example, psychologist Claude Steele (e.g., Purdie-Vaughns et al., 2008) has shown that many African Americans sabotage their own performance on intelligence tests because of *stereotype threat*. That is, rather than focus on the test items, they worry about the stereotype, or widespread belief, that African Americans are not as intelligent as European Americans. As a result of this anxiety, they hurt their own performance. According to Steele, this phenomenon can apply to any negatively stereotyped group.

Two other African American psychologists who have greatly influenced their profession are Nancy Boyd-Franklin and Tony Strickland. Boyd-Franklin (e.g., Boyd-Franklin & Lockwood, 2009) is on the faculty at Rutgers University and studies group and family therapy with African Americans. Strickland (e.g., Strickland, 2007) studies the effects of psychoactive drugs on individuals with and without psychological disorders. He has discovered that people from different ethnic groups may respond to drugs in different ways.

Latin American and Asian American psychologists have also made their mark. Jorge Sanchez was among the first to show how intelligence tests are culturally biased to the disadvantage of Mexican American children. Latina American psychologist Lillian Comas-Diaz (e.g., 2008) has edited a journal on multicultural mental health. Latina American psychologist Martha E. Bernal (1932–2002) studied the development of ethnic identity among Mexican American children. Asian American psychologist Stanley Sue (e.g., Sue & Zane, 2009) directed the National Research Center on Asian American Mental Health in Los Angeles and has shown that discrimination may be connected with racial differences in intelligence and achievement (see Chapter 7). Asian American psychologist Richard M. Suinn (e.g., 2001) studies mental health and the development of identity among Asians and Asian Americans.

The contributions of women and members of diverse ethnic and racial groups have broadened our understanding of the influences of gender and ethnicity on behavior and mental processes. They have taught us that what is true for men may not always be true for women (that is, what is sauce for the goose may not always be sauce for the gander). What is true for European Americans may not be true for Americans from other backgrounds. The presence of women and individuals from diverse ethnic backgrounds has given us the grand mosaic that is psychology today.

Like other scientists, psychologists rely on research to find answers to the questions that interest them. We explore methods of research in the following section.

LearningConnections • GENDER, ETHNICITY, AND PSYCHOLOGY: REAL PEOPLE IN THE REAL WORLD

ACTIVE REVIEW (20) _____ introduced the method of paired associates and discovered the primacy and recency effects. (21) Kenneth B. _____ influenced a key U.S. Supreme Court decision on desegregation in the schools.

REFLECT AND RELATE Consider your own gender and ethnic background. What would it have been like for you to try to study psychology in the United States a century ago?

CRITICAL THINKING Women now receive the majority of undergraduate and graduate degrees in psychology. Review the fields in psychology and speculate as to why this may be so.

 Go to Psychology CourseMate at **www.cengagebrain.com** for an interactive version of these questions.

CRITICAL THINKING: SORTING TRUTH FROM FICTION

Checking out at the supermarket, I see the usual tabloid headlines. The tabloids claim that extraterrestrials regularly kidnap us Earthlings. The aliens prod and poke us to figure out how we work—or don't work. What do we know about people who claim to have been abducted by aliens? How can we sort truth from fiction and decide whether we will believe the "kidnap victims"?

Psychologists who have studied reported alien kidnappings conclude that the kidnappings never occurred. **Truth or Fiction Revisited:** However, the people making the claims are not necessarily mentally ill, nor are they even lying (Clancy et al., 2002). By and large, these are people who have "remembered" their "experiences" while undergoing therapy, often under hypnosis. Tales of alien abduction are widely known throughout our culture, so it is not at all surprising that the "memories" of kidnap victims would tend to coincide (Meyersburg et al., 2009; Swami et al., 2009).

"Abductees" generally claim that they are awakened in their sleep by the aliens and unable to move. Psychologists know that many of our voluntary muscles—the ones involved in movement—are "paralyzed" when we sleep, which is why we usually don't thrash about when we dream (Clancy, 2008; Forrest, 2008). *Hallucinations*—that is, seeing and hearing things that are not really there—are quite common as we are waking from a sleep-paralyzed state, and it seems that the reported experiences of abductees fit the pattern.

Psychologists also know that people are quite open to suggestion (Bernstein & Loftus, 2009; Clark & Loftus, 1996). Memories are not perfect snapshots. When trial witnesses are asked leading questions—that is, questions that might encourage them to recall events in a certain way—the opposing attorney will usually object ("Leading the witness, your Honor"). Sometimes, the person interviewing the supposed kidnap victim asks leading questions, looking for experiences with aliens.

All in all, "UFO memories may be constructed from bits and pieces of sleep-related hallucinations, nightmares, and media attention and fixed solidly into place with the suggestion of hypnosis and the validation of support groups" (Clark & Loftus, 1996, p. 294). Abductees may also be trying to escape, temporarily, from their humdrum lives—like the buyers of supermarket tabloids (Clancy et al., 2002).

© Tim Boyle/Bloomberg via Getty Images

Typical Tabloids Found at Supermarket Checkout Counters Each week, there are 10 new sightings of Elvis and extraterrestrials. There are 10 new "absolutely proven" ways to take off weight and 10 new ways to conquer stress and depression. There are 10 new ways to tell if your partner has been cheating and, of course, 10 new predictions by astrologers and psychics. Should we believe them? How can we know?

Astronomer Carl Sagan (2005) noted that the evidence in favor of abduction is almost entirely anecdotal.

> Someone says something happened to them. . . . The fact that someone says something doesn't mean it's true. . . .To be taken seriously, you need physical evidence that can be examined at leisure by skeptical scientists: a scraping of the . . . ship, and the discovery that it contains [chemicals] that aren't present on Earth, . . . Or material of absolutely bizarre properties of many sorts. . . . There are many things like that that would instantly give serious credence to an account. But there [are] no scrapings, no interior photographs, no filched page from the captain's log book.

In sum, when we think critically about the stories in the supermarket tabloids, we usually find that they fall short of any reasonable requirements of evidence. In this section, we will see how scientists, as in the case of so-called alien abductions, sort out truth from fiction. Scientists, including psychologists, begin with an attitude of skepticism—a hallmark of **critical thinking**.

Question 18: What is critical thinking? Critical thinking has many meanings. On one level, it means taking nothing for granted—not believing things just because they are in print or because they were uttered by authority figures or celebrities. On another level, critical thinking refers to a process of thoughtfully analyzing and probing the questions, statements, and arguments of others. It means examining definitions of terms, examining the premises or assumptions behind arguments, and then scrutinizing the logic with which arguments are developed.

Principles of Critical Thinking

Let's consider some principles of critical thinking that can help you in college and beyond (Halpern, 2007; Sternberg, 2007):

1. *Be skeptical:* Keep an open mind. Politicians and advertisers try to persuade you. Even research reported in the media or in textbooks may take a certain slant. Extend this principle to yourself. Are some of your own attitudes and beliefs superficial or unfounded? Accept nothing as the truth until you have examined the evidence.

2. *Examine definitions of terms:* Some statements are true when a term is defined in one way but not when it is defined in another. Consider the statement "Head Start programs have raised children's IQs." The correctness of the statement depends on the definition of IQ. (You will see later in the text that *IQ* has a specific meaning and is not exactly the same as *intelligence*.)

3. *Examine the assumptions or premises of arguments:* Consider the statement that one cannot learn about human beings by engaging in research with animals. One premise in the statement seems to be that human beings are not animals. We are, of course. (Would you rather be a plant?)

4. *Be cautious in drawing conclusions from evidence:* For many years, studies had shown that most clients who receive psychotherapy improve. It was therefore generally assumed that psychotherapy worked. Some 40 years ago, however, psychologist Hans Eysenck pointed out that most psychologically troubled people who did *not* receive psychotherapy also improved. The question thus becomes whether people receiving psychotherapy are more likely to improve than those who do not. Current research on the effectiveness of psychotherapy therefore compares the benefits of therapy techniques to the benefits of other techniques or no treatment at all. Be especially skeptical of anecdotes. When you hear "I know someone who . . . ," ask yourself whether this person's reported experience is satisfactory as evidence.

5. *Consider alternative interpretations of research evidence:* Does alcohol cause aggression? Later in the chapter we report evidence that there is a *connection*, or correlation, between alcohol and aggression. But does the evidence show that drinking *causes* aggression? Might other factors, such as gender, age, or willingness to take risks, account for both drinking and aggressive behavior?

6. *Do not oversimplify:* Most human behavior involves complex interactions of genetic and environmental influences. For example, consider the issue of whether psychotherapy helps people with psychological problems. A broad answer to this

---

"Mental fight means thinking against the current, not with it. It is our business to puncture gas bags and discover the seeds of truth."

VIRGINIA WOOLF

"Faith requires, in Coleridge's formulation, a willing suspension of disbelief; I do it myself, all the time. But that is a different thing from the suspension of reason and critical intelligence—faculties that tell us that something is not necessarily the case simply because it is written down somewhere or repeated over and over."

JON MEACHEM

Critical thinking An approach to the examination of arguments based on skepticism, logical analysis, and insistence upon the importance of empirical evidence.

question—a simple yes or no—might be oversimplifying. It is more worthwhile to ask what *type* of psychotherapy, practiced by *whom*, is most helpful for *what kind of problem?*

7. *Do not overgeneralize:* Consider the statement that one cannot learn about humans by engaging in research with nonhuman animals. Is the truth of the matter an all-or-nothing issue? Are there certain kinds of information we can obtain about people from research with animals? What kinds of things are you likely to learn only through research with people?

    Apply critical thinking to all areas of life: A skeptical attitude and a demand for evidence are not only useful in college but are of value in all areas of life. Be skeptical when you are bombarded by TV commercials, when political causes try to sweep you up, and when you see the latest stories about Elvis and UFO sightings in supermarket tabloids.

    These are the kinds of principles that guide psychologists' thinking as they observe behavior, engage in research, or advise clients on how to improve their lives. Perhaps these principles will help you improve the quality of your own life, too.

> *"A great many people think they are thinking when they are merely rearranging their prejudices."*
>
> WILLIAM JAMES

LIFE CONNECTIONS   THINKING CRITICALLY ABOUT PSYCHOLOGICAL ADVICE ON THE INTERNET: ARE THERE ANY QUICK FIXES?

www.goaskalice.columbia.edu

www.cdc.gov

www.suicide.org

www.nimh.nih.gov/health/topics/index.shtml

http://panicdisorder.about.com

www.depression.com

www.apa.org

These are just a few of the websites offering psychological advice that have flooded the Internet in recent years. These happen to be reliable. However, many are not, and lonely people, anxious people, depressed people, confused people, and people with sexual problems surf the Internet every day in hope of finding the website that will provide the answer. How can they evaluate the merits of the websites they find?

There are no easy answers. Many of us believe the things we see posted, and anecdotes about how Tyrone lost 30 pounds in two months and how Maria learned to read her textbooks 10 times more rapidly—and increased her comprehension!—can have a powerful allure.

Be on guard. A price we pay for freedom of speech is that nearly anything can wind up posted on a website or in print (Wu, 2009). Authors can make extravagant claims with little fear of punishment. They can lie about the effectiveness of a new cure for acne or for feelings of depression as easily as they can lie about sightings of Elvis Presley or UFOs.

How can you protect yourself? Try some critical thinking:

1. In this instance, *do* "judge the book by its cover." Does the website look well organized? Do the links within the webpages work? A credible website will look professional and will be well maintained.

2. Ignore websites that make extravagant claims. If it sounds too good to be true, it probably is. No method helps everyone who tries it. Very few methods work overnight.

3. Check the credentials of the people who posted the information. Be suspicious if the author's title is "Dr." and is placed before the name. The degree could be a phony doctorate bought through the mail. It is better if the "doctor" has a Ph.D., Psy.D., M.D., or Ed.D. *after* her or his name.

4. Check authors' affiliations. Professionals who are affiliated with colleges, universities, clinics, and hospitals may have more to offer than those who are not.

5. Check the *evidence* reported on the website. Unscientific websites (and books) usually make extensive use of personal *anecdotes*—unsupported stories or case studies about fantastic results with one or a few individuals. Responsible helping professionals test the effectiveness of techniques with large numbers of people. They carefully measure the outcomes. They use cautious language. For example, they say, "It appears that . . ." or, "It may be that . . . ."

6. Check the reference citations for the evidence. Legitimate research is reported in the journals or on the websites you will find in the "References" section of this book. If there are no links to reference citations, or if the references look suspicious, you should be suspicious, too.

7. Ask your instructor for advice on what to do, where to go (electronically, perhaps), whom to talk to, what to read.

8. Talk to someone in your college or university counseling center.

© Getty Images/Inspirestock RF/Jupiterimages

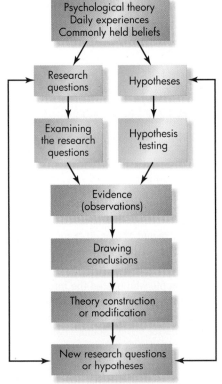

Figure 1.3 ■ The Scientific Method
The scientific method is a systematic way of organizing and expanding scientific knowledge.

"Science is a way of thinking much more than it is a body of knowledge."

CARL SAGAN

Empirical science A science that obtains evidence by experience or experimentation.

Scientific method An approach to acquiring or confirming knowledge that is based on gathering measurable evidence through observation and experimentation. Evidence is often obtained to test hypotheses.

HOW PSYCHOLOGISTS STUDY BEHAVIOR AND MENTAL PROCESSES

Consider some questions of interest to psychologists: Does alcohol cause aggression? Why do some people hardly ever think of food, whereas others are obsessed with it and snack all day long? Why do some unhappy people attempt suicide, whereas others seek ways of coping with their problems? Does having people of different ethnic backgrounds collaborate in their work serve to decrease or increase feelings of prejudice?

Many of us have expressed opinions on questions like these. Various psychological theories also suggest possible answers. Modern psychology aims to be an **empirical science**, however. In an empirical science, we cannot test assumptions about the behavior of cosmic rays, chemical compounds, cells, or people unless we observe and measure that behavior. Assumptions must be supported by evidence. Strong arguments, personal stories, reference to authority figures, and even tightly knit theories are not adequate as scientific evidence. The guiding principle behind this kind of skepticism is the *scientific method*.

The Scientific Method: Putting Ideas to the Test

Question 19: What is the scientific method? The **scientific method** is an organized way of using experience and testing ideas to expand and refine knowledge. Psychologists do not necessarily follow the steps of the scientific method as we might follow a recipe in a cookbook. However, modern research ideally is guided by certain principles.

Psychologists usually begin by *formulating a research question*. Research questions can have many sources. Our daily experiences, psychological theory, and even folklore all help generate questions for research. Consider some questions that may arise from daily experience. Daily experience in using day-care centers may motivate us to conduct research on whether day care affects the development of social skills or the bonds of attachment between children and their parents. Social-cognitive principles of observational learning may prompt research on the effects of TV violence. Research questions may also arise from common knowledge. Consider familiar adages such as "misery loves company" and "opposites attract." Psychologists may ask, *does* misery love company? *Do* opposites attract?

A research question may be studied as a question or reworded as a *hypothesis* (see Figure 1.3 ■). A **hypothesis** is a specific statement about behavior or mental processes that is testable through research. A nontestable hypothesis might be whether angels exist. A hypothesis about day care might be that preschoolers who are placed in day care will acquire greater social skills in relating to peers than preschoolers who are cared for in the home. A hypothesis about TV violence might be that elementary schoolchildren who watch more violent TV shows tend to behave more aggressively toward their peers.

Psychologists next examine the research question or *test the hypothesis* through controlled methods such as the *experiment*, which we'll discuss shortly. For example, we could take a group of preschoolers who attend day care and another group who do not, and introduce each to a new child in a controlled setting such as a child-research center. We could then observe how children in each group interact with the new acquaintance.

Psychologists draw conclusions about their research questions or the accuracy of their hypotheses on the basis of their observations or findings. When their observations do not bear out their hypotheses, they may modify the theories from which the hypotheses were derived. Research findings often suggest refinements to psychological theories and, consequently, new avenues of research. In our research on day care, we would probably find that children in day care show greater social skills than children who are cared for in the home (Belsky et al., 2001). We would probably also find that more aggressive children spend more time watching TV violence.

As psychologists draw conclusions from research evidence, they are guided by principles of critical thinking. For example, they try not to confuse **correlations**—or associations—between findings with cause and effect. Although more aggressive children apparently spend more time watching violent TV shows, it may be erroneous to conclude from this kind of evidence that TV violence *causes* aggressive behavior. Perhaps a **selection factor** is at work—because the children studied choose (select) for themselves what they will watch. Perhaps more aggressive children are more likely than less aggressive children to tune in to violent TV shows.

To better understand the effects of the selection factor, consider a study on the relationship between exercise and health. Imagine that we were to compare a group of people who exercised regularly with a group of people who did not. We might find that the exercisers were physically healthier than the couch potatoes. But could we conclude without doubt that exercise is a causal factor in good health? Perhaps not. The selection factor—the fact that one group chose to exercise and the other did not—could also explain the results. Perhaps healthier people are more likely to *choose* to exercise.

Some psychologists include the publication of research reports in professional journals as a crucial part of the scientific method. Researchers are obligated to provide enough details of their work so that others will be able to repeat, or **replicate**, it to see whether the findings hold up over time and with different participants. Publication of research also permits the scientific community at large to evaluate the methods and conclusions of other scientists.

Video Connections—Facial Analysis— The Scientific Method in Action

Will you soon be using your camera cell phone to snap a picture of someone, send it to a lab for analysis, and get a report back on the person? View the video to understand more about the scientific method in action.

Samples and Populations: Hitting the Target Population

Consider a piece of history that never quite happened: The Republican candidate Alf Landon defeated the incumbent president, Franklin D. Roosevelt, in 1936. Or at least Landon did so in a poll conducted by a popular magazine of the day, the *Literary Digest.* In the actual election, however, Roosevelt routed Landon by a landslide of 11 million votes. **Truth or Fiction Revisited:** It is true that you could survey millions of voters and still not predict the outcome of a presidential election. In effect, the *Digest* accomplished something like this when they predicted a Landon victory. How was so great a discrepancy possible?

The *Digest,* you see, had surveyed voters by phone. Today telephone sampling is a widely practiced and reasonably legitimate polling technique. But the *Digest* poll was taken during the Great Depression, when people who had telephones were much wealthier than those who did not. People at higher income levels are also more likely to vote Republican. No surprise, then, that the overwhelming majority of those sampled said they would vote for Landon.

Question 20: How do psychologists use samples to represent populations? The *Digest* poll failed because of its method of sampling. A **sample** is a segment of a **population** that is drawn with the goal of accurately *representing* that population. Only representative samples allow us to **generalize**—or *extend*—our findings from research samples to target populations, such as U.S. voters, and not subgroups such as southern Californians or European American members of the middle class.

PROBLEMS IN GENERALIZING FROM PSYCHOLOGICAL RESEARCH Many factors must be considered when interpreting the accuracy of the results of scientific research. One is the nature of the research sample.

Hypothesis Within the science of psychology, a specific statement about behavior or mental processes that is testable through research.

Correlation An association or relationship among variables, as we might find between height and weight or between study habits and school grades.

Selection factor A source of bias that may occur in research findings when participants are allowed to choose for themselves a certain treatment in a scientific study.

Replicate Repeat, reproduce, copy.

Sample Part of a population.

Population A complete group of organisms or events.

Generalize To extend from the particular to the general; to apply observations based on a sample to a population.

Later in the chapter, we consider research in which the participants were drawn from a population of college men who were social drinkers. That is, they tended to drink at social gatherings but not when alone. Whom do college men represent other than themselves? To whom can we extend, or generalize, the results?

Compared to the general adult male population, college men tend to be younger and score higher on intelligence tests. We cannot be certain that the findings extend to older men or to those with lower intelligence test scores, although it seems reasonable to assume they do. Social drinkers may also differ biologically and psychologically from alcoholics, who have difficulty controlling their drinking. Nor can we be certain that male college social drinkers represent people who do not drink at all.

By and large, we must also question whether findings of research with men can be generalized to women and whether research with European American men can be extended to members of ethnic minority groups. For example, personality tests completed by European Americans and by African Americans may need to be interpreted in diverse ways if accurate conclusions are to be drawn. The well-known Kinsey studies on sexual behavior (Kinsey et al., 1948; Kinsey et al., 1953) did not adequately represent African Americans, low-income people, older people, and numerous other groups.

RANDOM AND STRATIFIED SAMPLING One way to achieve a representative sample is by means of random sampling. In a **random sample**, each member of a population has an equal chance of being selected to participate. Researchers can also use a **stratified sample**, which is selected so that identified subgroups in the population are represented proportionately in the sample. For instance, 13% of the American population is African American. A stratified sample would thus be 13% African American. As a practical matter, a large randomly selected sample will show reasonably accurate stratification. A random sample of 1,500 people will represent the broad American population reasonably well. However, a sample of 20 million drawn either in the North or the South, or the East or the West, will not.

Large-scale magazine surveys of sexual behavior ask readers to fill out and return questionnaires. Although many thousands of readers complete the questionnaires and send them in, do the survey respondents represent the American population? Probably not. These and similar studies may be influenced by **volunteer bias**. People who offer, or volunteer, to participate in research studies differ systematically from people who do not. In the case of research on sexual behavior, volunteers may represent subgroups of the population—or of readers of the magazines in question—who are willing to disclose intimate information and therefore may also be likely to be more liberal in their sexual behavior (Rathus et al., 2011). Volunteers may also be more interested in research than other people, as well as have more spare time. How might such volunteers differ from the population at large? How might such differences slant, or bias, the research outcomes?

Another bias in the case-study and survey methods of research is *social desirability*. That is, many people involved in research studies tend to tell the interviewer what they think the interviewer would like to hear and not what they really think. You can gain insight into whether you tend to express your genuine feelings or instead tend to give socially desirable answers by completing the nearby Social-Desirability Scale.

Methods of Observation: The Better to See You With

Many people consider themselves experts on behavior and mental processes. How many times, for example, have you or someone else been eager to share a life experience that proves some point about human nature?

Indeed, we see much during our lifetimes. However, our personal observations tend to be fleeting and unsystematic. We sift through experience for the things that interest us. We often ignore the obvious because it does not fit our assumptions about the way things ought to be. Scientists, however, have devised more controlled ways of observing others. **Question 21: What methods of observation do psychologists use?** In this section, we consider methods of observation widely used by psychologists and other behavioral scientists: the case-study, survey, naturalistic-observation, and brain-imaging methods.

CASE STUDY We begin with the case-study method because our own informal ideas about human nature tend to be based on **case studies**, or information we collect about individuals and small groups through interviews, questionnaires, and psychological tests.

"All generalizations are dangerous, even this one."

ALEXANDRE DUMAS

Random sample A sample drawn so that each member of a population has an equal chance of being selected to participate.

Stratified sample A sample drawn so that identified subgroups in the population are represented proportionately in the sample.

Volunteer bias A source of bias or error in research reflecting the prospect that people who offer to participate in research studies differ systematically from people who do not.

Case study A carefully drawn biography that may be obtained through interviews, questionnaires, and psychological tests.

But most of us gather our information haphazardly. We often see only what we want to see. Ideally, psychologists attempt to gather information about individuals more carefully.

Case studies are sometimes used to investigate rare occurrences, as in the case of "Eve," immortalized in the film *The Three Faces of Eve*. Although case studies can provide compelling portraits of individuals, they also have some sources of inaccuracy. For example, there are gaps and factual inaccuracies in people's memories (Bernstein & Loftus, 2009). People may also distort their pasts due to social desirability or because they want to remember things in certain ways. Interviewers may also have certain expectations and may subtly encourage participants to fill in gaps in ways that are consistent with these expectations. Psychoanalysts, for example, have been criticized for guiding people who seek their help into viewing their own lives from the psychodynamic

SELF-ASSESSMENT

Dare You Say What You Think? The Social-Desirability Scale

One of the problems researchers encounter during surveys and case studies is that of social desirability. That is, people being interviewed may tell the researcher what they think the researcher wants to hear and not what they really believe. In doing so, they may provide the so-called *socially desirable answer*—the answer they believe will earn the approval of the researcher. Falling prey to social desirability may cause us to distort our beliefs and experiences in interviews and psychological tests. The bias toward responding in socially desirable directions is a source of error in the case-study and survey methods.

What about you? Do you say what you think, or do you tend to misrepresent your beliefs to earn the approval of others? Do you answer questions honestly, or do you say what you think other people want to hear?

You can complete the Social-Desirability Scale devised by Crowne and Marlowe to gain insight into whether you have a tendency to produce socially desirable responses.

Directions: Read each item and decide whether it is true (T) or false (F) for you. Try to work rapidly and answer each question by circling the T or the F. Then turn to the scoring key in the appendix to interpret your answers.

T F   1. Before voting, I thoroughly investigate the qualifications of all the candidates.

T F   2. I never hesitate to go out of my way to help someone in trouble.

T F   3. It is sometimes hard for me to go on with my work if I am not encouraged.

T F   4. I have never intensely disliked anyone.

T F   5. On occasions I have had doubts about my ability to succeed in life.

T F   6. I sometimes feel resentful when I don't get my way.

T F   7. I am always careful about my manner of dress.

T F   8. My table manners at home are as good as when I eat out in a restaurant.

T F   9. If I could get into a movie without paying and be sure I was not seen, I would probably do it.

T F   10. On a few occasions, I have given up something because I thought too little of my ability.

T F   11. I like to gossip at times.

T F   12. There have been times when I felt like rebelling against people in authority even though I knew they were right.

T F   13. No matter whom I'm talking to, I'm always a good listener.

T F   14. I can remember "playing sick" to get out of something.

T F   15. There have been occasions when I have taken advantage of someone.

T F   16. I'm always willing to admit it when I make a mistake.

T F   17. I always try to practice what I preach.

T F   18. I don't find it particularly difficult to get along with loudmouthed, obnoxious people.

T F   19. I sometimes try to get even rather than forgive and forget.

T F   20. When I don't know something I don't mind at all admitting it.

T F   21. I am always courteous, even to people who are disagreeable.

T F   22. At times I have really insisted on having things my own way.

T F   23. There have been occasions when I felt like smashing things.

T F   24. I would never think of letting someone else be punished for my wrongdoings.

T F   25. I never resent being asked to return a favor.

T F   26. I have never been irked when people expressed ideas very different from my own.

T F   27. I never make a long trip without checking the safety of my car.

T F   28. There have been times when I was quite jealous of the good fortune of others.

T F   29. I have almost never felt the urge to tell someone off.

T F   30. I am sometimes irritated by people who ask favors of me.

T F   31. I have never felt that I was punished without cause.

T F   32. I sometimes think that when people have a misfortune they only got what they deserved.

T F   33. I have never deliberately said something that hurt someone's feelings.

Source: D. P. Crowne and D. A. Marlowe, A new scale of social desirability independent of pathology, *Journal of Consulting Psychology, 24* (1960): 351. Copyright 1960 by the American Psychological Association. Reprinted by Permission.

TM & © 20th Century Fox Film Corp./ courtesy Everett Collection

perspective (Hergenhahn, 2009). No wonder, then, that many people provide "evidence" that is consistent with psychodynamic theory—such as, "My parents' inept handling of my toilet training is the source of my compulsive neatness." However, interviewers and other kinds of researchers who hold *any* theoretical viewpoint run the risk of indirectly prodding people into saying what they want to hear.

THE SURVEY In the good old days we had to wait until the wee hours of the morning to learn the results of local and national elections. Throughout the evening and early morning hours, suspense would build as ballots from distant neighborhoods and states were tallied. Nowadays we are barely settled with an after-dinner cup of coffee on election night when reporters announce that a computer has examined the ballots of a "scientifically selected sample" and predicted the next president of the United States. All of this may occur with less than 1% of the vote tallied.

© Photos 12/Alamy

Investigating Human Sexuality In the film biography *Kinsey*, Liam Neeson played Alfred Kinsey, the scientist who investigated human sexuality during a time when even talking about sex was considered indecent.

Just as computers and pollsters predict election results and report national opinion on the basis of scientifically selected samples, psychologists conduct **surveys** to learn about behavior and mental processes that cannot be observed in the natural setting or studied experimentally. Psychologists conducting surveys may employ questionnaires and interviews or examine public records. One of the advantages of the survey is that by distributing questionnaires and analyzing answers with a computer, psychologists can study many thousands of people at a time (Schwartz, 2007).

Alfred Kinsey of Indiana University and his colleagues published two surveys of sexual behavior, based on interviews, that shocked the nation. These were *Sexual Behavior in the Human Male* (1948) and *Sexual Behavior in the Human Female* (1953). Kinsey reported that masturbation was virtually universal in his sample of men at a time when masturbation was still widely thought to impair health. He also reported that about one woman in three who was still single at age 25 had had premarital sex.

Surveys, like case studies, have various sources of inaccuracy (Schwartz, 2007). People may recall their behavior inaccurately or purposefully misrepresent it. Some people try to ingratiate themselves with their interviewers by answering in what they perceive to be the socially desirable direction. The Kinsey studies all relied on male interviewers, for example. It has been speculated that female interviewees might have been more open and honest with female interviewers. Similar problems may occur when interviewers and the people surveyed are from different ethnic or socioeconomic backgrounds. Or some people may falsify their attitudes and exaggerate their problems to draw attention to themselves or even to intentionally foul up the results.

Consider some examples of survey measurement errors caused by inaccurate self-reports of behavior. If people brushed their teeth as often as they claimed and used the amount of toothpaste they indicated, three times as much toothpaste would be sold in the United States as is actually sold (Koerber et al., 2006). People also appear to overreport the degree to which they follow doctors' orders (Wilson et al., 2009) and to underreport how much they smoke (Swan et al., 2007). Why do you think this is so?

Survey A method of scientific investigation in which a large sample of people answer questions about their attitudes or behavior.

Internet Surveys Many surveys today are conducted over the Internet. The websites of magazines such as *Cosmopolitan* and *Elle* frequently encourage visitors to fill out online questionnaires, for example. Professional psychologists also use the Internet to conduct research.

One Internet study sought to determine which psychotherapists were considered most influential among practitioners of psychotherapy today (Cook, Biyanova, & Coyne, 2009). The research group emailed some 22,000 readers of a psychotherapy magazine, the *Psychotherapy Networker (PN)*. These were readers with listed e-mail addresses, representing about 40% of the total readership. The magazine editor also wrote letters to these readers, endorsing the survey. About 13% of those contacted (2,902 readers) consented to participate, and the responses of 2,647 readers were analyzed.

Cognitive therapist Aaron Beck was considered most influential by one in four (24%) of the readers who were psychologists. Carl Rogers was considered the most influential psychotherapist overall, with mentions by nearly one psychotherapist in five, whether psychologist or nonpsychologist. We will discuss Beck and Rogers in Chapter 13, "Methods of Therapy."

Let's say you're looking to be a critical thinker. Would you agree that the readers of any one magazine represent psychotherapists in general? Why or why not? How might readers who respond to magazine or Internet surveys differ from those who do not?

NATURALISTIC OBSERVATION You use naturalistic observation—that is, you observe people in their natural habitats—every day. Naturalistic observation has the advantage of allowing psychologists and other scientists to observe behavior where it happens, or "in the field." In doing so, researchers use unobtrusive measures to avoid interfering with the behaviors they are observing. For example, Jane Goodall has observed the behavior of chimpanzees in their natural environment to learn about their social behavior, sexual behavior, use of tools, and other facts of chimp life (Peterson, 2006; Pusey et al., 2008). Her observations have shown us that (1) we were incorrect to think that only humans use tools and (2) kissing on the lips, as a greeting, is used by chimps as well as humans.

Jane Goodall observed her chimpanzees with her own eyes. As we see next, other researchers have taken images of things going on in the brains of chimpanzees—and humans—while they are thinking.

IMAGING THE BRAIN "Gage is no longer Gage," said those who had known him before the accident. There are many key characters in the history of psychology, and some of them did not arrive there intentionally. One of these was a railroad worker, Phineas Gage, who was helping our young nation stretch from coast to coast. Gage was admired by friends and coworkers. But all that changed one day in 1848. While he was tamping down the blasting powder for a dynamite charge, Gage accidentally set the powder off. The metal tamping rod shot up through his cheek and brain and out the top of his head (see Figure 1.4 ■).

Naturalistic observation A scientific method in which organisms are observed in their natural environments.

© Bruce Coleman Inc./Alamy

What Can You Observe? Jane Goodall's naturalistic observations revealed that chimpanzees—like humans—use tools and greet one another with a kiss.

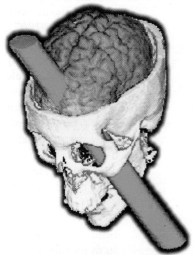
Reprinted with permission from Damasio, H., Grabowski, T., Frank, R., Galaburda, A. M., Damasio, A. R.: "The Return of Phineas Gage: Clues About the Brain from the Skull of a Famous Patient." *Science*, 264: 1102–1105, © 1994. Department of Neurology and Image Analysis Facility, University of Iowa.

© Collection of Jack and Beverly Wilgus.

Figure 1.4 ■ Two Views of Phineas Gage The drawing shows the trajectory of a tamping rod through his head. The photo shows him holding the rod, blinded in the left eye. "Here is business enough for you" Gage allegedly told the first doctor to treat him after a premature detonation on a railroad building site turned the rod into a missile.

Although Gage fell back in a heap, he was miraculously alive. He stood up a few moments later and spoke. While the local doctor marveled at the hole through Gage's head, Gage asked when he'd be able to return to work. Two months later, Gage's external wounds had healed, but the psychological wounds became obvious. Gage had become undependable, foul-mouthed, and ill-mannered.

Generations of researchers have wondered how the changes in Gage's personality might have been caused by the damage to his brain. When Gage had his accident, the only ways to look into the brain were to drill holes or crack it open, neither of which would have contributed to the well-being of the participant. But researchers today use computers to generate images of parts of the brain without invading it. A number of methods are in use.

As shown in Figure 1.5 ■, *computerized axial tomography,* or a *CAT scan,* passes a narrow X-ray beam through the head and measures the structures that reflect the X rays from various angles, generating a three-dimensional image of the brain. The CAT scan reveals deformities in shape and structure that are connected with blood clots, tumors, and other health problems. *Positron emission tomography (PET scan)* forms a computer-generated image of the activity of parts of the brain by tracing the amount of glucose used (or metabolized) by these parts. More glucose is metabolized in more active parts of the brain. In *functional magnetic resonance imaging (fMRI),* the person lies in a magnetic field and is exposed to radio waves that cause parts of the brain to emit signals. The fMRI relies on subtle shifts in blood flow. (More blood flows to more active parts of the brain, supplying them with oxygen.) The PET scan and fMRI have been used by researchers to see which parts of the brain are most active when we are, for example, listening to music, using language, or playing chess (Krueger et al., 2009; Newman et al., 2009; Stocco & Anderson, 2008). The fMRI has shown that people with the psychological disorder schizophrenia have smaller prefrontal regions (see Figure 1.5 again) of the cortex than other people but larger ventricles (hollow spaces) in the brain (Mata et al., 2009).

Research with PET scans and fMRIs suggests that the prefrontal part of the brain is where we do much of the work in making plans and solving problems (Gilbert et al., 2008; Wang et al., 2008). For this reason, the prefrontal cortex has been dubbed the brain's "executive center," where we think about problems and develop solutions.

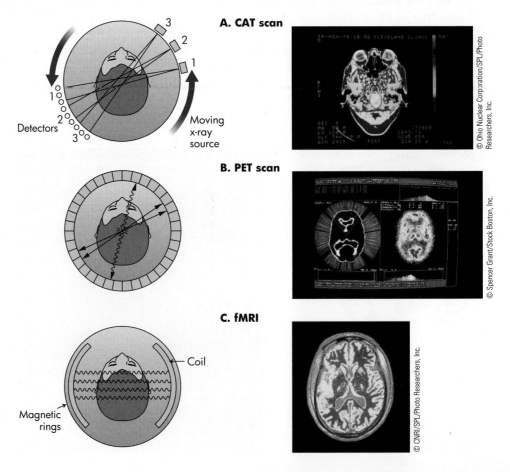

Figure 1.5 ■ Brain Imaging Techniques
Part A shows a CAT scan, part B a PET scan, and part C an fMRI.

Correlation: On How Things Go Together—or Not

Are people with higher intelligence more likely to do well in school? Are people with a stronger need for achievement likely to climb higher up the corporate ladder? What is the relationship between stress and health?

Such questions are often answered by means of the **correlational method**. **Question 22: What is the correlational method?** By using the correlational method, psychologists investigate whether observed behavior or a measured trait is related to, or correlated with, another. Consider the variables of intelligence and academic performance. These variables are assigned numbers such as intelligence test scores and academic averages. Then the numbers are mathematically related and expressed as a **correlation coefficient**. A correlation coefficient is a number between +1.00 and −1.00 that expresses the strength and direction (positive or negative) of the relationship between two variables

Studies report **positive correlations** between intelligence test scores and academic achievement, as measured, for example, by grade point averages. Generally speaking, the higher people score on intelligence tests, the better their academic performance is likely to be. The scores attained on intelligence tests tend to be positively correlated (about +0.30 to +0.60) with academic achievement (see Figure 1.6 ■). But factors *other* than performance on intelligence tests also contribute to academic success. These include desire to get ahead, self-discipline, ability to manage stress, and belief in one's ability to succeed (Duckworth & Seligman, 2005; Jennings et al., 2009; Thomas, 2008).

Many correlations are **negative correlations**; that is, as one variable increases, the other variable decreases. For example, there is a negative correlation between stress and health. As the amount of stress affecting us increases, the functioning of our immune system decreases. Under high levels of stress, many people show poorer health.

What kinds of correlations (positive or negative) would you expect to find among behavior patterns such as the following: Churchgoing and crime? Language ability and musical ability? Grades in school and delinquency? Why?

Correlational research may *suggest* but does not *prove* cause and effect. For instance, it may seem logical to assume that high intelligence makes it possible for children to profit from education. Research has also shown, however, that education contributes to higher scores on intelligence tests (Nisbett, 2009). Preschoolers who are placed in stimulating Head Start programs later attain higher scores on intelligence tests than age-mates who did not have this experience. The relationship between intelligence and academic performance may not be as simple as we think. What of the link between stress and health? Does stress impair health, or is it possible that people in poorer health encounter more stress? (See Figure 1.7 ■).

The Experimental Method: Trying Things Out

Question 23: What is the experimental method? Most psychologists agree that the preferred method for answering questions about cause and effect is the experiment.

Correlational method A mathematical method of determining whether one variable increases or decreases as another variable increases or decreases. For example, there is a correlation between intelligence test scores and grades in school.

Correlation coefficient A number between +1.00 and −1.00 that expresses the strength and direction (positive or negative) of the relationship between two variables.

Positive correlation A relationship between variables in which one variable increases as the other also increases.

Negative correlation A relationship between two variables in which one variable increases as the other decreases.

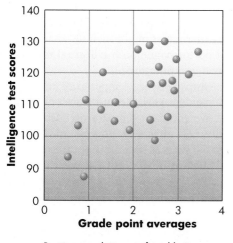

Positive correlation, as found between intelligence and academic achievement

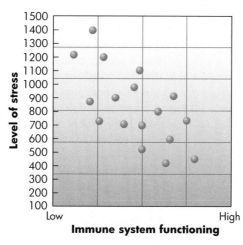

Negative correlation, as found between stress and functioning of the immune system

Figure 1.6 ■ Positive and Negative Correlations When there is a positive correlation between variables, as there is between intelligence and achievement, one increases as the other increases. By and large, the higher people score on intelligence tests, the better their academic performance is likely to be, as in the diagram to the left. (Each dot represents an individual's intelligence test score and grade point average.) But there is a negative correlation between stress and health. As the amount of stress we experience increases, the functioning of our immune system tends to decrease. Rathus. PSYCH 1/e.
© 2009 Cengage Learning.

Experiment A scientific method that seeks to confirm cause-and-effect relationships by introducing independent variables and observing their effects on dependent variables.

Treatment In experiments, a condition received by participants so that its effects may be observed.

Independent variable A condition in a scientific study that is manipulated so that its effects may be observed.

Dependent variable A measure of an assumed effect of an independent variable.

Experimental groups In experiments, groups whose members obtain the treatment.

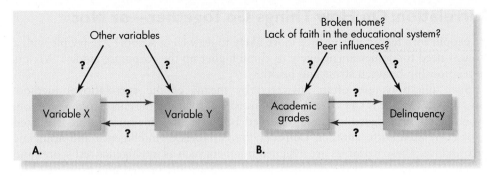

Figure 1.7 ■ Correlational Relationships, Cause, and Effect Correlational relationships may suggest but do not demonstrate cause and effect. In part A, there is a correlation between variables X and Y. Does this mean that either variable X causes variable Y or that variable Y causes variable X? Not necessarily. Other factors could affect both variables X and Y. Consider the examples of academic grades (variable X) and juvenile delinquency (variable Y) in part B. There is a negative correlation between the two. Does this mean that poor grades contribute to delinquency? Perhaps. Does it mean that delinquency contributes to poor grades? Again, perhaps. But there could also be other variables—such as a broken home, lack of faith in the educational system, or peer influences—that contribute both to poor grades and delinquency.

In an **experiment** a group of participants obtains a **treatment**, such as a dose of alcohol, a change in room temperature, or perhaps an injection of a drug. The participants are then observed to determine whether the treatment makes a difference in their behavior. Does alcohol alter the ability to take tests, for example? What about differences in room temperatures and level of background noise?

Experiments are used whenever possible because they allow psychologists to control the experiences of participants and thus draw conclusions about cause and effect (Roediger & McCabe, 2007). A psychologist may theorize that alcohol leads to aggression because it reduces fear of consequences or because it energizes the activity levels of drinkers (Sayette et al., 2009). She or he may then hypothesize that a treatment in which participants receive a specified dosage of alcohol will lead to increases in aggression. Let's follow the example of the effects of alcohol on aggression to further our understanding of the experimental method.

INDEPENDENT AND DEPENDENT VARIABLES In an experiment to determine whether alcohol causes aggression, participants are given an amount of alcohol and its effects are measured. In this case, alcohol is an **independent variable**. An independent variable is one that can be manipulated by the experimenters so that its effects may be determined. The independent variable of alcohol may be administered at different levels, or doses, from none or very little to enough to cause intoxication or drunkenness.

The measured results, or outcomes, in an experiment are called **dependent variables**. The nature of a dependent variable is determined by the independent variable or variables. In an experiment to determine whether alcohol influences aggression, aggressive behavior would be a dependent variable. Other dependent variables of interest might include sexual arousal, visual-motor coordination, and performance on intellectual tasks such as defining words or doing numerical computations.

In an experiment on the relationships between temperature and aggression, temperature would be an independent variable and aggressive behavior would be a dependent variable. We could set temperatures from below freezing to blistering hot and study their effects on aggression. We could also use a second independent variable such as social provocation. That is, we could insult some participants but not others and see whether insults affect their level of aggression. This method would allow us to study how two independent variables—temperature and social provocation—affect aggression, singly and/or together.

EXPERIMENTAL AND CONTROL GROUPS Ideal experiments use experimental groups and control groups. Participants in **experimental groups** obtain the treatment.

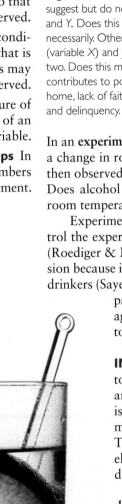

How Can We Run Experiments to Determine the Effects of Alcohol? One problem is that people who are drinking alcohol know they are doing so. How can we surmount this problem?

Members of **control groups** do not. Every effort is made to ensure that all other conditions are held constant for both groups. This method enhances the researchers' ability to draw conclusions about cause and effect. By use of control groups, researchers can be more confident that outcomes of the experiment are caused by the treatments and not by chance factors or chance fluctuations in behavior.

For example, in an experiment on the effects of alcohol on aggression, members of the experimental group would ingest alcohol, and members of the control group would not (Eriksson, 2008). The researcher would then measure how much aggression was expressed by each group. In a complex version of this experiment, different experimental groups might ingest different dosages of alcohol and be exposed to different types of social provocations as well.

BLINDS AND DOUBLE BLINDS One experiment on the effects of alcohol on aggression (Boyatzis, 1974) reported that men at parties where beer and liquor were served acted more aggressively than men at parties where only soft drinks were served. But participants in the experimental group knew they had drunk alcohol, and those in the control group knew they had not. Aggression that appeared to result from alcohol might not have reflected drinking per se. In other words, it might have reflected the participants' expectations about the effects of alcohol. People tend to act in stereotypical ways when they believe they have been drinking alcohol (Eriksson, 2008). For instance, men who have been drinking alcohol tend to become less anxious in social situations, more aggressive, and more sexually aroused. To what extent do these behavior patterns reflect the direct effects of alcohol on the body, and to what extent do they affect people's beliefs about the effects of alcohol?

In medicine, physicians have sometimes given patients **placebos** (or "sugar pills") when the patient insisted on having a medical cure but the physician did not believe that medicine was necessary. When patients report that placebos have helped them, it is because they expected the pills to be of help and not because of the direct effect of the pills on their bodies. Psychologists and other researchers have adopted the lore of the sugar pill to sort out the effects of actual treatments from people's expectations about the effects of those treatments. Placebos are not limited to pills made of sugar. When participants in psychological experiments are given placebos such as tonic water, but they think they have drunk alcohol, we can conclude that changes in their behavior stem from their *beliefs* about the effects of alcohol, not from the alcohol itself.

Well-designed experiments control for the effects of expectations by creating conditions under which participants are unaware of, or **blind** to, the treatment. Yet researchers may also have expectations. They may, in effect, be "rooting for" a certain treatment outcome, a phenomenon known as **experimenter bias**. For instance, tobacco company executives may wish to show that cigarette smoking is harmless. In such cases, it is useful if the people measuring the experimental outcomes are unaware of which participants have received the treatment. Studies in which neither the participants nor the experimenters know who has obtained the treatment are called **double-blind studies**.

Truth or Fiction Revisited: Neither the participants nor the researchers know who is receiving the real treatment in many experiments. For example, the Food and Drug Administration requires double-blind studies before it allows the marketing of new drugs. The drug and the placebo look and taste alike. Experimenters assign the drug or placebo to participants at random. Neither the participants nor the observers know who is taking the drug and who is taking the placebo. After the final measurements have been made, a neutral panel (a group of people who have no personal stake in the outcome of the study) judges whether the effects of the drug differed from those of the placebo.

In one **double-blind** study on the effects of alcohol, Alan Lang and his colleagues (1975) pretested a highball of vodka and tonic water to determine that it could not be discriminated by taste from tonic water alone. They recruited college men who described themselves as social drinkers to participate in the study. Some of the men drank vodka and tonic water. Others drank tonic water only. Of the men who drank vodka, half were misled into believing they had drunk tonic water only (see Figure 1.8 ■). Of those who drank tonic water only, half were misled into believing their drink contained vodka. Thus, half

Control groups In experiments, groups whose members do not obtain the treatment, while other conditions are held constant.

Placebo A bogus treatment that has the appearance of being genuine.

Blind In experimental terminology, being unaware of whether one has received a treatment or not.

Experimenter bias A condition in which a researcher expects or desires a certain outcome in a research study, possibly affecting the outcome.

Double-blind study A study in which neither the participants nor the observers know who has received the treatment.

Figure 1.8 ■ The Experimental Conditions in the Lang Study The taste of vodka cannot be discerned when vodka is mixed with tonic water. For this reason, it was possible for subjects in the Lang study on the effects of alcohol to be kept "blind" as to whether they had actually drunk alcohol. Blind studies allow psychologists to control for the effects of study participants' expectations. Source: Rathus. PSYCH 1/e. © 2009 Cengage Learning.

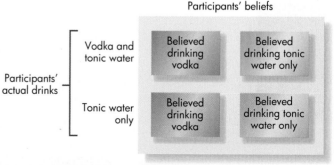

Method	What Happens	Comments
Case Study 	The researcher uses observations, interviews, and records to gather in-depth information about an individual or a small group.	The accuracy of case studies is compromised by gaps and mistakes in memory and by participants' tendency to present themselves in a socially desirable manner.
The Survey 	The researcher uses interviews, questionnaires, or public records to gather information about large numbers of people.	Surveys can include thousands of people but are subject to the same limitations as case studies. People who volunteer to participate in surveys may also differ from people who do not. There may thus be problems in generalization of results to people who do not participate.
Naturalistic Observation 	The researcher observes behavior where it happens—"in the field."	Researchers try to avoid interfering with the behaviors they are observing by using unobtrusive measures.
Brain Imaging 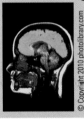	Researchers use methods such as the CAT scan, the PET scan, and fMRI to learn what is happening in the brain when a person is solving a problem, listening to music, and so on.	Contemporary brain imaging techniques are noninvasive—that is, they do not cause pain or discomfort. They have enabled researchers to gather new information from the biological perspective.
Correlation 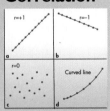	The researcher uses statistical (mathematical) methods to reveal positive and negative relationships between variables.	The correlational method does not show cause and effect. Correlation coefficients vary between $+1.00$ (a perfect positive correlation) and -1.00 (a perfect negative correlation).
Experiment 	The researcher manipulates independent variables and observes their effects on dependent variables.	Experimental groups obtain the treatment; control groups do not. Researchers use blinds to control for the effect of expectations. With double blinds, neither the participants nor the observers know which participant has received which treatment. The experimental method allows researchers to draw conclusions about cause and effect.

the participants were blind to their treatment. Experimenters who measured the men's aggressive responses were also blind concerning which participants had drunk vodka.

The research team found that men who believed that they had drunk vodka responded more aggressively to a provocation than men who believed that they had drunk tonic water only. The actual content of the drink was immaterial. That is, the men's *belief* about what they drank affected their aggressive behavior more than what they actually consumed. The results of the Lang study differ dramatically from those reported by Boyatzis, perhaps because the Boyatzis study did not control for the effects of expectations or beliefs about alcohol. The nearby Concept Review will enhance your understanding of all the research methods you have just learned about.

LearningConnections • HOW PSYCHOLOGISTS STUDY BEHAVIOR AND MENTAL PROCESSES

ACTIVE REVIEW (24) Samples must accurately represent the target _____. (25) In a _____ sample, each member of a population has an equal chance of being selected to participate. (26) A _____ study is a carefully drawn biography. (27) In the _____, a large sample of people answer questions about their attitudes or behavior. (28) Correlational research does not reveal _____ and effect. (29) In an experiment, the _____ variable is manipulated so that its effects may be determined. (30) Ideal experiments use experimental and _____ groups. (31) Well-designed experiments control for the effects of expectations by creating conditions under which subjects are unaware of, or _____ to, the treatment they have received.

REFLECT AND RELATE The next time you eat at a fast-food restaurant, look around. Pick out slender people and overweight people and note whether they eat differently—even when they select the same foods. Do overweight people eat more rapidly? Do they chew less frequently? Do they leave less food on their plates? What conclusions can you draw?

CRITICAL THINKING Can we use the experimental method to show that cigarette smoking causes lung cancer in people? The problem is that we cannot (ethically) assign some people to smoke cigarettes and others not to smoke. Because people decide whether to smoke, is it possible that the same factors that lead some people to smoke—selection factors—also lead to lung disease? What might such selection factors be?

 Go to Psychology CourseMate at **www.cengagebrain.com** for an interactive version of these questions.

● ETHICAL ISSUES IN PSYCHOLOGICAL RESEARCH AND PRACTICE

The researchers in the Lang study gave some participants alcohol to drink and deceived the entire group about the purposes and methods of the study. Was their method ethical? We'll return to this question, but let's first address a broader one. **Question 24: What are the ethical issues that concern psychological research and practice with humans?**

Psychologists adhere to a number of ethical standards that are intended to promote individual dignity, human welfare, and scientific integrity. The standards are also intended to ensure that psychologists do not undertake research methods or treatments that are harmful.

Research with Humans

If the Lang group were running their experiment today rather than in the 1970s, they would probably have been denied permission to do so by a university ethics review committee. Why? Because in virtually all institutional settings, including colleges, hospitals, and research foundations, ethics review committees help researchers consider the potential harm of their methods and review proposed studies according to ethical guidelines. When such committees find that proposed research might be unacceptably harmful to participants, they may withhold approval until the proposal has been modified. Ethics review committees also weigh the potential benefits of research against the potential harm.

"An act has no ethical quality whatever unless it be chosen out of several, all equally possible."

WILLIAM JAMES

Ethical Moral; referring to one's system of deriving standards for determining what is moral.

Informed consent A participant's agreement to participate in research after receiving information about the purposes of the study and the nature of the treatments.

Today individuals must provide **informed consent** before they participate in research (American Psychological Association, 2002). Having a general overview of the research and the opportunity to choose not to participate apparently gives them a sense of control and decreases the stress of participating (Fisher, 2009). Can you think of some reasons why the Lang research group should have obtained informed consent from potential participants in the study? For example, what if a participant was recovering from alcoholism? Can you think of a way participants in the Lang study could have provided informed consent without giving away so much information about the methods in the study that the study was invalidated?

Psychologists treat the records of research participants and clients as confidential (Fisher, 2009). This is because they respect people's privacy and also because people are more likely to express their true thoughts and feelings when they know that researchers or therapists keep their disclosures confidential. Sometimes conflicts of interest arise, however; for example, this can happen when a client threatens to harm someone, and the psychologist feels an obligation, and may be required by law, to warn that person (Follingstad & McCormick, 2002).

Ethics also limit the types of research that psychologists may conduct. For example, how can we determine whether early separation from one's mother impairs social development? One way would be to observe the development of children who were separated from their mothers at an early age for reasons such as the death of the mother or court-ordered protective custody. It is difficult to draw conclusions from such research, however, because of the selection factor. That is, the same factors that led to the separation—such as family tragedy or irresponsible parents—may have led to the outcome rather than the separation itself producing the outcome. Scientifically, it would be sounder to run experiments in which researchers separate children from their mothers at an early age and compare their development with that of other children. But psychologists would not undertake such research because of the ethical issues they pose. Yet, they run experiments in which infant animals are separated from their mothers, which has brought criticism from animal-rights groups.

THE STANFORD PRISON EXPERIMENT Also consider the Stanford Prison Experiment conducted by Philip Zimbardo in 1971. In this study, "mature, emotionally stable, normal, intelligent college students from middle-class homes throughout the United States and Canada" were randomly assigned the roles of "guard" or "prisoner" in a mock prison on the Stanford University campus. The study was planned to last two weeks, but it was ended early when it appeared that many "guards" were brutalizing "prisoners." The point of the study was to show that college students—as other groups—were likely to try to meet the demands of their social situations despite their personal values. The study revealed that normal people can act in brutal ways in brutal situations—as in warfare and interrogating prisoners (Lurigio, 2009; Zimbardo, 2007). The longer individuals are immersed in such a situation on the battlefield or in a prison, the more susceptible they become to humiliating and torturing others. A noted recent example occurred at the prison at Abu Ghraib in Iraq, where U.S. soldiers humiliated Iraqi prisoners (Zimbardo, 2008).

Although the information obtained in the Stanford Prison Study is useful and important, it has been considered unethical because it placed participants in a dehumanizing situation (Bigger, 2009). Guards began to view prisoners as less human than themselves—as real guards and soldiers may consider the perceived enemy to be "vermin" or "gooks"—and therefore felt free to treat prisoners in inhumane ways.

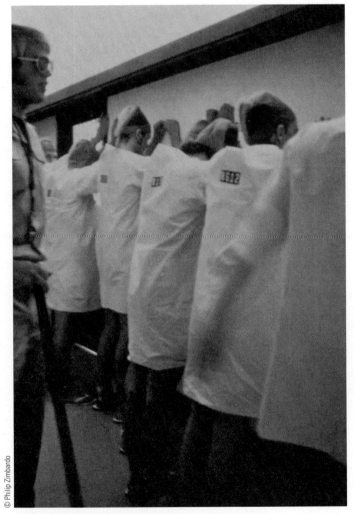

© Philip Zimbardo

A Scene from the Stanford Prison Experiment Zimbardo's experiment revealed important information about people's tendencies to meet the requirements of their social situations but has been called unethical due to the stress it placed on participants.

DECEPTION OF STUDY PARTICIPANTS Question 25: Is it ethical for psychologists to deceive research participants about the methods and objectives of their research? Some studies cannot be done if participants know what the researchers are trying to find out or which treatment they have received (for example, a new drug or a sugar pill). According to the American Psychological Association's (2002) *Ethical Principles of Psychologists and Code of Conduct,* psychologists may use deception only when they believe the benefits of the research outweigh its potential harm, when they believe the individuals might have been willing to participate if they had understood the benefits of the research, and when participants are **debriefed** afterward—that is, the purposes and methods of the research are explained.

Let's return to the Lang (Lang et al., 1975) study on alcohol and aggression. In this study, the researchers misinformed participants about what they were drinking and told them they were shocking other participants when they were actually only pressing switches on a dead control board. Students who believed they had drunk vodka were "more aggressive"—that is, selected higher levels of shock—than students who believed they had not.

What do you think? Was it ethical to deceive participants in the Lang study as to what they were drinking? Why or why not?

Debrief To elicit information about a completed procedure.

Research with Animals

Psychologists and other scientists frequently use animals to conduct research that cannot be carried out with humans. For example, as noted earlier, experiments on the effects of early separation from the mother have been done with monkeys and other animals (see Chapter 9). Such research has helped psychologists investigate the formation of parent–child bonds of attachment.

Question 26: What are the ethical issues that concern research with animals? Experiments with infant monkeys highlight some of the ethical issues faced by psychologists and other scientists who contemplate potentially harmful research. Psychologists and biologists who study the workings of the brain destroy sections of the brains of laboratory animals to learn how they influence behavior. For instance, a lesion in one part of a brain structure causes a rat to overeat. A lesion elsewhere causes the rat to go on a crash diet. Psychologists generalize to humans from experiments such as these in the hope of finding solutions to problems such as eating disorders (Mehta & Gosling, 2008). Proponents of the use of animals in research argue that major advances in medicine and psychology could not have taken place without them (Ringach & Jentsch, 2009). For example, we would know much less about how experimental drugs affect cancerous growths and the brain.

However, the majority of psychologists disapprove of research in which animals are exposed to pain or killed (Plous, 1996). According to the ethical guidelines of the American Psychological Association, animals may be harmed only when there is no alternative and when researchers believe that the benefits of the research justify the harm (American Psychological Association, 2002; Fisher, 2009).

LearningConnections • ETHICAL ISSUES IN PSYCHOLOGICAL RESEARCH AND PRACTICE

ACTIVE REVIEW (32) Psychologists adhere to _____ standards that help promote the dignity of the individual, maintain scientific integrity, and protect subjects or clients from harm. (33) To help avoid harm, human subjects must provide _____ consent. (34) Ethics require that subjects who are deceived be _____ afterward to help eliminate misconceptions and anxieties about the research.

REFLECT AND RELATE Do you believe it ethical to harm animals in conducting research when the results may be beneficial to humans? Why or why not?

CRITICAL THINKING Psychologists are expected to keep things that clients tell them confidential. However, if a client in therapy were to tell his psychologist that he was thinking of hurting you, should the psychologist tell you about it? Why or why not?

 Go to Psychology CourseMate at **www.cengagebrain.com** for an interactive version of these questions.

© BonkersAboutScience/Alamy

Psychology as a Science

1. What is psychology?
Psychology is the scientific study of behavior and mental processes.

2. What are the goals of psychology?
Psychology seeks to describe, explain, predict, and control behavior and mental processes.

What Psychologists Do: Something for Everyone?

3. Just what do psychologists do?
Psychologists engage in research, practice, and teaching. Research can be pure or applied.

Where Psychology Comes From: A History

4. Who were some of the ancient contributors to psychology?
The ancient Greek philosopher Aristotle declared that people are motivated to seek pleasure and avoid pain. Another Greek, Democritus, suggested that we could think of behavior in terms of a body and a mind

5. What is structuralism?
Structuralism, founded by Wilhelm Wundt, used introspection to study the objective and subjective elements of experience.

6. What is functionalism?
Functionalism dealt with observable behavior as well as conscious experience and focused on the importance of habit.

7. What is behaviorism?
Behaviorism, founded by John B. Watson, argues that psychology must limit itself to observable behavior and not attempt to deal with consciousness.

8. What is Gestalt psychology?
Gestalt psychology is concerned with perception and argues that the wholeness of human experience is more than the sum of its parts.

9. What is psychoanalysis?
Psychoanalysis asserts that people are driven by hidden impulses and that they distort reality to protect themselves from anxiety.

How Today's Psychologists View Behavior and Mental Processes

10. What is the evolutionary perspective?
The evolutionary perspective argues that in the age-old struggle for survival, only the fittest organisms reach maturity and reproduce, thereby transmitting the traits that enable them to survive to their offspring.

11. What is the biological perspective?
The biological perspective studies the links between behavior and mental processes, on the one hand, and the functioning of the brain, the endocrine system, and heredity on the other.

12. What is the cognitive perspective?
The cognitive perspective is concerned with how we learn, remember the past, plan for the future, solve problems, form judgments, make decisions, and use language.

13. What is the humanistic–existential perspective?
Humanistic–existential psychologists stress the importance of subjective experience and assert that people have the freedom to make choices.

14. What is the role of psychoanalysis today?
Contemporary psychoanalysts focus less on unconscious processes and more on conscious choice and self-direction.

15. What are the two major perspectives on learning?
The two key perspectives on learning are the behavioral perspective and the social-cognitive perspective.

16. What is the sociocultural perspective?
The sociocultural perspective focuses on the roles of ethnicity, gender, culture, and socioeconomic status in behavior and mental processes.

Gender, Ethnicity, and Psychology: Real People in the Real World

17. How have access to education and the field of psychology historically influenced the participation of women and people from certain ethnic and racial backgrounds?
Women have increasingly contributed to all areas of psychology. For example, Calkins studied memory and heightened awareness of prejudice against women. People from ethnic minority groups have likewise increasingly contributed to all areas of psychology, and some, like Kenneth Clark, Mamie Phipps Clark, and Jorge Sanchez, have heightened awareness of issues concerning their groups.

Critical Thinking: Sorting Truth from Fiction

18. What is critical thinking?
Critical thinking is associated with skepticism. It involves analyzing the questions, statements, and arguments of others. It means examining the definitions of terms, examining the assumptions behind arguments, and scrutinizing the logic with which arguments are developed.

How Psychologists Study Behavior and Mental Processes

19. What is the scientific method?
The scientific method is an organized way of expanding and refining knowledge. Psychologists reach conclusions about

their research questions or the accuracy of their hypotheses on the basis of their research observations or findings.

20. How do psychologists use samples to represent populations?
In a random sample, each member of a population has an equal chance of being selected to participate. A stratified sample is selected so that identified subgroups in the population are represented proportionately in the sample.

21. What methods of observation do psychologists use?
The methods used include the case study, the survey, naturalistic observation, and imaging of the brain.

22. What is the correlational method?
The correlational method reveals positive and negative relationships between variables but does not determine cause and effect.

23. What is the experimental method?
Experiments are used to discover cause and effect—that is, the effects of independent variables on dependent variables. Experimental groups receive a treatment whereas control groups do not. Blinds control for the effects of the expectations of the participants and the researchers.

Ethical Issues in Psychological Research and Practice

24. What are the ethical issues that concern psychological research and practice with humans?
The ethical standards of psychologists are intended to protect participants in research and clients in practice from harm. Human participants are required to give informed consent prior to participating in research. Records of human behavior are kept confidential.

25. Is it ethical for psychologists to deceive research participants about the methods and objectives of their research?
Deception is ethical only when research cannot be conducted without it. Deceived participants must be debriefed after a study.

26. What are the ethical issues that concern research with animals?
Ethical standards require that animals may be harmed only if there is no alternative and the benefits justify the harm.

KEY TERMS

Applied research (p. 5)
Behaviorism (p. 11)
Biological perspective (p. 14)
Blind (p. 31)
Case study (p. 24)
Cognition (p. 16)
Cognitive perspective (p. 14)
Control group (p. 31)
Correlation (p. 23)
Correlation coefficient (p. 29)
Correlational method (p. 29)
Critical thinking (p. 20)
Debrief (p. 35)
Dependent variable (p. 30)
Double-blind study (p. 31)
Empirical science (p. 22)
Ethical (p. 33)
Ethnic group (p. 16)
Evolutionary perspective (p. 14)

Existentialism (p. 15)
Experiment (p. 30)
Experimental group (p. 30)
Experimenter bias (p. 31)
Functionalism (p. 9)
Gender (p. 16)
Generalize (p. 23)
Gestalt psychology (p. 11)
Humanism (p. 15)
Hypothesis (p. 23)
Independent variable (p. 30)
Informed consent (p. 34)
Insight (p. 11)
Instinctive (p. 14)
Introspection (p. 8)
Naturalistic observation (p. 27)
Negative correlation (p. 29)
Placebo (p. 31)
Population (p. 23)

Positive correlation (p. 29)
Psychoanalysis (p. 13)
Psychology (p. 4)
Pure research (p. 5)
Random sample (p. 24)
Reinforcement (p. 11)
Replicate (p. 23)
Sample (p. 23)
Scientific method (p. 22)
Selection factor (p. 23)
Social-cognitive theory (p. 16)
Sociocultural perspective (p. 16)
Stratified sample (p. 24)
Structuralism (p. 8)
Survey (p. 26)
Theory (p. 5)
Treatment (p. 30)
Volunteer bias (p. 24)

ACTIVE LEARNING RESOURCES

Log in to **www.cengagebrain.com** to access the resources your instructor requires. For this book, you can access:

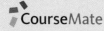 CourseMate brings course concepts to life with interactive learning, study, and exam preparation tools that support the printed textbook. A textbook-specific website, Psychology CourseMate includes an integrated interactive eBook and other interactive learning tools including quizzes, flashcards, videos, and more.

 Need help studying? This site is your one-stop study shop. Take a Pre-Test and CengageNOW will generate a Personalized Study Plan based on your test results. The Study Plan will identify the topics you need to review and direct you to online resources to help you master those topics. You can then take a Post-Test to determine the concepts you have mastered and what you still need to work on.

2 Biology and Psychology

© Colin Anderson/Getty Images

MAJOR TOPICS

Evolution and Evolutionary Psychology: "Survivor" Is More Than Just a TV Show 39

Heredity: The Nature of Nature 43

The Nervous System: On Being Wired 49

Video Connections—The Action Potential 52

The Brain: The Star of the Human Nervous System 59

The Endocrine System: Chemicals in the Bloodstream 70

FEATURES

A Closer Look: Charles Darwin 40

A Closer Look: Are You a Human or a Mouse? Some Fascinating Facts about Genes 46

A Closer Look: Mirror, Mirror, in the Brain: Who's the Fairest Imitator of Them All? 66

Concept Review 2.1: The Endocrine System 70

Life Connections: Coping with PMS 74

T F Charles Darwin was nearly excluded from the voyage that led to the development of his theory of evolution because the captain of the ship did not approve of the shape of his nose.

page 39

T F Neanderthals are not necessarily extinct; they may be lurking in your genes.

page 46

T F The human brain is larger than that of any other animal.

page 49

T F One cell can stretch all the way from your spine to your toe.

page 50

T F Messages travel in the brain by means of electricity.

page 52

T F A single brain cell can send out hundreds of messages every second—and manage to catch some rest in between.

page 53

T F Fear can give you indigestion.

page 58

T F If a surgeon were to electrically stimulate a certain part of your brain, you might swear that someone had stroked your leg.

page 65

T F A hormone turns a disinterested male rodent into a doting father.

page 71

Are these items truth or fiction? We will be revisiting them throughout the chapter.

He almost missed the boat. Literally. British naturalist Charles Darwin had volunteered to serve as the scientist for an expeditionary voyage on H.M.S. *Beagle,* but the captain, Robert Fitz-Roy, objected to Darwin because of the shape of his nose. **Truth or Fiction Revisited:** Thus, it is true that Darwin was nearly prevented from undertaking his historic voyage due to the shape of his nose. Fitz-Roy believed that you could judge a person's character by the outline of his facial features, and Darwin's nose didn't fit the . . . bill. But Fitz-Roy relented, and in the 1830s, Darwin undertook the voyage to the Galápagos Islands that led to the development of his theory of evolution.
Darwin would write,

> Afterwards, I heard that I had run a very narrow risk of being rejected [as the *Beagle*'s scientist], on account of the shape of my nose! [Fitz-Roy] was convinced that he could judge a man's character by the outline of his features; and he doubted whether anyone with my nose could possess sufficient energy and determination for the voyage. But I think he was afterwards well-satisfied that my nose had spoken falsely.

● EVOLUTION AND EVOLUTIONARY PSYCHOLOGY: "SURVIVOR" IS MORE THAN JUST A TV SHOW

In 1871, Darwin published *The Descent of Man,* which made the case that humans, like other species, were a product of evolution. He argued that the great apes (chimpanzees, gorillas, and so on) and humans shared a common primate ancestor (see Figure 2.1 ■). Many ridiculed Darwin's views because they were displeased with the notion that they might share ancestry with apes. Darwin's theory also contradicted the Book of Genesis, which stated that humans had been created in one day in the image of God.

At the Galápagos Islands, Darwin found himself immersed in the unfolding of a huge game of "Survivor." But here the game was for real, and the rewards had nothing to do with fame or fortune. The rewards were reaching sexual maturity, mating, and transmitting one's genes into subsequent generations. **Question 1: What are some of the basic concepts of the theory of evolution?**

The concept of a *struggle for existence* lies at the core of the theory of evolution. The universe is no bed of roses. Since the beginning of time, the universe has been changing. For billions of years, microscopic particles have been forming immense gas clouds in space. Galaxies and solar systems have been condensing from the clouds, sparkling for some eons, and then winking out. Change has brought life and death and countless challenges to survival. As described by evolutionary theory, some creatures have adapted

"I am turned into a sort of machine for observing facts and grinding out conclusions."

CHARLES DARWIN

Natural selection A core concept of the theory of evolution that holds that adaptive genetic variations among members of a species enable individuals with those variations to survive and reproduce. As a result, such variations tend to be preserved, whereas nonadaptive variations tend to drop out.

successfully to these challenges, and their numbers have increased. Others have not met the challenges and have fallen back into the distant mists of time. The species that prosper and those that fade away are thus determined by **natural selection**.

When we humans first appeared on planet Earth, our survival required a different sort of struggle than it does today. We fought or fled from predators such as leopards. We foraged across parched lands for food. We might have warred with humanoid creatures very much like ourselves—creatures who have since become extinct. But because of the evolution of our intellect, not fangs nor wings nor claws, we prevailed. Our numbers have increased. We continue to transmit the traits that led to our selection down through the generations by means of genetic material whose chemical codes are only now being cracked.

Just what is handed down through the generations? The answer is biological, or physiological, structures and processes. Our biology serves as the material base for our behaviors, emotions, and cognitions (our thoughts, images, and plans). Biology somehow gives rise to specific behavioral tendencies in some organisms, such as the chick's instinctive fear of the shadow of a hawk. But the behavior of many species, especially higher species such as humans, is flexible and affected by environmental factors and choice as well as by heredity.

A CLOSER LOOK : Charles Darwin

© The Granger Collection, New York

As far as I can judge of myself I worked to the utmost during the voyage [of the *Beagle*] from the mere pleasure of investigation, and from my strong desire to add a few facts to the great mass of facts in natural science.

—Charles Darwin

Charles Darwin was a dabbler who, in one of history's coincidences, was born on the same day as Abraham Lincoln (February 12, 1809). Darwin's father was a well-known physician, and his mother was Susannah Wedgwood of the chinaware family. His cousin was Sir Francis Galton, who made many innovations in psychological measurement. Unlike Galton, Darwin gave no early signs of genius. He did so poorly in school that his father feared he would disgrace himself and the family. Nevertheless, Darwin went on to change the face of modern thought.

Darwin enjoyed collecting and classifying plants, minerals, and animals. He tried medical school, entered Cambridge University to become an Anglican priest, and eventually graduated with a degree in science. Because he was independently wealthy, Darwin undertook the 5-year volunteer position aboard H.M.S. *Beagle*. The ship stopped at the Galápagos Islands, where Darwin observed how species of lizards, tortoises, and plants varied from island to island. Although Darwin undertook his voyage as a believer in the Book of Genesis account of creation, his observations convinced him that the organisms he observed shared common ancestors but had evolved in different directions.

In midlife, Darwin almost missed the boat again. From his observations of sea lions, tortoises, insects, and plants, he was ready to formulate his theory of evolution upon his return from his voyage. But because he was "anxious to avoid prejudice," Darwin did not want his theory of evolution to be published until after his death. He feared it would be immensely unpopular because it contradicted religious views, and it would bring scorn on his family. He shared his ideas with a few fellow scientists, but he finally published his ideas more broadly 20 years later when he learned that other scientists, including Alfred Russel Wallace, a scientist who had worked in the Amazon, were about to publish similar ideas on evolution. Papers by both Darwin and Wallace were read at the Linnaean Society, and Darwin's *On the Origin of Species by Natural Selection* (1859) was published shortly thereafter. The public's interest in evolutionary theory had been aroused, and the first printing of Darwin's book sold out on the first day. Later, Darwin would publish his book *The Descent of Man,* which claimed that modern-day humans were, like other species, a product of evolution and that humans and apes shared common ancestors. Needless to say, Darwin's views became better known than those of Wallace. (Have you ever heard of Wallace's theory of evolution?)

Darwin, of course, did meet with prejudice. The notion that humans and apes have common ancestors met with ridicule. In fact, many school boards in the United States object to the teaching of evolution to this day.

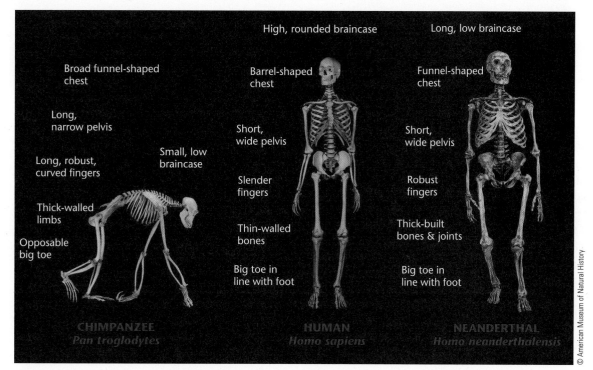

| CHIMPANZEE *Pan troglodytes* | HUMAN *Homo sapiens* | NEANDERTHAL *Homo neanderthalensis* |

Figure 2.1 ■ The Human Skeleton and the Skeletons of Some Relatives The idea that humans were genetically related to monkeys and other animals was so divergent from other 19th-century views of our species that Darwin was initially reluctant to discuss his theory of evolution. *The Descent of Man,* published in 1871, made the case that humans, like other species, were a product of evolution. Darwin believed that the great apes (chimpanzees, gorillas, and so on) shared a common primate ancestor. We did not descend from Neanderthals, but we coexisted with them for thousands of years. Neanderthals became extinct some 35,000 years ago.

Doing What Comes Naturally

According to the theory of evolution, there is a struggle for survival as various species and individuals compete for a limited quantity of resources. The combined genetic instructions from parents lead to variations among individuals. No one who ever lived, except, perhaps, for your identical twin, is exactly like you. There are also sharper divergences from parents caused by sudden changes in genetic material called **mutations.** Those individuals whose variations in traits are better adapted to their environments are more likely to survive (that is, to be naturally selected). Survival permits them to reach sexual maturity, to select mates, and to reproduce, thereby transmitting their features or traits to the next generation. What began as a minor variation, or a mutation, becomes embedded in more and more individuals over the generations—if it fosters survival. Chance variations that hinder survival are likely to disappear from the gene pool.

> *"My nose had spoken falsely."*
> CHARLES DARWIN

Mutation A sudden variation in an inheritable characteristic as distinguished from a variation that results from generations of gradual selection.

> *"It is not the strongest of the species that survives, nor the most intelligent that survives. It is the one that is the most adaptable to change."*
> CHARLES DARWIN

> *"The lion and the calf shall lie down together but the calf won't get much sleep."*
> WOODY ALLEN

Dinosaurs Long ago and right here on planet Earth, dinosaurs once ruled the day. However, they—along with 99.99% of all species that ever existed—are now extinct. Evidence that they existed, and when they existed, is found in the fossil record.

Evolutionary Psychology

Evolutionary psychology The branch of psychology that studies the ways adaptation and natural selection are connected with mental processes and behavior.

Species A category of biological classification consisting of related organisms that are capable of inter-breeding. *Homo sapiens*—humans—make up one species.

Instinct A stereotyped pattern of behavior triggered by a particular stimulus and nearly identical among members of a species, even when reared in isolation.

These same concepts of *adaptation* and *natural selection* have also been applied to psychological traits and are key concepts in **evolutionary psychology. Question 2: What is evolutionary psychology?** Evolutionary psychology studies the ways adaptation and natural selection are connected with mental processes and behavior (Buss, 2009a). Over the eons, evolution has provided organisms with advantages such as stronger fins and wings, sharper claws, and camouflage. Human evolution has given rise to various physical traits and also to such diverse activities as language, art, committed relationships, and warfare. Evolutionary psychologist David M. Buss (2009a) writes that the field attempts to answer questions such as why do so many struggles have to do with sex? Why is there so much social conflict? What are the mechanisms of the mind that define human nature?

One of the concepts of evolutionary psychology is that not only physical traits but also patterns of behavior, including social behavior, evolve and are transmitted genetically from generation to generation. In other words, behavior patterns that help an organism survive and reproduce are likely to be transmitted to the next generation (Buss, 2009a). Such behaviors are believed to include aggression, strategies of mate selection, and even altruism (that is, self-sacrifice of the individual to help perpetuate the family grouping) (Buss, 2009b; Lukaszewski & Roney, 2009). The behavior patterns are termed *instinctive* or *species-specific* because they evolved within certain **species.**

Question 3: What is an instinct? An **instinct** is a stereotyped pattern of behavior that is triggered in a specific situation. Instinctive behavior is nearly identical among the members of the species in which it appears. It tends to resist modification, even when it serves no purpose (as in the interminable barking of some breeds of dogs) or results in punishment. Instinctive behavior also appears when the individual is reared in isolation from others of its kind and thus cannot learn the behavior from experience.

Consider some examples of instinctive behavior. If you place an egg from the nest of a goose a few inches in front of her, she will roll it back to the nest with her beak. However, she won't retrieve it if it's farther away—in the "not my egg" zone. If you rear

"The very essence of instinct is that it's followed independently of reason."

CHARLES DARWIN

Instinctive Behavior The male stickleback instinctively attacks fish (or pieces of painted wood) with the kinds of red bellies that are characteristic of other male sticklebacks. Sticklebacks will show the stereotyped instinctive behavior even when they are reared in isolation from other members of their species. We rear an organism in isolation so that we can be certain that it is not learning the targeted behavior from another member of its species.

© David Thompson/OSF/Animals, Animals

a white-crowned sparrow in isolation from other sparrows, it will still sing a recognizable species-specific song when it matures. The male stickleback fish instinctively attacks fish (or pieces of painted wood) with the kinds of red bellies that are characteristic of other male sticklebacks (Dzieweczynski et al., 2009). Many psychologists consider language to be instinctive in humans, and psychologists are trying to determine whether aspects of human mate selection and aggression are instinctive. However, even instinctive behavior can be modified to some degree by learning, and most psychologists agree that the richness and complexity of human behavior are made possible by human learning ability.

LearningConnections • EVOLUTION AND EVOLUTIONARY PSYCHOLOGY: "SURVIVOR" IS MORE THAN JUST A TV SHOW

ACTIVE REVIEW (1) The concept of a struggle for _____ lies at the core of the theory of evolution. (2) Individuals whose traits are better _____ to their environments are more likely to survive and reproduce. (3) _____ psychology studies the ways adaptation and natural selection are connected with mental processes and behavior. (4) Stereotypical behavior patterns that have evolved within certain species are called _____.

REFLECT AND RELATE Have you known family pets that have engaged in instinctive behavior? What was the behavior? Why do you believe it was instinctive?

CRITICAL THINKING Do you believe that this textbook, and other textbooks, should present the theory of evolution? Why or why not?

 Go to Psychology CourseMate at **www.cengagebrain.com** for an interactive version of these questions.

Consider some facts of life:

- People cannot breathe underwater (without special equipment).
- People cannot fly (again, without rather special equipment).
- Fish cannot learn to speak French or do an Irish jig even if you rear them in enriched environments and send them to finishing school.
- Chimpanzees and gorillas can use sign language but cannot speak.

People cannot breathe underwater or fly (without oxygen tanks, airplanes, or other devices) because of their *heredity*. **Question 4: What is heredity?** Heredity defines one's *nature*—which is based on one's biological structures and processes. **Heredity** refers to the biological transmission of traits that have evolved from generation to generation. Fish are limited in different ways by their natural traits. Chimpanzees and gorillas can understand many spoken words and express some concepts through nonverbal symbol systems such as American Sign Language. However, apes cannot speak. They have probably failed to inherit humanlike speech areas of the brain. Their nature differs from ours. Our speech mechanisms have evolved differently.

Genetics and Behavioral Genetics

Heredity both makes behaviors possible and places limits on them. **Question 5: What is genetics?** Genetics is the subfield of biology that studies heredity. **Behavioral genetics** bridges the sciences of psychology and biology. It is concerned with the genetic transmission of traits that give rise to patterns of behavior.

The field of genetics looks at both species-specific behavior patterns (instincts) and individual differences among the members of a species. Behavioral genetics studies the effects of genetics on animal and human behavior. Psychologists are thinking in terms of behavioral genetics when they ask about the inborn reasons that individuals differ in their behavior and mental processes. For example, some children learn language more quickly than others. Part of the reason may lie in behavioral genetics—their heredity. But some children also experience a richer exposure to language at early ages.

Heredity appears to be a factor in almost all aspects of human behavior, personality, and mental processes (Plomin & Asbury, 2005; Plomin & Haworth, 2009). Examples include sociability, anxiety, social dominance, leadership, effectiveness as a parent or a therapist, happiness, and even interest in arts and crafts (Blum et al., 2009; Ebstein et al., 2010; Leonardo & Hen, 2006). **Question 6: What are the roles of genes and chromosomes in heredity?**

Genes and Chromosomes: The Building Blocks of Heredity

Genes are the most basic building blocks of heredity. They regulate the development of specific traits. It is estimated that your cells contain 20,000 to 25,000 genes (International Human Genome Sequencing Consortium, 2006).

Genes are segments of **chromosomes**. That is, chromosomes are made up of strings of genes. Each cell in the body contains 46 chromosomes arranged in 23 pairs. Chromosomes are large complex molecules of DNA (short for *deoxyribonucleic acid*), which has several chemical components. The tightly wound structure of DNA was first demonstrated in the 1950s by James Watson and Francis Crick. DNA takes the form of a double helix—a twisting molecular ladder (see Figure 2.2 ■). The "rungs" of the ladder are made up of chemicals called *nucleotides* whose names are abbreviated as A, T, C, and G. The nucleotide A always links up with T to complete a rung, and C always combines with G. Therefore, you can describe the *genetic code* in terms of the nucleotides you find along just one of the rungs—for example, CTGAGTCAC and so on. A single gene can contain hundreds of thousands of base pairs. So if you think of a gene as a word, it can be a few hundred thousand letters long and completely unpronounceable.

> *"It's necessary to be slightly underemployed if you are to do something significant."*
>
> JAMES D. WATSON,
> ONE OF THE DISCOVERERS OF DNA

Heredity The transmission of traits from parent to offspring by means of genes.

Genetics The area of biology that focuses on heredity.

Behavioral genetics The area of biology and psychology that focuses on the transmission of traits that give rise to behavior.

Gene A basic unit of heredity, which is found at a specific point on a chromosome.

Chromosome A microscopic rod-shaped body in the cell nucleus carrying genes that transmit hereditary traits from generation to generation.

DNA Abbreviation for deoxyribonucleic acid, the substance that forms the basic material of chromosomes. It takes the form of a double helix and contains the genetic code.

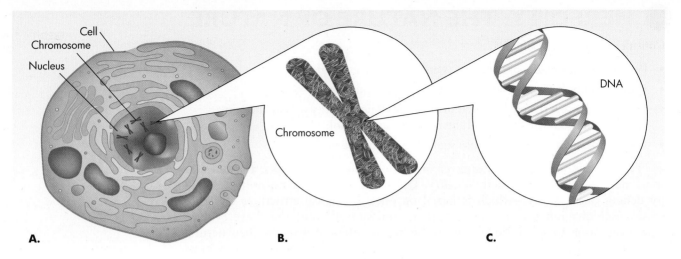

Figure 2.2 ■ Cells, Chromosomes, and DNA A. The nuclei of cells contain chromosomes. B. Chromosomes are made up of DNA. C. Segments of DNA are made up of genes that determine physical traits such as height, eye color, and whether pigs have wings (no, because of their genetic makeup, they don't). Genes are segments of chromosomes that are found with the nuclei of cells. The genetic code—that is, the order of the chemicals A, T, C, and G—determines your species and all those traits that can be inherited, from the color of your eyes to predispositions toward many psychological traits and abilities, including sociability and musical talent.

Polygenic Referring to traits that are influenced by combinations of genes.

Genotype One's genetic makeup based on the sequencing of the nucleotides we term A, C, G, and T.

Phenotype One's actual development and appearance based on one's genotype and environmental influences.

Nature The inborn, innate character of an organism.

Nurture The sum total of the environmental factors that affect an organism from conception onward. (In another usage, *nurture* refers to the act of nourishing and otherwise promoting the development of youngsters.)

Sex chromosomes The 23rd pair of chromosomes, whose genetic material determines the sex of the individual.

A group of scientists working together around the globe in an endeavor referred to as the Human Genome Project has learned that the sequencing of your DNA consists of about 3 billion DNA sequences spread throughout your chromosomes (Plomin & Schalkwyk, 2007). These sequences—the order of the chemicals we call A, T, C, and G—caused you to grow arms and not wings and skin rather than scales. Psychologists debate the extent to which genes influence complex psychological traits such as intelligence, aggressiveness, and happiness and the appearance of psychological disorders such as schizophrenia. Some traits, such as eye color, are determined by a single pair of genes. Other traits, especially complex psychological traits such as sociability and aggressiveness, are thought to be **polygenic**—that is, influenced by combinations of genes.

Your genetic code provides your **genotype**—that is, your full genetic potential as determined by the sequencing of the chemicals in your DNA. But the person you see in the mirror was also influenced by your early experiences in the home, injuries, adequacy of nourishment, educational experiences, and numerous other environmental influences. Therefore, you see the outer appearance of your *phenotype*, including the hairstyles of the day. Your **phenotype** is the way your genetic code manifests itself because of your experiences and environmental circumstances. Your genotype enables you to acquire language. Your phenotype reveals that you are likely to be speaking English if you were reared in the United States or Spanish if you were reared in Mexico (or both if you are Mexican American).

Your genotype provides what psychologists refer to as your **nature**. Your phenotype represents the interaction of you nature (heredity) and your **nurture** (environmental influences) in the origins of your behavior and mental processes. Psychologists are especially interested in the roles of nature and nurture in intelligence and psychological disorders. Our genotypes provide us with physical traits that set the stage for certain behaviors. But none of us is the result of heredity alone. Environmental factors such as nutrition, learning opportunities, cultural influences, exercise, and (unfortunately) accident and illness also determine our phenotypes and whether genetically possible behaviors will be displayed. Behavior and mental processes represent the interaction of nature and nurture. A potential Shakespeare who is reared in poverty and never taught to read or write will not create a *Hamlet*.

We normally receive 23 chromosomes from our father's sperm cell and 23 chromosomes from our mother's egg cell (ovum). When a sperm cell fertilizes an ovum, the chromosomes form 23 pairs (see Figure 2.3 ■). The 23rd pair consists of **sex chromosomes**, which determine whether we are female or male. We all receive an

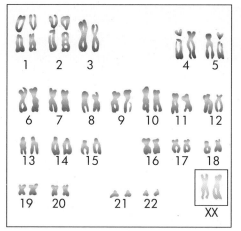
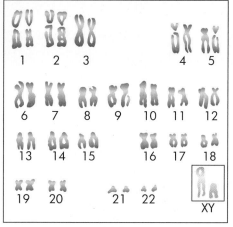

Female   Male

Figure 2.3 ■ The 23 Pairs of Human Chromosomes People normally have 23 pairs of chromosomes. Whether one is female or male is determined by the 23rd pair of chromosomes. Females have two X sex chromosomes, whereas males have an X and a Y sex chromosome.

X sex chromosome (so called because of the X shape) from our mother. If we also receive an X sex chromosome from our father, we develop into a female. If we receive a Y sex chromosome (named after its Y shape) from our father, we develop into a male. In the following section, we observe the unfortunate results that may occur when people do not receive the normal complement of chromosomes from their parents.

DOWN SYNDROME When people do not have the normal number of 46 chromosomes (23 pairs), physical and behavioral abnormalities may result. Most persons with Down syndrome, for example, have an extra, or third, chromosome on the 21st pair. The extra chromosome is usually contributed by the mother, and the condition becomes increasingly likely as the mother's age at the time of pregnancy increases. Persons with Down syndrome have a downward-sloping fold of skin at the inner corners of the eyes, a round face, a protruding tongue, and a broad, flat nose. They are cognitively impaired and usually have physical problems that cause death by middle age.

Kinship Studies: Is the Behavior of Relatives Related?

Question 7: What are kinship studies? In *kinship studies,* psychologists compare the presence of traits and behavior patterns in people who are biologically related or unrelated to help determine the role of genetic factors in their occurrence. The more *closely* people are related, the more *genes* they have in common. Identical twins share 100% of their genes. Parents and children have 50% of their genes in common, as do siblings (brothers and sisters). Aunts and uncles related by blood have a 25% overlap with nieces and nephews. First cousins share 12.5% of their genes. If genes are involved in a trait or behavior pattern, people who are more closely related should be more likely to show similar traits or behavior. Psychologists and behavioral geneticists are especially interested in running kinship studies with twins and adopted individuals (Plomin & Haworth, 2009).

TWIN STUDIES: LOOKING INTO THE GENETIC MIRROR The fertilized egg cell (ovum) that carries genetic messages from both parents is called a *zygote.* Now and then, a zygote divides into two cells that separate so that instead of developing into a single person, it develops into two people with the same genetic makeup. Such people are identical, or **monozygotic (MZ), twins.** If the woman releases two ova in the same month and they are both fertilized, they develop into fraternal, or **dizygotic (DZ), twins.** Dizygotic twins, like other siblings, share 50% of their genes. Monozygotic twins

© Michael Greenlar/The Image Works

Down Syndrome Down syndrome is caused by an extra chromosome on the 21st pair and becomes more likely to occur as the mother's age at the time of pregnancy increases. Persons with Down syndrome have characteristic facial features including downward-sloping folds of skin at the inner corners of the eyes, are intellectually deficient, and usually have health problems that lead to death by middle age.

Down syndrome A condition caused by an extra chromosome on the 21st pair and characterized by mental deficiency, a broad face, and slanting eyes.

Monozygotic (MZ) twins Twins that develop from a single fertilized ovum that divides in two early in prenatal development. MZ twins thus share the same genetic code. Also called *identical twins.*

Dizygotic (DZ) twins Twins that develop from two fertilized ova and who are thus as closely related as brothers and sisters in general. Also called *fraternal twins.*

A randomly selected sequence of your genetic code would overlap about 25% with a randomly selected sequence of the genetic code of a carrot. Don't be concerned. It doesn't mean you're going to turn orange, nor that you are about to enter your "salad days." So, to quote carrot maven Bugs Bunny, "What's up, Doc?" What's "up" is that your genetic code, like the genetic codes of other life forms, is a sequence of four chemicals. By chance alone, then, one of four in the sequence would be repeated in any randomly selected segments of carrot and human DNA.

That 0.1% of Difference Can Be Quite a Difference The genetic codes of humans overlap by 99.9% However, the remaining 0.1% can make quite a difference, as in the cases of cellist Yo Yo Ma (left) and professional football players (right).

The house mouse is not only in your pantry; much of it is in your genes. The genomes of humans and mice have been decoded, and of the 20,000 to 25,000 genes possessed by each, about 18,800 to 24,750 genes in one have some counterpart in the other (Gunter & Dhand, 2002; Lappalainen & Dermitzakis, 2010). The counterparts are not necessarily the same; for example, the mouse has more genes related to odor detection and thus a better sense of smell. The genetic difference between mice and humans results from some 75 million years of evolution along different paths from a common mammalian ancestor. When we consider how different we appear to be from the mouse, it is remarkable how similar we are in genetic makeup. But only a few hundred genes apparently explain why mice are pests (and pets). The overlap also makes mice—and their genetic cousins, rats—excellent stand-ins for humans in medical research.

Our closest genetic relatives are chimpanzees, with whom we may have shared a common ancestor some 6 to 9 million years ago. Only 1.58% of the genetic code of the chimpanzee differs from our own. Putting it another way, our genetic codes overlap with those of chimps by more than 98% (Xu et al., 2010; Zimmer, 2002–2003)!

The sequence of your own DNA also overlaps about 99.9% with that of other humans (Plomin & Crabbe, 2000). Yet the difference of 0.1% accounts for the differences between Mozart and Nelson Mandela and between Sandra Oh and Oprah Winfrey. Despite this enormous overlap, people differ greatly in their skin coloration, their body shape, and their psychological makeup, including their talents and skills. Some compose symphonies and others are tone-deaf. Some tackle differential equations and others cannot add or subtract. Some figure-skate in the Olympics, and others trip over their own feet. Even though we differ but 0.1% in genetic code from our fellows, it often seems easier to focus on how much we differ rather than on how much we have in common.

Truth or Fiction Revisited: Neanderthals and some other ancient humanoids may not be quite as extinct as has been believed. In fact, they may be "lurking" in your own genetic code. Analysis of DNA suggests that modern humans—that's us—probably interbred with other humanoids rather than simply replacing them (Forhan et al., 2008). When you misbehave, could you now say it's the Neanderthal in you? Of course, the truth could be quite the reverse.

are important in the study of the relative influences of nature (heredity) and nurture (the environment) because, since they share 100% of their genes, differences between such twins are the result of nurture. (They do not differ in their heredity—that is, their nature—because their genetic makeup is the same.)

Twin studies compare the presence of traits and behavior patterns in MZ twins, DZ twins, and other people to help determine the role of genetic factors in their occurrence. If MZ twins show greater similarity on a trait or behavior pattern than DZ twins, a genetic basis for the trait or behavior is suggested.

Twin studies show how strongly genetic factors influence physical features. Monozygotic twins are more likely to look alike, to be similar in height, and even to have more similar cholesterol levels than DZ twins (Souren et al., 2007). This finding holds even when the identical twins are reared apart and the fraternal twins are reared together (Stunkard et al., 1990).

Other physical similarities between pairs of MZ twins may be more subtle, but they are also strong. For example, research shows that MZ twin sisters begin to menstruate about 1 to 2 months apart, whereas DZ twins begin to menstruate about a year apart. Monozygotic twins are more alike than dizygotic twins in their blood pressure, brain wave patterns, and in their speech patterns, gestures, and mannerisms (Ambrosius et al., 2008; Lykken et al., 1992; Wessel et al., 2007).

Monozygotic twins also resemble one another more strongly than dizygotic twins in psychological traits, such as intelligence, and personality traits, such as sociability, anxiety, friendliness, conformity, and happiness (Lykken, 2007; Markon et al., 2002; McCrae et al., 2000; Veselka et al., 2009). David Lykken and Mike Csikszentmihalyi (2001) suggest that we inherit a tendency toward a certain level of happiness. Despite the ups and downs of life, we tend to drift back to our usual levels of cheerfulness (or irritability). Heredity is also a key contributor to developmental factors, such as cognitive functioning, and early signs of attachment, such as smiling, cuddling, and the expression of fear of strangers (Plomin & Haworth, 2009; Segal, 2009).

Twins Monozygotic twins share 100% of their genes, whereas dizygotic twins share 50% of their genes.

Monozygotic twins are more likely than dizygotic twins to share psychological disorders such as autism, depression, schizophrenia, and vulnerability to alcoholism (Dworzynski et al., 2009; Plomin, 2000; Veenstra-Vanderweele & Cook, 2003). In one study on autism, the agreement rate for MZ twins was about 60%. (That is, if one member of a pair of MZ twins was autistic, the other member had a 60% chance of being so.) The concordance rate for DZ twins was only 10% (Plomin et al., 1994).

Of course, twin studies are not perfect. Monozygotic twins may resemble each other more closely than dizygotic twins partly because they are treated more similarly. Monozygotic twins frequently are dressed identically, and parents sometimes have difficulty telling them apart.

One way to get around this difficulty is to find and compare MZ twins who were reared in different homes. Any similarities between MZ twins reared apart cannot be explained by a shared home environment and would appear to be largely a result of heredity. In the fascinating Minnesota Study of Twins Reared Apart (Lykken, 2007), researchers have been measuring the physiological and psychological characteristics of 56 sets of MZ adult twins who were separated in infancy and reared in different homes. Constance Holden (1980) wrote a progress report on the study when it had processed 9 pairs of MZ twins and was about to study 11 other pairs. A team of psychologists, psychiatrists, and other professionals analyzed the twins' life histories, including their interests, medical problems, abilities, and intelligence.

All in all, there were some uncanny similarities between the pairs, except when there were extreme differences in their environment. Consider one pair of twins, both of whom were named Jim. Both were married and divorced. Both had been trained to become police officers. They each named their first sons James Allan. They drove the same kind of car and vacationed at the same beach. They each mentioned carpentry as a hobby; each had constructed a bench around a tree in the yard. There are certainly coincidences in their histories, and they were chosen for this lengthy description because of them. However, the interests in police work and carpentry are probably more than coincidental.

In sum, MZ twins reared apart are about as similar as MZ twins reared together on a variety of measures of intelligence, personality, temperament, occupational and leisure-time interests, and social attitudes. These traits thus would appear to have a genetic underpinning.

ADOPTION STUDIES The interpretation of kinship studies can be confused when relatives share similar environments as well as genes. *Adoption studies* offer special insight into the roles of nature and nurture in the development of traits, especially when they compare children who have been separated from their parents at an early age (or in which identical twins are separated at an early age) and reared in different environments. Psychologists look for similarities between children and their adoptive and natural parents. When children reared by adoptive parents are more similar to their natural parents in a particular trait, strong evidence exists for a genetic role in the appearance of that trait.

In later chapters, we will see that psychologists have been particularly interested in the use of adoption studies to sort out the effects of nature and nurture in the development of personality traits, intelligence, and various psychological disorders. Such traits and disorders apparently represent the interaction of complex groupings of genes as well as environmental influences.

> *"I believe that every person is born with talent."*
>
> MAYA ANGELOU

> *"I have no special talent. I am only passionately curious."*
>
> ALBERT EINSTEIN

Genetic–Environmental Correlation: The Interaction of Nature and Nurture

One of the problems in sorting out the influences of heredity and environment, or nature and nurture, is that genes in part determine the environments to which people are exposed (Gottlieb, 2007; Narusyte et al., 2008). This aspect of development is termed *genetic–environmental correlation*. Not only do children's biological parents contribute genes to their offspring, but they also intentionally and unintentionally place them in certain kinds of environments. For example, artistically oriented parents are likely not only to transmit genes that predispose their children to have an interest in the arts but also to expose their children to artistic activities such as visits to museums and piano lessons. As we develop, we are more likely to take an active, conscious role in choosing or creating our environments. For example, adolescents may select after-school activities that are connected with their academic, artistic, or athletic interests. Choosing environments that allow us to develop inherited preferences is termed *niche-picking* (W. Johnson et al., 2009; Plomin & Daniels, 1987).

The Epigenetic Framework

The relationship between genetic and environmental influences is not a one-way street. Instead, it is bidirectional (Gottlieb, 2007; Narusyte et al., 2008). Although it is true that our genes affect the development of our traits and behaviors, our traits and behaviors also prompt certain kinds of responses from other people and lead us to place ourselves in certain environments. These environments—specialized schools, after-school activities, museums, the theater, certain films and television programs—all affect how genes are expressed. According to what developmental psychologists call **epigenesis**, or the *epigenetic framework*, our development reflects continuing bidirectional exchanges between our genetic heritages and the environments in which we find or place ourselves (Lickliter & Logan, 2007; Vercelli & Piattelli-Palmarini, 2009).

Genetic–Environmental Correlation Both of these girls are athletic, but the one to the left immediately felt at home during a ballet class and chose to continue. The one on the right was not at all tempted by dance, but she enjoyed soccer and was competitive, so she joined her school's soccer team.

© Brand X Pictures/Jupiterimages/Veer

© Rubberball/Veer

LearningConnections • HEREDITY: THE NATURE OF NATURE

ACTIVE REVIEW (5) _____ are the most basic building blocks of heredity. (6) Genes are segments of _____. (7) People with _____ syndrome have an extra chromosome on the 21st pair. (8) The behavior of _____ twins is of special interest to psychologists because their genetic endowment is the same.

REFLECT AND RELATE Which family members seem to be like you physically or psychologically? Which seem to be very different? How do you explain the similarities and differences?

CRITICAL THINKING Given that people have unique sets of genes (with the exception of identical twins), can people be said to be equal? If so, in what way?

 Go to Psychology CourseMate at **www.cengagebrain.com** for an interactive version of these questions.

As a child, I did not think it sounded like a good thing to have a "nervous" system. After all, if your system were not "nervous," or jittery, you might be less likely to jump at strange noises. Later, I learned that a nervous system is not a system that is nervous. It is a system of nerves involved in thought processes, heartbeat, visual–motor coordination, and so on.

I also learned that the human nervous system is more complex than that of any other animal and that our brains are larger than those of any other animal. Now, this last piece of business is not quite true. A human brain weighs about 3 pounds, but the brains of elephants and whales may be four times as heavy. **Truth or Fiction Revisited:** Thus, it is not true that the human brain is larger than that of any other animal. Still, our brains account for a greater part of our body weight than do those of elephants or whales. Our brains weigh about 1/60th of our body weight. Elephant brains weigh about 1/1,000th of their total weight, and whale brains are a paltry 1/10,000th of their weight. So humans win the brain-as-a-percentage-of-body-weight contest. Figure 2.4 ■ shows the human brain compared with the brains of some other mammals.

The brain is only one part of the nervous system, which, as we will see, serves as the material base for our behaviors, emotions, and cognitions (our thoughts, images, and plans). As the nervous system is composed of cells that are mostly neurons, we begin our study of it with an examination of those neurons.

Neurons: Into the Fabulous Forest

Within our brains lies a fabulous forest of nerve cells, or neurons. **Question 8: What are neurons? Neurons** are specialized cells of the nervous system that conduct impulses. These cells can be visualized as having branches, trunks, and roots—something like trees. As we voyage through the neuron forest, we see that many of them lie alongside one another like a thicket of trees. But neurons can also lie end to end, with their "roots" intertwined with the "branches" of the neurons that lie below. Whereas trees receive sunlight, water, and nutrients from the soil, neurons receive "messages" from a number of sources, such as the senses of vision and touch, and from other neurons, and they can pass these messages along in a complex biological dance.

We are born with more than 100 billion neurons. Most of them are found in the brain. The nervous system also contains glial cells, or **glia**. It has long been known that glia remove dead neurons and waste products from the nervous system, nourish neurons, and direct their growth (Filosa et al., 2009; Gordon et al., 2009). Now we know that glia also synchronize the transmission of messages of nearby neurons, enabling them to transmit messages in waves (Perea et al., 2009).

Neurons occupy center stage in the nervous system. The messages transmitted by neurons somehow account for phenomena ranging from the perception of an itch from a mosquito bite to the coordination of a skier's vision and muscles to the composition of a concerto to the solution of an algebraic equation.

Neurons vary according to their functions and their location. Neurons in the brain may be only a fraction of an inch in length, whereas others that transmit messages between the spinal cord and the toes are several feet long. **Truth or Fiction Revisited:** Thus, it is true that a single cell can stretch all the way from your spine to your toe. Neurons include a cell body, dendrites, and an axon (see Figure 2.5 ■). The cell body contains the core, or *nucleus,* of the cell. The nucleus uses oxygen and nutrients to generate the energy needed to carry out the work of the cell. Anywhere from a few to several hundred short fibers, or **dendrites**, extend like roots from the cell body to receive incoming messages from thousands of adjoining neurons. Each neuron has an **axon** that extends like a trunk from the cell body. Axons are microscopically thin, but those that carry messages from the toes to the spinal cord extend several feet.

Like tree trunks, axons can branch off in different directions. Axons end in small bulb-shaped structures called *terminals,* or *terminal buttons.* Neurons carry messages in one direction only: from the dendrites or cell body through the axon to the axon terminals. The messages are then transmitted from the terminal buttons to other neurons, muscles, or glands.

Epigenesis The fact that children's development reflects continuing bidirectional exchanges between their genetic heritage and the environments in which they find themselves or place themselves.

Neuron A specialized cell of the nervous system that transmits messages.

Glia Cells that nourish neurons, remove waste products from the nervous system, and help synchronize the messages sent by neurons.

Dendrites Rootlike structures, attached to the cell body of a neuron, that receive impulses from other neurons.

Axon A long, thin part of a neuron that transmits impulses to other neurons, an organ, or muscle from branching structures called *terminal buttons.*

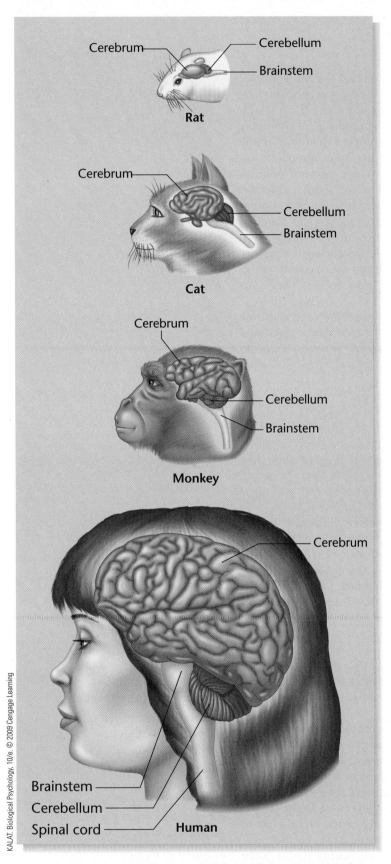

Figure 2.4 ■ Brains of Humans and of Some Other Mammals Other mammals have brains with parts that correspond to the human brain, although they differ in shape and size.

As a child matures, the axons of neurons become longer, and the dendrites and terminals proliferate, creating vast interconnected networks for the transmission of complex messages. The number of glial cells also increases as the nervous system develops, contributing to its dense appearance.

MYELIN The axons of many neurons are wrapped tightly with white, fatty **myelin** that makes them look like strings of sausages under the microscope (bratwurst, actually). The fat insulates the axon from electrically charged atoms, or ions, found in the fluids that surround the nervous system. This myelin sheath minimizes leakage of the electrical current being carried along the axon, thereby allowing messages to be conducted more efficiently.

Myelination is part of the maturation process that leads to the child's ability to crawl and walk during the first year. Infants are not physiologically "ready" to engage in visual–motor coordination and other activities until the coating process reaches certain levels. In people with the disease multiple sclerosis, myelin is replaced with a hard fibrous tissue that throws off the timing of nerve impulses and disrupts muscular control.

AFFERENT AND EFFERENT NEURONS: FROM THERE TO HERE AND HERE TO THERE If someone steps on your toes, the sensation is registered by receptors or sensory neurons near the surface of your skin. Then it is transmitted to the spinal cord and brain through **afferent neurons**, which are perhaps 2 to 3 feet long. In the brain, subsequent messages might be conveyed by associative neurons that are only a few thousandths of an inch long. You experience the pain through this process and perhaps entertain some rather nasty thoughts about the perpetrator, who is now apologizing and begging for understanding. Long before you arrive at any logical conclusions, however, motor neurons—**efferent neurons**—send messages to your foot so that you withdraw it and begin an impressive hopping routine. Other efferent neurons stimulate glands so that your heart is beating more rapidly, you are sweating, and the hair on the back of your arms has become erect! Being a good sport, you say, "Oh, it's nothing." But considering all the neurons involved, it really is something, isn't it?

In case you think that afferent and efferent neurons will be hard to distinguish because they sound pretty much the SAME to you, remember that they *are* the SAME. That is, *Sensory = Afferent* and *Motor = Efferent.*

The Neural Impulse: Let Us "Sing the Body Electric"[1]

In the 18th century, Italian physiologist Luigi Galvani (1737–1798) conducted a shocking experiment in a rainstorm. While his neighbors had the sense to remain indoors, Galvani and his wife were on the porch connecting

---

[1]From Walt Whitman's *Leaves of Grass.*

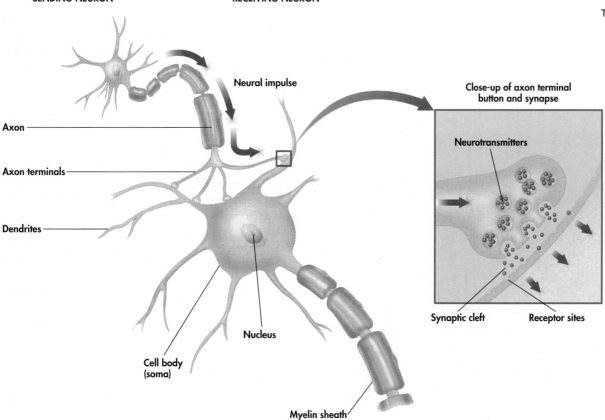

SENDING NEURON   RECEIVING NEURON

Neural impulse

Axon

Axon terminals

Dendrites

Nucleus

Cell body
(soma)

Myelin sheath

Close-up of axon terminal
button and synapse

Neurotransmitters

Synaptic cleft   Receptor sites

Figure 2.5 ■ The Anatomy of a Neuron "Messages" enter neurons through dendrites, are transmitted along the trunklike axon, and then are sent from axon terminal buttons to muscles, glands, and other neurons. Axon terminal buttons contain sacs of chemicals called *neurotransmitters*. Neurotransmitters are released into the synaptic cleft, where many of them bind to receptor sites on the dendrites of the receiving neuron. Dozens of neurotransmitters have been identified.

lightning rods to the heads of dissected frogs whose legs were connected by wires to a well of water. When lightning blazed above, the frogs' muscles contracted. This is not a recommended way to prepare frogs' legs. Galvani was demonstrating that the messages (*neural impulses*) that travel along neurons are electrochemical in nature.

Question 9: What are neural impulses? Neural impulses are messages that travel within neurons at somewhere between 2 miles an hour (in nonmyelinated neurons) and 225 miles an hour (in myelinated neurons). This speed is not impressive when compared with that of an electrical current in a toaster oven or a lamp, which can travel at close to the speed of light—more than 186,000 miles per second. Distances in the body are short, however, and a message will travel from a toe to the brain in perhaps 1/50th of a second.

AN ELECTROCHEMICAL VOYAGE The process by which neural impulses travel is electrochemical. Neurons generate electricity as a result of chemical changes that cause an electrical charge to be transmitted along the lengths of their axons. The interiors of axons are separated from surrounding fluids by the cell membrane. The fluids inside and outside the cell membranes contain positively or negatively charged atoms called *ions*. Ions with positive charges (sodium and potassium ions) and negative charges (chloride ions) can flow back and forth across the cell membrane. Yet the flow is not random. The cell membranes of axons have *selective permeability;* that is, gates open and close to allow the movement back and forth of certain ions. In a resting state— that is, when a neuron is not being stimulated by its neighbors—gates prevent the positively charged sodium ions from entering the axon, although potassium can flow. But the overall result is that the concentration of negatively charged chloride (Cl^-) ions inside the cell creates a negative charge in relation to the outside. The axon is said to

Myelin A fatty substance that encases and insulates axons, facilitating transmission of neural impulses.

Afferent neurons Neurons that transmit messages from sensory receptors to the spinal cord and brain. Also called *sensory neurons.*

Efferent neurons Neurons that transmit messages from the brain or spinal cord to muscles and glands. Also called *motor neurons.*

Neural impulse The electrochemical discharge of a nerve cell, or neuron.

be **polarized** with a negative **resting potential** of about −70 millivolts in relation to the body fluid outside the cell membrane.

When the resting neuron is adequately stimulated by other neurons, the so-called *sodium-potassium pump* goes into operation. The gates in the part of the axon closest to the cell body allow positively charged sodium ions to enter but also pump out some potassium ions. Since more sodium ions enter than potassium ions leave, there is a net gain in the charge inside the axon, **depolarizing** the area. The influx of sodium ions also positively charges the area with respect to the outside (see Figure 2.6 ■).

The inside of the axon at the disturbed area is said to have an **action potential** of 110 millivolts. This action potential, added to the −70 millivolts that characterize the resting potential, brings the axon's voltage to a positive charge of about +30 to +40 millivolts in the affected area (see Figure 2.6 again). The action potential causes the gates in the next part of the cell to open, or become permeable, to sodium ions. At the same time, positively charged sodium ions are being pumped out of the first area of the axon, which returns it to its negative resting potential. In this way, the neural impulse is transmitted continuously along an axon. Because the impulse is generated anew as it progresses, it does not lose strength.

Truth or Fiction Revisited: Thus, it is true that messages travel in the brain by means of electricity. These are messages *within* neurons. However, communication between neurons is carried out quite differently.

FIRING: HOW MESSAGES VOYAGE FROM NEURON TO NEURON The conduction of the neural impulse along the length of a neuron is what is meant by "firing." When a rifle fires, it sends a bullet speeding through its barrel and discharges it at more than

Video Connections—The Action Potential

A neuron's action potential is the electrical impulse that travels along its axon, enabling the conduction of a neural impulse. This concept is explained and illustrated in "The Action Potential" video on your Psychology CourseMate at www.cengagebrain.com.

Polarize To ready a neuron for firing by creating an internal negative charge in relation to the body fluid outside the cell membrane.

Resting potential The electrical potential across the neural membrane when it is not responding to other neurons.

Depolarize To reduce the resting potential of a cell membrane from about −70 millivolts toward zero.

Action potential The electrical impulse that provides the basis for the conduction of a neural impulse along an axon of a neuron.

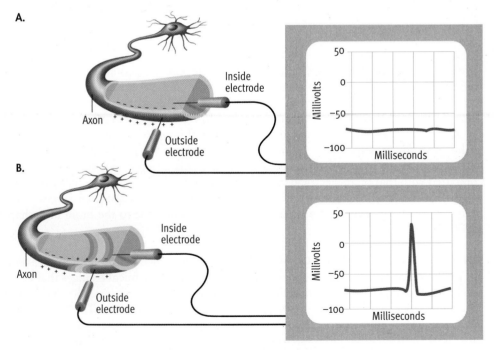

Figure 2.6 ■ Changes in Electrical Charges as a Neural Impulse Is Transmitted Along the Length of an Axon Electrical charges inside and outside axons are measured by microscopic glass tubes placed inside and outside the cell membranes of axons. As shown in part A, when an axon is at rest, it has a negative charge of about −70 millivolts. But when sodium ions enter and the area of entry is depolarized, as shown in part B, the charge in that part of the axon rises to +30 to +40 millivolts. The change causes the next part of the cell membrane to become permeable to sodium ions, continuing the transmission of the neural impulse along the axon.

Source: Weiten. *Psychology*, 8/e. Copyright © 2010, Cengage Learning.

1,000 feet per second. **Question 10: What happens when a neuron fires?** Neurons also fire, but instead of a barrel, a neuron has an axon. Instead of discharging a bullet, it releases neurotransmitters.

Some neurons fire in less than 1/1,000th of a second. When they fire, neurons transmit messages to other neurons, muscles, or glands. However, neurons will not fire unless the incoming messages combine to reach a certain strength, which is defined as the *threshold* at which it will fire. A weak message may cause a temporary shift in electrical charge at some point along the cell membrane, but this charge will dissipate if the neuron is not stimulated to its threshold.

Every time a neuron fires, it transmits an impulse of the same strength. This occurrence is known as the **all-or-none principle**. That is, either a neuron fires or it doesn't. Not only can a neuron fire in less than 1/1,000th of a second, but a neuron may also transmit several hundred messages each second. Neurons fire more often when they have been stimulated by larger numbers of other neurons. Stronger stimuli cause more frequent firing, but again, the strength of each firing remains the same.

For a few thousandths of a second after firing, a neuron is insensitive to messages from other neurons and will not fire. It is said to be in a **refractory period**. This period is a time of recovery during which sodium is prevented from passing through the neuronal membrane. When we realize that such periods of recovery might take place hundreds of times per second, it seems a rapid recovery and a short rest indeed. **Truth or Fiction Revisited:** It is therefore true that a single brain cell can send out hundreds of messages each second—and manage to catch some rest in between.

The facts that there are so many neurons and that they can fire so frequently begin to suggest how much information can be transmitted within the brain and to and from the brain. Just think: billions of cells can each fire hundreds of times per second, sending different kinds of messages to different groups of cells each time. How can any human-made computer we know of today begin to transmit such vast quantities of information? It apparently requires just such a complex system of information transmission to begin to understand the particularly human capacities for insight and intuition.

THE SYNAPSE: ON BEING WELL CONNECTED A neuron relays its message to another neuron across a junction called a *synapse*. **Question 11: What is a synapse?** A synapse consists of an axon terminal button from the transmitting neuron, a dendrite or the body of a receiving neuron, and a fluid-filled gap between the two that is called the *synaptic cleft* (refer again to Figure 2.4). Although the neural impulse is electrical, it does not jump across the synaptic cleft like a spark. Instead, when a nerve impulse reaches a synapse, axon terminals release chemicals into the synaptic cleft like myriad ships being cast into the sea. Scientists have identified a few dozen of these chemicals to date. In the following section, we consider a few of them that are usually of greatest interest to psychologists.

Neurotransmitters: The Chemical Keys to Communication

Sacs called *synaptic vesicles* in the axon terminals contain neurotransmitters. When a neural impulse (action potential) reaches the axon terminal, the vesicles release varying amounts of **neurotransmitters**—the chemical keys to communication—into the synaptic cleft. From there, they influence the receiving neuron. **Question 12: What do neurotransmitters do?**

Dozens of neurotransmitters have been identified. Each has its own chemical structure, and each can fit into a specifically tailored harbor, or **receptor site**, on the receiving cell. The analogy of a key fitting into a lock is often used to describe this process. Once released, not all molecules of a neurotransmitter find their way into receptor sites of other neurons. "Loose" neurotransmitters are usually either broken down or reabsorbed by the axon terminal (a process called *reuptake*).

Some neurotransmitters act to *excite* other neurons; that is, they cause other neurons to fire. Other neurotransmitters act to *inhibit* receiving neurons; that is, they prevent

All-or-none principle The fact that a neuron fires an impulse of the same strength whenever its action potential is triggered.

Refractory period A phase following firing during which a neuron is less sensitive to messages from other neurons and will not fire.

Synapse A junction between the axon terminals of one neuron and the dendrites or cell body of another neuron.

Neurotransmitters Chemical substances involved in the transmission of neural impulses from one neuron to another.

Receptor site A location on a dendrite of a receiving neuron tailored to receive a neurotransmitter.

Parkinson's Disease Boxer Muhammad Ali and actor Michael J. Fox are two of the better-known individuals who are afflicted with Parkinson's disease.

them from firing. The sum of the stimulation—excitatory and inhibitory—determines whether a neuron will fire and, if so, when neurotransmitters will be released.

Neurotransmitters are involved in physical processes such as muscle contraction and psychological processes such as thoughts and emotions. Excesses or deficiencies of neurotransmitters have been linked to psychological disorders such as depression and schizophrenia. Let's consider the effects of some neurotransmitters of interest to psychologists: acetylcholine (ACh), dopamine, norepinephrine, serotonin, GABA, and endorphins.

Acetylcholine (ACh) controls muscle contractions. It is excitatory at synapses between nerves and muscles that involve voluntary movement but inhibitory at the heart and some other locations. The effects of *curare* highlight the functioning of ACh. Curare is a poison that is extracted from plants by native South Americans and used in hunting. If an arrow tipped with curare pierces the skin and the poison enters the body, it prevents ACh from binding to the receptor sites on neurons. Because ACh helps muscles move, curare causes paralysis. The victim is prevented from contracting the muscles used in breathing and therefore dies from suffocation. Botulism, a disease that stems from food poisoning, prevents the release of ACh and has the same effect as curare.

Acetylcholine is also normally prevalent in a part of the brain called the **hippocampus**, a structure involved in the formation of memories. When the amount of ACh available to the brain decreases, memory formation is impaired, as in Alzheimer's disease (Packard, 2009). In one experiment, researchers decreased the ACh available to the hippocampus of laboratory rats. As a result, the rats were incapable of learning their way through a maze, apparently because they could not remember which way to turn at various choice points (Egawa et al., 2002).

Dopamine is involved at the level of the brain and affects voluntary movements, learning and memory, and emotional arousal. Deficiencies of dopamine are linked to Parkinson's disease, in which people progressively lose control over their muscles (Fuentes et al., 2009). They develop muscle tremors and jerky, uncoordinated movements. Muhammad Ali and Michael J. Fox are two of the better-known individuals who are afflicted with Parkinson's disease.

The psychological disorder *schizophrenia* is characterized by confusion and false perceptions, and it has been linked to dopamine. People with schizophrenia may have more receptor sites for dopamine in an area of the brain that is involved in emotional responding. For this reason, they may *overutilize* the dopamine available in the brain (Neve, 2009; Roth et al., 2009). This leads to hallucinations and disturbances of thought and emotion. The phenothiazines, a group of drugs used to treat schizophrenia, inhibit the action of dopamine by blocking some dopamine receptor sites (Neve, 2009). Because of their action, phenothiazines may have Parkinson-like side effects, which are usually treated by lowering the dose, prescribing additional drugs, or switching to another drug.

Norepinephrine is produced largely by neurons in the brain stem. It acts both as a neurotransmitter and as a hormone. It is an excitatory neurotransmitter that speeds up the heartbeat and other body processes and is involved in general arousal, learning and memory, and eating. Excesses and deficiencies of norepinephrine have been linked to mood disorders. Deficiencies of both ACh and norepinephrine are particularly impairing of memory (Qi & Gold, 2009).

The stimulants cocaine and amphetamines ("speed") create excesses of norepinephrine (as well as dopamine) in the nervous system, increasing the firing of neurons and leading to persistent arousal. Amphetamines act by facilitating the release of these neurotransmitters and also prevent their reabsorption by the releasing synaptic vesicles—that is, their reuptake. Cocaine also blocks reuptake.

Serotonin is involved in emotional arousal and sleep. Deficiencies of serotonin have been linked to eating disorders, alcoholism, depression, aggression, and insomnia (Polina et al., 2009; Risch et al., 2009). The drug LSD decreases the action of serotonin and may also increase the utilization of dopamine. Overutilization of

Acetylcholine (ACh) A neurotransmitter that controls muscle contractions.

Hippocampus A part of the limbic system of the brain that is involved in memory formation.

Dopamine A neurotransmitter that is involved in Parkinson's disease and that appears to play a role in schizophrenia.

Norepinephrine A neurotransmitter whose action is similar to that of the hormone epinephrine and that may play a role in depression.

Serotonin A neurotransmitter, deficiencies of which have been linked to affective disorders, anxiety, and insomnia.

Gamma-aminobutyric acid (GABA) An inhibitory neurotransmitter that apparently helps calm anxiety.

dopamine may give rise to hallucinations in both people with schizophrenia and users of LSD.

Gamma-aminobutyric acid (GABA) is another neurotransmitter of great interest to psychologists. One reason is that GABA is an inhibitory neurotransmitter that may help calm anxiety reactions (Cunningham et al., 2009). Tranquilizers and alcohol may quell anxiety by binding with GABA receptors and amplifying its effects. One class of antianxiety drug may also increase the sensitivity of receptor sites to GABA. Other studies link deficiencies of GABA to depression (Karolewicz et al., 2009).

Endorphins are inhibitory neurotransmitters. The word *endorphin* is the contraction of *endogenous morphine*. *Endogenous* means "developing from within." Endorphins occur naturally in the brain and in the bloodstream and are similar to the narcotic morphine in their functions and effects. They lock into receptor sites for chemicals that transmit pain messages to the brain. Once the endorphin "key" is in the "lock," the pain-causing chemicals are locked out. Endorphins may also increase our sense of competence, enhance the functioning of the immune system, and be connected with the pleasurable "runner's high" reported by many long-distance runners (Shah et al., 2009). Table 2.1 ■ reviews much of the information on neurotransmitters.

There you have it—a fabulous forest of neurons in which billions upon billions of axon terminals are pouring armadas of neurotransmitters into synaptic clefts at any given time. The process occurs when you are involved in strenuous activity. It is taking place this moment as you are reading this page. It will happen later on when you have a snack or passively watch television. Moreover, the process is repeated several hundred times every second. The combined activity of all these neurotransmitters determines which messages will be transmitted and which ones will not. You experience your sensations, your thoughts, and your control over your body as psychological events, but the psychological events somehow result from many billions of electrochemical events.

We can think of neurons as the microscopic building blocks of the nervous system. However, millions upon millions of neurons gather together to form larger visible structures that we think of as the parts of the nervous system. We discuss those parts next, including the most human part—the brain.

Endorphins Neurotransmitters that are composed of amino acids and that are functionally similar to morphine.

© Yellow Dog Productions/Getty Images

Runner's High Why have thousands of people taken up long-distance running? Running promotes cardiovascular conditioning, muscle strength, and weight control. But many long-distance runners also experience a "runner's high" that appears to be connected with the release of endorphins. Endorphins are naturally occurring substances that are similar in function to the narcotic morphine.

TABLE 2.1 ■ Key Neurotransmitters and Their Functions

Neurotransmitter	Functions	Comments
Acetylcholine (ACh)	Causes muscle contractions and is involved in formation of memories	Found at synapses between motor neurons and muscles; deficiencies of ACh linked with paralysis and Alzheimer's disease
Dopamine	Plays a role in movement, learning, attention, memory, and emotional response	Tremors of Parkinson's disease linked with low levels of dopamine; people with schizophrenia may *overutilize* dopamine
Norepinephrine	Accelerates the heart rate, affects eating, and is linked with activity levels, learning, and remembering	Imbalances linked with mood disorders such as depression and bipolar disorder
Serotonin	Is involved in behavior patterns and psychological problems, including obesity, depression, insomnia, alcoholism, and aggression	Drugs that block the reuptake of serotonin helpful in the treatment of depression
Gamma-aminobutyric acid (GABA)	An inhibitory neurotransmitter that may lessen anxiety	Tranquilizers and alcohol may counter anxiety by binding with GABA receptors or increasing the sensitivity of receptor sites to GABA
Endorphins	Inhibit pain by locking pain-causing chemicals out of their receptor sites	Endorphins may be connected with some people's indifference to pain, the painkilling effects of acupuncture, and the "runner's high" experienced by many long-distance runners

The Parts of the Nervous System

Question 13: What are the parts of the nervous system? The nervous system consists of the brain, the spinal cord, and the **nerves** linking them to the sensory organs, muscles, and glands. As shown in Figure 2.7 ■, the brain and spinal cord make up the **central nervous system.** If you compare your nervous system to a computer, your central nervous system would be your central processing unit (CPU).

The sensory (afferent) neurons, which receive and transmit messages to the brain and spinal cord, and the motor (efferent) neurons, which transmit messages from the brain or spinal cord to the muscles and glands, make up the **peripheral nervous system.** In the comparison of the nervous system to a computer, the peripheral nervous system makes up the nervous system's peripheral devices—keyboard, mouse, DVD drive, and so on. You would not be able to feed information to your computer's central processing unit without these *peripheral* devices. Other peripheral devices, such as your monitor and printer, allow you to follow what is happening inside your CPU and to see what it has accomplished.

THE PERIPHERAL NERVOUS SYSTEM: THE BODY'S PERIPHERAL DEVICES

Question 14: What are the divisions and functions of the peripheral nervous system? The peripheral nervous system consists of sensory and motor neurons that transmit messages to and from the central nervous system. Without the peripheral nervous system, our brains would be like isolated CPUs. There would be no keyboards, mouses, DVDs, or other ways of entering information. There would be no monitors, printers, modems, or other ways of displaying or transmitting information. We would be detached from the world: We would not be able to perceive it, and we would not be able to act on it. The two main divisions of the peripheral nervous system are the *somatic nervous system* and the *autonomic nervous system.*

The **somatic nervous system** contains sensory (afferent) and motor (efferent) neurons. It transmits messages about sights, sounds, smells, temperature, body positions, and so on to the central nervous system. As a result, we can experience the beauties and the horrors of the world, its physical ecstasies and agonies. Messages transmitted from the brain and spinal cord to the somatic nervous system control purposeful body movements such as raising a hand, winking, or running, as well as the tiny, almost imperceptible movements that maintain our balance and posture.

Autonomic means "acting independently"—without conscious control. The **autonomic nervous system (ANS)** regulates the glands and the muscles of internal organs. Thus, the ANS controls activities such as heartbeat, respiration, digestion, and dilation of the pupils of the eyes. These activities can occur automatically,

Nerve A bundle of axons from many neurons.

Central nervous system The brain and spinal cord.

Peripheral nervous system The part of the nervous system consisting of the somatic nervous system and the autonomic nervous system.

Somatic nervous system The division of the peripheral nervous system that connects the central nervous system with sensory receptors, skeletal muscles, and the surface of the body.

Autonomic nervous system (ANS) The division of the peripheral nervous system that regulates glands and activities such as heartbeat, respiration, digestion, and dilation of the pupils.

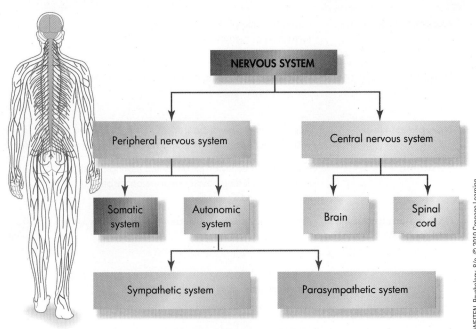

Figure 2.7 ■ The Divisions of the Nervous System The nervous system contains two main divisions: the central nervous system and the peripheral nervous system. The central nervous system consists of the brain and spinal cord. The peripheral nervous system contains the somatic and autonomic systems. In turn, the autonomic nervous system has sympathetic and parasympathetic divisions.

WEITEN, Psychology, 8/e. © 2010 Cengage Learning

while we are asleep. But some of them can be overridden by conscious control. You can breathe at a purposeful pace, for example. Methods like biofeedback and yoga also help people gain voluntary control of functions such as heart rate and blood pressure.

The ANS also has two branches, or divisions: *sympathetic* and *parasympathetic*. These branches have largely opposing effects. Many organs and glands are stimulated by both branches of the ANS (see Figure 2.8 ■). When organs and glands are simultaneously stimulated by both divisions, their effects can average out to some degree. In general, the **sympathetic** division is most active during processes that involve spending body energy from stored reserves, such as a fight-or-flight response to a predator or when you find out that your rent is going to be raised. The **parasympathetic** division is most active during processes that replenish reserves of energy, such as eating. When we are afraid, the sympathetic division of the ANS accelerates the heart rate. When we relax, the parasympathetic division decelerates the heart rate. The parasympathetic division stimulates digestive processes, but the sympathetic branch inhibits digestion.

Have you ever tried to eat a meal when you're worried or anxious about something, like a big test or a speech you will have to present to the class? At such times, food usually has no appeal, and if you force yourself to eat, it may seem to land in your stomach like a rock. This is the sympathetic division of your ANS in action. The sympathetic division of the ANS predominates when we feel fear or anxiety, and these feelings

Sympathetic The branch of the ANS that is most active during emotional responses— such as fear and anxiety—that spend the body's reserves of energy.

Parasympathetic The branch of the ANS that is most active during processes such as digestion that restore the body's reserves of energy.

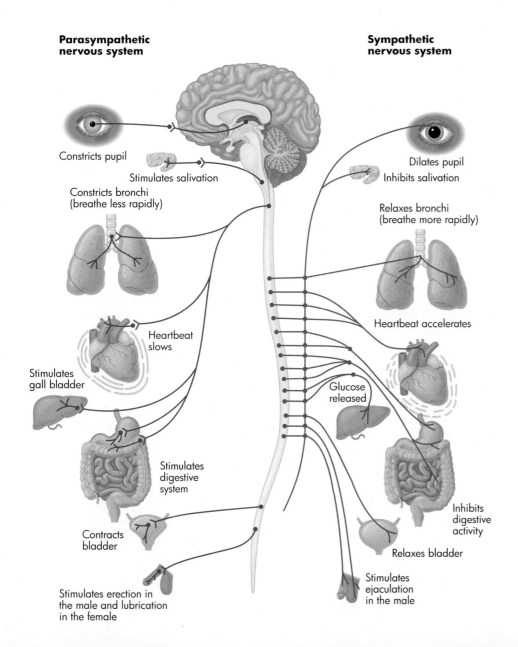

Parasympathetic nervous system

Constricts pupil

Stimulates salivation

Constricts bronchi
(breathe less rapidly)

Heartbeat slows

Stimulates gall bladder

Stimulates digestive system

Contracts bladder

Stimulates erection in the male and lubrication in the female

Sympathetic nervous system

Dilates pupil

Inhibits salivation

Relaxes bronchi
(breathe more rapidly)

Heartbeat accelerates

Glucose released

Inhibits digestive activity

Relaxes bladder

Stimulates ejaculation in the male

Figure 2.8 ■ The Branches of the Autonomic Nervous System (ANS)
The parasympathetic branch of the ANS generally acts to replenish stores of energy in the body. The sympathetic branch is most active during activities that expend energy. The two branches of the ANS frequently have antagonistic effects on the organs they service.

Source: Weiten. *Psychology*, 8/e. Copyright © 2010, Cengage Learning.

can therefore cause indigestion. **Truth or Fiction Revisited:** Therefore, it is true that fear can give you indigestion.

The ANS is of particular interest to psychologists because its activities are linked to various emotions such as anxiety and love. Some people seem to have overly reactive sympathetic nervous systems. In the absence of external threats, their bodies still respond as though they were faced with danger. Psychologists can often help them learn to relax when there is no external reason for them to feel so "wound up tight."

THE CENTRAL NERVOUS SYSTEM: THE BODY'S CENTRAL PROCESSING UNIT It is your central nervous system that makes you so special. Other species see more sharply, smell more keenly, and hear more acutely. Other species run faster, fly through the air, or swim underwater without the benefit of artificial devices such as airplanes and submarines. But it is your central nervous system that enables you to use symbols and language, the abilities that allow people not only to adapt to their environment but also to create new environments and give them names (Bandura, 1999).

Question 15: What are the divisions and functions of the central nervous system? As noted earlier, the central nervous system consists of the spinal cord and the brain.

The **spinal cord** is a true "information superhighway"—a column of nerves about as thick as a thumb. It transmits messages from sensory receptors to the brain and from the brain to muscles and glands throughout the body. The spinal cord is also capable of some "local government." That is, it controls some responses to external stimulation through **spinal reflexes.** A spinal reflex is an unlearned response to a stimulus that may involve only two neurons—a sensory (afferent) neuron and a motor (efferent) neuron (see Figure 2.9 ■). In some reflexes, a third neuron, called an **interneuron,** transmits the neural impulse from the sensory neuron through the spinal cord to the motor neuron.

The spinal cord (and the brain) consists of gray matter and white matter. The **gray matter** is composed of nonmyelinated neurons. Some of these are involved in spinal reflexes. Others send their axons to the brain. The **white matter** is composed of bundles of longer, myelinated (and thus whitish) axons that carry messages to and from the brain. As you can see in Figure 2.9, a cross section of the spinal cord shows that the gray matter, which includes cell bodies, is distributed in a butterfly pattern.

The spinal cord is also involved in reflexes. We have many reflexes: We blink in response to a puff of air in our faces. We swallow when food accumulates in the mouth. A physician may tap the leg below the knee to elicit the knee-jerk reflex, a sign that the nervous system is operating adequately. Urinating and defecating are reflexes that occur in response to pressure in the bladder and the rectum. Parents typically spend weeks or months toilet-training toddlers—in other words, teaching them to involve their brains in the process of elimination. Learning to inhibit these reflexes makes civilization possible.

Spinal cord A column of nerves within the spine that transmits messages from sensory receptors to the brain and from the brain to muscles and glands.

Spinal reflex A simple, unlearned response to a stimulus that may involve only two neurons.

Interneuron A neuron that transmits a neural impulse from a sensory neuron to a motor neuron.

Gray matter In the spinal cord, the grayish neurons and neural segments that are involved in spinal reflexes.

White matter In the spinal cord, axon bundles that carry messages from and to the brain.

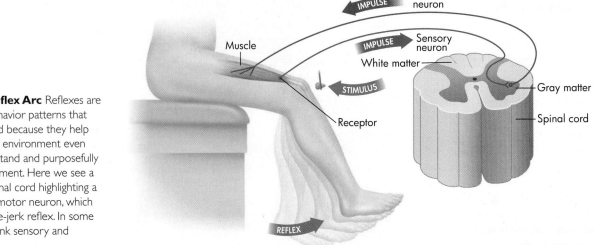

Figure 2.9 ■ The Reflex Arc Reflexes are inborn, stereotyped behavior patterns that have apparently evolved because they help individuals adapt to the environment even before they can understand and purposefully manipulate the environment. Here we see a cross section of the spinal cord highlighting a sensory neuron and a motor neuron, which are involved in the knee-jerk reflex. In some reflexes, interneurons link sensory and motor neurons.

Sexual response also involves many reflexes. Stimulation of the genital organs leads to the reflexes of erection in the male and vaginal lubrication in the female (reflexes that make sexual intercourse possible) and to the reflexive muscle contractions of orgasm. As reflexes, these processes need not involve the brain, but most often they do. Feelings of passion, memories of an enjoyable sexual encounter, and sexual fantasies usually contribute to sexual response by transmitting messages from the brain to the genitals through the spinal cord.

LearningConnections ● THE NERVOUS SYSTEM: ON BEING WIRED

ACTIVE REVIEW (9) Neurons transmit messages to other neurons by means of chemical substances called _____. (10) Neurons have a cell body, or soma; dendrites, which receive "messages"; and a(n)_____, which extends from the cell body. (11) The axons of many neurons have a fatty insulating sheath called _____. (12) A(n) _____ consists of an axon terminal, a dendrite, and a fluid-filled gap between them. (13) Acetylcholine (Ach) is normally prevalent in a brain structure essential to the formation of memories: the _____. (14) It is theorized that people with the psychological disorder _____ overutilize dopamine. (15) The _____ nervous system (ANS) regulates the glands and involuntary activities such as heartbeat and digestion.

REFLECT AND RELATE Reflexes are automatic, involuntary responses. Yet the great majority of the time we engage in sexual behavior voluntarily. How, then, do we explain the fact that sexual responses like erection, vaginal lubrication, and orgasm are reflexes?

CRITICAL THINKING Psychology is the study of behavior and mental processes. Why, then, are psychologists interested in the nervous system?

 Go to Psychology CourseMate at **www.cengagebrain.com** for an interactive version of these questions.

THE BRAIN: THE STAR OF THE HUMAN NERVOUS SYSTEM

Every show has a star, and the brain is the undisputed star of the human nervous system. The size and shape of your brain are responsible for your large, delightfully rounded head. In all the animal kingdom, you (and about 6 billion other people) are unique because of the capacities for learning and thinking residing in the human brain.

The brains of men are about 8% to 10% larger than those of women (Lenroot et al., 2007), which is related to the difference in body size. However, it may be that how well connected one is (in terms of synapses) is more important than size in the human brain. After all, Albert Einstein's brain was only average in size (Abraham, 2002). Moreover, women's brains "run hotter" than men's. Women metabolize more glucose (sugar) and appear to use more of their brains on a given task (Cosgrove et al., 2007; McCarthy et al., 2009).

Scientists who have engaged in brain research generally agree that the mind is a function of the brain (American Psychological Association, 2008; Block, 2009). **Question 16: How do researchers learn about the functions of the brain?**

Seeing the Brain Through the Eyes of the Psychologist

Philosophers and scientists have wondered about the functions of the brain throughout history. Sometimes, they have engaged in careful research that attempts to pinpoint exactly what happens in certain parts of the brain. At other times—as in the case of Phineas Gage, who, as you learned in Chapter 1, had the accident with the tamping rod—knowledge has almost literally fallen into their laps. From injuries to the head—some of them minimal, some horrendous—we have learned that brain damage can impair consciousness and awareness. Brain damage can result in loss of vision and hearing, confusion, or loss of memory. In some cases, the loss of large portions of the brain may result in little loss of function. Ironically, the loss of smaller portions in particularly sensitive locations can result in language problems, memory loss, or death.

"The Brain—is wider than the Sky—For—put them side by side—The one the other will contain With ease—and You—beside—"

EMILY DICKINSON

It has been known for about two centuries that damage to the left side of the brain is connected with loss of sensation or movement on the right side of the body, and vice versa. Thus, it has been assumed that the brain's control mechanisms must cross over from right to left, and vice versa, as they descend into the body.

Accidents provide unplanned and uncontrolled opportunities of studying the brain. Scientists have learned more about the brain, however, through methods like experimentation, use of the electroencephalograph, and brain scans.

EXPERIMENTING WITH THE BRAIN The results of disease and accidents have shown us that brain injuries can be connected with changes in behavior and mental processes. Scientists have also purposefully experimented with the brain to observe the results. For example, **lesioning** (damaging) part of the brain region called the *hypothalamus* causes rats to overeat. Damaging another part of the hypothalamus causes them to stop eating. It is as if parts of the brain contain on–off switches for certain kinds of behavior, at least in lower animals.

Surgeon Wilder Penfield (1969) stimulated parts of human brains with electrical probes, and as a result, his patients reported the occurrence of certain kinds of memories. Similar experiments in electrical stimulation of the brain have found that parts of the brain are connected with specific kinds of sensations (as of light or sound) or motor activities (such as movement of an arm or leg).

THE ELECTROENCEPHALOGRAPH AND BRAIN IMAGING TECHNIQUES
Penfield stimulated parts of the brain with an electrical current and asked people to report what they experienced as a result. Researchers have also used the *electroencephalograph (EEG)* to record the natural electrical activity of the brain. The EEG detects minute amounts of electrical activity—called *brain waves*—that pass between the electrodes. Certain brain waves are associated with feelings of relaxation and with the stages of sleep.

As described in Chapter 1, researchers today use the computer to generate images of the parts of the brain from various sources of radiation. *Computerized axial tomography (CAT scan)* passes an X-ray beam through the head and measures the structures that reflect the X rays from various angles, generating a three-dimensional image of the brain. *Positron emission tomography (PET scan)* forms a computer-generated image of the activity of parts of the brain by tracing the amount of glucose used (or metabolized) by these parts. More glucose is metabolized in more active parts of the brain. In *functional magnetic resonance imaging (fMRI),* the person lies in a magnetic field and is exposed to radio waves that cause parts of the brain to emit signals that are measured from various angles.

Imaging with the PET scan and fMRI suggests that the prefrontal cortex is the "executive center" of the brain—where we process much of the information involved in making plans and solving problems (Mansouri et al., 2009; Tanji & Hoshi, 2008). Figure 2.10 ■ shows the prefrontal cortex. One prefrontal region is found in each hemisphere, a bit above the outer edge of the eyebrow.

A Voyage Through the Brain: Revealing the Central Processing Unit

Perhaps you never imagined yourself as going off to foreign territory to unearth evidence about the history and functioning of the human species. But pack your traveling gear, because we are about to go off on a voyage of discovery—a voyage within your own skull. We will be traveling through your brain—a fascinating archeological site.

Your brain reveals much of what is so special about you. It also holds a record of your connectedness with animals that have walked, swum, and flown the Earth for hundreds of millions of years. In fact, the "older" parts of your brain—those that we meet first on our tour—are not all that different from the corresponding parts of the brains of other mammals. These parts of your brain, evolutionarily speaking, also have functions very similar to those of these other species. They are involved in basic survival functions such as breathing, feeding, and the regulation of cycles of sleeping and waking. **Question 17: What are the structures and functions of the brain?**

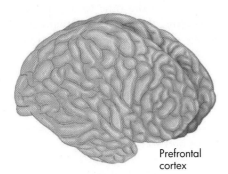

Prefrontal
cortex

Figure 2.10 ■ The Prefrontal Cortex of the Brain The prefrontal cortex comes in pairs. One is found in each hemisphere, a bit above the outer edge of the eyebrow. The prefrontal cortex is highly active during visual and spatial problem solving. Your sense of self—your continuous sense of being in and functioning in the world—may also reside largely in the prefrontal cortex.

"The brain is a wonderful organ; it starts working the moment you get up in the morning and does not stop until you get into the office."

ROBERT FROST

Lesion An injury that results in impaired behavior or loss of a function.

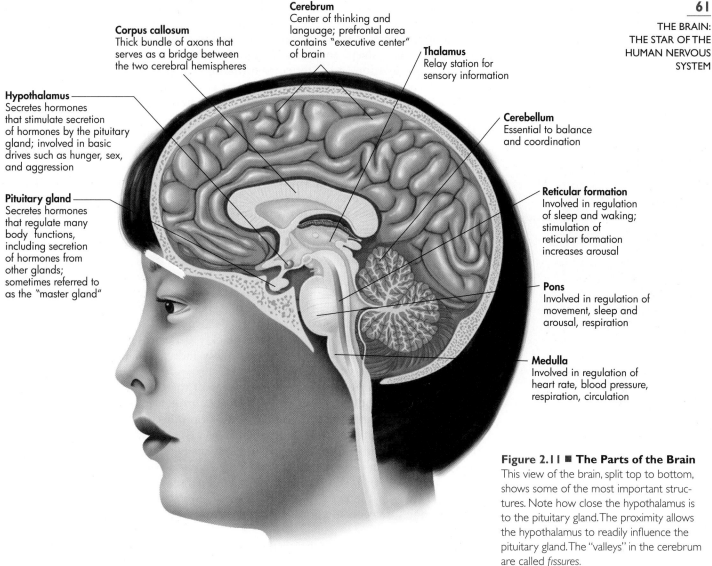

Cerebrum
Center of thinking and
language; prefrontal area
contains "executive center"
of brain

Corpus callosum
Thick bundle of axons that
serves as a bridge between
the two cerebral hemispheres

Thalamus
Relay station for
sensory information

Hypothalamus
Secretes hormones
that stimulate secretion
of hormones by the pituitary
gland; involved in basic
drives such as hunger, sex,
and aggression

Pituitary gland
Secretes hormones
that regulate many
body functions,
including secretion
of hormones from
other glands;
sometimes referred to
as the "master gland"

Cerebellum
Essential to balance
and coordination

Reticular formation
Involved in regulation
of sleep and waking;
stimulation of
reticular formation
increases arousal

Pons
Involved in regulation of
movement, sleep and
arousal, respiration

Medulla
Involved in regulation of
heart rate, blood pressure,
respiration, circulation

Figure 2.11 ■ The Parts of the Brain
This view of the brain, split top to bottom,
shows some of the most important structures. Note how close the hypothalamus is
to the pituitary gland. The proximity allows
the hypothalamus to readily influence the
pituitary gland. The "valleys" in the cerebrum
are called *fissures*.

Let's now begin our tour of the brain (see Figure 2.11 ■). We begin with the oldest part of our "archeological dig"—the hindbrain, where the spinal cord rises to meet the brain. Here we find three major structures: the medulla, the pons, and the cerebellum. Many pathways that connect the spinal cord to higher levels of the brain pass through the **medulla**. The medulla regulates vital functions such as heart rate, blood pressure, and respiration. The medulla also plays a role in sleeping, sneezing, and coughing. The **pons** is a bulge in the hindbrain that lies forward of the medulla. *Pons* is the Latin word for "bridge," so named because of the bundles of nerves that pass through it. The pons transmits information about body movement and is involved in functions related to attention, sleep and alertness, and respiration.

Behind the pons lies the **cerebellum** ("little brain" in Latin). The cerebellum has two hemispheres that are involved in maintaining balance and controlling motor (muscle) behavior. You may send a command from your forebrain to get up and walk to the refrigerator, but your cerebellum is key to organizing the information that enables you to engage in these movements. The cerebellum allows you to place one leg in front of the other and reach your destination without tipping over. Injury to the cerebellum may lead to lack of motor coordination, stumbling, and loss of muscle tone. Alcohol depresses the functioning of the cerebellum, so police often ask drivers suspected of drinking too much to engage in tasks that involve the cerebellum, such as touching their noses with their fingers or walking a straight line.

Medulla An oblong area of the hindbrain involved in regulation of heartbeat and respiration.

Pons A structure of the hindbrain involved in breathing, attention, sleep, and dreams.

Cerebellum A part of the hindbrain involved in muscle coordination and balance.

Walking the Line The cerebellum plays a key role in your ability to keep to the straight and narrow—that is, to walk a straight line. Because alcohol depresses the functioning of the cerebellum, police may ask suspected drivers to walk a straight line as a test of whether they have drunk too much to drive their cars safely.

Reticular formation A part of the brain involved in attention, sleep, and arousal.

Thalamus An area near the center of the brain involved in the relay of sensory information to the cortex and in the functions of sleep and attention.

Hypothalamus A bundle of nuclei below the thalamus involved in body temperature, motivation, and emotion.

Limbic system A group of structures involved in memory, motivation, and emotion that forms a fringe along the inner edge of the cerebrum.

As we tour the hindbrain, we also find the lower part of the **reticular formation**. That is where the reticular formation begins, but it ascends through the midbrain into the lower part of the forebrain. The reticular formation is vital in the functions of attention, sleep, and arousal. Injury to the reticular formation may result in a coma. Stimulation of the reticular formation causes it to send messages to the cerebral cortex (the large wrinkled mass that you think of as your brain), making us more alert to sensory information. In classic neurological research, Guiseppe Moruzzi and Horace Magoun (1949) discovered that electrical stimulation of the reticular formation of a sleeping cat caused it to awaken at once. But when the reticular formation was severed from higher parts of the brain, the animal fell into a coma from which it would not awaken. Drugs known as central nervous system depressants, such as alcohol, are thought to work, in part, by lowering reticular formation activity.

Sudden loud noises stimulate the reticular formation and awaken a sleeping animal or person. But the reticular formation may become selective through learning. That is, it comes to play a filtering role. It may allow some messages to filter through to higher brain levels and awareness while screening others out. For example, the parent who has primary responsibility for child care may be awakened by the stirring sounds of an infant, while the sounds of traffic or street noise are filtered out, even though they are louder. The other parent, in contrast, may sleep through loud crying by the infant. If the first parent must be away for several days, however, the second parent's reticular formation may quickly become sensitive to noises produced by the child. This sensitivity may rapidly fade again when the first parent returns.

Let's move onward and upward. Key areas of the forebrain are the *thalamus*, the *hypothalamus*, the *limbic system*, and the *cerebrum* (see Figures 2.11 and 2.12). The **thalamus** is located near the center of the brain. It consists of two joined egg- or football-shaped structures. The thalamus serves as a relay station for sensory stimulation. Nerve fibers from the sensory systems enter from below; the information carried by them is then transmitted to the cerebral cortex by way of fibers that exit from above. For instance, the thalamus relays sensory input from the eyes to the visual areas of the cerebral cortex. The thalamus is also involved in controlling sleep and attention in coordination with other brain structures, including the reticular formation.

The **hypothalamus** lies beneath the thalamus and above the pituitary gland. It weighs only 4 grams, yet it is vital in the regulation of body temperature, concentration of fluids, storage of nutrients, and various aspects of motivation and emotion. Experimenters learn many of the functions of the hypothalamus by implanting electrodes in parts of it and observing the effects of an electrical current. They have found that the hypothalamus is involved in hunger, thirst, sexual behavior, caring for offspring, and aggression. Among lower animals, stimulation of various areas of the hypothalamus can trigger instinctual behaviors such as fighting, mating, or even nest building.

Canadian psychologists James Olds and Peter Milner (1954) made a wonderful mistake in the 1950s. They were attempting to implant an electrode in a rat's reticular formation to see how stimulation of the area might affect learning. Olds, however, was primarily a social psychologist, not a biological psychologist. He missed his target and found a part of the animal's hypothalamus instead. Olds and Milner dubbed this area the "pleasure center" because the animal would repeat whatever it was doing when that area was stimulated. The term *pleasure center* is not used too frequently because it appears to attribute human emotions to rats. Yet the pleasure centers must be doing something right because rats stimulate themselves in these centers by pressing a pedal several thousand times an hour until they are exhausted (Olds, 1969).

The hypothalamus is just as important to humans as it is to lower animals. Unfortunately (or fortunately), our pleasure centers are not as clearly defined as those of the rat. Then, too, our responses to messages from the hypothalamus are less automatic and relatively more influenced by higher brain functions—that is, cognitive factors such as thought, choice, and value systems. It is all a part of being human.

The **limbic system** forms a fringe along the inner edge of the cerebrum and is fully evolved only in mammals. (Dig in from the surface a little to find it; see

Figure 2.12 ■). It is made up of several structures, including the *amygdala, hippocampus,* and parts of the *hypothalamus.* It is involved in memory and emotion and in the drives of hunger, sex, and aggression. People in whom surgical operations have damaged the hippocampus can retrieve old memories but cannot permanently store new information. As a result, they may, for example, reread the same newspaper day in and day out without recalling that they read it before. Or they may have to be perpetually reintroduced to people they have met just hours earlier (Squire, 1993, 1996).

The **amygdala** is near the bottom of the limbic system (see Figure 2.12). Studies using lesioning and electrical stimulation show that the amygdala is connected with aggressive behavior in monkeys, cats, and other animals. Early in the 20th century, Heinrich Klüver and Paul Bucy (1939) lesioned part of the amygdala of a rhesus monkey. Rhesus monkeys are normally a scrappy lot and try to bite or grab at intruders, but destruction of this animal's amygdala made it docile. No longer did it react aggressively to people. It even allowed people to poke and pinch it. Electrical stimulation of the part of the amygdala that Klüver and Bucy had destroyed, however, triggers a "rage response." For example, it causes a cat to hiss and arch its back in preparation to attack. The amygdala is also connected with a fear response (Ahs et al., 2009; Feinstein et al., 2010). If you electrically stimulate another part of the amygdala, the cat cringes in fear when you cage it with a mouse. Not very tigerlike.

The amygdala is also connected with vigilance. It is involved in emotions, learning, and memory, and it behaves like a spotlight, focusing attention on matters that are novel and important to know more about. In studies reported in 2000, researchers used fMRI to scan the amygdala while participants were shown faces of European Americans and African Americans. One study flashed the photos by four men and four women, half European American and half African American (Hart et al., 2000). The participants showed less activity in the amygdala when they viewed faces belonging to people of their own ethnic group, suggesting that they were more comfortable with "familiar" faces.

And now we journey upward to the cerebrum. The **cerebrum** is the crowning glory of the brain. Only in humans does the cerebrum make up such a large part of the brain (refer again to Figure 2.11). The cerebrum is responsible for thinking and language. The surface of the cerebrum—the **cerebral cortex**—is wrinkled, or convoluted, with ridges and valleys. The convolutions allow a great deal of surface area to be packed into the brain—and surface area is apparently connected with cognitive ability. Valleys in the cortex are called *fissures.* A key fissure almost divides the cerebrum in half, creating two hemispheres with something of the shape of a walnut. The hemispheres are connected by the **corpus callosum** (Latin for "thick body" or "hard body"), a bundle of some 200 million nerve fibers.

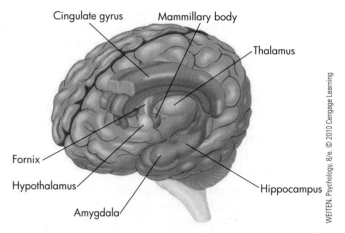

WEITEN. Psychology, 8/e. © 2010 Cengage Learning

Figure 2.12 ■ The Limbic System The limbic system is made up of structures that include the amygdala, the hippocampus, and parts of the hypothalamus. It is evolved fully only in mammals and forms a fringe along the inner edge of the cerebrum. The limbic system is involved in memory and emotion and in the drives of hunger, sex, and aggression.

"The brain is the organ that sets us apart from any other species. It is not the strength of our muscles or of our bones that makes us different, it is our brain."

PASKO T. RAKIC

The Cerebral Cortex: The "Bark" that Reasons

The cerebral cortex is the part of the brain that you usually think of as your brain. *Cortex* is a Latin word meaning "bark," as in the bark of a tree. Just as the bark is the outer coating of a tree, the cerebral cortex is the outer coating of the cerebrum. Despite its extreme importance and its creation of a world of civilization and culture, it is only about one-eighth of an inch thick. It is the outer edge of the brain that brings humans to their outer limits.

The cerebral cortex is involved in almost every bodily activity, including most sensations and most responses. It is also the part of the brain that frees people from the tyranny of genetic dictates and instinct. It is the seat of thinking and language, and it enables humans to think deeply about the world outside and make decisions. Other organisms run faster than we do, are stronger, or bite more sharply. Yet humans think faster, are intellectually "stronger," and, we might add, have a "biting" wit—all of which is made possible by the cerebral cortex. **Question 18: What are the parts of the cerebral cortex?**

Amygdala A part of the limbic system that apparently facilitates stereotypical aggressive responses.

Cerebrum The large mass of the forebrain, which consists of two hemispheres.

Cerebral cortex The wrinkled surface area (gray matter) of the cerebrum.

Corpus callosum A thick fiber bundle that connects the hemispheres of the cortex.

Frontal lobe The lobe of the cerebral cortex that lies in front of the central fissure.

Parietal lobe The lobe that lies just behind the central fissure.

Temporal lobe The lobe that lies below the lateral fissure, near the temples of the head.

Occipital lobe The lobe that lies behind and below the parietal lobe and behind the temporal lobe.

Somatosensory cortex The section of cortex in which sensory stimulation is projected. It lies just behind the central fissure in the parietal lobe.

The cerebral cortex has two hemispheres, left and right. Each of the hemispheres is divided into four lobes, as shown in Figure 2.13 ■. The **frontal lobe** lies in front of the central fissure, and the **parietal lobe** is behind it. The **temporal lobe** lies below the side, or lateral, fissure—across from the frontal and parietal lobes. The **occipital lobe** lies behind the temporal lobe and behind and below the parietal lobe.

When light strikes the eyes, neurons in the occipital lobe fire, and as a result, we "see" (that is, the image is projected in the brain). Direct artificial stimulation of the occipital lobe also produces visual sensations. If neurons in the occipital region of the cortex were stimulated with electricity, you would "see" flashes of light even if it were pitch black or your eyes were covered. The hearing or auditory area of the cortex lies in the temporal lobe along the lateral fissure. Sounds cause structures in the ear to vibrate. Messages are relayed from those structures to the auditory area of the cortex, and when you hear a noise, neurons in this area are firing.

Just behind the central fissure in the parietal lobe lies a sensory area called the **somatosensory cortex**, which receives messages from skin senses all over the body.

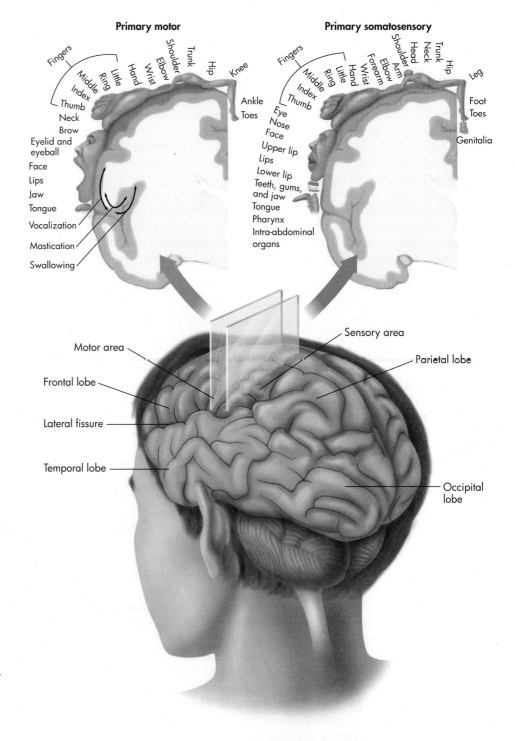

Figure 2.13 ■ The Geography of the Cerebral Cortex The cortex is divided into four lobes: frontal, parietal, temporal, and occipital. The visual area of the cortex is located in the occipital lobe. The hearing or auditory cortex lies in the temporal lobe. The sensory and motor areas face each other across the central fi ssure. What happens when a surgeon stimulates areas of the sensory or motor cortex during an operation?

These sensations include warmth and cold, touch, pain, and movement. Neurons in different parts of the sensory cortex fire depending on whether you wiggle your finger or raise your leg. **Truth or Fiction Revisited:** It is quite true that if a brain surgeon were to stimulate the proper area of your somatosensory cortex with an electrical probe, it might seem as if someone were touching your arm or leg. A Swedish MRI study found that just the expectation of being tickled in a certain part of the body activates the corresponding area of the somatosensory cortex (Carlsson et al., 2000).

But Figure 2.13 shows that the ways in which our bodies are situated or represented in the sensory area make for strange-looking humans indeed. Our faces and our hands are huge compared with, say, our trunk and our legs. This overrepresentation is one of the reasons that our face, head, and hands are more sensitive to touch than other parts of the body.

Many years ago, it was discovered that patients with injuries to one hemisphere of the brain would show sensory or motor deficits on the opposite side of the body below the head. This led to the recognition that sensory and motor nerves cross in the brain and elsewhere. The left hemisphere acts on, and receives inputs from, the right side of the body. The right hemisphere acts on, and receives inputs from, the left side of the body.

How do you make a monkey smile? One way is by inserting an electrical probe in its motor cortex and giving it a burst of electricity. Let's see what we mean by this.

The motor area of the cerebral cortex, or **motor cortex**, lies in the frontal lobe, just across the valley of the central fissure from the sensory area (the somatosensory cortex). Neurons firing in the motor area cause parts of our body to move. More than 100 years ago, German scientists electrically stimulated the motor cortex in dogs and observed that muscles contracted in response (Fritsch & Hitzig, 1870/1960). Since then, neuroscientists have mapped the motor cortex in people and lower animals by inserting electrical probes and seeing which muscles contract. For example, José Delgado (1969) caused one patient to make a fist even though he tried to prevent his hand from closing. The patient said, "I guess, doctor, that your electricity is stronger than my will" (Delgado, 1969, p. 114). Delgado also made a monkey smile in this manner many thousands of times in a row. If a surgeon were to stimulate a certain area of the right hemisphere of the motor cortex with an electrical probe, you would raise your left leg. This action would be sensed in the somatosensory cortex, and you might have a devil of a time trying to figure out whether you had intended to raise that leg!

We find the same overrepresentation of the face, head, and hands in the motor cortex as we find in the somatosensory cortex. The "detail" of these body parts on the cortex would appear to enable us to engage in fine muscle control over these areas of our bodies. Think of the possible human nuances of facial expression. Think of the fine motor (muscle) control we can exert as our fingers fly over the piano keyboard or the fine motor control of the surgeon engaged in a delicate operation.

THINKING, LANGUAGE, AND THE CORTEX Areas of the cerebral cortex that are not primarily involved in sensation or motor activity are called *association areas*. They make possible the breadth and depth of human learning, thought, memory, and language. **Question 19: What parts of the cerebral cortex are involved in thinking and language?** As noted earlier, the association areas in the prefrontal region of the brain—that is, in the frontal lobes, near the forehead—could be called the brain's executive center. It appears to be where we solve problems and make plans and decisions.

Executive functions like problem solving also require memory, like the memory in your computer. Moreover, association areas provide the core of your working memory (Rawley & Constantinidis, 2008). They are connected with various sensory areas in the brain and can tap whatever kind of sensory information is needed or desired. The prefrontal region of the brain thus retrieves visual, auditory, and other kinds of memories and manipulates them—similar to the way a computer retrieves information from files in storage and manipulates it in working memory.

Certain neurons in the visual area of the occipital lobe fire in response to the visual presentation of vertical lines. Others fire in response to the presentation of horizontal

Motor cortex The section of cortex that lies in the frontal lobe, just across the central fissure from the sensory cortex. Neural impulses in the motor cortex are linked to muscular responses throughout the body.

Mirror, Mirror, in the Brain: Who's the Fairest Imitator of Them All?

If we want to survive, we must understand the actions of others. Furthermore, without action understanding, social organization is impossible. In the case of humans, there is another faculty that depends on the observation of others' actions: imitation learning. Unlike most species, we are able to learn by imitation, and this faculty is at the basis of human culture.
— Rizzolatti and Craighero (2004)

According to Giacomo Rizzolatti and Laila Craighero (2004), social organization and human culture, as we know it, are made possible by the presence of certain kinds of neurons. And these neurons, like so many other important psychological discoveries, were found by accident.

A research team in Parma, Italy, headed by Vittorio Gallese and including Giacomo Rizzolatti (Gallese et al., 1996), was recording the activity of individual neurons in monkey's brains as the animals reached for objects. One of the researchers reached for an object that had been handled by a monkey, and quite to his surprise, a neuron in the monkey's brain fired in the same way it had fired when the animal had picked up the object. The research team followed up the phenomenon and discovered many such neurons in the frontal lobes of their monkeys, just before the motor cortex, which they dubbed *mirror neurons*. These *mirror neurons* in monkeys, and in humans, are activated by performing a motor act or by observing another monkey or human engage in the same act (Cattaneo & Rizzolatti, 2009; Cattaneo et al., 2010). Mirror neurons also operate in apes such as chimpanzees.

Mirror neurons are not limited to motor acts; in humans, they are also connected with emotions. Certain regions of the brain—particularly in the frontal lobe—are active when people experience emotions such as disgust, happiness, pain, and the like and also when they observe another person experiencing an emotion (Iacoboni, 2009a, 2009b). It thus appears that there is a neural basis for empathy—that is, the identification or vicarious experiencing of feelings in other people based on the observation of visual and other cues.

Some researchers believe that there is a connection between mirror neuron dysfunction and autistic disorders in children, which are characterized by impaired communication and emotional detachment from other people (Baron-Cohen & Belmonte, 2005). Activity in motor areas of the brain is suppressed in normal children when they observe another person move, which is thought to be an indication of mirror neuron activity. But such suppression is less prevalent in children with autism. Children with autistic disorders also show less mirror neuron activity when they imitate other people. This hypothesis has been developed further in that mirror neurons facilitate the modeling—or imitation—of the behavior of others by internally representing the bodily states linked to actions and emotions. Such internal representation could provide a direct way to experience and understand other people. Deficient minor neuron activity would prevent such understanding of other people and lead to the social deficits associated with autism.

It has also been suggested that mirror neurons are connected with the built-in human capacity to acquire language. In later chapters, we will see that mirror neurons are connected with observational learning and, perhaps, with sex differences in empathy (Cheng et al., 2008, 2009).

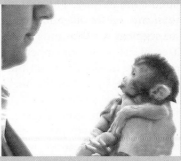

© Gross L (2006) Evolution of Neonatal Imitation. PLoS Biol 4(9): e311. doi:10.1371/journal. pbio.0040311

A Newborn Rhesus Monkey Imitates Protrusion of the Tongue, a Feat Made Possible by Mirror Neurons, Not by Learning

lines. Although one group of cells may respond to one aspect of the visual field and another group of cells may respond to another, association areas put it all together. As a result, we see a box or an automobile or a road map and not a confusing array of verticals and horizontals.

LANGUAGE FUNCTIONS In some ways, the left and right hemispheres of the brain duplicate each other's functions. In other ways, they differ. The left hemisphere contains language functions for nearly all right-handed people and for two of three left-handed people (Pinker, 2007). However, the brain remains "plastic," or changeable, through about the age of 13. As a result, children who lose the left hemisphere of the brain because of medical problems may largely transfer speech functions to the right hemisphere (Mbwana et al., 2008; Mercado, 2008).

Two key language areas lie within the hemisphere of the cortex that contains language functions (usually the left hemisphere): Broca's area and Wernicke's area (see Figure 2.14 ■). Damage to either area is likely to cause an **aphasia**—that is, a disruption of the ability to understand or produce language.

Wernicke's area lies in the temporal lobe near the auditory cortex. It responds mainly to auditory information (sounds). As you are reading this page, however, the visual information is registered in the visual cortex of your occipital lobe. It is then recoded as auditory information as it travels to Wernicke's area. Broca's area is located in the frontal lobe, near the section of the motor cortex that controls the muscles of the tongue, throat, and other areas of the face used when speaking. Broca's area processes the information and relays it to the motor cortex. The motor cortex sends the signals that cause muscles in your throat and mouth to contract. If you are "subvocalizing"— saying what you are reading "under your breath"—that is because Wernicke's area transmits information to Broca's area via nerve fibers.

People with damage to Wernicke's area may show **Wernicke's aphasia**, which impairs their abilities to comprehend speech. Even so, they usually speak freely and with proper syntax. Wernicke's area is essential to understanding the relationships between words and their meanings. When Broca's area is damaged, people usually understand language well enough but speak slowly and laboriously in simple sentences. This pattern is termed **Broca's aphasia**.

Some people with Broca's aphasia utter short, meaningful phrases that omit small but important grammatical words such as *is, and,* and *the*. Such an individual may laboriously say, "Walk dog." The phrase can have various meanings, such as, "I want to take the dog for a walk," or, "Take the dog out for a walk." Carroll (2004) reports the laborious, ungrammatical speech of one individual with Broca's aphasia: "Yes . . . ah . . . Monday . . . er Dad and Peter H. . . . (his own name), and Dad . . . er hospital . . . and ah . . . Wednesday . . . Wednesday nine o'clock . . . and oh . . . Thursday . . . ten o'clock, ah doctors . . . two . . . an' doctors . . . and er . . . teeth . . . yah."

A part of the brain called the *angular gyrus* lies between the visual cortex and Wernicke's area. The angular gyrus "translates" visual information, as in perceiving written words, into auditory information (sounds) and sends it on to Wernicke's area. Research using MRI suggests that problems in the angular gyrus can give rise to *dyslexia,* or serious impairment in reading, because it becomes difficult for the reader to segment words into sounds (Milne et al., 2002).

Left Brain, Right Brain?

We often hear of individuals being "left-brained" or "right-brained." **Question 20: What would it mean to be left-brained or right-brained?** The notion is that the hemispheres of the brain are involved in very different kinds of intellectual and emotional functions and responses. According to this view, left-brained people would be primarily logical and intellectual. Right-brained people would be intuitive, creative, and emotional. Those of us who are fortunate enough to have our brains "in balance" would presumably have the best of it—the capacity for logic combined with emotional richness.

Like so many other popular ideas, the left-brain–right-brain notion is at best exaggerated. Research does suggest that in right-handed individuals, the left hemisphere is relatively more involved in intellectual undertakings that require logical analysis and problem solving, language, and mathematical computation (Corballis, 2009). The other hemisphere (usually the right hemisphere) is usually superior in visual–spatial functions (it's better at putting puzzles together), recognition of faces, discrimination of colors, aesthetic and emotional responses, understanding metaphors, and creative mathematical reasoning. Despite these differences, the hemispheres of the brain do not act independently such that some people are truly left-brained and others right-brained (American Psychological Association, 2008; Baynes & Gazzaniga, 2000). The functions of the left and right hemispheres overlap to some degree, and they tend to respond simultaneously as we focus our attention on one thing or another.

Now let's consider another issue involving sidedness: left-handedness. People who are left-handed are different from people who are right-handed in terms of the way they write, throw a ball, and so on. But there are interesting questions as to whether people who are left-handed are also psychologically different from righties.

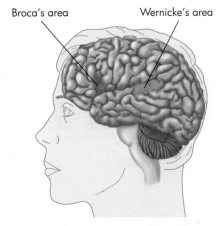

Broca's area   Wernicke's area

Figure 2.14 ■ Broca's and Wernicke's Areas of the Cerebral Cortex The areas that are most involved in speech are Broca's area and Wernicke's area. Damage to either area can produce an aphasia—a disruption of the ability to understand or produce language.

Aphasia A disruption in the ability to understand or produce language.

Wernicke's aphasia A language disorder characterized by difficulty comprehending the meaning of spoken language.

Broca's aphasia A language disorder characterized by slow, laborious speech.

Some Well-Known Lefties.

Oprah Winfrey   Bill Gates

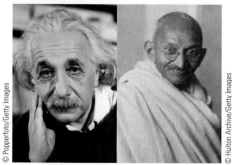

Albert Einstein   Mahatma Gandhi

"It seems that half of the scientific world sees the human animal as on a continuum with other animals, and others see a sharp break between animals and humans, see two distinct groups. The argument has been raging for years, and it surely won't be settled in the near future. After all, we humans are either lumpers or splitters. We either see the similarities or prefer to note the differences."

MICHAEL S. GAZZANIGA

Epilepsy Temporary disturbances of brain functions that involve sudden neural discharges.

Handedness: Is Being Right-Handed Right?

What do Michelangelo, Leonardo da Vinci, Angelina Jolie, and John McEnroe have in common? No, they are not all artists. Only one was a tennis player. But they are all left-handed. **Question 21: Does it matter whether one is left-handed?**

Despite the vast success of the individuals just named, being left-handed was once viewed as a deficiency. Left-handed students were compelled to learn to write with the right hand, and today the English language still swarms with slurs on lefties. We speak of "left-handed compliments," of having "two left feet," and of strange events as "coming out of left field." The word *sinister* means "left-hand or unlucky side" in Latin. *Gauche* is a French word that literally means "left," though in English it is used to mean clumsy. The English word *adroit,* meaning "skillful," derives from the French *à droit,* "to the right." Also consider positive usages such as "being righteous" or "being on one's right side."

Overall, 8 to 10% of us are lefties. Left-handedness is more common in boys than girls (Papadatou-Pastou et al., 2008). We are usually labeled right-handed or left-handed on the basis of our handwriting preferences, yet some people write with one hand and pass a football with the other. Some people even swing a tennis racket and pitch a baseball with different hands.

Being left-handed appears to provide a somewhat greater than average probability of language problems, such as dyslexia and stuttering, and health problems, such as migraine headaches and allergies (Fasmer et al., 2008; Goez & Zelnik, 2008; Lengen et al., 2008). But there may also be advantages to being left-handed. Left-handed people are more likely than right-handed people to be numbered among the ranks of artists, musicians, and mathematicians (Preti & Vellante, 2007). The downside of that creative tendency is a greater proneness to developing serious psychological disorders (Preti & Vellante, 2007).

Does handedness run in families? It does to some degree. In the English royal family, Queen Elizabeth II and Princes Charles and William are all left-handed, as was the Queen Mother. On the other hand, a recent study of more than 27,000 Dutch and Australian twin families found that heritability makes only about a 24% contribution to the likelihood of being right- or left-handed (Medland et al., 2008).

Whether we are talking about language functions, being left-brained or right-brained, or handedness, we are talking about people whose hemispheres of the cerebral cortex communicate back and forth. Now let's see what happens when the major avenue of communication between the hemispheres shuts down.

Split-Brain Experiments: How Many Brains Do You Have?

A number of people with severe cases of epilepsy have split-brain operations in which much of the corpus callosum is severed. The purpose of the operation is to confine seizures to one hemisphere of the cerebral cortex rather than allowing a neural tempest to reverberate. Split-brain operations do seem to help people with epilepsy. **Question 22: What happens when the brain is split in two?**

People who have undergone split-brain operations can be thought of as winding up with two brains, yet under most circumstances, their behavior remains ordinary enough. Still, some aspects of hemispheres that have stopped talking to each other are intriguing.

As reported by pioneering brain surgeon Joseph Bogen (1969, 2000), each hemisphere may have a "mind of its own." One split-brain patient reported that her hemispheres frequently disagreed on what she should be wearing. What she meant was that one hand might undo her blouse as rapidly as the other was buttoning it. A man reported that one hemisphere (the left hemisphere, which contained language functions) liked reading but the other one did not. If he shifted a book from his right hand to his left hand, his left hand would put it down. The left hand is connected with the right hemisphere of the cerebral cortex, which in most people—including this patient—does not contain language functions.

Another pioneer of split-brain research, Michael Gazzaniga (American Psychological Association, 2008), found that people with split brains whose eyes are closed may be able to verbally describe an object such as a key when they hold it in one hand but not when they hold it in the other hand. As shown in Figure 2.15 ■, if a person with a split brain handles a key with his left hand behind a screen, tactile impressions of the key are projected into the right hemisphere, which has little or no language ability. Thus, he will not be able to describe the key. If he holds it in his right hand, he will have no trouble describing it because sensory impressions are projected into the left hemisphere of the cortex, which contains language functions. To further confound matters, if the word *ring* is projected into the left hemisphere while the person is asked what he is handling, he will say "ring," not "key."

However, this discrepancy between what is felt and what is said occurs only in people with split brains. Even so, people who have undergone split-brain operations tend to lead largely normal lives. And for the rest of us, the two hemispheres work together most of the time, even when we are playing the piano or solving math problems.

Now that we have discussed the structures and the functioning of the brain, we will return to matters of chemistry. In the next section, we see the effects on behavior and mental processes of chemicals—*hormones*—that are secreted by glands and poured directly into the bloodstream.

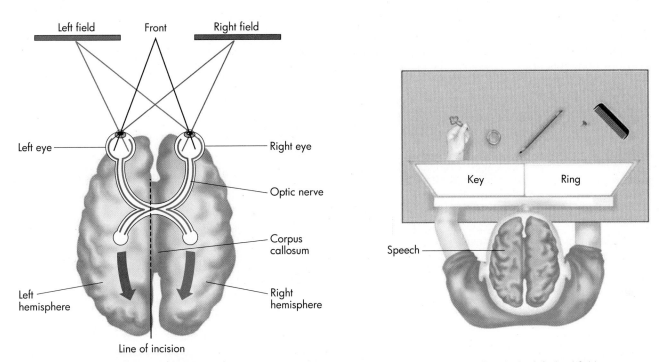

Figure 2.15 ■ A Divided-Brain Experiment In the drawing on the left, we see that visual sensations in the left visual field are projected in the occipital cortex of the right hemisphere. Visual sensations from the right visual field are projected in the occipital cortex in the left hemisphere. In the divided-brain experiment diagrammed on the right, a person with a severed corpus callosum handles a key with his left hand and perceives the written word "key" in his left visual field. The word "key" is projected in the right hemisphere. Speech, however, is usually a function of the left hemisphere. The written word "ring," perceived by the right visual field, is projected in the left hemisphere. So, when asked what he is handling, the divided-brain subject reports "ring," not "key."

LearningConnections ● THE BRAIN: THE STAR OF THE HUMAN NERVOUS SYSTEM

ACTIVE REVIEW (16) In functional magnetic _____ imaging, radio waves cause parts of the brain to emit signals. (17) The _____ is involved in balance and coordination. (18) The _____ is involved in body temperature, motivation, and emotion. (19) The hemispheres of the cerebrum are connected by the corpus _____. (20) The executive center of the brain is found in the _____ lobe. (21) Language areas are usually found in the (left or right?) hemisphere of the brain.

REFLECT AND RELATE Would you consider yourself to be more left-brained or right-brained? Explain.

CRITICAL THINKING Does the research evidence reported in this section demonstrate that the mind is a function of the brain? Why or why not?

 Go to Psychology CourseMate at **www.cengagebrain.com** for an interactive version of these questions.

THE ENDOCRINE SYSTEM: CHEMICALS IN THE BLOODSTREAM

The body contains two types of **glands**: glands with ducts and glands without ducts. A *duct* is a passageway that carries substances to specific locations. Saliva, sweat, tears, and breast milk all reach their destinations through ducts. **Question 23: What is the endocrine system?** The ductless glands constitute the **endocrine system**, and they secrete **hormones** (from the Greek *horman*, meaning "to stimulate" or "to excite"). Psychologists are interested in the substances secreted by ductless glands because of their behavioral effects.

Hormones are released into the bloodstream and circulate through the body. Like neurotransmitters, hormones have specific receptor sites. That is, they act only on receptors in certain locations. Some hormones that are released by the hypothalamus influence only the *pituitary gland*. Other hormones released by the pituitary influence the *adrenal cortex*; still others influence the testes and ovaries and so on (see Concept Review 2.1).

Much hormonal action helps the body maintain steady states, as in fluid levels, blood sugar levels, and so on. Bodily mechanisms measure current levels; when these levels deviate from optimal, they signal glands to release hormones. The maintenance of steady states requires feedback of bodily information to glands. This type of system is referred to as a *negative feedback loop*. That is, when enough of a hormone has been secreted, the gland is signaled to stop.

Gland An organ that secretes one or more chemical substances such as hormones, saliva, or milk.

Endocrine system The body's system of ductless glands that secrete hormones and release them directly into the bloodstream.

Hormone A substance secreted by an endocrine gland that regulates various body functions.

CONCEPT REVIEW 2.1 THE ENDOCRINE SYSTEM

Hypothalamus

- Releasing hormones or factors; e.g., growth hormone–releasing factor, corticotrophin releasing hormone (influences the pituitary gland to secrete corresponding hormones, e.g., growth hormone, adrenocorticotrophic hormone)

Pituitary

- Growth hormone (causes growth of muscles, bones, and glands)
- Adrenocorticotrophic hormone (ACTH) (regulates adrenal cortex)
- Thyrotrophin (causes thyroid gland to secrete thyroxin)
- Follicle-stimulating hormone (causes formation of egg and sperm cells)
- Luteinizing hormone (causes ovulation, maturation of egg and sperm cells)
- Prolactin (stimulates production of milk)
- Antidiuretic hormone (ADH) (inhibits production of urine)
- Oxytocin (stimulates uterine contractions during delivery and ejection of milk during nursing)

Pineal

- Melatonin (involved in regulation of sleep–wake cycle; possibly connected with aging)

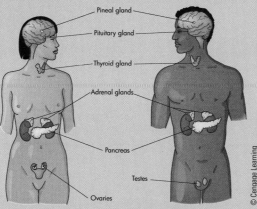

Pineal gland
Pituitary gland
Thyroid gland
Adrenal glands
Pancreas
Testes
Ovaries

© Cengage Learning

Pancreas

- Insulin (enables body to metabolize sugar; regulates storage of fats)

Thyroid

- Thyroxin (increases metabolic rate)

Adrenal

- Corticosteroids (increase resistance to stress; regulate carbohydrate metabolism)
- Epinephrine (adrenaline) (increases metabolic activity—heart and respiration rates, blood sugar level, etc.)
- Norepinephrine (noradrenaline) (raises blood pressure; acts as a neurotransmitter)

Testes

Testosterone (promotes development of male sex characteristics; involved in sex drive and aggressiveness)

Ovaries

Estrogen (regulates menstrual cycle; promotes development of female sex characteristics; connected with feelings of well-being)

The Hypothalamus: Master of the Master Gland

The hypothalamus secretes a number of releasing hormones, or factors, that influence the pituitary gland to secrete related hormones. For example, growth-hormone-releasing factor (hGRF) causes the pituitary to produce growth hormone. A dense network of blood vessels between the hypothalamus and the pituitary gland provides a direct route of influence for these factors.

The Pituitary Gland: The Pea-Sized Governor

The **pituitary gland** lies below the hypothalamus. Although the pituitary is only about the size of a pea, it produces so many hormones that it has been referred to as the *master gland*. (Because the hypothalamus regulates much pituitary activity, it could be dubbed the "master of the master gland.") The anterior (front) and posterior (back) lobes of the pituitary gland secrete many hormones. *Growth hormone* regulates the growth of muscles, bones, and glands. Children whose growth patterns are abnormally slow may catch up to their age-mates when they obtain growth hormone. *Prolactin* largely regulates maternal behavior in lower mammals such as rats and stimulates the production of milk in women. As a water conservation measure, *antidiuretic hormone (ADH)* inhibits production of urine when fluid levels in the body are low.

Oxytocin stimulates labor in pregnant women and is connected with maternal behavior (cuddling and caring for young) in some mammals (Champagne et al., 2009). Obstetricians may induce labor by injecting pregnant women with oxytocin. During nursing, stimulation of nerve endings in and around the nipples sends messages to the brain that cause the secretion of oxytocin. Oxytocin then causes the breasts to eject milk. Antidiuretic hormone and oxytocin are apparently also connected with stereotypical paternal behavior patterns in some mammals. **Truth or Fiction Revisited:** ADH and oxytocin can transform unconcerned male voles (mouselike rodents) into affectionate and protective mates and fathers (Donaldson & Young, 2008; Lim & Young, 2006; Parker et al., 2001). The hormone is not known to have such a powerful effect with humans, however.

The Pineal Gland

The pineal gland secretes the hormone *melatonin*, which helps regulate the sleep–wake cycle and may affect the onset of puberty. Some researchers speculate that melatonin is also connected with aging. In addition, it appears that melatonin is a mild sedative that fosters sleep, and some people use it as a sleeping pill (Ismail & Mowafi, 2009). Melatonin may also help people adjust to jet lag (Arendt, 2009).

The Thyroid Gland: The Body's Accelerator

The thyroid gland could be considered the body's accelerator. It produces *thyroxin*, which affects the body's *metabolism*—the rate at which the body uses oxygen and produces energy. Some people are overweight because of *hypothyroidism*, a condition that results from too little thyroxin. Thyroxin deficiency in children can lead to *cretinism*, a condition characterized by stunted growth and mental retardation. Adults who secrete too little thyroxin may feel tired and sluggish and may put on weight. People who produce too much thyroxin may develop *hyperthyroidism*, which is characterized by excitability, insomnia, and weight loss.

The Adrenal Glands: Coping with Stress

The adrenal glands, located above the kidneys, have an outer layer, or *cortex*, and an inner core, or *medulla*. The adrenal cortex is regulated by the pituitary hormone ACTH (adrenocorticotrophic hormone). The adrenal cortex secretes hormones known as *corticosteroids*, or cortical steroids. These hormones increase resistance to stress, promote muscle development, and cause the liver to release stored sugar, making more energy available in emergencies, as when you see another car veering toward your own. Epinephrine and norepinephrine are secreted by the adrenal medulla. *Epinephrine*, also known as *adrenaline*, is manufactured exclusively by the adrenal glands, but

"What is the cuddle hormone? The cuddle hormone is oxytocin, a chemical produced by the human body that has been linked to maternal affection and the feelings of attachment between couples."

CUDDLEHORMONE.COM

Pituitary gland The gland that secretes growth hormone, prolactin, antidiuretic hormone, and other hormones.

norepinephrine (*noradrenaline*) is also produced elsewhere in the body. (We saw that norepinephrine acts as a neurotransmitter in the brain.)

The sympathetic branch of the autonomic nervous system causes the adrenal medulla to release a mixture of epinephrine and norepinephrine that helps arouse the body to cope with threats and stress. Epinephrine is of interest to psychologists because it has emotional as well as physical effects. It intensifies most emotions and is crucial to the experience of fear and anxiety.

The Testes and the Ovaries

The testes and ovaries also produce steroids, among them testosterone and estrogen. If it were not for the secretion of the male sex hormone *testosterone* about 6 weeks after conception, we would all develop the external genital organs of females. Testosterone is produced not only by the testes but in smaller amounts by the adrenal glands. A few weeks after conception, testosterone causes the male sex organs to develop. During puberty, testosterone stokes the growth of muscle and bone and the development of primary and secondary sex characteristics. *Primary sex characteristics* such as the increased size of the penis and the sperm-producing ability of the testes are directly involved in reproduction. *Secondary sex characteristics* such as presence of a beard and a deeper voice differentiate males from females but are not directly involved in reproduction.

The ovaries produce *estrogen* and *progesterone* as well as small amounts of testosterone. Estrogen is also produced in smaller amounts by the testes. Estrogen fosters female reproductive capacity and secondary sex characteristics such as accumulation of fat in the breasts and hips. Progesterone stimulates growth of the female reproductive organs and prepares the uterus to maintain pregnancy.

Estrogen, like testosterone, has psychological as well as biological effects. For one thing, higher levels of estrogen seem to be connected with optimal cognitive functioning and feelings of well-being among women (Rocca et al., 2008; Wild, 2007). Women are also more interested in sexual activity when estrogen levels are high—particularly during ovulation, when they are fertile. Female mammals placed on estrogen replacement following menopause show improved memory functioning and visual–spatial abilities (Talboom et al., 2008; Voytko et al., 2009).

Estrogen and progesterone levels vary and regulate the woman's menstrual cycle. Following menstruation—the monthly sloughing off of the lining of the uterus—estrogen levels increase, leading to the ripening of an ovum (egg cell) and the growth of the lining of the uterus. Ovulation (release of the ovum by an ovary) occurs when estrogens reach peak blood levels. Then the lining of the uterus thickens in response to the secretion of progesterone, gaining the capacity to support an embryo if fertilization should occur. If the ovum is not fertilized, estrogen and progesterone levels drop suddenly, triggering menstruation once more.

STEROIDS, BEHAVIOR, AND MENTAL PROCESSES Steroids increase muscle mass, heighten resistance to stress, and increase the body's energy supply by signaling the liver to release sugar into the bloodstream. The steroid testosterone is connected with the sex drive in both males and females (females secrete some testosterone in the adrenal glands) (Roland & Incrocci, 2008).

Anabolic steroids (synthetic versions of the male sex hormone testosterone) have been used, sometimes in tandem with growth hormone, to enhance athletic prowess. Not only do they enhance athletic prowess, but they are also connected with self-confidence, aggressiveness, and even memory functioning (Janowsky et al., 2000). However, anabolic steroids are generally outlawed in sports. One reason has to do with the ethics of competition—the idea that athletes should "play fair." But steroid use is also linked to liver damage, other health problems, and possibly to outbursts of aggression that have been dubbed "'roid rage" (Kanayama et al., 2009).

Estrogen and testosterone even affect women's perceptions of who is attractive (Welling et al., 2008). Really! One study found that British women prefer feminized male faces, as shown in Figure 2.16B ■, during most phases of the menstrual cycle (Penton-Voak & Perrett, 2000). Women apparently associate such facial features with personality traits like warmth and honesty. However, they prefer the masculinized faces, as shown in Figure 2.16A ■, when estrogen levels are highest and they are ovulating.

> *"Testosterone does not have to be toxic."*
> ANNA QUINDLEN

Professional Wrestler Chris Benoit and Nancy Benoit—Before His Double Murder and Suicide That Took Their Lives and the Life of Their 7-Year-Old Son Benoit had a number of explosive outbursts, and it has been suggested that he might have been experiencing "'roid rage" due to his use of anabolic steroids to pump up his muscle mass and his competitiveness.

© George Napolitano/FilmMagic/Getty Images

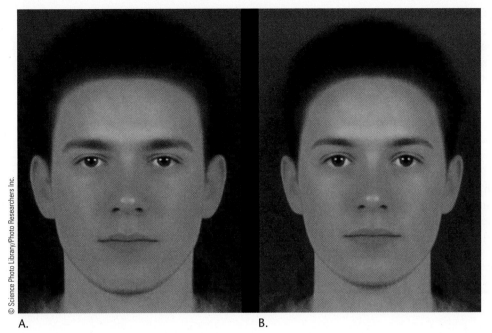

© Science Photo Library/Photo Researchers Inc.

A.   B.

Figure 2.16 ■ Which One Is Mr. Right?
The answer may depend on the phase of the woman's menstrual cycle. Women are apparently more attracted to men with masculinized features when they are capable of conceiving (part A) and men with more feminized features (part B) when they are not.

Perhaps they unconsciously interpret such features as indicative of reproductive capacity; that is, they instinctively see these men as more likely to father children.

PREMENSTRUAL SYNDROME (PMS) *Premenstrual syndrome (PMS)* is an important issue that is related to sex hormones. Psychologists study the effects of menstruation because of stereotypes about menstruating women and to help women with the discomfort that many experience. For several days prior to and during menstruation, according to the outmoded stereotype, "raging hormones" doom women to irritability and poor judgment. Even the ability of college women to focus on academic tasks during this period has been questioned.

Now for a few facts: Studies in the United States find that up to 90% of women of reproductive age have some symptoms of PMS (Fife & Schrager, 2009), such as depression, anxiety, and headaches, during the 4 to 6 days that precede menstruation (Clayton, 2008). However, only a small minority of women have symptoms severe enough to impair their academic, occupational, or social functioning.

Researchers have found that peak estrogen levels are connected with optimal cognitive functioning and psychological well-being in women (Talboom et al., 2008; Voytko et al., 2009). If peaks in female sex hormones are connected with psychological well-being, then perhaps the drop-off in hormones that precedes and accompanies menstruation is connected with PMS (De Berardis et al., 2007). But PMS is also linked with imbalances in neurotransmitters such as serotonin and beta-endorphins (Reed et al., 2008). Serotonin imbalances are linked to changes in appetite as well, so women with PMS tend to be hungrier during part of the cycle than other women. PMS may reflect an interaction between ovarian hormones and neurotransmitters (Clayton, 2008).

A generation ago, PMS was seen as something a woman must tolerate. Today, there are many treatment options. These include exercise, diet (for example, eating several small meals a day rather than two or three large meals; limiting salt and sugar; and taking vitamin supplements), hormone treatments (usually progesterone), and medications that affect levels of neurotransmitters in the nervous system. PMS is connected with drops in serotonin levels, and drugs called *selective serotonin reuptake inhibitors* (*SSRIs*) have helped many women with PMS (Brown et al., 2009). Women who use SSRIs to help with PMS do not take them continuously, as people do to fight depression, but rather for about 2 weeks each month.

Thus, there are important links between biological factors, behavior, and mental processes. Thoughts and mental images may seem to be intangible pictures that float in our heads, but they have substance. They involve billions of brain cells (neurons) and the transmission of thousands of chemicals from one neuron to another—repeated hundreds of times per second. These countless bits of microscopic activity give rise to feelings, plans, computation, art and music, and all the cognitive activities that make us human. We pour chemicals called hormones into our own bloodstreams, and they affect our activity levels, our anxiety levels, and even our sex drives. We inherit traits that make us human and that enable us to think more deeply and act more cleverly than any other organism (after all, we write the textbooks). An understanding of biology helps us grasp many psychological events that might otherwise seem elusive and without substance.

LearningConnections • THE ENDOCRINE SYSTEM: CHEMICALS IN THE BLOODSTREAM

ACTIVE REVIEW (22) The _____ secretes hormones that regulate the pituitary gland. (23) The pituitary hormone _____ regulates maternal behavior in lower animals and stimulates production of milk in women. (24) The thyroid hormone _____ affects the metabolism. (25) Epinephrine is secreted by the adrenal _____ and is involved in emotional arousal.

REFLECT AND RELATE Have you heard that adolescents are "hormonal" or affected by "glands"? If so, which glands would they be?

CRITICAL THINKING If so many behaviors and mental processes are affected by glands, do people have free will?

 Go to Psychology CourseMate at **www.cengagebrain.com** for an interactive version of these questions.

LIFE CONNECTIONS COPING WITH PMS

Most women experience some degree of menstrual discomfort. Women with persistent menstrual distress may profit from the following suggestions.

1. Don't blame yourself. Menstrual problems were once erroneously attributed to women's "hysterical" nature. This is nonsense. Researchers have not yet fully pinpointed the causal elements and patterns, but there is no evidence that women with PMS are hysterical.

2. Keep track of your menstrual symptoms to identify patterns.

3. Develop strategies for dealing with days on which you experience the most distress—strategies that will enhance pleasure and minimize stress. Go to a movie or get into that novel you've been meaning to read.

4. Ask yourself whether you harbor self-defeating attitudes that might be compounding distress. Do close relatives or friends see menstruation as an illness, a time of "pollution," or a "dirty thing"? Have you adopted any of these attitudes—if not verbally, then in ways that affect your behavior, as by restricting social activities during your period?

5. See a doctor about your symptoms. Pain can be caused or worsened by problems such as endometriosis and pelvic inflammatory disease (PID).

6. Develop healthful eating habits. Consider limiting intake of alcohol, caffeine, fats, salt, and sweets.

7. If you feel bloated, eat smaller meals or snacks throughout the day rather than a couple of highly filling meals.

8. Vigorous exercise—jogging, swimming, bicycling, fast walking, dancing, skating, jumping rope—helps relieve PMS in some women (Daley, 2009). Try it out.

9. Check with your doctor about herbal, vitamin, and mineral supplements (chaste berry, calcium, evening primrose, magnesium, vitamin E, wild yams, and so on) (Lloyd & Hornsby, 2009).

Exercise and PMS Many women find that vigorous exercise helps them manage premenstrual symptoms.

10. Over-the-counter anti-inflammatory medicines such as aspirin, acetaminophen, and ibuprofen may be helpful for cramping (Clayton, 2008). Prescription drugs such as tranquilizers (e.g., alprazolam) and SSRIs may be of help (Brown et al., 2009; Clayton, 2008). Ask your doctor for a recommendation.

11. Menstruation is triggered by a sharp drop-off in sex hormones. Some gynecologists prescribe estrogen replacement to relieve PMS, although this approach is not free of hazards. One method is simply to continue specialized oral contraceptives for 28 days rather than 21 days and thus to forego menstruation (Fife & Schrager, 2009).

12. Menstrual problems are time limited. Don't worry about getting through life or a career. Focus instead on the next couple of days.

Evolution and Evolutionary Psychology: "Survivor" Is More Than Just a TV Show

1. What are some of the basic concepts of the theory of evolution?
The "struggle for existence" refers to the competition among species and among members within a species to survive and reproduce. Variations among individuals, including mutations, affect organisms' ability to adapt. Changes that enhance survival are likely to be preserved. Natural selection refers to the finding that organisms that are better adapted to their environments tend to survive and transmit their genes to subsequent generations.

2. What is evolutionary psychology?
Evolutionary psychology studies the ways adaptation and natural selection are connected with mental processes and behavior. Evolutionary psychologists suggest that not only physical traits but also patterns of behavior, including social behavior, evolve and are transmitted from generation to generation.

3. What is an instinct?
An instinct is a stereotypical behavior pattern that is nearly identical among the members of a species in which it appears. It occurs even when the individual is reared in isolation from others of its kind.

Heredity: The Nature of Nature

4. What is heredity?
Heredity involves the biological transmission of traits from generation to generation.

5. What is genetics?
Genetics is the subfield of biology that studies heredity. Behavioral genetics is concerned with the genetic transmission of traits that give rise to behavior and focuses on individual differences.

6. What are the roles of genes and chromosomes in heredity?
Genes are the biochemical materials that regulate the development of traits. Genes are segments of chromosomes. Humans have 46 chromosomes arranged in 23 pairs. Chromosomes are molecules of DNA, which takes the form of a twisting ladder. We normally receive 23 chromosomes from each parent. People with Down syndrome have an extra chromosome on the 21st pair.

7. What are kinship studies?
Psychologists conduct kinship studies to help determine the influences of genetic and environmental factors on behavior and mental processes. Twin studies are useful because identical (monozygotic) twins share the same genetic code; therefore, differences reflect environmental factors. When children reared by adoptive parents are more similar to their natural parents in a particular trait, evidence exists for a genetic role in the expression of that trait.

The Nervous System: On Being Wired

8. What are neurons?
Neurons are cells that transmit information through neural impulses. Neurons have a cell body; dendrites, which receive messages; and trunklike axons, which conduct and then transmit messages to other cells by means of chemicals called neurotransmitters. Many neurons have a myelin coating that insulates their axons, allowing more efficient conduction of messages. Afferent neurons transmit sensory messages to the central nervous system. Efferent neurons conduct messages from the central nervous system that stimulate glands or cause muscles to contract.

9. What are neural impulses?
Neural impulses are electrical charges that are conducted along axons through processes that allow sodium ions to enter cells and then pump them out. The neuron has a resting potential of -70 millivolts and an action potential of about $+40$ millivolts.

10. What happens when a neuron fires?
Neurons fire (transmit messages to other neurons, muscles, or glands) by releasing neurotransmitters. They fire according to an all-or-none principle up to hundreds of times per second. Each firing is followed by a refractory period during which neurons are insensitive to messages from other neurons.

11. What is a synapse?
Neurons fire across synapses, which consist of an axon terminal from the transmitting neuron, a dendrite or the body of a receiving neuron, and a fluid-filled synaptic cleft between the two.

12. What do neurotransmitters do?
Acetylcholine is involved in muscle contractions and memory; imbalances of dopamine have been linked to Parkinson's disease and schizophrenia; norepinephrine accelerates the heartbeat and other body processes; serotonin is involved in eating, sleeping, and emotional arousal; GABA inhibits anxiety; and endorphins are naturally occurring painkillers.

13. What are the parts of the nervous system?
The nervous system is one of the systems that regulates the body. It is made up of neurons and divided into the central and peripheral nervous systems.

14. What are the divisions and functions of the peripheral nervous system?
The peripheral nervous system has two main divisions: somatic and autonomic. The somatic nervous system transmits sensory information about skeletal muscles, skin, and joints to the central nervous system. It also controls skeletal muscular activity. The autonomic nervous system (ANS) regulates the glands and activities such as heartbeat, digestion, and dilation of the pupils. The sympathetic division of the ANS helps expend the body's resources, such as when fleeing from a predator, and the parasympathetic division helps build the body's reserves.

15. What are the divisions and functions of the central nervous system?

The central nervous system consists of the brain and spinal cord. Reflexes involve the spinal cord but not the brain. The central nervous system has gray matter, which is composed of nonmyelinated neurons, and white matter, which is composed of bundles of myelinated (and thus whitish) axons.

The Brain: The Star of the Human Nervous System

16. How do researchers learn about the functions of the brain?

Researchers historically learned about the brain by studying the effects of accidents. They have also studied the effects of purposeful damage to the brain made by lesions. They have seen how animals and people respond to electrical stimulations of certain parts of the brain. They have studied the waves emitted by the brain with the electroencephalograph. With CAT scans, PET scans, and MRIs, computer-generated images are made by passing radiation of some sort through the brain.

17. What are the structures and functions of the brain?

The hindbrain includes the medulla, which regulates the heart rate, blood pressure, and respiration; the pons, which is involved in movement, attention, and respiration; and the cerebellum, which is involved in balance and coordination. The reticular formation, which is involved in wakefulness and sleep, begins in the hindbrain and continues through the midbrain into the forebrain. Important structures of the forebrain include the thalamus, which serves as a relay station for sensory stimulation; the hypothalamus, which regulates body temperature and various aspects of motivation and emotion, such as eating and sexual behavior; the limbic system, which is involved in memory, emotion, and motivation; and the cerebrum, which is the brain's center of thinking and language.

18. What are the parts of the cerebral cortex?

The outer fringe of the cerebrum is the cerebral cortex, which is divided into two hemispheres and four lobes: frontal, parietal, temporal, and occipital. When light strikes the eyes, neurons in the occipital lobe fire. The somatosensory cortex lies behind the central fissure in the parietal lobe, and the motor cortex lies in the frontal lobe, across the central fissure from the somatosensory cortex. The prefrontal cortex may be thought of as the executive center of the brain—making plans, solving problems, and drawing upon sensory information from other areas of the cortex as needed.

19. What parts of the cerebral cortex are involved in thinking and language?

Language areas of the cortex usually lie in the left hemisphere, near the intersection of the frontal, temporal, and parietal lobes. Wernicke's area, in the temporal lobe, responds mainly to auditory information. Broca's area, in the frontal lobe, is mainly responsible for speech. Damage to either area can result in an aphasia—a problem in understanding (Wernicke's aphasia) or producing (Broca's aphasia) language.

20. What would it mean to be left-brained or right-brained?

The left hemisphere is usually relatively more involved in cognitive functions involving logical analysis and problem solving, whereas the right hemisphere is usually superior in visual–spatial functions, aesthetic and emotional responses, and creative mathematical reasoning. But the notion that some people are left-brained (that is, only logical and lacking completely in functions involving visual–spatial responses and the like) and others are right-brained is exaggerated.

21. Does it matter whether one is left-handed?

About one person in ten is left-handed. Learning disabilities are somewhat more common among left-handed people, but so is creativity, as shown in the arts. Handedness appears to have a genetic component.

22. What happens when the brain is split in two?

For the most part, the behavior of people who have had split-brain operations (which sever most of the corpus callosum) is perfectly normal. However, an example of the type of change that occurs is that they cannot verbally describe a screened-off object such as a pencil held in the hand that is not connected to the hemisphere that contains language functions.

The Endocrine System: Chemicals in the Bloodstream

23. What is the endocrine system?

The endocrine system consists of ductless glands that secrete hormones. The pituitary gland secretes growth hormone; prolactin regulates maternal behavior in lower animals and stimulates production of milk in women; and oxytocin stimulates labor in pregnant women. The pineal hormone melatonin is connected with the sleep–wake cycle and the onset of puberty. Thyroxin affects the body's metabolism, and its deficiency in childhood is connected with mental retardation. The adrenal cortex produces steroids, which promote the development of muscle mass and increase activity levels. The adrenal medulla secretes epinephrine (adrenaline), which increases the metabolic rate and is involved in general emotional arousal. The sex hormones are responsible for prenatal sexual differentiation. Female sex hormones regulate the menstrual cycle.

KEY TERMS

Acetylcholine (ACh) (p. 54)
Action potential (p. 52)
Afferent neurons (p. 49)
All-or-none principle (p. 53)
Amygdala (p. 63)
Aphasia (p. 67)
Autonomic nervous system (ANS) (p. 56)
Axon (p. 49)
Behavioral genetics (p. 43)
Broca's aphasia (p. 67)
Central nervous system (p. 56)
Cerebellum (p. 61)
Cerebral cortex (p. 63)
Cerebrum (p. 63)
Chromosome (p. 43)
Corpus callosum (p. 63)
Dendrites (p. 49)
Depolarize (p. 52)
Dizygotic (DZ) twins (p. 45)
DNA (p. 43)
Dopamine (p. 54)
Down syndrome (p. 45)
Efferent neurons (p. 49)
Endocrine system (p. 70)
Endorphins (p. 55)
Epigenesis (p. 48)
Epilepsy (p. 68)
Evolutionary psychology (p. 42)

Frontal lobe (p. 64)
Gamma-aminobutyric acid (GABA) (p. 55)
Gene (p. 43)
Genetics (p. 43)
Genotype (p. 44)
Gland (p. 70)
Glia (p. 49)
Gray matter (p. 58)
Heredity (p. 43)
Hippocampus (p. 54)
Hormone (p. 70)
Hypothalamus (p. 62)
Instinct (p. 42)
Interneuron (p. 58)
Lesioning (p. 60)
Limbic system (p. 62)
Medulla (p. 61)
Monozygotic (MZ) twins (p. 45)
Motor cortex (p. 65)
Mutation (p. 41)
Myelin (p. 50)
Natural selection (p. 40)
Nature (p. 44)
Nerve (p. 56)
Neural impulse (p. 51)
Neuron (p. 49)
Neurotransmitters (p. 53)
Norepinephrine (p. 54)

Nurture (p. 44)
Occipital lobe (p. 64)
Parasympathetic (p. 57)
Parietal lobe (p. 64)
Peripheral nervous system (p. 56)
Phenotype (p. 44)
Pituitary gland (p. 71)
Polarize (p. 52)
Polygenic (p. 44)
Pons (p. 61)
Receptor site (p. 53)
Refractory period (p. 53)
Resting potential (p. 52)
Reticular formation (p. 62)
Serotonin (p. 54)
Sex chromosomes (p. 44)
Somatic nervous system (p. 56)
Somatosensory cortex (p. 64)
Species (p. 42)
Spinal cord (p. 58)
Spinal reflex (p. 58)
Sympathetic (p. 57)
Synapse (p. 53)
Temporal lobe (p. 64)
Thalamus (p. 62)
Wernicke's aphasia (p. 67)
White matter (p. 58)

ACTIVE LEARNING RESOURCES

Log in to **www.cengagebrain.com** to access the resources your instructor requires. For this book, you can access:

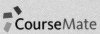 CourseMate brings course concepts to life with interactive learning, study, and exam preparation tools that support the printed textbook. A textbook-specific website, Psychology CourseMate includes an integrated interactive eBook and other interactive learning tools including quizzes, flashcards, videos, and more.

 Need help studying? This site is your one-stop study shop. Take a Pre-Test and CengageNOW will generate a Personalized Study Plan based on your test results. The Study Plan will identify the topics you need to review and direct you to online resources to help you master those topics. You can then take a Post-Test to determine the concepts you have mastered and what you still need to work on.

© Chung Sung-Jun/Getty Images

3 Sensation and Perception

MAJOR TOPICS

Sensation and Perception: Your Tickets of Admission to the World Outside 80

Vision: Letting the Sun Shine In 83

Visual Perception: How Perceptive? 91

Hearing: Making Sense of Sound 100

The Chemical Senses: Smell and Taste 104

The Skin Senses (Yes, It Does) 106

Kinesthesis and the Vestibular Sense 110

Extrasensory Perception: Is There Perception Without Sensation? 112

FEATURES

Concept Review 3.1: Monocular Cues for Depth Perception 97

Video Connections: The Ames Room 97

A Closer Look: iPods on Campus: The Sounds of Oblivion? 102

A Closer Look: Advances in Science? The Case of the Aromatic T-Shirts 106

Life Connections: Pain, Pain, Go Away—Don't Come Again Another Day 110

Concept Review 3.2: The Senses 113

T F People have five senses.

page 80

T F If we could see waves of light with slightly longer wavelengths, warm-blooded animals would glow in the dark.

page 81

T F People sometimes hear what they want to hear.

page 82

T F When we mix blue and yellow light, we obtain green light.

page 88

T F The bodies of catfish are covered with taste buds.

page 105

T F The skin is a sensory organ as well as a protective coating for the body.

page 106

T F Many people experience pain "in" limbs that have been amputated.

page 109

T F You have a sense that keeps you an upright person.

page 111

T F Some people can read other people's minds.

page 114

Are these items truth or fiction? We will be revisiting them throughout the chapter.

The tsunami that hit the coast of southern Asia in 2004 killed as many as one quarter of a million people. The people were caught off guard, but not the animals.

Along the western coast of Thailand, elephants giving rides to tourists began to trumpet agitatedly hours before the tsunami, just about when the earthquake that fractured the ocean floor sent the big waves rushing toward the shore. An hour before the waves slammed into the area, the elephants began wailing. Before the waves struck, they trooped off to higher ground. A survivor said, "Dogs are smarter than all of us. . . . [They] started running away up to the hilltops long before we even realized what was coming" (Oldenburg, 2005). Flamingos usually breed in low-lying areas at this time of year, but on the day of the tsunami, they abandoned their sanctuary on the coast of India and headed into safer forests before the waves hit shore. Rats evacuated buildings. Sparrows took flight. Elephants, tigers, leopards, deer, wild boar, water buffalo, monkeys, and reptiles in Sri Lanka's Yala National Park escaped the tsunami unharmed.

Animals appear to detect earthquakes, hurricanes, volcanic eruptions, and tsunamis before the earth starts shaking. Some animals are apparently supersensitive to sound, others to temperature, touch, or vibration, which gives them advance warning. Many animals seem to detect vibrations on land and in water, or electromagnetic changes in the atmosphere. Other animals have keen senses of hearing or smell that enable them to detect something approaching long before people can (Mott, 2005).

Elephants are particularly sensitive to ground vibrations and probably sensed the earthquake that caused the tsunami in their feet and trunks. Some birds, dogs, tigers, and elephants can sense sound waves whose frequencies are too low for humans to hear. Dogs' superior sense of smell might detect subtle chemical changes in the air that warn them of calamities.

Different animals, then, have different sensory equipment, and many sense things that people cannot sense. Just how do humans sense the world around them?

How did elephants sense the approaching tsunami, when people did not?

SENSATION AND PERCEPTION: YOUR TICKETS OF ADMISSION TO THE WORLD OUTSIDE

Question 1: What are sensation and perception? **Sensation** is the stimulation of sensory receptors and the transmission of sensory information to the central nervous system (the spinal cord or brain). Sensory receptors are located in sensory organs such as the eyes and ears, the skin, and elsewhere in the body. Stimulation of the senses is a mechanical process. It results from sources of energy, likee light and sound, or from the presence of chemicals, as in smell and taste.

Perception is not mechanical. It is an *active* process in which sensations are organized and interpreted to form an inner representation of the world (Hafemeister et al., 2010; Rouder & Morey, 2009). Perception may begin with sensation, but it also reflects our experiences and expectations as it makes sense of sensory stimuli. A person standing 15 feet away and a 12-inch-tall doll may cast similar-sized images on the back of your eye, but whether you interpret the shape to be a foot-long doll or a full-grown person 15 feet away is a matter of perception that depends on your experience with dolls, people, and distance.

In this chapter, you will see that your personal map of reality—your ticket of admission to a world of changing sights, sounds, and other sources of sensory input—depends largely on the so-called five senses: vision, hearing, smell, taste, and touch. We will see, however, that touch is just one of several "skin senses," which also include pressure, warmth, cold, and pain. There are also senses that alert you to your own body position without your having to watch every step you take. As we explore the nature of each of these senses, we will find that similar sensations may lead to different perceptions in different people—or within the same person in different situations. **Truth or Fiction Revisited:** People do have more than five senses.

Before we begin our voyage through the senses, let's consider a number of concepts that apply to all of them: *absolute threshold, subliminal stimulation, difference threshold, signal-detection theory, feature detectors,* and *sensory adaptation*. In doing so, we will learn why we can dim the lights gradually to near darkness without anyone noticing. (Sneaky?) We will also learn why we might become indifferent to the savory aromas of delightful dinners. (Disappointing?) **Question 2: How do we know when something is there?** How do we know when something has changed?

Absolute Threshold: So, Is It There or Not?

Gustav Fechner used the term **absolute threshold** to refer to the weakest amount of a stimulus that a person can distinguish. For example, the absolute threshold for light would be the minimum brightness (physical energy) required to activate the visual sensory system.

Psychophysicists look for the absolute thresholds of the senses by exposing individuals to progressively stronger stimuli until they find the minimum stimuli that the person can detect no more (and no less) than 50% of the time. However, it has been discovered that these absolute thresholds are not really absolute. That is, some people are more sensitive than others, and even the same person might have a slightly different response from one occasion to another (Rouder & Morey, 2009).

Nevertheless, under ideal conditions, our ability to detect stimuli is amazingly sensitive. The following are measures of the absolute thresholds for the senses of vision, hearing, taste, smell, and touch:

- *Vision:* a candle flame viewed from about 30 miles on a clear, dark night.
- *Hearing:* a watch ticking from about 20 feet away in a quiet room.
- *Taste:* 1 teaspoon of sugar dissolved in 2 gallons of water.
- *Smell:* about one drop of perfume diffused throughout a small house (1 part in 500 million).
- *Touch:* the pressure of the wing of a fly falling on a cheek from a distance of about 0.4 inch.

It's interesting to imagine how our lives would differ if the absolute thresholds for the human senses differed. For example, if your ears were more sensitive to sounds that

Sensation The stimulation of sensory receptors and the transmission of sensory information to the central nervous system.

Perception The process by which sensations are organized into an inner representation of the world.

Absolute threshold The minimal amount of energy that can produce a sensation.

are low in **pitch**, you might hear the collisions among molecules of air. If you could see light with slightly longer wavelengths, you would see infrared light waves. Your world would be transformed because heat generates infrared light. **Truth or Fiction Revisited:** Moreover, if we could see waves of light with slightly longer wavelengths, warm-blooded animals would glow in the dark. In addition, the worlds of those who are blind, deaf, or have other variations in their sensory capabilities can be substantially different. These different experiences of reality may not always be viewed as losses. For example, some deaf people have advocated against artificial restoration of hearing through surgical means because of the beauty and value of a world of silence and sign language (Berke, 2009).

Subliminal Stimulation

Do TV commercials contain words or sexual images that are flashed so briefly on the screen that we do not become conscious of them but they influence us? **Question 3: Would ads that show an appealing image or a command—such as "Buy!"—for only a fraction of a second influence us?** Perhaps they would.

Sensory stimulation that is below a person's absolute threshold for conscious perception is termed **subliminal stimulation**—and its perception is called *subliminal perception.* Visual stimuli can be flashed too briefly to enable us to process them. Auditory stimuli can be played at a volume too low for us to consciously hear or can be played backward.

Johan Karremans and his colleagues (2006) repeatedly flashed "Lipton Ice" for 24 milliseconds (about 1/50th of a second) on a computer screen that was viewed by an experimental group of participants. They flashed a message without a brand name to a control group. Thirsty participants in the experimental group showed a preference for Lipton Ice, but non-thirsty participants showed no such preference.

Even the most fleeting experiences can have emotional consequences. In one experiment, participants were shown fearful, happy, or neutral faces for 30 milliseconds (about 1/30th of a second), too briefly to recognize consciously (Sweeny et al., 2009). A day later, they were shown faces of the same people, all with neutral expressions. Faces that had been subliminally shown as happy were rated more positively by the participants, even though they had been flashed too rapidly for conscious recognition.

© LAYLANDMASUDA/Veer

Subliminal Stimulation Will flashing the word "buy" too briefly to enable conscious recognition influence you to buy a product in a TV commercial?

Difference Threshold: Is It the Same, or Is It Different?

How much of a difference in intensity between two lights is required before you will detect one as brighter than the other? The minimum difference in *magnitude* of two stimuli required to tell them apart is their **difference threshold**. As with the absolute threshold, psychologists have agreed to the criterion of a difference in magnitudes that can be detected 50% of the time.

Psychophysicist Ernst Weber discovered through laboratory research that the threshold for perceiving differences in the intensity of light is about 2% (actually closer to 1/60th) of their intensity. This fraction, 1/60th, is known as **Weber's constant** for light. A closely related concept is the **just noticeable difference (jnd)**, the minimum difference in stimuli that a person can detect. For example, at least 50% of the time, most people can tell if a light gets just 1/60th brighter or dimmer. Weber's constant for light holds whether we are comparing two quite bright lights or two moderately dull lights. However, it becomes inaccurate when we compare extremely bright or extremely dull lights.

Weber's constant for noticing differences in lifted weight is 1/53rd. (Round it off to 1/50th.) That means if you are strong enough to heft a 100-pound barbell, you would not notice that it was heavier until about 2 pounds were added. Yet if you are a runner who carries 1-pound dumbbells, you would definitely notice if someone slipped you dumbbells even a pound heavier because the increase would be 100%, not a small fraction.

What about sound? People are most sensitive to changes in the pitch (frequency) of sounds. The Weber constant for pitch is 1/333, meaning that on average, people can tell

Pitch The highness or lowness of a sound as determined by the frequency of the sound waves.

Subliminal stimulation Sensory stimulation that is below a person's absolute threshold for conscious perception.

Difference threshold The minimal difference in intensity required between two sources of energy so that they will be perceived as different.

Weber's constant The fraction of the intensity by which a source of physical energy must be increased or decreased so that a difference in intensity will be perceived.

Just noticeable difference (jnd) The minimal amount by which a source of energy must be increased or decreased so that a difference in intensity will be perceived.

when a tone rises or falls in pitch by an extremely small one-third of 1%. (Singers have to be right on pitch. The smallest error makes them sound sharp or flat.) Remember this when friends criticize your singing—you may not be "tone deaf" but just slightly off.

The sense of taste is much less sensitive. On average, people cannot detect differences in saltiness of less than 20%. That is why those low-salt chips that have 15% less salt than your favorite do not taste so bad.

Signal-Detection Theory: Is Being Bright Enough?

From the discussion so far, it might seem as if people are simply switched on by certain amounts of stimulation. This is not quite true. People are influenced by psychological factors as well as by external changes. Signal-detection theory considers the human aspects of sensation and perception. **Question 4: What is signal-detection theory?**

Signal Detection The detection of signals is determined not only by the physical characteristics of stimuli but also by psychological factors such as motivation and attention. The woman in this photo is engrossed by her newspaper, and the man is focusing on the PDA. Neither notices the people around them or the noise and buffeting about of the subway.

According to signal-detection theory, the relationship between a physical stimulus and a sensory response is not just mechanical (Gigerenzer, 2010). People's ability to detect stimuli such as meaningful blips on a radar screen depends not only on the intensity of the blips but also on their training (learning), motivation (desire to perceive meaningful blips), and psychological states such as fatigue or alertness (Rouder & Morey, 2009).

The intensity of the signal is just one factor that determines whether people will perceive sensory stimuli (signals) or a difference between signals. Another is the degree to which the signal can be distinguished from background noise. It is easier to hear a friend in a quiet room than in a room where people are talking loudly and clinking glasses. The sharpness or acuteness of a person's biological sensory system is still another factor. Is sensory capacity fully developed? Is it diminished by advanced age?

Truth or Fiction Revisited: It is true that people sometimes hear what they want to hear. That is, we tend to detect stimuli we are searching for. Signal-detection theory also considers psychological factors such as motivation, expectations, and learning. For example, the place where you are reading this book may be abuzz with signals. If you are outside, perhaps a breeze is blowing against your face. Perhaps the shadows of passing clouds darken the scene now and then. If you are inside, perhaps there are the occasional clanks and hums emitted by a heating system. Perhaps the aromas of dinner are hanging in the air, or the voices from a TV set suggest a crowd in another room. Yet you are focusing your attention on this page (I hope). Thus, the other signals recede into the background of your consciousness. One psychological factor in signal detection is the focusing or narrowing of attention to signals that the person deems important.

Feature Detectors in the Brain: Firing on Cue

Imagine you are standing by the curb of a busy street as a bus approaches. When neurons in your sensory organs—in this case, your eyes—are stimulated by the approach of the bus, they relay information to the sensory cortex in the brain. Nobel Prize winners David Hubel and Torsten Wiesel (1979) discovered that various neurons in the visual cortex of the brain fire in response to particular features of the visual input. **Question 5: What are feature detectors?** Many cells in the brain detect (that is, fire in response to) lines presented at various angles—vertical, horizontal, and in between. Other cells fire in response to specific colors. Because they respond to different aspects or features of a scene, these brain cells are termed feature detectors. In the example of the bus, visual feature detectors respond to the bus's edges, depth, contours, textures, shadows, speed, and kinds of motion (up, down, forward, and back). There are also feature detectors for other senses. Auditory feature detectors, for example, respond to the pitch, loudness, and other aspects of the sounds of the bus.

Signal-detection theory The view that the perception of sensory stimuli involves the interaction of physical, biological, and psychological factors.

Feature detectors Neurons in the sensory cortex that fire in response to specific features of sensory information such as lines or edges of objects.

Sensory Adaptation: Where Did It Go?

Our sensory systems are admirably suited to a changing environment. **Question 6: How do our sensory systems adapt to a changing environment?** Sensory adaptation refers to the processes by which we become more sensitive to stimuli of low magnitude and less sensitive to stimuli that remain the same (such as the background noises outside the window) (Lawless & Heymann, 2010).

Consider how the visual sense adapts to lower intensities of light. When we first walk into a darkened movie theater, we see little but the images on the screen. As we search for our seats, however, we become increasingly sensitive to the faces around us and to the features of the theater. The process of becoming more sensitive to stimulation is referred to as **sensitization**, or *positive adaptation*.

But we become less sensitive to constant stimulation. Sources of light appear to grow dimmer as we adapt to them. In fact, if you could keep an image completely stable on the retinas of your eyes—which is virtually impossible to accomplish without a motionless image and stabilizing equipment—the image would fade within a few seconds and be very difficult to see. Similarly, at the beach, we soon become less aware of the sound of the lapping of the waves. When we live in a city, we become desensitized to traffic sounds except for the occasional backfire or siren. And as you may have noticed from experiences with freshly painted rooms, sensitivity to disagreeable odors fades quite rapidly. The process of becoming less sensitive to stimulation is referred to as **desensitization**, or *negative adaptation*.

Our sensitivities to stimulation provide our brains with information that we use to understand and control the world outside. This information influences our behavior and mental processes. Therefore, it is not surprising that psychologists study the ways we sense and perceive this information—through vision, hearing, the chemical senses, and yet other senses, as we see throughout the remainder of the chapter.

Sensory adaptation The processes by which organisms become more sensitive to stimuli that are low in magnitude and less sensitive to stimuli that are constant or ongoing in magnitude.

Sensitization The type of sensory adaptation in which we become more sensitive to stimuli that are low in magnitude; also called positive adaptation.

Desensitization The type of sensory adaptation in which we become less sensitive to constant stimuli; also called negative adaptation.

LearningConnections ● SENSATION AND PERCEPTION: YOUR TICKETS OF ADMISSION TO THE WORLD OUTSIDE

ACTIVE REVIEW (1) _____ is a mechanical process that involves the stimulation of sensory receptors and the transmission of sensory information to the central nervous system. (2) _____ is the organization of sensations into an inner representation of the world; it reflects learning and expectations as well as sensations. (3) The _____ threshold for a stimulus, such as light, is the lowest intensity at which it can be detected. (4) The minimum difference in intensity that can be discriminated is the _____ threshold.

REFLECT AND RELATE Have you been so involved in something that you didn't notice the heat or the cold? Have you grown so used to sounds like those made by crickets or trains at night that you fall asleep without hearing them? How do these experiences relate to signal-detection theory?

CRITICAL THINKING Which factors in sensation and perception reflect our nature? Which reflect nurture?

 Go to Psychology CourseMate at **www.cengagebrain.com** for an interactive version of these questions.

● VISION: LETTING THE SUN SHINE IN

Our eyes are literally our "windows on the world." Vision is our most dominant sense. Vision provides the most reliable spatial information and plays the largest role in guiding goal-directed behavior (Fiehler et al., 2008; Hagler et al., 2007). Blindness, therefore, is considered by many to be the most debilitating type of sensory loss. To understand vision, let's first consider the nature of light.

Light: How Dazzling?

Light is fascinating stuff. It radiates. It illuminates. It dazzles. It glows. It beckons like a beacon. We speak of the "light of reason." We speak of genius as "brilliance." In almost all cultures, light is a symbol of goodness and knowledge. People who aren't in the know are said to be "in the dark." **Question 7: Just what is light?**

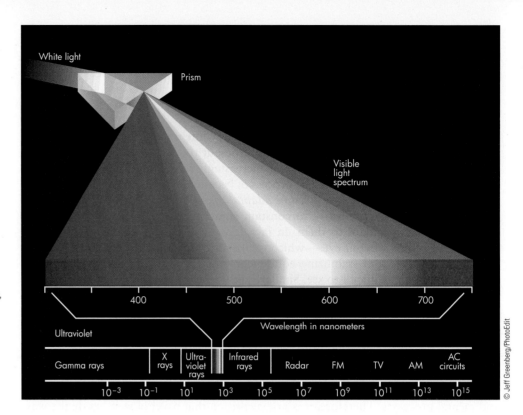

Figure 3.1 ■ The Visible Spectrum
By passing a source of white light, such as sunlight, through a prism, we break it down into the colors of the visible spectrum. The visible spectrum is just a narrow segment of the electromagnetic spectrum. The electromagnetic spectrum also includes radio waves, microwaves, X-rays, cosmic rays, and many others. Different forms of electromagnetic energy have wavelengths that vary from a few trillionths of a meter to thousands of miles. Visible light varies in wavelength from about 400 to 700 *billionths* of a meter. (1 meter = 39.37 inches.)

> *"It is a terrible thing to see and have no vision."*
>
> HELEN KELLER

Visible light The part of the electromagnetic spectrum that stimulates the eye and produces visual sensations.

Hue The color of light as determined by its wavelength.

Cornea Transparent tissue forming the outer surface of the eyeball.

Iris A muscular membrane whose dilation regulates the amount of light that enters the eye.

It is **visible light** that triggers visual sensations. Yet visible light is just one small part of a spectrum of electromagnetic energy that surrounds us (see Figure 3.1 ■). All forms of electromagnetic energy move in waves, and different kinds of electromagnetic energy have signature wavelengths as follows:

- *Cosmic rays:* The wavelengths of these rays from outer space are only a few *trillionths* of an inch long.
- *Radio waves:* Some radio signals extend for miles.
- *Visible light:* Different colors have different wavelengths, with violet the shortest at about 400 *billionths* of a meter in length and red the longest at 700 billionths of a meter.

Have you seen rainbows or light that has been broken down into several colors as it filtered through your windows? Sir Isaac Newton, the British scientist, discovered that sunlight could be broken down into different colors by means of a triangular solid of glass called a *prism* (refer again to Figure 3.1). When I took introductory psychology, I was taught to remember the colors of the spectrum, from longest to shortest wavelengths, by using the mnemonic device *Roy G. Biv* (red, orange, yellow, green, blue, indigo, violet). The wavelength of visible light determines its color, or **hue**. The wavelength for red is longer than the wavelength for orange and so on through the spectrum.

The Eye: The Better to See You With

Consider that magnificent invention called the camera, which records visual experiences. In traditional cameras, light enters an opening and is focused onto a sensitive surface, or film. Chemicals on film create a lasting impression of the image that entered the camera.

Question 8: How does the eye work? The eye—our living camera—is no less remarkable. Look at its major parts, as shown in Figure 3.2 ■. As with a film or TV camera, light enters through a narrow opening and is projected onto a sensitive surface. Light first passes through the transparent **cornea**, which covers the front of the eye's surface. (The "white" of the eye, or *sclera*, is composed of hard protective tissue.) The amount of light that passes through the cornea is determined by the size of the opening of the muscle called the **iris**, which is the colored part of the eye. The opening in

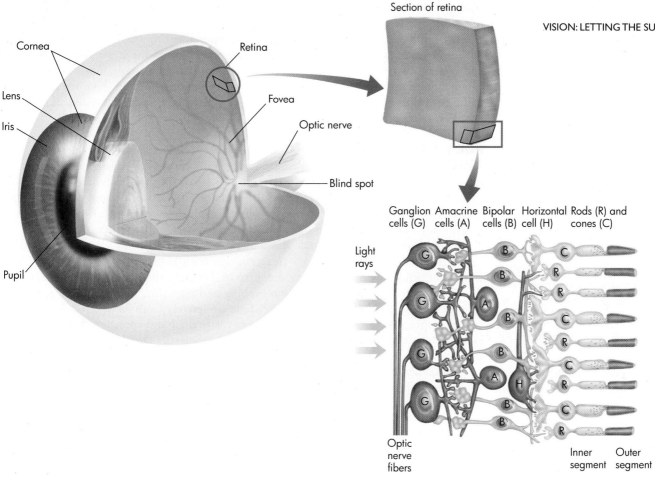

Figure 3.2 ■ The Human Eye In both the eye and a camera, light enters through a narrow opening and is projected onto a sensitive surface. In the eye, the photosensitive surface is called the retina, and information concerning the changing images on the retina is transmitted to the brain. The retina contains photoreceptors called rods and cones. Rods and cones transmit sensory input back through the bipolar neurons to the ganglion neurons. The axons of the ganglion neurons form the optic nerve, which transmits sensory stimulation through the brain to the visual cortex of the occipital lobe.

the iris is the **pupil**. The size of the pupil adjusts automatically to the amount of light present. Therefore, you do not have to purposefully open your eyes further to see better in low lighting conditions. The more intense the light, the smaller the opening. In a similar fashion, we adjust the amount of light allowed into a camera according to its brightness. Interestingly, pupil size is also sensitive to emotional response: we can be literally "wide-eyed with fear."

Once light passes through the iris, it encounters the **lens**. The lens adjusts or accommodates to the image by changing its thickness. Changes in thickness permit a clear image of the object to be projected onto the retina. These changes focus the light according to the distance of the object from the viewer. If you hold a finger at arm's length and slowly bring it toward your nose, you will feel tension in the eye as the thickness of the lens accommodates to keep the retinal image in focus. When people squint to bring an object into focus, they are adjusting the thickness of the lens. In contrast, the lens in a camera does not accommodate to the distance of objects. Instead, to focus the light that is projected onto the film, the camera lens is moved farther from the film or closer to it, as in a zoom lens.

The **retina** is like the film or image surface of the camera. However, the retina consists of cells called **photoreceptors** that are sensitive to light (photosensitive). There are two types of photoreceptors: *rods* and *cones*. The retina (refer again to Figure 3.2) contains several layers of cells: the rods and cones, **bipolar cells**, and **ganglion cells**. All of these cells are neurons. The rods and cones respond to light with chemical changes that create neural impulses that are picked up by the bipolar cells. These then activate the ganglion cells. The axons of the million or so ganglion cells in our retina converge

Pupil The apparently black opening in the center of the iris through which light enters the eye.

Lens A transparent body behind the iris that focuses an image on the retina.

Retina The area of the inner surface of the eye that contains rods and cones.

Photoreceptors Cells that respond to light.

Bipolar cells Neurons that conduct neural impulses from rods and cones to ganglion cells.

Ganglion cells Neurons whose axons form the optic nerve.

to form the **optic nerve.** The optic nerve conducts sensory input to the brain, where it is relayed to the visual area of the occipital lobe.

As if this were not enough, the eye has additional neurons to enhance this process. Amacrine cells and horizontal cells make sideways connections at a level near the rods and cones and at another level near the ganglion cells. As a result, single bipolar cells can pick up signals from many rods and cones, and in turn, a single ganglion cell is able to funnel information from multiple bipolar cells. In fact, rods and cones outnumber ganglion cells by more than 100 to 1.

RODS AND CONES Rods and **cones** are the photoreceptors in the retina (see Figure 3.3 ■). About 125 million rods and 6.4 million cones are distributed across the retina. The cones are most densely packed in a small spot at the center of the retina called the **fovea** (refer again to Figure 3.2). Visual acuity (sharpness and detail) is greatest at this spot. The fovea is composed almost exclusively of cones. Rods are densest just outside the fovea and thin out toward the periphery of the retina.

Rods allow us to see in black and white. Cones provide color vision. In low lighting, it is possible to photograph a clearer image with black-and-white film than with color film. Similarly, rods are more sensitive to dim light than cones. Therefore, as the illumination grows dim, as during the evening and nighttime hours, objects appear to lose their color well before their outlines fade completely from view.

In contrast to the visual acuity of the fovea is the **blind spot,** which is insensitive to visual stimulation. It is the part of the retina where the axons of the ganglion cells converge to form the optic nerve (see Figure 3.2 and 3.4 ■).

Visual acuity (sharpness of vision) is connected with the shape of the eye. People who have to be unusually close to an object to discriminate its details are *nearsighted.* People who see distant objects unusually clearly but have difficulty focusing on nearby objects are *farsighted.* Nearsightedness can result when the eyeball is elongated so that the images of distant objects are focused in front of the retina. When the eyeball is too short, the images of nearby objects are focused behind the retina, causing farsightedness. Eyeglasses or contact lenses can be used to help nearsighted people focus distant objects on their retinas. Laser surgery can correct vision by actually changing the shape of the eye. Farsighted people usually see well enough without eyeglasses until they reach their middle years, when they may need glasses for reading.

Beginning in their late 30s to the mid-40s, people's lenses start to grow brittle, making it more difficult to accommodate to, or focus on, objects. This condition is called **presbyopia,** from the Greek words for "old man" and "eyes," a slight misnomer because presbyopia occurs by middle adulthood, not late adulthood. Presbyopia makes

Optic nerve The nerve that transmits sensory information from the eye to the brain.

Rods Rod-shaped photoreceptors that are sensitive only to the intensity of light.

Cones Cone-shaped photoreceptors that transmit sensations of color.

Fovea An area near the center of the retina that is dense with cones and where vision is consequently most acute.

Blind spot The area of the retina where axons from ganglion cells meet to form the optic nerve.

Visual acuity Sharpness of vision.

Presbyopia A condition characterized by brittleness of the lens.

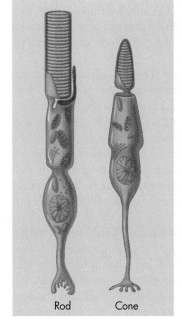

Figure 3.3 ■ Rods and Cones You have about 125 million rods and 6.4 million cones distributed across the retina of each eye as shown in the drawing (A) and photo (B). Only cones provide sensations of color. The fovea of the eye is almost exclusively populated by cones, which are then distributed more sparsely as you work toward the periphery of the retina.

Rod   Cone

A.

B. Each human retina contains two types of photoreceptor cells: rods and cones. As shown in this color-enhanced photo, the rods are rod-shaped in appearance and the cones are cone-shaped.

© Omikron/Photo Researchers, Inc.

Figure 3.4 ■ The Blind Spot To try a "disappearing act," close your left eye, hold the book close to your face, and look at the boy with your right eye. Slowly move the book away until the pie disappears. The pie disappears because it is being projected onto the blind spot of your retina, the point at which the axons of ganglion neurons collect to form the optic nerve. Note that when the pie disappears, your brain "fills in" the missing checkerboard pattern, which is one reason that you're not usually aware that you have blind spots.

it difficult to perceive nearby visual stimuli. People who had normal visual acuity in their youth often require corrective lenses to read in middle adulthood and beyond.

LIGHT ADAPTATION When we walk out onto a dark street, we may at first not be able to see people, trees, and cars clearly, but as time goes on, we are better able to discriminate the features of people and objects. The process of adjusting to lower lighting conditions is called **dark adaptation**.

Figure 3.5 ■ shows the amount of light needed for detection as a function of the amount of time spent in the dark. The cones and rods adapt at different rates. The cones, which permit perception of color, reach their maximum adaptation to darkness in about 10 minutes. The rods, which allow perception of light and dark only, are more sensitive to dim light and continue to adapt to darkness for up to about 45 minutes.

Adaptation to brighter lighting conditions takes place much more rapidly. When you emerge from the theater into the brilliance of the afternoon, you may at first be painfully surprised by the featureless blaze around you. The visual experience is not unlike turning the brightness of the TV set to its maximum setting, at which the edges of objects seem to dissolve into light. Within a minute or so of entering the street, however, the brightness of the scene dims, and objects regain their edges.

Color Vision: Creating an Inner World of Color

For most of us, the world is a place of brilliant colors—the blue-greens of the ocean, the red-oranges of the setting sun, the deepened greens of June, the glories of the purple rhododendron and red hibiscus. Color is an emotional and aesthetic part of our

Dark adaptation The process of adjusting to conditions of lower lighting by increasing the sensitivity of rods and cones.

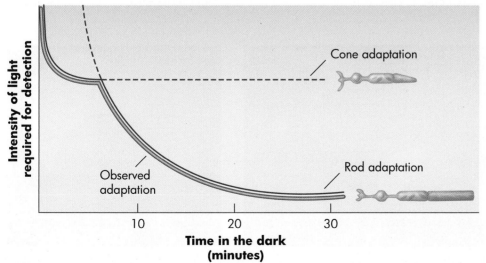
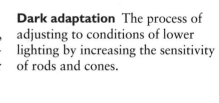
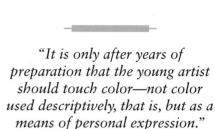

Figure 3.5 ■ Dark Adaptation This illustration shows the amount of light necessary for detection as a function of the amount of time spent in the dark. Cones and rods adapt at different rates. Cones, which permit perception of color, reach maximum dark adaptation in about 10 minutes. Rods, which permit perception of dark and light only, are more sensitive than cones. Rods continue to adapt for up to about 45 minutes.

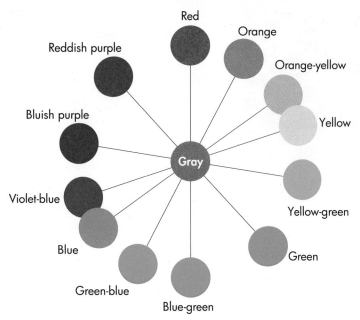

Figure 3.6 ■ **The Color Wheel** A color wheel can be formed by bending the colors of the spectrum into a circle and placing complementary colors across from one another. (A few colors between violet and red are not found in the spectrum and must be added to complete the circle.) When lights of complementary colors such as yellow and violet-blue are mixed, they dissolve into neutral gray. The afterimage of a color is its complement.

Complementary Descriptive of colors of the spectrum that when combined produce white or nearly white light.

everyday lives. In this section, we explore some of the dimensions of color and then examine theories about how we manage to convert different wavelengths of light into perceptions of color. **Question 9: What are some perceptual dimensions of color?** These dimensions of color include *hue*, *value*, and *saturation*.

The wavelength of light determines its color, or *hue*. The *value* of a color is its degree of lightness or darkness. The *saturation* refers to how intense a color appears to us. A fire-engine red will appear more saturated than a pale pinkish red.

Colors can also have psychological associations within various cultural settings. For example, in the United States, a bride may be dressed in white as a sign of purity. In traditional India, the guests would be shocked because white is the color for funerals. Here we mourn in black.

WARM AND COOL COLORS If we bend the colors of the spectrum into a circle, we create a color wheel, as shown in Figure 3.6 ■. Psychologically, the colors on the green-blue side of the color wheel are considered cool in temperature. Those colors on the yellow-orange-red side are considered warm. Perhaps greens and blues suggest the coolness of the ocean and the sky, whereas things that are burning tend to be red or orange. A room decorated in green or blue may seem more appealing on a hot July day than a room decorated in red or orange.

COMPLEMENTARY COLORS The colors across from one another on the color wheel are labeled **complementary**. Red–green and blue–yellow are the major complementary pairs. If we mix complementary colors together, they dissolve into gray. **Truth or Fiction Revisited:** It is true, therefore, that when we mix blue and yellow light, we obtain green light.

"But wait!" you say. "Blue and yellow cannot be complementary because by mixing pigments of blue and yellow we create green, not gray." True enough, but we have been talking about mixing *lights,* not *pigments.* Light is the source of all color. Pigments reflect and absorb different wavelengths of light selectively. The mixture of lights is an *additive* process. The mixture of pigments is *subtractive.* Figure 3.7 ■ shows mixtures of lights and pigments of various colors.

Pigments gain their colors by absorbing light from certain segments of the spectrum and reflecting the rest. For example, we see most plant life as green because the pigment in chlorophyll absorbs most of the red, blue, and violet wavelengths of light. The remaining green is reflected. A red pigment absorbs most of the spectrum but reflects red. White pigments reflect all colors equally. Black pigments reflect very little light.

In *Sunday Afternoon on the Island of La Grande Jatte* (see Figure 3.8 ■, part A), French painter Georges Seurat molded his figures and forms from dabs of color. Instead of mixing his pigments, he placed points of pure color next to one another. When the painting is viewed from very close (see the detail in part B), the sensations are of

Figure 3.7 ■ **Additive and Subtractive Color Mixtures Produced by Lights and Pigments** Thomas Young discovered that white light and all the colors of the spectrum could be produced by adding combinations of lights of red, green, and violet-blue and varying their intensities (see Part A). Part B shows subtractive color mixtures, which are formed by mixing pigments, not light.

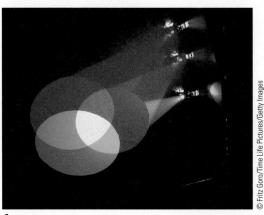

A.

B.

© Fritz Goro/Time Life Pictures/Getty Images

A. **B.**

Figure 3.8 ■ Sunday Afternoon on the Island of La Grande Jatte French painter Georges Seurat molded his figures and forms from dabs of color. Instead of mixing pigments, he placed points of pure color next to one another. When the viewer is close to the canvas (see the detail), the points of color are apparent. But from a distance, they create the impression of color mixtures.

Georges Seurat, French, 1859–1891, *A Sunday on La Grande Jatte—1884*, 1884–86, Oil on canvas, 81 3/4 x 121 1/4 in. (207.5 x 308.1 cm), Helen Birch Bartlett Memorial Collection, 1926.224, The Art Institute of Chicago. Photography © The Art Institute of Chicago.

pure color. But from a distance, the juxtaposition of pure colors creates the impression of mixtures of color.

AFTERIMAGES Before reading on, why don't you try a mini-experiment? Look at the strangely colored American flag in Figure 3.9 ■ for at least half a minute. Try not to blink as you are doing so. Then look at a sheet of white or gray paper. What has happened to the flag? If your color vision is working properly, and if you looked at the miscolored flag long enough, you should see a flag composed of the familiar red, white, and blue. The flag you perceive on the white sheet of paper is an **afterimage** of the first. (If you didn't look at the green, black, and yellow flag long enough the first time, try it again.) In afterimages, persistent sensations of color are followed by perception of the complementary color when the first color is removed. The same holds true for black and white. Staring at one will create an afterimage of the other. The phenomenon of afterimages has contributed to one of the theories of color vision, as we will see.

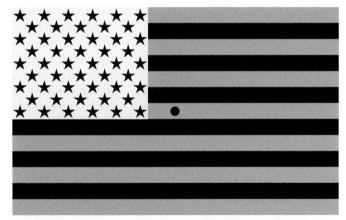

Figure 3.9 Three Cheers for the ... Green, Black, and Yellow? Don't be concerned. We can readily restore Old Glory to its familiar hues. Place a sheet of white paper beneath the book, and stare at the black dot in the center of the flag for at least 30 seconds. Then remove the book. The afterimage on the paper beneath will look familiar.

Theories of Color Vision: How Colorful?

Adults with normal color vision can discriminate many thousands of colors across the visible spectrum. Different colors have different wavelengths. Although we can vary the physical wavelengths of light in a continuous manner from shorter to longer, many changes in color are discontinuous. For example, our perception of a color shifts suddenly from blue to green even though the change in wavelength may be smaller than that between two blues.

Question 10: How do we perceive color? Our ability to perceive color depends on the eye's transmission of different messages to the brain when lights with different wavelengths stimulate the cones in the retina. There are two key theories of color vision: the *trichromatic theory* and the *opponent-process theory*.

Trichromatic theory is based on an experiment conducted by British scientist Thomas Young in the early 1800s. As in Figure 3.7, shown earlier, Young projected three lights of different colors onto a screen so that they partly overlapped. He found

Afterimage The lingering visual impression made by a stimulus that has been removed.

Trichromatic theory The theory that color vision is made possible by three types of cones, some of which respond to red light, some to green, and some to blue.

89

that he could create any color from the visible spectrum simply by varying the intensities of the lights. When all three lights fell on the same spot, they created white light, or the appearance of no color at all. The three lights manipulated by Young were red, green, and blue-violet.

German physiologist Hermann von Helmholtz saw in Young's discovery an explanation of color vision. Helmholtz suggested that the retina in the eye must have three different types of color photoreceptors, or cones. Some cones must be sensitive to red light, some to green, and some to blue. We see other colors when two different types of color receptors are stimulated. The perception of yellow, for example, would result from the simultaneous stimulation of receptors for red and green. The trichromatic theory is also known as the *Young–Helmholtz theory*.

In 1870, another German physiologist, Ewald Hering, proposed the **opponent-process theory** of color vision: there are three types of color receptors; however, they are sensitive not just to the simple hues of red, green, and blue as Helmholtz claimed. Hering suggested instead that afterimages (such as that of the American flag shown in Figure 3.9) are made possible by these three types of color receptors: red–green, blue–yellow, and a type that perceives differences in brightness. According to Hering, because a red–green cone could not transmit messages for red and green at the same time, if you stare at the green, black, and yellow flag for 30 seconds, that would disturb the balance of neural activity. The afterimage of red, white, and blue would represent the eye's attempt to reestablish a balance.

Research suggests that each theory of color vision is partially correct. In fact, color vision may be made possible by a two-stage process in which the cones are as Helmholtz says, and the transmission signals to the brain are as Hering proposes. For example, research shows that some cones are sensitive to blue, some to green, and some to red (see Figure 3.10 ■) (Pang et al., 2010). But studies of the bipolar and ganglion neurons suggest that messages from cones are transmitted to the brain and relayed by the thalamus to the occipital lobe in an opponent-process fashion (Yin et al., 2009).

A neural rebound effect apparently helps explain the occurrence of afterimages. That is, a green-sensitive ganglion that is excited by green light for half a minute or so might switch briefly to inhibitory activity when the light is shut off. The effect would be to perceive red even though no red light is present. Imagine looking at a green fir tree with red ornaments for a minute or so during the holidays and then turning your gaze to a white brick fireplace nearby. You just might see an image of a red tree with green ornaments!

These theoretical updates allow for the afterimage effects with the green, black, and yellow flag and are also consistent with Young's experiments in mixing lights of different colors.

Opponent-process theory The theory that color vision is made possible by three types of cones, some of which respond to red or green light, some to blue or yellow, and some to the intensity of light.

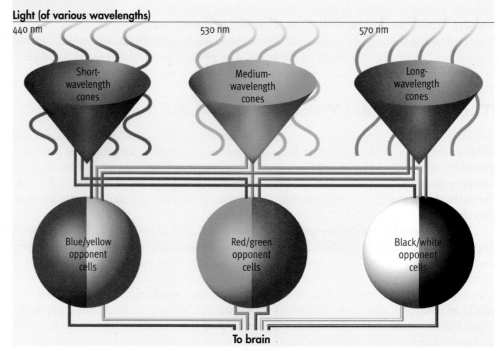

Figure 3.10 ■ The Perception of Color
Perception of color actually requires elements of both trichromatic and opponent-process theory. Cones in the retina are sensitive to either blue, green, or red. Color mixtures (such as yellow) require the simultaneous firing of groups of cones (in this case, green and red). But higher levels of visual processing occur in opponent-process fashion, explaining the occurrence of afterimages.

Light (of various wavelengths)

440 nm · 530 nm · 570 nm

Short-wavelength cones · Medium-wavelength cones · Long-wavelength cones

Blue/yellow opponent cells · Red/green opponent cells · Black/white opponent cells

To brain

Color-Blindness

If you can discriminate among the colors of the visible spectrum, you have normal color vision and are labeled a trichromat. This means that you are sensitive to red–green, blue–yellow, and light–dark. **Question 11: What is color-blindness, and why are some people color-blind?** People who are totally color-blind, called **monochromats**, are sensitive only to lightness and darkness. Total color-blindness is rare. Fully color-blind individuals see the world as trichromats would on a black-and-white TV set or in a black-and-white movie.

Partial color-blindness is a sex-linked trait that mostly affects males. Partially color-blind people are called **dichromats**. There are two kinds of dichromats. One kind cannot distinguish between red and green. The other kind cannot distinguish between blue and yellow. The first kind of dichromat might put on one red sock and one green sock, failing to recognize that they differ in hue, but would not mix red socks with blue socks. Monochromats, on the other hand, might put on socks of any color. They would not notice a difference as long as the socks' colors did not differ in intensity—that is, brightness.

© Getty Images/Purestock

© Sam Armstrong/Photographer's Choice/Getty Images

Red Braeburn and Green Granny Smith Apples as Seen by Trichromats (Top Row) and by Dichromats Who Have Difficulty Distinguishing Red from Green (Bottom Row) How might dichromatism impair driving?

LearningConnections • VISION: LETTING THE SUN SHINE IN

ACTIVE REVIEW (5) The color of visible light is determined by its _____. (6) Light enters the eye through the _____. (7) The _____ accommodates to an image by changing thickness and focusing light onto the retina. (8) The retina is made up of photoreceptors called _____ and _____. (9) The axons of ganglion cells make up the _____ nerve, which conducts visual information to the brain.

REFLECT AND RELATE Try a mini-experiment. Take a watch with a second hand and enter a walk-in closet that allows just the merest sliver of light to pass under the door. Close the door. How long does it take until you can see the objects in the closet?

CRITICAL THINKING What is the evidence for the different theories of color vision?

 Go to Psychology CourseMate at **www.cengagebrain.com** for an interactive version of these questions.

● VISUAL PERCEPTION: HOW PERCEPTIVE?

What do you see in Figure 3.11 ■? Do you see meaningless splotches of ink or a rider on horseback? If you perceive a horse and rider, it is not just because of the visual sensations provided by the drawing. Each of the blobs is meaningless in and of itself, and the pattern is vague. Despite the lack of clarity, however, you may still perceive a horse and rider.

Visual perception is the process by which we organize or make sense of the sensory impressions caused by the light that strikes our eyes. Visual perception involves our knowledge, expectations, and motivations. As noted earlier, whereas sensation may be thought of as a mechanical or passive process (that is, light stimulating the rods and cones of our retina), perception is an active process through which we interpret the world around us. **Question 12: How do we organize bits of visual information into meaningful wholes?** The answer has something to do with your general knowledge and your desire to fit incoming bits and pieces of information into familiar patterns.

Trichromat A person with normal color vision.

Monochromat A person who is sensitive to black and white only and hence color-blind.

Dichromat A person who is sensitive to black–white and either red–green or blue–yellow and hence partially color-blind.

Figure 3.11 ■ Closure Meaningless splotches of ink, or a horse and rider? This figure illustrates the Gestalt principle of closure.

Closure The tendency to perceive a broken figure as being complete or whole.

Perceptual organization The tendency to integrate perceptual elements into meaningful patterns.

In the case of the horse and rider, your integration of disconnected pieces of information into a meaningful whole also reflects what Gestalt psychologists (see Chapter 1) refer to as the principle of **closure**, or the tendency to perceive a complete or whole figure even when there are gaps in the sensory input. Put another way, in perception, the whole can be very much more than the mere sum of the parts. A collection of parts can be meaningless. It is their configuration that matters.

Perceptual Organization: Getting It Together

Early in the 20th century, Gestalt psychologists noted certain consistencies in the way we integrate bits and pieces of sensory stimulation into meaningful wholes. They attempted to identify the rules that govern these processes. Max Wertheimer, in particular, discovered many such rules. As a group, these rules are referred to as the laws of **perceptual organization**. We examine several of them here, beginning with those concerning figure–ground perception. Then we consider top-down and bottom-up processing.

FIGURE–GROUND PERCEPTION If you look out your window, you may see people, buildings, cars, and streets, or perhaps grass, trees, birds, and clouds. All these objects tend to be perceived as figures against grounds, or backgrounds. Individual cars seen against the background of the street are easier to pick out than cars piled on top of one another in a junkyard. Birds seen against the sky are more likely to be perceived than birds seen "in the bush."

When figure–ground relationships are *ambiguous,* or capable of being interpreted in various ways, our perceptions tend to be unstable, shifting back and forth (Bull et al., 2003). As an example, look for a while at Figure 3.12 ■. How many people, objects, and animals can you find? If your eye is drawn back and forth so that sometimes you are perceiving light figures on a dark background and at other time dark figures on a light background, you are experiencing figure–ground reversals. In other words, a shift is occurring in your perception of what is figure and what is ground. The artist was able to have some fun with us because of our tendency to try to isolate geometric patterns or figures from a background. However, in this case, the background is as meaningful and detailed as the figure. Therefore, our perceptions shift back and forth.

Figure 3.12 ■ Figure and Ground How many animals and demons can you find in this Escher print? Do we have white figures on a black background or black figures on a white background? Figure–ground perception is the tendency to perceive geometric forms against a background.

  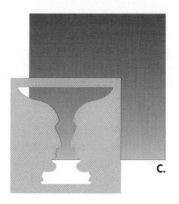

Figure 3.13 ■ The Rubin Vase This is a favorite drawing used by psychologists to demonstrate figure–ground perception. Part A is ambiguous, with neither the vase nor the profiles clearly the figure or the ground. In part B, the vase is the figure; in part C, the profiles are.

Figure 3.13 ■ shows a Rubin vase, one of psychologists' favorite illustrations of figure–ground relationships. The figure–ground relationship in part A of the figure is ambiguous. There are no cues that suggest which area must be the figure. For this reason, our perception may shift from seeing the vase to seeing two profiles. There is no such problem in part B. Because it seems that a white vase has been brought forward against a colored ground, we are more likely to perceive the vase than the profiles. In part C, we are more likely to perceive the profiles than the vase because the profiles are whole and the vase is broken against the background. Of course, if we wish to, we can still perceive the vase in part C because experience has shown us where it is. Why not have some fun with friends by covering up parts B and C and asking them what they see? (They'll catch on quickly if they can see all three drawings at once.)

The Necker Cube, shown in Figure 3.14 ■, is another ambiguous drawing that can lead to perceptual shifts. Hold this page at arm's length and stare at the center of the figure for 30 seconds or so. Try to allow your eye muscles to relax. (The feeling is of your eyes "glazing over.") After a while, you will notice a dramatic shift in your perception of the box. What was once a front edge is now a back edge, and vice versa. The perceptual shift is made possible by the fact that the outline of the drawing permits two interpretations.

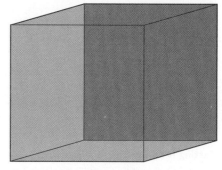

Figure 3.14 ■ The Necker Cube Ambiguity in the drawing of the cube makes perceptual shifts possible. Therefore, the darker tinted surface can become either the front or back of the cube.

OTHER GESTALT RULES FOR ORGANIZATION In addition to the law of closure, Gestalt psychologists have noted that our perceptions are guided by rules or laws of *proximity*, *similarity*, *continuity*, and *common fate*.

Let's try a mini-experiment. Without reading further, describe part A of Figure 3.15 ■. Did you say it consists of six lines or of three groups of two parallel lines? If you said three sets of lines, you were influenced by the **proximity**, or nearness, of some of the lines. There is no other reason for perceiving them in pairs or subgroups: All of the lines are parallel and equal in length.

Now describe part B of the figure. Did you perceive the figure as a 6 by 6 grid, or as three columns of x's and three columns of o's? According to the law of **similarity**, we perceive similar objects as belonging together. For this reason, you may have been more likely to describe part B in terms of columns than in terms of rows or a grid.

What about part C? Is it a circle with two lines stemming from it, or is it a (broken) line that goes through a circle? If you saw it as a single (broken) line, you were probably organizing your perceptions according to the rule of **continuity**. That is, we perceive a series of points or a broken line as having unity.

Proximity Nearness. The perceptual tendency to group together objects that are near one another.

Similarity The perceptual tendency to group together objects that are similar in appearance.

Continuity The tendency to perceive a series of points or lines as having unity.

 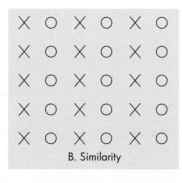 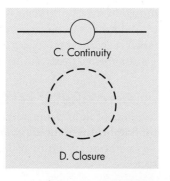

Figure 3.15 ■ Some Gestalt Laws of Perceptual Organization These drawings illustrate the Gestalt laws of proximity, similarity, continuity, and closure.

Putting It All Together Is it easier to complete a jigsaw puzzle when you have a picture of the completed cover on the box or when you only have the pieces? Why?

According to the law of **common fate**, elements seen moving together are perceived as belonging together. A group of people running in the same direction appears unified in purpose. Birds that flock together seem to be of a feather. (Did I get that right?) Part D of Figure 3.15 provides another example of the law of closure. The arcs tend to be perceived as a circle (or circle with gaps) rather than as just a series of arcs.

TOP-DOWN VERSUS BOTTOM-UP PROCESSING Imagine that you are trying to put together a thousand-piece jigsaw puzzle—a task I usually avoid. Now imagine that you are trying to accomplish it after someone has walked off with the box showing the picture formed by the completed puzzle.

When you have the box—when you know what the "big picture" or pattern looks like—cognitive psychologists refer to the task of assembling the pieces as **top-down processing**. The "top" of the visual system refers to the image of the pattern in the brain, and the top-down strategy for putting the puzzle together implies that you use the larger pattern to guide subordinate perceptual motor tasks such as hunting for particular pieces. Without knowledge of the pattern (without the box), the assembly process is referred to as **bottom-up processing**. You begin with bits and pieces of information and become aware of the pattern formed only after you have worked at it for a while (K. D. Wilson & Farah, 2003).

Top-down and bottom-up processing can be applied to many cognitive matters, even politics. If you consider yourself a liberal or a conservative, you can "fill in" your attitude toward many specific issues by applying the liberal or conservative position. That is top-down processing. But many people do not label themselves liberal or conservative. They look at issues and form positions on an issue-by-issue basis. Eventually, they may discover an overall pattern that places them more or less in the liberal or conservative camp. That is bottom-up processing.

Perception of Motion: Life on the Move

Moving objects—people, animals, cars, or boulders plummeting down a hillside—are vital sources of sensory information. Moving objects even capture the attention of newborn infants. **Question 13: How do we perceive movement?** To understand how we perceive movement, recall what it is like to be on a train that has begun to pull out of the station while the train on the adjacent track remains stationary. If your own train does not lurch as it accelerates, you might think at first that the other train is moving. Or you might not be certain whether your train is moving forward or the other train is moving backward.

The visual perception of movement is based on change of position relative to other objects. To early scientists, whose only tool for visual observation was the naked eye, it seemed logical that the Sun circled the Earth. You have to be able to imagine the movement of the Earth around the Sun as seen from a theoretical point in outer space; you cannot observe it directly.

How, then, do you determine which train is moving when your train is pulling out of the station (or the other train is pulling in)? One way is to look for objects that you know are stable, such as platform columns, houses, signs, or trees. If you are stationary in relation to them, your train is not moving. Observing people walking on the station platform may not provide the answer, however, because they are also changing their position relative to stationary objects. You might also try to sense the motion of the train in your body. You know from experience how to do these things quite well, although it may be difficult to phrase explanations for them.

We have been considering the perception of real movement. Psychologists have also studied several types of apparent movement, or **illusions** of movement. These include the *autokinetic effect, stroboscopic motion,* and the *phi phenomenon*.

THE AUTOKINETIC EFFECT If you were to sit quietly in a dark room and stare at a point of light projected onto the far wall, after a while it might appear that the light had begun to move, even if it actually remained quite still. The tendency to perceive a stationary point of light as moving in a dark room is called the **autokinetic effect**.

Common fate The tendency to perceive elements that move together as belonging together.

Top-down processing The use of contextual information or knowledge of a pattern to organize parts of the pattern.

Bottom-up processing The organization of the parts of a pattern to recognize, or form an image of, the pattern they compose.

Illusions Sensations that give rise to misperceptions.

Autokinetic effect The tendency to perceive a stationary point of light in a dark room as moving.

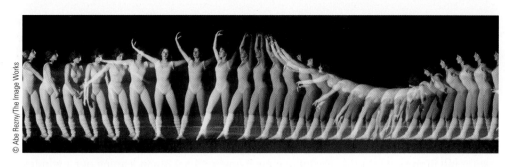

Stroboscopic Motion In a motion picture, viewing a series of stationary images at the rate of about 16 to 22 frames per second provides an illusion of movement termed stroboscopic motion. The actual movement that is occurring is the rapid switching of stationary images.

STROBOSCOPIC MOTION In **stroboscopic motion**, the illusion of movement is provided by the presentation of a rapid progression of images of stationary objects, as in so-called motion pictures. Motion pictures are not really made up of images that move. Rather, the audience is shown 16 to 22 pictures, or frames, per second. Each frame differs slightly from the preceding one. Showing the frames in rapid succession provides the illusion of movement. At the rate of at least 16 frames per second, the "motion" in a film seems smooth and natural. With fewer than 16 or so frames per second, the movement looks jumpy and unnatural. That is why slow motion is achieved by filming perhaps 100 or more frames per second. When they are played back at about 22 frames per second, the movement seems slowed down yet still smooth and natural.

THE PHI PHENOMENON Have you seen news headlines spelled out in lights that rapidly wrap around a building? Have you seen an electronic scoreboard in a baseball or football stadium? When the home team scores, some scoreboards suggest explosions of fireworks. What actually happens is that a row of lights is switched on and then off. As the first row is switched off, a second row is switched on, and so on for dozens, perhaps hundreds, of rows. When the switching occurs rapidly, the **phi phenomenon** occurs: the on–off process is perceived as movement.

Depth Perception: How Far Is Far?

Think of the problems you might have if you could not judge depth or distance. You might bump into other people, believing them to be farther away. An outfielder might not be able to judge whether to run toward the infield or the fence to catch a fly ball. You might give your front bumper a workout in stop-and-go traffic. **Question 14: How do we perceive depth?** It happens that *monocular* and *binocular cues* both help us perceive the depth of objects—that is, their distance from us.

MONOCULAR CUES Now that you have considered how difficult it would be to navigate through life without depth perception, ponder the problems of the artist who attempts to portray three-dimensional objects on a two-dimensional surface. Artists use a type of **monocular cue**—pictorial cues—to create an illusion of depth. These are cues that can be perceived by one eye (*mono-* means "one"). They include perspective, relative size, clearness, interposition, shadows, and texture gradient, and they cause certain objects to appear more distant from the viewer than others.

Distant objects stimulate smaller areas on the retina than nearby ones. The amount of sensory input from them is smaller, even though they may be the same size. The distances between far-off objects also appear smaller than equivalent distances between nearby objects. For this reason, the phenomenon known as **perspective** occurs. That is, we tend to perceive parallel lines as coming closer together, or converging, as they recede from us. However, as we will see when we discuss *size constancy,* experience teaches us that distant objects that look small are larger when they are close. In this way, their relative size also becomes a cue to their distance.

The engraving in Figure 3.16 ■ represents an impossible scene in which the artist uses principles of perspective to fool the viewer. Artists normally use *relative size*—the

Stroboscopic motion A visual illusion in which the perception of motion is generated by a series of stationary images that are presented in rapid succession.

Phi phenomenon The perception of movement as a result of sequential presentation of visual stimuli.

Monocular cues Stimuli suggestive of depth that can be perceived with only one eye.

Perspective A monocular cue for depth based on the convergence (coming together) of parallel lines as they recede into the distance.

FRONTISPIECE TO KERBY.

Figure 3.16 ■ What Is Wrong with This Picture? How does English artist William Hogarth use monocular cues for depth perception to deceive the viewer?

Figure 3.17 ■ The Effects of Interposition The four circles are all the same size. Which circles seem closer? The complete circles or the circles with chunks bitten out of them?

Figure 3.18 ■ Shadowing as a Cue for Depth Shadowing makes the circle on the right look three-dimensional.

Interposition A monocular cue for depth based on the fact that a nearby object obscures a more distant object behind it.

Shadowing A monocular cue for depth based on the fact that opaque objects block light and produce shadows.

Texture gradient A monocular cue for depth based on the perception that closer objects appear to have rougher (more detailed) surfaces.

Motion parallax A monocular cue for depth based on the perception that nearby objects appear to move more rapidly in relation to our own motion.

Binocular cues Stimuli suggestive of depth that involve simultaneous perception by both eyes.

Retinal disparity A binocular cue for depth based on the difference in the image cast by an object on the retinas of the eyes as the object moves closer or farther away.

Convergence A binocular cue for depth based on the inward movement of the eyes as they attempt to focus on an object that is drawing nearer.

Size constancy The tendency to perceive an object as being the same size even as the size of its retinal image changes according to the object's distance.

fact that distant objects look smaller than nearby objects of the same size—to suggest depth in their works. The paradoxes in *Frontispiece to Kerby* are made possible because more distant objects are *not* necessarily depicted as smaller than nearby objects. Thus, what at first seems to be background suddenly becomes foreground, and vice versa.

The *clearness* of an object also suggests its distance. Experience teaches us that we sense more details of nearby objects. For this reason, artists can suggest that objects are closer to the viewer by depicting them in greater detail. Note that the "distant" hill in the Hogarth engraving (refer to Figure 3.16 again) is given less detail than the nearby plants at the bottom of the picture. Our perceptions are mocked when a man "on" the distant hill in the background is shown conversing with a woman leaning out a window in the middle ground.

We also learn that nearby objects can block our view of more distant objects. Overlapping, or **interposition**, is the placing of one object in front of another. Experience teaches us that partly covered objects are farther away than the objects that obscure them (see Figure 3.17 ■). In the Hogarth engraving, which looks closer? The row of trees in the background or the moon sign hanging from the building (or is it buildings?) to the right? How does the artist use interposition to confuse the viewer?

Additional information about depth is provided by **shadowing** and is based on the fact that opaque objects block light and produce shadows. Shadows and highlights give us information about an object's three-dimensional shape and its relationship to the source of light. For example, the left part of Figure 3.18 ■ is perceived as a two-dimensional circle, but the right part tends to be perceived as a three-dimensional sphere because of the highlight on its surface and the shadow underneath. In the "sphere," the highlighted central area is perceived as closest to us, with the surface receding to the edges.

Another monocular cue is **texture gradient**. (A gradient is a progressive change.) Closer objects are perceived as having rougher textures. In the Hogarth engraving (refer again to Figure 3.16), the building just behind the large fisherman's head has a rougher texture and therefore seems to be closer than the building with the window from which the woman is leaning. And how can the moon sign be hanging from both buildings?

Motion cues also indicate depth. If you have ever driven in the country, you have probably noticed that distant objects such as mountains and stars appear to move along with you. Objects at an intermediate distance seem to be stationary, but nearby objects such as roadside markers, rocks, and trees seem to go by quite rapidly. The tendency of objects to seem to move backward or forward as a function of their distance is known as **motion parallax**. We learn that objects that seem to move with us are farther away.

BINOCULAR CUES Binocular cues involve both eyes and help us perceive depth. Two binocular cues are *retinal disparity* and *convergence*.

Try an experiment. Hold your right index finger at arm's length. Now hold your left index finger about a foot closer but in a direct line. If you keep your eyes relaxed as you do so, you will see first one finger, then the other. An image of each finger will be projected onto the retina of each eye, and each image will be slightly different because the finger will be seen from different angles. The difference between the projected images is referred to as **retinal disparity**. In the case of the closer finger, the "two fingers" look farther apart. Closer objects have greater retinal disparity.

If we try to maintain a single image of the closer finger, our eyes must turn inward, or converge on it, making us cross-eyed. **Convergence** causes feelings of tension in the eye muscles. The binocular cues of retinal disparity and convergence are strongest when objects are close.

Why are psychologists concerned with depth perception? On a fundamental level, sources of food and danger lie beyond, near or far, making depth perception important for obtaining the one and avoiding the latter. Evolutionary psychologists would note that organisms that have sophisticated systems for perceiving distance are more likely to survive into adulthood and reproduce, thus making these systems a stable element in their species. In the following section, you will see that our methods of perception also help us keep the world a stable place, even though the shapes and colors and other properties of objects are perpetually shifting.

Clearness leads us to perceive the trees and signs and people with greater detail as being closer to us.

Relative size leads us to perceive the bicycles and people that are larger as being closer to us.

Perspective leads us to perceive the parallel lines on the sidewalk as coming closer together, or converging, as they recede from us.

Texture gradient leads us to perceive the tree trunks and handlebars with rougher (more detailed) textures as being closer.

Shadowing leads us to perceive the shadows and highlights in the seats of the bicycles as giving them depth (and curved surfaces) although the picture we are viewing is two-dimensional.

Overlapping leads us to perceive the bicycles that block our view of parts of other bicycles as being closer to us.

© Richard Douglas Rose

Perceptual Constancies: Keeping the World a Stable Place

The world is a constantly shifting display of visual sensations. Think how confusing it would be if you believed that a door was a trapezoid and not a rectangle because it is ajar. Or what if we perceived a doorway to be a different doorway when seen from 6 feet away compared to 4 feet? As we neared it, we might think it was larger than the door we were seeking and become lost. Or consider the problems of the pet owner who recognizes his dog from the side but not from above because its shape is different when seen from above. Fortunately, these problems tend not to occur—at least with familiar objects—because perceptual constancies enable us to recognize objects even when their apparent shape or size differs. **Question 15: What are perceptual constancies?** For example, why do we perceive a door to be a rectangle even when it is partly open?

SIZE CONSTANCY One perceptual constancy is size constancy. We may say that people "look like ants" when viewed from the top of a tall building, but because of size constancy, we know they remain full-sized people even if the details of their forms are lost in the distance. Thus we perceive people to be the same size even when viewed from different distances. Likewise, the image

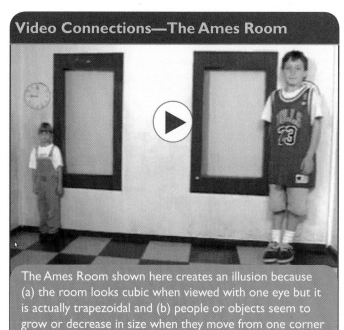

Video Connections—The Ames Room

The Ames Room shown here creates an illusion because (a) the room looks cubic when viewed with one eye but it is actually trapezoidal and (b) people or objects seem to grow or decrease in size when they move from one corner to the other. To understand how the Ames Room works, go to your Psychology CourseMate at **www.cengagebrain.com** to watch this video.

of a dog seen from 20 feet away occupies about the same amount of space on your retina as an inch-long insect crawling on your hand. Yet you do not perceive the dog to be as small as the insect. Through your visual experiences, you have acquired size constancy—that is, the tendency to perceive an object as the same size even though the size of its image on your retina varies as a function of its distance. Experience teaches us about perspective—that the same object seen at a distance appears to be smaller than when it is nearby (see Figure 3.19 ■).

A cross-cultural case study suggests that a person from another culture might indeed perceive people and cars to be insects from the vantage point of an airplane. It also emphasizes the role of experience in the development of size constancy. Anthropologist Colin Turnbull (1961) found that an African Pygmy, Kenge, thought that buffalo perceived across an open field were some form of insect. Turnbull had to drive Kenge down to where the animals were grazing to convince him that they were not insects. During the drive, as the buffalo gradually grew in size, Kenge muttered to himself and moved closer to Turnbull in fear. Even after Kenge saw that these animals were, indeed, familiar buffalo, he still wondered how they could grow large so quickly. Kenge, you see, lived in a thick forest and normally did not view large animals from great distances. For this reason, he had not developed size constancy for distant objects. However, Kenge had no difficulty displaying size constancy with objects placed at various distances in his home.

Figure 3.19 ■ Size Constancy Although this woman's hand looks as though it is larger than her head, we recognize that this is an illusion created by the fact that her hand is closer to us than her head.

COLOR CONSTANCY Color constancy is the tendency to perceive objects as retaining their color even though lighting conditions may alter their appearance. Your bright yellow car may edge toward gray as the hours wend their way through twilight. But when you finally locate the car in the parking lot, you may still think of it as yellow. You expect to find a yellow car and still judge it to be "yellower" than the (twilight-faded) red and green cars on either side of it.

BRIGHTNESS CONSTANCY Brightness constancy is similar to color constancy. Consider Figure 3.20 ■. The orange squares within the blue squares are equally bright, yet the one within the dark blue square is perceived as brighter. Why? Again, consider the role of experience. If it were nighttime, we would expect orange to fade to gray. The fact that the orange within the dark square stimulates the eye with equal intensity suggests that it must be much brighter than the orange within the lighter square.

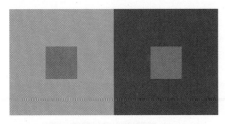

Figure 3.20 Brightness Constancy The orange squares within the blue squares are the same hue, yet the orange within the dark blue square is perceived as brighter. Why?

SHAPE CONSTANCY Shape constancy is the tendency to perceive objects as maintaining their shape, even if we look at them from different angles so that the shape of their image on the retina changes dramatically. You perceive the top of a coffee cup or a glass to be a circle even though it is a circle only when seen from above. When seen from an angle, it is an ellipse. When the cup or glass is seen on edge, its retinal image is the same as that of a straight line. So why do you still describe the rim of the cup or glass as a circle? Perhaps for two reasons: First, experience has taught you that the cup will look circular when seen from above. Second, you may have labeled the cup as circular or round. Experience and labels help make the world a stable place. Can you imagine the chaos that would prevail if we described objects as they appear, considering they stimulate our sensory organs with each changing moment?

Let's return to the door that "changes shape" when it is ajar. The door is a rectangle only when viewed straight on (Figure 3.21 ■). When we move to the side or open it, the left or right edge comes closer and appears larger, changing the retinal image to a trapezoid. Yet we continue to think of doors as rectangles.

Figure 3.21 ■ Shape Constancy When closed, the door is a rectangle. When open, the retinal image is trapezoidal. But because of shape constancy, we still perceive it as rectangular.

Visual Illusions: Is Seeing Believing?

The principles of perceptual organization make it possible for our eyes to play tricks on us. Psychologists, like magicians, enjoy pulling a rabbit out of a hat now and then. Let

© Enamul Hoque/Getty Images

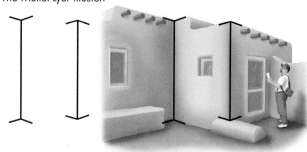

The Hering-Helmholtz Illusion

The Müller-Lyer Illusion

A.

B.

Figure 3.22 ■ The Hering–Helmholtz and Müller–Lyer Illusions In the Hering–Helmholtz illusion, are the horizontal lines straight or curved? In the Müller–Lyer illusion, are the vertical lines equal in length?

me demonstrate how the perceptual constancies trick the eye through *visual illusions.*

The *Hering–Helmholtz* and *Müller–Lyer illusions* (see Figure 3.22 ■, parts A and B) are named after the people who devised them. In the Hering–Helmholtz illusion, the horizontal lines are straight and parallel. However, the radiating lines cause them to appear to be bent outward near the center. The two lines in the Müller–Lyer illusion are the same length, but the line on the right, with its reversed arrowheads, looks longer.

Let's try to explain these illusions. Because of our experience and lifelong use of perceptual cues, we tend to perceive the Hering–Helmholtz drawing as three-dimensional. Because of our tendency to perceive bits of sensory information as figures against grounds, we perceive the blue area in the center as a circle in front of a series of radiating lines, all of which lie in front of a blue ground. Next, because of our experience with perspective, we perceive the radiating lines as parallel. We perceive the two horizontal lines as intersecting the "receding" lines, and we know that they would have to appear bent out at the center if they were to be equidistant at all points from the center of the circle.

Experience probably compels us to perceive the vertical lines in the Müller–Lyer illusion as the corners of a building (again, Figure 3.22, part B). We interpret the length of the lines based on our experience with corners of buildings.

Figure 3.23 ■ represents the *Ponzo illusion*. In this illusion, the two monsters are the same length. However, do you perceive the top monster as bigger? The rule of size constancy may give us some insight into this illusion as well. Perhaps the converging lines again strike us as being lines receding into the distance. The rule of size constancy tells us that if two objects appear to be the same size and one is farther away, the object that looks farther away must be larger. So we perceive the top monster as larger.

Figure 3.23 ■ A Monstrous Illusion The two monsters in this drawing are exactly the same height and width. Yet the top one appears to be much larger. Can you use the principle of size constancy to explain why?

Ponzo illusion illustration from Mind Sights by Roger N. Shepard. © 1990 by Roger N. Shepard. Reprinted by permission of Henry Holt and Company, LLC

LearningConnections ● VISUAL PERCEPTION: HOW PERCEPTIVE?

ACTIVE REVIEW (10) Perceptual organization concerns the grouping of bits of sensory stimulation into a meaningful _____. (11) Gestalt rules of perceptual organization refer to _____–ground relationships, proximity, similarity, continuity, common fate, and closure. (12) We perceive movement by sensing motion across the _____ of the eye and change of position in relation to other objects. (13) _____ motion, used in films, is an illusion of motion caused by the rapid presentation of a series of still images.

REFLECT AND RELATE Have you had the experience of being in a train and not knowing whether your train or the one on the next track was moving? How do you explain your confusion? How did you figure out which one was really moving?

CRITICAL THINKING How do creators of visual illusions use laws of perception to trick the eye? How do research findings concerning visual perception demonstrate the difference between sensation and perception?

 Go to Psychology CourseMate at **www.cengagebrain.com** for an interactive version of these questions.

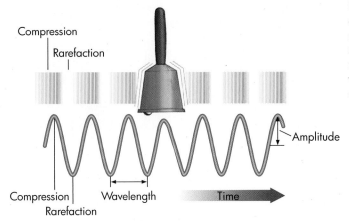

Figure 3.24 ■ Creation of Sound Waves The ringing of a bell compresses and expands (rarefies) air molecules, sending forth vibrations called sound waves that stimulate the sense of hearing.

"The empty vessel makes the loudest sound."

WILLIAM SHAKESPEARE

"Music is the movement of sound to reach the soul for the education of its virtue."

PLATO

"The temple bell stops but I still hear the sound coming out of the flowers."

BASHO

Color constancy The tendency to perceive an object as being the same color even though lighting conditions change its appearance.

Brightness constancy The tendency to perceive an object as being just as bright even though lighting conditions change its intensity.

HEARING: MAKING SENSE OF SOUND

Consider the advertising slogan for the classic science fiction film *Alien:* "In space, no one can hear you scream." It's true. Space is an almost perfect vacuum. Hearing requires a medium through which sound can travel, such as air or water. **Question 16: What is sound?**

Sound, or **auditory** stimulation, travels through the air like waves. If you could see sound waves, they would look something like the ripples in a pond when you toss in a pebble. You hear the splash even if you can't see it. The sound of the splash is caused by changes in air pressure. The air is alternately compressed and expanded like the movements of an accordion. If you were listening underwater, you would also hear the splash because of changes in the pressure of the water. In either case, the changes in pressure are vibrations that approach your ears in waves. These vibrations—sound waves—can also be created by a ringing bell (see Figure 3.24 ■), your vocal cords, guitar strings, or the slam of a book thrown down on a desk. A single cycle of compression and expansion is one wave of sound. Sound waves can occur many (many!) times in 1 second. The human ear is sensitive to sound waves with frequencies of from 20 to 20,000 cycles per second.

Pitch and Loudness

Pitch and loudness are two psychological dimensions of sound. The pitch of a sound is determined by its frequency, or the number of cycles per second as expressed in the unit **hertz (Hz)**. One cycle per second is 1 Hz. The greater the number of cycles per second (Hz), the higher the pitch of the sound.

The pitch of women's voices is usually higher than that of men's voices because women's vocal cords are usually shorter and therefore vibrate at a greater frequency. Also, the strings of a violin are shorter than those of a viola or bass viol. Pitch detectors in the brain allow us to tell differences in pitch.

The loudness of a sound roughly corresponds to the height, or amplitude, of sound waves. Figure 3.25 ■ shows records of sound waves that vary in frequency and amplitude. Frequency and amplitude are independent. That is, both high- and low-pitched sounds can be either high or low in loudness. The loudness of a sound is expressed in **decibels (dB)**. Zero dB is equivalent to the threshold of hearing—the lowest sound that the typical person can hear. How loud is that? It's about as loud as the ticking of a watch 20 feet away in a very quiet room.

The decibel equivalents of many familiar sounds are shown in Figure 3.26 ■. Twenty-five dB is equivalent in loudness to a whisper at 5 feet. Thirty dB is roughly the limit of loudness at which your librarian would like to keep your college library. You may suffer hearing damage if you are exposed to sounds of 85 to 90 dB for very long periods. This is why (careful) carpenters wear ear covers while they are hammering away, and why people risk permanent damage to their hearing when they attend loud rock concerts, which reach levels above 140 dB. (Bring earplugs.)

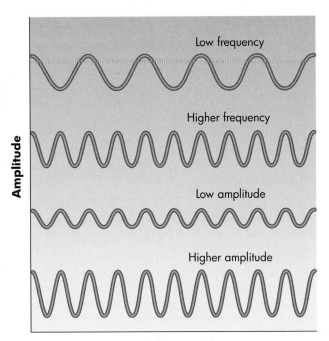

Figure 3.25 ■ Sound Waves of Various Frequencies and Amplitudes Which sounds have the highest pitch? Which are loudest?

Now let's turn our attention to the human ear—the marvelous instrument that senses all these different "vibes."

The Ear: The Better to Hear You With

The human ear is good for lots of things—including catching dust, combing your hair around, and hanging jewelry from. It is also well suited to sensing sounds. **Question 17: How does the ear work?** The ear is shaped and structured to capture sound waves, vibrate in sympathy with them, and transmit them to centers in the brain. In this way, you not only hear something, but you can also figure out what it is. The ear has three parts: the outer ear, middle ear, and inner ear (see Figure 3.27 ■).

The outer ear is shaped to funnel sound waves to the **eardrum**, a thin membrane that vibrates in response to sound waves and thereby transmits them to the middle and inner ears. The middle ear contains the eardrum and three small bones—the *hammer*, the *anvil*, and the *stirrup*—which also transmit sound by vibrating. These bones were given their names (actually the Latin *malleus*, *incus*, and *stapes* [pronounced STAY-peas], which translate as hammer, anvil, and stirrup) because of their shapes. The middle ear functions as an amplifier, increasing the pressure of the air entering the ear.

The stirrup is attached to another vibrating membrane, the *oval window*. This oval window works in conjunction with the round window, which balances the pressure in the inner ear. The round window pushes outward when the oval window pushes in and is pulled inward when the oval window vibrates outward.

The oval window transmits vibrations into the inner ear, the bony snail-shell-shaped tube called the **cochlea** (from the Greek word for "snail"). The cochlea contains two longitudinal membranes that divide it into three fluid-filled chambers. One of the membranes that lies coiled within the cochlea is called the **basilar membrane**. Vibrations in the fluids within the chambers of the inner ear press against the basilar membrane.

The **organ of Corti**, sometimes referred to as the "command post" of hearing, is attached to the basilar membrane. Some 16,000 receptor cells—called *hair cells* because they project like hair from the organ of Corti—are found in each ear (Hwang et al., 2010). Hair cells "dance" in response to the vibrations of the basilar membrane. Their up-and-down movements generate neural impulses, which are transmitted to the brain via the **auditory nerve**. Auditory input is then projected onto the hearing areas of the temporal lobes of the cerebral cortex.

Locating Sounds: Up, Down, and Around

How do you balance the loudness of a stereo set? You sit between the speakers and adjust the volume until the sound seems to be equally loud in each ear. If the sound to the right is louder, the musical instruments are perceived as being to the right rather than in front. **Question 18: How do we locate sounds?** There is a resemblance between balancing a stereo set and locating sounds. A sound that is louder in the right ear is perceived as coming from the right. A sound coming from the right also reaches the right ear first. Both loudness and the sequence in which the sounds reach the ears provide directional cues.

But it may not be easy to locate a sound coming from directly in front or in back of you or overhead. Such sounds are equally distant from each ear and equally loud. So what do we do? Simple—usually, we turn our head slightly to determine in which ear the sound increases. If you turn your head a few degrees to the right and the loudness increases in your left ear, the sound must be coming from in front of you. Of course, we

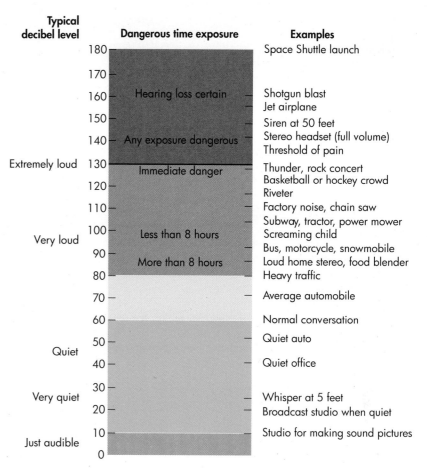

Typical decibel level	Dangerous time exposure	Examples
180		Space Shuttle launch
170	Hearing loss certain	
160		Shotgun blast
150		Jet airplane
		Siren at 50 feet
140	Any exposure dangerous	Stereo headset (full volume)
Extremely loud 130		Threshold of pain
	Immediate danger	Thunder, rock concert
120		Basketball or hockey crowd
110		Riveter
		Factory noise, chain saw
Very loud 100	Less than 8 hours	Subway, tractor, power mower
		Screaming child
90		Bus, motorcycle, snowmobile
	More than 8 hours	Loud home stereo, food blender
80		Heavy traffic
70		Average automobile
60		Normal conversation
Quiet 50		Quiet auto
40		Quiet office
30		
Very quiet 20		Whisper at 5 feet
		Broadcast studio when quiet
10		Studio for making sound pictures
Just audible 0		

Figure 3.26 ■ Decibel Ratings of Familiar Sounds Zero dB is the threshold of hearing. You may suffer hearing loss if you incur prolonged exposure to sounds of 85 to 90 dB.

Shape constancy The tendency to perceive an object as being as the same shape although the retinal image varies in shape as it rotates.

Auditory Having to do with hearing.

Hertz (Hz) A unit expressing the frequency of sound waves. One hertz equals one cycle per second.

Decibel (dB) A unit expressing the loudness of a sound.

Eardrum A thin membrane that vibrates in response to sound waves, transmitting the waves to the middle and inner ears.

Cochlea The inner ear; the bony tube that contains the basilar membrane and the organ of Corti.

A CLOSER LOOK — iPods on Campus: The Sounds of Oblivion?

iPods are extremely popular on campus. Two of three university students have them, and most others have another personal listening device (Danhauer, 2009). Because iPods and similar devices store so much music and are capable of producing outputs at 130 dB and higher, listeners may be at risk for hearing loss. To combat hearing loss, Fligor and Cox (2004) recommend the "60–60 rule"—that people should listen at no more than 60% of full volume for no more than 60 minutes per day. Other health professionals would allow listening levels up to 70% of full volume for 4 to 5 hours per day. However, most standard earphones do not block out ambient noise, so many listeners increase the volume when they encounter background noise (78%) or are exercising (61%). But there are other dangers. One is so-called iPod oblivion, in which listeners pay less attention to their environments when they are listening. Two pedestrian deaths in New York within 4 months were attributed to iPod oblivion (Kuntzman, 2007).

Jeffrey Danhauer (2009) undertook a survey with 607 students drawn from universities across the United States to learn about the use of iPods. The great majority (86%) were 18–21 years old, and 60% were female.

Two of three respondents reported using an iPod, and the largest number of students said they did so 1–2 hours per day. Their reasons for using an iPod included listening to music (95%), avoiding bothering other people with their music (77%), relaxing (75%), fighting boredom (74%), isolating themselves from the people around them (55%), and helping them concentrate on things such as schoolwork (46%).

The great majority (87%) admitted that using an iPod at high volume could cause hearing loss, yet 52% said they had no hearing problems (only 6% thought they had hearing loss due to iPod use). Five of six students said they did not know that Apple has a software download that enables listeners to protect their hearing by setting their maximum loudness. Nearly two respondents in five (38%) endorsed the 60–60 rule (another 42% might do so). If they had to choose, most students would lower the volume rather than curtail listening time.

iPod: Big MP3 Player on Campus
Two of three university students use iPods. Do they cause hearing loss? What can students due to lessen the risk of damage to hearing?

---

also use vision and general knowledge in locating the source of sounds. If you hear the roar of jet engines, most of the time you can bet that the airplane is overhead.

Perception of Loudness and Pitch

Sounds are heard because they cause vibration in parts of the ear, and information about these vibrations is transmitted to the brain. **Question 19: How do we perceive loudness and pitch?** The loudness and pitch of sounds appear to be related to the number of receptor neurons on the organ of Corti that fire and how often they fire. Psychologists generally agree that sounds are perceived as louder when more of these sensory neurons fire.

As discussed earlier, it takes two processes to explain perception of color: *trichromatic theory* and *opponent-process theory*. For pitch perception—that is, perception of sound waves with frequencies that vary from 20 to 20,000 cycles per second—it takes three processes: *place theory, frequency theory,* and the *volley principle*.

Hermann von Helmholtz helped develop the place theory of pitch discrimination as well as the Young–Helmholtz (trichromatic) theory of color vision. **Place theory** holds that the pitch of a sound is sensed according to the place along the basilar membrane that vibrates in response to it. In classic research with guinea pigs and cadavers that led to the award of a Nobel Prize, Georg von Békésy (1957) found evidence for place theory. He determined that receptors at different sites along the membrane fire in response to tones of differing frequencies. Receptor neurons appear to be lined up along the basilar membrane like piano keys. The higher the pitch of a sound, the closer the responsive neurons lie to the oval window (Erixon et al., 2009). However, place theory appears to apply only to pitches that are at least as high as 4000 Hz. But what about lower pitches? That's where frequency theory comes in.

Frequency theory notes that for us to perceive these lower pitches, we need the stimulation of neural impulses that match the frequency of the sound waves. That is, in response to low pitches—pitches of about 20 to 1,000 cycles per second—hair cells

Basilar membrane A membrane that lies coiled within the cochlea.

Organ of Corti The receptor for hearing that lies on the basilar membrane in the cochlea.

Auditory nerve The axon bundle that transmits neural impulses from the organ of Corti to the brain.

Place theory The theory that the pitch of a sound is determined by the section of the basilar membrane that vibrates in response to the sound.

Frequency theory The theory that the pitch of a sound is reflected in the frequency of the neural impulses that are generated in response to the sound.

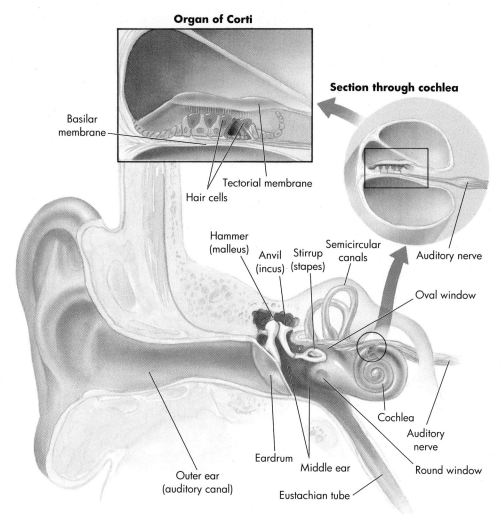

Organ of Corti

Section through cochlea

Basilar membrane

Tectorial membrane

Hair cells

Hammer (malleus)

Anvil (incus)

Stirrup (stapes)

Semicircular canals

Auditory nerve

Oval window

Cochlea

Auditory nerve

Round window

Eardrum

Middle ear

Outer ear (auditory canal)

Eustachian tube

Figure 3.27 ■ The Human Ear The outer ear funnels sound to the eardrum. Inside the eardrum, vibrations of the hammer, anvil, and stirrup transmit sound to the inner ear. Vibrations in the cochlea transmit the sound to the auditory nerve by way of the basilar membrane and the organ of Corti.

on the basilar membrane fire at the same frequencies as the sound waves. However, neurons cannot fire more than 1,000 times per second. Therefore, frequency theory can account only for perception of pitches between 20 and 1,000 cycles per second. In actuality, frequency theory appears to account only for pitch perception between 20 and a few hundred cycles per second.

The *volley principle* accounts for pitch discrimination between a few hundred and 4,000 cycles per second (Ebeling, 2008; Machery & Carlyon, 2010). In response to sound waves of these frequencies, groups of neurons take turns firing in the way that one row of soldiers used to fire rifles while another row knelt to reload. Alternating firing—that is, volleying—appears to transmit sensory information about pitches in the intermediate range.

Deafness: Navigating a World of Silence

More than 1 in 10 Americans has a hearing impairment, and 1 in 100 cannot hear at all (Erixon et al., 2009). Deaf people are deprived of a key source of information about the world around them. In recent years, however, society has made greater efforts to bring them into the mainstream of sensory experience. People are usually on hand to convert political and other speeches into hand signs (such as those of American Sign Language) for hearing-impaired members of the audience. Many TV shows are closed captioned so they can be understood by people with hearing problems. Also, as mentioned earlier, advocates for deaf people have emphasized the positive aspects of dwelling in a world of silence. **Question 20: What kinds of deafness are there?** What can we do about them?

The two major types of deafness are *conductive deafness* and *sensorineural deafness*. **Conductive deafness** stems from damage to the structures of the middle ear—either to the eardrum or to the three bones that conduct (and amplify) sound waves from the outer ear to the inner ear (Daud et al., 2010; Erixon et al., 2009). This is the hearing impairment often found among older people. People with conductive deafness often

Conductive deafness The forms of deafness in which there is loss of conduction of sound through the middle ear.

Sensorineural deafness The forms of deafness that result from damage to hair cells or the auditory nerve.

profit from hearing aids, which provide the amplification that the middle ear does not. Surgical treatment can be successful as well.

Sensorineural deafness usually stems from damage to the structures of the inner ear, most often the loss of hair cells, which normally do not regenerate. Sensorineural deafness can also stem from damage to the auditory nerve caused by factors such as disease or acoustic trauma (prolonged exposure to very loud sounds). In sensorineural deafness, people tend to be more sensitive to some pitches than to others. In the hearing impairment called Hunter's notch, the loss is limited to particular frequencies—in this case, the frequencies of the sound waves generated by a gun firing. Prolonged exposure to 85 dB can cause hearing loss. As noted earlier, people who attend rock concerts, where sounds may reach 140 dB, risk permanently damaging their ears, as do workers who run pneumatic drills or drive noisy vehicles. The ringing sensation that often follows exposure to loud sounds probably means that hair cells in the inner ear have been damaged. If you find yourself suddenly exposed to loud sounds, remember that your fingertips serve as good emergency ear protectors.

Cochlear implants, or *artificial ears*, contain microphones that sense sounds and electronic equipment that transmits sounds past damaged hair cells to stimulate the auditory nerve directly. Such implants have helped many people with sensorineural deafness (Tait et al., 2010). However, they cannot assume the functions of damaged auditory nerves.

LearningConnections • HEARING: MAKING SENSE OF SOUND

ACTIVE REVIEW (14) Sound waves alternatively _____ and expand molecules of a medium like air. (15) The human ear can hear sounds varying in frequency from 20 to _____ cycles per second (Hz). (16) The frequency of sound waves determines their _____. (17) The "command post" of hearing—called the _____—is attached to the basilar membrane.

REFLECT AND RELATE Do you know anyone with hearing problems? What is the cause? How does the person cope with them?

CRITICAL THINKING Are you familiar with the violin, viola, cello, and bass fiddle? How do their sounds differ? How can you use the information in this section to explain the differences?

Go to Psychology CourseMate at **www.cengagebrain.com** for an interactive version of these questions.

 THE CHEMICAL SENSES: SMELL AND TASTE

Smell and taste are the chemical senses. In the cases of vision and hearing, physical energy strikes our sensory receptors. With smell and taste, we sample molecules of the substances being sensed.

Smell: Sampling Molecules in the Air

"I judge people on how they smell, not how they look"

JENNIFER LOPEZ

"Smell is a potent wizard that transports you across thousands of miles and all the years you have lived."

HELEN KELLER

People are underprivileged when it comes to the sense of smell. Dogs, for instance, devote about seven times as much of the cerebral cortex as we do to the sense of smell. Male dogs sniff to determine where the boundaries of other dogs' territories leave off and whether female dogs are sexually receptive. Dogs have been selectively bred to enhance their sense of smell. Some now earn a living by sniffing out explosive devices or illegal drugs in suitcases.

Smell also has an important role in human behavior. It makes a crucial contribution to the **flavor** of foods, for example. If you did not have a sense of smell, an onion and an apple might taste the same to you! People's sense of smell may be deficient when we compare them to those of a dog, but we can detect the odor of 1-millionth of a milligram of vanilla in a liter of air.

Flavor A complex quality of food and other substances that is based on their odor, texture, and temperature as well as their taste.

Question 21: How does the sense of smell work? Smell is the sense that detects odors. An *odor* is a sample of the substance being sensed. Odors are detected by sites on receptor neurons in the *olfactory membrane* high in each nostril. Receptor neurons fire when a few molecules of the substance in gaseous form come into contact with them. Their firing transmits information about odors to the brain via the **olfactory nerve**. That is how the substance is smelled.

It is unclear how many basic kinds of odors there are. In any event, olfactory receptors may respond to more than one kind of odor. Mixtures of smell sensations also help produce the broad range of odors that we can perceive.

The sense of smell adapts rapidly to odors such that you lose awareness of them, even obnoxious ones. This might be fortunate if you are in a locker room or an outhouse. It might not be so fortunate if you are exposed to paint fumes or secondhand smoke because you may lose awareness of them while danger remains. Also, one odor can mask another, which is how air fresheners work.

Taste: Yes, You've Got Taste

Your cocker spaniel may jump at the chance to finish off your bowl of sherbet, but your Siamese cat may turn up her nose at the opportunity. Why? Dogs can perceive the taste quality of sweetness, as can pigs, but cats cannot. But when it comes to the sense of taste, the lowly catfish may well be the champ. Think of them as "swimming tongues." They can detect food through murky water and across long distances because their bodies are studded with nearly 150,000 taste buds (Rodrigues-Galdino et al., 2009). **Truth or Fiction Revisited:** So it is true that the bodies of catfish are covered with taste buds.

Taste is an extremely important sense because animals, including humans, use the sense of taste in acquiring nutrients and avoiding poisons. A food may look good from a distance. It may trigger fond memories. It may even smell good, but if it tastes bad, we are likely not to swallow it.

Question 22: How does the sense of taste work? As in the case of smell, taste involves sampling molecules of a substance. Taste is sensed through **taste cells**, which are receptor neurons located on **taste buds**. You have about 10,000 taste buds, most of which are located near the edges and back of your tongue. Taste buds tend to specialize a bit. Some, for example, are more responsive to sweetness, whereas others react to several tastes. Other taste receptors are found in the roof, sides, and back of the mouth and in the throat. Some taste buds are even found in the stomach, although we only perceive tastes in the mouth and top of the throat. Buds deep in the mouth are evolutionarily adaptive because they can warn of poisonous food as it is about to be swallowed (Brand, 2000).

Researchers generally agree on at least four primary taste qualities: sweet, sour, salty, and bitter. There also appears to be a fifth basic taste, which is termed *umami* in Japanese and means "meaty" or "savory" (Rolls, 2009). Others believe that there may be still more basic tastes (Schiffman, 2000; Yamamoto et al., 2009). Regardless of how many basic tastes there are, the flavor of a food involves its taste but is more complex than just taste. Although apples and onions are similar in taste, their flavors differ greatly. After all, you wouldn't chomp into a nice cold onion on a warm day, would you? The flavor of a food depends on its odor, texture, and temperature as well as on its taste. If it were not for odor, heated, tenderized shoe leather might pass for steak.

Just as some people see better than others, some people taste better than others—but their superiority may be limited to one or more basic tastes. Those of us with low sensitivity for the sweet taste may require twice the sugar to sweeten our food as others who are more sensitive to sweetness. Those of us who claim to enjoy very bitter foods may actually be taste blind to them. Sensitivities to different tastes apparently have a genetic component (Bartoshuk, 2000; Snyder & Bartoshuk, 2009).

By eating hot foods and scraping your tongue with forks and rough pieces of food, you regularly kill off many taste cells. But you need not be alarmed at this inadvertent oral aggression. Taste cells are the rabbits of the sense receptors. They reproduce rapidly enough to completely renew themselves about once a week.

Although older people often complain that their food has little or no "taste," they are more likely to experience a decline in the sense of smell. Because the flavor of a food represents both its tastes and its odors, or aromas, older people experience loss in the *flavor* of their food. Therefore, older people often spice their food heavily to enhance its flavor.

An Acute Sense of Smell Compared with humans, dogs devote more of their cerebral cortex to the sense of smell. Dogs have been trained to sniff out drugs, explosives, and specific people.

"A cucumber should be well sliced, and dressed with pepper and vinegar, and then thrown out."

DR. SAMUEL JOHNSON

"Americans can eat garbage, provided you sprinkle it liberally with ketchup, mustard, chili sauce, Tabasco sauce, cayenne pepper, or any other condiment which destroys the original flavor of the dish."

HENRY MILLER

Olfactory nerve The nerve that transmits information concerning odors from olfactory receptors to the brain.

Taste cells Receptor cells that are sensitive to taste.

Taste buds The sensory organs for taste. They contain taste cells and are located on the tongue.

A CLOSER LOOK   Advances in Science? The Case of the Aromatic T-Shirts

© Collage Photography/Veer

Readers may be familiar with perfume and cologne as aids to sexual attraction, but how about body odor? Body odor? Yes, body odor.

A group of researchers (Jacob et al., 2002) had a sample of men wear T-shirts for 2 days. Throughout that period, they kept their aromas "pure" by avoiding deodorants, spicy foods (no garlic, please), pets, and sex. They then placed the T-shirts in boxes where they could not be seen but could clearly be smelled. Women in the study proceeded to make a sacrifice for science that may have been much greater than the men's. They were asked to smell each of the boxes and choose the one they would be most willing to live with—that is, the one they would choose "if they had to smell it all the time."

Now, the women were kept blind (but not nasally blocked) as to the purpose of the study and also blind to the fact that they were smelling "ripe" T-shirts. By and large, the women rated the odors as mildly pleasant. The women had no difficulty telling the "boxes" apart and easily selected a favorite.

The T-shirt study apparently has something to do with evolution and genes. The shirts selected as favorites had been worn by men who were similar in genetic makeup to the women's fathers. The genes that seem to do the trick are called *M.H.C. genes*, and they produce proteins that identify cells within one's body as "self," not foreign. Cells that obtain the stamp of approval are not attacked by the body's immune system. But why the father? Here the researchers become speculative. Perhaps by finding odors that are suggestive of genetic similarity to the father, but not the mother, women are enticed to mate with men who are similar but not overly similar to themselves.

This is not to suggest that the major factor in mate selection is, well, nasal inspiration. Visual appearance, educational background, sharing of interests, and socioeconomic status may have more to do with it (Foster, 2008). But possibly, the nose also knows something about what it takes for a woman to live with a man year after year.

LearningConnections • THE CHEMICAL SENSES: SMELL AND TASTE

ACTIVE REVIEW (18) A(n)_____ is a sample of molecules of the substance being smelled. (19) Odors are detected by the _____ membrane in each nostril. (20) There are four primary taste qualities: sweet, sour, salty, and _____. (21) The receptor neurons for taste are called _____ cells, which are located in taste buds on the tongue.

REFLECT AND RELATE Has food ever lost its flavor when you had a cold or allergies? Why did it happen? Have you had the experience of growing accustomed to a noxious odor so that you have lost awareness of it?

CRITICAL THINKING Critical thinkers pay close attention to definitions. What is the difference between the *taste* of a food and its *flavor*?

 Go to Psychology CourseMate at **www.cengagebrain.com** for an interactive version of these questions.

"Once I knew only darkness and stillness. . . . My life was without past or future, . . . but a little word from the fingers of another fell into my hand that clutched at emptiness, and my heart leaped to the rapture of living."

HELEN KELLER

"At the touch of a lover, everyone becomes a poet."

PLATO

THE SKIN SENSES (YES, IT DOES)

The skin is much more than a protective coating for your body. As you may know from lying on the sand beneath a broiling sun, and perhaps from touching the person lying next to you, the skin also discriminates among many kinds of sensations. **Truth or Fiction Revisited:** It is true that the skin is a sensory organ as well as a protective coating for the body. **Question 23: What are the skin senses, and how do they work?** The skin senses include touch, pressure, warmth, cold, and pain. We have distinct sensory receptors for pressure, temperature, and pain, but some nerve endings may receive more than one type of sensory input. Here, let's focus on touch and pressure, temperature, and pain.

Touch and Pressure: Making Contact

Sensory receptors embedded in the skin fire when the surface of the skin is touched. There may be several kinds of receptors for touch—some that respond to constant pressure and others that respond to intermittent pressure, as in tapping the skin. *Active touching* means continually moving your hand along the surface of an object so that you continue to receive sensory input from the object. You may have noticed that if you are trying to get the feel of a fabric or the texture of a friend's hair, you must move your hand over it. Otherwise, the sensations quickly fade. If you pass your hand over the fabric or hair and then hold it still, again the sensations of touching will fade. Active touching receives information concerning not only touch per se but also pressure, temperature, and feedback from the muscles involved in movements of our hands.

You can assess the sensitivity of your sense of touch by trying a mini-experiment suggested by Cynthia O'Dell and Mark Hoyert (2002): set out a series of cookie-cutter outlines, close your eyes, and see how many you can identify from your sense of touch alone.

Different parts of the body are more sensitive to touch and pressure than others. If you take another look at Figure 2.13 on page 64, you'll see that the parts of the body that "cover" more than their fair share of somatosensory cortex are most sensitive to touch. These parts include the hands, face, and some other regions of the body.

Psychophysicists use methods such as the **two-point threshold** to assess sensitivity to pressure. This method determines the smallest distance by which two rods touching the skin must be separated before the (blindfolded) individual reports that there are two rods rather than one. With this method, psychophysicists have found that our fingertips, lips, noses, and cheeks are more sensitive than our shoulders, thighs, and calves. That is, the rods can be closer together but perceived as distinct when they touch the lips more than when they touch the shoulders. Why the difference in sensitivity? First, nerve endings are more densely packed in the fingertips and face than in other locations. Second, more sensory cortex is devoted to the perception of sensations in the fingertips and face (see Figure 2.13 once again).

The sense of pressure, like the sense of touch, undergoes rapid adaptation. For example, you may have undertaken several minutes of strategic movements to wind up with your hand on the arm or leg of your date, only to discover that adaptation to this delightful source of pressure reduces the sensation.

Temperature: Sometimes Everything Is Relative

The receptors for temperature are neurons located just beneath the skin. When skin temperature increases, the receptors for warmth fire. Decreases in skin temperature cause receptors for cold to fire.

Sensations of temperature are relative. When we are at normal body temperature, we might perceive another person's skin as warm. When we are feverish, though, the other person's skin might seem cool. We also adapt to differences in temperature. When we walk out of an air-conditioned house into the July sun, we feel intense heat at first. Then the sensations of heat tend to fade (although we may still be uncomfortable because of high humidity). Similarly, when we first enter a swimming pool, the water may seem cool or cold because it is below our body temperature. Yet after a few moments, an 80°F pool may seem quite warm. In fact, we may chide a newcomer for not diving right in.

Pain

For most people, pain is a frequent visitor. Headaches, backaches, toothaches—these are only a few of the types of pain that most of us encounter from time to time. According to a national Gallup survey of 2,002 adults in the United States (Arthritis Foundation, 2000), 89% experience pain at least once a month. More than half (55%) of people aged 65 and older say they experience pain daily. Sad to say, these people are most likely to attribute pain to getting older (88%), with the implication—that they can do nothing about disabilities such as arthritis. By contrast, people aged 18 to 34 are more likely to attribute pain to tension or stress (73%), to overwork (64%), or to their lifestyle (51%), all features of life that they can likely modify. When we assume that there is nothing we can do about pain, we are less apt to look for a solution. Yet 43% of Americans say that pain curtails their activities, and 50% say that pain puts them in a bad mood. There are also a number of gender differences

© Kathy Ferguson-Johnson/PhotoEdit Inc.

Sensational? The flavors of foods are determined not only by their taste but also by their odor, texture, and temperature.

Two-point threshold The least distance by which two rods touching the skin must be separated before the person will report that there are two rods, not one, on 50% of occasions.

"After great pain, a formal feeling comes. The Nerves sit ceremonious, like tombs."

EMILY DICKINSON

TABLE 3.1 ■ Gender Differences in Experiencing and Responding to Pain

Percentage Who Report ...	Women	Men
Experiencing daily pain	46	37
Feeling they have a great deal of control over their pain	39	48
Feeling that tension and stress are their leading causes of pain	72	56
Going to see the doctor about pain only when other people urge them to do it	27	38
Balancing the demands of work and family life to be the key cause of their pain	35	24
Frequent headaches	17	8
Frequent backaches	24	19
Arthritis	20	15
Sore feet	25	17

Why do you think women are more likely than men to experience pain? What is the gender difference in willingness to see the doctor about pain? How would you explain the gender difference in willingness to see the doctor?

Source of data: Arthritis Foundation (2000, April 6). Pain in America: Highlights from a Gallup survey. http://www.arthritis.org

in the experiencing of, and response to, pain, as shown in Table 3.1 ■. What is pain? What can we do about it?

Pain results from the stimulation of neurons in the skin called *nociceptors*. Evolutionary psychologists would point out that pain is adaptive, if unpleasant, because it motivates us to do something about it. For some of us, however, chronic pain—pain that lasts once injuries or illnesses have cleared—saps our vitality and interferes with the pleasures of everyday life (Fenton, 2010; Gatchel & Kishino, 2010).

We can sense pain throughout most of the body, but pain is usually sharpest where nerve endings are densely packed, as in the fingers and face. Pain can also be felt deep within the body, as in the cases of abdominal pain and back pain. Even though headaches may seem to originate deep inside the head, there are no nerve endings for pain in the brain. In fact, brain surgery can be done with a local anesthetic that prevents the patient from feeling the drilling of a small hole through the skull.

Pain usually originates at the point of contact, as when you bang a knee (see Figure 3.28 ■). But its reverberations throughout the nervous system are extensive. The pain message to the brain is initiated by the release of chemicals, including prostaglandins, bradykinin, and a chemical called *P* (yes, *P* stands for "pain"). Prostaglandins facilitate transmission of the pain message to the brain and heighten circulation to the injured area, causing the redness and swelling that we call inflammation. Inflammation serves the biological function of attracting infection-fighting blood cells to the affected area to protect it against invading germs. Pain-relieving drugs such as aspirin and ibuprofen work by inhibiting the production of prostaglandins.

The pain message is relayed from the spinal cord to the thalamus and then projected to the cerebral cortex, making us aware of the location and intensity of the damage. Ronald Melzack and Joel Katz (2006) speak of a "neuromatrix" that includes these chemical reactions but involves other aspects of physiology and psychology in our reaction to pain. For example, visual and other sensory inputs tell us what is happening and influence the cognitive interpretation of the situation. Our emotional response affects the degree of pain, and so do the ways we respond to stress. For example, if the pain derives from an object we fear, perhaps a knife or needle, we may experience more pain. If we perceive that there is nothing we can do to change the situation, perception of pain may increase. If we have self-confidence and a history of successful responding to stress, the perception of pain may diminish.

One of the more intriguing topics within the study of pain is that of phantom limb pain.

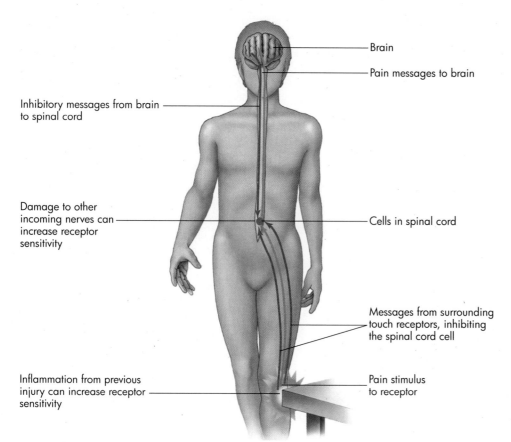

Brain

Pain messages to brain

Inhibitory messages from brain to spinal cord

Damage to other incoming nerves can increase receptor sensitivity

Cells in spinal cord

Messages from surrounding touch receptors, inhibiting the spinal cord cell

Inflammation from previous injury can increase receptor sensitivity

Pain stimulus to receptor

Figure 3.28 ■ Perception of Pain Pain originates at the point of contact, and the pain message to the brain is initiated by the release of prostaglandins, bradykinin, and substance P.

PHANTOM LIMB PAIN

[I was] suddenly aware of a sharp cramp in my left leg. I tried to get at it . . . with my single arm, but, finding myself too weak, hailed an attendant. "Just rub my left calf, . . . if you please." "Calf? . . . You ain't got none, pardner. It's took off."

The above is a true story from the U.S. Civil War as reported by Melzack (2006). The soldier had been wounded in battle. An arm had been amputated, with his knowledge, but he had also lost both legs, with no recollection of the operation. Yet he experienced pain "in" the amputated limbs.

Truth or Fiction Revisited: Many people do experience pain in limbs that have been amputated. For example, the majority of combat veterans with amputated limbs report feeling pain in such missing, or "phantom," limbs (Kooijman et al., 2000; Nampiaparampil, 2008). The limb may be gone, but the pain is real enough. It sometimes involves activation of nerves in the stump of the missing limb, but local anesthesia does not always eliminate the pain. The pain appears to result from activation of parts of the brain in which the pain was represented. Research shows that many people who experience phantom limb pain show neural activity in the motor and somatosensory cortex that is consistent with the pain (Melzack & Katz, 2006).

We consider what to do about pain in the nearby Life Connections feature.

LearningConnections ● THE SKIN SENSES (YES, IT DOES)

ACTIVE REVIEW (22) The _____ threshold method allows psychophysicists to assess sensitivity to pressure by determining the distance by which two rods touching the skin must be separated before a person will report that there are two rods, not one. (23) Our lips are (more or less?) sensitive to touch than our shoulders.

REFLECT AND RELATE Have you ever entered a swimming pool and felt cold even though the water temperature was in the 70s? How can you explain the experience?

CRITICAL THINKING Does it seem strange to think of the skin as a sensory organ? If it does, be my guest and check out the discussion of "functional fixedness" in Chapter 7.

 Go to Psychology CourseMate at **www.cengagebrain.com** for an interactive version of these questions.

The most common method of pain relief is to take a pill—aspirin, acetaminophen, ibuprofen, and so on. But these medicines have side effects, especially when they are used over prolonged periods. Psychologists, like medical doctors, are concerned about the control of pain, so let's have a look at some views on pain.

Gate Theory

Simple remedies like rubbing a banged knee frequently help relieve pain. Why? According to the *gate theory* of pain originated by Ronald Melzack and Patrick Wall, the nervous system can process only a limited amount of stimulation at a time. Rubbing the painful area transmits sensations to the brain that "compete" for the attention of neurons and prevents many nerves from transmitting pain messages to the brain. It shuts down a "gate" in the spinal cord, like flooding an area with cell phone calls.

Acupuncture

Thousands of years ago, the Chinese began mapping the body to learn where pins might be placed to deaden pain. Research shows that acupuncture may stimulate nerves that reach the hypothalamus and lead to release of endorphins and cortisol (Spelts & Gaynor, 2010). *Endorphins* are naturally occurring chemical mes-

© Fancy Photography/Veer

Treating Pain Pills are the most common method of treating pain. However, psychologists have devised many methods for coping with chronic pain.

sengers that are similar in effect to the narcotic morphine. *Cortisol* is a stress hormone.

Transcutaneous Electrical Nerve Stimulation (TENS)

Transcutaneous electrical nerve stimulation (TENS) is a noninvasive alternative to acupuncture (Binder & Baron, 2010). It applies electrodes to the skin, often at acupuncture points, and electrical currents are passed through the body from point to point. In a typical study of TENS, electrodes were placed at places commonly used to help pregnant women deliver their babies with less discomfort (Chao et al., 2007). The women reported less discomfort during delivery than did a control group.

Psychological Methods for Coping with Pain

Coping with that age-old enemy—pain—has traditionally been a medical issue. The primary treatment has been chemical, as in the use of drugs. However, psychology has expanded our arsenal of weapons for fighting the perception of pain.

Accurate Information

Simply giving people accurate information about a medical condition often helps them manage perception of pain (Turner & Turk,

⦿ KINESTHESIS AND THE VESTIBULAR SENSE

Try this mini-experiment. Close your eyes and then touch your nose with your finger. If you weren't right on target, I'm sure you came close. But how? You didn't see your hand moving, and you didn't hear your arm swishing through the air. Humans and many other animals have senses that alert them to their movements and body position without relying on vision, including *kinesthesis* and the *vestibular sense*.

Kinesthesis: How Moving?

Kinesthesis The sense that informs us about the positions and motion of parts of our bodies.

Vestibular sense The sense of equilibrium that informs us about our bodies' positions relative to gravity.

Question 24: What is kinesthesis? Kinesthesis is the sense that informs you about the position and motion of parts of the body. The term is derived from the ancient Greek words for "motion" *(kinesis)* and "perception" *(aisthesis)*. In kinesthesis, sensory information is fed back to the brain from sensory organs in the joints, tendons, and muscles. You were able to bring your finger to your nose easily by employing your kinesthetic sense. When you make a muscle in your arm, the sensations of tightness and hardness are also provided by kinesthesis.

Imagine going for a walk without kinesthesis. You would have to watch the forward motion of each leg to be certain you had raised it high enough to clear the curb. And if you had tried the nose-to-finger brief experiment without the kinesthetic sense,

2008). Most people in pain try *not* to think about why things hurt. Yet when uncomfortable treatment methods are used, such as chemotherapy for cancer, knowledge of the details of the treatment, including how long pain will last and how much pain there will be, can help people cope (Jaaniste et al., 2007).

Distraction and Fantasy: The X-Box Approach to Coping with Pain?

Psychologists frequently recommend distraction or fantasy as ways of lessening the perception of pain (Jaaniste et al., 2007). Imagine that you've injured your leg and you're waiting to see the doctor in an emergency room. You can distract yourself by focusing on details of your environment. You can count ceiling tiles or the hairs on the back of a finger. You can describe (or criticize) to yourself the clothes of medical personnel or passers-by. Playing video games distracts child cancer patients while they receive injections of nausea-producing chemicals (Dahlquist et al., 2009; Hoffman et al., 2008).

Hypnosis

Hypnosis is often used to reduce the perception of chronic pain (Jensen, 2009; Jensen & Patterson, 2006) and as an anesthetic in dentistry, childbirth, and even in some forms of

The Video-Game Approach to Coping with Pain? Psychologists find that distraction and fantasy help individuals manage pain. Yes, it may hurt, but that doesn't mean we must focus all of our attention on it.

surgery (Montgomery et al., 2000). In using hypnosis to lessen perception of pain, the hypnotist usually instructs the person that she feels nothing or that the pain is distant and slight. Hypnosis can also amplify distraction and fantasy. For example, the hypnotist can instruct the person to imagine that he is relaxing on a warm, exotic seashore.

Relaxation Training

When we are in pain, we often tense up. Tensing muscles is uncomfortable in itself; it also arouses the sympathetic nervous system and focuses our attention on perception of the pain. Relaxation counteracts these behavior patterns. Some psychological methods of relaxation focus on relaxing muscle groups. Some involve breathing exercises. Others use relaxing imagery. Relaxation training may be as effective as most medications for migraine headaches and for chronic pain in the lower back and jaw (Gatchel & Kishino, 2010).

Coping with Irrational Beliefs

Irrational beliefs can heighten pain (Gatchel & Kishino, 2010). For example, telling oneself that the pain is unbearable and that it will never cease increases discomfort. Cognitive therapy methods that challenge such beliefs may be of help (Dummett, 2010).

you would have had no sensory feedback until you felt the pressure of your finger against your nose (or cheek or eye or forehead), and you probably would have missed dozens of times.

Are you in the mood for another experiment? Close your eyes again. Then "make a muscle" in your right arm. Could you sense the muscle without looking at it or feeling it with your left hand? Of course you could. Kinesthesis also provides information about muscle contractions.

The Vestibular Sense: How Upright?

Truth or Fiction Revisited: It is true that you have a sense that keeps you an upright person. It is your **vestibular sense**, which provides your brain with information as to whether you are upright (physically, not morally). **Question 25: How does the vestibular sense work?** Sensory organs located in the **semicircular canals** and elsewhere in the ears monitor your body's motion and position in relation to gravity. They tell you whether you are falling and provide cues to whether your body is changing speed, such as when you are in an accelerating airplane or automobile. It is thus the vestibular sense that keeps us physically upright. Now, you may recall episodes when you have been spun around blindfolded at a party or in the spinning Teacups amusement park ride. Afterward, it might have been difficult for you to locate yourself in space (if you remained blindfolded) or to retain your balance. The reason is that the fluid in the

Kinesthesis These acrobats receive information about the position and movement of parts of their bodies through the sense of kinesthesis. Information is fed to the brain from sensory organs in the joints, tendons, and muscles.

semicircular canals was tossed about so fiercely that you lost your ability to monitor or control your position in relation to gravity.

The nearby Concept Review 3.2 summarizes key points about the senses.

LearningConnections • KINESTHESIS AND THE VESTIBULAR SENSE

ACTIVE REVIEW (24) Kinesthesis is the sensing of bodily _____ and movement. (25) The vestibular sense informs us whether we are in a(n) _____ position or changing speeds. (26) The vestibular sense is housed mainly in the _____ _____ of the ears.

REFLECT AND RELATE Can you walk upright with your eyes closed? How do you do it?

CRITICAL THINKING Why are some people "natural athletes"? Might there be genetic factors related to kinesthesis and the vestibular sense that contribute to their abilities?

 Go to Psychology CourseMate at **www.cengagebrain.com** for an interactive version of these questions.

EXTRASENSORY PERCEPTION: IS THERE PERCEPTION WITHOUT SENSATION?

"The major theoretical challenge for psi researchers is to provide an explanatory theory for the alleged phenomena that is compatible with physical and biological principles."

DARYL J. BEM

"It's craziness, pure craziness. I can't believe a major journal [allowed] this work in."

RAY HYMAN

Imagine the wealth you could amass if you had *precognition*, that is, if you were able to perceive future events in advance. Perhaps you would check the next week's stock market reports and know what to buy or sell. Or you could bet with confidence on who would win the next Super Bowl or World Series. Or think of the power you would have if you were capable of *psychokinesis*, that is, mentally manipulating or moving objects. Precognition and psychokinesis are two concepts associated with *extrasensory perception* (ESP). Two other theoretical forms of ESP are *telepathy*, or direct transmission of thoughts or ideas from one person to another, and *clairvoyance*, or the perception of objects that do not stimulate the known sensory organs. An example of clairvoyance is "seeing" what card will be dealt next, even though it is still in the deck and unseen even by the dealer.

Extrasensory perception (ESP)—also referred to as *parapsychological* or *psi phenomena*—refers to the perception of objects or events through means other than the known sensory organs. As suggested by the root *para*, meaning "alongside," *para*psychological (psi) means standing alongside psychology, not being a part of psychology. Psychological communication occurs verbally or by means of body language. Psi communication refers to the transfer of information through an irregular or unusual process—not through the usual senses.

Let's note that many psychologists do not believe ESP is an appropriate area for scientific inquiry. For example, a major psychology journal, the *Journal of Personality and Social Psychology*, published a research article on clairvoyance by Daryl J. Bem in 2011. Psychologist Ray Hyman (2011) objected: "It's craziness, pure craziness. I can't believe a major journal [allowed] this work in. I think it's just an embarrassment for the entire field." Psychologist Charles Judd (2011), the journal's editor, countered that the paper had met the journal's standards for carefully conducted research, even though "there was no [scientific] mechanism by which we could understand the results" (in Carey, 2011).

Scientists study natural events, but ESP smacks of the supernatural, even the occult. Extrasensory perception also has the flavor of a nightclub act in which a blindfolded "clairvoyant" calls out the contents of an audience member's pocketbook. Other psychologists, however, believe that there is nothing wrong with investigating ESP. The issue for them is not whether ESP is sensationalistic but whether its existence can be demonstrated in the laboratory. **Question 26: Is there really such a thing as extrasensory perception (ESP)?**

Semicircular canals Structures of the inner ear that monitor body movement and position.

Extrasensory perception (ESP) Perception of objects or events through means other than the recognized sensory organs.

Perhaps the best known of the ESP researchers was Joseph Banks Rhine of Duke University. Although he received his doctorate in botany, Rhine studied ESP for several decades beginning in the late 1920s (Viulli, 2008). In a typical experiment in

Sense	What We Sense	Receptor Organs	Nature of Sensory Receptors
Vision	Visible light (part of the spectrum of electromagnetic energy; different colors have different wavelengths)	**Eyes**	Photoreceptors in the retinas (rods, which are sensitive to the intensity of light, and cones, which are sensitive to color)
Hearing	Changes in air pressure (or in another medium, such as water) that result from vibrations called sound waves	**Ears**	Hair cells in the organ of Corti, which is attached to a membrane (the basilar membrane) within the inner ear (the cochlea)
Smell	Molecules of the substance	**Nose**	Receptor neurons in the olfactory membrane high in each nostril
Taste	Molecules of the substance	**Tongue**	Taste cells located on taste buds on the tongue
Touch, pressure	Pushing or pulling of the surface of the body	**Skin**	Nerve endings in the skin, some of which are located around the hair follicles
Kinesthesis	Muscle contractions	**Sensory organs in joints, tendons, and muscles** © RubberBall Photography/Veer	Receptor cells in joints, tendons, and muscles
Vestibular sense	Movement and position in relation to gravity	**Sensory organs in the ears (e.g., in the semicircular canals)**	Receptor cells in the ears

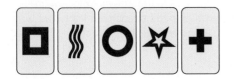

Figure 3.29 ■ Zener Cards Joseph Banks Rhine used these Zener cards in research on clairvoyance. Participants are asked to predict which card will be turned up.

clairvoyance, Rhine would use a pack of 25 Zener cards, which contained five sets of the cards shown in Figure 3.29 ■. Pigeons' pecking randomly to indicate which one was about to be turned up would be "correct" 20% of the time. Rhine found that some people guessed correctly significantly more often than the 20% chance rate. He concluded that these individuals might have some degree of ESP.

The *ganzfeld procedure* is a method for studying *telepathy* (direct communication between minds, without use of sensory perception) (Howard et al., 2009). In this method, one person acts as a "sender" and the other as a "receiver." The sender views randomly selected visual stimuli such as photographs or videotapes, while the receiver, who is in another room and whose eyes are covered and ears are blocked, tries to mentally tune in to the sender. After a session, the receiver is shown four visual stimuli and asked to select the one transmitted by the sender. A person guessing which stimulus was "transmitted" would be correct 25% of the time (1 time in 4) by chance alone. An analysis of 28 experiments using the ganzfeld procedure, however, found that receivers correctly identified the visual stimulus 38% of the time (Honorton, 1985), a percentage unlikely to be due to chance.

The article by Daryl Bem (2011), published in the *Journal of Personality and Social Psychology,* reported the results of nine experiments with more than 1,000 participants. The procedure of the first experiment involved showing 100 Cornell University students digital photos that depicted erotic or non-erotic scenes. They were then shown the photos again, in random order, but asked to predict, before each showing, whether a photo with erotic or non-erotic content was about to be displayed. Since half were erotic and half were not, a chance result would be 50–50. Participants correctly predicted the erotic photos 53.1% of the time, whereas their hit rate on predicting non-erotic photos was just 50–50, a chance result. Given the large number of participants and showings, the chances that the 53.1% success rate was due to chance alone was less than 1 in 20. Findings in the other experiments were similar: a correct prediction rate that excelled chance on interesting items, but nothing like 60% or 70%, let alone 100%.

Overall, there are many reasons for skepticism of ESP. First is the file-drawer problem (Howard et al., 2009). Buyers of supermarket magazines tend to forget "psychics'" predictions when they fail to come true (that is, they have "filed" them away). Similarly, ESP researchers are less likely to report research results that show failure. Then, too, it has not been easy to replicate experiments in ESP (Howard et al., 2009). People who have "demonstrated" ESP with one researcher have failed to do so with another researcher or have refused to participate in other studies.

It should also be noted, emphatically, that in all of these studies, *not one person has emerged who can reliably show ESP from one occasion to another and from one researcher to another.* **Truth or Fiction Revisited:** There is no adequate scientific evidence that people can read other people's minds. Research has not identified one single indisputable telepath or clairvoyant. In sum, most psychologists do not grant ESP research much credibility. They prefer to study perception that involves sensation. After all, what is life without sensation?

LearningConnections ● EXTRASENSORY PERCEPTION: IS THERE PERCEPTION WITHOUT SENSATION?

ACTIVE REVIEW (27) _____ refers to perception of objects or events through means other than sensory organs. (28) The ganzfeld procedure is currently used to study _____. (29) One reason for skepticism about ESP is the _____ problem; that is, researchers are less likely to report research results that show failure.

REFLECT AND RELATE Does anyone you know believe that some people are "psychics"? What kind of evidence is required to support the existence of ESP? Why do you think

many readers of this textbook will continue to believe in ESP despite the lack of scientific evidence?

CRITICAL THINKING Should psychologists conduct research into ESP? Why or why not?

 Go to Psychology CourseMate at **www.cengagebrain.com** for an interactive version of these questions.

Sensation and Perception: Your Tickets of Admission to the World Outside

1. What are sensation and perception?
Sensation is a mechanical process that involves the stimulation of sensory receptors (neurons) and the transmission of sensory information to the central nervous system. Perception is not mechanical. Perception is the active organization of sensations into a representation of the outside world, and it reflects learning and expectations.

2. How do we know when something is there?
We know something is there when the intensity of the stimulus, such as a light, exceeds the absolute threshold for that stimulus. The absolute threshold is the lowest intensity at which the stimulus can be detected. We know that something has changed when the change in intensity exceeds the difference threshold. The difference threshold is the minimum difference in intensity that can be discriminated. Difference thresholds are expressed in Weber's constants.

3. Would ads that show an appealing image or a command—such as "Buy!"—for only a fraction of a second influence us?
They might do so. Subliminal stimulation has been shown to have modest effects on behavior, especially when people are motivated in the direction of an ad or command.

4. What is signal-detection theory?
Signal-detection theory explains the ways that stimulus characteristics and psychological factors—for example, motivation, familiarity with a stimulus, and attention—interact to influence whether a stimulus will be detected.

5. What are feature detectors?
Feature detectors are neurons that fire in response to specific features of sensed stimuli. For example, detectors in the visual cortex fire in response to particular features of visual input, such as lines sensed at various angles or specific colors.

6. How do our sensory systems adapt to a changing environment?
We become more sensitive to stimuli of low magnitude and less sensitive to stimuli that remain the same (such as the background noises outside the window). Growing more sensitive to stimulation is termed sensitization, or positive adaptation. Growing less sensitive to continuous stimulation is called desensitization, or negative adaptation.

Vision: Letting the Sun Shine In

7. Just what is light?
Visible light is the part of the range of electromagnetic energy that triggers visual sensations. Light is made up of waves of energy; the color violet has the shortest wavelength, and red has the longest. White sunlight can be broken down into the colors of the rainbow by means of a prism.

8. How does the eye work?
The eye senses and transmits visual stimulation to the occipital lobe of the cerebral cortex. After light passes through the cornea, the size of the pupil determines the amount that can pass through the lens. The lens focuses light onto the retina, which is composed of photoreceptors (neurons) called rods and cones. Cones permit perception of color. Rods transmit sensations of light and dark only. Light is transmitted from the retina to the brain via the optic nerve, which is made up of the axons of retinal ganglion cells. Visual acuity is connected with the shape of the eye and age. As we age, the lenses grow brittle, making it difficult to focus; this condition is called presbyopia. Rods are more sensitive than cones to lowered lighting and continue to adapt to darkness once cones have reached their peak adaptation.

9. What are some perceptual dimensions of color?
Perceptual dimensions of color include hue, value, and saturation. The wavelength of light determines its hue. Yellow-orange-red colors are considered warm. Greens and blues are considered cool. Colors across from one another on the color wheel are complementary. In afterimages, persistent sensations of color are followed by perception of the complementary color when the first color is removed.

10. How do we perceive color?
There are two theories as to how we perceive color. According to the trichromatic theory, there are three types of cones—some sensitive to red, others to green, and still others to blue-violet. The opponent-process theory proposes three types of color receptors: red–green, blue–yellow, and light–dark. Opponent-process theory is supported by the appearance of afterimages. These two theories may actually reflect a two-step process.

11. What is color blindness and why are some people color-blind?
People with normal color vision are called trichromats. Monochromats see no color, and dichromats are blind to some parts of the spectrum. Partial color blindness is a sex-linked trait.

Visual Perception: How Perceptive?

12. How do we organize bits of visual information into meaningful wholes?
Perceptual organization involves recognizing patterns and processing information about relationships between parts and the whole. Gestalt rules of perceptual organization involve figure–ground relationships, proximity, similarity, continuity, common fate, and closure. Perception of a whole followed by perception of parts is termed top-down processing. Perception of the parts that leads to perception of a whole is termed bottom-up processing.

13. How do we perceive movement?

We visually perceive movement when the light reflected by moving objects moves across the retina and also when objects shift in relation to one another. Distant objects appear to move more slowly than nearby objects, and objects in the middle ground may give the illusion of moving backward. Stroboscopic motion, responsible for the illusion of motion pictures, occurs through the presentation of a rapid progression of images of stationary objects (frames).

14. How do we perceive depth?

Depth perception involves monocular and binocular cues. Monocular cues include pictorial cues, such as perspective, clearness, interposition, shadows, and texture gradient, and motion cues, such as motion parallax. Binocular cues include retinal disparity and convergence.

15. What are perceptual constancies?

Perceptual constancies are acquired through experience and make the world a stable place for us. For example, we learn to assume that objects retain their size, shape, brightness, and color despite their distance from us, their position, or changes in lighting conditions.

Hearing: Making Sense of Sound

16. What is sound?

To be transmitted, sound waves require a medium such as air or water. Sound waves alternatively compress and expand molecules of the medium, creating vibrations. The human ear can hear sounds varying in frequency from 20 to 20,000 cycles per second (Hz). The greater the frequency is, the higher the sound's pitch. The loudness of a sound roughly corresponds to the amplitude of sound waves measured in decibels (dB). We can experience hearing loss if we are exposed to protracted sounds of 85 to 90 dB or more.

17. How does the ear work?

The ear captures sound waves, vibrates in sympathy with them, and transmits auditory information to the brain. The outer ear funnels sound waves to the eardrum, which vibrates in sympathy with them and transmits the auditory information through the bones of the middle ear to the cochlea of the inner ear. The basilar membrane of the cochlea transmits those stimuli to the organ of Corti. From there, sound travels to the brain via the auditory nerve.

18. How do we locate sounds?

We locate sounds by determining in which ear they are louder. We may turn our heads to pin down that information.

19. How do we perceive loudness and pitch?

Sounds are perceived as louder when more sensory neurons fire. The place theory of pitch perception holds that the pitch of a sound is sensed according to the place along the basilar membrane that vibrates in response to it; it accounts for sounds whose frequencies exceed 4000 Hz. Frequency theory states that pitch perception depends on the stimulation of neural impulses that match the frequency of the sound waves

and accounts for frequencies of 20 to 1000 Hz. The volley principle accounts for pitch discrimination between a few hundred and 4,000 cycles per second.

20. What kinds of deafness are there?

Conductive deafness—common among older people—is caused by damage to the middle ear and is often ameliorated by hearing aids, which amplify sounds. Sensorineural deafness is usually caused by damage to neurons in the inner ear and can sometimes be corrected by cochlear implants.

The Chemical Senses: Smell and Taste

21. How does the sense of smell work?

The sense of smell is chemical. It samples molecules of substances called odors through the olfactory membrane in each nostril. Smell makes a key contribution to the flavor of foods.

22. How does the sense of taste work?

There are four primary taste qualities: sweet, sour, salty, and bitter. Flavor involves the odor, texture, and temperature of food, as well as its taste. Taste is sensed through taste cells, which are located in taste buds on the tongue.

The Skin Senses (Yes, It Does)

23. What are the skin senses, and how do they work?

The skin senses include touch, pressure, warmth, cold, and pain. Touches and pressure are sensed by receptors located around the roots of hair cells below the surface of the skin. We have separate receptors for warmth and cold beneath the skin. Pain generally results from the firing of nocioreceptors and the transmission of pain messages to the brain.

Kinesthesis and the Vestibular Sense

24. What is kinesthesis?

Kinesthesis is the sensation of body position and movement. It relies on sensory organs in the joints, tendons, and muscles.

25. How does the vestibular sense work?

The vestibular sense is mostly housed in the semicircular canals of the ears and tells us whether we are in an upright position.

Extrasensory Perception: Is There Perception Without Sensation?

26. Is there really such a thing as extrasensory perception (ESP)?

ESP, or psi communication, refers to the perception of objects or events through means other than sensory organs. Many psychologists do not believe that ESP is an appropriate area for scientific inquiry. The ganzfeld procedure studies telepathy by having one person (the sender) try to mentally transmit visual information to a receiver in another room. Because of the so-called file-drawer problem and lack of replication of positive results, there is no reliable evidence for the existence of ESP.

KEY TERMS

Absolute threshold (p. 80)
Afterimage (p. 89)
Auditory (p. 100)
Auditory nerve (p. 101)
Autokinetic effect (p. 94)
Basilar membrane (p. 101)
Binocular cues (p. 96)
Bipolar cells (p. 85)
Blind spot (p. 86)
Bottom-up processing (p. 94)
Brightness constancy (p. 98)
Closure (p. 92)
Cochlea (p. 101)
Color constancy (p. 98)
Common fate (p. 94)
Complementary (p. 88)
Conductive deafness (p. 103)
Cones (p. 86)
Continuity (p. 93)
Convergence (p. 96)
Cornea (p. 84)
Dark adaptation (p. 87)
Decibel (dB) (p. 100)
Desensitization (p. 83)
Dichromat (p. 91)
Difference threshold (p. 81)
Eardrum (p. 101)
Extrasensory perception (ESP) (p. 112)

Feature detectors (p. 82)
Flavor (p. 104)
Fovea (p. 86)
Frequency theory (p. 102)
Ganglion cells (p. 85)
Hertz (Hz) (p. 100)
Hue (p. 84)
Illusions (p. 94)
Interposition (p. 96)
Iris (p. 84)
Just noticeable difference (jnd) (p. 81)
Kinesthesis (p. 110)
Lens (p. 85)
Monochromat (p. 91)
Monocular cues (p. 95)
Motion parallax (p. 96)
Olfactory nerve (p. 105)
Opponent-process theory (p. 90)
Optic nerve (p. 86)
Organ of Corti (p. 101)
Perception (p. 80)
Perceptual organization (p. 92)
Perspective (p. 95)
Phi phenomenon (p. 95)
Photoreceptors (p. 85)
Pitch (p. 81)
Place theory (p. 102)
Presbyopia (p. 86)

Proximity (p. 93)
Pupil (p. 85)
Retina (p. 85)
Retinal disparity (p. 96)
Rods (p. 86)
Semicircular canals (p. 111)
Sensation (p. 80)
Sensitization (p. 83)
Sensorineural deafness (p. 104)
Sensory adaptation (p. 83)
Shadowing (p. 96)
Shape constancy (p. 98)
Signal-detection theory (p. 82)
Similarity (p. 93)
Size constancy (p. 97)
Stroboscopic motion (p. 95)
Subliminal stimulation (p. 81)
Taste buds (p. 105)
Taste cells (p. 105)
Texture gradient (p. 96)
Top-down processing (p. 94)
Trichromat (p. 91)
Trichromatic theory (p. 89)
Two-point threshold (p. 107)
Vestibular sense (p. 111)
Visible light (p. 84)
Visual acuity (p. 86)
Weber's constant (p. 81)

ACTIVE LEARNING RESOURCES

4 Consciousness

MAJOR TOPICS

The Many Meanings of
   Consciousness 119
Sleep and Dreams: Other Worlds
   Within? 121
Altering Consciousness Through
   Hypnosis, Meditation, and
   Biofeedback 131
Altering Consciousness Through
   Drugs 135

FEATURES

Self-Assessment: Are You Getting Your Z's? 128
Life Connections: Strategies for Coping with Insomnia 129
Self-Assessment: Do You Have a Problem with Alcohol? 140
A Closer Look: Dependence on Cocaine? Denial at Work 144
Video Connections—Why Is Nicotine So Addictive? 145
A Closer Look: On the Edge with Ecstasy 146
Life Connections: Is Marijuana Harmful? Should It Be Available
   as a Medicine? 148
Concept Review 4.1: Psychoactive Drugs and Their Effects 149

T F We act out our forbidden fantasies in our dreams.

page 126

T F Many people have insomnia because they try too hard to fall asleep at night.

page 128

T F It is dangerous to awaken a sleepwalker.

page 130

T F You can be hypnotized against your will.

page 132

T F The effects of hypnotism are due to a special trance state.

page 133

T F You can teach a rat to raise or lower its heart rate.

page 134

T F Substance abuse is on the rise in high schools.

page 136

T F More 12th graders smoke cigarettes than marijuana.

page 136

T F A drink a day is good for you.

page 141

T F Heroin was once used as a cure for addiction to morphine.

page 141

T F Many health professionals calm down hyperactive children by giving them a stimulant.

page 142

T F Coca-Cola once "added life" to its signature drink through the use of a powerful—but now illegal—stimulant.

page 142

T F The number of people who die from smoking-related causes is greater than the number lost to motor vehicle accidents, abuse of alcohol and all other drugs, suicide, homicide, and AIDS *combined.*

page 145

Are these items truth or fiction? We will be revisiting them throughout the chapter.

W

hen you talk to yourself, who talks and who listens?

This is the sort of question posed by philosophers and scientists who study consciousness. Although it might seem that psychologists, who study the brain and mental processes, would be best equipped to look into consciousness, for many years they banished the topic from their field. In 1904, for example, William James wrote an article with the intriguing title "Does Consciousness Exist?" James did not think consciousness was a proper area of study for psychologists because scientific methods could not directly observe or measure another person's consciousness.

John Watson, the "father of modern behaviorism," agreed. Watson insisted that only observable, measurable behavior is the province of psychology: "The time seems to have come when psychology must discard all references to consciousness" (1913, p. 163). When Watson became the president of the American Psychological Association in 1914, his view was further cemented in the minds of many psychologists.

But the past few decades have seen a cognitive revolution, and thousands of psychologists now believe we cannot capture the richness of human experience without referring to consciousness (Sternberg, 2009). We are flooded with studies of consciousness by psychologists, biologists, neuroscientists, physicists, even computer scientists. Yet we still cannot directly observe the consciousness of another person, and so we rely on self-reports of consciousness as we observe events such as neural activity in the brain.

● THE MANY MEANINGS OF CONSCIOUSNESS

Let's begin this most intriguing area of psychology by posing this question: **Question 1: What is consciousness?**

Consciousness as Awareness

One meaning of **consciousness** is *sensory awareness* of the environment. The sense of vision enables us to see, or be *conscious* of, the sun gleaming on the snow. Yet sometimes we are not aware of sensory stimulation. We may be unaware, or unconscious, of sensory stimulation when we do not pay attention to it. The world is abuzz with signals, yet you are conscious of, or focusing on, only the words on this page (I hope).

Therefore, another aspect of consciousness is **selective attention**. Selective attention means focusing one's consciousness on a particular stimulus. To keep your car on the road, you must pay more attention to driving conditions than to your hunger pangs.

"Consciousness comes in many flavors. Anyone who has taught an introductory psychology class, or attended one at eight o'clock Friday morning, has seen them all. There may be a couple of party-hearty frat boys in the back row, dozing after a long night spent celebrating the upcoming weekend. These two are not conscious. Up a couple of rows is the scammer checking out [someone] across the aisle and wondering if he can get a date. He is conscious, but not of you; nor are the three girls down the way who are passing notes to each other and suppressing their merriment. Another student has a tape recorder going and is finishing up a paper for another class, and he will be conscious of you later. The front-row kids are sippin' their coffee, taking notes furiously and occasionally nodding in agreement; at least they are conscious of you."

MICHAEL S. GAZZANIGA, 2008,
P. 277.

Consciousness A concept with many meanings, including sensory awareness of the world outside, direct inner awareness of one's thoughts and feelings, personal unity, and the waking state.

Selective attention The focus of one's consciousness on a particular stimulus.

Direct inner awareness Knowledge of one's own thoughts, feelings, and memories without the use of sensory organs.

Preconscious In psychodynamic theory, descriptive of material that is not in awareness but can be brought into awareness by focusing one's attention.

Unconscious In psychodynamic theory, descriptive of ideas and feelings that are not available to awareness.

Adaptation to our environment involves learning which stimuli must be attended to and which ones can be safely ignored. Selective attention makes our senses keener (Kerlin et al., 2010; McLachlan & Wilson, 2010). This is why we can pick out the speech of a single person across a room at a cocktail party—a phenomenon suitably termed the *cocktail party effect*.

Although we can decide where and when we will focus our attention, various kinds of stimuli also tend to capture attention. Among them are these:

- Sudden changes, as when a cool breeze enters a sweltering room or we receive a particularly high or low grade on an exam.
- Novel stimuli, as when a dog enters the classroom or a person shows up with an unusual hairdo.
- Intense stimuli, such as bright colors, loud noises, sharp pain, or extremely attractive people.
- Repetitive stimuli, as when the same TV commercial is played a dozen times throughout the course of a football game.

How do advertisers use these facts to get "into" our consciousness and our pocketbooks? Think of some TV commercials that captured your attention. What kinds of stimuli put them front and center in your awareness?

Yet another meaning of consciousness is **direct inner awareness**. Close your eyes and imagine spilling a can of bright red paint across a black tabletop. Watch it spread across the black, shiny surface and then drip onto the floor. Although this image may be vivid, you did not "see" it literally. Neither your eyes nor any other sensory organs were involved. You were *conscious* of the image through direct inner awareness.

We are conscious of—or have direct inner awareness of—our own thoughts, emotions, and memories. However, we may not be able to measure direct inner awareness scientifically. Nevertheless, many psychologists argue, "It is detectable to anyone that has it" (J. L. Miller, 1992, p. 180).

Conscious, Preconscious, Unconscious, and Nonconscious

Sigmund Freud, the founder of psychoanalysis, differentiated between the thoughts and feelings we are conscious, or aware, of and those that are preconscious and unconscious. **Preconscious** material is not currently in awareness but is readily available. For example, if you answer the following questions, you will summon up preconscious information: What did you eat for dinner yesterday? About what time did you wake up this morning? What is your phone number? You can make these preconscious bits of information conscious by directing your inner awareness, or attention, to them.

According to Freud, still other mental events are **unconscious**. This means that they are unavailable to awareness under most circumstances. Freud believed that some painful memories and sexual and aggressive impulses are unacceptable to us, so we *automatically* (unconsciously) eject them from our awareness. In other words, we *repress* them. **Repression** of these memories and impulses allows us to avoid feelings of anxiety, guilt, or shame.

People can also *choose* to stop thinking about unacceptable ideas or distractions. When we consciously eject unwanted mental events from awareness, we are engaging in **suppression**. We may, for example, suppress thoughts of an upcoming party when we need to study for a test. We may also try to suppress thoughts of a test while we are at the party!

Some bodily processes, such as the firings of neurons, are **nonconscious**. They cannot be experienced through sensory awareness or direct inner awareness. The growing of hair and the carrying of oxygen in the blood are nonconscious. We can see that our hair has grown, but we have no sense receptors that give us sensations of growing. We can feel the need to breathe but do not directly experience the exchange of carbon dioxide and oxygen.

Let's now journey all the way back to the most conscious aspect of our being—our sense of self.

Consciousness as Personal Unity: The Sense of Self

As we develop, we differentiate ourselves from what is not us. We develop a sense of being persons, individuals. There is a totality to our impressions, thoughts, and feelings that makes up our conscious existence—our continuing sense of self in a changing world. In this usage of the word, consciousness *is* self.

Consciousness as the Waking State

The word *conscious* also refers to the waking state as opposed, for example, to sleep. From this perspective, sleep, meditation, the hypnotic "trance," and the distorted perceptions that can accompany the use of consciousness-altering drugs are considered *altered states of consciousness*.

In the remainder of this chapter, we explore various types of altered states of consciousness. They include sleep and dreams; hypnosis, meditation, and biofeedback; and finally, the effects of psychoactive drugs.

The Sense of Self One of the meanings of consciousness is the continuing sense of self in a changing world.

LearningConnections ● THE MANY MEANINGS OF CONSCIOUSNESS

ACTIVE REVIEW (1) John B. Watson argued that only observable _____ should be studied by psychologists. (2) *Consciousness* has several meanings, including sensory awareness, the selective aspect of attention, direct inner _____, personal unity, and the waking state. (3) _____ differentiated among ideas that are conscious, preconscious, and unconscious.

REFLECT AND RELATE Are you conscious, or aware, of yourself and the world around you? How do you know?

CRITICAL THINKING Why do behaviorists object to studying consciousness? Why do cognitive psychologists pursue the study of consciousness?

 Go to Psychology CourseMate at **www.cengagebrain.com** for an interactive version of these questions.

● SLEEP AND DREAMS: OTHER WORLDS WITHIN?

Sleep is a fascinating topic. After all, we spend about one third of our adult lives asleep. Sleep experts recommend that adults get 8 hours of sleep a night, but according to the National Sleep Foundation (2009), adults in the United States typically get about 6.8 hours of sleep. About one third get 6 hours or less of sleep a night during the workweek. One third admit that lack of sleep impairs their ability to function during the day, and nearly one in five admits to falling asleep at the wheel.

Yes, we spend one third of our lives in sleep—or would if we could. As you can see in Figure 4.1 ■, however, some animals get much more sleep than we do, and some obtain much less. Why? It might have something to do with evolutionary forces. Animals that are most at risk of being hunted by predators tend to sleep less—an adaptive response to the realities of life, and death.

Biological and Circadian Rhythms

We and other animals are subject to rhythms, and they are related to the rotation and revolutions of the planet. Many birds (and people who can afford it!) migrate south

Repression In psychodynamic theory, the automatic (unconscious) ejection of anxiety-evoking ideas, impulses, or images from awareness.

Suppression The deliberate, or conscious, placing of certain ideas, impulses, or images out of awareness.

Nonconscious Descriptive of bodily processes, such as growing hair, of which we cannot become conscious. We may "recognize" that our hair is growing but cannot directly experience the biological process.

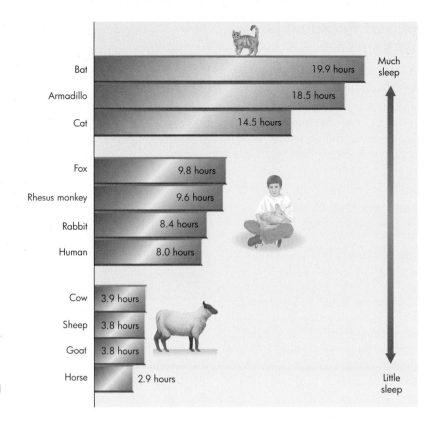

Figure 4.1 ■ Sleep Time for Mammals Different mammals require different amounts of sleep. Reasons remain uncertain, but evolution apparently plays a role: Animals more prone to being attacked by predators sleep less.

Circadian rhythm Referring to cycles that are connected with the 24-hour period of the Earth's rotation. (From the Latin *circa*, meaning "about," and *dia*, meaning "day.")

"Night Owl" Some of us—"night owl"— function best while our neighbors are sleeping soundly. For most of us, however, the traditional 9 to 5 is just fine.

in the fall and north in the spring. A number of animals hibernate for the winter and emerge when buds are again about to blossom.

Our alternating periods of wakefulness and sleep provide an example of an internally generated *circadian rhythm*. **Question 2: What is a circadian rhythm?** A **circadian rhythm** is a cycle that is connected with the 24-hour period of the Earth's rotation. A cycle of wakefulness and sleep is normally 24 hours long. However, when people are removed from cues that signal day or night, a cycle tends to extend to about 25 hours, and people sleep nearly 10 of them (National Sleep Foundation, 2000b). Why? We do not know. And within our periods of sleep, we typically undergo a number of 90-minute cycles during which we run through five stages of sleep.

Some of us function optimally in the morning, and others in the afternoon. Some of us are "night owls," who are at our best when most of our neighbors are sleeping soundly.

Your circadian rhythm can become disturbed when there is a mismatch between your sleep-schedule demands and your internal sleep–wake cycle. A disruption in sleep patterns can lead to trouble falling asleep—*insomnia*—or to getting too much sleep—*hypersomnia*. Jet lag is one kind of assault on your circadian rhythm. Frequent changes of time zones or frequent changes of work shifts (as encountered, for example, by nursing personnel) can induce more persistent or recurrent problems in your circadian rhythm. Treatment often includes gradual adjustments in your sleep schedule to allow your circadian system to become aligned with changes in your sleep–wake schedule.

Why do we sleep? Why do we dream? What are daydreams? Let's explore the nature of sleep, dreams, and sleep disorders.

The Stages of Sleep: How Do We Sleep?

When we sleep, we slip from consciousness to unconsciousness. When we are conscious, our brains emit waves characterized by certain *frequencies* (numbers of waves per second) and *amplitudes* (heights—an index of strength). Brain waves are rough indicators of the activity of large numbers of neurons. The strength, or energy, of brain waves is expressed in volts (an electrical unit). Likewise, when we sleep, our brains emit waves that differ from those emitted when we are conscious. The electroencephalograph, or EEG, has helped researchers identify the different brain waves during the waking state and when we are sleeping. Figure 4.2 ■ shows EEG patterns that reflect the frequency and strength of brain waves that occur during the waking state, when we are relaxed, and when we are in the various stages of sleep. Brain waves, like other waves, are cyclical. The printouts in Figure 4.2 show what happens during a period of 15 seconds or so. **Question 3: How do we describe the stages of sleep?**

High-frequency brain waves are associated with wakefulness. When we move deeper into sleep, their frequency decreases and their amplitude (strength) increases. When we close our eyes and begin to relax before going to sleep, our brains emit many **alpha waves**. Alpha waves are low-amplitude brain waves of about 8 to 13 cycles per second.

Figure 4.2 shows five stages of sleep. The first four sleep stages are considered **non-rapid-eye-movement (NREM) sleep**. These contrast with the fifth stage, which is called **rapid-eye-movement (REM) sleep** because our eyes dart back and forth quickly beneath our closed lids.

STAGE 1 As we enter stage 1 sleep, our brain waves slow down from the alpha rhythm and enter a pattern of **theta waves**. Theta waves, with a frequency of about 6 to 8 cycles per second, are accompanied by slow, rolling eye movements. The transition from alpha waves to theta waves may be accompanied by a **hypnagogic state**, during which we may experience brief dreamlike images that resemble vivid photographs. Stage 1 sleep is the lightest stage of sleep. If we are awakened from stage 1 sleep, we may deny that we were asleep or feel that we have not slept at all.

STAGES 2, 3, AND 4 After 30 to 40 minutes of stage 1 sleep, we undergo a rather steep descent into stages 2, 3, and 4 (see Figure 4.3 ■). During stage 2, brain waves are medium in amplitude with a frequency of about 4 to 7 cycles per second, but these are punctuated by *sleep spindles*—brief bursts of brain wave activity that signal the onset of REM sleep. Sleep spindles have a frequency of 12 to 16 cycles per second.

Alpha waves Rapid low-amplitude brain waves that have been linked to feelings of relaxation.

Non-rapid-eye-movement (NREM) sleep The first four stages of sleep.

Rapid-eye-movement (REM) sleep A stage of sleep characterized by rapid eye movements, which have been linked to dreaming.

Theta waves Slow brain waves sometimes accompanied by a hypnagogic state.

Hypnagogic state The drowsy interval between waking and sleeping characterized by brief, hallucinatory, dreamlike experiences.

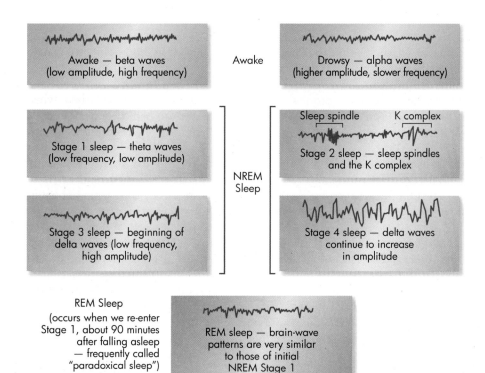

Figure 4.2 ■ The Stages of Sleep This figure illustrates typical EEG patterns for the stages of sleep. During REM sleep, EEG patterns resemble those of the waking state. For this reason, REM sleep is often termed paradoxical sleep. As sleep progresses from stage 1 to stage 4, brain waves become slower, and their amplitude increases. Dreams, including normal nightmares, are most vivid during REM sleep. More disturbing sleep terrors tend to occur during deep stage 4 sleep.

| Sleep stage | A | 1 | 2 | 3 | 4 | 3 | 2 | REM | 1 | 2 | 3 | 4 | 3 | 2 | 3 | 2 | REM |

Figure 4.3 ■ Sleep Cycles This figure illustrates the alternation of REM and non-REM sleep for the typical sleeper. There are about five periods of REM sleep during an eight-hour night. Sleep is deeper earlier in the night, and REM sleep tends to become prolonged toward morning.

During deep sleep stages 3 and 4, our brains produce slower **delta waves**, which reach relatively great amplitude compared with other brain waves. During stage 3, the delta waves have a frequency of 1 to 3 cycles per second. Stage 4 is the deepest stage of sleep, from which it is the most difficult to be awakened. During stage 4 sleep, the delta waves slow to about 0.5 to 2 cycles per second, and their amplitude is greatest.

REM SLEEP After perhaps half an hour of deep stage 4 sleep, we begin a relatively rapid journey back upward through the stages until we enter REM sleep (refer to Figure 4.3). REM sleep derives its name from the *rapid eye movements*, observable beneath the closed eyelids, that characterize this stage. During REM sleep, we produce relatively rapid, low-amplitude brain waves that resemble those of light stage 1 sleep. REM sleep is also called *paradoxical sleep* because the EEG patterns observed suggest a level of arousal similar to that of the waking state (see Figure 4.3 again). However, it is difficult to awaken a person during REM sleep. When people are awakened during REM sleep, as is the practice in sleep research, about 80% of the time they report that they have been dreaming. (We also dream during NREM sleep but less frequently. People report dreaming only about 20% of the time when awakened during NREM sleep.)

Each night, we tend to undergo five trips through the stages of sleep as shown in Figure 4.3. These trips include about five periods of REM sleep. Our first journey through stage 4 sleep is usually longest. Sleep tends to become lighter as the night wears on. Our periods of REM sleep tend to become longer, and toward morning, our last period of REM sleep may last close to half an hour.

The Functions of Sleep: Why Do We Sleep?

Question 4: Why do we sleep? Researchers do not have all the answers as to why we sleep, but sleep seems to serve a number of purposes: it rejuvenates the body, helps us recover from stress, helps us consolidate learning and memories, and in infants, it may even promote the development of the brain.

Consider the hypothesis that sleep helps rejuvenate a tired body. Most of us have had the experience of going without sleep for a night and feeling "wrecked" or "out of it" the following day. Perhaps the next evening, we went to bed early to "catch up on our sleep." What happens to you if you do not sleep for one night? For several nights?

Many students can pull "all-nighters" in which they cram for a test through the night and then perform reasonably well the following day. But they tend to show deficits in psychological functions such as attention, learning, and memory, especially if they go sleepless for more than one night (Dubiela et al., 2010; Ward et al., 2009).

Sleep deprivation also makes for dangerous driving (M. L. Jackson, 2009). It is estimated to be connected with 100,000 vehicular crashes and 1,500 deaths in the United States each year (S. Clark, 2009). A Swedish study of more than 10,000 traffic accidents concluded that early morning driving—particularly at 4:00 A.M.—is many times more dangerous than driving during the later morning or afternoon. The researchers controlled for the effects of alcohol consumption and darkness and attributed the greater number of accidents to sleepiness (Akerstedt et al., 2001). To combat sleep deprivation that occurs during the week, many people sleep late or nap on their days off (National Sleep Foundation, 2009).

"The woods are lovely, dark, and deep,
But I have promises to keep,
And miles to go before I sleep,
And miles to go before I sleep."

ROBERT FROST

Delta waves Strong, slow brain waves usually emitted during stage 3 and 4 sleep.

WHY DO YOU NEED THE AMOUNT OF SLEEP YOU NEED? The amount of sleep we need seems in part genetically determined (Cirelli, 2009). People also tend to need more sleep during periods of stress, such as a change of job, an increase in workload, or an episode of depression (Mayers et al., 2009; Rosekind et al., 2010). In fact, sleep seems to help us recover from stress.

Newborn babies may sleep 16 hours a day, and teenagers may sleep 12 hours or more ("around the clock"). It is widely believed that older people need less sleep than younger adults do, but sleep in older people is often interrupted by physical discomfort or the need to go to the bathroom. To make up for sleep lost at night, older people will often "nod off" during the day.

SLEEP, LEARNING, AND MEMORY REM sleep and deep sleep are both connected with the consolidation of learning and memory (Dubiela et al., 2010; Ward et al., 2009). In fact, fetuses have periods of waking and sleeping, and REM sleep may foster the development of the brain before birth (McCarley, 1992; Uhlhaas et al., 2010). REM sleep may also help maintain neurons in adults by "exercising" them at night. Researchers deprive study participants of REM sleep by monitoring their EEG records and eye movements and waking them during REM sleep. Under these conditions, animals and people learn more slowly and forget what they have learned more rapidly. In any event, people and other animals that are deprived of REM sleep tend to show *REM rebound*, meaning that they spend more time in REM sleep during subsequent sleep periods. That is, they catch up. It is mostly during REM sleep that we dream. Let's now consider dreams, a mystery about which philosophers, poets, and scientists have theorized for centuries.

Dreams: What Is the "Stuff" of Dreams?

To quote from Shakespeare's *The Tempest,* just what is the "stuff" of dreams? What are they "made on"? **Question 5: What are dreams?** Like memories and fantasies, dreams involve imagery in the absence of external stimulation and can seem very real. In college, I often had "anxiety dreams" the night before a test. I dreamed repeatedly that I had taken the test and it was all over. (Imagine the disappointment when I awakened and realized that the test still lay before me!)

Dreams are most likely to have vivid imagery during REM sleep, whereas images are vaguer and more fleeting during NREM sleep. Also, you tend to dream every time you are in REM sleep. Therefore, if you sleep for 8 hours and undergo five sleep cycles, you may have five dreams. Dreams may compress time the way a movie does by skipping over hours or days to a future time, but the actual action tends to take place in "real time." Fifteen minutes of events fill about 15 minutes of dreaming. Furthermore, your dream theater is quite flexible. You can dream in black and white or in full color.

Some dreams are nightmares. One common nightmare is that something heavy is sitting on your chest and watching you as you breathe. Another is that you are trying to run away from a terrible threat but cannot gain your footing or coordinate your leg muscles. Nightmares, like most pleasant dreams, are generally products of REM sleep.

Question 6: Why do we dream what we dream? There are many theories as to why we dream what we dream. Some are psychological, and others are more biologically oriented.

DREAMS AS REFLECTIONS OF "THE RESIDUE OF THE DAY" You may recall dreams involving fantastic adventures, but most dreams involve memories of the activities and problems of the day (Morewedge & Norton, 2009). If we are preoccupied with

125

Dreams What is "such stuff as dreams are made on"? Where do dreams come from? Why do they contain the imagery they contain? Are most dreams exciting adventures, dull recurrences of the events of the day, or plans for the following day?

"We all dream; we do not understand our dreams, yet we act as if nothing strange goes on in our sleep minds, strange at least by comparison with the logical, purposeful doings of our minds when we are awake."

ERICH FROMM

Activation–synthesis model The view that dreams reflect activation of cognitive activity by the reticular formation and synthesis of this activity into a pattern.

illness or death, sexual or aggressive urges, or moral dilemmas, we are likely to dream about them. The characters in our dreams are more likely to be friends and neighbors—subjects that have been referred to, poetically, as "the residue of the day"— than spies, monsters, or princes.

However, traumatic events can spawn nightmares, as reported in studies of the aftermath of the terrorist attacks on the World Trade Center and Pentagon in 2001 (Roberts et al., 2009; Singareddy & Balon, 2002). People who suffer frequent nightmares are more likely than other people to also suffer from anxiety, depression, and other kinds of psychological discomfort (Roberts et al., 2009).

DREAMS AS THE EXPRESSION OF UNCONSCIOUS DESIRES "A dream is a wish your heart makes" is a song lyric from the Disney film *Cinderella*. Freud theorized that dreams reflect unconscious wishes and urges. He argued that through dreams we can express impulses we would censor during the day. Moreover, he said that the content of dreams is symbolic of unconscious fantasized objects such as the genitals. A key part of Freud's method of psychoanalysis involved interpretation of his clients' dreams. **Truth or Fiction Revisited:** However, there is no evidence that we act out forbidden fantasies in our dreams.

DREAMS AS PROTECTING SLEEP Freud also believed that dreams "protect sleep" by providing imagery that helps keep disturbing, repressed thoughts out of awareness. The theory that dreams protect sleep has been challenged by the observation that disturbing events tend to be followed by disturbing dreams on the same theme—not by protective imagery (Hollan, 2009; Reiser, 2001). Our behavior in dreams is also generally consistent with our waking behavior. Most dreams, then, are unlikely candidates for the expression of repressed urges (even disguised). A person who leads a moral life tends to dream moral dreams.

THE ACTIVATION–SYNTHESIS MODEL OF DREAMS There are also biological views of the "meanings" of dreams. According to the **activation–synthesis model**, acetylcholine (a neurotransmitter) and the pons (a structure in the lower part of the brain) stimulate responses that lead to dreaming (Hobson, 2003, 2009; Stuart & Conduit, 2009). One effect is *activation* of the *reticular formation*, which arouses us, but not to waking. During the waking state, firing of these cells in the reticular formation is linked to movement, particularly the movements involved in walking, running, and other physical acts. During REM sleep, however, neurotransmitters generally inhibit activity, so we usually do not thrash about as we dream (Stuart & Conduit,

2009). In this way, we save ourselves (and our bed partners) some wear and tear. But the eye muscles are stimulated and thus show the rapid eye movement associated with dreaming. The reticular formation also stimulates neural activity in the parts of the cortex involved in memory. The cortex then *synthesizes,* or puts together, these sources of stimulation to some degree to yield the stuff of dreams. Yet research with the PET scan shows that the frontal lobes of the brain, which seem to be where we make sense of experience, are relatively inactive during sleep (Wade, 1998). Dreams are therefore more likely to be emotionally gripping than coherent in plot.

DREAMS AS HELPING US CONSOLIDATE MEMORIES Another view of dreams is that with the brain cut off from the world outside, learning experiences and memories are replayed and consolidated during sleep, although the evidence for this hypothesis is somewhat contradictory (Siegel, 2009). This view finds support in research showing a neural "replaying" of recent waking patterns of neural activity in the hippocampus (Zhang, 2009).

There may be no absolute agreement on the origins of the functions of sleep or the content of dreams, but many—perhaps most—of us either live with or encounter sleep disorders now and then.

Sleep Disorders

Although nightmares are unpleasant, they do not qualify as sleep disorders. The term *sleep disorders* is reserved for other problems that can seriously interfere with our functioning. **Question 7: What kinds of sleep disorders are there?** Some sleep disorders, like insomnia, are all too familiar, experienced by at least half of American adults. Others, like sleep apnea (pauses in breathing), affect as many as one quarter of us (National Sleep Foundation, 2009). In this section, we discuss insomnia and less common sleep disorders: narcolepsy, sleep apnea, and the so-called *deep-sleep disorders*—sleep terrors, bed-wetting, and sleepwalking.

INSOMNIA

I grew up in a family where the question "How'd you sleep?" was a topic of genuine reflection at the breakfast table. My five sisters and I each rated the last night's particular qualities—when we fell asleep, how often we woke, what we dreamed, if we dreamed. My father's response influenced the family's mood for the day: if "lousy," the rest of us felt lousy, too. If there's such a thing as an insomnia gene, Dad passed it on to me, along with his green eyes and Irish melancholy... .

Hayes, 2001, pp. 3–5

According to the National Sleep Foundation (2009), more than half of American adults and about two thirds of older adults are affected by insomnia in any given year. Women complain of insomnia more often than men do (Hale et al., 2009). Table 4.1 ■ shows a number of factors that contribute to insomnia according to gender.

TABLE 4.1 ■ Gender Differences in Factors That Disrupt Sleep

Factor	Percent of women reporting factor	Percent of men reporting factor
Stress (e.g., restlessness, muscle tension): 22% of adults overall	26	20
Pain: 20% of adults overall	25	13
Children: 17% of adults overall	21	12
Partner's snoring: 16% of adults overall	22	7
Pauses in partner's breathing: 8% of adults overall	11	2

Source: Based on data reported by the National Sleep Foundation, 2000b.

"Fatigue is the best pillow."
BENJAMIN FRANKLIN

"Man should forget his anger before he lies down to sleep."
MOHANDAS GANDHI

Truth or Fiction Revisited: It is true that many people have insomnia because they try too hard to fall asleep at night. People with insomnia tend to compound their sleep problems when they try to force themselves to fall asleep. Their concern heightens autonomic activity and muscle tension (Ong et al., 2009). You cannot force or will yourself to go to sleep. You can only set the stage for sleep by lying down and relaxing when you are tired. If you focus on sleep too closely, it will elude you.

You will find strategies for tackling insomnia in the nearby Life Connections feature.

NARCOLEPSY A person with **narcolepsy** falls asleep suddenly and irresistibly. Narcolepsy afflicts as many as 100,000 people in the United States and seems to run in families. The "sleep attack" may last about 15 minutes, after which the person awakens feeling refreshed. Nevertheless, these sleep episodes are dangerous and frightening. They can occur while a person is driving or working with sharp tools. They also may be accompanied by the sudden collapse of muscle groups or even of the entire body—a condition called *sleep paralysis*. In sleep paralysis, the person cannot move during the transition from the waking state to sleep, and hallucinations (such as of a person or object sitting on the chest) occur.

Although the causes are unknown, narcolepsy is thought to be a disorder of REM-sleep functioning. Stimulants and antidepressant drugs have helped many people with narcolepsy (Mamelak, 2009).

SLEEP APNEA Sleep apnea is a dangerous sleep disorder in which the air passages are obstructed. People with sleep apnea stop breathing periodically up to several hundred times per night. Obstruction may cause the sleeper to suddenly sit up and gasp for air before falling back asleep. People with sleep apnea are stimulated nearly, but not quite, to waking by the buildup of carbon dioxide. Sleep apnea is associated with obesity and chronic loud snoring. It is more than a sleep problem. It can lead to high blood pressure, heart attacks, and strokes (Sekizuka et al., 2010).

Causes of sleep apnea include anatomical deformities that clog the air passageways, such as a thick palate, and problems in the breathing centers in the brain. Sleep apnea is treated by such measures as weight loss, surgery, and continuous positive airway pressure (CPAP), which is supplied by a mask that provides air pressure that keeps the airway open during sleep.

Narcolepsy A "sleep attack" in which a person falls asleep suddenly and irresistibly.

Sleep apnea Temporary absence or cessation of breathing while asleep. (From Greek and Latin roots meaning "without" and "breathing.")

Do you have a problem with insomnia? The self-assessment on the previous page titled "Are You Getting Your Z's?" may offer some insight. If you decide that you have this problem, what can you do about it?

No question about it: the most common medical method for getting to sleep in the United States is taking pills (Carney et al., 2010). Sleeping pills may work—for a while. So may tranquilizers. They generally work by reducing arousal and also distract you from trying to get to sleep. Expectations of success may also help.

But there are problems with sleeping pills. First, many people may attribute success to the pill and not to themselves and come to depend on the pill. Second, a person may develop tolerance for many kinds of sleeping pills and, with regular use, need higher doses to achieve the same effects. Third, high doses of these chemicals can be dangerous, especially if mixed with alcohol. Fourth, sleeping pills do not enhance your skills at handling insomnia. Thus, when you stop taking them, insomnia is likely to return (Carney et al., 2010).

There are excellent psychological methods for coping with insomnia, which can be effective alternatives for many. Some methods like muscle relaxation exercises reduce tension directly. Psychological methods also divert us from the task of trying somehow to get to sleep, which, ironically, is one of the ways we keep ourselves awake (Carney et al., 2010). You can try any or all of the following psychological methods:

- *Relax:* Take a hot bath at bedtime or try meditating. Releasing muscle tension has been shown to reduce the amount of time needed to fall asleep and the incidence of waking up during the night (Ashworth et al., 2010; Ebben & Spielman, 2009).

- *Challenge exaggerated fears:* You need not be a sleep expert to realize that convincing yourself the day will be ruined unless you get to sleep *right now* may increase, rather than decrease, bedtime tension. However, cognitive–behavioral psychologists note that we often exaggerate the problems that will befall us if we do not sleep (Carney et al., 2010; Kaplan et al., 2009). Table 4.2 ■ shows some beliefs that increase bedtime tension and some alternatives.

- *Don't ruminate in bed:* Don't plan or worry about tomorrow while in bed (Kaplan et al., 2009). When you lie down for sleep, you may organize your thoughts for the next day for a few minutes, but then allow yourself to relax or engage in a soothing fantasy. If an important idea comes to you, jot it down on a handy pad so that you won't worry about forgetting

TABLE 4.2 ■ Beliefs That Increase Bedtime Tension and Alternatives

Beliefs that Increase Tension	Alternatives
If I don't get to sleep, I'll feel wrecked tomorrow.	Not necessarily. If I'm tired, I can go to bed early tomorrow night.
It's unhealthy for me not to get more sleep.	Not necessarily. Some people do very well on only a few hours of sleep.
I'll wreck my sleeping schedule for the whole week if I don't get to sleep very soon.	Not at all. If I'm tired, I'll just go to bed a bit earlier. I'll get up about the same time with no problem.
If I don't get to sleep, I won't be able to concentrate on that big test/conference tomorrow.	Possibly, but my fears may be exaggerated. I may just as well relax or get up and do something enjoyable for a while.

it. If thoughts or inspirations persist, however, get up and think about them elsewhere. Let your bed be a place for relaxation and sleep—not your second office. A bed—even a waterbed—should not be a think tank.

- *Establish a regular routine:* Sleeping late can end up causing problems falling asleep (sleep-onset insomnia). Set your alarm for the same time each morning and get up regardless of how long you have slept (Ebben & Spielman, 2009). By rising at a regular time, you'll encourage yourself to fall asleep at a regular time.

- *Try fantasy:* Fantasies or daydreams are almost universal and may occur naturally as we fall asleep. You can allow yourself to "go with" soothing, relaxing fantasies that occur at bedtime, or purposefully use pleasant fantasies to get to sleep. You may be able to ease yourself to sleep, for example, by focusing on a sun-drenched beach with waves lapping on the shore or on a walk through a mountain meadow on a summer day. You can construct your own "mind trips" and paint in the details.

Above all: Accept the idea that it really doesn't matter if you don't get to sleep early *this night.* You will survive. In fact, you'll do just fine.

SLEEP TERRORS It typically begins with a loud, piercing cry or scream in the night. Even the most soundly sleeping parents will be summoned to children's bedrooms as if shot from a cannon. Children (most cases involve children) may be sitting up, appearing frightened and showing signs of extreme arousal—profusely sweating with rapid heartbeat and respiration. They may start talking incoherently or thrash about wildly but remain asleep. If the children awaken fully, they may not recognize their parent or may attempt to push their parent away. After a few minutes, they fall back into a deep sleep and, upon awakening in the morning, remember nothing of the experience. These terrifying attacks are called **sleep terrors**.

Sleep terrors Frightening dreamlike experiences that occur during the deepest stage of NREM sleep. Nightmares, in contrast, occur during REM sleep.

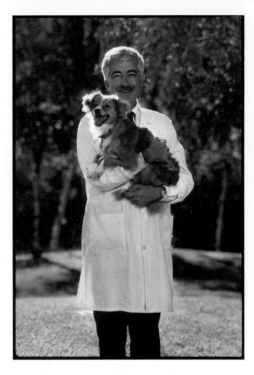

Narcolepsy In an experiment on narcolepsy, the dog barks, nods its head, and then falls suddenly asleep.

Sleep terrors occur during deep (stage 3 or 4) sleep, are more common among children, and may reflect immaturity of the nervous system (Kotagal, 2009; Nir & Tononi, 2010). Sleep terrors are similar to, but more severe than, nightmares. They usually occur during deep sleep, whereas nightmares take place during REM sleep. Sleep terrors usually occur during the first two sleep cycles of the night, whereas nightmares are more likely to occur during later sleep cycles. Although people experiencing sleep terrors may suddenly sit up, they are never fully awake, return to sleep, and may recall a vague image as of someone pressing on their chest. (Memories of nightmares tend to be more vivid.) Sleep terrors are often decreased by taking a minor tranquilizer at bedtime. The drug reduces the amount of time spent in stage 4 sleep.

BED-WETTING Bed-wetting also occurs during deep sleep. It is often seen as a stigma that reflects parental harshness or children's attempt to punish their parents, but this disorder, too, may stem from immaturity of the nervous system. In most cases, it resolves itself before adolescence, often by age 8. Behavior-therapy methods that condition children to awaken when they are about to urinate have been helpful (E. C. Jackson, 2009). The drug imipramine often helps, although the reason for its effectiveness is not fully understood. Sometimes, all that is needed is reassurance that no one is to blame for bed-wetting and that most children outgrow it.

SLEEP TALKING AND SLEEPWALKING

> All five of my sisters remember me as the family sleepwalker. [My sister] Shannon recalls helping Mom fold clothes in the den late one night when I appeared. Perhaps it was the fragrant smell of laundry, like incense, that drew me.
>
> Hayes, 2001, p. 99

Perhaps half of all children occasionally talk in their sleep. Surveys suggest that some 7% to 15% walk in their sleep (Cotton & Richdale, 2010; Li et al., 2009). Only about 2% of a random sample of nearly 5,000 people aged 15 to 100 did so (Ohayon et al., 1999). Sleepwalkers may roam about almost nightly while their parents fret about the accidents that could befall them. Sleepwalkers typically do not remember their excursions, although they may respond to questions while they are up and about.

Truth or Fiction Revisited: Contrary to myth, there is no evidence that sleepwalkers become violent if they are awakened, although they may be confused and upset. Mild tranquilizers and maturity typically put an end to sleepwalking.

> *"Some people talk in their sleep. Lecturers talk while other people sleep."*
>
> ALBERT CAMUS

© Louie Psihoyos/Science Faction/Corbis

● ALTERING CONSCIOUSNESS THROUGH HYPNOSIS, MEDITATION, AND BIOFEEDBACK

Perhaps you have seen films in which Count Dracula hypnotized resistant victims into a stupor. Then he could give them a bite in the neck with no further nonsense. Perhaps you have watched a fellow student try to place a friend in a "trance" after reading a book on hypnosis. Or perhaps you have seen an audience member hypnotized in a nightclub act. If so, chances are the person acted as if he or she had returned to childhood, imagined that a snake was about to have a nip, or lay rigid between two chairs for a while. In this section, we deal with what have been referred to as some of the "oddities" of psychology: hypnosis, meditation, and biofeedback. Each of these is an *altered state of consciousness* because they involve focusing on stimuli that are not common parts of our daily lives.

Hypnosis: On Being Entranced

Of these altered states, perhaps the one we hear of most is hypnosis. **Question 8: What is hypnosis? Hypnosis,** a term derived from the Greek word for "sleep," is an altered state of consciousness in which people appear to be highly suggestible and behave as though they are in a trance. Hypnosis has only recently become a respectable subject for psychological inquiry. Modern hypnosis evolved from the ideas of Franz Mesmer in the 18th century. Mesmer asserted that everything in the universe was connected by forms of magnetism—which actually may not be far from the mark. However, he incorrectly claimed that people, too, could be drawn to one another by "animal magnetism." (No bull's-eye here.) Mesmer used bizarre props to bring people under his "spell" and managed a respectable cure rate for minor ailments. Scientists now attribute his successes to the placebo effect, not to animal magnetism.

Today, hypnotism retains its popularity in nightclubs, but it is also used as an anesthetic in dentistry, childbirth, and various medical procedures, even surgery (Vanhaudenhuyse et al., 2009). Some psychologists use hypnosis to teach clients how to reduce anxiety or overcome fears (Dufresne et al., 2009). A study with 241 surgery patients in a Boston hospital shows how hypnosis can help people deal with pain and anxiety. The patients underwent procedures that used only local anesthetics (Lang et al., 2000). They could use as much pain medication as they desired by means of an intravenous tube. Patients who were hypnotized during these procedures needed less additional medication for pain and experienced less anxiety as measured by blood pressure and heart rate. The hypnotized patients focused on pleasant imagery rather than the details of the surgery.

Hypnosis as an aid in relaxation training also helps people cope with stress and enhances the functioning of their immune systems (Jensen et al., 2009; Kiecolt-Glaser et al., 2001). Research also shows that hypnosis can be a useful supplement to other

"Why do we love to change our consciousness, our appreciation and feelings about the world around us? We drink, we smoke, we do lattes, we seek painkillers, we may even get runner's high. We are always tampering with an aspect of our existence we still can't define: phenomenal conscious experience."

MICHAEL S. GAZZANIGA

Hypnosis An altered state of consciousness in which people appear to be highly suggestible and behave as though they are in a trance.

forms of therapy, especially in helping people control their weight and stop smoking (Tønnesen, 2009). The police also use hypnosis to prompt the memories of witnesses.

The state of consciousness called the *hypnotic trance* has traditionally been induced by asking people to narrow their attention to a small light, a spot on the wall, an object held by the hypnotist, or the hypnotist's voice. The hypnotist usually suggests that the person's limbs are becoming warm, heavy, and relaxed. People may also be told that they are becoming sleepy or falling asleep. Hypnosis is *not* sleep, however. This is shown by differences between EEG recordings for the hypnotic trance and the stages of sleep. But the word *sleep* is used with subjects because it is understood by them to suggest a hypnotic trance. It is also possible to induce hypnosis through instructions that direct subjects to remain active and alert (De Vos & Louw, 2009). So the effects of hypnosis probably cannot be attributed to relaxation. The key appears to be that the induction procedure encourages the subject to cooperate with the hypnotist (Barber, 2000).

People who are readily hypnotized are said to have *hypnotic suggestibility*. Part of "suggestibility" is knowledge of what is expected during the "trance state." Generally speaking, suggestible people are prone to fantasy, can compartmentalize unwanted memories, and want to cooperate with the hypnotist (Dienes et al., 2009). As a result, they pay close attention to the hypnotist's instructions. **Truth or Fiction Revisited:** It is therefore extremely unlikely that someone could be hypnotized against his or her will. However, in a nightclub act, the social pressure of the audience may further encourage the subject to play along with the suggestions of the hypnotist (Barber, 2000). Hypnotists and people who have been hypnotized report that hypnosis can bring about the changes shown in Table 4.3 ■.

TABLE 4.3 ■ Changes in Consciousness Attributed to Hypnosis[a]

Change	Comments
Passivity	Awaiting instructions and suspending planning.
Narrowed attention	Focusing on the hypnotist's voice or a spot of light and not attending to background noise or intruding thoughts.
Pseudomemories and hypermnesia	Reporting pseudomemories (false memories) or highly detailed memories (hypermnesia). Police hypnotists attempt to heighten witnesses' memories by instructing them to focus on details of a crime and reconstruct the scene. Some studies challenge the accuracies of such memories.
Suggestibility	Responding to suggestions that an arm is becoming lighter and will rise or that the eyelids are becoming heavier and must close.
Playing unusual roles	Playing roles calling for increased strength or alertness, such as riding a bicycle with less fatigue than usual. In *age regression,* people may play themselves as infants or children. A person may speak a language forgotten since childhood.
Perceptual distortions	Acting as though hypnotically induced hallucinations and delusions are real. Behaving as though one cannot hear loud noises, smell odors, or feel pain.
Posthypnotic amnesia	Acting as though one cannot recall events that took place under hypnosis.
Posthypnotic suggestion	Following commands given "under" hypnosis after one "awakens," such as falling quickly into a deep trance when given the command "Sleep!" or—in the case of a would-be quitter of smoking—finding cigarette smoke aversive.

[a]Research evidence in support of these changes in consciousness is mixed.
Sources: Barber, 2000; Lynn et al., 2008.

THEORETICAL VIEWS OF HYPNOSIS Hypnotism is no longer explained in terms of animal magnetism, but psychodynamic and learning theorists have offered explanations. According to Freud, hypnotized adults permit themselves to return to childish modes of responding that emphasize fantasy and impulse rather than fact and logic. Modern views of hypnosis are quite different. **Question 9: How do modern psychologists explain the effects of hypnosis?** Role, multifactorial, response set, and neodissociation theories, described as follows, have been proposed.

ROLE THEORY Theodore Sarbin offers a *role theory* view of hypnosis (Lynn et al. 2008; Sarbin & Coe, 1972). He points out that the changes in behavior attributed to the hypnotic trance can be successfully imitated when people are instructed to behave as though they are hypnotized. For example, people can lie rigid between two chairs whether they are hypnotized or not. Also, people cannot be hypnotized unless they are familiar with the hypnotic "role"—the behavior that constitutes the so-called trance. Sarbin is not saying that subjects fake the hypnotic role. Research evidence suggests that most people who are hypnotized are not faking (Lynn et al., 2008). Instead, Sarbin is suggesting that people allow themselves to enact this role under the hypnotist's directions.

MULTIFACTORIAL THEORY Nichola Spanos's *multifactorial theory* focuses on factors such as the beliefs, attitudes, imaginings, and expectancies of the person being hypnotized in the shaping of hypnotic behavior (Lynn et al., 2008). Spanos used the term *strategic role enactment* to explain how people transform their thoughts and feelings into behavior that is consistent with their view of how a "good" hypnotized subject should behave.

RESPONSE SET THEORY The *response set theory* of hypnosis is closely related to role theory and multifactorial theory. It suggests that response expectancies (the things we know we are expected to do) play a key role in the production of personal experiences and also in experiences suggested by the hypnotist (Lynn et al., 2008). Response set theory focuses on the ways that a positive response to each suggestion of the hypnotist sets the stage—creates a *response set*—in which the subject is more likely to follow subsequent suggestions.

NEODISSOCIATION THEORY Runners frequently get through the pain and tedium of long-distance races by *dissociating*—by imagining themselves elsewhere doing other things. (My students inform me that they manage the pain and tedium of *other* instructors' classes in the same way.) Ernest Hilgard (1904–2001) similarly explained hypnotic phenomena through *neodissociation theory* (Dell, 2010; Hilgard, 1994). This is the view that we can selectively focus our attention on one thing (like hypnotic suggestions) and dissociate ourselves from the things going on around us.

Although hypnotized people may be focusing on the hypnotist's suggestions and perhaps imagining themselves to be somewhere else, they still tend to perceive their actual surroundings peripherally. In a sense, we do this all the time. We are not fully conscious, or aware, of everything going on around us. Rather, at any given moment, we selectively focus on events such as tests, dates, or television shows that seem important or relevant.

Role theory, multifactorial theory, response set theory, and neodissociation theory do not suggest that the phenomena of hypnosis are phony. Instead, they suggest that we do not need to explain these events through an altered state of awareness called a trance. **Truth or Fiction Revisited:** It has not been shown that the effects of hypnotism are due to a special trance state. Role theory, multifactorial theory, and response set theory appear to be supported by research evidence that suggestible people want to be hypnotized, are good role players, have vivid and absorbing imaginations, and also know what is expected of them (Cavallaro et al., 2010; Lynn et al., 2008). Neodissociation theory offers still another explanation, but again, does not support the idea of a trance state.

One Type of Hypnotic Induction What is hypnotic suggestibility? Do you have it?

Meditation: On Letting the World Fade Away

Question 10: What is meditation? The dictionary defines *meditation* as the act or process of thinking. But the concept usually suggests thinking deeply about the universe or about one's place in the world, often within a spiritual context. As the term is commonly used by psychologists, however, meditation refers to various ways of focusing one's consciousness to alter one's relationship to the world. As used by psychologists, ironically, *meditation* can also refer to a process in which people seem to suspend thinking and allow the world to "fade away" from their consciousness.

Thus, the kinds of meditation that psychologists and other kinds of helping professionals speak of are *not* the first definition you find in the dictionary. Rather, they tend to refer to rituals, exercises, and even passive observation—activities that alter the normal relationship between the person and her or his environment. They are various methods of suspending problem solving, planning, worries, and awareness of the events of the day. These methods alter consciousness—that is, the normal focus of attention—and help people cope with stress by inducing feelings of relaxation.

The Effects of Meditation Meditation has been shown to lower blood pressure and induce other bodily changes associated with relaxation.

Let's consider one common form of meditation. **Transcendental meditation (TM)** is a simplified form of Far Eastern meditation that was brought to the United States by the Maharishi Mahesh Yogi in 1959. Hundreds of thousands of Americans practice TM by repeating and concentrating on *mantras*—words or sounds that are claimed to help the person achieve an altered state of consciousness. Transcendental meditation has a number of goals that cannot be assessed scientifically, such as expanding consciousness so that it encompasses spiritual experiences, but there are also measurable goals, such as reducing anxiety and normalizing blood pressure.

Question 11: What are the effects of meditation? In early research, Herbert Benson (1975) found that TM lowered the heart and respiration rates and also produced what he labeled a *relaxation response* (A. Taylor et al., 2010). The blood pressure of people with hypertension—a risk factor in cardiovascular disease—decreased. In fact, people who meditated twice daily tended to show more normal blood pressure through the day. Meditators produced more frequent alpha waves—brain waves associated with feelings of relaxation. Meditation has been shown to increase nighttime concentrations of the hormone melatonin, which is relaxing and helps people get to sleep (Rubia, 2009). Research in brain imaging has shown that meditation activates neural structures involved in attention and control of the autonomic nervous system as well, helping produce feelings of relaxation (Rubia, 2009).

Biofeedback: On Getting in Touch with the Untouchable

Let's begin our discussion of biofeedback by recounting some remarkable experiments in which psychologist Neal E. Miller (1909–2002) trained laboratory rats to increase or decrease their heart rates. His procedure was simple but ingenious. As discovered by psychologists James Olds and Peter Milner (1954), there is a "pleasure center" in the rat's hypothalamus. A small burst of electricity in this center is strongly reinforcing: rats learn to do what they can, such as pressing a lever, to obtain this stimulus.

N. E. Miller (1969) implanted electrodes in the rats' pleasure centers. Then some rats were given a burst of electricity in their brain's pleasure center (that is, rewarded) whenever their heart rate happened to increase. Other rats received the stimulus when their heart rate decreased. After a single 90-minute training session, the rats learned to alter their heart rates by as much as 20% in the direction for which they had been rewarded. **Truth or Fiction Revisited:** It is true that you can teach a rat to raise or lower its heart rate.

Transcendental meditation (TM) The simplified form of meditation brought to the United States by the Maharishi Mahesh Yogi and used as a method for coping with stress.

Biofeedback training (BFT) The systematic feeding back to an organism information about a bodily function so that the organism can gain control of that function.

Miller's research was an early example of **biofeedback training (BFT)**. **Question 12: What is biofeedback training?** Biofeedback is a system that provides, or "feeds back," information about a bodily function. Miller used electrical stimulation of the brain to feed back information to rats when they had engaged in a targeted bodily response (in this case, raised or lowered their heart rates). Somehow, the rats then used this information to raise or lower their heart rates voluntarily.

Similarly, people have learned to change various bodily functions voluntarily, including heart rate, that were once considered beyond their control. However, electrodes are not implanted in people's brains. Rather, people hear a "blip" or observe some other signal that informs them when the targeted response is being displayed.

Question 13: How is biofeedback training used? Biofeedback training has been used in many ways, including helping people combat stress, tension, and anxiety. For example, people can learn to emit alpha waves (and feel somewhat more relaxed) through feedback from an EEG. A blip may increase in frequency whenever alpha waves are being emitted. The psychologist's instructions are simply to "make the blip go faster." An **electromyograph (EMG)** monitors muscle tension. The EMG can be used to help paralyzed people who have lost afferent but not efferent nerves to limbs regain some control over those limbs. The EMG is also commonly used to help people become more aware of muscle tension in the forehead, fingers, and elsewhere and to learn to lower the tension (Pluess et al., 2009). Through the use of other instruments, people have learned to lower their heart rate, their blood pressure, and the amount of sweat in the palm of the hand (Greenhalgh et al., 2010). All of these changes are relaxing. Biofeedback is also widely used by sports psychologists to teach athletes how to relax muscle groups that are unessential to the task at hand so that they can control anxiety and tension.

Sleep, hypnosis, meditation, and biofeedback training all involve "natural" ways of deploying our attention or consciousness. Some altered states depend on the ingestion of psychoactive chemical substances we call "drugs." Let's now deploy our attention to the effects of alcohol and other drugs.

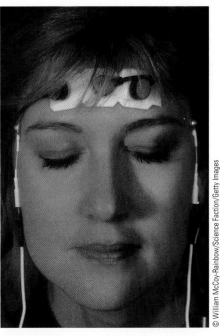

Biofeedback Biofeedback is a system that provides, or "feeds back," information about a bodily function to an organism. Through biofeedback training, people have learned to gain voluntary control over a number of functions that are normally automatic, such as heart rate and blood pressure.

LearningConnections • ALTERING CONSCIOUSNESS THROUGH HYPNOSIS, MEDITATION, AND BIOFEEDBACK

ACTIVE REVIEW (8) Hypnosis typically brings about the following changes in consciousness: passivity, narrowed attention, _____ (detailed memory), suggestibility, assumption of unusual roles, perceptual distortions, posthypnotic amnesia, and posthypnotic suggestion. (9) According to _____ set theory, knowledge of what one is expected to do is a key component of being hypnotized. (10) In meditation, one focuses passively on a _____ to alter the normal person–environment relationship. (11) Neal Miller taught rats to increase or decrease their _____ rates by giving them an electric shock in their so-called pleasure centers when they performed the targeted response.

REFLECT AND RELATE Has anybody ever tried to hypnotize you or someone you know? How did she or he do it? What were the results? How do the results fit with the theories of hypnosis discussed in this section?

CRITICAL THINKING Is it possible to explain the behavior of the rats in Miller's research on biofeedback by referring to what the animals were "thinking" when they learned to increase or decrease their heart rates? Explain.

 Go to Psychology CourseMate at **www.cengagebrain.com** for an interactive version of these questions.

ALTERING CONSCIOUSNESS THROUGH DRUGS

The world is a supermarket of **psychoactive substances**, or drugs. The United States is flooded with drugs that distort perceptions and change mood—drugs that take you up, let you down, and move you across town. Some of these drugs are legal, others illegal. Some are used recreationally, others medically. Some are safe if used correctly and dangerous if they are not. Some people use drugs because their friends do or because their

Electromyograph (EMG) An instrument that measures muscle tension.

Psychoactive substances Drugs that have psychological effects such as stimulation or distortion of perceptions.

135

"I can get prescription drugs from different places and don't ever have to see a doctor ... I have friends whose parents are pill addicts, and we "borrow" from them. Other times I have friends who have ailments who get lots of pills and sell them for cheap. As long as prescription pills are taken right, they're much safer than street drugs."

A HIGH SCHOOL STUDENT, CITED IN FRIEDMAN, 2006, P. 1448

Depressant A drug that lowers the rate of activity of the nervous system.

Stimulant A drug that increases the rate of activity of the nervous system.

Substance abuse Repeated use of a substance despite the fact that it is causing or compounding social, occupational, psychological, or physical problems.

Substance dependence Loss of control over use of a substance. Biologically speaking, dependence is typified by tolerance, withdrawal symptoms, or both.

© Noble Stock/Jupiterimages

parents tell them not to. Some are seeking pleasure; others are seeking inner truth or escape.

For better or worse, drugs are part of American life. Young people often become involved with drugs that impair their ability to learn at school and are connected with reckless behavior (Pani et al., 2009). Alcohol is the most popular drug on high school and college campuses (Johnston et al., 2010). More than one in six people of college age smokes marijuana regularly (Johnston et al., 2010). Many Americans take **depressants** to get to sleep at night and **stimulants** to get going in the morning. Karl Marx charged that "religion … is the opium of the people," but heroin is the real "opium of the people." Cocaine was once a toy of the well-to-do, but price breaks have brought it into the lockers of high school students.

Truth or Fiction Revisited: Substance use and abuse among high school students seems to be experiencing a slight decline in the early years of the 21st century. Ongoing surveys of high school students by the Institute of Social Research at the University of Michigan find that the use of illicit drugs by students in 8th through 12th grade has generally declined over the past few decades (Johnston et al., 2010).

How widespread is substance abuse among adolescents? Table 4.4 ■ compares self-reported substance abuse in 1999 with that in 2009 for 12th graders. There was a decline in the use of (any) illicit drug during the past 30 days (an index of regular use) from about 26% to a bit more than 23% among 12th graders.

The incidence of use of some drugs was relatively high: alcohol, cigarettes (nicotine is the drug in cigarettes), and marijuana. Some drugs have been used by fewer than 10% of 12th graders: MDMA (ecstasy), cocaine, LSD, steroids, PCP, and heroin. Perhaps the most heartening news in the survey results is that messages about the dangers of cigarette smoking have apparently been getting through to youngsters. In 2009, only about one in five 12th graders (20.1%) reported that they smoked cigarettes in the last month, as compared with more than one in three 12th graders (34.6%) in 1999. **Truth or Fiction Revisited:** It is not true that more 12th graders smoke cigarettes than marijuana. Although use of both substances has declined over the past decade, we have actually arrived at the point where more 12th graders use marijuana than cigarettes made of tobacco.

Table 4.5 ■ shows that about one in five young adults (aged 19–30) reports having used an illicit drug in the past 30 days, with men more likely than women to report such use. (Men are more likely than women to report the use of all drugs in Table 4.5, with the exception on amphetamines and sedatives.) As among 12th graders, the most commonly reported illicit drug is marijuana. Three male young adults in four (74.3%) and two women in three (66.8%) have used alcohol in the past 30 days, and nearly half of men (46.1%) have engaged in binge drinking (having five or more drinks in a row), as compared with three in ten women (29.4%).

Substance Abuse and Dependence: Crossing the Line

Where does drug use end and abuse begin? **Question 14: What are substance abuse and dependence?** The American Psychiatric Association (2000) defines **substance abuse** as repeated use of a substance despite the fact that it is causing or compounding social, occupational, psychological, or physical problems. If you are missing school or work because you are drunk or "sleeping it off," you are abusing alcohol. The amount you drink is not as crucial as the fact that your pattern of use disrupts your life. Binge drinking, for example, is abusive because it has been associated with health problems such as heart failure and inter-personal problems such as rape (McCauley et al., 2010; Zagrosek et al., 2010).

Substance dependence is more severe than substance abuse, having both behavioral and biological aspects (American Psychiatric Association, 2000). Behaviorally, dependence is often characterized by loss of control over one's use of the substance. Dependent people may organize their lives around getting and using a substance. Biological or physiological dependence is typified by tolerance, withdrawal symptoms, or

TABLE 4.4 ■ Percentage of 12th Graders Using Various Substances During the Past 30 Days

	1999	2009
Any illicit drug	25.9	23.3
Marijuana	26.4[a]	24.1[a]
Other hallucinogens	3.5	1.6
Ecstasy	2.5	1.8
Cocaine	2.6	1.3
Heroin	0.5	0.4
Narcotics other than heroin	2.6	4.1[b]
Amphetamines	4.5	3.0
Sedatives (barbiturates)	2.6	2.5
Tranquilizers	2.5	2.7
Alcohol	51.0	43.5
Cigarettes (daily usage)	34.6	20.1
Steroids	0.9	1.0

[a]Self-reported marijuana use exceeds self-reported use of "any illicit drug," possibly because of misunderstanding as to what the word "illicit" means.

[b]Increased use of narcotics other than heroin partly involves increased use of the painkillers Vicodin and OxyContin.

Source: Johnston, L. D., O'Malley, P. M., Bachman, J. G., & Schulenberg, J. E. (2010). *Monitoring the Future national survey results on drug use, 1975–2009. Volume II: College students and adults ages 19–50* (NIH Publication No. 10-7585). Bethesda, MD: National Institute on Drug Abuse, Table 2.3, pp. 50–54.

"The chains of habit are too weak to be felt until they are too strong to be broken."

DR. SAMUEL JOHNSON

both. **Tolerance** is the body's habituation to a substance so that, with regular usage, higher doses are required to achieve similar effects. There are characteristic withdrawal symptoms, or an **abstinence syndrome**, when the level of usage suddenly drops off. The abstinence syndrome for alcohol includes anxiety, tremors, restlessness, weakness, rapid pulse, and high blood pressure.

When living without a drug, people who are *psychologically* dependent show signs of anxiety (such as shakiness, rapid pulse, and sweating) that may be similar to

Tolerance Habituation to a drug, with the result that increasingly higher doses of the drug are needed to achieve similar effects.

Abstinence syndrome A characteristic cluster of symptoms that results from a sudden decrease in an addictive drug's level of usage.

TABLE 4.5 ■ Percentage of 19–30-Year-Olds Using Various Substances During the Past 30 Days

	Males	Females
Any illicit drug	22.1	17.1
Marijuana	20.1	13.7
Other hallucinogens	1.0	0.5
Ecstasy	0.8	0.5
Cocaine	2.3	1.4
Heroin	0.4	0.1
Narcotics other than heroin	3.4	3.2
Amphetamines	2.2	2.4
Sedatives (barbiturates)	1.1	1.2
Tranquilizers	3.0	2.7
Alcohol	74.3	66.8
5+ drinks in a row (in last 2 weeks)	46.1	29.4
Cigarettes (daily usage)	16.7	14.4
Steroids	0.4	0.1

Source: Johnston, L. D., O'Malley, P. M., Bachman, J. G., & Schulenberg, J. E. (2010). *Monitoring the Future national survey results on drug use, 1975–2009. Volume II: College students and adults ages 19–50* (NIH Publication No. 10-7585). Bethesda, MD: National Institute on Drug Abuse, Table 4.1, pp. 88–90.

abstinence syndromes. Because of these signs, they may believe that they are physiologically dependent on—or addicted to—a drug when they are actually psychologically dependent. But symptoms of abstinence from some drugs are unmistakably physiological. One symptom is *delirium tremens* ("the DTs") experienced by some chronic alcoholics when they suddenly lower their intake of alcohol. The DTs are characterized by heavy sweating, restlessness, general disorientation, and terrifying hallucinations—often of crawling animals.

Causal Factors in Substance Abuse and Dependence

Question 15: What are the causes of substance abuse and dependence? Substance abuse and dependence usually begin with experimental use in adolescence (Marlatt, 2010; Schulte et al., 2009). People experiment with drugs for various reasons, including curiosity, conformity to peer pressure, parental use, rebelliousness, escape from boredom or pressure, and the seeking of excitement or pleasure (T. T. Clark, 2010; Lindgren et al., 2009; Yang et al., 2009; Zilberman, 2009). People commonly try tranquilizing agents such as Valium (the generic name is diazepam) and alcohol on the basis of a recommendation or observation of others. Use of a substance may be reinforced by peers or by the drug's positive effects on mood and its reduction of unpleasant sensations such as anxiety, fear, and stress. Many people use drugs as a form of self-medication for anxiety and depression and even for feelings of low self-esteem.

For people who are physiologically dependent, avoidance of withdrawal symptoms is also reinforcing. Carrying a supply of the substance is reinforcing because one need not worry about going without it.

People may have a genetic predisposition toward physiological dependence on various substances, including alcohol, opioids, cocaine, and nicotine (Agrawal et al., 2009; Dick et al., 2009; Farrer et al., 2009; Kuo et al., 2010). For example, the biological children of alcoholics who are reared by adoptive parents seem more likely to develop alcohol-related problems than the natural children of the adoptive parents. An inherited tendency toward alcoholism may involve greater sensitivity to alcohol (that is, greater enjoyment of it) and greater tolerance of it (Radcliffe et al., 2009). College students with alcoholic parents exhibit better muscular control and visual–motor coordination when they drink than do college students whose parents are not alcoholics. They also feel less intoxicated when they drink (Pihl et al., 1990).

Now that we have learned about substance abuse and dependence, let's turn to a discussion of the different kinds of psychoactive drugs. Some are depressants, others stimulants, and still others hallucinogenics.

© Blend Images Photography/Veer

Why Do Young People Turn to Drugs? Some are bored, some are following recommendations of peers, some are experimenting, and others are rebelling.

"Wine is constant proof that God loves us and loves to see us happy."

BENJAMIN FRANKLIN

Depressants

Depressant drugs generally act by slowing the activity of the central nervous system. There are also effects that are specific to each depressant drug. In this section, we consider the effects of alcohol, opiates, and barbiturates.

ALCOHOL—THE SWISS ARMY KNIFE OF PSYCHOACTIVE SUBSTANCES

No drug has meant so much to so many as alcohol. Alcohol is our dinnertime relaxant, our bedtime sedative, our cocktail-party social facilitator. We use alcohol to celebrate holy days, applaud our accomplishments, and express joyous wishes. The young assert their maturity with alcohol. Alcohol is used with at least some regularity by the majority of college students and adults (Johnston et al., 2010). Alcohol even kills germs on surface wounds.

People use alcohol like a Swiss Army knife. It does it all. Alcohol is the all-purpose medicine you can buy without prescription. It is the relief from anxiety, depression, or loneliness that you can swallow in public without criticism or stigma. A man who takes a Valium tablet may look weak. A man who downs a bottle of beer may be perceived as "macho."

But the army knife also has a sharp blade. No drug has been so abused as alcohol. There are 10 million to 20 million people with alcoholism in the United States. In contrast, 750,000 to 1 million use heroin regularly, and about 800,000 use cocaine regularly (Johnston et al., 2010). Excessive drinking has been linked to lower productivity, loss of employment, and downward movement in social status. Yet half of all Americans use alcohol regularly.

What about alcohol on campus? A study by the National Institute of Alcohol Abuse and Alcoholism (Hingson et al., 2002) found that about four college students die each day due to alcohol-related causes, another 1,300 to 1,400 have alcohol-related injuries, and nearly 200 are raped by their dates after drinking. *Binge drinking*—defined as having five or more drinks in a row for a male or four or more for a female—is connected with aggressive behavior, poor grades, sexual promiscuity, and serious accidents (McCauley et al., 2010; Randolph et al., 2009; Swartout & White, 2010). About 79,000 accidents per year can be related to binge drinking (Naimi et al., 2010). Nevertheless, nearly half of college men and three in ten college women binge at least twice a month (Johnston et al., 2010). Males are more likely than females to binge, and they tend to drink more than females when they do (Naimi et al., 2010). The media seem to pay more attention to deaths due to heroin and cocaine overdoses, but many more college students die each year from causes related to drinking, including accidents and alcohol overdoses (Hingson et al., 2002; Hustad et al., 2010). Despite widespread marijuana use, alcohol remains the drug of choice among adolescents and adults.

Alcohol Is the Swiss Army Knife of Substances We use it to fight boredom, lubricate social interactions, lower anxieties, erase inhibitions, and celebrate joyous occasions.

Question 16: What are the effects of alcohol? The effects of alcohol vary with the dose and the duration of use. Low doses of alcohol may be stimulating because alcohol dilates blood vessels, which ferry sugars through the body. But higher doses of alcohol have a clear sedative effect, which is why alcohol is classified as a depressant. Alcohol relaxes people and deadens minor aches and pains. Alcohol also intoxicates: it impairs cognitive functioning, slurs the speech, and reduces motor coordination. Alcohol is involved in about half of the fatal automobile accidents in the United States.

Research with rats and humans shows that alcohol lowers inhibitions (Hoffman & Friese, 2008; S. B. Johnson et al., 2010; Lam et al., 2009). Because alcohol lessens inhibitions, drinkers may do things they would not do if they were sober, such as engage in sexual activity or have unprotected sex (Collins et al., 2010; Hoffman & Friese, 2008). When drunk, people may be less able to foresee the consequences of their behavior. They may also be less likely to summon up their moral beliefs. Then, too, alcohol induces feelings of elation and euphoria that may wash away doubts. Alcohol is also associated with a liberated social role in our culture. Drinkers may place the blame on alcohol ("It's the alcohol, not me"), even though they choose to drink.

Adolescent involvement with alcohol has repeatedly been linked to poor school grades and other stressors (Donovan, 2009; Wills et al., 2002). Drinking can, of course, contribute to poor grades and other problems, but adolescents may—ironically—drink to reduce academic and other stresses.

Men are more likely than women to become alcoholics. Why? A cultural explanation is that tighter social constraints are usually placed on women. A biological explanation is that alcohol hits women harder, discouraging them from overindulging. If you have the impression that alcohol "goes to women's heads" more quickly than to men's, you are probably right. Women seem more affected by alcohol because they have less of an enzyme—*aldehyde dehydrogenase*—that metabolizes alcohol in the stomach than men do (M. A. Miller et al., 2009; Oertelt-Prigione & Regitz-Zagrosek, 2009). Thus, alcohol reaches women's bloodstream and brain relatively intact. Women metabolize it mainly in the liver. According to one health professional, for women "drinking alcohol has the same effect as injecting it intravenously" (Lieber, 1990). Strong stuff indeed.

Levels of aldehyde dehydrogenase are also associated with levels of drinking in some ethnic groups. Asians and Asian Americans, who have lower levels of aldehyde dehydrogenase than Europeans do, are more likely than Europeans and European Americans to show a "flushing response" to alcohol, as evidenced by redness of the face, rapid heart rate, dizziness, and headaches (Kawano, 2010). Such sensitivity to alcohol may inhibit immoderate drinking among Asian Americans as well as women in general.

Culture is also connected with alcohol abuse. Native Americans and Irish Americans have the highest rates of alcoholism in the United States. Jewish Americans have relatively low rates, a fact for which a cultural explanation is usually offered. Jewish Americans tend to expose children to alcohol (wine) early in life, but they do so within a strong family or religious context. Wine is offered in small quantities, with consequent low blood alcohol levels. Alcohol therefore is not connected with rebellion, aggression, or failure in Jewish culture.

Regardless of how or why one starts drinking, regular drinking can lead to physiological dependence. People are then motivated to drink to avoid withdrawal symptoms. Still, even when alcoholics have "dried out"—withdrawn from alcohol—many return to drinking (Schuckit, 1996). Perhaps they still want to use alcohol as a way of coping with stress or as an excuse for failure (Laucht et al., 2009).

© Blend Images Photography/Veer

Women and Alcohol Women have less of an enzyme—aldehyde dehydrogenase—that metabolizes alcohol in the stomach than men do. Therefore, alcohol "goes to their heads" more quickly. Asians also have less of the enzyme than Europeans do, placing them at increased risk of a "flushing response" when they drink.

IS A DRINK A DAY GOOD FOR YOU? The effects of alcohol on health are complex. Light drinking can be beneficial. One effect of having a drink or two a day is to increase levels of high-density lipoprotein (HDL, or "good" cholesterol) in the bloodstream and thus decrease the risk of cardiovascular disorders (Mukamal & Rimm, 2008). Another positive effect is cognitive: A study of 400 older adults by researchers at the Institute of Psychiatry in London found that those who had been having a drink a day from before the age of 60 were less likely to see their cognitive abilities decline with age (Cervilla et al., 2000). A drink or two a day may even cut the risk of Alzheimer's disease (Panza et al., 2009). According to the London researchers (Cervilla et al., 2000), the path to positive cognitive results from alcohol may be through the heart: Small doses of alcohol may help maintain a healthful flow of oxygen-laden blood to the brain.

Now for the negative: As a food, alcohol is fattening. Even so, chronic drinkers may be malnourished. Although it is high in calories, alcohol does not contain nutrients such as vitamins and proteins. Moreover, it can interfere with the body's absorption of vitamins, particularly thiamine, a B vitamin. Thus, chronic drinking can lead to a number of disorders such as *cirrhosis of the liver*, which has been linked to protein deficiency, and *Wernicke–Korsakoff syndrome*, which has been linked to vitamin B deficiency. In cirrhosis of the liver, connective fibers replace active liver cells, impeding circulation of the blood. Wernicke–Korsakoff syndrome is a cluster of symptoms associated with

SELF-ASSESSMENT

Do You Have a Problem with Alcohol?

How can you tell whether you have a drinking problem? Answering the following four questions can help you figure it out (National Institute on Alcohol Abuse and Alcoholism, 2005). Just one "yes" answer suggests a possible alcohol problem. Two or more "yes"es make it highly likely that a problem exists. In either case, it is advisable to discuss your answers with your doctor or another health-care provider.

Yes	No	
Yes	No	Have you ever felt you should cut down on your drinking?
Yes	No	Have people annoyed you by criticizing your drinking?
Yes	No	Have you ever felt bad or guilty about your drinking?
Yes	No	Have you ever had a drink first thing in the morning (as an "eye opener") to steady your nerves or get rid of a hangover?

chronic alcohol abuse and characterized by confusion, memory impairment, and filling in gaps in memory with false information (confabulation).

Chronic heavy drinking has been linked to cardiovascular disorders and cancer. In particular, heavy drinking places women at increased risk for breast cancer (S. M. Zhang et al., 2009). Drinking by a pregnant woman may also harm the embryo.

Truth or Fiction Revisited: So, is a drink a day good for you? Apparently, yes (Mukamal & Rimm, 2008). However, most health professionals are reluctant to advise that people drink regularly for fear that they may become physiologically dependent.

In Chapter 13 we discuss the effectiveness of the peer-support group, Alcoholics Anonymous (AA), for treating alcoholism. We will compare AA to professional psychological methods of treating alcoholism. Research is also under way on the use of medicines in treating problem drinking, including naltrexone, nalmefene, acamprosate (unavailable in the United States), and disulfiram. People who take disulfiram experience symptoms such as nausea and vomiting if they drink (De Sousa et al., 2008), but it apparently only decreases the frequency of drinking, thus leading many users to focus on finding ways around it rather than returning to a nonalcoholic lifestyle. Naltrexone and acamprosate are apparently more effective because they reduce the craving for alcohol (Laaksonen et al., 2008).

OPIATES Opiates are a group of **narcotics** that are derived from the opium poppy, from which they obtain their name. **Opioids** are similar in chemical structure but are synthesized in a laboratory. The ancient Sumerians gave the opium poppy its name: it means "plant of joy." Opiates include morphine, heroin, codeine, Demerol (generic name meperidine), and similar drugs. **Question 17: What are the effects of opiates?** The major medical application of this group of drugs is relief from pain.

Heroin can provide a strong euphoric "rush." Users claim that it is so pleasurable it can eradicate any thought of food or sex. Although regular users develop tolerance for heroin, high doses can cause drowsiness and stupor, alter time perception, and impair judgment. With regular use of opiates, such as morphine and heroin, the brain stops producing the neurotransmitters that are chemically similar to opiates—that is, the pain-relieving endorphins. As a result, people can become physiologically dependent on opiates, and going without them can be an agonizing experience. Withdrawal syndromes may begin with flulike symptoms and progress through tremors, cramps, chills alternating with sweating, rapid pulse, high blood pressure, insomnia, vomiting, and diarrhea.

Because of their addictive properties, the nonmedical use of opiates has been criminalized. Penalties for possession or sale are high, so they are also expensive as street drugs. For this reason, many physiologically dependent people support their habit through dealing (selling heroin), prostitution, or selling stolen goods. This information seems to have gotten through to high school students; the great majority disapprove of using heroin (Johnston et al., 2010).

Heroin, by the way, was so named because it made people feel "heroic." **Truth or Fiction Revisited:** It was also hailed as the "hero" that would cure physiological dependence on morphine. In a way, it did: morphine addicts played "musical addictions" and became heroin addicts instead.

Methadone is a synthetic opioid. It has been used to treat physiological dependence on heroin in the same way that heroin was once used to treat physiological dependence on morphine. Methadone is slower acting than heroin and does not provide the thrilling rush, but it does prevent withdrawal symptoms. Some people are maintained on methadone indefinitely (Kakko et al., 2007), and many lead productive lives on methadone.

Prescription opioids can become drugs of abuse when they are used illicitly as street drugs (Friedman, 2006). About 7% of college students have used the prescription opioid Vicodin without a prescription (Srnick, 2007). Among 12th graders, about 5% report using another opioid, OxyContin, and 8% report taking Vicodin (Johnston et al., 2010).

BARBITURATES Question 18: What are the effects of barbiturates? Barbiturates like Nembutal and Seconal are depressants with several medical uses, including relief of anxiety and tension, relief from pain, and treatment of epilepsy, high blood pressure, and insomnia. With regular use, barbiturates lead rapidly to physiological and psychological dependence. Physicians therefore must provide these substances with care.

Opiates A group of narcotics derived from the opium poppy that provide a euphoric rush and depress the nervous system.

Narcotics Drugs used to relieve pain and induce sleep. The term is usually reserved for opiates.

Opioids Chemicals that act on opiate receptors but are not derived from the opium poppy.

Barbiturate An addictive depressant used to relieve anxiety or pain and to treat epilepsy, high blood pressure, and insomnia.

Barbiturates are popular as street drugs because they are relaxing and produce mild euphoria. High doses of barbiturates result in drowsiness, motor impairment, slurred speech, irritability, and poor judgment. A highly physiologically dependent person who is withdrawn abruptly from barbiturates may experience convulsions and die. Because of additive effects, it is dangerous to mix alcohol or other depressants with a barbiturate.

Stimulants

All stimulants increase the activity of the nervous system. Some of their effects can be positive. For example, amphetamines stimulate cognitive activity and apparently help rats (Hadamitzky & Koch, 2009) and humans (Wilner et al., 2009) control impulses. (The depressant alcohol, by contrast, can lower the inhibition of impulses.) Stimulants can be appealing as street drugs because many contribute to feelings of euphoria and self-confidence. But they also have their risks—sometimes quite serious risks. In this section, we discuss amphetamines, cocaine, and nicotine.

Amphetamines Stimulants derived from *alpha-methyl-beta-phenyl-ethyl-amine*.

Attention-deficit/hyperactivity disorder A disorder that begins in childhood and is characterized by a persistent pattern of lack of attention with or without hyperactivity and impulsive behavior.

"I can resist everything except temptation."

OSCAR WILDE (*LADY WINDERMERE'S FAN*)

AMPHETAMINES AND RELATED STIMULANTS Question 19: What are the effects of amphetamines? Amphetamines are a group of stimulants that were first used by soldiers during World War II to help them remain alert through the night. Truck drivers have also used them to stay awake all night. Amphetamines have become perhaps more widely known through students, who have used them for all-night cram sessions and to help "focus" on tests, and through dieters, who use them to reduce hunger.

Called *speed, uppers, bennies* (for Benzedrine), and *dexies* (for Dexedrine), these drugs are often abused for the euphoric rush they can produce in high doses. Some people swallow amphetamines in pill form or inject liquid Methedrine (methamphetamine hydrochloride), the strongest form, into their veins. As a result, they may stay awake and high for days on end. However, such highs must end. People who have been on prolonged highs sometimes "crash," or fall into a deep sleep or depression. Some people commit suicide when crashing.

On the other hand, physicians frequently prescribe stimulants in an effort to help hyperactive children control their behavior. **Truth or Fiction Revisited:** It is therefore true that many health professionals calm hyperactive children by giving them a stimulant. Stimulants such as Ritalin and Adderall are widely used to treat **attention-deficit/hyperactivity disorder** (ADHD) in children. These drugs have been shown to increase the attention span, decrease aggressive and disruptive behavior, and lead to academic gains (May & Kratochvil, 2010; Wanchoo et al., 2010). Why should stimulants calm children? Hyperactivity may be connected with immaturity of the cerebral cortex, and stimulants may stimulate the cortex to exercise control over more primitive centers in the brain. On the other hand, these stimulants place children—and adults who may continue to use them—at increased risk for sleep disorders and loss of appetite (Meijer et al., 2009).

Tolerance for amphetamines develops rapidly, and users can become dependent on them, especially when they use them to self-medicate themselves for depression. Regular use of the powerful amphetamine called methamphetamine may well be physically addictive (Embry et al., 2009), but the extent to which amphetamines cause physical addiction has been a subject of controversy. It is widely accepted, however, that high doses of amphetamines may cause restlessness, insomnia, loss of appetite, hallucinations, paranoid delusions (for example, false ideas that others are eavesdropping or intend to harm one), and irritability.

Now let's discuss some of the most widely abused stimulants.

COCAINE Cocaine is derived from coca leaves—the plant from which the soft drink took its name. Do you recall the commercials claiming that "Coke adds life"? Given its caffeine and sugar content, Coke—Coca-Cola, that is—should provide quite a lift. **Truth or Fiction Revisited:** It is true that Coca-Cola once "added life" through the use of a powerful, then legal but now illegal, stimulant: cocaine. But Coca-Cola hasn't been "the real thing" since 1906, when the company discontinued the use of cocaine in its formula.

Question 20: What are the effects of cocaine? Cocaine is a stimulant that produces euphoria, reduces hunger, deadens pain, and bolsters self-confidence

© David Young-Wolff/PhotoEdit Inc.

Snorting Cocaine Cocaine is a powerful stimulant that boosts self-confidence. However, health professionals have become concerned about its physical effects, including sudden rises in blood pressure, constriction of blood vessels, and acceleration of heart rate. Several athletes have died from cocaine overdoses.

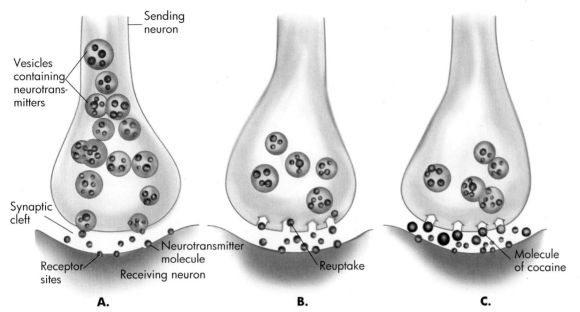

Figure 4.4 ■ How Cocaine Produces Euphoria and Why People "Crash" A. In the normal functioning of the nervous system, neurotransmitters are released into the synaptic cleft by vesicles in terminal buttons of sending neurons. Many are taken up by receptor sites in receiving neurons. **B.** In the process called reuptake, sending neurons typically reabsorb excess molecules of neurotransmitters. **C.** Molecules of cocaine bind to the sites on sending neurons that normally reuptake molecules of neurotransmitters. As a result, molecules of norepinephrine, dopamine, and serotonin remain longer in the synaptic cleft, increasing their typical mood-altering effects and providing a euphoric "rush." When the person stops using cocaine, the lessened absorption of neurotransmitters by receiving neurons causes his or her mood to "crash."

(see Figure 4.4 ■). About 1.3% of 12th graders have used cocaine in the past 30 days, down from 2.6% on 1999 (see Table 4.4; Johnston et al., 2010), apparently because most high school students believe that the use of cocaine is harmful (Johnston et al., 2010). It is used by about 2.3% of young adult males and 1.4% of young adult females (see Table 4.5).

Cocaine may be brewed from coca leaves as a tea, snorted in powder form, or injected in liquid form. Repeated snorting constricts blood vessels in the nose, drying the skin and sometimes exposing cartilage and perforating the nasal septum. These problems require cosmetic surgery. The potent cocaine derivatives known as "crack" and "bazooka" are inexpensive because they are unrefined.

Biologically speaking, cocaine stimulates sudden rises in blood pressure, constricts the coronary arteries, and thickens the blood (both of which decrease the oxygen supply to the heart), therefore quickening the heart rate (Kontak et al., 2009). These events occasionally result in respiratory and cardiovascular collapse (Lange & Hillis, 2010). The sudden deaths of a number of athletes have been caused in this way. Overdoses can lead to restlessness and insomnia, tremors, headaches, nausea, convulsions, hallucinations, and delusions. The use of crack has been connected with strokes.

Cocaine—also called *snow* and *coke*—has been used as a local anesthetic since the early 1800s. In 1884, it came to the attention of a young Viennese neurologist named Sigmund Freud, who used it to fight his own depression and published an article about it titled "Song of Praise." Freud's early ardor was tempered when he learned that cocaine is habit forming and can cause hallucinations and delusions. Cocaine causes physiological as well as psychological dependence.

NICOTINE

Nicotine is the stimulant found in cigarettes and cigars. **Question 21: What are the effects of nicotine?** Nicotine stimulates discharge of the hormone adrenaline and the release of many neurotransmitters, including noradrenaline, dopamine, and acetylcholine (Haustein & Groneberg, 2009). Adrenaline creates a burst of autonomic activity that disrupts normal heart rhythms, accelerates the heart rate, and pours sugar into the blood. Acetylcholine is vital in memory formation, and nicotine appears to enhance

Smoking: a "custome lothesome to the Eye, hatefull to the Nose, harmefull to the Braine, dangerous to the Lungs."

KING JAMES I, 1604

"As an example to others, and not that I care for moderation myself, it has always been my rule never to smoke when asleep, and never to refrain from smoking when awake."

MARK TWAIN

"Giving up smoking is the easiest thing in the world. I know because I've done it thousands of times."

MARK TWAIN

Dependence on Cocaine? Denial at Work

Denial Not me! People who are dependent on drugs frequently deny their situations.

The following clinical interview illustrates how denial can mask reality in substance abuse. A business executive was brought in by his wife for a consultation. She complained his once-successful business was jeopardized by his erratic behavior, he was grouchy and moody, and he had spent $7,000 in the previous month on cocaine.

CLINICIAN: Have you missed many days at work recently?

EXECUTIVE: Yes, but I can afford to, since I own the business. No-body checks up on me.

CLINICIAN: It sounds like that's precisely the problem. When you don't go to work, the company stays open, but it doesn't do very well.

EXECUTIVE: My employees are well trained. They can run the company without me.

CLINICIAN: But that's not happening.

EXECUTIVE: Then there's something wrong with them. I'll have to look into it.

CLINICIAN: It sounds as if there's something wrong with you, but you don't want to look into it.

EXECUTIVE: Now you're on my case. I don't know why you listen to everything my wife says.

CLINICIAN: How many days of work did you miss in the last two months?

EXECUTIVE: A couple.

CLINICIAN: Are you saying that you missed only two days of work?

EXECUTIVE: Maybe a few.

CLINICIAN: Only three or four days?

EXECUTIVE: Maybe a little more.

CLINICIAN: Ten? Fifteen?

EXECUTIVE: Fifteen.

CLINICIAN: All because of cocaine?

EXECUTIVE: No.

CLINICIAN: How many were because of cocaine?

EXECUTIVE: Less than fifteen.

CLINICIAN: Fourteen? Thirteen?

EXECUTIVE: Maybe thirteen.

CLINICIAN: So you missed thirteen days of work in the last two months because of cocaine. That's almost two days a week.

EXECUTIVE: That sounds like a lot but it's no big deal. Like I say, the company can run itself.

CLINICIAN: How long have you been using cocaine?

EXECUTIVE: About three years.

CLINICIAN: Did you ever use drugs or alcohol before that in any kind of quantity?

EXECUTIVE: No.

CLINICIAN: Then let's think back five years. Five years ago, if you had imagined yourself missing over a third of your workdays because of a drug, and if you had imagined yourself spending the equivalent of $84,000 a year on that same drug, and if you saw your once-successful business collapsing all around you, wouldn't you have thought that that was indicative of a pretty serious problem?

EXECUTIVE: Yes, I would have.

CLINICIAN: So what's different now?

EXECUTIVE: I guess I just don't want to think about it.

From Weiss, Mirin, and Bartell, 1994.

memory and attention, improve performance on simple repetitive tasks, and enhance the mood (Froeliger et al., 2009; Greenwood et al., 2009). Despite its stimulative properties, it also appears to relax people and reduce stress (A. Cohen et al., 2009).

Nicotine depresses the appetite and raises the metabolic rate. Thus, some people smoke cigarettes to control their weight (J. L. Johnson et al., 2009). People also tend to eat more when they stop smoking, causing some to return to the habit.

Nicotine may be as addictive as heroin or cocaine (Franklin et al., 2009). It is the agent that creates physiological dependence on tobacco products (Small et al., 2010).

It's no secret. Cigarette packs sold in the United States carry messages like "Warning: The Surgeon General Has Determined That Cigarette Smoking Is Dangerous to Your Health." Cigarette advertising has been banned on radio and television. Nearly 400,000 Americans die from smoking-related illnesses each year (American Lung Association, 2010). This is greater than the equivalent of two jumbo jets colliding in midair each day with all passengers lost. **Truth or Fiction Revisited:** Smoking-related deaths are higher than the number of people who die from motor vehicle accidents, alcohol and drug abuse, suicide, homicide, and AIDS *combined*.

The carbon monoxide in cigarette smoke impairs the blood's ability to carry oxygen, causing shortness of breath. The **hydrocarbons** ("tars") in cigarette and cigar smoke lead to lung cancer (American Lung Association, 2010). Smoking is responsible for about 90% of deaths from lung cancer (American Lung Association, 2010). Cigarette smoking also stiffens arteries (Campbell et al., 2010) and is linked to death from heart disease, chronic lung and respiratory diseases, and other health problems. Women who smoke show reduced bone density, increasing the risk of fracture of the hip and back (American Lung Association, 2010). Pregnant women who smoke have a higher risk of miscarriage, preterm births, low-birthweight babies, and stillborn babies (American Lung Association, 2010).

Passive smoking (also called *second-hand smoking*) is also connected with respiratory illnesses, asthma, and other health problems. Prolonged exposure to household tobacco smoke during childhood is a risk factor for lung cancer (American Cancer Society, 2010). Because of the noxious effects of secondhand smoke, smoking has been banished from many public places such as airplanes, restaurants, and elevators.

Video Connections—Why Is Nicotine So Addictive?

This video focuses on the role of reinforcement and how understanding cues may help people quit smoking. Go to Psychology CourseMate at www.cengagebrain.com to watch this video.

Hydrocarbons Chemical compounds consisting of hydrogen and carbon.

Passive smoking Inhaling smoke from the tobacco products and exhalations of other people; also called *secondhand smoking*.

The perils of cigarette smoking are widely known today. One surgeon general declared that cigarette smoking is the chief preventable cause of death in the United States. The numbers of Americans who die from smoking are comparable to the number of lives that would be lost if two jumbo jets crashed every day. If flying were that unsafe, would the government ground all flights? Would the public continue to make airline reservations?

© Stockbyte/Getty Images

TABLE 4.6 ■ Snapshot, USA: Gender, Level of Education, and Smoking

Factor	Group	Percent Who Smoke
Gender	Women	18.3
	Men	23.1
Level of education	Fewer than 12 years	27.5
	College graduate and above	10.6

Note: Data based on reports of persons aged 18 and above.
Source: Dube, S. R., Asman, K., Malarcher, A., & Carabollo, R. (2009). Cigarette smoking among adults and trends in smoking cessation—United States, 2008. *Morbidity and Mortality Weekly Report, 58*(44), 1227–1232.

Why, then, do people smoke? For many reasons—such as the desire to look sophisticated (although these days smokers may more likely be judged foolish than sophisticated), to have something to do with their hands, and—of course—to take in nicotine.

About one in five 12th graders and one in six or seven young adults uses cigarettes daily (Johnston et al., 2010). The incidence of smoking is connected with gender and level of education (see Table 4.6 ■) (Dube et al., 2009). Better-educated people are less likely to smoke and are more likely to quit if they do (Dube et al., 2009).

Hallucinogenics

Hallucinogenic drugs Substances that give rise to hallucinations.

Marijuana The dried vegetable matter of the *Cannabis sativa* plant.

Hallucinogenic drugs are so named because they produce hallucinations—that is, sensations and perceptions in the absence of external stimulation. But hallucinogenic drugs may also have additional effects such as relaxation, euphoria, or in some cases, panic.

MARIJUANA Marijuana is a substance that is produced from the *Cannabis sativa* plant, which grows wild in many parts of the world. **Question 22: What are the**

On the Edge with Ecstasy

© Houston Scott /Corbis Sygma

Ecstasy—A Popular Party Drug If Ecstasy—also known as MDMA—is enjoyable for most users, why are health professionals concerned about its possible short- and long-term effects?

Ecstasy—also known as MDMA (acronym for 3, 4-methylenedioxymethamphetamine)—is a popular "party drug" or "club drug." Ecstasy is "on the edge" in more ways than one. For example, its chemical formula has similarities both to amphetamines, which are stimulants, and to mescaline, which is a hallucinogen (Concar, 2002; Freese et al., 2002). As a result, it gives users the boost of a stimulant and, as a mild hallucinogen, also removes users a bit from reality. The combination appears to free users to some degree from inhibitions and awareness of the possible results of risky behavior, such as unprotected sex.

MDMA may also mean "living on the edge" because of its known risks and potential risks. Experiments with laboratory animals such as mice show that MDMA can increase anxiety (Navarro & Maldonado, 2002). These experiments show that MDMA reduces the activity of the neurotransmitters serotonin and dopamine in the brain, impairing the functioning of working memory (Cassaday et al., 2003; Taffe et al., 2002). MDMA also causes problems with eating, sleeping, and mood (leading to depression, for example). Some researchers are concerned that even occasional MDMA users could be setting themselves up for problems related to depletion of serotonin and dopamine later in life (Parrott, 2003; Taffe et al., 2002).

effects of marijuana? Marijuana helps some people relax and can elevate their mood. It also sometimes produces mild hallucinations, which is why we discuss it in this section on hallucinogenic, or *psychedelic,* drugs. The major psychedelic substance in marijuana is delta-9-tetrahydrocannabinol, or THC. It is found in the branches and leaves of the plant but is highly concentrated in the sticky resin. *Hashish,* or "hash," is derived from the resin and is more potent than marijuana.

In the 19th century, marijuana was used much as aspirin is used today for headaches and minor aches and pains. It could be bought without a prescription in any drugstore. Today, marijuana use and possession are illegal in most states. Marijuana also carries a number of health risks. For example, it impairs the perceptual–motor coordination used in driving and operating machines. It impairs short-term memory and slows learning (Egerton et al., 2006; Lamers et al., 2006). Although it causes positive mood changes in many people, there are also disturbing instances of anxiety and confusion and occasional reports of psychotic reactions (Bonn-Miller et al., 2007).

Some people report that marijuana helps them socialize at parties. Moderate to strong intoxication is linked to reports of heightened perceptions and increases in self-insight, creative thinking, and empathy for the feelings of others. Time seems to pass more slowly for people who are strongly intoxicated. A song might seem to last an hour rather than a few minutes. There is increased awareness of bodily sensations such as heartbeat. Marijuana smokers also report that strong intoxication heightens sexual sensations. Visual hallucinations are not uncommon, and strong intoxication may cause smokers to experience disorientation. If the smoker's mood is euphoric, loss of a sense of personal identity may be interpreted as being in harmony with the universe.

Some marijuana smokers have negative experiences. An accelerated heart rate and heightened awareness of bodily sensations leads some smokers to fear that their heart will "run away" with them. Some smokers find disorientation threatening and are afraid that they will not regain their identity. Strong intoxication sometimes causes nausea and vomiting.

People can become psychologically dependent on marijuana, but the use of marijuana had not been thought to lead to physiological dependence. Recent research, however, suggests that regular users of marijuana may experience tolerance and withdrawal symptoms (Budney et al., 2007).

LSD AND OTHER HALLUCINOGENICS LSD is the abbreviation for lysergic acid diethylamide, a synthetic hallucinogenic drug. **Question 23: What are the effects of LSD and other kinds of hallucinogenic drugs?** Users of "acid" (another term for LSD) claim that it "expands consciousness" and opens up new worlds to them. Sometimes, people believe they have achieved great insights while using LSD, but when it wears off, they often cannot apply or recall these discoveries. As a powerful hallucinogenic, LSD produces vivid and colorful hallucinations.

Some LSD users have **flashbacks**—distorted perceptions or hallucinations that mimic the LSD "trip" but occur days, weeks, or longer after usage. The experiencing of flashbacks is more technically termed *hallucinogen persisting perception disorder (HPPD)* by the American Psychiatric Association (2000), although some writers distinguish between the two terms. Over the years, both psychological and physiological explanations of HPPD have appeared. The psychological explanation of flashbacks, in a nutshell, is that people who would use LSD regularly are also more likely to allow flights of fancy. Yet research with people with HPPD suggests that following extensive use of LSD, the brain may fail to inhibit certain internal sources of visionlike experiences, especially when the eyes are closed (Catts & Catts, 2009).

© Fancy Photography/Veer

Marijuana Is the Most Popular Illicit Drug Marijuana helps some people socialize at parties and distorts the passage of time and other sensations. It also interferes with learning and impairs the sensorimotor coordination used in driving.

© Anne Marie Rousseau/The Image Works

An LSD Trip? This hallucinogenic drug can give rise to a vivid parade of colors and visual distortions. Some users claim to have achieved great insights while "tripping," but typically, they have been unable to recall or apply them afterward.

LSD Lysergic acid diethylamide. A hallucinogenic drug.

Flashbacks Distorted perceptions or hallucinations that occur days or weeks after LSD usage but mimic the LSD experience.

147

There are many controversies concerning marijuana. One is the issue of whether marijuana should be made available as a medicine to those who could benefit from it. Marijuana has been used to treat health problems, including glaucoma and the nausea experienced by cancer patients undergoing chemotherapy (Thomas, 2010). Supporters of marijuana for medical uses refer to it as an inexpensive, versatile, and reasonably safe medicine. Other medical researchers agree that marijuana has some positive effects, but the action of THC also has its negatives (Janero & Makriyannis, 2009). THC binds to a membrane receptor, 7TM, which is found in every cell. THC displaces the natural substance that would bind with the receptor and disrupts the receptor's signaling. As a result, the functioning of the brain, the immune system, and the cardiovascular and reproductive systems (for instance, it interferes with development of sperm and conception) is impaired to some degree.

Marijuana smoke also contains more hydrocarbons—a risk factor in cancer—than cigarette smoke does (Cobb et al., 2010). Smokers of marijuana often admit they know that marijuana smoke can be harmful, but they counter that compared with cigarette smokers, they smoke very few "joints" per day. Yet, as noted, marijuana elevates the heart rate and, in some people, the blood pressure. This higher demand on the heart and circulation poses a threat to people with hypertension and cardiovascular disorders.

Another issue is whether researchers and public figures exaggerate the dangers of marijuana to discourage people from using it. Does the information about marijuana in this textbook seem biased? Why or why not?

Marijuana has been with us for decades, but new research on its effects continues—with more sophisticated methods. And the findings are mixed. For example, some research has suggested that marijuana usage impairs learning, memory, and attention (Indlekofer et al., 2009), but it was assumed by many that the reason was that marijuana distracted people from learning tasks. Other laboratory research suggests a biological reason—that marijuana reduces the release of neurotransmitters involved in the consolidation of learning (Campolongo et al., 2009). Yet consider the results of a synthesis of 15 previously published studies on the long-term effects of marijuana on the cognitive performance of adults. The synthesis compared 704 long-term cannabis users with 484 nonusers (Grant et al., 2003). The cognitive measures included reaction time, attention, use of language, abstract thinking, perceptual–motor skills, and learning and forgetting. The only significant difference was that long-term marijuana users showed a small comparative deficit in learning new information. The importance of this difference is open to debate.

People who started using marijuana early may be generally smaller in height and weight than other people. Brain imaging studies suggest that males who began using marijuana in adolescence may have smaller brains and less gray matter than other males (Ashtari et al., 2009). These differences may reflect the effect of marijuana on pituitary and sex hormones.

More research is needed on the effects of marijuana. Some of the horror stories of the 1960s and 1970s may have been exaggerated, but a number of questions about potential harm remain. More research evidence—not more speculation—is needed.

Mescaline A hallucinogenic drug derived from the mescal (peyote) cactus.

Phencyclidine (PCP) Another hallucinogenic drug whose name is an acronym for its chemical structure.

Other hallucinogenic drugs include **mescaline** (derived from the peyote cactus) and **phencyclidine (PCP)**. Phencyclidine was developed as an anesthetic and a large-animal tranquilizer, and it goes by the street names "angel dust," "ozone," "wack," and "rocket fuel." The street terms "killer joints" and "crystal supergrass" refer to PCP that is combined with marijuana.

Regular use of hallucinogenics may lead to tolerance and psychological dependence. But hallucinogenics are not known to lead to physiological dependence. High doses may induce frightening hallucinations, impaired coordination, poor judgment, mood changes, and paranoid delusions.

LearningConnections • ALTERING CONSCIOUSNESS THROUGH DRUGS

ACTIVE REVIEW (12) Substance _____ is characterized by repeated use of a substance although it is impairing functioning. (13) Physiological dependence is evidenced by tolerance or by a(n) _____ syndrome when one discontinues use of the substance. (14) Women seem to be (more or less?) affected by alcohol than men. (15) Ritalin is used to treat _____-deficit/hyperactivity disorder in children. (16) _____ is a stimulant that boosts self-confidence but also triggers rises in blood pressure and constricts the coronary arteries. (17) Tobacco contains the stimulant _____. (18) _____ substances distort perceptions.

REFLECT AND RELATE The next time you are at a social occasion, note the behavior of people who are drinking and those who are not. What do you think are individuals' motives for drinking? Does drinking visibly affect their behavior? If you drink, how does it affect your behavior?

CRITICAL THINKING Does this textbook's presentation of information about the effects of drugs seem straightforward or biased? What is the evidence for your view?

 Go to Psychology CourseMate at **www.cengagebrain.com** for an interactive version of these questions.

Drug	Type	How Taken	Desired Effects	Tolerance	Abstinence Syndrome	Side Effects
Alcohol	Depressant	By mouth	Relaxation, euphoria, lowered inhibitions	Yes	Yes	Impaired coordination, poor judgment, hangover
Opiates	Depressants	Injected, smoked, by mouth	Relaxation, euphoria, relief from anxiety and pain	Yes	Yes	Impaired coordination and mental functioning, drowsiness, lethargy
Barbiturates	Depressant	By mouth, injected	Relaxation, sleep, euphoria, lowered inhibitions	Yes	Yes	Impaired coordination and mental functioning, drowsiness, lethargy
Amphetamines	Stimulants	By mouth, injected	Alertness, euphoria	Yes	?	Restlessness, loss of appetite, psychotic symptoms
Cocaine	Stimulant	By mouth, snorted, injected	Euphoria, self-confidence	Yes	Yes	Restlessness, loss of appetite, convulsions, strokes, psychotic symptoms
Nicotine	Stimulant	By tobacco (smoked, chewed, or sniffed)	Relaxation, stimulation, weight control	Yes	Yes	Cancer, heart disease, lung and respiratory diseases
Marijuana	Hallucinogenic	Smoked, by mouth	Relaxation, perceptual distortions, enhancement of experience	?	?	Impaired coordination and learning, respiratory problems, panic
LSD, Mescaline, PCP	Hallucinogenic	By mouth	Perceptual distortions, vivid hallucinations	Yes	No	Impaired coordination, psychotic symptoms, panic

The Many Meanings of Consciousness

1. What is consciousness?
The term *consciousness* has several meanings, including sensory awareness, direct inner awareness of cognitive processes, the selective aspect of attention, the sense of self, and the waking state.

Sleep and Dreams: Other Worlds Within?

2. What is a circadian rhythm?
A circadian rhythm is a cycle that is connected with the 24-hour period of the Earth's rotation, such as the sleep–wake cycle.

3. How do we describe the stages of sleep?
We undergo several stages of sleep. According to electroencephalograph (EEG) records, each stage of sleep is characterized by a different type of brain wave. There are four stages of non-rapid-eye-movement (NREM) sleep and one stage of REM sleep. Stage 1 sleep is the lightest, and stage 4 is the deepest.

4. Why do we sleep?
Sleep apparently serves a restorative function, but we do not know exactly how sleep restores us or how much sleep we need. Animals and people who have been deprived of REM sleep learn more slowly and forget what they have learned more rapidly.

5. What are dreams?
Dreams are a form of cognitive activity that occurs mostly while we are sleeping. Most dreaming occurs during REM sleep. Nightmares are dreams that tend to occur during REM sleep.

6. Why do we dream what we dream?
Freud believed that dreams reflected unconscious wishes and "protected sleep" by keeping unacceptable ideas out of awareness. The activation–synthesis hypothesis suggests that dreams largely reflect automatic biological activity by the pons and the synthesis of subsequent sensory stimulation by the frontal part of the brain. The content of most dreams is an extension of the events of the previous day.

7. What kinds of sleep disorders are there?
A common sleep disorder is insomnia, which is most often encountered by people who are anxious and tense. Deep sleep disorders include narcolepsy, sleep apnea, sleep terrors, bed-wetting, sleep-talking, and sleepwalking.

Altering Consciousness Through Hypnosis, Meditation, and Biofeedback

8. What is hypnosis?
Hypnosis is an altered state of consciousness in which people are suggestible and behave as though they are in a trance. People who are hypnotized may show passivity, narrowed attention, suggestibility, assumption of unusual roles, perceptual distortions, posthypnotic amnesia, and posthypnotic suggestion.

9. How do modern psychologists explain the effects of hypnosis?
Current theories of hypnosis deny the existence of a special trance state. Rather, they emphasize people's ability to role-play the trance (role theory), to strategically follow hypnotist's instructions (multifactorial theory), to do what is expected of them (response set theory), and to divide their consciousness (neodissociation theory).

10. What is meditation?
In meditation, one focuses "passively" on an object or a mantra to alter the normal relationship between oneself and the environment. In this way, consciousness (that is, the normal focus of attention) is altered.

11. What are the effects of meditation?
Meditation often has the effect of inducing relaxation. Transcendental meditation appears to reduce the blood pressure of hypertensive individuals.

12. What is biofeedback training?
Biofeedback is a method for increasing consciousness and control of bodily functions. The organism is continuously provided with information about a targeted biological response such as heart rate or emission of alpha waves.

13. How is biofeedback training used?
People and lower animals can learn to control their heart rate, blood pressure, and even the emission of certain brain waves through biofeedback training.

Altering Consciousness Through Drugs

14. What are substance abuse and dependence?
Substance abuse is the use of a substance that persists even though it impairs one's functioning. Dependence may be characterized by the organization of one's life around getting and using the substance and by the development of tolerance, withdrawal symptoms, or both.

15. What are the causes of substance abuse and dependence?
People usually try drugs out of curiosity, but usage can be reinforced by anxiety reduction and feelings of euphoria. People are also motivated to avoid withdrawal symptoms once they become physiologically dependent on a drug. People may have genetic predispositions to become physiologically dependent on certain substances.

16. What are the effects of alcohol?
Alcohol, the most widely used drug, is a depressant. It belongs to the group of substances that act by slowing the activity of the central nervous system. Alcohol is also intoxicating and can lead to physiological dependence.

17. What are the effects of opiates?
The opiates morphine and heroin are depressants that reduce pain, but they are also bought on the street because of the

euphoric "rush" they provide. Opiate use can lead to physiological dependence.

18. What are the effects of barbiturates?
Barbiturates are depressants. They have medical uses, including relaxation, pain management, and treatment of epilepsy, high blood pressure, and insomnia. Barbiturates lead rapidly to physiological dependence.

19. What are the effects of amphetamines?
Stimulants are substances that act by increasing the activity of the nervous system. Amphetamines are stimulants that produce feelings of euphoria when taken in high doses. But high doses may also cause restlessness, insomnia, psychotic symptoms, and a "crash" upon withdrawal. Amphetamines and a related stimulant, Ritalin, are commonly used to treat hyperactive children.

20. What are the effects of cocaine?
The stimulant cocaine provides feelings of euphoria and bolsters self-confidence. Physically, it spikes the blood pressure and constricts blood vessels. Overdoses can lead to restlessness, insomnia, psychotic reactions, and cardiorespiratory collapse.

21. What are the effects of nicotine?
Nicotine is the addictive stimulant in cigarettes that can paradoxically help people relax. Cigarette smoke also contains carbon monoxide and hydrocarbons. Smoking has been linked to death from heart disease, cancer, and other health problems.

22. What are the effects of marijuana?
Marijuana is a hallucinogenic substance whose active ingredients, including THC, may produce relaxation, heightened and distorted perceptions, feelings of empathy, and reports of new insights. Marijuana elevates the heart rate, and the smoke is harmful. Although it has some medical uses, it impairs learning and memory and may affect the growth of adolescents.

23. What are the effects of LSD and other kinds of hallucinogenic drugs?
LSD and other hallucinogenic drugs produce hallucinations. Some LSD users experience "flashbacks" to earlier experiences.

KEY TERMS

Abstinence syndrome (p. 137)
Activation–synthesis model (p. 126)
Alpha waves (p. 123)
Amphetamines (p. 142)
Attention-deficit/hyperactivity disorder (p. 142)
Barbiturate (p. 141)
Biofeedback training (BFT) (p. 134)
Circadian rhythm (p. 122)
Consciousness (p. 120)
Delta waves (p. 124)
Depressant (p. 136)
Direct inner awareness (p. 120)
Electromyograph (EMG) (p. 135)
Flashbacks (p. 147)
Hallucinogenic drugs (p. 146)
Hydrocarbons (p. 145)

Hypnagogic state (p. 123)
Hypnosis (p. 131)
LSD (p. 147)
Marijuana (p. 146)
Mescaline (p. 148)
Narcolepsy (p. 128)
Narcotics (p. 141)
Non-rapid-eye-movement (NREM) sleep (p. 123)
Nonconscious (p. 121)
Opiates (p. 141)
Opioids (p. 141)
Passive smoking (p. 145)
Phencyclidine (PCP) (p. 148)
Preconscious (p. 120)
Psychoactive substances (p. 135)

Rapid-eye-movement (REM) sleep (p. 123)
Repression (p. 121)
Selective attention (p. 120)
Sleep apnea (p. 128)
Sleep terrors (p. 129)
Stimulant (p. 136)
Substance abuse (p. 136)
Substance dependence (p. 136)
Suppression (p. 121)
Theta waves (p. 123)
Tolerance (p. 137)
Transcendental meditation (TM) (p. 134)
Unconscious (p. 120)

ACTIVE LEARNING RESOURCES

Log in to **www.cengagebrain.com** to access the resources your instructor requires. For this book, you can access:

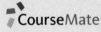 CourseMate brings course concepts to life with interactive learning, study, and exam preparation tools that support the printed textbook. A textbook-specific website, Psychology CourseMate includes an integrated interactive eBook and other interactive learning tools including quizzes, flashcards, videos, and more.

 Need help studying? This site is your one-stop study shop. Take a Pre-Test and CengageNOW will generate a Personalized Study Plan based on your test results. The Study Plan will identify the topics you need to review and direct you to online resources to help you master those topics. You can then take a Post-Test to determine the concepts you have mastered and what you still need to work on.

5 Learning

© Corbis Photography/Veer

MAJOR TOPICS

Learning: Experience and Change *153*
Classical Conditioning: Learning
  What Is Linked to What *154*
Operant Conditioning: Learning
  What Does What to What *163*
Cognitive Factors in Learning *173*

FEATURES

Video Connections: Little Albert *160*
Video Connections: Conditioning of Fear *161*
A Closer Look: Who Was "Little Albert"? *160*
Life Connections: Why Do Many Psychologists Disapprove of Punishment? *168*
A Closer Look: Robo Rats? Using Operant Conditioning to Teach Rats How to
  Search for Survivors of Disasters *169*
A Closer Look: Contingency Theory *174*
Video Connections: Mirror Neurons *175*
Life Connections: Teaching Children *Not* to Imitate Media Violence *177*
Concept Review 5.1: Kinds of Learning *178*

T F A single nauseating meal can give rise to a taste aversion that lasts for years.

page 156

T F Psychologists helped a young boy overcome his fear of rabbits by having him eat cookies while a rabbit was brought closer and closer.

page 161

T F During World War II, a psychologist created a guided missile that would use pigeons to take the missile to its target.

page 163

T F Punishment is ineffective at stopping unwanted behavior.

page 167

T F You can train a rat to climb a ramp, cross a bridge, climb a ladder, pedal a toy car, and do several other tasks—all in proper sequence.

page 171

T F You have to make mistakes to learn.

page 172

T F Despite all the media hoopla, no scientific connection has been established between TV violence and real-life aggression.

page 176

Are these items truth or fiction? We will be revisiting them throughout the chapter.

I was was showing my daughter Allyn how to teach our new dog, Phoebe, to fetch. I bought a soft yellow ball for the dog that squeaked when she bit into it. She enjoyed playing with it, and I assumed she would want to run after it. (Wrong!) I waved it under her nose. She sniffed at it, barked, and wagged her tail excitedly.

As my daughter watched, I tossed the ball about 20 feet away. "Fetch!" I said to Phoebe as the ball bounced invitingly in the grass.

Phoebe just stared.

My daughter scoffed. I ran after the ball, picked it up, and waved it under Phoebe's nose again. She barked and wagged her tail rapidly like a reed in a brisk wind.

"Fetch!" I said and tossed the ball again.

Again Phoebe refused to run. She barked and snapped at my legs again. "This is ridiculous," I muttered, and I went to get the ball. As I brought it back to Phoebe, Allyn said, "Don't you see what's happening?"

"What?"

"Phoebe's teaching you to fetch."

© Getty Images/Blend Images

LEARNING: EXPERIENCE AND CHANGE

One could say that Phoebe was teaching me what to do by showing excitement when I did the "right" thing—that is, fetch the ball. She was teaching, and I was learning. Learning is a key area in psychology. **Question 1: What is learning?**

Learning as defined in psychology is more than listening to teachers, honing skateboard jumps, or mastering the use of an iPod. From the behaviorist perspective, **learning** is a relatively permanent change in behavior that arises from practice or experience. The behavioral perspective plays down the roles of cognition and choice. It suggests that psychologists learn to run after balls because they have been rewarded or reinforced for doing so.

Cognitive psychologists define learning as the process by which organisms make relatively permanent changes in the way they represent the environment because of experience. These changes influence the organism's behavior but do not fully determine it. From this perspective, I knew that I would earn Phoebe's attention by running after the ball, but I could have chosen not to do it. Learning, for cognitive psychologists, may be *shown* by changes in behavior, but learning itself is a mental process. Cognitive psychologists

© Getty Images/Image Bank

Instinct The bird builds a nest on the basis of its genetic code. This is an example of instinctive behavior, which is not learned through experience.

Learning A relatively permanent change in behavior that results from experience.

Classical conditioning A simple form of learning in which an organism comes to associate or anticipate events. A neutral stimulus comes to evoke the response usually evoked by another stimulus by being paired repeatedly with the other stimulus. Also referred to as *respondent conditioning* or *Pavlovian conditioning.*

Reflex A simple unlearned response to a stimulus.

Stimulus An environmental condition that elicits a response.

suggest that people choose whether to imitate the aggressive and other behaviors they observe and that people are most likely to imitate behaviors that are consistent with their values.

In many animals, much behavior is instinctive, or inborn, rather than learned. For example, tadpoles start out life swimming, but after they develop legs, they hop on land in appropriate frog fashion—without taking hopping lessons. After they have spent sometimes years roaming the seas, salmon instinctively use their sense of smell to find, and return to spawn in, the stream where they were hatched. Robins instinctively know how to sing the song of their species and to build nests.

Among humans, however, the variety and complexity of behavior patterns are largely products of experience. We learn to read, to compute numbers, and to surf the Internet. It is natural to experience hunger and thus look for food, but humans learn to seek out foods that are preferred in their culture. We learn which behavior patterns are deemed socially acceptable and which are considered wrong. We also unfortunately learn prejudices and stereotypes and negative behaviors such as using violence to deal with conflict. Our families and communities use verbal guidance, set examples, and apply rewards and punishments to teach us and transmit cultural values.

Sometimes, learning experiences are direct, as when we are praised for doing something properly. But we can also learn from the experiences of others. Hence books and audiovisual media can help us learn from other people's experiences in the past, other people's cultures, and other people's knowledge. In this chapter, we consider various kinds of learning, including conditioning and learning in which cognition plays a more central role.

⬤ CLASSICAL CONDITIONING: LEARNING WHAT IS LINKED TO WHAT

Classical conditioning involves some of the ways we learn to associate events with other events. Consider this: We have a distinct preference for a grade of A rather than F. We are also (usually) more likely to stop for a red light than for a green light. Why? We are not born with instinctive attitudes toward the letters *A* and *F.* Nor are we born knowing that red means "stop" and green means "go." We learn the meanings of these symbols because they are associated with other events. A's are associated with instructor approval and the likelihood of getting into graduate school. Stopping at red lights is associated with avoiding accidents and traffic citations.

Question 2: What is classical conditioning? Classical conditioning is a simple form of associative learning in which organisms come to anticipate or associate events. If the name Ivan Pavlov rings a bell with us, it is most likely because of his research on learning in dogs. **Question 3: What is the contribution of Ivan Pavlov to the psychology of learning?** Ivan Pavlov (1927) made his great contribution to the psychology of learning by accident. Pavlov was attempting to identify neural receptors in the mouth that triggered a response from the salivary glands. But his efforts were hampered by the dogs' annoying tendency to salivate at undesired times, such as when a laboratory assistant was clumsy and banged the metal food trays.

Just as you salivate after you've taken a big bite of cake, a dog salivates if food (meat powder) is placed on its tongue. Pavlov was dosing his dogs with meat powder for his research because he knew that salivation in response to meat powder is a **reflex.** Reflexes are unlearned responses that are evoked by certain **stimuli.** Pavlov discovered that reflexes can also be learned, or *conditioned,* by association. His dogs began salivating in response to clanging food trays because clanging, in the past, had been repeatedly paired with the arrival of food. The dogs would also salivate when an assistant entered the laboratory. Why? In the past, the assistant had brought food.

© Bettmann/Corbis

Unconditioned stimulus (UCS)
A stimulus that elicits a response from an organism prior to conditioning.

Unconditioned response (UCR) An unlearned response to an unconditioned stimulus.

Orienting response An unlearned response in which an organism attends to a stimulus.

Conditioned stimulus (CS) A previously neutral stimulus that elicits a conditioned response because it has been paired repeatedly with a stimulus that already elicited that response.

Conditioned response (CR) A learned response to a conditioned stimulus.

Pavlov at first viewed the extra salivation of his dogs as a hindrance to his research. But then it dawned on him that this "problem" might be worth looking into. He found out that he could train, or condition, his dogs to salivate in response to any stimulus.

In his initial experiments, Pavlov trained dogs to salivate when he sounded a tone or a bell. Pavlov termed these trained salivary responses *conditional reflexes*. They were *conditional* upon the repeated pairing of a previously neutral stimulus (such as the clanging of a food tray) and a stimulus that evoked the target response (in this case, food served as the stimulus and salivation as the response). Today, conditional reflexes are generally referred to as *conditioned responses*.

Pavlov demonstrated conditioned responses by strapping a dog into a harness like the one shown in Figure 5.1 ■. When meat powder was placed on the dog's tongue, it salivated. Pavlov repeated the process several times, with one difference. He preceded the meat powder by half a second or so with the sound of a tone on each occasion. After several pairings of the meat powder and the tone, Pavlov sounded the tone but did *not* follow it with the meat powder. Still the dog salivated. It had learned to salivate in response to the tone.

Stimuli and Responses in Classical Conditioning

In Pavlov's experiment, the meat powder is an unlearned, or **unconditioned, stimulus (UCS)**. Salivation in response to the meat powder is an unlearned, or **unconditioned, response (UCR)**. The tone was at first a meaningless, or neutral, stimulus; it might have caused the dog to look in the direction of the sound—an **orienting response**. But the tone was not yet associated with food. Then, through repeated association with the meat powder, the tone became a learned, or **conditioned, stimulus (CS)** for the salivation response. Salivation in response to the tone (or conditioned stimulus) is a learned, or **conditioned, response (CR)**. Therefore, salivation can be either a conditioned response or an unconditioned response depending on the method used to evoke it (see Figure 5.2 ■).

Here is a mini-experiment that many adults have tried. They smile at infants, say something like "kitchie-coo" (don't ask me why), and then tickle the infant's foot. Perhaps the infant laughs; it also usually curls or retracts the foot. After a few repetitions—which psychologists call "trials"—the adult simply saying "kitchie-coo" is likely to be enough to cause the infant to laugh and retract its foot.

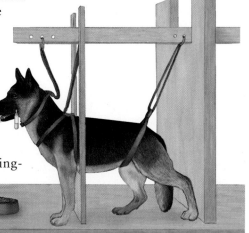

Figure 5.1 ■ Pavlov's Demonstration of Conditioned Reflexes in Laboratory Dogs From behind a one-way mirror, a laboratory assistant sounds a tone and then places meat powder on the dog's tongue. After several pairings, the dog salivates in response to the tone alone. A tube collects saliva and passes it to a vial. The quantity of saliva is taken as a measure of the strength of the animal's response.

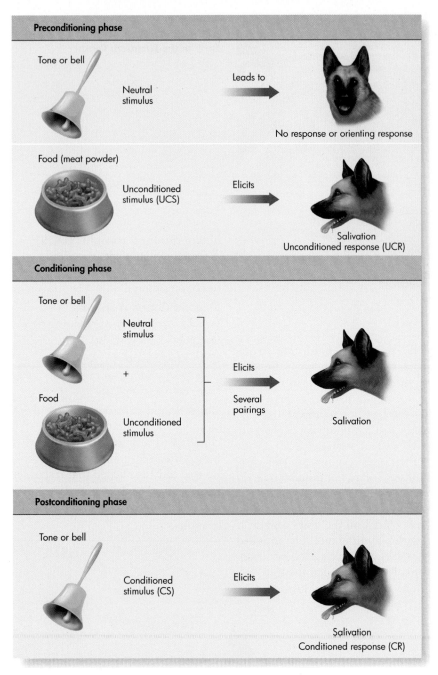

Preconditioning phase

Tone or bell

Neutral stimulus → Leads to → No response or orienting response

Food (meat powder)

Unconditioned stimulus (UCS) → Elicits → Salivation
Unconditioned response (UCR)

Conditioning phase

Tone or bell

Neutral stimulus

+

Food

Unconditioned stimulus

Elicits
Several pairings → Salivation

Postconditioning phase

Tone or bell

Conditioned stimulus (CS) → Elicits → Salivation
Conditioned response (CR)

Figure 5.2 ■ A Schematic Representation of Classical Conditioning Prior to conditioning, food elicits salivation. The tone, a neutral stimulus, elicits either no response or an orienting response. During conditioning, the tone is rung just before meat is placed on the dog's tongue. After several repetitions, the tone, now a CS, elicits salivation, the CR.

Taste Aversion: Are All Stimuli Created Equal?

When I was a child in the Bronx, my friends and I would go to the movies on Saturday mornings. One day, my friends dared me to eat two huge containers of buttered popcorn by myself. I had no problem with the first enormous basket of buttered popcorn. More slowly—much more slowly—I forced down the second basket. I felt bloated and nauseated. The taste of the butter, corn, and salt lingered in my mouth and nose, and my head spun. It was obvious to me that no one could talk me into even another handful of popcorn that day. But I was surprised that I couldn't face buttered popcorn again for a year.

Years later, I learned that psychologists refer to my response to buttered popcorn as a *taste aversion*. **Question 4: What is a taste aversion, and why are taste aversions of special interest to psychologists?**

Taste aversions are fascinating examples of classical conditioning. They are adaptive because they motivate organisms to avoid potentially harmful foods. Although taste aversions are acquired by association, they are of special interest because they differ from other kinds of classical conditioning in a couple of ways. First, only one association may be required. For example, many decades have now passed since the popcorn incident, but the distinctive odor of buttered popcorn still turns my stomach. **Truth or Fiction Revisited:** Thus, a single nauseating meal can give rise to a taste aversion that lasts for years. Second, whereas most kinds of classical conditioning require the unconditioned stimulus and conditioned stimulus to be close together in time, in taste aversion the unconditioned stimulus (in this case, nausea) can occur hours after the conditioned stimulus (in this case, the flavor of food).

THE EVOLUTION OF TASTE AVERSION Research on taste aversion also challenges the behaviorist view that organisms learn to associate any stimuli that are linked in time. In reality, not all stimuli are created equal. The evolutionary perspective suggests that animals (and humans) would be *biologically prepared* to develop aversions that are adaptive in their environmental settings (Bouton, 2010; Öhman & Mineka, 2001). That is, those of us who develop taste aversions quickly are less likely to feast on poisonous food, more likely to survive, and thus more likely to contribute our genes to future generations.

In a classic study, Garcia and Koelling (1966) conditioned two groups of rats. Each group was exposed to the same three-part conditioned stimulus: a taste of sweetened water, a light, and a clicker. Afterward, one group was presented with an unconditioned stimulus of nausea (induced by poison or radiation), and the other group was presented with an unconditioned stimulus of electric shock.

After conditioning, the rats who had been nauseated showed an aversion to sweetened water but not to the light or clicker. Although all three stimuli had been presented at the same time, *the rats had acquired only the taste aversion.* After conditioning, the rats that had been shocked avoided both the light and the clicker, *but they did not show a taste aversion to the sweetened water.* For each group of rats, the conditioning that took place was adaptive. In the natural scheme of things, nausea is more likely to stem from poisoned food than from lights or sounds. So, for nauseated rats, acquiring the taste aversion was appropriate. Sharp pain, in contrast, is more likely to stem from natural events involving lights (fire, lightning) and sharp sounds (twigs snapping, things falling). Therefore, it was more appropriate for the shocked animals to develop an aversion to the light and the clicker than to the sweetened water.

In classical conditioning, organisms learn to connect stimuli, such as the sound of a tone with food. Now let's consider various factors in classical conditioning beginning with what happens when the connection between stimuli is severed, an event termed *extinction.* This is of great interest to psychologists because, as we will see, psychologists have used extinction to help people overcome fears.

Extinction and Spontaneous Recovery

Extinction and *spontaneous recovery* are aspects of conditioning that help us adapt by updating our expectations or revising our thinking about (representations of) the changing environment. For example, a dog may have learned to associate a new scent (a conditioned stimulus) with the appearance of a dangerous animal. It can then take evasive action when it catches a whiff of that scent. A child may have learned to connect hearing a car pull into the driveway (a conditioned stimulus) with the arrival of his or her parents (an unconditioned stimulus). Thus, the child may begin to squeal with delight (squealing is a conditioned response) when the car is heard. Let's see how extinction and spontaneous recovery may enter the picture.

EXTINCTION Question 5: What is the role of extinction in classical conditioning?
Extinction can occur when the times—and the relationships between events—change. The once-dangerous animal may no longer be a threat to the dog. (What a puppy perceives as a threat may lose its fearsomeness once the dog matures.) After moving to a new house, the child's parents may commute by means of public transportation. The sound of a car in a nearby driveway may signal a neighbor's, not a parent's, homecoming. When conditioned stimuli (such as the scent of a dog or the sound of a car) are no longer followed by unconditioned stimuli (a dangerous animal, a parent's homecoming), they lose their ability to elicit conditioned responses. In this way, the organism adapts to a changing environment.

In classical conditioning, **extinction** is the process by which conditioned stimuli lose the ability to elicit conditioned responses because the conditioned stimuli are no longer associated with unconditioned stimuli. That is, the puppy loses its fear of the once-threatening animal's scent, or the toddler is no longer gleeful at the sounds of the car in the driveway. From the cognitive perspective, extinction changes the animal's mental representation of its environment because the conditioned stimulus no longer allows it to make the same prediction.

In experiments on the extinction of conditioned responses, Pavlov found that repeated presentations of the conditioned stimulus (in this case, the tone) without the unconditioned stimulus (in this case, meat powder) led to extinction of the conditioned response (salivation in response to the tone). Basically, the dog stopped salivating at the sound of the tone. Interestingly, Figure 5.3 ■ shows that after the initial conditioning, a dog's responsive salivation increased for a while and then leveled off. The dog was conditioned to begin to salivate in response to a tone after two or three pairings of the tone with meat powder. Continued pairings of the stimuli led to increased salivation (measured in number of drops of saliva). After seven or eight trials, salivation leveled off at 11 to 12 drops.

In the next series of experiments, salivation in response to the tone was extinguished through several trials in which the tone was presented without the meat powder. After about 10 extinction trials, the animal no longer salivated. That is, it no longer showed the conditioned response when the tone sounded.

Formation of a Taste Aversion? Taste aversions can be acquired by a single pairing of the UCS and the CS. Evolutionary psychologists hypothesize that the rapid acquisition of a taste aversion would make it more likely that an animal would not eat the repellent food again, would survive, and then reproduce, transmitting the genes for rapid acquisition of a taste aversion to the next generation.

Extinction The process by which stimuli lose their ability to evoke learned responses because the events that had followed the stimuli no longer occur. (The learned responses are said to be *extinguished.*)

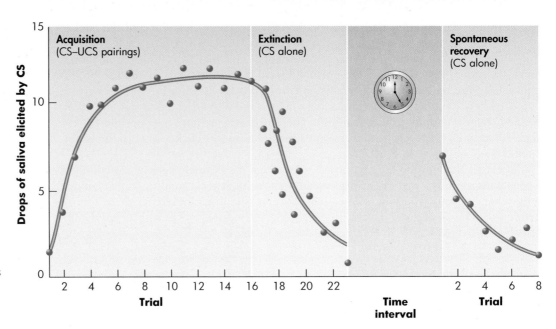

Figure 5.3 ■ Learning and Extinction Curves Actual data from Pavlov (1927) compose the jagged line, and the curved lines are idealized. In the acquisition phase, a dog salivates (shows a CR) in response to a tone (CS) after a few trials in which the tone is paired with meat powder (the UCS). Afterward, the CR is extinguished in about 10 trials during which the CS is not followed by the UCS. After a rest period, the CR recovers spontaneously. A second series of extinction trials leads to more rapid extinction of the CR.

Spontaneous recovery The recurrence of an extinguished response as a function of the passage of time.

Spontaneous Recovery of Approaching a Water Hole after Time Has Passed If a water hole dries up, animals' tendencies to visit the water hole in a given season may be extinguished. But when a new season rolls around, the tendency to visit the water hole may spontaneously recover. Evolution would favor the survival of animals that associate thirst with the water hole from time to time so that they are likely to revisit it when it again holds water.

Now, what will happen if we allow a couple of days to pass and then sound the tone again? **Question 6: What is the role of spontaneous recovery in classical conditioning?**

SPONTANEOUS RECOVERY We asked what would happen if we were to allow a day or two to pass after we had extinguished salivation in Pavlov's dog and then again sounded the tone. Where would you place your bet? Would the dog salivate or not?

If you bet that the dog would again show the conditioned response (in this case, salivation in response to the tone), you were correct. Organisms tend to show **spontaneous recovery** of extinguished conditioned responses merely as a function of the passage of time. For this reason, the term *extinction* may be a bit misleading. When a species of animal becomes extinct, all the members of that species capable of reproducing have died. The species vanishes. But the experimental extinction of conditioned responses does not lead to their permanent eradication. Rather, extinction merely *inhibits* the response. The response remains available for future performance under the "right" conditions.

Evolutionary psychologists note that spontaneous recovery, like extinction, is adaptive. What would happen if the child heard no car in the driveway for several months? Possibly, the next time a car entered the driveway, the child would associate the sounds with a parent's homecoming (rather than with the arrival of a neighbor). This expectation could be appropriate. After all, *something* had changed when no car entered the nearby driveway for so long. In the wild, a water hole may contain water for only a couple of months during the year. But evolution would favor the survival of animals that associate the water hole with the thirst drive from time to time so that they will return to it when it again holds water.

As time passes and the seasons change, things sometimes follow circular paths and arrive where they were before. Spontaneous recovery seems to function as a mechanism whereby organisms can adapt successfully to situations that recur from time to time.

Generalization and Discrimination

No two things are exactly alike. Traffic lights are hung at slightly different heights, and shades of red differ a little, as do shades of green. The barking of two dogs differs, and the sound of the same animal differs slightly from one bark to the next. Rustling sounds in the undergrowth differ, but evolution would favor the survival of rabbits and deer that flee when they perceive any one of many possible rustling sounds. Adaptation requires us to respond similarly (or *generalize*) to stimuli that are equivalent in function and to respond differently to (or *discriminate* between) stimuli that are not.

GENERALIZATION Question 7: What is the role of generalization in classical conditioning? Pavlov noted that responding to different stimuli as though they are functionally equivalent—*generalizing*—is adaptive for animals. Generalization is the tendency for a conditioned response to be evoked by stimuli that are similar to the stimulus to which the response was conditioned. Pavlov demonstrated generalization by first getting his dog to salivate when it was shown a circle. Later, the dog salivated in response to being shown closed geometric figures—even squares! The more closely the figure resembled a circle, however, the greater the strength of the response (as measured by drops of saliva).

But what happens if food follows the presentation of a circle but not a square?

DISCRIMINATION Question 8: What is the role of discrimination in classical conditioning? Organisms must also learn that (1) many stimuli perceived as being similar are functionally different, and (2) they must respond adaptively to each. During the first couple of months of life, for example, babies can discriminate their mother's voice from those of other women. They often stop crying when they hear their mother but not when they hear a stranger.

Pavlov showed that a dog conditioned to salivate in response to circles could be trained *not* to salivate in response to ellipses. After a while, the dog no longer salivated in response to the ellipses. Instead, it showed **discrimination:** It salivated only in response to circles. Pavlov found that increasing the difficulty of the discrimination task apparently tormented the dog. After the dog was trained to salivate in response to circles but not ellipses, Pavlov showed it a series of progressively rounder ellipses. Eventually, the dog could no longer distinguish the ellipses from circles. The animal was so stressed that it urinated, defecated, barked profusely, and snapped at laboratory personnel.

How do we explain the dog's belligerent behavior? In a classic work written more than 70 years ago, titled *Frustration and Aggression,* a group of behaviorally oriented psychologists suggested that frustration induces aggression (Dollard et al., 1939). Why is failure to discriminate circles from ellipses frustrating? For one thing, in such experiments, rewards—such as food—are usually contingent on correct discrimination. That is, if the dog errs, it doesn't get fed. Cognitive theorists, however, disagree (Rescorla, 1988). They would say that in Pavlov's experiment, the dog lost the ability to adjust its mental map of the environment as the ellipses grew more circular. Thus, it was frustrated.

Daily living requires appropriate generalization and discrimination. No two hotels are alike, but when we travel from one city to another, it is adaptive to expect to stay in a hotel. It is encouraging that a green light in Washington has the same meaning as a green light in Paris. But returning home in the evening requires the ability to discriminate between our home and those of others. And imagine the confusion that would occur if we could not discriminate our friends, mates, or coworkers from other people!

Higher Order Conditioning

Consider a child who is burned by touching a hot stove. After this experience, the sight of the stove may evoke fear. And because hearing the word "stove" may evoke a mental image of the stove, just hearing the word may evoke fear.

© Mike Kemp/Getty Images

Stop and Check This Out You have never seen this traffic light before and are unlikely to come across it. However, you would show excellent judgment to stop at it if you did— or at least we assume that you would. This is because of generalization from your other experiences with traffic lights.

Generalization In conditioning, the tendency for a conditioned response to be evoked by stimuli that are similar to the stimulus to which the response was conditioned.

Discrimination In conditioning, the tendency for an organism to distinguish between a conditioned stimulus and similar stimuli that do not forecast an unconditioned stimulus.

Recall the mini-experiment in which an adult smiles, says "kitchie-coo," and then tickles an infant's foot. After a few repetitions, just smiling at the infant may cause the infant to retract its foot. In fact, just walking into the room may have the same effect! The experiences with touching the hot stove and tickling the infant's foot are examples of higher order conditioning. **Question 9: What is higher order conditioning?**

In **higher order conditioning**, a previously neutral stimulus (for example, hearing the word "stove" or seeing the adult who had done the tickling enter the room) comes to serve as a learned or conditioned stimulus after being paired repeatedly with a stimulus that has already become a learned or conditioned stimulus (for example, seeing the stove or hearing the phrase "kitchie-coo"). Pavlov demonstrated higher order conditioning by first conditioning a dog to salivate in response to a tone. He then repeatedly paired the shining of a light with the sounding of the tone. After several pairings, shining the light (the higher order conditioned stimulus) came to evoke the response (salivation) that had been elicited by the tone (the first-order conditioned stimulus).

In the nearby Closer Look, we meet one of the celebrities of the science of psychology, "Little Albert." Albert did not seek his fame; after all, he was not even a year old at the time. At that tender age, he was conditioned by John B. Watson and Rosalie Rayner to fear rats and, by generalization, all furry animals.

Higher order conditioning A classical conditioning procedure in which a previously neutral stimulus comes to elicit the response brought forth by a *conditioned* stimulus by being paired repeatedly with that conditioned stimulus.

Biological preparedness Readiness to acquire a certain kind of conditioned response due to the biological makeup of the organism.

Video Connections—Little Albert

Watch the video to see the historic albeit unethical footage of John B. Watson and Rosalie Rayner conditioning Little Albert. You will learn more about the process of classical conditioning and have the opportunity to decide how you would go about reversing Albert's fear of rats. Go to Psychology CourseMate at www.cengagebrain.com to watch this video.

Preparedness and the Conditioning of Fear

Little Albert developed his fear of rats easily enough, but would Watson and Rayner have been able to condition him to fear flowers or potted plants? Perhaps not. **Question 10: Was Little Albert "prepared" to acquire his fear of rats?** As

A CLOSER LOOK   Who Was "Little Albert"?

People such as "Little Albert," who participate in well-known, controversial research studies, "have become unwilling protagonists whose stories are told over and over in psychology textbooks. So people become very curious. Who were they, and how did they feel about the experiment?"
—Cathy Faye, Archives of the History of American Psychology, University of Akron

© Archives of the History of American Psychology, the Center for the History of Psychology—The University of Akron

One of psychology's mysteries appears to have been recently solved (DeAngelis, 2010). An investigative team—led by Hall P. Beck and including Sharman Levinson and Gary Irons (2009)—pored over public records, conducted interviews with relatives of the lad they suspected of being Albert, and consulted facial recognition experts who compared the photos of the boy in the experiment to family photos. Ultimately, they determined that Little Albert, who was conditioned to fear furry objects before his first birthday, was the son of a wet nurse who had lived and worked at a Johns Hopkins campus pediatric hospital at the time of Watson and Rayner's famous experiment. Albert's actual name was Douglas Merritte, and his mother was

paid all of a dollar for her 9-month-old son's participation.

In 1920, the behaviorist John B. Watson and his future wife, Rosalie Rayner, published the report of their demonstration that emotional reactions can be acquired through classical conditioning. The subject of their demonstration became known as "Little Albert" (a counterpart to Freud's famous case study of "Little Hans"—see Chapter 12). Using a method that many psychologists have criticized as unethical, Watson startled Little Albert by clanging steel bars behind his head whenever the infant played with a laboratory rat. After repeated pairings, Albert showed fear of the rat even when the clanging was halted. Albert's fear also generalized to objects that were similar in appearance to the rat, such as a rabbit and the fur collar on a woman's coat. This study has become a hallmark in psychology, although Watson has also been criticized for not attempting to countercondition Albert's fear.

suggested by Arne Öhman and Susan Mineka (2003), humans (and other primates) may be **biologically prepared** by evolutionary forces to rapidly develop fears of certain animals, including snakes:

> Snakes are commonly regarded as slimy, slithering creatures worthy of fear and disgust.... Human fear of snakes and other reptiles may be a distant effect of the conditions under which early mammals evolved. In the world they inhabited, the animal kingdom was dominated by awesome reptiles, the dinosaurs, and so the prerequisite for early mammals to deliver genes to future generations was to avoid getting caught in the fangs of Tyrannosaurus rex and its relatives.
>
> Öhman and Mineka, 2003

People also seem to be prepared to fear other reptiles, spiders, thunder, threatening faces, sharp objects, darkness, and heights—all of which would have been sources of danger to our ancestors and which, to some degree, may still threaten us (Gerdes et al., 2009; Mineka & Oehlberg, 2008; Starratt & Shackelford, 2010). Susan Mineka and Arne Öhman (2002) ran an experiment in which they paired electric shock with slides of spiders, snakes, and other objects, including mushrooms, flowers, and firearms. Physiological monitoring of participants showed that the spiders and snakes produced more rapid conditioning, greater fear responses, and more resistance to having the fear responses extinguished. Therefore, it would seem that painful experiences with evolutionarily neutral objects—such as plant life, modern tools, hot stoves, and electrical appliances and outlets—are not as likely to lead to the development of severe fears.

Applications of Classical Conditioning

Watson did not attempt to eliminate Little Albert's fear of rats. However, soon afterward, a protégé of Watson carried out a well-known experiment in counterconditioning fears. In **counterconditioning**, an organism learns to respond to a stimulus in a way that is incompatible with a response that was conditioned earlier. For example, relaxation is incompatible with a fear response. Although the concept of counterconditioning did not do Little Albert any good, psychologists have used it to reduce fears in other people. Let's consider counterconditioning and other applications of classical conditioning.

COUNTERCONDITIONING The reasoning behind counterconditioning is this: if fears, as Watson has shown, can be conditioned by painful experiences, perhaps fears can be *counterconditioned* by substituting pleasant experiences. In 1924, Watson's protégé Mary Cover Jones attempted counterconditioning with a boy called Peter, 2 years and 10 months old, as a method of counteracting fear.

Peter had an intense fear of rabbits. Jones arranged for a rabbit to be gradually brought closer to Peter while he engaged in some of his favorite activities, such as munching on candy and cookies. **Truth or Fiction Revisited:** Thus, it is true that psychologists helped a young boy overcome his fear of rabbits by having him eat cookies while a rabbit was brought progressively closer. Jones first placed the rabbit in a far corner of the room while Peter munched and crunched. Peter cast a wary eye, but he continued to consume the

Counterconditioning A fear-reduction technique in which pleasant stimuli are associated with fear-evoking stimuli so that the fear-evoking stimuli lose their aversive qualities.

An Unlikely Encounter in the 21st Century Visitors to the Dinosaur Park in Kleinwelka, Germany, are walking past a model of a *Tyrannosaurus rex*. Preparedness theory suggests that we humans are likely to develop fears of snakes and other reptiles (the Tyrannosaurus was a reptile) because of events in our evolutionary history. Öhman and Mineka write: "The prerequisite for early mammals to deliver genes to future generations was to avoid getting caught in the fangs of Tyrannosaurus rex."

Flooding A behavioral fear-reduction technique based on principles of classical conditioning. Fear-evoking stimuli (CSs) are presented continuously in the absence of actual harm so that fear responses (CRs) are extinguished.

Systematic desensitization A behavioral fear-reduction technique in which a hierarchy of fear-evoking stimuli is presented while the person remains relaxed.

treat. Over a couple of months, the animal was brought gradually closer until, eventually, Peter ate treats and touched the rabbit at the same time. Jones theorized that the joy of eating was incompatible with fear and thus counterconditioned it.

FLOODING AND SYSTEMATIC DESENSITIZATION If Mary Cover Jones had simply plopped the rabbit on Peter's lap rather than bring it gradually closer, she would have been using the method of **flooding**. Had she done so, the cookies on the plate, not to mention those already eaten, might have decorated the walls—even if the method eventually worked.

Flooding, like counterconditioning, is a behavior therapy method for reducing fears. It is based on the classical conditioning principle of extinction (Mystkowski & Mineka, 2007). In flooding, the client is exposed to the fear-evoking stimulus until the fear response is extinguished. Little Albert, for example, might have been placed in close contact with a rat until his fear had become fully extinguished. In extinction, the conditioned stimulus (in this case, the rat) is presented repeatedly in the absence of the unconditioned stimulus (the clanging of the steel bars) until the conditioned response (fear) is no longer evoked. But note that according to preparedness theory, fear responses rooted in our evolutionary history can be very difficult to extinguish.

A German study of 75 people aged 18 to 54 evaluated the effectiveness of a flooding-type treatment for agoraphobia (fear of being out in busy open areas) (Fischer et al., 1998). Agoraphobic participants were exposed persistently—for 2 to 3 weeks, all day long—to densely populated open places. Participants were assessed immediately after treatment, then 6 months after treatment, and as much as 53 months after treatment. They showed significant reductions in anxiety and in avoidance of busy open places at each assessment. Although flooding is usually effective, it is unpleasant. (When you are fearful of rats, being placed in a small room with one is no picnic.) For this reason, behavior therapists frequently prefer to use **systematic desensitization**, in which the client is gradually exposed to fear-evoking stimuli under relaxing circumstances. For example, while feeling relaxed, Little Albert might have been given an opportunity to look at photos of rats or to see live rats from a distance before they were brought closer to him. Systematic desensitization takes longer than flooding but is not as unpleasant.

Will Fear of Busy Open Places Be Extinguished by Persistent Exposure?
Research results are encouraging. It seems that persistent exposure of agoraphobic individuals to busy open areas reduces their anxiety and their avoidance of such places.

© Pierre Perrin/Zoko/Sygma/Corbis

LearningConnections • CLASSICAL CONDITIONING: LEARNING WHAT IS LINKED TO WHAT

ACTIVE REVIEW (1) Behaviorists define learning in terms of a change in _____. (2) Cognitive psychologists define learning in terms of a change in the way organisms mentally _____ the environment. (3) A _____ is an environmental condition that evokes a response. (4) A response to an unconditioned stimulus (UCS) is called a(n) _____ response (UCR). (5) A response to a conditioned stimulus (CS) is termed a(n) _____ response (CR). (6) Repeated presentation of a CS (such as a tone) without the UCS (such as meat) will _____ the CR (salivation). (7) Extinguished responses often show _____ recovery as a function of the passage of time. (8) In stimulus _____, organisms learn to show a conditioned response in response to a limited range of stimuli. (9) John B. Watson and Rosalie Rayner used conditioning to teach "Little _____" to fear rats. (10) In the behavior-therapy method of _____, a client is continuously exposed to a fear-evoking stimulus until the fear response is extinguished.

REFLECT AND RELATE Have you heard or used the expression "That rings a bell"? If so, what do you think it means? Do you know where the expression comes from? Is the phrase historically accurate?

CRITICAL THINKING Critical thinkers pay attention to the definitions of terms. Psychologists disagree on the definition of learning. Behaviorists define learning as a relatively permanent change in behavior that arises from experience. Cognitive psychologists define learning as a change in the way an organism mentally represents the environment due to experience. Why do they have these different approaches?

 Go to Psychology CourseMate at **www.cengagebrain.com** for an interactive version of these questions.

Through classical conditioning, we learn to associate stimuli so that a simple, usually passive, response made to one stimulus is then made in response to the other. In the case of Little Albert, clanging noises were associated with presentation of a rat. As a result, the rat came to elicit the fear response caused by the clanging. However, classical conditioning is only one kind of learning that occurs in these situations. After Little Albert acquired his fear of the rat, his voluntary behavior changed. He avoided the rat as a way of reducing his fear. Thus, Little Albert had also engaged in another kind of learning—*operant conditioning*.

Question 11: What is operant conditioning? In operant conditioning, organisms learn to do things—or *not* to do things—because of the outcomes of their behavior. For example, I avoided buttered popcorn to prevent nausea. But we also seek fluids when we are thirsty, sex when we are aroused, and an ambient temperature of 68° to 70°F when we feel too hot or too cold. *Classical conditioning focuses on how organisms form anticipations about their environments. Operant conditioning focuses on what they* do *about them.*

We begin this section with the historic research of the psychologist Edward L. Thorndike. Then we will examine the more recent work of B. F. Skinner.

Edward L. Thorndike and the Law of Effect

In the 1890s, stray cats were mysteriously disappearing from the streets and alleyways of Harlem. Some of them, it turned out, were being brought to the quarters of Columbia University doctoral student Edward Thorndike. Thorndike was using the cats as subjects in experiments on the effects of rewards and punishments on learning.

Thorndike placed the cats in so-called puzzle boxes. If the animal managed to pull a dangling string, a latch would be released, allowing it to jump out and reach a bowl of food. When first placed in a puzzle box, a cat would try to squeeze through any opening and would claw and bite at the confining bars and wire. It would claw at anything it could reach. Through such random behavior, it might take 3 to 4 minutes for the cat to chance upon the response of pulling the string. Pulling the string would open the cage and allow the cat to reach the food. When placed back in the cage, it might again take several minutes for the animal to pull the string. But with repetition, it took the cat progressively less time. After seven or eight repetitions, the cat might pull the string immediately when placed back in the box.

Thorndike explained the cat's learning to pull the string in terms of his **law of effect. Question 12: What is the law of effect?** According to this law, a response (such as string pulling) is—to use Thorndike's term—"stamped in" (that is, strengthened) in a particular situation (such as being inside a puzzle box) by a reward (escaping from the box and eating). That is, **rewards** stamp in S–R (stimulus–response) connections. **Punishments**—using Thorndike's terminology once again—"stamp out" S–R connections. That is, organisms learn not to engage in behavior that brings on punishment. That is the law of effect, but later, we shall see that the effects of punishment on learning are not so certain.

B. F. Skinner and Reinforcement

When it comes to unusual war stories, few will top that of B. F. Skinner. One of Skinner's wartime efforts was "Project Pigeon." **Truth or Fiction Revisited:** During World War II, Skinner proposed that pigeons be trained to guide missiles to their targets. In their training, the pigeons would be **reinforced** with food pellets for pecking at targets projected onto a screen (see Figure 5.4 ■). Once trained, the pigeons would be placed in missiles. Their pecking at similar targets displayed on a screen would correct the missile's flight path, resulting in a "hit" and a sacrificed pigeon. However, plans for building the necessary missile—for some reason called the *Pelican* and not the *Pigeon*—were scrapped. The pigeon equipment was too bulky, and Skinner lamented his suggestion

"An American monkey, after getting drunk on brandy, would never touch it again, and thus is much wiser than most men."

CHARLES DARWIN

"It is an open question whether any behavior based on fear of eternal punishment can be regarded as ethical or should be regarded as merely cowardly."

MARGARET MEAD

"Your most unhappy customers are your greatest source of learning."

BILL GATES

"A man who carries a cat by the tail learns something he can learn in no other way."

MARK TWAIN

Law of effect Thorndike's view that pleasant events stamp in responses, and unpleasant events stamp them out.

Reward A pleasant stimulus that increases the frequency of the behavior it follows.

Punishment An unpleasant stimulus that suppresses the behavior it follows.

Reinforce To follow a response with a stimulus that increases the frequency of the response.

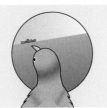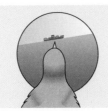

Figure 5.4 ■ Project Pigeon During World War II, B. F. Skinner suggested using operant conditioning to train pigeons to guide missiles to their targets. The pigeons would first be reinforced for pecking targets projected on a screen. Afterward, in combat, pecking the on-screen target would keep the missile on course.

Burrhus Frederic Skinner During his first TV appearance, psychologist B. F. Skinner (1904–1990) was asked, "Would you, if you had to choose, burn your children or your books?" He said with a wry smile that he would have chosen to burn his children because his contribution to the future lay more in his writings than in his genes. Skinner delighted in controversy and enjoyed shocking TV viewers with his irreverent wit.

"Education is what survives when what has been learned has been forgotten."

B. F. SKINNER

"Society attacks early, when the individual is helpless."

B. F. SKINNER

Operant behavior Behavior that operates on, or manipulates, the environment.

Operant conditioning A simple form of learning in which an organism learns to engage in certain behavior because it is reinforced.

Operant The same as an operant behavior.

was not taken seriously. Might one conclude that the Department of Defense decided that Project Pigeon was—forgive me—for the birds?

Question 13: What was the contribution of B. F. Skinner to the psychology of learning? Project Pigeon may have been scrapped, but the principles of learning that Skinner applied to the project have found wide application. Skinner taught pigeons and other animals to engage in **operant behavior**, behavior that operates on, or manipulates, the environment. In classical conditioning, involuntary responses such as salivation or eye blinks are often conditioned. In operant conditioning, *voluntary* responses such as pecking at a target, pressing a lever, or many of the skills required for playing tennis are acquired, or conditioned.

Operant conditioning is therefore defined as a simple form of learning in which an organism learns to engage in certain behavior because of the effects of that behavior. In operant conditioning, we learn to engage in operant behaviors, also known simply as **operants**, that result in presumably desirable outcomes such as food, a hug, an A on a test, attention, or social approval. For example, some children learn to conform their behavior to social rules to earn the attention and approval of their parents and teachers. Other children, ironically, may learn to "misbehave," because misbehavior also gets attention from other people. In particular, children may learn to be "bad" when their "good" behavior is routinely ignored. Some children who do not do well in school, in fact, seek reinforcement from deviant peers (Patterson et al., 2000).

Methods of Operant Conditioning

In his influential work *The Behavior of Organisms,* Skinner (1938) made many theoretical and technological innovations. Among them was his focus on discrete behaviors such as lever pressing as the *unit,* or type, of behavior to be studied (Glenn et al., 1992). Other psychologists might focus on how organisms think or "feel." Skinner focused on measurable things that they *do.* Many psychologists have found these kinds of behavior inconsequential, especially when it comes to explaining and predicting human behavior. But Skinner's supporters point out that focusing on discrete behavior creates the potential for helpful changes. For example, in helping people combat depression, one psychologist might focus on their "feelings." A Skinnerian psychologist would focus on cataloging (and modifying) the types of things that depressed people actually *do.* Directly modifying depressive behavior might also brighten clients' self-reports about their feelings of depression.

To study operant behavior efficiently, Skinner devised an animal cage (or "operant chamber") that has been dubbed the *Skinner box.* (Skinner himself repeatedly requested that his operant chamber *not* be called a Skinner box. History has thus far failed to honor his wishes, however.) Such a box is shown in Figure 5.5 ■. The cage is ideal for laboratory experimentation because experimental conditions can be carefully introduced and removed, and the effects on laboratory animals (defined as changes in rates of lever pressing) can be carefully observed.

The rat in Figure 5.5 was deprived of food and placed in a Skinner box with a lever at one end. At first, it sniffed its way around the cage and engaged in random behavior. The rat's first pressing of the lever was inadvertent. However, because of this action, a food pellet dropped into the cage. The arrival of the food pellet increased the probability that the rat would press the lever again. The pellet is thus said to have *reinforced* lever pressing.

Skinner's operant methodology even works when pigeons can fly in and out of Skinner boxes in the wild. Japanese researcher Ken'ichi Fuji (2002) poured commercial grain into the feeder, and several hundred pigeons flew in and out of the box over a 3-month period. Although the pigeons generally learned to peck a key to obtain the grain, one pair of pigeons showed a fascinating variation on the theme. One of them always did the pecking, while the other always ate the grain!

In operant conditioning, it matters little how the first response that is reinforced comes to be made. The animal can happen on it by chance, as in random learning. The animal can also be physically guided to make the response. You may command your dog to "Sit!" and then press its backside down until it is in a sitting position. Finally, you reinforce sitting with food or a pat on the head and a kind word. Animal trainers use physical guiding or coaxing to bring about the first "correct" response. Can you imagine how long it would take to train your dog if you waited for it to sit or roll over and then seized the opportunity to command it to sit or roll over? Both of you would age significantly in the process.

People, of course, can be verbally guided into desired responses when they are learning tasks such as spelling, adding numbers, or operating a machine. But they need to be informed when they have made the correct response. Knowledge of results often is all the reinforcement people need to learn new skills.

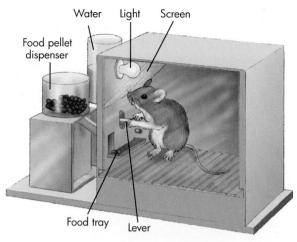

Figure 5.5 ■ The Effects of Reinforcement One of the celebrities of modern psychology, a laboratory rat, earns its keep in a Skinner box. The animal presses a lever because of reinforcement—in the form of food pellets—delivered through the feeder. The habit strength of this operant is the frequency of lever pressing.

Types of Reinforcers

Any stimulus that increases the probability that responses preceding it—whether pecking a button in a Skinner box or studying for a quiz—will be repeated serves as a reinforcer. Reinforcers include food pellets when an animal has been deprived of food, water when it has been deprived of liquid, the opportunity to mate, and the sound of a tone that has previously been associated with eating. **Question 14: What are the various kinds of reinforcers?** Skinner distinguished between *positive* and *negative* reinforcers and *primary* and *secondary* reinforcers.

POSITIVE AND NEGATIVE REINFORCERS Positive reinforcers increase the probability that a behavior will occur when they are applied. Food and approval usually serve as positive reinforcers. Negative reinforcers increase the probability that a behavior will occur when the reinforcers are removed (see Figure 5.6 ■). People often learn to plan ahead so that they need not fear things will go wrong. In such cases, fear acts as a negative reinforcer because removal of fear increases the probability that the behaviors preceding it (such as planning ahead) will be repeated.

Positive reinforcer A reinforcer that when *presented* increases the frequency of an operant.

Negative reinforcer A reinforcer that when *removed* increases the frequency of an operant.

Procedure	Behavior	Consequence	Change in behavior
Use of positive reinforcement	Behavior (Studying)	Positive reinforcer (Teacher approval) is *presented* when student studies	Frequency of behavior *increases* (Student studies more)
Use of negative reinforcement	Behavior (Studying)	Negative reinforcer (Teacher disapproval) is *removed* when student studies	Frequency of behavior *increases* (Student studies more)

Figure 5.6 ■ Positive versus Negative Reinforcers All reinforcers increase the frequency of behavior. However, negative reinforcers are aversive stimuli that increase the frequency of behavior when they are removed. In these examples, teacher approval functions as a positive reinforcer when students study harder because of it. Teacher disapproval functions as a negative reinforcer when its removal increases the frequency of studying. Can you think of situations in which teacher approval might function as a negative reinforcer?

Some reinforcers have more impact than others. For example, pigeons that learn one food tray has more food than another choose the tray with more food (Olthof & Roberts, 2000). Similarly, you would probably choose a job that paid $1,000 over a similar job that paid $10. (If not, get in touch with me—I have some chores for you.) With sufficient reinforcement, operants become *habits*. They have a high probability of recurrence in certain situations.

IMMEDIATE VERSUS DELAYED REINFORCERS Immediate reinforcers are more effective than delayed reinforcers. This means that the short-term consequences of behavior often provide more of an incentive than the long-term consequences.

For example, some students socialize when they should be studying because the pleasure of socializing is immediate. Studying may not pay off until the final exam or graduation. (This is why younger students do better with frequent tests.) It is difficult to quit smoking cigarettes because the reinforcement of nicotine is immediate and the health hazards of smoking are more distant. Focusing on short-term reinforcement is also connected with risky sexual behavior, such as engaging in sexual activity with a stranger or failing to use devices to prevent pregnancy and sexually transmitted infections (Castor et al., 2010; Shuper et al., 2010). One of the aspects of being human is the ability to foresee the long-range consequences of one's behavior and choices. But immediate reinforcers—such as those cookies staring a would-be dieter in the face—can be powerful temptations indeed.

Now versus Later? For those who are addicted to nicotine, smoking provides immediate reinforcement. Most of the negative consequences of smoking, such as respiratory illnesses, are off in the future. How can smokers who want to quit keep those long-term outcomes in mind?

PRIMARY AND SECONDARY REINFORCERS We can also distinguish between primary and secondary, or conditioned, reinforcers. **Primary reinforcers** are effective because of the organism's biological makeup. Food, water, warmth (positive reinforcers), and pain (a negative reinforcer) all serve as primary reinforcers. **Secondary reinforcers** acquire their value through being associated with established reinforcers. For this reason, they are also termed **conditioned reinforcers**. We may seek money because we have learned that it can be exchanged for primary reinforcers. Part of understanding others lies in the ability to predict what they will find reinforcing.

Extinction and Spontaneous Recovery in Operant Conditioning

Keisha's teacher writes "Good" on all of her homework assignments before returning them. One day, her teacher no longer writes anything on the assignments—the reinforcement ends. Reinforcers are used to strengthen responses. What happens when reinforcement stops? **Question 15: What is the role of extinction in operant conditioning?**

In Pavlov's experiment, the meat powder was the event that followed and confirmed the appropriateness of salivation. In operant conditioning, the ensuing events are reinforcers. In operant conditioning, the extinction of learned responses results from the repeated performance of operant behavior without reinforcement. If you go for a month without mail, you may stop checking the mailbox because the mail served as reinforcement. In other words, reinforcers maintain operant behavior or strengthen habitual behavior in operant conditioning.

Question 16: What is the role of spontaneous recovery in operant conditioning? Spontaneous recovery of learned responses occurs in operant conditioning as well as in classical conditioning. For example, checking the mailbox again after going without letters for a while is spontaneous recovery of checking the mailbox. Spontaneous recovery is adaptive in operant conditioning as well as in classical conditioning. Reinforcers may once again become available after time elapses, just as there are new tender sprouts on twigs when the spring arrives.

Primary reinforcer A reinforcer whose effectiveness is based on the biological makeup of the organism and not on learning.

Secondary reinforcer A stimulus that gains reinforcement value through association with established reinforcers.

Conditioned reinforcer Another term for a secondary reinforcer.

166

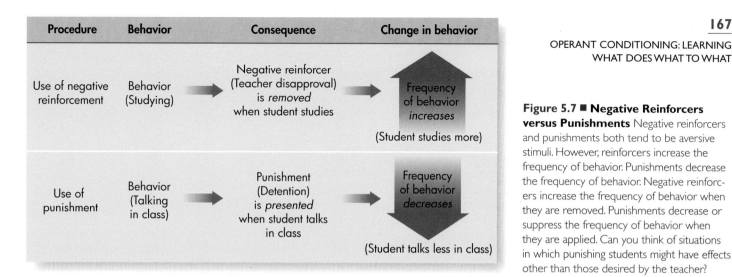

Procedure	Behavior	Consequence	Change in behavior
Use of negative reinforcement	Behavior (Studying)	Negative reinforcer (Teacher disapproval) is *removed* when student studies	Frequency of behavior *increases* (Student studies more)
Use of punishment	Behavior (Talking in class)	Punishment (Detention) is *presented* when student talks in class	Frequency of behavior *decreases* (Student talks less in class)

Figure 5.7 ■ Negative Reinforcers versus Punishments Negative reinforcers and punishments both tend to be aversive stimuli. However, reinforcers increase the frequency of behavior. Punishments decrease the frequency of behavior. Negative reinforcers increase the frequency of behavior when they are removed. Punishments decrease or suppress the frequency of behavior when they are applied. Can you think of situations in which punishing students might have effects other than those desired by the teacher?

Reinforcers versus Rewards and Punishments

Reinforcers are defined as stimuli that increase the frequency of behavior. **Question 17: Why did Skinner distinguish between reinforcers on the one hand and rewards and punishments on the other?** *Reinforcers* are known by their effects, whereas *rewards* and *punishments* are known by how they feel. Perhaps most reinforcers—food, hugs, having the other person admit to starting the argument, and so on—feel good, or are pleasant events. Yet things that we might assume would feel bad, such as a slap on the hand, disapproval from a teacher, even suspensions and detention may be positively reinforcing to some people—perhaps because such experiences confirm negative feelings toward teachers or one's belonging within a deviant subculture (Atkins et al., 2002).

Skinner preferred the concept of reinforcement to that of reward because reinforcement does not suggest trying to "get inside the head" of an organism (whether a human or lower animal) to guess what it would find pleasant or unpleasant. A list of reinforcers is arrived at scientifically, *empirically*—that is, by observing what sorts of stimuli increase the frequency of the behavior.

Whereas reinforcers—even negative reinforcers—increase the frequency of the behavior they follow, punishments decrease it (see Figure 5.7 ■). Punishment can rapidly suppress undesirable behavior (Gershoff, 2002) and may be warranted in "emergencies," such as when a child tries to run into the street. **Truth or Fiction Revisited:** Actually, punishment can work; that is, it can decrease the frequency of unwanted behavior.

Psychologists distinguish between *positive punishments* and *negative punishments*. Both kinds of punishments are aversive events, and both decrease the frequency of the behavior they follow (see Figure 5.8 ■). *Positive punishment* is

Procedure	Behavior	Consequence	Change in behavior
Use of positive punishment	Behavior (Parking illegally)	Positive punisher (Parking ticket) is presented—on driver's windshield	Frequency of behavior *decreases* (Driver parks illegally less often)
Use of negative punishment	Behavior (Using SmartPhone to text a friend while in class)	Negative punisher (Teacher removes student's SmartPhone during class)	Frequency of behavior *decreases* (Student stops using SmartPhone in class)

Figure 5.8 ■ Positive Punishments versus Negative Punishments Both positive and negative punishments decrease unwanted behavior. In the use of positive punishment, an aversive stimulus is presented. Negative punishment removes a desirable stimulus.

Although positive punishments can rapidly decrease the frequency of unwanted behavior, such as a child's running into the street without looking, many psychologists argue that punishment—especially corporal or physical punishment—often fails to achieve the goals of parents, teachers, and others. Psychologist Elizabeth Gershoff (2002) analyzed 88 studies of more than 36,000 children and found connections between physical punishment (for example, spanking) and various behavior patterns in childhood and adulthood. For example:

- Children who are physically punished are less likely to develop internal moral standards.

- Physical punishment is connected with poorer parent–child relationships.

- Physically punished children are more likely to be aggressive toward other children and to engage in criminal behavior later on.

- Physically punished children are more likely to abuse their spouses or their own children as adults.

Gershoff (2002) adds that punishment tends to suppress undesirable behavior only under circumstances when its delivery is guaranteed. It does not take children long to learn that they can "get away with murder" with one parent or teacher but not with another. Moreover, punishment does not in itself suggest an alternative acceptable form of behavior.

There are some other reasons not to use physical punishment:

- It hurts.

- Punished individuals may withdraw from the situation. Severely punished children may run away, cut class, or drop out of school.

- Children also *learn* responses that are punished. Whether or not children choose to perform punished responses, punishment rivets their attention on them.

To reward, or positively reinforce, children for desired behavior takes time and care. Avoiding the use of punishment is not enough. First, we must pay attention to children when they are behaving well. If we take their desirable behavior for granted and respond to them only when they misbehave, we may be encouraging misbehavior. Second, we must be certain that children are aware of, and capable of performing, desired behavior. It is harmful and fruitless merely to punish children for unwanted behavior. We must also carefully guide them, either physically or verbally, into making the desired responses and then reward them. We cannot teach children table manners by waiting for them to exhibit proper responses at random and then reinforcing them for their responses. Try holding a reward of ice cream behind your back and waiting for a child to exhibit proper manners. You will have a slippery dining room floor long before the child develops good table manners.

A Discriminative Stimulus You might not think that pigeons are very discriminating, yet they readily learn that pecking will not bring food in the presence of a discriminative stimulus such as a red light.

the application of an aversive stimulus to decrease unwanted behavior, such as spanking, scolding, or a parking ticket. *Negative punishment* is the removal of a pleasant stimulus, such as removing a student's opportunity to talk with friends in class by seating them apart, or removing a student's opportunity to mentally escape from class by taking her iPhone or iPad. Time out is a form of negative punishment because it places a misbehaving child in an environment in which he cannot experience rewards.

Discriminative Stimuli: Do You Step on the Accelerator When the Light Is Green or Red?

B. F. Skinner might not have been able to get his pigeons into the drivers' seats of missiles, but he had no problem training them to respond to traffic lights. Imagine yourself trying the following experiment.

You find a pigeon. Or you sit on a park bench, close your eyes, and one finds you. You place it in a Skinner box with a button on the wall. You drop a food pellet into the cage whenever the pigeon pecks the button. (Soon it will learn to peck the button whenever it has not eaten for a while.) Now you place a small green light in the cage and turn it on and off intermittently throughout the day. You reinforce button pecking with food whenever the green light is on but not when the light is off. It will not take long for this clever city pigeon to learn that it will gain as much by grooming itself or cooing and flapping around as it will by pecking the button when the light is off.

The green light has become a discriminative stimulus. **Question 19: What are discriminative stimuli?** Discriminative stimuli, such as green lights, act as signals or cues. They provide information about when an operant (in the case of the pigeon, pecking a button) will be reinforced (by a food pellet being dropped into the cage).

Operants that are not reinforced tend to be extinguished. For the pigeon in our experiment, the behavior of pecking the button *when the light is off* is extinguished.

A moment's reflection will suggest many ways that discriminative stimuli influence our behavior. Isn't it more efficient to answer the telephone when it is ringing? Do you think it is wise to ask someone for a favor when she or he is displaying anger and disapproval toward you?

We noted that a pigeon learns to peck a button if food drops into its cage when it does so. What if you want the pigeon to continue to peck the button, but you're running out of food? Do not despair. (Worse things have happened.) As we see in the following section, you can keep that bird pecking away indefinitely, even as you hold up on most of the food.

Time out Removal of an organism from a situation in which reinforcement is available when unwanted behavior is shown.

Discriminative stimulus In operant conditioning, a stimulus that indicates that reinforcement is available.

Robo Rats? Using Operant Conditioning to Teach Rats How to Search for Survivors of Disasters

A CLOSER LOOK

City dwellers know that rats rustle through garbage, but will we one day use rats to search through rubble where people cannot go to find survivors of disasters? The results of a study carried out in Brooklyn suggest that this is a real possibility.

Sanjiv Talwar and his colleagues (2002) used operant conditioning to guide rats through mazes by means of "remote control." They were inspired by an earthquake in India and the terrorist attacks of September 11, 2001, to test the method. The Haitian earthquake of 2010 provides an additional incentive for experimentation with new methods for finding out where people might be buried alive and in need of assistance.

The researchers outfitted five rats with electrodes in their brains and backpacks containing various electronic devices. One goal was to inform the rats whether they should turn right or left. Another was to reinforce them for doing so. To point the rats in the right direction, the team sent electric signals to brain regions that receive sensations from whiskers. The researchers inserted electrodes in the animals' pleasure centers to provide reinforcement.

The researchers placed the rats in a maze. As the animals approached a choice point where they could turn left or right, the researchers stimulated their brains as would a whisker touch on the left or right side of the head. When the animals turned in the direction of the "virtual touches," the researchers zapped their brains' pleasure centers.

Not only did the bursts of electricity teach the rats which way to turn, but they also apparently motivated the rats to move faster, even if it meant climbing steps or hopping from a shelf. The rat is apparently seeking the next burst. Talwar says that "the rats figure it out in 5 or 10 minutes" (Milius, 2002). The researchers steered the rats across a jagged pile of concrete, through an area so brightly lit that rats would normally avoid it, and even up a tree.

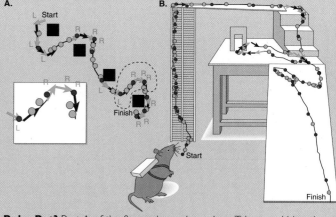

Robo Rat? Part A of the figure above shows how Talwar and his colleagues guided a rat through a zigzag course. They cued the rat to turn left (L) or right (R) and then reinforced it with a burst of electricity in the rat's pleasure center for doing so. Part B shows a more complex 3-D course through which a rat was guided. The goal is to shape rats to rustle through rubble to help find survivors of a disaster.

Source: "Behavioral neuroscience: Rat navigation guided by remote control" by Sanjiv K. Talwar et al., *Nature, 417* (2002), fig. 1, p. 37. Reprinted by permission of Nature Publishing Group.

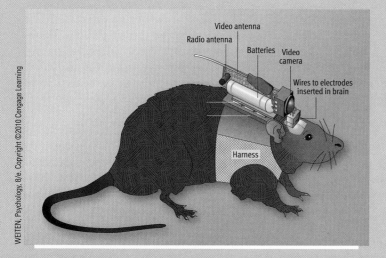

WEITEN, Psychology, 8/e. Copyright ©2010 Cengage Learning

Schedules of Reinforcement: How Often? Under What Conditions?

Continuous reinforcement A schedule of reinforcement in which every correct response is reinforced.

Partial reinforcement One of several reinforcement schedules in which not every correct response is reinforced.

Fixed-interval schedule A schedule in which a fixed amount of time must elapse between the previous and subsequent times that reinforcement is available.

Variable-interval schedule A schedule in which a variable amount of time must elapse between the previous and subsequent times that reinforcement is available.

Fixed-ratio schedule A schedule in which reinforcement is provided after a fixed number of correct responses.

Variable-ratio schedule A schedule in which reinforcement is provided after a variable number of correct responses.

Shaping A procedure for teaching complex behaviors that at first reinforces approximations of the target behavior.

Successive approximations Behaviors that are progressively closer to a target behavior.

In operant conditioning, some responses are maintained by means of **continuous reinforcement**. You probably become warmer every time you put on heavy clothing. You probably become less thirsty every time you drink water. Yet if you have ever watched people toss their money down the maws of slot machines, you know that behavior can also be maintained by means of **partial reinforcement**.

Folklore about gambling is based on solid learning theory. You can get a person "hooked" on gambling by fixing the game so as to allow heavy winnings at first. Then you gradually space out the winnings (reinforcements) until gambling is maintained by infrequent winning—or even no winning at all. Partial-reinforcement schedules can maintain gambling, like other behavior, for a great deal of time, even though it goes unreinforced (Pulley, 1998).

New operants, or behaviors, are acquired most rapidly through continuous reinforcement or, in some cases, through "one-trial learning" that meets with great reinforcement. People who cannot control their gambling often had big wins at the racetrack or casino or in the lottery in their late teens or early 20s (Greene, 1982). But once the operant has been acquired, it can be maintained by tapering off to a schedule of partial reinforcement.

Responses that have been maintained by partial reinforcement are more resistant to extinction than responses that have been maintained by continuous reinforcement (Rescorla, 1999). From the cognitive perspective, we could suggest that organisms that have experienced partial reinforcement do not expect reinforcement every time they engage in a response. Therefore, they are more likely to persist in the absence of reinforcement.

Question 20: What are the various schedules of reinforcement? How do they affect behavior? There are four basic types of reinforcement schedules. They are determined by changing either the *interval* of time that must elapse between correct responses before reinforcement occurs or the *ratio* (number) of responses that must occur before reinforcement is provided. If reinforcement of responses is immediate (zero seconds), the reinforcement schedule is continuous. A larger interval of time, such as 1 or 30 seconds, is one kind of partial-reinforcement schedule. A one-to-one (1:1) ratio of correct responses to reinforcements is also a continuous-reinforcement schedule. A higher ratio such as 2:1 or 5:1 creates another kind of partial-reinforcement schedule.

More specifically, the four basic reinforcement schedules are *fixed-interval*, *variable-interval*, *fixed-ratio*, and *variable-ratio* schedules, which we discuss next.

INTERVAL SCHEDULES In a fixed-interval schedule, a fixed amount of time—say, a minute—must elapse before the correct response will result in a reinforcer. With a fixed-interval schedule, an organism's response rate falls off after each reinforcement and then picks up again as the time of reinforcement approaches. For example, in a 1-minute fixed-interval schedule, a rat is reinforced with, say, a food pellet for the first operant—for example, the first pressing of a lever—that occurs after a minute has elapsed. After each reinforcement, the rat's rate of lever pressing slows down, but as the end of the 1-minute interval draws near, lever pressing increases in frequency, as suggested in Figure 5.9 ■. It is as if the rat has learned that it must wait a while before it is reinforced. The resultant record on the *cumulative recorder* shows a series of characteristic upward-moving waves, or scallops, which are referred to as *fixed-interval scallops*.

Car dealers use fixed-interval reinforcement schedules when they offer incentives for buying up the remainder of the year's line every summer and fall. In a sense, they are suppressing buying at other times, except for consumers whose current cars are in their death throes or those with little self-control. Similarly, you learn to check your e-mail for a certain person's correspondence only at a certain time of day if that is when it usually arrives.

Reinforcement is more unpredictable in a **variable-interval schedule**. Therefore, the response rate is lower. But it is also steadier. If the boss calls us in for a weekly report, we probably work hard to pull things together just before the report is to be given, just as we might cram the night before a weekly quiz. But if we know that

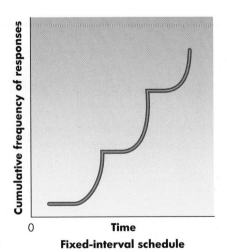

Figure 5.9 ■ The "Fixed-Interval Scallop" Organisms that are reinforced on a fixed-interval schedule tend to slack off responding after each reinforcement. The rate of response picks up as they near the time when reinforcement will become available. The results on the cumulative recorder look like upward-moving waves, or scallops.

the boss might call us in for a report on the progress of a certain project at any time (variable-interval schedule), we are likely to keep things in a state of reasonable readiness at all times. However, our efforts are unlikely to have the intensity they would in a fixed-interval schedule (for example, a weekly report). Similarly, we are less likely to cram for unpredictable pop quizzes than we are to study for regularly scheduled quizzes. But we are likely to do at least some studying on a regular basis in preparation for pop quizzes. Likewise, if you receive e-mail from your correspondent irregularly, you are likely to check your e-mail regularly for his or her communication, but with less eagerness.

RATIO SCHEDULES In a fixed-ratio schedule, reinforcement is provided after a fixed number of correct responses have been made. In a **variable-ratio schedule,** reinforcement is provided after a variable number of correct responses have been made. In a 10:1 variable-ratio schedule, the mean number of correct responses that would have to be made before a subsequent correct response would be reinforced is 10, but the ratio of correct responses to reinforcements might be allowed to vary from, say, 1:1 to 20:1 on a random basis.

Fixed- and variable-ratio schedules both maintain a high response rate. With a fixed-ratio schedule, it is as if the organism learns that it must make several responses before being reinforced. It then "gets them out of the way" as rapidly as possible. Consider the example of piecework. If a worker must sew five shirts to receive $10, he or she is on a fixed-ratio (5:1) schedule and is likely to sew at a uniformly high rate, although there might be a brief pause after each reinforcement. With a variable-ratio schedule, reinforcement can come at any time. This unpredictability also maintains a high response rate. Slot machines tend to pay off on variable-ratio schedules, and players can be seen popping coins into them and yanking their "arms" with barely a pause. I have seen players who do not even stop to pick up their winnings. Instead, they continue to pop in the coins, whether from their original stack or from the winnings tray.

© Fuse/Getty Images

Slot Machines Pay Off on Unpredictable Variable-Ratio Schedules Because reinforcement from these "one-armed bandits" is unpredictable, people tend to maintain a high response rate—that is, to drop coins into them in rapid succession.

Shaping

If you are teaching hip-hop to people who have never danced, do not wait until they have performed it precisely before telling them they're on the right track. The foxtrot will be back in style before they have learned a thing.

We can teach complex behaviors by shaping. **Question 21: How can we use shaping to teach complex behavior patterns?** Shaping reinforces progressive steps toward the behavioral goal. At first, for example, it may be wise to smile and say, "Good," when a reluctant newcomer gathers the courage to get out on the dance floor, even if your feet are flattened by his initial clumsiness. If you are teaching someone to drive a car with a standard shift, at first generously reinforce the learner simply for shifting gears without stalling.

But as training proceeds, we come to expect more before we are willing to provide reinforcement. We reinforce **successive approximations** of the goal. If you want to train a rat to climb a ladder, first reinforce it with a food pellet when it turns toward the ladder. Then wait until it approaches the ladder before giving it a pellet. Then do not drop a pellet into the cage until the rat touches the ladder. In this way, the rat will reach the top of the ladder more quickly than if you had waited for the target behavior to occur at random.

Truth or Fiction Revisited: Through the use of shaping, one

© Corbis/Fuse/Jupiterimages

Shaping Complex Behavior We can shape complex behavioral sequences, such as those found in hip-hop, by reinforcing small progressive steps toward the behavioral goal. Nature also plays a role, of course. Some would-be dancers do not possess adequate balance and coordination.

can indeed train a rat to climb a ramp, cross a bridge, climb a ladder, and so on in a desired sequence.

Learning to drive a standard-shift automobile to a new location also involves a complex sequence of operant behaviors. At first, we actively seek out all the discriminative stimuli or landmarks that give us cues for when to turn—signs, buildings, hills, valleys. We also focus on shifting to a lower gear as we slow down so the car won't stall. After many repetitions, these responses, or *chains of behavior*, become habitual, and we need to pay very little attention to them.

Have you ever driven home and suddenly realized that you couldn't recall exactly how you got there? Your entire trip may seem "lost." How could you allow such a thing to happen? You might have been in great danger without even realizing it! Actually, your driving and your responses to the demands of the route may have become so habitual that you did not have to focus on them. As you drove, you were able to think about dinner, work, or the weekend. But if something unusual had occurred on the way, such as an engine problem or a rainstorm, you would have devoted as much attention to your driving as was needed to arrive home. Your trip was probably quite safe after all.

Applications of Operant Conditioning

Operant conditioning, like classical conditioning, is not just an exotic laboratory procedure. We use it every day to influence other people. Parents and peers induce children to acquire so-called gender-appropriate behavior patterns through rewards and punishments. Peers influence peers by playing with those who are generous and nonaggressive and by avoiding those who are not (Warman & Cohen, 2000). Adults often reward children for expressing attitudes that coincide with their own and punish or ignore them for expressing contradictory attitudes.

Behavior modification Therapy techniques based on principles of learning that teach adaptive behavior and extinguish or discourage maladaptive behavior.

Programmed learning A method of teaching that breaks down tasks into small steps, each of which is reinforced and then combined to form the correct behavioral chain.

BIOFEEDBACK TRAINING *Biofeedback training (BFT)* is based on operant conditioning. It has enabled people and lower animals to learn to control autonomic responses to attain reinforcement (N. E. Miller, 1969; Vernon et al., 2003). In BFT, people receive reinforcement in the form of *information*. For example, we can learn to emit alpha waves—the kind of brain wave associated with relaxation—through feedback from an electroencephalograph, which measures brain waves. People use other instruments to learn to lower muscle tension, heart rates, and blood pressure.

BEHAVIOR MODIFICATION Remember that reinforcers are not defined as pleasant events but rather as stimuli that increase the frequency of behavior. Ironically, adults frequently reinforce undesirable behavior in children by paying attention to them, or punishing them, when that behavior occurs but ignoring them when they behave in desirable ways. Similarly, teachers who raise their voices when children misbehave may be unintentionally conferring hero status on those pupils in the eyes of their peers. To the teacher's surprise, some children may then go out of their way to earn disapproval. But teachers can learn to use **behavior modification** to reinforce appropriate behavior in children and, when possible, to extinguish misbehavior by ignoring it.

Teachers also frequently use time out from positive reinforcement to discourage misbehavior. In this method, children are placed in a drab environment for a specified period, usually about 10 minutes, when they are disruptive. While isolated, they cannot earn the attention of peers or teachers.

Time Out Teachers may use time out from positive reinforcement as a way of maintaining classroom discipline. This young student has been assigned some time on a special "time out" chair.

PROGRAMMED LEARNING B. F. Skinner developed an educational method called **programmed learning** that is based on operant conditioning. This method assumes that any complex task can be broken down into a number of small steps. These steps can be shaped individually and then combined in sequence to form the correct behavioral chain. Programmed learning does not punish errors. Instead, correct responses are reinforced. **Truth or Fiction Revisited:** Actually, one can learn without making mistakes.

ACTIVE REVIEW (11) Thorndike originated the law of _____ in learning. (12) Skinner developed the concept of _____ as an alternative to the concepts of reward and punishment. (13) _____ reinforcers increase the probability that operants will occur when they are removed. (14) _____ reinforcers, such as money, acquire their value through association with established reinforcers. (15) In operant conditioning, repeated performance of a learned response in the absence of reinforcement leads to _____ of that response. (16) A _____ stimulus indicates when an operant will be reinforced. (17) In a(n) _____ schedule, a specific amount of time must elapse since a previous correct response before reinforcement again becomes available. (18) _____ learning breaks down learning tasks into small steps and reinforces correct performance of each step.

REFLECT AND RELATE How have teachers in your own experience maintained—or failed to maintain—control over their classrooms? Has the information in this chapter helped you understand what they did right or wrong?

CRITICAL THINKING Every time I tell my classes that many psychologists frown on the use of punishment, students chide me for being unrealistic and "goody-goody." Let's try some critical thinking: What are the effects of punishment? Does it stop undesirable behavior? If so, when? Are there other ways of encouraging desirable behavior? Which is preferable? How can we judge?

 Go to Psychology CourseMate at **www.cengagebrain.com** for an interactive version of these questions.

● COGNITIVE FACTORS IN LEARNING

Classical and operant conditioning were originally conceived of as relatively simple forms of learning. Much of conditioning's appeal is that it can be said to meet the behaviorist objective of explaining behavior in terms of observable events—in this case, laboratory conditions. Building on this theoretical base, some psychologists have suggested that the most complex human behavior involves the summation of a series of instances of conditioning. However, many psychologists believe that conditioning is too mechanical a process to explain all instances of learned behavior, even in laboratory rats (Weiner, 2006). They turn to cognitive factors to describe and explain additional findings in the psychology of learning. **Question 22: How do we explain what happens during classical conditioning from a cognitive perspective?**

In addition to concepts such as *association* and *reinforcement*, cognitive psychologists use concepts such as *mental structures, schemas, templates,* and *information processing.* Cognitive psychologists see people as searching for information, weighing evidence, and making decisions. Let's consider some classic research that points to cognitive factors in learning as opposed to mechanical associations. These cognitive factors are not limited to humans—although, of course, humans are the only species that can talk about them.

Latent Learning: Forming Cognitive Maps

Many behaviorists argue that organisms acquire only responses, or operants, for which they are reinforced. E. C. Tolman (1886–1959), however, showed that rats also learn about their environment in the *absence* of reinforcement. In doing so, he demonstrated that rats must form **cognitive maps** of their surroundings. **Question 23: What is the evidence that people and other animals form cognitive maps of their environments?**

Tolman trained some rats to run through mazes for standard food goals. Other rats were permitted to explore the same mazes for several days without food goals or other rewards. After the unrewarded rats had been allowed to explore the mazes for 10 days, food rewards were placed in a box at the far end of the maze. The previously unrewarded rats reached the food box as quickly as the rewarded rats after only one or two reinforced trials (Tolman & Honzik, 1930).

Tolman concluded that rats learned about mazes in which they roamed even when they were unrewarded for doing so. He distinguished between *learning* and *performance.* Rats would acquire a cognitive map of a maze. Even though they would not be motivated to follow an efficient route to the far end, they would learn rapid routes from one end to the other just by roaming about within the maze. Yet this learning might remain hidden, or be considered **latent learning**, until they were motivated to follow the rapid routes to obtain food goals.

"Soap and education are not as sudden as a massacre, but they are more deadly in the long run."

MARK TWAIN

Cognitive map A mental representation of the layout of one's environment.

Latent learning Learning that is hidden, or concealed.

Observational Learning: Monkey See, Monkey May *Choose* to Do?

How many things have you learned from watching other people in real life, in films, and on television? From films and television, you may have gathered vague ideas about how to skydive, ride a surfboard, climb sheer cliffs, run a pattern to catch a touchdown pass in the Super Bowl, and dust for fingerprints, even if you have never tried these activities yourself. **Question 24: How do people learn by observing others?**

When we sit in a classroom, check out the behavior of other people in a high-class restaurant, go to a film, or watch television, we are seeking to learn or to be entertained. Our behavior is intentional; it has purpose. One of the theoretical lures of conditioning is that it allows scientists to explain behavior in mechanical terms—without resorting to concepts such as wants or desires. We can say that a rat presses a lever in a Skinner box because lever pressing is reinforced with food pellets. We need not try to "get into" the rat's mind and speculate on its motives. We need not even say that the rat was hungry; we can note, instead, that it had been deprived of food for a certain amount of time.

In the terminology of **observational learning**, a person who engages in a response to be imitated is a **model**. When observers see a model being reinforced for displaying an operant, the observers are said to be *vicariously* reinforced. Display of the operant thus becomes more likely for the observer as well as for the model.

Observational learning A form of cognitive learning in which we learn by observing others—regardless of whether we perform what we have learned or not.

Model An organism that engages in a response that is then imitated by another organism.

MIRROR NEURONS AND OBSERVATIONAL LEARNING Could some observational learning indeed be mechanical? Is there something in us (and monkeys and apes) that leads us to automatically imitate the behavior of others? The answer is

A CLOSER LOOK — Contingency Theory

Behaviorists and cognitive psychologists interpret the conditioning process in different ways. Behaviorists explain it in terms of the pairing of stimuli. Cognitive psychologists explain classical conditioning in terms of the ways stimuli provide information that allows organisms to form and revise mental representations of their environment (Stewart & Watt, 2008). Robert Rescorla conducted research in an effort to demonstrate which view is more accurate. His viewpoint, *contingency theory,* suggests that learning occurs only when the conditioned stimulus provides information about the unconditioned stimulus.

In classical conditioning experiments with dogs, Rescorla (1967) obtained some results that are difficult to explain without reference to cognitive concepts. Each phase of his work paired a tone (a conditioned stimulus) with an electric shock (an unconditioned stimulus) but in different ways. With one group of animals, the shock was consistently presented after the tone. That is, the unconditioned stimulus followed on the heels of the conditioned stimulus, as in Pavlov's studies. The dogs in this group learned to show a fear response when the tone was presented.

A second group of dogs heard an equal number of tones and received an equal number of electric shocks, but the shock never immediately followed the tone. That is, the tone and the shock were not paired. Now, from the behaviorist perspective, the dogs should not have learned to associate the tone and the shock because one did not predict the other. Actually, the dogs learned quite a lot: They learned that they had nothing to fear when the tone was sounded! They showed vigilance and fear when the

laboratory was quiet—for the shock could apparently come at any time—but they were calm in the presence of the tone.

The third group of dogs also received equal numbers of tones and shocks, but the stimuli were presented at purely random intervals. Occasionally, they were paired, but most often, they were not. According to Rescorla, behaviorists might argue that intermittent pairing of the tones and shocks should have brought about some learning. Yet it did not. The animals showed no fear in response to the tone. Rescorla suggests that the animals in this group learned nothing because the tones did not allow them to make predictions about electric shock.

Rescorla concluded that *contiguity*—that is, the coappearance of the unconditioned stimulus and the conditioned stimulus—cannot in itself explain classical conditioning. Learning occurs only when the conditioned stimulus (in this case, the tone) provides information about the unconditioned stimulus (in this case, the shock). According to contingency theory, learning occurs because a conditioned stimulus indicates that the unconditioned stimulus is likely to follow (Balsam et al., 2006).

Behaviorists might counter, of course, that for the second group of dogs the absence of the tone became the signal for the shock. Shock may be a powerful enough event that the fear response becomes conditioned to the laboratory environment. For the third group of dogs, the shock was as likely to occur in the presence of the neutral stimulus as in its absence. Therefore, many behaviorists would expect no learning to occur.

apparently yes. We are referring to *mirror neurons*—the neurons that fire both when an animal acts and when the animal observes the same action performed by another—discovered in rhesus monkeys in the 1990s (see Chapter 2; Gallese et al., 1996). Mirror neurons are apparently involved when newborn babies return the favor if their caregivers stick out their tongues at them (Meltzoff & Prinz, 2002; see Figure 5.10 ■). Mirror neurons also allow us—as children and adults—to anticipate other people's intentions when they reach for things. Neurons in our brains fire to mimic the firing in the brains of the actors, and the chambers of our memories flood our minds with the likely outcomes—not always correctly. For example, it occasionally tragically happens that a police officer or soldier erroneously responds to the movements of another person when that person appears to be pulling out a weapon but isn't (Cañal-Bruland et al., 2010).

We also yawn when other people yawn. We may laugh or feel the urge to laugh when other people laugh. We apparently *learn* what other people are feeling when we pick up cues that lead our own mirror neurons to fire in the ways that mirror neurons are firing in the brains of others.

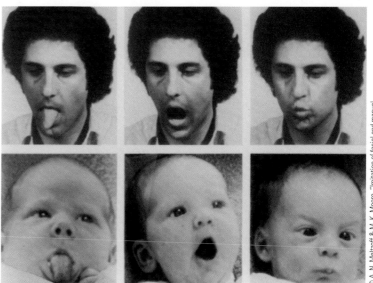

Video Connections—Mirror Neurons

See the video for an explanation of the action of "mirror neurons" while exploring the case of a person with Asperger's syndrome. Go to Psychology CourseMate at **www.cengagebrain.com** to watch this video.

Media Violence and Aggression

The debate as to whether violence in media such as films, television, and video games fuels violence in the real world has been going on for more than 50 years. However, research strongly suggests that media violence is a risk factor for increasing emotional arousal, aggressive behavior, and violent thoughts (Anderson et al., 2008; Dubow et al., 2010; Fanti et al., 2009).

One reason to be particularly concerned about violent video games is that they require audience participation (Anderson et al., 2008). Players don't just watch; they *participate*. Violent games like *Grand Theft Auto* have grown increasingly popular. Some games reward players for killing police, prostitutes, or bystanders. Virtual weapons include guns, knives, flamethrowers, swords, clubs, cars, hands, and feet. Sometimes, the player assumes the role of a hero, but it is also common for the player to assume the role of a criminal.

Much human learning occurs through observation. We learn by observing parents and peers, attending school, reading books, and watching media such as television and films. Nearly all of us have been exposed to television, videotapes, and films in the classroom. Children in day-care centers often watch *Sesame Street*. There are filmed and electronic versions of great works of literature portrayed by actors, such as Orson Welles's *Macbeth* or Laurence Olivier's *Hamlet*. Nearly every school shows films of laboratory experiments. Sometimes, we view "canned lectures" by master teachers.

But what of our exposure to these media *outside* the classroom? Television is one of our major sources of informal observational learning. Children are routinely exposed to scenes of murder, beating, and sexual assault—just by turning on the TV set (Huesmann et al., 2003; Potter, 2008). If children watch 2 to 4 hours of TV a day, they will have seen 8,000 murders and another 100,000 acts of violence *by the time they have finished elementary school* (Eron, 1993). Are kids less likely to be exposed to violence by going to the movies? No. One study found that virtually all G-rated animated films have scenes of violence, with a mean duration of 9 to 10 minutes per film (Yokota & Thompson, 2000). Other media that contain violence include movies, music, music videos, advertising, video games, the Internet—even comic books.

© A. N. Meltzoff & M. K. Moore, "Imitation of facial and manual gestures by human neonates," *Science, 1977, 198, 75–78.*

Figure 5.10 ■ Imitation in Infants These 2- to 3-week-old infants are imitating the facial gestures of an adult experimenter. How are we to interpret these findings? Can we say that the infants are *learning* to stick out their tongues? That they *know* what the experimenter is doing and *choose* to imitate the behavior? That the response is *instinctive* or *reflexive?* The biological truth of the matter apparently has to do with mirror neurons.

© Dimitri Vervitsiotis/Getty Images

What Do We Learn from Playing Violent Video Games?

BANDURA'S RESEARCH ON THE EFFECTS OF VIOLENCE IN THE MEDIA A classic experiment by Bandura, Ross, and Ross (1963) suggests the powerful influence of televised models on children's aggressive behavior. One group of preschool children observed a film of an adult model hitting and kicking an inflated Bobo doll, while a control group saw an aggression-free film. The experimental and control children were then left alone in a room with the same doll as hidden observers recorded their behavior. The children who had observed the aggressive model showed significantly more aggressive behavior toward the doll themselves (see Figure 5.11 ■). Many children imitated bizarre attack behaviors devised for the model in this experiment—behaviors that they would not have thought up themselves. **Truth or Fiction Revisited:** Actually, a scientific connection has been established between violence in the media and real-life aggression (Bushman & Anderson, 2007).

The children exposed to the aggressive model also showed aggressive behavior patterns that had not been modeled. Observing the model, therefore, not only led to imitation of modeled behavior patterns but also apparently disinhibited previously learned aggressive responses. The results were similar whether children observed human or cartoon models on film.

Violence tends to be glamorized in the media. For example, in one cartoon show, superheroes battle villains who are trying to destroy or take over the world. Violence is often shown to have only temporary or minimal effects. (How often has Wile E. Coyote fallen from a cliff and been pounded into the ground by a boulder, only to bounce back and pursue the Road Runner once more?) In the great majority of violent TV shows, there is no remorse, criticism, or penalty for violent behavior (Potter, 2008). Few TV programs show harmful long-term consequences of aggressive behavior. Seeing the perpetrator of the violence go unpunished increases the chances that the child will act aggressively (Potter, 2008). Children may not even view death as much of a problem. How many times do video-game characters "die"—only to be reborn to fight again because the children have won multiple lives for them?

Why all this violence? Simple: Violence sells. But does violence do more than sell? That is, does media violence *cause* real violence? If so, what can parents and educators do to prevent the fictional from spilling over into the real world?

CONSENSUS ON THE EFFECTS OF VIOLENCE IN THE MEDIA? In any event, most organizations of health professionals agree that media violence does contribute to aggression (Bushman & Anderson, 2007). This relationship has been found for girls and boys of different ages, social classes, ethnic groups, and

© Albert Bandura

Figure 5.11 ■ Classic Research on the Imitation of Aggressive Models Albert Bandura and his colleagues showed that children frequently imitate the aggressive behavior that they observe. In the top row, an adult model strikes a clown doll. The lower rows show a boy and a girl imitating the aggressive behavior.

cultures (Huesmann et al., 2003). Consider a number of ways that depictions of violence make such a contribution (Anderson et al., 2010; Bushman & Anderson, 2007):

- *Observational learning:* Children learn from observation. Television violence supplies *models* of aggressive "skills," which children may acquire. In fact, children are more likely to imitate what their parents do than to heed what they say. If adults say that they disapprove of aggression but smash furniture or slap each other when frustrated, children are likely to develop the notion that aggression is the way to handle frustration.

- *Disinhibition:* Punishment inhibits behavior. Conversely, media violence may disinhibit aggressive behavior, especially when media characters "get away" with violence or are rewarded for it.

- *Increased emotional arousal:* Media violence and aggressive video games increase viewers' level of emotional arousal. That is, television "works them up." We are more likely to be aggressive when we are highly aroused.

- *Priming of aggressive thoughts and memories:* Media violence "primes," or arouses, aggressive ideas and memories.

- *Habituation:* We become "habituated to," or used to, repeated stimuli. Repeated exposure to TV violence may decrease viewers' sensitivity to real violence. If children come to perceive violence as the norm, they may become more tolerant of it and place less value on restraining aggressive urges.

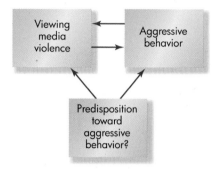

Violent video games are also connected with aggressive behavior, including juvenile delinquency (Dubow et al., 2010). Playing violent video games increases aggressive thoughts and behavior in the laboratory (Anderson et al., 2010). However, males are relatively more likely than females to act aggressively after playing violent video games and are more likely to see the world as a hostile place. Students who obtain higher grades are also less likely to behave aggressively following exposure to violent video games. Thus, cultural stereotyping of males and females, possible biological sex differences, and moderating variables like academic achievement also figure into the effects of media violence. There is no simple one-to-one connection between media violence and violence in real life.

There seems to be a circular relationship between exposure to media violence and aggressive behavior (Anderson et al., 2010). Yes, TV violence and violent video games contribute to aggressive behavior, but aggressive youngsters are also more likely to seek out this kind of "entertainment." Figure 5.12 ■ explores the possible connections between TV violence and aggressive behavior among viewers.

Aggressive children are frequently rejected by age mates who are not aggressive—at least in middle-class culture (Eron, 1982; Warman & Cohen, 2000). Aggressive children may watch more television because their peer relationships are less fulfilling and because the high incidence of TV violence tends to confirm their view that aggressive behavior is normal (Eron, 1982). Studies find that parental substance abuse, parental rejection, parental physical punishments, and single motherhood also contribute to the likelihood of aggression in childhood (Jester et al., 2008; Wareham et al., 2009). A harsh home life may also confirm the TV viewer's vision of the world as a violent place.

It would be of little use to discuss *how* we learn if we were not capable of remembering *what* we learn from second to second, from day to day, or in many cases, for a lifetime. In the next chapter, we turn our attention to the subject of memory. In Chapter 7, we will see how learning is intertwined with thinking, language, and intelligence.

Figure 5.12 ■ What Are the Connections Between Media Violence and Aggressive Behavior? Does media violence cause aggressive behavior? Do aggressive children prefer to tune in to violent shows? Or do other factors, such as personality traits that create a disposition toward aggression, contribute both to aggressive behavior and to the observation of violent shows?

LIFE CONNECTIONS   TEACHING CHILDREN *NOT* TO IMITATE MEDIA VIOLENCE

Children are going to be exposed to media violence—if not in Saturday morning cartoon shows, then in evening dramas and in the news. Or they'll hear about violence from friends, watch other children get into fights, or read about violence in the newspapers. If all those sources of violence were somehow hidden from view, they would learn about violence in *Hamlet, Macbeth,* and the Bible. The notion of preventing children from being exposed to violent models may be impractical.

What, then, should be done? Parents and educators can do many things to tone down the impact of media violence (Huesmann et al., 2003; Potter, 2008). Children who watch violent shows act less aggressively when they are informed that

- The violent behavior they observe in the media does *not* represent the behavior of most people.

- The apparently aggressive behaviors they watch are not real. They reflect camera tricks, special effects, and stunts.

- Most people resolve conflicts by nonviolent means.

- The real-life consequences of violence are harmful to the victim and, often, the aggressor.

Despite our history of evolutionary forces, and despite the fact that in most species successful aggression usually wins individuals the right to transmit their genes to future generations, humans are thinking beings. If children consider violence to be inappropriate for them, they will be less likely to act aggressively, even when they have acquired aggressive skills from exposure to the media or other sources.

Kind of Learning	What Is Learned	How It Is Learned
Classical conditioning Major proponents: • Ivan Pavlov (known for basic research with dogs) • John B. Watson (known as originator of behaviorism) 	Association of events; anticipations, signs, expectations; automatic responses to new stimuli.	A neutral stimulus is repeatedly paired with a stimulus (an unconditioned stimulus, or UCS) that elicits a response (an unconditioned response, or UCR) until the neutral stimulus produces a response (conditioned response, or CR) that anticipates and prepares for the unconditioned stimulus. At this point, the neutral stimulus has become a conditioned stimulus (CS).
Operant conditioning Major proponent: • B. F. Skinner 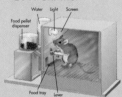	Behavior that operates on, or affects, the environment to produce outcomes.	A response is rewarded or reinforced so that it occurs with greater frequency in similar situations.
Observational learning Major proponents: • Albert Bandura • Julian Rotter • Walter Mischel 	Expectations, knowledge, and skills. May also acquire fears and other emotions displayed by others.	A person observes the behavior of another person (live or through media such as films, television, or books) and its effects.

LearningConnections • COGNITIVE FACTORS IN LEARNING

ACTIVE REVIEW (19) Tolman's work with rats suggests that they develop _____ maps of the environment. (20) Tolman labels learning without performing _____ learning. (21) According to _____ theory, learning occurs because a CS indicates that the UCS is likely to follow.

REFLECT AND RELATE Have you ever studied an atlas, a road map, a cookbook, or a computer manual for the pleasure of doing so? What kind of learning were you engaging in?

CRITICAL THINKING How do the results of research into cognitive factors in learning challenge behaviorist principles? Refer to contingency theory, latent learning, and observational learning in your answer.

 Go to Psychology CourseMate at **www.cengagebrain.com** for an interactive version of these questions.

Learning: Experience and Change

1. What is learning?
Learning is the process by which experience leads to modified representations of the environment (the cognitive perspective) and relatively permanent changes in behavior (the behavioral perspective).

Classical Conditioning: Learning What Is Linked to What

2. What is classical conditioning?
Classical conditioning is a simple form of associative learning in which a previously neutral stimulus (the conditioned stimulus, or CS) comes to elicit the response evoked by a second stimulus (the unconditioned stimulus, or UCS) as a result of repeatedly being paired with the second stimulus.

3. What is the contribution of Ivan Pavlov to the psychology of learning?
Russian physiologist Ivan Pavlov happened upon conditioning by chance when he was studying salivation in laboratory dogs. Pavlov discovered that reflexes can be learned, or conditioned, through association.

4. What is a taste aversion, and why are taste aversions of special interest to psychologists?
Taste aversions are examples of classical conditioning in which organisms learn that a food is noxious on the basis of a nauseating experience. Taste aversions are of special interest because learning may occur on the basis of a single association and because the unconditioned stimulus (in this case, nausea) can occur hours after the conditioned stimulus (in this case, the flavor of food).

5. What is the role of extinction in classical conditioning?
Extinction is the process by which conditioned stimuli lose the ability to elicit conditioned responses because the conditioned stimuli are no longer associated with unconditioned stimuli. Extinction helps organisms adapt to environmental changes.

6. What is the role of spontaneous recovery in classical conditioning?
Extinguished responses may show spontaneous recovery as a function of the time that has elapsed since extinction occurred. Spontaneous recovery is adaptive in that environmental conditions may have reverted to what they were before.

7. What is the role of generalization in classical conditioning?
Generalization is the tendency for a conditioned response to be evoked by stimuli that are similar to the stimulus to which the response was conditioned.

8. What is the role of discrimination in classical conditioning?
In discrimination, organisms learn to show a CR in response to a more limited range of stimuli by pairing only the limited stimulus with the UCS.

9. What is higher order conditioning?
In higher order conditioning, a previously neutral stimulus comes to serve as a CS after being paired repeatedly with a stimulus that has already become a CS.

10. Was Little Albert "prepared" to acquire his fear of rats?
Evolutionary theorists believe that humans are indeed prepared, biologically, to readily develop fears of objects and situations that threatened our survival in our evolutionary history.

Operant Conditioning: Learning What Does What to What

11. What is operant conditioning?
Operant conditioning is a simple form of learning in which organisms learn to engage in behavior that is reinforced.

12. What is the law of effect?
This is Thorndike's view that responses are "stamped in" by rewards and "stamped out" by punishments.

13. What was the contribution of B. F. Skinner to the psychology of learning?
Skinner developed the concept of reinforcement and encouraged the study of discrete behaviors such as lever pressing by rats. He was also involved in the development of behavior modification and programmed learning.

14. What are the various kinds of reinforcers?
These include positive, negative, primary, and secondary reinforcers. Positive reinforcers increase the probability that a behavior will occur when they are applied. Negative reinforcers increase the probability that a behavior will occur when they are removed. Primary reinforcers (such as food and water) have their value because of the organism's biological makeup. Secondary reinforcers (such as money and approval) acquire their value through association with established reinforcers.

15. What is the role of extinction in operant conditioning?
Extinction is adaptive in operant conditioning. Learned responses are extinguished as a result of repeated performance in the absence of reinforcement.

16. What is the role of spontaneous recovery in operant conditioning?
As in classical conditioning, spontaneous recovery occurs as a function of the passage of time, which is adaptive because things may return to the way they once were.

17. Why did Skinner distinguish between reinforcers on the one hand and rewards and punishments on the other?
Rewards and punishments are defined, respectively, as pleasant and aversive events that affect behavior. Skinner preferred the concept of reinforcement because its definition does not rely on getting inside the head of the organism.

18. Why do many psychologists disapprove of punishment?

Many psychologists recommend not using punishment because it hurts, it does not suggest acceptable behavior, it may create feelings of hostility, and it may only suppress behavior in the specific situation in which it is used.

19. What are discriminative stimuli?

Discriminative stimuli (such as green lights) act as signals or cues that indicate when an operant (such as pecking a button) will be reinforced (such as with food).

20. What are the various schedules of reinforcement?

Continuous reinforcement leads to the most rapid acquisition of new responses, but operants are maintained most economically through partial reinforcement. There are four basic schedules of reinforcement. In a fixed-interval schedule, a specific amount of time must elapse after a previous correct response before reinforcement again becomes available. In a variable-interval schedule, the amount of time is allowed to vary. In a fixed-ratio schedule, a fixed number of correct responses must be performed before one is reinforced. In a variable-ratio schedule, this number is allowed to vary. Ratio schedules maintain high response rates.

21. How can we use shaping to teach complex behavior patterns?

In shaping, successive approximations of the target response are reinforced, leading to the performance of a complex sequence of behaviors.

Cognitive Factors in Learning

22. How do we explain what happens during classical conditioning from a cognitive perspective?

From the cognitive perspective, in classical conditioning a new stimulus provides information about how events are related. According to contingency theory, organisms learn associations between stimuli only when stimuli provide new information about each other.

23. What is the evidence that people and other animals form cognitive maps of their environments?

Some evidence is derived from Tolman's research on latent learning. He demonstrated that rats can learn—that is, they can modify their cognitive map of the environment—in the absence of reinforcement.

24. How do people learn by observing others?

Bandura has shown that people can learn to do things simply by observing others; it is not necessary that they emit responses that are reinforced to learn. Some learning of motor acts and emotional responses by observation appears to be automatic and enabled by mirror neurons.

KEY TERMS

Behavior modification (p. 172)
Biological preparedness (p. 160)
Classical conditioning (p. 154)
Cognitive map (p. 173)
Conditioned reinforcer (p. 166)
Conditioned response (CR) (p. 155)
Conditioned stimulus (CS) (p. 155)
Continuous reinforcement (p. 170)
Counterconditioning (p. 161)
Discrimination (p. 159)
Discriminative stimulus (p. 168)
Extinction (p. 157)
Fixed-interval schedule (p. 170)
Fixed-ratio schedule (p. 171)
Flooding (p. 162)
Generalization (p. 159)

Higher order conditioning (p. 160)
Latent learning (p. 173)
Law of effect (p. 163)
Learning (p. 153)
Model (p. 174)
Negative reinforcer (p. 165)
Observational learning (p. 174)
Operant (p. 164)
Operant behavior (p. 164)
Operant conditioning (p. 164)
Orienting response (p. 155)
Partial reinforcement (p. 170)
Positive reinforcer (p. 165)
Primary reinforcer (p. 166)
Programmed learning (p. 172)
Punishment (p. 163)

Reflex (p. 154)
Reinforce (p. 163)
Reward (p. 163)
Secondary reinforcer (p. 166)
Shaping (p. 171)
Spontaneous recovery (p. 158)
Stimuli (p. 154)
Successive approximations (p. 171)
Systematic desensitization (p. 162)
Time out (p. 168)
Unconditioned response (UCR) (p. 155)
Unconditioned stimulus (UCS) (p. 155)
Variable-interval schedule (p. 170)
Variable-ratio schedule (p. 171)

ACTIVE LEARNING RESOURCES

Log in to **www.cengagebrain.com** to access the resources your instructor requires. For this book, you can access:

CourseMate CourseMate brings course concepts to life with interactive learning, study, and exam preparation tools that support the printed textbook. A textbook-specific website, Psychology CourseMate includes an integrated interactive eBook and other interactive learning tools including quizzes, flashcards, videos, and more.

 **CENGAGENOW** Need help studying? This site is your one-stop study shop. Take a Pre-Test and CengageNOW will generate a Personalized Study Plan based on your test results. The Study Plan will identify the topics you need to review and direct you to online resources to help you master those topics. You can then take a Post-Test to determine the concepts you have mastered and what you still need to work on.

6 Memory: Remembrance of Things Past—and Future

© J. Price/Getty Images

MAJOR TOPICS

Kinds of Memory: Pressing the "Rewind" and "Fast-Forward" Buttons *184*

Processes of Memory: Processing Information in Our Most Personal Computers *189*

Stages of Memory: Making *Sense* of the *Short* and the *Long* of It *191*

Forgetting: Will You Remember How We Forget? *204*

The Biology of Memory: The Brain as a Living Time Machine *212*

FEATURES

Self-Assessment: Five Challenges to Your Memory *184*

A Closer Look: Will You Remember Your Psychology Grade in 2062? *187*

Concept Review 6.1: The Relationships among the Various Kinds of Memories *188*

A Closer Look: Can We Trust Eyewitness Testimony? *199*

Video Connections: Reconstructive Memory *200*

A Closer Look: Do People Really Recover Repressed Memories of Childhood? *208*

Life Connections: Using the Psychology of Memory to Enhance Your Memory *210*

T F   A woman who could not remember who she was automatically dialed her mother's number when the police gave her a telephone.

page 186

T F   Learning must be meaningful if we are to remember it.

page 190

T F   Oh say, can you see? If the answer is yes, you have a photographic memory.

page 193

T F   It may be easier for you to recall the name of your first-grade teacher than the name of someone you just met at a party.

page 194

T F   All of our experiences are permanently imprinted on the brain, so the proper stimulus can cause us to remember them exactly.

page 197

T F   You may always recall where you were and what you were doing on the morning of September 11, 2001.

page 201

T F   If you study with the stereo on, you would probably do better to take the test with the stereo on.

page 203

T F   Learning Spanish can make it harder to remember French—and vice versa.

page 207

T F   After part of his hippocampus was surgically removed, a man could not form new memories. Each time he was reminded of his uncle's death, he grieved as he had when he first heard about it.

page 209

T F   You may improve your memory by sniffing antidiuretic hormone.

page 213

Are these items truth or fiction? We will be revisiting them throughout the chapter.

Jeff would never forget his sudden loss of memory. He watched in horror as his cell phone slipped from his pocket and fell to the floor of the Blockbuster store in Boston. Before he could grab it, it shattered into pieces. A New York college student, Jeff experienced the trauma of phone loss on his winter break.

Why was the loss traumatic? Why was it a memory problem? Simple: there was no way for Jeff to retrieve his phone book. "I was at the store and it was snowing out and I suddenly realized that I had no way of getting in touch with anyone," he explains (Metz, 2005). The worst part of the loss was that Jeff had been seeing someone in New York, and because her cell phone was her only phone, he now had no way to contact her. A day later, he showed up on her doorstep, hoping she wouldn't think he had been avoiding her calls. She forgave him but had him write her number down—*on paper*. Still, Jeff would not forget the day his cell phone lost its memory. After all, he also had his family, his friends, his pizza-delivery service, his tutor, and his mother's pet groomer in it.

Jeff now copies every cell-phone entry into a little black book—made of paper. Other people back up their phone books—and their pictures and downloads—on servers provided by cellular telephone operating companies or cell-phone manufacturers. iPhones have backups available. Verizon's method is called Backup Assistant. Most people transfer their memories from their old cell phone to the new one when they make a change.

Jeff's cell-phone memory is electronic. Information is stored on a chip smaller than a fingernail. His own memory is much more complex—involving biological structures as well as chemical and electrical processes.

This chapter is all about the "backup assistant" in your brain—your memory. Without your memory, there is no past. Without your memory, experience is trivial and learning is lost. Let's see what psychologists have learned about the ways we remember things—other than keying them into a cell phone's memory chip. However, first try to meet the challenges to your memory we pose in the Self-Assessment on the next page. We'll be talking about your responses throughout the chapter.

⬤ KINDS OF MEMORY: PRESSING THE "REWIND" AND "FAST-FORWARD" BUTTONS

Jeff remembered things he had personally done, like dropping his cell phone in Boston and showing up at his girlfriend's doorstep on a blustery day in January. Remembering a dropped cell phone is an *episodic memory*—a memory of an event in one's life. According to psychologists who have extensively researched memory, episodic memory is one kind of memory system (Carver & Cluver, 2009; Dickerson & Eichenbaum, 2009). And when I learned of Jeff's experience, I tried to remind myself repeatedly not to forget to jot down notes about it and write it up as soon as I could. (I was trying to jog my *prospective memory*—remembering to do something in the future.) Let's consider several memory systems.

SELF-ASSESSMENT
Five Challenges to Your Memory

Before you read further, let's challenge your memory. This is not an actual memory test of the sort used by psychologists to determine whether people's memory functioning is within normal limits. Instead, it will provide you with some insight into how your memory works and may also be fun.

Directions: Find four sheets of blank paper and number them 1 through 4. Also use a watch with a second hand. Then follow these instructions:

1. Following are 10 letters. Look at them for 15 seconds. Later in the chapter, I will ask you if you can write them on sheet number 1. (No cheating! Don't do it now.)

THUNSTOFAM

2. Look at these nine figures for 30 seconds. Then try to draw them in the proper sequence on sheet number 2. (Yes, right after you've finished looking at them. We'll talk about your drawings later, on page 196.)

3. Okay, here's another list of letters, 17 this time. Look at the list for 60 seconds and then see whether you can reproduce it on sheet number 3. (I'm being generous this time—a full minute.)

GMC–BSI–BMA–TTC–IAF–BI

4. Which of these pennies is an accurate reproduction of the Lincoln penny you see every day? This time there's nothing to draw on another sheet; just circle or put a checkmark by the penny that you think resembles the ones you throw in the back of the drawer.

A	B	C	D	E	F

5. Examine the following drawings for 1 minute. Then copy the names of the figures on sheet number 4. When you're finished, just keep reading. Soon I'll be asking you to draw those figures.

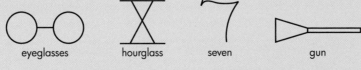

eyeglasses   hourglass   seven   gun

That's it. You'll find out about the results of this Self-Assessment as you read through the chapter.

Explicit Memory: When Memory Is Out in the Open

Question 1: What is explicit memory? Explicit memory—also referred to as *declarative memory*—is memory for specific information. Things that are explicit are clear, or clearly stated or explained. The use of the term *declarative* indicates that these memories state or reveal (that is, declare) specific information. The information may be autobiographical or refer to general knowledge. ("Well, I declare!") There are two kinds of explicit memories described by psychologist Endel Tulving (1985; Tulving & Markowitsch, 1998): episodic and semantic. They are identified according to the type of information they hold.

EPISODIC MEMORY Question 2: What is episodic memory? Episodic memories are kinds of explicit memories. They are memories of the things that happen to us or take place in our presence (Dickerson & Eichenbaum, 2009; Grillon et al., 2010). Episodic memory is also referred to as *autobiographical memory*. Your memories of what you ate for breakfast and of what your professor said in class this afternoon are examples of episodic memory.

It is common for us to build, or "reconstruct," inaccurate memories that have a bit of this and a bit of that. These memories might reflect autobiographical experience, such as things we hear about from family members and others, the stuff we read about or see in the media, and even things that other people suggest might have happened to us. These memories are fiction, as we see in novels, but we may believe that they are truly autobiographical (Mori, 2008).

SEMANTIC MEMORY: ON *NOT* GETTING PERSONAL Question 3: What is semantic memory? General knowledge is referred to as **semantic memory**. *Semantics* concerns meanings. You can "remember" that the United States has 50 states without visiting them and personally adding them up. You "remember" who authored *Hamlet,* although you were not looking over Shakespeare's shoulder as he did so. These are examples of semantic memory.

Your future recollection that there are several kinds of memory is more likely to be semantic than episodic. That is, you are more likely to "know" that there are several types of memory than to recall the date on which you learned about them, where you were, how you were sitting, and whether you were also thinking about dinner at the time. We tend to use the phrase "I remember ..." when we are referring to episodic memories, as in "I *remember* the blizzard of 1998." But we are more likely to say "I know ..." in reference to semantic memories, as in "I *know* about ..." (or "I heard about ...") "... the blizzard of 1898." Put another way, you may *remember* that you wrote to your mother, but you *know* that Shakespeare wrote *Hamlet.*

> *"If any one faculty of our nature may be called more wonderful than the rest, I do think it is memory. There seems something more speakingly incomprehensible in the powers, the failures, the inequalities of memory, than in any other of our intelligences. The memory is sometimes so retentive, so serviceable, so obedient; at others, so bewildered and so weak; and at others again, so tyrannic, so beyond control!"*
>
> JANE AUSTEN

> *"For the sense of smell, almost more than any other, has the power to recall memories and it is a pity that you use it so little."*
>
> RACHEL CARSON

Implicit Memory: When Remembering Is Doing

Question 4: What is implicit memory? Implicit memory—also referred to as *nondeclarative memory*—is memory of how to perform a task. It is the act itself; it is doing something (Schacter, 1992). As the term *implicit* implies (should I start this sentence again?), implicit memories are suggested (or implied) but not plainly stated or expressed (not declared). Implicit memories are illustrated by the things people *do* but not by the things they state clearly. Implicit memories involve skills, both cognitive and physical; they reveal habits; and they involve the effects of conditioning. My taste aversion to buttered popcorn—which I described in Chapter 5—is an implicit memory. Because I was once nauseated by buttered popcorn, I still feel somewhat queasy when I smell it. It's a conditioned response. I don't have to think about it. (And I don't want to think about it, to tell you the truth. I wrote about it here because of my deep commitment to you.)

Here are some other examples of implicit memories: You have learned and now remember how to speak at least one language, how to ride a bicycle, how to swim or swing a bat, how to type, how to turn on the lights, and how to drive a car. It is said that you never "forget" how to ride a bicycle. This is because implicit memories can persist even when we have not used them for many years. Getting to class "by habit"—without paying attention to landmarks or directions—is another instance of

Explicit memory Memory that clearly and distinctly expresses (explicates) specific information; also referred to as *declarative memory.*

Episodic memory Memories of events that happen to a person or that take place in the person's presence.

Semantic memory General knowledge, as opposed to episodic memory.

Implicit memory Memory that is suggested (implied) but not plainly expressed, as illustrated in the things that people *do* but do not state clearly; also referred to as *nondeclarative memory.*

implicit memory. If someone asked you what 2 times 2 equals, the number 4 would probably "jump" into your mind without much thought or conscious calculation. After going over the alphabet or multiplication tables hundreds of times, our memory of them becomes automatic, or implicit. We don't have to pay conscious attention to them to remember them.

Your memory of the alphabet or the multiplication tables is the result of a great deal of repetition that makes associations automatic, a phenomenon which psychologists refer to as **priming**. Studies involving brain imaging reveal that priming makes it possible for people to carry out a mental task with less neural activity (Koenig et al., 2008; Spencer et al., 2009). Years of priming help people make complete words out of word fragments (Friedrich et al., 2009; Schacter et al., 2007). Even though the perceptual cues in the following word fragments are limited, you may very well make them into words:

PYGY   MRCA   TXT   BUFL

(Sample answers would be "pygmy," "merchant," "text," and "buffalo.") Let's jump ahead to the next chapter ("Thinking, Language, and Intelligence") to mention a couple of factors that will be involved in how many words you can make out of these fragments. One is your expertise with the English language. If English is your second language, you will probably make fewer associations to these fragments than if English is your first language. In fact, you might not perceive any complete words. Another factor could be creativity. Can you think of other factors?

Daniel Schacter (1992) also illustrates implicit memory with the story of a woman with amnesia who was wandering the streets. The police picked her up and discovered that she could not remember who she was or any other fact about her life, and she had no identification. After extensive fruitless interviewing, the police hit on the idea of asking her to dial phone numbers—just any number at all. Even though the woman did not "know" what she was doing, she dialed her mother's number.

Truth or Fiction Revisited: It is true that a woman who could not remember who she was automatically dialed her mother's number when the police gave her a telephone. When asked for the phone numbers of people she knew, the woman had no answer. She could not *declare* her mother's phone number. She could not make the number *explicit*. She could not even remember her mother's name or whether she had a mother. All this explicit information was gone. But dialing her mother's phone number was apparently a habit, and she did it "on automatic pilot." We can assume that she had been *primed* for this task by dialing the number hundreds of times, perhaps many thousands of times. Implicit memory reveals the effects of experience when we are not specifically trying to recall information.

Retrospective Memory versus Prospective Memory

Question 5: What is the difference between retrospective memory and prospective memory? Retrospective memory is the recalling of information that has been previously learned. *Episodic, semantic,* and *implicit memories* all involve remembering things that were learned.

Prospective memory involves remembering to do things in the future (Klein et al., 2010). Tasks that depend on prospective memory include remembering to brush your teeth before going out, to pay your bills (yuck), to take out some cash, and to make the list of things to do so that you won't forget what to do! And if one does make a list of things to do, one must remember to use it. Most of us have had failures of prospective memory when we have the feeling that we were supposed to do something, but we can't remember what. Prospective memory tends to fail when we are preoccupied (caught up on the Internet or fantasizing about you-know-who), distracted (we get a phone call just as we are about to get going on something), or feeling the stress of time pressure (Knight & Titov, 2009).

There are various kinds of prospective memory tasks. For example, *habitual tasks* such as getting to class on time are easier to remember than occasional tasks such as meeting someone for coffee at an arbitrary time (Henry et al., 2004). But motivation also plays a role. You are more likely to remember the coffee date if the person you are meeting is extremely attractive and someone you are interested in getting to know

Priming The activation of specific associations in memory, often as a result of repetition and without making a conscious effort to access the memory.

Retrospective memory Memory for past events, activities, and learning experiences, as shown by explicit (episodic and semantic) and implicit memories.

Prospective memory Memory to perform an act in the future, as at a certain time or when a certain event occurs.

Will You Remember Your Psychology Grade in 2062?

Will you remember your grade in this course when there is gray in your hair and the hint of a creak in your bones? When, considering inflation, your salary is $1.2 million per year but gasoline costs $400 a gallon?

Perhaps you will, especially now that we've drawn your attention to the task. Harry Bahrick and his colleagues (2008) recruited 276 alumni of Ohio Wesleyan University who had graduated 1 to 50 years earlier. Participants were asked to recall their college grades, and their recollections were checked against their actual grades. They found that the alumni accurately recalled 3,025 of 3,967 college grades. As you can see in Figure 6.1 ■, the number of correct recollections fell off with the age of the respondent, generally due to errors of omission—that is, leaving items blank rather than entering the wrong grade. But graduates who were out of school more than 40 years made no more errors of commission—that is, entered no more wrong grades—on average, than those who were out of school 8 years or so. Students who received better grades made fewer errors. The more confident alumni were that they were correct, the more likely it was that they were.

Chances are also that if you recall your grade inaccurately, you will have bumped it up a notch or two. Eighty-one percent of errors of commission inflated the grade. The researchers suggest that we

bring in relevant generic memories to fill in gaps ("I was sort of a good student; I got a B+.") after our actual episodic memory fails and that most of us distort our memories in a more emotionally gratifying fashion. Some of us, unfortunately, expect the worst and fill in the gaps with the worst. Of course, it will be difficult to distort your A or A+ "in a more emotionally gratifying fashion."

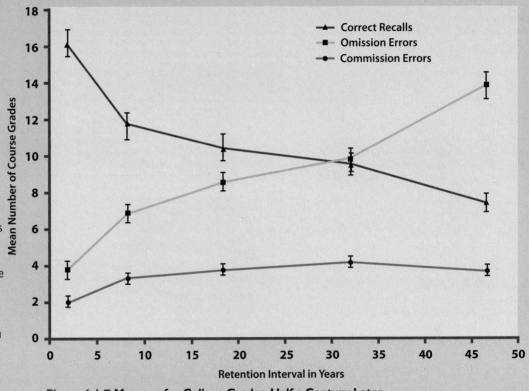

Figure 6.1 ■ Memory for College Grades, Half a Century Later.

better. Psychologists also distinguish between event-based and time-based prospective memory tasks. *Event-based tasks* are triggered by events, such as remembering to take one's medicine at breakfast or to brush one's teeth after eating. *Time-based tasks* are performed at a certain time or after a certain amount of time has elapsed between occurrences, such as tuning in to a favorite news program at 7:30 P.M. or taking a pill every 4 hours.

There is an age-related decline in both retrospective and prospective memory (Old & Naveh-Benjamin, 2008). Generally speaking, the decline in older adults often appears to be related to the speed of cognitive processing rather than "loss" of memory per se. In the case of prospective memory, older adults seem to be about as aware of specific cues or reminders as young adults; however, it takes them longer to respond to the cues or reminders (Old & Naveh-Benjamin, 2008). That is, if they meet with a friend, they are likely to remember that they were supposed to ask something, but it may take longer for them to remember the particular question. However, older adults with greater verbal ability and occupational status and more social involvement are better able to keep their intentions in mind (Engelhardt et al., 2010; Hughes et al., 2008).

Moods and attitudes have an effect on prospective memory. For example, negative emotional states such as depression also impair prospective memory. Depressed people are less likely to push to remind themselves to do what they intend to do (Altgassen et al., 2008). On the other hand, older people who are confident in their ability to remember to carry out tasks are more likely to actually remember to do them (McDonald-Miszczak et al., 1999; Pansky et al., 2009). The various kinds of memory are summarized in the nearby Concept Review.

Before proceeding to the next section, why don't you turn to the piece of paper on which you wrote the names of the four figures—that is, sheet 4—and draw them from memory as exactly as you can. Hold on to the drawings. We'll talk about them a bit later.

CONCEPT REVIEW 6.1 THE RELATIONSHIPS AMONG THE VARIOUS KINDS OF MEMORIES

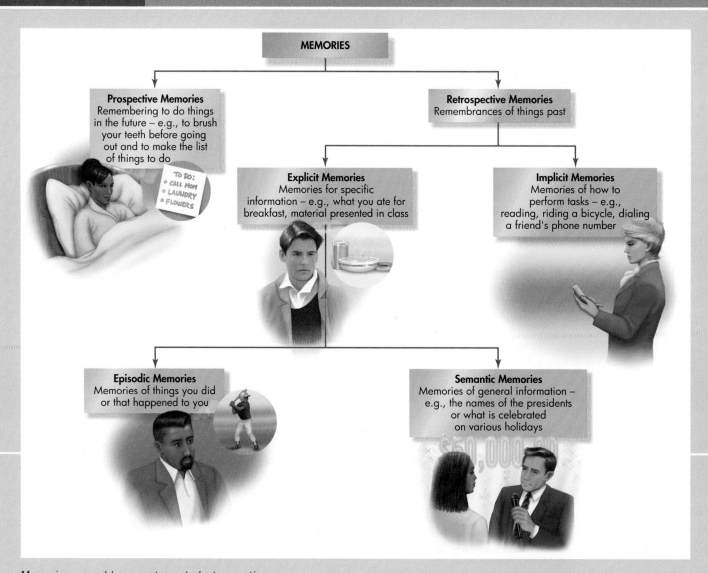

Memories can address past events (*retrospective memories*) or future events (*prospective memories*). Memories of the past can be *explicit* (declarative) or *implicit* (nondeclarative). Explicit memories include memories of personal episodes (which are called *episodic or autobiographical memories*) or of general information (*semantic memories*).

ACTIVE REVIEW (1) _____ memories are memories of specific information. (2) Memories of the events that happen to a person are _____ memories. (3) _____ memories concern generalized knowledge.

REFLECT AND RELATE Try a mini-experiment. Take out a pen or pencil and write your name. (Or if you are using a keyboard, type your name.) Now reflect: You remembered how to hold and write with the pen or pencil or how to type. What type of memory was this?

CRITICAL THINKING Definitions matter. Should this chapter be called *Memory* or *Memories?* You have retrospective versus prospective memories, implicit versus explicit memories, and so on. Do they represent different *systems* of memory, or are they just different examples of memory?

 Go to Psychology CourseMate at **www.cengagebrain.com** for an interactive version of these questions.

● PROCESSES OF MEMORY: PROCESSING INFORMATION IN OUR MOST PERSONAL COMPUTERS

Both psychologists and computer scientists speak of processing information. Think of using a computer to write a term paper. Once the system is up and operating, you begin to enter information. You can enter information into the computer's memory by, for example, typing letters on a keyboard or—in the case of voice recognition technology—speaking. If you were to do some major surgery on your computer and open up its memory, however, you wouldn't find these letters or sounds inside it. This is because the computer is programmed to change the letters or sounds—that is, the information you have entered—into a form that can be placed in its electronic memory. Similarly, when we perceive information, we must convert it into a form that can be remembered if we are to place it in our memory.

Encoding: The Memory's "Transformer"

Information about the outside world reaches our senses in the form of physical and chemical stimuli. The first stage of information processing is changing information so that we can place it in memory: encoding. **Question 6: What is the role of encoding in memory?** When we encode information, we transform it into psychological formats that can be represented mentally. To do so, we commonly use visual, auditory, and semantic codes.

Let's illustrate the uses of coding by referring to the list of letters you first saw in the section on challenges to memory. Try to write the letters on sheet 1. Go on, take a minute, and then come back.

Okay, now: If you had used a visual code to try to remember the list, you would have mentally represented it as a picture. That is, you would have maintained—or attempted to maintain—a mental image of the letters. Some artists and art historians seem to maintain marvelous visual mental representations of works of art. This enables them to quickly recognize whether a work is authentic.

You may also have decided to read the list of letters to yourself—that is, to silently say them in sequence: "t," "h," "u," and so on. By so doing, you would have been using an **acoustic code**, or representing the stimuli as a sequence of sounds. You may also have read the list as a three-syllable word, "thun-sto-fam." This is an acoustic code, but it also involves the "meaning" of the letters in the sense that you are interpreting the list as a word. This approach has elements of a semantic code.

Semantic codes represent stimuli in terms of their meaning. Our 10 letters were meaningless in and of themselves. However, they can also serve as an *acronym*—a term made up of the first letters of a phrase—for the familiar phrase "THe UNited STates OF AMerica." This observation lends them meaning.

Encoding Modifying information so that it can be placed in memory; the first stage of information processing.

Visual code Mental representation of information as a picture.

Acoustic code Mental representation of information as a sequence of sounds.

Semantic code Mental representation of information according to its meaning.

Storage: The Memory's "Save" Function

The second memory process is storage. **Question 7: What is the role of storage in memory?** Storage means maintaining information over time. If you were given the task of storing the list of letters—that is, told to remember it—how would you attempt to place it in storage? One way would be by **maintenance rehearsal**—by mentally repeating the list, or saying it to yourself (see Figure 6.2 ■). Our awareness of the functioning of our memory, referred to by psychologists as **metamemory**, becomes more sophisticated as we develop.

You could also have condensed the amount of information you were rehearsing by reading the list as a three-syllable word; that is, you could have rehearsed three syllables (said "thun-sto-fam" over and over again) rather than 10 letters. In either case, repetition would have been the key to memory. (We talk more about such condensing, or *chunking*, very soon.)

However, you could also encode the list of letters by relating it to something that you already know. This coding is called **elaborative rehearsal**. You are "elaborating," or extending the semantic meaning of the letters you are trying to remember. For example, did you recognize that the list of 10 letters is an acronym for "The United States of America"? (That is, you take the first two letters of each of the words in the phrase and string them together to make up the 10 letters of THUNSTOFAM.) If you had recognized this, storage of the list of letters might have been almost instantaneous, and it would probably have been permanent.

However, adequate maintenance rehearsal can do the job. **Truth or Fiction Revisited:** Therefore, it is not necessarily true that learning must be meaningful if we are to remember it.

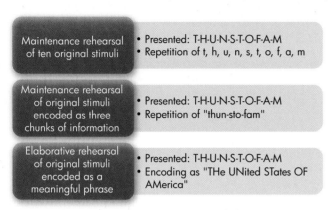

Figure 6.2 ■ Ways of Remembering T-H-U-N-S-T-O-F-A-M To remember this series of letters, one might try to repeat the entire series rapidly until it was committed to memory (pure maintenance rehearsal). One might break it into three chunks and repeat those chunks, attempting to remember how to "spell" each chunk. One could also convert the series into a meaningful phrase and try to remember the rule for converting back to the original series (elaborative rehearsal, using the first two letters of each word in the phrase). Which strategy would probably be most effective? Why?

Storage The maintenance of information over time; the second stage of information processing.

Maintenance rehearsal Mental repetition of information to keep it in memory.

Metamemory Self-awareness of the ways memory functions, allowing the person to encode, store, and retrieve information effectively.

Elaborative rehearsal The kind of coding in which new information is related to information that is already known.

Retrieval The process of locating stored information and returning it to consciousness; the third stage of information processing.

Retrieval cue A clue or prompt that can be used to enable, or trigger, the recovery of a memory in storage.

Memory The processes by which information is encoded, stored, and retrieved.

Retrieval: The Memory's "Find" Function

The third memory process is retrieval. **Question 8: What is the role of retrieval in memory?** The retrieval of stored information means locating it and returning it to consciousness. With well-known information such as our names and occupations, retrieval is effortless and, for all practical purposes, immediate. But when we are trying to remember massive quantities of information, or information that is not perfectly understood, retrieval can be tedious and not always successful. It is easiest to retrieve information stored in a computer by using the name of the file. Similarly, retrieval of information from our memories requires knowledge of the proper **retrieval cues**.

If you had encoded THUNSTOFAM as a three-syllable word, your retrieval strategy would involve recollection of the word and rules for decoding. That is, you would say the "word" *thun-sto-fam* and then decode it by spelling it out. You might err in that "thun" sounds like "thumb" and "sto" could also be spelled "stow." However, using the semantic code, or recognition of the acronym for "The United States of America," could lead to flawless recollection.

I predicted that you would immediately and permanently store the list if you recognized it as an acronym. Here, too, there would be recollection (of the name of our country) and rules for decoding. That is, to "remember" the ten letters, you would have to envision the phrase ("The United States of America") and read off the first two letters of each word. Because using this semantic code is more complex than simply seeing the entire list (using a visual code), it may take a while to recall (actually, to reconstruct) the list of 10 letters. But by using the phrase, you are likely to remember the list of letters permanently.

Now, what if you were not able to remember the list of 10 letters? What would have gone wrong? In terms of the three processes of memory, perhaps you had (a) not encoded the list in a useful way, (b) not entered the encoded information into storage, or (c) stored the information but lacked the proper cues for remembering it—such as the phrase "The United States of America" or the rule for decoding the phrase.

By now, you may have noticed that I have discussed three kinds of memory and three processes of memory, but I have not yet *defined* memory. No apologies—we weren't ready for a definition yet. Now that we have explored some basic concepts, let's give it a try: memory is the processes by which information is encoded, stored, and retrieved.

ACTIVE REVIEW (4) _____ is the transforming of information so that we can remember it. (5) One way of storing information is by _____ rehearsal, or by mentally repeating it. (6) Another way of storing information is by _____ rehearsal, when we relate new information to things we already know.

REFLECT AND RELATE As you read this page, are you using acoustic coding to transform the sensory stimulation? Are you surprised that you "know" how to do this? How do you remember how to spell the words *receive* and *retrieve*?

CRITICAL THINKING Why would an author—like me—compare the functioning of memory to the functioning of a computer? Do you find the comparison useful, or is it misleading?

 Go to Psychology CourseMate at **www.cengagebrain.com** for an interactive version of these questions.

STAGES OF MEMORY: MAKING *SENSE* OF THE *SHORT* AND THE *LONG* OF IT

The world is a continual display of sights, sounds, and other sources of sensory stimulation, but only some of these things are remembered. Psychologists Richard Atkinson and Richard Shiffrin (1968) suggested a model for how some stimuli are lost immediately, others held briefly, and still others held for a lifetime. **Question 9: What is the Atkinson–Shiffrin model of memory?** Atkinson and Shiffrin proposed that there are three stages of memory and suggested that the progress of information through these stages determines whether (and how long) it is retained (see Figure 6.3 ■). These stages are *sensory memory, short-term memory (STM)*, and *long-term memory (LTM)*.

There is a saying that when you cover a topic completely, you are talking about "the long and the short of it." In the case of the stages of memory, we could say that we are trying to "make *sense* of the *short* and the *long* of it."

Sensory Memory: Flashes on the Mental Monitor

When we look at a visual stimulus, our impressions may seem fluid enough. Actually, however, they consist of a series of eye fixations referred to as **saccadic eye movements**. These movements jump from one point to another about four times each second. Yet the visual sensations seem continuous, or streamlike, because of sensory memory. Sensory memory is the type or stage of memory that is first encountered by a stimulus. Although sensory memory holds impressions briefly, it is long enough so that a series of perceptions seem connected. **Question 10: How does sensory memory function?**

To explain the functioning of sensory memory, let's return to our list of letters: THUNSTOFAM. If the list were flashed on a screen for a fraction of a second, the visual impression, or **memory trace**, of the stimulus would also last for only a fraction of a second afterward. Psychologists speak of the memory trace of the list as being held in a visual **sensory register**.

If the letters had been flashed on a screen for, say, 1/10 of a second, your ability to remember them on the basis of sensory memory alone would be limited. Your memory would be based on a single eye fixation, and the trace of the image would vanish before a single second had passed. A century ago, psychologist William McDougall (1904) engaged in research in which he showed people one to twelve letters arranged in rows—just long enough to allow a single eye fixation. Under these conditions, people could typically remember only four or five letters. Thus, recollection of THUNSTOFAM, a list of 10 letters arranged in a single row, would probably depend on whether one had encoded it so that it could be processed further.

George Sperling (1960) modified McDougall's experimental method and showed that there is a difference between what people can see and what they can report. McDougall had used a *whole-report procedure*, in which people were asked to report every letter they saw in the array. Sperling used a modified *partial-report procedure*,

> "*Consciousness … does not appear to itself chopped up in bits. A "river" or a "stream" are the metaphors by which it is most naturally described. In talking of it hereafter, let us call it the stream of thought, of consciousness, or of subjective life.*"
>
> WILLIAM JAMES

Saccadic eye movement The rapid jumps made by a person's eyes as they fixate on different points.

Sensory memory The type or stage of memory first encountered by a stimulus. Sensory memory holds impressions briefly, but long enough so that series of perceptions are psychologically continuous.

Memory trace An assumed change in the nervous system that reflects the impression made by a stimulus. Memory traces are said to be "held" in sensory registers.

Sensory register A system of memory that holds information briefly, but long enough so that it can be processed further. There may be a sensory register for every sense.

191

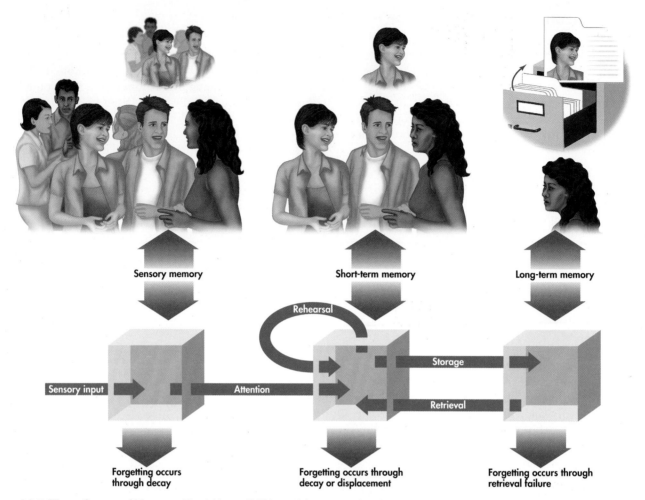

Figure 6.3 ■ Three Stages of Memory The Atkinson–Shiffrin model proposes that there are three distinct stages of memory. Sensory information impacts upon the registers of sensory memory, where memory traces are held briefly before decaying. If we attend to the information, much of it is transferred to short-term memory (STM). Information in STM may decay or be displaced if it is not transferred to long-term memory (LTM). We can use rehearsal or elaborative strategies to transfer memories to LTM. If information in LTM is organized poorly, or if we cannot find cues to retrieve it, it may be lost.

> *"The stream of thought flows on, but most of its elements fall into the bottomless pit of oblivion. Of some, no element survives the instant of their passage. Of others, it is confined to a few moments, hours, or days. Others, again, leave vestiges which are indestructible, and by means of which they may be recalled as long as life endures."*
>
> WILLIAM JAMES

in which people were asked to report the contents of one of three rows of letters. In a typical procedure, Sperling flashed three rows of letters like the following on a screen for 50 milliseconds (1/20 of a second):

A G R E

V L S B

N K B T

Using the whole-report procedure, people could report an average of four letters from the entire display (one of three). But if immediately after presenting the display Sperling pointed an arrow at a row he wanted viewers to report, they usually reported most of the letters in the row successfully.

If Sperling presented six letters arrayed in two rows, people could usually report either row without error. If people were flashed three rows of four letters each—a total of twelve—they reported correctly an average of three of four letters in the designated row, suggesting that about nine of the twelve letters had been perceived.

Sperling found that the amount of time that elapsed before indicating the row to be reported was crucial. If he delayed pointing the arrow for a few fractions of a second after presenting the letters, people were much less successful in reporting the letters in the target row. If he allowed a full second to elapse, the arrow did not aid recall at all. From these data, Sperling concluded that the memory trace of visual stimuli *decays* within a second in the visual sensory register (see Figure 6.3 again). With a single eye fixation, people can *see* most of a display of 12 letters clearly, as shown by their ability to immediately read off most of the letters in a designated row. Yet as the fractions of a single second are elapsing, the memory trace of the letters is fading. By the time a second has elapsed, the trace has vanished.

ICONIC MEMORY Psychologists believe we possess a sensory register for each one of our senses. The mental representations of visual stimuli are referred to as **icons**. The sensory register that holds icons is labeled **iconic memory**. Iconic memory is one kind of sensory memory. Iconic memories are accurate photographic memories. **Truth or Fiction Revisited:** Those of us who can see and mentally represent visual stimuli do have "photographic memories." However, these memories are brief. What most of us usually think of as a photographic memory—the ability to retain *exact mental* representations of visual stimuli over long periods of time—is technically termed **eidetic imagery**. Although all people who can see have photographic memories (that is, iconic memory), only a few have the capacity for eidetic imagery.

ICONIC MEMORY AND SACCADIC EYE MOVEMENTS Iconic memory smoothes out the bumps in the visual ride. Saccadic eye movements occur about four times every second. Iconic memory, however, holds icons for up to a second. As a consequence, the flow of visual information seems smooth and continuous. Your impression that the words you are reading flow across the page, rather than jump across in spurts, is a product of your iconic memory. Similarly, motion pictures present 16 to 22 separate frames, or still images, each second. Iconic memory allows you to perceive the imagery in the film as being seamless (Demeyer et al., 2009).

ECHOIC MEMORY Mental representations of sounds, or auditory stimuli, are called **echoes**. The sensory register that holds echoes is referred to as **echoic memory**.

The memory traces of auditory stimuli (that is, echoes) can last for several seconds, many times longer than the traces of visual stimuli (icons). The difference in the duration of traces is probably based on biological differences between the eye and the ear. This difference is one of the reasons why acoustic codes aid in the retention of information that has been presented visually—or why saying the letters or syllables of THUNSTOFAM makes the list easier to remember.

Yet echoes, like icons, fade with time. If they are to be retained, we must pay attention to them. By selectively attending to certain stimuli, we sort them out from the background noise. For example, in studies on the development of patterns of processing information, young children have been shown photographs of rooms full of toys and then been asked to recall as many of the toys as they can. One such study found that 2-year-old boys are more likely to attend to and remember toys such as cars, puzzles, and trains; 2-year-old girls are more likely to attend to and remember dolls, dishes, and teddy bears (C. F. Miller et al., 2009; Renninger & Wozniak, 1985). Even by this early age, the things that children attend to frequently fall into stereotypical patterns.

Short-Term Memory: Keeping Things "in Mind"

Imagine you are completing a writing assignment, and you key or speak words and phrases into your word-processing program. They appear on your monitor as a sign that your computer has them in *memory.* Your word-processing program allows you to add words, delete words, see if they are spelled correctly, add images, and move paragraphs from place to place. So you can manipulate the information in your computer's memory, but it isn't saved. It hasn't been entered into storage. If the program or

Icon A mental representation of a visual stimulus that is held briefly in sensory memory.

Iconic memory The sensory register that briefly holds mental representations of visual stimuli.

Eidetic imagery The maintenance of detailed visual memories over several minutes.

Echo A mental representation of an auditory stimulus (sound) that is held briefly in sensory memory.

Echoic memory The sensory register that briefly holds mental representations of auditory stimuli.

"The true art of memory is the art of attention."

DR. SAMUEL JOHNSON

© Comstock Images/Getty Images

Memorizing a Script by Rehearsing Echoic Memories As these actors work to memorize their scripts, they first encode visual information (printed words) as echoes (the corresponding sounds within their brains). They then commit the echoes to memory by rehearsing (repeating) them. They refer to the visual information as often as needed.

the computer crashes, the information is gone. The computer's memory is a short-term affair. To maintain a long-term connection with the information, you need to save it. Saving it means giving it a name—ideally, a name that you will remember so that you can later find and retrieve the information—and instructing your computer to save it (keep it in storage until told otherwise).

If you focus on a stimulus in the sensory register, you will tend to retain it in your own **short-term memory**—also referred to as **working memory**—for a minute or so after the trace of the stimulus decays. **Question 11: How does short-term memory function?** As one researcher describes it, "Working memory is the mental glue that links a thought through time from its beginning to its end" (Goldman-Rakic, 1995). When you are given a phone number by the information operator and write it down or immediately dial the number, you are retaining the number in your short-term memory. When you are told the name of someone at a party and then use that name immediately when addressing that person, you are retaining the name in short-term memory. In short-term memory, the image tends to fade significantly after 10 to 12 seconds if it is not repeated or rehearsed. It is possible to focus on maintaining a visual image in short-term memory, but it is more common to encode visual stimuli as sounds, or auditory stimuli. Then the sounds can be rehearsed, or repeated.

Most of us know that one way of retaining information in short-term memory—and possibly storing it permanently—is to rehearse it. When an information operator tells me a phone number, I usually rehearse it continuously while I am dialing it or running around frantically searching for a pencil and a scrap of paper so that I can save it. The more times we rehearse information, the more likely we are to remember it. We have the capacity (if not the will or the time) to rehearse information and thereby keep it in short-term memory indefinitely.

Once information is in our short-term memories, we can work on it. Like the information in the word-processing program, we can manipulate it. But it isn't necessarily saved. If we don't do something to save it (like write down that telephone number on a scrap of paper or key it into your cell phone), it can be gone forever. We can try to reconstruct it, but it may never be the same. Getting *most* of the digits in someone's phone number right doesn't get you a date for the weekend—at least not with the person you were thinking of!

Truth or Fiction Revisited: It is true that it may be easier for you to recall the name of your first-grade teacher than the name of someone you just met at a party. You need to rehearse new information to save it, but you may only need the proper cue to retrieve information from long-term memory.

KEEPING *THUNSTOFAM* IN SHORT-TERM MEMORY Let's now return to the task of remembering the first list of letters in the challenges to memory at the beginning of the chapter. If you had encoded the letters as the three-syllable "word" THUN-STO-FAM, you would probably have recalled them by mentally rehearsing (saying to yourself) the three-syllable word and then spelling it out from the sounds. A few minutes later, if someone asked whether the letters had been uppercase (THUNSTOFAM) or lowercase (thunstofam), you might not have been able to answer with confidence. You used an acoustic code to help recall the list, and uppercase and lowercase letters sound alike.

Because it can be pronounced, THUNSTOFAM is not too difficult to retain in short-term memory. But what if the list of letters had been TBXLFNTSDK? This list of letters cannot be pronounced as it is. You would have to find a complex acronym to code these letters and do so within a fraction of a second—most likely an impossible task. To aid recall, you would probably choose to try to repeat the letters rapidly—to read each one as many times as possible before the memory trace fades. You might visualize each letter as you say it and try to get back to it (that is, to run through the entire list) before it decays.

Let's assume that you encoded the letters as sounds and then rehearsed the sounds. When asked to report the list, you might mistakenly say T-V-X-L-F-N-T-S-T-K. This would be an understandable error because the incorrect V and T sounds are similar to the correct B and D sounds.

THE SERIAL-POSITION EFFECT If asked to recall the list of letters TBXLFNTSDK, you would be likely to recall the first and last letters in the series, T and K, more

Short-term memory The type or stage of memory that can hold information for up to a minute or so after the trace of the stimulus decays; also called *working memory*.

Working memory Same as *short-term memory*.

Question 12: Why are we most likely to remember the first and last items in a list? The tendency to recall the first and last items in a series is known as the **serial-position effect**. This effect may occur because we pay more attention to the first and last stimuli in a series. They serve as the visual or auditory boundaries for the other stimuli. In addition, the first items are likely to be rehearsed more frequently (repeated more times) than other items. The last items are likely to have been rehearsed most recently and hence are most likely to be retained in short-term memory.

According to cognitive psychologists, the tendency to recall the initial items in a list is referred to as the **primacy effect**. Social psychologists have also noted a powerful primacy effect in our formation of impressions of other people. That is, first impressions tend to last. The tendency to recall the last items in a list is referred to as the **recency effect**. If we are asked to recall the last items soon after we have been shown the list, they may still be in short-term memory. As a result, they can be "read off." Earlier items, in contrast, may have to be retrieved from long-term memory.

CHUNKING

Rapidly rehearsing 10 meaningless letters is not an easy task. With TBXLFNTSDK, there are 10 discrete elements, or **chunks**, of information that must be kept in short-term memory. When we encode THUNSTOFAM as three syllables, there are only three chunks to swallow at once—a memory task that is much easier on the digestion.

George Miller (1956) noted that the average person is comfortable with digesting about seven integers at a time, the number of integers in a telephone number. **Question 13: Is seven a magic number, or did the phone company get lucky?** Research shows that most people have little trouble recalling five chunks of information, as in a zip code. Some can remember nine, which is, for all but a few, an upper limit. So seven chunks, plus or minus one or two, is a "magic" number in the sense that the typical person can manage to remember that many chunks of information but not a great deal more.

So how, you ask, do we manage to include area codes in our recollections of telephone numbers, hence making them 10 digits long? The truth of the matter is that we usually don't. We tend to recall the area code as a single chunk of information derived from our general knowledge of where a person lives. So we are more likely to remember (or "know") the 10-digit numbers of acquaintances who reside in locales with area codes that we use frequently.

Businesses pay the phone company hefty premiums to obtain numbers with two or three zeroes or repeated digits—for example, 592-2000 or 277-3333. These numbers include fewer chunks of information and hence are easier to remember. Customer recollection of business phone numbers increases sales. One financial services company uses the toll-free number CALL-IRA, which reduces the task to two chunks of information that also happen to be meaningfully related (semantically coded) to the nature of the business. Similarly, a clinic that helps people quit smoking arranged for a telephone number that can be reached by dialing the letters NO SMOKE.

Return to the third challenge to memory presented earlier. Were you able to remember the six groups of letters? Would your task have been simpler if you had grouped them differently? How about moving the dashes forward by a letter so that they read GM-CBS-IBM-ATT-CIA-FBI? If we do this, we have the same list of letters, but we also have six chunks of information that can be coded semantically (according to what they mean). You may have also been able to generate the list by remembering a rule, such as "big corporations and government agencies."

If we can recall seven or perhaps nine chunks of information, how do children remember the alphabet? The alphabet contains 26 discrete pieces of information. How do children learn to encode the letters of the alphabet, which are visual symbols, as spoken sounds? There is nothing about the shape of an A that suggests its sound. Nor does the visual stimulus B sound "B-ish." Children learn to associate letters with their spoken names by **rote**. It is mechanical associative learning that takes time and repetition. If you think that learning the alphabet by rote is a simple task, try learning the Russian alphabet.

If you had recognized THUNSTOFAM as an acronym for the first two letters of each word in the phrase "THe UNited STates OF AMerica," you would also have reduced the number of chunks of information that had to be recalled. You could have considered the phrase to be a single chunk of information. The rule that you must use the first two letters of each word of the phrase would be another chunk.

My problem is that I have been persecuted by an integer [[the number seven]]. For seven years this number has followed me around, has intruded in my most private data, and has assaulted me from the pages of our most public journals.... The persistence with which this number plagues me is far more than a random accident. There is ... a design behind it, some pattern governing its appearances. Either there really is something unusual about the number or else I am suffering from delusions of persecution. (George Miller, 1956, p. 81).

Serial-position effect The tendency to recall more accurately the first and last items in a series.

Primacy effect The tendency to recall the initial items in a series of items.

Recency effect The tendency to recall the last items in a series of items.

Chunk A stimulus or group of stimuli that is perceived as a discrete piece of information.

Rote Mechanical associative learning that is based on repetition.

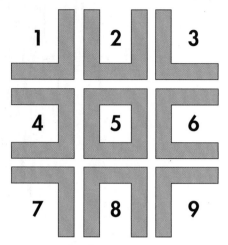

Figure 6.4 ■ A Familiar Grid The nine drawings in the second challenge to memory form this familiar tic-tac-toe grid when the numbers are placed inside them and they are arranged in order. This method for recalling the shapes collapses nine chunks of information into two. One is the tic-tac-toe grid. The second is the rule for decoding the drawings from the grid.

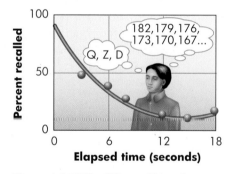

Figure 6.5 ■ The Effect of Interference on Short-Term Memory In this experiment, college students were asked to remember a series of three letters while they counted backward by threes. After just 3 seconds, retention was cut by half. The ability to recall the letters was almost completely lost by 15 seconds.

Displace In memory theory, to cause information to be lost from short-term memory by adding new information.

Long-term memory The type or stage of memory capable of relatively permanent storage.

Repression In Freud's psychodynamic theory, the ejection of anxiety-evoking ideas from conscious awareness.

Reconsider the second challenge to memory presented earlier. You were asked to remember nine chunks of visual information. Perhaps you could have used the acoustic codes "L" and "Square" for chunks 3 and 5, but no obvious codes are available for the seven other chunks. Now look at Figure 6.4 ■. If you had recognized that the elements in the challenge could be arranged as the familiar tic-tac-toe grid, remembering the nine elements might have required only two chunks of information. The first would have been the mental image of the grid, and the second would have been the rule for decoding: Each element corresponds to the shape of a section of the grid if read like words on a page (from upper left to lower right). The number sequence 1 through 9 would not in itself present a problem because you learned this series by rote many years ago and have rehearsed it in countless calculations since then.

INTERFERENCE IN SHORT-TERM MEMORY I mentioned that I often find myself running around looking for a pencil and a scrap of paper to write down a telephone number that has been given to me. If I keep on rehearsing the number while I'm looking, I'm okay. But I have also often cursed myself for failing to keep a pad and pencil by the telephone, and sometimes, this has interfered with my recollection of the number. (The moral of the story? Avoid self-reproach.) It has also happened that I have actually looked up a phone number and been about to dial it when someone has asked me for the time or where I said we were going to dinner. Unless I say, "Hold on a minute!" and manage to jot down the number on something, it's back to the phone book. Attending to distracting information, even briefly, prevents me from rehearsing the number, so it falls through the cracks of my short-term memory.

In an experiment with college students, Lloyd and Margaret Peterson (1959) demonstrated how prevention of rehearsal can wreak havoc with short-term memory. They asked students to remember three-letter combinations such as HGB—normally, three easy chunks of information. They then had the students count backward from an arbitrary number, such as 182, by threes (that is, 182, 179, 176, 173, and so on). The students were told to stop counting and to report the letter sequence after the intervals of time shown in Figure 6.5 ■. The percentage of letter combinations that were recalled correctly fell precipitously within seconds. Counting backward for 18 seconds dislodged the letter sequences in almost all of these bright students' memories.

Psychologists say that the appearance of new information in short-term memory **displaces** the old information. Remember, only a few bits of information can be retained in short-term memory at the same time. (Unfortunately, we cannot upgrade our human memories from, say, 512 megabytes to 8 gigabytes.) Think of short-term memory as a shelf or workbench. Once it is full, some things fall off when new items are shoved on. Here we have another possible explanation for the recency effect: The most recently learned bit of information is least likely to be *displaced* by additional information.

Displacement occurs at cocktail parties, and I'm not referring to jostling by the crowd. The point is this: When you meet Linda or Latrell at the party, you should have little trouble remembering the name. But then you may meet Tamara or Timothy and, still later, Keith or LaToya. By that time, you may have a hard time dredging up Jennifer or Jonathan's name—unless, of course, you were very, very attracted to one of them. A passionate response would set a person apart and inspire a good deal of selective attention. According to *signal-detection theory* (see Chapter 3), if you were enamored enough, you might "detect" the person's name (sensory signals) with a vengeance, and the other names would dissolve into background noise.

Long-Term Memory: Your Memory's "Hard Drive"

Long-term memory is the third stage of information processing. Think of your long-term memory as a vast storehouse of information containing names, dates, places, what Johnny did to you in second grade, and what Susan said about you when you were 12.

Question 14: How does long-term memory function?

Some psychologists (Freud was one) believed that nearly all of our perceptions and ideas are stored permanently. We might not be able to retrieve all of them. Some memories might be "lost" because of lack of proper cues, or they might be kept unconscious by the forces of **repression** (which we'll discuss in more detail in a bit). Adherents to this view often pointed to the work of neurosurgeon Wilder Penfield (1969). When parts of the brains of Penfield's patients were electrically stimulated, many reported the appearance of images that had something of the feel of memories.

Today, most psychologists view this notion as exaggerated. Memory researcher Elizabeth Loftus, for example, notes that the "memories" stimulated by Penfield's probes lacked detail and were sometimes incorrect (e.g., Bernstein & Loftus, 2009). **Truth or Fiction Revisited:** Therefore, it has not been shown that all of our experiences are permanently imprinted on the brain. Now let's consider some other questions about long-term memory.

HOW ACCURATE ARE LONG-TERM MEMORIES? Psychologist Elizabeth Loftus notes that our memories are distorted by our biases and needs—by the ways we conceptualize our worlds. We represent much of our world in the form of **schemas.**

To understand what the term *schema* means, consider the problems of travelers who met Procrustes, the legendary highwayman of ancient Greece. Procrustes had a quirk. He was interested not only in travelers' pocketbooks but also in their height. He had a concept—a schema—of how tall people should be, and when people did not fit his schema, they were in trouble. You see, Procrustes also had a bed, the famous "Procrustean bed." He made his victims lie down in the bed, and if they were too short for it, he stretched them to make them fit. If they were too long for the bed, he practiced surgery on their legs.

Although the myth of Procrustes may sound absurd, it reflects a quirky truth about each of us. We all carry our cognitive Procrustean beds around with us—our unique ways of perceiving the world—and we try to make things and people fit them. Let me give you an example. "Retrieve" the fourth sheet of paper you prepared according to the Self-Assessment at the beginning of the chapter. You drew the figures "from memory" according to instructions on page 184. Now look at Figure 6.6 ■. Are your drawings closer in form to those in group 1 or to those in group 2? I wouldn't be surprised if they were more like those in group 1—if, for example, your first drawing looked more like eyeglasses than a dumbbell. After all, they were labeled like the drawings in group 1. The labels serve as *schemas* for the drawings—ways of organizing your knowledge of them—and these schemas may have influenced your recollections. By the way, take out a penny and look at it. Did you pick the correct penny when you answered the challenges to memory?

Consider another example of the power of schemas in processing information. Loftus and Palmer (1974) showed people a film of a car crash and then asked them to fill out questionnaires that included a question about how fast the cars were going at the time. The language of the question varied in subtle ways, however. Some people were asked to estimate how fast the cars were going when they "hit" each other. Others were asked to estimate the cars' speed when they "smashed into"

Schema A way of mentally representing the world, such as a belief or an expectation, that can influence perception of persons, objects, and situations.

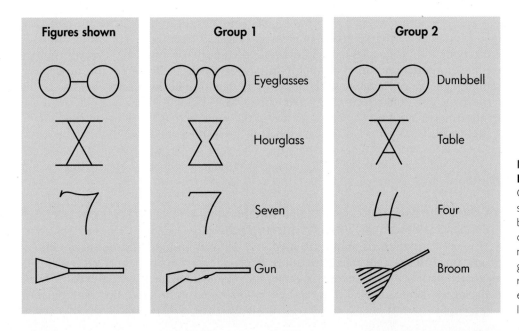

Figure 6.6 ■ Memory as Reconstructive In their classic experiment, Carmichael, Hogan, and Walter (1932) showed people the figures in the left-hand box and made remarks as suggested in the other boxes. For example, the experimenter might say, "This drawing looks like eyeglasses [or a dumbbell]." When people later reconstructed the drawings, they were influenced by the labels. What did your drawings look like?

How Fast Were These Cars Moving When They Collided? Our schemas influence our processing of information. When shown photos such as these, people who were asked how fast the cars were going when they *smashed* into each other offered higher estimates than people who were asked how fast they were going when they *hit* each other.

Elizabeth Loftus Loftus's research on memory is so widely recognized that the April 2002 issue of *Review of General Psychology* ranked her as the first woman on the list of the top 100 psychologists of the 20th century. For three decades, Loftus has been demonstrating that memories are not snapshots but instead are changeable and susceptible to bias and suggestion. In her research with people in the laboratory, she has implanted "memories" of seeing barns in barren fields or of being lost in a mall as a child. After the implanting, the people painted in "recalled" details of the events that never happened.

each other. On average, people who reconstructed the scene on the basis of the cue "hit" estimated a speed of 34 mph. People who watched the same film but reconstructed the scene on the basis of the cue "smashed" estimated a speed of 41 mph! Hence, the use of the word *hit* or *smashed* caused people to organize their knowledge about the crash in different ways. That is, the words served as diverse schemas that fostered the development of very different ways of processing information about the crash.

Subjects in the same study were questioned again a week later: "Did you see any broken glass?" Because there was no broken glass shown in the film, an answer of "yes" would be wrong. Of those who had earlier been encouraged to process information about the accident in terms of one car "hitting" the other, 14% incorrectly answered yes. But 32% of the subjects who had processed information about the crash in terms of one car "smashing into" the other reported, incorrectly, that they had seen broken glass.

Another experiment reported by Elizabeth Loftus (1979) shows that people may reconstruct their experiences according to their prejudices. Subjects in the study were shown a picture that contained an African American man who was holding a hat and a European American man who was holding a razor. Later, when they were asked what they had seen, many subjects erroneously recalled the razor as being in the hands of the African American. The subjects recalled information that was consistent with their schemas, but it was wrong.

HOW MUCH INFORMATION *CAN* BE STORED IN LONG-TERM MEMORY?

How many terabytes of storage are there in your most personal computer—your brain? Unlike a computer, the human ability to store information is, for all practical purposes, unlimited (Voss, 2009; Y. Wang et al., 2009). Even the largest hard drives fill up quickly when we save web pages, pictures, or videos. Yet how many movies of the past have you saved in your own long-term memory? How many thousands of scenes and stories can you rerun at will? And assuming that you have an intact sensory system, the movies in your personal storage bins have not only color and sound but also aromas, tactile sensations, and much more. *Your long-term memory is a biochemical "hard drive" with no known limits on the terabytes of information it can store.*

Yes, new information may replace older information in short-term memory, but there is no evidence that long-term memories—those in "storage"—are lost by displacement. Long-term memories may endure for a lifetime. Now and then, it may seem that we have forgotten, or "lost," a long-term memory such as the names of our elementary or high school classmates. Yet possibly, we cannot find the proper cues to help us retrieve them. It is like forgetting a file name when working with a computer. If long-term memories are lost, they may be lost in the same way that a misplaced object or computer file is lost. It is lost, but we sense that it is still somewhere in the room or on the hard drive. For example, you may drive by your elementary school and suddenly recall the long-lost names of elementary schoolteachers and of the streets in your old neighborhood.

TRANSFERRING INFORMATION FROM SHORT-TERM TO LONG-TERM MEMORY: USING THE "SAVE" FUNCTION How can you transfer information from short-term to long-term memory? By and large, the more often chunks of information are rehearsed, the more likely they are to be transferred to long-term memory. As noted earlier, repeating information frequently to prevent it from decaying or being displaced is termed *maintenance rehearsal*. But maintenance

Can We Trust Eyewitness Testimony?

Jean Piaget, the investigator of children's cognitive development, distinctly remembered an attempt to kidnap him from his baby carriage as he was being wheeled along the Champs Élysées. He recalled the excited throng, the abrasions on the face of the nurse who rescued him, the police officer's white baton, and the flight of the assailant. Although they were graphic, Piaget's memories were false. Years later, the nurse admitted that she had made up the tale. Piaget had fallen victim to an example of what psychologists term the **misinformation effect**. The false information provided by his nurse became implanted in his own memory.

Can eyewitness testimony be trusted? Is there reason to believe that the statements of eyewitnesses are any more factual than Piaget's?

One problem with eyewitness testimony is that the words chosen by an experimenter—and those chosen by a lawyer interrogating a witness—have been shown to influence the reconstruction of memories (Cutler & Kovera, 2010). For example, as in the experiment described earlier, an attorney for the plaintiff might ask the witness, "How fast was the defendant's car going when it *smashed into* the plaintiff's car?" In such a case, the car might be reported as going faster than if the question had been "How fast was the defendant's car going when the accident occurred?" (Loftus & Palmer, 1974). Could the attorney for the defendant claim that the use of the word *smashed* biased the witness? What about jurors who heard the word *smashed?* Would they be biased toward assuming that the driver had been reckless?

Children tend to be more suggestible witnesses than adults, and preschoolers are more suggestible than older children (Ceci et al., 2007; Cutler & Kovera, 2010; Krähenbühl et al., 2009). But when questioned properly, even young children may provide accurate and useful testimony (Ceci et al., 2007; Krähenbühl et al., 2009).

There are also problems in the identification of criminals by eyewitnesses. For one thing, witnesses may pay more attention to the suspect's clothing than to more meaningful characteristics such as facial features, height, and weight. In one experiment, viewers of a videotaped crime incorrectly identified a man as the criminal because he wore the eyeglasses and T-shirt that had been worn by the perpetrator on the tape. The man who had actually committed the crime was identified less often (Sanders, 1984).

Other problems with eyewitness testimony include the following (Cutler & Kovera, 2010):

- Identification is less accurate when suspects belong to ethnic or racial groups that differ from that of the witness.

- Identification of suspects is compromised when interrogators make misleading suggestions.

Eyewitness Testimony? How trustworthy is eyewitness testimony? Memories are reconstructive rather than photographic. The wording of questions also influences the content of the memory. Attorneys therefore are sometimes instructed not to phrase questions in such a way that they "lead" the witness.

- Witnesses are seen as more credible when they claim to be certain in their testimony, but there is little evidence that claims of certainty are accurate.

Thus, there are many problems with eyewitness testimony. Yet even Elizabeth Loftus (e.g., Wright & Loftus, 2008), who has extensively studied the accuracy of eyewitness testimony, agrees that it is a valuable tool in the courtroom. After all, identifications made by eyewitnesses are frequently correct, and what, Loftus asks, would be the alternative to the use of eyewitnesses? If we were to prevent eyewitnesses from testifying, how many criminals would go free?

---

rehearsal does not give meaning to information by linking it to past learning. Thus, it is not considered the best way to permanently store information (Callan & Schweighofer, 2009).

A more effective method is to make information more meaningful—to purposefully relate new information to things that are already well known (Craik & Lockhart, 2008). For example, to better remember the components of levers, physics students might use seesaws, wheelbarrows, and oars as examples. The nine chunks of information in our second challenge to memory were made easier to reconstruct once they were

Misinformation effect The shaping of bogus or slanted memories by providing inaccurate information as, for example, in the form of "leading questions."

associated with the familiar tic-tac-toe grid in Figure 6.4. As noted earlier, relating new material to well-known material is known as *elaborative rehearsal*. For example, have you seen the following word before?

F U N T H O S T A M

Say it aloud. Do you know it? If you had used an acoustic code alone to memorize THUNSTOFAM, the list of letters you first saw on page 184, it might not have been easy to recognize FUNTHOSTAM as an incorrect spelling. Let's assume, however, that by now you have used elaborative rehearsal and encoded THUNSTOFAM semantically (according to its "meaning") as an acronym for "The United States of America." Then you would have been able to scan the spelling of the words in the phrase "The United States of America" to determine that FUNTHOSTAM is an incorrect spelling.

Rote repetition of a meaningless group of syllables, such as *thun-sto-fam*, relies on maintenance rehearsal for permanent storage. The process might be tedious (continued rehearsal) and unreliable. Elaborative rehearsal, on the other hand—as in tying THUNSTOFAM to the name of a country—might make storage instantaneous and retrieval practically foolproof.

LEVELS OF PROCESSING INFORMATION People who use elaborative rehearsal to remember things are *processing information at a deeper level* than people who use maintenance rehearsal. **Question 15: What is the levels-of-processing model of memory?** Fergus Craik and Robert Lockhart (2008) pioneered the *levels-of-processing model of memory*, which holds that memories tend to endure when information is processed *deeply*—attended to, encoded carefully, pondered, and related to things we already know. Remembering relies on how *deeply* people process information, not on whether memories are transferred from one *stage* of memory to another.

Evidence for the importance of levels of processing information is found in a classic experiment with three groups of college students, all of whom were asked to study a picture of a living room for 1 minute (Bransford et al., 1977). The groups' examination of the picture entailed different approaches. Two groups were informed that small x's were imbedded in the picture. The first of these groups was asked to find the x's by scanning the picture horizontally and vertically. The second group was informed that the x's could be found in the edges of the objects in the room and was asked to look for them there. The third group was asked, instead, to think about how members would use the objects pictured in the room. As a result of the divergent sets of instructions, the first two groups (the x hunters) processed information about the objects in the picture superficially. But the third group rehearsed the objects elaboratively; that is, members of this group thought about the objects in terms of their meanings and uses. It should not be surprising that the third group remembered many more objects than the first two groups.

Language arts teachers encourage students to use new vocabulary words in sentences to process the words more deeply. Each new usage is an instance of elaborative rehearsal. Usage helps build semantic codes that make it easier to retrieve the meanings of words in the future. When I was in high school, teachers of foreign languages told us that learning classical languages "exercises the mind" so that we understand English better. Not exactly. The mind is not analogous to a muscle that responds to exercise. However, the meanings of many English words are based on foreign words. A person who recognizes that *retrieve* stems from roots meaning "again" *(re-)* and "find" *(trouver* in French) is less likely to forget that *retrieval* means "finding again" or "bringing back."

Think, too, of all the algebra and geometry problems we were asked to solve in high school. Each problem is an application of a procedure and, perhaps, of certain formulas and theorems. By repeatedly applying the procedures, formulas, and theorems in different contexts, we rehearse them elaboratively (Callan & Schweighofer, 2009). As a consequence, we are more likely to remember them. Knowledge of the ways a formula or an equation is used helps us remember the formula. Also, by building one geometry theorem on another, we relate new theorems to ones that we already understand. As a result, we process information about them more deeply and remember them better.

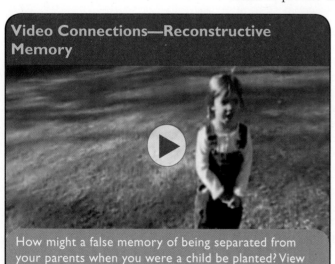

Video Connections—Reconstructive Memory

How might a false memory of being separated from your parents when you were a child be planted? View the video and learn why reconstructive memory is not like viewing a snapshot of an event. Go to Psychology CourseMate at **www.cengagebrain.com** to watch this video.

There is also a good deal of biologically oriented research that connects deep processing with activity in certain parts of the brain, notably the prefrontal area of the cerebral cortex (Barbey & Barsalou, 2009; Luo & Craik, 2009). One reason why older adults show memory loss is that they tend not to process information quite as deeply as younger people do (Craik & Bialystok, 2006; Schneider-Garces et al., 2010). Deep processing requires sustained attention, and older adults, along with people who have suffered brain injuries and strokes, are apparently not capable of focusing their attention as well as they had previously (Willmott et al., 2009).

Before proceeding to the next section, go back three paragraphs and cover it with your hand. Which of the following words is spelled correctly: *retrieval* or *retreival*? The spellings sound alike, so an acoustic code for reconstructing the correct spelling would fail. Yet a semantic code, such as the spelling rule "i before e except after c," would allow you to reconstruct the correct spelling: retr*ie*val.

FLASHBULB MEMORIES: "TO LEAVE A SCAR UPON THE CEREBRAL TISSUES" Truth or Fiction Revisited: It is true that

many of us will never forget where we were or what we were doing when we learned of the attacks on the World Trade Center and the Pentagon on September 11, 2001 (Jhangiani, 2010). Some of us will recall the day in 1997 when Britain's Princess Diana died in an automobile accident. Some of us who are older will recall where we were and what we were doing when President John F. Kennedy was assassinated (Holland & Kensinger, 2010). We may have a detailed memory of what we were doing when we learned of a relative's death.

Question 16: Why can some events, like the attack of September 11, 2001, be etched in memory for a lifetime? It appears that we tend to remember events that are surprising, important, and emotionally stirring more clearly. Such events can create **flashbulb memories**, which preserve experiences in detail (Hirst et al., 2009), even if those details are sometimes reconstructed, as is the case with other memories (Kvavilashvili et al., 2009). Why is the memory etched when the "flashbulb" goes off? One factor is the distinctness of the memory. It is easier to discriminate stimuli that stand out. Such events are striking in themselves. The feelings caused by them are also special. It is thus relatively easy to pick them out from the storehouse of memories. Another factor is that major events such as the assassination of a president or the loss of a close relative tend to have important effects on our lives. We are likely to dwell on them and form networks of associations. That is, we are likely to rehearse them elaboratively. Our rehearsal may include great expectations or deep fears for the future.

Biology is intimately connected with psychology. Strong feelings are connected with the secretion of stress hormones, and stress hormones help etch events into our memory—"as almost to leave a scar upon the cerebral tissues," wrote William James.

ORGANIZATION IN LONG-TERM MEMORY The storehouse of long-term memory is usually well organized. Items are not just piled on the floor or thrown into closets. **Question 17: How is knowledge organized in long-term memory?** We tend to gather information about rats and cats into a certain section of the storehouse, perhaps the animal or mammal section. We put information about oaks, maples, and eucalyptuses into the tree section. Such categorization of stimuli is a basic cognitive function. It allows us to make predictions about specific instances and to store information efficiently.

We also tend to organize information according to a *hierarchical structure*, as shown in Figure 6.7 ∎. In a *hierarchy*, items (or chunks of information) are grouped according to common or distinct features and then these groups or classes are ordered from lowest to highest. As we work our way up the hierarchy shown in Figure 6.7, we find more encompassing, or *superordinate*, classes to which the items below them belong. For example, all mammals are animals, but there are many types of animals other than mammals.

When items are correctly organized in long-term memory, you are more likely to recall—or know—accurate information about them. For instance, do you "remember" whether whales breathe underwater? If you did not know that whales are mammals

AP Photo/Carmen Taylor

Flashbulb Memories Where were you and what were you doing on the morning of September 11, 2001? Many older Americans never forgot where they were and what they were doing when they learned about the attack on Pearl Harbor on December 7, 1941. Major events can illuminate everything that occurred so that we recall everything that was happening at the time.

"*The attention which we lend to an experience is proportional to its vivid or interesting character; and it is a notorious fact that what interests us most vividly at the time is, other things equal, what we remember best. An impression may be so exciting emotionally as almost to leave a scar upon the cerebral tissues.*"

WILLIAM JAMES

Flashbulb memory A memory that is highly detailed and strongly emotionally elaborated because of its great and unusual significance.

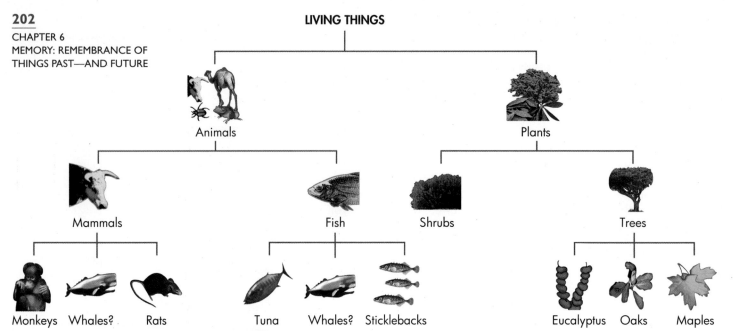

Figure 6.7 ■ The Hierarchical Structure of Long-Term Memory Where are whales filed in the hierarchical cabinets of your memory? Your classification of whales may influence your answers to these questions: Do whales breathe underwater? Are they warm-blooded? Do they nurse their young? A note to biological purists: This figure is not intended to represent phyla, classes, orders, and so on accurately. Rather, it shows how an individual's classification scheme might be organized.

(or, as shown in Figure 6.7, *subordinate* to mammals) or if you knew nothing about mammals, a correct answer might depend on some remote instance of rote learning. That is, you might be depending on chancy episodic memory rather than on reliable semantic memory. For example, you might recall some details from a TV documentary on whales. If you *did* know that whales are mammals, however, you would also know—or remember—that whales do not breathe underwater. Why? You would reconstruct information about whales from your knowledge about mammals, the group to which whales are subordinate. Similarly, you would know, or remember, that because they are mammals, whales are warm-blooded, nurse their young, and are a good deal more intelligent than, say, tunas and sharks, which are fish. Had you incorrectly classified whales as fish, you might have searched your memory and constructed the incorrect answer that they do breathe underwater.

Your memory is thus organized according to a remarkably complex filing system that has a certain internal logic. If you place a piece of information into the wrong file, it is probably not the fault of the filing system itself. Nevertheless, you may "lose" the information in the sense of not being able to find the best cues to retrieve it.

THE TIP-OF-THE-TONGUE PHENOMENON Having something on the tip of your tongue can be a frustrating experience. It is like reeling in a fish but having it drop off the line just before it breaks the surface of the water. Psychologists term this experience the tip-of-the-tongue (TOT) phenomenon, also called the **feeling-of-knowing** experience. **Question 18: Why do we sometimes feel that the answer to a question is on the tip of our tongue?**

Research provides insight into the TOT phenomenon (R. Brown & McNeill, 1966; Galdo-Alvarez et al., 2009; Schwartz, 2008). In classic research, Brown and McNeill (1966) defined some rather unusual words for students, such as *sampan*, a small riverboat used in China and Japan. The students were then asked to recall the words they had learned. Some of the students often had the right word "on the tip of their tongue" but reported words with similar meanings such as *junk, barge,* or *houseboat*. Still other students reported words that sounded similar, such as *Saipan, Siam, sarong,* and *sanching*. Why?

To begin with, the words were unfamiliar, so elaborative rehearsal did not take place. The students did not have an opportunity to relate the words to other things they knew. Brown and McNeill also suggested that our storage systems are indexed according to cues that include both the sounds and the meanings of words—that is,

Tip-of-the-tongue (TOT) phenomenon The feeling that information is stored in memory although it cannot be readily retrieved; also called the *feeling-of-knowing experience*.

Feeling-of-knowing experience Same as *tip-of-the-tongue phenomenon*.

according to both acoustic and semantic codes. By scanning words similar in sound and meaning to the word on the tip of the tongue, we sometimes find a useful cue and retrieve the word for which we are searching.

The feeling-of-knowing experience also seems to reflect incomplete or imperfect learning. In such cases, our answers may be "in the ballpark" if not on the mark. In some feeling-of-knowing experiments, people are often asked trivia questions. When they do not recall an answer, they are then asked to guess how likely it is that they will recognize the right answer if it is among a group of possibilities. People turn out to be very accurate in their estimations about whether or not they will recognize the answer. Similarly, Brown and McNeill found that the students in their TOT experiment proved to be very good at estimating the number of syllables in words they could not recall. The students often correctly guessed the initial sounds of the words. They occasionally recognized words that rhymed with them.

Sometimes, an answer seems to be on the tip of our tongue because our learning of the topic is incomplete. We may not know the exact answer, but we know something. (As a matter of fact, if we have good writing skills, we may present our incomplete knowledge so forcefully that we earn a good grade on an essay question on the topic!) At such times, the problem lies not in retrieval but in the original processes of learning and memory—that is, encoding and storage.

"It's déjà vu all over again."
YOGI BERRA

CONTEXT-DEPENDENT MEMORY: BEEN THERE, DONE THAT? The context in which we acquire information can also play a role in retrieval. I remember walking down the halls of the apartment building where I had lived as a child. Cooking odors triggered a sudden assault of images of playing under the staircase, of falling against a radiator, of the shrill voice of a former neighbor calling for her child at dinnertime. Have you ever walked the halls of an old school building and been assaulted by memories of faces and names that you had thought would be lost forever? Odors, it turns out, are particularly likely to trigger related memories (Lee et al., 2009).

My experience was an example of a **context-dependent memory**. My memories were particularly clear in the context in which they were formed. **Question 19: Why may it be useful to study in the room in which we will be tested?** One answer is that being in the proper context—for example, studying in the exam room or under the same conditions, either in silence or with the stereo on—can dramatically enhance recall (Isarida & Isarida, 2006). **Truth or Fiction Revisited:** Therefore, if you study with the stereo on, you would probably do better to take the test with the stereo on. One classic experiment in context-dependent memory included a number of people who were "all wet." Members of a university swimming club were asked to learn lists of words either while they were submerged or while they were literally high and dry (Godden & Baddeley, 1975). Students who learned the list underwater showed superior recall of the list when immersed. Similarly, those who had rehearsed the list ashore showed better retrieval on terra firma.

Should This Student Bring the TV to Class to Take the Test? Research on context-dependent memory suggests that we remember information better when we attempt to recall it in the context in which we learned it. If we study with the TV or stereo on, should we also take the test within the "context" of the TV or stereo?

According to a study with 20 bilingual Cornell students, the "context" for memory extends to language (Marian & Neisser, 2000). The students emigrated from Russia at an average age of 14 and were an average of about 22 years old at the time of the experiment. They were asked to recall the details of experiences in Russia and the United States. When they were interviewed in Russian, they were better able to retrieve experiences from their lives in Russia. Similarly, when they were interviewed in English, they were better able to recall events that had happened in the United States.

When police are interviewing witnesses to crimes, they ask the witnesses to paint the scene verbally as vividly as possible, or they visit the scene of the crime with the witnesses. People who mentally place themselves in the context in which they encoded and stored information frequently retrieve it more accurately.

One of the eerier psychological experiences is *déjà vu* (French for "already seen"). Sometimes, we meet someone new or find ourselves in a strange place, yet we have the feeling that we know this person or have been there before (Kovacs et al., 2009). All in all, about 60% of us believe we have had a déjà vu experience (A.S. Brown, 2003). The *déjà vu* experience seems to occur when we are in a context

Context-dependent memory Information that is better retrieved in the context in which it was encoded and stored, or learned.

similar to one we have been in before—or when we meet someone who has a way of talking or moving similar to that of someone we know or once knew. Yet we do not recall the specific place or person. Nevertheless, familiarity with the context leads us to think, "I've been here before." Other explanations for the *déjà vu* experience run from the neurological (for example, a disruption in normal neural transmission) to the cognitive (for example, dual cognitive processes that are temporarily out of synchrony) (A. S. Brown, 2003). In any event, the sense that one has been there before, or done this before, can be so strong that one just stands back and wonders.

STATE-DEPENDENT MEMORY State-dependent memory is an extension of context-dependent memory. Sometimes, we retrieve information better when we are in a physiological or emotional state that is similar to the one in which we encoded and stored the information. Feeling the rush of love may trigger images of other times we fell in love. The grip of anger may prompt memories of incidents of frustration and rage. The research in this area even extends to states in which we are sober or inebriated!

Gordon Bower (Bower et al., 2007) ran experiments in which happy or sad moods were induced by hypnotic suggestion. The subjects then learned lists of words. People who learned a list while in a happy mood showed better recall when a happy state was induced again. But people who learned the list while in a sad mood showed superior recall when they were saddened again.

Psychologists suggest that in day-to-day life, a happy mood influences us to focus on positive events (Koo & Oishi, 2009). As a result, we have better recall of these events in the future. A sad mood, unfortunately, leads us to focus on and recall the negative. Happiness may feed on happiness, but under extreme circumstances, sadness can develop into a vicious cycle and lead to depression.

Recognition In information processing, the easiest memory task, involving identification of objects or events encountered before.

Recall Retrieval or reconstruction of learned material.

Paired associates Nonsense syllables presented in pairs in experiments that measure recall.

Relearning A measure of retention. Material is usually relearned more quickly than it is learned initially.

LearningConnections ● STAGES OF MEMORY: MAKING *SENSE* OF THE *SHORT* AND THE *LONG* OF IT

ACTIVE REVIEW (7) The Atkinson–Shiffrin model hypothesizes three stages of memory: _____, _____, and _____. (8) _____ imagery is the ability to retain exact mental representations of visual stimuli over long amounts of time. (9) According to the _____-position effect, we are most likely to recall the first and last items in a series. (10) The Petersons showed that information can be displaced from short-term memory by means of _____. (11) Detailed memories of surprising, important, and emotional events are termed _____ memories. (12) The _____-of-the-tongue phenomenon is most likely due to incomplete learning.

REFLECT AND RELATE Pause the next time you experience the tip-of-the-tongue phenomenon. Note the words or ideas that come to mind as you try to recall the information. What do they have in common? If you eventually recall the missing information, consider how the words and ideas that came to mind relate to it.

CRITICAL THINKING Were you ever convinced that you were remembering something accurately, only to discover later that your memory was incorrect? Can we know whether our own memories are accurate?

 Go to Psychology CourseMate at **www.cengagebrain.com** for an interactive version of these questions.

State-dependent memory Information that is better retrieved in the physiological or emotional state in which it was encoded and stored, or learned.

Nonsense syllables Meaningless sets of two consonants, with a vowel sandwiched between, that are used in the study of memory.

● FORGETTING: WILL YOU REMEMBER HOW WE FORGET?

What do DAL, RIK, BOF, and ZEX have in common? They are all nonsense syllables. Nonsense syllables are meaningless sets of two consonants with a vowel sandwiched between. They were first used by Hermann Ebbinghaus to study memory and forgetting. Because nonsense syllables are intended to be meaningless, remembering them should depend on simple acoustic coding and maintenance rehearsal rather than on elaborative rehearsal, semantic coding, or other ways of making learning meaningful. They are thus well suited for use in the measurement of forgetting. **Question 20: What types of memory tasks are used in measuring forgetting?**

Memory Tasks Used in Measuring Forgetting

Three basic memory tasks have been used by psychologists to measure forgetting: recognition, recall, and relearning. Nonsense syllables have been used in studying each of them. The study of these memory tasks has led to several conclusions about the nature of forgetting.

RECOGNITION One aspect of forgetting is failure to recognize something we have experienced. There are many ways of measuring **recognition**. In numerous studies, psychologists ask subjects to read a list of nonsense syllables. The subjects then read a second list of nonsense syllables and indicate whether they recognize any of the syllables as having appeared on the first list. Forgetting is defined as failure to recognize a syllable that has been read before.

In another kind of recognition study, Harry Bahrick and his colleagues (1975) studied high school graduates who had been out of school for various lengths of time. They interspersed photos of the graduates' classmates with four times as many photos of strangers. Recent graduates correctly recognized former classmates 90% of the time. Those who had been out of school for 40 years recognized former classmates 75% of the time. A chance level of recognition would have been only 20% (one photo in five was of an actual classmate). Thus, even older people showed rather solid long-term recognition ability.

Recognition is the easiest type of memory task. This is why multiple-choice tests are easier than fill-in-the-blank or essay tests. We can recognize correct answers more easily than we can recall them unaided.

RECALL In his studies of **recall**, another kind of memory task, Ebbinghaus would read lists of nonsense syllables aloud to the beat of a metronome and then see how many he could produce from memory. After reading through a list once, he usually would be able to recall seven syllables—the typical limit for short-term memory.

Psychologists also often use lists of pairs of nonsense syllables, called **paired associates**, to measure recall. A list of paired associates is shown in Figure 6.8 ■. Subjects read through the lists pair by pair. Later, they are shown the first member of each pair and asked to recall the second. Recall is more difficult than recognition. In a recognition task, one simply indicates whether an item has been seen before or which of a number of items is paired with a stimulus (as in a multiple-choice test). In a recall task, the person must retrieve a syllable with another syllable serving as a cue.

Retrieval is made easier if the two syllables can be meaningfully linked—that is, encoded semantically—even if the "meaning" is stretched a bit. Consider the first pair of nonsense syllables in Figure 6.8. The image of a WOMan smoking a CEG-arette may make CEG easier to retrieve when the person is presented with the cue WOM.

It is easier to recall vocabulary words from foreign languages if you can construct a meaningful link between the foreign and English words (Atkinson, 1975). The *peso,* pronounced *pay-so,* is a unit of Mexican money. A link can be formed by finding a part of the foreign word, such as the *pe-* (pronounced *pay*), and constructing a phrase such as "You pay with money." When you read or hear the word *peso* in the future, you recognize the *pe-* and retrieve the link or phrase. From the phrase, you then reconstruct the translation, "a unit of money."

RELEARNING: IS LEARNING EASIER THE SECOND TIME AROUND? Relearning is a third method of measuring retention. Do you remember having to learn all of the state capitals in grade school? What are the capitals of Wyoming and Delaware? Even when we cannot recall or recognize material that had once been learned, such as Cheyenne for Wyoming and Dover for Delaware, we can relearn it more rapidly the

© CW Images/Alamy

Recognition versus Recall In going through a photo album or a yearbook, it is easier to recognize people from years past than it is to recall what one did with whom in a given year—or to recall people's names.

Figure 6.8 ■ Paired Associates Psychologists often use paired associates to measure recall. Retrieving CEG in response to the cue WOM is made easier by an image of a WOMan smoking a "CEG-arette."

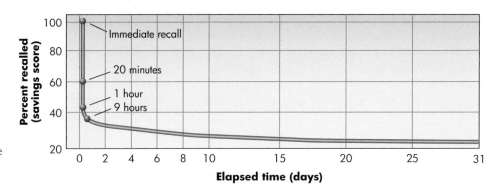

Figure 6.9 ■ Ebbinghaus's Classic Curve of Forgetting Recollection of lists of words drops by half during the first hour after learning. Losses of learning then become more gradual. It takes a month (31 days) for retention to be cut in half again.

Method of savings A measure of retention in which the difference between the number of repetitions originally required to learn a list and the number of repetitions required to relearn the list after a certain amount of time has elapsed is calculated.

Savings The difference between the number of repetitions originally required to learn a list and the number of repetitions required to relearn the list after a certain amount of time has elapsed.

Interference theory The view that we might forget stored material because other learning interferes with it.

Retroactive interference The interference of new learning with the ability to retrieve material learned previously.

Interference In retroactive interference, new learning interferes with the retrieval of old learning. In proactive interference, older learning interferes with the capacity to retrieve more recently learned material. For example, high school French may "pop in" when you are trying to retrieve Spanish words learned in college.

second time. Similarly, as we go through our 30s and 40s, we may forget a good deal of our high school French or geometry. Yet the second time around, we could learn what previously took months or years much more rapidly.

To study the efficiency of relearning, Ebbinghaus (1885/1913) devised the **method of savings**. First he recorded the number of repetitions required to learn a list of nonsense syllables or words. Then he recorded the number of repetitions required to relearn the list after a certain amount of time had elapsed. Next he computed the difference in the number of repetitions to determine the **savings**. If a list had to be repeated 20 times before it was learned and 20 times again after a year had passed, there were no savings. Relearning, that is, was as tedious as the initial learning. However, if the list could be learned with only 10 repetitions after a year had elapsed, half the number of repetitions required for learning had been saved.

Figure 6.9 ■ shows Ebbinghaus's classic curve of forgetting. As you can see, there was no loss of memory as measured by savings immediately after a list had been learned. However, recollection dropped quite a bit, by half, during the first hour after learning a list. Losses of learning then became more gradual. It took a month (31 days) for retention to be cut in half again. So forgetting occurred most rapidly right after material was learned. We continue to forget material as time elapses but at a slower pace.

Before leaving this section, I have one question for you: What are the capitals of Wyoming and Delaware?

Interference Theory

When we do not attend to, encode, and rehearse sensory input, we may forget it through decay of the trace of the image. Material in short-term memory, like material in sensory memory, can be lost through decay. It can also be lost through displacement, as may happen when we try to remember several new names at a party.

Question 21: Why can learning Spanish make it harder to remember French? The answer may be found in **interference theory**. According to this view, we also forget material in short-term and long-term memory because newly learned material interferes with it. The two basic types of interference are retroactive interference (also called *retroactive inhibition*) and proactive interference (also called *proactive inhibition*).

RETROACTIVE INTERFERENCE In retroactive interference, new learning interferes with the retrieval of old learning. For example, a medical student may memorize the names of the bones in the leg through rote repetition. Later, he or she may find that learning the names of the bones in the arm makes it more difficult to retrieve the names of the leg bones, especially if the names are similar in sound or in relative location on each limb.

PROACTIVE INTERFERENCE In proactive interference, older learning interferes with the capacity to retrieve more recently learned material. High school Spanish may pop in when you are trying to retrieve college French or Italian words. All three are Romance languages with similar roots and spellings. Previously learned Japanese words probably would not interfere with your ability to retrieve more recently learned French or Italian because the roots and sounds of Japanese differ considerably from those of the Romance languages. Truth or Fiction Revisited: It is therefore true that learning Spanish can make it harder to remember French—and vice versa.

Consider motor skills. You may learn to drive a standard shift on a car with three forward speeds and a clutch that must be let up slowly after shifting. Later, you may learn to drive a car with five forward speeds and a clutch that must be released rapidly. For a while, you may make errors on the five-speed car because of proactive interference. (Old learning interferes with new learning.) If you return to the three-speed car after driving the five-speed car has become natural, you may stall it a few times. This is because of retroactive interference. (New learning interferes with the old.)

Repression: Ejecting the Unwanted from Consciousness

According to Freud, we are motivated to forget painful memories and unacceptable ideas because they produce anxiety, guilt, and shame. **Question 22: What is the Freudian concept of repression?** Repression, according to Freud, is the automatic ejection of painful memories and unacceptable urges from conscious awareness. It is motivated by the desire to avoid facing painful memories and emotions. Psychoanalysts suggest that repression is at the heart of disorders such as dissociative amnesia (see Chapter 12). There is a current controversy in psychology as to whether repression (motivated forgetting) actually exists and, if it does, how it works. One interesting finding is that stress hormones—the kind we secrete when we experience extremes of anxiety, guilt, and shame—*heighten* memory formation (Clayton & Williams, 2000; McGaugh et al., 2002). But supporters of the concept of repression do not claim that repressed memories were ill-formed; they say, rather, that we do not focus on them.

There is much research on repression, often in the form of case studies in psychoanalytic journals (e.g., Eagle, 2000). Much has been made of case studies in which veterans have supposedly forgotten traumatic battlefield experiences, developed posttraumatic stress disorder (once called "battlefield neurosis"), and then "felt better" once they recalled and discussed the traumatic events. Critics argue that the evidence for such repression and recovery of memories is weak and that this kind of "memory" can be implanted by the suggestions of interviewers (Loftus & Davis, 2006; A. K. Thomas & Loftus, 2002; van de Wetering et al., 2002). The issue remains controversial, as we see in the nearby Closer Look box.

Infantile Amnesia: Why Can't Johnny Remember?

Question 23: Can children remember events from the first couple of years of life? When he interviewed people about their early experiences, Freud discovered that they could not recall episodes that had happened prior to the age of 3 or so and that recall was cloudy through the age of 5. This phenomenon is referred to as infantile amnesia.

Infantile amnesia has little to do with the fact that the episodes occurred in the distant past. Middle-aged and older people have vivid memories from the ages of 6 and 10, yet the events happened many decades ago. But 18-year-olds show steep declines in memory when they try to recall episodes that occurred earlier than the age of 6, even though they happened fewer than 18 years earlier (Wetzler & Sweeney, 1986).

Freud believed that young children have aggressive impulses and perverse lusts toward their parents. He attributed infantile amnesia to repression of these impulses. However, the episodes lost to infantile amnesia are not weighted in the direction of such "primitive" impulses. In fact, infantile amnesia probably reflects the interaction of physiological and cognitive factors. For example, a structure of

> *"I've learned that people will forget what you said, people will forget what you did, but people will never forget how you made them feel."*
>
> MAYA ANGELOU

Proactive interference The interference of old learning with the ability to retrieve material learned recently.

Dissociative amnesia Amnesia thought to stem from psychological conflict or trauma.

Infantile amnesia Inability to recall events that occurred prior to the age of 3 or so; also termed *childhood amnesia*.

A CLOSER LOOK

Do People Really Recover Repressed Memories of Childhood Sexual Abuse?

There is apparently little doubt that the memory of traumatic events can be repressed. But as we see in this section, there is also little doubt that many so-called recovered memories, particularly memories of childhood sexual abuse, are sometimes induced by a therapist.

A young woman in psychotherapy recovered the memory that at age 13 she was raped by her teacher, became pregnant, and underwent an abortion. No corroborating evidence for this event existed. In fact, the woman had not reached menarche until 15, so the pregnancy was impossible. Still, she filed criminal charges against the teacher, who spent his life savings to defend himself against the false accusation. Eventually, the court ruled that recovery of a repressed memory lacked sufficient scientific foundation to be admissible evidence. This *false memory syndrome* has also resulted in many family tragedies: alienation of children from their parents, loss of jobs, ostracism, and divorces.

"We don't know what percent of these recovered memories are real and what percent are pseudomemories," said psychiatrist Harold Lief, who was one of the first to question these induced memories. "But we do know there are hundreds, maybe thousands of cases of pseudomemories and that many families have been destroyed by them. We also know that many therapists who track down these memories and focus on them fail to deal with the patient's real problems." Indeed, many adults who had in treatment recovered a memory of childhood sexual abuse and accused the supposed perpetrator later retracted the claim.

How can someone tell if a recovered memory is false? Serious questions should be raised when corroborating evidence is lacking, when the so-called memory occurs before a child is able to remember, and when details of the memory are preposterous (like a rape by aliens), said psychiatrist Paul McHugh. McHugh also questioned the reliability of methods typically used to elicit these "memories." Among the most common are hypnosis and guided imagery, during which a therapist may introduce the notion that

Recovered Memories People may see a therapist because of distress, the origins of which are not completely clear. Some people have apparently been encouraged in therapy to recover memories of traumatic experiences, often of childhood sexual abuse, that may never have happened.

sexual abuse had occurred and ask the patient to try to remember the circumstances and who the perpetrator might have been.

Psychologist Elizabeth Loftus (Loftus & Davis, 2006) cited numerous studies that demonstrated how easy it was to implant a false memory. By asking a series of leading questions and by having a supposed "witness" talk about the made-up experience, it was often possible to convince someone that the event actually happened. In one study, researchers easily convinced half the adult participants that they had been hospitalized in severe pain as children or that they had been lost in a shopping mall at age 5. Several people with these false memories provided detailed embellishments.

the limbic system (the **hippocampus**) that is involved in the storage of memories does not become mature until we are about 2 years old (Shrager et al., 2008; Wais et al., 2006). In addition, myelination of brain pathways is incomplete for the first few years, contributing to the inefficiency of information processing and memory formation.

There are also cognitive explanations for infantile amnesia (Piolino et al., 2009; Q. Wang, 2008):

- Infants are not particularly interested in remembering the past.

- Infants, in contrast to older children, tend not to weave episodes together into meaningful stories of their own lives. Information about specific episodes thus tends to be lost. Research shows that when parents reminisce about the past with children, infants' memories are strengthened. (Of course, one could question the accuracy of some of these reminiscences.)

Hippocampus A structure in the limbic system that plays an important role in the formation of new memories.

- Infants do not make reliable use of language to symbolize or classify events. Their ability to *encode* sensory input—that is, to apply the auditory and semantic codes that facilitate memory formation—is therefore limited. Yet research shows that young infants can recall events throughout the period when infantile amnesia is presumed to occur if they are now and then exposed to objects they played with or photos of events.

In sum, we are unlikely to remember episodes from the first 2 years of life unless we are reminded of them from time to time as we develop. Many of the early childhood memories that seem clear today are likely to be reconstructed, and they may hold many inaccuracies. They might also be memories of events that occurred later than the period to which we attribute them. Yet there is no evidence that such early memories are systematically repressed.

Adults also experience amnesia, although usually for biological reasons, as in the cases of anterograde and retrograde amnesia (Kikuchi et al., 2010).

Anterograde and Retrograde Amnesia

Question 24: Why do people frequently have trouble recalling being in accidents? In so-called **anterograde amnesia**, there are memory lapses for the period following a trauma such as a blow to the head, an electric shock, or an operation. In some cases, the trauma seems to interfere with all the processes of memory. The ability to pay attention, the encoding of sensory input, and rehearsal are all impaired. A number of investigators have linked certain kinds of brain damage—such as damage to the hippocampus—to amnesia (Epp et al., 2008; Travis et al., 2010).

Consider the classic case of a man with the initials H. M. Parts of the brain are sometimes lesioned to help people with epilepsy. In H. M.'s case, a section of the hippocampus was removed (Squire, 2009). Right after the operation, H. M.'s mental functioning appeared normal. As time went on, however, it became clear that he had problems processing new information. For example, 2 years after the operation, H. M. believed he was 27—his age at the time of the operation. When his family moved to a new address, H. M. could not find his new home or remember the new address. He responded with appropriate grief to the death of his uncle, yet he then began to ask about his uncle and why he did not visit. **Truth or Fiction Revisited:** It is true that a man could not form new memories after part of his hippocampus was surgically removed (see Figure 6.10 ■). Each time he was reminded of his uncle's passing, he grieved as if he were hearing it for the first time. H. M.'s operation apparently prevented him from transferring information from short-term to long-term memory.

In **retrograde amnesia**, the source of trauma prevents people from remembering events that took place before the accident (Wheeler & McMillan, 2001). A football player who is knocked unconscious or a person in an auto accident may be unable to recall events that occurred for several minutes prior to the trauma. The football player may not recall taking the field. The person in the accident may not recall entering the car. It also sometimes happens that the individual cannot remember events that occurred for several years prior to the trauma.

Anterograde amnesia Failure to remember events that occurred after physical trauma because of the effects of the trauma.

Retrograde amnesia Failure to remember events that occurred prior to physical trauma because of the effects of the trauma.

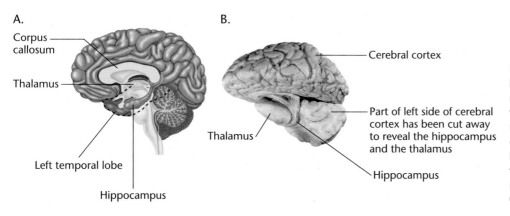

A.
Corpus callosum
Thalamus
Left temporal lobe
Hippocampus

B.
Cerebral cortex
Part of left side of cerebral cortex has been cut away to reveal the hippocampus and the thalamus
Thalamus
Hippocampus

Figure 6.10 ■ The Hippocampus The hippocampus is essential to the formation of new memories. Part A shows the location of the hippocampus in the brain. In Part B, the upper part of the left side of the cerebral cortex has been cut away, revealing the hippocampus. The hippocampus loops over the thalamus, runs behind it, and then runs underneath it.

Courtesy of Dana Copeland

Humans have survived the Ice Age, the Stone Age, the Iron Age, and a bit more recently, the Industrial Revolution. Now we are trying to cope with the so-called Information Age and its explosion of information. Computers have been developed to process it. Humans, too, process information, and there is more of it to process than ever before. Fortunately, psychologists have helped devise methods for improving memory.

Drill and Practice: "A, B, C, D ..."

Repetition (rote maintenance rehearsal) helps transfer information from short-term to long-term memory. This is how you learned the alphabet and how to count. Schoolchildren write spelling words over and over to remember them. Athletes repeat motions so that they will become an implicit memory. Some students use flash cards to help them remember facts. For example, they might write "The originator of modern behaviorism is _____" on one side of the card and "John Broadus Watson" on the flip side.

Relate New Information to What Is Already Known

Relating new information to what is already known is a form of elaborative rehearsal. You can better remember the name of a new acquaintance by thinking of a rhyme for it. Now you have done some thinking about the name, and you also have two tags for the person, not one. If you are trying to retrieve the spelling of the word *retrieve*, do so by retrieving the rule "i before e except after c." There are exceptions, of course: Remember that *weird* doesn't follow the rule because it's a "weird" word.

Form Unusual, Exaggerated Associations

Psychologist Charles L. Brewer uses an interesting method to teach psychology students the fundamentals of shaping:

Dr. Brewer first danced on his desk, then bleated like a sheep, and finally got down on "all fours and oinked like a pig," he said. His antics were in response to a session he

teaches on "successive approximation"—shaping behavior into a desired response. To get students to "shape" him, he told them he would try to figure out what they wanted him to do. If he guessed wrong, they'd "boo and hiss," whereas if he did what they wanted, they'd applaud him—which is why he eventually acted like a pig. "I'll do anything to get them to learn," he said. (DeAngelis, 1994a, p. 40).

Use the Method of Loci: Meat Loaf in the Pocket

Another way to form unusual associations is the *method of loci* (pronounced LOW-sigh). Select a series of related images such as the parts of your body or the furniture in your home. Then imagine an item from your shopping list, or another list you want to remember, as being attached to each image. Consider this meaty application: remember your shopping list by imagining meat loaf in your jacket pocket and balancing a breakfast plate on your head.

By placing meat loaf or a favorite complete dinner in your pocket rather than a single item such as ground beef, you can combine several items into one chunk of information (see Figure 6.11 ■). At the supermarket, you recall the ingredients for meat loaf and consider whether you need each one. The breakfast plate can remind you whether you need juice, bread for toast, eggs, cereals, fruit for the cereals, coffee or tea, milk for the coffee or lemons for the tea, and so on.

Figure 6.11 ■ The Method of Loci By imagining meat loaf in your jacket pocket, you can combine several items into a single chunk of information. Once at the supermarket, recall the ingredients for meat loaf and ask yourself which ones you need to buy.

Use Mediation: Build a Conceptual Bridge

The method of mediation also relies on forming associations: You link two items with a third one that ties them together. What if you are having difficulty remembering that John's wife's name is Tillie? You can mediate between John and Tillie as follows. Reflect that *john* is a slang term for bathroom. Bathrooms often have ceramic *tiles. Tiles,* of course, sounds like *Tillie.* So it goes: John → bathroom tiles → Tillie.

In one well-known case of retrograde amnesia, a man received a head injury in a motorcycle accident (Baddeley, 1982). When he regained consciousness, he had lost memory for all events that had occurred after the age of 11. In fact, he appeared to believe that he was still 11 years old. During the next few months, he gradually recovered more knowledge of his past. He moved toward the present year by year, up until

Use Mnemonic Devices: "Soak Her Toe"

Broadly speaking, methods for jogging memory can all be termed *mnemonics,* or systems for remembering information. But so-called *mnemonic devices* usually combine chunks of information into a format such as an acronym, jingle, or phrase. (By the way, the word *mnemonic* is derived from Mnemosyne, the Greek goddess of memory. Her name is pronounced *nee-MOS-uh-nee.* How can you remember the pronunciation? Why not think of the goddess getting down on her two knees *[[nee-nee]]* to worship? End of commercial for mnemonic devices.) For example, recalling the phrase "Every Good Boy Does Fine" has helped many people remember the lines in the musical staff: E, G, B, D, F. In Chapter 2, we saw that the acronym *SAME* serves as a mnemonic device for distinguishing between afferent and efferent neurons. In Chapter 3, we noted that most psychology students use the acronym *Roy G. Biv* to remember the colors of the rainbow.

Acronyms have found applications in many disciplines. Consider geography. The acronym *HOMES* stands for the Great Lakes: *Huron, Ontario, Michigan, Erie,* and *Superior.* You can remember that Dromedary camels have one hump while Bactrian camels have two by turning the letters D and B on their sides. Table 6.1 ■ lists some of my favorite mnemonic devices.

Finally, how can you remember how to spell *mnemonics?* Easy—be willing to grant "a*MN*esty" to those who cannot.

TABLE 6.1 ■ Mnemonic Devices

Mnemonic Device	Encoded Information
HOMES	The names of the Great Lakes: Huron, Ontario, Michigan, Erie, and Superior
No Plan Like Yours to Study History Wisely.	The royal houses of England: Norman, Plantagenet, Lancaster, York, Tudor, Stuart, Hanover, and Windsor
X shall stand for playmates Ten. V for Five stalwart men. I for One, D for Five. M for a Thousand soldiers true. And L for Fifty, I'll tell you.	The value of the Roman numerals. "D for Five" means D = 500
Mary Eats Peanut Butter.	The first four hydrocarbons of the alkane class: methane, ethane, propane, and butane, in ascending order of the number of carbon atoms in their chains
These Ten Valuable Amino acids Have Long Preserved Life In Man.	Ten vital amino acids: threonine, tryptophan, valine, arginine, histidine, lysine, phenylalanine, leucine, isoleucine, methionine
All Hairy Men Will Buy Razors.	Constituents of soil: air, humus, mineral salts, water, bacteria, rock particles
Soak Her Toe.	Translates into SOHCAHTOA, or: Sine = Opposite/Hypotenuse Cosine = Adjacent/Hypotenuse Tangent = Opposite/Adjacent
Krakatoa Positively Casts Off Fumes; Generally Sulfurous Vapors.	Biological classifications in descending order: kingdom, phylum, class, order, family, genus, species, variety
Never Lower Tillie's Pants; Mother Might Come Home.	The eight bones of the wrist: navicular, lunate, triangular, pisiform, multangular greater, multangular lesser, capitate, hamate
Roy G. Biv	The colors of the spectrum: red, orange, yellow, green, blue, indigo, violet
Lazy French Tarts Sit Naked In Anticipation.	The nerves that pass through the superior orbital fissure of the skull: lachrymal, frontal, trochlear, superior, nasal, inferior, abducent

the critical motorcycle ride. But he never did recover the events just prior to the accident. The accident had apparently prevented the information that was rapidly unfolding before him from being transferred to long-term memory. In terms of stages of memory, perhaps our perceptions and ideas need to consolidate, or rest undisturbed for a while, if they are to be transferred to long-term memory (Nader et al., 2000).

● THE BIOLOGY OF MEMORY: THE BRAIN AS A LIVING TIME MACHINE

Joel and Clementine didn't meet on Match.com. In fact, they are anything but well matched. In the film *Eternal Sunshine of the Spotless Mind,* Joel (Jim Carrey) is a sort of cautious, depressed male who runs into Clementine (Kate Winslet), a volatile and offbeat book clerk. Clementine divides her time between dyeing her hair blue and dyeing it blood orange. When the relationship fails, Clementine is miserable. She visits a doctor who erases all memory of Joel from her mind—making it "spotless"—so that she will feel the warmth of the sun once more rather than the lonely dread of darkness. Joel is dumbfounded by Clementine's failure to recognize him. He learns of the process she underwent and decides to have Clementine erased from his mind as well.

Engram An assumed electrical circuit in the brain that corresponds to a memory trace.

The main part of the film follows the erasing process that takes place inside Joel's mind. One image of Clementine after another dissolves as the world around them dissolves as well. Erasure is possible because the doctor has "mapped" Joel's memories of Clementine. They are all interconnected, and he can follow their paths through the brain and sort of zap them.

Are memories in fact interconnected in the brain? Psychologists know that mental processes such as the encoding, storage, and retrieval of information—that is, memory—are accompanied by changes in the brain (Kandel, 2006). Early in the 20th century, many psychologists used the concept of the **engram** in their study of memory. Engrams were viewed as electrical circuits in the brain that corresponded to memory traces—neurological processes that paralleled experiences. Yet biological psychologists such as Karl Lashley (1950) spent many fruitless years searching for such circuits or the structures of the brain in which they might be housed. Much current research on the biology of memory focuses on the roles of stimulants, neurons, neurotransmitters, hormones, and structures in the brain.

Would You Want to Erase Troublesome Memories? Kate Winslet and Jim Carrey play a pair of mismatched lovers in *Eternal Sunshine of the Spotless Mind.* When the relationship doesn't work out, Winslet has memories of Carrey mapped and erased from her brain. Carrey follows suit. Can memories be mapped? Can they be erased?

Neural Activity and Memory: "Better Living Through Chemistry"

Question 25: What neural events are connected with memory? The story of Joel and Clementine is fictional but may hold a kernel of truth. Rats that are reared in stimulating environments provide some answers. The animals develop more dendrites and synapses in the cerebral cortex than rats reared in impoverished environments (Kolb et al., 2009). Moreover, visually stimulating rats increases the number of synapses in their visual cortex (Inaba et al., 2009). Therefore, the storage of experience does involve avenues of communication among brain cells.

Information received through other senses is just as likely to lead to corresponding changes in the cortical regions that represent them. For example, sounds may similarly cause changes in the auditory cortex. Experiences perceived by several senses are apparently stored in numerous parts of the cortex. The recall of sensory experiences evidently involves neural activity in related regions of the brain.

Research with sea snails such as *Aplysia* and *Hermissenda* offers more insight into the biology of memory. *Aplysia* has only some 20,000 neurons compared with humans' *billions*. As a result, researchers have been able to study how experience is reflected at the synapses of specific neurons. The sea snail reflexively withdraws its gills when it receives electric shock in the same way a person reflexively withdraws a hand from a hot stove or a thorn. In one kind of experiment, researchers precede the shock with a squirt of water. After a few repetitions, the sea snail becomes conditioned to withdraw its gills when squirted with the water. When sea snails are conditioned, they release more serotonin at certain synapses. As a consequence, transmission at these synapses becomes more efficient as trials (learning) progress (Mechner, 2009; Squire & Kandel, 2008). This greater efficiency is termed **long-term potentiation (LTP)**. As shown in Figure 6.12 ■, dendrites can also participate in LTP by sprouting new branches that attach to the transmitting axon. Rats that are given substances that enhance LTP learn mazes with fewer errors; that is, they are less likely to turn down the wrong alley (Adams et al., 2009; Uzakov et al., 2005).

Serotonin and many other naturally occurring chemical substances—including adrenaline, noradrenaline, acetylcholine, glutamate, antidiuretic hormone, and even the sex hormone estrogen—have been shown to play roles in memory:

- *Serotonin.* This neurotransmitter increases the efficiency of conditioning in sea snails (Rajasethupathy et al., 2009; Squire & Kandel, 2008). It is released when stimuli are paired repeatedly, increasing the efficiency of neural transmission (LTP) at certain synapses and creating neural circuits that contain the information.

- *Acetylcholine (ACh).* This neurotransmitter is vital in memory formation; low levels of ACh are connected with Alzheimer's disease. Increased levels of ACh promote conditioning in mice and rats (Gulledge et al., 2009; Valenzuela et al., 2010).

- *Glutamate.* Glutamate, like serotonin, increases the efficiency of conditioning. Agents that increase the action of glutamate promote conditioning in mice and chicks (Barber et al., 2010; Goddyn et al., 2008).

- *Adrenaline and noradrenaline (also called epinephrine and norepinephrine).* The hormone adrenaline and the related hormone and neurotransmitter noradrenaline both strengthen memory when they are released into the bloodstream following learning. Stressful events stimulate release of stress hormones from the adrenal glands—adrenaline and steroids—which, in turn, stimulate a structure in the limbic system (the amygdala) to release noradrenaline. The hormones and neurotransmitter, acting together, heighten memory for stressful events (Ferry & McGaugh, 2008).

- *Vasopressin.* Also known as *antidiuretic hormone,* vasopressin affects fluid retention. Like many other chemical substances in the body, it has multiple tasks, one of which is facilitating memory functioning, particularly working memory (Caldwell et al., 2008). **Truth or Fiction Revisited:** Sniffing vasopressin in the form of a nasal spray generally benefits memory functioning (Born et al., 2002).

- *Estrogen and testosterone.* The sex hormones estrogen and testosterone boost working memory in females and males, respectively (Shansky et al., 2009; Spritzer et al., 2008). Estrogen replacement may help older, postmenopausal women retain cognitive functioning.

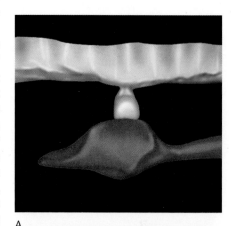

A.

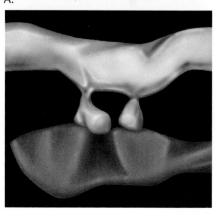

B.

Figure 6.12 ■ One Avenue to Long-Term Potentiation (LTP) LTP can occur via the action of neurotransmitters such as serotonin and glutamate at synapses. Structurally, LTP can also occur as shown in Parts A and B, when dendrites sprout new branches that connect with transmitting axons, increasing the amount of stimulation they receive.

Long-term potentiation (LTP) Enhanced efficiency in synaptic transmission that follows brief, rapid stimulation.

Brain Structures and Memory

Question 26: What structures in the brain are connected with memory? There is no single storage cabinet in the brain. As suggested in *Eternal Sunshine of the Spotless Mind,* memory relies on complex neural networks that draw on various parts of the brain.

But some parts of the brain play more specific roles in memory. The hippocampus is vital for storing new information even if we can retrieve old information without it (Squire, 2009). But the hippocampus is not a storage bin. Rather, it is involved in relaying sensory information to parts of the cortex.

Where are the storage bins? The brain stores parts of memories in the appropriate areas of the sensory cortex. Sights are stored in the visual cortex, sounds in the auditory cortex, and so on. The limbic system is largely responsible for integrating these pieces of information when we recall an event. However, the frontal lobes apparently store information about where and when events occur (Chafee & Goldman-Rakic, 2000; C. R. E. Wilson et al., 2008).

But what of the decision to try to recall something? What of the spark of consciousness that drives us to move backward in time or to strive to remember to do something in the future? The prefrontal cortex is the executive center in memory (Christ et al., 2009; Wheeler & Treisman, 2002). It appears to empower people with consciousness—the ability to mentally represent and become aware of experiences that occur in the past, present, and future. It enables people to mentally travel back in time to reexperience the personal, autobiographical past. It enables people to focus on the things they intend to do in the future, such as mail a letter on the way to class or brush their teeth before going to bed.

The hippocampus is also involved in the where and when of things (Eichenbaum & Fortin, 2003). The hippocampus does not become mature until we are about 2 years old. Immaturity may be connected with infantile amnesia. Adults with hippocampal damage may be able to form new procedural memories, even though they cannot form new episodic ("where and when") memories (Fields, 2005). They can develop new skills even though they cannot recall the practice sessions (Squire & Kandel, 2008).

The thalamus (see Figure 6.10) is involved in the formation of verbal memories. Part of the thalamus of an Air Force cadet known as N. A. was damaged in a fencing accident. Afterward, N. A. could no longer form verbal memories, but he could form visual memories (Squire, 2004). (One might measure visual memory by showing people pictures, allowing time to pass, and then asking them to point out those they have been shown.)

The encoding, storage, and retrieval of information thus involve biological activity. As we learn, new synapses are developed, and changes occur at existing synapses. Parts of the brain are also involved in the formation of memories. In the next chapter, we see how people manipulate information they have stored to adapt to the environment or create new environments.

LearningConnections ● THE BIOLOGY OF MEMORY: THE BRAIN AS A LIVING TIME MACHINE

ACTIVE REVIEW (17) Experience enhances the avenues of communication among brain cells by development of dendrites and _____. (18) Conditioning of sea snails causes more of the neurotransmitter _____ to be released at certain synapses, making transmission at these synapses more efficient. (19) The hippocampus appears vital to the storage of (new or old?) information. (20) The _____ seems to be involved in the formation of verbal memories.

REFLECT AND RELATE How would you design an experiment to explore whether a chemical had an effect on mem-

ory functioning? How would you determine a safe dose of the chemical? How would you measure memory functioning? How might your research differ depending on whether you were using people or other animals?

CRITICAL THINKING This is a *psychology* course. Why do you think we discuss the *biology* of memory?

 Go to Psychology CourseMate at **www.cengagebrain.com** for an interactive version of these questions.

Kinds of Memory: Pressing the "Rewind" and "Fast-Forward" Buttons

1. What is explicit memory?
An explicit memory contains specific information—information that can be clearly stated or declared. The information can be autobiographical or general.

2. What is episodic memory?
An episodic memory is a memory of a specific event that one has observed or participated in.

3. What is semantic memory?
Semantic memory is general knowledge, as in remembering that the United States has 50 states.

4. What is implicit memory?
Implicit memory means knowing how to do things like write with a pencil or ride a bicycle.

5. What is the difference between retrospective memory and prospective memory?
Retrospective memory concerns events in the past. Such memories can be explicit or implicit. Prospective memory involves remembering to do things in the future.

Processes of Memory: Processing Information in Our Most Personal Computers

6. What is the role of encoding in memory?
Encoding information means transforming it so that we can place it in memory. We use visual, auditory, and semantic codes to convert physical stimulation into psychological formats that we can remember.

7. What is the role of storage in memory?
Storage means the maintenance of information over time. The main methods of storing information are maintenance rehearsal (rote repetition) and elaborative rehearsal (relating it to things we already know).

8. What is the role of retrieval in memory?
Retrieval means locating stored information and bringing it back into consciousness. Retrieval requires the use of the proper cues (just as we need to know the file name to retrieve information stored on a hard drive).

Stages of Memory: Making *Sense* of the *Short* and the *Long* of It

9. What is the Atkinson–Shiffrin model of memory?
Atkinson and Shiffrin propose that there are three stages of memory—sensory memory, short-term memory, and long-term memory—and that the progress of information through these stages determines how long it is remembered.

10. How does sensory memory function?
The senses have sensory registers that briefly hold the *memory traces* of stimuli in sensory memory. The traces then *decay*. Visual sensory memory makes discrete visual sensations—produced by saccadic eye movements—seem continuous. Some people, usually children, can maintain icons over long periods of time and are said to have eidetic imagery. Echoes can be held in sensory memory for several seconds.

11. How does short-term memory function?
Focusing on a stimulus allows us to maintain it in short-term memory—also called *working memory*—for a minute or so after the trace decays. Rehearsal allows us to maintain information indefinitely. The appearance of new information in short-term memory can *displace* old information.

12. Why are we most likely to remember the first and last items in a list?
The serial-position effect states that we remember the initial items in a list because they are rehearsed most often. We remember the final items in a list because they are least likely to have been displaced by new information.

13. Is seven a magic number, or did the phone company get lucky?
Seven may not be a magic number, but it seems that the typical person can keep about seven chunks of information in short-term memory.

14. How does long-term memory function?
There is no known limit to the amount of information that can be stored in long-term memory, and memories can be stored for a lifetime. Long-term memories are frequently biased because they are reconstructed according to our schemas. The memories of eyewitnesses can be distorted by leading questions. Information is usually transferred from short-term to long-term memory by maintenance rehearsal and elaborative rehearsal.

15. What is the levels-of-processing model of memory?
This model hypothesizes that we encode, store, and retrieve information more efficiently when we have processed it more deeply.

16. Why are some events, like the attack of September 11, 2001, etched in memory for a lifetime?
So-called *flashbulb memories*, such as those of the terrorist attack of September 11, 2001, tend to occur within a web of unusual and emotionally arousing circumstances.

17. How is knowledge organized in long-term memory?
We tend to classify or arrange chunks of information into hierarchies of groups or classes according to common features.

18. Why do we sometimes feel that the answer to a question is on the tip of our tongue?
Research suggests that the tip-of-the-tongue phenomenon often reflects incomplete learning.

19. Why may it be useful to study in the room in which we will be tested?
This is because we often retrieve information more efficiently when we are in the same context as when we

acquired it. State dependence refers to the finding that we often retrieve information better when we are in the same state of consciousness or mood as when we learned it.

Forgetting: Will You Remember How We Forget?

20. What types of memory tasks are used in measuring forgetting?

Retention is often tested through three types of memory tasks: recognition, recall, and relearning.

21. Why can learning Spanish make it harder to remember French?

This is an example of retroactive interference, in which new learning interferes with old learning. In proactive interference, on the other hand, old learning interferes with new learning.

22. What is the Freudian concept of repression?

Freud suggested that we are motivated to forget (repress) painful memories or unacceptable ideas.

23. Can children remember events from the first couple of years of life?

Probably not. Modern psychologists believe that "infantile amnesia" reflects immaturity of the hippocampus and failure to use acoustic and semantic codes to help remember information.

24. Why do people frequently have trouble recalling being in accidents?

Physical trauma can interfere with memory formation. In anterograde amnesia, a traumatic event such as damage to the hippocampus prevents the formation of new memories. In retrograde amnesia, shock or other trauma prevents previously known information from being retrieved.

The Biology of Memory: The Brain as a Living Time Machine

25. What neural events are connected with memory?

Learning is apparently connected with the proliferation of dendrites and synapses in the brain. Learning and memory are also connected with the release of the neurotransmitters serotonin and acetylcholine and the hormones adrenaline and vasopressin.

26. What structures in the brain are connected with memory?

The hippocampus relays sensory information to the cortex and is therefore vital in the formation of new memories. Visual memories appear to be stored in the visual cortex, auditory memories in the auditory cortex, and so on. The thalamus is connected with the formation of visual memories.

KEY TERMS

Acoustic code (p. 189)
Anterograde amnesia (p. 209)
Chunk (p. 195)
Context-dependent memory (p. 203)
Displace (p. 196)
Dissociative amnesia (p. 207)
Echo (p. 193)
Echoic memory (p. 193)
Eidetic imagery (p. 193)
Elaborative rehearsal (p. 190)
Encoding (p. 189)
Engram (p. 212)
Episodic memory (p. 185)
Explicit memory (p. 185)
Feeling-of-knowing experience (p. 202)
Flashbulb memory (p. 201)
Hippocampus (p. 208)
Icon (p. 193)
Iconic memory (p. 193)
Implicit memory (p. 185)

Infantile amnesia (p. 207)
Interference theory (p. 206)
Long term memory (p. 196)
Long-term potentiation (LTP) (p. 213)
Maintenance rehearsal (p. 190)
Memory (p. 190)
Memory trace (p. 191)
Metamemory (p. 190)
Method of savings (p. 206)
Misinformation effect (p. 199)
Nonsense syllables (p. 204)
Paired associates (p. 204)
Primacy effect (p. 195)
Priming (p. 186)
Proactive interference (p. 207)
Prospective memory (p. 186)
Recall (p. 204)
Recency effect (p. 195)
Recognition (p. 204)
Relearning (p. 204)
Repression (p. 196)

Retrieval (p. 190)
Retrieval cue (p. 190)
Retroactive interference (p. 206)
Retrograde amnesia (p. 209)
Retrospective memory (p. 186)
Rote (p. 195)
Saccadic eye movement (p. 191)
Savings (p. 206)
Schema (p. 197)
Semantic code (p. 189)
Semantic memory (p. 185)
Sensory memory (p. 191)
Sensory register (p. 191)
Serial-position effect (p. 195)
Short-term memory (p. 194)
State-dependent memory (p. 204)
Storage (p. 190)
Tip-of-the-tongue (TOT) phenomenon (p. 202)
Visual code (p. 189)
Working memory (p. 194)

ACTIVE LEARNING RESOURCES

Log in to **www.cengagebrain.com** to access the resources your instructor requires. For this book, you can access:

 CourseMate brings course concepts to life with interactive learning, study, and exam preparation tools that support the printed textbook. A textbook-specific website, Psychology CourseMate includes an integrated interactive eBook and other interactive learning tools including quizzes, flashcards, videos, and more.

CENGAGENOW Need help studying? This site is your one-stop study shop. Take a Pre-Test and CengageNOW will generate a Personalized Study Plan based on your test results. The Study Plan will identify the topics you need to review and direct you to online resources to help you master those topics. You can then take a Post-Test to determine the concepts you have mastered and what you still need to work on.

7

Thinking, Language, and Intelligence

MAJOR TOPICS

Thinking: Reasoning about
   Reasoning *220*
Language: Of Signs, Grammar, and
   Many Things *231*
Intelligence: The Most Controversial
   Concept in Psychology? *237*

FEATURES

Self-Assessment: Puzzles, Problems, and Just Plain Fun *223*
Video Connections: Problem Solving *225*
A Closer Look: "Motherese"—Of "Yummy Yummy" and "Kitty Cats" *236*
A Closer Look: Emotional Intelligence and Social Intelligence *241*
Concept Review 7.1: Theories of Intelligence *242*
Self-Assessment: The Remote Associates Test *243*
Life Connections: Enhancing Intellectual Functioning *251*

© Tetra Images/Getty Images

T F   Only humans can use insight to solve problems.

page 227

T F   You are most likely to find the answer to a frustrating problem by continuing to plug away at it.

page 227

T F   If a couple has five sons, the sixth child is likely to be a daughter.

page 228

T F   People change their opinions when they are shown to be wrong.

page 230

T F   Crying is a child's first use of language.

page 234

T F   Young children say things like "Daddy goed away" and "Mommy sitted down" because they *do* understand rules of grammar.

page 235

T F   "Street smarts" are a sign of intelligence.

page 241

T F   Creative people are highly intelligent.

page 243

T F   Highly intelligent people are creative.

page 243

T F   Two children can answer exactly the same items on an intelligence test correctly, yet one child can be above average in IQ, and the other can be below average.

page 245

Are these items truth or fiction? We will be revisiting them throughout the chapter.

W

hat form of life is so adaptive that it can survive in desert temperatures of 120°F or Arctic climes of −40°F? What form of life can run, walk, climb, swim, live underwater for months on end, and fly to the moon and back? I won't keep you in suspense any longer. We are that form of life. Yet our unclad bodies do not allow us to adapt to these extremes of temperature. Brute strength does not allow us to live underwater or travel to the moon. Rather, it is our cognitive processes of thinking, language, and intelligence that permit us to adapt to these conditions and to challenge our physical limitations.

Our cognitive processes are the key assets that have enabled humans to survive and prosper. Other species may be stronger, run faster, smell more keenly, even live longer, but only humans have produced literature, music, mathematics, and science. Our cognitive processes have made these achievements possible. In this chapter, we look at these three related areas of **cognition**: thinking, language, and intelligence.

Out for a Walk It is not our brawn that boosts us into outer space and enables us to withstand its cold and lack of oxygen. It is rather our capacities for thought and language—our intelligence—that makes possible those achievements that are particularly human.

● THINKING: REASONING ABOUT REASONING

The Greek philosopher Aristotle pointed out that people differ from lower organisms in their capacity for rational thinking. Thinking enables us to build skyscrapers, create computers, and scan the interior of the body without surgery. Some people even manage to keep track of their children and balance their checkbooks.

Question 1: What *is* thinking? Thinking means attending to information, representing it mentally, reasoning about it, and making judgments and decisions about it. It refers to conscious, *planned* attempts to make sense of the world and change it. Mental processes such as dreaming and daydreaming may be unplanned and seem to proceed more or less on their own.

In this chapter, we explore thinking and the related topics of language and intelligence. Humans tend to use language not only in communicating but also in thinking. Intelligence provides the foundation for our capacity to think and solve problems. We begin with the subject of *concepts*, which provide many of the building blocks for thinking.

Cognition Mental activity involved in understanding, processing, and communicating information.

Thinking Paying attention to information, mentally representing it, reasoning about it, and making decisions about it.

Concept A mental category that is used to class together objects, relations, events, abstractions, ideas, or qualities that have common properties.

Concepts: Building Blocks of Thinking

Here's a riddle from my childhood: "What's black and white and read all over?" Because this riddle was spoken, not written, and involved the colors black and white, you would probably assume that "read" meant "red." Thus, in seeking an answer, you might scan your memory for an object that was red although it also somehow managed to be black and white. The answer to the riddle, "newspaper," was usually met with a groan.

The word *newspaper* is a concept. *Red, black,* and *white* are also concepts—color concepts. **Question 2: What are concepts?** Concepts are mental categories used to group together objects, relations, events, abstractions, ideas, or qualities that have common properties. Concepts are crucial to cognition.

Words and Concepts, Concepts and Words Circles, squares, and triangles are found only rarely in nature and not among the Himba of northern Namibia. It is not surprising, then, that they have no words for these concepts.

© Ariadne Van Zandbergen/Getty Images

They can represent objects, events, and activities—and visions of things that never were or cannot be measured, such as Middle Earth in Tolkien's *Lord of the Rings* novels or the Land of Oz in *The Wizard of Oz*.

Labels for objects depend on experience with them and on one's cultural setting (Sloman et al., 2002). Concepts such as *square, circle,* and *triangle* are not all that common in nature, and some peoples who do not construct houses with these shapes, such as the Himba of northern Namibia, have no words for them (Davidoff et al., 2008; Roberson et al., 2002). Yet these concepts are basic to geometry. Much thinking has to do with categorizing new concepts and manipulating relationships among concepts, as in geometric proofs.

We tend to organize concepts in *hierarchies* (see Figure 7.1 ■). The *newspaper* category includes objects such as your school paper and the *Los Angeles Times*. Newspapers, college textbooks, novels, and merchandise catalogs can be combined into higher order categories such as *printed matter* or *printed devices that store information*. If you add iPods and DVDs, you can create a still higher category, *objects that store information*. Now consider a question that requires categorical thinking: How are a newspaper and a DVD alike? Answers to such questions entail supplying the category that includes both objects. In this case, we can say that both objects store information. Their functions are alike, even if their technology differs.

Prototypes are examples that best match the key features of categories (Machery, 2009). Which animal seems more birdlike to you: a robin or an ostrich? Why? Which better fits the prototype of a fish: a seahorse or a tuna? Why?

Many simple prototypes, such as *dog* and *red*, are taught by means of specific examples, or **exemplars**. Research suggests that it is more efficient for most of us to learn what *fruits* and *vegetables* are from experience with exemplars of each rather than by working from definitions of them (Freund, 2009; Voorspoels et al., 2008). We point to a dog and tell a child "dog" or "This is a dog." Dogs are *positive instances* of the dog concept. We then show the child *negative instances*—things that are *not* dogs—and say, "This is *not* a dog." Negative instances of one concept may be positive instances of another. So in teaching a child, we may be more likely to say, "This is not a dog—it's a cat" than simply, "This is not a dog."

"I think; therefore I am. (Cogito ergo sum.)"

RENÉ DESCARTES

"Those who know how to think need no teachers."

MAHATMA GANDHI

"You can only understand something when you know what it is not."

STEVEN PINKER

Prototype A concept of a category of objects or events that serves as a good example of the category.

Exemplar A specific example.

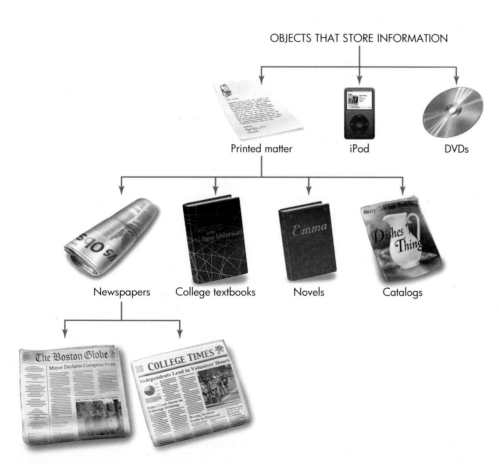

OBJECTS THAT STORE INFORMATION

Printed matter   iPod   DVDs

Newspapers   College textbooks   Novels   Catalogs

Figure 7.1 ■ Organization of Concepts into Hierarchies People may have a concept "objects that store information." This concept may include concepts such as iPod, DVD, and printed matter. Within the concept of printed matter, people may include newspapers, college textbooks (certainly the most important object that stores information!), novels, and catalogs. The concept of newspaper may include one's school newspaper and various commercial newspapers.

A Goat or a Dog? Yes, you know the answer, but at first, young children may include goats, horses, and other four-legged animals within the dog concept. Later, they come to understand the differences between the animals.

"I think and think for months and years. Ninety-nine times the conclusion is false. The hundredth time I am right."

ALBERT EINSTEIN

"[People] fear thought as they fear nothing else on earth, more than ruin, more even than death. Thought is subversive and revolutionary, destructive and terrible, thought is merciless to privilege, established institutions, and comfortable habit. Thought looks into the pit of hell and is not afraid. Thought is great and swift and free, the light of the world, . . ."

BERTRAND RUSSELL

Children may at first include horses and other four-legged animals within the dog concept until the differences between dogs and horses are pointed out. In language development, such overinclusion of instances in a category (reference to horses as dogs) is labeled *overextension*. Children's prototypes become refined after they are shown positive and negative instances and given explanations. Abstract concepts such as *bachelor* or *square root* tend to be formed through explanations that involve more basic concepts.

Problem Solving: Getting from Here to There

Problem solving is an important aspect of thinking. Here's a problem for you to solve. What are the next two letters in this series?

$$O \ T \ T \ F \ F \ S \ S \ E \ \_\_ \ ?$$

How did you try to find the answer? Did you search your personal memory banks and ask yourself what *O* can stand for, then *T*, and so on? Did you try to think of some phrase the letters might represent? Perhaps the first letters of the stars in a constellation? (You can check Appendix B for the answer.)

This section is about the ways in which we solve problems, but first, I would like to share something personal with you. One of the pleasures I derived from my own introductory psychology course lay in showing friends the textbook and getting them involved in the problems in the section on problem solving. First, of course, I struggled with them myself. Now it's your turn. Get some scrap paper, take a breath, and have a go at the problems in the nearby Self-Assessment. The answers will be discussed in the following pages, but don't peek. *Try* to solve the problems first.

Question 3: What tools do people use to solve problems? To answer this question, begin by considering the steps you used to try to solve parts a and b of problem 1 in the Self-Assessment. Did you first make sure you understood the problem by rereading the instructions? Or did you dive in as soon as you saw them on the page? Perhaps the solutions to 1a and 1b came easily, but I'm sure you studied 1c very carefully. Let's review what you may have been thinking when you attempted to solve these problems and how your cognitive processes might have led you to or away from solutions.

After you believed you understood what was required in each problem, you probably tried to discover the structure of the cycles in each series. Series 1a has repeated cycles of two letters: *AB, AB,* and so on. Series 1b may be seen as having four cycles of two consecutive letters: *AB, DE, BC,* and so on.

Again, did you solve 1a and 1b in a flash of insight, or did you try to find rules that govern each series? In series 1a, the rule is simply to repeat the cycle. Series 1b is more complicated, and different sets of rules can be used to describe it. One correct set of rules is that odd-numbered cycles (*1 and 3*, or *AB* and *BC*) simply repeat the last letter of the previous cycle (in this case *B*) and then advance by one letter in the alphabet. The same rule applies to even-numbered cycles (*2 and 4*, or *DE* and *EF*).

If you found rules for problems 1a and 1b, you used them to produce the next letters in the series: *AB* in series 1a and *CD* in series 1b. Perhaps you then evaluated the effectiveness of your rules by checking your answers against the solutions in the preceding paragraphs.

Now, the question is whether your solutions to problems 1a and 1b helped you to understand 1c or whether they interfered with your ability to solve 1c. Let's consider what psychologists mean by "understanding" a problem. Then let's see whether you applied an *algorithm* to solve 1a and 1b. As we read on, we'll also consider the roles of *heuristics, insight,* and *mental sets,* among other cognitive processes. You'll see that solving 1a and 1b might have made it more difficult rather than less difficult to solve 1c.

UNDERSTANDING THE PROBLEM Let's begin our discussion of understanding problems by considering a bus driver problem my 9-year-old daughter Jordan asked me to solve. Because I believe in exposing students to the tortures I have endured, see what you can do with it:

Are you ready for some mind benders? Following are a number of problems I came across in my own psychology courses. They were challenging and mostly enjoyable, except that I think I scratched my head a bit too hard over a couple of them. (The hair still hasn't grown back, although people unfamiliar with my past attribute it to male-pattern baldness.)

Have some fun with them. If the answer doesn't come immediately, why not stand back from the problem for a while and see if the answer comes to you in a "flash of insight." (I confess that I was suffering from a deficiency of insight when I tried to solve them.)

You will find the answers to problems 1a and 1b as you read along in the text. You will find the answers to the others, including 1c, on page 512.

1. Provide the next two letters in the series for each of the following:
   a. ABABABAB??
   b. ABDEBCEF??
   c. OTTFFSSE??
2. Draw straight lines through all the points in part A of Figure 7.2 ■ using only *four* lines. Do not lift your pencil from the paper or retrace your steps. (See Appendix B, p. 512, for the answer.)
3. Move three matches in part B of Figure 7.2 to make four squares of the same size. You must use *all* the matches. (See p. 512 for the answer.)
4. You have three jars—A, B, and C—which hold the amounts of water, in ounces, shown in the table below. For each of the seven problems, use the jars in any way you wish to arrive at the indicated amount of water. Fill or empty any jar as often as you wish. How do you obtain the desired amount of water in each problem? (The solutions are discussed on p. 512.)

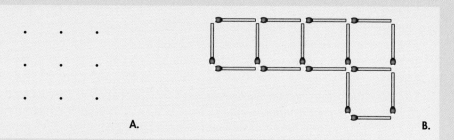

A.   **B.**

Figure 7.2 ■ Two Problems Draw straight lines through all the points in part A using only four lines. Do not lift your pencil or retrace your steps. Move three matches in part B to make four squares equal in size. Use all the matches. See page B-00 for the answers.

Water Jar Problems

Three Jars Are Present with the Listed Capacities (in Ounces)

Problem	Jar A	Jar B	Jar C	Goal
1	21	127	3	100
2	14	163	25	99
3	18	43	10	5
4	9	42	6	21
5	20	59	4	31
6	23	49	3	20
7	10	36	7	3

Source: Adapted from *Rigidity of Behavior* (p. 109), by Abraham S. Luchins and Edith H. Luchins, 1959, Eugene: University of Oregon Press.

How Do You Go about Understanding a Problem? This student is apparently seeking to boost her storehouse of background knowledge. Will doing so help her focus on the answer efficiently?

"When we think well, we feel good. Understanding is a kind of ecstasy."

CARL SAGAN

Algorithm A systematic procedure for solving a problem that works invariably when it is correctly applied.

Systematic random search An algorithm for solving problems in which each possible solution is tested according to a particular set of rules.

You're driving a bus that's leaving from Pennsylvania. To start off with, there were 32 people on the bus. At the next bus stop, 11 people got off, and 9 people got on. At the next bus stop, 2 people got off, and 2 people got on. At the next bus stop, 12 people got on, and 16 people got off. At the next bus stop, 5 people got on, and 3 people got off. What color are the bus driver's eyes?

I was not about to be fooled when I was listening to this problem. Although it seemed that I should tracking the number of people on the bus, I sensed there was a trick. Therefore, I told myself to remember that the bus was leaving from Pennsylvania. Being clever, I also kept track of the number of stops rather than the number of people getting on and off. When I was finally hit with the question about the bus driver's eyes, I was at a loss. I protested that Jordan had said nothing about the bus driver's eyes, but she insisted that she had given me enough information to answer the question.

One of the requirements of problem solving is attending to relevant information. To do that, you need some familiarity with the type of problem. I classified the bus driver problem as a trick question and paid attention to silly details, but I wasn't remotely on target.

How about you? What color were the bus driver's eyes?

If we assume it is crucial to keep track of the number of people getting on and off the bus, we focus on information that turns out to be unessential. In fact, it distracts us from the key information.

When we are faced with a novel problem, how can we know which information is relevant and which is not? Background knowledge helps. If you are given a chemistry problem, it helps if you have taken courses in chemistry. If Jordan gives you a problem, it is helpful to expect the unexpected. (In case you still haven't gotten it, the critical information you need to solve the bus driver problem is provided in the first sentence.)

Successfully understanding a problem generally requires three features:

1. *The parts, or elements, of our mental representation of the problem relate to one another in a meaningful way.* If we are trying to solve a problem in geometry, our mental triangles, like actual triangles, should have angles that total 180 degrees.

2. *The elements of our mental representation of the problem correspond to the elements of the problem in the outer world.* If we are meeting a patient in the emergency room of a hospital, we want to arrive at a diagnosis of what might be wrong before we make a treatment plan. To do so, we take the patient's vital signs, including heart rate, temperature, and blood pressure, so that our mental picture of the patient conforms to what is going on in his or her body.

3. *We have a storehouse of background knowledge that we can apply to the problem.* We have the necessary experience or course work to solve the problem.

THE USE OF ALGORITHMS: FINDING THE RIGHT FORMULA An algorithm is a specific procedure for solving a type of problem. An algorithm invariably leads to the solution—if it is used properly, that is. Mathematical formulas like the Pythagorean theorem are examples of algorithms. They yield correct answers to problems *as long as the right formula is used.* Finding the right formula to solve a problem may require scanning one's memory for all formulas that contain variables that represent one or more of the elements in the problem. The Pythagorean theorem concerns right triangles. Therefore, it is appropriate to consider using this formula for problems concerning right triangles but not others.

If you are going to be meeting someone for the first time and want to make a good impression, you consider the nature of the encounter (for example, a job interview or a blind date) and then consider how to dress and behave for the encounter. If it's a job interview, the algorithm may be to dress neatly, to be well groomed, and not to wear too much cologne or perfume. If it's a date, you may ditch the suit but hike up the cologne or perfume a notch. In either case, smile and make eye contact—it's all part of the formula.

Anagrams are words with scrambled letters. *Korc* is an anagram for *rock* or *cork*. The task in anagram problems is to try to reorganize jumbles or groups of letters into words. Some anagram problems require us to use every letter from the pool of letters; others allow us to use only some of the letters. How many words can you make from the pool of letters *DWARG?* If you were to use the **systematic random search** algorithm, you would list every possible letter combination, using from one to all five letters. You could use a dictionary or a spell-checking program to see whether each result is, in fact, a word. The method might take a while, but it would work.

THE USE OF HEURISTIC DEVICES: IF IT WORKS, JUST DO IT? Question 4: Is it best to use a tried-and-true formula to solve a problem? Sometimes, people use shortcuts to "jump to conclusions," and these are often correct conclusions. The shortcuts are called **heuristics,** or heuristic devices—rules of thumb that help us simplify and solve problems and make decisions. Heuristics are often based on strategies that worked in the past for similar kinds of problems (Mair et al., 2009).

In contrast to algorithms, heuristics do not guarantee a correct solution. But when they work, they permit more rapid solutions. A heuristic device for solving the anagram problem would be to look for familiar letter combinations and then check the remaining letters for words that include these combinations. In *DWARG,* for example, we find some familiar combinations: *dr* and *gr.* We may then quickly find *draw, drag,* and *grad.* The drawback to this method is that we might miss some words.

One type of heuristic device is **means–end analysis.** In using this heuristic device, we assess the difference between our current situation and our goals and do what we can to reduce this difference. Let's say that you are in your car and have gotten lost. One heuristic device based on analysis of what you need to do to reach your destination might be to ask for directions. This approach requires no "sense of direction." An algorithm might be more complicated and require some geographical knowledge. For example, let's say that you know your destination is west of your current location and on the other side of the railroad tracks. You might therefore drive toward the setting sun (west) and, at the same time, watch for railroad tracks. If the road comes to an end and you must turn left or right, you can scan in both directions for tracks. If you don't see any, turn right or left, but at the next major intersection, turn toward the setting sun. Eventually, you should get there. If not, you can ask for directions.

THE USE OF ANALOGIES: THIS IS JUST LIKE …? An *analogy* is a partial similarity among things that are different in other ways. The analogy heuristic applies the solution of an earlier problem to the solution of a new one. We use the analogy heuristic whenever we try to solve a new problem by referring to a previous problem (Mair et al., 2009; Wang & Chiew, 2010). Consider the water jar problems on page 223. Problem 2 is analogous to problem 1. Therefore, the approach to solving problem 1 works with problem 2. (Later, we consider what happens when the analogy heuristic fails.)

Let's see whether you can use the analogy heuristic to your advantage in the following number series problem: To solve letter problems 1a, 1b, and 1c of the Self-Assessment on page 223, you had to figure out the rules that govern the order of the letters. Scan the following series of numbers and find the rule that governs their order:

$$8, 5, 4, 9, 1, 7, 6, 3, 2, 0$$

This is rather abstract and mathematical. Actually, you use the analogy heuristic regularly. For example, when you begin a new term with a new instructor, you probably consider whom the instructor reminds you of. Then, perhaps, you recall the things that helped you get along with the analogous instructor and try them on the new one. We tend to look for things that helped us in the past in similar situations.

FACTORS THAT AFFECT PROBLEM SOLVING: MAKING RUTS, CLIMBING OUT The way you approach a problem is central to how effective you are at solving it. Other factors also influence your effectiveness. **Question 5: What factors make it**

Video Connections—Problem Solving

Move the matches to form four equal-sided triangles.

Can you solve these riddles and explain the psychological processes behind them? Watch the video to see the riddles and the role of insight in problem solving. Go to Psychology CourseMate at **www.cengagebrain .com** to watch this video.

Heuristics Rules of thumb that help us simplify and solve problems.

Means–end analysis A heuristic device in which we try to solve a problem by evaluating the difference between the current situation and the goal.

easier or harder to solve problems? These factors include level of expertise, mental sets, insight, incubation, and functional fixedness.

Expertise To appreciate the role of expertise in problem solving, unscramble the following anagrams taken from Novick and Coté (1992). In each case, use all of the letters to form an actual English word:

DNSUO
RCWDO
IASYD

How long did it take you to unscramble each anagram (*sound*, *crowd*, and *daisy*)? Would a person whose native language is English—that is, an "expert"—unscramble each anagram more efficiently than a bilingual person who spoke another language in the home? Why or why not?

Experts solve problems more efficiently and rapidly than novices do. Generally speaking, people who are experts at solving a certain kind of problem share the following characteristics:

- They know the particular subject area well (Mair et al., 2009).
- They have a good memory for the elements in the problems (Mair et al., 2009).
- They form **mental images**, or representations, that facilitate problem solving (Szala, 2002).
- They relate the problem to similar problems (Gorodetsky & Klavir, 2003; Nokes & VanLehn, 2008).
- They are goal directed and have efficient methods for problem solving (Gorodetsky & Klavir, 2003).

These factors are interrelated. Art historians, for example, acquire a database that permits them to understand the intricacies of artworks. As a result, their memory for details of artworks expands.

Novick and Coté (1992) found that the solutions to the anagram problems seemed to "pop out" in less than 2 seconds among experts. The experts apparently used more efficient methods than the novices. Experts seemed to use *parallel processing*. That is, they dealt simultaneously with two or more elements of the problems. In the case of DNSUO, for example, they may have played with the order of the vowels (UO or OU) at the same time that they tested which consonant (D, N, or S) was likely to precede them, arriving quickly at *sou* and *sound*. Novices were more likely to engage in *serial processing*—that is, to handle one element of the problem at a time.

Mental Sets Jordan hit me with another question: "A farmer had 17 sheep. All but 9 died. How many sheep did he have left?" Being a victim of a **mental set**, I assumed that this was a subtraction problem and gave the answer 8. She gleefully informed me that she hadn't said "9 died." She had said *"all but 9* died." Therefore, the correct answer was 9. (Get it?) Put it another way: I had not *understood* the problem. My mental representation of the problem did not correspond to the actual elements of the problem.

Return to problem 1, part c, in the Self-Assessment (p. 223). To try to solve this problem, did you seek a pattern of letters that involved cycles and the alphabet? If so, it may be because this approach worked in solving parts a and b.

The tendency to respond to a new problem with the same approach that helped solve similar problems is termed a **mental set**. Mental sets usually make our work easier, but they can mislead us when the similarity between problems is illusory, as in part c of problem 1. Here is a clue: part c is not an alphabet series. Each letter in the series *stands for* something. If you can discover what each stands for (that is, if you can discover the rule), you will be able to generate the 9th and 10th letters. (See page 512 for the answer.)

Insight: Aha! To gain **insight** into the role of insight in problem solving, consider the following problem posed by Metcalfe (1986):

A stranger approached a museum curator and offered him an ancient bronze coin. The coin had an authentic appearance and was marked with the date 544 BCE.

Mental image An internal image or visual representation that is used in thinking and memory.

Mental set The tendency to respond to a new problem with an approach that was successfully used with similar problems.

Insight In Gestalt psychology, a sudden perception of relationships among elements of the mentally represented elements of a problem that permits its solution.

The curator had happily made acquisitions from suspicious sources before, but this time he promptly called the police and had the stranger arrested. Why?

I'm not going to give you the answer to this problem just yet. (You'll find it in Appendix B on p. 512 under Puzzles, Problems, and Just Plain Fun.) But I'll make a guarantee. When you arrive at the solution, it will hit you all at once. You'll think, "Of course!" (or something less polite). It will seem as though the pieces of information in the problem have suddenly been reorganized so that the solution leaps out—in a flash.

Bismarck, one of psychologist N. R. F. Maier's rats, provided evidence of insight in his species (Maier & Schneirla, 1935). Bismarck had been trained to climb a ladder to a tabletop where food was placed. On one occasion, Maier used a mesh barrier to prevent the rat from reaching his goal. But, as shown in Figure 7.3 ■, a second ladder was provided and was visible to the animal. At first, Bismarck sniffed and scratched and tried to find a path through the mesh. Then he spent some time washing his face, an activity that may signal frustration in rats. Suddenly, he jumped into the air, turned, ran down the familiar ladder and around to the new ladder, ran up the new ladder, and claimed his just desserts. Did Bismarck suddenly perceive the relationships between the elements of the problem so that the solution occurred by insight? He seems to have had what Gestalt psychologists have termed an "Aha! experience." **Truth or Fiction Revisited:** It thus appears that not only humans use insight to solve problems.

Incubation Let's return to the problems in the Self-Assessment. How did you do with problem 1, part c, and problems 2 and 3? Students tend to fiddle around with them for a while. The solutions, when they come, appear to arrive in a flash. Students set the stage for the flash of insight by studying the elements in the problems carefully, repeating the rules to themselves, and trying to imagine what a solution might look like. If you tried solutions that did not meet the goals, you may have become frustrated and thought, "The heck with it! I'll come back to it later." **Truth or Fiction Revisited:** Standing back from the problem, rather than continuing to plug away at it, may allow for the **incubation** of insight. An incubator warms chicken eggs so that they will hatch. Incubation in problem solving refers to standing back from the problem for a while as some process within may continue to work on it. Later, the answer may come in a flash of insight. Standing back from the problem may help by distancing us from unprofitable but persistent mental sets (Kohn & Smith, 2009; Sio & Ormerod, 2009).

Have another look at the role of incubation in helping us overcome mental sets. Consider the seventh water jar problem on page 223. What if we had tried several solutions involving the three water jars and none had worked? We could distance ourselves from the problem for a day or two. At some point, we might recall a 10, a 7, and a 3— three elements of the problem—and suddenly realize that we can arrive at the correct answer by using only two water jars!

Functional Fixedness The tendency toward **functional fixedness** may hinder problem solving. For example, first ask yourself what a pair of pliers is. Is it a tool for grasping, a paperweight, or a weapon? A pair of pliers could function as any of these, but your tendency to think of it as a grasping tool is fostered by your experience with it. You have probably used pliers only for grasping things. Functional fixedness is the tendency to think of an object in terms of its name or its familiar function. It can be similar to a mental set because it makes it difficult to use familiar objects to solve problems in novel ways.

Now that you know what functional fixedness is, try to overcome it by solving the Duncker candle problem. You find these objects on a table: a candle, a box of matches, and some thumbtacks (see Figure 7.4 ■). How do you use the objects on the table to attach the candle to the wall of the room so that it will burn properly. (See the answer on page 512.)

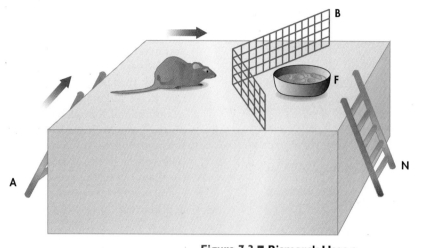

Figure 7.3 ■ Bismarck Uses a Cognitive Map to Claim His Just Desserts Bismarck has learned to reach dinner by climbing ladder A. But now the food goal (F) is blocked by a wire mesh barrier B. Bismarck washes his face for a while, but then, in an apparent flash of insight, he runs back down ladder A and up new ladder N to reach the goal.

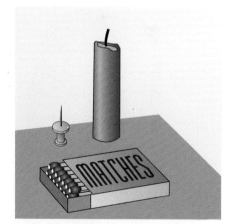

Figure 7.4 ■ The Duncker Candle Problem Can you use the objects shown on the table to attach the candle to the wall of the room so that it will burn properly?

Incubation In problem solving, a process that may sometimes occur when we stand back from a frustrating problem for a while and the solution "suddenly" appears.

Functional fixedness The tendency to view an object in terms of its name or familiar usage.

Judgment and Decision Making

Decisions, decisions. Should you go to breakfast before classes begin or catch a few extra winks? Should you rent or buy? For whom should you vote? What should you eat? Should you take a job or go on for advanced training when you complete your college program? If you opt for the job, cash will soon be jingling in your pockets. Yet later, you may wonder if you have enough education to reach your full potential. By furthering your education, you may have to delay independence and gratification, but you may find a more fulfilling position later on. Decisions, decisions.

Question 6: How do people make judgments and decisions? You might like to think that people are so rational that they carefully weigh the pros and cons when they make judgments or decisions. Or you might think that they insist on finding and examining all the relevant information. Actually, people make most of their decisions on the basis of limited information. They take shortcuts. They use heuristic devices—rules of thumb—in judgments and decision making just as they do in problem solving (Gigerenzer et al., 2008). For example, they may let a financial advisor select stocks for them rather than research the companies themselves. Or they may see a doctor recommended by a friend rather than look at the doctor's credentials. In this section, we consider various factors in judgment and decision making.

HEURISTICS IN DECISION MAKING: IF IT WORKS, MUST IT BE LOGICAL?

Imagine that you flip a coin six times. In the following three possible outcomes, H stands for heads and T for tails. Circle the most likely sequence of six tosses:

H H H H H H

H H H T T T

T H H T H T

Did you select T H H T H T as the most likely sequence of events? Most people do. Why? There are two reasons. First, people recognize that the sequence of six heads in a row is unlikely. (The probability of achieving it is $\frac{1}{2} \times \frac{1}{2} \times \frac{1}{2} \times \frac{1}{2} \times \frac{1}{2} \times \frac{1}{2}$, or 1/64.) Three heads and three tails are more likely than six heads (or six tails). Second, people recognize that the sequence of heads and tails ought to appear random. T H H T H T has a random look to it, whereas H H H T T T does not.

People tend to select T H H T H T because of the **representativeness heuristic**. According to this decision-making heuristic, people make judgments about events (samples) according to the populations of events that they appear to represent (Nilsson et al., 2008). In this case, the sample of events is six coin tosses. The "population" is an infinite number of random coin tosses. But guess what? *Each sequence is equally likely* (or unlikely). If the question had been whether the outcome six heads or three heads and three tails is more likely, the correct answer would have been three and three. If the question had been whether heads and tails are more likely to be consecutive or in random order, the correct answer would have been random order. But each of the three sequences is a *specific* sequence. What is the probability of obtaining the specific sequence T H H T H T? The probability that the first coin toss will result in a tail is $\frac{1}{2}$. The probability that the second will result in a head is $\frac{1}{2}$, and so on. Thus, the probability of obtaining the exact sequence T H H T H T is identical to that of achieving any other specific sequence: $\frac{1}{2} \times \frac{1}{2} \times \frac{1}{2} \times \frac{1}{2} \times \frac{1}{2} \times \frac{1}{2}$, or 1/64. (Don't just sit there. Try this out on a friend.)

Or consider this question: If a couple has five children, all of whom are boys, is their sixth child more likely to be a boy or a girl? Use of the representativeness heuristic might lead us to imagine that the couple is due for a girl. That is, five boys and one girl are closer to the assumed random distribution that accounts for roughly equal numbers of boys and girls in the world. But people with some knowledge of reproductive biology might predict that another boy is actually more likely because five boys in a row may be too many to be a random biological event.

Truth or Fiction Revisited: Therefore, it is not true that the sixth child of a couple with five sons is likely to be a daughter. If the couple's conception of a boy or girl were random, however,

How Do You Choose a Doctor? Do you go by reputation or the advice of a friend or family member? Do you check out his or her credentials online? Or is the choice foreclosed because you are on campus or in a particular health insurance plan?

© Jose Luis Pelaez Inc./Blend Images

what would be the probability of conceiving another boy? Answer: ½.

Another heuristic device used in decision making is the **availability heuristic.** According to this heuristic, our estimates of frequency or probability are based on how easy it is to find examples of relevant events. Let me ask you whether there are more art majors or sociology majors at your college. Unless you are familiar with the enrollment statistics, you will probably answer on the basis of the numbers of art majors and sociology majors that you know.

The **anchoring and adjustment heuristic** suggests that there can be a good deal of inertia in our judgments. In forming opinions or making estimates, we have an initial view, or presumption. This is the anchor. As we receive additional information, we make adjustments, sometimes grudgingly. That is, if you grow up believing that one religion or one political party is the "right" one, that belief serves as a cognitive anchor. When inconsistencies show up in your religion or political party, you may adjust your views of them but perhaps not very willingly.

Practicing His Faith—Early Can you use the anchoring and adjustment heuristic to explain why most people grow up believing that their religion is the right religion?.

Let's illustrate further by means of a math problem. Write each of the following multiplication problems on a separate piece of paper:

A. $8 \times 7 \times 6 \times 5 \times 4 \times 3 \times 2 \times 1$

B. $1 \times 2 \times 3 \times 4 \times 5 \times 6 \times 7 \times 8$

Show problem A to a few friends. Give them each 5 seconds to estimate the answer. Show problem B to some other friends and give them 5 seconds to estimate the answer.

The answers to the multiplication problems are the same because the order of quantities being multiplied does not change the outcome. However, when Amos Tversky and Daniel Kahneman (1982, 2003) showed these problems to high school students, the average estimate given by students who were shown version A was significantly higher than that given by students shown version B. Students who saw 8 in the first position offered an average estimate of 2,250. Students who saw 1 in the first position gave an average estimate of 512. That is, the estimate was larger when 8 served as the anchor. By the way, what is the correct answer to the multiplication problems? Can you use the anchoring and adjustment heuristic to explain why both groups were so far off?

THE FRAMING EFFECT: SAY THAT AGAIN? If you were on a low-fat diet, would you be more likely to choose an ice cream that is 97% fat free or one whose fat content makes up 10% of its calorie content? On one shopping excursion, I was impressed with an ice cream package's claims that the product was 97% fat free. Yet when I read the label closely, I noticed that a 4-ounce serving had 160 calories, 27 of which were contributed by fat. Fat, then, accounted for 27/160, or about 17%, of the ice cream's calorie content. But fat accounted only for 3% of the ice cream's *weight*. The packagers of the ice cream knew all about the *framing effect*. They understood that labeling the ice cream as "97% fat free" would make it sound more healthful than "Only 17% of calories from fat." This is an example of the framing effect.

Question 7: What is the framing effect? The **framing effect** refers to the way in which wording, or the context in which information is presented, affects decision making (Li & Chapman, 2009; Tetlock & McGraw, 2005). Political groups, like advertisers, are aware of the framing effect and choose their words accordingly. For example, proponents of legalized abortion refer to themselves as "pro-choice," and opponents refer to themselves as "pro-life." Each group frames itself in a positive way ("pro" something) and refers to a popular value (choice or life).

Parents also use the framing effect. My preschooler, Taylor, was invited to a play date at Abigail's house. I asked Taylor, "Would you like to play with Abigail at her house?" The question met with a resounding no. I thought things over and reframed the question: "Would you like to play at Abigail's house and have a real fun time? She has lots of toys and games, and I'll pick you up really soon." This time Taylor said yes.

Representativeness heuristic A decision-making heuristic in which people make judgments about samples according to the populations they appear to represent.

Availability heuristic A decision-making heuristic in which our estimates of frequency or probability of events are based on how easy it is to find examples.

Anchoring and adjustment heuristic A decision-making heuristic in which a presumption or first estimate serves as a cognitive anchor. As we receive additional information, we make adjustments but tend to remain in the proximity of the anchor.

Framing effect The influence of wording, or the context in which information is presented, on decision making.

229

OVERCONFIDENCE: IS YOUR HINDSIGHT 20-20? Whether our decisions are correct or incorrect, most of us tend to be overconfident about them. Overconfidence applies to judgments as wide ranging as whether one will be infected by the virus that causes AIDS, predicting the outcome of elections, boasting that one's answers on a test are correct, and selecting stocks (Blavatsky, 2009). **Truth or Fiction Revisited:** It is not true that people change their opinions when they are shown to be wrong. (Have you ever known someone to maintain unrealistic confidence in a candidate who was far behind in the polls?)

We also tend to view our situations with 20-20 hindsight. When we are proven wrong, we frequently find a way to show that we "knew it all along." We also become overconfident that we would have known the actual outcome if we had access to information that became available after the event. For example, if we had known that a key player would pull a hamstring muscle, we would have predicted a different outcome for the football game. If we had known that it would be blustery on Election Day, we would have predicted a smaller voter turnout and a different outcome.

Question 8: Why do people tend to be convinced that they are right even when they are clearly wrong? There are several reasons for overconfidence even when our judgments are wrong. Here are some of them:

- We tend to be unaware of how flimsy our assumptions may be.
- We tend to focus on examples that confirm our judgments and ignore those that do not.
- Because our working memories have limited space, we tend to forget information that runs counter to our judgments.
- We work to bring about the events we believe in, so they sometimes become self-fulfilling prophecies.

Before leaving the section on thinking, I have a final problem for you:

> You're driving a bus that's leaving from Pennsylvania. To start off with, there were 32 people on the bus. At the next bus stop, 11 people got off, and 9 people got on. At the next bus stop, 2 people got off, and 2 people got on. At the next bus stop, 12 people got on, and 16 people got off. At the next bus stop, 5 people got on, and 3 people got off. How many people are now on the bus?

> *"Doctors will opt for a cautious public-health program . . . when it is framed as saving the lives of 200 people out of 600 who are vulnerable, but will eschew the same program when it is framed as resulting in the deaths of 400 people out of the 600."*
>
> STEVEN PINKER

LearningConnections • THINKING: REASONING ABOUT REASONING

ACTIVE REVIEW (1) _____ are mental categories used to class objects, relations, or events with common properties. (2) A(n) _____ is a specific procedure for solving a type of problem. (3) _____ devices are rules of thumb that serve as shortcuts to rapid solutions. (4) A _____ set is the tendency to respond to a new problem with the same approach that helped solve similar problems. (5) Some problems are solved by rapid "perception of relationships" among the elements of the problem, which is called _____.

REFLECT AND RELATE Have you or anyone you know used the framing effect in an argument? Which term is more appealing, "pro-life" or "anti-choice"? Why?

CRITICAL THINKING Research suggests that people are reluctant to change their views, even when they are shown to be incorrect. What are the implications of these research findings for professors who desire to encourage their students to become critical thinkers?

 Go to Psychology CourseMate at **www.cengagebrain.com** for an interactive version of these questions.

● LANGUAGE: OF SIGNS, GRAMMAR, AND MANY THINGS

> *"The time has come," the Walrus said, "To talk of many things*
> *Of shoes—and ships—and sealing wax—Of cabbages—and kings—*
> *And why the sea is boiling hot—And whether pigs have wings."*
>
> LEWIS CARROLL, *THROUGH THE LOOKING-GLASS*

Lewis Carroll wasn't quite telling the truth. The sea is not boiling hot. At the risk of alienating walrus fans across the land, let me boldly assert that walruses neither speak nor use other forms of language to communicate. On the other hand, the time has come indeed to talk of how talking—of how language—permits us to communicate about shoes and ships and . . . you get the idea.

Going Ape over Language?

In recent years, our exclusive claim to language has been questioned because apes have been taught to use symbols to communicate. (*Symbols* such as words stand for or represent objects, events, or ideas.) Chimpanzees and gorillas have been taught to communicate by making signs with their hands.

Chimpanzees are our closest genetic relatives, sharing an estimated 98.42% of their genetic code with humans (Zimmer, 2002–2003). Magnetic resonance imaging (MRI) studies with chimpanzees and gorillas reveal that most of them, like humans, show enlargement in the left hemisphere of the cerebral cortex in part of Broca's area (Cantalupo & Hopkins, 2001; Keller et al., 2009). (See Figure 7.5 ■.) The differences that remain between humans and chimps are at least in part associated with capabilities such as fine control of the mouth and larynx that are not found in apes (Sherwood et al., 2008). The genetic differences between chimps and humans probably explain why chimps cannot articulate speech but also apparently give chimps and other apes some meaningful ability to use language (Sherwood et al., 2008).

Question 9: Do apes really use language? Although apes do not speak, they have been taught to use American Sign Language and other symbol systems. For example, a chimpanzee named Washoe, who was a pioneer in the effort to teach apes to use language, was using 181 signs by the age of 32 (King, 2008). A baby chimp adopted by Washoe, Loulis, gained the ability to use signs just by observing Washoe and some other chimps who had been trained in sign language. Other chimps have used plastic symbols or have pressed keys on a computer keyboard to communicate.

Sue Savage-Rumbaugh and her colleagues (Segerdahl et al., 2006; Washburn et al., 2007) believe that pygmy chimpanzees can understand some of the **semantic** subtleties of language. She claims that one chimp, Kanzi, picked up language from observing another chimp being trained and has the grammatical abilities of a 2 1/2-year-old child. Kanzi also understands several spoken words (spoken by humans, that is). Kanzi held a toy snake to a toy dog's mouth when asked to make the dog bite the snake.

Critics of the view that apes can learn to produce language, such as Herbert Terrace (Terrace & Metcalfe, 2005) and Steven Pinker (1994b), note that:

- Apes can string together signs in a given sequence to earn rewards, but animals lower on the evolutionary ladder, such as pigeons, can also peck buttons in a certain sequence to obtain a reward.

- It takes apes longer to learn new signs than it takes children to learn new words.

"Man invented language to satisfy his deep need to complain."

LILY TOMLIN

"Language is the dress of thought."

DR. SAMUEL JOHNSON

Semantic Having to do with the meanings of words and symbols.

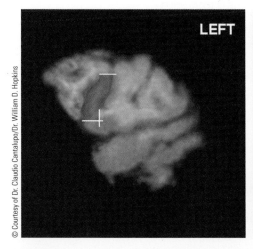
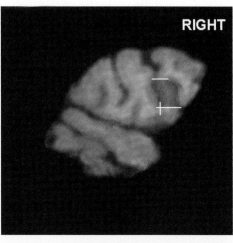

LEFT
RIGHT

© Courtesy of Dr. Claudio Cantalupo/Dr. William D. Hopkins

Figure 7.5 ■ MRI Results of the Left and Right Hemispheres of the Cerebral Cortexes of a Great Ape In their MRI study of the brains of 25 chimpanzees and 2 gorillas, Cantalupo and Hopkins found that the great majority, 20, showed larger areas similar to Broca's area in the left hemisphere. So do most humans. Six apes showed larger areas in the right hemisphere. Only one showed no difference. It would thus appear that chimpanzees and gorillas have some rudimentary language structures in their brains, even if they are not prewired for speech.

A Chimpanzee Uses Signs to Communicate
We share more than 98% of our genetic code with chimpanzees and apparently also some ability to communicate using symbols. Although chimpanzees and other apes cannot articulate speech, they have enlarged areas on the left side of the brain that correspond to Broca's area in humans. There is no question that chimpanzees learn signs for objects and actions; however, many psychologists and linguists question whether they share the inborn human ability to order those signs according to rules of grammar.

"It seems to me that the controversy [as to whether chimpanzees and gorillas have the capacity for language] is about whether [they] have grammar in their communications. And to be honest, I'm not interested in whether or not they have a grammar. Why would they?"

JANE GOODALL

Language The communication of information by means of symbols arranged according to rules of grammar.

Semanticity Meaning. The quality of language in which words are used as symbols for objects, events, or ideas.

Infinite creativity The capacity to combine words into original sentences.

- Apes are unreliable in their sequencing of signs, suggesting that by and large they do not comprehend rules of grammar.
- People observing apes sign may be subject to *observer bias* or *experimenter bias*—that is, they may be seeing what they want to see.

Scientists will continue to debate how well chimpanzees and gorillas understand and produce language, but there is little doubt that they have learned to use symbols to communicate (Segerdahl et al., 2006). Moreover, it is clear that chimps understand many of the subtleties of communication. For example, when they are behind a human, they make noises to get the person's attention. As soon as the person turns to them, they begin to sign (Bodamer & Gardner, 2002). Yet most researchers continue to consider that language emerges spontaneously only in people (Dominguez & Rakic, 2009).

What Is Language?

As you can see from the discussion of apes and language, the way one defines language is no small matter. **Question 10: Just how do we define language?** If we simply define language as a system of communication, many animals have language, including the birds and the bees. Dogs may communicate their possession of a territory by barking at an intruder, but they are not saying, "Excuse me—you are too close for comfort." Birds warn other birds of predators. And through particular chirps and shrieks, they may communicate that they have taken possession of a tree or bush. The waggle dances of bees inform other bees of the location of a food source or a predator. Vervet monkeys make sounds that signal the distance and species of predators. All of these are instinctive communication patterns but not what we mean by language.

With language, sounds or signs are symbols for objects and actions. There is apparently no doubt that apes have learned to use symbols to communicate. But is the use of symbols to communicate an adequate definition of language? Many language experts require one more piece. They define **language** as the communication of thoughts and feelings by means of symbols *that are arranged according to rules of grammar*. Instinctive waggle dances and barks have no symbols and no grammar, even though, in the case of a dog that needs to go for a walk, they may carry hints of desperation. By this rigorous definition, only humans clearly use language. Whether or not apes can handle rules of grammar is under debate.

Language makes it possible for one person to communicate knowledge to another and for one generation to communicate to another. It creates a vehicle for recording experiences. It allows us to put ourselves in the shoes of other people, to learn more than we could learn from direct experience. Language also provides many units of thinking.

Question 11: What are the properties of a "true" language? True language is distinguished from the communication systems of lower animals by properties such as semanticity, infinite creativity, and displacement (Hoff, 2005).

- **Semanticity:** The sounds (or signs) of a language have meaning. Words serve as symbols for actions, objects, relational concepts (*over*, *in*, *more*, and so on), and other ideas. The communication systems of the birds and the bees do not use words and symbols. Therefore, they lack semanticity.
- **Infinite creativity:** The capacity to create rather than imitate sentences.
- **Displacement:** The capacity to communicate information about events and objects in another time or place. Language makes it possible to transmit knowledge from one person to another and from one generation to another, furthering human adaptation.

Language and Cognition: Do We Need Words to Think?

Let's discuss language in terms of the broader picture: **Question 12: What are the relationships between language and thinking?** The relationships between language and thinking are complex and not always obvious. For example, can you think *without* using language? (The answer seems to be yes, but of course, you would not be able to use thoughts that entail symbols that are arranged according to rules of grammar.) Would you be able to solve problems without using words or sentences? (That depends on the problem.)

Jean Piaget (Inhelder & Piaget, 1958) believed that language reflects knowledge of the world but that much knowledge can be acquired without language. For example, it is possible to understand the concepts of roundness and redness even when we do not know or use the words *round* and *red*.

Language and Culture

Different languages have different words for the same concepts, and concepts do not necessarily overlap. As noted earlier, concepts expressed in our own language (such as *square* and *triangle*) may not exist in the language of another culture—and vice versa. **Question 13: Is it possible for English speakers to share all the thoughts experienced by people who speak other languages?** The answer is probably yes in many or most cases, but in some cases, no. In any event, the question brings us to the linguistic-relativity hypothesis.

THE LINGUISTIC-RELATIVITY HYPOTHESIS The linguistic-relativity hypothesis was proposed by Benjamin Lee Whorf (1956). Whorf believed that language structures the way we perceive the world. That is, the categories and relationships we use to understand the world are derived from our language. Therefore, speakers of various languages conceptualize the world in different ways.

Thus, most English speakers' ability to think about snow may be limited compared with that of the Inuit (Eskimos). We have only a few words for snow, whereas the Inuit have many. The Inuit's words differ according to whether the snow is hard packed, falling, melting, covered by ice, and so on. When we think about snow, we have fewer words to choose from and have to search for descriptive adjectives. The Inuit, however, can readily find a single word that describes a complex weather condition. Is it therefore easier for them to think about this variety of snow? Similarly, the Hanunoo people of the Philippines use 92 words for rice, depending on whether the rice is husked or unhusked and on how it is prepared. And whereas we have one word for camel, Arabs have more than 250.

In English, we have hundreds of words to describe colors. There is about a 95% overlap in perception and labeling of colors among English speakers and Chinese people (Moore et al., 2002). It has been pointed out, however, that Shona-speaking people use only three words for colors, and Bassa speakers use only two, corresponding to light and dark. Nevertheless, studies of languages spoken in nonindustrialized societies find overlaps for white, black, red, green, yellow, and blue (Regier, 2005; Tohidian, 2009). Moreover, people who use only a few words to distinguish among colors seem to perceive the same color variations as people with more words. For example, the Dani of New Guinea have just two words for colors: one that refers to yellows and reds and one that refers to greens and blues. Yet performance on matching and memory tasks shows that the Dani can discriminate the many colors of the spectrum.

The Hopi Indians had two words for flying objects, one for birds and an all-inclusive word for anything else that might be found traveling through the air. Does this mean that the Hopi were limited in their ability to think about bumblebees and airplanes? Are English

"Language shapes the way we think, and determines what we can think about."

BENJAMIN LEE WHORF

"Change your language and you change your thoughts."

KARL ALBRECHT

Displacement The quality of language that permits one to communicate information about objects and events in another time and place.

Linguistic-relativity hypothesis The view that language structures the way we view the world.

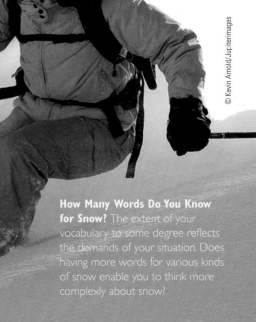

How Many Words Do You Know for Snow? The extent of your vocabulary to some degree reflects the demands of your situation. Does having more words for various kinds of snow enable you to think more complexly about snow?

speakers limited in their ability to think about skiing conditions? Probably not. English-speaking skiers who are concerned about different skiing conditions have developed a comprehensive vocabulary about snow, including the terms *powder, slush, ice, hard packed,* and *corn snow.* This allows them to communicate and think about snow with the facility of the Inuit. When a need to expand a language's vocabulary arises, the speakers of that language apparently have little trouble meeting the need.

Most cognitive scientists no longer accept the linguistic-relativity hypothesis (Pinker, 2007). For one thing, adults use images and abstract logical propositions, as well as words, as units of thought. Infants, moreover, display considerable intelligence before they have learned to speak. Another criticism is that a language's vocabulary suggests the range of concepts that the speakers of the language have traditionally found important, not their cognitive limits. For example, if people were magically lifted from the 19th century and placed inside an airplane, they probably would not think they were flying inside a bird or a large insect, even if their language lacked a word for airplane.

Language Development: The 2-Year Explosion

Question 14: How does language develop? Languages around the world develop in a specific sequence of steps beginning with the *prelinguistic* vocalizations of crying, cooing, and babbling. These sounds are not symbols. That is, they do not represent objects or events. Therefore, they are *pre*linguistic, not linguistic.

PRELINGUISTIC VOCALIZATIONS: THE MEANING OF AN ABSENCE OF MEANING As parents are well aware, newborn children have one inborn, highly effective form of verbal expression: crying—and more crying. **Truth or Fiction Revisited:** But crying does not represent language; it is a prelinguistic event. During the 2nd month, babies begin *cooing,* another form of prelinguistic expression which appears to be linked to feelings of pleasure. By the 5th or 6th month, children begin to *babble.* Children babble sounds that occur in many languages, including the throaty German *ch,* the clicks of certain African languages, and rolling *r*'s. Babies' babbling frequently combines consonants and vowels, as in "ba," "ga," and sometimes, the much-valued "dada" (McCardle et al., 2009). "Dada" at first is purely coincidental (sorry, dads), despite the family's delight over its appearance.

Babbling, like crying and cooing, is inborn and prelinguistic. Deaf children babble, and children from cultures whose languages sound very different all seem to babble the same sounds (Hoff, 2005). But children single out the sounds used in the home within a few months. By the age of 9 or 10 months, they are repeating them regularly, and foreign sounds are dropping out. In fact, early experience in acquiring the phonemes (that is, meaningful units of sound) native to one's own language can make it difficult to pronounce and even discriminate the phonemes used in other languages later in life (Iverson et al., 2003).

The first word—which represents *linguistic* speech—is typically spoken between 11 and 13 months, but a range of 8 to 18 months is normal (McCardle et al., 2009; Tamis-LeMonda et al., 2006). Parents often miss the first word because it is not pronounced clearly or because pronunciation varies from one usage to the next. The growth of vocabulary is slow at first. It may take children 3 to 4 months to achieve a 10-word vocabulary after they have spoken their first word. By about 18 months, children are producing a couple of dozen words.

DEVELOPMENT OF GRAMMAR The first linguistic utterances of children around the globe are single words that can express complex meanings. These initial utterances of children are called **holophrases.** For example, *mama* may be used by the child to signify meanings as varied as "There goes Mama," "Come here, Mama," and "You are my Mama." Similarly, *cat* can signify "There is a cat," "That stuffed animal looks just like my cat," or "I want you to give me my cat right now!" Most children readily teach their parents what they intend by augmenting their holophrases with gestures, intonations, and reinforcers. That is, they act delighted when parents do as requested and howl when they do not.

Crying: A Prelinguistic Event Although crying can effectively communicate discomfort and the desire to have a caregiver present—now—cries do not possess symbols and are thus not an example of true language.

Holophrase A single word used to express complex meanings.

Toward the end of the 2nd year, children begin to speak two-word sentences. These sentences are termed *telegraphic speech* because they resemble telegrams. Telegrams cut out the "unnecessary" words. "Home Tuesday" might stand for "I expect to be home on Tuesday." Two-word utterances seem to appear at about the same time in the development of all languages (Saffran, 2009; Slobin, 1983). Two-word utterances are brief but grammatically correct. The child says, "Sit chair" to tell a parent to sit in a chair, not "Chair sit." The child says, "My shoe," not "Shoe my," to show possession. "Mommy go" means Mommy is leaving. "Go Mommy" expresses the wish for Mommy to go away.

There are different kinds of two-word utterances. Some, for example, contain nouns or pronouns and verbs ("Daddy sit"). Others contain verbs and objects ("Hit ball"). The sequence of emergence of the various kinds of two-word utterances is also apparently the same in all languages—languages as diverse as English, Luo (an African tongue), German, Russian, and Turkish (Slobin, 1983). The invariance of this sequence has implications for theories of language development, as we will see.

OVERREGULARIZATION: ON FOLLOWING THE (APPARENT) RULES Overregularization is an important development for understanding the roles of nature and nurture in language development (E. V. Clark & Nikitina, 2009). In English, we add *d* or *ed* to make the past tense of regular verbs and *s* or *z* sounds to make regular nouns plural. Thus, *walk* becomes *walked,* and *look* becomes *looked. Cat* becomes *cats,* and *doggy* becomes *doggies.* There are also irregular verbs and nouns. For example, *see* becomes *saw, sit* becomes *sat,* and *go* becomes *went. Sheep* remains *sheep* (plural), and *child* becomes *children.*

At first, children learn irregular verbs and nouns by imitating older people. Two-year-olds tend to form them correctly—at first! Then they become aware of the grammatical rules for forming the past tense and plurals. As a result, they tend to make charming errors (Pinker, 1997). A 3- to 5-year-old, for example, may be more likely to say "I seed it" than "I saw it," and more likely to say "Mommy sitted down" than "Mommy sat down." They are likely to talk about the "gooses" and "sheeps" they "seed" on the farm and about all the "childs" they ran into at the playground. This tendency to regularize the irregular is what is meant by overregularization. **Truth or Fiction Revisited:** Young children do say things like "Daddy goed away" and "Mommy sitted down" because they understand rules of grammar.

Should parents be concerned about overregularization? Not at all. Overregularization reflects knowledge of grammar, not faulty language development. In another year or two, *mouses* will be boringly transformed into *mice,* and Mommy will no longer have *sitted* down. Parents might as well enjoy overregularization while they can.

OTHER DEVELOPMENTS By the age of 6, children's vocabularies have expanded to 10,000 words, give or take a few thousand. (Vocabulary can grow for a lifetime.) By 7 to 9, most children realize that words can have more than one meaning, and they are entertained by riddles and jokes that require some sophistication with language ("What's black and white and read all over?").

Nature and Nurture in Language Development: Why Houseplants Don't Talk

Billions of children have acquired the languages spoken by their parents and passed them down, with minor changes, from generation to generation. Language development, like many other areas of development, apparently reflects the interactions between nature and nurture. **Question 15: What are the roles of nature and nurture in language development?**

LEARNING THEORY AND LANGUAGE DEVELOPMENT: INFANT HEAR, INFANT SAY? Learning theorists see language as developing according to laws of learning (Hoff, 2005). They usually refer to the concepts of *imitation* and *reinforcement.* From a social-cognitive perspective, parents serve as *models.* Children learn language, at least in part, through observation and imitation. Many words,

Overregularization The application of regular grammatical rules for forming inflections (e.g., past tense and plurals) to irregular verbs and nouns.

One way that adults attempt to prompt the language development of young children is through the use of baby talk, or "motherese," referred to more technically as *infant-directed speech (IDS)* (Meltzoff & Brooks, 2009; Singh et al., 2009). Motherese is a limiting term because grandparents, fathers, siblings, and unrelated people have also been observed using IDS (Braarud & Stormark, 2008). Moreover, women (but usually not men) often talk to their pets as if they were infants (Prato-Previde et al., 2006). Infant-directed speech is used in languages as diverse as Arabic, English, Comanche, Italian, French, German, Xhosa (an African tongue), Japanese, Mandarin Chinese, and even a Thai sign language (Lee et al., 2009; Nonaka, 2004).

Researchers have found that IDS has the following characteristics (Braarud & Stormark, 2008; Meltzoff & Brooks, 2009):

- It is spoken more slowly and at a higher pitch than speech addressed to adults. There are distinct pauses between ideas.

- Sentences are brief, and adults try to speak in a grammatically correct manner.

- Sentences are simple in **syntax**. The focus is on nouns, verbs, and just a few modifiers.

- Key words are placed at the ends of sentences and spoken in a higher and louder voice.

- The diminutive morpheme *y* is frequently added to nouns. *Dad* becomes *Daddy,* and *horse* becomes *horsey.*

- Adults repeat sentences several times, sometimes using minor variations, as in "Show me your nose." "Where is your nose?" "Can you touch your nose?" Adults also rephrase children's utterances to expand children's awareness of

their expressive opportunities. If the child says, "Baby shoe," the mother may reply, "Yes, that's your shoe. Shall Mommy put the shoe on baby's foot?"

- It includes duplication. *Yummy* becomes *yummy-yummy. Daddy* may alternate with *Da-da.*

- Much IDS focuses on naming objects (Meltzoff & Brooks, 2009). Vocabulary is concrete and refers to the child's environment. For example, stuffed lions may be called "kitties."

- Objects may be overdescribed with compound labels. Rabbits may become "bunny rabbits," and cats may become "kitty cats." Users of IDS try to ensure that they are using at least one label that the child will recognize.

- Parents speak for the children, as in "Is baby tired?" "Oh, we're so tired." "We want to take our nap now, don't we?" Parents seem to be helping children express themselves by offering them models of sentences they can use.

Does IDS encourage communication and foster language development? Research supports its use. Infants as young as 2 days old prefer IDS to adult talk (N. A. Smith & Trainor, 2008). The short, simple sentences and high pitch are more likely to produce a response from the child and enhance vocabulary development than complex sentences and those spoken in a lower pitch (Singh et al., 2009). Children who hear their utterances repeated and recast seem to learn from adults who are modeling new expressions (Singh et al., 2009; N. A. Smith & Trainor, 2008). Repetition of children's vocalizations appears to encourage vocalizing.

© Rubberball

"Since all normal humans talk but no house pets or house plants do, no matter how pampered, heredity must be involved in language. But since a child growing up in Japan speaks Japanese whereas the same child brought up in California would speak English, the environment is also crucial."

STEVEN PINKER, *THE LANGUAGE INSTINCT,* 1994

especially nouns and verbs (including irregular verbs), are apparently learned by imitation.

As explained earlier, at first children accurately repeat the irregular verb forms they observe (imitation), but later they begin to overregularize irregular verb forms as a result of their gaining knowledge of rules of grammar. This first, accurate repetition of irregular verb forms can probably be explained by modeling, but modeling does not explain all the events involved in learning. Nor does imitative learning explain how children come to utter phrases and sentences they have *not* observed. Parents, for example, are unlikely to model utterances such as "Bye-bye sock" and "All gone Daddy," but children say them.

Learning theory cannot account for the unchanging sequence of language development and the spurts in children's language acquisition. Even the types of two-word utterances emerge in a consistent pattern in diverse cultures. Although timing differs from one child to another, the types of questions used, passive versus active sentences, and so on all emerge in the same order.

THE NATIVIST APPROACH TO LANGUAGE DEVELOPMENT: SPEAKING FROM THE GENES? The nativist theory of language development holds that innate factors—which make up children's *nature*—cause children to attend to and acquire language in certain ways. From this perspective, children bring neurological "prewiring" to language learning (A. Clark & Misyak, 2009; Pinker, 2007).

According to **psycholinguistic theory**, language acquisition involves the interaction of environmental influences—such as exposure to parental speech and reinforcement—and the inborn tendency to acquire language. Noam Chomsky (see Cherniak, 2009) refers to the inborn tendency as a **language acquisition device (LAD)**. Evidence for an LAD is found in the universality of human language abilities and in the specific sequence of language development (Cherniak, 2009; A. Clark & Misyak, 2009).

The LAD prepares the nervous system to learn grammar. On the surface, languages differ a great deal. However, the LAD serves children all over the world because languages share what Chomsky refers to as a *universal grammar*—an underlying set of rules for turning ideas into sentences (Pinker, 2007). Consider an analogy with computers: According to psycholinguistic theory, the universal grammar that resides in the LAD is the same as a computer's basic operating system (M. C. Baker, 2001). The particular language that a child learns to use is the same as a word-processing program.

In the following section, we see that some aspects of language development—particularly vocabulary development—are strongly related to intelligence.

"Colorless green ideas sleep furiously."

NOAM CHOMSKY (DEMONSTRATING THAT FAMILIAR SYNTAX CAN MAKE EVEN NONSENSICAL STATEMENTS SOUND AS IF THEY ARE LADEN WITH MEANING)

Syntax The rules for forming grammatical phrases and sentences in a language.

LearningConnections • LANGUAGE: OF SIGNS, GRAMMAR, AND MANY THINGS

ACTIVE REVIEW (6) Apes (have or have not?) been taught to use symbols to communicate. (7) Language is the communication of thoughts and feelings by means of symbols that are arranged according to rules of _____. (8) According to the _____-relativity hypothesis, language structures (and limits) the way we perceive the world. (9) _____ are one-word utterances that have the meanings of sentences. (10) Children's use of sentences such as "I standed up" and "Mommy sitted down" are examples of _____. (11) Chomsky refers to the inborn tendency to develop language as a language _____ device (LAD).

REFLECT AND RELATE Have you ever known someone to claim that a pet could "speak" or "understand" English or another language? Did the pet really speak? Did the pet understand language? What was the nature of the evidence?

CRITICAL THINKING Critical thinkers pay close attention to the definitions of terms. How do scientists distinguish true language from the communication systems of lower animals?

 Go to Psychology CourseMate at **www.cengagebrain.com** for an interactive version of these questions.

INTELLIGENCE: THE MOST CONTROVERSIAL CONCEPT IN PSYCHOLOGY?

Intelligence may well be the most controversial topic in psychology. **Question 16: Just what is intelligence?** The concept of intelligence is closely related to thinking. Whereas thinking involves the understanding and manipulating of information, intelligence is considered to be the underlying ability to understand the world and cope with its challenges (Cornoldi, 2006; Sternberg et al., 2005). That is, intelligence is seen as making thinking possible.

Although these concepts overlap, psychologists tend to be concerned with *how* we think, but people are more concerned with *how much* intelligence we have. At an

Psycholinguistic theory The view that language learning involves an interaction between environmental factors and an inborn tendency to acquire language.

Language acquisition device (LAD) In psycholinguistic theory, neural "prewiring" that facilitates the child's learning of grammar.

Intelligence A general mental capability that involves the ability to reason, plan, solve problems, think abstractly, comprehend complex ideas, learn quickly, and learn from experience.

early age, we gain impressions of how intelligent or bright we are compared to other people.

Intelligence provides the basis for academic achievements. It allows people to think—to understand complex ideas, reason, and solve problems—and to learn from experience and adapt to the environment (Gottfredson & Saklofske, 2009). As we see in architecture and space travel, intelligence also permits people to create environments. Although intelligence, like thinking, cannot be directly seen or touched, psychologists tie the concept to achievements such as school performance and occupational status (Nisbett, 2009; Pind et al., 2003).

Psychologists have engaged in thousands of studies on intelligence, yet they do not quite agree on what it is. They have therefore developed theories to help them understand and define intelligence. In this section, we discuss these theories of the nature of intelligence. Then we see how intelligence is measured and discuss group differences in intelligence. Finally, we examine the determinants of intelligence: heredity and the environment. Along the way, you'll see why intelligence may just be the most controversial concept in the science of psychology. **Question 17: What are the various theories of intelligence?**

Theories of Intelligence

Theories of intelligence have taken the concept apart and then put it back together again. But like Humpty Dumpty, the pieces don't necessarily fit together easily. Let's begin with factor theories.

FACTOR THEORIES Many investigators have viewed intelligence as consisting of one or more *factors*. Factor theories argue that intelligence is made up of a number of mental abilities, ranging from one kind of ability to hundreds.

In 1904, British psychologist Charles Spearman suggested that the behaviors we consider intelligent have a common underlying factor. He labeled this factor *g,* for "general intelligence," or broad reasoning and problem-solving abilities. Spearman supported his view by noting that people rarely score very high in one area (such as knowledge of the meaning of words) and very low in another (such as the ability to compute numbers). People who excel in one area are also likely to excel in others. But he also noted that even the most capable people are relatively superior in some areas—such as music or business or poetry—as compared to others. For this reason, he suggested that specific, or *s,* factors account for specific abilities.

To test his views, Spearman developed **factor analysis**—a statistical technique that allows researchers to determine which items on tests seem to be measuring the same things. When he compared relationships among test scores of verbal, mathematical, and spatial reasoning, Spearman repeatedly found evidence supporting the existence of *s* factors. The evidence for *g* was more limited. Interestingly, more than 100 years later, researchers continue to find a key role for *g* in performance on many intelligence tests (Gottfredson & Saklofske, 2009). A number of cognitive psychologists (e.g., Colom et al., 2003; Saggino et al., 2006) find evidence that connects *g* with *working memory*— that is, the ability to keep various elements of a problem in mind at once. Psychologists continue to use the term *g* in research, speaking, for example, of the extent to which they believe a particular kind of test, such as the SAT, measures *g* (Lubinski & Benbow, 2006).

American psychologist Louis Thurstone (1938) used factor analysis with tests of specific abilities and concluded that Spearman had oversimplified intelligence. Thurstone's data suggested the presence of nine specific factors, which he labeled **primary mental abilities** (see Table 7.1 ■). Thurstone's primary mental abilities contain the types of items measured on the most widely used intelligence tests today. The question remains as to whether his primary mental abilities are distinct or whether they are different ways of assessing *g*.

THE THEORY OF MULTIPLE INTELLIGENCES Thurstone wrote about various factors, or components, of intelligence. Howard Gardner's (1983/1993, 2009) **theory of multiple intelligences** proposes, instead, that there are a number of *intelligences*, not just one. Gardner refers to each kind of intelligence in his theory as "an intelligence" because they can differ so much (see Figure 7.6 ■). He also believes that each kind

g Spearman's symbol for general intelligence, which he believed underlay more specific abilities.

s Spearman's symbol for *specific* factors, or *s factors,* which he believed accounted for individual abilities.

Factor analysis A statistical technique that allows researchers to determine the relationships among a large number of items, such as test items.

Primary mental abilities According to Thurstone, the basic abilities that make up intelligence.

Theory of multiple intelligences Gardner's view that there are several intelligences, not just one.

TABLE 7.1 ■ Primary Mental Abilities, According to Thurstone

Ability	Definition
Visual and spatial abilities	Visualizing forms and spatial relationships
Perceptual speed	Grasping perceptual details rapidly, perceiving similarities and differences between stimuli
Numerical ability	Computing numbers
Verbal meaning	Knowing the meanings of words
Memory	Recalling information (words, sentences, etc.)
Word fluency	Thinking of words quickly (rhyming, doing crossword puzzles, etc.)
Deductive reasoning	Deriving examples from general rules
Inductive reasoning	Inferring general rules from examples

of intelligence is based in a different part of the brain. Two of these intelligences are familiar ones: language ability and logical-mathematical ability. However, Gardner also refers to bodily-kinesthetic talents (of the sort shown by dancers and athletes), musical talent, spatial-relations skills, and two kinds of personal intelligence: awareness of one's own inner feelings and sensitivity to other people's feelings. Gardner (2001) more recently added naturalist intelligence and existential intelligence to his list. *Naturalist intelligence* refers to the ability to look at natural events, such as kinds of animals and plants or the stars above and to develop insights into their nature and the laws that govern their behavior. *Existential intelligence* means dealing with the larger philosophical issues of life. According to Gardner, one can compose symphonies or advance mathematical theory yet be average in, say, language and personal skills. (Are not some academic "geniuses" foolish in their personal lives?)

Figure 7.6 ■ Gardner's Theory of Multiple Intelligences According to Gardner, there are several intelligences, not one, each based in a different area of the brain. Language ability and logic are familiar aspects of intelligence. But Gardner also refers to bodily talents, musical ability, spatial-relations skills, and two kinds of personal intelligence—sensitivity to one's own feelings (intrapersonal sensitivity) and sensitivity to the feelings of others (interpersonal sensitivity) as intelligences. Gardner's critics ask whether such special talents are truly "intelligences" or specific talents.

Critics of Gardner's view agree that people function more intelligently in some aspects of life than in others. They also agree that many people have special talents, such as bodily-kinesthetic talents, even if their overall intelligence is average. But they question whether such special intellectual skills are best thought of as intelligences or, rather, special talents (Neisser et al., 1996). Language skills, reasoning ability, and the ability to solve math problems seem to be more closely related than musical or gymnastic talent to what most people mean by intelligence. If people have no musical ability, do we really think of them as *unintelligent*? It is difficult to define intelligence in a way that everyone agrees on.

THE TRIARCHIC THEORY OF INTELLIGENCE Psychologist Robert Sternberg (2000; Sternberg et al., 2006) has constructed a three-pronged, or **triarchic, theory of intelligence** that resembles a view proposed by the Greek philosopher Aristotle (Tigner & Tigner, 2000). The three prongs include *analytical, creative,* and *practical intelligence* (see Figure 7.7 ■).

Analytical intelligence is similar to Aristotle's "theoretical intelligence" and can be defined as academic ability. It enables us to solve problems and acquire new knowledge. It is the type of intelligence measured by standard intelligence tests. Problem-solving skills include encoding information, combining and comparing bits of information, and generating a solution. Consider Sternberg's analogy problem:

Washington is to *1* as *Lincoln* is to (a) 5, (b) 10, (c) 15, (d) 50?

To solve the analogy, we must first correctly *encode* the elements—*Washington, 1,* and *Lincoln*—by identifying them and comparing them to other information. We can first encode *Washington* and *Lincoln* as the names of presidents and then try to combine *Washington* and *1* in a meaningful manner. (There are other possibilities: Both are also the names of memorials and cities, for example.) If we do encode the names as presidents, two possibilities quickly come to mind. Washington was the first president, and his picture is on the $1 bill. We can then generate two possible solutions and try them out. First, was Lincoln the 5th, 10th, 15th, or 50th president? Second, on what bill is Lincoln's picture found? (Do you need to consult a history book or peek into your wallet at this point?) The answer is (a) 5, because Lincoln's likeness is found on the $5 bill. (He was the nation's 16th president, not the 15th.)

Triarchic theory of intelligence Sternberg's theory that intelligence has three prongs, consisting of analytical, creative, and practical intelligence ("street smarts").

Analytical intelligence
(Academic ability)
Abilities to solve problems, compare and contrast, judge, evaluate, and criticize

Creative intelligence
(Creativity and insight)
Abilities to invent, discover, suppose, or theorize

Practical intelligence
("Street smarts")
Abilities to adapt to the demands of one's environment and apply knowledge in practical situations

Figure 7.7 ■ Sternberg's Theory of Intelligence According to Robert Sternberg, there are three types of intelligence: analytical (academic ability), creative, and practical ("street smarts"). Psychologists discuss the relationships between intelligence and creativity, but within Sternberg's model, creativity is a type of intellectual functioning.

Creative intelligence is similar to Aristotle's "productive intelligence" and is defined by the abilities to cope with novel situations and generate many possible solutions to problems. It is creative to quickly relate novel situations to familiar situations (that is, to perceive similarities and differences). Psychologists who consider creativity to be separate from analytical intelligence or academic ability find there is only a moderate relationship between academic ability and creativity (Simonton, 2009). However, to Sternberg, creativity *is* a form of intelligence.

Aristotle and Sternberg both speak of *practical intelligence*, or "street smarts." **Truth or Fiction Revisited:** It is therefore true that street smarts are a sign of intelligence—at least according to Aristotle and Sternberg. Practical intelligence enables people to deal with people, including difficult people, and to meet the demands of their environment. For example, keeping a job by adapting one's behavior to the employer's requirements is adaptive. But if the employer is making unreasonable demands, finding a more suitable job is also adaptive. Street smarts appear to help people get by in the real world, especially with other people, but are not particularly predictive of academic success (Heng, 2000).

> *"Intelligence is the ability to take in information from the world and to find patterns in that information that allow you to organize your perceptions and understand the external world."*
>
> BRIAN GREENE, PHYSICIST

A CLOSER LOOK

Emotional Intelligence and Social Intelligence

Psychologists Peter Salovey and John Mayer developed the *theory of emotional intelligence*, which was popularized by the *New York Times* writer Daniel Goleman (1995). The theory holds that social and emotional skills are a form of intelligence, just as academic skills are (Mayer et al., 2008; Salovey et al., 2008). Emotional intelligence resembles two of Gardner's intelligences—awareness of one's inner feelings and sensitivity to the feelings of others. It also involves control, or regulation, of one's emotions. The theory suggests that self-awareness and social awareness are best learned during childhood. Failure to develop emotional intelligence is connected with childhood depression and aggression.

Is emotional intelligence a form of intelligence? Psychologist Ulric Neisser (1997b) wrote, "The skills that Goleman describes . . . are certainly important for determining life outcomes, but nothing is to be gained by calling them forms of intelligence."

Ten years later, Goleman stirred the controversy anew by returning with another best seller, *Social Intelligence* (2006). This time around, Goleman described how an American commander prevented a confrontation between his troops and an Iraqi mob by ordering the troops to point their rifles at the ground and smile. Although there was a language barrier, the aiming of the weapons downward and the smiles were a form of universal language that was understood by the Iraqis, who then smiled back. Conflict was avoided. According to Goleman, the commander had shown *social intelligence*—the ability to read the Iraqis' social concerns and solve the social problem by coming up with a useful social response. Social intelligence, like emotional intelligence, also corresponds to Gardner's intelligences, and critics ask whether it brings anything new to the table (Landy, 2006).

Goleman (and Gardner before him) suggests that we may be genetically "prewired" to connect with other people. The purpose of social intelligence, as Goleman sees it, is not to manipulate other people but rather to understand them, feel what they are feeling, and develop mutually nourishing relationships with them.

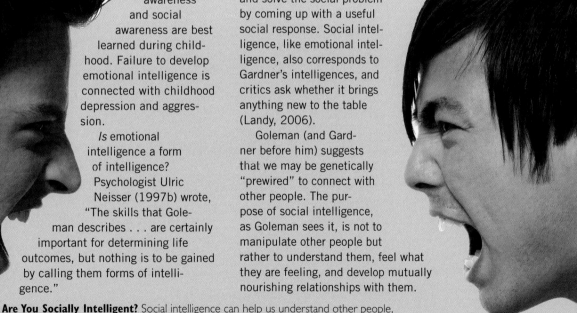

Are You Socially Intelligent? Social intelligence can help us understand other people, feel what they are feeling, and develop productive relationships with them.

© Mike Kemp/Rubberball

There are thus many views of what intelligence is and how many kinds of intelligence there may be. We do not yet have the final word on the nature of intelligence, but I would like to share Linda Gottfredson's definition:

"[Intelligence is] a very general mental capability that, among other things, involves the ability to reason, plan, solve problems, think abstractly, comprehend complex ideas, learn quickly and learn from experience. It is not merely book learning, a narrow academic skill, or test-taking smarts. Rather it reflects a broader and deeper capability for comprehending our surroundings— 'catching on,' 'making sense' of things, or 'figuring out what to do.'"

LINDA GOTTFREDSON IN NISBETT, 2009, P. 4

Creativity and Intelligence

Think of artists, musicians, poets, scientists who devise innovative research methods, and other creative individuals. **Question 18: What is creativity, and how is it related to intelligence?**

The concept of creativity has been difficult to define, just as the concept of intelligence has been. One issue is whether creativity is distinct from intelligence or is, as

CONCEPT REVIEW 7.1   THEORIES OF INTELLIGENCE

Theory	Basic Information	Comments
General versus specific factors (main proponent: Charles Spearman) © Archives of the History of American Psychology, The Center for the History of Psychology—The University of Akron	• Spearman created factor analysis to study intelligence. • There is strong evidence for the general factor (*g*) in intelligence. • *s* factors are specific abilities, skills, talents.	• Concept of *g* remains in use today—a century later.
Primary mental abilities (proponent: Louis Thurstone) © George Skadding/Time & Life Pictures/Getty Images	• Thurstone used factor analysis. • There are many "primary" abilities. • All abilities and factors are academically oriented.	• Other researchers (e.g., Guilford) claim to have found hundreds of factors. • The more factors that are claimed, the more they overlap.
Triarchic theory (proponent: Robert Sternberg) © Robert Sternberg/Tufts University	• Intelligence has three prongs—analytical, creative, and practical intelligence. • Analytical intelligence is analogous to academic ability.	• The theory coincides with the views of Aristotle. • Critics do not view creativity as a component of intelligence.
Multiple intelligences (proponent: Howard Gardner) © 2003 J. Gardner	• Gardner theorized distinct "intelligences." • Intelligences include academic intelligences, personal and social intelligences, talents, and philosophical intelligences. • The theory posits different bases in the brain for different intelligences.	• Proponents continue to expand the number of intelligences. • Critics see little value to theorizing "intelligences" versus aspects of intelligence. • Most critics consider musical and bodily skills to be special talents, not intelligences.

Sternberg suggests, a type of intelligence. For example, we would not ask the question, "Do creative people tend to be intelligent?" unless we saw creativity as distinct from intelligence. **Truth or Fiction Revisited:** The answer to whether an intelligent person is creative or a creative person is intelligent thus partly depends on definitions. If you consider creativity an aspect of intelligence, then the two concepts—intelligence and creativity—overlap. But if you think of intelligence as more closely related to academic ability, it is not always true that a highly intelligent person is creative or that a creative person is highly intelligent. Research findings suggest that the relationship between intelligence test scores and standard measures of creativity is only moderate (Simonton, 2009).

Within his triarchic theory, Sternberg (2007) defines **creativity** as the ability to do things that are novel and useful. Other psychologists note that creative people can solve problems to which there are no preexisting solutions, no tried and true formulas (Simonton, 2009). Creative people share a number of qualities (Milgram & Livne, 2006; Sternberg, 2006; Sternberg et al., 2009). They take chances. They refuse to accept limitations. They appreciate art and music. They use common materials to make unique things. They challenge social norms and take unpopular stands. They challenge ideas that other people accept at face value.

Creative problem solving demands divergent rather than convergent thinking. In **convergent thinking**, thought is limited to present facts; the problem solver narrows his or her thinking to find the best solution. (You use convergent thinking to arrive at the right answer to a multiple-choice question.) In **divergent thinking**, the problem solver associates freely to the elements of the problem, allowing "leads" to run a nearly limitless course. (You may use divergent thinking when you are trying to generate ideas to answer an essay question.) Problem solving can involve both kinds of thinking. At first, divergent thinking helps generate many possible solutions. Convergent thinking is then used to select likely solutions and reject others. The nearby Remote Associates Test may afford you insight into your creativity.

Intelligence test questions usually require analytical, convergent thinking to focus in on the one right answer. Tests of creativity determine how flexible a person's thinking is (Simonton, 2009). Here is an item from a test used by Getzels and Jackson (1962) to measure *associative ability*, a factor in creativity: "Write as many meanings as you can for each of the following words: (a) duck; (b) sack; (c) pitch; (d) fair." Those who write several meanings for each word, rather than only one, are rated as potentially more creative.

Another measure of creativity asks people to produce as many words as possible that, say, begin with T and end with N within a minute. Still another item might give

What Is Creativity? How is creativity related to intelligence?

Creativity The ability to generate novel and useful solutions to problems.

Convergent thinking A thought process that narrows in on the single best solution to a problem.

Divergent thinking A thought process that attempts to generate multiple solutions to problems.

SELF-ASSESSMENT
The Remote Associates Test

One aspect of creativity is the ability to associate freely to all aspects of a problem. Creative people take far-flung ideas and piece them together in novel combinations. Following are items from the Remote Associates Test, which measures the ability to find words that are distantly related to stimulus words. For each set of three words, try to think of a fourth word that is related to all three words. For example, the words *rough, resistance,* and *beer* suggest the word *draft*, as in the phrases *rough draft, draft resistance,* and *draft beer*. The answers are given in Appendix B.

1. food	catcher	hot	_____
2. hearted	feet	bitter	_____
3. dark	shot	sun	_____
4. Canadian	golf	sandwich	_____
5. tug	gravy	show	_____

6. attorney	self	spending	_____
7. magic	pitch	power	_____
8. arm	coal	peach	_____
9. type	ghost	story	_____

people a minute to classify a list of names in as many ways as possible. How many ways can you group the following names?

MARTHA   PAUL   JEFFRY   SALLY   PABLO   JOAN

One way would be to classify them as men's names or women's names. Another would be English names versus Spanish names. Still another would be six-letter names, five-letter names, and four-letter names. The ability to do well on these kinds of items is connected with scores on standard intelligence tests, but only moderately so.

Now that we have begun speaking of scores on intelligence tests, let's see how psychologists go about measuring intelligence. We will also see how psychologists attempt to *validate* their measures of intelligence—that is, how they try to demonstrate that they are in fact measuring intelligence.

The Measurement of Intelligence

Although psychologists disagree about the nature of intelligence, laypeople and educators are concerned with how much intelligence people have because the issue affects educational and occupational choices. In this section, we consider two of the most widely used intelligence tests.

THE STANFORD–BINET INTELLIGENCE SCALE Many of the concepts of psychology have their origins in common sense. The commonsense notion that academic achievement depends on children's intelligence led Alfred Binet and Theodore Simon to invent measures of intelligence.

Question 19: What is the Stanford–Binet Intelligence Scale? Early in the 20th century, the French public school system was looking for a test that could identify children who were unlikely to benefit from regular classroom instruction. If these children were identified, they could be given special attention. The first version of that test, the Binet–Simon scale, came into use in 1905. Since that time, it has undergone extensive revision and refinement. The current version is the *Stanford–Binet Intelligence Scale (SBIS)*.

Binet assumed that intelligence increases with age, so older children should get more items right than younger children. He therefore included a series of age-graded questions, as in Table 7.2 ■, arranged in order of difficulty.

The Binet–Simon scale yielded a score called a **mental age (MA)**. The MA shows the intellectual level at which a child is functioning. For example, a child with an MA of 6 is functioning intellectually like the average 6-year-old. In taking the test, children earned "months" of credit for each correct answer. Their MA was determined by adding up the years and months of credit they attained.

Louis Terman adapted the Binet–Simon scale for use with American children at Stanford University. The first version of the resultant Stanford–Binet Intelligence Scale (SBIS) was published in 1916. The SBIS included more items than the original test and was used with children aged 2 to 16. It also yielded an **intelligence quotient (IQ)** rather than an MA. As a result, American educators developed interest in learning the IQs of their pupils. The SBIS is used today with children from the age of 2 upward and with adults.

The IQ reflects the relationship between a child's mental age and his or her actual or *chronological age (CA)*. Use of this ratio reflects the fact that the same MA score has different implications for children of different ages. That is, an MA of 8 is an above-average score for a 6-year-old but below average for a 10-year-old. In 1912, German psychologist Wilhelm Stern suggested the IQ as a way to deal with this problem. Stern computed IQ using the formula

$$IQ = \frac{\text{Mental Age (MA)}}{\text{Chronological Age (CA)}} \times 100$$

Mental age (MA) The accumulated months of credit that a person earns on the Stanford–Binet Intelligence Scale.

Intelligence quotient (IQ) (a) Originally, a ratio obtained by dividing a child's score (or mental age) on an intelligence test by chronological age. (b) Generally, a score on an intelligence test.

According to this formula, a child with an MA of 6 and a CA of 6 would have an IQ of 100. Younger children who can handle intellectual problems as well as older children have IQs above 100. For instance, an 8-year-old who does as well on the SBIS as the average 10-year-old would attain an IQ of 125. Children who do not answer as many items correctly as other children of the same age attain MAs lower than their CAs. Thus, their IQ scores are below 100.

TABLE 7.2 ■ Items Similar to Those on the Stanford–Binet Intelligence Scale

Level (Years)	Item
2	1. Children show knowledge of basic vocabulary words by identifying parts of a doll, such as the mouth, ears, and hair. 2. Children show counting and spatial skills along with visual-motor coordination by building a tower of four blocks to match a model.
4	1. Children show word fluency and categorical thinking by filling in the missing words when they are asked questions such as "Father is a man; mother is a _____?" "Hamburgers are hot; ice cream is _____?" 2. Children show comprehension by answering correctly when they are asked questions such as "Why do people have automobiles?" "Why do people have medicine?"
9	1. Children can point out verbal absurdities, as in this question: "In an old cemetery, scientists unearthed a skull which they think was that of George Washington when he was only 5 years of age. What is silly about that?" 2. Children display fluency with words, as shown by answering these questions: "Can you tell me a number that rhymes with snore?" "Can you tell me a color that rhymes with glue?"
Adult	1. Adults show knowledge of the meanings of words and conceptual thinking by correctly explaining the differences between word pairs like "sickness and misery," "house and home," and "integrity and prestige." 2. Adults show spatial skills by correctly answering questions like "If a car turned to the right to head north, in what direction was it heading before it turned?"

IQ scores on the SBIS today are derived by comparing the test-takers' results to those of other people of the same age. People who answer more items correctly than the average for people of the same age attain IQ scores above 100. People who answer fewer items correctly than the average for their age attain scores below 100. **Truth or Fiction Revisited:** Therefore, two children can answer exactly the same items on an intelligence test correctly, yet one can be above average and the other below average in IQ. This is because the ages of the children may differ. The more intelligent child would be the younger of the two.

THE WECHSLER SCALES David Wechsler developed a series of scales for use with children and adults. **Question 20: How do the Wechsler scales of intelligence differ from the Stanford–Binet?** The Wechsler scales group test questions into a number of separate subtests (see Figure 7.8 ■). Each subtest measures a different intellectual task. For this reason, the test shows how well a person does on one type of task (such as defining words) compared with another (such as using blocks to construct geometric designs). In this way, the Wechsler scales highlight children's relative strengths and weaknesses as well as measure overall intellectual functioning.

© SSPL/The Image Works

The Stanford–Binet Intelligence Scale In 1905, Alfred Binet and Theodore Simon in France introduced the idea of measuring intelligence. This version of the test was produced in 1937 by Lewis Terman and Maude Merrill in the United States and was specifically designed for younger children.

Wechsler described some of his scales as measuring *verbal* tasks and others as assessing *performance* tasks. In general, verbal subtests require knowledge of verbal concepts, whereas performance subtests require familiarity with spatial-relations concepts. But it is not that easy to distinguish between the two groupings. For example, recognizing the name of the object being assembled (the puzzle) in subtest 11 is a sign of word fluency and general knowledge as well as of spatial-relations ability, and it helps the person piece together the puzzle more rapidly. In any event, Wechsler's scales permit the computation of verbal and performance IQs. Nontechnically oriented college

Figure 7.8 ■ Items Similar to Those on the Wechsler Adult Intelligence Scale

Verbal Subtests

1. *Information:* "What is the capital of the United States?" "Who was Shakespeare?"
2. *Comprehension:* "Why do we have ZIP codes?" "What does 'A stitch in time saves 9' mean?"
3. *Arithmetic:* "If 3 candy bars cost 25 cents, how much will 18 candy bars cost?"

4. *Similarities:* "How are good and bad alike?" "How are peanut butter and jelly alike?"
5. *Digit span:* Repeating a series of numbers forwards and backwards.
6. *Vocabulary:* "What does canal mean?"

Performance Subtests

7. *Digit Symbol:* Learning and drawing meaningless figures that are associated with numbers. The faster a person memorizes the correlations, the higher he or she scores on this subtest.

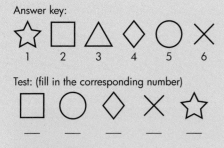

8. *Picture completion:* Pointing to the missing part of a picture.

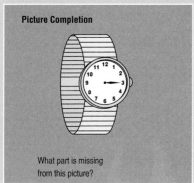

9. *Block design:* Copying pictures of geometric designs using multicolored blocks.

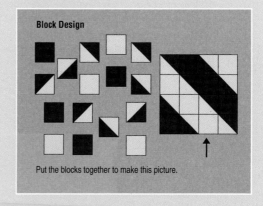

10. *Picture arrangement:* Arranging cartoon pictures in sequence so that they tell a meaningful story.

11. *Object assembly:* Putting pieces of a puzzle together so that they form a meaningful object.

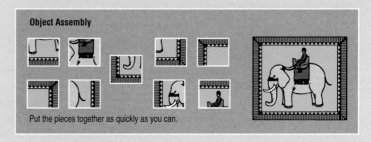

students often attain higher verbal than performance IQs. Less-well-educated people often obtain higher performance than verbal IQs.

Wechsler also introduced the concept of the *deviation IQ*. Instead of dividing mental age by chronological age to compute an IQ, he based IQ scores on how a person's answers compared with those given by people in the same age group. The average test result at any age level is defined as an IQ score of 100. Wechsler distributed IQ scores so that the middle 50% were defined as the "broad average range" of 90 to 110.

As you can see in (Figure 7.9 ■), IQ scores cluster around the average. Only 4% of the population obtain IQ scores above 130 or below 70.

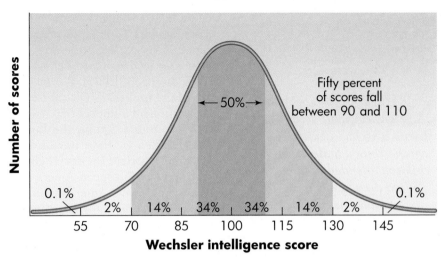

Figure 7.9 ■ Approximate Distribution of IQ Scores Wechsler defined the deviation IQ so that 50% of scores fall within the broad average range of 90 to 110. This bell-shaped curve is referred to as a normal curve by psychologists. It describes the distribution of many traits, including height.

GROUP TESTS The SBIS and Wechsler scales are administered to one person at a time. This one-to-one ratio is optimal because it allows the examiner to observe the test taker closely. Examiners are alerted to factors that impair performance, such as language difficulties, illness, or a noisy or poorly lit room. But large institutions with few trained examiners, such as the public schools and armed forces, require tests that can be administered simultaneously to large groups.

Group tests for children were first developed during World War I. At first, these tests were hailed as remarkable instruments because they helped school administrators place children. However, as the years passed, group tests came under attack because many administrators relied on them exclusively and did not seek other sources of information about children's abilities.

At their best, intelligence tests provide just one source of information about individual children. Numbers alone, and especially IQ scores, cannot adequately define children's special abilities and talents.

THE RELIABILITY AND VALIDITY OF INTELLIGENCE TESTS Over the years, the SBIS and the Wechsler scales have been shown to be reliable and valid. In terms of **reliability**, the scores are rather consistent from testing to testing. (After all, we would not trust a bathroom scale that yielded different results each time we weighed ourselves—unless we had stuffed or starved ourselves between weighings.) This kind of reliability is called *test–retest reliability*.

The tests also show **validity** in that the scores correlate moderately to highly with the variables they are supposed to predict, such as school performance, even though motivation and adjustment to the school setting are also involved (Kaplan & Saccuzzo, 2008; Roid & Tippin, 2009).

"The question of whether there are innate differences in intelligence between blacks and whites goes back more than a thousand years, to the time when the Moors [who were from North Africa] invaded Europe. The Moors speculated that Europeans might be congenitally incapable of abstract thought."

RICHARD E. NESBITT, 2009, P. 93

Differences in Intellectual Functioning

The average IQ score in the United States is very close to 100. Yet for some socioeconomic and ethnic groups in the United States, the average is higher, and for others, it is lower. Questions have also been raised as to whether males or females are more intelligent overall and as to whether there are gender differences in the kinds of intellectual or cognitive skills valued in society. Tests of intellectual functioning have thus been seen as divisive and as maintaining a class system or social order that is based on prejudices and "tradition" as much as on science. In this section, we discuss (a) socioeconomic and ethnic differences and (b) sex differences in cognitive skills.

SOCIOECONOMIC AND ETHNIC DIFFERENCES

There is a body of research suggestive of differences in intelligence—or more precisely, intelligence test scores—between socioeconomic and ethnic groups. **Question 21: What are the socioeconomic and ethnic differences in intelligence?** Lower-class U.S. children obtain IQ scores some 10 to 15 points lower than those obtained

Reliability The consistency of a method of measurements, as, for example, shown by obtaining similar scores on different testing occasions.

Validity The extent to which a method of measurement measures what it is supposed to measure, as, for example, shown by the extent to which test scores predict or are related to an external standard. In the case of intelligence tests, the external standard might involve academic performance.

"I used the phrase 'Asian overachievement' to a Korean friend who had just spent a year in the United States, where his children attended public schools. 'What do you mean by "Asian overachievement"?' he [said].

'You should say "American underachievement"!' He told me that he was astonished when he attended ceremonies at the end of the year for his daughter's school and discovered that an award was given for having done all of the homework assignments. His daughter was one of two recipients of the award. To him, giving an award for doing homework was about as preposterous as giving an award for eating lunch."

RICHARD E. NESBITT, 2009, P. 157

"If the Aborigine drafted an I.Q. test, all of Western civilization would presumably flunk it."

STANLEY GARN

© Nicholas Prior/Stone+/Getty Images

Who's Smart? Asian American children outperform all other groups of American children in school. Is it because they are more intelligent or because they work harder?

by middle- and upper-class children. African American children tend to obtain IQ scores some 15 points lower than those obtained by their European American age-mates (Helms, 2006; Neisser et al., 1996). Latin American and Native American children also tend to score below the norms for European Americans (Neisser et al., 1996; Sternberg, 2007).

Many studies of IQ confuse the factors of social class and ethnicity because disproportionate numbers of African Americans, Latin Americans, and Native Americans are found among the lower socioeconomic classes (Helms, 2006; Nisbett, 2009). When we limit our observations to particular ethnic groups, however, we still find an effect for social class. That is, middle-class European Americans outscore poorer European Americans. Middle-class African Americans, Latin Americans, and Native Americans also outscore poorer members of their own ethnic groups. *Washington Post* columnist Eugene Robinson (2011) notes that "a gap has opened between an educated middle-class black America and a poor, undereducated black America." In addition, he notes, there are recent immigrants with an African background and there are mixed-race individuals. You cannot lump all African Americans together any more than you can lump all European Americans together.

There may also be intellectual differences between Asian Americans and European Americans. Asian Americans, for example, frequently outscore European Americans on the math portion of the Scholastic Aptitude Test. Students in China (Taiwan) and Japan also outscore European Americans on achievement tests in math and science (Nisbett, 2009). In the United States, moreover, people of Asian Indian, Korean, Japanese, Filipino, and Chinese descent are more likely than European Americans, African Americans, and Latin Americans to graduate from high school and complete college (Sternberg, 2007; Xie & Goyette, 2003; Yeh & Chang, 2004). Asian Americans are also highly overrepresented in the most competitive U.S. colleges and universities (Knapp et al., 2011; Liu, 2009). For example, Asian Americans make up 12% of the population of California, but they comprise 41% of the state's top-ranked public university: the University of California at Berkeley.

There are differences in mathematical ability between high school students in Germany and Japan, with Japanese students outscoring German students (Randel et al., 2000). Most psychologists believe that such ethnic differences reflect cultural attitudes toward education rather than inborn racial differences (Nisbett, 2009). That is, Asian students may be more motivated to work in school. Research shows that Chinese and Japanese students and their mothers tend to attribute academic successes to hard work (Bae et al., 2008). European Americans are more likely to attribute their children's academic successes to "natural" ability (Bae et al., 2008).

These ethnic differences lead us to ask, **Question 22: Do intelligence tests contain cultural biases against ethnic minority groups and immigrants?** Are the tests valid when used with ethnic minority groups or people who are poorly educated? Some psychologists and social critics argue that intelligence tests measure many things other than intelligence—including familiarity with the dominant middle-class culture—and motivation to perform well (Steinmayr & Spinath, 2009).

Intelligence tests may be said to have a **cultural bias** because children reared in African American or Latin American neighborhoods are at a cultural disadvantage in intelligence testing (Dotson et al., 2009). Many psychologists, including Raymond B. Cattell (1949) and Florence Goodenough (1926), have tried to construct culture-free intelligence tests. Cattell's *Culture-Fair Intelligence Test (CFIT)* evaluates reasoning through the child's ability to understand and use the rules that govern a progression of geometric designs (see Figure 7.10 ■). Goodenough's *Draw-A-Person test* is based on the premise that children from all cultural backgrounds have had the opportunity to observe people and note the relationships between the parts and the whole. Her instructions simply require children to draw a picture of a man or woman.

Ironically, European American children outperform African American children on "culture-fair" tests (Rushton et al., 2003), perhaps because they are more likely to be familiar with materials such as blocks and pencils and paper. They are more likely than disadvantaged children to have played with blocks (which is relevant to the Cattell test) and to have sketched animals, people, and things (which is relevant to the Goodenough test). Nor have culture-fair tests predicted academic success as well as other intelligence tests. Yet psychologists are still working to develop culture-fair intelligence tests (e.g., Fagan & Holland, 2009).

SEX DIFFERENCES It was once widely believed that males, because of their greater knowledge of world affairs and their skills in science and industry, were more intelligent than females. But these differences did not reflect differences in cognitive ability. Rather, they reflected exclusion of females from world affairs, science, and industry. Indeed, intelligence tests do not show overall gender differences in cognitive abilities (Halpern & LaMay, 2000).

Question 23: Do males and females differ in intellectual functioning? However, studies suggest that girls are somewhat superior to boys in verbal abilities, such as vocabulary, ability to generate sentences and words that are similar in meaning to other words, spelling, knowledge of foreign languages, and pronunciation (Andreano & Cahill, 2009; Lohman & Lakin, 2009). Girls seem to acquire language somewhat faster than boys do. Also, in the United States, more boys than girls have reading problems ranging from reading below grade level to severe disabilities (Brun et al., 2009).

Males seem to do somewhat better than females at manipulating visual images in working memory. Males as a group excel in visual-spatial abilities of the sort used in math, science, and reading maps (Andreano & Cahill, 2009; Yazzie, 2010). One study compared the navigation strategies of 90 male and 104 female university students (Dabbs et al., 1998). In giving directions, men more often referred to miles and directional coordinates (north, south, east, and west). Women were more likely to refer to landmarks and turning right or left. The implication in the Dabbs study, and in recent studies that use computer-generated virtual environments (Castelli et al., 2008; Chai & Jacobs, 2009), is that males have a slight advantage in visualizing distances and coordinates.

For half a century or more, it has been believed that male adolescents generally outperform females in mathematics, and research has tended to support that belief (Collaer & Hill, 2006; Halpern et al., 2007). But a recent study by Janet Hyde and her colleagues (2008) of some 7 million children in second through eleventh grade found no sex differences for performance in mathematics on standardized tests. Nevertheless, most Americans have different expectations for boys and girls, and these expectations may still dissuade some math-proficient girls from entering so-called STEM (science, technology, engineering, and mathematics) fields (Hyde & Mertz, 2009).

Regarding differences in verbal abilities and spatial-relations skills, note that the reported gender differences are *group* differences. There is greater variation in these skills among individuals *within* the groups than between males and females (Halpern, 2003). Millions of females outdistance the "average" male in math and spatial abilities. Men have produced their verbally adept Shakespeares. Moreover, in most cases, differences in cognitive skills are small (Hyde & Plant, 1995).

Thus, there is reason to believe that women have the capacity to be entering STEM fields in greater numbers. So why, in the 21st century in the United States, do women remain underrepresented in STEM fields? According to psychologists Stephen Ceci, Wendy Williams, and Susan Barnett (2009), the reasons are likely as follow:

- Women who are proficient in math are more likely than math-proficient men to prefer careers that do not require skills in math.
- More males than females obtain extremely high scores on the SAT mathematics test and the quantitative reasoning sections of the Graduate Record Exam.
- Women who are proficient in math are more likely than men with this proficiency to have high verbal competence as well, which encourages many such women to choose careers other than those in STEM fields.
- In some STEM fields, women with children find themselves penalized in terms of promotions.

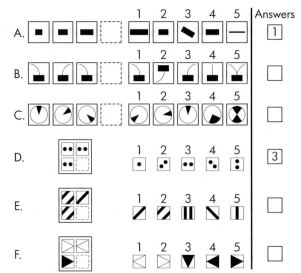

Figure 7.10 ■ Examples of Types of Items Found on CFIT (Cattell's Culture-Fair Intelligence Test)
Culture-fair tests attempt to use items that do not discriminate against ethnic groups on the basis of their cultural background. For each item above, which answer (1, 2, 3, 4, or 5) completes the series? Answers are shown in Appendix B.

Source: Sample Items from Cattell's Culture-Fair Intelligence Test. Copyright © 1949, 1960. Reproduced with permission from the publishers, Hogrefe Ltd, from Culture Fair Scale 2, Test A by R. B. Cattell and A. K. S. Cattell. The UK version of this test is soon to be updated and restandardized.

[Interviewer: Do you think SAT scores define intelligence?] "No. They define the capacity to answer questions on an SAT test."

BRIAN GREENE, PHYSICIST

Cultural bias A factor that provides an advantage for test takers from certain cultural backgrounds, such as using test items that are based on middle-class culture in the United States.

249

TABLE 7.3 ■ Percentage of Bachelor's and Doctoral Degrees Women Earned, by Field of Study: Academic Years 1990–1991, 1995–1996, and 2005–2006

	1990–1991	1995–1996	2005–2006
BACHELOR'S DEGREES			
Health professions & related clinical sciences	83.9	81.5	86.0
Biological & biomedical sciences	50.8	52.6	61.5
Physical sciences & science technologies	31.6	36.0	41.8
Mathematics & statistics	47.3	46.1	45.1
Engineering & engineering technologies	14.1	16.2	17.9
DOCTORAL DEGREES			
Health professions & related clinical sciences	57.7	60.3	72.5
Biological & biomedical sciences	36.9	41.8	49.2
Physical sciences & science technologies	19.6	22.9	30.0
Mathematics & statistics	19.2	20.6	29.5
Engineering & engineering technologies	9.3	12.6	20.2

Source: U.S. Department of Education, National Center for Education Statistics (NCES). *Digest of Education Statistics, 2007* (NCES 2008-022), tables 258, 286, 288, 290–294, 296, 299–301, 303, 305, and 307, data from U.S. Department of Education, NCES, 1990–91, 1995–96, and 2005–06 Integrated Postsecondary Education Data System, "Completions Survey" (IPEDS-C:91–96), and IPEDS, Fall 2006. Table 27.1.

"Twins have a special claim upon our attention; it is, that their history affords means of distinguishing between the effects of tendencies received at birth, and those that were imposed by the special circumstances of their after lives."

SIR FRANCIS GALTON, 19TH-CENTURY BEHAVIORAL GENETICS PIONEER, *INQUIRIES INTO HUMAN FACULTY AND ITS DEVELOPMENT,* 1875

Women's preferences may well be the strongest reason why there are more men entering and remaining in STEM fields today. Even so, women are in fact entering STEM fields in increasing numbers (Cox & Alm, 2005; Park et al., 2008) (see Table 7.3 ■).

Nature and Nurture in Intelligence: Where Does Intelligence Come From?

If different ethnic groups tend to score differently on intelligence tests, psychologists—like educators and other people involved in public life—want to know why. We will see that this is one debate that can make use of key empirical findings. Psychologists can point with pride to a rich mine of research on the roles of nature (genetic influences) and nurture (environmental influences) in the development of intelligence.

GENETIC INFLUENCES ON INTELLIGENCE Question 24: What are the genetic influences on intelligence? Research on genetic influences on intelligence has employed kinship studies, twin studies, and adoptee studies. Let's consider each of these to see whether heredity affects intellectual functioning.

Kinship and Twin Studies We can examine the IQ scores of closely and distantly related people who have been reared together or apart. If heredity is involved in human intelligence, closely related people ought to have more similar IQs than distantly related or unrelated people, even when they are reared separately (Petrill et al., 2010).

Figure 7.11 ■ is a composite of the results of studies on IQ and heredity in human beings (McGue et al., 1993; Plomin & Spinath, 2004; Plomin et al., 2008). The IQ scores of identical (monozygotic, or MZ) twins are more alike than scores for any other pairs, even when the twins have been reared apart. There are moderate correlations between the IQ scores of fraternal (dizygotic, or DZ) twins, between those of siblings, and between those of parents and their children. Correlations between the scores of children and their foster parents and between those of cousins are weak.

LIFE CONNECTIONS — ENHANCING INTELLECTUAL FUNCTIONING

Does enhancing intellectual functioning sound like an impossible dream? It does only if you believe that intelligence is a fixed commodity—a sort of "knob in the head." Actually, intelligence—or intellectual functioning—changes with age, experiences in the home, education, and many other factors, including day-to-day differences in responding to items on intelligence tests. Research into the effects of the home environment and early educational experiences suggests that there are many things you can do to enhance your children's intellectual functioning—and your own:

- Provide a safe, organized home for your children.

- Be emotionally and verbally responsive to your children. Provide appropriate and stimulating play materials. Get involved in their play.

- Provide a variety of experiences. Take your children to local museums and cultural events. Do whatever traveling your budget and time will allow.

- Encourage your children to be independent, to try to solve their own problems, and to do as much of their schoolwork on their own as they can.

- Make sure your children know the educational basics. Expose them to materials and activities that include letters and words, numbers, books, exercises in drawing, pegs and pegboards, puzzles, toy animals, and dolls.

- Consider giving your children training in music. It may also enhance their spatial-relations skills.

And what about you? It is not too late to enhance your own intellectual functioning, even if you are a grandparent. Psychologist Walter Schaie and his colleagues (Schaie, 1994) have been studying the cognitive development of adults for four decades and discovered factors that contribute to intellectual functioning across the life span:

- *General health*: People in good health tend to retain higher levels of intellectual functioning into late adulthood. Therefore, paying attention to one's diet, exercising, and having regular medical checkups contribute to intellectual functioning as well as physical health.

- *Socioeconomic status (SES)*: People with high SES tend to maintain intellectual functioning more adequately than people with low SES. High SES is also connected with above-average income and levels of education, a history of stimulating occupational pursuits, maintenance of intact families, and better health.

- *Stimulating activities*: Cultural events, travel, participation in professional organizations, and extensive reading contribute to intellectual functioning.

To enhance children's intellectual functioning, provide a safe home environment, be verbally responsive to their comments and questions, and involve them in stimulating activities in educational and cultural facilities.

- *A relationship with a partner with a high level of intellectual functioning*: The partner whose level of intellectual functioning is lower at the beginning of a long-term relationship tends to increase in intellectual functioning as time goes by. Perhaps that partner is continually challenged by the other.

- *Openness to new experience*: Being open to new challenges of life apparently helps keep us young—at any age.

None of these measures is a guarantee, of course. But regardless of how they affect intelligence, they will certainly lead to a more stimulating life—both for your children and for you.

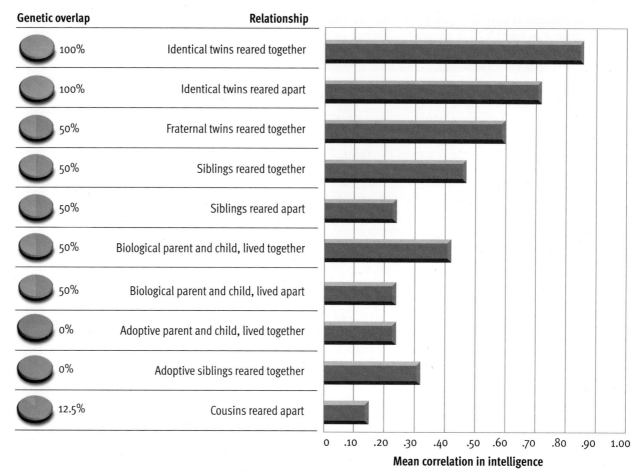

Genetic overlap	Relationship	
100%	Identical twins reared together	
100%	Identical twins reared apart	
50%	Fraternal twins reared together	
50%	Siblings reared together	
50%	Siblings reared apart	
50%	Biological parent and child, lived together	
50%	Biological parent and child, lived apart	
0%	Adoptive parent and child, lived together	
0%	Adoptive siblings reared together	
12.5%	Cousins reared apart	

Mean correlation in intelligence

Figure 7.11 ■ Findings of Studies of the Relationship Between IQ Scores and Heredity The data represent a composite of several studies. By and large, correlations are higher between people who are more closely related, yet people who are reared together have more similar IQ scores than people who are reared apart. Such findings suggest that both genetic and environmental factors contribute to IQ scores.

Source: From Weiten. *Psychology*, 8/e. Copyright © 2010 Wadsworth, a part of Cengage Learning, Inc. Reproduced by permission. www.cengage.com/permissions

The results of large-scale twin studies are consistent with the data in Figure 7.11 (e.g., Haworth et al., 2009). A classic study of 500 pairs of MZ and DZ twins in Louisville, Kentucky (R. S. Wilson, 1983), found that the correlations in intelligence between MZ twins were higher than those for DZ twins, as shown in Figure 7.11. The correlations in intelligence between DZ twin pairs were the same as those between other siblings. The MacArthur Longitudinal Twin Study examined the intellectual abilities of 200 fourteen-month-old pairs of twins (Oliver & Plomin, 2007). It found that MZ twins were more similar than DZ twins in spatial memory, ability to categorize things, and word comprehension.

In sum, studies generally suggest that the **heritability** of intelligence is between 40% and 60% (Haworth et al., 2009; Neisser et al., 1996). That is, about half of the difference between your IQ score and the IQ scores of other people can be explained by heredity.

Note, too, that genetic pairs (such as MZ twins) who were reared together show higher correlations in their IQ scores than similar genetic pairs (such as other MZ twins) who were reared apart. This finding holds for DZ twins, siblings, parents and their children, and unrelated people. Being reared together is therefore associated with similarities in IQ. *For this reason, the same group of studies used to demonstrate a role for the heritability of IQ scores also suggests that the environment plays a role in determining IQ scores.*

Heritability The degree to which the variations in a trait from one person to another can be attributed to, or explained by, genetic factors.

Adoptee Studies Another strategy for exploring genetic influences on intelligence is to compare the correlations between the IQ scores of adopted children and those of their biological and adoptive parents. When children are separated from their biological parents at an early age, one can argue that strong relationships between their IQs and those of their natural parents reflect genetic influences. Strong relationships between their IQs and those of their adoptive parents might reflect environmental influences. Several studies with 1- and 2-year-old children in Colorado (L. A. Baker et al., 1983), Texas (Horn, 1983), and Minnesota (Scarr & Weinberg, 1983) have found a stronger relationship between the IQ scores of adopted children and those of their biological parents than between the children's scores and those of their adoptive parents.

ENVIRONMENTAL INFLUENCES ON INTELLIGENCE Question 25: What are the environmental influences on intelligence? To answer this question, we must consider studies that employ a variety of research strategies. These include observation of the role of the home environment and evaluation of the effects of educational programs.

The Home Environment Research shows that the home environment and styles of parenting affect IQ scores (Bradley, 2006). Children of parents who are emotionally and verbally responsive, furnish appropriate play materials, are involved with their children, encourage independence, and provide varied daily experiences obtain higher IQ scores later on (Bradley, 2006). Other studies support the view that children's early environment is linked to IQ scores and academic achievement. For example, Victoria Molfese and her colleagues (1997) found that the home environment was the single most important predictor of scores on IQ tests among children aged 3 to 8.

Education Although intelligence is viewed as permitting people to profit from education, education also apparently contributes to intelligence. Government-funded efforts to provide preschoolers with enriched early environments such as Head Start enhance the IQ scores, the achievement test scores, and the academic skills of disadvantaged children (Bierman et al., 2008) by exposing them to materials and activities that middle-class children take for granted. These include letters and words, numbers, books, exercises in drawing, pegs and pegboards, puzzles, toy animals, and dolls. On the other hand, many children's IQ scores and achievements tend to decrease again in the years following the Head Start experience if they return to the less intellectually stimulating environment that preceded Head Start (Nisbett, 2009).

Later schooling also contributes to IQ. When children of about the same age start school a year apart because of admissions standards related to their date of birth, children who have been in school longer obtain higher IQ scores (Neisser et al., 1996). Moreover, test scores tend to decrease during the summer vacation (Neisser et al., 1996).

The findings on intelligence, the home environment, and educational experiences show that much can be done to enhance intellectual functioning in children. Now let's return to research on the intellectual development of adopted children.

Adoptee Studies As mentioned earlier, the Minnesota adoption studies reported by Scarr and Weinberg suggest a genetic influence on intelligence. But the same studies (Scarr & Weinberg, 1976, 1977) also suggest a role for environmental influences. African American children who were adopted during their first year by European American parents with above-average income and education obtained IQ scores some 15 to 25 points higher than those obtained by African American children reared by their natural parents (Scarr & Weinberg, 1976).

All in all, intellectual functioning appears to reflect the interaction of a complex web of genetic, physical, personal, and sociocultural factors (Bartels et al., 2002; Bishop et al., 2003), as suggested by Figure 7.12 ∎.

Perhaps we need not be so concerned with whether we can sort out exactly how much of a person's IQ is due to heredity and how much is due to environmental influences. Psychology has traditionally supported the dignity of the individual. It might be more appropriate for us to try to identify children *of all ethnic groups* whose environments place them at risk for failure and do what we can to enrich their

"Some recent philosophers seem to have given their moral approval to these deplorable verdicts that affirm that the intelligence of an individual is a fixed quantity, a quantity that cannot be augmented. We must protest and react against this brutal pessimism; we will try to demonstrate that it is founded on nothing."

ALFRED BINET

Genetic factors

Health

Socioeconomic status
Stimulating home environment
Possession of academic basics
Flexible personality
Achievement motivation
Academic/educational adjustment
Belief that intellectual functioning
is a key to fulfillment

Figure 7.12 ■ The Complex Web of Factors That Appears to Affect Intellectual Functioning Intellectual functioning appears to be influenced by the interaction of genetic factors, health, personality, and sociocultural factors.

environments. As noted by Paul Ehrlich (2000), professor of biology and population studies at Stanford University,

> There is no such thing as a fixed human nature, but rather an interaction between our genotypes—the genetic information we have—and the different environments we live in, with the result that all our natures are unique.

LearningConnections • INTELLIGENCE: THE MOST CONTROVERSIAL CONCEPT IN PSYCHOLOGY?

ACTIVE REVIEW (12) Spearman suggested that intelligent behaviors have a common underlying factor, which he labeled _____, and specific factors that account for specific abilities. (13) Gardner proposes the existence of _____ intelligences, each of which is based in a different area of the brain. (14) Sternberg constructed a "triarchic" model of intelligence, including analytical, creative, and _____ intelligence. (15) The Stanford–Binet Intelligence Scale yields a score called a(n) _____ _____ (IQ). (16) The _____ scales have verbal and performance subtests.

REFLECT AND RELATE When did you form an impression of how intelligent you are? How has this impression affected you?

CRITICAL THINKING Do the talents of dancers, gymnasts, artists, and musicians strike you as kinds of intelligences? Why or why not?

 Go to Psychology CourseMate at **www.cengagebrain.com** for an interactive version of these questions.

Thinking: Reasoning about Reasoning

1. What is thinking?
Thinking is conscious mental activity that involves attending to information, representing it mentally, reasoning about it, and making judgments about it.

2. What are concepts?
Concepts are mental categories for grouping objects, relations, events, abstractions, ideas, or qualities with common properties.

3. What tools do people use to solve problems?
People first try to understand the problem. Then they use strategies such as algorithms, heuristic devices, and analogies.

4. Is it best to use a tried-and-true formula to solve a problem?
Not necessarily. Heuristic devices—rules of thumb—can help us "jump" to right answers.

5. What factors make it easier or harder to solve problems?
Key factors include level of expertise, mental sets, insight, incubation, functional fixedness, and insight.

6. How do people make judgments and decisions?
People sometimes make decisions by weighing the pluses and minuses, but most make decisions with limited information and heuristic devices.

7. What is the framing effect?
People often phrase, or frame, arguments in such a way as to persuade others.

8. Why do people tend to be convinced that they are right even when they are clearly wrong?
People tend to retain their convictions because they are unaware of the flimsiness of their assumptions, they focus on examples that confirm their judgments, and they work to bring about results that fit their judgments.

Language: Of Signs, Grammar, and Many Things

9. Do apes really use language?
Apes can be said to "use" language in that they learn signs for objects and actions and produce these signs to communicate. However, critics argue that apes' use of grammar is inadequate to fulfill the requirements for true language.

10. How do we define language?
Language is the communication of thoughts and feelings by means of symbols that are arranged according to rules of grammar.

11. What are the properties of a "true" language?
True language is distinguished by properties such as semanticity, infinite creativity, and displacement.

12. What are the relationships between language and thinking?
Language is not necessary for thinking, but language makes possible cognitive activity that involves the use of symbols arranged according to rules of grammar.

13. Is it possible for English speakers to share the thoughts experienced by people who speak other languages?
Perhaps it is. According to the linguistic-relativity hypothesis, the concepts we use to understand the world are derived from our language. But the vocabulary of a language may suggest the range of concepts users find to be useful, not their cognitive limits.

14. How does language develop?
Children make the prelinguistic sounds of crying, cooing, and babbling before true language develops. Single-word utterances occur at about 1 year, two-word utterances by 2 years. Early language is characterized by overextension and overregularization.

15. What are the roles of nature and nurture in language development?
The two main theories of language development are learning theories and nativist theories. Learning theories focus on reinforcement and imitation. Nativist theories assume that innate factors enable children to attend to and perceive language.

Intelligence: The Most Controversial Topic in Psychology?

16. What is intelligence?
Gottfredson defines intelligence as "a very general mental capability that . . . involves the ability to reason, plan, solve problems, think abstractly, comprehend complex ideas, learn quickly and learn from experience."

17. What are the various theories of intelligence?
Spearman believed that a common factor, g, underlies all intelligent behavior but that people also have specific abilities, or s factors. Gardner believes that people have several intelligences, and that each is based in a different area of the brain. Sternberg proposes three kinds of intelligence: academic ability, creativity, and practical intelligence.

18. What is creativity, and how is it related to intelligence?
Creative people take chances, defy limits, and appreciate art and music. Creative problem solving involves divergent thinking. Creativity is only moderately related to academic ability.

19. What is the Stanford–Binet Intelligence Scale?
This is the test originated by Binet in France and developed by Terman at Stanford University. It includes age-graded questions and compares mental age with chronological age.

20. How do the Wechsler scales of intelligence differ from the Stanford–Binet?
The Wechsler scales use deviation IQs, which compare a person's performance with that of age-mates. The Wechsler scales contain verbal and performance subtests.

21. What are the socioeconomic and ethnic differences in intelligence?
Middle- and upper-class children outscore lower-class children by 10 to 15 points on intelligence tests. Asian Americans tend to outscore European Americans, and European Americans tend to outscore African Americans and Latin Americans.

22. Do intelligence tests contain cultural biases against ethnic minority groups and immigrants?
Many psychologists believe that intelligence tests are biased against African Americans and people in the lower classes because they require familiarity with concepts that reflect middle-class European American culture.

23. Do males and females differ in intellectual functioning?
Females would appear to excel in verbal skills, and males in spatial relations. However, these group differences are small and narrowing. Moreover, many males excel in verbal skills, and many females excel in math and spatial relations.

24. What are the genetic influences on intelligence?
The heritability of intelligence is estimated at 40% to 60%. Kinship studies find a stronger relationship between the IQ scores of adopted children and their biological parents than between the children's scores and those of their adoptive parents.

25. What are the environmental influences on intelligence?
Environmental influences on intelligence include, among other things, the home environment and education.

KEY TERMS

Algorithm (p. 224)
Anchoring and adjustment heuristic (p. 229)
Availability heuristic (p. 229)
Cognition (p. 220)
Concept (p. 220)
Convergent thinking (p. 243)
Creativity (p. 243)
Cultural bias (p. 249)
Displacement (p. 233)
Divergent thinking (p. 243)
Exemplar (p. 221)
Factor analysis (p. 238)
Framing effect (p. 229)
Functional fixedness (p. 227)
g (p. 238)

Heritability (p. 252)
Heuristics (p. 225)
Holophrase (p. 234)
Incubation (p. 227)
Infinite creativity (p. 232)
Insight (p. 226)
Intelligence (p. 237)
Intelligence quotient (IQ) (p. 244)
Language (p. 232)
Language acquisition device (LAD) (p. 237)
Linguistic-relativity hypothesis (p. 233)
Means–end analysis (p. 225)
Mental age (MA) (p. 244)
Mental image (p. 226)
Mental set (p. 226)

Overregularization (p. 235)
Primary mental abilities (p. 238)
Prototype (p. 221)
Psycholinguistic theory (p. 237)
Reliability (p. 247)
Representativeness heuristic (p. 229)
s (p. 238)
Semantic (p. 231)
Semanticity (p. 232)
Syntax (p. 237)
Systematic random search (p. 224)
Theory of multiple intelligences (p. 238)
Thinking (p. 220)
Triarchic theory of intelligence (p. 240)
Validity (p. 247)

ACTIVE LEARNING RESOURCES

Log in to **www.cengagebrain.com** to access the resources your instructor requires. For this book, you can access:

CourseMate CourseMate brings course concepts to life with interactive learning, study, and exam preparation tools that support the printed textbook. A textbook-specific website, Psychology CourseMate includes an integrated interactive eBook and other interactive learning tools including quizzes, flashcards, videos, and more.

 Need help studying? This site is your one-stop study shop. Take a Pre-Test and CengageNOW will generate a Personalized Study Plan based on your test results. The Study Plan will identify the topics you need to review and direct you to online resources to help you master those topics. You can then take a Post-Test to determine the concepts you have mastered and what you still need to work on.

8 Motivation and Emotion

MAJOR TOPICS

The Psychology of Motivation: The *Whys* of Why 260

Theories of Motivation: Which Why Is Which? 261

Hunger: Do You Go by "Tummy-Time"? 265

Sexual Motivation and Sexual Orientation: Pressing the START Button and Finding Direction 273

Aggression 280

Achievement Motivation: "Just Do It"? 283

Emotion: Adding Color to Life 284

FEATURES

Self-Assessment: The Sensation-Seeking Scale 263

Video Connections: Childhood Obesity 267

Life Connections: The Skinny on Weight Control 268

Video Connections: Anorexia Nervosa 270

Self-Assessment: Eating Disorders Quiz 273

A Closer Look: Is the Human Sex Drive Affected by Pheromones? 275

Life Connections: "Come On! Get Happy!" A Possible or Impossible Dream? 287

A Closer Look: Just What Do Lie Detectors Detect? 292

T F Siamese fighting fish that have been reared without ever seeing another fish assume stereotypical threatening postures and attack other males when they are introduced into their tanks.

page 261

T F Getting away from it all by going on a vacation from all sensory input for a few hours is relaxing.

page 262

T F People feel hunger due to contractions ("pangs") in the stomach.

page 265

T F More than half of adult Americans are overweight.

page 266

T F Dieting accelerates the body's metabolic rate so that dieters are more likely than nondieters to burn calories rapidly.

page 267

T F You can never be too rich or too thin.

page 270

T F Checking out the Victoria's Secret catalog can contribute to eating disorders among women.

page 272

T F Education is a liberating influence on sexual behavior.

page 276

T F Money can't buy you happiness.

page 287

T F You may be able to fool a lie detector by squiggling your toes.

page 292

Are these items truth or fiction? We will be revisiting them throughout the chapter.

The Seekers had received word that the world was coming to an end on December 21. A great flood would engulf their city and the rest of the Earth. Now they were gathered around their leader, Marian Keech, in her home, as she recorded messages that she said were sent to her by the Guardians from outer space. The messages were received through "automatic writing"; that is, the Guardians communicated through Ms. Keech, who wrote down their words while in a kind of semiconscious trance. Another message brought good news, however. Because of their faith, the Seekers would be saved by flying saucers at the stroke of midnight on the 21st.

In their classic observational study, Leon Festinger and his colleagues (1956) described how they managed to be present in Ms. Keech's household at the fateful hour by pretending to belong to the group. Their purpose was to observe the behavior of the Seekers during and following the prophecy's failure.

The cognitive theory of motivation that Festinger was working on—*cognitive-dissonance theory*—suggested that there would be a discrepancy or conflict between two key cognitions: (a) Ms. Keech is a prophet, and (b) Ms. Keech is wrong.

© Fuse/Getty Images

When Prophecy Failed Believing Earth was in peril, "the Seekers" waited for flying saucers that their leader said would rescue them. (Don't worry, the flying saucer in the photo is Photoshopped, not real.) Needless to say, the saucers never arrived. How did the group react?

How might the conflict be resolved? One way would be for the Seekers to lose faith in Ms. Keech. But the researchers expected that according to their theory, the Seekers could also be motivated to resolve the conflict by going out to spread the word and find additional converts. Otherwise, the group would be painfully embarrassed.

Let's return to the momentous night. Many members of the group had quit their jobs and gone on spending sprees before the anticipated end. Now, as midnight approached, they fidgeted while awaiting the flying saucers. Midnight came, but there were no saucers. Anxious glances were exchanged. There was silence, and then some coughs. Minutes passed. Watches were checked, more glances exchanged.

At 4:00 A.M., a bitter and frantic Ms. Keech complained that she sensed members of the group were doubting her. At 4:45 A.M., however, she seemed suddenly relieved. Another message was arriving, and Ms. Keech was spelling it out through automatic writing! The Seekers, it turned out, had saved the world through their faith. The universal powers had decided to let the world travel on its sinful way for a while longer. Why? Because of the faith of the Seekers, there was hope!

With their faith restored, the followers called wire services and newspapers to spread the word. The three psychologists from the University of Minnesota went home, weary but enlightened. They wrote a book titled *When Prophecy Fails*, which serves as a key document of their theory.

Mr. Keech? He was a tolerant sort. He slept through it all.

"When I was young I thought that money was the most important thing in life; now that I am old I know that it is."

OSCAR WILDE

"No man but a blockhead ever wrote except for money."

DR. SAMUEL JOHNSON

THE PSYCHOLOGY OF MOTIVATION: THE *WHYS* OF WHY

The psychology of **motivation** is concerned with the *whys* of behavior. Why do we eat? Why do some of us strive to get ahead? Why do some of us ride motorcycles at breakneck speeds, while others look on in horror? Why are some people aggressive? Why were the Seekers in a state of discomfort when the prophecy failed?

To answer these questions, psychologists use concepts such as *motives, needs, drives,* and *incentives.* **Question 1: What are motives, needs, drives, and incentives?** Motives are hypothetical states that activate behavior, propelling one toward goals. We call them "hypothetical states" because motives are not seen and measured directly; they are inferred from behavior. May we infer that Ms. Keech was motivated to continue to earn the adulation of her followers when the flying saucers failed to arrive? Motives can take the form of *needs, drives,* and *incentives,* which are also inferred from behavior.

Psychologists speak of physiological and psychological needs. We must meet physiological needs to survive. Examples include the needs for oxygen, food, drink, pain avoidance, proper temperature, and elimination of waste products. Some physiological needs, such as hunger and thirst, are states of physical deprivation. When we have not eaten or drunk for a while, we develop needs for food and water. Psychological needs include needs for achievement, power, self-esteem, approval, and belonging. The Seekers certainly needed one another's approval, to belong to the group and to maintain their self-esteem in the light of the failed prophecy. Psychological needs may be acquired through experience, or learned, whereas physiological needs reside in the physical makeup of the organism. People share similar physiological needs, but we are also influenced by our social and cultural settings. All of us need food, but some prefer a vegetarian diet whereas others prefer meat.

Needs give rise to **drives.** Depletion of food gives rise to the hunger drive, and depletion of liquids gives rise to the thirst drive. Physiological drives are the counterparts of physiological needs. When we have gone without food and water, our body may *need* these substances. However, our *experience* of drives is psychological. Drives arouse us to action. Drives tend to be stronger when we have been deprived longer. Psychological needs for approval, achievement, and belonging also give rise to drives. We can have a drive to get ahead in the business world just as we have a drive to eat. We can also be driven by *incentives.*

An incentive is an object, person, or situation that is viewed as capable of satisfying a need or as desirable for its own sake. Money, food, a sexually attractive person, social approval, and attention can all act as incentives that motivate behavior.

Motivation The state in which an organism experiences an inducement or incentive to do something.

Motive A hypothetical state within an organism that propels the organism toward a goal.

Need A state of deprivation.

Drive A condition of arousal in an organism that is associated with a need.

Incentive An object, person, or situation perceived as capable of satisfying a need or as desirable for its own sake.

ACTIVE REVIEW (1) _____ are hypothetical states that activate behavior and direct organisms toward goals. (2) Some physiological needs reflect states of physical _____. (3) A(n) _____ is an object, person, or situation that is perceived as capable of satisfying a need.

REFLECT AND RELATE What are some of the key motives in your own life? Can you think of any needs or drives that motivate you but might not motivate other people?

CRITICAL THINKING If we observe a person behaving in a certain way, are we justified in assuming that the person is motivated to behave in that way? For example, if we see one person acting aggressively toward another, can we assume that the motive is aggression or that the person is an aggressive individual?

 Go to Psychology CourseMate at **www.cengagebrain.com** for an interactive version of these questions.

● THEORIES OF MOTIVATION: WHICH WHY IS WHICH?

Although psychologists agree that it is important to understand why humans and lower animals do things, they do not agree about the precise nature of motivation. Let's consider various theoretical perspectives on motivation.

The Evolutionary Perspective: The Fish, the Spiders, and the Bees

The evolutionary perspective notes that many animals are neurally *prewired*—that is, born with preprogrammed tendencies—to respond to certain situations in certain ways (Burghardt, 2009; Confer et al., 2010). **Truth or Fiction Revisited:** It is true that Siamese fighting fish reared in isolation from other fish assume stereotypical threatening postures and attack other males when they are introduced into their tank. Spiders spin webs instinctively. Bees "dance" instinctively to communicate the location of food to other bees.

These instinctive behaviors are found in particular species. They are *species-specific*. **Question 2: What are species-specific behaviors?** Species-specific behaviors are also called **instincts**, or *fixed-action patterns (FAPs)*. Such behavior patterns are inborn, meaning that they are genetically transmitted from generation to generation.

Psychologists have asked whether humans have instincts and, if so, how many. More than a century ago, psychologists William James (1890) and William McDougall (1908) argued that humans have instincts that foster survival and social behavior. James numbered love, sympathy, and modesty among his social instincts. McDougall compiled 12 "basic" instincts, including hunger, sex, and self-assertion. Other psychologists have made longer lists, and still others deny that people have instincts. The question of whether people have instincts—and which instincts—remains unresolved.

A Fixed Action Pattern In the presence of another male, Siamese fighting fish (*Betta splendens*) assume stereotypical threatening postures in which they extend their fins and gills and circle one another. If neither male retreats, there will be conflict.

Instinct An inherited disposition to activate specific behavior patterns that are designed to reach certain goals.

Drive-Reductionism and Homeostasis: "Steady, Steady . . ."

Freud believed that tension motivates us to behave in ways that restore us to a resting state. His views are similar to those of the **drive-reduction theory**, as set forth by psychologist Clark Hull in the 1930s. **Question 3: What is drive-reduction theory?**

According to Hull, **primary drives** such as hunger, thirst, and avoidance of pain trigger arousal (tension) and activate behavior. We learn to engage in behaviors that reduce the tension. We also acquire drives through experience. These drives are called

Drive-reduction theory The view that organisms learn to engage in behaviors that have the effect of reducing drives.

Primary drives Unlearned, or physiological, drives.

© George Diebold/Photodisc/Getty Images

"Such is the state of life, that none are happy but by the anticipation of change: the change itself is nothing; when we have made it, the next wish is to change again."

DR. SAMUEL JOHNSON

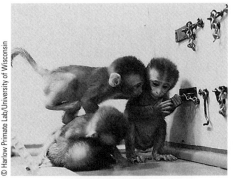

Monkeying Around Do organisms have innate drives to obtain sensory stimulation, manipulate objects (like these young rhesus monkeys), and explore the environment? The monkeys appear to monkey around with gadgets just for the fun of it. No external incentives are needed. Children similarly enjoy manipulating gadgets that honk, squeak, rattle, and buzz, even though the resultant honks and squeaks do not satisfy physiological drives such as hunger or thirst.

Acquired drives Drives acquired through experience or that are learned.

Homeostasis The tendency of the body to maintain a steady state.

Stimulus motive A state within an organism that propels it toward increasing the amount of stimulation it obtains.

acquired drives. We may acquire a drive for money because money enables us to obtain food, drink, and homes, which protect us from predators and extremes of temperature. We might acquire drives for social approval and affiliation because other people, and their goodwill, help us reduce primary drives, especially when we are infants. In all cases, reduction of tension is the goal. Yet some people appear to acquire what could be considered excessive drives for money or affiliation. They gather money long after their material needs have been met, and some people find it difficult to be alone, even briefly.

Primary drives like hunger are triggered when we are in a state of deprivation. Sensations of hunger motivate us to act in ways that will restore the bodily balance. This tendency to maintain a steady state is called **homeostasis**. Homeostasis works much like a thermostat. When the temperature in a room drops below this *set point*, the heating system is triggered. The heat stays on until the set point is reached. Similarly, most animals eat until they are no longer hungry.

The Search for Stimulation: Is Downtime a Downer?

Physical needs give rise to drives like hunger and thirst. In such cases, we are motivated to *reduce* the tension or stimulation that impinges on us. **Question 4: Are all motives aimed at the reduction of tension?** No, in the case of **stimulus motives**, organisms seek to *increase* stimulation.

A classic study conducted at McGill University in Montreal during the 1950s suggests the importance of sensory stimulation and activity. Some "lucky" students were paid $20 a day (which, with inflation, would now be well above $100) for doing nothing—literally. Would you like to "work" by doing nothing for $100 a day? Don't answer too quickly. According to the results of classic research on sensory deprivation, you might not like it at all.

In that experiment, student volunteers were placed in quiet cubicles and blindfolded (Bexton et al., 1954). Their arms were bandaged so that they felt little if anything with their hands. They could hear nothing but the dull, monotonous hum of air conditioning. Many slept for a while, but after a few hours of sensory-deprived wakefulness, most felt bored and irritable. As time went on, many grew more uncomfortable. Many students quit the experiment during the first day despite the financial incentive. **Truth or Fiction Revisited:** Therefore, it is not necessarily true that going on a vacation from all sensory input is relaxing. Many of those who remained for a few days found it hard to concentrate on simple problems for days afterward. For many, the experiment did not provide a relaxing vacation. Instead, it produced boredom and disorientation.

Lower animals and humans appear motivated to seek novel stimulation. Even when they have been deprived of food, rats may explore unfamiliar arms of mazes rather than head straight for the spot where they have learned to expect food. Animals that have just copulated and thereby reduced their primary sex drives often show renewed interest in sexual behavior when presented with a new sex partner— a novelty. People (and lower animals) tend to take in more calories at buffets and smorgasbords than when they have fewer kinds of food available (Szentirmai et al., 2010). Children spend hour after hour manipulating the controls of video games for the pleasure of zapping video monsters. Similarly, infants prolong their play with "busy boxes" filled with objects that honk, squeak, rattle, and buzz when manipulated.

Although it is normal enough to seek stimulation, some people—"thrill seekers"— seek unusual amounts of stimulation. Are you one of them? Check out the nearby self-assessment to find out.

Stimulus motives provide an evolutionary advantage. Animals that are active and motivated to learn about and manipulate their environment are more likely to survive. If you know where the nearest tall tree is, you're more likely to be able to escape from a lion. If you've explored where to find food and water, you're more likely to pass your genes on to future generations.

But note that survival is more or less a question of defending oneself or one's group against dangers of one kind or another. In the following section, we see that many psychologists believe people are also motivated to develop their unique potentials, even in the absence of any external threat.

Some people seek higher levels of stimulation and activity than others. John is a couch potato, content to sit by the TV all evening. Marsha doesn't feel right unless she's out on the tennis court or jogging. What about you? Are you content to read or watch television all day? Or must you catch the big wave or bounce the bike across the dunes of the Mojave Desert?

Marvin Zuckerman and his colleagues have identified four factors that are involved in sensation seeking: (a) seeking thrill and adventure, (b) disinhibition (that is, a tendency to express impulses), (c) seeking experience, and (d) susceptibility to boredom. People who are high in sensation seeking are also less tolerant of sensory deprivation. They are more likely to use drugs and become involved in sexual experiences, to be drunk in public, and to volunteer for high-risk activities and unusual experiments (Cooper, 2006; Self et al., 2007).

Sensation-seeking scales measure the level of stimulation or arousal a person will seek. A shortened version of one of Zuckerman's scales follows. To gain insight into your own sensation-seeking tendencies, circle the choice that best describes you. Then compare your answers to those in the answer key in Appendix B.

1. A. I would like a job that requires a lot of traveling.
   B. I would prefer a job in one location.
2. A. I am invigorated by a brisk, cold day.
   B. I can't wait to get indoors on a cold day.
3. A. I get bored seeing the same old faces.
   B. I like the comfortable familiarity of everyday friends.
4. A. I would prefer living in an ideal society in which everyone is safe, secure, and happy.
   B. I would have preferred living in the unsettled days of our history.

5. A. I sometimes like to do things that are a little frightening.
   B. A sensible person avoids activities that are dangerous.
6. A. I would not like to be hypnotized.
   B. I would like to have the experience of being hypnotized.
7. A. The most important goal in life is to live it to the fullest and experience as much as possible.
   B. The most important goal in life is to find peace and happiness.
8. A. I would like to try parachute jumping.
   B. I would never want to try jumping out of a plane, with or without a parachute.
9. A. I enter cold water gradually, giving myself time to get used to it.
   B. I like to dive or jump right into the ocean or a cold pool.
10. A. When I go on a vacation, I prefer the change of camping out.
    B. When I go on a vacation, I prefer the comfort of a good room and bed.
11. A. I prefer people who are emotionally expressive even if they are a bit unstable.
    B. I prefer people who are calm and even tempered.
12. A. A good painting should shock or jolt the senses.
    B. A good painting should give one a feeling of peace and security.
13. A. People who ride motorcycles must have some kind of unconscious need to hurt themselves.
    B. I would like to drive or ride a motorcycle.

Source: From M. Zuckerman, "Sensation Seeking" in *Dimensions of Personality*, H. London and J. Exner, eds., © 1980 John Wiley & Sons. Reprinted by permission.

Humanistic Theory: "I've Got to Be Me"?

Humanistic psychologists, particularly Abraham Maslow (1908–1970), suggest that human behavior is not just mechanical and aimed toward survival and the reduction of tension. **Question 5: How does humanistic theory differ from other theories of motivation?** As a humanist, Maslow believed that people are also motivated by the conscious desire for personal growth. Humanists note that people tolerate pain, hunger, and other sources of tension to obtain personal fulfillment.

Maslow believed that we are separated from so-called lower animals by our capacity for **self-actualization**, or self-initiated striving to become whatever we believe we are capable of being. Maslow considered self-actualization to be as important a need in humans as hunger. The need for self-actualization pushes people to strive to become concert pianists, chief executive officers, or best-selling authors—even when a person has plenty of money to live on.

Maslow (1970) organized human needs into a hierarchy. **Question 6: What is Maslow's hierarchy of needs?** Maslow's hierarchy of needs ranges from physiological needs such as hunger and thirst through self-actualization (see Figure 8.1 ■). He believed that we naturally strive to travel up through this hierarchy.

Critics of Maslow's theory argue that there is too much individual variation for the hierarchy of motives to apply to everyone (Cooke, 2008). Some people whose physiological, safety, and love needs are met show little interest in achievement

Self-actualization According to Maslow and other humanistic psychologists, self-initiated striving to become what one is capable of being. The motive for reaching one's full potential, for expressing one's unique capabilities.

Hierarchy of needs Maslow's ordering of needs from most basic (physiological needs such as hunger and thirst) to most elaborate and sophisticated (self-actualization).

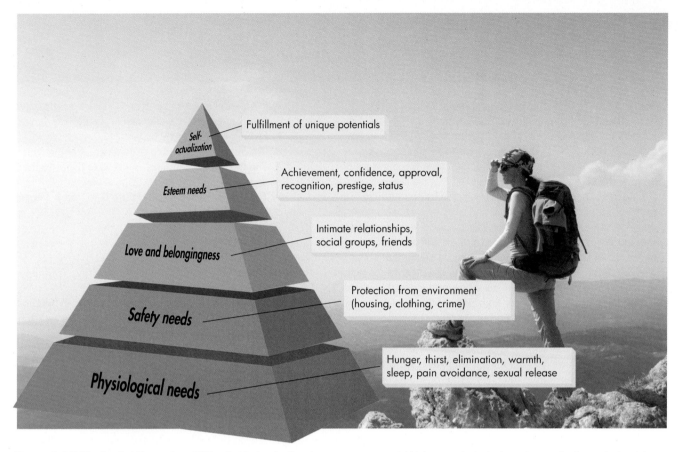

Figure 8.1 ■ Maslow's Hierarchy of Needs Maslow believed we progress toward higher psychological needs once basic survival needs have been met. Where do you fit in this picture?

"A musician must make music, an artist must paint, a poet must write, if he is to be ultimately at peace with himself."

ABRAHAM MASLOW

and recognition. And some visual and performing artists devote themselves fully to their craft, even if they have to pass up the comforts of a warm home, live in an unsafe part of town, and alienate their friends. Thus, many people seek distant, self-actualizing goals, even while their other needs, as outlined by Maslow, have not yet been met.

Each theory of motivation may have something to offer. Drive-reduction theory may explain why we drink when thirsty, but stimulus motives might explain why we go out to a club and drink alcohol. Each theory might apply to certain aspects of behavior. As the chapter progresses, we will describe research that lends support to each theory.

LearningConnections ● THEORIES OF MOTIVATION: WHICH WHY IS WHICH?

ACTIVE REVIEW (4) According to the _____ perspective, animals are born with instinctive tendencies to behave in certain ways. (5) Drives help the body maintain a steady state, a tendency that is called _____. (6) Studies in sensory _____ show that lack of stimulation is aversive and irritating. (7) Humanistic psychologist Maslow argued that people have a hierarchy of needs, the highest of which is the need for _____.

REFLECT AND RELATE Where would you place yourself in Maslow's hierarchy? Where do you see yourself as being headed? Why?

CRITICAL THINKING How does rearing an animal in isolation from others of its kind help researchers learn about instinctive behaviors? Would it be possible to run such an experiment with humans? Why or why not?

 Go to Psychology CourseMate at **www.cengagebrain.com** for an interactive version of these questions.

HUNGER: DO YOU GO BY "TUMMY-TIME"?

We need food to survive, but for many of us, food means more than survival. Food is a symbol of family togetherness and caring. We associate food with the nurturance of the parent–child relationship and with visits home during holidays. Friends and relatives offer us food when we enter their homes, and saying no may be viewed as a personal rejection. Bacon and eggs, coffee with cream and sugar, meat and mashed potatoes—all seem to be part of sharing American values and abundance.

Biological Influences on Hunger

Question 7: What bodily mechanisms regulate the hunger drive? In considering the bodily mechanisms that regulate hunger, let's begin with the mouth, where we get signals of **satiety** that regulate our eating. We also get signals of satiety from the digestive tract, although it takes longer for these signals to reach the brain. Therefore, if we did not receive signals of satiety from chewing and swallowing, we might eat for a long time after we had taken in enough food.

In classic *sham feeding* experiments with dogs, researchers implanted a tube in the animals' throats so that any food swallowed fell out of the body. Even though no food reached the stomach, the animals stopped feeding after a while (Janowitz & Grossman, 1949). Thus, sensations of chewing and swallowing must provide some feelings of satiety. However, the dogs in the study resumed feeding sooner than animals whose food did reach the stomach. Let's proceed to the stomach, too, as we seek further regulatory factors in hunger.

An empty stomach leads to stomach contractions, which we call *hunger pangs*. Classic research suggested that stomach contractions are crucial to hunger. A man (A. L. Washburn) swallowed a balloon that was inflated in his stomach. His stomach contractions squeezed the balloon, so the contractions could be recorded by observers. Washburn also pressed a key when he felt hungry, and the researchers found a correspondence between his stomach contractions and his feelings of hunger (Cannon & Washburn, 1912).

Truth or Fiction Revisited: It is true that pangs in the stomach are connected with feelings of hunger, *but* stomach contractions are not as influential as formerly thought. (We apparently go by more than "tummy-time.") Medical observations and classic research also find that people and animals whose stomachs have been removed still regulate food intake so as to maintain their normal weight (Tsang, 1938). (Food is absorbed through their intestines.) This finding led to the discovery of many other mechanisms that regulate hunger, including the hypothalamus, blood sugar level, and even receptors in the liver. When we are deprived of food, the level of sugar in the blood drops. The drop in blood sugar is communicated to the hypothalamus and apparently indicates that we have been burning energy and need to replenish it by eating.

If you were just reviving from a surgical operation, fighting your way through the fog of the anesthesia, food would probably be the last thing on your mind. But when a researcher uses a probe to destroy the **ventromedial nucleus (VMN)** of a rat's hypothalamus, the rat will grope toward food as soon as its eyes open (Fetissov & Meguid, 2010). Then it eats vast quantities of Purina Rat Chow or whatever is available.

The VMN seems to function like a "stop-eating center" in the rat's brain. If the VMN is electrically stimulated—that is, "switched on"—the rat stops eating until the current is turned off. When the VMN is destroyed, the rat becomes **hyperphagic** (see Figure 8.2 ■). That is, it continues to eat until it has about doubled its normal weight. Then it will level off its eating rate and maintain the higher weight. It is as if the set point of the stop-eating center has been raised to a higher level, like turning up the thermostat in a house from 65°F to 70°F. Hyperphagic rats are also more finicky. They eat more fats or sweet-tasting food and less salty or bitter food. Some people develop tumors near the base of the brain, damaging the VMN and apparently causing them to overeat and grow obese (Chance et al., 2007).

"I go by tummy-time and I want my dinner."

SIR WINSTON CHURCHILL

"In general my children refuse to eat anything that hasn't danced on television."

ERMA BOMBECK

"There is no sincerer love than the love of food."

GEORGE BERNARD SHAW

"The two biggest sellers in any bookstore are the cookbooks and the diet books. The cookbooks tell you how to prepare the food and the diet books tell you how not to eat any of it."

ANDY ROONEY

© Alloy Photography/Veer

What Triggers Your Hunger Drive? Are you only interested in eating when your blood sugar level falls, or do the sights and aromas of foods stimulate you to eat?

Satiety The state of being satisfied; fullness.

Ventromedial nucleus (VMN) A central area on the underside of the hypothalamus that appears to function as a stop-eating center.

Hyperphagic Characterized by excessive eating.

Figure 8.2 ■ A Hyperphagic Rat This rodent winner of the basketball look-alike contest went on a binge after it received a lesion in the ventromedial nucleus (VMN) of the hypothalamus. It is as if the lesion pushed the set point for body weight up several notches; the rat's weight is now about five times normal. But now it eats only enough to maintain its pleasantly plump figure, so you need not be concerned that it will eventually burst. If the lesion had been made in the lateral hypothalamus, the animal might have become the Calista Flockhart of the rat world.

> *"We are in real trouble. Having a culture bombarded with rushed lifestyles, fast foods, and physical inactivity has caught up with us."*
>
> CARMEN NEVAREZ, BERKELEY, CALIFORNIA, PUBLIC HEALTH INSTITUTE

Lateral hypothalamus An area at the side of the hypothalamus that appears to function as a start-eating center.

Aphagic Characterized by undereating.

The **lateral hypothalamus** may function like a "start-eating center." If you electrically stimulate the lateral hypothalamus, the rat starts to eat (N. E. Miller, 1995). If you destroy the lateral hypothalamus, the rat may stop eating altogether—that is, become **aphagic.** If you force-feed an aphagic rat for a while, however, it begins to eat on its own and levels off at a relatively low body weight. It is as if you have lowered the rat's set point. It is like turning down the thermostat from, say, 70°F to 40°F.

Are physiological influences the whole story in explaining hunger? **Question 8: What psychological factors are connected with the hunger drive?**

Psychological Influences on Hunger

How many times have you been made hungry by the sight or aroma of food? How many times have you eaten not because you were hungry but because you were at a relative's home or hanging around in a cafeteria? Or because you felt anxious or bored? Although many areas of the body work in concert to regulate the hunger drive, psychological as well as physiological factors play an important role.

One study confirmed what most of us already assumed—that watching television increases the amount of food we eat (Higgs & Woodward, 2009). One reason is that watching television can distract us from bodily changes that signal fullness and from awareness of how much we have eaten. The same reason seems to hold true for gorging on popcorn, candy, and soft drinks at the movies. Watching television also interferes with memory formation of how much we have eaten, making us vulnerable to overeating at subsequent meals.

Being Overweight: A Serious and Pervasive Problem

Consider some facts about being overweight:

- More than two of three adult Americans are overweight, according to the national *body mass index (BMI)* guidelines, and one in three are obese (Flegal et al., 2010). **Truth or Fiction Revisited:** It is therefore true that more than half of adult Americans are overweight.

- Problems with unhealthy weight gain have been on the upswing in the United States; for example, 68% of Americans were overweight in 2008 compared with 60% in 1988–1994 (Flegal et al., 2010).

- More than 78% of African American women and 81% of Latina Americans age 40 and older are overweight, and about half are obese (Flegal et al., 2010).

- Obesity is a risk in various chronic medical conditions including type 2 diabetes, hypertension (high blood pressure), high cholesterol, stroke, heart disease, some cancers, arthritis, and respiratory problems (Apovian, 2010; Flegal et al., 2010).

- Weight control is elusive for most people, who regain most of the weight they have lost even when they have dieted "successfully" (Apovian, 2010; Heber, 2010).

Studies using data obtained by the federal government find that extremely obese people, whose BMIs are greater than or equal to 40, live shorter lives than people who are normal in weight (Finkelstein et al., 2010) (see Table 8.1 ■). Fortunately, research has contributed to our understanding of obesity and what can be done about it.

FACTORS IN BEING OVERWEIGHT Question 9: Why are people overweight? Numerous biological and psychological factors are involved in being overweight. On the biological side, we can point to the influences of heredity, adipose tissue (body fat), and metabolism (the rate at which the individual converts calories to energy).

Being overweight runs in families. It was once assumed that overweight parents encouraged their children to become overweight by serving fattening foods and setting poor examples. However, a study of Scandinavian adoptees by Albert Stunkard and his

TABLE 8.1 ▪ Years of Life Lost by an Extremely Obese, Non-Smoking 40-Year-Old Compared with a Normal-Weight Person of the Same Age

	European American	African American
Male	9 years	8 years
Female	7 years	5 years

Source of data: Finkelstein, E.A., Brown, D. S., Wrage, L. A., Allaire, B. T., & Hoerger, T. J. (2010). Individual and aggregate years-of-life-lost associated with overweight and obesity. *Obesity, 18*(2), 333–339.

colleagues (1990) found that children bear a closer resemblance in weight to their biological parents than to their adoptive parents. Today, it is widely accepted that heredity plays a role in obesity in humans (Bouchard, 2010) and other animals, including monkeys and rats (Felsted et al., 2010).

The efforts of overweight people to maintain a slender profile may be sabotaged by microscopic units of life within their own bodies: fat cells (Apovian, 2010). No, fat cells are not overweight cells. They are *adipose tissue*, or cells that store fat. Hunger might be related to the amount of fat stored in these cells. As noted earlier, as time passes after a meal, the blood sugar level drops. Fat is then drawn from these cells to provide nourishment. At some point, referred to as the **set point**, fat deficiency in these cells is communicated to the hypothalamus in the brain, triggering the hunger drive.

People with more adipose tissue than others feel food-deprived earlier, even though they may be equal in weight (Heber, 2010). This might occur because more signals are being sent to the brain. Obese and *formerly* obese people tend to have more adipose tissue than people of normal weight. Thus, many people who have lost weight complain that they are always hungry when they try to maintain normal weight levels.

Fatty tissue also metabolizes (burns) food more slowly than muscle does. For this reason, a person with a high fat-to-muscle ratio metabolizes food more slowly than a person of the same weight with a lower fat-to-muscle ratio (Apovian, 2010; Heber, 2010). Thus, two people who are identical in weight may metabolize food at different rates depending on the distribution of muscle and fat in their bodies. Overweight people therefore are doubly disadvantaged in their efforts to lose weight—not only by their extra weight but by the fact that much of their body is composed of adipose tissue.

The normal distribution of fat cells is different for men and women. The average man is 40% muscle and 15% fat. The average woman is 23% muscle and 25% fat. If a man and a woman with typical distributions of muscle and fat are of equal weight, therefore, the woman—who has more fat cells—must eat less to maintain that weight.

Truth or Fiction Revisited: It is not true that dieting accelerates the body's metabolic rate. Ironically, the very act of dieting can make it progressively more difficult to lose weight. This is because the metabolic rates of people on diets and those who have lost substantial amounts of weight slow down; that is, they burn fewer calories (Apovian, 2010; Heber, 2010). From an evolutionary perspective, the slowing of the metabolic rate—also known as *adaptive thermogenesis*—appears to be a built-in mechanism that helps preserve life in times of famine (Doucet et al., 2007; Major et al., 2007). However, adaptive thermogenesis makes it more difficult for dieters in our modern era to continue to lose weight (Heber, 2010; Wijers et al., 2009). The pounds seem to come off more and more reluctantly.

We also live in an *obesogenic environment* (Apovian, 2010; Heber, 2010). Foods high in sugar and fat are everywhere. Children in the United States are exposed to an average of 10,000 food commercials a year. More than nine of ten of these commercials are for fast foods, sugared cereals, candy, and soft drinks (Harris et al., 2009; Sixsmith & Furnham, 2010). Psychological factors, such as observational learning, stress, and emotional states, also "bombard" us and play a role in obesity (Apovian, 2010). Situations contribute as well. Family celebrations, watching television, arguments, and tension at work can

© Ashley Cooper/CORBIS

Overweight in Childhood: Like Mother, Like Daughter? Weight problems run in families, but environmental as well as genetic factors appear to be involved.

Set point A weight range that one's body is programmed to maintain such that the body will increase or decrease its metabolic rate according to the amount of calories one consumes.

Video Connections—Childhood Obesity

Why are so many children overweight? Does being overweight in childhood predict being overweight in adulthood? Go to Psychology CourseMate at **www.cengagebrain.com** to watch this video.

You can do many things to control your weight, but first be advised that psychologists warn that not everyone should try to slim down. Women in the United States today are under social pressure to conform to an unnaturally slender female ideal. As a result, they tend to set unrealistic weight loss goals (Nordgren et al., 2008). Moreover, many attempts to lose weight are ineffective (Heber, 2010). For many obese people, however, especially those who are severely obese, shedding excess pounds lowers the risks of health problems such as type 2 diabetes and heart disease.

Research on motivation and on methods of therapy has enhanced our knowledge of healthful ways to lose weight. Sound weight-control programs do not involve fad diets such as fasting, eliminating carbohydrates, or eating excessive amounts of one particular food (Heber, 2010). They involve improving nutritional knowledge, decreasing calorie intake, exercising, and changing eating habits (see Table 8.2 ■).

Most health experts believe that people in the United States eat too much fat and not enough fruits and vegetables (Heber, 2010). Eating foods low in saturated fats and cholesterol is not only good for the heart but can also contribute to weight loss. Taking in fewer calories results in lower weight. Eating fewer calories does not just mean eating smaller portions. It means switching to some lower-calorie foods—relying more on fresh, unsweetened fruits and vegetables (eating apples rather than apple pie), fish and poultry, and skim milk and cheese. It can mean cutting down on—or eliminating—butter, margarine, oils, and sugar. It appears that the same foods that help control weight also reduce the risk of heart disease and some other illnesses.

Dieting plus exercise is more effective than dieting alone for shedding pounds and keeping them off. Exercise burns calories and builds muscle tissue, which metabolizes more calories than fatty tissue does (Heber, 2010).

Cognitive-behavioral methods have also provided many strategies for losing weight. Among them are the following:

- Establish calorie-intake goals and keep track of whether you are meeting them. Get a book that shows how many calories are found in foods.

- Substitute low-calorie foods for high-calorie foods. Fill your stomach with celery rather than cheesecake. Eat planned low-calorie snacks instead of binge-eating ice cream.

- Take a 5-minute break between helpings. Ask yourself, "Am I still hungry?" If not, stop eating.

- Avoid temptations that have sidetracked you in the past. When shopping at the mall, take your lunch break at the Alfalfa Sprout Café, not the Cheesecake Factory. Plan your meal before entering a restaurant. Attend to your own plate, not to the sumptuous dish at the next table. Walk briskly

© Mike Kemp/Rubberball/Getty Images

all lead to overeating or going off a diet. Efforts to diet may also be impeded by negative emotions such as depression and anxiety, which can lead to binge eating (Ricca et al., 2009).

While millions of Americans are eating too much and putting on more weight than is healthful for them, hundreds of thousands of people—mainly adolescent girls and young women but boys and men as well—are eating less than is healthful. We consider their problems in the following section.

Eating Disorders: Is It True That "You Can Never Be Too Rich or Too Thin"?

Consider some facts about eating and eating disorders in the United States as reported by the National Eating Disorders Association (2010):

through the supermarket, preferably after dinner when you're no longer hungry. and shop from a list. Don't be sidetracked by pretty packages (fattening things may come in them). Don't linger in the kitchen. Study, watch TV, or write letters elsewhere. Don't bring fattening foods into the house. Prepare only enough food to keep within your calorie goals.

- Exercise to burn more calories and increase your metabolic rate. Reach for your mate, not your plate (to coin a phrase). Take a brisk walk instead of eating an unplanned snack. Build exercise routines by adding a few minutes each week.

- Reward yourself for meeting calorie goals (but not with food). When you meet your weekly calorie goal, put cash in the bank toward a vacation or a new camera.

- Use imagery to help yourself lose weight. Tempted by a fattening dish? Imagine that it's rotten, that you would be nauseated by it and have a sick taste in your mouth for the rest of the day.

- Mentally walk through solutions to problem situations. Consider what you will do when cake is handed out at the office party. Rehearse your next visit to relatives and imagine how you will politely refuse seconds and thirds, despite their objections.

- Above all, if you slip from your plan for a day, don't blow things out of proportion. Dieters are often tempted to binge, especially when they rigidly see themselves either as perfect successes or as complete failures or when they experience powerful emotions—either positive or negative. Consider the weekly or monthly trend, not just a single day. If you do binge, resume dieting the next day.

Losing weight—and keeping it off—is not easy, but it can be done. Making a commitment to losing weight and establishing a workable plan for doing so are two of the keys.

TABLE 8.2 ■ American Heart Association Diet Recommendations

Vegetables and Fruits	At least four servings a day. Vegetables and fruits are high in vitamins, minerals, and fiber—and they're low in calories. Eating a variety of fruits and vegetables may help you control your weight and your blood pressure.
Grains	Choose whole grains, high fiber. Unrefined whole-grain foods contain fiber that can help lower your blood cholesterol and help you feel full, which may help you manage your weight.
Fish	At least two servings a week. Eating oily fish containing omega-3 fatty acids (for example, salmon, trout, and herring) may help lower your risk of death from coronary artery disease.
Fats	Select fat-free, 1% fat, and low-fat dairy products. Aims: • Cholesterol: <300 mg per day • Trans fat: <1% of total calorie intake. Cut back on foods containing partially hydrogenated vegetable oils to reduce trans fat in your diet. • Saturated fats: <7% of total calorie intake
Salt	Choose and prepare foods with little or no salt. Aim to eat less than 1,500 milligrams of sodium per day (less than one teaspoon).
Sugar	Minimize sugary foods and drinks to fewer than five servings per week.
Alcohol	If you drink alcohol, drink in moderation. That means one drink per day if you're a woman and two drinks per day if you're a man.

These guidelines will not only help you control your weight, they will also contribute to your heart health.

Source: American Heart Association. (2010, December 7). www.americanheart.org/presenter.jhtml?identifier=851

- More than half of teenage girls and nearly one third of teenage boys use unhealthful methods to try to control their weight, including fasting, skipping meals, smoking, vomiting, and taking laxatives.

- About two of five first- through third-grade girls would like to be thinner.

- More than four of five 10-year-old girls report fear of being fat.

- Nearly half of 9- to 11-year-old girls are "sometimes" or "very often" dieting.

- More than 90% of college women have dieted at some time.

- The average American woman is about 5' 4" tall and weighs about 140 pounds. The typical American model is 5' 11" and weighs 117 pounds.

Question 10: What are eating disorders? Eating disorders are characterized by persistent, gross disturbances in eating patterns. In this section, we focus on an eating disorder in which individuals are too thin, *anorexia nervosa*, and one in which the person may be normal in weight but not in the methods used to maintain that weight, *bulimia nervosa*.

Eating disorders A group of disorders marked by persistent, gross disturbances in eating patterns.

269

ANOREXIA NERVOSA The Duchess of Windsor once said, "You can never be too rich or too thin." **Truth or Fiction Revisited:** Most people make no objection to having a fat bank account, but the fact is that one can most certainly be too skinny, as in the case of anorexia nervosa. **Anorexia nervosa** is a life-threatening eating disorder characterized by extreme fear of being too heavy, dramatic weight loss, a distorted body image, and resistance to eating enough to reach or maintain a healthful weight.

Anorexia nervosa afflicts mainly women during adolescence and young adulthood (Ackard et al., 2007). The typical person with anorexia is a young European American female of higher socioeconomic status. Affluent females have greater access to fitness centers and are more likely to read the magazines that idealize slender bodies and to shop in the boutiques that cater to females with svelte figures. All in all, they are regularly confronted with unrealistically high standards of slimness that make them unhappy with their own physiques (Ackard et al., 2007).

The incidences of anorexia nervosa and bulimia nervosa have increased markedly in recent years. We also find eating disorders among some males, particularly among males who are compelled by their chosen activities—for example, wrestling or dancing—to keep their weight within a certain range or to remain very slender (Cobb, 2008; Lock, 2009). However, women with these disorders greatly outnumber the men who have them by more than six to one, although we lack precise data on their prevalence because so many people deny their disorder (Ackard et al., 2007). A study of 985 European American women and 1,061 African American women found that 1.5% of the European Americans and none of the African Americans had met the diagnostic standards for anorexia nervosa at some time during their lives (Striegel-Moore et al., 2003) (see Table 8.3 ■).

Females with anorexia nervosa can drop 25% or more of their weight within a year. Severe weight loss triggers abnormalities in the endocrine system (that is, with hormones) that prevent ovulation (Andersen & Ryan, 2009). General health deteriorates. Nearly every system in the body is affected. There are problems with the respiratory (Gardini et al., 2009) and cardiovascular systems (Papadopoulos et al., 2009). Females with anorexia are also at risk for premature development of osteoporosis, a condition characterized by loss of bone density that usually afflicts people in late adulthood (Andersen & Ryan, 2009). Given all these problems, it is not surprising that the mortality rate for females with anorexia nervosa is approximately 5%.

In one common pattern, the girl sees that she has gained weight after reaching puberty, and she resolves she must lose it. But even after the weight is gone, she maintains her pattern of dieting and, in many cases, exercises at a fever pitch. This pattern continues as she plunges below her "desirable" weight—according to standardized weight charts—and even after others tell her she is becoming all skin and bones.

Denial is a huge part of anorexia nervosa. Girls with the disorder tend to deny that they are losing too much weight. They are in denial about any health problems, pointing to their feverish exercise routines as evidence of their strength. Distortion of the body image—seeing oneself as heavier than one is—is a major feature of the disorder (Hrabosky et al., 2009; Miyake et al., 2010).

Video Connections—Anorexia Nervosa

Eating disorders affect many Americans, especially women. Why? Watch the video to hear this woman's story of battling her eating disorder. Go to Psychology CourseMate at **www.cengagebrain.com** to watch this video.

Anorexia nervosa A life-threatening eating disorder characterized by dramatic weight loss and a distorted body image.

TABLE 8.3 ■ Incidence of Anorexia Nervosa and Bulimia Nervosa among African American Women and European American Women

	Anorexia Nervosa	Bulimia Nervosa
African Americans	0%	0.4%
European Americans	1.5%	2.3%

In their study of 985 European American women and 1,062 African American women who had participated in the 10-year National Heart, Lung, and Blood Institute (NHLBI) Growth and Health Study, Ruth Striegel-Moore and her colleagues (2003) found that the incidence of eating disorders was higher among European Americans than African Americans.

Ironically, individuals with anorexia do not literally distance themselves from food. They may become as preoccupied with food as they are with their own body shape. They may develop a fascination with cookbooks, shop for their families, and prepare gourmet feasts—for other people, that is.

BULIMIA NERVOSA Bulimia nervosa is sort of a companion disorder to anorexia nervosa. Bulimia nervosa also tends to afflict women during adolescence and young adulthood (Bravender et al., 2010). It entails repeated cycles of binge eating and purging. Binge eating often follows on the heels of food restriction—as in dieting (Cifani et al., 2009; White et al., 2009). There are various methods of purging. Some people vomit. Other avenues include strict dieting or fasting, the use of laxatives, and engaging in demanding, prolonged exercise regimens. Individuals with eating disorders tend to be perfectionists about their bodies. They will not settle for less than their idealized body shape and weight (Franco et al., 2009; Watson et al., 2010). Bulimia, like anorexia, triggers hormonal imbalances: Studies find that many females with bulimia nervosa have irregular menstrual cycles (Mendelsohn, & Warren, 2010).

Eating disorders are upsetting and dangerous in themselves, of course, but they are also often connected with deep depression (Wilson et al., 2010). However, it seems that depression is more likely to co-occur with eating disorders than to be caused by them (Wade et al., 2000).

Every night that I throw up I can't help but be afraid that my heart might stop or something else happen. I just pray and hope I can stop this throwing up before it kills me. I hate this bulimia and I won't stop. It's hard for me to binge and throw up now (refrigerator is locked) and I just can't do it anymore. I just can't race through so much food so fast and then throw it up. I don't really want to. There are times that I do but not often. My new pattern is sure leaving me with an awful feeling in the morning. I eat dinner and kind of keep eating (snacking) afterwards to the point where I either feel too full or think (know) I've eaten too much, then I fall asleep (one hour or so) wake up and think I have to throw up. Half of me doesn't want to, the other half does and I always find myself throwing up. I try falling back asleep but it always seems like eventually sometime during the night I always throw up.

Costin, 1996, pp. 62–63

ORIGINS OF EATING DISORDERS Question 11: What are the origins of eating disorders? Health professionals have done a great deal of research into the origins of eating disorders. Yet they will be the first to admit that many questions about these disorders remain unanswered.

According to some psychoanalysts, anorexia nervosa may symbolize a young woman's efforts to cope with sexual fears, especially fear of pregnancy. Anorexia is connected with *amenorrhea* (lack of menstruation) (Mendelsohn & Warren, 2010); therefore, some psychoanalysts interpret anorexia as a female's attempt to regress to her lifestyle prior to puberty. Anorexia nervosa prevents some adolescents from separating from their families and assuming adult responsibilities. Their breasts and hips flatten again due to the loss of fatty tissue. In the adolescent's fantasies, perhaps, she remains a sexually undifferentiated child.

Many parents are obsessed with getting their children—especially their infants—to eat. Thus, some psychoanalysts suggest that children now and then refuse to eat as a way of engaging in warfare with their parents. ("You have to eat something!" "I'm not hungry!") It often seems that warfare does occur in the families of adolescents with eating disorders. Parents in such families are often unhappy with the family's functioning. They frequently have issues with eating and dieting themselves. They also "act out" against their daughters—letting them know that they consider them unattractive and, prior to the development of the eating disorder, letting them know that they think they should lose weight (Cooper et al., 2001; Crittenden & Dallos, 2009).

A particularly disturbing risk factor for eating disorders in adolescent females is a history of child abuse, particularly sexual abuse (Leung et al., 2010; Maniglio, 2009). One study found a history of childhood sexual abuse in about half of women with bulimia as opposed to a rate of about 7% among women without the disorder (Deep et al., 1999). Another study compared 45 pairs of sisters, one of whom was diagnosed with anorexia (Karwautz et al., 2001). Those with anorexia were significantly more likely to be exposed to high parental expectations *and* to sexual abuse.

We must also consider sociocultural factors that may contribute to eating disorders. Slimness is idealized in the United States, but when you check out *Cosmopolitan* or the Victoria's Secret catalog, you are looking at models who, on average, are 9%

Bulimia nervosa An eating disorder characterized by repeated cycles of binge eating and purging.

taller and 16% thinner than the typical female—and who still manage to have ample bust lines. Miss America, the annually renewed American role model, has also been slenderizing herself over the years. Over the past 80 years, the winner has added only 2% in height but has lost 12 pounds in weight. In the early days of the 1920s, Miss America's weight relative to her height yielded a body mass index (BMI[1]) of 20 to 25, which is considered normal by the World Health Organization (WHO). The WHO labels people as malnourished when their BMIs are lower than 18.5. However, recent Miss Americas come in at a BMI near 17 (Schick et al., 2009).

Truth or Fiction Revisited: Thus, it is true that checking out the Victoria's Secret catalog can contribute to eating disorders among women. As the cultural ideal slenderizes, women with desirable body weights according to the health charts feel overweight, and overweight women feel gargantuan (Schick et al., 2009).

Many individuals with eating disorders are involved in activities that demand weight limits, such as dancing, acting, and modeling. As noted earlier, male wrestlers and other athletes also feel the pressure to stay within an "acceptable" weight range (Lock, 2009). Men, like women, experience pressure to create an ideal body, one with power in the upper torso and a trim abdomen (Lock, 2009).

Eating disorders tend to run in families, which raises the possibility of the involvement of genetic factors (J. H. Baker et al., 2009). Genetic factors might be involved in the obsessionist and perfectionist personality traits that often accompany the need to be super thin (Altman & Shankman, 2009; Ansell et al., 2010). Genetically inspired perfectionism, cultural emphasis on slimness, self-absorption, and family conflict may create a perfect recipe for the development of eating disorders (Altman & Shankman, 2009; J. H. Baker et al., 2009).

Do you have an eating disorder, or are you at risk of developing one? The nearby Eating Disorders Quiz might provide some insight.

The Model Figure for the 2010s? The great majority of women who compare themselves to the idealized embodiment of the tall, slender model are likely to be disappointed. Their body mass index (BMI) is about 17, and nearly two of three American women have a BMI in excess of 25.

[1]You can calculate your body mass index as follows. Write down your weight in pounds. Multiply it by 703. Divide the product by your height in inches squared. For example, if you weigh 160 pounds and are 5' 8" tall, your BMI is $(160 \times 703) / 68^2$, or 24.33. A BMI of 25 or higher is defined as overweight. A BMI of 30 or higher is defined as obese.

© Kristian Dowling/Getty Images

The following are some questions that may help identify the presence of or potential for an eating disorder. These are not a substitute for evaluation by a professional in the field.

1. Are you preoccupied about your weight or shape? (Note: some concern is normal in our society.)
2. If you are dieting, have you lost a significant amount of weight or have you lost weight rapidly?
3. If you answered yes to question 2, are your family, friends, or your doctor concerned about your weight loss?
4. If you answered yes to question 2, is your weight more than 10% under a healthy weight for your age and height?
5. If you answered yes to question 2, do you feel colder than your friends or family?
6. If you answered yes to question 2, has your energy level decreased significantly?
7. If you answered yes to question 2, and if you are female, have your periods stopped or become irregular?
8. If you answered yes to question 2, and if you are still growing, have you failed to increase weight as you have become taller and older?
9. Do you experience binge eating or "grazing" with a sense of loss of control that causes physical or psychological distress?
10. Do you purge after eating by inducing vomiting, using laxatives, taking water pills, using diet pills, skipping meals, or do you compensate in other ways for eating more than you thought you should?
11. Do you compulsively exercise—to the point where your friends or family are concerned, your coach is concerned, or you have medical symptoms from excessive exercise?
12. Are you using any bodybuilding steroids to increase your muscle mass?
13. Do you experience yo-yo (up and down) weights on a regular basis?
14. Do you have a significant increase in carbohydrate craving or binge eating or grazing in the fall and winter months?
15. Do you have a continuing negative attitude toward your body weight or shape to the extent that it interferes with the quality of daily life or preoccupies you much of the time?

The above questions address only some of the signs and symptoms of an eating disorder. If you answered "yes" to any of the questions, there is a possibility that you have an eating disorder, so you may want to seek assistance. If you answered "yes" to five or more items, you should seriously consider seeking professional advice.

Source: University of Iowa Hospitals and Clinics. Department of Psychiatry. (2007). Accessed February 6, 2009. www.uihealthcare.com/depts/med/psychiatry/divisions/eatingdisorders/quiz.html

LearningConnections • HUNGER: DO YOU GO BY "TUMMY-TIME"?

ACTIVE REVIEW (8) Biological factors in hunger include _____ contractions. (9) The _____ nucleus (VMN) of the hypothalamus functions as a stop-eating center. (10) As time passes after a meal, the _____ sugar level drops, and fat is drawn from fat cells to provide nourishment. (11) _____ nervosa is a life-threatening eating disorder characterized by dramatic weight loss and a distorted body image. (12) _____ nervosa involves repeated cycles of binge eating and purging.

REFLECT AND RELATE Why do you eat? Have you ever eaten because you were anxious or bored or because you passed a bakery window with some enticing pastries? What are the effects on your health?

CRITICAL THINKING Since genetic factors are involved in the development of eating disorders, is there any purpose in trying to challenge the cultural idealization of the extremely thin female? Explain.

 Go to Psychology CourseMate at **www.cengagebrain.com** for an interactive version of these questions.

● SEXUAL MOTIVATION AND SEXUAL ORIENTATION: PRESSING THE START BUTTON AND FINDING DIRECTION

In a TV comedy, a mother referred to her teenage son as "a hormone with feet." She recognized that her son had become obsessed with sex, which is normal enough for adolescents in our culture. It is also now widely understood that the adolescent preoccupation with sex is strongly related to the surge in sex hormones that occurs at puberty. The phrase "a hormone with feet" implies movement as well as motivation, and movement means direction. We will see that sex hormones tend to propel us in certain directions as well as provide the driving force. **Question 12: How do sex hormones affect sexual motivation?**

Hormones and Sexual Motivation: Adding Fuel to the Fire

Sex hormones can be said to fuel the sex drive. Research with men who produce little testosterone—due to age or health problems—shows that their sex drive is increased when they receive testosterone replacement therapy (Muraleedharan et al., 2010). The most common sexual problem among women is lack of sexual desire or interest, and the sex drive in women is also connected with testosterone levels (Downey, 2009). Although men produce 7 to 10 times the testosterone produced by women, women produce androgens ("male" sex hormones) in the adrenal glands and the ovaries. Testosterone injections, patches, or pills can heighten the sex drive in women who do not produce enough of it (Brand & van der Schouw, 2010).

Sex hormones promote the development of male and female sex organs and regulate the menstrual cycle. They also have *activating* and *organizing* effects on sexual behavior. They affect the sex drive and promote sexual response; these are **activating effects**. Female mice, rats, cats, and dogs are receptive to males only during **estrus**, when female sex hormones are plentiful. During estrus, female rats respond to males by hopping, wiggling their ears, and arching their backs with their tails to one side, thus enabling males to penetrate them. But, as noted by Kimble (1988),

> [I]f we were to observe this same pair of animals one day [after estrus], we would see very different behaviors. The male would still be interested (at least at first), but his advances would not be answered with hopping, ear wiggling, and [arching of the back]. The female would be much more likely to "chatter" her teeth at the male (a sure sign of hostility if you are a rat). If the male were to be slow to grasp her meaning, she might turn away from him and kick him in the head, mule fashion. Clearly, it is over between them. (p. 271)

The nearby Closer Look box suggests that pheromones, like hormones, may play a role in human sexual behavior.

Sexual Response and Sexual Behavior

Although we may consider ourselves sophisticated about sex, it is surprising how little most of us know about sexual biology. For example, how many male readers know that women have different orifices for urination and sexual intercourse? How many readers know that the erect penis—sometimes referred to by the slang term "boner"—contains no bones? In this section, we fill in some gaps in knowledge. We first consider how females and males respond to sexual stimulation—that is, the so-called *sexual response cycle*. Then we discuss some forms of sexual behavior in the United States today.

THE SEXUAL RESPONSE CYCLE Although we may be more culturally attuned to focus on gender differences rather than similarities, William Masters and Virginia Johnson (1966) found that the biological responses of males and females to sexual stimulation—that is, their sexual response cycles—are quite similar. **Question 13: What is the sexual response cycle?** Masters and Johnson use the term **sexual response cycle** to describe the changes that occur in the body as men and women become sexually aroused. They divide the sexual response cycle into four phases: *excitement, plateau, orgasm,* and *resolution.* Some observers argue for a fifth (initial) phase: desire (e.g., Wylie & Manoun, 2009).

The sexual response cycle is characterized by *vasocongestion* and *myotonia.* **Vasocongestion** is the swelling of the genital tissues with blood. **Myotonia** is muscle tension. It causes facial grimaces, spasms in the hands and feet, and the spasms of orgasm.

Vasocongestion during the **excitement phase** causes erection in men. The testes increase in size and become elevated. In the female, excitement is characterized by vaginal lubrication. Vasocongestion swells the clitoris, flattens and spreads

---

Activating effect The arousal-producing effects of sex hormones that increase the likelihood of sexual behavior.

Estrus The periodic sexual excitement of many female mammals as governed by levels of sex hormones.

Sexual response cycle Masters and Johnson's model of sexual response, which consists of four stages or phases: excitement, plateau, orgasm, and resolution.

Vasocongestion Engorgement of blood vessels with blood, which swells the genitals and breasts during sexual arousal.

Myotonia Muscle tension.

Excitement phase The first phase of the sexual response cycle, which is characterized by muscle tension, increases in the heart rate, and erection in the male and vaginal lubrication in the female.

Is the Human Sex Drive Affected by Pheromones?

"Pheromones have been found across the animal kingdom, sending messages between courting lobsters, alarmed aphids, suckling rabbit pups, mound-building termites and trail-following ants."

—T. D. Wyatt, 2009

For centuries, people have searched for a love potion—a magical formula that could make other people fall in love with them or be strongly attracted to them. Some scientists suggest that such potions may already exist in the form of chemical secretions known as pheromones. **Pheromones** are odorless chemicals that may enhance people's moods, have effects on fertility, and provide a basis for sexual communication below the level of conscious awareness (T. Wyatt, 2009). They are detected through a "sixth sense"—the *vomeronasal organ (VNO),* located in the mucous lining of the nose (Touhara & Vosshall, 2009; T. Wyatt, 2009). The VNO may detect pheromones and transmit information about them to the hypothalamus, possibly affecting sexual response (Cutler, 1999). Infants might use them to recognize their mothers, and adults might respond to them in seeking a mate. Research clearly shows that lower animals use pheromones to stimulate sexual response, organize food gathering, maintain pecking orders, sound alarms, and mark territories (T. Wyatt, 2009).

So, what about humans? In a typical study, Winnifred Cutler and her colleagues (1998) had men wear a suspected male pheromone, whereas a control group wore a placebo. At the end of the study, the men using the pheromone increased their frequency of sexual intercourse with their female partners. The researchers conclude that the substance increased the attractiveness of the men.

Ah, for the Sake of Science! Research suggests that pheromones in men's sweat can amp up the heart rate of women, put them in a better mood, and help stimulate sexual arousal. (No, this does not mean that men should discontinue showering.)

A couple of double-blind studies exposed men and women to steroids (androstadienone produced by males and estratetraenol produced by females) suspected of being pheromones. They found that both steroids enhanced the moods of women but not of men; the substances also apparently reduced feelings of nervousness and tension in women but, again, not in men (Grosser et al., 2000; Jacob & McClintock, 2000). The findings about estratetraenol are not terribly surprising. This substance is related to estrogen, and women tend to function best during ovulation, when estrogen levels are highest (Ross et al., 2000).

Do pheromones enhance the moods of women and thus make them more receptive to sexual advances? In any event, pheromones do not directly stimulate sexual behavior in humans as they do with lower animals. Perhaps the higher we climb the evolutionary ladder, the less important is the role of instinctive behavior.

---

the vaginal lips, and expands the inner part of the vagina. The breasts enlarge, and blood vessels near the surface become more prominent, taking on a reddish hue. The nipples may become erect in both sexes. Heart rate and blood pressure increase.

The level of sexual arousal remains somewhat stable during the **plateau phase** of the cycle. Vasocongestion causes some increase in the circumference of the head of the penis, which also takes on a purplish hue. The testes increase in size and are elevated into position for **ejaculation**. In women, vasocongestion swells the outer part of the vagina, and the inner vagina expands further. The clitoris withdraws beneath the clitoral hood. Breathing becomes rapid. Heart rate may increase to 100 to 160 beats per minute. Blood pressure continues to rise.

During **orgasm** in the male, muscle contractions propel the ejaculate out of the body. Sensations of pleasure tend to be related to the strength of the contractions and the amount of seminal fluid present. The first three to four contractions are generally most intense and occur at 0.8-second intervals (five contractions every 4 seconds) in both genders. Additional contractions occur more slowly. Orgasm in the female is manifested by three to fifteen contractions of the pelvic muscles that surround the vaginal barrel. As in the male, contractions produce pleasure and release sexual tension. Blood pressure and heart rate peak, with up to 180 beats per minute.

Pheromone A chemical secretion detected by other members of the same species that stimulates a certain kind of behavior.

Plateau phase The second phase of the sexual response cycle, which is characterized by increases in vasocongestion, muscle tension, heart rate, and blood pressure in preparation for orgasm.

Ejaculation The process of propelling seminal fluid (semen) from the penis.

Orgasm The height, or climax, of sexual excitement, involving involuntary muscle contractions, release of sexual tensions, and usually, subjective feelings of pleasure.

275

After orgasm, in the **resolution phase**, the body returns to its unaroused state. Men enter a **refractory period** during which they cannot experience another orgasm or ejaculate. Women do not undergo a refractory period and can become quickly rearoused to the point of repeated (multiple) orgasms if they desire and receive continued sexual stimulation.

The sexual response cycle describes what happens when females and males are exposed to sexual stimulation. But what kinds of sexual experiences do people seek?

SOME SURVEYS OF SEXUAL BEHAVIOR: PEERING INTO PRIVATE LIVES

Question 14: What do we know about the sex lives of people in the United States?
What is normal in the United States, at least in the statistical sense? There are many difficulties in gathering data, such as the refusal of many individuals to participate in research. People who return surveys differ from those who do not in that they are more willing to disclose intimate information and are possibly also more liberal in their sexual behavior (Rathus et al., 2011).

The well-known Kinsey reports (Kinsey et al., 1948, 1953) carefully interviewed 5,300 males and 5,940 females in the United States between 1938 and 1949. Interviewers asked about sexual experiences, including masturbation, oral sex, and premarital sex. The nation was astounded to learn that the majority of males masturbated and had engaged in sexual intercourse prior to marriage. Moreover, 20% to 50% of females reported engaging in these behaviors.

A more recent survey—The National Health and Social Life Survey (NHSLS; Laumann et al., 1994)—interviewed 3,432 people and may offer the most accurate information we have. The NHSLS team identified sets of households in various locales and obtained an overall participation rate of close to 80%. The NHSLS considered the factors of level of education, religion, and race/ethnicity in many aspects of people's sexual behavior, including their number of sex partners (see Table 8.4 ■). Males in the survey report having higher numbers of sex partners than females do. For example, one male in three (33%) reports having 11 or more sex partners since the age of 18. This compares with fewer than one woman in ten (9%). One the other hand, most people in the United States appear to limit their numbers of sex partners to a handful or fewer. This finding has been corroborated by many surveys over the years.

Level of education is connected with sexual behavior. **Truth or Fiction Revisited:** Generally speaking, it would appear that education is a liberating influence on sexual

Resolution phase The fourth phase of the sexual response cycle, during which the body gradually returns to its prearoused state.

Refractory period In the sexual response cycle, a period of time following orgasm during which an individual is not responsive to sexual stimulation.

Sex (Sex?) in the 1950s The Kinsey reports showed that there was much more premarital sex than one would have expected in the late 1940s and early 1950s.

© George Marks/Hulton Archives/Getty Images

TABLE 8.4 ■ Number of Sex Partners Since Age 18 as Found in the NHSLS[a]

Sociocultural Factors	Number of Sex Partners					
	0	1	2–4	5–10	11–12	21+
	Percents					
Sex						
Male	3%	20%	21%	23%	16%	17%
Female	3	32	36	20	6	3
Education						
Less than high school	4	27	36	19	9	6
High school graduate	3	30	29	20	10	7
Some college	2	24	29	23	12	9
College graduate	2	24	26	24	11	13
Advanced degree	4	25	20	23	10	13
Religion						
None	3	16	29	20	16	16
Liberal, moderate Protestant	2	23	31	23	12	8
Conservative Protestant	3	30	30	20	10	7
Catholic	4	27	29	23	8	9
Race/Ethnicity						
European American	3	26	29	22	11	9
African American	2	18	34	24	11	11
Latin American	3	36	27	17	8	9
Asian American[b]	6	46	25	14	6	3
Native American[b]	5	28	35	23	5	5

[a]National Health and Social Life Survey, conducted by a research team centered at the University of Chicago.

[b]These sample sizes are quite small.

Source: Adapted from *The Social Organization of Sexuality: Sexual Practices in the United States* (Table 5.1C, p. 179), by E. O. Laumann, J. H. Gagnon, R. T. Michael, & S. Michaels, 1994, Chicago: University of Chicago Press.

"Bisexuality immediately doubles your chances for a date on Saturday night."

WOODY ALLEN

behavior. People with some college education, or who have completed college, are likely to report having more sex partners than those who attended grade school or high school only. But if education has a liberating influence on sexuality, conservative religious experience appears to be a restraining factor.

Ethnicity is also connected with sexual behavior. The research findings in Table 8.4 suggest that European Americans and African Americans have the highest numbers of sex partners. Latin Americans, who report having fewer partners, are mostly Catholic. Perhaps Catholicism provides a restraint on sexual behavior. Asian Americans would appear to be the most sexually restrained ethnic group.

The NHSLS found that 63% of the men and 42% of the women sampled reported masturbating during the past year. Women may be less motivated to masturbate than men are, or they may be more responsive to cultural constraints (Chivers et al., 2007).

Surveys find that about half of the high school students in the United States are sexually active. According to the National Survey of Family Growth (Mosher et al., 2005), the number of adolescents who have had vaginal intercourse increases each year between the ages of 15 and 19.

The following section does not focus on sexual behavior but rather on whom we wish to have as partners.

Sexual Orientation: Which Way Is Love?

Earlier we discussed that sex hormones have *activating* effects. However, they also have directional, or **organizing, effects.** That is, they predispose lower animals toward masculine or feminine mating patterns. Sex hormones are thus likely candidates for influencing the development of sexual orientation (De Rooij et al., 2009). **Question 15: What is sexual orientation?**

One's **sexual orientation** refers to the direction of her or his sexual and romantic interests—toward people of the other sex or toward people of the same sex. The

Organizing effect The directional effect of sex hormones—for example, along typical male or female patterns of mating.

Sexual orientation The directionality of one's sexual and romantic interests; that is, whether one is sexually attracted to, and desires to form a romantic relationship with, members of the other sex or of one's own sex.

great majority of people have a **heterosexual** orientation. That is, they are sexually attracted to, and interested in forming romantic relationships with, people of the other sex. However, some people have a **homosexual** orientation. They are attracted to and interested in forming romantic relationships with people of their own sex. Males with a homosexual orientation are referred to as *gay males*. Females with a homosexual orientation are referred to as *lesbians*. *Bisexual* people are attracted to both females and males.

Heterosexual Referring to people who are sexually aroused by, and interested in forming romantic relationships with, people of the other sex.

Homosexual Referring to people who are sexually aroused by, and interested in forming romantic relationships with, people of the same sex. (Derived from the Greek *homos*, meaning "same," not from the Latin *homo*, meaning "man.")

© Plush Studios/Bill Reitzel/Jupiterimages

THE ORIGINS OF SEXUAL ORIENTATION About 7% of American women and men define themselves as being "other than heterosexual," but the behavior of the other 93% doesn't exactly match up with the way in which people label themselves. For example, nearly twice as many people—about 14%—say they have had oral sex with a person of the same sex (Herbenick et al., 2010a, 2010b, 2010c; Reece et al., 2010). Theories of the origins of sexual orientation look both at nature and nurture—the biological makeup of the individual and environmental factors. Some theories bridge the two. **Question 16: What do we know about the origins of gay male and lesbian sexual orientations?**

Social-cognitive theorists look for the roles of factors such as reinforcement and observational learning. From this perspective, reinforcement of sexual behavior with members of one's own sex—as in reaching orgasm with them when members of the other sex are unavailable—might affect one's sexual orientation. Similarly, childhood sexual abuse by someone of the same sex could lead to a pattern of sexual activity with people of one's own sex and affect sexual orientation. Observation of others engaged in enjoyable male–male or female–female sexual encounters could also affect the development of sexual orientation. But critics point out that most individuals become aware of their sexual orientation before they experience sexual contacts with other people of either sex (Savin-Williams & Cohen, 2007). Moreover, in a society that generally condemns homosexuality, young people are unlikely to believe that male–male or female–female relationships will have positive effects for them.

There is evidence for genetic factors in sexual orientation (Dawood et al., 2009; Ramagopalan et al., 2010). About 52% of identical (MZ) twin pairs are *concordant* (in agreement) for a gay male sexual orientation compared with 22% for fraternal (DZ) twins and 11% for adoptive brothers (Dawood et al., 2009). Monozygotic (MZ) twins fully share their genetic heritage, whereas dizygotic (DZ) twins, like other pairs of siblings, overlap 50%.

In a search for possible differences in the brain among heterosexuals, gay men, and lesbians, Swedish researchers (Savic & Lindström, 2008) conducted MRI scans of the brains of 90 subjects—50 heterosexual men and women and 40 gay men and lesbians. They found that the brains of the heterosexual men and the lesbians were slightly asymmetrical; the right hemisphere was slightly larger than the left hemisphere. Other studies have found that the right hemisphere is usually larger in men than women and that its relative size may be connected with sex differences in spatial-relations ability (Andreano & Cahill, 2009; Hugdahl et al., 2006). (Researchers control for the typically larger brains of males.)

This difference in the sizes of the hemispheres was not found among the brains of gay men and heterosexual women. The researchers also measured the blood flow to the amygdala, an area of the brain involved in the emotional response to threats. They found that the amygdala was wired similarly in gay men and heterosexual women and also in lesbians and heterosexual men (see Figure 8.3 ■). The researchers admitted that their methodology cannot show whether the differences in brain shape and interconnectivity are inherited or due to environmental factors such as exposure to testosterone in the womb. Nor can they conclude that the differences in the brain are responsible for sexual orientation. But even at this stage in the research, it would appear that the brains of many heterosexuals and gay males and lesbians *might* differ in ways that are consistent with their sexual orientations.

RESEARCH WITH NONHUMANS In many families of animals, such as rodents, there is little room for thinking about sex and deciding whether an individual will pursue sexual relationships with males or females. Sexual orientation comes under the almost complete governance of sex hormones (Henley et al., 2010; Piffer et al., 2009).

Heterosexual men | Heterosexual women | Homosexual men | Homosexual women

Left amygdala

Right amygdala

0 ▬▬ 6.0

Figure 8.3 ■ PET Scans of the Amygdalas of Heterosexuals and Homosexuals The amygdalas of homosexual men and heterosexual women appear to have similar patterns of blood flow, as shown by PET scanning. Moreover, the patterns of blood flow of the amygdalas of homosexual women and heterosexual men also appear to be similar.

Source: Figure I from Savic, Ivanka, Per Lindstro. 2008. PET and MRI show differences in cerebral asymmetry and functional connectivity between homo- and heterosexual subjects. *PNAS* (June): I–3. Copyright 2010 National Academy of Sciences, U.S.A.

Furthermore, much sexual orientation is determined by whether the brains and sex organs of fetuses are bathed in large doses of testosterone in the uterus. In male fetuses, testosterone is normally produced by the developing testes. Yet female fetuses may also be exposed to testosterone. They can be flooded with testosterone naturally if they share the uterus with many male siblings. Researchers can also inject male sex hormones into the uterus. When female embryos are bathed in testosterone, the sex organs become masculinized in appearance, and their brains become organized in the male direction, creating a tendency toward female–female mating efforts and other masculine-typed behavior patterns at maturity (Phoenix, 2009). Basically, the rodents become male, although they are infertile.

BACK TO HUMANS It has been demonstrated repeatedly that sex hormones predispose lower animals toward stereotypical masculine or feminine mating patterns. But sexual orientation has not been reliably connected with adolescent or adult levels of sex hormones in humans (Lonstein & Auger, 2009). But might sex hormones influence the developing human embryo and fetus in the way that they affect rodents (Garcia-Falgueras & Swaab, 2010)? The evidence is somewhat mixed, and this possibility continues to receive intensive study (Dawood et al., 2009). And if prenatal hormone levels affect the sexual orientation of the fetus, what causes the fluctuation in hormone levels? Hormone levels in utero can be affected by genetic factors, maternal stress, drinking alcohol, and other factors.

LearningConnections ● SEXUAL MOTIVATION AND SEXUAL ORIENTATION: PRESSING THE START BUTTON AND FINDING DIRECTION

ACTIVE REVIEW (13) The hormone _____ is connected with sex drive in both males and females. (14) Masters and Johnson divide the sexual response cycle into four phases: the _____, plateau, orgasm, and resolution phases. (15) Sex hormones have activating and _____ effects on sexual behavior. (16) A person's sexual _____ involves whether he or she is sexually attracted to, and interested in forming romantic relationships with, people of the same or the other sex. (17) Sex hormones (do or do not?) predispose lower animals toward stereotypical masculine or feminine mating patterns.

REFLECT AND RELATE Have you heard the term *sexual preference*? Do you believe that people prefer, or decide, whether to be heterosexual or homosexual?

CRITICAL THINKING In general, people who attribute sexual orientation to biological causes are more accepting of gay male and lesbian sexual orientations. Why do you think this is so?

 Go to Psychology CourseMate at **www.cengagebrain.com** for an interactive version of these questions.

AGGRESSION

A murder trial took place in the library of anthropologist Raymond Dart. His guest, Robert Ardrey, held the evidence in his hand—the smashed jawbone of an adolescent. Dart had deduced that the adolescent had been struck in the head with a leg bone of an antelope. The angle of the blow and its intensity swept aside any possibility that the death was accidental.

What struck Ardrey was that the murder had taken place more than 500,000 years ago. The victim belonged to a species that was not a direct ancestor of humans but shared a branch on the evolutionary tree with humans. The murderer belonged to the same species. In this murder, Ardrey found an explanation of human aggression: Murder and warfare were instinctive. Here in the dawn of time, close relatives of humans had stalked antelopes, baboons, and each other with weapons.

Critical thinking teaches us to search for rival explanations for the behavior we observe—whether we observe it in the present or its record from the distant past, and whether we observe it in humans or other species. One possibility is that aggressive behavior among humans (and perhaps among more primitive apes) is and was learned—by trial and error and by observing others. In Chapter 6, for example, we noted evidence that observing violence in the media is connected with violent behavior among viewers. The idea of an instinct also suggests that a behavior pattern occurs automatically, without thinking, without decision making. Many—perhaps most—psychologists believe that violence between people is not automatic but involves evaluation of one's situation and choosing among possible patterns of behavior.

Still, we cannot ignore the fact that humans are aggressive—today. There are armed conflicts of one kind or another on nearly every continent of planet Earth. There is murder, and there is battering, often by people's most intimate partners. There is rape. Ardrey's evidence for a killer instinct is flawed, but there is evidence of a role for biology in aggression, even among humans. **Question 17: What have psychologists and other scientists learned about the biological and psychological origins of aggressive behavior?**

Biology, Chemistry, and Aggression

Evolutionary psychologists believe that "genetic whisperings" influence aggression (Buss, 2009; Confer et al., 2010). Numerous biological structures and chemicals appear to be involved in aggression. In response to certain stimuli, many lower animals show

> "Human nature is potentially aggressive and destructive and potentially orderly and constructive."
>
> MARGARET MEAD

> "The tendency to aggression is an innate, independent, instinctual disposition in man... it constitutes the powerful obstacle to culture."
>
> SIGMUND FREUD

A Speculative View of the Primate Past from the Film 2001 Researchers have unearthed evidence that the ancestors and relatives of humans used weapons against each other as well as prey. In the film *2001*, a fictitious primate—similar in appearance to a relative but not an ancestor of humans—uses a bone from an antelope as a weapon.

© The Everett Collection

instinctive aggressive reactions (Archer, 2009). This behavior is automatic, although it can be modified somewhat by learning. For example, the male robin responds aggressively to the red breast of another robin. The hypothalamus appears to be involved in this inborn reaction pattern. Electrical stimulation of part of the hypothalamus triggers stereotypical aggressive behaviors in many lower animals. However, in humans, whose brains are more complex, other brain structures apparently moderate possible aggressive instincts.

Chemistry is also involved in aggression, especially in the form of the male sex hormone testosterone. Testosterone appears to affect the tendencies to dominate and control other people. Men have higher testosterone levels than women do and are also (usually) more aggressive than women, especially with male strangers (Archer & Parker, 2006; Crofoot & Wrangham, 2010; Pradhan et al., 2010). For example, aggressive boys and adolescents are likely to have higher testosterone levels than their less aggressive peers (Popma et al., 2007). James Dabbs and his colleagues (1996) found that members of so-called rambunctious fraternities have higher testosterone levels, on average, than members of more "well-behaved" fraternities. Testosterone levels also vary with the occasion: men's testosterone levels tend to be higher when they are "winning"—whether in athletic competitions such as football or in chess (Carré et al., 2009; Carré & Putnam, 2010).

Another reason that males are more likely than females to behave aggressively is that females are more likely to empathize with the victim—to put themselves in the victim's place (Proverbio et al., 2010; Yamasue et al., 2008). Empathy encourages helping behavior, not aggression.

Psychological Aspects of Aggression

Psychologists have recognized the importance of understanding (and curbing) human aggression for many generations. Let's consider various psychological views of aggression.

PSYCHODYNAMIC THEORY AND AGGRESSION Sigmund Freud, the originator of psychodynamic theory, believed that aggression is natural and instinctive. But Freud viewed aggressive impulses as inevitable reactions to the frustrations of daily life. He was not thinking so much in terms of the evolutionary history of humans. According to Freud, children (and adults) naturally desire to vent aggressive impulses on other people, including parents, because even the most attentive parents cannot gratify all of their demands immediately. Yet children also fear punishment and loss of love, so they repress most aggressive impulses and store them in the unconscious recesses of the mind. Instinctive behavior is thus modified by experience.

COGNITIVE PSYCHOLOGY AND AGGRESSION Cognitive psychologists assert that it is natural for people to attempt to understand their environments and make decisions. From this perspective, our behavior is influenced by our values, by how we interpret situations, and by choice. People who believe that aggression is sometimes necessary and justified—as during wartime—are likely to act aggressively. People who believe that a particular war or act of aggression is unjust, or who oppose aggression regardless of the circumstances, are less likely to behave aggressively (Hurka, 2010; Maxwell et al., 2009).

One cognitive theory suggests that frustration and discomfort trigger unpleasant feelings (Archer, 2009). These feelings, in turn, prompt aggression. Aggression is *not* automatic, however. Cognitive factors intervene (Berkowitz, 1994; Fischer et al., 2008). People *decide*—sometimes making split-second decisions—whether they will strike out or not on the basis of factors such as their previous experiences with aggression and their interpretation of the other person's motives.

Researchers also find that many individuals who act aggressively distort other people's motives for their behavior. For example, they assume that other people wish them harm when they actually do not (Dodge, 2006; Ellis et al., 2009). Cognitive therapists note that we are more likely to respond aggressively to a provocation when we magnify the importance of the "insult" or otherwise stir up feelings of anger (Ellis et al., 2009). How do you respond when someone bumps into you? If you view it as an intentional insult to your honor, you may respond with aggression. If you view it

"It is impossible to overlook the extent to which civilization is built upon a renunciation of instinct."

SIGMUND FREUD

as an accident or as a social problem in need of a solution, you are less likely to act aggressively.

From the cognitive perspective, in sum, it is natural for people to appraise their situations. Whether or not they behave aggressively depends on the outcome of that appraisal.

LEARNING AND AGGRESSION What do the behavioral and social-cognitive perspectives have to say about aggression? From the behavioral perspective, learning is acquired through reinforcement. Organisms that are reinforced for aggressive behavior are more likely to behave aggressively in situations similar to those in which reinforcement occurs. Environmental consequences make it more likely that an animal will be rewarded for aggression if it attacks a smaller, weaker animal. Strong, agile organisms are likely to be reinforced for aggressive behavior.

Among lower animals, reinforcement is usually physical—for example, food, mating, or escaping a predator. Humans respond to such reinforcements but also to other reinforcers, such as social approval. Research shows that children are less likely to behave aggressively when teachers and classmates communicate strong disapproval of aggressive behavior (Henry, 2008; Simon et al., 2009).

The behavioral perspective would describe aggressive behaviors as instinctive, as in the case of many lower animals, or as acquired by means of reinforcement. From the social-cognitive perspective, aggressive skills are mainly acquired by the observation of other people acting aggressively. Most behaviorists would see aggressive behavior as being mechanical even in humans either because it is inborn or because the learning of aggressive behaviors is controlled by reinforcements. However, social-cognitive theorists—like other cognitive theorists—believe that consciousness and choice play key roles in aggressive behavior among humans. Social-cognitive theorists believe that we are not likely to act aggressively unless we believe that aggression is appropriate under the circumstances and likely to be reinforced.

Situational Factors and Aggression

Situational factors can contribute to aggression. For example, aggression sometimes takes place within the context of a mob. When people act as individuals, fear of consequences and awareness of their moral values tend to prevent them from hurting other people. But in a mob, they may experience *deindividuation,* which is a state of reduced self-awareness with less of a focus on one's values. Factors that lead to deindividuation include anonymity, sharing of responsibility for aggressive behavior (also called *diffusion of responsibility*), a high level of emotional arousal due to noise and crowding, and a focus on the group's norms rather than on one's own concepts of right and wrong (McKimmie et al., 2009). Under these circumstances, crowd members behave more aggressively than they would as individuals.

LearningConnections ● AGGRESSION

ACTIVE REVIEW (18) Electrical stimulation of part of the brain structure called the _____ triggers stereotypical aggressive behaviors in many lower animals. (19) The male sex hormone _____ affects tendencies to dominate and control other people. (20) Cognitive psychologists assert that our behavior is influenced by our values, by how we _____ situations, and by choice.

REFLECT AND RELATE Consider people you would label "explosive." Do you believe that they actually decide where and when to behave violently or that they have no control over their outbursts?

CRITICAL THINKING What can we deduce about humans from the murder trial in Dart's library? Yes, one humanlike animal may have killed another and used a weapon to do so. People have also killed other people and used weapons to do so. But do these incidents provide evidence that aggressive behavior is instinctive? Why or why not?

 Go to Psychology CourseMate at **www.cengagebrain.com** for an interactive version of these questions.

ACHIEVEMENT MOTIVATION: "JUST DO IT"?

Many students persist in studying despite being surrounded by distractions. Many people strive relentlessly to get ahead, to "make it," to earn large sums of money, to invent, to accomplish the impossible. **Question 18: Why do some people strive to get ahead while others do not?** Psychological research has pointed to these people having something called *achievement motivation*.

Psychologist David McClelland (1958) helped pioneer the assessment of achievement motivation through the evaluation of fantasies. One method involves the *Thematic Apperception Test (TAT)* developed by Henry Murray. The TAT contains cards with pictures and drawings that are subject to various interpretations. Individuals are shown one or more TAT cards and asked to construct stories about the pictured theme: to indicate what led up to it, what the characters are thinking and feeling, and what is likely to happen.

One TAT card is similar to that in Figure 8.4 ■. The meaning of the card is ambiguous—unclear. Is the girl nodding off, thinking about the book, wishing she were out with friends? Consider two stories that could be told about this card:

- *Story 1:* "She's upset that she's got to read the book because she's behind in her assignments and doesn't particularly like to work. She'd much rather be out with her friends, and she may very well sneak out to do just that."

- *Story 2:* "She's thinking, 'Someday I'll be a great scholar. I'll write books like this, and everybody will be proud of me.' She reads all the time."

The second story suggests the presence of more achievement motivation than the first. Research finds that people with high achievement motivation earn higher grades than people with comparable learning ability but lower achievement motivation (E. A. Turner et al., 2009). They are more likely to envision themselves as becoming successful and work harder to achieve success (Story et al., 2009; E. A. Turner et al., 2009).

McClelland (1965) used the TAT to sort college students into two groups: students with high achievement motivation and students with low achievement motivation. He found that 83% of college graduates with high achievement motivation found jobs in occupations characterized by risk, decision making, and the chance for great success, such as business management, sales, or self-employment. Most (70%) of the graduates who chose nonentrepreneurial positions showed low achievement motivation. People with high achievement motivation seem to prefer challenges and are willing to take moderate risks to achieve their goals.

What Flavor Is Your Achievement Motivation?

Do you want to do well in this course? If you do, why? Carol Dweck (2009; Dweck & Master, 2008) finds that achievement motivation can be driven by different forces. Are you motivated mainly by performance goals? For example, is your grade in this course of most importance? If so, it may be in part because your motives concern tangible rewards such as getting into graduate school, landing a good job, reaping approval from parents or your instructor, or avoiding criticism. Performance goals are usually met through **extrinsic rewards** such as prestige and income. Parents of children who develop performance goals are likely to respond to good grades with tangible rewards such as toys or money and to respond to poor grades with anger and removal of privileges.

Or do learning goals mainly motivate you to do well? That is, is your central motive to enhance your knowledge and skills—your ability to understand and master the subject matter? Learning goals usually lead to **intrinsic rewards**, such as self-satisfaction. Students who develop learning goals often have parents with strong achievement

"Work is the curse of the drinking classes."

OSCAR WILDE

Figure 8.4 ■ Tapping Fantasies in Personality Research This picture is similar to a Thematic Apperception Test card used to measure the need for achievement. What is happening in this picture? What is the person thinking and feeling? What is going to happen? Your answers to these questions reflect your own needs as well as the content of the picture itself.

Extrinsic rewards The rewards associated with performance goals, such as a good salary, health care, and retirement benefits.

Intrinsic rewards The rewards associated with learning goals, such as self-esteem and increased understanding and insight.

motivation who encourage their children to think and act independently from an early age. They help their children develop learning goals by showing warmth and praising them for their efforts to learn, exposing them to novel and stimulating experiences, and encouraging persistence (Dweck, 2006; 2009). Children of such parents frequently set high standards for themselves, associate their achievements with self-worth, and attribute their achievements to their own efforts rather than to genetic factors, chance, or the intervention of others.

Many of us strive to meet both performance and learning goals in our courses as well as in other areas of life. Grades are important because they are connected with (very) tangible benefits, but learning for its own sake is also of value.

LearningConnections • ACHIEVEMENT MOTIVATION: "JUST DO IT"?

ACTIVE REVIEW (21) McClelland used the Thematic _____ Test to measure achievement motivation. (22) Students with _____ goals are mainly motivated by factors such as good grades, rewards from parents, and the prospect of landing a good job.

REFLECT AND RELATE Do you seem to be driven mainly by performance goals or learning goals in this course and in your other courses? Explain.

CRITICAL THINKING Some people strive harder to get ahead than others. Is it circular reasoning to "explain" the difference in terms of more or less achievement motivation?

Go to Psychology CourseMate at **www.cengagebrain.com** for an interactive version of these questions.

EMOTION: ADDING COLOR TO LIFE

Emotions color our lives. We are green with envy, red with anger, blue with sorrow. Positive emotions such as love and desire can fill our days with pleasure. Negative emotions such as fear, depression, and anger can fill us with dread and make each day a chore. Sometimes, our emotions "lurk in the background." Sometimes, they seize control of the day. And as noted by Solomon (2008), emotion can be hard to define.

Question 19: Just what is an emotion? An emotion can be a response to a situation in the way that fear is a response to a threat. An emotion can motivate behavior (for example, anger can motivate us to act aggressively). An emotion can also be a goal in itself. We may behave in ways that will lead us to experience happiness or feelings of love. Emotions are thus intertwined with motivation. We are driven by emotions, and meeting—or failing to meet—our needs can have powerful emotional results.

Emotions are feeling states with physiological, cognitive, and behavioral components (Solomon, 2008). In terms of physiology, strong emotions arouse the **autonomic nervous system** but also involve the limbic system and other parts of the brain (LeDoux & Phelps, 2008) (see Chapter 3). The greater the arousal, the more intense the emotion. It also appears that the type of arousal affects the emotion being experienced. Although the word *emotion* might seem to be about feeling and not about thinking, cognitions—particularly interpretations of the meanings of events—are important aspects of emotions. *Fear,* which usually occurs in response to a threat, involves cognitions that one is in danger as well as arousal of the **sympathetic nervous system** (rapid heartbeat and breathing, sweating, muscle tension) and significant activity on the part of the limbic system—the **amygdala** (LeDoux & Phelps, 2008). The amygdala sends messages to the hypothalamus that control the autonomic responses related to fear, as in increasing blood pressure. The amygdala receives pain messages as well as visual and auditory information, so it is well suited to the conditioning of fear responses (see Figure 8.5 ■).

Emotions also involve behavioral tendencies. Fear is connected with behavioral tendencies to avoid or escape from a particular situation (see Table 8.5 ■). As a response to a social provocation, *anger* involves cognitions involving revenge, arousal of both the sympathetic and **parasympathetic nervous systems**, and tendencies to approach the object of the anger—that is, to attack (Carver & Harmon-Jones, 2009). *Depression* usually

> "*Emotions have always lurked in the background—often as a threat to reason. . . . One of the most enduring metaphors of reason and emotion has been the metaphor of master and slave, with the wisdom of reason firmly in control and the dangers of emotion safely suppressed, channeled, or (ideally) in harmony with reason. But the question "What is an emotion?" has proved to be as difficult to resolve as the emotions have been to master.*"

ROBERT C. SOLOMON, 2008, P. 3

Emotion A state of feeling that has cognitive, physiological, and behavioral components.

Autonomic nervous system (ANS) The division of the peripheral nervous system that regulates glands and activities such as heartbeat, respiration, digestion, and dilation of the pupils.

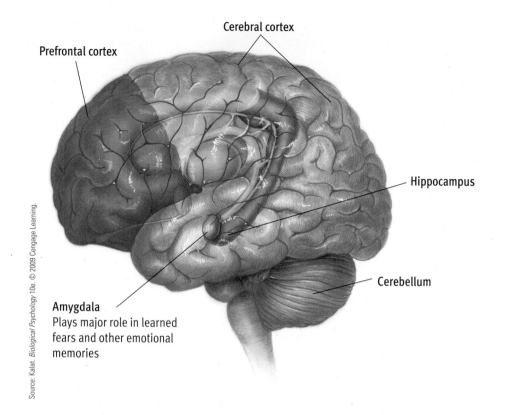

Prefrontal cortex

Cerebral cortex

Hippocampus

Cerebellum

Amygdala
Plays major role in learned fears and other emotional memories

Source: Kalat. *Biological Psychology* 10e. © 2009 Cengage Learning.

Figure 8.5 ■ The Amygdala and the Learning of Fears The amygdala is significantly involved in the learning of fears. The basolateral part of the amygdala receives visual and auditory information and then transmits messages to the central amygdala. The central amygdala, in turn, transmits messages to the gray matter in the midbrain, which relays the messages to the part of the pons that is responsible for the startle reflex.

TABLE 8.5 ■ Components of Emotions

Emotion	Physiological	Cognitive	Behavioral
Fear	Sympathetic arousal	Belief that one is in danger	Avoidance tendencies
Anger	Sympathetic and parasympathetic arousal	Frustration or belief that one is being mistreated	Attack tendencies
Depression	Parasympathetic arousal	Thoughts of helplessness, hopelessness, worthlessness	Inactivity, possible self-destructive tendencies

involves cognitions of helplessness and hopelessness, parasympathetic arousal, and tendencies toward inactivity—or sometimes, self-destruction. *Happiness, grief, jealousy, disgust, embarrassment,* and *liking* all have cognitive, physiological, and behavioral components as well.

The Expression of Emotions: The Smile Seen Round the World?

Happiness and sadness are found in all cultures, but, **Question 20: Do people around the world express emotions in the same way?** It turns out that the expression of many emotions may be universal (Ekman, 2003). Smiling is apparently a universal sign of friendliness and approval. Baring the teeth, as noted by Charles Darwin (1872) in the 19th century, may be a universal sign of anger. As the originator of the theory of evolution, Darwin believed that the universal recognition of facial expressions would have survival value. For example, in the absence of language, facial expressions could signal the approach of enemies (or friends).

Most investigators concur that certain facial expressions suggest the same emotions in people who are reared in different cultures (e.g., Matsumoto et al., 2008; Sebe et al., 2007). Moreover, people in diverse cultures recognize the emotions manifested by certain facial expressions, such that there is some immediate cross-cultural communication of feelings. In a classic study, Paul Ekman (1980) took photographs of people exhibiting anger, disgust, fear, happiness, sadness, and surprise (see Figure 8.6 ■). He then asked

Sympathetic nervous system The branch of the autonomic nervous system that is most active during processes that spend body energy from stored reserves, such as in a fight-or-flight reaction to a predator or when you are anxious about a big test. When people experience fear, the sympathetic nervous system accelerates the heart rate, raises blood pressure, tenses muscles, and so on.

Amygdala An almond-shaped structure in the frontal part of the temporal lobe that is part of the limbic system and involved in processing and expressing emotions, particularly fear.

Parasympathetic nervous system The branch of the autonomic nervous system that is most active during processes that restore reserves of energy to the body, such as relaxing and eating. When people relax, the parasympathetic nervous system decelerates the heart rate, normalizes blood pressure, relaxes muscles, and so on. The parasympathetic division also stimulates digestion.

 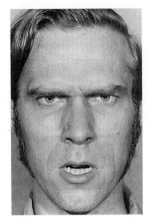  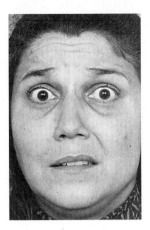

Figure 8.6 ■ Photographs Used in Research by Paul Ekman Ekman's research suggests that the facial expressions connected with several important emotions such as happiness, anger, surprise, and fear are universally recognized.

people around the world to indicate what emotions were being depicted. Those queried ranged from European college students to members of the Fore, a tribe that dwells in the New Guinea highlands. All groups, including the Fore, who had almost no contact with Western culture, agreed on the emotions being portrayed. The Fore also displayed familiar facial expressions when asked how they would respond if they were the characters in stories that called for basic emotional responses. Ekman and his colleagues (1987) obtained similar results in a study of 10 cultures. In that study, participants were allowed to identify more than one emotion in facial expressions. The participants generally agreed on which two emotions were shown and which emotion was more intense.

On the other hand, there is no perfect one-to-one relationship between facial expressions and emotions (Matsumoto et al., 2008). Facial expressions sometimes occur in the absence of the emotion they are thought to accompany (Porter & ten Brinke, 2008). As noted by psychologist Joseph Campos (2000), the voice, posture, and gestures also provide clues as to what people are feeling and about to do.

Many psychologists help individuals cope with negative emotions such as fear, anger, and depression. But psychologists have also studied positive emotions, such as happiness, and considered ways people might increase their feelings of happiness.

> *"How to gain, how to keep, how to recover happiness is in fact for most men at all times the secret motive of all they do, and of all they are willing to endure."*
>
> WILLIAM JAMES

"Is Evvvvrybody Happy?" An Excursion into Positive Psychology

Ted Lewis, the Great Depression–era bandleader, used to begin his act by asking, "Is evvvvrybody happy?" Well, everybody is not happy, but surveys do suggest that the majority of people in developed nations are satisfied with their lives (Cummins & Nistico, 2002). Many people might think that psychologists are only interested in negative emotions such as anxiety, depression, and anger. Not at all. An area of psychology called positive psychology deals with positive emotions such as happiness and love, optimism and hope, and joy and sensual pleasures.

Question 21: What factors contribute to happiness? Are some people just "born happy," or do life experiences determine happiness? What factors interfere with happiness? Some psychologists, such as David Lykken (Lykken & Csikszentmihalyi, 2001), believe that genetic factors play a powerful role in happiness. They note that happiness tends to run in families and that we tend to have a rather stable level of happiness throughout much of our lives (W. Johnson & Krueger, 2006). Positive events such as learning that the person we love also loves us or receiving recognition for our work can certainly raise the level of happiness we experience at the moment. Similarly, negative life events such as the loss of a loved one, financial reverses, or injuries can depress us. Yet we may tend to revert to our characteristic level of happiness after an event that makes us either happier or sadder than usual. Actor Christopher Reeve, for example, eventually bounced back to his characteristically happy nature following the accident that paralyzed him.

Positive psychology The field of psychology that is about personal well-being and satisfaction; joy, sensual pleasure, and happiness; and optimism and hope for the future.

Which life experiences contribute to happiness? **Truth or Fiction Revisited:** Despite the saying that "Money can't buy you happiness," surveys in the United States, Russia, China, and Latin America suggest that people tend to be happier when they live in affluent societies and earn decent incomes (W. Johnson & Krueger, 2006). Perhaps money doesn't make people happy in itself, but when we have enough money, at least we don't have to worry about it. Money aside, Chinese college students tend to think about happiness in terms of feelings of contentment, inner harmony, personal achievement, physical wellness, spiritual enrichment, hopefulness about the future, generosity, and self-development (Lu, 2001).People who are married (Waite et al., 2009) and people in enduring gay and lesbian relationships (Wienke & Hill, 2009) tend to be happier than loners. There is a difference, of course, between loneliness and solitude, and maybe people who are extraverted and who have the skills to maintain social relationships are generally more capable of finding life satisfaction. Happy people also tend to be open to new experiences; they are more willing to risk becoming involved in new relationships (Demir & Weitekamp, 2007).

Then there are the attitudinal aspects of happiness. People at any income level can make themselves miserable when they compare their incomes to higher ones(Cheung & Leung, 2008). Happiness also tends to be accompanied by optimism—a cognitive bias toward assuming that things will work out (Ho et al., 2010; Wilhelm et al., 2010). But the bias is not groundless because happy people often believe in their ability to effect change. Thus, they try harder. And, consequently, they often produce the changes that make their lives happier. They are also willing to pat themselves on the back for their successes and are not quick to blame themselves when things go wrong. These attitudes contribute to self-esteem, yet another factor in happiness.

The Facial-Feedback Hypothesis: Does Smiling Make You Happy?

The face has a special place among visual stimuli. Social animals like humans need to differentiate and recognize members of their group, and for people, the face is the most distinctive key to identity (Parr et al., 2000). Faces are also a key to social communication. Facial expressions reflect emotional states, and our ability to "read" these expressions enables us to interact appropriately with other people.

It is known that various emotional states give rise to certain patterns of electrical activity in the facial muscles and in the brain (Davis et al., 2009; Porter & ten Brinke, 2008). But can it work the other way around? The facial-feedback hypothesis argues that facial expressions can also affect our emotional state; that is, the causal relationship between emotions and facial expressions can work in the opposite direction. **Question 22: Can smiling give rise to feelings of goodwill? (Can frowning produce anger?)** Perhaps they can.

Christopher Reeve The actor who played Superman in several films turned out not to be invulnerable when he was thrown from a horse. The accident paralyzed Reeve but did not destroy his fighting spirit or his general tendency toward happiness.

Facial-feedback hypothesis The view that stereotypical facial expressions can contribute to stereotypical emotions.

LIFE CONNECTIONS "COME ON! GET HAPPY!" A POSSIBLE OR IMPOSSIBLE DREAM?

Are there lessons for you in research findings on happiness? Perhaps. They do not clearly show cause and effect when it comes to money, for example, but there is no harm in placing oneself within groups of people who are more likely to be happy. Here are some suggestions:

- Take advantage of your education to develop knowledge and skills that can help you be free from want. Even if money doesn't make you happy, you won't have to worry about money.

- Do not let the fact that other people have more stop you from enjoying what you have.

- Value friendships and other relationships. Be open to new relationships.

- Think about whether you can make your life more meaningful to yourself.

- Consider whether you are generally optimistic or pessimistic. If you are pessimistic, examine the reasons. If you cannot find reasons for your pessimism, challenge yourself to change your outlook.

- Consider whether you blame yourself too much when things go wrong or give yourself too little credit when things go right.

Psychological research has yielded some interesting findings concerning the facial-feedback hypothesis. Inducing people to smile, for example, leads them to report more positive feelings and to rate cartoons as more humorous (Soussignan, 2002; Strack et al., 1988) (see Figure 8.7 ■, part A). When induced to frown, as by holding the pen between their lips, they rate cartoons as more aggressive (see Figure 8.7, part B). When they exhibit pain through facial expressions, they rate electric shocks as more painful. An interesting study found that women's college yearbook pictures predicted life outcomes for many women as much as 30 years later. LeeAnne Harker and Dacher Keltner (2001) found that women who showed more positive emotions in yearbook photos—as by smiling—were more likely to show social competence, personal well-being, and even happier marriages as the years went by. By the way, their physical attractiveness did not seem to matter; it was the display of positive emotions that told the lifelong tale.

What are the possible links between facial feedback and emotion? One is arousal. Intense contraction of facial muscles such as those used in signifying fear heightens arousal, which, in turn, boosts emotional response. Feedback from the contraction of facial muscles may also induce emotions. Engaging in the *Duchenne smile*, characterized by "crow's feet wrinkles around the eyes and a subtle drop in the eye cover fold so that the skin above the eye moves down slightly toward the eyeball" (Ekman, 2003), can induce pleasant feelings (Soussignan, 2002).

You may have heard the British expression "Keep a stiff upper lip" as a recommendation for handling stress. Perhaps a "stiff" lip suppresses emotional response—as long as the lip is relaxed rather than quivering with fear or tension. But when the lip is stiffened through strong muscle tension, facial feedback may heighten emotional response.

Theories of Emotion: *"How Do You Feel?"*

David, 32, is not sleeping well. He wakes before dawn and cannot get back to sleep. His appetite is off, his energy level is low, he has started smoking again. He has a couple of drinks at lunch and muses that it's lucky that any more alcohol makes him sick to his stomach—otherwise, he'd probably be drinking too much, too. Then he thinks, "So what difference would it make?" Sometimes he is sexually frustrated; at other times he wonders whether he has any sex drive left. Although he's awake, each day it's getting harder to drag himself out of bed in the morning. This week he missed one day of work and was late twice. His supervisor has suggested in a nonthreatening way that he "do something about it." David knows that her next warning will not be unthreatening. It's been going downhill since Sue walked out. Suicide has even crossed David's mind. He wonders if he's going crazy.

The author's files

David is experiencing the emotion of depression, seriously so. Depression is to be expected following a loss, such as the end of a relationship, but David's feelings have lingered. His friends tell him that he should get out and do things, but David is so down

Figure 8.7 ■ We May Smile When We Are Pleased, but Can Smiling Make Us Feel Good about Things? According to the facial-feedback hypothesis, smiling just might have that effect. When people are compelled to smile because they are holding a pen between their teeth, they are more likely to rate comic strips as funny (see part A). Holding the pen between their lips forces a frown, and the rating of the cartoons plummets (part B).

A.

B.

that he hasn't the motivation to do much of anything at all. After much prompting by family and friends, David consults a psychologist who, ironically, also pushes him to get out and do things—the things he used to enjoy. The psychologist also shows David that part of his problem is that he sees himself as a failure who cannot make meaningful changes.

Question 23: How do the physiological, situational, and cognitive components of emotions interact to produce feelings and behavior? Some psychologists argue that physiological arousal comes first. It is more central to emotional response than cognition is. Moreover, the type of arousal we experience strongly influences our cognitive appraisal and our labeling of the emotion (e.g., Izard, 1984). For these psychologists, the body takes precedence over the mind. Do David's bodily reactions—for example, his loss of appetite and energy—take precedence over his cognitions? Other psychologists argue that cognitive appraisal and physiological arousal are so strongly intertwined that cognitive processes may determine the emotional response. Are David's ideas that he is helpless to make meaningful changes more at the heart of his feelings of depression?

The "commonsense theory" of emotions is that something happens (a situation) that is cognitively appraised (interpreted) by the person, and the feeling state (a combination of arousal and thoughts) follows. For example, you meet someone new, appraise that person as delightful, and feelings of attraction follow. Or as in the case of David, a social relationship comes to an end, you recognize your loss, feel powerless to change it, and feel down in the dumps.

However, both historical and contemporary theories of how the components of emotions interact are at variance with this commonsense view. Let's consider a number of theories and see whether we can arrive at some useful conclusions.

THE JAMES–LANGE THEORY A century ago, William James suggested that our emotions follow, rather than cause, our behavioral responses to events. At about the same time, this view was also proposed by the Danish physiologist Karl G. Lange. It is therefore termed the **James–Lange theory** of emotion.

According to James and Lange, certain external stimuli instinctively trigger specific patterns of arousal and action, such as fighting or fleeing (see Figure 8.8 ■, part A). We then become angry *because* we are acting aggressively or become afraid *because* we are running away. Emotions are simply the cognitive representations (or by-products) of automatic physiological and behavioral responses.

The James–Lange theory is consistent with the facial-feedback hypothesis. That is, smiling apparently can induce pleasant feelings, even if the effect may not be strong enough to overcome feelings of sadness (Ekman, 1993). The theory also suggests that we may be able to change our feelings by changing our behavior. Changing one's behavior to change one's feelings is one aspect of behavior therapy. When David's psychologist

James–Lange theory of emotion The view that certain external stimuli instinctively trigger specific patterns of arousal and action, such as fighting or fleeing. This theory says that we experience emotions as a consequence of our physiological and behavioral responses.

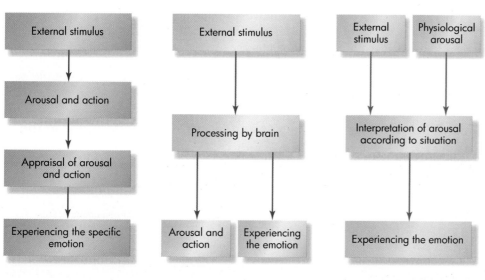

A. James–Lange **B. Cannon–Bard** **C. Cognitive appraisal**

Figure 8.8 ■ Parts A, B and C: The James–Lange Theories of Emotion Several theories of emotion have been advanced, each of which proposes a different role for the components of emotional response. According to the James–Lange theory (part A), events trigger specific arousal patterns and actions. Emotions result from our appraisal of our body responses. According to the Cannon–Bard theory (part B), events are first processed by the brain. Body patterns of arousal, action, and our emotional responses are then triggered simultaneously. According to the theory of cognitive appraisal (part C), events and arousal are appraised by the individual. The emotional response stems from the person's appraisal of the situation and his or her level of arousal.

urges him to get out and do things, she is assuming that by changing his behavior, David can have a positive effect on the way he feels.

Walter Cannon (1927) criticized the James–Lange assertion that each emotion has distinct physiological correlates. He argued that the physiological arousal associated with emotion A is not as distinct from the arousal associated with emotion B as the theory asserts. Note that the James–Lange view downplays the importance of human cognition; it denies the roles of cognitive appraisal, personal values, and personal choice in our behavioral and emotional responses to events.

THE CANNON–BARD THEORY Cannon (1927) was not content to criticize the James–Lange theory. Along with Philip Bard (1934), he suggested that an event might simultaneously trigger bodily responses (arousal and action) and the experience of an emotion. As shown in Figure 8.8, part B, when an event is perceived (processed by the brain), the brain stimulates autonomic and muscular activity (arousal and action) and cognitive activity (experience of the emotion). Thus, according to the **Cannon–Bard theory of emotion**, emotions *accompany* bodily responses. They are not *produced* by bodily changes, as in the James–Lange theory.

The central criticism of the Cannon–Bard theory focuses on whether bodily responses (arousal and action) and emotions are actually stimulated simultaneously. For example, pain or the perception of danger may trigger arousal before we begin to feel distress or fear. Also, many of us have had the experience of having a "narrow escape" and becoming aroused and shaky afterward, when we have had time to consider the damage that might have occurred. What is needed is a theory that allows for an ongoing interaction of external events, physiological changes (such as autonomic arousal and muscular activity), and cognitive activities.

THE THEORY OF COGNITIVE APPRAISAL More recent theoretical approaches to emotion have stressed cognitive factors. Stanley Schachter asserts that many emotions have similar patterns of bodily arousal but that the labels we give them depend largely on our cognitive appraisal of our situations (see Figure 8.8, part C). Given the presence of other people, we engage in social comparison to arrive at an appropriate response.

In a classic experiment, the investigators told participants that they wanted to determine the effects of a vitamin on vision (Schacter & Singer, 1962). Half of the participants received an injection of adrenaline, a hormone that increases the arousal of the sympathetic branch of the autonomic nervous system. A control group received an injection of an inactive solution. Those who had been given adrenaline then received one of three "cognitive manipulations," as shown in Table 8.6 ■. Group 1 was told nothing about possible emotional effects of the "vitamin." Group 2 was deliberately misinformed; members of this group were led to expect itching, numbness, or other irrelevant symptoms. Group 3 was informed accurately about the increased arousal they would experience. Group 4 was a control group injected with an inactive substance and given no information about its effects.

After receiving injections and cognitive manipulations, the participants were asked to wait in pairs while the experimental apparatus was being set up. The participants did not know that the person with whom they were waiting was a confederate of the

Cannon–Bard theory of emotion The view that emotions *accompany* bodily responses but are not caused by them.

TABLE 8.6 ■ Injected Substances and Cognitive Manipulations in the Schachter–Singer Study

Group	Substance	Cognitive Manipulation
1	Adrenaline	No information given about effects
2	Adrenaline	Misinformation given: itching, numbness, etc.
3	Adrenaline	Accurate information given: physiological arousal
4	Inactive	None

Source: Schachter and Singer, 1962

experimenter. The confederate's purpose was to display behavior that the individual would believe was caused by the injection.

Some of those who took part in the experiment waited with a confederate who acted in a happy-go-lucky manner. He flew paper airplanes about the room and tossed paper balls into a wastebasket. Other participants waited with a confederate who acted angry. He complained about the experiment and left the "waiting room" in a huff. As the confederates worked for their Oscar awards, the real participants were observed through a one-way mirror.

The people in groups 1 and 2 were likely to imitate the confederate. Those who were exposed to the happy-go-lucky confederate acted jovial and content. Those who were exposed to the angry confederate complained and acted aggressively. But those in groups 3 and 4 were less influenced by the confederate's behavior.

Schachter and Singer concluded that participants in groups 1 and 2 were in an ambiguous situation. They felt arousal from the adrenaline injection but couldn't label it as a specific emotion. Social comparison with a confederate led them to attribute their arousal either to happiness or to anger. Members of group 3 expected arousal from the injection, with no particular emotional consequences. These participants did not imitate the confederate's display of happiness or anger because they were not in an ambiguous situation; they knew their arousal was caused by the shot of adrenaline. Members of group 4 had no physiological arousal for which they needed an attribution. Like those in group 3, they did not imitate the behavior of the confederate.

Now, happiness and anger are quite different emotions. Happiness is a positive emotion, whereas anger, for most of us, is a negative emotion. Yet Schachter and Singer suggest that the bodily differences between these two emotions are so slight that different views of the situation can lead one person to label arousal as happiness and another person to label it as anger.

In science, it must be possible to replicate experiments and attain identical or similar results for a theory to be considered valid. The Schachter and Singer study has been replicated but with *different* results (Ekman, 1993). For instance, a number of studies found that participants were less likely to imitate the behavior of the confederate and were likely to perceive unexplained arousal in negative terms, attributing it to nervousness, anger, even jealousy (Zimbardo et al., 1993).

EVALUATION OF THE THEORIES What can we make of all this? Research suggests that the patterns of arousal connected with various emotions are more specific than suggested by Schachter and Singer—although less so than suggested by James and Lange (Larsen et al., 2008). Research with brain imaging suggests that different emotions, such as happiness and sadness, involve different structures within the brain (Lane et al., 2009; Pollatos et al., 2007; Suslow et al., 2010). Even so, researchers have not found brain cells that respond to but a single emotion. The emotion of disgust apparently has the most specific brain location, in the primary taste cortex. It makes sense that an emotion that derives from distasteful experiences would be centered here (Murphy, 2003).

Regarding the Schachter and Singer study, Zimbardo and his colleagues (1993) note that lack of control over our emotions and lack of understanding of what is happening to us are disturbing experiences. Thus, our cognitive appraisals of situations apparently do affect our emotional responses, even if not quite in the way envisioned by Schachter.

In sum, various components of an experience—cognitive, physiological, and behavioral—contribute to our emotional responses. Our bodies may become aroused in a given situation, but people also appraise those situations so that arousal in itself may not directly cause one emotion or another. The fact that none of the theories of emotion we have discussed applies to all people in all situations is comforting. Apparently, our emotions are not quite as easily understood, manipulated, or—as in the case of the lie detector—even detected as some theorists have suggested.

The nearby Closer Look box considers the polygraph or, as it is more commonly known, the lie detector.

The connection between autonomic arousal and emotions has led to the development of many kinds of "lie detectors," but are there specific emotional responses that signify lies? Let's take a closer look at the problem of lying.

Lying—for better or worse—is a part of life. People admit to lying in 14% of their e-mails, 27% of their face-to-face interactions, and 37% of their phone calls (Hancock, 2007). Political leaders lie to get elected. When people communicate with online "matches," men are most likely to lie about their personal assets and their goals for a relationship (Hall et al., 2010). Women are most likely to lie about their weight (Hall et al., 2010). The great majority of people lie to their lovers—most often about other relationships (Rowatt et al., 1999; Toma et al., 2008). People also lie about their qualifications to obtain jobs, and of course, some people lie in denying guilt for crimes.

Facial expressions often offer clues to deceit, but some people can lie with a straight face—or a smile. As Shakespeare pointed out in *Hamlet,* "One may smile, and smile, and be a villain." The use of devices to detect lies has a long, if not laudable, history:

> The Bedouins of Arabia . . . until quite recently required conflicting witnesses to lick a hot iron; the one whose tongue was burned was thought to be lying. The Chinese, it is said, had a similar method for detecting lying: Suspects were forced to chew rice powder and spit it out; if the powder was dry, the suspect was guilty. A variation of this test was used during the Inquisition. The suspect had to swallow a "trial slice" of bread and cheese; if it stuck to the suspect's palate or throat he or she was not telling the truth.
>
> Kleinmuntz & Szucko, 1984, pp. 766–767

These methods may sound primitive, even bizarre, but they are broadly consistent with modern psychological knowledge.

Anxiety about being caught in a lie is linked to arousal of the sympathetic division of the autonomic nervous system. One sign of sympathetic arousal is lack of saliva, or dryness in the mouth. The emotions of fear and guilt are also linked to sympathetic arousal and, hence, to dryness in the mouth.

Question 24: How do lie detectors work? Modern lie detectors, or polygraphs, monitor indicators of sympathetic arousal while a witness or suspect is being examined. These indicators include heart rate, blood pressure, respiration rate, and electrodermal response (sweating). Questions have been raised about the validity of assessing truth or fiction in this way, however (Iacono, 2008).

The American Polygraph Association claims that use of the polygraph is 85% to 95% accurate. Critics find polygraph testing to be less accurate and claim that it is sensitive to more than lies (Iacono, 2008). Factors such as tense muscles, drugs, and previous experience with polygraph tests can significantly reduce the accuracy rate. In one experiment, people were able to reduce the accuracy of polygraph-based judgments to about 50% by biting their tongue (to produce pain) or by pressing their toes against the floor (to tense muscles) while being interviewed (Fiske & Borgida, 2008; Honts et al., 1985). Hence, you might give the examiner the impression that you are lying even when you are telling the truth, throwing off the test's results. **Truth or Fiction Revisited:** Thus, it is true that you might be able to fool a lie detector by wiggling your toes.

It appears that no identifiable pattern of bodily responses pinpoints lying (Gronau et al., 2005; Iacono, 2008). Because of validity problems, results of polygraph examinations are no longer admitted as evidence in many courts.

LearningConnections • EMOTION: ADDING COLOR TO LIFE

ACTIVE REVIEW (23) The expression of emotions such as anger, fear, happiness, and surprise appears to be (culture-specific or universal?). (24) Genetic factors (do or do not?) appear to be involved in happiness. (25) According to the James–Lange theory, emotions have specific patterns of arousal and _____. (26) According to the theory of _____ appraisal, the emotion a person will experience reflects his or her appraisal of the situation.

REFLECT AND RELATE Have you ever been able to change the way you feel by doing something? For example, have you ever purposefully worked yourself up into a rage? Or have you ever done something enjoyable to elevate your mood? How do your personal experiences relate to the various theories of emotion?

CRITICAL THINKING Should lie detectors be used in screening candidates for mortgages or jobs?

Go to Psychology CourseMate at **www.cengagebrain.com** for an interactive version of these questions.

The Psychology of Motivation: The *Whys* of Why

1. What are motives, needs, drives, and incentives?
The psychology of motivation is concerned with why people behave in certain ways. Motives are hypothetical states within an organism that propel the organism toward goals. Physiological needs include those for oxygen and food. Psychological needs include those for achievement and self-esteem. Needs give rise to drives; for example, depletion of food gives rise to the hunger drive.

Theories of Motivation: Which Why Is Which?

2. What are species-specific behaviors?
According to the evolutionary perspective, organisms are born with preprogrammed tendencies—called instincts—to behave in certain ways in certain situations.

3. What is drive-reduction theory?
According to drive-reduction theory, we are motivated to engage in behavior that reduces drives. Primary drives such as hunger and thirst are based on the biological makeup of the organism. Acquired drives such as the drive for money are learned. The body has a tendency called homeostasis to maintain a steady state.

4. Are all motives aimed at the reduction of tension?
Apparently not all motives are aimed at reducing tension. Stimulus motives aim to increase rather than decrease stimulation. Sensory-deprivation studies suggest that inactivity and lack of stimulation are aversive in humans.

5. How does humanistic theory differ from other theories of motivation?
Instincts and drives are mainly defensive, aimed at survival and reproduction. Humanistic psychologists argue that people are self-aware and that behavior can be growth oriented; people are motivated to strive for self-actualization.

6. What is Maslow's hierarchy of needs?
Maslow hypothesized that people have a hierarchy of needs. Once lower-level physiological and safety needs are met, people strive to meet needs for love, esteem, and self-actualization.

Hunger: Do You Go by "Tummy-Time"?

7. What bodily mechanisms regulate the hunger drive?
Hunger is regulated by several internal factors, including stomach contractions, blood sugar level, receptors in the mouth and liver, and the hypothalamus. The ventromedial nucleus in the hypothalamus functions as a stop-eating center. The lateral hypothalamus may function as a start-eating center. Chewing and swallowing provide some satiety.

8. What psychological factors are connected with the hunger drive?
External stimuli such as the aroma of food can trigger hunger. One can also experience hunger due to the time of day. ("If it's lunchtime, I must be hungry.")

9. Why are people overweight?
Research shows that genetic factors are involved in being overweight. Americans also live in an environment that is conducive to being overweight, with fast foods and foods high in sugar and fats. Efforts to diet may be hindered by adaptive thermogenesis.

10. What are eating disorders?
Eating disorders, including anorexia nervosa and bulimia nervosa, involve gross disturbances in normal patterns of eating.

11. What are the origins of eating disorders?
Cultural idealization of the slender female—and the pressure that such idealization places on young women—may be the major contributor to eating disorders. Yet many females with eating disorders have a history of child sexual abuse, and eating disorders may have a genetic component.

Sexual Motivation and Sexual Orientation: Pressing the START Button and Finding Direction

12. How do sex hormones affect sexual motivation?
Sex hormones have activating and organizing effects on behavior. "Male" sex hormones appear to fuel the sex drive, even in women, who produce much less of them.

13. What is the sexual response cycle?
The sexual response cycle describes the body's response to sexual stimulation. It is generally characterized by vasocongestion and myotonia and consists of four phases: excitement, plateau, orgasm, and resolution. Following orgasm, males enter a refractory period during which they are temporarily unresponsive to sexual stimulation.

14. What do we know about the sex lives of people in the United States?
In the United States, males are generally more likely than females to masturbate, engage in premarital sex, and have a large number of sex partners. Education appears to have a liberating influence on sexual behavior, whereas conservative religious beliefs appear to constrain it.

15. What is sexual orientation?
Sexual orientation refers to the direction of one's erotic interests. Gay males and lesbians are sexually attracted to people of their own sex.

16. What do we know about the origins of gay male and lesbian sexual orientations?
Social-cognitive theorists focus on the role of reinforcement of early patterns of sexual behavior. Evidence of a genetic contribution to sexual orientation is accumulating. Prenatal sex hormones may play a role in determining sexual orientation.

Aggression

17. What have psychologists and other scientists learned about the biological and psychological origins of aggressive behavior?

Many lower animals show instinctive aggressive reactions. Electrical stimulation of part of the hypothalamus triggers stereotypical aggressive behaviors in many animals. Testosterone appears to affect the tendencies to dominate and control other people and is also involved in aggression. Cognitive psychologists assert that our behavior is influenced by our values, our interpretation of situations, and by choice. From the social-cognitive perspective, aggressive skills are mainly acquired by observation.

Achievement Motivation: "Just Do It"?

18. Why do some people strive to get ahead while others do not?

One factor may be achievement motivation. McClelland used TAT cards to study achievement motivation. Academic achievement may be motivated by performance or learning goals. Performance goals are tangible rewards, such as getting into graduate school. Learning goals involve the enhancement of knowledge or skills

Emotion: Adding Color to Life

19. Just what is an emotion?

An emotion is a state of feeling with physiological, cognitive, and behavioral components. Emotions motivate behavior and also serve as goals.

20. Do people around the world express emotions in the same way?

According to Ekman, the expression of several basic emotions is recognized in cultures around the world. Darwin believed that universal recognition of facial expressions had survival value.

21. What factors contribute to happiness?

Happiness may have a genetic component, but affluence helps, and so do social relationships, a sense of meaning, optimism, and self-esteem.

22. Can smiling give rise to feelings of goodwill? (Can frowning produce anger?)

Facial expressions might influence one's experience of emotion. The contraction of facial muscles might be influential.

23. How do the physiological, situational, and cognitive components of emotions interact to produce feelings and behavior?

According to the James–Lange theory, emotions are associated with specific patterns of arousal and action that are triggered by certain external events. The emotion follows the behavioral response. The Cannon–Bard theory proposes that processing of events by the brain gives rise simultaneously to feelings and bodily responses; that is, feelings accompany bodily responses. According to Schachter and Singer's theory of cognitive appraisal, emotions are associated with similar patterns of arousal. The emotion a person experiences reflects a person's appraisal of the situation.

24. How do lie detectors work?

Lie detectors—also called polygraphs—monitor indicators of sympathetic arousal: heart rate, blood pressure, respiration rate, and sweating while a person is being questioned. These responses are presumed to indicate the presence of emotions—anxiety and/or guilt—that might be caused by lying. Critics find polygraph testing to be unreliable.

KEY TERMS

Acquired drives (p. 262)
Activating effect (p. 274)
Amygdala (p. 285)
Anorexia nervosa (p. 270)
Aphagic (p. 266)
Autonomic nervous system (p. 284)
Bulimia nervosa (p. 271)
Cannon–Bard theory of emotion (p. 290)
Drive (p. 260)
Drive-reduction theory (p. 261)
Eating disorders (p. 269)
Ejaculation (p. 275)
Emotion (p. 284)
Estrus (p. 274)
Excitement phase (p. 274)
Extrinsic rewards (p. 283)
Facial-feedback hypothesis (p. 287)

Heterosexual (p. 278)
Hierarchy of needs (p. 263)
Homeostasis (p. 262)
Homosexual (p. 278)
Hyperphagic (p. 265)
Incentive (p. 261)
Instinct (p. 261)
Intrinsic rewards (p. 283)
James–Lange theory of emotion (p. 289)
Lateral hypothalamus (p. 266)
Motivation (p. 260)
Motive (p. 260)
Myotonia (p. 274)
Need (p. 260)
Organizing effect (p. 277)
Orgasm (p. 275)
Parasympathetic nervous system (p. 285)

Pheromone (p. 275)
Plateau phase (p. 275)
Positive psychology (p. 286)
Primary drives (p. 261)
Refractory period (p. 276)
Resolution phase (p. 276)
Satiety (p. 265)
Self-actualization (p. 263)
Set point (p. 267)
Sexual orientation (p. 277)
Sexual response cycle (p. 274)
Stimulus motive (p. 262)
Sympathetic nervous system (p. 285)
Vasocongestion (p. 274)
Ventromedial nucleus (VMN) (p. 265)

ACTIVE LEARNING RESOURCES

Log in to **www.cengagebrain.com** to access the resources your instructor requires. For this book, you can access:

 CourseMate brings course concepts to life with interactive learning, study, and exam preparation tools that support the printed textbook. A textbook-specific website, Psychology CourseMate includes an integrated interactive eBook and other interactive learning tools including quizzes, flashcards, videos, and more.

CENGAGENOW Need help studying? This site is your one-stop study shop. Take a Pre-Test and CengageNOW will generate a Personalized Study Plan based on your test results. The Study Plan will identify the topics you need to review and direct you to online resources to help you master those topics. You can then take a Post-Test to determine the concepts you have mastered and what you still need to work on.

9 The Voyage Through the Life Span

MAJOR TOPICS

How Psychologists Study Human Development *297*

Prenatal Development: The Beginning of Our Life Story *299*

Childhood: On the Edge of Reason? *301*

Adolescence: "Neither Fish nor Fowl"? *317*

Emerging Adulthood: A New Stage of Development? *323*

Early Adulthood: Becoming Established *324*

Middle Adulthood: The "Sandwich Generation"? *325*

Late Adulthood: Of Wisdom, Decline, and Compensation *328*

On Death and Dying: The Final Chapter *332*

FEATURES

Video Connections: Prenatal Assessment *301*

Video Connections: The Visual Cliff *305*

A Closer Look: Is Development Continuous or Discontinuous? *305*

Video Connections: Piaget's Sensorimotor Stage *307*

Life Connections: Day Care: Blessing, Headache, or Both? *316*

Video Connections: Piaget's Formal Operational Stage: Hypothetical Propositions *319*

A Closer Look: Are There Gender Differences in Moral Development? *320*

A Closer Look: Aging, Gender, and Ethnicity *330*

Self-Assessment: How Long Will You Live? The Life-Expectancy Scale *330*

© Blend Images Photography/Veer

TRUTH OR FICTION?

T F Your heart started beating when you were only one fifth of an inch long and weighed a fraction of an ounce.

page 299

T F Prior to 6 months or so of age, "out of sight" is literally "out of mind."

page 305

T F Child abusers were frequently abused themselves as children.

page 316

T F It is normal for male adolescents to think of themselves as action heroes and to act as though they are made of steel.

page 319

T F Adolescents are in a constant state of rebellion against their parents.

page 321

T F Scores on the verbal subtests of standardized intelligence tests can increase for a lifetime.

page 326

T F Most parents suffer from the "empty-nest syndrome" when their youngest child leaves home.

page 327

Are these items truth or fiction? We will be revisiting them throughout the chapter.

W**e have a story to tell.** It is a fascinating story about the remarkable voyage you have already taken through childhood and adolescence. It is about the unfolding of your adult life. Billions have made this voyage before. Yet you are unique, and things will happen to you that have never happened before.

Let's watch as Ling and Patrick Chung begin such a story by conceiving a child. On a summerlike day in October, Ling and Patrick rush to their jobs as usual. While Ling, a trial attorney, is preparing a case to present in court, a very different drama is unfolding in her body. Hormones are causing a follicle (egg container) in one of her ovaries to ovulate—that is, to rupture and release an egg cell, or ovum. How this particular ovum was selected to ripen and be released this month is unknown. But in any case, Ling will be capable of becoming pregnant for only a couple days following ovulation.

When it is released, the ovum begins a slow voyage down a 4-inch-long Fallopian tube to the uterus. Within this tube, one of Patrick's sperm cells will unite with the egg. The fertilized ovum, or zygote, is 1/175 of an inch across—a tiny stage for the drama that is about to unfold.

Developmental psychologists are interested in studying Patrick and Ling's new child's voyage through the life span for several reasons. The discovery of early influences and developmental sequences helps psychologists understand adults. Psychologists are also interested in the effects of genetic and environmental factors on traits such as aggression and intelligence. Developmental psychologists seek to learn the causes of developmental abnormalities. For instance, should pregnant women abstain from smoking and drinking? (Yes.) What factors contribute to child abuse? Other developmental psychologists focus on adult development. For example, what can we expect as we voyage through our 30s, 40s, 50s, and beyond? The information developmental psychologists acquire can help us make decisions about how we rear our children and, in general, lead our lives.

In the next section we will see how developmental psychologists go about their work. Then we will turn to prenatal developments—the changes that occur between conception and birth.

● HOW PSYCHOLOGISTS STUDY HUMAN DEVELOPMENT

Although developmental psychologists use the types of research conducted by other psychologists—such as case studies, surveys, naturalistic observation, and experiments—the processes of development occur over time, so researchers have devised

"There is no cure for life or death save to enjoy the interval."

GEORGE SANTAYANA

Longitudinal research The study of developmental processes by taking repeated measures of the same group of people at various stages of development.

Cross-sectional research The study of developmental processes by taking measures of people of different age groups at the same time.

Cohort effect Similarities in behavior that stem from the fact that group members are approximately the same age.

additional strategies for studying them. **Question 1: How do researchers study development over time?** In longitudinal research, the same people are observed repeatedly over time, and changes in development, such as gains in height or changes in approaches to problem solving, are recorded. In cross-sectional research, people of different ages are observed and compared. It is assumed that when a large number of people are chosen at random, the differences found in the older age groups reflect how the younger people will develop, given time.

Longitudinal Studies

Some ambitious longitudinal studies have followed the development of children and adults for more than half a century. One, the Fels Longitudinal Study, began in 1929. Children were observed twice a year in their homes and twice a year in the Fels Institute nursery school. In this way, researchers have been able to observe, for example, the development of intelligence. They found that intelligence test scores at ages 3 and 18 were significantly related to intellectual and occupational status after the age of 26 (McCall, 1997). Results are still being gleaned from this study (e.g., Chumlea et al., 2009; Li et al., 2009). Note, however, that most longitudinal studies span months or a few years, not decades.

Longitudinal studies do have drawbacks. It can be difficult to enlist volunteers to participate in a study that will last a lifetime. Many participants fall out of touch as the years pass; others die. Researchers must also be patient. To compare 3-year-olds with 6-year-olds, they must wait 3 years. In the early stages of such a study, the idea of comparing 3-year-olds with 21-year-olds remains a distant dream. When the researchers themselves are middle-aged or older, they must hope that the candle of yearning for knowledge will be kept lit by a new generation of researchers.

Is Listening to an iPod While Studying an Activity That Illustrates the Cohort Effect? Children and adults of different ages experience cultural and other events unique to their age group. This is known as the *cohort effect*. For example, today's children—unlike their parents—are growing up taking video games, the Internet, and rap stars for granted.

Cross-Sectional Studies

Because of the drawbacks of longitudinal studies, most research that compares children of different ages is cross-sectional. That is, most investigators gather data on what the "typical" 6-month-old is doing by finding children who are 6 months old today. When they expand their research to the behavior of typical 12-month-olds, they seek another group of children, and so on.

The **cohort effect** is a major challenge to cross-sectional research. A *cohort* is a group of people born at about the same time. As a result, they experience cultural and other events unique to their age group. However, children and adults of different ages (different cohorts) probably have not shared similar cultural backgrounds. People who are 80 years old today, for example, grew up without television, and today's 50-year-olds grew up without computers. Today's children are growing up taking iPods and the Internet for granted. Children of past generations also grew up with different expectations about gender roles and appropriate behavior. Women in the Fels study generally chose motherhood over careers. Today, the great majority of mothers are in the workforce, and their attitudes about women's roles have changed.

Today's 80-year-olds are not today's 5-year-olds as seen 75 years later. The times change, and their influence on development also changes. In longitudinal studies, we study the same individuals as they develop over the years. In cross-sectional research, we can only hope that the groups will be comparable.

© RubberBall/Veer

ACTIVE REVIEW (1) In _____ research, the same people are observed repeatedly over time. (2) In _____ research, people of different ages are observed and compared. (3) The _____ effect defines similarities among peers that stem from the fact that group members are approximately the same age.

REFLECT AND RELATE How would you describe the cohort to which your parents belong? How does it differ from your cohort?

CRITICAL THINKING Which type of research—longitudinal or cross-sectional—is less likely to be tainted by the cohort effect? Explain.

 Go to Psychology CourseMate at **www.cengagebrain.com** for an interactive version of these questions.

● PRENATAL DEVELOPMENT: THE BEGINNING OF OUR LIFE STORY

The most dramatic gains in height and weight occur during prenatal development. **Question 2: What developments occur from conception through birth?** Within 9 months, the newly conceived organism develops from a nearly microscopic cell to a **neonate** (newborn) about 20 inches long. Its weight increases a billionfold!

During the months following conception, the single cell formed by the union of sperm and egg—the **zygote**—multiplies, becoming two cells, then four, then eight, and so on. By the time the infant is ready to be born, it contains trillions of cells.

The zygote divides repeatedly as it proceeds on its 3- to 4-day voyage to the uterus. The ball-like mass of multiplying cells wanders about the uterus for another 3 to 4 days before beginning to implant in the uterine wall. Implantation takes another week or so. The period from conception to implantation is called the **germinal stage**, or the *period of the ovum*.

The **embryonic stage** lasts from implantation until about the eighth week of development. During this stage, the major body organ systems take form. The growth of the organs—heart, lungs, and so on—precedes the growth of the extremities. The relatively early **maturation** of the brain and the organs allows them to participate in the nourishment and development of the embryo. **Truth or Fiction Revisited:** During the fourth week, the heart begins to beat and pump blood—in an organism that is one fifth of an inch long.

By the end of the second month, the head has become rounded and the facial features distinct—in an embryo that is about 1 inch long and weighs $\frac{1}{30}$th of an ounce. During the second month, the nervous system begins to transmit messages. By 5 to 6 weeks, the embryo is only a quarter to half an inch long, yet nondescript sex organs have formed. By about the seventh week, the genetic code (XY or XX) begins to assert itself, causing the sex organs to differentiate. If a Y sex chromosome is present, testes form and begin to produce **androgens** (male sex hormones), which further masculinize the sex organs. In the absence of these hormones, the embryo develops sex organs that appear to be typical of the female regardless of its genetic code. However, apparently female individuals with a male (XY) genetic code would be sterile.

As it develops, the embryo is suspended within a protective **amniotic sac** in the mother's uterus. The sac is surrounded by a clear membrane and contains amniotic fluid. The fluid is a shock absorber; it allows the child to move or jerk around without injury. It also helps maintain an even temperature.

From now until birth, the embryo exchanges nutrients and wastes with the mother through the **placenta**. The embryo is connected to the placenta by the **umbilical cord**. The placenta is connected to the mother by blood vessels in the uterine wall.

The **fetal stage** lasts from the beginning of the third month until birth. By the end of the third month, the major organ systems and the fingers and toes have formed. In the middle of the fourth month, the mother usually detects the first fetal movements. By the end of the sixth month, the fetus moves its limbs so vigorously that mothers may

Neonate A newly born child.

Zygote A fertilized ovum (egg cell).

Germinal stage The first stage of prenatal development, during which the dividing mass of cells has not become implanted in the uterine wall.

Embryonic stage The baby from the third through the eighth weeks following conception, during which time the major organ systems undergo rapid differentiation.

Maturation The process of development as guided by the unfolding of the genetic code.

Androgens Male sex hormones.

Amniotic sac A sac within the uterus that contains the embryo or fetus.

Placenta A membrane that permits the exchange of nutrients and waste products between the mother and her developing child but does not allow the maternal and fetal bloodstreams to mix.

Umbilical cord A tube between the mother and her developing child through which nutrients and waste products are conducted.

Fetal stage The baby from the third month following conception through childbirth, during which time there is maturation of organ systems and dramatic gains in length and weight.

feel that they are being kicked. The fetus opens and shuts its eyes, sucks its thumb, and alternates between periods of wakefulness and sleep.

During the last 3 months, the organ systems of the fetus continue to mature. The heart and lungs become increasingly capable of sustaining independent life. The fetus gains about 5½ pounds and doubles in length. Newborn boys average about 7½ pounds and newborn girls about 7 pounds.

Environmental Influences on Prenatal Development

Although the fetus develops in a protective "bubble"—the amniotic sac—it is subject to many environmental hazards. **Question 3: What environmental hazards face embryos and fetuses?** Teratogens are environmental agents that can harm the embryo or fetus. Exposure to particular teratogens is most harmful during **critical periods** that correspond to times when vulnerable organs are developing. Because the major organ systems differentiate during the embryonic stage, the embryo is generally at greater risk than the fetus. Let's look at some of the most common teratogens:

Fetal Alcohol Syndrome (FAS) The children of many mothers who drank alcohol during pregnancy exhibit FAS. This syndrome is characterized by developmental lags and such facial features as an underdeveloped upper jaw, a flattened nose, and widely spaced eyes.

- *Alcohol:* Because alcohol passes through the placenta, drinking by a pregnant woman poses risks for the embryo and fetus. Some children of heavy drinkers develop **fetal alcohol syndrome** (FAS) (Connor et al., 2006; Floyd et al., 2005). They are often smaller than normal, and so are their brains. They have distinct facial features: widely spaced eyes, an underdeveloped upper jaw, and a flattened nose. There may be malformation of the limbs and cardiovascular problems. A number of psychological characteristics are also connected with FAS, including hyperactivity and learning disabilities (Connor et al., 2006; Guerrini et al., 2007).

- *Nicotine:* Cigarette smoke contains nicotine and carbon monoxide, which pass through the placenta. Nicotine stimulates the fetus, but its long-term effects are uncertain. Carbon monoxide decreases the amount of oxygen available to the fetus, which is connected with cognitive and behavioral problems (Spencer, 2006). The babies of pregnant women who smoke are more likely to be smaller, be stillborn, or die soon after birth (Cnattingius, 2004).

- *Illicit Drugs:* Smoking marijuana during pregnancy poses risks for the fetus, including slower growth (Hurd et al., 2005), immature development of the nervous system (Huestis, 2002), low birthweight (Visscher et al., 2003), and impaired cognitive skills (Huizink & Mulder, 2006). Maternal addiction to heroin or methadone is linked to low birthweight, prematurity, and toxemia. The fetuses of women who use these drugs regularly can also become addicted (Lejeune et al., 2006). Pregnant women who use cocaine increase the risk of stillbirth, low birthweight, and birth defects, and their infants are often excitable, irritable, or lethargic (Schuetze et al., 2006).

- *Prescription Drugs:* Certain prescription drugs, such as thalidomide (previously used as a treatment for insomnia; Ances, 2002) and accutane (prescribed for acne; Fisher et al., 2008), are connected with birth deformities. Even high doses of vitamins A and D have been associated with nervous system damage and heart defects (National Institutes of Health, 2002). Therefore, if a woman is pregnant or thinks she may be, she should consult her obstetrician before taking any drugs, including aspirin, not just prescription medications.

Teratogens Environmental influences or agents that can damage the embryo or fetus.

Critical period In prenatal development, a period during which an embryo is particularly vulnerable to a certain teratogen. In infancy, the term is usually used to refer to a period during which infants are most likely to form bonds of attachment with caregivers.

Fetal alcohol syndrome (FAS) A cluster of symptoms caused by maternal drinking of alcohol, in which the child shows developmental lags and characteristic facial features such as an underdeveloped upper jaw, flattened nose, and widely spaced eyes.

- *Caffeine:* Some studies report no adverse findings, but others have found that pregnant women who take in a good deal of caffeine are more likely to have a miscarriage or a low-birthweight baby (e.g., Cnattingius et al., 2000; Weng et al., 2008).

In addition to these teratogens, there are many others that are toxic to the embryo and fetus, including heavy metals such as lead and mercury (Heindel & Lawler, 2006; Mayes & Ward, 2003) and disease-causing organisms (*pathogens*) such as bacteria and viruses (Mandal et al., 2010; Smith et al., 2007). Maternal infection with rubella can cause deafness, intellectual deficiency, heart disease, and blindness (Food and Drug Administration, 2004). Some maternal disorders, such as *toxemia* (or *preeclampsia*), are not transmitted to the embryo or fetus but adversely affect the environment in which it develops. Women who have toxemia often have premature or undersized babies (Rumbold et al., 2006). In *Rh incompatibility*, antibodies produced by the mother are transmitted to a fetus or newborn and cause brain damage or death.

In addition, certain sexually transmitted infections can affect the fetus or newborn. For example, HIV, the virus that causes AIDS, can be transmitted during childbirth and breast feeding. About one fourth of babies born to HIV-infected mothers become infected themselves (Coovadia, 2004).

Finally, malnutrition in the mother has been linked to low birthweight, prematurity, stunted growth, cognitive and behavioral problems, and cardiovascular disease (Giussani, 2006; Guerrini et al., 2007; Morton, 2006). Maternal obesity is linked with a higher risk of stillbirth and neural tube defects (Fernandez-Twinn & Ozanne, 2006).

Genetic Counseling and Prenatal Testing

Researchers have enabled parents to detect genetic abnormalities that are responsible for hundreds of diseases. For example, prenatal testing can indicate whether the fetus is carrying genetic abnormalities. The following are common testing methods:

- *Amniocentesis* is usually performed on the mother 14–16 weeks after conception. A syringe (needle) is used to withdraw fluid from the amniotic sac. This fluid contains fetal cells that are then examined for abnormalities.

- *Chorionic villus sampling (CVS)* is carried out between the ninth and twelvth week of pregnancy. In CVS, a syringe is inserted through the vagina into the uterus. The syringe sucks out threadlike projections (villi) from the membrane that envelops the amniotic sac. CVS has not been used as frequently as amniocentesis because studies have shown it carries a slightly greater risk of miscarriage.

- In *ultrasound,* a computer uses high-frequency sound waves to generate a picture, or *sonogram,* of the fetus. Ultrasound is used to track the growth of the fetus, to determine fetal age and sex, and to detect multiple pregnancies and structural abnormalities.

- Parental *blood tests* can reveal the presence of recessive genes for a variety of disorders, such as sickle-cell anemia, Tay-Sachs disease, and cystic fibrosis.

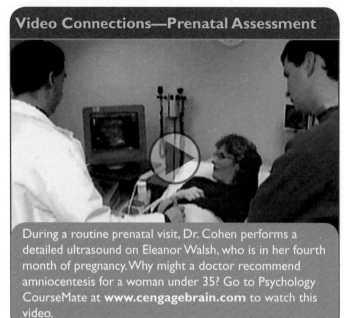

Video Connections—Prenatal Assessment

During a routine prenatal visit, Dr. Cohen performs a detailed ultrasound on Eleanor Walsh, who is in her fourth month of pregnancy. Why might a doctor recommend amniocentesis for a woman under 35? Go to Psychology CourseMate at **www.cengagebrain.com** to watch this video.

LearningConnections • PRENATAL DEVELOPMENT: THE BEGINNING OF OUR LIFE STORY

ACTIVE REVIEW (4) It is possible to become pregnant for a day or so after _____. (5) The _____ permits the embryo to exchange nutrients and wastes with the mother. (6) Heavy maternal use of alcohol is linked to _____ alcohol syndrome (FAS). (7) Women who smoke cigarettes during pregnancy deprive their fetuses of _____, sometimes resulting in stillbirth and persistent academic problems.

REFLECT AND RELATE During the 4th month of pregnancy, most mothers begin to detect their baby's movements and feel that their baby is "alive." What is your view on when a baby is alive? Explain.

CRITICAL THINKING Many researchers use terms like *zygote, embryo,* and *fetus* to refer to the human organism as it undergoes prenatal development. How do these terms differ in meaning from commonly used terms such as *baby* and *unborn child?*

 Go to Psychology CourseMate at **www.cengagebrain.com** for an interactive version of these questions.

● CHILDHOOD: ON THE EDGE OF REASON?

Let's now chronicle the events of childhood. The most obvious aspects of child development are physical, so let's begin with the physical development of newborns, or neonates.

Neonates: In the New World

In this section, we describe the characteristics of neonates. **Question 4: What behaviors can we expect from newborn babies?** We begin with reflexes.

Neonate A newborn child, especially during the first month.

Reflex A simple inborn response to a stimulus.

Rooting The turning of an infant's head toward a touch, such as by the mother's nipple.

REFLEXES: ENTERING THE WORLD PREWIRED Soon after you were born, a doctor or nurse probably pressed her fingers against the palms of your hands. Most likely you grasped the fingers firmly—so firmly that you could have been lifted from your cradle! Grasping at birth is inborn, an example of one of the neonate's many reflexes. **Reflexes** are simple, inborn responses elicited by specific stimuli. They do not involve higher brain functions. Rather, they occur automatically—without thinking.

Newborn children do not know that it is necessary to eat to survive. Fortunately, they have reflexes that cause them to eat. For example, they automatically turn their head toward stimuli that prod or stroke the cheek, chin, or corner of the mouth (such as a nipple). This is termed **rooting**. They also automatically suck objects that touch their lips.

Neonates also withdraw from painful stimuli (the *withdrawal reflex*). They draw up their legs and arch their backs in response to sudden noises, bumps, or loss of support while being held. This is the *startle*, or *Moro*, *reflex*. They grasp objects that press against the palms of their hands (the *grasp*, or *palmar*, *reflex*). They fan their toes when the soles of their feet are stimulated (the *Babinski reflex*). Pediatricians assess babies' neural functioning by testing these reflexes.

Babies also breathe, sneeze, cough, yawn, and blink reflexively. And it is guaranteed that you will learn about the sphincter (anal muscle) reflex if you hold an undiapered **neonate** on your lap for a while.

SENSORY CAPABILITIES In 1890, William James wrote that the neonate must sense the world "as one great blooming, buzzing confusion." The neonate emerges from being literally suspended in a temperature-controlled environment to being—again, in James's words—"assailed by eyes, ears, nose, skin, and entrails at once." In this section, we describe the sensory capabilities of neonates, and we see that James, for all his eloquence, probably exaggerated their disorganization.

Neonates can see, but they tend to be nearsighted; that is, they focus better on nearby than distant objects (Kellman & Arterberry, 2006). They can visually detect movement, and many neonates can track movement the first day after birth.

Fetuses respond to sound months before they are born, and normal neonates hear well unless their middle ears are clogged with amniotic fluid (Priner et al., 2003). The sense of hearing may play a role in the formation of bonds of affection between neonates and their mothers. Research indicates that neonates prefer their mothers' voices to those of other women, but they do not show similar preferences for the voices of their fathers (DeCasper & Prescott, 1984; Freeman et al., 1993). Because they are predominantly exposed to prenatal sounds produced by their mothers, learning appears to play a role in neonatal preferences.

Neonates can discriminate distinct odors, and their preferences are quite similar to those of older children and adults (Werner & Bernstein, 2001). When a cotton swab saturated with the odor of rotten eggs is passed beneath their noses, neonate infants spit, stick out their tongues, wrinkle their noses, and blink their eyes. However, they smile and lick when presented with the odors of chocolate, strawberry, vanilla, butter, bananas, and honey. Neonates are also sensitive to tastes, and their preferences, as suggested by their response to various fluids, appear similar to those of adults (Werner & Bernstein, 2001).

Physical Development: The Drama Continues

Physical development includes gains in height and weight, maturation of the nervous system, and development of bones, muscles, and organs. **Question 5: What physical developments occur during childhood?**

During the first 2 years of childhood, there are dramatic gains in height and weight. Babies usually double their birthweight in about 5 months and triple it by their first birthday (Kuczmarski et al., 2000). Their height increases by about 10 inches in the first year. Children grow another 4 to 6 inches during the second year and gain some

© Dan Bryant

The Rooting Reflex.

4 to 7 pounds. After that, they gain 2 to 3 inches a year until they reach the adolescent growth spurt. Weight gains also remain fairly even at about 4 to 6 pounds per year until the spurt begins. Other aspects of physical development in childhood include reflexes and perceptual development, as previously discussed.

BRAIN DEVELOPMENT Throughout childhood, the brain makes gains in size and weight. It forms neurons, a process that is completed by birth. Infant spurts in brain development are due primarily to the proliferation of dendrites and axon terminals—parts of neurons discussed in Chapter 2 (see Figure 9.1 ■). Infants' abilities are also related to myelination of neurons in parts of their brains.

The brain develops more quickly than any other organ in early childhood. At 2 years of age, the brain already has attained 75% of its adult weight. By age 5, the brain has reached 90% of its adult weight, even though the total body weight of the 5-year-old is barely one third of what it will be as an adult (Tanner, 1989).

The frontal part of the brain is most highly involved in the so-called executive functions of planning and self-regulation. And it is here that dramatic developments take place in middle childhood (Bell et al., 2007). Executive functioning has several aspects: control of attention, cognitive flexibility, goal setting, logical thinking, and problem solving. Executive functioning appears to undergo an important period of development during the ages of 7 to 9 and to be relatively mature by about age 12—setting the stage for the cognitive advances of adolescence (Anderson, 2002; Ferrer et al., 2009).

Nature and Nurture in Brain Development Development of the areas of the brain that control sensation and movement begins as a result of maturation, but sensory stimulation and physical activity during early infancy also spur their development. Sensory stimulation in this case refers to social interaction with caregivers—being held and spoken to, and the like (Fox & Rutter, 2010; Fox et al., 2010).

Research with rats shows how sensory stimulation sparks growth of the cortex. In these studies, rats exposed to more complex environments—those with toys such as ladders and platforms—develop heavier brains with more synapses per neuron (Briones et al., 2004). On the other hand, animals reared in darkness show shrinkage of the visual cortex, impaired vision, and impaired visual-motor coordination (Klintsova & Greenough, 1999). If they don't use it, they lose it.

MOTOR DEVELOPMENT The motor development of the child—the progression from simple acts like lifting the head to running around—offers psychologists a wondrous laboratory for sorting out genetic and environmental influences on development (Brown et al., 2009; Spittle et al., 2009). So much seems to happen so quickly during the first year. Children gain the capacity to move about through a sequence of activities that includes rolling over, sitting up, crawling, creeping, walking, and running. The ages at which infants first engage in these activities vary, but the sequence generally remains the same (see Figure 9.2 ■). Some children skip a step. For example, an infant may walk without ever having crawled. But by and large, the sequence remains intact. Invariant sequences are usually interpreted as reflecting the unfolding of the genetic code (maturation).

Note that the role of maturation in motor development is clear, but environmental factors are also involved. Children may have certain genetic potentials for body size and growth rates, but they do not reach them unless environmental factors such as nutrition, relatively clean air, and so on are available.

PERCEPTUAL DEVELOPMENT The visual preferences of infants are measured by the amount of time, termed **fixation time**, they spend looking at one stimulus instead of another. In classic research by Robert Fantz (1961), 2-month-old infants preferred visual stimuli that resembled the human face to other patterns such as a bull's-eye and featureless red, white, and yellow disks. At this age, the complexity of facelike patterns may be more important than their content. But by 15 to 20 weeks, the organization of the pattern also matters. At that age, babies dwell longer on facelike patterns (e.g., Haaf et al., 1983). Infants thus seem to have an inborn preference for complex visual stimuli. However, preference for faces may not emerge until infants have had experience with people.

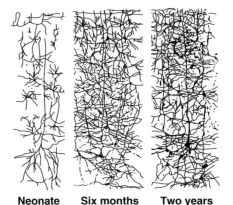

Neonate   Six months   Two years

Figure 9.1 ■ Increase in Neural Connections in the Brain A major growth spurt in the brain occurs between the 25th week of prenatal development and the end of the 2nd year after birth. This growth spurt is due primarily to the proliferation of dendrites and axon terminals.

Source: Reprinted by permission of the publisher from *The Postnatal Development of the Human Cerebral Cortex*, Vols. I–VIII by Jesse LeRoy Conel, Cambridge, MA: Harvard University Press, Copyright © 1939, 1941, 1947, 1951, 1955, 1959, 1963, 1967 by the President and Fellows of Harvard College. Copyright © renewed 1967, 1969, 1975, 1979, 1983, 1987, 1991

Fixation time The amount of time spent looking at a visual stimulus.

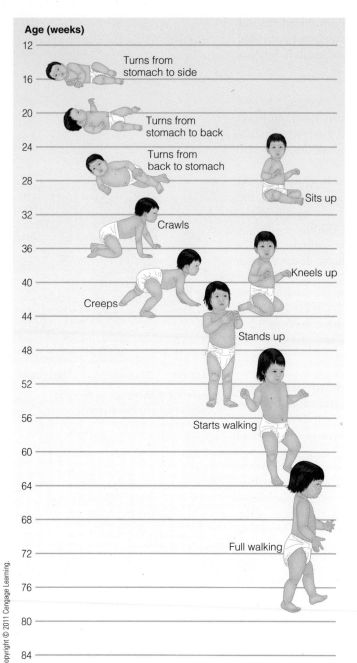

Age (weeks)

Turns from stomach to side

Turns from stomach to back

Turns from back to stomach

Sits up

Crawls

Kneels up

Creeps

Stands up

Starts walking

Full walking

Copyright © 2011 Cengage Learning.

Figure 9.2 ■ Motor Development in Infancy Motor development proceeds in an orderly sequence, but there is considerable variation in the timing of the marker events shown in this figure. An infant who is a bit behind will most likely develop without problems, and a precocious infant will not necessarily become a rocket scientist.

Source: From Rathus. *Childhood and Adolescence*, 4/e. © 2011 Cengage Learning.

Assimilation According to Piaget, the inclusion of a new event into an existing schema.

Schema According to Piaget, a hypothetical mental structure that permits the classification and organization of new information.

Classic research has shown that infants tend to respond to cues for depth by the time they are able to crawl (at about 6 to 8 months). Most also have the good sense to avoid crawling off ledges and tabletops into open space (Campos et al., 1978). In the classic "visual cliff" experiment run by Walk and Gibson (1961), an 8-month-old crawls freely above the portion of the glass with a checkerboard pattern immediately beneath it. But the infant hesitates to crawl over the portion of the glass beneath which the checkerboard has been lowered a few feet. Because the glass would support the infant, this is a visual cliff, not an actual cliff.

Cognitive Development: On the Edge of Reason?

This section explores the ways children mentally represent and think about the world—that is, their *cognitive development*. **Question 6: What cognitive developments occur during childhood?** Let's consider three views of cognitive development. We begin with Jean Piaget's stage theory of cognitive development. Next we turn to the views of Russian psychologist Lev Semenovich Vygotsky (1896–1934). Then we focus on Lawrence Kohlberg's theory of moral development.

JEAN PIAGET'S COGNITIVE–DEVELOPMENTAL THEORY Swiss biologist and psychologist Jean Piaget contributed significantly to our understanding of children's cognitive development. Piaget hypothesized that children's cognitive processes develop in an orderly sequence of stages. Although some children may be more advanced than others at particular ages, the developmental sequence remains the same. Piaget (1963) identified four major stages of cognitive development: sensorimotor, preoperational, concrete-operational, and formal-operational (see Table 9.1 ■).

Assimilation and Accommodation Piaget described human thought, or intelligence, in terms of two concepts: assimilation and accommodation. **Assimilation** means responding to a new stimulus through a reflex or existing habit. Infants, for example, usually try to place new objects in their mouth to suck, feel, or explore. Piaget would say that the child is assimilating a new toy to the sucking schema. A **schema** is a pattern of action or a mental structure involved in acquiring or organizing knowledge.

Piaget regarded children as natural physicists who seek to learn about and control their world. In the Piagetian view, when children squish their food and laugh, they are often acting as budding scientists. In addition to enjoying the responses of their parents, they are studying the texture and consistency of their food. **Accommodation** is the creation of new ways of responding to objects or looking at the world. With accommodation, children transform existing schemas—action patterns or ways of organizing knowledge—to incorporate new events. For example, children who study biology learn that whales cannot be assimilated into the "fish" schema. They accommodate by constructing new schemas, such as "mammals without legs that live in the sea."

Most of the time, newborns assimilate environmental stimuli according to reflexive schemas, although adjusting the mouth to contain the nipple is a primitive kind of accommodation. Reflexive behavior, to Piaget, is not "true" intelligence. True intelligence involves adapting to the world through a fluid balancing of the processes of assimilation and accommodation. Let's now apply these concepts to the stages of cognitive development.

The Sensorimotor Stage The newborn infant is capable of assimilating novel stimuli only to existing reflexes (or ready-made schemas) such as the rooting and sucking reflexes. But by the time infants reach the age of 1 month, they already show purposeful behavior by repeating behavior patterns that are pleasurable, such as sucking their hands. During the first month or so, infants apparently do not connect stimuli perceived through different senses. Reflexive turning toward sources of auditory and olfactory stimulation cannot be considered purposeful searching. But within the first few months, they begin to coordinate vision with grasping to look at the object being held or touched.

Infants of 3 or 4months of age may be fascinated by their own hands and legs. They may become absorbed in watching themselves open and close their fists. They become increasingly interested in acting on the environment to make interesting results (such as the sound of a rattle) last longer or recur. Behavior becomes progressively intentional and purposeful. Between 4 and 8 months of age, they explore cause-and-effect relationships such as the way kicking can cause a hanging toy to bounce.

Truth or Fiction Revisited: It is true that "out of sight" is literally "out of mind" prior to the age of 6 months or so. For most infants younger than 6 months, objects are not yet represented mentally. For this reason, as you can see in Figure 9.3 ■, a child makes no effort to search for an object that has been removed or placed behind a screen. By the age of 8 to 12 months, however, infants apparently realize that objects removed from sight still exist because they attempt to find them. They show what is known as **object permanence**, thereby making it possible to play peekaboo.

Between 1 and 2 years of age, children begin to show an interest in how things are constructed. Toward the end of the second year, children begin to engage in mental trial and error before they try out overt behaviors. For instance, when they look for an object you have removed, they will no longer begin their search in the last place they saw it. Rather, they may follow you, assuming you are carrying the object even though it is not visible. It is as though they are anticipating failure in searching for the object in the place they last saw it.

Because the first stage of development is dominated by learning to coordinate perception of the self and of the environment with motor (muscular) activity, Piaget termed it the **sensorimotor stage**. This stage comes to a close with the acquisition of language basics at about age 2.

Video Connections—The Visual Cliff

Do infants have to experience some of life's "bumps" before they avoid "going off the deep end," or does fear of heights "mature" at about the same time infants gain the ability to move around? Go to Psychology CourseMate at www.cengagebrain.com to watch this video.

Accommodation According to Piaget, the modification of schemas so that information inconsistent with existing schemas can be integrated or understood.

Object permanence Recognition that objects removed from sight still exist, as demonstrated in young children by continued pursuit.

Sensorimotor stage The first of Piaget's stages of cognitive development, characterized by coordination of sensory information and motor activity, early exploration of the environment, and lack of language.

A CLOSER LOOK   Is Development Continuous or Discontinuous?

Do developmental changes tend to occur gradually (continuously)? Or do they tend to occur in major leaps (discontinuously) that dramatically alter our bodies and behavior? John B. Watson and other behaviorists viewed development as a mainly continuous process in which the effects of learning mount gradually. Maturational theorists, however, argue that people are prewired to change dramatically at certain times of life. They point out that the environment, even when enriched, profits us little until we are ready, or mature enough, to develop in a certain direction. For example, aided practice in "walking" during the first few months after birth does not significantly accelerate the date when the child can walk on her or his own.

Stage theorists, such as Jean Piaget—whose theory of cognitive development we discuss next—and Sigmund Freud, saw

development as *dis*continuous. Both theorists saw biological changes as providing the potential for psychological changes.

From the age of 2 to the onset of puberty (that is, the period of development during which reproduction becomes possible), growth appears to be continuous as children gradually grow larger. Then the adolescent growth spurt—triggered by hormones—leads to rapid changes in structure and function (as in the development of the sex organs) as well as size.

Psychologists disagree more strongly on whether aspects of development such as cognition, attachment, and gender typing occur in stages. But as we see next, Jean Piaget believed that cognitive development was discontinuous and consisted of four stages of development.

TABLE 9.1 ■ Piaget's Stages of Cognitive Development

Stage	Approximate Age	Comments
Sensorimotor	Birth–2 years	At first, the child lacks language and does not use symbols or mental representations of objects. In time, reflexive responding ends, and intentional behavior begins. The child develops the object concept and acquires the basics of language.
Preoperational	2–7 years	The child begins to represent the world mentally, but thought is egocentric. The child does not focus on two aspects of a situation at once and therefore lacks conservation. The child shows animism, artificialism, and objective responsibility for wrongdoing.
Concrete-operational	7–12 years	The child develops conservation concepts, can adopt the viewpoint of others, can classify objects in series, and shows comprehension of basic relational concepts (such as one object being larger or heavier than another).
Formal-operational	12 years and older	Mature, adult thought emerges. Thinking is characterized by deductive logic, consideration of various possibilities (mental trial and error), abstract thought, and the formation and testing of hypotheses.

Preoperational stage The second of Piaget's stages, characterized by illogical use of words and symbols, spotty logic, and egocentrism.

Egocentrism According to Piaget, the assumption that others view the world as one does oneself.

Conservation According to Piaget, recognition that basic properties of substances such as weight and mass remain the same when superficial features change.

Jean Piaget Piaget's first love was biology, and he published his first scientific article at the age of 10. In 1920, he obtained a job at the Binet Institute in Paris, where he tried out intelligence tests on children in various age groups to see whether they could arrive at correct answers. He became intrigued by the children's wrong answers, which reflected consistent, if illogical, cognitive processes. Piaget's observations led to his influential theory of cognitive development.

The Preoperational Stage The **preoperational stage** is characterized by the use of words and symbols to represent objects and relationships among them. But be warned—any resemblance between the logic of 2- to 7-year-old children and your own logic is often purely coincidental. Preoperational children tend to think one-dimensionally—to focus on one aspect of a problem or situation at a time.

One consequence of one-dimensional thinking is **egocentrism**. Preoperational children cannot understand that other people do not see things the same way they do. When my daughter Allyn was 2½, I asked her to tell me about a trip to the store with her mother. "You tell me," she replied. Upon questioning, it seemed she did not understand that I could not see the world through her eyes.

To egocentric preoperational children, all the world's a stage that has been erected to meet their needs and amuse them. When asked, "Why does the sun shine?" they may say, "To keep me warm." If asked, "Why is the sky blue?" they may respond, "'Cause blue's my favorite color." Preoperational children also show *animism*. They attribute life and consciousness to physical objects like the sun and the moon. In addition, they show *artificialism*. They believe that environmental events like rain and thunder are human inventions. Asked why the sky is blue, 4-year-olds may answer, "'Cause Mommy painted it." Examples of egocentrism, animism, and artificialism appear in Table 9.2. ■

To gain further insight into preoperational thinking, find a 3- or 4-year-old and try these mini-experiments:

- Pour water from a tall, thin glass into a short, wide glass. Now ask the child whether the short, wide glass contains more, less, or the same amount of water that was in the tall, thin glass. If the child says they hold the same amount (with exceptions for spillage and evaporation), the child is correct. But if the child errs, why do you think this happens?

- Flatten a ball of clay into a pancake, and ask the child whether you wind up with more, less, or the same amount of clay. If the child errs, why do you think this happens?

To arrive at the correct answers to these questions, children must understand the law of **conservation**. This law holds that basic properties of substances such as mass,

Figure 9.3 ■ Development of Object Permanence To the infant who is in the early part of the sensorimotor stage, out of sight is truly out of mind. Once a sheet of paper is placed between the infant and the toy monkey (top two photos), the infant loses all interest in the toy. From evidence of this sort, Piaget concluded that the toy is not mentally represented. The bottom series of photos shows a child in a later part of the sensorimotor stage. This child does mentally represent objects and pushes through a towel to reach an object that has been screened from sight.

weight, and volume remain the same—that is, are *conserved*—when one changes superficial properties such as their shape or arrangement.

Conservation requires the ability to think about, or **center** on, two aspects of a situation at once, such as height and width. Conserving the mass, weight, or volume of a substance requires the recognition that a change in one dimension can compensate for a change in another. But the preoperational boy in Figure 9.4 ■ focuses on only one dimension at a time. First, he is shown two short, wide glasses of water and agrees that they contain the same amount of water. Then, while he watches, water is poured from a short, wide glass into a tall, thin glass. Now he is asked which glass contains more water. After mulling over the problem, he points to the tall, thin glass. Why? Because when he looks at the glasses, he is "overwhelmed" by the fact that the thinner glass is taller. The preoperational child focuses on the most apparent dimension of the situation—in this case, the greater height of the thinner glass. He does not realize that the increased width of the squat glass compensates for the decreased height.

Piaget (1932) found that the moral judgment of preoperational children is also one-dimensional. The 5-year-olds he observed were slaves to rules and authority. When you ask them why something should be done in a certain way, they may insist, "Because that's the way to do it!" or "Because my Mommy says so!" Right is right and wrong is wrong. Why? "Because!"—that's why.

According to most older children and adults, an act is a crime only when there is criminal intent. Accidents may be hurtful, but the perpetrators are usually seen as blameless. But in the court of the one-dimensional, preoperational child, there is **objective responsibility**. People are sentenced on the basis of the amount of damage they do, not because of their intentions. To demonstrate objective responsibility, Piaget would tell children stories and ask them which character was naughtier and why. John, for instance, accidentally breaks 15 cups when he opens a cabinet door. Henry breaks 1 cup when he sneaks into a kitchen cabinet to find forbidden jam. The preoperational child usually judges John to be naughtier. Why? Because he broke more cups.

The Concrete-Operational Stage By about age 7, the typical child is entering the **concrete-operational stage**. In this stage, which lasts until about age 12, children

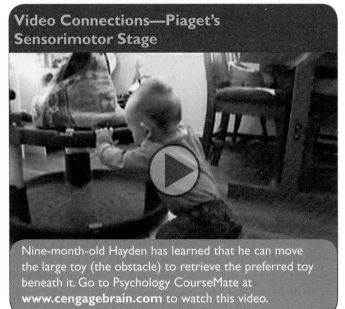

Video Connections—Piaget's Sensorimotor Stage

Nine-month-old Hayden has learned that he can move the large toy (the obstacle) to retrieve the preferred toy beneath it. Go to Psychology CourseMate at **www.cengagebrain.com** to watch this video.

Center According to Piaget, to focus one's attention.

Objective responsibility According to Piaget, the assignment of blame according to the amount of damage done rather than the motives of the actor.

Concrete-operational stage Piaget's third stage, characterized by logical thought concerning tangible objects, conservation, and subjective morality.

307

TABLE 9.2 ■ Examples of Preoperational Thought

Type of Thought	Sample Questions	Typical Answers
Egocentrism—seeing oneself as the center of things; not viewing things from other perspectives	Why does it get dark out? Why does the sun shine? Why is there snow?	So I can go to sleep. To keep me warm. For me to play in.
Animism—attributing life and consciousness to physical objects	Why do trees have leaves? Why do stars twinkle? Why does the sun move in the sky?	To keep them warm. Because they're happy. To follow me and hear what I say.
Artificialism—assuming that environmental events are human inventions	Why is the sky blue? What is the wind? What causes thunder?	Somebody painted it. A man blowing. A man grumbling.

show the beginnings of the capacity for adult logic. However, their logical thoughts, or *operations,* generally involve tangible objects rather than abstract ideas. Concrete-operational children are capable of **decentration**; they can center on two dimensions of a problem at once.

Children now become **subjective** in their **moral judgments.** When assigning guilt, they center on the motives of wrongdoers as well as on the amount of damage done. Concrete-operational children judge Henry more harshly than John because John's misdeed was an accident.

Concrete-operational children understand the laws of conservation. The boy in Figure 9.4, now a few years older, would say that the tall glass still contains the same amount of water. If asked why, he might reply, "Because you can pour it back into the other one." Such an answer also suggests awareness of the concept of **reversibility**—the recognition that many processes can be reversed so that things are restored to their previous condition. The boy now recognizes that the loss in width compensates for the gain in height.

Children in this stage are less egocentric. They are able to take on the roles of others and to view the world, and themselves, from other people's perspectives. They recognize that people see things in different ways because of different situations and sets of values.

During the concrete-operational stage, children's own sets of values begin to emerge and acquire stability. Children come to understand that feelings of love between them and their parents can endure even when someone feels angry at a particular moment. (We continue our discussion of Piaget's theory—his stage of *formal operations*—in the section on adolescence.)

Evaluation of Piaget's Theory A number of questions have been raised concerning the accuracy of Piaget's views. Among them are these:

- *Was Piaget's timing accurate?* Some critics argue that Piaget's methods led him to underestimate children's abilities (Bjorklund, 2000; Meltzoff & Gopnik, 1997). Researchers using different methods have found, for example, that preschoolers are less egocentric than Piaget thought.

Decentration Simultaneous focusing on more than one dimension of a problem so that flexible, reversible thought becomes possible.

Subjective moral judgment According to Piaget, moral judgment that is based on the motives of the perpetrator.

Reversibility According to Piaget, recognition that processes can be undone, and things can be made as they were.

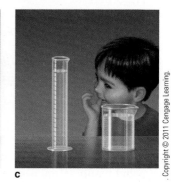

Figure 9.4 ■ Conservation (a) The boy in this illustration agreed that the amount of water in two identical containers is equal. (b) He then watched as water from one container was poured into a tall, thin container. (c) When asked whether the amounts of water in the two containers are now the same, he says no.

Source: From RATHUS. *Childhood and Adolescence,* 4/e. © 2011 Cengage Learning.

a   b   c

- *Does cognitive development occur in stages?* Cognitive events such as egocentrism and conservation appear to develop more continuously than Piaget thought—that is, they may not occur in stages (Bjorklund, 2000; Flavell, 2000).

- *Are developmental sequences always the same?* Here, Piaget's views have fared better. It seems there is no variation in the sequence in which cognitive developments occur.

In sum, Piaget's theoretical edifice has been rocked, but it has not been reduced to rubble. Now let's consider the views of Vygotsky. Unlike Piaget, Vygotsky is not a stage theorist. Instead, he sees the transmission of knowledge from generation to generation as cumulative and focuses on the ways that children's interactions with their elders enhance their cognitive development.

LEV VYGOTSKY'S SOCIOCULTURAL THEORY The term *sociocultural theory* has different meanings in psychology. In Chapter 1, we saw that the term can refer to the roles of factors such as ethnicity and gender in behavior and mental processes. But Vygotsky's sociocultural theory focuses instead on the ways children's cognitive development is influenced by the culture in which they are reared and the individuals who help transmit information about that culture.

Vygotsky's (1978) theory focuses on the transmission of information and cognitive skills from generation to generation. The transmission of skills involves teaching and learning, but Vygotsky does not view learning as a mechanical process that can be described in terms of conditioning. Rather, he focuses more generally on how the child's social interaction with adults organizes a child's learning experiences in such a way that the child can obtain cognitive skills—such as computation or reading skills—and use them to acquire information. Like Piaget, Vygotsky sees the child's functioning as adaptive (Piaget & Smith, 2000), and the child adapts to his or her social and cultural interactions.

Key concepts in Vygotsky's theory include the *zone of proximal development* and *scaffolding*. The word *proximal* means "nearby" or "close," as in the words *approximate* and *proximity*. The **zone of proximal development (ZPD)** refers to a range of tasks that a child can carry out with the help of someone who is more skilled (Haenen, 2001). The "zone" refers to the relationship between the child's own abilities and what she or he can do with help from others. Adults or older children best guide the child through this zone by gearing their assistance to the child's capabilities (Flavell et al., 2002).

Within the zone, the child works with and learns from others (Meijer & Elshout, 2001). When learning with others, the child tends to internalize—or bring inward—the conversations and explanations that help him or her gain skills (Murata & Fuson, 2006; Umek et al., 2005). Outer speech becomes inner speech. What was the teacher's becomes the child's. What was a social and cultural context becomes embedded within the child—thus the term *sociocultural theory*.

A *scaffold* is a temporary skeletal structure that enables workers to fabricate a building, bridge, or other more permanent structure. Cognitive **scaffolding** refers to the temporary support provided by a parent or teacher to a child who is learning to perform a task. The amount of guidance decreases as the child becomes more skilled and self-sufficient. In Vygotsky's theory, teachers and parents provide children with problem-solving methods that serve as cognitive scaffolding while the child gains the ability to function independently.

Piaget's focus was largely maturational. It assumed that maturation of the brain allowed the child to experience new levels of insights and suddenly develop new kinds of problem solving. Vygotsky focused on the processes in the teacher–learner relationship. To Vygotsky, cognitive development was about culture and social interaction (Montero & De Dios, 2006; Norton & D'Ambrosio, 2008). Let's now turn to another aspect of cognitive development—the ways children (and adults) arrive at judgments as to what is right and what is wrong.

LAWRENCE KOHLBERG'S THEORY OF MORAL DEVELOPMENT Cognitive-developmental theorist Lawrence Kohlberg studied the development of the ways in which children made judgments of right and wrong. He used the following tale in his research into children's moral reasoning.

Zone of proximal development (ZPD) Vygotsky's term for the situation in which a child carries out tasks with the help of someone who is more skilled, frequently an adult who represents the culture in which the child develops.

Scaffolding Vygotsky's term for temporary cognitive structures or methods of solving problems that help the child as he or she learns to function independently.

© Brand X Pictures/Jupiterimages

Scaffolding According to Vygotsky's theory, teachers and parents provide children with problem-solving methods that serve as cognitive scaffolding.

In Europe a woman was near death from a special kind of cancer. There was one drug that the doctors thought might save her. It was a form of radium that a druggist in the same town had recently discovered. The drug was expensive to make, but the druggist was charging ten times what the drug cost him to make. He paid $200 for the radium and charged $2,000 for a small dose of the drug. The sick woman's husband, Heinz, went to everyone he knew to borrow the money, but he could only get together about $1,000, which was half of what it cost. He told the druggist that his wife was dying and asked him to sell it cheaper or let him pay later. But the druggist said: "No, I discovered the drug, and I'm going to make money from it." So Heinz got desperate and broke into the man's store to steal the drug for his wife.

Kohlberg, 1969

Heinz was caught in a moral dilemma. A legal or social rule (in this case, the law that forbids stealing) was pitted against a strong human need (his desire to save his wife). Children and adults arrive at yes or no answers for different reasons. According to Kohlberg, the reasons can be classified according to their level of moral development.

As a stage theorist, Kohlberg argues that the stages of moral reasoning follow a specific sequence (see Table 9.3 ■). Children progress at different rates, and not all children (or adults) reach the highest stage. But the sequence is the same: Children must go through stage 1 before they enter stage 2 and so on. According to Kohlberg, there are three levels of moral development and two stages within each level.

When it comes to the dilemma of Heinz, Kohlberg believed that people could justify Heinz's stealing the drug or his decision not to steal it by the reasoning of any level or stage of moral development. Thus, Kohlberg was not as interested in the eventual yes or no as he was in *how a person reasoned* to arrive at yes or no.

Lawrence Kohlberg

TABLE 9.3 ■ Kohlberg's Levels and Stages of Moral Development

	Stage of Development	Examples of Moral Reasoning That Support Heinz's Stealing the Drug	Examples of Moral Reasoning That Oppose Heinz's Stealing the Drug
Level I: Preconventional	STAGE 1: Judgments guided by obedience and prospect of punishment (consequences of behavior)	It isn't wrong to take the drug. Heinz did try to pay for it, and it's only worth $200, not $2,000.	Taking things without paying is wrong because it's against the law. Heinz will get caught and go to jail.
	STAGE 2: Naively egoistic, instrumental orientation (things are right when they satisfy people's needs)	Heinz ought to take the drug because his wife really needs it. He can always pay the druggist back.	Heinz shouldn't take the drug. If he gets caught and winds up in jail, it won't do his wife any good.
Level II: Conventional	STAGE 3: Good-boy orientation (moral behavior helps others and is socially approved)	Stealing is a crime, so it's bad, but Heinz should take the drug to save his wife or else people would blame him for letting her die.	Stealing is a crime. Heinz shouldn't just take the drug because his family will be dishonored and they will blame him.
	STAGE 4: Law-and-order orientation (moral behavior is doing one's duty and showing respect for authority)	Heinz must take the drug to do his duty to save his wife. Eventually, he has to pay the druggist for it, however.	If everyone took the law into his or her own hands, civilization would fall apart, so Heinz shouldn't steal the drug.
Level III: Postconventional	STAGE 5: Contractual, legalistic orientation (one must weigh pressing human needs against society's need to maintain social order)	This thing is complicated because society has a right to maintain law and order, but Heinz has to take the drug to save his wife. ■	I can see why Heinz feels he has to take the drug, but laws exist for the benefit of society as a whole and can't simply be cast aside.
	STAGE 6: Universal ethical principles orientation (people must follow universal ethical principles and their own conscience, even if it means breaking the law)	In this case, the law comes into conflict with the principle of the sanctity of human life. Heinz must take the drug because his wife's life is more important than the law.	If Heinz truly believes that stealing the drug is worse than letting his wife die, he should not take it. People have to make sacrifices to do what they think is right.

The Preconventional Level The preconventional level applies to most children through about the age of 9. Children at this level base their moral judgments on the consequences of behavior. For instance, stage 1 is oriented toward obedience and punishment. Good behavior is obedient and allows one to avoid punishment. However, a child in stage 1 can decide that Heinz should or should not steal the drug.

In stage 2, good behavior allows people to satisfy their needs and those of others. (Heinz's wife needs the drug; therefore, stealing the drug—the only way of obtaining it—is not wrong. But there is also a stage 2 reason for not stealing the drug: Stealing could lead to Heinz's being punished.)

The Conventional Level In the conventional level of moral reasoning, right and wrong are judged by conformity to conventional (familial, religious, societal) standards of right and wrong. According to the stage 3, "good-boy orientation," moral behavior is that which meets the needs and expectations of others. Moral behavior is what is "normal"—what the majority does. (Heinz should steal the drug because that is what a "good husband" would do. It is "natural" or "normal" to try to help one's wife. *Or* Heinz should *not* steal the drug because "good people do not steal.")

In stage 4, moral judgments are based on rules that maintain the social order. Showing respect for authority and doing one's duty are valued highly. (Heinz *must* steal the drug; it would be his fault if he let his wife die. He would pay the druggist later, when he had the money.) Many people do not mature beyond the conventional level.

The Postconventional Level Postconventional moral reasoning is more complex and focuses on dilemmas in which individual needs are pitted against the need to maintain the social order and on personal conscience. We discuss the postconventional level in the section on adolescence.

Social and Emotional Development

Social relationships are crucial to us as children. **Question 7: What social and emotional developments occur during childhood?** When we are infants, our very survival depends on them. Later in life, they contribute to our feelings of happiness and satisfaction. In this section, we discuss many aspects of social development, starting with Erikson's theory of psychosocial development.

ERIK ERIKSON'S STAGES OF PSYCHOSOCIAL DEVELOPMENT According to Erik Erikson, we undergo several stages of psychosocial development (see Table 9.4 ■).

> "We find delight in the beauty and happiness of children that makes the heart too big for the body."
>
> RALPH WALDO EMERSON

> "Insanity is hereditary; you get it from your children."
>
> SAM LEVENSON

Preconventional level According to Kohlberg, a period during which moral judgments are based largely on expectation of rewards or punishments.

Conventional level According to Kohlberg, a period during which moral judgments largely reflect social conventions; a "law and order" approach to morality.

TABLE 9.4 ■ Erikson's Stages of Psychosocial Development

Time Period	Life Crisis	The Developmental Task
Infancy (0–1)	Trust versus mistrust	Coming to trust the parent and the environment—to associate surroundings with feelings of inner goodness
Early childhood (1–3)	Autonomy versus shame and doubt	Developing the wish to make choices and the self-control to exercise choice
Preschool years (4–5)	Initiative versus guilt	Adding planning and "attacking" to choice: becoming active and on the move
Elementary school years (6–12)	Industry versus inferiority	Becoming eagerly absorbed in skills, tasks, and productivity; mastering the fundamentals of technology
Adolescence	Identity versus role diffusion	Connecting skills and social roles to formation of career objectives; developing a sense of who one is and what one stands for
Young adulthood	Intimacy versus isolation	Committing the self to another; engaging in sexual love
Middle adulthood	Generativity versus stagnation	Needing to be needed; guiding and encouraging the younger generation; being creative
Late adulthood	Integrity versus despair	Accepting the time and place of one's life cycle; achieving wisdom and dignity

During Erikson's first stage, *trust versus mistrust*, we depend on our primary caregivers (usually our parents) and come to expect that our environments will—or will not—meet our needs. Toddlers through about the age of 3 are said to be in the stage of *autonomy versus shame and doubt*. During this period, their relationships with parents and friends can encourage the development of self-direction and initiative, or feelings of shame and guilt. Children in this stage need to develop feelings of self-control over physical functions—such as toileting—and a sense of independence. One of the ways that many children demonstrate their growing autonomy, much to the dismay of their parents, is by refusing to comply with parental requests or commands. Erikson believed that children are in the stage of *initiative versus guilt* through about the age of 5, in which they begin to assert control over the environment and strive to master adult skills. Erikson labeled the years of about 6 to 12 the stage of *industry versus inferiority*, during which children meet academic and social challenges in school. A positive outcome contributes to a sense of industry, whereas setbacks can lead to feelings of inferiority. Later we will see that Erikson's theory includes four more stages and straddles the life span.

ATTACHMENT: TIES THAT BIND At the age of 2, my daughter Allyn almost succeeded in preventing me from finishing a book. When I locked myself into my study, she positioned herself outside the door and called, "Daddy, oh Daddy." At other times, she would bang on the door or cry outside. When I would give in (several times a day) and open the door, she would run in and say, "I want you to pick up me" and hold out her arms or climb into my lap. Although we were separate human beings, it was as though she were very much *attached* to me.

Psychologist Mary D. Salter Ainsworth (1913–1999) defined **attachment** as an emotional tie that is formed between one animal or person and another specific individual. Attachment keeps organisms together—it is vital to the survival of the infant—and it tends to endure. The behaviors that define attachment include (a) attempts to maintain contact or nearness and (b) displays of anxiety when separated. Babies and children try to maintain contact with caregivers to whom they are attached. They engage in eye contact, pull and tug at them, ask to be picked up, and may even jump in front of them in such a way that they will be "run over" if they are not picked up!

Mary D. Salter Ainsworth Salter and her colleagues observed infants in many societies, including the African country of Uganda. She noted the efforts of infants to maintain contact with the mother, their protests when separated from her, and their use of her as a base for exploring their environment.

The Strange Situation and Patterns of Attachment The ways infants behave in strange situations are connected with their bonds of attachment with their caregivers. Given this fact, Ainsworth and her colleagues (1978) innovated the *strange situation method* to learn how infants respond to separations and reunions with a caregiver (usually the mother) and a stranger. Using this method, Ainsworth and her colleagues (1978) identified three major types of attachment:

1. *Secure attachment:* Securely attached infants mildly protest their mother's departure, seek interaction upon reunion, and are readily comforted by her.

2. *Avoidant attachment:* Infants who show avoidant attachment are the least distressed by their mother's departure. They play by themselves without fuss and ignore their mothers when they return.

3. *Ambivalent/resistant attachment:* Infants with ambivalent/resistant attachment are the most emotional. They show signs of severe distress when their mother leaves and show ambivalence by alternatively clinging to and pushing their mother away when she returns.

Attachment is connected with the quality of care infants receive. The parents of securely attached children are more likely to be affectionate and reliable caregivers (Posada et al., 2002). Securely attached children are happier, more sociable with unfamiliar adults, and more cooperative with parents; they get along better with peers and are better adjusted in school (Belsky, 2006a; McCartney et al., 2004; Spieker et al., 2003). Insecure attachment in infancy predicts psychological disorders during adolescence (Lee & Hankin, 2009; Sroufe, 1998; Steele, 2005).

Stages of Attachment Ainsworth also studied phases in the development of attachment. At first, infants show *indiscriminate attachment*. That is, they prefer being

Attachment The enduring affectional tie that binds one person to another.

held or being with someone to being alone but show no preferences for particular people. Specific attachment to the primary caregiver begins to develop at about 4 months of age and becomes intense by about 7 months. Ainsworth identified three stages of attachment:

1. The *initial-preattachment phase*, which lasts from birth to about 3 months and is characterized by indiscriminate attachment.

2. The *attachment-in-the-making phase*, which occurs at about 3 or 4 months and is characterized by preference for familiar figures.

3. The *clear-cut-attachment phase*, which occurs at about 6 or 7 months and is characterized by intensified dependence on the primary caregiver.

John Bowlby (1988), a colleague of Ainsworth, believed that attachment is also characterized by fear of strangers (*stranger anxiety*). That is, at about 8 to 10 months of age, children may cry and cling to their parents when strangers try to befriend them. But not all children develop fear of strangers. It therefore does not seem necessary to include fear of strangers as an essential part of the process of attachment.

Theoretical Views of Attachment Early in the 20th century, behaviorists argued that attachment is acquired through experience. Caregivers feed their infants and tend to their other physiological needs. Thus, infants associate their caregivers with gratification of needs and learn to approach them to meet their needs. The feelings of gratification associated with the meeting of basic needs generalize into feelings of security when the caregiver is present.

Classic research by psychologist Harry F. Harlow suggests that skin contact may be more important than learning. Harlow noted that infant rhesus monkeys reared without mothers or companions became attached to pieces of cloth in their cages. They maintained contact with them and showed distress when separated from them. Harlow (1959) conducted a series of experiments to find out why.

In one study, Harlow placed infant rhesus monkeys in cages with two surrogate mothers, as shown in Figure 9.5 ■. One "mother" was made of wire mesh from which a baby bottle was extended. The other surrogate mother was made of soft cloth. The infant monkeys spent most of their time clinging to the cloth mother, even though "she" did not gratify their need for food. Harlow concluded that monkeys—and perhaps humans—have an inborn need for **contact comfort** that is as basic as the need for food. Gratification of the need for contact comfort, rather than food, might be why infant monkeys (and humans) cling to their mothers.

Harlow and Zimmerman (1959) found that a surrogate mother made of cloth could also serve as a comforting base from which an infant monkey could explore its

Contact comfort A hypothesized primary drive to seek physical comfort through contact with another.

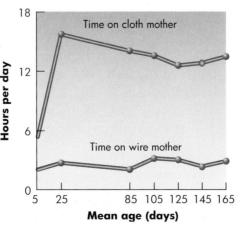

Mean age (days)

Figure 9.5 ■ Attachment in Infant Monkeys Although this rhesus monkey infant is fed by the wire "mother," it spends most of its time clinging to the soft, cuddly, terry cloth "mother." It knows where to get a meal, but contact comfort is apparently more important than food in the development of attachment in infant monkeys (and infant humans?).

Figure 9.6 ■ Security With its terry cloth surrogate mother nearby, this infant rhesus monkey apparently feels secure enough to explore the "bear monster" placed in its cage. But infants with wire surrogate mothers or no mother all cower in a corner when such monsters are introduced.

Imprinting A process occurring during a critical period in the development of an organism, in which that organism responds to a stimulus in a manner that will afterward be difficult to modify.

Figure 9.7 ■ Konrad Lorenz and His Family of Geese Lorenz may not look like Mommy to you, but these goslings became attached to him because he was the first moving object they perceived and followed after they hatched. This type of attachment process is termed imprinting.

environment (see Figure 9.6 ■). Toys such as stuffed bears were placed in cages with infant rhesus monkeys and their surrogate mothers. When the infants were alone or had wire surrogate mothers for companions, they cowered in fear as long as the "bear monster" was present. But when the cloth mothers were present, the infants clung to them for a while and then explored the intruding "monster." With human infants, too, the bonds of mother–infant attachment appear to provide a secure base from which infants feel encouraged to explore their environments.

Other researchers, such as Konrad Lorenz, note that for many animals, attachment is an instinct. Attachment, like other instincts, is theorized to occur in the presence of a specific stimulus and during a *critical period* during which the animal is sensitive to the stimulus Some animals become attached to the first moving object they encounter. It is as if the image of the moving object becomes "imprinted" on the young animal. The formation of an attachment in this manner is therefore called **imprinting**.

Lorenz (1981) became well known when pictures of his "family" of goslings were made public (see Figure 9.7 ■). How did Lorenz acquire his following? He was present when the goslings hatched and during their critical period, and he allowed them to follow him. The critical period for geese and some other animals is bounded, at the younger end, by the age at which they first walk and, at the older end, by the age at which they develop fear of strangers. The goslings followed Lorenz persistently, ran to him when they were frightened, honked with distress at his departure, and tried to overcome barriers between them. If you substitute crying for honking, it all sounds rather human.

Ainsworth and Bowlby (1991) consider attachment to be instinctive—that is, a process that is inborn—in humans. However, among humans, attachment is relatively less mechanical than it is in nonhuman animals—less likely to be related to issues such as locomotion and fear of strangers (which is not experienced by all humans). Moreover, as shown when people adopt children who are in early childhood or older, a "critical period" with humans would be quite extended. In other words, children are not limited to developing strong attachments in infancy, and parents are not limited to developing attachments according to some specified amount of time following childbirth.

Another issue in social and emotional development is parenting styles, which we discuss next.

PARENTING STYLES: STRICTLY SPEAKING? Many psychologists have studied the relationships between parenting styles and the personality development of the child. Diana Baumrind (1989, 2005) and her colleagues have been interested in the connections between parental behavior and the development of instrumental competence in their children. *Instrumental competence* refers to the ability to manipulate the environment to achieve one's goals. Baumrind has largely focused on four aspects of parental behavior: (a) restrictiveness; (b) demands for mature behavior; (c) communication; and (d) warmth and support. She labeled the three most important parenting styles as *authoritative, authoritarian,* and *permissive.* Other researchers have identified the *uninvolved* style. The four parenting styles are as follows:

- *Authoritative parents:* The parents of the most competent children rate high in all four areas of behavior (see Table 9.5 ■). They are strict (restrictive) and demand mature behavior. However, they temper their strictness and demands with willingness to reason with their children and with warmth—love and support. They expect a lot, but they explain why and offer help.

- *Authoritarian parents:* Authoritarian parents have strict guidelines about what is right and wrong, and they demand that their children follow those guidelines. Both authoritative and authoritarian parents adhere to strict standards of conduct. However, authoritative parents explain their demands and are supportive, whereas authoritarian parents rely on force and communicate poorly with their children. Authoritarian parents do not respect their children's points of view, and they may be cold and rejecting.

- *Permissive parents:* Permissive parents are generally easygoing with their children. As a result, the children do pretty much whatever they wish. Permissive parents are warm and supportive but poor at communicating.

- *Uninvolved parents:* Uninvolved parents tend to leave their children on their own. They make few demands and show little warmth or encouragement.

Research shows that the children of warm parents are more likely to be socially and emotionally well adjusted (Lau et al., 2006; Murray et al., 2009). They are also more likely to internalize moral standards—that is, to develop a conscience (Bender et al., 2007; Lau et al., 2006).

Strictness seems to pay off, if tempered with reason and warmth. Children of authori*tative* (versus authori*tarian*) parents have greater self-reliance, self-esteem, social competence, and achievement motivation than other children (Grusec, 2006). Children of authori*tarian* parents are often withdrawn or aggressive and usually do not do as well in school as children of authoritative parents (Paulussen-Hoogeboom et al., 2007; Rudy & Grusec, 2006). Children of permissive parents seem to be the least mature. They are often impulsive, moody, and aggressive. In adolescence, lack of parental monitoring is often linked to delinquency and poor academic performance. Children of uninvolved parents tend to obtain poorer grades than children whose parents make demands on them (Ginsburg & Bronstein, 1993). The children of uninvolved parents also tend to be more likely to hang out with crowds who party a good deal and use drugs (Durbin et al., 1993). The message? Children appear to profit when their parents make reasonable demands, show warmth and encouragement, and spend time with them.

CHILD ABUSE: BROKEN BONDS The incidence of child abuse is underreported, but it is estimated that nearly 3 million children in the United States are neglected or abused by parents or caregivers each year (Kaiser, & Miller-Perrin, 2009; Runyan et al., 2009). More than half a million suffer serious injuries; thousands die.

Children who are abused are quite likely to develop personal and social problems such as anxiety, depression, conduct disorders, low self-esteem, and substance abuse (Kaiser & Miller-Perrin, 2009; Wilson & Widom, 2009). They are less likely than other

"I don't think my parents liked me. They put a live teddy bear in my crib."

WOODY ALLEN

"Children begin by loving their parents; as they grow older they judge them; sometimes they forgive them."

OSCAR WILDE

TABLE 9.5 ■ Parenting Styles

Style of Parenting	Parental Behavior			
	Restrictiveness	**Demands for Mature Behavior**	**Communication**	**Warmth and Support**
Authoritative	High (use of reasoning)	High	High	High
Authoritarian	High (use of force)	Moderate	Low	Low
Permissive	Low (easygoing)	Low	Low	High
Uninvolved	Low (uninvolved)	Low	Low	Low

Note: Research suggests that the children of authoritative parents develop as the most competent.

children to venture out to explore the world. As adults, they are more likely to be violent toward their dates and spouses.

Many children are also victims of sexual abuse. Sexually abused children are more likely to develop physical and psychological health problems than unabused children (Saywitz et al., 2000). Child sexual abuse can also have lasting effects on people's relationships.

Many factors contribute to child abuse: stress, acceptance of violence as a way of coping with stress, substance abuse, and rigid attitudes toward child rearing (Babb et al., 2009; Lee et al., 2009). Unemployment and low socioeconomic status are common stressors that lead to abuse (Strathearn et al., 2009). Research also shows that child abuse runs in families to some degree (Belsky et al., 2009; Conger et al., 2009). **Truth or Fiction Revisited:** It is true that child abusers were frequently abused themselves as children. Even so, most children who are abused do *not* abuse their own children as adults (Conger et al., 2009).

Why does abuse sometimes run in families? There are several hypotheses. One is the generalization that child abuse is part of a poor parenting environment and that children reared in such an environment are less likely to have the resources that contribute to a better environment for their own parenting (Belsky et al., 2009). Another is that parents serve as role models; for example, spanking teaches children to hit people who are doing something you don't like (Straus, 1995). A third is that exposure to violence in their own home leads some children to view abuse as normal. A fourth is that being abused can create feelings of hostility that are then expressed against others, including one's own children (Conger et al., 2009).

LIFE CONNECTIONS — DAY CARE: BLESSING, HEADACHE, OR BOTH?

Not many American families still fit the conventional model where the father works and the mother stays at home to care for the children. Most mothers are now in the workforce, and one child in six under the age of 5 is placed in day care (ChildStats, 2009). These parents, and psychologists, are vitally concerned about the effects of day care. Let's examine some research findings:

- *Attachment:* Some studies find that infants placed in day care are more likely to be insecure (Aviezer & Sagi-Schwartz, 2008), but most infants, whether cared for in the home or in day care, are securely attached (Timmerman, 2006).

- *Social, emotional, and cognitive development:* Infants with day-care experience are more peer oriented and play at higher developmental levels. They are more independent, self-confident, outgoing, affectionate, and cooperative

(Belsky et al., 2007). High-quality day care—defined as richness of the learning environment and ratio of caregivers to children—is associated with greater language and cognitive skills (Belsky, 2009; Thompson, 2008).

- *Aggression:* About 17% of children placed in day care are rated as moderately more aggressive toward peers and adults than children reared at home by their mother (Belsky, 2001). Might the difference in part reflect competition for limited resources?

The effects of day care, then, are mixed. The best workable strategy for parents who place their children in day care may be to seek a center with a high ratio of caregivers to children, a wealth of books and toys, and a solid safety record.

LearningConnections • CHILDHOOD: ON THE EDGE OF REASON?

ACTIVE REVIEW (8) Neonates show _____, which are simple, unlearned, stereotypical responses elicited by specific stimuli. (9) Piaget's _____-operational period is characterized by conservation and reversibility. (10) Vygotsky used the concepts of scaffolding and the _____ of proximal development to explain cognitive development. (11) Ainsworth identified three stages of attachment: The _____ phase, the attachment-in-the-making phase, and the clear-cut-attachment phase. (12) The Harlow studies with monkeys suggest that _____ comfort is more important than conditioning in the development of attachment.

REFLECT AND RELATE Would you say that your caregivers were basically authoritative, authoritarian, or permissive? Explain.

CRITICAL THINKING Which aspects of child development provide evidence for the concept of stages of development?

 Go to Psychology CourseMate at **www.cengagebrain.com** for an interactive version of these questions.

Except for infancy, more changes occur during adolescence than during any other time of life. In our society, adolescents are "neither fish nor fowl," as the saying goes—neither children nor adults. Adolescents may be old enough to reproduce and be as large as their parents, yet they are required to remain in school through age 16 and cannot attend R-rated films unless accompanied by an adult. Given the restrictions placed on adolescents, their growing yearning for independence, and a sex drive heightened by high levels of sex hormones, it is not surprising that adolescents occasionally are in conflict with their parents.

Adolescence is a time of transition from childhood to adulthood. Like childhood, adolescence entails physical, cognitive, social, and emotional changes. Let's begin with physical changes.

Physical Development: Fanning the Flames

Question 8: What physical developments occur during adolescence? One of the most noticeable physical developments of adolescence is a growth spurt. The adolescent growth spurt lasts 2 to 3 years and ends the stable patterns of growth in height and weight that characterize most of childhood. Within this short span of years, adolescents grow some 8 to 12 inches, with most boys winding up taller and heavier than most girls.

PUBERTY: MORE THAN "JUST A PHASE"? Puberty is the period during which the body becomes sexually mature. It heralds the onset of adolescence. Puberty begins with the appearance of **secondary sex characteristics** such as body hair, deepening of the voice in males, and rounding of the breasts and hips in females. In boys, pituitary hormones stimulate the testes to increase the output of testosterone, which in turn causes enlargement of the penis and testes and the appearance of body hair. By the early teens, erections become common, and boys may ejaculate. Ejaculatory ability usually precedes the presence of mature sperm by at least a year. Ejaculation thus is not evidence of reproductive capacity.

In girls, a critical body weight in the neighborhood of 100 pounds is thought to trigger a cascade of hormonal secretions in the brain that cause the ovaries to secrete higher levels of the female sex hormone, estrogen (Frisch, 1997). Estrogen stimulates the growth of breast tissue and fatty and supportive tissue in the hips and buttocks. Thus, the pelvis widens, rounding the hips. Small amounts of androgens produced by the adrenal glands, along with estrogen, spur the growth of pubic and underarm hair. Estrogen and androgens together stimulate the development of female sex organs. Estrogen production becomes cyclical during puberty and regulates the menstrual cycle. The beginning of menstruation, or **menarche**, usually occurs between the ages of 11 and 14. Girls cannot become pregnant until they begin to ovulate, however, and ovulation may begin as much as 2 years after menarche.

BRAIN DEVELOPMENT What happens to the brains of adolescents who spend hours a day practicing the piano or the violin? Their learning translates physically into increases in the thickness of the parts of the cerebral cortex that are being used (Bermudez et al., 2009; Johnson et al., 2008). The gains in thickness of the cerebral cortex represent increases in gray matter, which consists of associative neurons that transmit messages back and forth in the brain when we are engaged in thought and sensorimotor activities.

Many adolescents show poor judgment, at least from time to time, and take risks that most adults would avoid, such as excessive drinking, reckless driving, violence, disordered eating behavior, and unprotected sexual activity (Berten & Rossem, 2009). Brain immaturity may play a role. Deborah Yurgelun-Todd and her colleagues (Sava & Yurgelun-Todd, 2008) showed pictures of people with fearful expressions to adolescents ranging in age from 11 to 17 while the adolescents'

Adolescence The period of life bounded by puberty and the assumption of adult responsibilities.

Puberty The period of physical development during which sexual reproduction first becomes possible.

Secondary sex characteristics Characteristics that distinguish females and males, such as distribution of body hair and depth of voice, but that are not directly involved in reproduction.

Menarche The beginning of menstruation.

© Photodisc Photography/Veer

Brain Development and Violin Practice
This adolescent musician is not only learning to play the violin but also thickening the parts of her cerebral cortex that are being used in the effort. Associative neurons are sprouting new axon tips and dendrites, creating new synapses, and enhancing the flow of information.

brains were scanned by functional magnetic resonance imaging (fMRI). Compared to adults, the adolescents' frontal lobes (the seat of executive functioning) were less active, and their amygdalas (a part of the limbic system involved in discriminating emotions, including fear) were more active. The adolescents often misread the facial expressions, with those younger than 14 more often inferring sadness, anger, or confusion rather than fear. The researchers suggest that one reason many adolescents fail to show the judgment, insight, and reasoning ability of adults is immaturity of the frontal lobes (Yurgelun-Todd, 2007).

Cognitive Development: The Age of Reason?

The adolescent thinker approaches problems very differently from the elementary school child. **Question 9: What cognitive developments occur during adolescence?**

Let's begin by comparing the child's thought processes to that of the adolescent. The child sticks to the facts, to concrete reality. Speculating about abstract possibilities and what might be is very difficult. The adolescent, on the other hand, is able to deal with the abstract and the hypothetical. Adolescents realize that one does not have to believe in the truth or justice of something to argue for it (Flavell et al., 2002). In this section, we explore some of the cognitive developments of adolescence by referring to the theories of Jean Piaget and Lawrence Kohlberg.

THE STAGE OF FORMAL OPERATIONS The formal operational stage is the final stage in Piaget's theory of cognitive development, and it represents cognitive maturity. For many children in Western societies, formal-operational thought begins at about the beginning of adolescence—the age of 11 or 12. However, not all people enter the stage at this time, and some never reach it.

The major achievements of the stage of formal operations involve classification, logical thought, and the ability to hypothesize. Central features are the ability to think about ideas as well as objects and to group and classify ideas—symbols, statements, entire theories. The flexibility and reversibility of operations, when applied to statements and theories, allow adolescents to follow arguments from premises to conclusions and back again. Several features of formal-operational thought give the adolescent a generally greater capacity to manipulate and appreciate the outer environment and the world of the imagination: hypothetical thinking, the ability to use symbols to stand for symbols, and deductive reasoning.

Formal-operational adolescents (and adults) think abstractly. They become capable of solving geometric problems about circles and squares without reference to what the circles and squares may represent in the real world. Adolescents in this stage derive rules for behavior from general principles and can focus, or center, on many aspects of a situation at once in arriving at judgments and solving problems.

During the stage of formal operations, adolescents become capable of dealing with hypothetical situations. They realize that situations can have different outcomes, and they think ahead, experimenting with different possibilities. Adolescents also conduct "experiments" to determine whether their hypotheses are correct. They may try out different tones of voice and ways of carrying themselves and of treating others to see what works best for them.

ADOLESCENT EGOCENTRISM: "YOU JUST DON'T UNDERSTAND!" Adolescents in the formal-operational stage can reason deductively, or draw conclusions about specific objects or people once they have been classified accurately. Adolescents can be somewhat proud of their new logical abilities, and so a new sort of egocentrism can develop in which adolescents emotionally press for acceptance of their logic without recognizing the exceptions or practical problems that are often considered by adults. Consider this example: "It is wrong to hurt people. Company A occasionally hurts people (perhaps through pollution). Therefore, Company A must be severely punished or shut down." This thinking is logical. By impatiently pressing for immediate major changes or severe penalties, however, one may not fully consider various practical problems such as the thousands of workers who would be laid off if the company were shut down. Adults frequently have undergone life experiences that lead them to see shades of gray in situations rather than just black or white.

"Unlike infants, whose brain activity is completely determined by their parents and environment, [adolescents] may actually be able to control how their own brains are wired and sculpted... . This argues for doing a lot of things as a teenager... . You are hard-wiring your brain in adolescence. Do you want to hard-wire it for sports and playing music and doing mathematics or for lying on the couch in front of the television?"

NEUROSCIENTIST JAY GIEDD OF THE NIMH

Formal-operational stage Piaget's fourth stage, characterized by abstract logical thought; deduction from principles.

Imaginary audience An aspect of adolescent egocentrism; the belief that other people are as concerned with our thoughts and behaviors as we are.

The thought of preschoolers is characterized by *egocentrism*; they cannot take another's point of view. Adolescent thought is marked by another sort of egocentrism; adolescents can understand the thoughts of others but still have trouble separating things that are of concern to others and those that are of concern only to themselves (Elkind, 1967, 1985). Adolescent egocentrism gives rise to two cognitive developments: the *imaginary audience* and the *personal fable*.

The **imaginary audience** refers to the belief that other people are as concerned with our thoughts and behavior as we are. As a result, adolescents see themselves as the center of attention and assume that other people are about as preoccupied with their appearance and behavior as they are (Milstead et al., 1993). Indeed, adolescents may feel as if they are in a sense on stage, with all eyes focused on them.

The concept of the imaginary audience may fuel the intense adolescent desire for privacy. It helps explain why adolescents are so self-conscious about their appearance and why they worry about every facial blemish. Self-consciousness seems to peak at about the age of 13 and then decline. Furthermore, girls tend to be more self-conscious than boys (Elkind & Bowen, 1979).

The **personal fable** is the belief that our feelings and ideas are special, even unique, and that we are invulnerable. **Truth or Fiction Revisited:** It is true that it is normal for male adolescents to think of themselves as action heroes and to act as though they are made of steel. The personal fable seems to underlie adolescent behavior patterns such as showing off and taking risks (Alberts et al., 2007). Some adolescents adopt an "it can't happen to me" attitude; they assume they can smoke without risk of cancer or engage in sexual activity without risk of *sexually transmitted infections (STIs)* or pregnancy. Another aspect of the personal fable is the idea that no one else has experienced or can understand one's "unique" feelings such as being in love. The personal fable may underlie the common teenage lament, "You just don't understand me!"

THE POSTCONVENTIONAL LEVEL OF MORAL REASONING Recall that Laurence Kohlberg's theory of moral reasoning involves three levels: preconventional, conventional, and postconventional. Individuals can arrive at the same decision—for example, as to whether Heinz should save his wife by taking the drug without paying for it—but they would be doing so for a different kind of reason. (Deciding not to take the drug for fear of punishment is cognitively less complex than not taking the drug because of the belief that doing so could have negative consequences for the social order.)

None of Kohlberg's levels is tied precisely to a person's age. Although postconventional reasoning is the highest level, for example, most adolescents and adults reason conventionally. However, when postconventional reasoning does emerge, it usually does so in adolescence. Kohlberg's (1969) research showed that postconventional moral judgments were clearly absent among 7- to 10-year-olds. But by age 16, stage 5 reasoning is shown by about 20% of adolescents, and stage 6 reasoning is shown by about 5% of adolescents.

At the **postconventional level**, moral reasoning is based on the person's own moral standards. In each instance, moral judgments are derived from personal values, not from conventional standards or authority figures. In the contractual, legalistic orientation characteristic of stage 5, it is recognized that laws stem from agreed-upon procedures and that the rule of law is in general good for society; therefore, laws should not be violated. But under exceptional circumstances, laws cannot bind the individual. (Although it is illegal for Heinz to steal the drug, in this case it is the right thing to do.)

Stage 6 moral reasoning demands adherence to supposed universal ethical principles such as the sanctity of human life, individual dignity, justice, and the Golden Rule ("Do unto others as you would have them do unto you"). If a law is unjust or contradicts the rights of the individual, it is wrong to obey it.

People at the postconventional level look to their conscience as the highest moral authority. This point has created confusion. To some, it suggests that it is right to break

Imaginary Audience One aspect of adolescent egocentrism is the belief that others around us are as concerned with our thoughts and behaviors as we are.

I am a college student of extremely modest means. Some crazy psychologist interested in something called "formal operational thought" has just promised to pay me $20 if I can make a coherent logical argument for the proposition that the federal government should under no circumstances ever give or lend more to needy college students. Now what could people who believe that possibly say by way of supporting argument? Well, I suppose they could offer this line of reasoning ...

ADAPTED FROM FLAVELL ET AL., 2002

Personal fable Another aspect of adolescent egocentrism; the belief that our feelings and ideas are special and unique and that we are invulnerable.

Postconventional level According to Kohlberg, a period during which moral judgments are derived from moral principles and people look to themselves to set moral standards.

319

the law when it is convenient. But Kohlberg means that people at this level of moral reasoning must do what they believe is right even if this action runs counter to social rules or laws or requires personal sacrifice.

Cognitive development blossoms during adolescence. Social and emotional development also tends to change dramatically, as we discuss next.

Video Connections—Piaget's Formal Operational Stage: Hypothetical Propositions

Researchers asked children and adolescents of different ages, "What if people had no thumbs?" Formal-operational adolescents, such as the boy on the left, can answer hypothetically, contrasting it with reality. The younger boy at the right still has difficulty imagining a world without thumbs. Go to Psychology CourseMate at **www.cengagebrain. com** to watch this video.

Social and Emotional Development: Storm and Stress, Smooth Sailing, or Both?

Adolescents differ from children in their social and emotional development. **Question 10: What social and emotional developments occur during adolescence?** A century ago, psychologist G. Stanley Hall described adolescence as a time of *Sturm und Drang*—"storm and stress" in German. Yet research shows that many adolescents experience a rather calm and joyous period of development (Griffin, 2001). Jeffrey Arnett (1999) argues that we need to consider individual differences and cultural variations.

Certainly, many American teenagers abuse drugs, get pregnant, contract STIs, become involved in violence, fail in school, even attempt suicide (Minñiño, 2010). The U.S. Centers for Disease Control and Prevention (Minñiño, 2010) reported that 73% of all deaths among people aged 12 to 19 years result from three

A CLOSER LOOK

Are There Gender Differences in Moral Development?

Some researchers claim that males reason at higher levels of moral development than females in terms of responses to Heinz's dilemma. For example, Kohlberg and Kramer (1969) reported that the average stage of moral development for men was stage 4, which emphasizes justice, law, and order. The average stage for women was reported to be stage 3, which emphasizes caring and concern for others.

Since Kohlberg's cognitive-developmental theory is largely maturational, it might seem that it is "natural" for males to reason at higher levels than females. However, Carol Gilligan (Gilligan, 1977, 1982; Gilligan & Attanucci, 1988) argues that this gender difference reflects patterns of socialization that are in keeping with gender stereotypes rather than maturation. To make her point, Gilligan notes that 11-year-old Jake views Heinz's dilemma as a math problem. He sets up an equation showing that life has greater value than property. Heinz should thus steal the drug. But 11-year-old Amy notes that stealing the drug and letting Heinz's wife die would both be wrong. Amy searches for alternatives,

such as getting a loan, stating that it would profit Heinz's wife little if he went to jail and was no longer around to help her.

Although Gilligan sees Amy's pattern of reasoning as being as sophisticated as Jake's, it would be rated at a lower level of development in Kohlberg's system. Gilligan asserts that Amy, like other girls, has been socialized into focusing on the needs of others and foregoing simplistic judgments of right and wrong. Jake, by contrast, has been socialized into making judgments based on logic. To him, clear-cut conclusions are derived from a set of premises. Amy was aware of the logical considerations that struck Jake, but she processed them as one source of information—not as the sole source.

Kohlberg, Gilligan, and other researchers tend to agree that in making moral judgments, females are more likely to show a caring orientation, whereas males are more likely to assume a justice orientation (Jorgensen, 2006). But there remains a dispute as to whether this difference means that girls reason at a lower level than boys do (Gottschalk, 2007; Jorgensen, 2006).

Males vs. Females? According to Lawrence Kohlberg and Carol Gilligan, males and females often see right and wrong in different ways. Males have typically scored "higher" in Kohlberg's system, but Gilligan has said, "Not so fast!" Kohlberg's response?—modifying his system.

© RubberBall/Veer

causes: accidents (48%), homicide (13%), and suicide (12%). Numerous high school students engage in risky behavior:

- About one in six rarely or never wears seat belts, and one in three rides with drivers who have been drinking alcohol.
- One in six carries weapons.
- Half drink alcohol and one-quarter use marijuana regularly.
- Nearly one in twelve had attempted suicide in the past year.
- Half have engaged in sexual intercourse, and two in five did not use a condom during their latest sexual encounter.

Hall attributed the conflicts of adolescence to biological changes. Research evidence suggests that hormonal changes affect activity levels, mood swings, and aggressive tendencies, but sociocultural influences have a greater effect (Buchanan et al., 1992).

Adolescence Is adolescence a time of storm and stress, or is it much more complicated than that?

RELATIONSHIPS WITH PARENTS AND PEERS Adolescents spend much less time with their parents than they did as children (Halpern, 2005; Staff et al., 2004). Adolescents interact more with their mothers than with their fathers and therefore also have more conflict with their mothers. But they also view their mothers as more supportive and more likely to accept their opinions (Costigan et al., 2007; Sheeber et al., 2007).

The decrease in time spent with family may reflect a striving to become more independent. Yet most adolescents maintain love, loyalty, and respect for their parents (Collins & Laursen, 2006). And adolescents who feel close to their parents are more likely to show greater independence, higher self-esteem, better school performance, and fewer psychological problems (Costigan et al., 2007; Flouri & Buchanan, 2003).

Parent–adolescent conflict is greatest during puberty and declines in later adolescence (Smetana et al., 2003, 2006). Conflicts typically center on the everyday details of family life, such as chores, homework, curfews, personal appearance, finances, and dating. On the other hand, parents and adolescents are usually quite similar in their values and beliefs regarding social, political, religious, and economic issues (Collins & Laursen, 2006). **Truth or Fiction Revisited:** Thus, adolescents are not in a constant state of rebellion against their parents. As adolescents grow older, parents are more likely to relax controls and are less likely to use punishment (Smetana et al., 2006).

Although relationships with parents generally remain positive, the role of peers as a source of activities, influence, and support increases during the teen years (Kirke, 2009). Adolescents stress the importance of acceptance, self-disclosure, mutual understanding, and loyalty in their friendships (González et al., 2004). Adolescents and their friends are typically the same age and the same race (Castelli et al., 2009). Friends are also often alike in their school attitudes, educational aspirations, school achievement, and attitudes about drinking, drug use, and sexual activity (Hartup, 1993; Snijders et al., 2007).

Parents often worry that their teenage children will fall in with the wrong crowd and be persuaded by their peers to engage in behaviors that are self-destructive or go against the parents' wishes. But research shows that most adolescents' friends are not bad influences (Allen & Antonishak, 2008; Reis & Youniss, 2004). Many peers reinforce positive behaviors, such as academic achievement (Allen & Antonishak, 2008).

EGO IDENTITY VERSUS ROLE DIFFUSION: "WHO AM I?" According to Erik Erikson (1963), individuals undergo eight stages of psychosocial development, each of which is characterized by a certain "crisis." (Refer again to Table 9.4. ■) Four stages, beginning with that of *trust versus mistrust*, occur during childhood. The fifth stage, that of *ego identity versus role diffusion*, occurs during adolescence.

Ego identity is a firm sense of who one is and what one stands for. Adolescents who do not develop ego identity may experience *role diffusion*. They may spread themselves thin, running down one blind alley after another and placing themselves at the mercy of leaders who promise to give them the sense of identity they cannot find for themselves.

"Adolescents are not monsters. They are just people trying to learn how to make it among the adults of the world, who are probably not so sure themselves."

VIRGINIA SATIR

"To an adolescent there is nothing in the world more embarrassing than a parent."

DAVE BARRY

"The best way to keep children home is to make the home atmosphere pleasant—and let the air out of the tires."

DOROTHY PARKER

"Friendships in childhood are usually a matter of chance, whereas in adolescence they are most often a matter of choice."

DAVID ELKIND

321

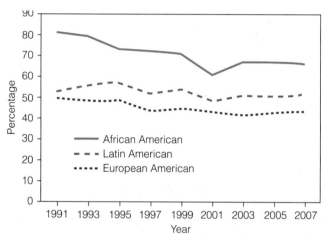

Figure 9.8 ■ Percentage of High School Students Who Have Ever Had Sexual Intercourse, by Race/Ethnicity and Year–United States

Source: Youth Risk Behavior Survey, United States, 1991–2007. In Gavin, L. et al. (2009, July 17). Sexual and reproductive health of persons aged 10–24 years—United States, 2002–2007. Figure 2. *Morbidity and Mortality Weekly Report*, 58 (27), 1–58.

In Western society, in which adolescents generally have a good deal of choice in determining what they will become, the creation of an adult identity is a key challenge. Much of this challenge involves learning about one's interests and abilities and connecting them with an occupation or a role in life. But identity also involves sexual, political, and religious beliefs and commitments.

ADOLESCENT SEXUALITY—WHEN? WHAT? (HOW?) WHO? WHERE? AND WHY?—NOT TO MENTION, "SHOULD I?" Because of the flood of sex hormones, many or most adolescents experience a powerful sex drive. In addition, they are bombarded with sexual messages in the media, including scantily clad pop stars and ads for barely there underwear (McGeal, 2009). Teenagers are strongly motivated to follow the crowd, yet they are also influenced by the views of their parents and teachers. So what is a teen to do?

Masturbation—sexual self-stimulation—is the most common sexual outlet in adolescence. Surveys indicate that most adolescents masturbate at some time. Masturbation is very common among male adolescents but less common among female adolescents (Petersen & Hyde, 2010). It is unclear whether this difference reflects a stronger sex drive in boys (Lippa, 2009), greater social constraints on girls, or both.

Petting is practically universal among American adolescents. Adolescents use petting to express affection, satisfy their curiosities, heighten their sexual arousal, and reach orgasm while avoiding pregnancy and maintaining virginity. Many adolescents do not see themselves as having sex if they stop short of vaginal intercourse. Girls are more likely than boys to be coerced into petting and to feel guilty about it (Gavin et al., 2009).

Since the early 1990s, the percentage of high school students who have engaged in sexual intercourse has been gradually declining for African American teenagers and holding near 50% for European American and Latin American teenagers (see Figure 9.8 ■). Male high school students are somewhat more likely than girls to be sexually active. The incidences of kissing, "making out," oral sex, and sexual intercourse all increase with age.

Adolescent girls and boys usually obtain little advice at home or in school about how to handle their emerging sexuality. Some initiate sex at very early ages, when they are least likely to use contraception (Buston et al., 2007). Many adolescent girls, especially younger adolescents, do not have access to contraceptive devices. Among those who do, fewer than half use them reliably (Buston et al., 2007).

TEENAGE PREGNANCY About 750,000 teenage girls in the United States are impregnated each year (Buston et al., 2007). However large this number may sound, 10 to 20 years ago, about 1 million girls became pregnant each year. The Centers for Disease Control and Prevention attribute the drop-off to educational efforts by schools, the media, religious institutions, and communities (America's Children, 2007).

Most pregnant teenagers will become single mothers (America's Children, 2007). The medical, social, and economic costs of unplanned or unwanted pregnancies among adolescents are enormous both to the mothers and to the children. Adolescent mothers are more likely to experience medical complications during the months of pregnancy, and their labor is likely to be prolonged. The babies are at greater risk of being premature and of low birthweight (Mathews & MacDorman, 2007). These medical problems are not necessarily due to the age of the mother but rather to the fact that teenage mothers—especially those at the lower end of the socioeconomic spectrum—are less likely to have prenatal care.

Teenage mothers are also less likely to graduate from high school or move on to college. Their deficit in education means that they earn less and are in greater need of public assistance (Bunting & McAuley, 2004). Children born to teenage mothers also are at a disadvantage. As early as the preschool years, they show lower levels of cognitive functioning and more behavioral and emotional problems.

ACTIVE REVIEW (13) Puberty begins with the appearance of _____ sex characteristics, such as the deepening of the voice in males and rounding of the breasts and hips in females. (14) _____-operational thought is characterized by hypothetical thinking and deductive logic. (15) Adolescent egocentrism gives rise to the _____ audience and the personal fable. (16) In stage 6 moral reasoning, people consider behavior that is consistent with _____ ethical standards as right. (17) Erik Erikson considers the life crisis of adolescence to be ego identity versus role _____.

REFLECT AND RELATE There is a saying: "Adolescents are neither fish nor foul." Does this saying apply to your own experiences as an adolescent?

CRITICAL THINKING Is adolescence is a distinct stage of life? Explain.

 Go to Psychology CourseMate at **www.cengagebrain.com** for an interactive version of these questions.

● EMERGING ADULTHOOD: A NEW STAGE OF DEVELOPMENT?

By and large, adulthood is usually defined in terms of what people do rather than how old they are. Over the years, marriage has been a key standard to be considered an adult (Carroll et al., 2007). Other criteria for adult status include holding a full-time job and living independently (not with one's parents). Today, the transition to adulthood is mainly marked by adjustment issues, such as deciding on one's values and beliefs, accepting self-responsibility, becoming financially independent, and establishing an equal relationship with one's parents (Arnett, 2007; Gottlieb et al., 2007).

Adulthood itself has been divided into stages, and the first of these, early adulthood, has been seen largely as the period of life when people focus on establishing their careers or pathways in life. However, many individuals in their late teens and early 20s remain dependent on their parents and are reluctant or unable to make enduring commitments in terms of either identity formation or the development of intimate relationships. The question is whether we can speak of the existence of another stage of development, one that bridges adolescence and early adulthood. A number of developmental theorists, such as Jeffrey Arnett (2007), believe that we can.

Question 11: What is emerging adulthood? Emerging adulthood is theorized to be a distinct period of development, roughly spanning the ages of 18 to 25, found in societies that allow young people an extended opportunity to explore their roles in life. These tend to be affluent societies, such as those found in developed nations. Parents in the United States are often affluent enough to continue to support their children throughout college and graduate school. When parents cannot do the job, the government often steps in to help—for example, through student loans. These supports allow young people the luxury of sorting out identity issues and creating meaningful life plans—even if some still do not know where they are going after they graduate from college.

Although there are pluses to taking time to formulate one's identity, there are downsides, too. For example, remaining dependent on parents can compromise an individual's self-esteem. Taking out loans for school means that there is more to pay back; many individuals mortgage their own lives as they invest in their futures. Women who focus on their educations and careers may marry and bear children later than they would otherwise do. Although many people appreciate children more when they bear them later in life, they also become less fertile and may find themselves in a race with their "biological clock."

Young people in the United States seem to be generally aware of the issues involved in defining the transition from adolescence to adulthood. Arnett (2000) reported what people say when they are asked whether they think they have become adults. The most common answer of 18- to 25-year-olds was something like "in some respects yes and in other respects no" (see Figure 9.9 ■). Many think they have developed beyond the conflicts and exploratory voyages of adolescence, but they may not yet have the ability to assume the financial and interpersonal responsibilities they associate with adulthood.

And then, of course, there are those who remain adolescents forever.

A New Stage of Development? Some researchers suggest that affluent societies like ours have spawned a new stage of development, emerging adulthood.

Emerging adulthood A theoretical period of development, spanning the ages of about 18 to 25, in which young people in developed nations engage in extended role exploration or preparation.

"*Human beings are the only creatures on earth that allow their children to come back home.*"

BILL COSBY

"*I take a very practical view of raising children. I put a sign in each of their rooms: 'Checkout Time is 18 years.'*"

ERMA BOMBECK

323

ACTIVE REVIEW (18) Emerging adults tend to be found in (affluent or poor?) nations. (19) When Americans are asked "Do you feel that you have reached adulthood," the largest group of people aged 18–25 respond _____.

REFLECT AND RELATE Are you or are people in your class emerging adults? Explain.

CRITICAL THINKING How would students in your class react to being called "adolescents"? Why?

 Go to Psychology CourseMate at **www.cengagebrain.com** for an interactive version of these questions.

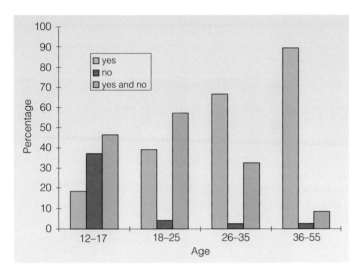

Figure 9.9 ■ People's Responses When Asked Whether They Have Become Adults Between the ages of 18 and 25, most respondents are likely to say, in effect, "In some ways, yes; in other ways, no."

Source: Arnett, J. J. (2000). Emerging adulthood. *American Psychologist, 55*(5), 469–480.

"*I've yet to be on a campus where most women weren't worrying about some aspect of combining marriage, children, and a career. I've yet to find one where many men were worrying about the same thing.*"

GLORIA STEINEM

EARLY ADULTHOOD: BECOMING ESTABLISHED

Early adulthood overlaps with emerging adulthood, beginning at about the age of 20, and is usually considered to end by about age 40. Most psychologists agree that early adulthood is generally a time of feeling strong, growing more aware of the differences between ideals and realities, striving intensely, becoming established, and often, settling in.

Physical Development

Question 12: What physical developments occur during early adulthood? Physical development peaks in early adulthood. Most people are at their height of sensory sharpness, strength, reaction time, and cardiovascular fitness. Young adults are at their tallest, and height remains stable through middle adulthood, declining somewhat in late adulthood. Physical strength in both men and women peaks in the 20s and early 30s and then slowly declines (Markham, 2006). Most athletes experience a decline in their 30s, and most athletes retire by age 40. Sexually speaking, most people in early adulthood become readily aroused. They tend to attain and maintain erections as desired and to lubricate readily.

Cognitive Development

Question 13: What cognitive developments occur during early adulthood? As with physical development, people are at the height of their cognitive powers during early adulthood. Most verbal and quantitative capacities of the sort measured by the SAT and the ACT tend to have developed by late adolescence, emerging adulthood, or early adulthood.

William Perry (1981, 1970/1998) points out that young adults often enter college or adult life assuming that there are right and wrong answers and that the world can be divided easily into black versus white, good versus bad, and us versus them. After a while, in a multicultural society or on a college campus, students may realize that judgments of good or bad are often made from a certain belief system, such as a religion or a particular cultural background, so that their thinking grows more complex and less absolute (Vukman, 2005).

Gisella Labouvie-Vief (2006) notes that adults must typically narrow possibilities into practical choices, whether the choices are about careers, graduate school, or life partners. The "cognitively healthy" young adult is more willing than the egocentric adolescent to compromise and cope within the world as it is, not the world as she or he would like it to be. Adults need to develop a complexity that enables them to harbor both positive and negative feelings about their career choices ("I may never get rich, but I'll look forward to what I'm doing that day") and their partners ("He may not be a hunk, but he's stable and kind") (Labouvie-Vief & González, 2004).

In sum, young adults are less likely to see the world in black and white than those in "emerging adulthood." They are more relativistic but ideally capable of making commitments in their relativistic worlds. Despite the advances in cognitive development of early adulthood, Piaget did not propose a **postformal** stage of cognitive development, one that would extend beyond the stage of formal operations. Nor do all developmental psychologists agree on whether they should consider the cognitive abilities of young adults to be a fifth stage of cognitive development.

Social and Emotional Development

Question 14: What social and emotional developments take place during early adulthood? Many theorists suggest that early adulthood is the period of life during which people tend to establish themselves as independent members of society.

At some point during their 20s, many people strive to advance in their careers. Those who seek professional careers may spend much of their 20s acquiring the skills that will enable them to succeed professionally (Levinson et al., 1978; Levinson, 1996). It is largely during the 20s that people become generally responsible for their own support, make their own choices, and are free from parental influences. Many young adults adopt what theorist Daniel Levinson and his colleagues (1978) call *the Dream*—the drive to "become" someone, to leave their mark on history—which serves as a tentative blueprint for their life.

Erik Erikson (1963) characterized early adulthood as the stage of *intimacy versus isolation*. Erikson saw the establishment of intimate relationships as central to early adulthood. Young adults may not be able to commit themselves to others until they have achieved *ego identity*—that is, established stable life roles. They may not be able to gauge the extent to which their developing values may conflict with those of a potential intimate partner. Erikson suggested that in our society, which values compatibility in relationships, lack of ego identity is connected with the high divorce rate in teenage marriages. Once passion fades a bit, conflicting ways of looking at the world may be too abrasive to bear. Erikson argued that young adults who do not reach out to develop intimate relationships risk retreating into isolation and loneliness.

Levinson labeled the ages of 28 to 33 the *age-30 transition*. For men and women, the late 20s and early 30s are commonly characterized by reassessment: "Where is my life going?" During our 30s, we often find that the lifestyles we adopted during our 20s do not fit as comfortably as we had expected. Many psychologists find that the later 30s are characterized by settling down or planting roots. Many young adults feel a need to make a financial and emotional investment in their home. Their concerns become more focused on promotion or tenure, career advancement, and mortgages.

Postformal stage A proposed stage of cognitive development in which the individual has achieved knowledge that judgments of people and behavior are made within certain value systems, has begun to narrow infinite possibilities into practical choices, and has overcome the egocentrism of adolescence.

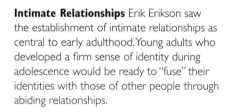

© RubberBall

Intimate Relationships Erik Erikson saw the establishment of intimate relationships as central to early adulthood. Young adults who developed a firm sense of identity during adolescence would be ready to "fuse" their identities with those of other people through abiding relationships.

LearningConnections ● EARLY ADULTHOOD: BECOMING ESTABLISHED

ACTIVE REVIEW (20) Perry points out that young adults are (more or less?) likely than adolescents to realize that judgments of good or bad are often made from a certain belief system, so their thinking grows more complex and less absolute. (21) Young adults are (more or less?) egocentric than adolescents.

REFLECT AND RELATE Where do you see yourself as fitting in the chronicle of adolescent and adult life?

CRITICAL THINKING How would *you* define adulthood? Explain.

 Go to Psychology CourseMate at **www.cengagebrain.com** for an interactive version of these questions.

● MIDDLE ADULTHOOD: THE "SANDWICH GENERATION"?

Middle adulthood spans the ages of 40 to 60 or 65. It is a period of being sort of "sandwiched" between early and late adulthood. Yet it is a most fruitful period of life, and for many, as the saying goes, it is the "prime of life."

Physical Development

Question 15: What physical developments occur during middle adulthood? In our middle years, we are unlikely to possess the strength, coordination, and stamina that we had during our 20s and 30s. Still, the years between 40 and 60 are reasonably stable. There is gradual physical decline, but it is minor and likely to be of concern only if a person competes with young adults—or with idealized memories of oneself. Because the physical decline in middle adulthood is gradual, people who begin to eat more nutritious diets and to exercise may find themselves looking and feeling better than they did in early adulthood.

For women, **menopause** is usually considered the single most important change of life that occurs during middle adulthood. It usually occurs during the late 40s or early 50s. Menopause is the final phase of the *climacteric,* which is caused by a decline in secretion of female sex hormones. Ovulation draws to an end, and there is some loss of breast tissue and skin elasticity. During the climacteric, many women experience hot flashes, loss of sleep, and some anxiety and depression. Women's experiences during and following the climacteric reflect the intensity of their physical symptoms—which vary considerably—and the extent to which their self-concept was wrapped up with their reproductive capacity (Rathus et al., 2011).

Cognitive Development

Menopause The cessation of menstruation.

Crystallized intelligence One's lifetime of intellectual achievement as shown largely through vocabulary and knowledge of world affairs.

Fluid intelligence Mental flexibility as shown in learning rapidly to solve new kinds of problems.

Question 16: What cognitive developments occur in middle adulthood? As we approach middle adulthood, it becomes useful to think in terms of two types of intellectual functioning: *crystallized intelligence* and *fluid intelligence.* Crystallized intelligence is defined as a cluster of knowledge and skills that depend on accumulated information and experience, awareness of social conventions, and the capacity to make good decisions. Crystallized intelligence includes knowledge of the specialized vocabulary in a field; in English, for example, one might know the meaning of the terms *iambic pentameter* and *onomatopoeia.*

Fluid intelligence involves a person's skills at processing information. Let's do a quick comparison to a computer. Your crystallized intelligence is like the amount of information you have in storage. Your fluid intelligence is more like the sizes of your processor and your memory (that is, *working memory*—how much you can keep in mind at once), which work together to access and manipulate information and arrive at answers quickly and accurately. Whereas researchers suggest a powerful role for environmental factors in the genesis of crystallized intelligence, they theorize a relatively stronger role for neurological factors in fluid intelligence (Horn & Noll, 1997; Salthouse & Davis, 2006).

Crystallized intelligence tends to increase with age through middle adulthood. **Truth or Fiction Revisited:** In the absence of senile dementias, crystallized intelligence commonly increases throughout the life span, along with scores on verbal subtests of standardized intelligence tests. The same studies that indicate that crystallized intelligence tends to increase throughout adulthood tend to show a decline for fluid intelligence (Escorial et al., 2003; Salthouse, 2001). K. Warner Schaie's (1994) longitudinal data (see Figure 9.10 ■) show that perceptual speed, which is most strongly related to fluid intelligence, drops off most dramatically from early adulthood to late adulthood. Verbal ability and inductive reasoning are more closely related to crystallized intelligence, and these show gains through middle adulthood and hold up in late adulthood.

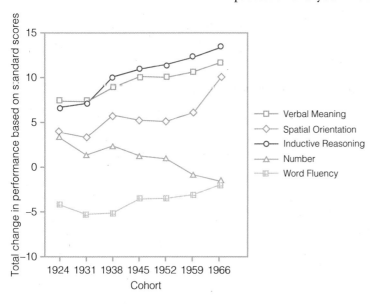

Figure 9.10 ■ Longitudinal Changes in Six Intellectual Abilities, Ages 25–88 Most intellectual abilities show gains or remain largely unchanged through middle adulthood. Numerical ability shows a modest decline throughout middle adulthood, and perceptual speed shows a more dramatic drop-off.

Source: K. Warner Schaie. The course of adult intellectual development. *American Psychologist, 49,* 304–313, Figure 6. Copyright © 1994 American Psychological Association. Reprinted by permission.

Figure 9.10 reveals group trends; there are interindividual variations. Schaie and his colleagues (2004) found that circumstances such as good physical health, intellectual activity, and favorable conditions such as decent housing stem cognitive decline in late adulthood.

Social and Emotional Development

Question 17: What social and emotional developments occur during middle adulthood? Erikson (1963) labeled the life crisis of the middle years *generativity versus* *stagnation*. Generativity involves things such as rearing children, producing on the job, or making the world a better place, for example, through church or civic groups. Generativity enhances self-esteem. Stagnation means treading water, as in keeping the same job at the same rate of pay for 30 years or neglecting to rear one's children. Stagnation hurts self-esteem.

According to Levinson and colleagues (1978), whose research involved case studies of 40 men, there is a *midlife transition* at about age 40 to 45 characterized by a shift in psychological perspective. Previously, men had thought of their age in terms of the number of years that had elapsed since birth. Now they begin to think of their age in terms of the number of years they have left. They mourn the passing of their youth and begin to adjust to the specter of old age. Research suggests that women may undergo a midlife transition earlier than men do (Stewart & Ostrove, 1998). Why? Much of it is related to the winding down of the "biological clock"—their ability to bear children. Yet many women today are having children in their 40s and, now and then, beyond.

In both women and men, according to Levinson, the midlife transition may trigger a *midlife crisis*. The middle-aged businessperson looking ahead to another 10 to 20 years of grinding out accounts in a cubbyhole may encounter depression. The homemaker with two teenagers and an empty house from 8 A.M. to 4 P.M. may feel that she or he is coming apart at the seams.

While some theorists present portraits of middle-aged people suddenly focusing on "gloom and doom," others find people to be in or entering the "prime of life" (Almeida & Horn, 2004; Lachman, 2004). As noted earlier, most people in middle adulthood encounter little decline in physical prowess. Intellectually, there is some loss in fluid intelligence, but crystallized intelligence is often growing. Middle-aged adults are also often earning more money than young adults.

RELATIONSHIPS IN MIDDLE ADULTHOOD The term *middle adulthood* is a convenient way of describing people whose ages lie between early adulthood and late adulthood. In terms of their family relationships, their generation is in the middle in another way—often "sandwiched," as we will see, between their own children (and grandchildren) and their parents.

Empty-nest syndrome A sense of depression and loss of purpose felt by some parents when the youngest child leaves home.

Sandwich generation People in middle adulthood who are responsible for meeting the needs of their children yet also burdened by the needs of aging parents.

The "Empty-Nest Syndrome": Fact or Fiction? In earlier decades, psychologists placed great emphasis on the so-called **empty-nest syndrome**. This concept was applied most often to women. It was assumed that women experience a profound sense of loss when their youngest child goes off to college, gets married, or moves out of the home (Stewart & Ostrove, 1998). **Truth or Fiction Revisited:** However, it is *not* generally true that parents suffer from the empty-nest syndrome when the youngest child leaves home. Certainly, there can be a sense of loss when the children have left home, and the loss applies to both parents. However, once their children become adults, most parents in the United States are content to "launch" their children to live on their own. Many mothers report increased marital satisfaction and personal changes such as greater mellowness, self-confidence, and stability once the children have left home (Etaugh & Bridges, 2006). Moreover, in many cases, the children remain at least partly financially dependent on their parents, sometimes for years (Aquilino, 2005; Roberts, 2009), and if they have been close to their parents, they may also remain somewhat emotionally dependent once they are out on their own.

Middle-Aged Children and Aging Parents: The "Sandwich Generation" Because of increasing life expectancy, more than half of the middle-aged people in developed nations have at least one living parent, and they frequently go on to late adulthood together (Callahan, 2007; U.S. Bureau of the Census, 2008). Twothirds of aging American parents have a residence near a child (U.S. Bureau of the Census, 2008), and there are frequent visits and phone calls. The relationships between middle-aged and older parents can grow quite close, especially as tensions and expectations from earlier years tend to slip into history. If the aging parents require assistance, the task usually falls to a middle-aged daughter, who then becomes what has been dubbed part of the **sandwich generation**. She is sandwiched between caring for or contributing to the support of her children or grandchildren at the same time she is caring for her parents (Grundy & Henretta, 2006). Given that she is also likely to be in the workforce, her role overload is multiplied (Gans & Silverstein, 2006).

© 2008 Eric Lowenbach/Getty Images

Sandwich Generation The woman pushing the wheelchair may be thought of being in the "sandwich generation." She is "sandwiched" between the needs of her adolescent children and those of her aging parents.

ACTIVE REVIEW (22) _____ intelligence refers to one's lifetime of intellectual achievement as shown by vocabulary and general knowledge. (23) _____ intelligence is mental flexibility as shown by the ability to solve new kinds of problems. (24) Research shows that most parents (do or do not?) suffer from the empty-nest syndrome. (25) Many people in middle adulthood are considered part of the _____ generation because they may be subject to the needs of their children and their aging parents.

REFLECT AND RELATE Are people in your extended family part of the sandwich generation? Explain.

CRITICAL THINKING Do you see middle adulthood as a time of decline or as being in the prime of life? Explain.

 Go to Psychology CourseMate at **www.cengagebrain.com** for an interactive version of these questions.

Life span The maximum amount of time a person can live under optimal conditions.

Life expectancy The amount of time a person can be expected to live in a given setting.

"Sooner or later I'm going to die, but I'm not going to retire."

MARGARET MEAD

● LATE ADULTHOOD: OF WISDOM, DECLINE, AND COMPENSATION

An *agequake* is coming. People age 65 and older are the most rapidly growing segment of the U.S. population (National Center for Health Statistics, 2009). In 1900, only one person in twenty-five was over the age of 65. Today, that figure has more than tripled to one in eight. By mid-century, more than one in five Americans will be 65 years of age or older (National Center for Health Statistics, 2009) (see Figure 9.11 ■).

One's **life span**, or *longevity,* is the length of time one can live under the best of circumstances. The life span of a species, including humans, depends on its genetic programming. With the right genes and environment and with the good fortune to avoid serious accidents or illnesses, people have a life span of about 115 years.

One's **life expectancy** refers to the number of years a person in a given population group can expect to live. The average European American child born 100 years ago in the United States could expect to live 47 years. The average African American could expect a shorter life of 35.5 years (Andersen & Taylor, 2009). High infant mortality rates due to diseases such as German measles, smallpox, polio, and diphtheria contributed to the lower life expectancy rates of a century ago. These diseases have been brought under control or eradicated. Other major killers, including bacterial infections such as tuberculosis, are now largely controlled by antibiotics. Factors that contribute to longevity include safer water supplies, improved dietary habits, and health care.

Today, the average American newborn can expect to live to about 78 years, but there are important differences in life expectancy according to gender, race, geographical location, and health-related behavior (Ezzati et al., 2008). For example, the life expectancy for an Asian American woman living in an upscale county is in the upper 80s. The life expectancy for an African American male living in an urban environment with a high risk of homicide is in the 60s (Murray et al., 2006).

Despite the increases in life expectancy, our health and some cognitive processes decline during late adulthood. Also, many of the social expectations and institutions with which we are familiar—such as the retirement age and social security—were shaped at times when we did not live so long. Therefore, the retirement age is being pushed back. On a psychological level, aging requires adjusting to inevitable physical changes and financial limitations and, for many, seeking new age-appropriate challenges and optimizing the opportunities that remain.

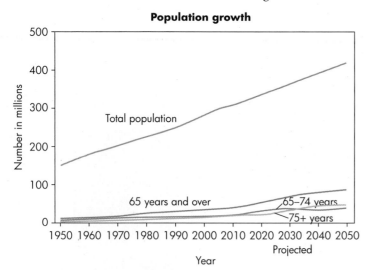

Population growth

Figure 9.11 ■ Projected Population Growth of the U.S. Population and of People Aged 65 and Over Through 2050.

Source: National Center for Health Statistics. (2009). Health, United States, 2008 with Chartbook, Figure 1. Hyattsville, MD. Library of Congress Catalog Number 76–641496. U.S. Government Printing Office, Washington, DC 20402.

Physical Development

Question 18: What physical changes occur as people advance to late adulthood? The skin becomes less elastic and is subject to wrinkles and folds in late adulthood (see Figure 9.12 ■). Hair tends to thin. Reaction time—the amount of time required to respond to a stimulus—increases. Older drivers, for example, need more time to respond to changing road conditions. As we grow older, our immune system functions less effectively, leaving us more vulnerable to disease. The metabolism slows, frequently leading to weight gain. Muscle strength also tends to decline.

SENSORY CHANGES Beginning in middle age, the lenses of the eyes become brittle—a condition called *presbyopia*. Chemical changes of aging can lead to vision disorders such as cataracts and glaucoma. Cataracts cloud the lenses of the eyes, reducing vision. Glaucoma is a buildup of fluid pressure inside the eyeball. It can lead to tunnel vision (lack of peripheral vision) or blindness.

The sense of hearing, especially the ability to hear higher frequencies, also declines with age (Sommers, 2008). Taste and smell become less acute as we age. We also lose taste buds in the tongue with aging. As a result, foods must be more strongly spiced to yield the same flavor.

CHANGES IN BONE DENSITY Bones lose density as we progress through adulthood, becoming more brittle and vulnerable to fracture. Bones in the spine, hip, thigh, and forearm lose the most density. In osteoporosis, bones lose so much calcium that they become prone to breakage. Hip fractures often result in hospitalization, loss of mobility, and, often in people in advanced late adulthood, death from complications.

Osteoporosis can shorten one's stature and deform one's posture. Both men and women are at risk of osteoporosis, but it poses a greater threat to women. Men typically have a larger bone mass, which provides them with more protection.

CHANGES IN SEXUALITY Sexual daydreaming, sex drive, and sexual activity all tend to decline with age, but sexual satisfaction may remain high (Barnett & Dunning, 2003). Older people with partners usually remain sexually active and report that they like sex (Laumann et al., 2006). Sexual activity among older people is influenced not only by physical changes but also by psychological well-being and feelings of intimacy (Laumann et al., 2006; Trudel et al., 2007).

Many of the physical changes in older women stem from a decline in estrogen production. The vaginal walls lose much of their elasticity; thus, sexual activity may become painful. The vaginal opening constricts, and penile entry may become difficult. Following menopause, women also produce less vaginal lubrication—a key reason for painful sex. Orgasm may feel less intense, even though the experience may remain satisfying.

Age-related changes occur more gradually in men and are not clearly connected with any one biological event (Barnett & Dunning, 2003). After about age 50, men take progressively longer to achieve erection. Erections become less firm, perhaps because of lowered testosterone levels (Laumann et al., 2006). Testosterone production usually declines from about age 40 to age 60 and then levels off. An adolescent may require but a few minutes to regain erection and ejaculate again after a first orgasm, whereas past age 50, regaining erection may require several hours. Older men produce less ejaculate, and the contractions of orgasm become weaker and fewer.

WHY DO WE AGE? Theories of aging fall into two broad categories: *Programmed theories* see aging as the result of genetic instructions, Such theories propose that aging and longevity are determined by a biological clock that ticks at a rate governed by genes. Evidence supporting a genetic link to aging comes in part from studies showing that longevity tends to run in families (Terry et al., 2008).

Cellular damage theories propose that internal bodily changes and external environmental assaults (such as carcinogens and toxins) cause cells and organ systems to malfunction, leading to death. For example, the *wear-and-tear theory* suggests that over the years, our bodies—as machines that wear out through use—become less capable of repairing themselves.

Cognitive Development

Question 19: What cognitive developments take place during late adulthood? Cognitive development in late adulthood has many aspects—creativity, memory functioning, and intelligence. People can be creative for a lifetime, and some have flowered in late adulthood.

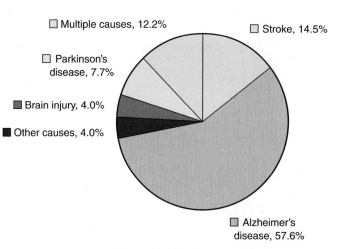

☐ Multiple causes, 12.2%
☐ Parkinson's disease, 7.7%
■ Brain injury, 4.0%
■ Other causes, 4.0%
☐ Stroke, 14.5%
☐ Alzheimer's disease, 57.6%

Figure 9.12 ■ Causes of Dementia
Source: Lippa, R. A. (2008). The relationship between childhood gender nonconformity and adult masculinity–femininity and anxiety in heterosexual and homosexual men and women. *Sex Roles, 59*(9–10), 684–693.

© BlendImages/Jupiterimages

329

Although Americans in general are living longer, there are gender and ethnic differences in life expectancy. Women outlive men, and European Americans and Asian Americans outlive Latin, African, and Native Americans (Miniño et al., 2010). For example, women in our society outlive men by 5 to 6 years (Miniño et al., 2010).

Why do women in the United States outlive men? For one thing, heart disease—the nation's leading killer—tends to develop later in women than in men. Men are also more likely to die because of accidents, cirrhosis of the liver, strokes, suicide, homicide, AIDS, and cancer (Miniño et al., 2010). Many such deaths reflect excessive drinking and other risky behavior. Many men are also reluctant to have regular physical exams or to talk to their doctors about their health issues.

There is a 7-year difference in life expectancy between people in the highest income brackets and those in the lowest, and members of certain minority groups in our society are more likely to be in the lowest. Poor people tend to eat less nutritious diets, encounter more stress, and have less access to health care (Wong et al., 2009; Yang et al., 2009). We cannot control our gender and ethnic background, but we can choose whether to engage in more healthful behavior.

SELF-ASSESSMENT

How Long Will You Live? The Life-Expectancy Scale

The life-expectancy scale is one of several used to estimate how long people will live. Scales such as these are far from precise—which is a good thing, if you think about it. But they make "guesstimates" based on our heredity, medical histories, and lifestyles.

Directions: To complete the scale, begin with the age of 72. Then add or subtract years according to the directions for each item.

72 = STARTING POINT

PERSONAL FACTS

_____ 1. If you are male, **subtract 3**.

_____ 2. If female, **add 4**.

_____ 3. If you live in an urban area with a population over 2 million, **subtract 2**.

_____ 4. If you live in a town with under 10,000 people or on a farm, **add 2**.

_____ 5. If any grandparent lived to 85, **add 2**.

_____ 6. If all four grandparents lived to 80, **add 6**.

_____ 7. If either parent died of a stroke or heart attack before the age of 50, **subtract 4**.

_____ 8. If any parent, brother, or sister under 50 has (or had) cancer or a heart condition, or has had diabetes since childhood, **subtract 3**.

_____ 9. Do you earn over $75,000[a] a year? If so, **subtract 2**.

_____ 10. If you finished college, **add 1**. If you have a graduate or professional degree, **add 2 more**.

_____ 11. If you are 65 or over and still working, **add 3**.

_____ 12. If you live with a spouse or friend, **add 5**. If not, **subtract 1** for every 10 years alone since age 25.

LIFESTYLE STATUS

_____ 13. If you work behind a desk, **subtract 3**.

_____ 14. If your work requires regular, heavy physical labor, **add 3**.

_____ 15. If you exercise strenuously (tennis, running, swimming, etc.) five times a week for at least a half-hour, **add 4**. If two or three times a week, **add 2**.

_____ 16. Do you sleep more than 10 hours each night? **Subtract 4.**

_____ 17. Are you intense, aggressive, easily angered? **Subtract 3.**

_____ 18. Are you easygoing and relaxed? **Add 3**.

_____ 19. Are you happy? **Add 1**. Unhappy? **Subtract 2**.

_____ 20. Have you had a speeding ticket in the last year? **Subtract 1**.

_____ 21. Do you smoke more than two packs a day? **Subtract 8**. One or two packs? **Subtract 6**. One-half to one? **Subtract 3**.

_____ 22. Do you drink the equivalent of 1½ oz. of liquor a day? **Subtract 1**.

_____ 23. Are you overweight by 50 lbs. or more? **Subtract 8**. By 30 to 50 lbs.? **Subtract 4**. By 10 to 30 lbs.? **Subtract 2**.

_____ 24. If you are a man over 40 and have annual checkups, **add 2**.

_____ 25. If you are a woman and see a gynecologist once a year, **add 2**.

AGE ADJUSTMENT

_____ 26. If you are between 30 and 40, **add 2**.

_____ 27. If you are between 40 and 50, **add 3**.

_____ 28. If you are between 50 and 70, **add 4**.

_____ 29. If you are over 70, add 5.

_____ **TOTAL = YOUR LIFE EXPECTANCY**

[a]This figure is an inflation-adjusted estimate.

Source: From Robert F. Allen with Shirley Linde. (1986). *Lifegain*. Human Resources Institute Press, Tempe Wick Road, Morristown, NJ.

For example, Pablo Picasso was painting in his 90s, and Frank Lloyd Wright designed New York's spiral-shaped Guggenheim Museum when he was 89 years old. "Grandma" Moses began her painting career in her 70s. Memory functioning does, however, decline with age. Yet declines in memory are not usually as large as people assume. Older people show better memory functioning in areas in which they can apply their experience, especially their specialties, to new challenges. For example, who would do a better job of remembering how to solve problems in chemistry—a college history major or a retired chemistry professor?

One of the most severe assaults on intellectual functioning, especially among older people, is Alzheimer's disease.

DEMENTIA AND ALZHEIMER'S DISEASE Dementia is a condition characterized by dramatic deterioration of mental abilities involving thinking, memory, judgment, and reasoning. It is not a consequence of normal aging but of disease processes that damage brain tissue. Causes of dementia include brain infections, such as meningitis, HIV infection, and encephalitis, and chronic alcoholism, infections, strokes, and tumors (see Figure 9.13 ■). The most common cause of dementia is **Alzheimer's disease (AD)**, a progressive and irreversible brain disease affecting 4–5 million Americans.

About one in ten Americans between the ages of 65 and 74 is diagnosed with AD, jumping to more than one in two among those in the 75- to 84-year-old category (Henderson, 2009). Alzheimer's disease is rare in people younger than 65.

Alzheimer's disease progresses in several stages. At first, there are subtle cognitive and personality changes, and people with AD have trouble managing finances and recalling recent events. As AD progresses, people find it harder to manage daily tasks, recall names and addresses, and drive. Later, they have trouble maintaining hygiene. They no longer recognize family and friends or speak in full sentences. People with AD may eventually become unable to walk or communicate.

Both environmental and genetic factors may be involved in AD (Goldman et al., 2008; Tomiyama et al., 2008). An accumulation of plaque in the nervous system may cause the memory loss and other symptoms of AD; however, experiments with nonhumans suggest that memory deficits may precede the formation of significant deposits of plaque (Jacobsen et al., 2006).

Social and Emotional Development

Question 20: What social and emotional developments occur during late adulthood? Research suggests that many individuals in late adulthood maintain a firm sense of who they are and what they stand for (Webster, 2003). The Greek philosopher Plato

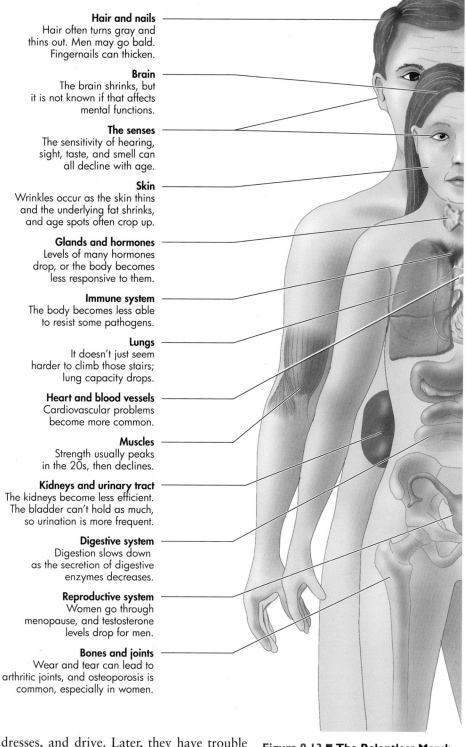

Hair and nails
Hair often turns gray and thins out. Men may go bald. Fingernails can thicken.

Brain
The brain shrinks, but it is not known if that affects mental functions.

The senses
The sensitivity of hearing, sight, taste, and smell can all decline with age.

Skin
Wrinkles occur as the skin thins and the underlying fat shrinks, and age spots often crop up.

Glands and hormones
Levels of many hormones drop, or the body becomes less responsive to them.

Immune system
The body becomes less able to resist some pathogens.

Lungs
It doesn't just seem harder to climb those stairs; lung capacity drops.

Heart and blood vessels
Cardiovascular problems become more common.

Muscles
Strength usually peaks in the 20s, then declines.

Kidneys and urinary tract
The kidneys become less efficient. The bladder can't hold as much, so urination is more frequent.

Digestive system
Digestion slows down as the secretion of digestive enzymes decreases.

Reproductive system
Women go through menopause, and testosterone levels drop for men.

Bones and joints
Wear and tear can lead to arthritic joints, and osteoporosis is common, especially in women.

Figure 9.13 ■ The Relentless March of Time A number of physical changes occur during late adulthood.

Dementia A condition characterized by deterioration of cognitive functioning.

Alzheimer's disease A progressive form of mental deterioration characterized by loss of memory, language, problem solving, and other cognitive functions.

331

"It's never too late to be what you might have been."

GEORGE ELIOT

was so optimistic about late adulthood that he argued one could achieve great pleasure in one's later years, engage in meaningful public service, and also achieve wisdom (McKee & Barber, 2001).

According to psychologist Erik Erikson, late adulthood is the stage of *ego integrity versus despair.* The basic challenge is to maintain the belief that life is meaningful and worthwhile as one faces the inevitability of death. Erikson, like Plato, spoke of the importance of wisdom. He believed that ego integrity derives from wisdom, which can be defined as expert knowledge about the meaning of life, balancing one's own needs and those of others, and pushing toward excellence in one's behavior and achievements (Baltes & Staudinger, 2000; Sternberg, 2000). Erikson also believed that wisdom enables people to accept their life span as occurring at a certain point in the sweep of history and as being limited. We spend most of our lives accumulating objects and relationships, and Erikson argues that adjustment in the later years requires the ability to let go of them. Other views of late adulthood stress the importance of creating new challenges; however, biological and social realities may require older people to become more selective in their pursuits.

SUCCESSFUL AGING Despite the changes that accompany aging, the majority of Americans in their 70s report being generally satisfied with their lives (Volz, 2000). According to a national poll by the *Los Angeles Times* of some 1,600 adults, 75% of older people say they feel younger than their years (Stewart & Armet, 2000).

There have been many definitions of "successful aging." One journal article identified 28 studies with 29 definitions of the concept (Depp & Jeste, 2006). By and large, the definitions included physical activity, social contacts, self-rated good health, the absence of cognitive impairment and depression, nonsmoking, and the absence of disabilities and chronic diseases such as arthritis and diabetes. According to these common criteria, 35% of the older people sampled in these studies could be said to be aging successfully.

According to the principle of **selective optimization with compensation**, put forth by Margaret Baltes and Laura Carstensen (2003), successful agers tend to seek emotional fulfillment by reshaping their lives to concentrate on what they find to be important and meaningful. Research with people aged 70 and older reveals that successful agers form emotional goals that bring them satisfaction (Löckenhoff & Carstensen, 2004). They no longer compete in certain athletic or business activities (Bajor & Baltes, 2003; Freund & Baltes, 2002). Instead, they focus on matters that allow them to maintain a sense of control over their own lives. Retaining social contacts and building new ones also contribute to a positive outlook, as does continuing with physical, artistic, and cultural activities. In sum, successful agers seek to optimize their strengths and compensate for their weaknesses.

Selective optimization with compensation Reshaping of one's life to concentrate on what one considers important and meaningful in the face of physical decline and possible cognitive impairment.

ON DEATH AND DYING: THE FINAL CHAPTER

When we are young and our bodies are supple and strong, it may seem that we will live forever. But death can occur at any age—by accident, violence, or illness. Death can also affect us deeply at any stage of life through the loss of others.

LearningConnections • LATE ADULTHOOD: OF WISDOM, DECLINE, AND COMPENSATION

ACTIVE REVIEW (26) According to _____ theories of aging, aging is determined by a genetic biological clock. (27) During late adulthood, the senses become less acute and reaction time (increases or decreases?) (28) Alzheimer's disease (is or is not?) a normal feature of the aging process. (29) Successful agers optimize their strengths, and they _____ for their weaknesses.

REFLECT AND RELATE Would you characterize the older people in your life as successful agers? Explain.

CRITICAL THINKING How do the factors that contribute to longevity demonstrate the roles of nature and nurture?

 Go to Psychology CourseMate at **www.cengagebrain.com** for an interactive version of these questions.

Question 21: What are psychological perspectives on death and dying? In her work with terminally ill patients, Elisabeth Kübler-Ross found some common responses to news of impending death. She identified five stages of dying through which many patients pass, and she suggested that older people who suspect that death is approaching may undergo similar stages:

1. *Denial:* In the denial stage, people feel that "it can't be happening to me. The diagnosis must be wrong."

2. *Anger:* Denial usually gives way to anger and resentment toward the young and healthy and, sometimes, toward the medical establishment—"It's unfair. Why me?"

3. *Bargaining:* Next, people may try to bargain with God to postpone their death, promising, for example, to do good deeds if they are given another 6 months or another year to live.

4. *Depression:* With depression come feelings of loss and hopelessness—grief at the inevitability of leaving loved ones and life itself.

5. *Final acceptance:* Ultimately, an inner peace may come, a quiet acceptance of the inevitable. Such "peace" does not resemble contentment. It is nearly devoid of feeling.

Much current "death education" suggests that hospital staff and family members can help support dying people by understanding the stages they are going through, by not imposing their own expectations on patients, and by helping patients achieve final acceptance when patients are ready to do so. But critics note that staff may be imposing Kübler-Ross's expectations on dying patients.

"Lying Down to Pleasant Dreams …"

American poet William Cullen Bryant is best known for his poem "Thanatopsis," which he composed at the age of 18. "Thanatopsis" expresses Erik Erikson's goal of ego integrity—optimism that we can maintain a sense of trust through life. By meeting squarely the challenges of our adult lives, perhaps we can take our leave with dignity. When our time comes to "join the innumerable caravan"—the billions who have died before us—perhaps we can depart life with integrity.

> *"Live," wrote the poet, so that*
> *… when thy summons comes to join*
> *The innumerable caravan that moves*
> *To that mysterious realm, where each shall take*
> *His chamber in the silent halls of death,*
> *Thou go not, like the quarry-slave at night,*
> *Scourged to his dungeon, but, sustained and soothed*
> *By an unfaltering trust, approach thy grave*
> *Like one that wraps the drapery of his couch*
> *About him, and lies down to pleasant dreams.*

Bryant, of course, wrote "Thanatopsis" at age 18, not at 85, the age at which he died. At that advanced age, his feelings—and his verse—might have differed. But literature and poetry, unlike science, need not reflect reality. They can serve to inspire and warm us.

> *"It's only when we truly know and understand that we have a limited time on earth—and that we have no way of knowing when our time is up, we will then begin to live each day to the fullest, as if it was the only one we had. "*
>
> ELISABETH KÜBLER-ROSS

> *"Dying is one of the few things that can be done as easily lying down."*
>
> WOODY ALLEN

LearningConnections • ON DEATH AND DYING: THE FINAL CHAPTER

ACTIVE REVIEW (30) Kübler-Ross's stages of dying include _____, anger, bargaining, depression, and final acceptance. (31) Kübler-Ross conducted her research with _____ ill patients.

REFLECT AND RELATE Do your own experiences with people in the final days of life fit in with the views of Kübler-Ross?

CRITICAL THINKING Do you believe that acceptance of death is a sign of wisdom? Why or why not?

 Go to Psychology CourseMate at **www.cengagebrain.com** for an interactive version of these questions.

How Psychologists Study Human Development

1. How do researchers study development over time?
Developmental psychologists use the methods of other psychologists but also use longitudinal and cross-sectional studies to learn how people develop over time.

Prenatal Development: The Beginning of Our Life Story

2 What developments occur from conception through birth?
Prenatal development occurs in the germinal, embryonic, and fetal stages. During the germinal stage, the zygote divides as it travels through the Fallopian tube and becomes implanted in the uterine wall. The major organ systems are formed during the embryonic stage.

3. What environmental hazards face embryos and fetuses?
Teratogens are environmental agents that can harm the embryo or fetus. Maternal use of alcohol is linked to fetal alcohol syndrome. Parental smoking is linked with low birthweight, stillbirth, and intellectual deficiency. Maternal use of illicit drugs is linked to low birthweight, prematurity, and toxemia. Other teratogens include certain prescription drugs, caffeine, certain heavy metals, and maternal infections, among others.

Childhood: On the Edge of Reason?

4. What behaviors can we expect from newborn babies?
Reflexes are inborn responses to stimuli that in many cases are essential to the survival of the infant. Examples include sucking and swallowing. Neonates are nearsighted. Hearing develops prior to birth.

5. What physical developments occur during childhood?
The brain gains in size and weight through prenatal development and childhood, mainly by proliferating dendrites and axon terminals and by myelination. Infants are capable of depth perception by the time they can crawl. Locomotion develops in an invariant sequence.

6. What cognitive developments occur during childhood?
Piaget proposed four stages of cognitive development: sensorimotor, preoperational, concrete-operational, and formal-operational. Vygotsky's key concepts include the zone of proximal development (ZPD) and scaffolding. Kohlberg hypothesized that children's moral reasoning develops through preconventional, conventional, and postconventional levels.

7. What social and emotional developments occur during childhood?
Erikson hypothesizes that there are eight stages of psychosocial development. According to Ainsworth, there are three stages of attachment: the initial-preattachment phase, the attachment-in-the-making phase, and the clear-cut-attachment phase. Harlow's research suggests that contact comfort is a key to attachment. There are critical developmental periods during which animals such as geese and ducks become attached instinctively to (or imprinted on) an object that they then follow. The children of authoritative parents are the most achievement oriented and well adjusted.

Adolescence: "Neither Fish nor Fowl"?

8. What physical developments occur during adolescence?
Increased levels of hormones spur changes that lead to reproductive capacity and secondary sex characteristics in adolescents. During the adolescent growth spurt, young people may grow 6 or more inches a year. Adolescents' frontal lobes are less active than those of adults, and their amygdalas are more active—differences that may underlie adolescents' poorer judgment and higher risk taking compared to adults.

9. What cognitive developments occur during adolescence?
Formal-operational thinking appears in adolescence, but not everyone reaches it. Two consequences of adolescent egocentrism are the imaginary audience and the personal fable.

10. What social and emotional developments occur during adolescence?
Adolescents and parents are often in conflict because adolescents desire more independence and may experiment with things that can jeopardize their health. According to Erikson, adolescents strive to forge an ego identity.

Emerging Adulthood: A New Stage of Development?

11. What is emerging adulthood?
Emerging adulthood is found in more affluent societies and is an extended period of time from age 18 to 25 during which individuals explore their roles in life.

Early Adulthood: Becoming Established

12. What physical developments occur during early adulthood?
Most people are at their height of sensory sharpness, strength, reaction time, and cardiovascular fitness during early adulthood.

13. What cognitive developments occur during early adulthood?
According to Perry, young adults may come to realize that judgments of good or bad are often made from a particular belief system. Labouvie-Vief notes that young adults often learn to narrow endless possibilities into practical choices.

14. What social and emotional developments take place during early adulthood?
Early adulthood is generally characterized by efforts to advance in the business world and the development of intimate ties. Many young adults reassess their lives during the "age-30 transition."

Middle Adulthood: The "Sandwich Generation"?

15. What physical developments occur during middle adulthood?
Middle adulthood is characterized by a gradual decline in strength. Research suggests that most women go through menopause without great difficulty.

16. What cognitive developments occur in middle adulthood?
Crystallized intelligence—one's vocabulary and accumulated knowledge—generally increases with age. Fluid intelligence—the ability to process information rapidly—declines.

17. What social and emotional developments occur during middle adulthood?
Erikson speaks of generativity versus stagnation as the key "crisis" of middle adulthood. Many middle adults are "sandwiched" between the needs of their children and their aging parents. Only a minority of middle-aged adults experience an "empty-nest syndrome" when their youngest child leaves home.

Late Adulthood: Of Wisdom, Decline, and Compensation

18. What physical changes occur as people advance to late adulthood?
Older people show less sensory acuity, and their reaction time lengthens. The immune system weakens. There is loss of bone density. Sexual response declines.

19. What cognitive developments take place during late adulthood?
Memory functioning declines with age, as does processing speed. Verbal skills may remain high—or increase—for a lifetime. Alzheimer's disease is characterized by cognitive deterioration in memory, language, and problem solving.

20. What social and emotional developments occur during late adulthood?
"Successful agers" optimize their strengths and compensate for their weaknesses—reshaping their lives to focus on what they find important.

On Death and Dying: The Final Chapter

21. What are psychological perspectives on death and dying?
Kübler-Ross hypothesized five stages of dying among people who are terminally ill: denial, anger, bargaining, depression, and final acceptance.

KEY TERMS

Accommodation (p. 305)
Adolescence (p. 317)
Alzheimer's disease (p. 331)
Amniotic sac (p. 299)
Androgens (p. 299)
Assimilation (p. 304)
Attachment (p. 312)
Center (p. 307)
Cohort effect (p. 298)
Concrete-operational stage (p. 307)
Conservation (p. 306)
Contact comfort (p. 313)
Conventional level (p. 311)
Critical Period (p. 300)
Cross-sectional research (p. 298)
Crystallized intelligence (p. 326)
Decentration (p. 308)
Dementia (p. 331)
Egocentrism (p. 306)
Embryonic stage (p. 299)
Emerging adulthood (p. 323)

Empty-nest syndrome (p. 327)
Fetal alcohol syndrome (p. 300)
Fetal stage (p. 299)
Fixation time (p. 303)
Fluid intelligence (p. 326)
Formal operational stage (p. 318)
Germinal stage (p. 299)
Imaginary audience (p. 319)
Imprinting (p. 314)
Intimacy versus isolation (p. 000)
Life expectancy (p. 328)
Life span (p. 328)
Longitudinal research (p. 298)
Maturation (p. 299)
Menarche (p. 317)
Menopause (p. 326)
Neonate (p. 299)
Object permanence (p. 305)
Objective responsibility (p. 307)
Personal fable (p. 319)
Placenta (p. 299)

Postconventional level (p. 319)
Postformal stage (p. 325)
Preconventional level (p. 311)
Preoperational stage (p. 306)
Puberty (p. 317)
Reflex (p. 302)
Reversibility (p. 308)
Rooting (p. 302)
Sandwich generation (p. 327)
Scaffolding (p. 309)
Schema (p. 304)
Secondary sex characteristics (p. 317)
Selective optimization with
    compensation (p. 332)
Sensorimotor stage (p. 305)
Subjective moral judgment (p. 308)
Teratogens (p. 300)
Umbilical cord (p. 299)
Zone of proximal development (ZPD)
    (p. 309)
Zygote (p. 299)

ACTIVE LEARNING RESOURCES

Log in to **www.cengagebrain.com** to access the resources your instructor requires. For this book, you can access:

 CourseMate brings course concepts to life with interactive learning, study, and exam preparation tools that support the printed textbook. A textbook-specific website, Psychology CourseMate includes an integrated interactive eBook and other interactive learning tools including quizzes, flashcards, videos, and more.

Need help studying? This site is your one-stop study shop. Take a Pre-Test and CengageNOW will generate a Personalized Study Plan based on your test results. The Study Plan will identify the topics you need to review and direct you to online resources to help you master those topics. You can then take a Post-Test to determine the concepts you have mastered and what you still need to work on.

Personality: Theory and Measurement

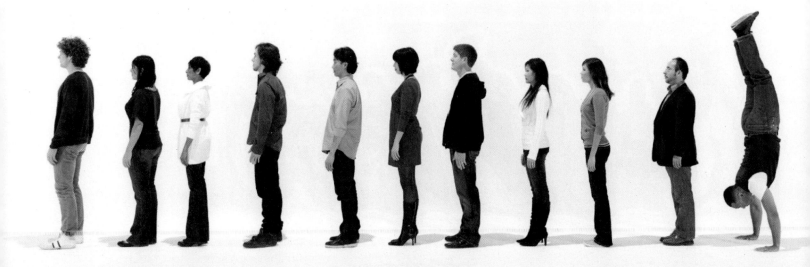

© Fancy Photography/Veer

MAJOR TOPICS

The Psychodynamic Perspective:
Excavating the Iceberg 340
The Trait Perspective: The
Five-Dimensional Universe 346
Learning-Theory Perspectives:
All the Things You Do 350
The Humanistic–Existential
Perspective: How Becoming? 356
The Sociocultural Perspective:
Personality in Context 360
Measurement of Personality 362

FEATURES

A Closer Look: Virtuous Traits—Positive Psychology and Trait Theory 348
Video Connections: Personality Theories and Measurement 348
Self-Assessment: Will You Be a Hit or a Miss? The Expectancy for Success Scale 353
A Closer Look: Biology, Social Cognition, and Gender-Typing 354
Self-Assessment: Do You Strive to Be All That You Can Be? 357
Life Connections: Enhancing Self-Esteem 358
Concept Review 10.1: Perspectives on Personality 362

T F Biting one's fingernails or smoking cigarettes as an adult is a sign of conflict experienced during early childhood.

page 345

T F Bloodletting and vomiting were once recommended as ways of coping with depression.

page 346

T F About 2,500 years ago, a Greek physician devised a way of looking at personality that—with a little "tweaking"—remains in use today.

page 347

T F Actually, there are no basic personality traits. We are all conditioned by society to behave in certain ways.

page 353

T F The most well-adjusted immigrants are those who abandon the language and customs of their country of origin and become like members of the dominant culture in their new host country.

page 361

T F There is a psychological test made up of ink-blots, and test-takers are asked to say what the blots look like to them.

page 365

Are these items truth or fiction? We will be revisiting them throughout the chapter.

Nearly 1,000 years ago, an Islamic theologian told his pupils the fable of the Blind Men and the Elephant:

> Once upon a time, a group of blind men heard that an unusual animal called an elephant had come to their country. Since they had no idea what an elephant looked like and had never even heard its name, they resolved that they would obtain a "picture" of sorts, and the knowledge they sought, by feeling the animal. After all, that was the only possibility available to them. They sought out the elephant, and its handler kindly permitted them to touch the beast. One blind man stroked its leg, the other a tusk, the third an ear, and believing that they now had knowledge of the elephant, they returned home satisfied. But when they were questioned by others, they provided very different descriptions.
>
> The one who had felt the leg said that the elephant was firm, strong, and upright, like a pillar. The one who had felt the tusk disagreed. He described the elephant as hard and smooth, clearly not as stout as a pillar, and sharp at the end. Now spoke the third blind man, who had held the ear of the elephant. "By my faith," he asserted, "the elephant is soft and rough." It was neither pillar-like nor hard and smooth. It was broad, thick, and leathery. And so the three argued about the true nature of the beast. Each was right in part, but none grasped the real nature of the elephant. Yet each was fervent in his belief that he knew the animal.

Each of the blind men had come to know the elephant from a different angle. Each was bound by his first experience and blind to the beliefs of his fellows and to the real nature of the beast—not only because of his physical limitations but also because his initial encounter led him to think of the elephant in a certain way.

Our own conceptions about people, and about ourselves, may be similarly bound up with our own perspectives and initial beliefs.

Some think of personality as consisting of the person's most striking traits, as in "This person has an outgoing personality" or "That person has an agreeable personality." But many psychological theorists look deeper. Those schooled in the Freudian tradition look at personality as consisting of underlying mental structures that jockey for supremacy outside the range of our ordinary awareness. Other theorists focus on how personality is shaped by learning. And to the humanistic theorists, personality is not something people have but rather something they create to give their lives meaning and direction.

Sometimes, psychologists are subject to the influence of initial beliefs by preferring the first theory of personality they learn about. The Islamic theologian taught his pupils the legend of the blind men and the elephant to foster tolerance and to illustrate that no person can have a complete view of the truth; therefore, we need to be

Sigmund Freud Sigmund Freud was a mass of contradictions. He has been lauded as one of the greatest thinkers of the 20th century; he has been criticized as overrated. He preached liberal views of sexuality but was himself a model of sexual restraint. He invented a popular form of psychotherapy but experienced lifelong psychologically related problems such as migraine headaches, bowel problems, fainting under stress, hatred of the telephone, and an addiction to cigars. He smoked 20 cigars a day and could not (or would not) break the habit even after he developed cancer of the jaw.

"Freud found sex an outcast in the outhouse, and left it in the living room an honored guest."

W. BERTRAM WOLFE

Personality The reasonably stable patterns of emotions, motives, and behavior that distinguish one person from another.

Psychodynamic theory Sigmund Freud's perspective, which emphasizes the importance of unconscious motives and conflicts as forces that determine behavior. *Dynamic* refers to the concept of (psychological) forces in motion.

Conscious Self-aware.

Preconscious Capable of being brought into awareness by the focusing of attention.

Unconscious In psychodynamic theory, not available to awareness by simple focusing of attention.

flexible in our thinking and open to new ideas. It is possible that none of the views of personality presented in this chapter offer the one true portrait of personality, but each may have something to contribute to our understanding. So let's approach our study with an open mind, because years from now psychologists may well be teaching new ideas about personality.

Before we examine these different theoretical views, let's define our subject matter. **Question 1: What is personality?** Psychologists define **personality** as the reasonably stable patterns of emotions, motives, and behavior that distinguish one person from another. In this chapter, we lay the foundations for the understanding of personality. We also discuss personality tests—the methods used by psychologists to touch the untouchable.

THE PSYCHODYNAMIC PERSPECTIVE: EXCAVATING THE ICEBERG

There are several **psychodynamic theories** of personality, and each owes its origin to the thinking of Sigmund Freud. These theories have a number of features in common. Each teaches that personality is characterized by conflict—by a dynamic struggle. At first, the conflict is external: drives like sex, aggression, and the need for superiority come into conflict with laws, social rules, and moral codes. But at some point, laws and social rules are brought inward, or *internalized*. After that, the conflict is between opposing inner forces. At any given moment, our behavior, thoughts, and emotions represent the outcome of these inner contests. **Question 2: What is Freud's theory of psychosexual development?**

Sigmund Freud's Theory of Psychosexual Development

Sigmund Freud was trained as a physician. Early in his practice, he was astounded to find that some people apparently experience loss of feeling in a hand or paralysis of the legs in the absence of any medical disorder. These odd symptoms often disappear once the person has recalled and discussed stressful events and feelings of guilt or anxiety that seem related to the symptoms. For a long time, these events and feelings have lain hidden beneath the surface of awareness. Even so, they have the capacity to influence behavior.

From this sort of clinical evidence, Freud concluded that the human mind is like an iceberg. Only the tip of an iceberg rises above the surface of the water; the great mass of it is hidden in the depths (see Figure 10.1 ■). Freud came to believe that people, similarly, are aware of only a small portion of the ideas and impulses that dwell within their minds. He argued that a much greater portion of the mind—our deepest images, thoughts, fears, and urges—remains beneath the surface of conscious awareness, where little light illumines them.

Freud labeled the region that pokes through into the light of awareness the **conscious** part of the mind. He called the regions below the surface the *preconscious* and the *unconscious*. The **preconscious** mind contains elements of experience that are out of awareness but can be made conscious simply by focusing on them. The **unconscious** mind is shrouded in mystery. It contains biological instincts such as sex and aggression. Some unconscious urges cannot be experienced consciously because mental images and words cannot portray them in all their color and fury. Other unconscious urges may be kept below the surface through repression.

Repression is the automatic ejection of anxiety-evoking ideas from awareness. Research evidence suggests that many people repress bad childhood experiences (Myers & Brewin, 1994). Perhaps "something shocking happens, and the mind pushes it into some inaccessible corner of the unconscious" (Loftus, 1993, p. 518). Repression may also protect us from perceiving morally unacceptable impulses.

In the unconscious mind, primitive drives seek expression, while internalized values try to keep them in check. The conflict can arouse emotional outbursts and psychological problems. To explore the unconscious mind, Freud engaged in a form of mental detective work called **psychoanalysis**. Thus, his theory of personality is referred to as *psychoanalytic theory*. In psychoanalysis, people are prodded to talk about anything that pops into their mind while they remain comfortable and relaxed.

THE STRUCTURE OF PERSONALITY Freud spoke of mental, or **psychic**, **structures** to describe the clashing forces of personality. Psychic structures cannot be seen or measured directly, but their presence is suggested by behavior, expressed thoughts, and emotions. Freud believed that there are three psychic structures: the id, the ego, and the superego.

The id is present at birth. It represents physiological drives and is entirely unconscious. Freud described the id as "a chaos, a cauldron of seething excitations" (1927/1964, p. 73). The conscious mind might find it inconsistent to love and hate the same person, but Freud believed that conflicting emotions could dwell side by side in the id. In the id, one can feel hatred for one's mother for failing to gratify immediately all of one's needs while also feeling love for her. The id follows what Freud termed the *pleasure principle*. It demands instant gratification of instincts without consideration of law, social custom, or the needs of others.

The **ego** begins to develop during the first year, in part because a child's demands for gratification cannot all be met immediately. The ego stands for reason and good sense, for rational ways of coping with frustration. It curbs the appetites of the id and makes plans that fit social conventions. Thus, a person can find gratification yet avoid social disapproval. The id informs you that you are hungry, but the ego decides to microwave enchiladas. The ego is guided by the *reality principle*. It takes into account what is practical along with what is urged by the id. The ego also provides the person's conscious sense of self.

Although most of the ego is conscious, some of its business is carried out unconsciously. For instance, the ego also acts as a censor that screens the impulses of the id. When the ego senses that improper impulses are rising into awareness, it may use psychological defenses to prevent them from surfacing. Repression is one such psychological defense, or **defense mechanism**. Several defense mechanisms are described in Table 10.1 ■.

The **superego** develops throughout early childhood as the child incorporates the moral standards and values of parents and important members of the community. The child does so through *identification*—that is, by trying to become like these people. The superego functions according to the *moral principle*. It holds forth shining examples of an ideal self and also acts like the conscience, an internal moral guardian. Throughout life, the superego monitors the intentions of the ego and hands out judgments of right and wrong. It floods the ego with feelings of guilt and shame when the verdict is negative.

The ego hasn't an easy time of it. It stands between the id and the superego, striving to satisfy the demands of the id and the moral sense of the superego. From the Freudian perspective, a healthy personality has found ways to gratify most of the id's remaining unfulfilled demands without seriously offending the superego. Most of these demands are contained or repressed. If the ego is not a good problem solver or if the superego is too stern, the ego suffers. According to psychodynamic theory, identification is a means by which people usually incorporate the moral standards and values of parents and important members of the community.

STAGES OF PSYCHOSEXUAL DEVELOPMENT Freud stirred controversy by arguing that sexual impulses are a central factor in personality development, even among children. He believed that sexual feelings are closely linked to children's basic ways of relating to the world, such as sucking their mother's breasts and moving their bowels.

Freud believed that a major instinct, which he termed *eros*, is aimed at preserving and perpetuating life. Eros is fueled by psychological, or psychic, energy, which Freud labeled *libido*. Libidinal energy involves sexual impulses, so Freud considered it *psychosexual*. As the child develops, libidinal energy is expressed through sexual

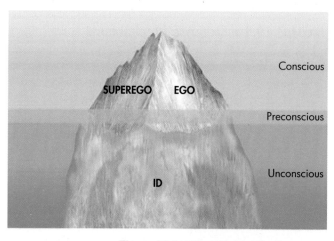

Figure 10.1 ■ The Human Iceberg According to Freud According to psychodynamic theory, only the tip of human personality rises above the surface of the mind into conscious awareness. Material in the preconscious can become conscious if we direct our attention to it. Unconscious material tends to remain shrouded in mystery.

"All these primary impulses, not easily described in words, are the springs of man's actions."

ALBERT EINSTEIN

"Denial ain't just a river in Egypt."

MARK TWAIN

Psychoanalysis Freud's method of exploring human personality.

Psychic structure In psychodynamic theory, a hypothesized mental structure that helps explain different aspects of behavior.

Id The psychic structure, present at birth, that represents physiological drives and is fully unconscious.

Ego The second psychic structure to develop, characterized by self-awareness, planning, and delay of gratification.

Defense mechanism In psychodynamic theory, an unconscious function of the ego that protects it from anxiety-evoking material by preventing accurate recognition of this material.

Superego The third psychic structure, which functions as a moral guardian and sets forth high standards for behavior.

TABLE 10.1 ■ Defense Mechanisms

Defense Mechanism	Definition	Examples
Repression	Ejection of anxiety-evoking ideas from awareness	• A person in therapy forgets an appointment when anxiety-evoking material is to be discussed.
Regression	The return, under stress, to a form of behavior characteristic of an earlier stage of development	• An adolescent cries when forbidden to use the family car. • An adult becomes highly dependent on his parents after the breakup of his marriage.
Rationalization	The use of self-deceiving justifications for unacceptable behavior	• A student blames her cheating on her teacher's leaving the room during a test. • A man explains his cheating on his income tax by saying "Everyone does it."
Displacement	The transfer of ideas and impulses from threatening or unsuitable objects to less threatening objects	• A worker picks a fight with her spouse after being sharply criticized by her supervisor.
Projection	The thrusting of one's own unacceptable impulses onto others so that others are assumed to have those impulses	• A hostile person perceives the world as a dangerous place. • A sexually frustrated person interprets innocent gestures as sexual advances.
Reaction formation	Engaging in behavior that opposes one's genuine impulses to keep those impulses repressed	• A person who is angry with a relative behaves in a "sickly sweet" manner toward that relative. • A sadistic individual becomes a physician.
Denial	The refusal to face the true nature of a threat	• Belief that one will not contract cancer or heart disease even though one smokes heavily.
Sublimation	The channeling of primitive impulses into positive, constructive efforts	• A person paints nudes for the sake of "beauty" and "art." • A hostile person becomes a tennis star.

"Most people do not really want freedom, because freedom involves responsibility, and most people are frightened of responsibility."

SIGMUND FREUD

"Flowers are restful to look at. They have neither emotions nor conflicts."

SIGMUND FREUD

Erogenous zone An area of the body that is sensitive to sexual sensations.

Psychosexual development In psychodynamic theory, the process by which libidinal energy is expressed through different erogenous zones during different stages of development.

feelings in different parts of the body, or **erogenous zones**. To Freud, human development involves the transfer of libidinal energy from one erogenous zone to another. He hypothesized five periods of **psychosexual development**: oral, anal, phallic, latency, and genital.

During the first year of life, a child experiences much of his or her world through the mouth. If it fits, into the mouth it goes. This is the *oral stage*. Freud argued that oral activities such as sucking and biting give the child sexual gratification as well as nourishment.

Freud believed that children encounter conflict during each stage of psychosexual development. During the oral stage, conflict centers on the nature and extent of oral gratification. Early weaning (cessation of breast feeding) could lead to frustration. Excessive gratification, on the other hand, could lead an infant to expect that it will routinely be given anything it wants. Either insufficient or excessive gratification in any stage could lead to *fixation* in that stage and to the development of traits characteristic of that stage. Oral traits include dependence, gullibility, and excessive optimism or pessimism.

Freud theorized that adults with an *oral fixation* could experience exaggerated desires for "oral activities," such as smoking, overeating, alcohol abuse, and nail biting. Like the infant whose very survival depends on the mercy of an adult, adults with oral fixations may be disposed toward clinging, dependent relationships.

During the *anal stage,* sexual gratification is attained through contraction and relaxation of the muscles that control elimination of waste products from the body. Elimination, which was controlled reflexively during most of the first year of life, comes under voluntary muscular control, even if such control is not reliable at first. The anal stage is said to begin in the second year of life.

During the anal stage, children learn to delay the gratification that comes from eliminating as soon as they feel the urge. The general issue of self-control may become a source of conflict between parent and child. *Anal fixations* may stem from this conflict and lead to two sets of traits in adulthood. So-called *anal-retentive* traits involve excessive use of self-control. They include perfectionism, a strong need for order, and exaggerated neatness and cleanliness. *Anal-expulsive* traits, on the other hand, "let it all hang out." They include carelessness, messiness, even sadism.

Children enter the *phallic stage* during the third year of life. During this stage, the major erogenous zone is the phallic region (the penis in boys and the clitoris in girls). Parent–child conflict is likely to develop over masturbation, to which parents may respond with threats or punishment. During the phallic stage, children may develop strong sexual attachments to the parent of the other gender and begin to view the parent of the same gender as a rival for the other parent's affection.

It is difficult for children to deal with feelings of lust and jealousy. These feelings, therefore, remain unconscious, but their influence is felt through fantasies about marriage with the parent of the other gender and hostility toward the parent of the same gender. In boys, this conflict is labeled the **Oedipus complex**, after the legendary Greek king who unwittingly killed his father and married his mother. Similar feelings in girls give rise to the **Electra complex**. According to Greek legend, Electra was the daughter of King Agamemnon. She longed for him after his death and sought revenge against his slayers—her mother and her mother's lover.

The Oral Stage? According to Freud, during the first year, the child is in the oral stage of development. If it fits, into the mouth it goes. What, according to Freud, are the effects of too little or too much gratification during the oral stage? Is there evidence to support his views?

The Oedipus and Electra complexes are resolved by about the age of 5 or 6. Children then repress their hostilities toward the parent of the same gender and begin to identify with her or him. Identification leads them to play the social and gender roles of that parent and to internalize his or her values. Sexual feelings toward the parent of the other gender are repressed for a number of years. When the feelings emerge again during adolescence, they are *displaced,* or transferred, to socially appropriate members of the other gender.

Freud believed that by the age of 5 or 6, children have been in conflict with their parents over sexual feelings for several years. The pressures of the Oedipus and Electra complexes cause them to repress all sexual urges. In so doing, they enter a period of *latency,* during which their sexual feelings remain unconscious. During the latency phase, it is not uncommon for children to prefer playmates of their own gender.

Freud believed that we enter the final stage of psychosexual development, the *genital stage,* at puberty. Adolescent males again experience sexual urges toward their mother, and adolescent females experience such urges toward their father. However, the *incest taboo* causes them to repress these impulses and displace them onto other adults or adolescents of the other gender. Boys might seek girls "just like the girl that married dear old Dad." Girls might be attracted to boys who resemble their fathers.

People in the genital stage prefer to find sexual gratification through intercourse with a member of the other gender. In Freud's view, oral or anal stimulation, masturbation, and homosexuality all represent pregenital fixations and immature forms of sexual conduct.

> "Even a happy life cannot be without a measure of darkness, and the word happy would lose its meaning if it were not balanced by sadness. It is far better to take things as they come along with patience and equanimity."
>
> CARL JUNG

Neo-Freudians

Several personality theorists—*neo-Freudians*—are among Freud's intellectual heirs. Their theories, like his, include dynamic movement of psychological forces, conflict, and defense mechanisms. In other respects, their theories differ considerably. **Question 3: What are the views of neo-Freudians?**

Oedipus complex A conflict of the phallic stage in which the boy wishes to possess his mother sexually and perceives his father as a rival in love.

Electra complex A conflict of the phallic stage in which the girl longs for her father and resents her mother.

343

Karen Horney Horney, like many of Freud's intellectual descendants, took issue with Freud on many issues. For one thing, Horney did not believe that little girls had penis envy or felt inferior to boys in any other way. She also believed that children's social relationships are more important in their development than unconscious sexual and aggressive impulses.

Analytical psychology Jung's psychodynamic theory, which emphasizes the collective unconscious and archetypes.

Collective unconscious Jung's hypothesized store of vague racial memories.

Archetypes Basic, primitive images or concepts hypothesized by Jung to reside in the collective unconscious.

Inferiority complex Feelings of inferiority hypothesized by Adler to serve as a central motivating force.

CARL JUNG Carl Jung (1875–1961) was a Swiss psychiatrist who had been a member of Freud's inner circle. He fell into disfavor with Freud when he developed his own psychodynamic theory—**analytical psychology**. In contrast to Freud, Jung downplayed the importance of the sexual instinct. He saw it as just one of several important instincts.

Jung, like Freud, was intrigued by unconscious processes. He believed that we have not only a personal unconscious that contains repressed memories and impulses but also an inherited **collective unconscious**. The collective unconscious contains primitive images, or **archetypes**, that reflect the history of our species. Examples of archetypes are the all-powerful God, the young hero, the fertile and nurturing mother, the wise old man—even fairy godmothers, wicked witches, and themes of rebirth or resurrection. Archetypes themselves remain unconscious, but Jung declared that they influence our thoughts and emotions and cause us to respond to cultural themes in stories and films.

ALFRED ADLER Alfred Adler (1870–1937), another follower of Freud, also felt that Freud had placed too much emphasis on sexual impulses. Adler believed that people are basically motivated by an **inferiority complex**. In some people, feelings of inferiority may be based on physical problems and the need to compensate for them. Adler believed, however, that all of us encounter some feelings of inferiority because of our small size as children and that these feelings give rise to a **drive for superiority**. As a child, Adler was crippled by rickets and suffered from pneumonia, and it may be that his theory developed in part from his own childhood striving to overcome repeated bouts of illness.

Adler believed that self-awareness plays a major role in the formation of personality. He spoke of a **creative self**, a self-aware aspect of personality that strives to overcome obstacles and develop the individual's potential. Because each person's potential is unique, Adler's views have been termed **individual psychology**.

KAREN HORNEY Karen Horney (1885–1952) was drummed out of the New York Psychoanalytic Institute because she took issue with the way psychoanalytic theory portrayed women. Early in the 20th century, psychoanalytic theory taught that a woman's place was in the home. Women who sought to compete with men in the business world were assumed to be suffering from unconscious *penis envy*. Psychoanalytic theory taught that little girls feel inferior to boys when they learn that boys have a penis and they do not. Horney argued that little girls do not feel inferior to boys and that these views were founded on Western cultural prejudice, not scientific evidence.

Trained in psychoanalysis, Horney agreed with Freud that childhood experiences are important factors in the development of adult personality. Like other neo-Freudians, however, she asserted that unconscious sexual and aggressive impulses are less important than social relationships in children's development. She also believed that genuine and consistent love can alleviate the effects of even the most traumatic childhood.

ERIK ERIKSON Like many other modern psychoanalysts, Erik Erikson (1902–1994) believed that Freud had placed undue emphasis on sexual instincts. He asserted that social relationships are more crucial determinants of personality than sexual urges. To Erikson, the nature of the mother–infant relationship is more important than the details of the feeding process or the sexual feelings that might be stirred by contact with the mother. Erikson also argued that to a large extent we are the conscious architects of our own personalities. In Erikson's theory, it is possible for us to make real choices. In Freud's theory, we may think that we are making choices but may merely be rationalizing the compromises forced on us by internal conflicts.

Erikson, like Freud, is known for devising a comprehensive theory of personality development. But whereas Freud proposed stages of psycho*sexual* development, Erikson proposed stages of psycho*social* development. Rather than label stages for various erogenous zones, Erikson labeled them for the traits that might be developed during stages of development (see Table 9.4 in Chapter 9). Each stage is named according to its possible outcomes. For example, the first stage of **psychosocial development** is labeled the stage of *trust versus mistrust* because of its two possible outcomes: (a) A warm, loving relationship with the mother (and others) during infancy might lead to a sense of basic trust in people and the world. (b) On the other hand, a cold, ungratifying relationship might generate a pervasive sense of mistrust. Erikson believed that most people would wind up with some blend of trust and mistrust. A basic sense of mistrust could interfere with the formation of relationships unless it was recognized and challenged.

For Erikson, the goal of adolescence is the attainment of **ego identity**, not genital sexuality. The focus is on whom we see ourselves as being and what we stand for, not on sexual interests.

Evaluation of the Psychodynamic Perspective

Psychodynamic theories have tremendous appeal. They involve many concepts and explain many varieties of human behavior and traits. **Question 4: What are the strengths and weaknesses of the psychodynamic perspective?**

Today, concepts such as *the id* and *libido* strike many psychologists as unscientific, but Freud was fighting for the idea that human personality and behavior are subject to scientific analysis. He developed his theories when many people still viewed psychological problems as signs of possession by the devil or evil spirits, as they had during the Middle Ages. Freud argued that psychological disorders stem from problems within the individual—not evil spirits. His thinking contributed to the development of compassion for people with psychological disorders and methods for helping them.

Psychodynamic theory has also focused on the far-reaching effects of childhood events. Freud and other psychodynamic theorists are to be credited for suggesting that personality and behavior are the result of a developmental process and that it is important for parents to be aware of the emotional needs of their children. **Truth or Fiction Revisited:** However, there is no adequate evidence that biting one's nails in adulthood or smoking cigarettes is a sign of an oral fixation.

Freud has helped us recognize that sexual and aggressive urges are common and that admitting to them is not the same thing as acting on them. On the other hand, his views of girls and women have been seen as sexist, as noted by Karen Horney.

Freud also noted that people have defensive ways of looking at the world. His defense mechanisms have become part of everyday speech. Because defense mechanisms are unconscious, they have been difficult to assess and were rejected by academic psychologists in the 1950s and 1960s. However, the cognitive revolution of more recent years has again made them the subject of scientific investigation, and cognitive, developmental, and personality psychologists have found some evidence for their existence (Cramer, 2009; Somerfield & McCrae, 2000). The debate is unresolved.

A number of critics note that "psychic structures" such as the id, ego, and superego are too vague to measure scientifically (Hergenhahn, 2009). They cannot be used to predict behavior with precision. They are little more than useful fictions—poetic ways to express inner conflict. The stages of psychosexual development have also not escaped criticism. Children begin to masturbate as early as the first year, not in the phallic stage. As parents know from discovering their children play "doctor," the latency stage is not as sexually latent as Freud believed. Much of Freud's thinking about the Oedipus and Electra complexes remains little more than speculation. The evidence for some of Erikson's developmental views seems somewhat sturdier. For example, people who fail to develop ego identity in adolescence seem to encounter problems developing intimate relationships later.

Freud's method of gathering evidence from clinical sessions is also suspect (Hergenhahn, 2009). In subtle ways, therapists may influence clients to produce memories and feelings they expect to find. Therapists may also fail to separate what they are told from their own interpretations. Furthermore, Freud and many other psychodynamic theorists restricted their evidence gathering to case studies with individuals who sought help for psychological problems. Their clients were mostly European and European American and from the middle and upper classes. People who seek therapy differ from the general population.

Erik Erikson As a child, Erikson faced religious identity issues. As he matured, Erikson faced another identity issue: 'What am I to do in life?' His stepfather encouraged him to attend medical school, but Erikson sought his own path. As a youth, he studied art and traveled through Europe, leading a Bohemian life. Erikson came to label this period of soul-searching an identity crisis. As a result of his own search for identity, he became oriented toward his life's work—psychotherapy. He left his wanderings and plunged into psychoanalytic training under the supervision of Sigmund Freud's daughter, Anna Freud.

Drive for superiority Adler's term for the desire to compensate for feelings of inferiority.

Creative self According to Adler, the self-aware aspect of personality that strives to achieve its full potential.

Individual psychology Adler's psychodynamic theory, which emphasizes feelings of inferiority and the creative self.

Psychosocial development Erikson's theory of personality and development, which emphasizes social relationships and eight stages of growth.

Ego identity A firm sense of who one is and what one stands for.

ACTIVE REVIEW (1) According to Freud, the unconscious psychic structure called the _____ is present at birth and operates according to the pleasure principle. (2) The _____ is the sense of self and operates according to the reality principle. (3) The _____ is the moral sense and develops by internalizing the standards of parents and others. (4) The stages of psychosexual development include the oral, _____, phallic, latency, and genital stages. (5) Jung believed that in addition to a personal unconscious mind, people also have a(n) _____ unconscious. (6) Adler believed that people are motivated by a(n) _____

complex. (7) Karen _____, like Freud, saw parent–child relationships as paramount in importance.

REFLECT AND RELATE If you were fixated in a stage of psychosexual development, which stage would it be? Explain.

CRITICAL THINKING If Freud's theory is riddled with scientific shortcomings, why do you think it remains popular in the general population?

Go to Psychology CourseMate at **www.cengagebrain.com** for an interactive version of these questions.

THE TRAIT PERSPECTIVE: THE FIVE-DIMENSIONAL UNIVERSE

The notion of *traits* is familiar enough. If I asked you to describe yourself, you would probably do so in terms of traits such as bright, sophisticated, and witty. (That is you, is it not?) We also describe other people in terms of traits. **Question 5: What are traits?**

Traits are reasonably stable elements of personality that are inferred from behavior. If you describe a friend as shy, perhaps it's because you have observed social anxiety or withdrawal in that person's encounters with others. Traits are assumed to account for consistent behavior in diverse situations. You probably expect your shy friend to be retiring in most social confrontations—"all across the board," as the saying goes. The concept of traits is also found in other approaches to personality. Freud linked the development of certain traits to children's experiences in each stage of psychosexual development.

"In most of us by the age of thirty, the character has set like plaster, and will never soften again."

WILLIAM JAMES

"Humans recognize unique individuals, and also pigeonhole them into categories. They distinguish stable categories that capture an individual's essence from transitory and superficial properties they may happen to possess."

STEVEN PINKER

From Hippocrates to the Present

Question 6: What is the history of the trait perspective? The trait perspective dates back at least to the Greek physician Hippocrates (ca. 460–377 B.C.E.). Hippocrates believed that traits were embedded in bodily fluids, which gave rise to certain types of personalities. In his view, an individual's personality depends on the balance of four basic fluids, or "humors," in the body. Yellow bile is associated with a choleric (quick-tempered) disposition; blood with a sanguine (warm, cheerful) temperament; phlegm with a phlegmatic (sluggish, calm, cool) disposition; and black bile with a melancholic (gloomy, pensive) temperament. Disease was believed to reflect an imbalance among the humors. Methods such as bloodletting and vomiting were recommended to restore the balance (Lander & Pritchett, 2009). **Truth or Fiction Revisited:** Therefore, it is true that bloodletting and vomiting were recommended as ways of coping with depression. Although Hippocrates' theory was speculative, the terms choleric, sanguine, and so on are still used in descriptions of personality.

More enduring theories assume that traits are heritable and are embedded in the nervous system. These theories rely on the mathematical technique of *factor analysis*, developed by Charles Spearman to study intelligence (see Chapter 7), to help determine which traits are basic.

Sir Francis Galton was among the first scientists to suggest that many of the world's languages use single words to describe fundamental differences in personality. Nearly 75 years ago, Allport and Odbert (1936) cataloged some 18,000 human traits from a search through word lists like dictionaries. Some were physical traits such as *short, black*, and *brunette*. Others were behavioral traits such as *shy* and *emotional*. Still others were moral traits such as *honest*. This exhaustive list has served as the basis for personality research by many other psychologists. **Question 7: How have contemporary psychologists reduced the universe of traits to more manageable lists?**

Trait A relatively stable aspect of personality that is inferred from behavior and assumed to give rise to consistent behavior.

Hans Eysenck's Trait Theory: A Two-Dimensional View

British psychologist Hans J. Eysenck (1916–1997) focused much of his research on the relationships between two personality traits: introversion–extraversion and emotional stability–instability (Eysenck & Eysenck, 1985). (Emotional *in*stability is also known as neuroticism). Carl Jung was first to distinguish between

Unstable

Moody
Anxious
Rigid
Sober
Pessimistic
Reserved
Unsociable
Quiet

Touchy
Restless
Aggressive
Excitable
Changeable
Impulsive
Optimistic
Active

Melancholic | Choleric

Introverted | **Extraverted**

Phlegmatic | Sanguine

Passive
Careful
Thoughtful
Peaceful
Controlled
Reliable
Even-tempered
Calm

Sociable
Outgoing
Talkative
Responsive
Easygoing
Lively
Carefree
Leadership

Stable

introverts and extraverts. Eysenck added the dimension of emotional stability–instability to introversion–extraversion. He cataloged various personality traits according to where they are situated along these dimensions or factors (see Figure 10.2 ■). For instance, an anxious person would be high in both introversion and neuroticism—that is, preoccupied with his or her own thoughts and emotionally unstable.

Eysenck acknowledged that his scheme is similar to Hippocrates' system. According to Eysenck's dimensions, the choleric type would be extraverted and unstable; the sanguine type, extraverted and stable; the phlegmatic type, introverted and stable; and the melancholic type, introverted and unstable. **Truth or Fiction Revisited:** It is therefore true that some 2,500 years ago, Hippocrates, the Greek physician, devised a way of looking at personality that could be said to remain in use today.

Figure 10.2 ■ Eysenck's Personality Dimensions and Hippocrates' Personality Types Various personality traits shown in the outer ring fall within the two major dimensions of personality suggested by Hans Eysenck. The inner circle shows how Hippocrates' four major personality types—choleric, sanguine, phlegmatic, and melancholic—fit within Eysenck's dimensions.

The "Big Five": The Five-Factor Model

More recent research suggests that there may be five basic personality factors, not two. These include the two found by Eysenck—*extraversion* and *neuroticism*—along with *conscientiousness*, *agreeableness*, and *openness to experience* (see Table 10.2 ■). Many personality theorists, especially Robert McCrae and Paul T. Costa Jr., have played a role in the development of the *five-factor model*. Cross-cultural research has found that these five factors appear to define the personality structure of American,

TABLE 10.2 ■ The "Big Five": The Five-Factor Model

Factor	Name	Traits
I	Extraversion	Contrasts talkativeness, assertiveness, and activity with silence, passivity, and reserve
II	Agreeableness	Contrasts kindness, trust, and warmth with hostility, selfishness, and distrust
III	Conscientiousness	Contrasts organization, thoroughness, and reliability with carelessness, negligence, and unreliability
IV	Neuroticism	Contrasts nervousness, moodiness, and sensitivity to negative stimuli with coping ability
V	Openness to experience	Contrasts imagination, curiosity, and creativity with shallowness and lack of perceptiveness

Introversion A trait characterized by tendencies to direct one's interests inward and to inhibit impulses.

Extraversion A trait characterized by tendencies to be socially outgoing and to express feelings and impulses freely.

Neuroticism Eysenck's term for emotional instability.

© Mike Kemp/Jupiterimages

© Rubberball/Jupiterimages

German, Portuguese, Hebrew, Chinese, Korean, Japanese, and Philippine people (Katigbak et al., 2002; McCrae & Costa, 1997). A study of more than 5,000 German, British, Spanish, Czech, and Turkish people suggests that the factors are related to people's basic temperaments, which are considered to be largely inborn (McCrae et al., 2000). The researchers interpret the results to suggest that our personalities tend to mature rather than be shaped by environmental conditions, although the expression of personality traits is certainly affected by culture. (A person who is basically open to new experience is likely to behave less openly in a restrictive society than in an open society.)

The five-factor model—also known as the *Big Five model*—is fueling a great deal of research now. Hundreds of studies are correlating scores on the five factors, according to a psychological test constructed by Costa and McCrae (the NEO Five-Factor Inventory), with various behavior patterns, psychological disorders, and kinds of "personalities." Consider driving. Significant negative correlations have been found between the numbers of tickets people get and accidents people get into, on the one hand, and the factor of agreeableness on the other (Cellar et al., 2000). As we have long suspected, it's safer to share the freeway with agreeable people. People who are not judgmental—who will put up with your every whim—tend to score low on conscientiousness (they don't examine you too closely) and high on agreeableness (you can be yourself) (Bernardin et al., 2000). A firm handshake is positively correlated with extraversion and negatively correlated with neuroticism (Chaplin et al., 2000).

Researchers have also found relationships between the five-factor model of personality and health. For example, the factors of openness to experience, extraversion, and conscientiousness are negatively correlated with the progression of HIV disease (Ironson et al., 2008). That is, people who are more open to treatment, more assertive, more positive in their attitudes and emotions (extraversion), and more likely to follow doctors' orders (conscientious) are more likely to take their medicine and adopt a healthful lifestyle. In an Italian study, conscientiousness (about diet and lifestyle) was associated with lower levels of unhealthful cholesterol (Sutin et al., 2010). Being neurotic—but also conscientious—is associated with a relatively low body weight; impulsivity and lack of conscientiousness, on the other hand, are connected with being overweight and obese (Terracciano et al., 2009).

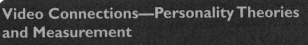

Video Connections—Personality Theories and Measurement

The "person-in-the-situation" phenomenon offers one explanation of why we may be shy in one situation and uninhibited in another. See the video for discussion of patterns of behavior, personality traits, and how to understand "if-then" signatures. Go to Psychology CourseMate at **www.cengagebrain.com** to watch this video.

A CLOSER LOOK
Virtuous Traits—Positive Psychology and Trait Theory

Curious. Open-minded. Persistent. Zestful. Kind. Fair. Modest. Hopeful. Humorous. That's you, isn't it?

Trait theory has found applications within *positive psychology*, an approach that studies character strengths and virtues such as those just listed. Psychologists are also developing psychological methods that help people increase their happiness and life satisfaction (Sheldon, 2009; Shyrack et al., 2010).

Psychologists list six major virtues that were found in countries as different as Azerbaijan and Venezuela, along with the United States and other developed nations (Peterson & Seligman, 2004; Snyder et al., 2010):

Wisdom and knowledge: Creativity, curiosity, open-mindedness, love of learning, perspective (ability to provide other people with sound advice)

Courage: Authenticity (speaking one's mind), bravery, persistence, zest

Humanity: Kindness, love, social intelligence

Justice: Fairness, leadership, teamwork

Temperance: Forgiveness, modesty, prudence, self-regulation

Transcendence: Appreciation of beauty and excellence, gratitude (when appropriate), hope, humor, religiosity (having a belief system about the meaning of life)

These virtues were traitlike in that they were reasonably stable individual differences (Seligman et al., 2005). Research has also found that these virtues are related to life satisfaction and personal fulfillment (Gillham et al., 2011; Peterson et al., 2005). In addition, these virtues are defined by a number of character strengths. The strengths of zest, gratitude, hope, and love were most closely related to life satisfaction. Although the researchers did not isolate the causes of the development of these virtues, they did find that they were widely recognized and valued despite cultural and religious differences and that they were generally promoted by institutions in the cultures studied (Park et al., 2005).

Is He on the Path to Developing an Antisocial Personality? Children who are developing antisocial personalities show low responses to threats and stressors, deceit, callous disregard for the feelings of others, and lack of interest in conforming to social rules. Adrian Raine has suggested that antisocial personality development may involve parts of the brain including the ventral (lower) part of the prefrontal cortex and the amygdala.

Biology and Traits

Researchers have also been investigating biological factors that are connected with, and may give rise to, personality traits. For example, researchers estimate that the heritability of the extraverted personality is 40% to 60% (Smillie et al., 2009). Research suggests that brain levels of the neurotransmitter dopamine are involved with extraversion and that levels tend to be higher in extraverts than in introverts (Smillie et al., 2009; Wacker et al., 2009).

Jerome Kagan and other researchers (Kagan & Saudino, 2001; Dai et al., 2003) have also found evidence that genetic factors are part of a child's basic temperament and are involved in shyness and behavioral inhibition. The **antisocial personality** is the other side of the coin when it comes to personality. Whereas shy children readily acquire fears and are highly reactive to stress, children who are on the path to developing antisocial personalities show low responses to threats and stressors (Gao et al., 2010; Isen et al., 2010). As children, they show a pattern of deceit, callous disregard for the feelings of others, and lack of interest in conforming their behavior to social rules (Raine, 2008). As adults, they are likely to become involved in criminal activity.

Adrian Raine (2008) has extensively studied the intersection of biology and the antisocial personality. In a review of the literature, he found a number of brain impairments that are related to the development of an antisocial personality in the ventral prefrontal cortex (part of the so-called executive center of the brain) and the amygdala (part of the limbic system)—see Chapter 12.

Experiences with animals also support the connections between biology and personality. People have been selectively breeding dogs for various traits for thousands of years (Wong et al., 2009). There are more than 400 breeds of dogs today, bred not only for behavioral traits but also for shape, size, and the quality of fur (Zhang et al., 2009). All of them, from the most nervous Chihuahua to the calmest and least aggressive golden retriever, are descended from and belong to the same species as *Canis lupus*—the wolf. People have bred dogs to hunt with them, to work (as in pulling sleds and herding sheep), and to keep them company (Driscoll et al., 2009).

Antisocial personality A personality descriptive of an individual who is in frequent conflict with society yet who is undeterred by punishment and experiences little or no guilt or anxiety.

Canis lupus—**the Wolf** All dogs, from the most aggressive German shepherds and pit bulls to the mildest golden retrievers and Labrador retrievers, from the largest Newfoundlands to the smallest toy poodles, are descended from—and can interbreed with—wolves.

There is also research into the "personalities" of dogs—defined as consistent patterns of behavior recorded by their owners (Helton et al., 2010). Perhaps in a bow to the Big Five model of personality, one group of researchers has developed a five-factor assessment of dogs' personalities (Ley et al., 2008, 2009). These factors include extraversion, motivation, trainability, amicability, and neuroticism. The investigators found that larger breeds tend to be less neurotic than smaller breeds and that working and hunting dogs tend to be more extraverted and trainable than the average. Gender matters: female dogs are more affectionate and sociable than males (Kubinyi et al., 2009).

Research with dogs suggests that biological differences can be related to personality. Perhaps it also shows that despite the fierceness of our ancestors, our personalities can develop along different paths and that perhaps the human species, like *Canis lupus,* is capable of unexpected and even surprising outcomes. And as with *Canis lupus,* environmental influences also matter. Just as there may be different outcomes for dogs who are adopted by humans at various ages and who are trained, there may be different outcomes for genetically similar people who have different early social and academic experiences.

Evaluation of the Trait Perspective

Question 8: What are the strengths and weaknesses of trait theory? Trait theorists have focused much attention on the development of personality tests. They have also given rise to theories about the fit between personality and certain kinds of jobs (Gottfredson, 2009). The qualities that suit a person for various kinds of work can be expressed in terms of abilities, personality traits, and interests.

One limitation of trait theory is that it has tended to be more descriptive than explanatory. It has historically focused on describing traits rather than on tracing their origins or finding out how they may be modified.

LearningConnections ● THE TRAIT PERSPECTIVE: THE FIVE-DIMENSIONAL UNIVERSE

ACTIVE REVIEW (8) _____ are personality elements that endure and account for behavioral consistency. (9) Eysenck used factor analysis to derive two basic traits: introversion–extraversion and emotional _____. (10) Five-factor theory suggests that there are five basic personality factors: extraversion, neuroticism, _____, agreeableness, and openness to experience. (11) Raine found brain impairments that are related to the development of a(n) _____ personality

REFLECT AND RELATE How would you describe yourself in terms of traits? Where would you place yourself in Eysenck's two-dimensional scheme? Where would you stand according to the five-factor model? Are you pleased with your self-evaluation? Why or why not?

CRITICAL THINKING The trait theories of Hippocrates and Eysenck are similar. Is one more scientific than the other?

 Go to Psychology CourseMate at **www.cengagebrain.com** for an interactive version of these questions.

● LEARNING-THEORY PERSPECTIVES: ALL THE THINGS YOU DO

Trait theory focused on enduring personality characteristics that were generally presumed to be embedded in the nervous system. Learning theorists tend not to theorize in terms of traits. They focus instead on behaviors and presume that those behaviors are largely learned. That which is learned is also, in principle, capable of being unlearned. As a result, learning theory and personality theory may not be a perfect fit. Nevertheless, learning theorists—both behaviorists and social-cognitive theorists—have contributed to the discussion of personality. **Question 9: What does behaviorism contribute to our understanding of personality?**

Behaviorism: On Being Easy in One's Harness?

In 1924, at Johns Hopkins University, John B. Watson raised the battle cry of the behaviorist movement:

> Give me a dozen healthy infants, well-formed, and my own specified world to bring them up in and I'll guarantee to take any one at random and train him to become any type of specialist I might suggest—doctor, lawyer, merchant-chief and, yes, even beggar-man and thief, regardless of his talents, penchants, tendencies, abilities, vocations, and the race of his ancestors. (p. 82)

What Does This Child Want, and Why Does He Want It? According to B. F. Skinner, societies socialize individuals into wanting what is good for society. Are the music, the color, and all the excitement socializing this child into wanting to belong to the group?

This proclamation underscores the behaviorist view that personality is plastic. Situational variables or environmental influences—not internal individual variables—are the key shapers of human preferences and behaviors. In contrast to the psychoanalysts and structuralists of his day, Watson argued that unseen, undetectable mental structures must be rejected in favor of what can be seen and measured. Furthermore, Watson's view is extreme and inconsistent with evidence suggesting that personality traits are to some degree heritable. Nevertheless, in the 1930s, Watson's battle cry was taken up by B. F. Skinner, who agreed that psychologists should avoid trying to see into the "black box" of the organism and instead emphasized the effects that reinforcements have on behavior.

The views of Watson and Skinner largely ignored the notions of personal freedom, choice, and self-direction. Most of us assume that our wants originate within us. Watson and Skinner suggested that environmental influences such as parental approval and social custom shape us into wanting certain things and not wanting others.

In his novel *Walden Two*, Skinner (1948) described a Utopian society where people are happy and content because they are allowed to do as they please, yet from early childhood have been trained or conditioned to cooperate. Because of their reinforcement histories, they want to behave in decent, kind, and unselfish ways. They see themselves as free because society makes no effort to force them to behave in particular ways. American poet Robert Frost wrote, "You have freedom when you're easy in your harness." Society in Skinner's *Walden Two* made children "easy" in their "harnesses," but the harnesses did exist.

Some object to behaviorist notions because they downplay the importance of consciousness and choice. Also, many argue that humans are not ruled by reinforcers (that is, rewards and punishments). In some circumstances, people have rebelled against the so-called necessity of survival by choosing pain and hardship over pleasure or death over life. Many people have sacrificed their own lives to save those of others. The behaviorist defense might be that the apparent choice of pain or death is forced on altruistic individuals just as conformity to social custom is forced on others. In other words, the altruist is still shaped by external influences, even if those influences differ from those that affect most people.

Social-Cognitive Theory: Is Determinism a Two-Way Street?

Social-cognitive theory was developed by Albert Bandura (1986, 2008) and other psychologists. It focuses on the importance of learning by observation and on cognitive processes that underlie individual differences. **Question 10: How does social-cognitive theory differ from the behaviorist view?** Social-cognitive theorists differ from behaviorists in that they see people as influencing their environment just as their environment influences them. Bandura terms this mutual pattern of influence reciprocal determinism. To social-cognitive theorists, people are not simply at the mercy of the environment. Instead, they are self-aware and purposefully engage in learning. They seek to learn about their environment and to alter it to make reinforcers available.

One goal of psychological theory is the prediction of behavior. We cannot predict behavior from *situational variables*—rewards and punishments—alone. Whether a person will behave in a certain way also depends on *person variables* (variables within people), including *expectancies* about the outcomes of that behavior and the perceived or *subjective values* of those outcomes (see Figure 10.3 ■). Self-efficacy expectations also come into play; these are beliefs that we can accomplish certain things, such as speaking before a group or solving math problems (Bandura, 2008; Bandura & Locke, 2003). People with positive self-efficacy expectations have higher self-esteem and are more likely to try difficult tasks than are people who do not believe that they can master those tasks (Rodin et al., 2009; Sherman et al., 2009).

Competencies are another aspect of social-cognitive theories; these include our knowledge and skills. In addition, different people *encode* (symbolize or represent) similar stimuli in different ways. For example, some people make themselves miserable by encoding events in self-defeating ways, as in encoding an unsuccessful date as a sign of their social incompetence. Social-cognitive theorists believe that we tend to regulate our own behavior, even in the absence of observers and external constraints. We set our own goals and standards, and we make plans to achieve them (Bandura, 2008; Bandura & Locke, 2003).

OBSERVATIONAL LEARNING Observational learning (also termed **modeling** or *cognitive learning*) is one of the foundations of social-cognitive theory. It refers to acquiring knowledge by observing others. For operant conditioning to occur, an organism must first engage in a response, and that response must then be reinforced. However, observational learning occurs even when the learner does not *perform* the observed behavior. Observing others extends to reading about them or seeing what they do and what happens to them in books and on TV, film, and the Internet.

Evaluation of the Learning Perspective

Learning theorists have contributed to the scientific understanding of behavior, but they have left some psychologists dissatisfied. **Question 11: What are the strengths and weaknesses of learning theories as they apply to personality?**

Psychodynamic theorists and trait theorists propose the existence of psychological structures that cannot be seen and measured directly. Learning theorists—particularly behaviorists—have dramatized the importance of referring to publicly observable variables, or behaviors, if psychology is to be accepted as a science.

Similarly, psychodynamic theorists and trait theorists focus on internal variables such as unconscious conflict and traits to explain and predict behavior. Learning theorists emphasize the importance of environmental conditions, or *situational variables*, as determinants of behavior. They have shown that we can learn to do things because of reinforcements and that many behavior patterns are acquired by observing others.

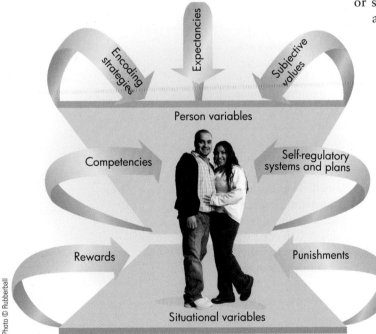

Photo © Rubberball

Figure 10.3 ■ Person Variables and Situational Variables in Social-Cognitive Theory According to social-cognitive theory, person variables and situational variables interact to influence behavior.

SELF-ASSESSMENT

Will You Be a Hit or a Miss? The Expectancy for Success Scale

Life is filled with opportunities and obstacles. What happens when you are faced with a difficult challenge? Do you rise to meet it, or do you back off? Social-cognitive theorists note that our self-efficacy expectancies influence our behavior. When we believe that we are capable of succeeding through our own efforts, we marshal our resources and apply ourselves.

The following scale can give you insight as to whether you believe that your own efforts are likely to meet with success. You can compare your own expectancies for success with those of other undergraduates taking psychology courses by turning to the scoring key in Appendix B.

Directions: Indicate the degree to which each item applies to you by circling the appropriate number according to this key:

1 = highly improbable
2 = improbable
3 = equally improbable and probable, not sure
4 = probable
5 = highly probable

IN THE FUTURE, I EXPECT THAT I WILL:

1. Find that people don't seem to understand what I'm trying to say   1 2 3 4 5
2. Be discouraged about my ability to gain the respect of others   1 2 3 4 5
3. Be a good parent   1 2 3 4 5
4. Be unable to accomplish my goals   1 2 3 4 5
5. Have a stressful marital relationship   1 2 3 4 5
6. Deal poorly with emergency situations   1 2 3 4 5
7. Find my efforts to change situations I don't like are ineffective   1 2 3 4 5
8. Not be very good at learning new skills   1 2 3 4 5
9. Carry through my responsibilities successfully   1 2 3 4 5
10. Discover that the good in life outweighs the bad   1 2 3 4 5
11. Handle unexpected problems successfully   1 2 3 4 5
12. Get the promotions I deserve   1 2 3 4 5
13. Succeed in the projects I undertake   1 2 3 4 5
14. Not make any significant contributions to society   1 2 3 4 5
15. Discover that my life is not getting much better   1 2 3 4 5
16. Be listened to when I speak   1 2 3 4 5
17. Discover that my plans don't work out too well   1 2 3 4 5
18. Find that no matter how hard I try, things just don't turn out the way I would like   1 2 3 4 5
19. Handle myself well in whatever situation I'm in   1 2 3 4 5
20. Be able to solve my own problems   1 2 3 4 5
21. Succeed at most things I try   1 2 3 4 5
22. Be successful in my endeavors in the long run   1 2 3 4 5
23. Be very successful working out my personal life   1 2 3 4 5
24. Experience many failures in my life   1 2 3 4 5
25. Make a good first impression on people I meet for the first time   1 2 3 4 5
26. Attain the career goals I have set for myself   1 2 3 4 5
27. Have difficulty dealing with my superiors   1 2 3 4 5
28. Have problems working with others   1 2 3 4 5
29. Be a good judge of what it takes to get ahead   1 2 3 4 5
30. Achieve recognition in my profession   1 2 3 4 5

Source: "The Generalized Expectancy for Success Scale," B. Fibel and W. D. Hale, *Journal of Consulting and Clinical Psychology, 46*, 1978, pp. 924–931. Copyright © 1978 by the American Psychological Association. Reprinted by permission.

On the other hand, behaviorism does not describe, explain, or suggest the richness of inner human experience. We experience thoughts and feelings and browse our inner maps of the world, but behaviorism does not deal with these. To be fair, the limitations of behaviorism are self-imposed. Personality theorists have traditionally dealt with thoughts, feelings, and behavior, whereas behaviorism, which studies only what is observable and measurable, deals with behavior alone.

Critics of social-cognitive theory cannot accuse its supporters of denying the importance of cognitive activity and feelings. But they often contend that social-cognitive theory has not come up with satisfying statements about the development of traits. **Truth or Fiction Revisited:** Actually, there may be some basic personality traits, as suggested by trait theory. We may be conditioned by society to behave in certain ways, but conditioning is unlikely to fully explain individual differences in personality.

Reciprocal determinism Bandura's term for the social-cognitive view that people influence their environment just as their environment influences them.

Self-efficacy expectations Beliefs to the effect that one can handle a task.

Modeling In social-cognitive theory, exhibiting behaviors that others will imitate or acquire through observational learning.

Gender-typing is the process by which males and females come to develop personality traits and behavior patterns that society considers to be consistent with their gender, male or female—at least most of the time. Researchers who investigate people's perceptions of gender differences in personality traits tend to find groups of "masculine" and "feminine" traits such as those shown in Table 10.3 ■. According to evolutionary psychologists, gender differences were fashioned by natural selection in response to problems in adaptation that were repeatedly encountered over thousands of generations (Buss, 2009, Schmitt, 2008). Men, who have generally been the hunters, breadwinners, and warriors, are more likely to be seen as *adventurous, aggressive,* and *assertive* (Amanatullah & Morris, 2010; Guzzetti, 2010; Lippa, 2010). Women, who have more often been the homemakers and caretakers, are more likely to be seen as *affectionate, agreeable,* and *emotional.*

A study using the "Big Five Inventory" investigated gender differences in personality in 55 nations, with a sample size of 17,637 (Schmitt et al., 2008). Responses revealed that women reported higher levels of neuroticism, extraversion, agreeableness, and conscientiousness than men did in most nations.

Biology and Gender-Typing

Researchers suggest that the development of gender differences in personality, along with the development of anatomical gender differences, may be related to prenatal levels of sex hormones. Although results of many studies attempting to correlate prenatal sex hormone levels with subsequent gender-typed play have been mixed, a study of 212 pregnant women conducted by Bonnie Auyeung and her colleagues (2009) found that fetal testosterone was related to masculine- or feminine-typed play at the age of 8½ years. Other studies show that children display gender-typed preferences—with boys preferring transportation toys and girls preferring dolls—as early as the age of 13 months (Knickmeyer et al., 2005). Another study investigated the gender-typed visual preferences of 30 human infants at the early ages of 3 to 8 months (Alexander et al., 2009). The researchers assessed interest in a toy truck and a doll by using eye-tracking technology to indicate the direction of visual attention. Girls showed a visual preference for the doll over the truck (that is, they made a greater number of visual fixations on the doll), and boys showed a visual preference for the truck.

Getting Ready for Female and Male Twins What do these children have to look forward to in terms of gender-role stereotypes? Would you prefer that this mother hold up yellow and green boxes—and use a green skirt in the crib—rather than blue or pink? Why or why not?

TABLE 10.3 ■ Stereotypical Masculine and Feminine Traits: Are They Accurate?

Masculine	Feminine
Adventurous	Affectionate
Aggressive	Agreeable
Assertive	Appreciative
Capable	Artistic
Coarse	Cautious
Confident	Dependent
Courageous	Emotional
Determined	Fearful
Disorderly	Fickle
Enterprising	Gentle
Hardheaded	Kind
Independent	Nurturant
Intelligent	Patient
Pleasure-seeking	Prudish
Quick	Sensitive
Rational	Sentimental
Realistic	Shy
Reckless	Softhearted
Sensation-seeking	Submissive
Scientific	Suggestible
Stern	Talkative
Tough	Unambitious

Sources: Amanatullah & Morris, 2010; Guzzetti, 2010; Lippa, 2010; Schmitt et al., 2008.

© Hill Street Studios/Blend Images/Getty Images

Acquiring Gender Roles How do gender roles develop? What contributions do evolutionary and genetic factors make? What is the role of experience? Social-cognitive theory notes that children obtain information as to what kinds of preferences and behaviors are considered masculine or feminine in their cultures. This information plus some use of rewards and punishments by family members and others apparently encourages most children to imitate the behavior of people of the same gender. But is learning the whole story, or does learning interact with evolutionary and genetic factors to fashion likes and dislikes and patterns of behavior?

Social Cognition and Gender-Typing

Social-cognitive theorists find roles for learning in gender-typing, and they suggest that children learn what is considered masculine or feminine in their societies by means of observational learning and socialization (Golombok et al., 2008; Zosuls et al., 2009). Children observe the behavior of adult role models and may come to assume that their behavior should conform to that of adults of the same gender. In social-cognitive theory, rewards and punishments influence children to imitate adult models of the same gender. The child not only imitates the behavior of the model but also tries to become broadly like the model—that is, she or he *identifies* with the model.

Almost from the moment a baby comes into the world, she or he is treated in ways that are consistent with gender stereotypes. Parents tend to talk more to baby girls, and fathers especially engage in more roughhousing with boys. When children are old enough to speak, caregivers and even other children begin to tell them how they are expected to behave. Parents may reward children for behavior they consider gender appropriate and punish (or fail to reinforce) them for behavior they consider inappropriate. Girls are encouraged to practice caregiving, which is intended to prepare them for traditional feminine adult roles. Boys are handed Legos or doctor sets to help prepare them for traditional masculine adult roles.

The Gender-Schema Theory of Gender-Typing

Gender-schema theory emphasizes the role of cognition in gender-typing (Martin et al., 2002; Martin & Ruble, 2004). Gender-schema theory proposes that children develop a **gender schema** as a means of organizing their perceptions of the world. A gender schema is a cluster of ideas about masculine and feminine physical traits. Gender becomes important because of society's emphasis on it.

According to gender-schema theory, once children come to see themselves as female or male, they begin to seek information concerning gender-typed traits and try to live up to them (Grace et al., 2008; Most et al., 2007; Tenenbaum et al., 2010). Jack will retaliate when provoked because boys are expected to do so. Jill will be "sugary and sweet" if such is expected of little girls.

Today, most scholars would agree that both biology and social cognition interact to affect most areas of behavior and mental processes—including the complex processes involved in gender-typing.

Gender-typing The process by which people acquire a sense of being female or male and acquire the traits considered typical of females or males within a cultural setting.

Gender-schema A concept of the distribution of behavior patterns into feminine and masculine roles that motivate and guide the gender-typing of the child.

Humanism The view that people are capable of free choice, self-fulfillment, and ethical behavior.

Existentialism The view that people are completely free and responsible for their own behavior.

"You are unique, and if that is not fulfilled, then something has been lost."

MARTHA GRAHAM

THE HUMANISTIC–EXISTENTIAL PERSPECTIVE: HOW BECOMING?

Humanists and existentialists dwell on the meaning of life. Self-awareness is the hub of the humanistic–existential search for meaning. **Question 12: What are humanism and existentialism?**

The term **humanism** has a long history and many meanings. As a counterpoint (or "third force") to the predominant psychodynamic and behavioral models, it puts self-awareness at the center of consideration and argues that people are capable of free choice, self-fulfillment, and ethical behavior. Humanism also represented a reaction to the "rat race" spawned by industrialization and automation. The humanistic views of Abraham Maslow and Carl Rogers emerged from these concerns.

Existentialism in part reflects the horrors of mass destruction of human life through war and genocide, frequent events in the 20th century. The European existentialist philosophers Jean-Paul Sartre and Martin Heidegger saw human life as trivial in the grand scheme of things. But psychiatrists like Viktor Frankl, Ludwig Binswanger, and Medard Boss argued that seeing human existence as meaningless could give rise to withdrawal and apathy—even suicide. Psychological salvation therefore requires giving personal meaning to things and making personal choices (McDonald, 2008).

Abraham Maslow and the Challenge of Self-Actualization

Humanists see Freud as preoccupied with the "basement" of the human condition. Freud wrote that people are basically motivated to gratify biological drives and that their perceptions are distorted by their psychological needs. **Question 13: How do humanistic psychologists differ from psychodynamic theorists?** Humanistic psychologist Abraham Maslow argued that people also have a conscious need for **self-actualization**—to become all that they can be—and that people's perceptions can be quite accurate. Because people are unique, they must follow unique paths to self-actualization. People are not at the mercy of unconscious, primitive impulses. Rather, one of the main threats to individual personality development is control by other people. We must each be free to get in touch with and actualize our selves. But self-actualization requires taking risks. Many people prefer to adhere to the tried and ... what may be untrue for them. Those who do adhere to the "tried and true" may find their lives degenerating into monotony and predictability.

Let's learn more about the nature of the self by examining Carl Rogers's *self theory*. Rogers offers insights into the ways the self develops—or fails to develop—in the real social world.

Carl Rogers's Self Theory

Humanistic psychologist Carl Rogers (1902–1987) wrote that people shape themselves through free choice and action. **Question 14: What is the *self*?** Rogers

Are you a self-actualizer? Do you strive to be all that you can be? Psychologist Abraham Maslow attributed the following eight characteristics to the self-actualizing individual. How many of them describe you? Why not check them "yes" or "no" and undertake some self-evaluation?

YES NO

____ ____   **1.** Do you fully experience life in the present—the here and now? (Self-actualizers do not focus excessively on the lost past or wish their lives away as they stride toward distant goals.)

____ ____   **2.** Do you make growth choices rather than fear choices? (Self-actualizers take reasonable risks to develop their unique potentials. They do not bask in the dull life of the status quo. They do not "settle.")

____ ____   **3.** Do you seek to acquire self-knowledge? (Self-actualizers look inward. They search for values, talents, and meaningfulness. It might be enlightening to take an *interest inventory*—a test frequently used to help make career decisions—at your college testing and counseling center.)

____ ____   **4.** Do you strive toward honesty in interpersonal relationships? (Self-actualizers strip away the social facades and games that stand in the way of self-disclosure and the formation of intimate relationships.)

____ ____   **5.** Do you behave self-assertively and express your own ideas and feelings, even at the risk of occasional social disapproval? (Self-actualizers do not bottle up their feelings for the sake of avoiding social disapproval.)

YES NO

____ ____   **6.** Do you strive toward new goals? Do you strive to be the best that you can be in a chosen life role? (Self-actualizers do not live by the memory of past accomplishments. Nor do they present second-rate efforts.)

____ ____   **7.** Do you seek meaningful and rewarding life activities? Do you experience moments of actualization that humanistic psychologists call *peak experiences*? (Peak experiences are brief moments of rapture filled with personal meaning. Examples might include completing a work of art, falling in love, redesigning a machine tool, suddenly solving a complex problem in math or physics, or having a baby. Note that we differ as individuals; one person's peak experience might bore another person silly.)

____ ____   **8.** Do you remain open to new experiences? (Self-actualizers do not hold themselves back for fear that novel experiences might shake their views of the world or of right and wrong. Self-actualizers are willing to revise their expectations, values, and opinions.)

---

defined the *self* as the center of experience. Your self is your ongoing sense of who and what you are, your sense of how and why you react to the environment and how you choose to act on the environment. Your choices are made on the basis of your values, and your values are also part of your self. **Question 15: What is self theory?** Rogers's *self theory* focuses on the nature of the self and the conditions that allow the self to develop freely. Two of his major concerns are the self-concept and self-esteem.

THE SELF-CONCEPT AND FRAMES OF REFERENCE Our self-concepts consist of our impressions of ourselves and our evaluations of our adequacy. Rogers believed that we all have unique ways of looking at ourselves and the world—that is, unique **frames of reference**. Perhaps we each use a different set of dimensions in defining ourselves and judge ourselves according to different sets of values. To one person, *achievement–failure* may be the most important dimension. To another person, the most important dimension may be *decency–indecency*. A third person may not even think in terms of decency.

SELF-ESTEEM AND POSITIVE REGARD Rogers assumed that we all develop a need for self-regard, or self-esteem, as we develop and become aware of

> *"Always remember that you are absolutely unique. Just like everyone else."*
>
> MARGARET MEAD

Self-actualization In humanistic theory, the innate tendency to strive to realize one's potential.

Frame of reference One's unique patterning of perceptions and attitudes according to which one evaluates events.

Unconditional positive regard An enduring expression of esteem for the essential value of a person.

Conditional positive regard Judgment of another person's value on the basis of the acceptability of that person's behaviors.

Conditions of worth Standards by which the value of a person is judged.

Self-ideal A mental image of what we believe we ought to be.

ourselves. At first, self-esteem reflects the esteem in which others hold us. Parents help children develop self-esteem when they show them **unconditional positive regard**—that is, when they accept them as having intrinsic merit regardless of their behavior at the moment. But when parents show children **conditional positive regard**—that is, when parents accept them only when they behave in a desired manner—children may develop **conditions of worth**. Therefore, children may come to think that they have merit only if they behave as their parents wish them to behave.

Because each individual is thought to have a unique potential, children who develop conditions of worth must be somewhat disappointed in themselves. We cannot fully live up to the wishes of others and remain true to ourselves. Children in some families learn that it is bad to have ideas of their own, especially about sexual, political, or religious matters. When they perceive their caregivers' disapproval, they may come to see themselves as rebels and label their feelings as selfish, wrong, or evil. If they wish to retain a consistent self-concept and self-esteem, they may have to deny many of their feelings or disown aspects of themselves. In this way, the self-concept becomes distorted. According to Rogers, anxiety often stems from recognition that people have feelings and desires that are inconsistent with their distorted self-concept. Because anxiety is unpleasant, people may deny the existence of their genuine feelings and desires.

According to Rogers, the path to self-actualization requires getting in touch with our genuine feelings, accepting them, and acting on them. This is the goal of Rogers's method of psychotherapy, *client-centered therapy*. Rogers also believed that we have mental images of what we are capable of becoming. These are termed **self-ideals**. We are motivated to reduce the discrepancy between our self-concepts and our self-ideals.

LIFE CONNECTIONS | ENHANCING SELF-ESTEEM

Few of us are as attractive as the models in the Abercrombie's and Victoria's Secret catalogs. Should that disturb our self-esteem? Research shows that one of the psychological boulders that can crush our self-esteem is self-comparison to people who are superior to us in a way that matters to us. For some of us, the crusher may be superior intellectual ability, for others, athletic ability, and for still others, physical appearance. That is unfortunate because self-esteem can buffer the effects of stress and help provide the courage to deal with it (Sherman et al., 2009).

How to Enhance Your Self-Esteem

There are many things you can do to enhance your self-esteem. Broadly speaking, they involve changing the things you can change and having the wisdom to accept what you cannot change.

Improve Yourself: For example, are you miserable because of excess dependence on another person? Perhaps you can enhance your social skills or your vocational skills in an effort to become more independent. Are you too heavy? Perhaps you can follow some of the suggestions for losing weight discussed in Chapter 8.

Just Doing It Many males tie their self-esteem to prowess in sports.

© Pierre Tostee/ASP via Getty Images

Evaluation of the Humanistic–Existential Perspective

Question 16: What are the strengths and weaknesses of humanistic–existential theory? Humanistic–existential theories have tremendous appeal for college students because of their focus on the importance of personal experience. We tend to treasure our conscious experiences (our "selves") and those of the people we care about. For lower organisms, to be alive is to move, to process food, to exchange oxygen and carbon dioxide, and to reproduce. But for human beings, an essential aspect of life is conscious experience—the sense of oneself as progressing through space and time.

Ironically, the primary strength of the humanistic–existential approaches—their focus on conscious experience—is also their main weakness. Conscious experience is private and subjective. Therefore, the validity of formulating theories in terms of consciousness has been questioned.

Self-actualization, like trait theory, yields circular explanations for behavior. When we see someone engaging in what seems to be positive striving, we gain little insight by attributing this behavior to a self-actualizing force. We have done nothing to account for the origins of the force. And when we observe someone who is not engaging in growth-oriented striving, it seems arbitrary to "explain" this outcome by suggesting that the self-actualizing tendency has been blocked or frustrated.

Humanistic–existential theories, like learning theories, have little to say about the development of traits and personality types. They assume we are all unique, but they do not predict the sorts of traits, abilities, and interests we will develop.

"No one can make you feel inferior without your consent."

ELEANOR ROOSEVELT

When it comes to self-improvement, there may or may not be things you can do about your facial features, your hair, and your body. It is not a good idea to compete with the cultural ideal as exemplified by chiseled facial features and a tight, slender body, but there may be some minor adjustments you can make. One "minor" but important change is to smile more often. As you will see in Chapter 14, people are perceived as more attractive when they are smiling.

Challenge the Realism of Your Ideal Self: Cognitive psychologists note that our internal list of "oughts" and "shoulds" can create perfectionist standards. We constantly fall short of these standards and experience frustration. Challenge your perfectionist demands on yourself and, when appropriate, revise them. It may be harmful to abolish worthy and realistic goals, even if we do have trouble measuring up now and then. However, some of our goals or values may not stand up to scrutiny.

Stop Comparing Yourself to Others! It is self-defeating to compare ourselves to other people who surpass us in traits or achievements that we deem important. You can be a respectable scientist without being an Einstein or a Madame Curie. You can be a good writer without being a Maya Angelou or a Shakespeare. You can be a worthy athlete without being a Serena Williams or a Peyton Manning. You can also make a good appearance without landing work for print ads in clothing catalogs. You can earn a decent living even if you are not making as much money as _____ (you fill in the blank).

Substitute Realistic Goals for Unattainable Goals: Perhaps we will never be as artistic, as tall, or as graceful as we would like to be. We can work to enhance our drawing skills, but if it becomes clear that we will not become Michelangelos, perhaps we can enjoy our scribblings for what they are and also find satisfaction elsewhere. We cannot make ourselves taller (except by wearing elevator shoes or high heels), but we can take off 5 pounds and cut our time for running the mile. We can learn to whip up a great fettuccine Alfredo.

Build Self-Efficacy Expectations: Our self-efficacy expectations affect our willingness to take on challenges and persist in efforts to meet them. We can build self-efficacy expectations by selecting tasks that are consistent with our interests and abilities and working at them. We can also build self-efficacy expectations by working at hobbies or charitable causes. Use realistic self-assessment, realistic goals, and a reasonable schedule for improvement. Perhaps you will never run a 5-minute mile, but after a few months of workouts, you might be able to put a few 8- to 10-minute miles back to back. (You might even enjoy them.)

ACTIVE REVIEW (14) The humanistic view argues that people (are or are not?) capable of free choice and self-fulfillment. (15) Maslow argued that people have growth-oriented needs for self-_____. (16) According to Rogers, we see the world through unique frames of _____.

REFLECT AND RELATE Try a mini-experiment: Think of how your own frame of reference is unique, how it differs from those of family members, friends, and (perhaps), love interests. Then consider some of the things that earn the

approval or disapproval of these important people in your life. Can you explain their responses to you in terms of their frames of reference?

CRITICAL THINKING If humanistic–existential theory is less scientific than some other views of personality, how do you explain its enduring popularity?

 Go to Psychology CourseMate at **www.cengagebrain.com** for an interactive version of these questions.

● THE SOCIOCULTURAL PERSPECTIVE: PERSONALITY IN CONTEXT

Thirteen-year-old Hannah brought her lunch tray to the table in the cafeteria. Her mother, Julie, eyed with horror the french fries, the plate of mashed potatoes in gravy, the bag of potato chips, and the large paper cup brimming with soda. "You can't eat that!" she said. "It's garbage!"

"Oh come on, Mom! Chill, okay?" Hannah rejoined before taking her tray to sit with some friends rather than with her mother.

I used to spend Saturdays with my children at the Manhattan School of Music. Not only did they study voice and piano, they—and I—widened our cultural perspective by relating to families and students from all parts of the world.

Julie and Hannah are Korean Americans. Flustered, Julie shook her head and said, "I've now been in the United States longer than I was in Korea, and I still can't get used to the way children act here." When she talks that way, it's embarrassing. I vaguely recall making some unhelpful comments about the ketchup on the french fries having antioxidants and some slightly helpful comments about what is typical of teenagers in the United States. But as I thought about Hannah, I realized that in our multicultural society, personality cannot be understood without reference to the **sociocultural perspective**. Different ethnic groups within the United States have different attitudes, beliefs, norms, self-definitions, and values (Phinney, 2006; Schwartz et al., 2010). Hannah was strongly influenced by her peers—she was completely at home with blue jeans and french fries. She was also a daughter in an Asian American immigrant group that views education as the key to success in our culture (Leppel, 2002; Magno, 2010). Belonging to this ethnic group had contributed to her ambition but had not prevented her from becoming an outspoken American teenager.

Let's consider how sociocultural factors can affect one's sense of self.

Individualism versus Collectivism: Who Am I (in This Cultural Setting)?

Sociocultural perspective The view that focuses on the roles of ethnicity, gender, culture, and socioeconomic status in personality formation, behavior, and mental processes.

Individualist A person who defines herself or himself in terms of personal traits and gives priority to her or his own goals.

Collectivist A person who defines himself or herself in terms of relationships to other people and groups and gives priority to group goals.

One could say that Julie's complaint was that Hannah saw herself as an individual and an artist to a greater extent than as a family member and a Korean girl. **Question 17: What do individualism and collectivism mean?** Cross-cultural research reveals that people in the United States and many northern European nations tend to be individualistic. **Individualists** tend to define themselves in terms of their personal identities and to give priority to their personal goals (Brewer & Chen, 2007; Triandis, 2006). When asked to complete the statement "I am … ," they are likely to respond in terms of their personality traits ("I am outgoing," "I am artistic") or their occupations ("I am a nurse," "I am a systems analyst") (Triandis & Suh, 2002). In contrast, many people from cultures in Africa, Asia, and Central and South America tend to be collectivistic (Brewer & Chen, 2007; Triandis, 2006). **Collectivists** tend to define themselves in terms of the groups to which they belong and to give priority to the group's goals (Triandis, 2006).

They feel complete in terms of their relationships with others (Triandis, 2006) (see Figure 10.4 ■). They are more likely than individualists to conform to group norms and judgments (Brewer & Chen, 2007; Triandis & Suh, 2002). When asked to complete the statement "I am... ," they are more likely to respond in terms of their families, gender, or nation ("I am a father," "I am a Buddhist," "I am Japanese") (Triandis, 2001).

The seeds of individualism and collectivism are found in the culture in which a person grows up. The capitalist system fosters individualism to some degree. The traditional writings of the East have exalted people who resist personal temptations in order to do their duty and promote the welfare of the group.

Another issue from the sociocultural perspective is *acculturation*. Just how much acculturation is good for you? **Question 18: How does acculturation affect the psychological well-being of immigrants and their families?**

A. Independent View of Self

B. Interdependent View of Self

Figure 10.4 ■ The Self in Relation to Others from the Individualist and Collectivist Perspectives To an individualist, the self is separate from other people (part A). To a collectivist, the self is complete only in terms of relationships to other people (part B). Based on Markus and Kitayama, 1991.

Acculturation, Adjustment, and Self-Esteem: Just How Much Acculturation Is Enough?

Self-esteem is connected with patterns of **acculturation** among immigrants (Phinney, 2006). Some immigrants are completely assimilated by the dominant culture. They lose the language and customs of their country of origin and become like the dominant culture in the new host country. Others maintain almost complete separation. They retain the language and customs of their country of origin and never acclimate to those of the new country. Still others become bicultural. They remain fluent in the language of their country of origin but become conversant in the new language. They blend the customs and values of both cultures Schwartz et al., 2010). They can switch "mental gears"—apply the values of one culture under some circumstances and apply the values of the other culture under different circumstances (Phinney, 2006). Perhaps they relate to other people in one way at work or in school and in another way at home or in the neighborhood.

Truth or Fiction Revisited: Research evidence suggests that people who identify with the bicultural pattern, and not those who surrender their traditional backgrounds, have the highest self-esteem (David et al., 2009; Schwartz et al., 2010). For example, Mexican Americans and Asian Americans who are proficient in English as well as the languages of their countries of origin are less likely to be anxious and depressed than less-proficient Mexican and Asian Americans (Kim et al., 2003; Weisskirch, 2007).

Evaluation of the Sociocultural Perspective

The sociocultural perspective provides insights into the roles of ethnicity, gender, culture, and socioeconomic status in personality formation. Sociocultural factors are external forces that are internalized. They touch many aspects of our cognitions, motives, emotions, and behavior. Without reference to sociocultural factors, we are not able to understand how individuals think, behave, and feel about themselves within a given cultural setting. The sociocultural perspective enhances our sensitivity to cultural differences and expectations and allows us to appreciate the richness of human behavior and mental processes.

Acculturation The process of adaptation in which immigrants and native groups identify with a new, dominant culture by learning about that culture and making behavioral and attitudinal changes.

LearningConnections ● THE SOCIOCULTURAL PERSPECTIVE: PERSONALITY IN CONTEXT

ACTIVE REVIEW (17) _____ define themselves in terms of their personal identities and give priority to their personal goals. (18) _____ define themselves in terms of the groups to which they belong and give priority to group goals. (19) Immigrants who identify with the bicultural pattern of assimilation have the (highest or lowest?) self-esteem.

REFLECT AND RELATE Do you see yourself as an individualist or collectivist? Explain.

CRITICAL THINKING Can one "believe in" more than one theory of personality? For example, could one accept the sociocultural perspective along with another perspective?

 Go to Psychology CourseMate at **www.cengagebrain.com** for an interactive version of these questions.

Psychodynamic Perspective

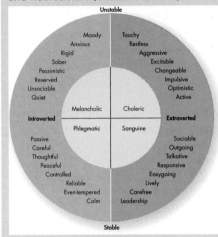

Preconscious and unconscious elements drive personality.

Trait Perspective

Personality is determined by a limited number of fundamental inherent traits. Hippocrates divides these traits into four types (inner circle), while Eysenck groups them into two major dimensions: introversion–extraversion and neuroticism (unstable–stable).

THE BIG FIVE

Extraversion
Neuroticism
Conscientiousness
Agreeableness
Openness to Experience

The current five-factor theory includes the two factors found by Eysenck, along with conscientiousness, agreeableness, and openness to experience.

	Psychodynamic Perspective	Trait Perspective
Key Theorists	Sigmund Freud (1856–1939) Carl Jung (1875–1961) Alfred Adler (1870–1937) Karen Horney (1885–1952) Erik Erikson (1902–1994) Margaret Mahler (1897–1985)	Hippocrates (ca. 460–377 b.c.e.) Hans Eysenck (1916–1997) Paul T. Costa Jr. Robert McCrae
Focus of Research	• Unconscious conflict • Drives such as sex, aggression, and the need for superiority come into conflict with laws, social rules, and moral codes	• Use of mathematical techniques to catalog and organize basic human personality traits
View of Personality	• Three structures of personality—id, ego, superego • Five stages of psychosexual development—oral, anal, phallic, latency, genital • Ego analysts—or neoanalysts—focus more on the role of the ego in making meaningful conscious decisions	• Based on theory of Hippocrates and work of Gordon Allport • Eysenck's two-dimensional model: Introversion–extraversion and emotional stability–instability • Current emphasis is on the five-factor model (the "Big Five")—extraversion, agreeableness, conscientiousness, neuroticism, and openness to experience

 ## MEASUREMENT OF PERSONALITY

Now that we have explored different perspectives on personality, let us see how psychologists measure personality. Methods of personality assessment use a sample of behavior to predict future behavior. Standardized interviews are often used. Some psychologists use computers to conduct routine interviews.

Question 19: What are the characteristics of scientific personality tests? The **validity** of a test is the extent to which it measures what it is supposed to measure. We usually assess the validity of personality tests by comparing test results to external criteria or standards. For example, a test of hyperactivity might be compared with teachers' reports as to whether children in their classes are hyperactive. The **reliability**

Validity In psychological testing, the degree to which a test measures what it is supposed to measure.

Reliability In psychological testing, the consistency, or stability, of test scores from one testing to another.

Learning-Theory Perspective	Humanistic–Existential Perspective	Sociocultural Perspective
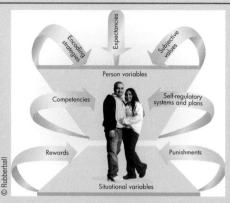 Situational and person variables influence behavior.	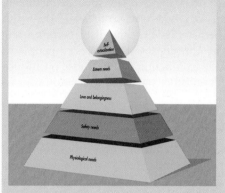 Maslow believed we progress toward higher psychological needs once basic survival needs have been met.	 One of the concerns of sociocultural theorists has to do with the effects of individualistic versus collective societies. People from individualistic societies have a more independent view of themselves and others.
John B. Watson (1878–1958) B. F. Skinner (1904–1990) Albert Bandura	Abraham Maslow (1908–1970) Carl Rogers (1902–1987)	Martha Bernal Beverly Greene Jean Phinney Harry Triandis Lillian Comas-Diaz Stanley Sue Richard Suinn
• Behaviorist focus on situational factors that determine behavior • Social-cognitive emphasis on observational learning	• The experiences of being human and developing one's unique potential within an often hostile environment	• The roles of ethnicity, gender, culture, and socioeconomic status in personality formation and behavior
• Watson saw personality as plastic and determined by external situational variables. • Skinner believed that society conditions individuals into wanting what is good for society. • Bandura believes in reciprocal determinism.	• People have inborn drives to become what they are capable of being. • Unconditional positive regard leads to self-esteem, which facilitates individual growth and development.	• Development differs in individualist and collectivist societies. • Discrimination, poverty, and acculturation affect the self-concept and self-esteem.

of a test is the stability of test results from one testing to another. We usually determine the reliability of tests by comparing testing results on different occasions or at different ages. A reliable IQ test should provide scores during childhood that remain reasonably similar in adolescence and adulthood. Test **standardization** is a process that checks out the scores, validity, and reliability of a test with people of various ages and from various groups.

Behavior-rating scales assess behavior in settings such as classrooms or mental hospitals. With behavior-rating scales, trained observers usually check off each occurrence of a specific behavior, such as talking to another student during class or biting a fingernail, within a certain time frame—say, 15 minutes. Behavior-rating scales are growing in popularity, especially for use with children (Kamphaus et al., 2000). However,

Standardization In psychological testing, the process by which one obtains and organizes test scores from various population groups, so that the results of a person completing a test can be compared to those of others of his or her sex, in his or her age group, and so on.

Behavior-rating scale A systematic means for recording the frequency with which target behaviors occur.

standardized objective and projective tests are used more frequently, and we focus on them in this section.

Question 20: How are measures of personality used? Measures of personality are used to make important decisions, such as whether a person is suited for a certain type of work, a particular class in school, or a drug to reduce agitation. As part of their admissions process, graduate schools often ask professors to rate prospective students on scales that assess traits such as intelligence, emotional stability, and cooperation. Students may take tests to measure their **aptitudes** and interests so as to gain insight into whether they are suited for certain occupations. It is assumed that students who share the aptitudes and interests of people who function well in certain positions are also likely to function well in those positions.

Let's consider objective tests and projective tests.

Objective Tests

Question 21: What are objective personality tests? Objective tests present respondents with a standardized group of test items in the form of a questionnaire. Respondents are limited to a specific range of answers. One test might ask respondents to indicate whether items are true or false for them. Another might ask respondents to select the preferred activity from groups of three.

Some tests have a **forced-choice format** in which respondents are asked to indicate which of two statements is truer for them or which of several activities they prefer. The respondents are not usually given the option of answering "none of the above." Forced-choice formats are frequently used in interest inventories, which help predict whether the person would function well in a certain occupation. The following item is similar to those found in occupational interest inventories:

I would rather

a. be a forest ranger.
b. work in a busy office.
c. play a musical instrument.

The *Minnesota Multiphasic Personality Inventory (MMPI)*[1] contains hundreds of items presented in a true–false format. The MMPI is designed for use by clinical and counseling psychologists to help diagnose psychological disorders. Accurate measurement of an individual's problems should point to appropriate treatment. The MMPI is the most widely used psychological test in clinical work and the most widely used instrument for personality measurement in psychological research.

The MMPI scales were constructed empirically—that is, on the basis of actual clinical data rather than on the basis of psychological theory. A test-item bank of several hundred items was derived from questions that are often asked in clinical interviews. Here are some examples of the kinds of items that were used:

My father was a good man.	T	F
I am very seldom troubled by headaches.	T	F
My hands and feet are usually warm enough.	T	F
I have never done anything dangerous for the thrill of it.	T	F
I work under a great deal of tension.	T	F

The items were administered to people with previously identified symptoms, such as depressive or schizophrenic symptoms. Items that successfully set these people apart were included on scales named for these conditions. Confidence in the MMPI has developed because of its extensive use.

Now that we have defined objective tests and surveyed the MMPI, we may ask—
Question 22: How do projective tests differ from objective tests?

Is This Test Taker Telling the Truth? How can psychologists determine whether or not people answer test items honestly? What are the validity scales of the MMPI?

Aptitude A natural ability or talent.

Objective tests Tests whose items must be answered in a specified, limited manner. Tests whose items have concrete answers that are considered correct.

Forced-choice format A method of presenting test questions that requires a respondent to select one of a number of possible answers.

---

[1] Currently the updated MMPI-2.

Projective Tests

Projective tests have no clearly specified answers. People are shown ambiguous stimuli such as inkblots or ambiguous drawings and asked to say what they look like or to tell stories about them. Or they are asked to complete sentences or to draw pictures of persons. There is no one correct response. It is assumed that people project their own personalities into their responses. The meanings they attribute to these stimuli are assumed to reflect their personalities as well as the drawings or blots themselves.

THE RORSCHACH INKBLOT TEST **Truth or Fiction Revisited:** There are a number of psychological tests made up of inkblots, and test-takers are indeed asked to say what the blots look like to them. The best known and most widely used of these is the Rorschach inkblot test, named after its originator, Hermann Rorschach (Archer et al., 2006).

In the Rorschach test, people are given the inkblots, one by one, and are asked what they look like or what they could be. A response that reflects the shape of the blot is considered a sign of adequate **reality testing**. A response that richly integrates several features of the blot is considered a sign of high intellectual functioning. Supporters of the Rorschach believe it provides insight into a person's intelligence, interests, cultural background, personality traits, psychological disorders, and many other variables. Critics argue that there is little empirical evidence to support the test's validity (Garb et al., 2005). Even when the Rorschach is being severely challenged as a method of obtaining diagnoses of psychological disorders, researchers continue to claim that it has uses in many other areas, including the hiring and selection of personnel in organizations (Del Giudice, 2010), determination of whether individuals are suitable to have child custody (Weiner, 2006), and even the assessment of children in schools (Hojnoski et al., 2006).

Although there is no single "correct" response to the Rorschach inkblot shown in Figure 10.5 ■, some responses are not in keeping with the features of the blots. The figure could be a bat or a flying insect, the pointed face of an animal, the face of a jack-o'-lantern, or many other things. But responses like "an ice cream cone," "diseased lungs," or "a metal leaf in flames" are not suggested by the features of the blot and may indicate personality problems.

Figure 10.5 ■ A Rorschach Inkblot The Rorschach is the most widely used projective personality test. What does this inkblot look like to you? What could it be?

THE THEMATIC APPERCEPTION TEST The *Thematic Apperception Test (TAT)* was developed in the 1930s by Henry Murray and Christiana Morgan. It consists of drawings, like the one in Figure 8.4 (see p. 000), that are open to a variety of interpretations. Individuals are given the cards one at a time and asked to make up stories about them.

The TAT is widely used in research on motivation and in clinical practice (Archer et al., 2006; Hojnoski et al., 2006). The notion is that we are likely to project our own needs into our responses to ambiguous situations, even if we are unaware of them or reluctant to talk about them. The TAT is also widely used to assess attitudes toward other people, especially parents, lovers, and spouses.

Projective test A psychological test that presents ambiguous stimuli onto which the test-taker projects his or her own personality in making a response.

Reality testing The capacity to perceive one's environment and oneself according to accurate sensory impressions.

LearningConnections • MEASUREMENT OF PERSONALITY

ACTIVE REVIEW (20) Personality tests sample _____ to predict future behavior. (21) _____ tests present standardized sets of test items in the form of questionnaires. (22) The MMPI is an objective test that uses a(n) _____–false format to assess psychological disorders. (23) Projective tests present _____ stimuli and permit the respondent a broad range of answers. (24) The foremost projective technique is the _____ inkblot test.

REFLECT AND RELATE Have you ever taken a personality test? What were the results? Do you believe the results were valid? Why or why not?

CRITICAL THINKING Do you think personality tests should be required as part of completing a job application? Why or why not?

 Go to Psychology CourseMate at **www.cengagebrain.com** for an interactive version of these questions.

The Psychodynamic Perspective: Excavating the Iceberg

1. What *is* personality?
Personality is defined as the reasonably stable patterns of emotions, motives, and behavior that distinguish one person from another.

2. What is Freud's theory of psychosexual development?
Freud's theory is termed psycho*dynamic* because it assumes we are driven largely by the movement of unconscious forces within our minds. People experience conflict as basic instincts come up against social pressures to follow laws, rules, and moral codes. The id represents psychological drives and seeks instant gratification. The ego, or the sense of self or "I," develops through experience and takes into account what is practical in gratifying the impulses of the id. Defense mechanisms such as repression protect the ego from anxiety. The superego, or conscience, develops largely through identification with others. There are five stages of psychosexual development: oral, anal, phallic, latency, and genital.

3. What are the views of neo-Freudians?
Carl Jung's analytical psychology features a collective unconscious and numerous archetypes. Alfred Adler's individual psychology features the inferiority complex and the compensating drive for superiority. Karen Horney's theory focuses on parent–child relationships and the possible development of feelings of anxiety and hostility. Erik Erikson's theory of psychosocial development highlights social relationships.

4. What are the strengths and weaknesses of the psychodynamic perspective?
Freud fought for the idea that personality is subject to scientific analysis at a time when many people still viewed psychological problems as signs of demonic possession. But there is no evidence for the existence of psychic structures, and his theory is fraught with inaccuracies about child development.

The Trait Perspective: The Five-Dimensional Universe

5. What are traits?
Traits are personality elements that are inferred from behavior and that account for behavioral consistency.

6. What is the history of the trait perspective?
Hippocrates, an ancient Greek physician, believed that personality reflected the balance of fluids ("humors") in the body. Galton in the 19th century and Allport in the 20th century surveyed traits by studying words that referred to them in dictionaries.

7. How have contemporary psychologists reduced the universe of traits to more manageable lists?
Hans Eysenck used factor analysis to arrive at two personality dimensions: introversion–extraversion and emotional stability–instability (neuroticism). More recent mathematical analyses point to the existence of five key factors (five-factor theory): extraversion, neuroticism, agreeableness, conscientiousness, and openness to experience.

8. What are the strengths and weaknesses of trait theory?
Trait theorists have helped develop personality tests and used them to predict adjustment in various lines of work. Critics argue that trait theory is descriptive, not explanatory.

Learning-Theory Perspectives: All the Things You Do

9. What does behaviorism contribute to our understanding of personality?
Behaviorists believe that we should focus on observable behavior and emphasize the situational determinants of behavior. John B. Watson rejected notions of mind and personality altogether. B. F. Skinner argued that environmental contingencies can shape people into wanting to do the things that are required of them.

10. How does social-cognitive theory differ from the behaviorist view?
Social-cognitive theory has a cognitive orientation and focuses on learning by observation. To predict behavior, social-cognitive theorists consider situational variables and person variables.

11. What are the strengths and weaknesses of learning theories as they apply to personality?
Learning theorists have highlighted the importance of referring to publicly observable behaviors in theorizing. However, learning theory does not suggest the richness of inner human experience or persuasively account for the development of traits.

The Humanistic–Existential Perspective: How Becoming?

12. What are humanism and existentialism?
Humanism argues that we are capable of free choice, self-fulfillment, and ethical behavior. Existentialists argue that our lives have meaning when we give them meaning.

13. How do humanistic psychologists differ from psychodynamic theorists?
Whereas Freud wrote that people are motivated to gratify unconscious drives, humanistic psychologists believe that people have a conscious need for self-actualization.

14. What is the *self*?
According to Rogers, the self is an organized and consistent way a person perceives his or her "I" in relation to others.

15. What is self theory?
Self theory begins by assuming the existence of the self and each person's unique frame of reference. The self can develop its unique potential when the person receives unconditional positive regard.

16. What are the strengths and weaknesses of humanistic–existential theory?
Humanistic–existential theory is appealing because of its focus on self-awareness and freedom of choice, but critics argue that concepts such as conscious experience and self-actualization are unscientific.

The Sociocultural Perspective: Personality in Context

17. What do individualism and collectivism mean?
Individualists give priority to their personal goals. Collectivists give priority to the group's goals. Many Western societies are individualistic and foster individualism in personality.

18. How does acculturation affect the psychological well-being of immigrants and their families?
Immigrants who retain the customs and values of their country of origin but also learn those of their new country, and blend the two, tend to have higher self-esteem than immigrants who become completely assimilated or who maintain complete separation from the new, dominant culture.

Measurement of Personality

19. What are the characteristics of scientific personality tests?
Scientific personality tests have adequate validity, reliability, and standardization.

20. How are measures of personality used?
Personality measures assess psychological disorders, predict the likelihood of adjustment in various lines of work, measure aptitudes, and determine academic placement.

21. What are objective personality tests?
Objective tests present test-takers with a standardized set of test items to which they must respond in specific, limited ways (as in multiple-choice or true–false tests).

22. How do projective tests differ from objective tests?
Projective tests present ambiguous stimuli and allow the test-taker to give a range of responses that reflect individual differences.

KEY TERMS

Acculturation (p. 361)
Analytical psychology (p. 344)
Antisocial personality (p. 349)
Aptitude (p. 364)
Archetypes (p. 344)
Behavior-rating scale (p. 363)
Collective unconscious (p. 344)
Collectivist (p. 361)
Conditional positive regard (p. 358)
Conditions of worth (p. 358)
Conscious (p. 340)
Creative self (p. 345)
Defense mechanism (p. 341)
Drive for superiority (p. 345)
Ego (p. 341)
Ego identity (p. 345)
Electra complex (p. 343)
Erogenous zone (p. 342)
Existentialism (p. 356)

Extraversion (p. 347)
Forced-choice format (p. 364)
Frame of reference (p. 357)
Gender-typing (p. 355)
Gender schema (p. 355)
Humanism (p. 356)
Id (p. 341)
Individual psychology (p. 345)
Individualist (p. 360)
Inferiority complex (p. 344)
Introversion (p. 347)
Modeling (p. 353)
Neuroticism (p. 347)
Objective test (p. 364)
Oedipus complex (p. 343)
Personality (p. 340)
Preconscious (p. 340)
Projective test (p. 365)
Psychic structure (p. 341)

Psychoanalysis (p. 341)
Psychodynamic theory (p. 340)
Psychosexual development (p. 342)
Psychosocial development (p. 345)
Reality testing (p. 365)
Reciprocal determinism (p. 353)
Reliability (p. 362)
Self-actualization (p. 357)
Self-efficacy expectations (p. 353)
Self-ideal (p. 358)
Sociocultural perspective (p. 360)
Standardization (p. 363)
Superego (p. 341)
Trait (p. 346)
Unconditional positive regard (p. 358)
Unconscious (p. 340)
Validity (p. 362)

ACTIVE LEARNING RESOURCES

Log in to **www.cengagebrain.com** to access the resources your instructor requires. For this book, you can access:

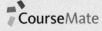
CourseMate brings course concepts to life with interactive learning, study, and exam preparation tools that support the printed textbook. A textbook-specific website, Psychology CourseMate includes an integrated interactive eBook and other interactive learning tools including quizzes, flashcards, videos, and more.

Need help studying? This site is your one-stop study shop. Take a Pre-Test and CengageNOW will generate a Personalized Study Plan based on your test results. The Study Plan will identify the topics you need to review and direct you to online resources to help you master those topics. You can then take a Post-Test to determine the concepts you have mastered and what you still need to work on.

Stress, Health, and Coping

© Blend Images Photography/Veer

MAJOR TOPICS

Stress: What It Is, Where It Comes From *370*

Psychological Moderators of Stress *378*

Stress and the Body: The War Within *382*

Psychology and Health *388*

FEATURES

Self-Assessment: Going Through Changes—How Stressful Is Your Life? *372*

A Closer Look: Stress in America *375*

Self-Assessment: Are You Type A or Type B? *377*

Self-Assessment: The Locus of Control Scale *380*

A Closer Look: "Fight or Flight" or "Tend and Befriend"? Do Men and Women Respond Differently to Stress? *384*

Video Connections: Health and Stress *385*

Life Connections: Preventing and Coping with Stress *386*

Concept Review 11.1: Factors in Heart Disease and Cancer *389*

Life Connections: Preventing and Coping with Headaches *391*

Life Connections: Reducing the Risk of CHD Through Behavior Modification *393*

Life Connections: Preventing and Coping with Cancer *395*

T F Because variety is the spice of life, the more change the better.

page 371

T F Making new friends is stressful.

page 373

T F Searching for social approval or perfection is an excellent way of making yourself miserable.

page 377

T F "A merry heart doeth good like a medicine."

page 379

T F At any given moment, countless microscopic warriors within our bodies are carrying out search-and-destroy missions against foreign agents.

page 385

T F People who exercise regularly live 2 years longer, on average, than their sedentary counterparts.

page 387

T F Blowing things out of proportion can give you a headache.

page 389

T F African Americans are more likely than European Americans to contract cancer and more likely to die from it when they do.

page 394

T F Ketchup (ketchup?) is a health food.

page 395

Are these items truth or fiction? We will be revisiting them throughout the chapter.

The Earth moved. Or, a bit more precisely, in March of 2011, two immense walls of rock that had been pressing against each other finally budged. As in other places we call "faults," such as California's San Andreas Fault, they had been rubbing against each other for millions of years, trying to pass in opposite directions. Nobody saw it happen, because this particular confrontation occurred at the bottom of the ocean, off the northern coast of Japan. But the energy released caused the greatest earthquake experienced in Japan in 140 years, and it drove a wall of water 33 feet high—a tsunami—into the coast of Japan.

The earthquake and its aftershocks were felt in Tokyo, 250 miles down the coast. A 26-year-old office worker said, "I thought I was going to die when the earthquake hit. At first the shaking was not so great, but then it grew more violent and we all ducked under our desks. Ceiling tiles dropped on us, and machines and reams of paper were hurled at us from shelves."

That was the least of it. The tsunami hit the shore and swept away boats, houses, cars, trucks, and people, turning villages and small cities into garbage heaps and graveyards. One fishing boat captain, Koji Haga, rode the tsunami inland like a rider clutching to the back of some prehistoric whale, struggling to keep his pitching vessel upright. Somehow he survived, but nearly 30,000 others did not. They were swept out to sea or buried in rubble. And some were poisoned by radiation.

The tsunami also smashed six reactors at a coastal nuclear power plant. Volunteer workers braved exposure to radiation to try to keep overheated, melting fuel rods cooled with water—succeeding here, failing there. They received overdoses of radiation and face radiation poisoning and potential early demise from cancer. Despite the workers' heroism, hundreds of thousands of people had to be evacuated from the area many miles around the plants. Many of them made up a new group of people in an affluent, well-organized society—the homeless.

Disasters like the tsunami take an emotional as well as a physical toll (Mason et al., 2010; Weems et al., 2010). Studies of communities devastated by earthquakes, oil spills, fires, tsunamis, hurricanes, and other disasters suggest that most survivors eventually adjust to the stress of living with their memories and their grief. But many others have a bundle of symptoms that we call *posttraumatic stress disorder*: lingering nightmares, flashbacks, depression, and irritability that suggest deeper effects of stress.

This chapter is about stress—its origins, its psychological and physical effects, and ways of coping with it. **Question 1: What is stress?**

⊙ STRESS: WHAT IT IS, WHERE IT COMES FROM

In physics, *stress* is defined as a pressure or force exerted on a body. Tons of rock pressing on the earth, one car smashing into another, a rubber band stretching—all are types of physical stress. Psychological forces, or **stressors**, also press, push, or pull. We may feel "crushed" by the weight of a big decision, "smashed" by adversity, or "stretched" to the point of snapping. In the case of the victims of the earthquake and tsunami in Japan, physical events had both psychological and physical consequences. As we will see throughout the chapter, those psychological consequences can also affect our health.

Psychologists define **stress** as the demand made on an organism to adapt, cope, or adjust. Some stress is healthful and necessary to keep us alert and occupied. Stress researcher Hans Selye (1907–1982) referred to such healthful stress as **eustress**. We may experience eustress when we begin a sought-after job or are trying to choose the color of an iPod. But intense or prolonged stress, such as that caused by a natural disaster or by social or financial problems, can overtax our ability to adjust, affect our moods, impair our ability to experience pleasure, and harm the body (S. L. Baker et al., 2006; Gotlieb & Joormann, 2010; Saul et al., 2008).

A study by the UCLA Higher Education Research Institute found that college freshmen are now encountering a record level of stress. Figure 11.1 ■ shows that over the past 25 years, fewer and fewer college freshmen have been reporting that their emotional health is "above average." During the same period, more and more college freshmen have been reporting that they felt overwhelmed during their senior year at high school. Either freshmen are being more open about their feelings or we have been living in more and more stressful times—or both.

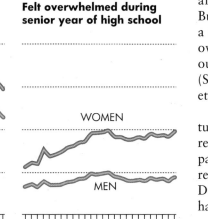

Emotional health was above average

Felt overwhelmed during senior year of high school

Figure 11.1 ■ College Freshmen's Emotional Health Freshmen's self-assessment of their emotional health hit a 25-year low in 2010, according to an annual report. A much larger share of students said they had felt frequently overwhelmed with all they had to do as high school seniors. Women were twice as stressed as men. Source: Tamar Lewin (2011, January 27). Record level of stress found in college freshmen. *The New York Times* online.

Stress is one of the key topics in health psychology. **Question 2: What is health psychology?** Health psychology studies the relationships between psychological factors (for example, attitudes, beliefs, situational influences, and behavior patterns) and the prevention and treatment of physical health problems. Health psychologists investigate how

- psychological factors such as stress, behavior patterns, and attitudes can lead to or aggravate illness;
- people can cope with stress;
- stress and disease-causing organisms such as bacteria and viruses interact to influence the immune system;
- people decide whether to seek health care; and
- psychological interventions such as health education (concerning nutrition, smoking, and exercise, for example) and behavior modification can contribute to physical health.

In this chapter, we consider sources of stress, factors that moderate the impact of stress, and the body's response to stress. We consider various physical health issues that overlap with the science of psychology, including headaches, heart disease, and cancer. We have seen how disasters create stress. Let's consider less severe but more common sources of stress: daily hassles, life changes, conflict, irrational beliefs, and Type A behavior.

Daily Hassles: The Stress of Everyday Life

Which straw will break the camel's back? The last straw, according to the saying. Similarly, stresses can pile up until we can no longer cope with them. Some of these stresses are daily hassles (Back et al., 2008; Henderson et al., 2010). **Question 3: What are**

Stressor An event that gives rise to feelings of stress.

Stress The demand that is made on an organism to adapt, cope, or adjust.

Eustress (YOU-stress). Stress that is healthful.

Health psychology The field of psychology that studies the relationships between psychological factors (e.g., attitudes, beliefs, situational influences, and behavior patterns) and the prevention and treatment of physical illness.

daily hassles? Daily hassles are regularly occurring conditions and experiences that can threaten or harm our well-being. Lazarus and his colleagues (1985) found that daily hassles could be grouped as follows:

1. *Household hassles:* preparing meals, shopping, and home maintenance
2. *Health hassles:* physical illness, concern about medical treatment, and side effects of medication
3. *Time-pressure hassles:* having too many things to do, too many responsibilities, and not enough time
4. *Inner concern hassles:* being socially isolated, lonely
5. *Environmental hassles:* crime, neighborhood deterioration, and traffic noise
6. *Financial responsibility hassles:* concern about owing money such as mortgage payments and loan installments
7. *Work hassles:* job dissatisfaction, not liking one's duties at work, and problems with coworkers
8. *Security hassles:* concerns about job security, terrorism, taxes, property investments, stock market swings, and retirement

The opposite of daily hassles are **uplifts,** such as pleasant family outings, good grades, enjoyable TV shows, and tasty meals. An Israeli study of Israeli Jews and Arabs found that uplifts were related to family satisfaction (Lavee & Ben-Ari, 2003). Daily hassles, by contrast, are linked to variables such as nervousness, worrying, feelings of sadness, and feelings of loneliness.

Life Changes: Variety May Be the Spice of Life, But Does Too Much Spice Leave a Bad Taste?

You might think that marrying Mr. or Ms. Right, finding a good job, and moving to a better neighborhood all in the same year would propel you into a state of bliss. It might. **Truth or Fiction Revisited:** Although variety adds spice to life, *too much* variety might lead to physical illness. **Question 4: How can too much of a good thing make you ill?** It is because the events that add variety to life are changes. Even pleasant changes require adjustment. Piling one atop the other, even positive changes can lead to headaches, high blood pressure, and other health problems.

Life changes differ from daily hassles in two key ways:

1. Many life changes are positive and desirable; hassles, by definition, are negative.
2. Hassles occur regularly, whereas life changes occur at irregular intervals.

The nearby Self-Assessment on "Going Through Changes" was

Daily hassles Notable daily conditions and experiences that are threatening or harmful to a person's well-being.

Uplifts Notable pleasant daily conditions and experiences.

Daily Hassles Daily hassles are notable conditions and experiences that are threatening or harmful to a person's well-being. This person is apparently overworked. Perhaps he works so hard because of financial hassles. He probably has time-pressure hassles and health hassles, or given his diet, health hassles may be forthcoming. His work environment also seems to be crashing in on him.

Going Through Changes: How Stressful Is Your Life?

The College Life Stress Inventory measures the level of life stress experienced by college students. The inventory consists of various life events, or life changes, that are scaled according to their perceived degrees of stress. To evaluate your level of stress, select the items you have experienced during the past year. Calculate your overall stress level by adding up the ratings of the selected items.

Event	(√) Experienced During Past Year	Life Event Stress Rating
Being raped		100
Finding out that you are HIV positive		100
Being accused of rape		98
Death of a close friend		97
Death of a close family member		96
Contracting a sexually transmitted infection (other than HIV/AIDS)		94
Concerns about being pregnant		91
Finals week		90
Concerns about your partner being pregnant		90
Oversleeping for an exam		89
Flunking a class		89
Having a boyfriend or girlfriend cheat on you		85
Ending a steady dating relationship		85
Serious illness in a close friend or family member		85
Financial difficulties		84
Writing a major term paper		83
Being caught cheating on a test		83
Being charged with drunk driving		82
Sense of overload in school or work		82
Two exams in one day		80
Cheating on your boyfriend or girlfriend		77
Getting married		76
Negative consequences of drinking or drug use		75
Depression or crisis in your best friend		73
Difficulties with parents		73
Talking in front of a class		72

Event	(√) Experienced During Past Year	Life Event Stress Rating
Lacking sleep		69
Changing your housing situation (hassles, moves)		69
Competing or performing in public		69
Getting in a physical fight		66
Difficulties with a roommate		66
Job changes (applying, new job, work hassles)		65
Declaring a major or having concerns about future plans		65
A class you hate		62
Drinking or using drugs		61
Confrontations with professors		60
Starting a new semester		58
Going on a first date		57
Registration		55
Maintaining a steady dating relationship		55
Commuting to campus or work, or both		54
Peer pressures		53
Being away from home for the first time		53
Getting sick		52
Concerns about your appearance		52
Getting straight A's		51
A difficult class that you love		48
Making new friends; getting along with friends		47
Fraternity or sorority rush		47
Falling asleep in class		40
Attending an athletic event (e.g., football game)		20

Source: Renner, M. J., and Mackin, R. S. A Life Stress Instrument for Classroom Use. *Teaching of Psychology*, 25 © 1998 Taylor and Francis, Reprinted by permission.

Scoring Key: Compare your total stress rating (total score) with those of a sample of 257 introductory psychology students. The average (mean) score in the sample was 1,247. About two out of three of the students obtained stress rating scores ranging from 806 to 1,688. Your total stress score can help you gauge how stressful your life has been during the preceding year, but it cannot reveal how stress may be affecting you.

constructed to measure the impact of life changes on college students. Being raped and finding out that one is HIV positive were rated as the two most stressful life events (each received a stress rating of 100). Flunking a course (89 units) and getting married (76 units) were also considered highly stressful, even though marriage is generally considered to be a positive event. Making new friends (47 units) also made the list. **Truth or Fiction Revisited:** Although friends and social support can be good for your health (Gump & Matthews, 2000), making new friends remains a life change that requires adjustment.

Hassles, Life Changes, and Health Problems

Hassles and life changes—especially negative life changes—can cause us to worry and affect our moods (McLaughlin et al., 2009; O'Driscoll & Brough, 2010). Hassles and life changes also predict health problems such as heart disease and cancer, even athletic injuries (Perna et al., 2003). Holmes and Rahe (1967) found that people who "earned" 300 or more life-change units within a year, according to their own scale, were at greater risk for health problems. Eight of ten developed health problems compared with only one of three people whose totals of life-change units for the year were below 150.

Moreover, people who remain married to the same person live longer than people who experience marital breakups and remarry (Wood et al., 2007). Apparently, the life changes of divorce and remarriage—or the instability associated with them—can be harmful to our health.

How Are Daily Hassles and Life Changes Connected with Health Problems?

The links among daily hassles, life changes, and health problems are supported by research. But what leads to what? Although it may appear obvious that hassles and life changes should *cause* health problems, what is obvious can be wrong. Let's consider a number of limitations in the research on the connections among daily hassles, life changes, and health problems:

1. *The nature of the links:* Because the data supporting the links among daily hassles, life changes, and illness is correlational, rival explanations are possible (see Figure 11.2 ■). Hassles and life changes may cause stress, but it is also possible that people who are *predisposed* toward medical or psychological problems encounter more hassles and amass more life-change units (Ewedemi & Linn, 2006; Harkness & Stewart, 2009). For example, undiagnosed medical disorders may contribute to sexual problems, arguments with spouses or in-laws, and changes in living conditions and sleeping habits.

2. *Positive versus negative life changes:* Other aspects of the research on the relationship between life changes and illness have also been challenged. For instance, *positive* life changes may be less disturbing than daily hassles and negative life changes, even though the number of life-change units assigned to them is high (Lefcourt et al., 1981).

3. *Personality differences:* People with different personalities respond to stress in different ways. People who are easygoing or psychologically hardy are less likely to become ill under the impact of stress. Optimism also helps people cope with stress, as by marshaling social support (Brydon et al., 2009; Feder et al., 2010).

4. *Cognitive appraisal:* The same event can have different meanings to different people and be a source of stress to some and of uplift to others (Buchanan et al., 2010; David et al., 2010). Pregnancy, for example, can be a positive or negative life change depending on whether you want and are prepared to have a child. In responding to the hassles, traumatic experiences, and life changes that we encounter, we take into account their perceived danger, our values and goals, our beliefs in our coping ability, our social support, and so on. The same event will be less taxing to someone with more coping ability and social support.

"Mental tensions, frustrations, insecurity, aimlessness are among the most damaging stressors, and … studies have shown how they cause migraine headache, peptic ulcers, heart attacks, hypertension, mental disease, suicide, or just hopeless unhappiness."

HANS SELYE

"Be willing to have it so. Acceptance of what has happened is the first step to overcoming the consequences of any misfortune."

WILLIAM JAMES

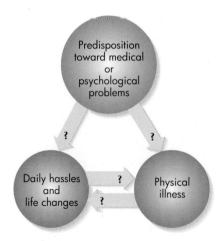

Figure 11.2 ■ What Are the Relationships Among Daily Hassles, Life Changes, and Physical Illness? Do daily hassles and life events cause illness, or do people who are predisposed toward medical or psychological problems encounter or generate more hassles and amass more life-change units?

Conflict: Darned If You Do, Darned If You Don't

Should you eat dessert or try to stick to your diet? Should you live on campus, which is more convenient, or should you rent an apartment, where you may have more independence? Choices like these can place us in conflict. **Question 5: What is conflict?** In psychology, **conflict** is the feeling of being pulled in two or more directions by opposing motives. Conflict is stressful. Psychologists often classify conflicts into four types: approach–approach, avoidance–avoidance, approach–avoidance, and multiple approach–avoidance.

Classic experimental research by Neal E. Miller (1944) and others suggests that the **approach–approach conflict** (see Figure 11.3 ■, part A) is the least stressful type. Here, each of two goals is desirable, and both are within reach. You may not be able to decide between pizza or tacos or a trip to Nassau or Hawaii. I recently had such a conflict in which I was "forced" to choose between triple-chocolate fat-free frozen yogurt and coffee-chocolate-chip fat-free frozen yogurt. Such conflicts are usually resolved by making a decision (I took the triple-chocolate!). Those who experience this type of conflict may vacillate until they make a decision.

Avoidance–avoidance conflict (see Figure 11.3 ■, part B) is more stressful because you are motivated to avoid each of two negative goals, yet avoiding one of them requires approaching the other. You may be fearful of visiting the dentist but also afraid that your teeth will decay if you do not. You may not want to contribute to the Association for the Advancement of Lost Causes, but you fear that your friends will consider you cheap or uncommitted if you do not. When an avoidance–avoidance conflict is highly stressful and no resolution is in sight, some people withdraw from the conflict by focusing on other matters or doing nothing. Highly conflicted people have been known to refuse to get up in the morning and start the day.

When the same goal produces both approach and avoidance motives, we have an **approach–avoidance conflict** (see Figure 11.3 ■, part C). People and things have their pluses and minuses, their good points and their bad points. Cheesecake may be delicious, but oh, the calories! Goals that produce mixed motives may seem more

Conflict Being torn in different directions by opposing motives. Feelings produced by being in conflict.

Approach–approach conflict A type of conflict in which the goals that produce opposing motives are positive and within reach.

Avoidance–avoidance conflict A type of conflict in which the goals are negative, but avoidance of one requires approaching the other.

Approach–avoidance conflict A type of conflict in which the same goal produces approach and avoidance motives.

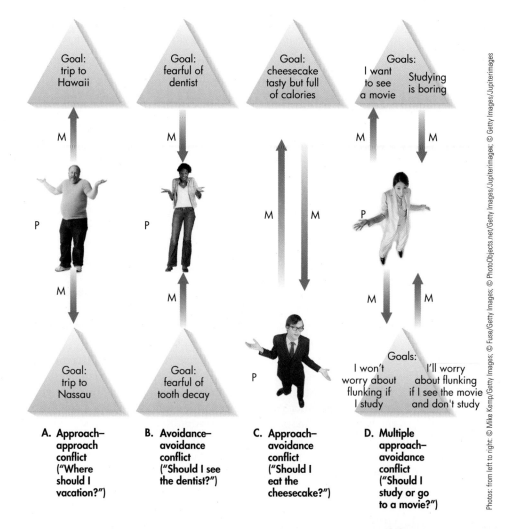

Figure 11.3 ■ Models for Conflict Part A shows an approach–approach conflict in which a person (P) has motives (M) to reach two goals (G) that are desirable, but approach of one requires exclusion of the other. Part B shows an avoidance–avoidance conflict in which both "goals" are negative, but avoiding one requires approaching the other. Part C shows an approach–avoidance conflict in which the same goal has desirable and undesirable properties. Part D shows a double approach–avoidance conflict, which is the simplest kind of multiple approach–avoidance conflict. In a multiple approach–avoidance conflict, two or more goals have mixed properties.

attractive from a distance but undesirable up close (Elliot & Mapes, 2005). Many couples repeatedly break up and then reunite. When they are apart and lonely, they may recall each other fondly and think they could make the relationship work if they got together again. But after they spend time together again, they may find themselves thinking, "How could I ever have believed that this so-and-so would change?"

The most complex form of conflict is the **multiple approach–avoidance conflict** in which each of several alternative courses of action has pluses and minuses. An example with two goals is shown in Figure 11.3 ▪, part D. This sort of conflict might arise on the eve of an examination, when you are faced with the choice of studying or, say, going to a film. Each alternative has both positive and negative aspects: "Studying's a bore, but I won't have to worry about flunking. I'd love to see the movie, but I'd just be worrying about how I'll do tomorrow."

Research has connected internal conflict with various health problems (Freitas et al., 2009). In one study (Emmons & King, 1988), the researchers enlisted 88 college undergraduates and surveyed their personal goals and the degree of conflict experienced between them. They used diaries to assess the students' emotional lives and physical symptoms. Students who reported more conflict and more ambivalence about conflict more often reported feeling anxious and depressed, reported more physical complaints, and made significantly more visits to the college health center over the course of 2 years.

Irrational Beliefs: Ten Doorways to Distress

Psychologist Albert Ellis (1913–2007) noted that our *beliefs* about events, not just the events themselves, can be stressors (David et al., 2010; Ellis, 2005). Consider a case in which a person is fired from a job and is anxious and depressed about it. It may seem logical that losing the job is responsible for the misery, but Ellis points out that an individual's beliefs about the loss may compound his or her misery.

Multiple approach–avoidance conflict A type of conflict in which each of a number of goals produces approach and avoidance motives.

Stress in America

Each year, the American Psychological Association has been commissioning surveys of stress in America. In 2010, as you see in Figure 11.4 ▪, the respondents overwhelmingly reported that money and work were their major sources of stress. We will see later that "job strain" is a key contributor to heart disease. When we add in the costs of housing, which are mentioned by nearly half the sample, we find another area in which finances contribute to stress. Health is also a major area of concern, mentioned in various ways by more than half of the sample. Intimate relationships are also sources of stress for more than half (55%) of the sample. One might think that intimate relationships would serve as a buffer against external sources of stress for people, and *perhaps they do.* (Life is complex.) However, these relationships can also contribute to stress.

Respondents reported many physical and psychological symptoms of stress. Nearly half (45%) reported that stress made them irritable or angry. Stress made more than two in five (41%) tired, and more than one-third (36%) reported having headaches. More than one in four (26%) had indigestion, and almost one in four (23%) felt tense. About one-third felt depressed (34%) or as though they could cry (30%).

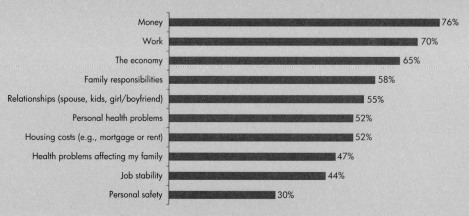

Figure 11.4. ▪ Sources of Stress. Percent of respondents who say that the source of stress is somewhat or very significant.

Source: American Psychological Association. (2010). *Stress in America 2011: Executive Summary.* (Accessed February 1, 2011). http://www.apa.org/news/press/releases/stress-exec-summary.pdf. Page 8. © 2011 by American Psychological Association. Reprinted by permission.

The most commonly reported methods of coping with stress were listening to music (49%), exercising or going for walks (48%), spending time with friends or family (46%), and reading (45%). Watching TV or movies was close behind (38%). About one-third reported praying (37%) or napping (34%). One in six (16%) drank alcohol, and one in seven (13%) smoked—not a healthful choice.

Catastrophize To interpret negative events as being disastrous; to "blow things out of proportion."

Question 6: How do irrational beliefs create or compound stress? Let's examine this situation according to Ellis's A → B → C approach: Losing the job is an *activating event* (A). The eventual outcome, or *consequence* (C), is misery. Between the activating event (A) and the consequence (C), however, lie *beliefs* (B), such as, "This job was the most important thing in my life," "What a no-good failure I am," "My family will starve," "I'll never find a job as good," "There's nothing I can do about it." Such beliefs compound misery, foster helplessness, and divert us from planning and deciding what to do next. The belief that "There's nothing I can do about it" fosters helplessness. The belief that "I am a no-good failure" internalizes the blame and may be an exaggeration. The belief that "My family will starve" may also be an exaggeration. We can diagram the situation like this:

Activating events → Beliefs → Consequences

or

A → B → C

Anxieties about the future and depression over a loss are normal and to be expected. However, the beliefs of the person who lost the job, such as those just expressed, tend to **catastrophize** the extent of the loss and contribute to anxiety and depression—and thus raise blood pressure (David et al., 2010; DiGiuseppe, 2009). By heightening the individual's emotional reaction to the loss and fostering feelings of helplessness, these beliefs also impair coping ability.

Ellis proposes that many of us carry the irrational beliefs shown in Figure 11.5. ∎ These irrational beliefs are our personal doorways to distress. In fact, they can give rise to problems in themselves. When problems assault us from other sources, these beliefs can magnify their effect.

Ellis finds it understandable that we would want the approval of others but irrational to believe that we cannot survive without it. It would be nice to be competent in everything we do, but it's unreasonable to expect it. Sure, it would be nice to serve and volley like a tennis pro, but most of us haven't the time or natural ability to perfect the

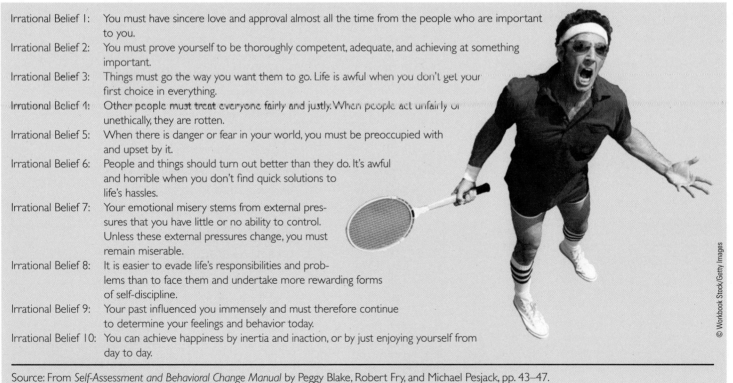

Irrational Belief 1:	You must have sincere love and approval almost all the time from the people who are important to you.
Irrational Belief 2:	You must prove yourself to be thoroughly competent, adequate, and achieving at something important.
Irrational Belief 3:	Things must go the way you want them to go. Life is awful when you don't get your first choice in everything.
Irrational Belief 4:	Other people must treat everyone fairly and justly. When people act unfairly or unethically, they are rotten.
Irrational Belief 5:	When there is danger or fear in your world, you must be preoccupied with and upset by it.
Irrational Belief 6:	People and things should turn out better than they do. It's awful and horrible when you don't find quick solutions to life's hassles.
Irrational Belief 7:	Your emotional misery stems from external pressures that you have little or no ability to control. Unless these external pressures change, you must remain miserable.
Irrational Belief 8:	It is easier to evade life's responsibilities and problems than to face them and undertake more rewarding forms of self-discipline.
Irrational Belief 9:	Your past influenced you immensely and must therefore continue to determine your feelings and behavior today.
Irrational Belief 10:	You can achieve happiness by inertia and inaction, or by just enjoying yourself from day to day.

Source: From *Self-Assessment and Behavioral Change Manual* by Peggy Blake, Robert Fry, and Michael Pesjack, pp. 43–47. Copyright © 1984 by Peggy Blake. Reprinted by permission of McGraw-Hill Companies.

© Workbook Stock/Getty Images

Figure 11.5. ∎ **Irrational Beliefs:** Cognitive Doorways to Distress.

game. Demanding perfection prevents us from going out on the court on weekends and batting the ball back and forth for fun. Irrational belief number 5 is a prescription for perpetual emotional upheaval. Irrational beliefs 7 and 9 lead to feelings of helplessness and demoralization. Sure, Ellis might say, childhood experiences can explain the origins of irrational beliefs, but it is our own cognitive appraisal—here and now—that makes us miserable.

Truth or Fiction Revisited: Research findings confirm the connections between irrational beliefs (such as excessive dependence on social approval and perfectionism) and feelings of anxiety and depression (Davies, 2008; DiGiuseppe, 2009; Wiebe & McCabe, 2002).

The Type A Behavior Pattern: Burning Out from Within?

Some people create stress for themselves through the Type A behavior pattern. **Question 7: What is Type A behavior?** Type A people are highly driven, competitive, impatient, and aggressive—so much so that they are prone to getting into vehicle accidents (Ben-Zur, 2002; Yamada et al., 2008). They feel rushed and under pressure and keep one eye firmly glued to the clock. They are not only prompt for appointments but often early. They eat, walk, and talk rapidly and become restless when others work slowly. They attempt to dominate group discussions. Type A people find it difficult

Type A behavior The Type A behavior pattern is characterized by a sense of time urgency, competitiveness, and hostility.

© Bill Bachman/The Image Works

SELF-ASSESSMENT

Are You Type A or Type B?

Complete the questionnaire by placing a check mark under Yes if the behavior pattern described is typical of you and under No if it is not. Then read the section on Type A behavior and turn to the scoring key in Appendix B.

Yes	No	Do You...
___	___	1. Strongly accent key words in your everyday speech?
___	___	2. Eat and walk quickly?
___	___	3. Believe that children should be taught to be competitive?
___	___	4. Feel restless when watching a slow worker?
___	___	5. Hurry other people to get on with what they're trying to say?
___	___	6. Find it highly aggravating to be stuck in traffic or waiting for a seat at a restaurant?
___	___	7. Continue to think about your own problems and business even when listening to someone else?
___	___	8. Try to eat and shave, or drive and jot down notes at the same time?
___	___	9. Catch up on your work while on vacations?
___	___	10. Bring conversations around to topics of concern to you?
___	___	11. Feel guilty when you spend time just relaxing?
___	___	12. Find that you're so wrapped up in your work that you no longer notice office decorations or the scenery when you commute?

Yes	No	Do You...
___	___	13. Find yourself concerned with getting more things rather than developing your creativity and social concerns?
___	___	14. Try to schedule more and more activities into less time?
___	___	15. Always appear for appointments on time?
___	___	16. Clench or pound your fists or use other gestures to emphasize your views?
___	___	17. Credit your accomplishments to your ability to work rapidly?
___	___	18. Feel that things must be done now and quickly?
___	___	19. Constantly try to find more efficient ways to get things done?
___	___	20. Insist on winning at games rather than just having fun?
___	___	21. Interrupt others often?
___	___	22. Feel irritated when others are late?
___	___	23. Leave the table immediately after eating?
___	___	24. Feel rushed?
___	___	25. Feel dissatisfied with your current level of performance?

to surrender control or share power. They are often reluctant to delegate authority, and consequently, they increase their own workloads. Type A people find it difficult just to go out on the tennis court and have fun. They watch their form, perfect their strokes, and strive for continual self-improvement. They demand perfect competence and achievement of themselves in everything they undertake.

Type B people, in contrast to Type A people, relax more readily and focus more on the quality of life. They show lower blood pressure than Type A people in response to stressors, which is a key reason that Type A behavior is also referred to as the *coronary-prone behavior pattern* (Glass et al., 2007; Manuck et al., 2007). Type B people are less ambitious and less impatient, and they pace themselves. Type A people earn higher grades and more money than Type Bs who are equal in intelligence.

LearningConnections ● STRESS: WHAT IT IS, WHERE IT COMES FROM

ACTIVE REVIEW (1) Daily _____ are regularly occurring conditions and experiences that threaten or harm our well-being. (2) Life changes, even pleasant ones, are stressful because they require _____. (3) The feeling of being pulled in two or more directions by opposing motives is called _____. (4) Albert _____ notes that our beliefs about events, as well as the events themselves, can be stressors.

REFLECT AND RELATE How many daily hassles do you experience? What can you do about them?

CRITICAL THINKING Life changes are stressful. Should people therefore avoid life changes?

Go to Psychology CourseMate at **www.cengagebrain.com** for an interactive version of these questions.

● PSYCHOLOGICAL MODERATORS OF STRESS

Psychological factors can influence, or *moderate,* the effects that stressors have on us. In this section, we discuss several psychological moderators of stress: self-efficacy expectations, psychological hardiness, humor, predictability and control, and social support.

Self-Efficacy Expectations: "The Little Engine That Could"

Self-efficacy is the ability to make things happen. Our self-efficacy expectations—our beliefs that we can bring about desired changes through our own efforts—affect our ability to withstand stress (Luszczynska et al., 2009; Pietrzak et al., 2010). **Question 8: How do our self-efficacy expectations affect our ability to withstand stress?**

In a classic experiment, Albert Bandura and his colleagues (1985) assessed participants' self-efficacy, exposed them to fearful stimuli, and monitored the levels of adrenaline and noradrenaline in their bloodstreams as they did so. Adrenaline and noradrenaline are secreted when we are under stress. They arouse the body in several ways, such as accelerating the heart rate and releasing glucose from the liver. As a result, we may have "butterflies in the stomach" and feel nervous. Excessive arousal can distract us from coping with the tasks at hand. Bandura and his colleagues exposed participants to fear-inducing objects and found that high self-efficacy expectations are accompanied by relatively lower levels of adrenaline and noradrenaline in the bloodstream. People with higher self-efficacy expectations thus have biological as well as psychological reasons for remaining calmer.

Research has also shown that people who have higher self-efficacy expectations are less disturbed by adverse events (Maddi, 2008). People with higher self-efficacy expectations are more likely to lose weight or quit smoking and less likely to relapse afterward (Kalavana et al., 2010; Martinez et al., 2010), They are better able to function in spite of pain (Howard et al., 2010). A study of

© Ocean Photography/Veer

Native Americans found that alcohol abuse was correlated with self-efficacy expectations (M. J. Taylor, 2000). That is, individuals with feelings of powerlessness were more likely to abuse alcohol, perhaps as an unhealthful way of reducing stress.

Psychological Hardiness: Tough Enough?

Psychological hardiness also helps people resist stress (Maddi et al., 2009; Pietrzak et al., 2010). Our understanding of this phenomenon is derived largely from the pioneering work of Suzanne Kobasa (Maddi, 2008). Kobasa and her colleagues studied business executives who seemed able to resist illness despite stress. In one phase of the research, executives completed a battery of psychological tests, and the researchers found that the psychologically hardy executives had three key characteristics. **Question 9: What characteristics are connected with psychological hardiness?** These include commitment, challenge, and control (Maddi et al., 2009):

1. *Commitment:* Psychologically hardy executives tended to involve themselves in, rather than feel alienated from, what they were doing or encountering.
2. *Challenge:* Psychologically hardy executives believed that change, rather than stability, is normal in life. They appraised change as an interesting incentive to personal growth, not a threat to security.
3. *Control:* Psychologically hardy executives were high in perceived control over their lives (Pietrzak et al., 2010). Psychologically hardy people tend to have what psychologist Julian B. Rotter (1990) termed an internal **locus of control** (Weiner, 2010). The nearby "Locus of Control" Self-Assessment will offer you insight into whether you see yourself as in control over your own life.

Psychologically hardy people in business and in the military are more resistant to stress because they *choose* to face it (Bartone et al., 2008; Maddi et al., 2009). They also interpret stress as making life more interesting. For example, they see a conference with a supervisor as an opportunity to persuade the supervisor rather than as a risk to their position.

Sense of Humor: "A Merry Heart Doeth Good Like a Medicine"

The idea that humor lightens the burdens of life and helps people cope with stress has been with us for millennia. Consider the biblical maxim "A merry heart doeth good like a medicine" (Proverbs 17:22).

> **Question 10: Is there any evidence that "A merry heart doeth good like a medicine"? Truth or Fiction Revisited:** Research suggests that humor can moderate the effects of stress (Marziali et al., 2008). In early research into humor as a means of coping with stress, students completed a checklist of negative life events and a measure of mood disturbance (Martin & Lefcourt, 1983). The measure of mood disturbance also yielded a stress score. In addition, the students were asked to try to produce humor in an experimental stressful situation, and their ability to do so was rated by the researchers. Students who were capable of producing humor were less affected by the stress than other students. Later experimentation found that exposing students to humorous videotapes raised the level of immunoglobulin A (a measure of the functioning of the immune system) in their saliva (Lefcourt, 1997; K. L. Smith, 2009).

> How does humor help people cope with stress? There are many possibilities. One is that laughter stimulates the output of endorphins, which might enhance the functioning of the immune system. Another is that the benefits of humor may be explained in terms of positive cognitive shifts and the positive emotions that accompany them. Humor also appears to be associated with social support and self-efficacy, two other factors that help us cope with stress (Marziali et al., 2008).

Predictability and Control: "If I Can Stop the Roller Coaster, I Don't Want to Get Off"

The ability to predict a stressor apparently moderates its impact. **Question 11: How do predictability and control help us cope with stress?** Predictability allows us to brace

---

"[People] should not try to avoid stress any more than [they] would shun food, love or exercise."

HANS SELYE

"Humor is the great thing, the saving thing. The minute it crops up, all our irritations and resentments slip away and a sunny spirit takes their place."

MARK TWAIN

"Total absence of humor renders life impossible."

COLETTE

Self-efficacy expectations Our beliefs that we can bring about desired changes through our own efforts.

Psychological hardiness A cluster of traits that buffer stress and are characterized by commitment, challenge, and control.

Locus of control The place (locus) to which an individual attributes control over the receiving of reinforcers—either inside or outside the self.

SELF-ASSESSMENT

The Locus of Control Scale

Psychologically hardy people tend to have an internal locus of control. They believe that they are in control of their own lives. In contrast, people with an external locus of control tend to see their fate as being out of their hands.

Are you "internal" or "external"? To learn more about your perception of your locus of control, respond to this questionnaire, which was developed by Nowicki and Strickland (1973). Place a check mark in either the Yes or the No column for each question. When you are finished, turn to the answer key in Appendix B.

Yes   No

1. Do you believe that most problems will solve themselves if you just don't fool with them?
2. Do you believe that you can stop yourself from catching a cold?
3. Are some people just born lucky?
4. Most of the time, do you feel that getting good grades means a great deal to you?
5. Are you often blamed for things that just aren't your fault?
6. Do you believe that if somebody studies hard enough he or she can pass any subject?
7. Do you feel that most of the time it doesn't pay to try hard because things never turn out right anyway?
8. Do you feel that if things start out well in the morning, it's going to be a good day no matter what you do?
9. Do you feel that most of the time parents listen to what their children have to say?
10. Do you believe that wishing can make good things happen?
11. When you get punished, does it usually seem it's for no good reason at all?
12. Most of the time, do you find it hard to change a friend's opinion?
13. Do you think cheering more than luck helps a team win?
14. Did you feel that it was nearly impossible to change your parents' minds about anything?
15. Do you believe that parents should allow children to make most of their own decisions?
16. Do you feel that when you do something wrong there's very little you can do to make it right?
17. Do you believe that most people are just born good at sports?
18. Are most other people your age stronger than you are?
19. Do you feel that one of the best ways to handle most problems is just not to think about them?
20. Do you feel that you have a lot of choice in deciding who your friends are?
21. If you find a four-leaf clover, do you believe that it might bring you good luck?

Yes   No

22. Did you often feel that whether or not you did your homework had much to do with what kind of grades you got?
23. Do you feel that when a person your age is angry with you, there's little you can do to stop him or her?
24. Have you ever had a good luck charm?
25. Do you believe that whether or not people like you depends on how you act?
26. Did your parents usually help you if you asked them to?
27. Have you ever felt that when people were angry with you, it was usually for no reason at all?
28. Most of the time, do you feel that you can change what might happen tomorrow by what you did today?
29. Do you believe that when bad things are going to happen they are just going to happen no matter what you try to do to stop them?
30. Do you think that people can get their own way if they just keep trying?
31. Most of the time do you find it useless to try to get your own way at home?
32. Do you feel that when good things happen, they happen because of hard work?
33. Do you feel that when somebody your age wants to be your enemy there's little you can do to change matters?
34. Do you feel that it's easy to get friends to do what you want them to do?
35. Do you usually feel that you have little to say about what you get to eat at home?
36. Do you feel that when someone doesn't like you, there's little you can do about it?
37. Did you usually feel it was almost useless to try in school, because most other children were just plain smarter than you were?
38. Are you the kind of person who believes that planning ahead makes things turn out better?
39. Most of the time, do you feel that you have little to say about what your family decides to do?
40. Do you think it's better to be smart than to be lucky?

ourselves for the inevitable and, in many cases, plan ways of coping with it. Control allows us to feel that we are not at the mercy of the fates (Folkman & Moskowitz, 2000b; Yartz et al., 2008). There is also a relationship between the desire to assume control over one's situation and the usefulness of information about impending stressors. Predictability is of greater benefit to **internals**—that is, to people who believe they have control over the events in their lives—than to **externals**. People who want information about medical procedures and what they will experience cope better with pain when they undergo those procedures (Ludwick-Rosenthal & Neufeld, 1993; Thompson, 2009).

Do You Want to Get Off the Roller Coaster? If you feel that you are in control, the answer is probably no.

Social Support: On Being in It Together

People are social beings, and social support seems to act as a buffer against the effects of stress (Folkman & Moskowitz, 2000a; Pietrzak et al., 2010). There are many aspects to social support:

1. *Emotional concern:* listening to people's problems and expressing feelings of sympathy, caring, understanding, and reassurance.

2. *Instrumental aid:* the material supports and services that facilitate adaptation. For example, after a disaster, relief organizations may provide food, medicine, and temporary living quarters.

3. *Information:* guidance and advice that enhance people's ability to cope.

4. *Appraisal:* feedback from others about how one is doing. This kind of support helps people interpret, or "make sense of," what has happened to them.

5. *Socializing:* simple conversation, recreation, even going shopping with another person. Socializing has beneficial effects, even when it is not oriented specifically toward solving problems.

Question 12: Is there evidence that social support helps people cope with stress? Yes, there is. Introverts, people who lack social skills, and people who live by themselves seem more prone to developing infectious diseases such as colds under stress (S. Cohen & Williamson, 1991; Pressman & Cohen, 2005). Social support helps people cope with the stresses of cancer and other health problems (Kahana et al., 2009). Social support helps people cope with the stresses of natural disasters such as hurricanes and earthquakes (Hu et al., 2010; X. Wang et al., 2000). Social support helps women cope with the aftermath of rape (Fisher et al., 2008). Stress is also less likely to lead to high blood pressure or alcohol abuse in people who have social support (Dennis et al., 2008; Rodriguez et al., 2008).

How does stress contribute to the development of physical health problems? In the next section, we'll gain insight into this question by examining the effects of stress on the body.

"One of the oldest human needs is having someone to wonder where you are when you don't come home at night."

MARGARET MEAD

"Time spent with cats is never wasted."

SIGMUND FREUD

Internals People who perceive the ability to attain reinforcements as largely within themselves.

Externals People who perceive the ability to attain reinforcements as largely outside themselves.

LearningConnections • PSYCHOLOGICAL MODERATORS OF STRESS

ACTIVE REVIEW (5) People with (higher or lower?) self-efficacy expectations tend to cope better with stress. (6) Psychologically hardy executives are high in _____, challenge, and control. (7) Being able to predict and control the onset of a stressor (increases or decreases?) its impact on us.

REFLECT AND RELATE Do you seek or avoid challenges? What does your answer suggest about your psychological hardiness?

CRITICAL THINKING Social support helps most people cope with stress. What does this research finding suggest about human nature?

 Go to Psychology CourseMate at **www.cengagebrain.com** for an interactive version of these questions.

STRESS AND THE BODY: THE WAR WITHIN

Stress is more than a psychological event. It is more than "knowing" it is there. It is more than "feeling" pushed and pulled. Stress also has effects on the body, which, as we will see, can impair our psychological and physical health. Stress researcher Hans Selye outlined a number of the bodily effects in his *general adaptation syndrome (GAS)*.

The General Adaptation Syndrome

General adaptation syndrome (GAS) Selye's term for a hypothesized three-stage response to stress.

Alarm reaction The first stage of the GAS, which is triggered by the impact of a stressor and characterized by sympathetic activity.

Fight-or-flight reaction A possibly innate adaptive response to the perception of danger.

Selye suggested that under stress the body is like a clock with an alarm that does not shut off until the clock shakes apart or its energy has been depleted. The body's response to various stressors shows certain similarities whether the stressor is a bacterial invasion, perceived danger, or a major life change (Selye, 1976). For this reason, Selye labeled this response the **general adaptation syndrome (GAS)**. **Question 13: What is the general adaptation syndrome?** The GAS is a group of bodily changes triggered by stressors. These bodily changes occur in three stages: an alarm reaction, a resistance stage, and an exhaustion stage. These changes mobilize the body for action and—like the alarm that goes on ringing—can eventually wear out the body.

THE ALARM REACTION The alarm reaction is triggered by perception of a stressor. This reaction mobilizes or arouses the body, biologically speaking. Early in the last century, Walter B. Cannon (1932) argued that this mobilization was the basis for an instinctive fight-or-flight reaction. But contemporary psychologists question whether the fight-or-flight reaction is instinctive in humans. Scheff (2007) writes, "It is generally recognized that outer behavior is not determined by instinctual drives. In this respect, humans differ from other mammals, whose behavior is largely instinctual" (p. 104). In any event, the alarm reaction involves bodily changes that are initiated by the brain and regulated by the endocrine system and the sympathetic division of the autonomic nervous system (ANS).

Are Their Alarm Systems Going Off as They Take Out a Loan? The alarm reaction of the general adaptation syndrome can be triggered by daily hassles and life changes—such as taking out a large loan—as well as by physical threats. When the stressor persists, diseases of adaptation may develop.

© Keith Brofsky/Photodisc/Getty Images

Stress has a domino effect on the *endocrine system*—the system of ductless glands that secrete hormones (Lupien et al., 2009) (see Figure 11.6 ■). The hypothalamus secretes corticotrophin-releasing hormone (CRH). CRH causes the pituitary gland to secrete adrenocorticotrophic hormone (ACTH). ACTH then causes the adrenal cortex to secrete the hormone cortisol and other corticosteroids (steroidal hormones). Corticosteroids help protect the body by combating allergic reactions (such as difficulty breathing) and producing inflammation. (However, corticosteroids can be harmful to the cardiovascular system, which is one reason why chronic stress can impair one's health and why athletes who use steroids to build muscle mass can experience cardiovascular problems.) Inflammation increases circulation to parts of the body that are injured. It ferries in hordes of white blood cells to fend off invading pathogens.

The adrenal medulla secretes two other hormones that play a major role in the alarm reaction. The sympathetic division of the ANS activates the adrenal medulla, causing it to release a mixture of adrenaline and noradrenaline (also known as epinephrine and norepinephrine). This mixture arouses the body by accelerating the heart rate and causing the liver to release glucose (sugar). These bodily changes fuel the fight-or-flight reaction, which mobilizes the body to fight or flee from a predator.

The fight-or-flight reaction apparently stems from a time in human prehistory when many stressors were

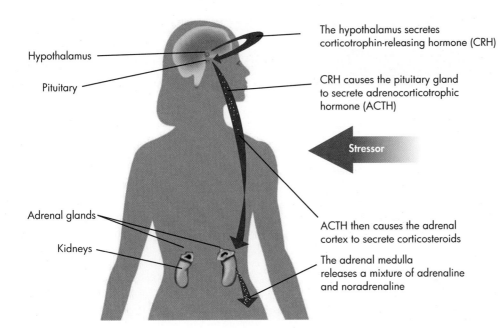

The hypothalamus secretes corticotrophin-releasing hormone (CRH)

Hypothalamus

Pituitary

CRH causes the pituitary gland to secrete adrenocorticotrophic hormone (ACTH)

Stressor

Adrenal glands

Kidneys

ACTH then causes the adrenal cortex to secrete corticosteroids

The adrenal medulla releases a mixture of adrenaline and noradrenaline

Figure 11.6 ■ **Stress and the Endocrine System** Stress has a domino effect on the endocrine system, leading to the release of corticosteroids and a mixture of adrenaline and noradrenaline. Corticosteroids combat allergic reactions (such as difficulty in breathing) and cause inflammation. Adrenaline and noradrenaline arouse the body to cope by accelerating the heart rate and providing energy for the fight-or-flight reaction. Source: From Rathus. PSYCH, 1/e. Copyright © 2009 Cengage Learning. Reproduced by permission.

life threatening. It was triggered by the sight of a predator at the edge of a thicket or by a sudden rustling in the undergrowth. Today, it may be aroused when you are caught in stop-and-go traffic or learn that your mortgage payments are going to increase. Once the threat is removed, the body returns to a lower state of arousal. Many of the bodily changes that occur in the alarm reaction are outlined in Figure 11.7 ■.

In the nearby Closer Look, Shelley Taylor and her colleagues report evidence that many women experience a "tend-and-befriend" response to threats rather than a fight-or-flight response. Margaret Kemeny (2009) also observes that some people attempt to respond productively to stress by pulling back from the situation to better appraise it and conserve their resources while doing so. This response pattern to stress is described by two theories that are currently under development: *cognitive adaptation theory* and *conservation of resources theory*.

Components of the Alarm Reaction

Corticosteroids are secreted.
Adrenaline is secreted.
Noradrenaline is secreted.
Respiration rate increases.
Heart rate increases.
Blood pressure increases.
Muscles tense.
Blood shifts from internal organs to the skeletal musculature.
Digestion is inhibited.
Sugar is released from the liver.
Blood coagulability increases.

A CLOSER LOOK

"Fight or Flight" or "Tend and Befriend"? Do Men and Women Respond Differently to Stress?

Nearly a century ago, physiologist Walter Cannon labeled the body's response to stress the "fight-or-flight" reaction. He believed that the body was prewired to become mobilized for combat when faced with a predator or a competitor, or if the predator was threatening enough, that "discretion"—a "strategic retreat"—would sometimes be the "better part of valor." The fight-or-flight reaction includes bodily changes that involve the brain (perceptions, neurotransmitters), the endocrine system (hormones), and the sympathetic division of the autonomic nervous system (rapid heartbeat, rapid breathing, muscle tension). The sum of these bodily changes pumps us up to fight like demons or, when advisable, to beat a hasty retreat.

Or does it?

According to reviews of the literature by psychologist Shelley E. Taylor and her colleagues (Taylor, 2006; Taylor et al., 2000b), women under stress are more likely to tend to the kids or "interface" with family and friends than to fight or flee. Taylor's research was prompted by a student who had noticed that nearly all of the rats in studies of the effects of stress on animals were male. Taylor did an overview of the research on stress with humans and noted that prior to 1995, when federal agencies began requiring more equal representation of women if they were to fund research, only 17% of the participants were female.

Taylor and her colleagues dug more deeply into the literature and found that "[m]en and women do have some reliably different responses to stress" (S. E. Taylor, 2000). The "woman's response" to stress can be called the "tend-and-befriend" response. It involves nurturing and seeking the support of others rather than fighting or fleeing. The studies that were reviewed showed that when females faced a predator, a disaster, or even a bad day at the office, they often responded by caring for their children and seeking social support, particularly other women. After a bad day at the office, men are more likely to withdraw from the family or start arguments.

This response may be prewired in female humans and in females of other mammalian species. Evolutionary psychologists might suggest that the tend-and-befriend response may have become sealed in our genes because it promotes the survival of females who are tending to their offspring. (Females who choose to fight may die or be otherwise separated from their offspring—no evolutionary brass ring here.)

Gender differences in behavior are frequently connected with gender differences in hormones and other biological factors. This one is no different. Taylor (2006) points to the effects of the pituitary hormone oxytocin. Oxytocin is connected with nurturing behaviors such as affiliating with and cuddling one's young in many mammals (S. E. Taylor, 2006). The literature shows that when oxytocin is released during stress, it tends to have a calming effect on both rats and humans. It makes them less afraid and more social.

But wait a minute! Men also release oxytocin when they are under stress. So why the gender difference? The answer may lie in the presence of other hormones—the sex hormones estrogen and testosterone. Female have more estrogen than males do, and estrogen appears to enhance the effects of oxytocin. Males, on the other hand, have more testosterone than females, and testosterone may mitigate the effects of oxytocin by pumping up feelings of self-confidence and fostering aggression (S. E. Taylor, 2006).

It is thus possible that males are more aggressive than females under stress because of the genetic balance of hormones in their bodies, whereas females are more affiliative and nurturant. Due to these differences, women tend to outlive men. "Men are more likely than women to respond to stressful experiences by developing certain stress-related disorders, including high blood pressure, aggressive behavior, or abuse of alcohol or hard drugs," Taylor added in a UCLA press release in May 2000. "Because the tend-and-befriend regulatory system may, in some ways, protect women against stress, this biobehavioral pattern may provide insights into why women live an average of seven and a half years longer than men."

"Fight-or-Flight" or "Tend-and-Befriend"? Walter Cannon labeled the body's response to stress the "fight-or-flight" reaction. He thought that evolution "prewired" the body to become mobilized in preparation for combat or rapid retreat when faced with a threat. It has been assumed that this reaction applies to both men and women, but research by Shelley Taylor and her colleagues suggests that women may be prewired to take care of others ("tend") or affiliate with others ("befriend") when they encounter threats.

Resistance stage The second stage of the GAS, characterized by prolonged sympathetic activity in an effort to restore lost energy and repair damage; also called the *adaptation stage.*

THE RESISTANCE STAGE According to Selye's theory, if the alarm reaction mobilizes the body and the stressor is not removed, we enter the adaptation, or **resistance, stage** of the GAS. Levels of endocrine and sympathetic activity are lower here than in the alarm reaction but still higher than normal. (It's as if the alarm is still on but a bit softer.) But make no mistake: The individual feels tense, and there continues to be a heavy burden on the body.

THE EXHAUSTION STAGE If the stressor is still not dealt with adequately, we may enter the **exhaustion stage** of the GAS. The muscles become fatigued. The body is depleted of the resources required for combating stress. With exhaustion, the parasympathetic division of the ANS may predominate. As a result, our heartbeat and respiration rate slow down, and many aspects of sympathetic activity are reversed. It might sound as if we would profit from the respite, but remember that we are still under stress—possibly an external threat. Continued stress in the exhaustion stage may lead to what Selye terms *diseases of adaptation*. These reactions are connected with constriction of blood vessels and alteration of the heart rhythm and can range from allergies to hives and heart disease—and ultimately, to death.

Discussion of the effects of stress on the immune system paves the way for understanding the links between psychological factors and physical illness.

Effects of Stress on the Immune System

Psychologists, biologists, and medical researchers have combined their efforts in a field of study called **psychoneuroimmunology** that addresses the relationships among psychological factors, the nervous system, the endocrine system, the immune system, and disease. One of its major concerns is the effect of stress on the immune system (Kemeny, 2009). Research shows that stress suppresses the immune system, as measured by the presence of various substances in the blood that make up the immune system (Calcagni & Elenkov, 2006). **Question 14: How does the immune system work?**

The **immune system** has several functions that combat disease (Iwasaki & Medzhitov, 2010). One of these is the production of white blood cells, which engulf and kill pathogens such as bacteria, fungi, viruses, worn-out body cells, and cancerous cells. The technical term for white blood cells is **leukocytes**. **Truth or Fiction Revisited:** Leukocytes carry on microscopic warfare. They engage in search-and-destroy missions in which they "recognize" and eradicate foreign agents and unhealthy cells.

Leukocytes recognize foreign substances by their shapes. The foreign substances are termed **antigens** because the body reacts to them by generating specialized proteins, or **antibodies**. Antibodies attach themselves to the foreign substances, deactivating them and marking them for destruction. The immune system "remembers" how to battle antigens by maintaining their antibodies in the bloodstream, often for years.[1]

Inflammation is another function of the immune system. When injury occurs, blood vessels in the area first contract (to stem bleeding) and then dilate. Dilation increases the flow of blood, cells, and natural chemicals to the damaged area, causing the redness, swelling, and warmth that characterize inflammation. The increased blood supply also floods the region with white blood cells to combat invading microscopic life forms such as bacteria, which otherwise might use the local damage as a port of entry into the body.

Question 15: How does stress affect the functioning of the immune system? One of the reasons stress eventually exhausts us is that it stimulates the production of corticosteroids. Steroids suppress the functioning of the immune system. Suppression has negligible effects when steroids are secreted occasionally. But persistent secretion of steroids decreases inflammation and interferes with the formation of antibodies. As a consequence, we become more vulnerable to various illnesses, including the

Exhaustion stage The third stage of the GAS, characterized by weakened resistance and possible deterioration.

Psychoneuroimmunology The field that studies the relationships between psychological factors (e.g., attitudes and overt behavior patterns) and the functioning of the immune system.

Immune system The system of the body that recognizes and destroys foreign agents (antigens) that invade the body.

Leukocytes White blood cells.

Antigen A substance that stimulates the body to mount an immune system response to it. (*Antigen* is the contraction of *anti*body *gen*erator.)

Antibodies Substances formed by white blood cells that recognize and destroy antigens.

Inflammation Increased blood flow to an injured area of the body, resulting in redness, warmth, and an increased supply of white blood cells.

---

[1] A vaccination introduces a weakened form of an antigen (usually a bacterium or virus) into the body to stimulate the production of antibodies. Antibodies can confer immunity for many years, in some cases for a lifetime.

PREVENTING AND COPING
WITH STRESS

"If you don't like something, change it. If you can't change it, change your attitude."

—Maya Angelou

Stress is a part of life, but excesses of stress are discomforting in themselves and connected with health problems such as headaches, heart disease, and cancer. There are two major ways of coping with stress: *problem-focused coping* and *emotion-focused coping*:

- Problem-focused coping seeks to manage stress directly by changing either the stressor itself or the ways we respond to the stressor. If you are having difficulty with a college subject, you can study harder or more efficiently, talk to your professor to find ways to perform better, or consult a tutor.

- Emotion-focused coping attempts to reduce the effects of a stressor by avoiding it, ignoring it, or managing the emotional needs connected with your reaction to the stressor. Some students drop out of college when they encounter academic or social stress. Other students, more usefully, seek out their friends and families to help them manage their emotional needs.

Because stress depresses the functioning of the immune system, it may be that alleviating stress has beneficial effects on the immune system, thus making us less vulnerable to some health problems. Psychologists have devised a number of methods collectively referred to as *stress management*. We will discuss stress management techniques that are examples of problem-focused coping—ways of changing your responses to stressors.

Controlling Irrational Thoughts—How to Change Your Mind for the Better

People often feel stressed because of their own thoughts. For example, if you have difficulty with the first item on a test, you might become convinced that you will flunk. Or if you haven't been able to get to sleep for 15 minutes, you might assume that you will lie awake all night and feel "wrecked" in the morning.

If you have had these or similar experiences, it may be because you harbor some of the irrational beliefs identified by Albert Ellis (see Figure 11.5). How do we change the irrational thoughts that create and compound stress? The answer is deceptively simple: we just change them. However, this may require work. Moreover, before we can change our thoughts, we must become aware of them. Table 11.1 ■ will help you become aware of irrational beliefs and how to change them.

TABLE 11.1 ■ Controlling Irrational Beliefs and Thoughts

Irrational (Upsetting) Thoughts	Rational (Calming) Thoughts
"Oh my God, I'm going to completely lose control!"	"This is painful and upsetting, but I don't have to go to pieces over it."
"This will never end."	"This will end even if it's hard to see the end right now."
"It'll be awful if Mom gives me that look again."	"It's more pleasant when Mom's happy with me, but I can live with it if she isn't."
"How can I go out there? I'll look like a fool."	"So you're not perfect. That doesn't mean that you're going to look stupid. And so what if someone thinks you look stupid? You can live with that, too. Just stop worrying and have some fun."
"My heart's going to leap out of my chest! How much can I stand?"	"Easy—hearts don't leap out of chests. Stop and think! Distract yourself. Breathe slowly, in and out."
"What can I do? There's nothing I can do!"	"Easy—stop and think. Just because you can't think of a solution right now doesn't mean there's nothing you can do. Take it a minute at a time. Breathe easy."

Do irrational beliefs or catastrophizing thoughts compound your feelings of anxiety and tension? Cognitive psychologists suggest that you can cope with stress by becoming aware of your irrational, upsetting thoughts and replacing them with rational, calming thoughts.

common cold (Aich et al., 2009). By weakening the immune system, stress may also be connected with a more rapid progression of HIV infection to AIDS (Scott-Sheldon et al., 2008).

Studies with college students have shown that the stress of exams depresses the immune system's response to the Epstein-Barr virus, which causes fatigue and other problems (Glaser et al., 1993). Students who were lonely showed greater suppression of the immune system than students who had more social support. The Epstein-Barr virus remains dormant in 90% of people who recover from an episode. Stress elevates blood levels of cortisol and adrenaline (epinephrine) and heightens the probability that the virus will be reactivated (Coskun et al., 2010).

Lowering Arousal: Turning Down the Inner Alarm

Stress tends to trigger intense activity in the sympathetic branch of the autonomic nervous system—that is, overarousal. Overarousal is a sign that something may be wrong, but once we are aware that a stressor is acting on us and have developed a plan to cope with it, it is no longer helpful to have blood pounding fiercely through our arteries.

Psychologists and other scientists have developed many methods for teaching people to reduce arousal. These include progressive relaxation and meditation. In progressive relaxation, people purposefully tense a particular muscle group before relaxing it. This sequence allows them to develop awareness of their muscle tensions and also to differentiate between feelings of tension and relaxation.

The following instructions will help you try meditation as a means for lowering the arousal connected with stress:

1. Begin by meditating once or twice a day for 10 to 20 minutes.

2. In meditation, what you *don't* do is more important than what you *do* do. Adopt a passive, "what happens happens" attitude.

3. Create a quiet, nondisruptive environment. For example, don't face a light directly.

4. Do not eat for 1 hour beforehand; avoid caffeine for at least 2 hours.

5. Assume a comfortable position. Change it as needed. It's okay to scratch or yawn.

6. As a device to aid concentrating, you may focus on your breathing or seat yourself before a calming object such as a plant or burning incense. Stress researcher Herbert Benson suggests "perceiving" the word *one* on every outbreath rather than saying it aloud. Others suggest thinking or perceiving the word *in* as you inhale and *out,* or *ah-h-h,* as you exhale.

7. If you are using a mantra (like the syllable "om," pronounced *oammm*), you can prepare for meditation and say the mantra out loud several times. Enjoy it. Then say it more and more softly. Close your eyes and only think the mantra. Allow yourself to perceive, rather than actively think, the mantra. Again, adopt a passive attitude. Continue to perceive the mantra. It may grow louder or softer, disappear for a while, and then return.

8. If disruptive thoughts enter your mind as you are meditating, you can allow them to "pass through." Don't get wrapped up in trying to squelch them, or you may raise your level of arousal.

9. Allow yourself to drift. (You won't go too far.) What happens happens.

10. Above all, take what you get. You cannot force the relaxing effects of meditation. You can only set the stage for them and allow them to happen.

Exercising: Run for Your Life?

"I like long walks, especially when they are taken by people who annoy me."

—Fred Allen

Exercise, particularly aerobic exercise, enhances the functioning of the immune system, contributes to our psychological well-being, and helps us cope with stress (Paffenbarger et al., 2007; Richardson & Rothstein, 2008).

Exercise helps people cope by enhancing their physical fitness, or "condition." Fitness includes muscle strength; muscle endurance; suppleness or flexibility; and a higher ratio of muscle to fat (usually due to both building muscle and reducing fat). Fitness enhances our natural immunity and boosts our levels of endorphins (Jonsdottir et al., 2000). Sustained physical activity reduces hypertension and the risk of heart attacks and strokes (Hu et al., 2000; Kurth et al., 2006; Li et al., 2006). Exercise keeps the arteries more supple, even among older adults; that is, it counters the hardening of the arteries that comes with age (Van Guilder et al., 2007). It raises blood levels of high-density lipoproteins (HDL, or "good cholesterol") (Buyukyazi et al., 2010). HDL, in turn, lowers the amount of low-density lipoproteins (LDL, or "bad cholesterol") in the blood.

In one research program, Ralph Paffenbarger and his colleagues (2009) have been tracking Harvard University alumni by means of university records and questionnaires. **Truth or Fiction Revisited:** They have discovered that alumni who burn at least 2,000 calories a week through exercise live 2 years longer, on average, than their sedentary counterparts.

Exercise may also have positive psychological effects. People who exercise regularly are less likely to be depressed and/or to commit suicide (Paffenbarger et al., 2007).

LearningConnections • STRESS AND THE BODY: THE WAR WITHIN

ACTIVE REVIEW (8) The GAS has three stages: _____, resistance, and exhaustion. (9) Cannon dubbed the alarm reaction the _____ reaction. (10) Under stress, pituitary ACTH causes the adrenal cortex to release _____ that help the body respond to stress by fighting inflammation and allergic reactions. (11) Women may show a tend-and-_____ response to stress rather than fight-or-flight. (12) Two hormones that play a role in the alarm reaction are secreted by the adrenal medulla: _____ and noradrenaline.

REFLECT AND RELATE What do you experience in your body when you are under stress? How do those sensations fit the description of the GAS?

CRITICAL THINKING Prolonged stress is connected with health problems. Must you avoid stress to remain healthy, or can you do something to become psychologically hardy?

 Go to Psychology CourseMate at **www.cengagebrain.com** for an interactive version of these questions.

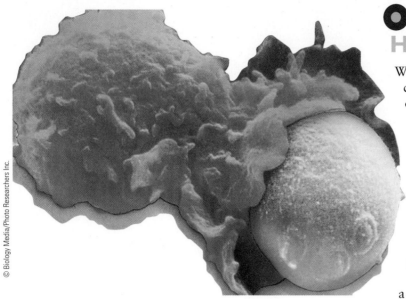

Microscopic Warfare The immune system helps us to combat disease. It produces white blood cells (leukocytes), such as that shown here, which routinely engulf and kill pathogens like bacteria and viruses.

"The only way to keep your health is to eat what you don't want, drink what you don't like, and do what you'd rather not."

MARK TWAIN

"There is this kind of fatalistic approach to genes that the general public seems to have now—that if your mom, dad, sister or brother had something [then] you're doomed to have it too"

ROBERT N. HOOVER, NATIONAL CANCER INSTITUTE

PSYCHOLOGY AND HEALTH

Why do people become ill? Why do some people develop cancer? Why do others have heart attacks? Why do still others seem to be immune to these illnesses? Why do some of us seem to come down with everything that is going around, while others ride out the roughest winters with nary a sniffle? **Question 16: What is the biopsychosocial approach to health?** The biopsychosocial approach recognizes that biological, psychological, and sociocultural factors are involved in health—and illness. The likelihood of contracting an illness—be it a case of the flu or cancer—can reflect the interaction of many factors, including genetic (biological) factors.

Factors such as pathogens, injuries, age, gender, and a family history of disease may strike us as the most obvious causes of illness. Genetics, in particular, tempts some people to assume there is little they can do about their health. It is true that there are some severe health problems that are unavoidable for people with certain genes. However, in many cases, especially with cardiovascular problems and cancer, genes only create *predispositions* toward the health problem.

Genetic predispositions interact with the environment (Benke & Fallin, 2010; Hunter, 2005). A problematic family medical history is not always a portent of doom. For example, genetic factors are involved in breast cancer. However, rates of breast cancer among women who have recently immigrated to the United States from rural Asia are similar to those in their countries of origin and nearly 80% lower than the rates among third-generation Asian American women, whose rates are similar to those of European American women (Hoover, 2000; Wu et al., 2009). Therefore, it would seem that one's lifestyle is also intimately connected with the risk of breast cancer—and most other kinds of cancer.

As shown in the nearby Concept Review 11.1, biological factors (such as genetics and obesity), psychological factors (such as behaviors and personality), sociocultural factors (such as socioeconomic status), environmental factors, and stressors all play roles in health problems such as heart disease and cancer.

Many health problems are affected by psychological factors, such as attitudes and emotions (Frasure-Smith & Lespérance, 2008; Kiecolt-Glaser et al., 2002b). Psychological states such as anxiety and depression can impair the functioning of the immune system, rendering us more vulnerable to physical disorders ranging from viral infections to cancer (Weinstein et al., 2010). Behavior is another psychological factor that affects physical health. Figure 11.8 ■ reveals that nearly 1 million deaths each year in the United States are preventable. Modifying our behavior—stopping smoking, eating right, exercising, and controlling alcohol use—would prevent nearly 80% of these preventable deaths.

Let's now discuss some health problems, including headaches, heart disease, and cancer. Each of them involves biological, psychological, and sociocultural factors. Although these are medical problems, we will explore the ways psychologists have contributed to their prevention and treatment.

Headaches: When Stress Presses and Pounds

Headaches are among the most common stress-related physical ailments. Nearly 20% of people in the United States suffer severe headaches. **Question 17: How has psychology contributed to the understanding and treatment of headaches?** To answer this question, let's consider the common muscle-tension headache and the more severe migraine headache.

HEART DISEASE

Biological:

Family history

Physiological conditions:
  Obesity
  High serum cholesterol
  Hypertension

Psychological (personality and behavior):

Type A behavior

Hostility and holding in feelings of anger

Job strain

Chronic fatigue, stress, anxiety, depression, and emotional strain

Patterns of consumption:

  Heavy drinking (but a drink a day may be helpful with heart disease)

  Smoking

  Overeating

Sudden stressors

Physical inactivity

Sociocultural:

African Americans are more prone to hypertension and heart disease than European Americans

Access to health care

Timing of diagnosis and treatment

© GoodShoot/Jupiterimages

CANCER

Biological:

Family history

Physiological conditions:
  Obesity

Psychological (personality and behavior):

Patterns of consumption:
  Smoking

  Drinking alcohol (especially in women)

Eating animal fats?

Sunbathing (skin cancer)

Prolonged depression

Stress? Especially prolonged stress

Sociocultural:

Socioeconomic status

Access to health care

Timing of diagnosis and treatment

Higher death rates are found in nations with higher rates of fat intake

---

MUSCLE-TENSION HEADACHE The single most frequent kind of headache is the muscle-tension headache. During the first two stages of the GAS, we are likely to contract muscles in the shoulders, neck, forehead, and scalp. Persistent stress can lead to constant contraction of these muscles, causing muscle-tension headaches. **Truth or Fiction Revisited:** Psychological factors, such as the tendency to catastrophize negative events—that is, to blow them out of proportion—can bring on a tension headache (Cathcart, 2009). Tension headaches usually come on gradually. They are most often characterized by dull, steady pain on both sides of the head and feelings of tightness or pressure.

MIGRAINE HEADACHE A migraine headache usually has a sudden onset and is identified by severe throbbing pain on one side of the head. Migraines affect one American

Migraine headaches Throbbing headaches that are connected with changes in the supply of blood to the head.

389

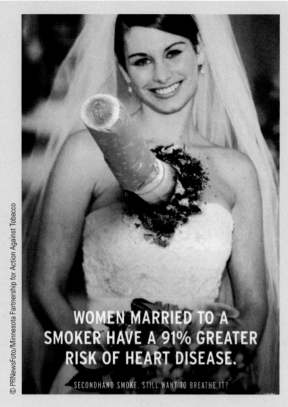

WOMEN MARRIED TO A
SMOKER HAVE A 91% GREATER
RISK OF HEART DISEASE.

SECONDHAND SMOKE. STILL WANT TO BREATHE IT?

Figure 11.8 ■ Annual Preventable Deaths in the United States

- Elimination of tobacco use could prevent 400,000 deaths each year from cancer, heart and lung diseases, and stroke.

- Improved diet and exercise could prevent 300,000 deaths from conditions like heart disease, stroke, diabetes, and cancer.

- Control of underage and excess drinking of alcohol could prevent 100,000 deaths from motor vehicle accidents, falls, drownings, and other alcohol-related injuries.

- Immunizations for infectious diseases could prevent up to 100,000 deaths.

- Safer sex or sexual abstinence could prevent 20,000 deaths from sexually transmitted infections (STIs).

in ten. They may last for hours or days. Sensory and motor disturbances often precede the pain; a warning "aura" may include vision problems and the perception of unusual odors. The migraines themselves are often accompanied by sensitivity to light, loss of appetite, nausea, vomiting, sensory and motor disturbances such as loss of balance, and changes in mood. Imaging techniques suggest that when something triggers a migraine, neurons at the back of the brain fire in waves that ripple across the top of the head, then down to the brain stem, the site of many pain centers.

Triggers for migraines include barometric pressure; pollen; certain drugs; monosodium glutamate (MSG), a chemical often used to enhance flavor; chocolate; aged cheese; beer, champagne, and red wine; and the hormonal changes connected with menstruation (Hauge et al., 2010; Levy et al., 2009).

The behaviors connected with migraine headaches serve as a mini-textbook in health psychology. For example, the Type A behavior pattern apparently contributes to migraines. In one study, 53% of people who had migraine headaches showed the Type A behavior pattern compared with 23% of people who had muscle-tension headaches (Rappaport et al., 1988). A study of 232 migraine sufferers found that those who catastrophized their symptoms were more likely to have impaired daily functioning and a lower quality of life (Holroyd et al., 2007).

Regardless of the source of the headache, we can unwittingly propel ourselves into a vicious cycle. Headache pain is a stressor that can lead us to increase, rather than relax, muscle tension in the neck, shoulders, scalp, and face.

Coronary Heart Disease: Taking Stress to Heart

Coronary heart disease (CHD) is the leading cause of death in the United States, most often from heart attacks (Arias et al., 2010). **Question 18: What are the major risk factors for coronary heart disease?**

RISK FACTORS Let's begin by considering the biological risk factors for CHD (Glynn, 2010).

Biological Risk Factors There are a number of biological risk factors for CHD, including

Headaches Can Pound Away Mercilessly What kinds of headaches are there? What can we do about them?

Because many headaches are related to stress, one way to fight headaches is to reduce the stress in your life. Challenging irrational beliefs, lowering the physical alarm, and exercising all may be of help. Biofeedback training has also helped many people with tension-type headaches and with migraine headaches, sometimes by enabling sufferers to move blood away from their heads and into their hands and feet (Mullally et al., 2009; Nestoriuc et al., 2008).

Aspirin, acetaminophen, ibuprofen, and many prescription drugs are also used to fight headache pain. Some inhibit the production of the prostaglandins that help initiate transmission of pain messages to the brain. Newer prescription drugs can help prevent many migraines. People who are sensitive to MSG or red wine can request meals without MSG and switch to white wine.

- *Family history:* People with a family history of CHD are more likely to develop the disease themselves.

- *Physiological conditions:* Obesity, high **serum cholesterol** levels, and **hypertension** (high blood pressure) are risk factors for CHD. About one American in five has hypertension, which can lead to CHD. *Essential hypertension*—that is, hypertension without an identifiable cause—has a genetic component. However, blood pressure is also connected with emotions like depression and anxiety. In addition, it rises when we inhibit the expression of strong feelings or are angry or on guard against threats. When we are under stress, we may believe that we can feel our blood pressure "pounding through the roof," but most people cannot sense hypertension. Therefore, it is important to check blood pressure regularly.

- *A physically inactive lifestyle.*

- *Patterns of consumption:* Risky patterns include heavy drinking, smoking, and overeating. On the other hand, a little alcohol seems to be good for the heart.

Psychological Risk Factors The following are some psychological risk factors for CHD:

- *Type A behavior:* Most studies suggest that there is at least a modest relationship between Type A behavior and CHD. Hostility seems to be the component of the Type A behavior pattern that is most harmful to physical health (Chida & Steptoe, 2009). People who are highly prone to anger are about three times as likely as other people to have heart attacks (J. E. Williams et al., 2000). The stress hormones connected with anger can constrict blood vessels to the heart, which can lead to the attack.

- *Job strain:* Overtime work, assembly line labor, and exposure to conflicting demands can all contribute to CHD. High-strain work, which makes heavy demands on workers but gives them little personal control, puts workers at the highest risk (Aboa-Éboulé et al., 2007; Krantz et al., 1988). As shown in Figure 11.9 ■, the work of waiters and waitresses fits this description well.

- *Chronic fatigue, stress, anxiety, depression, and emotional strain.* Depression is connected with irregularities in the heart rate and may make blood platelets "sticky," which may, in turn, cause clots that lead to CHD (Kramer, 2003).

- *Sudden stressors, such as natural disasters.*

Sociocultural Risk Factors African Americans are more likely than European Americans to have heart attacks and to die from them (Harper et al., 2007; National Center for Health Statistics, 2009). Figure 11.10 ■ compares the death rates from heart disease of American men and women of various ethnic backgrounds. Asian Americans, Native Americans, and Latin Americans are less likely than European or African Americans to die from heart disease. Early diagnosis and treatment might help decrease the racial gap. However, African Americans with heart disease are less

Serum cholesterol Cholesterol in the blood.

Hypertension High blood pressure.

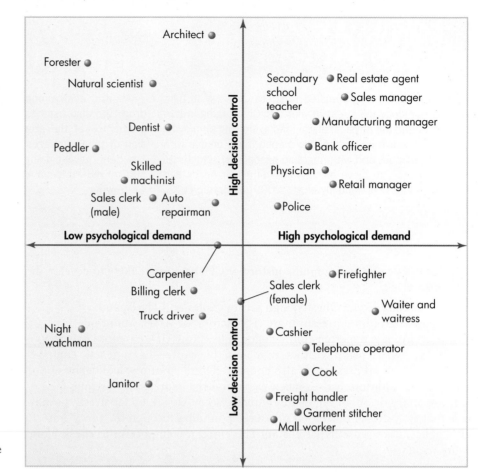

Figure 11.9 ■ The Job-Strain Model
This model highlights the psychological demands made by various occupations and the amount of personal (decision) control they allow. Occupations characterized by high demand and low decision control place workers at greatest risk for heart disease.

likely than European Americans to obtain procedures such as bypass surgery and to take a daily aspirin tablet, even when they would benefit equally from them (Mehta et al., 2010).

There are also significant differences among Europeans (Reaney, 2000). French, Spanish, and Portuguese people enjoy the lowest death rates from coronary heart

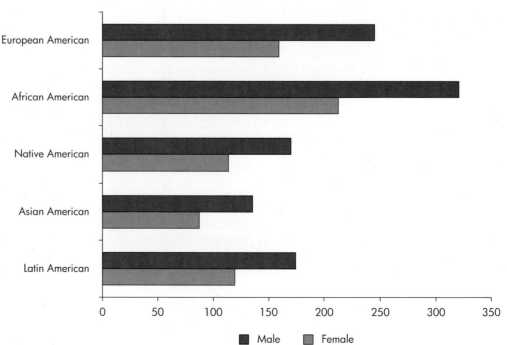

Figure 11.10 ■ Deaths from Heart Disease per 100,000 People, All Ages
Source: National Center for Health Statistics. Health, United States, 2009: With Special Feature on Medical Technology. Hyattsville, MD. 2010. Table 32. (Accessed October 8, 2010.) http://www.cdc.gov/ nchs/data/hus/ hus09.pdf#032

Once CHD has been diagnosed, a number of medical treatments, including surgery and medication, are available. However, people who have not had CHD (as well as those who have) can profit from behavior modification techniques designed to reduce the risk factors. These methods include

- *Stopping smoking.*
- *Dietary change:* Most health experts agree on three dietary strategies that are helpful in preventing CHD: Substitute nonhydrogenated unsaturated fats for saturated fats; increase consumption of omega-3 fatty acids, which are found in fish, fish oil supplements, and plant sources; and eat a diet high in fruits, vegetables, nuts (unsalted), and whole grains.

- *Reducing hypertension:* There is medication for reducing hypertension, but behavioral changes can help: meditation, aerobic exercise, and dietary changes, including consuming less salt.
- *Lowering low-density lipoprotein (LDL) serum cholesterol:* There is also medication for lowering LDL, and behavioral methods involve exercise and cutting down on foods that are high in cholesterol and saturated fats.
- *Modifying Type A behavior.*
- *Managing feelings of anger.*
- *Exercising:* Sustained physical activity helps protect people from CHD as well as helping them cope with stress.

disease and also eat diets that are relatively low in fat and high in fruits and vegetables. People in Ireland, Finland, and Britain suffer the most deaths from CHD and also eat high-fat diets and relatively fewer fruits and vegetables.

Cancer: Swerving Off Course

Cancer is characterized by the development of abnormal, or mutant, cells that may take root anywhere in the body: in the blood, bones, digestive tract, lungs, and sex organs. If their spread is not controlled early, the cancerous cells may *metastasize*—that is, establish colonies elsewhere in the body. The incidence of cancer has been declining in recent years in the United States due largely to decreases in breast and colorectal cancer in women and in lung, prostate, and colorectal cancer in men (Jemal et al., 2009). Even so, cancer remains the second leading cause of death in the United States behind heart disease (Jemal et al., 2009).

It appears that our bodies develop cancerous cells frequently. However, these are normally destroyed by the immune system. People whose immune system is damaged by physical or psychological factors may be more likely to develop tumors or have them progress to more deadly stages (Antoni & Lutgendorf, 2007; Mantovani & Sica, 2010). **Question 19: What are the major risk factors for cancer?**

RISK FACTORS As with CHD, the risk factors for cancer are biological, psychological, and sociocultural.

Biological Risk Factors. As with many other disorders, people can inherit a disposition toward cancer (Santarius et al., 2010). So-called carcinogenic genes remove the brakes from cell division, allowing cells to multiply wildly. Or they may allow mutations to accumulate unchecked.

Behavior patterns that heighten the risk for cancer include smoking, having more than a drink or two a day (especially for women), eating animal fats, and sunbathing (which may cause skin cancer due to exposure to ultraviolet light).

Psychological Risk Factors. Researchers have uncovered possible links between stress and cancer (Antoni & Lutgendorf, 2007; Gross et al., 2010). Stress may lower levels of cortisol and impair the ability of the immune system to destroy cancer cells (Yehuda, 2003). Prolonged depression may heighten the risk of some kinds of cancer by depressing the functioning of the immune system (Gross et al., 2010).

Experimental research that could not be conducted with humans has been carried out using rats and other animals. In one type of study, animals are injected with cancerous cells or with viruses that cause cancer and are then exposed to various conditions. In this way, researchers can determine which conditions influence the likelihood that the animals' immune systems will be able to fend off the disease. Such experiments suggest that once cancer has developed, stress can influence its course. In a classic study, for example, rats were implanted with small numbers of cancer cells so that their own immune systems would have a chance to combat them (Visintainer et al., 1982). Some of the rats were then exposed to inescapable shocks. Others were exposed to escapable shocks or to no shock. The rats that were exposed to the most stressful condition—the inescapable shock—were half as likely as the other rats to reject the cancer and twice as likely to die from it.

Sociocultural Risk Factors Truth or Fiction Revisited: African Americans are also more likely than European Americans to contract most forms of cancer (National Center for Health Statistics, 2009). Once they contract cancer, African Americans are more likely than European Americans to die from it. The results for African Americans are connected with lower socioeconomic status and relative lack of access to health care (Orsi et al., 2010).

Also consider cultural differences in health. Death rates from cancer are higher in such nations as the Netherlands, Denmark, England, Canada, and—yes—the United States, where average rates of daily fat intake are high (Bagchi & Preuss, 2007). Death rates from cancer are lower in such nations as Thailand, the Philippines, and Japan, where fat intake is lower. Thailand, the Philippines, and Japan are Asian nations, but do not assume that the difference is racial! The diets of Japanese Americans are similar in fat content to those of other Americans—and so are their rates of death from cancer.

PSYCHOLOGICAL FACTORS IN THE TREATMENT OF CANCER People with cancer not only must cope with the biological aspects of their illnesses. They may also face psychological problems such as feelings of anxiety and depression about treatment methods and the eventual outcome, changes in body image after the removal of a breast or testicle, feelings of vulnerability, and family problems (Reich et al., 2008). Some families actually criticize cancer patients for feeling sorry for themselves or not fighting the disease hard enough (Andersen et al., 1994, 2008). Psychological stress due to cancer can weaken the immune system, setting the stage for other health problems, such as respiratory tract infections (Andersen, 2002).

There are also psychological treatments for the nausea that often accompanies chemotherapy. People undergoing chemotherapy who obtain relaxation training and guided imagery techniques experience less nausea and vomiting (Richardson et al., 2006). Distraction helps (L. L. Cohen, 2002). Studies with children find that playing video games reduces the discomfort of chemotherapy (Windich-Biermeier et al., 2007). As they play, the children focus on battling computer-generated enemies rather than on the side effects of the drugs.

Of course, cancer is a medical disorder. However, health psychologists have improved the methods used to treat people with cancer. For example, a crisis like cancer can lead people to feel that life has spun out of control (Brooks, 2008). Since control is a factor in psychological hardiness, feelings of loss of control can heighten stress and impair the immune system. Health psychology

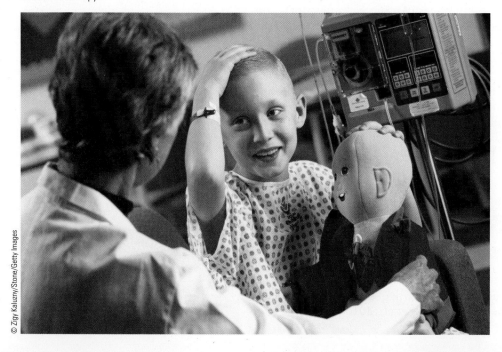

How Have Health Psychologists Helped This Youngster Cope with Cancer? Cancer is a medical disorder, but psychologists have contributed to the treatment of people with cancer. For example, psychologists help people with cancer remain in charge of their lives, combat feelings of hopelessness, manage stress, and cope with the side effects of chemotherapy.

© Zigy Kaluzny/Stone/Getty Images

Cancer is a frightening disease, and in many cases, there may be little that can be done about its eventual outcome. However, we are not helpless in the face of cancer. We can

- Limit exposure to behavioral risk factors for cancer.
- Modify diet by reducing intake of fats and increasing intake of fruits and vegetables. **Truth or Fiction Revisited:** Tomatoes (especially cooked tomatoes, such as we find in tomato sauce and ketchup—yes, ketchup!), broccoli, cauliflower, and cab-

bage appear especially helpful (Herr & Büchler, 2010; Seren et al., 2008). (Yes, Grandma was right about veggies.)
- Exercise regularly. (Exercise not only helps us cope with stress; it also lowers the risk of developing CHD and cancer. Just do it.)
- Have regular medical checkups so that cancer will be detected early. Cancer is most treatable in the early stages.
- Regulate exposure to stress.

therefore stresses the value of encouraging people with cancer to remain in charge of their lives (Brooks, 2008). Encouraging physicians to listen more attentively, convey warmth, and provide feedback (as opposed to saying nothing) can also help (Andersen, 2002).

Psychologists are teaching coping skills to people with cancer to relieve psychological distress as well as pain. One study of 235 women with metastatic breast cancer found that group therapy that provided social support and helped them express their feelings enhanced their moods and decreased their pain (Goodwin et al., 2001). Unfortunately, the therapy did not affect their survival rate. But psychological methods such as relaxation training, meditation, biofeedback training, and exercise can all help patients cope with their disorders (Andersen, 2002).

Yet another psychological application is helping people undergoing chemotherapy keep up their strength by eating. The problem is that chemotherapy often causes nausea. Nausea then becomes associated with foods eaten during the day of the chemotherapy, causing taste aversions (Ward, 2007). So people with cancer, who may already be losing weight because of their illness, may find that taste aversions aggravate the problems caused by lack of appetite. To combat these conditions, patients can eat unusual foods prior to chemotherapy. If taste aversions develop, they will not be associated with the patient's normal diet.

LearningConnections • PSYCHOLOGY AND HEALTH

ACTIVE REVIEW (13) Psychological states such as anxiety and depression impair the functioning of the _____ system, rendering us more vulnerable to health problems. (14) The _____ headache has a sudden onset and is identified by throbbing pain on one side of the head. (15) Risk factors for coronary heart disease include family history, obesity, hypertension, high levels of serum _____, heavy drinking, smoking, hostility, Type A behavior, and job strain. (16) Genetic factors (play or do not play?) a role in cancer.

REFLECT AND RELATE Does coronary heart disease or cancer run in your family? If so, what can you do about it?

CRITICAL THINKING What are the roles of psychologists in understanding and treating health problems such as headaches, coronary disorders, and cancer?

 Go to Psychology CourseMate at **www.cengagebrain.com** for an interactive version of these questions.

Stress: What It Is, Where It Comes From

1. What is stress?
Stress is the demand made on an organism to adapt, cope, or adjust. Some stress is desirable to keep us alert and occupied, but too much stress can tax our capacities to adjust and impair our health.

2. What is health psychology?
Health psychology studies the relationships between psychological factors and the prevention and treatment of physical health problems.

3. What are daily hassles?
Daily hassles are regularly occurring experiences that threaten or harm our well-being.

4. How can too much of a good thing make you ill?
Too many positive life changes can affect one's health because life changes require adjustment, whether they are positive or negative.

5. What is conflict?
Conflict is the stressful feeling of being pulled in two or more directions by opposing motives. There are four kinds of conflict: approach–approach, avoidance–avoidance, approach–avoidance, and multiple approach–avoidance.

6. How do irrational beliefs create or compound stress?
Albert Ellis showed that negative activating events (A) can have even more aversive consequences (C) when irrational beliefs (B) compound their effects. People often catastrophize negative events.

7. What is Type A behavior?
Type A behavior is connected with hostility, competitiveness, and impatience. Type B people relax more readily.

Psychological Moderators of Stress

8. How do our self-efficacy expectations affect our ability to withstand stress?
Self-efficacy expectations encourage us to persist in difficult tasks and to endure discomfort.

9. What characteristics are connected with psychological hardiness?
Kobasa and her colleagues found that psychological hardiness among business executives is characterized by commitment, challenge, and control.

10. Is there any evidence that "A merry heart doeth good like a medicine"?
Yes. Research evidence shows that humor can moderate the effects of stress.

11. How do predictability and control help us cope with stress?
Predictability allows us to brace ourselves for the inevitable and, in many cases, plan ways of coping with it. Control allows us to feel that we are not at the mercy of fate.

12. Is there evidence that social support helps people cope with stress?
Social support has been shown to help people resist infectious diseases such as colds. It also helps people cope with the stress of cancer and other health problems.

Stress and the Body: The War Within

13. What is the general adaptation syndrome?
The GAS is a cluster of bodily changes triggered by stressors. It consists of three stages: an alarm reaction, a resistance stage, and an exhaustion stage. Corticosteroids help resist stress by fighting inflammation and allergic reactions. Adrenaline arouses the body by activating the sympathetic nervous system, which is highly active during the alarm and resistance stages of the GAS.

14. How does the immune system work?
Leukocytes (white blood cells) engulf and kill pathogens, worn-out body cells, and cancerous cells. The immune system "remembers" how to battle antigens by maintaining their antibodies in the bloodstream.

15. How does stress affect the functioning of the immune system?
Stress depresses the functioning of the immune system by stimulating the release of corticosteroids. Steroids counter inflammation and interfere with the formation of antibodies.

Psychology and Health

16. What is the biopsychosocial approach to health?
The biopsychosocial view recognizes that many factors, including biological, psychological, sociocultural, and environmental factors, affect our health.

17. How has psychology contributed to the understanding and treatment of headaches?
Psychologists participate in research concerning the origins of headaches, including stress and tension. Psychologists help people alleviate headaches by showing them how to reduce tension.

18. What are the major risk factors for coronary heart disease?
The major risk factors for coronary heart disease include family history; physiological conditions such as hypertension and high levels of serum cholesterol; behavior patterns such as heavy drinking, smoking, eating fatty foods, and Type A behavior; job strain; chronic tension and fatigue; and physical inactivity.

19. What are the major risk factors for cancer?
The major risk factors for cancer include family history, smoking, excessive drinking, eating animal fats, sunbathing, and stress.

KEY TERMS

Alarm reaction (p. 382)
Antibodies (p. 385)
Antigen (p. 385)
Approach–approach conflict
  (p. 374)
Approach–avoidance conflict (p. 374)
Avoidance–avoidance conflict
  (p. 374)
Catastrophize (p. 376)
Conflict (p. 374)
Daily hassles (p. 371)
Eustress (p. 370)
Exhaustion stage (p. 385)

Externals (p. 381)
Fight-or-flight reaction (p. 382)
General adaptation syndrome (GAS)
  (p. 382)
Health psychology (p. 370)
Hypertension (p. 391)
Immune system (p. 385)
Inflammation (p. 385)
Internals (p. 381)
Leukocytes (p. 385)
Locus of control (p. 379)
Migraine headaches (p. 389)

Multiple approach–avoidance conflict
  (p. 375)
Psychological hardiness (p. 379)
Psychoneuroimmunology (p. 385)
Resistance stage (p. 384)
Self-efficacy expectations (p. 378)
Serum cholesterol (p. 391)
Stress (p. 370)
Stressor (p. 370)
Type A behavior (p. 377)
Uplifts (p. 371)

ACTIVE LEARNING RESOURCES

Log in to **www.cengagebrain.com** to access the resources your instructor requires. For this book, you can access:

 CourseMate brings course concepts to life with interactive learning, study, and exam preparation tools that support the printed textbook. A textbook-specific website, Psychology CourseMate includes an integrated interactive eBook and other interactive learning tools including quizzes, flashcards, videos, and more.

CENGAGENOW Need help studying? This site is your one-stop study shop. Take a Pre-Test and CengageNOW will generate a Personalized Study Plan based on your test results. The Study Plan will identify the topics you need to review and direct you to online resources to help you master those topics. You can then take a Post-Test to determine the concepts you have mastered and what you still need to work on.

12 Psychological Disorders

© Katrina Wittkamp/Taxi/Getty Images

MAJOR TOPICS

What Are Psychological
   Disorders? *399*
Anxiety Disorders: Real-Life
   "Fear Factors" *404*
Dissociative Disorders: Splitting
   Consciousness *410*
Somatoform Disorders: When
   the Body Expresses Stress *411*
Mood Disorders: Up, Down, and
   Around *412*
Schizophrenia: When Thinking Runs
   Astray *418*
Personality Disorders: Making
   Oneself or Others Miserable *425*

FEATURES

Self-Assessment: Are You Depressed? *413*
A Closer Look: The Case of Women and Depression *414*
Life Connections: Preventing Suicide *418*
A Closer Look: When the "Fatty Acid" Places Soda Off Limits *420*
Video Connections: Schizophrenia *421*
A Closer Look: Should We Ban the Insanity Plea? *424*
Concept Review 12.1: Psychological Disorders *428*

T F A man shot the president of the United States in front of millions of television witnesses, yet he was found not guilty by a court of law.

page 399

T F It is abnormal to feel anxious.

page 400

T F In the Middle Ages, innocent people were drowned to prove that they were not possessed by the Devil.

page 401

T F Some people have more than one identity, and each one may have different allergies and eyeglass prescriptions.

page 410

T F Feeling "up" is not always a good thing.

page 413

T F People who threaten to commit suicide are only seeking attention.

page 416

T F People with schizophrenia may see and hear things that are not really there.

page 419

T F Some people can kill or maim others with no feelings of guilt at all.

page 426

Are these items truth or fiction? We will be revisiting them throughout the chapter.

D

uring one long fall semester, the Ohio State campus lived in terror. Four college women were abducted, forced to cash checks or obtain money from automatic teller machines, and then raped. A mysterious phone call led to the arrest of a 23-year-old drifter—let's call him "William"—who had been dismissed from the Navy.

William was not the boy next door.

Psychologists and psychiatrists who interviewed William concluded that 10 personalities—8 male and 2 female—resided within him (Scott, 1994). His personality had been "fractured" by an abusive childhood. His several personalities displayed distinct facial expressions, speech patterns, and memories. They even performed differently on psychological tests.

Arthur, the most rational personality, spoke with a British accent. Danny and Christopher were quiet adolescents. Christine was a 3-year-old girl. Tommy, a 16-year-old, had enlisted in the Navy. Allen was 18 and smoked. Adelena, a 19-year-old lesbian personality, had committed the rapes. Who had made the mysterious phone call? Probably David, 9, an anxious child.

The defense claimed that William's behavior was caused by a psychological disorder termed *dissociative identity disorder* (previously referred to as *multiple personality disorder*). Several distinct identities or personalities dwelled within him. Some of them were aware of the others. Some believed that they were unique. Billy, the core identity, had learned to sleep as a child to avoid his father's abuse. A psychiatrist asserted that Billy had also been "asleep," or in a "psychological coma," during the abductions. Billy, it was argued, should therefore be found not guilty by reason of **insanity**.

William was found not guilty. He was committed to a psychiatric institution and released 6 years later.

Truth or Fiction Revisited: In 1982, John Hinckley was found not guilty of an assassination attempt on President Reagan's life, even though the shooting was witnessed on television by millions. Expert witnesses testified that he should be diagnosed with *schizophrenia*. Hinckley, too, was committed to a psychiatric institution.

William and Hinckley were diagnosed with psychological disorders. **Question 1: What are psychological disorders?**

● WHAT ARE PSYCHOLOGICAL DISORDERS?

Psychology is the study of behavior and mental processes. **Psychological disorders** are behaviors or mental processes—like those of William and John Hinckley—that are connected with various kinds of distress or significant impairment in functioning. However, they are not predictable responses to specific events.

Radioactive Cats © 1980 Sandy Skoglund

Hallucinations Hallucinations are a feature of schizophrenia. They are perceptions that occur in the absence of external stimulation, as in "hearing voices" or "seeing things." Hallucinations cannot be distinguished from real perceptions. Are the cats in this Sandy-Skoglund photograph real or hallucinatory?

Insanity A legal term descriptive of a person judged to be incapable of recognizing right from wrong or of conforming his or her behavior to the law.

Psychological disorders Patterns of behavior or mental processes that are connected with emotional distress or significant impairment in functioning.

Hallucination A perception that occurs in the absence of sensory stimulation and is confused with reality.

Ideas of persecution Erroneous beliefs that one is being victimized or persecuted.

Truth or Fiction Revisited: Some psychological disorders are characterized by anxiety, but many people are anxious now and then without being considered disordered. It might seem rather strange if one were not at least a little bit nervous before an important date or on the eve of a midterm exam. When, then, are feelings like anxiety deemed to be abnormal or signs of a psychological disorder? For one thing, anxiety may suggest a disorder when it is not appropriate to the situation. It is inappropriate to be anxious when entering an elevator or looking out a fourth-story window. The magnitude of the problem may also suggest disorder. Some anxiety is usual before a job interview. However, feeling that your heart is pounding so intensely that it might leap out of your chest—and then avoiding the interview—are not usual.

Behavior or mental processes suggest psychological disorders when they meet some combination of the following criteria:

1. *They are unusual:* Rarity, or statistical deviance, is one standard, though it may not be sufficient for behavior or mental processes to be labeled abnormal. After all, only a few people obtain a score of 700 or more on the verbal part of the SAT, but that achievement is not considered disordered. Only a few "see things" or "hear things" as Hinckley did, and those behaviors are deemed disordered because of their bizarre quality. We must also consider the situation. Although many of us feel "panicked" when we realize that a term paper or report is due the next day, most of us do not have panic attacks "out of the blue." Unpredictable panic attacks thus are suggestive of psychological disorder.

2. *They suggest faulty perception or interpretation of reality:* Our society considers it normal to be inspired by religious beliefs but abnormal to believe that God is literally speaking to you. "Hearing voices" and "seeing things" are considered **hallucinations**. Similarly, **ideas of persecution**, such as believing that the Mafia or the FBI is "out to get you," are considered signs of disorder. (Unless, of course, they *are* out to get you.) Hinckley testified that he believed he would be impressing a popular young actress, Jodie Foster, by killing the president—an idea that was delusional.

3. *They suggest severe personal distress:* Anxiety, exaggerated fears, and other psychological states cause personal distress, and severe personal distress may be considered abnormal. William and Hinckley were in distress—although, of course, they victimized other people.

4. *They are self-defeating:* Behavior or mental processes that cause misery rather than happiness and fulfillment may suggest psychological disorder. Those who have serious anxiety or depressive disorders suffer a great deal. We might also note that chronic drinking and cigarette smoking may be deemed abnormal because they threaten one's health and, in the case of drinking, one's social and vocational life.

5. *They are dangerous:* Behavior or mental processes that are hazardous to the self or others may be considered suggestive of psychological disorders. People who threaten or attempt suicide may be considered abnormal, as may people who threaten or attack others, like William and Hinckley.

6. *The individual's behavior is socially unacceptable:* We must consider the cultural context of a behavior pattern in judging whether it is normal (Lopez & Guarnaccia, 2000). In the United States, it is deemed normal to be aggressive in sports and in combat; in fact, aggression in these situations is applauded. In other situations, warmth and tenderness are valued. Many people in the United States admire women who are self-assertive, yet Latino and Latina American, Asian American, and "traditional" European American groups may see outspoken women as being disrespectful and having personality problems.

Perspectives on Psychological Disorders

Question 2: How have people viewed psychological disorders? If the standards for defining psychological disorders are complex and influenced by one's cultural background, so too are the explanations of their origins.

THE DEMONOLOGICAL MODEL If William and John Hinckley had lived in the 17th and 18th centuries, they might have been hanged as witches. At that time, most people assumed that the strange behaviors that were associated with psychological disorders were caused by possession by the Devil. Possession could stem from retribution, in which God caused the Devil to possess a person's soul as punishment for committing certain kinds of sins. Possession was also believed to result from deals with the Devil, in which people traded their souls for earthly gains. So-called witches were held responsible for unfortunate events ranging from a neighbor's infertility to a poor harvest. In Europe, as many as 500,000 accused witches were killed during the 17th and 18th centuries (Hergenhahn, 2009). A score of people were also executed in Salem, Massachusetts, in the late 1600s for allegedly practicing the arts of Satan.

Exorcism This medieval woodcut represents the practice of exorcism, in which a demon is expelled from a person who has been "possessed."

Truth or Fiction Revisited: A document authorized by Pope Innocent VIII, *The Hammer of Witches,* proposed "diagnostic" tests to identify those who were possessed. The water-float test was based on the principle that pure metals sink to the bottom during smelting. Impurities float to the surface. Suspects were thus placed in deep water. Those who sank to the bottom and drowned were judged to be pure. Those who managed to keep their heads above water were assumed to be "impure" and in league with the Devil. Then they were in real trouble. This ordeal is the origin of the phrase "damned if you do, and damned if you don't."

In fact, throughout all of recorded human history, people have attributed unusual behavior and psychological disorders to demons. The ancient Greeks believed that the gods punished humans by causing confusion and madness. An exception was the physician Hippocrates, who made the radical suggestion that psychological disorders are caused by an abnormality of the brain. The notion that biology could affect thoughts, feelings, and behavior was to lie dormant for about 2,000 years.

Few people in the United States today would argue that unusual or unacceptable behavior is caused by demons. Still, we continue to use "demonic" language. How many times have you heard the expressions "Something got into me" and "The Devil made me do it"?

THE MEDICAL MODEL The demonological model led to brutal "treatments"—from drilling holes in the skull to permit evil spirits to escape, as in prehistoric times, to burning at the stake and hanging, as practiced during the Middle Ages. In more modern times, as during the Age of Reason, many health professionals, such as Philippe Pinel (1745–1826) in France, began to view psychological disorders as diseases of the mind, and they encouraged humane treatment. During the 1800s, it was discovered that the late stages of the sexually transmitted infection syphilis can distort the workings of the mind as well as destroy the body. Since that time, researchers have assumed that other physical abnormalities can have psychological effects, and the search has been on to find the causes of other psychological disorders.

The so-called medical model assumes that illnesses have physical or biological causes that can be identified and that people afflicted by them are to be cured through treatment or therapy. Note the widespread use of medical terminology in the study and treatment of psychological disorders: People without psychological disorders are said to be in good mental *health.* The disorders themselves are termed mental *illnesses* or psycho-*pathology.* Disorders are *diagnosed* according to the *symptoms* shown by mental *patients.* Most patients are *outpatients;* that is, they remain out of the hospital and are seen as necessary; some are *admitted* to mental *hospitals,* where they become *inpatients.* Patients may be *prescribed* medication and psycho*therapy.*

401

The search for biological and physical causes of some psychological disorders has borne much fruit. Throughout the chapter, we will see they may be caused, at least in part, by abnormalities in the brain and in the autonomic and endocrine systems. Yet psychological factors such as conditioning and traumatic stress may also make their contributions.

CONTEMPORARY PSYCHOLOGICAL MODELS Many contemporary psychologists have joined in the search for biological and physical contributors to psychological disorders. However, they tend to invoke the *diathesis–stress model* or the *biopsychosocial model* rather than the medical model in explaining psychological disorders.

The diathesis–stress model assumes that there may be biological differences between individuals—diatheses—that explain why some people develop certain psychological disorders under stress, whereas others do not (Belsky & Pluess, 2009; Eberhart & Hammen, 2010). In the case of schizophrenia, as we will see, the diathesis (or biological difference) would appear to be a genetic vulnerability to schizophrenia.

The biopsychosocial model (or *interactionist model*) explains psychological disorders in terms of a combination of (a) biological vulnerabilities; (b) psychological factors such as conditioning, exposure to stress, and self-defeating thoughts about stressors; and (c) sociocultural factors such as family relationships, unemployment, and cultural beliefs and expectations (Gilbert, 2009; Levine & Schmelkin, 2006) (see Figure 12.1 ■). For example, schizophrenia and depression are found around the world, which appears to support other evidence for biological contributors to these disorders. Yet psychological factors such as family stresses and losses can also play roles in their development.

Some disorders, on the other hand, appear to be **culture-bound**, reflecting local customs and traditions:

Figure 12.1 ■ The Biopsychosocial Model

- Australian Aborigines believe they can communicate with the spirits of their ancestors and that people, especially close relatives, share their dreams (Clarke, 2009). These beliefs are considered normal within Aboriginal culture, but in ours, they would likely be deemed delusions.

- Being reared in the Dominican Republic and some other Caribbean cultures is connected with *susto,* which is characterized by agitation and a fear of voodoo (black magic) (Quinlan, 2010).

- Many traditional Native Americans distinguish between illnesses that are believed to arise from outside influences, called "white man's sicknesses," such as alcoholism and drug addiction, and those that emanate from a lack of harmony with traditional tribal life and thought, which are called "Indian sicknesses" (D. R. M. Beck, 2010).

- Japanese and Japanese Americans are prone to developing *taijin-kyofusho,* which is characterized by extreme anxiety over other people's perceptions of one's appearance and thus heightens the cultural tendency to avoid direct eye contact (Lim, 2009). In the dominant U.S. culture, eye contact—without glaring!—shows interest and normal self-assurance.

Therefore, according to the biopsychosocial model, biological, psychological, and sociocultural factors may all come into play in the development of psychological disorders. But again, different factors take on different importance among different people. For example, if your siblings, parents, grandparents, and cousins never had a brush with schizophrenia, you are also unlikely to have one regardless of how much stress you experience. Others, whose families are deeply afflicted, may develop schizophrenia despite the best of circumstances. Many others are in between, with a slight to moderate genetic vulnerability. They may incur intermittent episodes of schizophrenia, especially under stress, but they tend to be readily treated, if not "cured." As in the case of schizophrenia, psychologists today frequently speak of the interaction between the biological *nature* of the individual and his or her life experiences, or *nurture*.

Diathesis–stress model The view that psychological disorders can be explained in terms of an underlying vulnerability (diathesis) and problems that create pressure or tension (stress).

Biopsychosocial model The view that psychological disorders can be explained by a combination of (a) possible biological vulnerabilities; (b) psychological factors such as stress and self-defeating thoughts; and (c) sociocultural factors such as family relationships and cultural beliefs and expectations.

Culture-bound Determined by the experiences of being reared within a certain cultural setting.

Classifying Psychological Disorders

Classification is at the heart of science. Without classifying psychological disorders, investigators would not be able to communicate with each other, and scientific progress in the field would come to a halt. The most widely used classification for psychological disorders is the *Diagnostic and Statistical Manual (DSM)* of the American Psychiatric Association (2000). **Question 3: How are psychological disorders grouped or classified?**

The *DSM* provides information about a person's overall functioning as well as a diagnosis. People may receive diagnoses for clinical syndromes, personality disorders, or both. The *DSM* also includes information about people's medical conditions and psychosocial and environmental problems, as well as a "global assessment" of functioning. Medical conditions include health problems that may affect people's response to psychotherapy or medicines. Psychosocial and environmental problems include difficulties that may affect the diagnosis, treatment, or outcome of a psychological disorder. The global assessment of functioning allows the clinician to compare the client's current level of functioning with her or his highest previous level of functioning to help set goals for restoring functioning.

Although the *DSM* is widely used, researchers have some concerns about it. Two of them involve the **reliability** and **validity** of the diagnostic standards. The *DSM* might be considered *reliable* if different interviewers or raters make the same diagnosis when they evaluate the same people. The *DSM* might be considered *valid* if the diagnoses described in the manual correspond to clusters of behaviors observed in the real world. A specific type of validity—**predictive validity**—means that if a diagnosis is valid, then we should be able to predict what will happen to the person over time (that is, the *course* of the disorder) and what type of treatment may be of help.

DSM standards for assessing psychological disorders are strict—so strict that some actual cases of disorders might be left out. On the other hand, the *DSM* has also been accused of "pathologizing" some behavior patterns that may be of concern but are probably not abnormal. For example, perhaps some children, especially boys, who are bored silly by school and normally energetic (have their "motors running") might be diagnosed with attention-deficit/hyperactivity disorder. The diagnosis of "binge eating disorder" is controversial because it describes people (too many of us!) who have episodes of overeating and then fail to take off the extra pounds through more regular eating patterns (Striegel-Moore & Franco, 2008). Moreover, the reliability and validity of various diagnoses differ (Hilsenroth et al., 2004; S. W. Smith et al., 2009). For example, the diagnosis of schizophrenia is more reliable and valid than the diagnosis of borderline personality disorder (Johansen et al., 2004). All in all, when evaluating the *DSM,* we should consider whether it improves clinical decision making and whether it enhances the clinical outcome for people with psychological disorders. The *DSM* is about to enter another edition.

Prevalence of Psychological Disorders

Question 4: How common are psychological disorders? At first glance, psychological disorders might seem to affect only a few of us. Relatively few people are admitted to psychiatric hospitals. Most people will never seek the help of a psychologist or psychiatrist. Many of us have "eccentric" relatives or friends, but most of them are not considered "crazy." But psychological disorders actually affect us all in one way or another.

About half of us will meet the criteria for a *DSM* disorder at some time or another in our lives, with the disorder most often beginning in childhood or adolescence (Kessler et al., 2005a) (see Table 12.1 ■). Slightly more than a fourth of us will experience a psychological disorder in any given year (Kessler et al., 2005b; see Table 12.1). But if we include the problems of family members, friends, and coworkers, add in those who foot the bill in health insurance and taxes, and factor in increased costs due to lost productivity, then perhaps everyone is affected in one way or another.

Let's now consider the kinds of psychological disorders. Some of them, like anxiety disorders, are common. Others, like dissociative identity disorder (the disorder with which William was diagnosed), are rare.

Reliability The consistency of a method of assessment, such as a psychological test or (in this case) a manual describing the symptoms of psychological disorders.

Validity The extent to which a method of assessment, such as a psychological test or (in this case) a manual describing the symptoms of psychological disorders, measures the traits or clusters of behavior it is supposed to assess.

Predictive validity The extent to which a diagnosis permits one to predict the course of a disorder and the type of treatment that may be of help.

TABLE 12.1 ■ Past-Year and Lifetime Prevalences of Psychological Disorders

	Anxiety Disorders	Mood Disorders	Substance Use Disorders	Any Disorder
Prevalence during past year	18.1%	9.5%	3.8%	26.2%
Lifetime prevalence	28.8%	20.8%	14.6%	46.4%
Median age of onset	11 years	30 years	20 years	14 years

Sources: Kessler et al., 2005a; Kessler et al., 2005b.
The data in this table are based on a nationally representative sample of 9,282 English-speaking U.S. residents aged 18 and above. Respondents could report symptoms of more than one type of disorder. For example, anxiety and mood disorders are often "comorbid"—that is, occur together. Anxiety and mood disorders are discussed in this chapter. Substance abuse is discussed in Chapter 4.

LearningConnections ● WHAT ARE PSYCHOLOGICAL DISORDERS?

ACTIVE REVIEW (1) In the Middle Ages, Europeans largely explained psychological disorders in terms of _____ by the Devil. (2) Terms such as *psychopathology* and *mental patient* suggest the influences of the _____ model. (3) Behavior is labeled abnormal when it is unusual, is socially unacceptable, involves faulty _____ of reality (as with hallucinations), or is dangerous, self-defeating, or distressing. (4) The _____ perspective explains psychological disorders in terms of biological, psychological, and sociocultural factors.

REFLECT AND RELATE Have you ever heard anyone say, "Something got into me" or "The Devil made me do it"? What were the circumstances? Was the person trying to evade responsibility for wrongdoing?

CRITICAL THINKING When does a psychological problem become a "psychological disorder"? Is the border clearly defined?

Go to Psychology CourseMate at **www.cengagebrain.com** for an interactive version of these questions.

ANXIETY DISORDERS: REAL-LIFE "FEAR FACTORS"

Imagine allowing spiders to crawl all over your body or clinging to a beam swinging hundreds of feet above the ground. These are the types of experiences to which many people were exposed on the "reality TV" show *Fear Factor*. What made the show so riveting to some viewers? Possibly the fact that many of us, perhaps most of us, could not imagine participating in such activities for nearly any amount of fame or fortune. Discomfort with spiders and extreme heights is common enough, and also sensible. However, there are extreme, irrational fears of objects and situations, such as hypodermic needles and public speaking, that are examples of *phobias*—a type of anxiety disorder.

Anxiety disorders have psychological and physical symptoms. The psychological symptoms include worrying, fear of the worst happening, fear of losing control, nervousness, and inability to relax. The physical symptoms reflect arousal—or "overarousal"—of the sympathetic branch of the autonomic nervous system: trembling, sweating, a pounding or racing heart, elevated blood pressure (a flushed face), and faintness. Anxiety is an appropriate response to a real threat, but it can be abnormal when it is excessive, when it comes out of nowhere (that is, when events do not seem to warrant it), and when it prevents us from doing important things such as going for medical exams or working with other people. Some anxiety disorders even prevent people from leaving home. **Question 5: What kinds of anxiety disorders are there?**

Anxiety disorders Disorders characterized by excessive worrying, fear of losing control, nervousness, and inability to relax.

Types of Anxiety Disorders

The anxiety disorders include *phobic disorders*, *panic disorder*, *generalized anxiety*, *obsessive–compulsive disorder*, and *stress disorders*.

This will sound crazy, but I wouldn't get married because I couldn't stand the idea of getting the blood test. [Blood tests for syphilis were required at the time.] [My doctor] said that getting tested for marriage was likely to be one of my small life problems. He told me about minor medical problems that could arise and make it necessary for blood to be drawn, or to have an IV in my arm, so his message was I should try to come to grips with my fear. I nearly fainted while he was talking about these things, so he gave it up.

The story has half a "happy" ending. We finally got married in [a state] where we found out they no longer insisted on blood tests. But if I…need a blood test for some other reason, even if it's life-threatening, I really don't know what I'll do.

Alan, from the author's files

There are several types of phobic disorders, including *specific phobias, social phobia,* and *agoraphobia.* Some of them, such as social phobia, can be highly detrimental to one's quality of life (Ohayon & Schatzberg, 2010). **Specific phobias** are excessive, irrational fears of specific objects or situations, such as spiders, snakes, or heights. One specific phobia is fear of elevators. Some people will not enter elevators despite the hardships they incur as a result (such as walking up six flights of steps). Yes, the cable *could* break. The ventilation *could* fail. One *could* be stuck in midair waiting for repairs. These problems are uncommon, however, and it does not make sense for most people to walk up and down several flights of stairs to elude them.

Similarly, some people, like Alan, with a specific phobia for hypodermic needles, will not have injections, even to treat profound illness. Injections can be painful, but most people with a phobia for needles would gladly suffer an even more painful pinch if it would help them fight illness. Alan said,

People have me wrong, you know. They think I'm scared of the pain. I don't like pain—I'm not a masochist—but pain has nothing to do with it. You could pinch my arm till I turned black and blue and I'd tolerate it. I wouldn't like it, but I wouldn't start shaking and sweating and faint on you. But even if I didn't feel the needle at all—just the knowledge that it was in me is what I couldn't take.

Other specific phobias include **claustrophobia** (fear of tight or enclosed places), **acrophobia** (fear of heights), and fear of mice, snakes, and other creepy-crawlies. (Fear of spiders is technically called *arachnophobia.*) Fears of animals and imaginary creatures are common among children and therefore not considered abnormal.

Social phobias are persistent fears of scrutiny by others or of doing something that will be humiliating or embarrassing. Excessive fear of public speaking is a common social phobia.

Agoraphobia may affect 3% to 4% of adults (Kessler et al., 2005). Agoraphobia is derived from the Greek words meaning "fear of the marketplace," or fear of being out in open, busy areas. Some people who receive this diagnosis refuse to venture out of their homes, especially alone. They find it difficult to hold a job or to maintain an ordinary social life.

A Hypodermic Syringe Phobias are excessive irrational fears that can interfere with a person's life. A phobia for needles can prevent a person from obtaining needed medical care.

PANIC DISORDER

It happened while I was sitting in the car at a traffic light. I felt my heart beating furiously fast, like it was just going to explode. It just happened, for no reason. I started breathing really fast but couldn't get enough air. It was like I was suffocating and the car was closing in around me. I felt like I was going to die right then and there. I was trembling and sweating heavily. I thought I was having a heart attack. I felt this incredible urge to escape, to just get out of the car and get away.

Michael, in Nevid et al., 2011

Panic disorder is an abrupt anxiety attack that is apparently unrelated to specific objects or situations. People with panic disorder experience strong cardiac-related sensations: shortness of breath, heavy sweating, tremors, and pounding of the heart (Blechert et al., 2010). Many think they are having a heart attack. Levels of cortisol (a stress hormone) in the saliva are elevated during attacks (Bandelow et al., 2000). Many fear suffocation. People

Specific phobia Persistent fear of a specific object or situation.

Claustrophobia Fear of tight, small places.

Acrophobia Fear of high places.

Social phobia An irrational, excessive fear of public scrutiny.

Agoraphobia Fear of open, crowded places.

Panic disorder The recurrent experiencing of attacks of extreme anxiety in the absence of external stimuli that usually elicit anxiety.

with the disorder may also experience choking sensations, nausea, numbness or tingling, flushes or chills, and fear of going crazy or losing control. Panic attacks may last minutes or hours. Afterward, the person usually feels drained.

Many people panic now and then. The diagnosis of panic disorder is reserved for those who undergo multiple attacks or live in fear of attacks. Panic attacks seem to come from nowhere. Thus, some people who have had them stay home for fear of having an attack in public. They are diagnosed as having *panic disorder with agoraphobia* (Schmidt et al., 2010).

People with panic disorder live in fear of fear, a state known more technically as *anxiety sensitivity (AS)* (Naragon-Gainey, 2010). Anxiety sensitivity intensifies fear reactions to cues of bodily arousal. People with high AS fear that their emotions and the discomfort in their bodies will get out of hand, leading to disastrous consequences such as a heart attack. They tend to interpret the physical symptoms of anxiety, such as a racing heart or shortness of breath, as signs of impending doom, which in turn intensifies their physical symptoms and may bring on a full-blown panic attack.

Just as people in panic may fear they are having heart attacks, people with heart problems may sometimes misinterpret their symptoms as anxiety. For this reason, psychologists typically recommend that people experiencing the symptoms of panic disorder have a medical checkup.

GENERALIZED ANXIETY DISORDER

Generalized anxiety disorder Feelings of dread and foreboding and sympathetic arousal of at least 6 months' duration.

Obsessive–compulsive disorder (OCD) An anxiety disorder defined by recurrent, anxiety-provoking thoughts or images that seem irrational and beyond control (obsessions) and seemingly irresistible urges to engage in thoughts or behaviors that tend to reduce the anxiety (compulsions).

Earl was a 52-year-old supervisor at an automobile plant. His hands trembled as he spoke. His cheeks were pale. He was successful in his work, and his marriage was in "reasonably good shape." The mortgage on the house was not a burden, but "I don't know what it is—I think about money all the time." His three children were doing well, but "with everything going on these days, I'm up for hours worrying about them."

Earl shook his head. "I swear I'll find myself worrying when there's nothing in my head. It's like I'm worrying first and then there's something in my head to worry about. Then the shakes come, and I'm worrying about worrying."

From the author's files

Earl was diagnosed with generalized anxiety disorder. The central symptom of **generalized anxiety disorder** is persistent anxiety. As with panic disorder, the anxiety cannot be attributed to a phobic object, situation, or activity. Rather, it seems to be free floating. The core of the disorder appears to be pervasive worrying about numerous stressors (Behar et al., 2009). Symptoms include motor tension (shakiness, inability to relax, furrowed brow, fidgeting); autonomic overarousal (sweating, dry mouth, racing heart, light-headedness, frequent urinating, diarrhea); and excessive vigilance, as shown by irritability, insomnia, and a tendency to be easily distracted.

OBSESSIVE–COMPULSIVE DISORDER

Anne had her husband conform to her routines for removing the garbage: She would have him turn on the water and leave it on, because if her husband touched the garbage and then the spigot, she would feel that the spigot had been contaminated. She had him take a garbage bag in one hand, stand several feet from the dumpster so as to be certain not to touch it, and toss the bag in. Then she had him unlock the door to the house, slip off his shoes, enter, and wash his hands with soap from a pump. The pump enabled him to use his clean wrist to pump soap into the palm of his hand without contaminating the dispenser. She had him go through this routine for each bag, perhaps 20 on a given day. If she believed that he had been contaminated during any step, as by some liquid on the outside of a bag wetting his shirt, "I'd have to go over the scene again and again in my mind until I could...convince myself that I wasn't really in danger of getting a disease.... If I couldn't shake the fear, I'd ask him to go through [all the bags] to find the contaminated bag and try to identify the liquid. He was usually pretty against this, so...I'd talk about it for hours, and I guess in an effort to just shut me up he'd relent."

Adapted from Colas, 1999, p. 71

Anne's Obsessive–Compulsive Disorder Led Her to Compel Her Husband to Conform to Many Routines Concerning Disposal of Garbage

© Stuart Paton/Stone/Getty Images

Obsessive–compulsive disorder (OCD) is characterized by recurrent, anxiety-provoking thoughts or images that seem irrational and beyond control (*obsessions*) and seemingly irresistible urges to engage in thoughts or behaviors that tend to reduce the anxiety (*compulsions*). Obsessions are so compelling and recurrent that they disrupt daily life. They may include doubts about whether one has locked the doors and shut the windows or images such as one mother's repeated fantasy that her children had been run over on the way home from school.

Compulsions are urges to engage in specific acts, often repeatedly, such as Anne's compulsion to have her husband "decontaminate" himself after handling the garbage or elaborate washing after using the bathroom. The impulse is recurrent and forceful, interfering with daily life.

STRESS DISORDERS

Darla, who lives in Oregon, dreamed that she was trapped in a World Trade Center tower when it was hit by an airplane on September 11, 2001. Kelly, a Californian, dreamed of a beautiful bald eagle that was suddenly transformed into a snarling bird with glowing red eyes.

"Sleepers Suffer WTC Nightmares," 2001

The nightmarish events of September 11 caused many people to have bad dreams. Such dreams are part of the experience of *posttraumatic stress disorder.*

Posttraumatic Stress Disorder People diagnosed with posttraumatic stress disorder (PTSD) typically show a rapid heart rate and feelings of anxiety and helplessness following a disturbing experience. Such experiences may include a natural or human-made disaster, a threat or assault, or witnessing a death. PTSD may occur months or years after the event. It frequently occurs among firefighters, combat veterans, and people whose homes and communities have been swept away by natural disasters or who have been victims of accidents or interpersonal violence (Chard et al., 2010; McCauley et al., 2010).

The traumatic event is revisited in the form of intrusive memories, recurrent dreams, and flashbacks—the feeling that the event is recurring (McDevitt-Murphy et al., 2010). People with PTSD typically try to avoid thoughts and activities connected to the traumatic event. They may also find it more difficult to enjoy life, and they often have sleep problems, irritable outbursts, difficulty concentrating, extreme vigilance, and an intensified "startle" response. The terrorist attacks of September 11, 2001, took their toll on sleep. According to a poll taken by the National Sleep Foundation (2001) 2 months after the attacks, nearly half of Americans had difficulty falling asleep compared with about one-quarter of Americans before the attacks (see Figure 12.2 ■). Women, who are more likely than men to ruminate about stressors (Nolen-Hoeksema et al., 2008), were also more likely than men to report difficulty falling asleep (50% versus 37%).

Acute Stress Disorder Like PTSD, acute stress disorder is characterized by feelings of anxiety and helplessness that are caused by a traumatic event. However, PTSD can occur 6 months or more after the traumatic event and tends to persist. Acute stress disorder occurs within a month of the event and lasts from 2 days to 4 weeks. Women who have been raped, for example, experience acute distress that tends to peak in severity about 3 weeks after the assault (Bryant, 2006). Yet the same women may go on to experience PTSD (Kilpatrick et al., 2007; Koss et al., 2002).

Posttraumatic stress disorder (PTSD) A disorder that follows a distressing event outside the range of normal human experience and that is characterized by features such as intense fear, avoidance of stimuli associated with the event, and reliving of the event.

Acute stress disorder A disorder, like PTSD, that is characterized by feelings of anxiety and helplessness and caused by a traumatic event. Acute stress disorder occurs within a month of the event and lasts from 2 days to 4 weeks.

Robin—A Case of PTSD PTSD is often associated with combat and natural disasters, but Robin Hutchins developed the disorder after being raped in her first year of college by a man she knew. The following year she was pinned to a wall by a drunken male student, and it sent her into a tailspin. Anxiety would strike her without warning, and the prospect of leaving her dorm terrified her. Rather than seeking help, she left college. After learning that "emotional support" dogs can be trained to help people with PTSD, Hutchins adopted a dog, Dexter, from a shelter. Dexter helps Hutchins remain calm on airplanes and pushes her to go outside for long walks.

© Béatrice de Géa/New York Times/Redux

Origins of Anxiety Disorders

There are thus several kinds of anxiety disorders. **Question 6: What is known about the origins of anxiety disorders?**

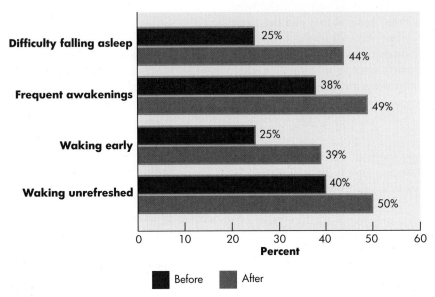

Difficulty falling asleep 25% / 44%

Frequent awakenings 38% / 49%

Waking early 25% / 39%

Waking unrefreshed 40% / 50%

Percent (0 10 20 30 40 50 60)

■ Before   ■ After

Figure 12.2 ■ Sleep Problems Among Americans Before and 2 Months After September 11, 2001 Insomnia is one of the symptoms of stress disorders. A poll by the National Sleep Foundation found that Americans had a greater frequency of sleep problems after the terrorist attacks of September 11.

PSYCHOLOGICAL VIEWS According to the psychodynamic perspective, *phobias* symbolize conflicts originating in childhood. Psychodynamic theory explains *generalized anxiety* as persistent difficulty in repressing primitive impulses. *Obsessions* are explained as leakage of unconscious impulses, and *compulsions* are seen as acts that allow people to keep such impulses partly repressed. For example, fixation in the anal stage is theorized to be connected with development of traits such as excessive neatness of the sort that could explain some cases of obsessive–compulsive disorder.

Some learning theorists, particularly behaviorists, consider phobias to be conditioned fears that were acquired in early childhood. Avoidance of feared stimuli is reinforced by the reduction of anxiety. Observational learning may also play a role in the acquisition of fears (Mineka & Oehlberg, 2008). If parents squirm, grimace, and shudder at the sight of mice, blood, or dirt on the kitchen floor, children might assume that these stimuli are awful and imitate their parents' behavior.

Cognitive theorists note that people's appraisals of the magnitude of threats help determine whether they are traumatic and can lead to PTSD (Koster et al., 2009). People with panic attacks tend to misinterpret bodily cues and to view them as threats. Obsessions and compulsions may serve to divert attention from more frightening issues, such as "What am I going to do with my life?" When anxieties are acquired at a young age, we may later interpret them as enduring traits and label ourselves as "someone who fears _____" (you fill it in). We then live up to the labels. We also entertain thoughts that heighten and perpetuate anxiety, such as "I've got to get out of here" or "My heart is going to leap out of my chest." Such ideas intensify physical signs of anxiety, disrupt planning, make stimuli seem worse than they really are, motivate avoidance, and decrease self-efficacy expectations. The belief that we will not be able to handle a threat heightens anxiety. The belief that we are in control reduces anxiety (Bandura et al., 1985).

BIOLOGICAL VIEWS Biological factors play key roles in anxiety disorders. They involve genetic factors, evolution, the autonomic nervous system, and the endocrine system.

Genetic Factors Genetic factors are implicated in most psychological disorders, including anxiety disorders (Bienvenu et al., 2007; Hettema et al., 2005). For one thing, anxiety disorders tend to run in families. Twin studies find much higher concordance rates for anxiety disorders among identical (MZ) twins than among fraternal (DZ) twins (Kendler et al., 2001). Studies of adoptees who are anxious also show that the biological parent places the child at greater risk for anxiety and related traits than does the adoptive parent.

Some researchers suggest that the actions of specific genes affect chemical balances that lead to an overarousal of brain circuitry, dubbed the "worry circuit," contributing to the development of obsessive–compulsive disorder (Fineberg & Craig, 2009). In obsessive-compulsive disorder, the brain may be sending continual but bogus messages to the so-called worry circuit, signaling erroneously that something is wrong and requires immediate attention. This leads to obsessive, worrisome thoughts and repetitive, compulsive behaviors. The worry circuit incorporates

Concordance Agreement.

structures in the limbic system, including the amygdala, which is involved in processing threatening stimuli.

Natural Selection Evolutionary psychologists suggest that anxiety may reflect natural selection. Humans (and nonhuman primates) are genetically predisposed ("biologically prepared") to fear stimuli that may have posed a threat to their ancestors (Gerdes et al., 2009; Mineka & Oehlberg, 2008; Starratt & Shackelford, 2010). Evolutionary forces would have favored the survival of individuals who were predisposed toward acquiring fears of large animals, spiders, snakes, heights, entrapment, sharp objects, and strangers. Thus, the individuals who fearlessly encounter potentially harmful stimuli may be at a disadvantage, evolutionarily speaking, rather than at an advantage.

The Autonomic Nervous System and the Endocrine System It is possible that a predisposition toward anxiety—in the form of a highly reactive autonomic nervous system—can be inherited (Beesdo et al., 2010; Binder & Nemeroff, 2009). What might make a nervous system "highly reactive"? The hypothalamus of people with anxiety disorders may secrete excessive amounts of corticotrophin-releasing hormone (CRH), which in turn causes the adrenal glands to secrete high levels of stress hormones. The autonomic nervous system may stimulate the production of excessive quantities of adrenaline (epinephrine) and noradrenaline (norepinephrine). These chemicals normally pump up the body in preparation for the fight-or-flight response—both sides of which, fight or flight, can serve as self-preserving responses to threats. But sometimes their production is so intense that they flood the body, making a person sweat profusely and feel shaky, incapable of doing anything useful.

Evolutionary Forces at Work? Why do so many people fear spiders?

Anxiety disorders may also involve the excitatory neurotransmitter glutamate, and receptor sites in the brain may not be sensitive enough to gamma-aminobutyric acid (GABA), an inhibitory neurotransmitter that may counterbalance glutamate (Martin et al., 2009). The benzodiazepines, a class of drugs that reduce anxiety, may work by increasing the sensitivity of receptor sites to GABA.

According to the biopsychosocial perspective, biological imbalances may initially trigger attacks in panic disorder. But subsequent fear of attacks—and of the bodily cues that signal their onset—may heighten discomfort and give one the idea there is nothing one can do about them (Olatunji & Wolitzky Taylor, 2009). Feelings of helplessness increase fear. People with panic disorder therefore can be helped by psychological methods that provide ways of reducing physical discomfort—including regular breathing—and show them that there are, after all, things they can do to cope with attacks (Olatunji & Wolitzky-Taylor, 2009).

LearningConnections ● ANXIETY DISORDERS: REAL-LIFE "FEAR FACTORS"

ACTIVE REVIEW (5) A(n) _____ is an irrational, excessive fear. (6) _____ disorder is characterized by sudden attacks in which people typically fear that they may be losing control or going crazy. (7) In obsessive–_____ disorder, people are troubled by intrusive thoughts or impulses to repeat some activity. (8) Anxiety disorders (do or do not?) tend to run in families.

REFLECT AND RELATE Have you ever felt anxious? Did your anxiety strike you as being normal under the circumstances? Why or why not?

CRITICAL THINKING Critical thinkers attend to the definitions of terms. For example, is anxiety abnormal? What is the difference between run-of-the-mill anxiety and an *anxiety disorder*?

 Go to Psychology CourseMate at **www.cengagebrain.com** for an interactive version of these questions.

DISSOCIATIVE DISORDERS: SPLITTING CONSCIOUSNESS

William's disorder, described at the beginning of the chapter, was a dissociative disorder. In the dissociative disorders, mental processes such as thoughts, emotions, memory, consciousness, even knowledge of one's own identity—the processes that make a person feel whole—may seem to be split off from one another. **Question 7: What kinds of dissociative disorders are there?**

Types of Dissociative Disorders

The *DSM* lists several dissociative disorders. Among them are *dissociative amnesia*, *dissociative fugue*, and *dissociative identity disorder* (previously termed *multiple personality disorder*).

DISSOCIATIVE AMNESIA A person with **dissociative amnesia** is suddenly unable to recall important personal information (that is, explicit episodic memories). The loss of memory cannot be attributed to organic problems such as a blow to the head or alcoholic intoxication. It is thus a psychological dissociative disorder and not an organic one. In the most common form, the person cannot recall events for a number of hours after a stressful incident, as in warfare or in the case of an uninjured survivor of an accident. In *generalized* dissociative amnesia, people forget their entire lives. Amnesia may last for hours or years.

DISSOCIATIVE FUGUE A person with **dissociative fugue** abruptly leaves his or her home or place of work and travels to another place, having lost all memory of his or her past life. While at the new location, the person either does not think about the past or reports a past filled with invented memories. The new personality is often more outgoing and less inhibited than the "real" identity. Following recovery, the events that occurred during the fugue are not recalled.

DISSOCIATIVE IDENTITY DISORDER Dissociative identity disorder (DID) (formerly termed **multiple personality disorder**) is the name given to William's disorder. In dissociative identity disorder, two or more identities or personalities, each with distinct traits and memories, "occupy" the same person. Each identity may or may not be aware of the others or of events experienced by the others (Huntjens et al., 2003).

Truth or Fiction Revisited: The identities of an individual with dissociative identity disorder can be very different from one another. They might even have different eyeglass prescriptions (Braun, 1988). Braun reports cases in which assorted identities even showed different allergic responses. In one person, an identity named Timmy was not sensitive to orange juice. But when other identities gained control over him and drank orange juice, he would break out with hives. Hives would also erupt if another identity emerged while the juice was being digested. If Timmy reappeared when the allergic reaction was present, the itching of the hives would cease, and the blisters would start to subside. In other cases reported by Braun, different identities within a person might show various responses to the same medicine. Or one identity might exhibit color blindness while others have normal color vision.

Origins of Dissociative Disorders

The dissociative disorders are some of the odder psychological disorders. **Question 8: What is known about the origins of dissociative disorders?**

Psychologists of different theoretical persuasions have offered hypotheses about the origins of dissociative identity disorder and other dissociative disorders. According to psychodynamic theory, for example, people with dissociative

Dissociative disorders Disorders in which there are sudden, temporary changes in consciousness or self-identity.

Dissociative amnesia A dissociative disorder marked by loss of memory or self-identity; skills and general knowledge are usually retained.

Dissociative fugue A dissociative disorder in which one experiences amnesia and then flees to a new location.

Dissociative identity disorder A disorder in which a person appears to have two or more distinct identities or personalities that may alternately emerge.

Multiple personality disorder The previous term for *dissociative identity disorder.*

© SHOWTIME/Landov

Showtime for Dissociative Identity Disorder In the Showtime series *United States of Tara*, Toni Collette plays Tara Gregson, a homemaker with two children and several other personalities. Tara has dissociative identity disorder, and within her "reside" the flirty "T," a suburban housewife plucked from the 1950s, and a beer-guzzling Vietnam veteran named "Buck."

disorders use massive repression to prevent them from recognizing improper impulses or remembering ugly events (Berlin & Koch, 2009). In dissociative amnesia and fugue, the person forgets a profoundly disturbing event or impulse. In dissociative identity disorder, the person expresses unacceptable impulses through alternative identities.

According to learning theorists, people with dissociative disorders have learned not to think about bad memories or disturbing impulses to avoid feelings of anxiety, guilt, and shame. Both psychodynamic and learning theories suggest that dissociative disorders help people keep disturbing memories or ideas out of mind. Of what could such memories be? Research suggests that many—perhaps most—cases involve memories of sexual or physical abuse during childhood, usually by a relative or caregiver (Foote et al., 2006; Ross, 2006; Simeon et al., 2007).

Whereas some disorders—major depressive disorder and schizophrenia among them—are found around the world, most cases of dissociative disorders have been limited to the United States and Canada (Ross, 2006). Perhaps dissociative disorders, especially DID, are culture-bound. It might also be the case, as suggested by skeptics, that many people who claim to have multiple personalities are misrepresenting (Kong et al., 2008).

LearningConnections • DISSOCIATIVE DISORDERS: SPLITTING CONSCIOUSNESS

ACTIVE REVIEW (9) People with generalized dissociative _____ forget their own identities. (10) In dissociative _____ disorder, the person behaves as if distinct personalities occupy the body. (11) Many people with dissociative disorders have a history of physical or sexual _____.

REFLECT AND RELATE Have you seen a film or a TV show in which a character was supposed to have dissociative identity disorder (perhaps it was called "multiple personality")? Did the character's behavior seem consistent with the description of the disorder described in this text?

CRITICAL THINKING Can you think of a way to determine whether someone who claims to have a dissociative disorder is telling the truth?

 Go to Psychology CourseMate at **www.cengagebrain.com** for an interactive version of these questions.

⬤ SOMATOFORM DISORDERS: WHEN THE BODY EXPRESSES STRESS

People with **somatoform disorders** complain of physical problems such as paralysis, pain, or a persistent belief that they have a serious disease. Yet no evidence of a physical abnormality can be found.

Types of Somatoform Disorders

Question 9: What kinds of somatoform disorders are there? In this section, we discuss two somatoform disorders: *conversion disorder* and *hypochondriasis*.

CONVERSION DISORDER Conversion disorder is characterized by a major change in, or loss of, physical functioning, although there are no medical findings to explain the loss of functioning. The behaviors are not intentionally produced. That is, the person is not faking. Conversion disorder is so named because it appears to "convert" a source of stress into a physical difficulty.

If you lost the ability to see at night or if your legs became paralyzed, you would understandably show concern. But some people with conversion disorder show indifference to their symptoms, a symptom termed la belle indifférence. The lack of concern suggests awareness, on some level, that the physical problems have their benefits.

During World War II, some bomber pilots developed night blindness. They could not carry out their nighttime missions, although no damage to the optic nerves was found. In rare cases, women with large families have been reported to become paralyzed

> *"The trouble with being a hypochondriac these days is that antibiotics have cured all the good diseases."*
>
> CASKIE STINNETT

Somatoform disorders Disorders in which people complain of physical (somatic) problems even though no physical abnormality can be found.

Conversion disorder A disorder in which anxiety or unconscious conflicts are "converted" into physical symptoms that often have the effect of helping the person cope with anxiety or conflict.

La belle indifférence A French term descriptive of the lack of concern sometimes shown by people with conversion disorder.

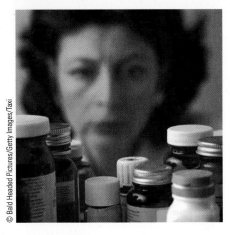

Hypochondriasis People with hypochondriasis are irrationally concerned that they have contracted illnesses. Such people appear to be unusually sensitive to physical sensations. Do they also focus on their physical symptoms as an alternative to dealing with the social and other problems in their lives?

in the legs, again with no medical findings. More recently, a Cambodian woman who had witnessed atrocities became blind as a result.

HYPOCHONDRIASIS Another, more common type of somatoform disorder is hypochondriasis (also called *hypochondria*). People with this disorder insist that they are suffering from a serious physical illness, even though no medical evidence of illness can be found. They become preoccupied with minor physical sensations and continue to believe that they are ill despite the reassurance of physicians that they are healthy. They may run from doctor to doctor, seeking the one who will find the causes of the sensations. Fear of illness may disrupt their work or home life.

Origins of Somatoform Disorders

Question 10: What is known about the origins of somatoform disorders?
There is evidence that people with conversion disorder are susceptible to being hypnotized (R. J. Brown et al., 2007). In fact, some investigators consider conversion disorder to be a form of self-hypnosis in which people focus so intently on an imaginary physical problem that they exclude conflicting information. Research evidence suggests that people who develop hypochondriasis are particularly sensitive to bodily sensations and tend to ruminate about them (Marcus et al., 2008).

LearningConnections • SOMATOFORM DISORDERS: WHEN THE BODY EXPRESSES STRESS

ACTIVE REVIEW (12) In _____ disorders, people complain of physical problems or persist in believing they have a serious disease, even though no medical problem can be found. (13) In _____ disorder, there is a major change in or loss of physical functioning with no organic basis.

REFLECT AND RELATE Have you heard anyone referred to as "hysterical"? What was the usage of the word intended to

mean? Now that you know the origin of the term, do you feel it was used appropriately?

CRITICAL THINKING Why have somatoform disorders been considered "hysterical"? What are the social problems in labeling them as hysterical?

 Go to Psychology CourseMate at **www.cengagebrain.com** for an interactive version of these questions.

⬤ MOOD DISORDERS: UP, DOWN, AND AROUND

Mood disorders are characterized by disturbance in expressed emotions. The disruption generally involves sadness or elation. Most instances of sadness are normal, or "run-of-the-mill." If you have failed an important test, if you have lost money in a business venture, or if your closest friend becomes ill, it is understandable and fitting for you to be sad about it. It would be odd, in fact, if you were *not* affected by adversity.

Hypochondriasis Persistent belief that one is ill despite lack of medical findings.

Mood disorder A disturbance in expressed emotions, generally involving excessive or inappropriate sadness or elation.

Major depressive disorder A serious to severe depressive disorder in which the person may show loss of appetite, psychomotor retardation, and in extreme cases, delusions of worthlessness.

Types of Mood Disorders

Question 11: What kinds of mood disorders are there? In this section, we discuss two mood disorders: *major depressive disorder* and *bipolar disorder*.

MAJOR DEPRESSIVE DISORDER Depression is the common cold of psychological problems. People with run-of-the-mill depression may feel sad, blue, or "down in the dumps." They may complain of lack of energy, loss of self-esteem, difficulty concentrating, loss of interest in activities and other people, pessimism, crying, and thoughts of suicide.

These feelings are more intense in people with **major depressive disorder**. According to a nationally representative sample of more than 9,000 adults in the United States, major depressive disorder affects 5% to 7% of us within any given year and one person in six or seven over the course of our lives (Hasin et al., 2005; Kessler et al., 2003). About half of those with major depressive disorder experience severe symptoms such as

SELF-ASSESSMENT

Are You Depressed?

This self-assessment, offered by the organizers of the National Depression Screening Day, can help you assess whether you are suffering from depression. It is not intended for you to diagnose yourself but rather to raise your awareness of concerns you may want to discuss with a professional.

	YES	NO
1. I feel downhearted, blue, and sad.	_____	_____
2. I don't enjoy the things that I used to.	_____	_____
3. I feel that others would be better off if I were dead.	_____	_____
4. I feel that I am not useful or needed.	_____	_____
5. I notice that I am losing weight.	_____	_____

	YES	NO
6. I have trouble sleeping through the night.	_____	_____
7. I am restless and can't keep still.	_____	_____
8. My mind isn't as clear as it used to be.	_____	_____
9. I get tired for no reason.	_____	_____
10. I feel hopeless about the future.	_____	_____

Check Appendix B to rate your responses.

Source: Adapted from J. E. Brody, "Myriad masks hide an epidemic of depression," *The New York Times*, September 30, 1992, p. C12.

poor appetite, serious weight loss, and agitation or **psychomotor retardation.** They may be unable to concentrate and make decisions. They may say that they "don't care" anymore and in some cases attempt suicide. A minority may display faulty perception of reality—so-called psychotic behaviors. These include delusions of unworthiness, guilt for imagined wrongdoings, even the notion that one is rotting from disease. There may also be delusions, as of the Devil administering deserved punishment, or hallucinations, as of strange bodily sensations. The nearby Self-Assessment will afford you insight into whether you are experiencing feelings of depression.

BIPOLAR DISORDER

[Bipolar disorder] is about buying a dozen bottles of Heinz ketchup and all eight bottles of Windex in stock at the Food Emporium on Broadway at 4 A.M., flying from Zurich to the Bahamas and back to Zurich in three days to balance the hot and cold weather…, carrying $20,000 in $100 bills in your shoes into the country on your way back to Tokyo, and picking out the person sitting six seats away at the bar to have sex with only because he or she happens to be sitting there. It's about blips and burps of madness, moments of absolute delusion, bliss, and irrational and dangerous choices made in order to heighten pleasure and excitement and to ensure a sense of control. . . .

From *Electroboy* by Andy Behrman

But then you crash—hard. You not only return to normal; you fall well beneath it and hope—unless you're too hopeless to hope—that you will rise back to normal again.

Truth or Fiction Revisited: It is true that feeling "up" is not always a good thing. People with **bipolar disorder,** formerly known as *manic–depressive disorder,* have mood swings from ecstatic elation to deep depression. The cycles seem to be unrelated to external events. In the elated, or **manic,** phase, the person may show excessive excitement or silliness, carrying jokes too far. The manic person may be argumentative. Like "Electroboy," he or she may show poor judgment, making foolish purchases, shoplifting, destroying property, making huge contributions to charity, or giving away expensive possessions. People often find manic individuals abrasive and avoid them. They are often oversexed and too restless to sit still or sleep restfully. They often speak rapidly (showing *pressured speech)* and jump from topic to topic (showing **rapid flight of ideas**). It can be hard to get a word in edgewise.

Depression is the other side of the coin. People with bipolar depression often sleep more than usual and are lethargic. People with major (or unipolar) depression are more likely to have insomnia and agitation. Those with bipolar depression also exhibit social withdrawal and irritability. Some people with bipolar disorder attempt suicide when the mood shifts from the elated phase toward depression (Jamison, 2000). They will do almost anything to escape the depths of depression that lie ahead.

Psychomotor retardation Slowness in motor activity and (apparently) in thought.

Bipolar disorder A disorder in which the mood alternates between two extreme poles (elation and depression); also referred to as *manic–depression.*

Manic Elated; showing excessive excitement.

Rapid flight of ideas Rapid speech and topic changes, characteristic of manic behavior.

Bipolar Disorder. In 2011, actress Catherine Zeta-Jones revealed that she was seeking treatment for bipolar disorder.

413

Women are about twice as likely as men to be diagnosed with depression (Kessler, 2003; Kramer et al., 2008). Many people assume that biological gender differences largely explain why women are more likely to become depressed. Low levels of estrogen are widely seen as the culprit. Estrogen levels plummet prior to menstruation. How often do we hear degrading remarks such as "It must be that time of the month" when a woman expresses feelings of anger or irritation? But part of the gender difference may be due to the fact that men are less likely than women to admit to depression or seek treatment for it. "I'm the John Wayne generation," admitted one man, a physician. "'It's only a flesh wound'; that's how you deal with it. I thought depression was a weakness—there was something disgraceful about it. A real man would just get over it" (cited in Wartik, 2000).

It was once assumed that depression was most likely to accompany menopause in women because women could no longer carry out their "natural" function of childbearing. However, women are more likely to encounter severe depression during the childbearing years (Depression Research, 2000).

Yes, hormonal changes may contribute to depression in women (Soares & Zitek, 2008). The bodies and brains of males, on the other hand, are stoked by testosterone, especially in adolescence and early adulthood. High testosterone levels are connected with feelings of self-confidence, high activity levels, and aggression—a cluster of traits and behaviors that are more connected with elation (even if sometimes misplaced) than with depression (Mehta & Beer, 2009).

Cognitive psychologists also note that people who ruminate about feelings of depression are more likely to prolong them (Hughes et al., 2008; Wisco & Nolen-Hoeksema, 2009). Women are more likely than men to ruminate about such feelings (Grabe et al., 2007; Wisco & Nolen-Hoeksema, 2009). Men seem more likely to try to fend off negative feelings by distracting themselves, as by turning to alcohol and aggression when they don't feel right (Nolen-Hoeksema, 2001). But then they expose themselves and their families to additional problems.

Origins of Mood Disorders

Question 12: What is known about the origins of mood disorders?
Depression may be a reaction to losses and stress (Cowen, 2002; Mazure et al., 2000). Sources of chronic strain such as marital discord, physical discomfort, incompetence, and failure or pressure at work all contribute to feelings of depression. We tend to be more depressed by things we bring on ourselves, such as academic problems, financial problems, unwanted pregnancy, conflict with the law, arguments, and fights (Greenberger et al., 2000). However, some people recover from depression less readily than others. People who remain depressed have lower self-esteem (Andrews, 1998; Sherrington et al., 2001), are less likely to solve social problems (Reinecke et al., 2001), and have less social support.

> *"Concern should drive us into action, not into a depression."*
>
> KAREN HORNEY

> *"I didn't know my mother had it. I think a lot of women don't know their mothers had it; that's the sad thing about depression. You know, you don't function anymore. You shut down. You feel like you are in a void."*
>
> MARIE OSMOND

PSYCHOLOGICAL VIEWS Psychoanalysts suggest various explanations for mood disorders. For example, from the psychodynamic perspective, people who are at risk for depression are overly concerned about hurting other people's feelings or losing their approval. As a result, they hold in feelings of anger rather than express them. Anger is turned inward and experienced as misery and self-hatred. From the psychodynamic perspective, *bipolar disorder* may be seen as alternating states in which the personality is dominated first by the ego and then by the superego. It is a classic case of excess followed by self-recrimination: The ascendant ego produces elation and irrational seeking of gratification. Then the superego passes judgment, producing exaggerated ideas of wrongdoing and feelings of guilt and shame.

Many learning theorists suggest that depressed people behave as though they cannot obtain reinforcement. For example, they appear to be inactive and apathetic. Many people with depressive disorders have an *external locus of control*. That is, they do not believe they can control events so as to achieve reinforcements (Tong, 2001; Weinmann et al., 2001).

Learned helplessness A model for the acquisition of depressive behavior based on findings that organisms in unchangeable aversive situations may learn to do nothing.

Learned Helplessness Research conducted by learning theorists has also found links between depression and learned helplessness. In classic research, psychologist Martin Seligman (1975) taught dogs that they were helpless to escape an electric shock. The dogs were prevented from leaving a cage in which they received repeated shocks. Later, a barrier to a safe compartment was removed, offering the animals a way out.

When they were shocked again, however, the dogs made no effort to escape. They had apparently learned that they were helpless. Seligman's dogs were also, in a sense, reinforced for doing nothing. That is, the shock *eventually* stopped when the dogs were showing helpless behavior—inactivity and withdrawal. "Reinforcement" might have increased the likelihood of repeating the "successful behavior"—that is, doing nothing—in a similar situation. This helpless behavior resembles that of people who are depressed.

Cognitive factors also contribute to depression. For example, perfectionists set themselves up for depression by making irrational demands on themselves. They are likely to fall short of their (unrealistic) expectations and to feel depressed as a result (Flett et al., 2007).

Attributions for Failure and Depression Still other cognitions involve the ways people explain their failures and shortcomings to themselves. Seligman (1996) suggests that when things go wrong, we may think of the causes of failure as either *internal* or *external*, *stable* or *unstable*, *global* or *specific*. These various **attributional styles** can be illustrated using the example of having a date that does not work out. An internal attribution involves self-blame (as in "I really loused it up"). An external attribution places the blame elsewhere (as in "Some couples just don't take to each other," or "She was the wrong sign for me"). A stable attribution ("It's my personality") suggests a problem that cannot be changed. An unstable attribution ("It was because I had a head cold") suggests a temporary condition. A global attribution of failure ("I have no idea what to do when I'm with other people") suggests that the problem is quite large. A specific attribution ("I have problems making small talk at the beginning of a relationship") chops the problem down to a manageable size. How does this connect to depression? Research has shown that people who are depressed are more likely to attribute the causes of their failures to internal, stable, and global factors—factors that they are relatively powerless to change (Safford et al., 2007).

BIOLOGICAL FACTORS Researchers are also searching for biological factors in mood disorders. Depression, for example, is often associated with the trait of **neuroticism**, which is heritable (Dunkley et al., 2009). Anxiety is also connected with neuroticism, and mood and anxiety disorders are frequently found in the same person (Spinhoven et al., 2010).

Twin and adoption studies support a role for genetic factors in bipolar disorder (Willcutt & McQueen, 2010). Such genetic factors may heighten the activity of the neurotransmitter dopamine during the manic phase, which is characterized by high activity levels, restlessness, and greater than normal sexual activity (Boora et al., 2009; Einat, 2007). Dopamine is produced in several places in the brain and is believed to play key roles in cognition, motivation, punishment and reward, sexual gratification, sleep, mood, and learning and memory. The release of dopamine normally has the effects of rewarding sexual activity, eating, and substance use and abuse.

Research into depression focuses on underutilization of the neurotransmitter serotonin in the brain (Artigas, 2008; Leach, 2008). It has been shown, for example, that learned helplessness is connected with lower serotonin levels in rats' brains (Wu et al., 1999). Moreover, people with severe depression often respond to drugs (selective serotonin reuptake inhibitors, or SSRIs) that heighten the action of serotonin (Leonard, 2008).

Suicide

Each year about 33,000 people in the United States take their own lives (Centers for Disease Control and Prevention, 2009). Suicide is the third leading cause of death among 15- to 24-year-olds, behind accidents and assaults (Heron & Tejada-Vera, 2009).

We discuss suicide in the section on mood disorders because most suicides are linked to feelings of depression and hopelessness (Dwivedi, 2010; Zaitsoff & Grilo,

Attributional style The tendency to attribute one's behavior to internal or external factors, stable or unstable factors, and global or specific factors.

Neuroticism A personality trait characterized largely by persistent anxiety.

Why Did He Miss That Basket? This basketball player is compounding his feelings of depression by attributing his shortcomings on the court to factors he cannot change. For example, he tells himself that he missed the basket out of stupidity and lack of athletic ability. He ignores the facts that his coaching was poor and his teammates failed to support him.

2010). My daughter Jill Rathus and her colleagues (A. L. Miller et al., 2007) have found that suicidal adolescents experience four kinds of psychological problems: (a) confusion about the self, (b) impulsiveness, (c) emotional instability, and (d) interpersonal problems. Some suicidal teenagers, like suicidal adults, are highly achieving, rigid perfectionists who have set impossibly high expectations for themselves (A. L. Miller et al., 2007).

Many people throw themselves into feelings of depression and hopelessness by comparing themselves negatively with others, even when the comparisons are inappropriate (Barber, 2001). Contributors to suicidal behavior among adolescents include concerns over sexuality, sexual abuse, grades, problems at home, and substance abuse (Duke et al., 2010; A. L. Miller et al., 2007; Zayas et al., 2010). It is not always a stressful event itself that precipitates suicide but the individual's anxiety or fear of being "found out" about something, such as failing a course or getting arrested (Marttunen, 1998). People who consider suicide are apparently less capable of solving problems, especially social problems, than others (A. L. Miller et al., 2007). They are thus less likely to find productive ways of changing the stressful situation. They want a magical solution to problems that require work or else a quick way out (Shneidman, 2001).

There is a tendency for suicide to run in families (Goldston & Compton, 2010). Many suicide attempters have family members with serious psychological problems, and about 25% have family members who have taken their own lives (Sorensen & Rutter, 1991). The causal connections are unclear, however. Do people who attempt suicide inherit disorders that can lead to suicide? Does the family environment subject family members to feelings of hopelessness? Does the suicide of a family member give a person the idea of committing suicide or create the impression that he or she is "fated" to commit suicide?

SOCIOCULTURAL FACTORS IN SUICIDE Suicide is connected not only with feelings of depression and stressful events but also with age, educational status, ethnicity, and gender. Suicide is more common among college students than among people of the same age who are not in college. Each year, about 10,000 college students attempt suicide. Although teenage suicides loom large in the media spotlight, older people are more likely to commit suicide (Centers for Disease Control and Prevention, 2009). The suicide rate among older people who are unmarried or divorced is double that of older people who are married.

Rates of suicide and suicide attempts also vary among different ethnic groups and according to gender. For example, about one in every six Native Americans (17%) has attempted suicide—a rate higher than that for other Americans (Centers for Disease Control and Prevention, 2009). About one in eight Latin Americans has attempted suicide, and three in ten have considered it. European Americans are next, with 8% attempting and 28% contemplating suicide. African Americans are least likely to attempt suicide (6.5%) or to think about it (20%). The actual suicide rates for African Americans are about two-thirds of those for European Americans, despite the fact that African Americans are more likely to live in poverty and suffer from discrimination (Centers for Disease Control and Prevention, 2009).

How can we explain this "disconnect" between hope for the future and suicide rates? One possibility is that when African Americans are feeling low, they tend to blame social circumstances, including discrimination. Many European Americans, on the other hand, may feel that there is no one to blame but themselves.

About three times as many females as males attempt suicide, but about five times as many males succeed (Centers for Disease Control and Prevention, 2009). Males are more likely to "succeed" because they use deadlier and quicker-acting methods: Males are more likely to shoot or hang themselves; females more often use drugs, such as overdoses of tranquilizers or sleeping pills, or poisons. It takes a while for drugs to work, giving people the opportunity to find them and intervene.

MYTHS ABOUT SUICIDE You may have heard that individuals who threaten suicide are only seeking attention—those who are serious just do it. **Truth or Fiction Revisited:** It is not true that people who threaten suicide are only seeking attention. Most people who commit suicide give warnings about their intentions (Jackson & Nuttall, 2001; Waters, 2000).

Suicide Why are women more likely than men to attempt suicide? Why are men more likely to "succeed"?

© Andrew Bret Wallis/Stock Image/Getty Images

Some believe that those who fail at suicide attempts are only seeking attention. But many people who commit suicide have made prior attempts (Bakst et al., 2009). Contrary to widespread belief, discussing suicide with a person who is depressed does not prompt the person to attempt suicide (Centers for Disease Control and Prevention, 1995). Extracting a promise not to commit suicide before calling or visiting a helping professional seems to prevent some suicides.

Some believe that only "insane" people (meaning people who are out of touch with reality) would take their own lives. However, suicidal thinking is not necessarily a sign of psychosis, neurosis, or personality disorder. Instead, people may consider suicide when they think they have run out of options (Nock & Kazdin, 2002; Townsend et al., 2001).

WARNING SIGNS OF SUICIDE The majority of people who commit suicide send out signals about their impending act (Rudd, 2008). But these signals often are overlooked, sometimes because other people do not recognize them and sometimes because other people don't know whom to call (Rudd, 2008). Here are clues that a person may be at risk of committing suicide (Bongar, 2002; Hendin et al., 2001):

- Changes in eating and sleeping patterns.
- Difficulty concentrating on school or the job.
- A sharp decline in performance and attendance at school or on the job.
- Loss of interest in previously enjoyed activities.
- Giving away prized possessions.
- Complaints about physical problems when no medical basis can be found.
- Withdrawal from social relationships.
- Personality or mood changes.
- Talking or writing about death or dying.
- Abuse of drugs or alcohol.
- A previously attempted suicide.
- Availability of a handgun.
- A precipitating event such as an argument, a broken romantic relationship, academic difficulties, problems on the job, loss of a friend, or trouble with the law.
- In the case of adolescents, knowing or hearing about another teenager who has committed suicide (which can lead to so-called cluster suicides).
- Threatening to commit suicide.

The nearby Life Connections feature offers advice on things you can do if someone tells you that she or he is considering suicide.

LearningConnections ● MOOD DISORDERS: UP, DOWN, AND AROUND

ACTIVE REVIEW (14) _____ depressive disorder can reach psychotic proportions, with delusional ideas of worthlessness. (15) In bipolar disorder, there are mood swings between _____ and depression. (16) Manicky people may have grand delusional schemes and show rapid _____ of ideas. (17) Seligman and his colleagues have explored links between depression and learned _____. (18) Depressed people are more likely than other people to make (internal or external?) attributions for failures. (19) Mood disorders (do or do not?) tend to run in families. (20) Depression is connected with underutilization of the neurotransmitter _____.

REFLECT AND RELATE When you fall short of your goals, do you tend to be merciless in your self-criticism, or do you tend to blame other people or "circumstances"?

CRITICAL THINKING Under what circumstances is depression considered a psychological disorder? How does bipolar disorder differ from responses to the normal "ups and downs" of life?

 Go to Psychology CourseMate at **www.cengagebrain.com** for an interactive version of these questions.

Imagine you are having a heart-to-heart talk with Jamie, one of your best friends. Things haven't been going well. Jamie's grandmother died a month ago, and they were very close. Jamie's course work has been suffering, and her love life has also been going to the dogs. But you are not prepared when Jamie looks you in the eye and says, "I've been thinking about this for days, and I've decided that the only way out is to kill myself."

If someone tells you that he or she is considering suicide, you may become frightened and flustered or feel that an enormous burden has been placed on you. You are right: it has. In such a case, your objective should be to encourage the person to consult a health-care provider, or to consult one yourself, as soon as possible. But if the person refuses to talk to anyone else and you feel that you can't break free for a consultation, there are a number of things you can do (Joffe, 2008; Shneidman, 2001):

1. Keep talking. Encourage the person to talk to you or to some other trusted person. Draw the person out with questions like "What's happening?" "Where do you hurt?" "What do you want to happen?" Questions like these may encourage the person to express frustrated needs and provide some relief. They also give you time to think.

2. Be a good listener. Be supportive with people who express suicidal thoughts or feel depressed, hopeless, or worthless. They may believe their condition is hopeless and will never improve, but let them know that you are there for them and willing to help them get help. Show that you understand how upset the person is. Do *not* say, "Don't be silly."

3. Suggest that something other than suicide might solve the problem, even if it is not evident at the time. Many suicidal people see only two solutions—death or a magical resolution of their problems. Therapists try to "remove the mental blinders" from suicidal people.

4. Emphasize as concretely as possible how the person's suicide would be devastating to you and to other people who care.

5. Ask how the person intends to commit suicide. People with concrete plans and a weapon are at greater risk. Ask if you might hold on to the weapon for a while. Sometimes, the answer is yes.

6. Suggest that the person go *with you* to obtain professional help *now*. The emergency room of a general hospital, the campus counseling center or infirmary, or the campus or local police station will do. Some campuses have hotlines you can call. Some cities have suicide prevention centers with hotlines that people can use anonymously.

7. Extract a promise that the person will not commit suicide before seeing you again. Arrange a specific time and place to meet. Get professional help as soon as you are apart.

8. Do *not* tell people threatening suicide that they're silly or crazy. Do *not* insist on contact with specific people, such as parents or a spouse. Conflict with these people may have led to the suicidal thinking in the first place.

● SCHIZOPHRENIA: WHEN THINKING RUNS ASTRAY

Jennifer was 19. Her husband, David, brought her into the emergency room because she had cut her wrists. When she was interviewed, she seemed distracted by things in the air or something she might be hearing. She explained that she had cut her wrists because the "hellsmen" had told her to. Then she seemed frightened. Later she said that the hellsmen had warned her not to reveal their existence. She had been afraid that they would punish her for talking about them.

David and Jennifer had been married for about a year. At first, they had lived in an apartment in town. But Jennifer didn't want to be near other people and had convinced Dave to move to the country. There she would make drawings of goblins and monsters during the day. Now and then, she would act as if invisible things were giving her instructions. She would begin to jumble her words. David would try to convince her to go to the hospital, but she would refuse. Then the wrist-cutting would begin. David thought he had made the cottage safe by removing knives and blades, but Jennifer would always find something.

Then Jennifer would be brought to the hospital, have stitches put in, and be kept under observation and medicated. She would explain that she cut herself because the hellsmen had told her that she was bad and must die. After a few days, she would deny hearing the hellsmen, and she would insist on leaving the hospital. David would take her home. The pattern continued.

From the author's files

When the emergency room staff examined Jennifer's wrists and heard that she believed she had been following the orders of "hellsmen," they suspected that she could be diagnosed with schizophrenia. **Question 13: What is schizophrenia?**

Schizophrenia is a severe psychological disorder that touches every aspect of a person's life. It is characterized by disturbances in thought and language, perception and attention, motor activity, and mood, as well as withdrawal and absorption in daydreams or fantasy.

Schizophrenia has been referred to as the worst psychological disorder affecting human beings. It afflicts nearly 1% of the population worldwide. Its onset occurs relatively early in life, and its adverse effects tend to endure.

Symptoms of Schizophrenia

In schizophrenia, whatever can go wrong, psychologically, seems to go wrong. There are disturbances in thinking, language, perception, motor behavior, and social interaction. People with schizophrenia may have *positive symptoms, negative symptoms,* or both. **Positive symptoms** are the inappropriate kinds of behavior we find in afflicted people, including, for example, agitated behavior, vivid hallucinations, unshakable delusions, disorganized thinking, and nonsensical speech. **Negative symptoms** are those that reflect the absence of appropriate behavior. We see them in flat, emotionless voices; blank faces; rigid, motionless bodies; and **mutism**.

PROBLEMS IN THINKING AND LANGUAGE Schizophrenia has been called a *thought disorder* because people with schizophrenia have problems in thinking, language, memory, and attention (Cellard et al., 2010). Their thinking and communication ability become unraveled. Their speech may be jumbled. They may combine parts of words into new words or make meaningless rhymes. They may jump from topic to topic, conveying little useful information. They usually do not recognize that their thoughts and behavior are abnormal.

Many people with schizophrenia have unshakeable **delusions** of grandeur, persecution, or reference (Freeman et al., 2010). In the case of *delusions of grandeur*, a person may believe that he is a famous historical figure such as Jesus or a person on a special mission. He may have grand, illogical plans for saving the world. People with *delusions of persecution* may believe that they are sought by the Mafia, CIA, FBI, or some other group. Paranoid individuals tend to jump to conclusions that people intend to do them harm based on little evidence (Lincoln et al., 2010). People with *delusions of reference* erroneously believe that other people are talking about them or referring to them. For example, a woman with delusions of reference said that news stories contained coded information about her. A man with such delusions complained that neighbors had "bugged" his walls with "radios." Other people with schizophrenia have had delusions that they had committed unpardonable sins, that they were rotting away from disease, or that they or the world did not exist.

PROBLEMS IN PERCEPTION: "DAGGERS OF THE MIND"? Truth or Fiction Revisited: It is true that people with schizophrenia may see and hear things that are not really there. Their perceptual problems often include hallucinations—imagery in the absence of external stimulation that the person cannot distinguish from reality. In Shakespeare's *Macbeth,* for example, after killing King Duncan, Macbeth apparently experiences a hallucination:

> Is this a dagger which I see before me,
> The handle toward my hand? Come, let me clutch thee:
> I have thee not, and yet I see thee still.
> Art thou not, fatal vision, sensible
> To feeling as to sight? or art thou but
> A dagger of the mind, a false creation,
> Proceeding from the heat-oppressed brain?

Jennifer apparently hallucinated the voices of "hellsmen." Other people who experience hallucinations may see colors or even obscene words spelled out in midair. Auditory hallucinations are the most common type.

"If you talk to God, you are praying. If God talks to you, you have schizophrenia."

THOMAS SZASZ

"Schizophrenia cannot be understood without understanding despair."

R. D. LAING

Schizophrenia A psychotic disorder characterized by loss of control of thought processes and inappropriate emotional responses.

Positive symptoms Those symptoms of schizophrenia that indicate the presence of inappropriate behavior, such as hallucinations, delusions, agitation, and inappropriate giggling.

Negative symptoms Those symptoms of schizophrenia that reflect the absence of appropriate behavior, such as blank faces, monotonic voices, and motionless bodies.

Mutism Refusal to talk.

Delusions False, persistent beliefs that are unsubstantiated by sensory or objective evidence.

The *Schizophrenia Bulletin* invited people to print their own first-person accounts of psychological disorders. This is what Thomas (Campbell, 2000), who was diagnosed with both schizophrenia and major depression, wrote:

> I finally had an episode…that I couldn't get out of and one that was making me too miserable. This was several months after a front-page automatic weapons robbery in North Hollywood, near my residence, and during a change in my supervisors. My paranoia made me think I was somehow tied to the first, and real stress came from the change of supervisors. The voices, human sounding, and sounding from a short distance outside my apartment, were slowly turning nearly all bad. I could hear them jeering me, plotting against me, singing songs sometimes that would only make sense later in the day when I would do something wrong at work or at home. I began sleeping on the floor of my living room because I was afraid a presence in the bedroom was torturing good forces around me. If I slept in the bedroom, the nightly torture would cause me to make mistakes during the day. A voice, calling himself Fatty Acid, stopped me from drinking soda. Another voice allowed me only one piece of bread with my meals. These two voices called themselves "professionals." I was forced to stop smoking, too. If I smoked, I would hit a pedestrian with my car.

Stupor A condition in which the senses, thought, and movement are dulled.

Paranoid schizophrenia A type of schizophrenia characterized primarily by delusions—commonly of persecution—and by vivid hallucinations.

Disorganized schizophrenia A type of schizophrenia characterized by disorganized delusions and vivid hallucinations.

Catatonic schizophrenia A type of schizophrenia characterized by striking motor impairment.

Schizophrenia in *A Beautiful Mind* In the film *A Beautiful Mind,* Russell Crowe played the role of mathematician John Forbes Nash Jr. Nash struggled with schizophrenia for more than three decades and was eventually awarded a Nobel Prize for work he had done as a graduate student decades earlier.

PROBLEMS IN ACTIONS, EMOTIONS, AND SOCIAL INTERACTION For individuals with schizophrenia, motor activity may become wild or so slowed that the person is said to be in a **stupor**—that is, a condition in which the senses, thought, and movement are inhibited. There may be strange gestures and facial expressions. The person's emotional responses may be flat or blunted or completely inappropriate—as in giggling upon hearing bad news. People with schizophrenia tend to withdraw from social contacts and become wrapped up in their own thoughts and fantasies (Horan et al., 2010; Mathews & Barch, 2010). **Question 14: What kinds of schizophrenia are there?**

Types of Schizophrenia

All types of schizophrenia involve a thought disorder. However, the three major types of schizophrenia—*paranoid*, *disorganized*, and *catatonic schizophrenia*—have distinct features.

PARANOID TYPE People with **paranoid schizophrenia** can have complex delusions and, frequently, related auditory hallucinations. They usually have delusions of grandeur and persecution, but they may also have delusions of jealousy, in which they believe that a spouse or lover has been unfaithful—again, jumping to conclusions with very little evidence (Lincoln et al., 2010). They may show agitation, confusion, and fear and may experience vivid hallucinations that are consistent with their delusions. People with paranoid schizophrenia often construct complex or systematized delusions involving themes of wrongdoing or persecution. John Nash, the character in the true story *A Beautiful Mind,* believed that the government was recruiting him to decipher coded messages sent by our Cold War enemies.

DISORGANIZED TYPE People with **disorganized schizophrenia** show incoherence, disorganized behavior, disorganized delusions, hallucinations, and flat or inappropriate emotional responses. Extreme social impairment is common. People with this type of schizophrenia may also exhibit silliness and giddiness of mood, giggling, and nonsensical speech. They may neglect their appearance and personal hygiene and lose control of their bladder and bowels.

CATATONIC TYPE Catatonic schizophrenia is one of the most unusual psychological disorders. People with **catatonic schizophrenia** show striking impairment in motor activity. It is characterized by a slowing of activity into a stupor that may suddenly change into an agitated phase. Catatonic individuals may maintain unusual, sometimes difficult postures for hours, even as their limbs grow swollen or stiff. A striking feature of this condition is **waxy flexibility,** in which the person maintains positions into which he or she has been manipulated by others. Catatonic individuals may also show mutism, but afterward, they usually report that they heard what others were saying at the time.

OTHER TYPES OF SCHIZOPHRENIA Two other types of schizophrenia are the undifferentiated type and the residual type. People with the *undifferentiated type* show abundant and varied symptoms that may be drawn from the major types. People with the *residual type* predominantly show social withdrawal after delusions and hallucinations have faded.

Origins of Schizophrenia

Question 15: What is known about the origins of schizophrenia? Psychologists have investigated various factors that may contribute to schizophrenia. They include psychological, sociocultural, and biological factors.

PSYCHOLOGICAL VIEWS According to the psychodynamic perspective, schizophrenia occurs because the ego is overwhelmed by sexual or aggressive impulses from the id. Under this barrage, the person regresses to an early phase of the oral stage in which the infant has not yet learned that it and the world are separate. Fantasies become confused with reality, giving rise to hallucinations and delusions. Yet critics point out that schizophrenic behavior is not the same as infantile behavior.

Most learning theorists have explained schizophrenia in terms of conditioning and observational learning. They have suggested that people engage in schizophrenic behavior when it is more likely to be reinforced than normal behavior. This may occur when a person is reared in a socially unrewarding or punitive situation. Inner fantasies then become more reinforcing than social realities. Patients in a psychiatric hospital may learn what is "expected" by observing others. Hospital staff may reinforce schizophrenic behavior by paying more attention to patients who behave bizarrely. This view is consistent with folklore that the child who disrupts the class attracts more attention from the teacher than the "good" child.

SOCIOCULTURAL VIEWS Many investigators have considered whether and how social and cultural factors such as poverty, poor parenting, discrimination, and overcrowding contribute to schizophrenia—especially among people who are genetically vulnerable to the disorder. Although quality of parenting is connected with the development of schizophrenia (Buckley et al., 2000), critics note that many people who are reared in socially punitive settings are apparently immune to the disorder. Classic research in New Haven, Connecticut, showed that the rate of schizophrenia was twice as high in the lowest socioeconomic class as in the next higher class on the socioeconomic ladder (Hollingshead & Redlich, 1958). It appears that poor-quality housing contributes to psychological disorders (Dunn, 2008). Some sociocultural theorists therefore suggest that treatment of schizophrenia requires alleviation of poverty and other social ills rather than changing people whose behavior is deviant.

Critics of this view suggest that low socioeconomic status may be a result, rather than a cause, of schizophrenia. People with schizophrenia may drift downward in social status because they lack the social skills and cognitive abilities to function at higher levels. Thus, they wind up in poor neighborhoods in disproportionately high numbers.

Although many researchers continue to seek psychological and social risk factors for the development of schizophrenia,

© Grunnitis/Photo Researchers, Inc.

Catatonic Schizophrenia People with catatonic schizophrenia show striking motor impairment and may hold unusual positions for hours.

Waxy flexibility A feature of catatonic schizophrenia in which people can be molded into postures that they maintain for quite some time.

Video Connections—Schizophrenia

Schizophrenia is considered the most severe of the psychological disorders and afflicts about 1% of the population. Etta suffers from schizophrenia. See the video to view a conversation between Etta and a therapist. Through Etta's plight you will realize how devastating this disorder is. Go to Psychology CourseMate at **www.cengagebrain. com** to watch this video.

research has not discovered any environmental causes that will lead to the development of schizophrenia in people who are unrelated to people with the disorder. Because of this lack of evidence, much focus today is on the biological aspects of schizophrenia—on its nature as a brain disease and on its likely biological origins. Once we have outlined the nature of the biological differences between schizophrenic people and normal people, we will turn to genetic and other biological factors that may produce schizophrenia.

BIOLOGICAL VIEWS Many studies have shown that the brains of schizophrenic people differ from those of normal people. Studies have focused on the amount of gray matter in the brain (see Figure 12.3 ■), the size of ventricles (hollow spaces), activity levels in the brain, and brain chemistry (for example, neurotransmitters).

Brain Deficits Associated with Schizophrenia One avenue of brain research connects the major deficits we find in schizophrenia—problems in attention, working memory, abstract thinking, and language—with dysfunction in the prefrontal cortex of the brain. Imaging of the brain has shown that people with schizophrenia generally have less gray matter than other people, which suggests deficiencies in associative processes (Takahashi et al., 2009). "Loose associations" is a key feature of schizophrenia; that is, people with schizophrenia are less likely than normal people to think logically and arrive at sensible conclusions. People with schizophrenia have smaller brains than normal people and, in particular, a smaller prefrontal region of the cortex (Shirayama et al., 2010). PET scans reveal that people with schizophrenia also tend to have a lower level of activity in the prefrontal cortex—the region responsible for executive functions such as planning and decision making (Farzan et al., 2010; Meyer-Lindenberg et al., 2001).

Still other research connects the lower activity levels with a loss in synapses (the structures that permit communication between neurons) in the region (Glantz et al., 2010), further decreasing the likelihood that people with schizophrenia will transmit neural messages efficiently. People with schizophrenia also tend to have larger ventricles than other people, suggestive of a process of deterioration (Keller et al., 2003; Puri, 2010). Enlarged ventricles are not only associated with schizophrenia; they are also predictive of development of the disorder.

What might account for differences in brain structure and brain functioning? Research evidence suggests that there are a number of biological risk factors for schizophrenia, such as heredity, complications during pregnancy and birth, and birth during winter.

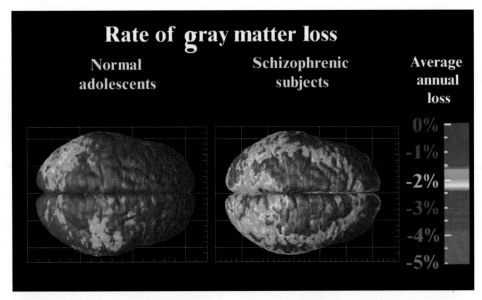

Figure 12.3 ■ Average Rates of Loss of Gray Matter Among Normal Adolescents and Adolescents Diagnosed with Schizophrenia High-resolution MRI scans show rates of gray matter loss in normal 13- to 18-year-olds and among adolescents of the same age diagnosed with schizophrenia. Maps of brain changes reveal profound, progressive loss in schizophrenia (right). Loss also occurs in normal adolescents (left) but at a slower rate. Source: P. M. Thompson et al. (2001). Mapping adolescent brain change reveals dynamic waves of accelerated gray matter loss in very early-onset schizophrenia. *Proceedings of the National Academy of Sciences of the USA*, 98(20), 11650–11655.

The Genetics of Schizophrenia Schizophrenia, like many other psychological disorders, runs in families (Bolinskey & Gottesman, 2010; Chan & Gottesman, 2008; Pogue-Geile & Gottesman, 2007). People with schizophrenia make up about 1% of the global population, yet children with one schizophrenic parent have about a 6% chance of being diagnosed with it themselves (see Figure 12.4 ■). There is about a 48% concordance rate for the diagnosis among pairs of identical (MZ) twins, whose genetic codes are the same, compared with a 17% rate among pairs of fraternal (DZ) twins (Gottesman, 1991). Moreover, adoptee studies find that the biological parent typically places the child at greater risk for schizophrenia than the adoptive parent—even though the child has been reared by the adoptive parent (Gottesman, 1991). Many studies have been carried out to try to isolate the gene or genes involved in schizophrenia. Some studies find locations for multiple genes on several chromosomes.

The importance of heredity is underscored by research findings that suggest individuals unrelated to people with schizophrenia will not develop it despite the worst of environments. Other people appear to be so genetically vulnerable to schizophrenia that they will probably not be able to avoid it despite the best of environments.

Other Biological Risk Factors in Schizophrenia In many cases of schizophrenia, a genetic vulnerability may be a necessary factor but insufficient to cause its development. The mothers of many people who develop schizophrenia have undergone complications during pregnancy and birth (Spencer et al., 2008). For example, many mothers had the flu during the sixth or seventh month of pregnancy (A. S. Brown & Sherkits, 2010; Short et al., 2010). Complications during childbirth, especially prolonged labor, seem to be connected with the larger ventricles we find among people with schizophrenia (Spencer et al., 2008). Poor maternal nutrition has been implicated as well (Stein et al., 2009; Susser et al., 2009).

People with schizophrenia are also somewhat more likely to have been born during winter than would be predicted by chance; cold weather might heighten the risk of viral and other infections in the mother during late pregnancy and early infancy (Polanczyk et al., 2010). Considering genetics and these other biological risk factors, it seems implausible to avoid the conclusion that schizophrenia involves atypical development of the central nervous system. Problems in the nervous system may involve brain chemistry as well as brain structures, and research along these lines has led to the dopamine theory of schizophrenia.

The Dopamine Theory of Schizophrenia Numerous chemical substances, including the neurotransmitter dopamine, have been suspected of playing a role in schizophrenia. According to the dopamine theory, people with schizophrenia overutilize dopamine (use more of it than other people do), although they may not produce more of it (Fatemi & Folsom, 2009; Tost et al., 2009). Why? Research suggests that they have increased concentrations of dopamine at the synapses in the brain and also larger numbers of dopamine receptors (Kegeles et al., 2010). It's a sort of "double hit" of neural transmission that may be connected with the confusion that characterizes schizophrenia.

Figure 12.5 ■ outlines the biopsychosocial model of schizophrenia. According

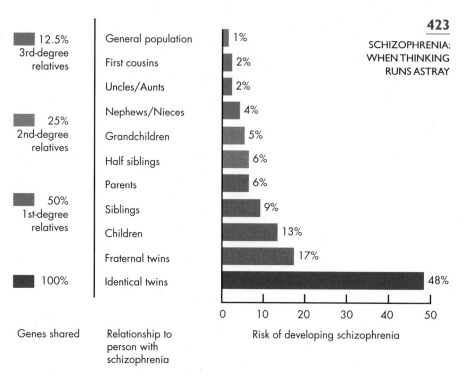

Figure 12.4 ■ Relationship to a Person Diagnosed with Schizophrenia and Likelihood of Being Diagnosed with Schizophrenia Oneself
Source: Gottesman, I. I. (1991). Schizophrenia genesis: The origins of madness. New York: W. H. Freeman.

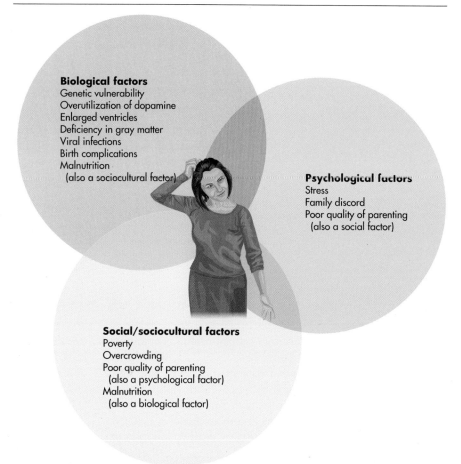

Figure 12.5 ■ The Biopsychosocial Model of Schizophrenia According to the biopsychosocial model of schizophrenia, people with a genetic vulnerability to the disorder experience increased risk for schizophrenia when they encounter problems such as viral infections, birth complications, stress, and poor parenting. People without the genetic vulnerability would not develop schizophrenia despite such problems.

Should We Ban the Insanity Plea?

During his trial, John Hinckley Jr. looks on while his father cries and claims responsibility for "John's tragedy" because he prevented his son from coming home when he desperately needed help.

John Hinckley was found not guilty of a 1981 assassination attempt on President Ronald Reagan by reason of insanity. Hinckley was diagnosed with schizophrenia and was committed to a psychiatric institution rather than given a prison term. In pleading insanity, lawyers use the M'Naghten rule, named after Daniel M'Naghten, who tried to assassinate British Prime Minister Robert Peel in 1843. M'Naghten had delusions that Peel was persecuting him, and he killed the minister's secretary in the attempt. The court found M'Naghten not guilty by reason of insanity. That is, the defendant did not understand what he was doing at the time of the act or did not realize it was wrong. The insanity plea is still used in much the same way (Zapf et al., 2009).

Many people would like to ban the insanity plea. They worry that "people are literally getting away with murder." Yet surveys show that people tend to exaggerate the extent to which the insanity please is used and how successful it is in obtaining acquittals (see Table 12.2 ■). Moreover, people found not guilty by reason of insanity are institutionalized for indefinite terms—supposedly until they are no longer insane. Hinckley remains institutionalized more than two decades after he tried to kill President Reagan, although he has had family visits on the outside. If he had been convicted of attempted murder, he might already have served his time in jail.

TABLE 12.2 ■ Use of the Insanity Defense

	Public Belief	Reality
Percent of felony indictments involving the insanity plea	37%	0.9%
Percent of pleas resulting in acquittal	44%	26%

Source: Cirincione, C., Steadman, H. J., & McGreevy, M.A. (1995).

to this model, genetic factors create a predisposition toward—or vulnerability to—schizophrenia. Genetic vulnerability to the disorder interacts with other factors, such as complications of pregnancy and birth, and perhaps psychological factors, such as stress and the quality of parenting, to give rise to the disorder (Bishop, 2009).

Because the perceptions and judgment of people with schizophrenia are impaired, the diagnosis is sometimes associated with the insanity plea in the criminal courts. The nearby Closer Look offers insight into the insanity plea.

LearningConnections ● SCHIZOPHRENIA: WHEN THINKING RUNS ASTRAY

ACTIVE REVIEW (21) Paranoid schizophrenia is characterized by paranoid _____. (22) _____ schizophrenia is characterized by impaired motor activity and waxy flexibility. (23) Schizophrenia (does or does not?) tend to run in families. (24) The prefrontal region of the brain of people with schizophrenia has (more or fewer?) synapses than that of other people. (25) People with schizophrenia utilize more of the neurotransmitter _____ than other people do.

REFLECT AND RELATE There is evidence for genetic factors in schizophrenia. What would you tell the son or daughter of a person with schizophrenia about the likelihood of his or her developing the disorder? Explain.

CRITICAL THINKING Agree or disagree with the following statement, and support your answer: Schizophrenia is a disease of the brain.

 Go to Psychology CourseMate at **www.cengagebrain.com** for an interactive version of these questions.

● PERSONALITY DISORDERS: MAKING ONESELF OR OTHERS MISERABLE

Personality disorders, like personality traits, are characterized by enduring patterns of behavior. Personality disorders, however, are inflexible and maladaptive. They impair personal or social functioning and are a source of distress to the individual or to other people. **Question 16: What kinds of personality disorders are there?**

Types of Personality Disorders

There are a number of personality disorders. These include *paranoid, schizotypal, schizoid, borderline, antisocial,* and *avoidant personality disorders.*

PARANOID PERSONALITY DISORDER The defining trait of the **paranoid personality disorder** is a tendency to interpret other people's behavior as threatening or demeaning. People with the disorder do not show the grossly disorganized thinking of paranoid schizophrenia. However, they are mistrustful of others, and their relationships suffer for it. They may be suspicious of coworkers and supervisors, but they can generally hold a job.

SCHIZOTYPAL PERSONALITY DISORDER Schizotypal personality disorder is characterized by peculiarities of thought, perception, or behavior, such as excessive fantasy and suspiciousness, feelings of being unreal, or the odd use of words. There are no complex delusions, no hallucinations, and no unusual motor activities, so this disorder is schizo*typal,* not schizophrenic.

THE SCHIZOID PERSONALITY Schizoid personality disorder is characterized by indifference to relationships and flat emotional response. People with this disorder are "loners." They do not develop warm, tender feelings for others. They have few friends and rarely maintain long-term relationships. Some people with schizoid personality disorder do very well on the job provided that continuous social interaction is not required. They do not have hallucinations or delusions.

BORDERLINE PERSONALITY DISORDER People with **borderline personality disorder** show instability in their relationships, self-image, and mood and a lack of control over impulses (Stanley & Siever, 2010). They tend to be uncertain of their values, goals, loyalties, careers, choices of friends, and sometimes even their sexual orientations (Roepke et al., 2010). Instability in self-image or identity may leave them with feelings of emptiness and boredom. Many cannot tolerate being alone and make desperate attempts to avoid feelings of abandonment. They may be clinging and demanding in social relationships, and their clinging often pushes away the people on whom they depend. They alternate between extremes of adulation in their relationships (when their needs are met) and loathing (when they feel scorned). They tend to view other people as all good or all bad, shifting abruptly from one extreme to the other. As a result, they may flit from partner to partner in brief and stormy relationships. They tend to idealize people, then treat them with contempt when those people appear to have failed them.

Instability of moods is a central characteristic of borderline personality disorder. Moods run the gamut from anger and irritability to depression and anxiety, with each lasting from a few hours to a few days. People with the disorder have difficulty controlling anger and are prone to fights or smashing things. They often act on impulse, like eloping with someone they have just met. This impulsive and unpredictable behavior is often self-destructive and linked to a risk of suicidal attempts and gestures. It may involve spending sprees, gambling, drug abuse, engaging in unsafe sexual activity,

Personality disorders Enduring patterns of maladaptive behavior that are sources of distress to the individual or others.

Paranoid personality disorder A personality disorder characterized by persistent suspiciousness but not involving the disorganization of paranoid schizophrenia.

Schizotypal personality disorder A personality disorder characterized by oddities of thought and behavior but not involving bizarre psychotic behaviors.

Schizoid personality disorder A personality disorder characterized by social withdrawal.

Borderline personality disorder A personality disorder characterized by instability in relationships, self-image, and mood, plus lack of impulse control.

A Person with Borderline Personality Disorder? Many well-known individuals such as Marilyn Monroe (seen here with her husband, playwright Arthur Miller) may have had borderline personality disorder. The disorder is characterized by instability in relationships, self-image, and mood and by problems in impulse control.

reckless driving, binge eating, or shoplifting. People with the disorder may also engage in self-mutilation, such as scratching their wrists or burning cigarettes on their arms (Zanarini et al., 2010). Self-mutilation is sometimes a means of manipulating others, particularly in times of stress. Frequent self-mutilation is also associated with suicide attempts.

ANTISOCIAL PERSONALITY DISORDER Truth or Fiction Revisited: It is true that some people can kill or maim others with no feelings of guilt at all. When these people also persistently violate the rights of others and are in repeated conflict with the law, they may be diagnosed with **antisocial personality disorder** (see Table 12.3 ■). People with antisocial personality disorder often show a superficial charm and are at least average in intelligence. They do not form meaningful bonds with other people, and they fail to learn to improve their behavior from punishment (Kumari et al., 2009; Romero et al., 2001). Though they are often heavily punished by their parents and rejected by peers, they continue in their impulsive, careless styles of life. Whereas women are more likely than men to have anxiety and depressive disorders, antisocial personality disorder is more common among men (McCormick et al., 2007).

> **Antisocial personality disorder** The diagnosis given a person who is in frequent conflict with society, yet who is undeterred by punishment and experiences little or no guilt and anxiety.

AVOIDANT PERSONALITY DISORDER People with avoidant personality disorder are generally unwilling to enter a relationship without some assurance of acceptance because they fear rejection and criticism. As a result, they may have few close relationships outside their immediate families. Unlike people with schizoid personality disorder, however, they have some interest in, and feelings of warmth toward, other people.

> **Avoidant personality disorder** A personality disorder in which the person is unwilling to enter relationships without assurance of acceptance because of fears of rejection and criticism.

Origins of Personality Disorders

Question 17: What is known about the origins of personality disorders? Many theoretical explanations of personality disorders are derived from the psychodynamic model. Traditional Freudian theory focuses on Oedipal problems as the source of many

---

TABLE 12.3 ■ Areas of the Brain Frequently Impaired in People with Antisocial Personality Disorder and Possible Consequences

Processes/Risk Factors	Possible Outcome
Ventral Prefrontal Cortex	
Regulation of emotion	Poor control over anger
Mediation of emotional responses guiding behavior	Poor control over behavior
Empathy/concern for others	Callous regard for the feelings or situation of others
Amygdala	
Fear conditioning	Lack of affect and poor development of conscience
Social-emotion judgments	Misinterpreting other people's motives and feelings
Moral emotion	Noncompliance with societal rules
Judging trustworthiness	Hypersociability and victimization of others

Adapted from Table 1, page 326. Raine, A. (2008). From genes to brain to antisocial behavior. *Current Directions in Psychological Science, 17*(5), 323–328.

psychological disorders, including personality disorders. Faulty resolution of the Oedipus complex might lead to lack of guilt because conscience, or superego, is thought to depend on proper resolution of the complex. Although lack of guilt may occur more often among children who are rejected and punished by parents rather than given affection (Fowles & Dindo, 2009), the view that such treatment causes Oedipal problems remains speculative.

Cognitive psychologists find that antisocial adolescents tend to interpret other people's behavior as threatening, even when it is not (Dodge, 2006; Ellis et al., 2009). Aggressive individuals often find it difficult to solve social problems in useful ways (Fontaine et al., 2010).

BIOLOGICAL VIEWS OF ANTISOCIAL PERSONALITY DISORDER Genetic factors are apparently involved in some personality disorders (Jang et al., 2007; Livesley & Jang, 2008). Personality traits are to some degree heritable, and many personality disorders seem to be extreme variations of normal personality traits. An analysis of 51 twin and adoption studies estimated that genetic factors were the greatest influences on antisocial behavior (Rhee & Waldman, 2002). Referring to the five-factor model of personality (see Chapter 10), people with schizoid personalities tend to be highly introverted (Widiger & Simonsen, 2005). People with avoidant personalities tend to be both introverted and emotionally unstable (neurotic) (Widiger & Simonsen, 2005).

Perhaps the genetics of antisocial personality involves the prefrontal cortex of the brain, which is connected with emotional responses. There is some evidence that people with antisocial personality, as a group, have less gray matter (associative neurons) in the prefrontal cortex—especially on the underside, or ventral part, of the prefrontal cortex—than other people do (Narayan et al., 2007; Raine et al., 2009). Adrian Raine (2008) suggests that specific genes lead to this impairment and also predispose people to antisocial behavior. He notes that a common change in one gene has been connected with antisocial behavior, on the one hand, and with reductions in the volume of the ventral prefrontal cortex and also the amygdala, on the other hand. Table 12.3 outlines findings concerning the impairments that have been found in these parts of the brain and the possible emotional and behavioral consequences.

Although the causes of many psychological disorders remain in dispute, various methods of therapy have been devised to deal with them. Those methods are the focus of Chapter 13.

LearningConnections ● PERSONALITY DISORDERS: MAKING ONESELF OR OTHERS MISERABLE

ACTIVE REVIEW (26) _____ disorders are inflexible, maladaptive behavior patterns that impair personal or social functioning and are a source of distress to the individual or to others. (27) Research suggests that people with antisocial personalities have (higher or lower?) than normal levels of arousal than most people.

REFLECT AND RELATE Do you know anyone whom you consider to have a personality disorder? What characteristics lead you to describe him or her in this way?

CRITICAL THINKING Within the medical model, sick people are often excused from school or work. If some criminals are "sick" in the sense of being diagnosed with antisocial personality disorder, does the disorder relieve them of responsibility for their behavior? Explain.

 Go to Psychology CourseMate at **www.cengagebrain.com** for an interactive version of these questions.

Anxiety Disorders	Dissociative Disorders	Somatoform Disorders
	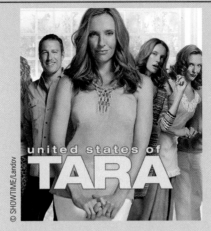	

Major Subtypes

• Phobic disorders • Panic disorder • Generalized anxiety disorder • Obsessive–compulsive disorder • Stress disorders	• Dissociative amnesia • Dissociative fugue • Dissociative identity disorder (multiple personality disorder)	• Conversion disorder • Hypochondriasis

Symptoms

• Worrying • Fear of the worst happening • Fear of losing control • Nervousness • Inability to relax	• Separation of mental processes such as thoughts, emotions, identity, memory, or consciousness	• Complaints of physical problems such as paralysis or pain • Persistent belief that one has a serious disease in the absence of medical findings

Possible Origins

• Phobias symbolize conflicts originating in childhood (psychodynamic theory). • Phobias may have been acquired in early childhood by conditioning or observational learning (learning theory). • People with anxiety disorders may be biased toward attending too much to threats (cognitive theory). • Genetic factors are implicated. • Phobias may have contributed to survival of human species (evolutionary perspective). • Receptor sites in the brain may not be sensitive enough to the neurotransmitter GABA, which quells anxiety reactions (neurological perspective).	• People with dissociative disorders use massive repression to prevent recognition of improper impulses or ugly memories (psychodynamic theory). • People with dissociative disorders learn not to think about improper impulses or ugly memories, such as childhood sexual abuse (learning theory).	• People with somatoform disorders have the capacity to focus on imagined physical problems, a form of self-hypnosis. • People with somatoform disorders have a special sensitivity to bodily symptoms.

Mood Disorders	Schizophrenia	Personality Disorders

• Major depression • Bipolar disorder	• Paranoid schizophrenia • Disorganized schizophrenia • Catatonic schizophrenia	• Paranoid personality disorder • Schizotypal personality disorder • Schizoid personality disorder • Borderline personality disorder • Antisocial personality disorder • Avoidant personality disorder
• Disturbance in expressed emotions	• Disturbances in language and thought (e.g., delusions, loose associations), attention and perception (e.g., hallucinations) • Disturbances in motor activity • Disturbances in mood • Withdrawal from reality and absorption in daydreams or fantasy	• Inflexible and maladaptive patterns of behavior • Impairment in personal or social functioning • A source of distress to oneself or others
• Depression may be anger turned inward due to holding in rather than expressing feelings of anger; bipolar disorder may be due to alternate domination by the ego and superego (psychodynamic theory). • People with depression learn that they are helpless to change their situations (learning theory). • Perfectionism, rumination, and attributional style—internal, stable, and global attributions for failures and shortcomings—lead to depression (cognitive theory). • Depression is connected with neuroticism, which is believed to be heritable (genetic). • Depression is connected with underutilization of the neurotransmitter serotonin (neurological).	• In people with schizophrenia, the ego may be overwhelmed by the id (psychodynamic theory). • Schizophrenic behavior can be imitated in the hospital setting and reinforced by staff attention (learning theory). • Poor parenting and poverty may contribute to schizophrenia (sociocultural). • Schizophrenia runs in families, with a high concordance rate among MZ twins (genetic). • People with schizophrenia may have larger ventricles, smaller prefrontal cortexes, and fewer synapses than others; complications during pregnancy and childbirth and overutilization of the neurotransmitter dopamine are also connected with schizophrenia (neurological).	• Faulty resolution of Oedipus complex may lead to personality disorders (psychodynamic theory). • People with personality disorders may have learned maladaptive ways of relating to other people in childhood (learning theory). • Antisocial people may misinterpret other people's behavior as threatening (cognitive theory). • Exaggerated personality traits, which are partly heritable (genetic), may be involved in the origin of personality disorders. • Antisocial individuals may have less gray matter in the brain, which might lower arousal and thus inhibit feelings of guilt and reduce the effects of punishment (neurological).

What Are Psychological Disorders?

1. What are psychological disorders?
Psychological disorders are characterized by unusual behavior, socially unacceptable behavior, faulty perception of reality, personal distress, dangerous behavior, or self-defeating behavior.

2. How have people viewed psychological disorders?
Psychological disorders were once viewed from a demonological perspective. In modern times, the medical model grew into prominence. Today, many psychologists view psychological disorders from the biopsychosocial perspective.

3. How are psychological disorders grouped or classified?
The most widely used classification is found in the *Diagnostic and Statistical Manual (DSM)* of the American Psychiatric Association.

4. How common are psychological disorders?
Nearly half (46%) of us will have some psychological disorder during our lifetime. We are most likely to develop depression and anxiety disorders; schizophrenia will affect about 1% of us.

Anxiety Disorders: Real-Life "Fear Factors"?

5. What kinds of anxiety disorders are there?
Anxiety disorders are characterized by feelings of dread and by overarousal of the sympathetic branch of the autonomic nervous system. These disorders include phobias, panic disorder, generalized anxiety disorder, obsessive–compulsive disorder, and stress disorders.

6. What is known about the origins of anxiety disorders?
Many learning theorists view phobias as conditioned fears. Cognitive theorists focus on ways people interpret threats. We may be "biologically prepared" to acquire certain kinds of fears. Anxiety disorders tend to run in families. Faulty regulation of neurotransmitters such as GABA may be involved in anxiety disorders.

Dissociative Disorders: Splitting Consciousness

7. What kinds of dissociative disorders are there?
Dissociative disorders are characterized by sudden, temporary changes in consciousness or self-identity. They include dissociative amnesia, dissociative fugue, and dissociative identity disorder (multiple personality disorder).

8. What is known about the origins of dissociative disorders?
Many psychologists suggest that dissociative disorders help people keep disturbing memories or ideas out of their mind. These memories may involve episodes of childhood sexual or physical abuse.

Somatoform Disorders: When the Body Expresses Stress

9. What kinds of somatoform disorders are there?
People with somatoform disorders complain of physical problems although no medical evidence can be found. In conversion disorder, stress is "converted" into a physical symptom. People diagnosed with hypochondriasis believe they have serious health problems that nobody can detect or explain.

10. What is known about the origins of somatoform disorders?
Somatoform disorders may reflect the relative benefits of focusing on physical symptoms rather than fears and conflicts.

Mood Disorders: Up, Down, and Around

11. What kinds of mood disorders are there?
Mood disorders involve disturbances in expressed emotions. They include major depression and bipolar disorder.

12. What is known about the origins of mood disorders?
Research emphasizes possible roles for learned helplessness, attributional styles, and underutilization of serotonin in depression. People who are depressed are more likely than other people to make internal, stable, and global attributions for failures.

Schizophrenia: When Thinking Runs Astray

13. What is schizophrenia?
Schizophrenia is a severe psychological disorder that is characterized by disturbances in thought and language, in perception and attention, in motor activity, in mood, and in social interaction.

14. What kinds of schizophrenia are there?
The major types of schizophrenia are paranoid, disorganized, and catatonic. Paranoid schizophrenia is characterized largely by delusions, disorganized schizophrenia by incoherence, and catatonic schizophrenia by motor impairment.

15. What is known about the origins of schizophrenia?
Schizophrenia is connected with smaller brains and larger ventricles. Genetic vulnerability to schizophrenia may interact with factors such as stress, complications during pregnancy and childbirth, and quality of parenting, to cause the disorder to develop. According to the dopamine theory of schizophrenia, people with schizophrenia utilize more dopamine than other people do.

Personality Disorders: Making Oneself or Others Miserable

16. What kinds of personality disorders are there?
Personality disorders are inflexible, maladaptive behavior patterns that impair personal or social functioning and

cause distress for the individual or others. They include paranoid personality disorder, schizotypal personality disorders, schizoid personality disorder, borderline personality disorder, antisocial personality disorder, and avoidant personality disorder.

17. What is known about the origins of personality disorders?
Genetic factors may be involved in some personality disorders. People diagnosed with antisocial personality disorder apparently have less gray matter in the prefrontal cortex of the brain, which may provide lower than normal levels of arousal.

KEY TERMS

Acrophobia (p. 405)
Acute stress disorder (p. 407)
Agoraphobia (p. 405)
Antisocial personality disorder (p. 426)
Anxiety disorders (p. 404)
Attributional style (p. 415)
Avoidant personality disorder (p. 426)
Biopsychosocial model (p. 402)
Bipolar disorder (p. 413)
Borderline personality disorder (p. 425)
Catatonic schizophrenia (p. 420)
Claustrophobia (p. 405)
Concordance (p. 408)
Conversion disorder (p. 411)
Culture-bound (p. 402)
Delusions (p. 419)
Diathesis–stress model (p. 402)
Disorganized schizophrenia (p. 420)
Dissociative amnesia (p. 410)
Dissociative disorders (p. 410)

Dissociative fugue (p. 410)
Dissociative identity disorder (p. 410)
Generalized anxiety disorder (p. 406)
Hallucination (p. 400)
Hypochondriasis (p. 412)
Ideas of persecution (p. 400)
Insanity (p. 399)
La belle indifférence (p. 411)
Learned helplessness (p. 414)
Major depressive disorder (p. 412)
Manic (p. 413)
Mood disorder (p. 412)
Multiple personality disorder (p. 410)
Mutism (p. 419)
Negative symptoms (p. 419)
Neuroticism (p. 415)
Obsessive–compulsive disorder (OCD) (p. 407)
Panic disorder (p. 405)
Paranoid personality disorder (p. 425)

Paranoid schizophrenia (p. 420)
Personality disorders (p. 425)
Positive symptoms (p. 419)
Posttraumatic stress disorder (PTSD) (p. 407)
Predictive validity (p. 403)
Psychological disorders (p. 399)
Psychomotor retardation (p. 413)
Rapid flight of ideas (p. 413)
Reliability (p. 403)
Schizoid personality disorder (p. 425)
Schizophrenia (p. 419)
Schizotypal personality disorder (p. 425)
Social phobia (p. 405)
Somatoform disorders (p. 411)
Specific phobia (p. 405)
Stupor (p. 420)
Validity (p. 403)
Waxy flexibility (p. 421)

ACTIVE LEARNING RESOURCES

Log in to **www.cengagebrain.com** to access the resources your instructor requires. For this book, you can access:

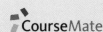 CourseMate brings course concepts to life with interactive learning, study, and exam preparation tools that support the printed textbook. A textbook-specific website, Psychology CourseMate includes an integrated interactive eBook and other interactive learning tools including quizzes, flashcards, videos, and more.

 Need help studying? This site is your one-stop study shop. Take a Pre-Test and CengageNOW will generate a Personalized Study Plan based on your test results. The Study Plan will identify the topics you need to review and direct you to online resources to help you master those topics. You can then take a Post-Test to determine the concepts you have mastered and what you still need to work on.

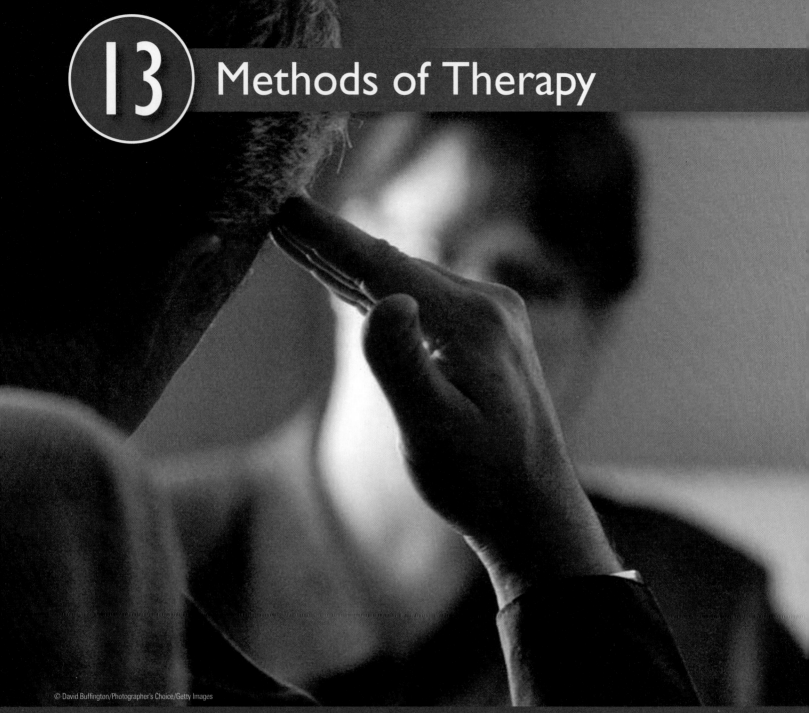

13 Methods of Therapy

© David Buffington/Photographer's Choice/Getty Images

MAJOR TOPICS

What Is Psychotherapy? *434*

Psychodynamic Therapies: Digging Deep Within *436*

Humanistic Therapies: Strengthening the Self *439*

Behavior Therapy: Adjustment Is What You Do *442*

Cognitive Therapies: Adjustment Is What You Think (and Do) *447*

Group Therapies: On Being in It Together *450*

Does Psychotherapy Work? *452*

Biological Therapies *456*

FEATURES

Video Connections: Virtual Reality Therapy *434*

Self-Assessment: Do You Speak Your Mind or Wimp Out? The Assertiveness Schedule *445*

A Closer Look: Eye-Movement Desensitization and Reprocessing *447*

A Closer Look: Contemporary Psychosurgery for Treatment-Resistant Obsessive–Compulsive Disorder and Depression *459*

Life Connections: Alleviating Depression: Getting Out of the Dumps *460*

Concept Review 13.1: Methods of Therapy *462*

T F Residents of London used to visit the local insane asylum for a fun night out on the town.

page 435

T F Some psychotherapists interpret clients' dreams.

page 438

T F Some psychotherapists let their clients take the lead in psychotherapy.

page 440

T F Other psychotherapists challenge their clients to make the tough choices in life.

page 441

T F Still other psychotherapists tell their clients exactly what to do.

page 442

T F Lying in a reclining chair and fantasizing can be an effective way of confronting fears.

page 443

T F Smoking cigarettes can be an effective method for helping people…stop smoking cigarettes.

page 443

T F You might be able to put an end to bad habits merely by keeping a record of where and when you practice them.

page 446

T F The same kind of drug is used to treat depression, panic disorder, obsessive–compulsive disorder, even eating disorders.

page 457

T F The originator of a surgical technique intended to reduce violence learned that it was not always successful…when one of his patients shot him.

page 458

T F People with psychological disorders should always say no to drugs.

page 458

Are these items truth or fiction? We will be revisiting them throughout the chapter.

Joanne Cartwright (dubbed "Miss Muffet" by her therapist) had a spider phobia. "I washed my truck every night before I went to work in case there were webs," she said (cited in Robbins, 2000). "I put all my clothes in plastic bags and taped duct tape around my doors so spiders couldn't get in. I thought I was going to have a mental breakdown. I wasn't living." She checked every crack in the sidewalk for spiders—if she could push herself to go outside at all. Finally, her crippling phobia made it all but impossible for her to leave the house. After years of misery, she sought help.

Fortunately for "Miss Muffet," she wound up in the University of Washington's Human Interface Technology Laboratory, where she worked with psychologist Hunter Hoffman. Writing in *Scientific American,* Hoffman (2004) describes a virtual environment called *SpiderWorld* that helps people with spider phobias overcome their aversion by gradually approaching virtual spiders and reaching out to touch them. A toy spider and a device that tracks the patient's hand movements provide tactile sensations akin to touching a real spider.

Twelve virtual therapy desensitization sessions changed Cartwright's life. "I'm amazed," she notes, "because I am doing all this stuff I could never do," such as camping and hiking.

University of Southern California psychologist Albert Rizzo has developed scenes from classrooms and parties to help people overcome social anxieties. "To help people deal with their problems, you must get them exposed to what they fear most," says Rizzo (Rizzo & Schultheis, 2002).

Atlanta-based company Virtually Better has developed scenes of a bridge and a glass elevator to desensitize patients to fear of heights, a virtual airplane cabin for people who fear flying, and a virtual thunderstorm to help people reduce their fear of tempestuous weather (DeAngelis, 2009). They are creating programs to help soldiers returning from combat zones. One, Virtual Iraq, is a virtual Iraqi city, complete with sounds of explosions and gunfire, sights of people in the streets, and a scent machine that conjures up the aromas of Middle Eastern spices, burning rubber, and rotting garbage (Miyahira et al., 2010).

Virtually Better is also working on programs to help treat addictions. Psychologists are studying whether virtual exposure to alcohol, drugs, and cigarettes can evoke cravings that patients can learn to resist. Virtually Better's contributions include scenes of a virtual crack house and a virtual bar.

Joanne Cartwright received virtual therapy to learn to cope with her phobia of spiders. If she had chosen a different kind of therapist, she might have been

- Lying on a couch, talking about anything that popped into awareness, trying to unearth the possible symbolic meaning of spiders.
- Sitting face to face with a warm, gentle therapist who expressed faith in Joanne's ability to cope with her fears.

Psychologist Hunter Hoffman Uses Virtual Therapy to Treat "Miss Muffet" *Miss Muffet* is the name playfully given by Hoffman to a woman with a phobia for spiders. She is wearing virtual reality headgear and sees the scene displayed on the monitor, which shows a large and hairy—but virtual—tarantula.

- Listening to a frank, straightforward therapist assert that she was catastrophizing the awfulness of spiders and compounding her problem by ruminating about it.
- Taking medication.
- Participating in some combination of these approaches.

These methods, although different, all represent methods of therapy. In this chapter, we explore various methods of psychotherapy and biological therapy. **Question 1: What is psychotherapy?**

Psychotherapy A systematic interaction between a therapist and a client that brings psychological principles to bear on influencing the client's thoughts, feelings, and/or behavior to help that client overcome psychological disorders, adjust to problems in living, or develop as an individual.

● WHAT IS PSYCHOTHERAPY?

There are many kinds of psychotherapy, but they all have certain common characteristics. **Psychotherapy** is a systematic interaction between a therapist and a client that applies psychological principles to affect the client's thoughts, feelings, and/or behavior to help the client overcome psychological disorders, adjust to problems in living, or develop as an individual.

Quite a mouthful? True. But note the essentials:

1. *Systematic interaction:* Psychotherapy is a systematic interaction between a client and a therapist. The therapist's theoretical point of view interacts with the client's to determine how the therapist and client relate to each other.

2. *Psychological principles:* Psychotherapy is based on psychological theory and research in areas such as personality, learning, motivation, and emotion.

3. *Thoughts, feelings, and behavior:* Psychotherapy influences clients' thoughts, feelings, and behavior. It can be aimed at any or all of these aspects of human psychology.

4. *Psychological disorders, adjustment problems, and personal growth:* Psychotherapy is often used with people who have psychological disorders. Other people seek help for problems such as shyness, overeating, and adjusting to loss of a life partner. Still other clients want to learn more about themselves and to reach their full potential as individuals, parents, or creative artists.

Video Connections—Virtual Reality Therapy

Virtual reality therapy helps people overcome fears like that of the subway and other enclosed spaces. View the video to learn more about how psychologists use virtual reality and why they might use different treatment methods for people with the same kind of problems. Go to Psychology CourseMate at **www.cengagebrain.com** to watch this video.

The History of Therapies

Historically speaking, "treatments" of psychological disorders often reflected the assumption that people who behaved in strange ways were possessed by demons. **Question 2: How, then, have people with psychological problems and disorders been treated throughout the ages?** Because of this belief, treatment tended to involve cruel practices such as exorcism and even execution. Some people who could not meet the demands of everyday life were tossed into prisons. Others begged in the streets, stole food, or became prostitutes. A few found their way to monasteries or other retreats that offered a kind word and some support. Generally speaking, they died early.

ASYLUMS Asylums originated in European monasteries. They were the first institutions meant primarily for people with psychological disorders. But their function was warehousing, not treatment. As their inmate populations mushroomed, the stresses created by noise, overcrowding, and disease aggravated the problems they were meant to ease. Inmates were frequently chained and beaten.

The word *bedlam* derives from St. Mary's of *Bethlehem*, the London asylum that opened its gates in 1547. Here unfortunate people with psychological disorders were chained, whipped, and allowed to lie in their own waste. **Truth or Fiction Revisited:** And here the ladies and gentlemen of the British upper class might stroll on a lazy afternoon to be amused by inmates' antics. The price of admission was one penny.

Humanitarian reform movements began in the 18th century. In Paris, the physician Philippe Pinel unchained the patients at La Salpêtrière. Rather than running amok as had been feared, most patients profited from kindness and freedom. Many eventually reentered society. Later, movements to reform such institutions were led by William Tuke in England and Dorothea Dix in America.

MENTAL HOSPITALS In the United States, mental hospitals gradually replaced asylums. In the mid-1950s, more than a million people resided in state, county, Veterans Administration, or private facilities. (The number has dropped to about 200,000 today.) The mental hospital's function is treatment, not warehousing. Still, because of high patient populations and understaffing, many patients receive little attention even today. Despite somewhat improved conditions, one psychiatrist may be responsible for the welfare of several hundred residents on a weekend when other staff members are absent.

The Unchaining of the Patients at La Salpêtrière Philippe Pinel sparked the humanitarian reform movement by unchaining the patients at this asylum in Paris.

Philippe Pinel (1745–1826) releasing lunatics from their chains at the Salpetriere asylum in Paris in 1795 (color litho), Robert-Fleury, Tony (1837–1912) (after)/Bibliotheque des Arts Decoratifs, Paris, France/Archives Charmet/ The Bridgeman Art Library International.

THE COMMUNITY MENTAL HEALTH MOVEMENT Since the 1960s, efforts have been made to maintain people with serious psychological disorders in their communities. Community mental health centers attempt to maintain new patients as outpatients and to serve patients who have been released from mental hospitals. Today, most people with chronic psychological disorders live in the community, not the hospital. Social critics note that many people who had resided in hospitals for decades were suddenly discharged to "home" communities that seemed foreign and forbidding to them. Many do not receive adequate follow-up care. Many join the ranks of the homeless (Drury, 2003).

Asylum An institution for the care of the mentally ill.

● PSYCHODYNAMIC THERAPIES: DIGGING DEEP WITHIN

Psychodynamic therapies are based on the thinking of Sigmund Freud, the founder of psychodynamic theory. Such therapies assume that psychological problems reflect early childhood experiences and internal conflicts. According to Freud, these conflicts involve the shifting of psychic, or libidinal, energy among the three psychic structures—the id, ego, and superego. These shifts of psychic energy determine our behavior. When primitive urges threaten to break through from the id or when the superego floods us with excessive guilt, defenses are established to protect us from these feelings; yet they are not completely eliminated, so we may experience some distress. Freud's psychodynamic therapy method—*psychoanalysis*—aims to modify the flow of energy among these structures, largely to bulwark the ego against the torrents of energy loosened by the id and the superego. With impulses and feelings of guilt and shame placed under greater control, clients are freer to develop adaptive behavior. **Question 3: How, then, do psychoanalysts conduct a traditional Freudian psychoanalysis?**

> *"Freud is the father of psychoanalysis. It has no mother."*
>
> GERMAINE GREER

Traditional Psychoanalysis: "Where Id Was, There Shall Ego Be"

> Canst thou not minister to a mind diseas'd,
> Pluck out from the memory a rooted sorrow,
> Raze out the written troubles of the brain,
> And with some sweet oblivious antidote
> Cleanse the stuff'd bosom of that perilous stuff
> Which weighs upon the heart?
>
> Shakespeare, *Macbeth*

In this passage, Macbeth asks a physician to help Lady Macbeth after she has gone mad. In the play, her madness is caused partly by events—namely, her role in murders designed to seat her husband on the throne of Scotland. There are also hints of mysterious, deeply rooted problems, such as conflicts about infertility.

If Lady Macbeth's physician had been a traditional psychoanalyst, he might have asked her to lie on a couch in a slightly darkened room. He would have sat behind her and encouraged her to talk about anything that came to mind, no matter how trivial, no matter how personal. To avoid interfering with her self-exploration, he might have said little or nothing for session after session. That would have been par for the course. A traditional psychoanalysis can extend for months, or years.

Psychoanalysis is the clinical method devised by Freud for plucking "from the memory a rooted sorrow," for razing "out the written troubles of the brain." It aims to provide *insight* into the conflicts that are presumed to lie at the roots of a person's problems. Insight means many things, including knowledge of the experiences that lead to conflicts and maladaptive behavior, recognition of unconscious feelings and conflicts, and conscious evaluation of one's thoughts, feelings, and behavior.

Psychodynamic therapy A type of psychotherapy that is based on Freud's thinking and that assumes that psychological problems reflect early childhood experiences and internal conflicts.

Psychoanalysis Freud's method of psychotherapy.

Psychoanalysis also aims to help the client express feelings and urges that have been repressed. By so doing, Freud believed that the client spilled forth the psychic energy that had been repressed by conflicts and guilt. He called this spilling forth **catharsis**. Catharsis would provide relief by alleviating some of the forces assaulting the ego.

Freud was also fond of saying, "Where id was, there shall ego be." In part, he meant that psychoanalysis could shed light on the inner workings of the mind. He also sought to replace impulsive and defensive behavior with coping behavior. In this way, for example, a man with a phobia for knives might discover that he had been repressing the urge to harm someone who had taken advantage of him. He might also find ways to confront the person verbally.

A View of Freud's Consulting Room Freud would sit in a chair by the head of the couch while a client free-associated. The basic rule of free association is that no thought is censored. Freud did not believe that free association was really "free"; he assumed that significant feelings would rise to the surface and demand expression.

FREE ASSOCIATION Freud used **free association** to break through the walls of defense that block a client's insight into unconscious processes. In free association, the client is made comfortable—for example, by lying on a couch—and asked to talk about any topic that comes to mind. No thought is to be censored—that is the basic rule. Psychoanalysts ask their clients to wander "freely" from topic to topic, but they do not believe that the process occurring *within* the client is fully free. Repressed impulses clamor for release.

The ego persists in trying to repress unacceptable impulses and threatening conflicts. As a result, clients might show **resistance** to recalling and discussing threatening ideas. A client about to entertain such thoughts might claim, "My mind is blank." The client might accuse the analyst of being demanding or inconsiderate. He might "forget" the next appointment when threatening material is about to surface.

The therapist observes the dynamic struggle between the client's compulsion to utter certain thoughts and, at the same time, her resistance to uttering them. Through discreet remarks, the analyst tips the balance in favor of utterance. A gradual process of self-discovery and self-insight ensues. Now and then, the analyst offers an **interpretation** of an utterance, showing how it suggests resistance or deep-seated feelings and conflicts.

TRANSFERENCE Freud believed that clients not only responded to him as an individual but also in ways that reflected their attitudes and feelings toward other people in their lives. He labeled this process **transference**. For example, a young woman client might respond to Freud as a father figure and displace her feelings toward her father onto Freud, perhaps seeking affection and wisdom.

Analyzing and working through transference have been considered key aspects of psychoanalysis. Freud believed that clients reenact their childhood conflicts with their parents when they are in therapy. For example, a client may interpret a suggestion by the therapist as a criticism and see it as a devastating blow, transferring feelings of self-hatred that he had repressed because his parents had rejected him in childhood. Transference can also distort clients' relationships with other people here and now, such as relationships with spouses or employers. The following therapeutic dialogue illustrates the way an analyst may interpret a client's inability to communicate his needs to his wife as a function of transference. The purpose is to provide his client, a Mr. Arianes, with insight into how his relationship with his wife has been colored by his childhood relationship with his mother:

ARIANES: I think you've got it there, Doc. We weren't communicating. I wouldn't tell [my wife] what was wrong or what I wanted from her. Maybe I expected her to understand me without saying anything.

Catharsis In psychoanalysis, the expression of repressed feelings and impulses to allow the release of the psychic energy associated with them.

Free association In psychoanalysis, the uncensored uttering of all thoughts that come to mind.

Resistance The tendency to block the free expression of impulses and primitive ideas—a reflection of the defense mechanism of repression.

Interpretation In psychoanalysis, an explanation of a client's utterance according to psychoanalytic theory.

Transference Responding to one person (such as a spouse or the psychoanalyst) in a way that is similar to the way one responded to another person (such as a parent) in childhood.

THERAPIST:	Like the expectations a child has of its mother.
ARIANES:	Not my mother!
THERAPIST:	Oh?
ARIANES:	No, I always thought she had too many troubles of her own to pay attention to mine. I remember once I got hurt on my bike and came to her all bloodied up. When she saw me she got mad and yelled at me for making more trouble for her when she already had her hands full with my father.
THERAPIST:	Do you remember how you felt then?
ARIANES:	I can't remember, but I know that after that I never brought my troubles to her again.
THERAPIST:	How old were you?
ARIANES:	Nine, I know that because I got that bike for my ninth birthday. It was a little too big for me still, that's why I got hurt on it.
THERAPIST:	Perhaps you carried this attitude into your marriage.
ARIANES:	What attitude?
THERAPIST:	The feeling that your wife, like your mother, would be unsympathetic to your difficulties. That there was no point in telling her about your experiences because she was too preoccupied or too busy to care.
ARIANES:	But she's so different from my mother. I come first with her.
THERAPIST:	On one level you know that. On another, deeper level there may well be the fear that people—or maybe only women, or maybe only women you're close to—are all the same, and you can't take a chance at being rejected again in your need.
ARIANES:	Maybe you're right, Doc, but all that was so long ago, and I should be over that by now.
THERAPIST:	That's not the way the mind works. If a shock or a disappointment is strong enough it can permanently freeze our picture of ourselves and our expectations of the world. The rest of us grows up—that is, we let ourselves learn about life from experience and from what we see, hear, or read of the experiences of others, but that one area where we really got hurt stays unchanged. So what I mean when I say you might be carrying that attitude into your relationship with your wife is that when it comes to your hopes of being understood and catered to when you feel hurt or abused by life, you still feel very much like that nine-year-old boy who was rebuffed in his need and gave up hope that anyone would or could respond to him. (Basch, 1980, pp. 29–30)

DREAM ANALYSIS Truth or Fiction Revisited: Some therapists do interpret clients' dreams. Freud would ask clients to jot down their dreams upon waking so that they could discuss them in therapy. Freud considered dreams the "royal road" to the unconscious. He believed that the content of dreams is determined by unconscious processes as well as by the events of the day. Unconscious impulses tend to be expressed in dreams as a form of **wish fulfillment.**

In dreams, unacceptable sexual and aggressive impulses are likely to be displaced onto objects and situations that reflect the client's era and culture. These objects become symbols of unconscious wishes. For example, long, narrow dream objects might be **phallic symbols,** but whether the symbol takes the form of a spear, rifle, stick shift, or spacecraft partially reflects the dreamer's cultural background.

In Freud's theory, the perceived content of a dream is called its visible, or **manifest, content.** Its presumed hidden, or symbolic, content is its **latent content.** If a man dreams he is flying, flying is the manifest content of the dream. Freud usually interpreted flying as symbolic of erection, so concerns about sexual potency might make up the latent content of the dream.

"Sometimes a cigar is just a cigar."

SIGMUND FREUD

"Dreams are often most profound when they seem the most crazy."

SIGMUND FREUD

"The interpretation of dreams is the royal road to a knowledge of the unconscious activities of the mind."

SIGMUND FREUD

Wish fulfillment In dreams, the acting out of ideas and impulses that are repressed when one is conscious.

Phallic symbol A sign that represents the penis.

Manifest content In psychodynamic theory, the reported content of dreams.

Latent content In psychodynamic theory, the symbolized or underlying content of dreams.

Modern Psychodynamic Approaches

Some psychoanalysts continue to engage in protracted therapy that relies on free association, interpretation of dreams, and other traditional methods. In recent years, however, more modern forms of psychodynamic therapy have been devised. **Question 4: How do modern psychodynamic approaches differ from traditional psychoanalysis?** Modern psychodynamic therapy is briefer and less intense, and it makes treatment available to clients who do not have the time or money for long-term therapy.

Some modern psychodynamic therapies continue to focus on revealing unconscious material and breaking through psychological defenses. Nevertheless, they differ from traditional psychoanalysis in several ways. First of all, the client and therapist usually sit face to face (the client does not lie on a couch) (Prochaska & Norcross, 2010). Modern therapists are usually directive as well. They suggest helpful behavior instead of focusing on insight alone. Finally, there is usually more focus on the ego as the "executive" of personality and less emphasis on the id. For this reason, many modern psychodynamic therapists are considered **ego analysts.**

Many of Freud's followers, called *neoanalysts,* from Jung and Adler to Horney and Erikson, believed that Freud had placed too much emphasis on unconscious conflict and underestimated the role of the ego. Erik Erikson, for example, spoke to clients directly about their values and concerns, and encouraged them to develop more productive behavior. Even Freud's daughter, the psychoanalyst Anna Freud (1895–1982), was more concerned with the ego than with unconscious forces and conflicts.

Learning Connections • PSYCHODYNAMIC THERAPIES: DIGGING DEEP WITHIN

ACTIVE REVIEW (3) Freud's method of psychoanalysis attempts to shed light on _____ conflicts that are presumed to lie at the roots of clients' problems. (4) Freud believed that psychoanalysis would promote _____, that is, the spilling forth of repressed psychic energy. (5) The chief psychoanalytic method is _____ association. (6) Freud considered _____ to be the "royal road" to the unconscious.

REFLECT AND RELATE Does it make you or other people you know feel good to talk with someone about your problems? If so, why?

CRITICAL THINKING Can you think of a way to demonstrate scientifically whether an unacceptable idea has been repressed?

 Go to Psychology CourseMate at **www.cengagebrain.com** for an interactive version of these questions.

⬤ HUMANISTIC THERAPIES: STRENGTHENING THE SELF

Psychodynamic therapies focus on internal conflicts and unconscious processes. **Humanistic therapies** focus on the quality of the client's subjective, conscious experience. Traditional psychoanalysis focuses on early childhood experiences. Humanistic therapies usually focus on what clients are experiencing "here and now."

These differences, however, are mainly a matter of emphasis. The past has a way of influencing us in the present. Carl Rogers, the originator of *client-centered therapy,* believed that childhood experiences gave rise to the conditions of worth that troubled his clients here and now. He and Fritz Perls, the originator of *Gestalt therapy*, recognized that early incorporation of other people's values often leads clients to "disown" parts of their own personalities.

Client-Centered Therapy: Removing Roadblocks to Self-Actualization

Question 5: What is Carl Rogers's method of client-centered therapy? Carl Rogers (1902–1987) believed that we are free to make choices and control our destinies despite the burdens of the past. He also believed that we have natural tendencies toward

Ego analyst A psychodynamically oriented therapist who focuses on the conscious, coping behavior of the ego instead of the hypothesized, unconscious functioning of the id.

Humanistic therapy A form of psychotherapy that focuses on the client's subjective, conscious experience in the "here and now."

Carl Rogers In discussing his professional development, Rogers noted that, "In my early professional years I was asking the question: How can I treat, or cure, or change this person? Now I would phrase the question in this way: How can I provide a relationship which this person may use for his own personal growth?"

Client-centered therapy Carl Rogers's method of psychotherapy, which emphasizes the creation of a warm, therapeutic atmosphere that frees clients to engage in self-exploration and self-expression.

Unconditional positive regard In client-centered therapy, the acceptance of the value of another person, although not necessarily acceptance of everything the person does.

Empathic understanding In client-centered therapy, the ability to perceive a client's feelings from the client's frame of reference.

Frame of reference In client-centered therapy, one's unique patterning of perceptions and attitudes, according to which one evaluates events.

Genuineness In client-centered therapy, openness and honesty in responding to the client.

Gestalt therapy Fritz Perls's form of psychotherapy, which attempts to integrate conflicting parts of the personality through directive methods designed to help clients perceive their whole selves.

health, growth, and fulfillment. Psychological problems arise from roadblocks placed in the path of *self-actualization*, which Rogers believed was an inborn tendency to strive to realize one's potential. If, when we are young, other people approve of us only when we are doing what they want us to do, we may learn to disown the parts of ourselves to which they object. As a result, we may experience stress and discomfort and the feeling that we—or the world—are not real.

Client-centered therapy aims to provide insight into the parts of us that we have disowned so that we can feel whole. It creates a warm, therapeutic atmosphere that encourages self-exploration and self-expression. The therapist's acceptance of the client is thought to foster self-acceptance and self-esteem. Self-acceptance frees the client to make choices that develop his or her unique potential.

Client-centered therapy is nondirective. **Truth or Fiction Revisited:** It is true that in this type of therapy, the client takes the lead by stating and exploring problems. An effective client-centered therapist has several qualities:

- **Unconditional positive regard:** Respect for clients as human beings with unique values and goals.

- **Empathic understanding:** Recognition of the client's experiences and feelings. Therapists view the world through the client's **frame of reference** by setting aside their own values and listening closely.

- **Genuineness:** Openness and honesty in responding to the client. Client-centered therapists must be able to tolerate differentness, based on the belief that every client is different in important ways.

The following excerpt from a therapy session shows how Carl Rogers uses empathetic understanding and paraphrases a client's (Jill's) feelings. His goal is to help her recognize feelings that she has partially disowned:

JILL: I'm having a lot of problems dealing with my daughter. She's 20 years old; she's in college; I'm having a lot of trouble letting her go....And I have a lot of guilt feelings about her; I have a real need to hang on to her.

C. R.: A need to hang on so you can kind of make up for the things you feel guilty about. Is that part of it?

JILL: There's a lot of that....Also, she's been a real friend to me, and filled my life....And it's very hard....a lot of empty places now that she's not with me.

C. R.: The old vacuum, sort of, when she's not there.

JILL: Yes. Yes. I also would like to be the kind of mother that could be strong and say, you know, "Go and have a good life," and this is really hard for me, to do that.

C. R.: It's very hard to give up something that's been so precious in your life, but also something that I guess has caused you pain when you mentioned guilt.

JILL: Yeah. And I'm aware that I have some anger toward her that I don't always get what I want. I have needs that are not met. And, uh, I don't feel I have a right to those needs. You know....she's a daughter; she's not my mother. Though sometimes I feel as if I'd like her to mother me...it's very difficult for me to ask for that and have a right to it.

C. R.: So, it may be unreasonable, but still, when she doesn't meet your needs, it makes you mad.

JILL: Yeah I get very angry, very angry with her.

C. R.: (Pauses) You're also feeling a little tension at this point, I guess.

JILL: Yeah. Yeah. A lot of conflict....(C. R.: Mmm-hmm.) A lot of pain.

C. R: A lot of pain. Can you say anything more about what that's about? (Farber et al., 1996, pp. 74–75)

Client-centered therapy is practiced widely in college and university counseling centers, not just to help students experiencing, say, anxieties or depression but also to help them make decisions. Many college students have not yet made career choices, or they wonder whether they should become involved with particular people or engage in sexual activity. Client-centered therapists do not tell clients what to do. Instead, they help clients arrive at their own decisions.

Gestalt Therapy: Getting It Together

Fritz Perls (1893–1970) originated gestalt therapy. **Question 6: What is Fritz Perls's method of Gestalt therapy?** Like client-centered therapy, Gestalt therapy assumes that people disown parts of themselves that might meet with social disapproval or rejection. People also don social masks, pretending to be things they are not. Therapy aims to help individuals integrate conflicting parts of their personality. Perls used the term *Gestalt* to signify his interest in giving the conflicting parts of the personality an integrated form or shape. He wanted his clients to become aware of inner conflict, accept the reality of conflict rather than deny it or keep it repressed, and make productive choices despite misgivings and fears. **Truth or Fiction Revisited:** People in conflict frequently find it difficult to make choices, and Perls firmly challenged them to do so.

Perls focuses on the here and now. In Gestalt therapy, clients perform exercises to heighten their awareness of their current feelings and behavior rather than exploring the past. Perls also believed, along with Rogers, that people are free to make choices and to direct their personal growth. But the charismatic and forceful Perls was temperamentally unlike the gentle and accepting Rogers (Prochaska & Norcross, 2010). Thus, unlike client-centered therapy, Gestalt therapy is highly directive. The therapist leads clients through experiences to heighten their awareness of inner conflict and take responsibility for their behavior.

The following excerpt from a therapy session with "Max" shows how Perls would make clients take responsibility for what they experience. One of his techniques is to show how clients are treating something they are doing (a "verb") like something that is just out there and beyond their control (a "noun"):

MAX:	I feel the tenseness in my stomach and in my hands.
PERLS:	The tenseness. Here we've got a noun. Now the tenseness is a noun. Now change the noun, the thing, into a verb.
MAX:	I am tense. My hands are tense.
PERLS:	Your hands are tense. They have nothing to do with you.
MAX:	I am tense.
PERLS:	You are tense. How are you tense? What are you doing?
MAX:	I am tensing myself.
PERLS:	That's it. (Perls, 1971, p. 115)

Once Max understands that he is tensing himself and takes responsibility for it, he can choose to stop tensing himself. The tenseness is no longer something out there that is victimizing him; it is something he is doing to himself.

Freud viewed dreams as the "royal road" to the unconscious. Perls saw the content of dreams as representing disowned parts of the personality. He would often ask clients to role-play elements of their dreams to get in touch with these parts of their personality.

> *"I do my thing and you do yours. I am not in this world to live up to your expectations, and you are not in this world to live up to mine. You are you and I am I, and if by chance we find each other, then it is beautiful. If not, it can't be helped."*
>
> FRITZ PERLS

www.fritzperls.com

Fritz Perls Known to friends, clients, and peers alike as "Fritz," Perls put clients through structured experiences to help them understand how their feelings might be in conflict. He believed that people had to accept responsibility for making choices in their lives.

LearningConnections • HUMANISTIC THERAPIES: STRENGTHENING THE SELF

ACTIVE REVIEW (7) _____ therapies focus on clients' subjective, conscious experience. (8) Client-centered therapy is a (directive or nondirective?) method that provides clients with an accepting atmosphere that enables them to overcome roadblocks to self-actualization. (9) Gestalt therapy provides (directive or nondirective?) methods that are designed to help clients accept responsibility and integrate conflicting parts of the personality.

REFLECT AND RELATE Rogers believed that our psychological well-being is connected with our freedom to develop our unique frames of reference. Do you think you can separate your "real self" from your sociocultural experiences and religious training?

CRITICAL THINKING Why are the therapies of Rogers and Perls placed in the same category? What do they have in common? How do they differ?

 Go to Psychology CourseMate at **www.cengagebrain.com** for an interactive version of these questions.

BEHAVIOR THERAPY: ADJUSTMENT IS WHAT YOU DO

Psychodynamic and humanistic forms of therapy tend to focus on what people think and feel. Behavior therapists tend to focus on what people do. **Question 7: What is behavior therapy?** Behavior therapy—also called *behavior modification*—applies principles of learning to directly promote desired behavioral changes. Behavior therapists rely heavily on principles of conditioning and observational learning. They help clients discontinue self-defeating behavior patterns such as overeating, smoking, and phobic avoidance of harmless stimuli. They also help clients acquire adaptive behavior patterns such as the social skills required to start social relationships or to say no to insistent salespeople. **Truth or Fiction Revisited:** In both cases, behavior therapists may use specific procedures—telling their clients what to do.

Behavior therapists may build warm, therapeutic relationships with clients, but they see the efficacy of behavior therapy as deriving from specific learning-based procedures (Rachman, 2009). They insist that their methods be established by experimentation and that the outcomes be assessed in terms of measurable behavior. In this section, we consider some frequently used behavior-therapy techniques.

Fear-Reduction Methods

Behavior therapy Systematic application of the principles of learning to the direct modification of a client's problem behaviors.

Many people seek therapy because of fears and phobias that interfere with their functioning. This is one of the areas in which behavior therapy has made great inroads. **Question 8: What are some behavior-therapy methods for reducing fears?** Fear-reduction methods include *flooding, systematic desensitization*, and *modeling*.

FLOODING Flooding is a kind of exposure therapy in which the client is exposed to the fear-evoking stimulus until the fear response is extinguished. The rationale is that the fear-evoking stimulus is not causing pain or harm. Therefore, perception of the stimulus is not being associated with physically aversive stimulation and will fade with time. Examples include exposing a person to an actual spider or snake (a harmless snake!) or preventing a person with obsessive–compulsive disorder from washing her hands.

SYSTEMATIC DESENSITIZATION

Adam has a phobia for receiving injections. His behavior therapist treats him as he reclines in a comfortable padded chair. In a state of deep muscle relaxation, Adam observes slides projected on a screen. A slide of a nurse holding a needle has just been shown three times, 30 seconds at a time. Each time Adam has shown no anxiety. So now a slightly more discomforting slide is shown: one of the nurse aiming the needle toward someone's bare arm. After 15 seconds, our armchair adventurer notices twinges of discomfort and raises a finger as a signal (speaking might disturb his relaxation). The projector operator turns off the light, and Adam spends 2 minutes imagining his "safe scene"—lying on a beach beneath the tropical sun. Then the slide is shown again. This time Adam views it for 30 seconds before feeling anxiety.

From the author's files

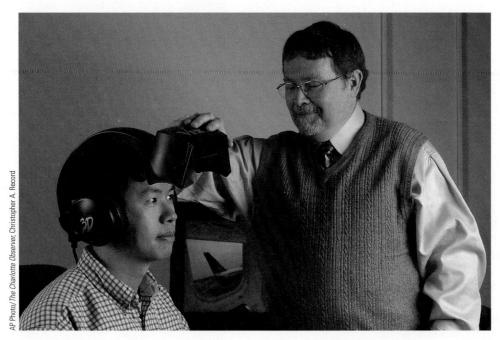

Overcoming Fear of Flying One way behavior therapists help clients overcome phobias is by having them gradually approach the feared object or situation while they remain relaxed. This man is gradually reducing his fear of being in an airplane and flying.

AP Photo/*The Charlotte Observer*, Christopher A. Record

Truth or Fiction Revisited: Adam is in effect confronting his fear while lying in a recliner and relaxing. Adam is undergoing **systematic desensitization**, a method for reducing phobic responses originated by psychiatrist Joseph Wolpe (1915–1997). Systematic desensitization is a gradual process in which the client learns to handle increasingly disturbing stimuli while anxiety to each one is being counterconditioned. About 10 to 20 stimuli are arranged in a sequence, or *hierarchy*, according to their capacity to elicit anxiety. In imagination or by being shown photos, the client travels gradually up through this hierarchy, approaching the target behavior. In Adam's case, the target behavior was the ability to receive an injection without undue anxiety.

Wolpe developed systematic desensitization on the assumption that anxiety responses, like other behaviors, are learned, or conditioned (Rachman, 2009). He reasoned that they can be unlearned by means of counterconditioning, or extinction. In counterconditioning, a response that is incompatible with anxiety is made to appear under conditions that usually elicit anxiety. Muscle relaxation is incompatible with anxiety. For this reason, Adam's therapist is teaching him to relax in the presence of (usually) anxiety-evoking slides of needles.

Remaining in the presence of phobic imagery, rather than running away from it, is also likely to enhance self-efficacy expectations (Deacon et al., 2010). Self-efficacy expectations are negatively correlated with levels of adrenaline in the bloodstream (Bandura et al., 1985). Raising clients' self-efficacy expectations thus may help lower their adrenaline levels and reduce their feelings of nervousness.

MODELING In modeling, clients observe, and then imitate, people who approach and cope with the objects or situations that the clients fear. Albert Bandura and his colleagues (1969) found that modeling worked as well as systematic desensitization—and more rapidly—in reducing fear of snakes. Modeling also increases self-efficacy expectations in coping with feared stimuli.

Aversive Conditioning

Many people also seek behavior therapy because they want to break bad habits, such as smoking, excessive drinking, nail biting, and the like. One behavior-therapy approach to helping people do so is **aversive conditioning**. **Question 9: How do behavior therapists use aversive conditioning to help people break bad habits?** Aversive conditioning is a controversial procedure that pairs painful or aversive stimuli with unwanted impulses to make the impulse less appealing. For example, to help people control alcohol intake, tastes of different alcoholic beverages can be paired with drug-induced nausea and vomiting or with electric shock.

Aversive conditioning has been used with problems as diverse as cigarette smoking and sexual abuse. *Rapid smoking* is an aversive-conditioning method designed to help smokers quit. With this method, the would-be quitter inhales every 6 seconds. In another method, the hose of a hair dryer is hooked up to a chamber containing several lit cigarettes. Smoke is blown into the quitter's face as he or she also smokes a cigarette. A third method uses branching pipes so that the smoker draws in smoke from several cigarettes at the same time. With these methods, overexposure makes once-desirable cigarette smoke aversive. The quitter becomes motivated to avoid, rather than seek, cigarettes. **Truth or Fiction Revisited:** Therefore, smoking can be a way to stop smoking. However, interest in aversive conditioning for quitting smoking has waned because of side effects such as raising blood pressure and the availability of nicotine-replacement techniques.

Aversive conditioning has also been used in the treatment of alcoholism. In one study, 63% of the 685 people treated remained abstinent for 1 year afterward, and about a third remained abstinent for at least 3 years (Wiens & Menustik, 1983).

Operant-Conditioning Procedures

We usually prefer to relate to people who smile at us rather than those who ignore us, and we prefer to take the kind of courses in which we usually do well rather than those

Aversive Conditioning In aversive conditioning, unwanted behaviors take on a noxious quality as a result of being repeatedly paired with aversive stimuli. Overexposure is making cigarette smoke aversive to this smoker.

Systematic desensitization Wolpe's method for reducing fears by associating a hierarchy of images of fear-evoking stimuli with deep muscle relaxation.

Modeling A behavior-therapy technique in which a client observes and imitates a person who approaches and copes with feared objects or situations.

Aversive conditioning A behavior-therapy technique in which undesired responses are inhibited by pairing repugnant or offensive stimuli with them.

in which we are likely to fail. We tend to repeat behavior that is reinforced. Behavior that is not reinforced tends to become extinguished. Behavior therapists have used these principles of operant conditioning with psychotic patients as well as with clients with milder problems. **Question 10: How do behavior therapists apply principles of operant conditioning in behavior modification?**

The staff at one mental hospital was at a loss about how to encourage withdrawn schizophrenic patients to eat regularly. Psychologists observed that staff members were making the problem worse by coaxing patients into the dining room and even feeding them. Staff attention apparently reinforced the patients' lack of cooperation. Some rules were changed (Dickerson et al., 2005). Patients who did not arrive at the dining hall within 30 minutes after serving were locked out. Staff were told to refrain from interacting with patients at mealtime. With uncooperative behavior no longer reinforced, patients quickly changed their eating habits. Then patients were required to pay one penny to enter the dining hall. Pennies were earned by interacting with other patients and showing other socially appropriate behaviors. These target behaviors also became more frequent.

Health professionals are concerned about whether people who are, or have been, dependent on alcohol can exercise control over their drinking. One study showed that rewards for remaining abstinent from alcohol can exert a powerful effect (Petry et al., 2000). In the study, one group of alcohol-dependent veterans was given a standard treatment while another group received the treatment *plus* the chance to win prizes for remaining alcohol-free, as measured by a Breathalyzer test. By the end of the 8-week treatment period, 84% of the veterans who could win prizes remained in the program compared with 22% of the standard treatment group. The prizes had an average value of $200, far less than what alcohol-related absenteeism from work and other responsibilities can cost.

THE TOKEN ECONOMY Many psychiatric wards and hospitals now use **token economies** in which patients must use tokens such as poker chips to purchase TV viewing time, extra visits to the canteen, or a private room (Dickerson et al., 2005). The tokens are reinforcements for productive activities such as making beds, brushing teeth, and socializing. Token economies have not eliminated all symptoms of schizophrenia but have enhanced patient activity and cooperation even in these patients. Tokens have also been used to modify the behavior of children with conduct disorders.

Token economy A controlled environment in which people are reinforced for desired behaviors with tokens (such as poker chips) that may be exchanged for privileges.

Successive approximations In operant conditioning, a series of behaviors that gradually become more similar to a target behavior.

Social skills training A behavior-therapy method for helping people in their interpersonal relations that uses self-monitoring, behavior rehearsal, and feedback.

SUCCESSIVE APPROXIMATIONS The operant-conditioning method of **successive approximations** is often used to help clients build good habits. Let's use a (not uncommon!) example: You want to study 3 hours each evening but can concentrate for only half an hour. Rather than attempting to increase your study time all at once, you could do so gradually by adding, say, 5 minutes each evening. After every hour or so of studying, you could reinforce yourself with 5 minutes of people watching in a busy section of the library.

SOCIAL SKILLS TRAINING In social skills training, behavior therapists decrease social anxiety and build social skills through operant-conditioning procedures that employ *self-monitoring* (keeping a record of one's own behavior to identify problems and record successes), coaching, modeling, role-playing, *behavior rehearsal* (practicing), and *feedback* (receiving information about the effectiveness of behavior). Social skills training has been used to help formerly hospitalized mental patients maintain jobs and apartments in the community. For example, a worker

Social Skills Training Social skills training is effective in groups. Group members can role-play key people—such as parents, spouses, or potential dates—in the lives of other members.

Part of social skills training is the teaching of clients to use assertive behavior. Assertive behavior means expressing one's genuine feelings, standing up for one's legitimate rights, and refusing unreasonable requests. It means resisting undue social influences, disobeying *arbitrary* authority figures, and resisting conformity to *arbitrary* group standards. But many feelings such as love and admiration are positive, so assertive behavior also means expressing positive feelings ("That was great!" "You're wonderful!"). The Assertiveness Schedule will give you insight into how assertive you are as part of the process of deciding whether to become more assertive. Once you have finished, turn to Appendix B to find out how to calculate and interpret your score. A table in the appendix will also allow you to compare your assertiveness to that of a sample of 1,400 students drawn from 35 college campuses across the United States.

Directions: Indicate how well each item describes you by using this code:

3 very much like me
2 rather like me
1 slightly like me
−1 slightly unlike me
−2 rather unlike me
−3 very much unlike me

__ 1. Most people seem to be more aggressive and assertive than I am.*

__ 2. I have hesitated to make or accept dates because of "shyness."*

__ 3. When the food served at a restaurant is not done to my satisfaction, I complain about it to the waiter or waitress.

__ 4. I am careful to avoid hurting other people's feelings, even when I feel that I have been injured.*

__ 5. If a salesperson has gone to considerable trouble to show me merchandise that is not quite suitable, I have a difficult time saying "No."*

__ 6. When I am asked to do something, I insist upon knowing why.

__ 7. There are times when I look for a good, vigorous argument.

__ 8. I strive to get ahead as well as most people in my position.

__ 9. To be honest, people often take advantage of me.*

__ 10. I enjoy starting conversations with new acquaintances and strangers.

__ 11. I often don't know what to say to people who are sexually attractive to me.*

__ 12. I will hesitate to make phone calls to business establishments and institutions*

__ 13. I would rather apply for a job or for admission to a college by writing letters than by going through with personal interviews.*

__ 14. I find it embarrassing to return merchandise.*

__ 15. If a close and respected relative were annoying me, I would smother my feelings rather than express my annoyance.*

__ 16. I have avoided asking questions for fear of sounding stupid.*

__ 17. During an argument I am sometimes afraid that I will get so upset that I will shake all over.*

__ 18. If a famed and respected lecturer makes a comment which I think is incorrect, I will have the audience hear my point of view as well.

__ 19. I avoid arguing over prices with clerks and salespeople.*

__ 20. When I have done something important or worthwhile, I manage to let others know about it.

__ 21. I am open and frank about my feelings.

__ 22. If someone has been spreading false and bad stories about me, I see him or her as soon as possible and "have a talk" about it.

__ 23. I often have a hard time saying "No."*

__ 24. I tend to bottle up my emotions rather than make a scene.*

__ 25. I complain about poor service in a restaurant and elsewhere.

__ 26. When I am given a compliment, I sometimes just don't know what to say.*

__ 27. If a couple near me in a theater or at a lecture were conversing rather loudly, I would ask them to be quiet or to take their conversation elsewhere.

__ 28. Anyone attempting to push ahead of me in a line is in for a good battle.

__ 29. I am quick to express an opinion.

__ 30. There are times when I just can't say anything.*

Reprinted from Rathus, 1973, pp. 398–406.
*Asterisks are explained in the answer key.

can rehearse politely asking a supervisor for assistance or asking a landlord to fix the plumbing in an apartment.

Social skills training is effective in groups. Group members can role-play key people—such as parents, spouses, or potential dates—in the lives of other members.

BIOFEEDBACK TRAINING Through biofeedback training (BFT), therapists help clients become more aware of, and gain control over, various bodily functions. Therapists attach devices to clients that measure bodily functions such as heart rate. "Bleeps" or other signals are used to indicate (and thereby reinforce) changes in the desired direction—for example, a slower heart rate. (Knowledge of results is a

Biofeedback training (BFT) The systematic feeding back to an organism of information about a bodily function so that the organism can gain control of that function.

powerful reinforcer.) One device, the electromyograph (EMG), monitors muscle tension. It has been used to augment control over muscle tension in the forehead and elsewhere, thereby alleviating anxiety, stress, and headaches.

BFT also helps clients voluntarily regulate functions once thought to be beyond conscious control, such as heart rate and blood pressure. Hypertensive clients use a blood pressure cuff and electronic signals to gain control over their blood pressure. The electroencephalograph (EEG) monitors brain waves and can be used to teach people how to produce alpha waves, which are associated with relaxation. Some people have overcome insomnia by learning to produce the brain waves associated with sleep.

Functional analysis A systematic study of behavior in which one identifies the stimuli that trigger problem behavior and the reinforcers that maintain it.

Self-Control Methods

Do mysterious forces sometimes seem to be at work in your life? Do these forces delight in wreaking havoc on New Year's resolutions and other efforts to put an end to your bad habits? Just when you go on a diet, that juicy pizza stares at you from the TV set. **Question 11: How can you— yes, *you*—use behavior therapy to deal with temptation and enhance your self-control?**

Behavior therapists usually begin with a **functional analysis** of the problem behavior. In this way, they help determine the stimuli that trigger the behavior and the reinforcers that maintain it. Then clients are taught how to manipulate the antecedents and consequences of their behavior and how to increase the frequency of desired responses and decrease the frequency of undesired responses. You can use a diary to jot down each instance of a problem behavior. Note the time of day, location, your activity at the time (including your thoughts and feelings), and reactions (yours and others'). Such functional analysis makes you more aware of the environmental context of your behavior and can increase your motivation to change. **Truth or Fiction Revisited:** For these reasons, keeping a record of where and when you engage in "bad habits" can help you end them (Drossel et al., 2008).

© Royalty-Free/Corbis

Getting Some Help from the Situation
Principles of operant conditioning suggest that we can improve our study habits by gradually building the amount of time we study and placing ourselves in situations with few distractions.

LearningConnections • BEHAVIOR THERAPY: ADJUSTMENT IS WHAT YOU DO

ACTIVE REVIEW (10) Behavior therapy applies principles of _____ to bring about desired behavioral changes. (11) Behavior-therapy methods for reducing fears include flooding; systematic _____, in which a client is gradually exposed to more fear-arousing stimuli; and modeling. (12) _____-conditioning methods reinforce desired responses and extinguish undesired responses. (13) In self-control methods, clients first engage in a(n) _____ analysis of problem behavior. (14) Clients are then taught how to change the behavior by manipulating its antecedents and _____.

REFLECT AND RELATE Would any of the methods for reducing fears be helpful to you in your life? If so, which method would you prefer? Explain.

CRITICAL THINKING Behavior therapists argue that their methods are more scientific than those of other therapists. How do they attempt to ensure that their methods are scientific?

 Go to Psychology CourseMate at **www.cengagebrain.com** for an interactive version of these questions.

Helping professionals are often inspired to develop therapy methods based on their personal experiences. As Francine Shapiro (1989) paints it, she had troubling thoughts on her mind when she entered a park. But as her eyes darted about, taking in the scene, she found her troubled thoughts disappearing. Thus, she developed a therapy method called *eye-movement desensitization and reprocessing (EMDR)* to join the arsenal of therapeutic weapons against stress disorders. With this method, clients are asked to imagine a traumatic scene while the therapist moves a finger rapidly back and forth before their eyes for about 20–30 seconds. The clients follow the finger while keeping the troubling scene in mind. They tell the therapist what they were thinking and how they felt during the procedure. The procedure is repeated until the clients' feelings of anxiety are dissipated. Treatment takes about three 90-minute sessions.

Evidence from a number of studies suggests that EMDR helps decrease the anxiety associated with traumatic events (Engelhard et al., 2010; Van der Kolk et al., 2007). One study, for example, compared the effectiveness of EMDR with two alternative treatments: exposure therapy (as in virtual therapy for spider phobia) and relaxation training (Taylor et al., 2003). Another study looked at the effectiveness of EMDR on numerous people following September 11 (Silver et al., 2005). These studies and others suggest that EMDR is effective, but it remains unclear how effective EMDR is and why it works (May, 2005; Schubert & Lee, 2009). Devilly (2002) allows that EMDR is often effective, but his review finds other exposure therapies are more effective. Research also challenges the idea that eye movements are necessary (Devilly, 2002; Schubert & Lee, 2009).

Perhaps the effects of EMDR can be attributed to a combination of nonspecific therapy factors and to exposure. Clients receiving EMDR may profit from their relationship with the therapist and from expectations of success. Moreover, clients are to some degree exposed to the trauma that haunts them under circumstances in which they believe they will be able to manage the trauma.

Conclusion? Exposure helps people cope with trauma. Eye movements may not be needed.

● COGNITIVE THERAPIES: ADJUSTMENT IS WHAT YOU THINK (AND DO)

"There is nothing either good or bad, but thinking makes it so."

SHAKESPEARE, *HAMLET*

In this line from *Hamlet,* Shakespeare did not mean to suggest that injuries and misfortunes are painless or easy to manage. Rather, he meant that our appraisals of unfortunate events can heighten our discomfort and impair our coping ability. In so doing, Shakespeare was providing a kind of motto for cognitive therapists. **Question 12: What is cognitive therapy?**

Cognitive therapy focuses on changing the beliefs, attitudes, and automatic types of thinking that create and compound their clients' problems (Butler et al., 2006; David et al., 2010). Cognitive therapists, like psychodynamic and humanistic therapists, attempt to foster self-insight, but they aim to heighten insight into *current cognitions* as well as those of the past. Cognitive therapists also aim to directly change maladaptive cognitions to reduce negative feelings, provide insight, and help the client solve problems. Let's look at the approaches and methods of some major cognitive therapists.

Aaron Beck's Cognitive Therapy: Correcting Cognitive Errors

Cognitive therapy is the name of a general approach to therapy as well as Aaron Beck's specific methods. **Question 13: What is Aaron Beck's method of cognitive therapy?** Beck focuses on clients' cognitive distortions (see Butler et al., 2006). He encourages clients to become their own personal scientists and challenge beliefs that are not supported by evidence.

Beck's approach to therapy is active. He questions people in a way that encourages them to see the irrationality of their ways of thinking. For example, depressed people tend to minimize their accomplishments and to assume that the worst will happen. Both cognitive distortions heighten feelings of depression. Such distortions can be fleeting and automatic, difficult to detect (Walker & Bright, 2009). Beck's therapy methods help

Cognitive therapy A form of therapy that focuses on how clients' cognitions (expectations, attitudes, beliefs, etc.) lead to distress and may be modified to relieve distress and promote adaptive behavior.

Cognitive Therapy Cognitive therapists aim to directly change maladaptive cognitions to reduce negative feelings, provide insight, and help the client solve problems. They may frankly challenge clients' ways of looking at their lives and problems.

clients become aware of these distortions and challenge them.

Beck notes how cognitive distortions or errors contribute to clients' miseries:

1. Clients may *selectively perceive* the world as a harmful place and ignore evidence to the contrary.

2. Clients may *overgeneralize* on the basis of a few examples. For instance, they may perceive themselves as worthless because they were laid off at work or as unattractive because they were refused a date.

3. Clients may *magnify,* or blow out of proportion, the importance of negative events. They may catastrophize failing a test by assuming they will flunk out of college or catastrophize losing a job by believing that they will never find another and that serious harm will befall their family as a result.

4. Clients may engage in *absolutist thinking,* or looking at the world in black and white rather than in shades of gray. In doing so, a rejection on a date takes on the meaning of a lifetime of loneliness; an uncomfortable illness takes on life-threatening proportions.

The concept of pinpointing and modifying cognitive distortions or errors may become clearer from the following excerpt from a case of a 53-year-old engineer who obtained cognitive therapy for severe depression. The engineer had left his job and become inactive. As reported by Beck and his colleagues, the first goal of treatment was to foster physical activity—even things like raking leaves and preparing dinner—because activity is incompatible with depression. Then:

[The engineer's] cognitive distortions were identified by comparing his assessment of each activity with that of his wife. Alternative ways of interpreting his experiences were then considered.

In comparing his wife's résumé of his past experiences, he became aware that he had (1) undervalued his past by failing to mention many previous accomplishments, (2) regarded himself as far more responsible for his "failures" than she did, and (3) concluded that he was worthless since he had not succeeded in attaining certain goals in the past. When the two accounts were contrasted, he could discern many of his cognitive distortions. In subsequent sessions, his wife continued to serve as an "objectifier."

In midtherapy, [he] compiled a list of new attitudes that he had acquired since initiating therapy. These included:

1. "I am starting at a lower level of functioning at my job, but it will improve if I persist."

2. "I know that once I get going in the morning, everything will run all right for the rest of the day."

3. "I can't achieve everything at once."

4. "I have my periods of ups and downs, but in the long run I feel better."

5. "My expectations from my job and life should be scaled down to a realistic level."

6. "Giving in to avoidance [e.g., staying away from work and social interactions] never helps and only leads to further avoidance."

He was instructed to reread this list daily for several weeks even though he already knew the content.

From Rush et al., 1975

The engineer gradually became less depressed and returned to work and an active social life. Along the way, he learned to combat inappropriate self-blame for problems, perfectionist expectations, magnification of failures, and overgeneralization from failures.

Becoming aware of cognitive errors and modifying catastrophizing thoughts helps us cope with stress. As we saw in Chapter 12, internal, stable, and global attributions of failure lead to depression and feelings of helplessness. Cognitive therapists also alert clients to cognitive errors such as these so that the clients can change their attitudes and pave the way for more effective overt behavior.

Aaron Beck (left) and Albert Ellis (right) chatting at a professional meeting.

Albert Ellis's Rational-Emotive Behavior Therapy: Overcoming "Musts" and "Shoulds"

Psychologist Albert Ellis (1913–2007) was originally trained in psychoanalysis but became frustrated with the slow rate of progress made by clients. He also found himself uncomfortable with the psychoanalyst's laid-back approach. Instead, he took to confronting clients with the ways that their irrational beliefs—especially those that give rise to excessive needs for social approval and perfect performance—make them miserable.

In **rational-emotive behavior therapy (REBT)**, Ellis pointed out that our beliefs *about* events, not only the events themselves, shape our responses to them. Moreover, many of us harbor a number of irrational beliefs that can give rise to problems or magnify their impact. Two of the most important are the belief that we must have the love and approval of people who are important to us and the belief that we must prove ourselves to be thoroughly competent, adequate, and achieving. **Question 14: What is Albert Ellis's method of rational-emotive behavior therapy?**

Ellis's REBT methods are active and directive. He urged clients to seek out their irrational beliefs. When Ellis saw clients behaving according to irrational beliefs, he refuted the beliefs by asking, "Where is it written that you must…?" or "What evidence do you have that…?" According to Ellis, we need less misery and less blaming in our lives and more action.

Ellis straddled behavioral and cognitive therapies. He originally dubbed his method of therapy *rational-emotive therapy* because he focused on the cognitive—irrational beliefs and how to change them. However, Ellis also promoted behavioral changes to cement cognitive changes. Thus, he eventually changed the name of rational-emotive therapy to rational-emotive *behavior* therapy.

Cognitive-Behavior Therapy

Many theorists consider cognitive therapy to be a collection of techniques that are part of the overall approach known as behavior therapy. Some members of this group use the term "cognitive-*behavioral* therapy." Others argue that the term *behavior therapy* is broad enough to include cognitive techniques. Many cognitive therapists and behavior therapists differ in focus, however. Behavior therapists deal with client cognitions to change *overt* behavior. Cognitive therapists also see the value of tying treatment outcomes to observable behavior, but they believe that cognitive change, not just behavioral change, is a key goal in itself.

The following case shows how behavioral techniques (exposure to fearful situations) and cognitive techniques (changing maladaptive thoughts) were used in the treatment of a case of *agoraphobia,* a type of anxiety disorder characterized by excessive fears of venturing out in public.

> [Ms._____] was a 41-year-old woman with a 12-year history of agoraphobia. She feared venturing into public places alone and required her husband or children to accompany her from place to place. In vivo (actual) exposure sessions were arranged in a series of progressively more fearful encounters (a fear-stimulus hierarchy). The first step in the hierarchy…involved taking a shopping trip while accompanied by the therapist. After accomplishing this task,

"I get people to truly accept themselves unconditionally, whether or not their therapist or anyone loves them."

ALBERT ELLIS

"The best years of your life are the ones in which you decide your problems are your own. You do not blame them on your mother, the ecology, or the president. You realize that you control your own destiny."

ALBERT ELLIS

Rational-emotive behavior therapy (REBT) Albert Ellis's form of therapy that encourages clients to challenge and correct irrational beliefs and maladaptive behaviors.

[Ms. _____] gradually moved upward in the hierarchy. By the third week of treatment, she was able to complete the last step in her hierarchy: shopping by herself in a crowded supermarket.

Cognitive restructuring was conducted along with [exposure. She] was asked to imagine herself in various fearful situations and to report [her thoughts]. The therapist helped her identify disruptive [thoughts] such as, "I am going to make a fool of myself." The therapist [asked] whether it was realistic to believe that she would actually lose control and [disputed] the belief that the consequences of losing control…would truly be disastrous. [Ms. _____] progressed rapidly…

Adapted from Biran, 1988, pp. 173–176

Cognitive-behavioral therapy has been effective in treating a wide range of psychological disorders, including anxiety disorders, depression, and personality disorders (e.g., Butler et al., 2006; Gibbons et al., 2010; Rachman, 2009; Stewart & Chambless, 2009). It has been used to help individuals with anorexia and bulimia challenge their perfectionism and their attitudes toward their bodies (Cooper & Shafran, 2008). It has also been used to systematically reinforce appropriate eating behavior.

LearningConnections ● COGNITIVE THERAPIES: ADJUSTMENT IS WHAT YOU THINK (AND DO)

ACTIVE REVIEW (15) _____ therapists focus on the beliefs, attitudes, and automatic thoughts that create and compound their clients' problems. (16) Beck notes four types of cognitive errors that contribute to clients' miseries: selective abstraction of the world as a harmful place; overgeneralization; magnification of the importance of negative events, and _____ thinking, or looking at the world in black and white rather than shades of gray. (17) Ellis's REBT confronts clients with the ways in which _____ beliefs contribute to anxiety and depression.

REFLECT AND RELATE Do you believe that you must always have the love and approval of people who are important to you? Do you believe that you must prove yourself to be thoroughly competent, adequate, and achieving? If you do, do these beliefs make you miserable? What can you do about them?

CRITICAL THINKING Many therapists call themselves cognitive-behavioral therapists. Does it seem possible to combine behavior therapy and cognitive therapy?

 Go to Psychology CourseMate at **www.cengagebrain.com** for an interactive version of these questions.

● GROUP THERAPIES: ON BEING IN IT TOGETHER

When a psychotherapist has several clients with similar problems—anxiety, depression, adjustment to divorce, lack of social skills—it often makes sense to treat them in a group rather than in individual sessions. The methods and characteristics of the group reflect the needs of the members and the theoretical orientation of the leader. In group psychoanalysis, clients might interpret one another's dreams. In a client-centered group, they might provide an accepting atmosphere for self-exploration. Members of behavior therapy groups might be jointly desensitized to anxiety-evoking stimuli or might practice social skills together.

Question 15: What are the advantages and disadvantages of group therapy?
Group therapy has the following advantages:

1. It is economical (Prochaska & Norcross, 2010). It allows the therapist to work with several clients at once.

2. Compared with one-to-one therapy, group therapy provides more information and life experience for clients to draw upon.

3. Appropriate behavior receives group support. Clients usually appreciate an outpouring of peer approval.

4. When we run into troubles, it is easy to imagine that we are different from other people or inferior to them. Affiliating with people who have similar problems is reassuring.

5. Group members who show improvement provide hope for other members.

6. Many individuals seek therapy because of problems in relating to other people. People who seek therapy for other reasons also may be socially inhibited. Members of groups have the opportunity to practice social skills in a relatively nonthreatening atmosphere. In a group consisting of men and women of different ages, group members can role-play one another's employers, employees, spouses, parents, children, and friends. Members can role-play asking one another out on dates, saying no (or yes), and so on.

Benefits of Group Therapy Group therapy is more economical than individual therapy, group members can practice social skills with one another, and members can learn from the experiences of others.

Yet group therapy is not for everyone. Some clients fare better with individual treatment. Many prefer not to disclose their problems to a group. They may be overly shy or want individual attention. It is the responsibility of the therapist to insist that group disclosures be kept confidential, to establish a supportive atmosphere, and to ensure that group members obtain the attention they need.

Many types of therapy can be conducted either individually or in groups. Couple therapy and family therapy are conducted only in groups.

Couple Therapy

Question 16: What is couple therapy? Couple therapy helps couples enhance their relationship by improving their communication skills and helping them manage conflict (Prochaska & Norcross, 2010). There are often power imbalances in relationships, and couple therapy helps individuals find "full membership" in the couple. Correcting power imbalances increases happiness and can decrease the incidence of domestic violence. Ironically, in situations of domestic violence, the partner with *less* power in the relationship is usually the violent one. Violence sometimes appears to be a way of compensating for an inability to share power in other aspects of the relationship (Rathus & Sanderson, 1999).

Today, the main approach to couple therapy is cognitive-behavioral (Rathus & Sanderson, 1999). It teaches couples communications skills (such as how to listen and how to express feelings), ways of handling feelings like depression and anger, and ways of solving problems.

Family Therapy

Question 17: What is family therapy? Family therapy is a form of group therapy in which one or more families constitute the group. Family therapy may be undertaken from various theoretical viewpoints. One is the *systems approach*, in which family interaction is studied and modified to enhance the growth of individual family members and of the family unit as a whole (Prochaska & Norcross, 2010).

Family members with low self-esteem often cannot tolerate different attitudes and behaviors in other family members. Faulty communication within the family also creates problems. In addition, it is not uncommon for the family to present an "identified patient"—that is, the family member who has *the* problem and is *causing* all the trouble. Yet family therapists usually assume that the identified patient is a scapegoat for other problems within and among family members. It is a sort of myth: change the bad apple—or identified patient—and the barrel—or family—will be functional once more.

The family therapist—often a specialist in this field—attempts to teach the family to communicate more effectively and encourage growth and autonomy in each family member.

Couple therapy A form of therapy in which a couple is treated as the client and helped to improve communication skills and manage conflict.

Family therapy A form of therapy in which the family unit is treated as the client.

451

Self-Help and Support Groups

Millions of people in the United States and elsewhere are involved in self-help and support groups that meet in person, online, or even by telephone. **Question 18: What do we know about self-help and support groups, such as AA?** Some self-help and support groups enable people who have been treated for psychological disorders to reach out to others who have had similar experiences (Greidanus & Everall, 2010). These groups tend to be quite specific, such as those in which members help one another cope with dental anxiety (Barak et al., 2008). Other groups help people cope with problems with children and other people in their lives—for example, groups for parents of children with autistic disorders, intellectual deficiency, or Down syndrome. Members share problems and possible solutions.

The best known of self-help and support groups is Alcoholics Anonymous (AA), whose 12-step program has been used by millions of people in the United States and around the world. The group has a religious orientation, with the initial members being Protestants. However, the members are now drawn from all religious or nonreligious backgrounds. Members meet regularly and call other members between meetings when they are tempted to "fall off the wagon" and drink. The 12 steps require admitting before the group that one's drinking is out of control, calling upon a "higher power" for strength, examining errors and injurious behavior, and attempting to make amends for injurious behavior under the influence.

Does AA work? The organization itself admits that the majority of new recruits drop out within a year. Of greater concern is a meta-analysis that concluded that AA is actually less effective than no treatment at all (Kownacki & Shadish, 1999). But most analyses suggest that AA is as effective as other forms of treatment. It has been compared with therapies such as motivational enhancement, relapse prevention training (strategies for *not* falling off the wagon), aversive conditioning, psychodynamic treatment, behavioral self-control training, and others (Imel et al., 2008; Project MATCH Research Group, 1997). When treatments, including AA, are effective, it seems to be because alcoholics remain in treatment for many years (Moos & Moos, 2006), are successful in alleviating feelings of depression (Kelly et al, 2010), and are able to heighten their confidence that they can navigate the challenges of the world without drinking (Forcehimes & Tonigan, 2008).

LearningConnections • GROUP THERAPIES: ON BEING IN IT TOGETHER

ACTIVE REVIEW (18) In the _____ approach to family therapy, family interaction is modified to enhance the growth of family members and the family unit as a whole. (19) Most analyses of Alcoholics Anonymous find it to be (less, more, or about as?) effective as other forms of treatment of alcoholism.

REFLECT AND RELATE Do you think you could share your intimate problems with a group of strangers? Can you see any advantages or disadvantages to doing so?

CRITICAL THINKING Why would you think that various forms of treatment for alcoholism are about equally effective?

 Go to Psychology CourseMate at **www.cengagebrain.com** for an interactive version of these questions.

DOES PSYCHOTHERAPY WORK?

In 1952, British psychologist Hans Eysenck published a review of psychotherapy research—"The Effects of Psychotherapy"—that sent shock waves through the psychotherapy community. On the basis of his review of the research, Eysenck concluded that the rate of improvement among people in psychotherapy was no greater than the rate of "spontaneous remission"—that is, the rate of improvement that would be shown by people with psychological disorders who received no treatment at all. Eysenck was not addressing the subject of people with schizophrenia, who typically profit from biological forms of therapy, but he argued that whether or not people with problems such as anxiety and depression received therapy, two of three reported substantial improvement within 2 years.

That was more than half a century ago. Since that time, sophisticated research studies—many of them employing a statistical averaging method called **meta-analysis**—have strongly suggested that psychotherapy is, in fact, effective. Before we report on the research dealing with the effectiveness of therapy, let's review some of the problems of this kind of research (Shadish, 2002). **Question 19: What kinds of problems do researchers encounter when they conduct research on psychotherapy?**

Problems in Conducting Research on Psychotherapy

It is not easy to evaluate the effectiveness of psychotherapy. Many problems bedevil the effort.

PROBLEMS IN RUNNING EXPERIMENTS ON PSYCHOTHERAPY In well-run experiments, people are assigned at random to experimental and control groups. A true experiment on psychoanalysis would require randomly assigning people seeking therapy to psychoanalysis and to a control group or other kinds of therapy for comparison. But a person may have to remain in traditional psychoanalysis for years to attain beneficial results. Can researchers wait all this time or compare traditional psychoanalysis to briefer treatment methods? Probably not.

In an ideal experiment, participants and researchers are "blind" with regard to the treatment the participants receive so that researchers can control for participants' expectations. In an ideal experiment on therapy, individuals would be blind regarding the type of therapy they are obtaining—or whether they are obtaining a placebo. But can researchers mask the type of therapy clients are obtaining? How would they manage that?

PROBLEMS IN MEASURING OUTCOMES OF THERAPY Consider the problems we run into when measuring outcomes of therapy (Shadish, 2002). Behavior therapists define their goals in behavioral terms—such as a formerly phobic individual being able to obtain an injection or look out of a 20th-story window. But client-centered therapists foster insight and self-actualization, which are not so easily measured.

DOES THERAPY HELP BECAUSE OF THE METHOD OR BECAUSE OF "NONSPECIFIC FACTORS"? Sorting out the benefits of a specific therapy method from broader aspects of the therapy situation is a staggering task. These broader aspects are termed *nonspecific factors,* and they refer to features that are found in most therapies, such as the instillation of hope, empathy, and the development of an effective working relationship (Baldwin et al., 2007).

WHAT IS THE EXPERIMENTAL TREATMENT IN PSYCHOTHERAPY OUTCOME STUDIES? We may also ask, what exactly is the experimental "treatment" being evaluated? Various therapists may say they are practicing psychoanalysis, but they differ as individuals and in their training. How can we specify just what is happening in the therapeutic session?

Analyses of the Effectiveness of Psychotherapy

Question 20: What, then, do we know about the effectiveness of psychotherapy? Despite these evaluation problems, research on the effectiveness of therapy has been encouraging (Driessen et al., 2010; Shedler, 2010).

In their classic early use of meta-analysis, Mary Lee Smith and Gene Glass (1977) analyzed the results of dozens of studies and concluded that people who obtained psychodynamic therapy showed greater well-being, on the average, than 70% to 75% of those who did not obtain treatment. Similarly, nearly 75% of the clients who obtained client-centered therapy were better off than people who did not obtain treatment. Psychodynamic and client-centered therapies appear to be most effective with well-educated, verbal, strongly motivated clients who report problems with anxiety, depression (of light to moderate

Does Psychotherapy Work? To answer this question, psychologists must first deal with the problems in running experiments on the effects of psychotherapy.

Meta-analysis A method for combining and averaging the results of individual research studies.

453

Is Psychotherapy Effective? They're talking over problems, but is it of any help? How would we determine the answer?

Evidence-based practices A method of therapy that has been shown effective in experiments in which participants are assigned at random to the treatment under investigation or to another treatment or placebo, and in which the methods being tested are clearly outlined.

proportions), and interpersonal relationships. Neither form of therapy appears to be effective with people with psychotic disorders such as major depression, bipolar disorder, and schizophrenia. Smith and Glass (1977) found that people who obtained Gestalt therapy showed greater well-being than about 60% of those who did not obtain treatment.

Smith and Glass (1977) did not include cognitive therapies in their meta-analysis because at the time of their study, many cognitive approaches were relatively new. Because behavior therapists incorporate many cognitive techniques, it can be difficult to sort out which aspects—cognitive or otherwise—of behavioral treatments are most effective. However, many meta-analyses of cognitive-behavioral therapy have been conducted, and their results are encouraging.

Studies of cognitive therapy have shown that modifying irrational beliefs of the type described by Albert Ellis helps people with problems such as anxiety and depression (David et al., 2010). Modifying self-defeating beliefs of the sort outlined by Aaron Beck also frequently alleviates anxiety and depression (Butler et al., 2006). Cognitive therapy may help people with severe depression, who had been thought responsive only to biological therapies (Hollon & Shelton, 2001; Simons et al., 1995). Cognitive therapy has also helped people with personality disorders (A. T. Beck et al., 2001; Trull et al., 2003).

Behavioral and cognitive therapies have provided strategies for treating anxiety disorders, social skills deficits, and problems in self-control (DeRubeis & Crits-Christoph, 1998). These therapies have helped couples and families in distress (Baucom et al., 2002). Moreover, they have modified behaviors related to health problems such as headaches (Verhagen et al., 2009), smoking, chronic pain, and bulimia nervosa (Agras et al., 2000; Butler et al., 2006). Cognitive-behavior therapists have innovated treatments for sexual dysfunctions for which there previously were no effective treatments.

Interestingly, different forms of psychotherapy for mild to moderate depression—including cognitive-behavior therapy, nondirective therapy, behavior therapy, and psychodynamic psychotherapy—seem to produce nearly equivalent effects when they are compared to one another (Cuijpers et al., 2008b).

Evidence-Based Practices

Experimentation is the gold standard for research in psychology, and a number of methods of therapy have been shown to be effective in carefully conducted, *random controlled experiments (RCEs)*—that is, experiments in which participants are assigned at random to a specific treatment or to a control treatment. The researchers in many of these studies also rely on treatment manuals that concretely outline the treatment methods. Treatment methods that survive these grueling tests are called **evidence-based practices** (Anchin & Pincus, 2010; Bruce & Sanderson, 2004). Table 13.1 ■ shows a number of evidence-based practices and the problems for which they have been found effective. Other treatments might eventually be added to this list as more evidence accumulates.

TABLE 13.1 ■ Examples of Evidence-Based Practices

Treatment	Condition for Which Treatment Is Effective
Cognitive therapy	Depression Headache
Behavior therapy or behavior modification	Depression Developmental disabilities Enuresis (bed-wetting)
Cognitive-behavior therapy	Panic disorder with and without agoraphobia Generalized anxiety disorder Bulimia nervosa
Exposure treatment	Agoraphobia Other specific phobias
Exposure and response prevention	Obsessive–compulsive disorder
Interpersonal psychotherapy	Depression Personality disorders
Parent training programs	Children with oppositional behavior

Many therapists argue that evidence-based practices favor cognitive-behavioral therapies because they are more readily standardized in treatment manuals and can be followed more accurately by practitioners in experiments (Kazdin, 2008; Levy & Ablon, 2009). Alternative treatments, such as psychodynamic therapy, are not so easily standardized or practiced. Therefore, they may not hold up as well in controlled trials. Second, critics assert that most studies supportive of evidence-based practices do not capture the complexity and uniqueness of real clients seen in community settings (Westen et al., 2006).

As we see in the following section on ethnicity and psychotherapy, we must also consider the sociocultural features of clients in determining how to make therapy most effective.

Ethnicity and Psychotherapy

Americans from ethnic minority groups are less likely than European Americans to seek therapy (Chen & Rizzo, 2010; Sue et al., 2009). Reasons for their lower participation rate include

- Lack of awareness that therapy would help
- Lack of information about the availability of professional services or inability to pay for them
- Distrust of professionals, particularly European American professionals and (for women) male professionals
- Language barriers
- Reluctance to open up about personal matters to strangers—especially strangers who are not members of one's own ethnic group
- Cultural inclinations toward other approaches to problem solving, such as religious approaches and psychic healers
- Negative experiences with professionals and authority figures

There are thus many reasons that clinicians need to be sensitive to the cultural heritage, language, and values of their clients. In other words, they need to develop multicultural competence (Sue et al., 2009). Let's consider some of the issues involved in conducting psychotherapy with African Americans, Asian Americans, Latin Americans, and Native Americans.

African Americans often are reluctant to seek psychological help because of cultural assumptions that people should manage their own problems (González et al., 2010; Jackson & Greene, 2000). Many African Americans are also suspicious of therapists of ethnic groups other than their own—especially European Americans (Mohr et al., 2010). They may withhold personal information because of society's history of racial discrimination (Dana, 2002).

Asian Americans tend to stigmatize people with psychological disorders. As a result, they may deny problems and refuse to seek help for them (Spencer et al., 2010). Asian Americans, especially recent immigrants, also may not understand or believe in Western approaches to psychotherapy. For example, Western psychotherapy typically encourages people to express their feelings. This mode of behavior may conflict with the Asian tradition of public restraint. Furthermore, many Asians experience psychological problems as physical symptoms (Kim & Omizo, 2003; Sue et al., 2009). Therefore, rather than thinking of themselves as anxious, they may focus on physical features of anxiety such as a pounding heart and heavy sweating. Therapists need to be aware of potential conflicts between the traditional Latin American value of interdependence in the family and the typical European American belief in independence and self-reliance (Garza & Watts, 2010).

Many psychological disorders experienced by Native Americans involve the disruption of their traditional culture caused by European colonization (Olson, 2003; Viets et al., 2009). Loss of cultural identity and social

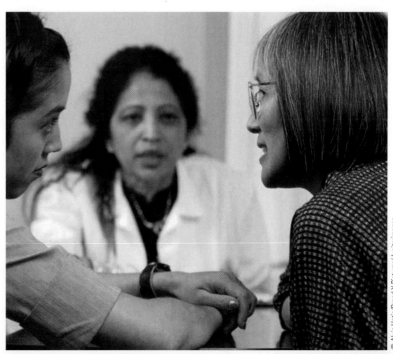

Sensitivity Psychologists need to be sensitive to the cultural heritages, languages, and values of their clients.

disorganization have set the stage for problems such as alcoholism, substance abuse, and depression. Efforts to prevent psychological disorders do well to focus on strengthening Native American cultural identity, pride, and cohesion.

Psychotherapy is most effective when therapists attend to and respect people's cultural as well as individual differences. Although it is the individual who experiences psychological anguish, the fault can often be traced to cultural issues.

LearningConnections ● DOES PSYCHOTHERAPY WORK?

ACTIVE REVIEW (20) Smith and Glass used the method of _____-analysis to analyze the results of dozens of outcome studies of various types of therapies. (21) Current research shows that psychotherapy (is or is not?) effective in the treatment of psychological disorders.

REFLECT AND RELATE If a medical doctor or a psychotherapist recommended a course of treatment for a problem, would you have any difficulty asking that medical doctor or psychotherapist about evidence as to whether that form of treatment has been shown effective? Why or why not?

CRITICAL THINKING Justin swears he feels much better because of psychoanalysis. Deborah swears by her experience with Gestalt therapy. Are such anecdotal endorsements acceptable as scientific evidence? Why or why not?

 Go to Psychology CourseMate at **www.cengagebrain.com** for an interactive version of these questions.

● BIOLOGICAL THERAPIES

The kinds of therapy we have discussed are psychological in nature—forms of *psycho*-therapy. Psychotherapies apply *psychological* principles to treatment, principles based on psychological knowledge of matters such as learning and motivation. However, people with psychological disorders are also often treated with biological therapies. Biological therapies apply what is known of people's *biological* structures and processes to the amelioration of psychological disorders. For example, they may work by altering events in the nervous system, such as by changing the action of neurotransmitters. In this section, we discuss three biological, or medical, approaches to treating people with psychological disorders: drug therapy, electroconvulsive therapy, and psychosurgery. **Question 21: What kinds of drug therapy are available for psychological disorders?**

Drug Therapy: In Search of the Magic Pill?

Some years ago, Fats Domino popularized the song "My Blue Heaven." Fats was singing about the sky and happiness. Today, "blue heavens" is one of the street names for the 10-milligram dose of the antianxiety drug Valium. Clinicians prescribe Valium and other drugs for people with various psychological disorders.

ANTIANXIETY DRUGS Most antianxiety drugs (also called minor tranquilizers) belong to the chemical class known as benzodiazepines. Valium (diazepam) is a benzodiazepine. Other benzodiazepines include lorazepam (Ativan), oxazepam (Serax), and alprazolam (Xanax). Valium and other antianxiety drugs depress the activity of the central nervous system (CNS). The CNS, in turn, decreases sympathetic activity, reducing the heart rate,

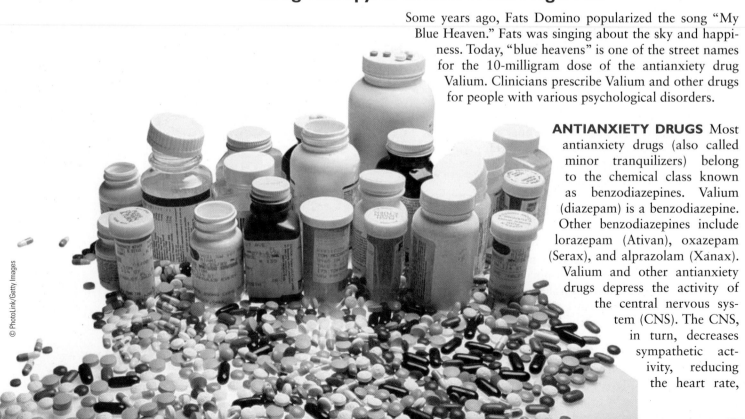

respiration rate, and feelings of nervousness and tension. Many people come to tolerate antianxiety drugs very quickly. When tolerance occurs, dosages must be increased for the drug to remain effective.

Sedation (resulting in feelings of being tired or drowsy) is the most common side effect of antianxiety drugs and the reason that many people use them as sleeping pills. Problems associated with withdrawal from these drugs include **rebound anxiety**. That is, some people who have been using these drugs regularly report that their anxiety becomes worse than before once they discontinue them. Antianxiety drugs can induce physical dependence, as evidenced by withdrawal symptoms such as tremors, sweating, insomnia, and rapid heartbeat.

ANTIPSYCHOTIC DRUGS People with schizophrenia are often given antipsychotic drugs (also called major tranquilizers). In most cases, these drugs reduce agitation, delusions, and hallucinations. Many antipsychotic drugs, including phenothiazines (for example, Thorazine) and clozapine (Clozaril) are thought to act by blocking dopamine receptors in the brain (Porsolt et al., 2010). Research along these lines supports the theory that schizophrenia is connected with overactivity of the neurotransmitter dopamine.

ANTIDEPRESSANTS People with major depression often take so-called **antidepressant** drugs. **Truth or Fiction Revisited:** These drugs are also helpful for some people with eating disorders, panic disorder, obsessive–compulsive disorder, and social phobia (Zohar & Westenberg, 2007). Problems in the regulation of noradrenaline and serotonin may be involved in eating and panic disorders as well as in depression. Antidepressants are believed to work by increasing levels of one or both of these neurotransmitters, which can affect both depression and the appetite (Dagyte et al., 2010).

There are various antidepressants. Each increases the concentration of noradrenaline or serotonin in the brain (Dagyte et al., 2010). *Monoamine oxidase (MAO) inhibitors* block the activity of an enzyme that breaks down noradrenaline and serotonin. *Tricyclic and tetracyclic antidepressants* prevent the reuptake of noradrenaline and serotonin by the axon terminals of the transmitting neurons. **Selective serotonin-reuptake inhibitors (SSRIs)** such as Lexapro, Prozac, and Zoloft also block the reuptake of serotonin by presynaptic neurons. As a result, serotonin remains in the synaptic cleft longer, influencing receiving neurons. SSRIs appear to be more effective than other antidepressants.

LITHIUM The ancient Greeks and Romans were among the first to use the metal lithium as a psychoactive drug. They prescribed mineral water—which contains lithium—for people with bipolar disorder. They had no inkling as to why this treatment sometimes helped. A salt of the metal lithium (lithium carbonate), in tablet form, flattens out cycles of manic behavior and depression in most people. Lithium can also be used to strengthen the effects of antidepressant medication (Redrobe & Bourin, 2009).

People with bipolar disorder may have to use lithium indefinitely, as a person with type 1 diabetes must use insulin to control the illness. Lithium has been shown to have side effects such as hand tremors, memory impairment, and excessive thirst and urination (Porsolt et al., 2010). Memory impairment is reported as the main reason people discontinue lithium.

Electroconvulsive Therapy

Question 22: What is electroconvulsive therapy (ECT)? Electroconvulsive therapy (ECT) is a biological form of therapy for psychological disorders that was introduced by the Italian psychiatrist Ugo Cerletti in 1939. Cerletti had noted that some slaughterhouses used electric current to render animals unconscious. The shocks also produced convulsions. Along with other European researchers of the period, Cerletti erroneously believed that convulsions were incompatible with schizophrenia and other major psychological disorders.

ECT was originally used for a variety of psychological disorders. Because of the advent of antipsychotic drugs, however, it is now used mainly for people with major depression who do not respond to antidepressants (Piccinni et al., 2009). People typically obtain one ECT treatment three times a week for up to 10 sessions. Electrodes are attached to the temples and an electrical current strong enough to produce a convulsion is induced. The shock causes unconsciousness, so the patient does not recall it. Nevertheless, patients are given a **sedative** so that they are asleep during the treatment.

Rebound anxiety Anxiety that can occur when one discontinues use of a tranquilizer.

Antidepressant Acting to relieve depression.

Selective serotonin-reuptake inhibitors (SSRIs) Antidepressant drugs that work by blocking the reuptake of serotonin by presynaptic neurons.

Electroconvulsive therapy (ECT) Treatment of disorders like major depression by passing an electric current (that causes a convulsion) through the head.

Sedative A drug that relieves nervousness or agitation or puts one to sleep.

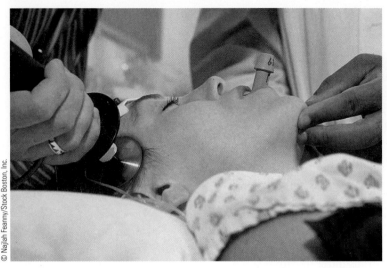

Electroconvulsive Therapy With ECT, electrodes are placed on each side of the patient's head and a current is passed between them, inducing a seizure. ECT is used mainly in cases of major depression when antidepressant drugs and psychotherapy are not sufficient.

Psychosurgery Surgery intended to promote psychological changes or to relieve disordered behavior.

Prefrontal lobotomy The severing or destruction of a section of the frontal lobe of the brain.

TABLE 13.2 ■ Average Percentage of Participants Responding to Treatments for Depression

Selective Serotonin-Reuptake Inhibitors	47.9%
Cognitive-behavior therapy	55.5%
Placebo	32.5%

Source: J. J. Wagner. (2005). A meta-analysis/literature review comparing the effectiveness of SSRI antidepressants, cognitive behavioral therapy, and placebo for the treatment of depression. *Dissertation Abstracts International: Section B: The Sciences and Engineering.* 66(4-B), pp. 2319.

ECT is controversial for many reasons, one being that many professionals are distressed by the thought of passing an electric current through a patient's head and producing convulsions. There are also side effects, including memory problems (Gregory-Roberts et al., 2010). However, research suggests that for most people, cognitive impairment from ECT tends to be temporary (Rayner et al., 2009). One study followed up ten adolescents who had received ECT an average of 3½ years earlier. Six of the ten had complained of memory impairment immediately after treatment, but only one complained of continued problems at the follow-up. Moreover, psychological tests did not reveal any differences in cognitive functioning between severely depressed adolescents who had received ECT and others who had not (D. Cohen et al., 2000).

Psychosurgery

Psychosurgery is more controversial than ECT. **Question 23: What is psychosurgery?** The most famous—or infamous—technique, **prefrontal lobotomy**, has been used with people with severe disorders. In this method, a picklike instrument severs the nerve pathways that link the prefrontal lobes of the brain to the thalamus. This method was pioneered by the Portuguese neurologist Antonio Egas Moniz and was brought to the United States in the 1930s. The theoretical rationale for the operation was vague and misguided, and Moniz's reports of success were exaggerated. Nevertheless, by 1950, prefrontal lobotomies had been performed on more than a thousand people in an effort to reduce their violence and agitation. **Truth or Fiction Revisited:** Anecdotal evidence of the method's unreliable outcomes is found in an ironic footnote to history: one of Dr. Moniz's "failures" shot the doctor, leaving a bullet lodged in his spine and paralyzing his legs. Thus, it is true that the originator of a surgical technique intended to reduce violence learned that it was not always successful…when one of his patients shot him.

Prefrontal lobotomy also has a host of side effects, including hyperactivity and distractibility, impaired learning ability, overeating, apathy and withdrawal, epileptic-type seizures, reduced creativity, and now and then, death. Because of these side effects and because of the advent of antipsychotic drugs, this method has been largely discontinued in the United States.

Does Biological Therapy Work?

There are thus a number of biological approaches to the therapy of psychological disorders. **Question 24: What do we know about the effectiveness of biological therapies?**

There is little question that drug therapy has helped many people with severe psychological disorders. Antipsychotic drugs largely account for the reduced need for the use of restraint and supervision (padded cells, straitjackets, hospitalization, and so on) with people diagnosed with schizophrenia. Antipsychotic drugs have allowed hundreds of thousands of former mental hospital residents to lead largely normal lives in the community, hold jobs, and maintain family lives. Most of the problems related to these drugs concern their side effects. **Truth or Fiction Revisited:** Therefore, people with psychological disorders should *not* always say no to drugs.

Comparisons of the effectiveness of psychotherapy and pharmacotherapy (medicine) for depression have yielded mixed results. Studies from the 1990s concluded that cognitive therapy is as effective as, or more effective than, antidepressants (Antonuccio, 1995; Muñoz et al., 1994). Cognitive therapy provides coping skills that reduce the risk of recurrence of depression once treatment ends (Hollon & Shelton, 2001). However, a meta-analysis of 30 randomized controlled experiments concluded that SSRIs may be more effective than psychological methods in the treatment of major depressive disorder, although the differences were small and, according to the researchers, might not have much clinical meaning (Cuijpers et al., 2008a). Still another analysis of the literature—in this case, analysis of 14 experiments and 5 meta-analyses—concluded that both SSRIs and cognitive-behavior therapy were more effective than placebos in treating depression (Wagner, 2005) (see Table 13.2 ■).

A CLOSER LOOK

Contemporary Psychosurgery for Treatment-Resistant Obsessive–Compulsive Disorder and Depression

"It got so bad, I didn't want any contact with people," said Ross, now in his 20s. "I couldn't hug my own parents" (in Carey, 2009).

At the age of 12, Ross realized that it took him longer than other people to wash his hands. He changed his clothes several times a day. After a while, he remained in his room whenever he could, being careful about touching things when he came out.

"I just looked horrible," said Leonard, another sufferer of obsessive-compulsive disorder (OCD), now in his sixties. "I had a big, ugly beard. My skin turned black. I was afraid to be seen out in public. I looked like a street person. If you were a policeman, you would have arrested me."

Leonard had been a successful businessman. Then the phobia for spiders and insects descended upon him. Although he dealt with the phobias, he developed powerful aversions to shaving, brushing his teeth, and washing himself.

Ross and Leonard tried psychotherapy and drug therapy to no avail. Ross said that drugs worked for a while but did not last. "I just thought my life was over."

With their disorders deemed severe and disabling, with standard treatments exhausted, Ross and Leonard were guided to current methods of psychosurgery, specifically *gamma knife surgery* in which physicians beam radiation into the skull. The beams cause no damage except where they converge, destroying spots of tissue in circuits believed to be overactive in severe OCD (Tyagi et al., 2010).

In addition to gamma knife surgery, three other psychosurgery procedures are being tried with caution (Bear et al., 2010). In *cingulotomy*, physicians drill through the skull and thread wires into the anterior cingulate of the limbic system (see Figure 13.1 ■). There they destroy small areas of tissue that connect the emotional centers of the brain to the frontal cortex, the brain's executive center. These areas seem to be overactive in people with the most severe OCD, and the surgery apparently calms that activity. There are occasional side effects of seizures (Read & Greenberg, 2009).

In a *capsulotomy,* surgeons go into the internal capsule and destroy tissue believed to be overactive. A 25-year follow-up of capsulotomy found positive effects but also some side effects such as weight gain, apathy, and problems in decision making and planning (Rcuk et al., 2008).

In *deep brain stimulation,* surgeons sink electrodes into the internal capsule and leave them there. A device sends an electric current to the area, disrupting circuits believed to be overactive in people with OCD (and in people with deep depression). A recent study found that four of six deep-brain-stimulation patients showed improvement in OCD and in depressive symptoms (Goodman et al., 2010).

Two years after his surgery, Ross, in college, was appreciative. "It saved my life," he said. "I really believe that."

Leonard, however, saw no benefits. "I still don't leave the house," he said.

Darin D. Dougherty, M.D., director of neurotherapeutics at Massachusetts General Hospital, one of the few hospitals that carries out these forms of psychosurgery, acknowledged some treatment failures. Because of the history of disturbing side effects and failed psychosurgical methods, he voiced concern that "if this effort somehow goes wrong, it'll shut down this approach for another hundred years."

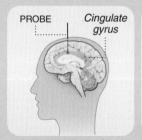

Cingulotomy
Probes are inserted into the brain to destroy a spot on the anterior cingulate gyrus, to disrupt a circuit that connects the emotional and conscious planning centers of the brain.

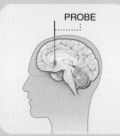

Capsulotomy
Probes are inserted deep into the brain and heated to destroy part of the anterior capsule, to disrupt a circuit thought to be overactive in people with severe O.C.D.

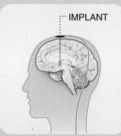

Deep brain stimulation
As an alternative to capsulotomy, an electrode is permanently implanted on one or both sides of the brain. A pacemaker-like device then delivers an adjustable current.

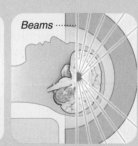

Gamma knife surgery
An M.R.I.-like device focuses hundreds of small beams of radiation at a point within the brain, destroying small areas of tissue.

Figure 13.1.■ Contemporary Methods of Psychosurgery Being Tried in Cases of Obsessive–Compulsive Disorder and Major Depressive Disorder That Do Not Respond to Other Treatments. A handful of medical centers have been conducting several experimental brain surgeries as a last resort for severe obsessive-compulsive disorders that are beyond the range of standard treatment.

Source: From Benedict Carey, "Surgery for Mental Ills Offers Both Hope and Risk," *New York Times,* 11/26/09. Copyright © 2009 by The New York Times. Reprinted by permission.

Pim Cuijpers and his colleagues (2009b) undertook a meta-analysis of randomly controlled experiments to attempt to answer the question of whether there was a difference in effectiveness of the treatment of depression when an antidepressant drug was added to a psychological treatment. They found that a treatment package that included psychotherapy and pharmacotherapy was more effective than psychological treatment alone, but it was not clear that the antidepressants offered much of an advantage.

In some cases, cognitive-behavior therapy appears to have helped relieve the positive symptoms of schizophrenia (Gregory, 2010; Wykes et al., 2008). Cognitive-behavior

"Be not afraid of life. Believe that life is worth living and your belief will help create the fact."

—William James

Depression is characterized by inactivity, feelings of sadness, and cognitive distortions. When we suspect that our feelings may fit the picture of a major depressive episode or bipolar disorder, it might be helpful to talk things over with our instructor or visit the college counseling or health center. Some of us may also want to try to get at the deep-seated roots of our feelings of depression, and doing so in some cases might require long-term talk therapy. On the other hand, cognitive-behavioral therapists have pointed out that there are many things we can do on our own to cope with milder feelings of depression. These methods attempt to directly reverse the characteristics of depression:

- Engaging in pleasant events
- Thinking rationally
- Exercising

Engaging in Pleasant Events

Make a list—perhaps with a friend or family member who knows you well—of things you used to enjoy before feelings of depression came along. Items might include things like watching or talking about sports or shows, reading poetry or novels, camping, playing cards or board games, lunching with friends, woodworking, singing, taking a bath, sitting in the sun, collecting stamps, people watching, walking in the city or county, or bicycling. Then try the following:

1. Engage in at least three pleasant events each day.

2. Record your activities in a diary. Add other activities and events that strike you as pleasant, even if they are unplanned.

3. Toward the end of each day, rate your response to each activity, using a scale like this one:

   +3 Wonderful

   +2 Very nice

   +1 Somewhat nice

    0 No particular response

   −1 Somewhat disappointing

   −2 Rather disappointing

   −3 The pits

4. After a week or so, check the items in the diary that received positive ratings.

5. Repeat successful activities and experiment with new ones.

Thinking Rationally

"Public opinion is a weak tyrant compared with our own private opinion. What a man thinks of himself, that it is which determines...his fate."

—Henry David Thoreau, *Walden*

Depressed people tend to blame themselves for failures and problems, even when they are not at fault. They *internalize* blame and see their problems as *stable* and *global*—as all but impossible to change. Depressed people also make cognitive errors such as *catastrophizing* their problems and *minimizing* their accomplishments.

Column 1 in Table 13.3 ■ illustrates a number of irrational, depressing thoughts. How many of them have you had? Column 2 indicates the type of cognitive error being made (such as internalizing or catastrophizing), and column 3 shows examples of rational alternatives.

You can pinpoint irrational, depressing thoughts by identifying the kinds of thoughts you have when you feel low. Look for the fleeting thoughts that can trigger mood changes. It helps to jot them down. Then challenge their accuracy. Do you characterize difficult situations as impossible and hopeless? Do you expect too much from yourself and minimize your achievements? Do you internalize more than your fair share of blame?

You can use Table 13.3 to classify your cognitive errors and construct rational alternatives. Write these next to each irrational thought. Review them from time to time. When you are alone, you can read the irrational thought aloud. Then follow it by saying to yourself firmly, "No, that's irrational!" Then read the rational alternative aloud twice, *emphatically*.

After you have thought or read aloud the rational alternative, say to yourself, "That makes more sense! That's a more accurate view of things! I feel better now that I have things in perspective."

therapy is apparently more effective, however, when it is combined with medication in the treatment of schizophrenia (Chadwick & Lowe, 1990).

Many psychologists and psychiatrists are comfortable with the short-term use of antianxiety drugs in helping clients manage periods of unusual anxiety or tension. However, many people use antianxiety drugs routinely to dull the arousal stemming from anxiety-producing lifestyles or interpersonal problems. Rather than make the often painful decisions required to confront their problems and change their lives, they prefer to take a pill.

Despite the controversies surrounding ECT, it helps many people who do not respond to antidepressant drugs (Piccinni et al., 2009). ECT may be a useful "last resort" when other treatment methods are of no avail.

In sum, drug therapy and perhaps ECT seem to be effective for some disorders that do not respond to psychotherapy alone. Yet common sense and research evidence suggest that psychotherapy is preferable for problems such as anxiety and mild depression. No chemical can show a person how to change an idea or solve an interpersonal problem.

Exercising

Exercise not only fosters physical health, but it can enhance psychological well-being and help us cope with depression as well. Depression is characterized by inactivity and feelings of helplessness. Exercise is, in a sense, the opposite of inactivity. It might also help alleviate feelings of helplessness. In one experiment, 156 adult volunteers who were depressed were randomly assigned to 4 months of either aerobic exercise, antidepressant medication, or a combination of the two (Babyak et al., 2000). Following treatment, all three groups showed comparable relief from depression. But at a further 6-month follow-up, subjects from the exercise groups who had continued to exercise showed the greatest improvement. Other experiments also find that exercise alleviates feelings of depression (Krogh et al., 2010; Mead et al., 2009). It has also been shown to decrease feelings of anxiety (Herring et al., 2010).

Perhaps the strategies presented here will work for you. If they don't, why not talk things over with your professor or visit the college health or counseling center?

TABLE 13.3 ■ Irrational, Depressing Thoughts and Rational Alternatives

Irrational Thought	Type of Thought	Rational Alternative
"There's nothing I can do."	Catastrophizing (the size of the problem), minimizing (one's coping ability), stabilizing (making into a permanent problem)	"I can't think of anything to do right now, but if I work at it, I may."
"I'm no good."	Internalizing, globalizing, stabilizing	"I did something I regret, but that doesn't make me evil or worthless as a person."
"This is absolutely awful."	Catastrophizing	"This is pretty bad, but it's not the end of the world."
"I just don't have the brains for college."	Stabilizing, globalizing	"I guess I really need to go back over the basics in that course."
"I just can't believe I did something so disgusting!"	Catastrophizing	"That was a bad experience. Well, I won't be likely to try that again soon."
"I can't imagine ever feeling right."	Stabilizing, catastrophizing	"This is painful, but if I try to work it through step by step, I'll probably eventually see my way out of it."
"It's all my fault."	Internalizing	"I'm not blameless, but I wasn't the only one involved. It may have been my idea, but he went into it with his eyes open."
"I can't do anything right."	Globalizing, stabilizing, catastrophizing, minimizing	"I sure screwed this up, but I've done a lot of things well, and I'll do other things well."
"I hurt everybody who gets close to me."	Internalizing, globalizing, stabilizing	"I'm not totally blameless, but I'm not responsible for the whole world. Others make their own decisions, and they have to live with the results, too."
"If people knew the real me, they would have it in for me."	Globalizing, minimizing (the positive in yourself)	"I'm not perfect, but nobody's perfect. I have positive as well as negative features, and I am entitled to self-interests."

Many of us create or compound feelings of depression because of cognitive errors such as those in this table. Have you had any of these irrational, depressing thoughts? Are you willing to challenge them?

LearningConnections ● BIOLOGICAL THERAPIES

ACTIVE REVIEW (22) (Minor or Major?) tranquilizers are usually prescribed for people who complain of anxiety or tension. (23) Major tranquilizers that belong to the chemical class of phenothiazines are thought to work by blocking the action of the neurotransmitter _____. (24) Antidepressants heighten the action of the neurotransmitters _____ and noradrenaline. (25) ECT is mainly used to treat severe cases of _____. (26) The best-known psychosurgery technique is the _____ lobotomy.

REFLECT AND RELATE In your experience, do people from your sociocultural background express any particular attitudes toward people who use antianxiety drugs or antidepressants? Explain.

CRITICAL THINKING Are there times when it is appropriate to prescribe medical treatment for a psychological disorder? How would you make that decision?

 Go to Psychology CourseMate at **www.cengagebrain.com** for an interactive version of these questions.

Psychodynamic Therapies	Humanistic Therapies	Behavior Therapies
Assume disorders stem from unresolved unconscious conflict	Assume that disorders reflect feelings of alienation from one's genuine beliefs and feelings.	Assume disorders reflect learning of maladaptive responses (such as maladaptive fear responses, or phobias) or failure to acquire adaptive responses (such as social skills).

Freud's Consulting Room

Client-centered therapists provide a warm atmosphere in which clients feel free to explore their genuine feelings.

One way behavior therapists help clients overcome phobias is to have them gradually approach the feared object or situation while they remain relaxed.

Goals

To strengthen the ego; to provide self-insight into unconscious conflict	To help clients get in touch with parts of themselves that they have "disowned" and actualize their unique desires and abilities	To use principles of learning to help clients engage in adaptive behavior and discontinue maladaptive behavior

Methods

Traditional psychoanalysis is lengthy and nondirective and involves methods such as free association and dream analysis.	Client-centered therapy is nondirective. It provides an atmosphere of "unconditional positive regard" from the therapist in which clients can engage in self-exploration without fear. Gestalt therapy uses highly directive methods to help clients integrate conflicting parts of the personality into a healthy "Gestalt," or whole.	Behavior therapy is directive and uses fear-reduction methods (including systematic desensitization) to overcome phobias such as fear of flying, aversive conditioning (to help clients discontinue bad habits), operant conditioning procedures (e.g., social skills training), and self-control methods (beginning with functional analysis of behavior).

Comments

Most effective with verbal, "upscale" clients. Modern ego-analytic approaches are briefer and more directive than traditional psychoanalysis.	Client-centered therapy is practiced widely in college and university counseling centers to help students make academic and personal decisions.	Behavior therapists have developed treatment for problems (e.g., smoking, phobias, sexual dysfunctions) for which there previously were no effective treatment methods.
Principal proponent: Sigmund Freud (1856–1939) formulated his psychodynamic theory of personality a century ago. His method of therapy, psychoanalysis, achieved greatest prominence in the 1940s and 1950s.	**Principal proponents:** Carl Rogers (1902–1970) developed client-centered therapy in the mid-20th century. Fritz Perls (1893–1970) originated Gestalt therapy, which reached its greatest prominence in the 1960s	**Principal proponents:** Joseph Wolpe (1915–1997) introduced systematic desensitization in the late 1950s. Albert Bandura integrated behavioral and cognitive factors in forming his therapeutic methods, such as modeling.

Sigmund Freud

Carl Rogers

Fritz Perls

Albert Bandura

Cognitive Therapies

Assume disorders reflect cognitive errors such as excessive self-blame, pessimism, and selective focus on negative events.

The therapist seeks to guide the client to correct cognitive errors and recognize irrational beliefs.

Goals

To make clients aware of the beliefs, attitudes, and automatic types of thinking that create and compound their problems; to help them correct these kinds of thinking to reduce negative feelings and solve problems

Methods

Aaron Beck's cognitive therapy helps people recognize and correct cognitive errors such as selective perception, overgeneralization, magnification of negative events, and absolutist thinking. Rational emotive behavior therapists show clients how irrational beliefs catastrophize events and make them miserable.

Comments

Many theorists consider cognitive therapy to be part of behavior therapy, and some call it cognitive-*behavioral* therapy.

Principal proponents: Aaron Beck introduced his approach, *cognitive therapy*" in the 1960s. Albert Ellis first developed what he called *rational–emotive therapy (RET)* in the late 1950s and 1960s. More recently, he changed the name to *rational emotive behavior therapy (REBT)*.

Aaron Beck and Albert Ellis

Biological Therapies

Assume that disorders reflect the interaction of genetic vulnerability with other factors, such as imbalances of neurotransmitters or hormones or situational stressors; for example, depression may reflect interaction of genetic vulnerability with low levels of serotonin and with a personal failure.

Many drugs have been used to combat psychological disorders.

To decrease anxiety, alleviate depression, lessen mood swings in bipolar disorder, eliminate or lessen symptoms of schizophrenia

Antianxiety drugs (also known as *anxiolytic* drugs or "minor tranquilizers"), antidepressant drugs, lithium and other drugs for treatment of bipolar disorder, antipsychotic drugs ("major tranquilizers"), electroconvulsive shock therapy (ECT) for treatment of depression that is unresponsive to drug therapy, psychosurgery

Most psychologists prefer psychotherapy to biological therapies as being more helpful in developing strategies for solving problems. There is controversy as to whether cognitive therapy is as effective as biological therapy for depression. Most psychologists agree that biological therapies may be appropriate when disorders are severe and unresponsive to psychotherapy.

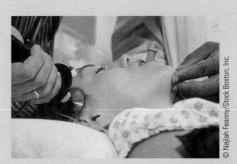

Electroconvulsive therapy is used mainly in cases of major depression after other therapies have failed.

463

What Is Psychotherapy?

1. What is psychotherapy?
Psychotherapy is a systematic interaction between a therapist and a client that applies psychological principles to affect the client's thoughts, feelings, and/or behavior to help the client overcome psychological disorders, adjust to problems in living, or develop as an individual.

2. How have people with psychological problems and disorders been treated throughout the ages?
It was once assumed that psychological disorders represented possession by the devil, and cruel methods were used to try to rid the person of evil spirits. Asylums were the first institutions for people with psychological disorders, and eventually mental hospitals and the community mental health movement came into being.

Psychodynamic Therapies: Digging Deep Within

3. How do psychoanalysts conduct a traditional Freudian psychoanalysis?
The main method in Freudian psychoanalysis is free association, but dream analysis and interpretations are used as well.

4. How do modern psychodynamic approaches differ from traditional psychoanalysis?
Modern psychodynamic approaches are briefer and more directive than traditional psychoanalysis, and the therapist and client usually sit face to face.

Humanistic Therapies: Strengthening the Self

5. What is Carl Rogers's method of client-centered therapy?
Client-centered therapy uses unconditional positive regard, empathic understanding, and genuineness to help clients overcome obstacles to self-actualization.

6. What is Fritz Perls's method of Gestalt therapy?
Perls's highly directive method of Gestalt therapy aims to make clients aware of conflict, accept responsibility, and make choices despite fear.

Behavior Therapy: Adjustment Is What You Do

7. What is behavior therapy?
Behavior therapy relies on learning principles to help clients develop adaptive behavior patterns and discontinue maladaptive ones.

8. What are some behavior-therapy methods for reducing fears?
Behavior therapy methods for reducing fear include flooding, systematic desensitization, and modeling.

9. How do behavior therapists use aversive conditioning to help people break bad habits?
Aversive conditioning discourages undesirable behaviors by repeatedly pairing clients' self-defeating impulses (for example, alcohol, cigarette smoke, deviant sex objects) with aversive stimuli so that the impulses become aversive rather than tempting.

10. How do behavior therapists apply principles of operant conditioning in behavior modification?
Principles of operant conditioning are applied in behavior-therapy methods that foster adaptive behavior through reinforcement. Examples include token economies, successive approximations, social skills training, and biofeedback training.

11. How can you use behavior therapy to deal with temptation and enhance your self-control?
Behavior-therapy self-control methods begin with functional analysis of the problem behavior, then modifying the antecedents and consequences of behavior along with the behavior itself.

Cognitive Therapies: Adjustment Is What You Think (and Do)

12. What is cognitive therapy?
Cognitive therapies aim to modify irrational beliefs and cognitive distortions.

13. What is Aaron Beck's method of cognitive therapy?
Beck notes that clients develop emotional problems such as depression because of cognitive distortions or errors that lead them to minimize accomplishments and catastrophize failures. He teaches clients to dispute cognitive errors.

14. What is Albert Ellis's method of rational-emotive behavior therapy?
Ellis holds that people's beliefs *about* events, not only the events themselves, shape people's responses to them. Ellis showed how irrational beliefs, such as the belief that we must have social approval, can worsen problems.

Group Therapies: On Being in It Together

15. What are the advantages and disadvantages of group therapy?
Group therapy is more economical than individual therapy. Moreover, group members benefit from the social support and experiences of other members. But some clients cannot disclose feelings in the group setting.

16. What is couple therapy?
Couple therapy addresses the couple as the unit of treatment and focuses on helping couples enhance their relationship by improving communication skills and helping them manage conflict

17. What is family therapy?
In family therapy, one or more families make up the group. Family therapy modifies family interactions to enhance the growth of individuals in the family and the family as a whole.

18. What do we know about self-help and support groups, such as AA?
Most analyses suggest that AA is about as effective as other forms of treatment in helping alcoholics remain abstinent.

Does Psychotherapy Work?

19. What kinds of problems do researchers encounter when they conduct research on psychotherapy?
It is difficult and perhaps impossible to randomly assign clients to therapy methods such as traditional psychoanalysis. Moreover, clients cannot be kept blind as to the treatment they are receiving. Further, it can be difficult to sort out the effects of nonspecific therapeutic factors from the effects of specific methods of therapy.

20. What do we know about the effectiveness of psychotherapy?
Meta-analyses show that people who obtain most forms of psychotherapy fare better than people who do not. Cognitive and behavior therapies are probably most effective.

Biological Therapies

21. What kinds of drug therapy are available for psychological disorders?
Antianxiety drugs help alleviate feelings of anxiety in people with anxiety disorders. Antipsychotic drugs help many people with schizophrenia. Antidepressants often help people with severe depression, apparently by raising levels of serotonin available to the brain. Lithium often helps people with bipolar disorder.

22. What is electroconvulsive therapy (ECT)?
In ECT, an electrical current is passed through the temples, inducing a seizure and frequently relieving severe depression. ECT is controversial because of side effects such as loss of memory.

23. What is psychosurgery?
The best-known psychosurgery technique, prefrontal lobotomy, has been largely discontinued because of side effects. However, other surgical techniques remain under study, including several for obsessive–compulsive disorder (OCD).

24. What do we know about the effectiveness of biological therapies?
Drugs do not teach people how to solve problems and build relationships, yet antidepressants may be of use when psychotherapy does not help people with depression. ECT appears to be helpful in some cases when neither psychotherapy nor drug therapy (antidepressants) is of help. Antipsychotic drugs benefit many people with schizophrenia.

KEY TERMS

Antidepressant (p. 457)
Asylum (p. 435)
Aversive conditioning (p. 443)
Behavior therapy (p. 442)
Biofeedback training (BFT) (p. 445)
Catharsis (p. 437)
Client-centered therapy (p. 440)
Cognitive therapy (p. 447)
Couple therapy (p. 451)
Ego analyst (p. 439)
Electroconvulsive therapy (ECT) (p. 457)
Empathic understanding (p. 440)
Evidence-based practices (p. 454)
Family therapy (p. 451)
Frame of reference (p. 440)

Free association (p. 437)
Functional analysis (p. 446)
Genuineness (p. 440)
Gestalt therapy (p. 441)
Humanistic therapy (p. 439)
Interpretation (p. 437)
Latent content (p. 438)
Manifest content (p. 438)
Meta-analysis (p. 453)
Modeling (p. 443)
Phallic symbol (p. 438)
Prefrontal lobotomy (p. 451)
Psychoanalysis (p. 436)
Psychodynamic therapy (p. 458)
Psychosurgery (p. 458)
Psychotherapy (p. 434)

Rational-emotive behavior therapy (REBT) (p. 449)
Rebound anxiety (p. 451)
Resistance (p. 437)
Sedative (p. 457)
Selective serotonin-reuptake inhibitors (SSRIs) (p. 457)
Social skills training (p. 444)
Successive approximations (p. 444)
Systematic desensitization (p. 443)
Token economy (p. 444)
Transference (p. 437)
Unconditional positive regard (p. 440)
Wish fulfillment (p. 438)

ACTIVE LEARNING RESOURCES

Log in to **www.cengagebrain.com** to access the resources your instructor requires. For this book, you can access:

 **CourseMate** brings course concepts to life with interactive learning, study, and exam preparation tools that support the printed textbook. A textbook-specific website, Psychology CourseMate includes an integrated interactive eBook and other interactive learning tools including quizzes, flashcards, videos, and more.

CENGAGENOW Need help studying? This site is your one-stop study shop. Take a Pre-Test and CengageNOW will generate a Personalized Study Plan based on your test results. The Study Plan will identify the topics you need to review and direct you to online resources to help you master those topics. You can then take a Post-Test to determine the concepts you have mastered and what you still need to work on.

© Steve Raymer/Corbis

14 Social Psychology

MAJOR TOPICS

Attitudes: "The Good, the Bad, and the Ugly" *468*

Prejudice: A Particularly Troublesome Attitude *474*

Interpersonal Attraction: On Liking and Loving *477*

Social Perception: Looking Out, Looking Within *483*

Social Influence: Are You an Individual or One of the Crowd? *486*

Group Behavior: Is a Camel a Horse Made by a Committee? *492*

FEATURES

A Closer Look: The Foot-in-the-Door Technique *473*

Video Connections: Stereotype Threat *475*

Life Connections: Combating Prejudice *476*

A Closer Look: When It Comes to Sex, Red May Mean "Go" *479*

Self-Assessment: The Triangular Love Scale *482*

A Closer Look: Who Are the Suicide Terrorists? A Case of the Fundamental Attribution Error? *485*

T F People vote their consciences.

page 468

T F Airing a TV commercial repeatedly turns off the audience and decreases sales.

page 470

T F We appreciate things more when we have to work for them.

page 474

T F Being compelled by the law to recycle can change a person's attitude toward recycling.

page 474

T F People have condemned billions of other people without ever meeting them or learning their names.

page 474

T F Beauty is in the eye of the beholder.

page 477

T F When you're smiling, people perceive you as more attractive.

page 478

T F Opposites attract.

page 480

T F You should just "be yourself" in a job interview. There's no point to getting dressed up and watching your language.

page 483

T F We tend to hold others responsible for their misdeeds but to see ourselves as victims of circumstances when we misbehave.

page 484

T F Most people will torture an innocent person just because they are ordered to do so.

page 488

T F Seeing is believing.

page 491

T F Nearly 40 people stood by and did nothing while a woman was being stabbed to death.

page 496

Are these items truth or fiction? We will be revisiting them throughout the chapter.

C

onsider some news items from the early years of the 21st century:

- 2011: A suicide bomber drove a car laden with explosives up to a Coptic Christian church in Egypt as worshipers exited a New Year's mass. The bomb killed 21 people and wounded at least 80 more.

- 2007: Benazir Bhutto, the two-time prime minister of Pakistan, was killed by a suicide bomber during a political rally as she was campaigning to obtain that post for a third time.

- 2005: Four suicide bombers blew themselves up aboard three London commuter trains and a bus, killing more than 50 people and wounding 700.

- 2001: And of course, on September 11, 2001, 19 suicide terrorists in the United States used fully fueled airplanes as bombs, flying them into the World Trade Center and the Pentagon, killing nearly 3,000 people.

As noted by political scientist Mark Danner, "There have been suicide truck bombs, suicide tanker bombs, suicide police cars, suicide bombers on foot, suicide bombers posing as police officers, suicide bombers posing as soldiers, even suicide bombers on bicycles" (2005, p. 52).

Although you might think of suicide terrorism as a recent development, it dates back thousands of years (Kazim et al., 2008). But we have become most recently aware of suicide terrorism by strikes throughout the Muslim world, in Israel, and—with the attacks on New York, Washington, Madrid, and London—in the Western world. The word *suicide* in the phrase "suicide bomber" leads people to turn to psychologists for understanding, with the idea that something must be psychologically wrong with these terrorists. But many social scientists assert that suicide terrorists have no telltale psychological profile (Consortium of Social Science Associations, 2003; Leenaars, 2006). Ariel Merari and his colleagues (2010) at the University of Tel Aviv could not interview "successful" suicide bombers, but they interviewed and tested would-be suicide bombers—Palestinians who had been caught in the act and arrested. They report that they found two groups among the would-be suicide terrorists: Some were dependent types with a tendency to follow leaders and public influences. Others were emotionally unstable and impulsive. And among both types, some were depressed but would not warrant a diagnosis of major depressive disorder. We still have no clear profile of the suicide terrorist.

Because of the difficulty in identifying suicide terrorists, social psychologist Philip Zimbardo (2004) argues that we must look to the psychology of social influence to understand them. As we will see, social psychologist Stanley Milgram (1974), who conducted famous—some would say "infamous"—studies on obedience to authority some 50 years ago, concluded, "Often, it is not so much the kind of person a man is, as the kind of situation in which he finds himself that determines how he will act."

Question 1: What is social psychology? Social psychology is the field of psychology that studies the nature and causes of behavior and mental processes in social situations. Social psychologists study the ways people can be goaded by social influences into doing things that are not necessarily consistent with their personalities. In particular, Zimbardo (2007) has investigated the relative ease with which "ordinary" men and women can be incited by social influence to behave in evil ways. He dubbed the transformation the *Lucifer effect*. The social psychological topics we discuss in this chapter include attitudes, social perception, social influence, and group behavior. As we explore each of these, we will ask what they might offer to those of us who have difficulty imagining why people would surrender their own lives to take the lives of others.

We begin with attitudes.

London, July 7, 2005 Commuters coming into London on this summer morning were accompanied by four suicide bombers, who detonated the bombs, and themselves, at the peak of rush hour on three subway trains and aboard a bus. More than 50 people died, along with the bombers, and 700 were wounded. The bombers were apparently expressing their displeasure over Britain's support of the United States in Iraq.

● ATTITUDES: "THE GOOD, THE BAD, AND THE UGLY"

How do you feel about abortion, amnesty for illegal immigrants, and exhibiting the Ten Commandments in public buildings such as courthouses? These are hot-button topics because people have strong attitudes toward them. They each give rise to cognitive evaluations (such as approval or disapproval), feelings (liking, disliking, or something stronger), and behavioral tendencies (such as approach or avoidance). **Question 2: What are attitudes?** Attitudes are enduring behavioral and cognitive tendencies that are expressed by evaluating particular people, places, or things with favor or disfavor (Eagly & Chaiken, 2007). Although I asked how you "feel" about things, attitudes are not just feelings or emotions. Many psychologists view thinking—or judgment—as more basic to attitudes. They believe that feelings and behavior follow cognition.

Attitudes are largely learned. For example, if you learn that an Apple iPad is a wonderful "toy," you may feel the urge to buy one. Attitudes can foster love or hate. They can give rise to helping behavior or to mass destruction. They can lead to social conflict or to the resolution of conflicts. Attitudes can change, but not easily.

The A–B Problem: Do We Act in Accord with Our Beliefs?

Our definition of *attitude* implies that our behavior is consistent with our cognitions—that is, with our beliefs and feelings. **Question 3: Do people do as they think?** (For example, do people really vote their consciences?) When we are free to do as we wish, our behavior is often consistent with our cognitions. But, as suggested by the term A–B problem, there are exceptions. **Truth or Fiction Revisited:** In fact, the links between attitudes (A) and behaviors (B) tend to be weak to moderate (Petty et al., 2009a, 2009b). People do not always vote "their consciences." Moreover, research reveals that people who say that drinking alcohol, smoking, and drunken driving are serious threats to their health do not necessarily curb these activities (Kiviniemi & Rothman, 2010).

It also appears that we tend to live up to our **stereotypes**—even our stereotypes of ourselves. For example, when older people are reminded that they are "elderly," they tend to walk more slowly (Wheeler & Petty, 2001).

A number of factors influence the likelihood that we can predict behavior from attitudes:

1. *Specificity:* We can better predict specific behavior from specific attitudes than from global attitudes. For example, we can better predict church attendance by

Social psychology The field of psychology that studies the nature and causes of behavior and mental processes in social situations.

Attitude An enduring mental representation of a person, place, or thing that typically evokes an emotional response and related behavior.

A–B problem The issue of how well we can predict behavior on the basis of attitudes.

Stereotype A fixed, conventional idea about a group.

knowing people's attitudes toward church attendance than by knowing whether they are Christian.

2. *Strength of attitudes:* Strong attitudes are more likely to determine behavior than weak attitudes (DeMarree et al., 2007). A person who believes that the nation's destiny depends on Republicans taking control of Congress is more likely to vote than a person who leans toward the Republican Party but does not think that elections make much difference.

3. *Vested interest:* People are more likely to act on their attitudes when they have a vested interest in the outcome (Lehman & Crano, 2002). People are more likely to vote for (or against) unionization of their workplace, for example, when they believe that their job security depends on the outcome.

4. *Accessibility:* People are more likely to behave in accord with their attitudes when they are accessible—that is, when they are brought to mind (DeMarree et al., 2007). This is why politicians attempt to "get out the vote" by means of media blitzes just prior to an election. Attitudes with a strong emotional impact are more accessible, which is one reason politicians strive to get their supporters "worked up" over the issues.

Origins of Attitudes

You were not born a Republican or a Democrat. You were not born a Christian, a Jew, a Muslim, or a Hindu, although your parents may have practiced one of these religions when you came along. **Question 4: Where do attitudes come from?** Political, religious, and other attitudes are learned or derived from cognitive processes. In this section, we describe some of the processes that result in acquiring attitudes.

Do People Always Vote Their "Conscience"? The A–B problem refers to the research finding that people do not always act in accord with their attitudes.

CONDITIONING Conditioning may play a role in acquiring attitudes. Experiments have shown that attitudes toward national groups can be influenced by associating them with positive words (such as *gift* or *happy*) or negative words (such as *ugly* or *failure*) (De Houwer et al., 2001). Parents often reward children for saying and doing things that agree with their own attitudes. Patriotism is encouraged by showing approval to children when they sing the national anthem or wave the flag.

OBESERVATIONAL LEARNING Attitudes formed through direct experience may be stronger and easier to recall, but we also acquire attitudes by observing others. The approval or disapproval of peers leads adolescents to prefer certain styles of clothes and music. Children and adolescents also acquire attitudes from their parents and other adults in their communities. The media inform us that body odor and bad breath are dreaded diseases—and, perhaps, that people who use harsh toilet paper are somehow un-American.

COGNITIVE APPRAISAL Despite what we have said, the acquisition of attitudes is not so mechanical. People are also motivated to have a valid understanding of reality so that they can make predictions and exercise some control over their environment (Wood, 2000). Thus, people evaluate information and form or change attitudes, including stereotypes, on the basis of new information (Petty et al., 2009a, 2009b). For example, we may believe that a car is more reliable than we had thought if a survey by *Consumer Reports* finds that it has an excellent repair record. We may check out reviewers' attitudes toward movies and books before we attend or read them ourselves.

Elaboration likelihood model The view that persuasive messages are evaluated (elaborated) on the basis of central and peripheral cues.

Central route In persuasive arguments, providing substantive information about the issues involved.

Peripheral route In persuasive arguments, associating viewpoints with tangential issues, such as who endorses a product, rather than the qualities of the product itself.

Fear appeal A type of persuasive communication that influences behavior on the basis of arousing fear instead of rational analysis of the issues.

Selective avoidance Turning one's attention from information that is inconsistent with one's attitudes.

Selective exposure Deliberately seeking and attending to information that is consistent with one's attitudes.

Even so, initial attitudes act as *cognitive anchors* (Wegener et al., 2001; Wood, 2000). We often judge new ideas in terms of how much they deviate from our existing attitudes. Accepting larger deviations requires more information processing—that is, more intellectual work (Petty et al., 2009a, 2009b). For this reason, perhaps, great deviations—such as changes from liberal to conservative attitudes, or vice versa—are apt to be resisted.

Changing Attitudes Through Persuasion: How Persuasive?

Rogers's comment (at left) sounds on the mark, but he was probably wrong. It does little good to have a wonderful product if its existence remains a secret. **Question 5: Can you really change people—their attitudes and behavior, that is?**

CENTRAL AND PERIPHERAL ROUTES TO PERSUASION The elaboration likelihood model describes the ways people respond to persuasive messages (Petty et al., 2009a). Consider two routes to persuading others to change their attitudes. The **central route** to persuasion inspires thoughtful consideration of arguments and evidence. Politicians might present the details of a tax bill before Congress to the public and explain how it will affect citizens in various income groups. The **peripheral route** to persuasion associates objects with positive or negative cues. Politicians may avow, "This bill is supported by Nancy Pelosi (or John Boehner)" without explaining what it will actually do, evoking, from some, predictable, knee-jerk reactions without careful consideration of the bill's merits. Other peripheral routes to persuasion are rewards (such as a smile or a hug), punishments (such as parental disapproval), and such factors as the trustworthiness and attractiveness of the communicator.

Advertisements, which are a form of persuasive communication, also rely on central and peripheral routes. Some ads focus on the quality of the product; that is, they take the central route. Some ads for Total cereal highlight its nutritional benefits, providing information about the quality of the product. Other ads take the peripheral route; they attempt to associate the product with appealing images. Ads that show football players heading to Walt Disney World or choosing a brand of beer offer little information about the product but may persuade us nonetheless.

In this section, we look at one central factor in persuasion—the nature of the message. We also examine three peripheral factors—the communicator of the message, the context of the message, and the audience.

THE NATURE OF THE PERSUASIVE MESSAGE: SAY WHAT? SAY HOW? SAY HOW OFTEN? How do we respond when TV commercials are repeated until we have memorized every dimple on the actors' faces? Research suggests that familiarity breeds content, not contempt (Förster, 2009; Macrae et al., 2002).

The strange words *zebulon* and *afworbu* might not elicit much of a reaction the first time you hear them, but psychologist Robert Zajonc (1968) found that people began to react favorably toward them on the basis of repeated exposure, even though the people still had no idea what they might mean. **Truth or Fiction Revisited:** It appears that repeated exposure to people and things as diverse as the following enhances their appeal (Banaji & Heiphetz, 2008; Tormala & Petty, 2007):

- Political candidates (who are seen in repeated TV commercials)
- Photographs of African Americans
- Photographs of college students
- Abstract art
- Classical music

Research suggests that the more complex the stimuli, the more likely frequent exposure will have favorable effects (Ohlsson, 2005; G. F. Smith & Dorfman, 1975). The 100th playing of a Bach fugue may be less tiresome than the 100th performance of a pop tune.

When trying to persuade people, is it helpful or self-defeating to alert them to the arguments presented by the opposition? In two-sided arguments, the communicator recounts the arguments of the opposition to refute them. In research concerning a mock trial, college undergraduates were presented with two-sided arguments—those of the prosecution and those of the defendant (McKenzie et al., 2002). When one argument was weak, the college "jurors" expressed more confidence in their decision than when they did not hear the other side at all. Theologians and politicians sometimes forewarn their followers about the arguments of the opposition and then refute each one. Forewarning creates a kind of psychological immunity to them (Eisend, 2007; Taber et al., 2009).

It would be nice to think that people are too sophisticated to be persuaded by a message's **fear appeal**. However, many women who are warned of the dire risk they run if they fail to be screened for breast cancer are more likely to obtain mammograms than women who are informed of the *benefits* of mammography (Ruiter et al., 2001). Interestingly, although suntanning has been shown to increase the likelihood of skin cancer, warnings against suntanning were shown to be more effective when students were warned of risks to their *appearance* (premature aging, wrinkling, and scarring of the skin) than when the warning dealt with the risk to their health (J. L. Jones & Leary, 1994). That is, students informed of tanning's cosmetic effects were more likely to say they would protect themselves from the sun than were students informed about the risk of cancer. Fear appeals are most effective when the audience believes that the risks are serious—as in causing wrinkles!—and that the audience members can change their behavior to avert the risks—as in preventing cancer or wrinkling (de Hoog et al., 2007; Thompson et al., 2009).

Audiences also tend to believe arguments that appear to run counter to the vested interests of the communicator (Lehman & Crano, 2002). If the president of Chrysler or General Motors said that Toyotas and Hondas were superior, you can bet that we would prick up our ears.

THE COMMUNICATOR OF THE MESSAGE: WHOM DO YOU TRUST?

Would you buy a used car from a person who had been convicted of larceny? Would you leaf through fashion magazines featuring homely models? Probably not. Research shows that persuasive communicators are characterized by expertise, trustworthiness, attractiveness, or similarity to their audiences (Petty et al., 2009a, 2009b).

People find it painful when they are confronted with information that discredits their own opinions (Garrett, 2009). Therefore, they often show **selective avoidance** and **selective exposure** (Bryant & Davies, 2006). That is, they switch channels when the news coverage runs counter to their own attitudes. They also seek communicators whose outlook coincides with their own. Whom would you prefer to listen to? Rush Limbaugh and Sean Hannity or Chris Matthews and Keith Olbermann?

THE CONTEXT OF THE MESSAGE: "GET 'EM IN A GOOD MOOD"

You are too shrewd to let someone persuade you by buttering you up, but perhaps someone you know would be influenced by a sip of wine, a bite of cheese, and a sincere compliment. Aspects of the immediate environment, such as music, increase the likelihood of persuasion. When we are in a good mood, we apparently are less likely to evaluate the situation carefully (Briñol et al., 2007; Park & Banaji, 2000).

It is also counterproductive to call your dates fools when they differ with you—even though their ideas are bound to be foolish if they do not agree with yours. Agreement and praise are more effective ways to encourage others to embrace your views. Appear sincere, or else your compliments will look manipulative. (It seems unfair to share this advice with you and not everyone.)

© Ethan Miller/Getty Images

© John W. McDonough/Sports Illustrated/Getty Images

"Arguments are to be avoided: they are always vulgar and often convincing."

OSCAR WILDE

Most Valuable Players or Most Valuable Endorsers? Advertisers use a combination of central and peripheral cues to sell their products. What factors contribute to the persuasiveness of messages? To the persuasiveness of communicators? Why are endorsements by race-car driver Danica Patrick (left) and basketball player LeBron James (right) so eagerly sought by advertisers?

Chris Matthews (left) and Rush Limbaugh (right)
From whom would you rather get your news and political options, Chris Matthews or Rush Limbaugh?
Would you switch the channel if you saw one of them speaking out? Which one? Why?

THE PERSUADED AUDIENCE Why are some people capable of saying no to salespeople? Why do others enrich the lives of every door-to-door salesperson? Perhaps people with high self-esteem and low concern about how strangers will evaluate them are more likely to resist social pressure (Ellickson et al., 2001).

A classic study by Schwartz and Gottman (1976) reveals the cognitive nature of the social anxiety that can make it difficult for some people to refuse requests. The researchers found that people who comply with unreasonable requests are more apt to report thoughts like the following:

- "I was worried about what the other person would think of me if I refused."
- "It is better to help others than to be self-centered."
- "The other person might be hurt or insulted if I refused."

People who refuse unreasonable requests reported thoughts like these:

- "It doesn't matter what the other person thinks of me."
- "I am perfectly free to say no."
- "This request is unreasonable."

Which group of thoughts is more characteristic of your reaction when someone tries to sell you something? Are you satisfied with your sales resistance? The nearby Closer Look will afford you insight into how salespeople try to get their foot in the door—literally and figuratively.

Changing Attitudes and Behavior by Means of Cognitive Dissonance: "I Think, Therefore I Am ... Consistent"?

Cognitive-dissonance theory The view that we are motivated to make our cognitions, or beliefs, consistent with each other and with our behavior.

Question 6: What is cognitive-dissonance theory? According to cognitive-dissonance theory, people are thinking creatures who seek consistency in their behaviors and their attitudes—their views of the world (Harmon-Jones & Harmon-Jones,

472

2008). People apparently must mentally represent the world accurately to predict and control events. Consistency in beliefs, attitudes, and behavior helps make the world seem like a predictable place. Therefore, if we find ourselves in the uncomfortable spot where two cherished ideas conflict, we are motivated to reduce the discrepancy—just as the Seekers did when their prophet, Marian Keech, was shown to be in error when the flying saucers she said were coming did not land on schedule (see Chapter 8).

In the first and still one of the best-known studies on cognitive dissonance, one group of participants received $1 (worth $5 to $10 today) for telling someone else that a boring task was interesting (Festinger & Carlsmith, 1959). Members of a second group received $20 (worth $100 to $200 today) to describe the chore positively. Both groups were paid to engage in **attitude-discrepant behavior**—that is, behavior that ran counter to what they actually thought. After presenting their fake enthusiasm for the boring task, the participants were asked to rate their own liking for it. Ironically, those who were paid *less* rated the task as more interesting than their better-paid colleagues reported.

EFFORT JUSTIFICATION Learning theorists might predict that the more we are reinforced for doing something (as with more money), the more we should like it (not find the task quite as boring, that is). But that is not what happened in the example of attitude-discrepant behavior just related. Cognitive-dissonance theorists rightly predicted this outcome. Because the ideas (cognitions) of (a) "I was paid very little" and (b) "I told someone that this assignment was interesting" are dissonant, people will tend to engage in **effort justification**. The discomfort of cognitive dissonance motivates people to explain their behavior to themselves in such a way that unpleasant undertakings seem worth it (Harmon-Jones et al., 2009). Participants who were paid only $1 may have justified their lie by concluding that they may not have been lying in the first place. **Truth or Fiction Revisited:** It also turns out

> *"The brain within its groove*
> *Runs evenly and true . . ."*
>
> EMILY DICKINSON

Attitude-discrepant behavior Behavior inconsistent with an attitude that may have the effect of modifying an attitude.

Effort justification In cognitive-dissonance theory, the tendency to seek justification (acceptable reasons) for strenuous efforts.

Foot-in-the-door technique A method for inducing compliance in which a small request is followed by a larger request.

A CLOSER LOOK   The Foot-in-the-Door Technique

You might suppose that contributing money to door to door solicitors for charity will get you off the hook. Perhaps they'll take the cash and leave you alone for a while. Actually, the opposite is true. The next time they mount a campaign, they may call on you to go door to door on their behalf! Organizations compile lists of people they can rely on. Because they have gotten their "foot in the door," this is known as the **foot-in-the-door technique**.

Consider a classic experiment by Freedman and Fraser (1966). Groups of women received phone calls from a consumer group requesting that they let a six-person crew come to their home to catalog their household products. The job could take hours. Only 22% of one group acceded to this irksome request. But 53% of another group of women assented to a visit. Why was the second group more compliant? They had been phoned a few days earlier and had agreed to answer a few questions about the soap products they used. Thus, they had been primed for the second request: The caller had gotten a foot in the door.

Research suggests that people who accede to small requests become more amenable to larger ones for a variety of reasons, including conformity and self-perception as the kind of people who help in this way (Burger, 2009). Regardless of how the foot-in-the-door technique works, if you want to say no, it may be easier to do so (and stick to your guns) the first time a request is made. Later may be too late.

to be true that we usually appreciate things more when we have to work for them (Stone & Fernandez, 2008). After all, we may want to tell ourselves, we didn't do all that hard work for nothing.

It also seems that behavioral changes can lead to changes in attitudes. Recycling laws were at first quite unpopular because they required people to change their years-long habits for disposing of wastes. **Truth or Fiction Revisited:** However, being compelled by the law to recycle actually led to more positive attitudes toward recycling as time went on (Stone & Fernandez, 2008). Recyclers apparently reduced the cognitive dissonance between what they were doing (recycling) and their attitudes (opposition to recycling) by changing their attitudes (becoming supportive of recycling).

LearningConnections • ATTITUDES: "THE GOOD, THE BAD, AND THE UGLY"

ACTIVE REVIEW (1) A(n) _____ is a behavioral and cognitive tendency expressed by evaluating people, places, or things with favor or disfavor. (2) Attitudes are acquired through conditioning, observational learning, and _____ appraisal. (3) Early attitudes serve as _____ anchors. (4) According to cognitive-_____ theory, we are motivated to make our cognitions consistent with one another and with our behavior.

REFLECT AND RELATE Here's a mini-experiment: Keep a log of radio or TV commercials you hear or see for a few days. Which ones grab your attention? Why? Which ones do you believe? Why? Which ones tempted you to consider buying or trying a product? Why?

CRITICAL THINKING How can you use the information in this section to develop sales resistance?

 Go to Psychology CourseMate at **www.cengagebrain.com** for an interactive version of these questions.

PREJUDICE: A PARTICULARLY TROUBLESOME ATTITUDE

Truth or Fiction Revisited: It is true that people have condemned billions of other people without ever meeting them—without ever learning their names. In this section, we discuss some of the reasons for this. We will be dealing with a particularly troubling kind of attitude: prejudice. **Question 7: What are prejudice and discrimination?**

Prejudice is an attitude toward a group that leads people to evaluate members of that group negatively—even though they have never met them. On a cognitive level, prejudice is linked to expectations that members of the target group will behave badly, say, in the workplace, or engage in criminal behavior. On an emotional level, prejudice is associated with negative feelings such as fear, dislike, or hatred. In behavioral terms, it is connected with avoidance, aggression, and discrimination. Prejudice is the most troubling kind of attitude. It is connected with the genocide of millions of people.

Prejudice involves stereotyping—that is, erroneous assumptions that all members of a group share the same traits or characteristics. Have people you know characterized African Americans as superstitious and musical? What about gays and lesbians? Are they unfit for military service? Stereotypes may lead people to view members of groups in a biased fashion.

On the other hand, some stereotypes are positive, such as stereotypes about physically attractive people. By and large, we assume that "good things come in pretty packages." Attractive children and adults are judged and treated more positively than their unattractive peers (Langlois et al., 2000). We expect attractive people to be poised, sociable, popular, intelligent, mentally healthy, fulfilled, persuasive, and successful in their jobs and marriages (Griffin & Langlois, 2006). Research shows that attractiveness is positively correlated with popularity, social skills, and sexual experience (Griffin & Langlois, 2006; Langlois et al., 2000). Attractive people are more likely to be judged innocent of crimes in mock jury experiments, and when

Prejudice An attitude toward a group that leads people to evaluate members of that group negatively.

they are found guilty, they are handed down less severe sentences (Sporer & Goodman-Delahunty, 2009). Perhaps we assume that attractive people have less need to resort to deviant behavior to achieve their goals. Even when they have erred, perhaps they will be more likely to change their evil ways.

Discrimination

Discrimination is a hostile behavior that results from prejudice. Many groups living in the United States have experienced discrimination—women, gays and lesbians, older people, and ethnic groups such as African Americans, Asian Americans, Latin Americans, Irish Americans, Jewish Americans, and Native Americans. Discrimination takes many forms, including denial of access to jobs, the voting booth, and housing.

The U.S. Department of Housing and Urban Development (HUD) has been tracking discrimination in the availability of housing for ethnic minority groups and the extent to which landlords and real estate agents encourage people from ethnic minority groups to rent an advertised apartment or house. Many landlords prefer to rent to European Americans rather than African Americans and Latin Americans. However, HUD found that housing discrimination against African Americans decreased by 18% between 1989 and 2000 (U.S. Department of Housing and Urban Development, 2002). There was no such decline in housing discrimination against Latin Americans.

AUTOMATIC PREJUDICE Many people in the United States endorse racial equality and yet still continue to hold negative views of people from other ethnic groups—views they might not be aware of (Dovidio et al., 2009). They respond without racial bias in explicit or overt tasks, such as expressing non-prejudicial attitudes both in interviews and on survey questions. Yet to be completely without prejudice, they may have to overcome years of exposure to prejudiced information from their families, peer groups, and the media (Devine et al., 2002; Plant & Devine, 2009). As a result, they may show *implicit* prejudiced attitudes on responses that they are less able to control. They may choose to sit next to a European American rather than an African American on a bus or train or at a table in a college cafeteria. Or they may provide "logical reasons" why immigration laws should be tightened or why gays and lesbians should not be allowed to serve in the military without realizing that prejudice is coloring their attitudes.

A Gay Pride March in Manila Gays and lesbians marched to protest discrimination and to campaign against the spread of sexually transmitted infections.

© Jay Directo/AFP/Getty Images

Sources of Prejudice

Question 8: What are the sources of prejudice? The sources of prejudice are many and varied:

1. *Dissimilarity:* We are apt to like people who share our attitudes (Cunningham, 2008). People of different religions and races often have different backgrounds, giving rise to dissimilar attitudes. Consequently, even when people of different races share values, people may assume that they do not.

Discrimination Hostile behavior that is directed against groups toward whom one is prejudiced.

475

2. *Social conflict:* There is often social and economic conflict between people of different races and religions. For example, for many decades, European Americans and African Americans competed for jobs in the American South, giving rise to negative attitudes, even to the point of lynchings by the ones with the most power, the European Americans (Reid, 2008).

3. *Social learning:* Children tend to imitate their parents, and parents reinforce their children for doing so. In this way, prejudices can be transmitted from generation to generation. The mass media also perpetuate stereotypes. TV commercials tend to portray European Americans, especially men, as more prominent and wielding more authority than African Americans (Coltraine & Messineo, 2000; Ramasubramanian & Oliver, 2007). Women are portrayed as more likely than men to seek romantic and domestic fulfillment. In general, European American men tend to be portrayed as powerful, European American women as sex objects, African American men as aggressive, and African American women as unimportant.

4. *Information processing:* One cognitive view is that prejudices act as cognitive filters through which we perceive the social world. The brain tends to automatically place people into categories such as "familiar" and "foreign" and "good" and "bad." Such categorization may then bias people's feelings and reactions

LIFE CONNECTIONS   COMBATING PREJUDICE

Prejudice has been with us throughout history, and it is unlikely that a miracle cure is at hand. Yet we need not stand idly by when we witness prejudice. We can create millions of mini-miracles—changes in those of us who wish to end prejudice. Here are some things we can do to combat prejudice:

1. *Encourage intergroup contact and cooperation.* Prejudice encourages us to avoid other groups, which is unfortunate because intergroup contact is one way of breaking down prejudices (Baron et al., 2009). Intergroup contact heightens awareness of individual variation, and this knowledge can lead us to abandon stereotypical thinking. Intergroup contact is especially effective when people are striving to meet common goals, such as playing on the same team or working together on a yearbook.

2. *Present examples of admired individuals within groups that are often stigmatized.* Nilanjana Dasgupta and Anthony G. Greenwald (2001) found that they could modify negative attitudes toward African Americans by presenting photographs of admired African American individuals. Verbal reminders should work as well.

3. *Attack discriminatory behavior.* It is sometimes easier to change people's behavior than to alter their feelings. Yet cognitive-dissonance theory suggests that when we change people's behavior, their feelings may follow along (Guadagno & Cialdini, 2010; Heitland & Bohner, 2010). It is illegal to deny access to education, jobs, and housing on the basis of gender, religion, race, or disability. Seek legal remedies if you have been discriminated against.

4. *Hold discussion forums.* Many campuses conduct workshops and discussion groups on gender, race, and diversity. Talk to your dean of students about holding such workshops.

5. *Examine your own beliefs.* Prejudice isn't "out there." It dwells within us. It is easy to focus on the prejudices of others, but what about our own? Have you examined your own attitudes and rejected stereotyping and prejudice?

© George Disario

Intergroup Contact Intergroup contact can reduce feelings of prejudice when people work together toward common goals.

Even if we do not personally harbor feelings of racial or religious enmity, are we doing anything to counter such feelings in others? Do we confront people who make prejudiced remarks? Do we belong to organizations that deny access to members of other racial and religious groups? Do we strike up conversations with people from other groups or avoid them? College is meant to be a broadening experience, and we deny ourselves much of the education we could be receiving when we limit our encounters to people who share our own backgrounds.

toward others (Azar, 2002). If you believe that Californians are airheads, it may be easier to recall TV images of surfing than of scientific conferences at Cal Tech and Berkeley.

5. *Social categorization:* A second cognitive perspective focuses on the tendency to divide our social world into "us" and "them." People usually view those who belong to their own groups—the "in-group"—more favorably than those who do not—the "out-group" (Park & Judd, 2005). Moreover, there is a tendency to assume that members of the out-group are more similar in their attitudes and behavior than members of our own groups (Mussweiler & Bodenhausen, 2002). Our isolation from the out-group makes it easier to maintain our stereotypes.

LearningConnections • PREJUDICE: A PARTICULARLY TROUBLESOME ATTITUDE

ACTIVE REVIEW (5) _____ is hostile behavior toward a group of people, such as denial of access to housing. (6) Prejudice may be based on factors such as social _____, or the tendency to divide the world into us and them.

REFLECT AND RELATE How do you feel when people around you make prejudiced remarks against ethnic minority groups?

CRITICAL THINKING Why do you think people tend to be prejudiced against others who are different from them?

 Go to Psychology CourseMate at **www.cengagebrain.com** for an interactive version of these questions.

INTERPERSONAL ATTRACTION: ON LIKING AND LOVING

Humans are social beings. Developmental psychology informs us that the psychologically healthful development of the child requires social interactions with caregivers. As adolescents and adults, we normally also come to be attracted to others for sexual and romantic reasons. Feelings of **attraction** can lead to liking, perhaps to loving, and to an enduring relationship. **Question 9: What factors contribute to attraction in our culture?** Among the factors contributing to attraction are physical appearance, similarity, and reciprocity.

Attraction In social psychology, an attitude of liking or disliking (negative attraction).

Physical Appearance: How Important Is Looking Good?

Physical appearance is a key factor in attraction and in the consideration of romantic partners (Sprecher et al., 2008). What determines physical allure? Are our standards subjective—that is, "in the eye of the beholder"? Or is there general agreement on what is appealing?

Truth or Fiction Revisited: Standards for beauty are apparently not so flexible that beauty is fully "in the eye of the beholder." Many standards for beauty appear to be cross-cultural (Buss, 2009). For example, a study of people in England and Japan found that both British and Japanese men consider women with large eyes, high cheekbones, and narrow jaws the most attractive (Perret, 1994). In his research, Perret created computer composites of the faces of 60 women and, as shown in part A of Figure 14.1 ■ on page 478, of the 15 women who were rated the most attractive. He then used computer enhancement to exaggerate the differences between the composite of the 60 and the composite of the 15 most attractive women. He arrived at the image shown in part B of Figure 14.1. Part B, which shows higher cheekbones and a narrower jaw than part A, was rated as the more attractive image. Similar results were found for the image of a Japanese woman. Works of art suggest that the ancient Greeks and Egyptians favored similar facial features.

Looking Good How important is physical attractiveness in interpersonal attraction and social and vocational success?

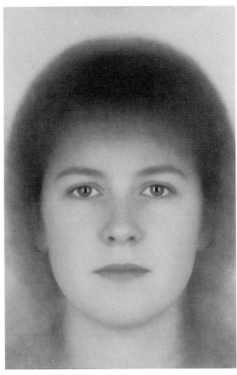 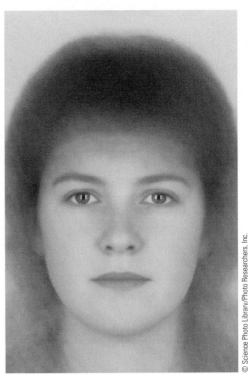

A. **B.**

Figure 14.1 ■ What Features Contribute to Facial Attractiveness? In both England and Japan, features such as large eyes, high cheekbones, and narrow jaws contribute to perceptions of the attractiveness of women. Part A shows a composite of the faces of 15 women rated as the most attractive of a group of 60. Part B is a composite in which the features of these 15 women are exaggerated—that is, developed further in the direction that separates them from the average of the entire 60.

In our society, tallness is an asset for men (Furnham, 2009; Kurzban & Weeden, 2005). Although women may be less demanding than men concerning a variety of physical features, height—that is, tallness—is more important to women in the selection of dates and mates than any height preference is to men.

Although preferences for facial features may transcend time and culture, preferences for body weight and shape may be more culturally determined. For example, plumpness has been valued in many cultures. Grandmothers who worry that their granddaughters are starving themselves often come from cultures where stoutness is or was acceptable or desirable. In contemporary Western society, there is pressure on both genders to be slender (Furnham, 2009). Women generally favor men with a V-taper—broad shoulders and a narrow waist.

An examination of the Internet dating profiles of 5,810 Yahoo personal ads shows that "thin" is more "in" in the expressed preferences for partners of European Americans and males (Glasser et al., 2009). European American males are more likely than African American and Latinos to want to date slender and buff women. African American and Latino men are significantly more likely to be interested in women with large or thick bodies.

"PRETTY IS AS PRETTY DOES?" Truth or Fiction Revisited: People are perceived as more attractive when they are smiling (Meier et al., 2010; Penton-Voak & Chang, 2008). When you're smiling, observers expect to have positive social interactions with you (Harker & Keltner, 2001). There is thus ample reason to, as the song goes, "put on a happy face" when you are meeting people or looking for a date.

Other aspects of behavior also affect interpersonal attraction. Women who are shown videotapes of prospective dates or asked to describe ideal partners tend to prefer men who are outgoing, assertive, and confident (Burger & Cosby, 1999).

The Attraction-Similarity Hypothesis: Do "Opposites Attract" or Do "Birds of a Feather Flock Together"?

Attraction-similarity hypothesis The view that people tend to choose persons similar to themselves in attractiveness and attitudes in the formation of interpersonal relationships.

Although we may rate highly attractive people as most desirable, most of us are not left to blend in with the wallpaper. According to the **attraction-similarity hypothesis**, we tend to date people who are similar to ourselves in physical attractiveness rather

When you go to buy a box of Valentine's Day candy, what color will the box be? Green? Blue? The answer, of course, is red. What is the most popular color of women's lipstick? Yellow? Brown? Again, the answer is red (Elliot et al., 2007). Red has been the most popular lipstick color since the hot days that saw the construction of the pyramids in ancient Egypt (Elliot & Niesta, 2008). Red is similarly the most popular color for women's lingerie.

At a traffic light, the color red means stop. But when it comes to sexual attraction, the color red is more likely to mean go.

But why is the color red associated with feelings of attraction? Could the answer be cultural conditioning? Anthropologists have found evidence that females used red ochre as a face and body paint in rituals carried out before the dawn of history (Lee, 2006). We find red used in ancient myths and folklore as a symbol of passion and fertility (Hutchings, 2004). Red has been associated with lust in literature, most notably in Nathaniel Hawthorne's novel of illicit romance and its consequences—*The Scarlet Letter*. Red has been used as a symbol of prostitution for centuries, as in the term *red-light district*.

The link between red and physical attraction may also be rooted in our biological heritage. Many nonhuman female primates, including baboons, chimpanzees, gorillas, and rhesus monkeys, show reddened genital regions and sometimes on their chest and face when they are nearing ovulation—the time of the month when they are fertile (Barelli et al., 2008). Reddening of the skin is caused by elevated estrogen levels (relative to progesterone), which increase the flow of blood under the surface of the skin. It is widely believed that reddish skin tones are a sexual signal that attracts mates (Huchard et al., 2009). Research has found that male primates are in fact especially attracted to females when they display red, as shown by attempts at sexual relations (Waitt et al., 2006).

As in the case of other female primates, women's estrogen levels relative to progesterone are elevated near ovulation, enhancing the flow of blood beneath the surface of the skin (Lynn et al., 2007). At this time of the month, women also tend to choose clothing that leaves more skin visible (Durante et al., 2008) and are more readily sexually aroused (Rupp et al., 2009). For men, then, as with other male primates, the reddening of a woman's skin at the time of ovulation may be a sexual signal.

Andrew Elliot and Daniela Niesta (2008) ran a series of experiments in which men did, indeed, rate the same woman as more attractive when her photograph was shown against a red background compared with a variety of other background colors. One experiment revealed that the red-related difference in attractiveness was found in male raters but not in female raters. As you can see in Figure 14.2 ■, male raters found women more attractive when they were shown with red backgrounds as opposed to white, but female raters did not show the same preference.

Andrew Elliot and his colleagues (2010) also ran experiments with women and found that they rated photos of men as being more attractive when the photos were bordered in red or the men were wearing red clothing. Women are more interested in the status of potential partners than men are, and it seems that they connect the color red with status in males. Cross-cultural research links the color red in males with power and social dominance, and the Elliot group found that women rated males in red as having more status than males in white, blue, or green. The color red had no effect on women's ratings of males as being likeable, agreeable, or outgoing—status was the lone association. But, as with men viewing women, red is "sexy."

A biological possibility as to why women are more attracted to males who are associated with the color red is that testosterone is involved in oxygenating blood and increasing its flow to the skin—giving off a reddish hue—and to the genitals, leading to sexual excitement. Red coloration can also be an indicator of health, because highly oxygenated blood levels can be maintained only by organisms in good health (Elliot et al., 2010).

© Fancy Photography/Veer

Why Did They Deck Her Out in Red? Cultural conditioning and the human biological heritage provide two good answers.

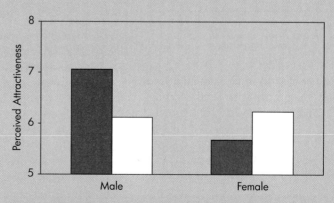

Figure 14.2 ■ Rated Attractiveness of a Woman Shown in a Photograph as a Function of the Color of the Background of the Photo and the Sex of the Rater

than the local Robert Pattinson or Zoe Saldana look-alike. **Truth or Fiction Revisited:** Despite the familiar saying "Opposites attract," it seems that people who are similar are more likely than opposites to be attracted to one another (Montoya et al., 2008; van Straaten et al., 2009).

The quest for similarity extends beyond physical attractiveness. Our marital and sex partners tend to be similar to us in race and ethnicity, age, level of education, and religion (Amodio & Showers, 2005). Note that nearly 95% of marriages and 80% to 90% of cohabiting unions were between partners of the same race at the time of the 2010 U.S. census (U.S. Census Bureau, 2011). Even so, highly educated people are more likely than poorly educated people to marry people of other races (Batson et al., 2006).

Why do most people have partners from the same background as their own? One reason is that marriages are made in the neighborhood and not in heaven (Sprecher & Felmlee, 2008). We tend to live among people who are similar to us in background, and we therefore come into contact with them more often. Another reason is that we are drawn to people whose attitudes are similar to ours (Fehr, 2008). People from similar backgrounds are more likely to share similar attitudes.

Other Factors in Attraction: Reciprocity and the Nearness of You?

Has anyone told you how good-looking, brilliant, and mature you are? That your taste is refined? That all in all, you are really something special? If so, have you been impressed by his or her fine judgment? Reciprocity is a powerful determinant of attraction (Fehr, 2008). We tend to be more open, warm, and helpful when we are interacting with people who seem to like us (Sprecher et al., 2008).

Deb Levine (2000), writing in the journal *CyberPsychology and Behavior,* compares attraction online ("virtual attraction") with attraction in the real world. She notes that proximity, or nearness, is a factor online and offline, but proximity online can mean visiting the same chat room a number of times even though individuals live thousands of miles apart. Self-disclosure and reciprocity occur more quickly online, perhaps because people think they are operating from a safe distance. It is more difficult, she asserts, to check out similarities in interests because people are more or less free to present themselves as they wish.

Whether online of offline, feelings of attraction are influenced by factors such as physical appearance and similarity. Let's explore what we mean when we say that feelings of attraction have blossomed into love.

Love: The Emotion That Launched a Thousand Ships?

Love—the ideal for which we make great sacrifice. Love—the sentiment that launched a thousand ships and led to the Trojan War in Homer's epic poem *The Iliad*. Through the millennia, poets have sought to capture the meaning of love in words. Dante, the Italian poet, wrote of "the love that moves the sun and the other stars." The Scottish poet Robert Burns wrote that his love was like "a red, red rose." Love is beautiful and elusive. Passion and romantic love are also lusty, surging with sexual desire (Berscheid, 2009). **Question 10: Just what is love?**

There are a number of theories about the nature of love. Let's look at Robert Sternberg's (1988) **triangular model of love**, which can be thought of as a love triangle. This love triangle does not refer to two men wooing the same woman. It refers to Sternberg's view that love can include combinations of three components: intimacy, passion, and commitment (see Figure 14.3 ■).

Intimacy refers to a couple's closeness, to their mutual concern and sharing of feelings and resources. **Passion** means romance and sexual feelings. **Commitment** means deciding to enhance and maintain the relationship. Passion is most crucial in short-term relationships. Intimacy and commitment are more important in enduring relationships.

The Attraction-Similarity Hypothesis Do opposites attract, or do we tend to pair off with people who are similar to us in level of physical attractiveness, attitudes, and tastes? From looking at these couples, it seems that similarity often runs at least skin deep.

"One should always be in love. That is the reason one should never marry."

OSCAR WILDE

"One is very crazy when in love."

SIGMUND FREUD

Reciprocity In interpersonal attraction, the tendency to return feelings and attitudes that are expressed about us.

Triangular model of love Sternberg's view that love involves combinations of three components: intimacy, passion, and commitment.

480

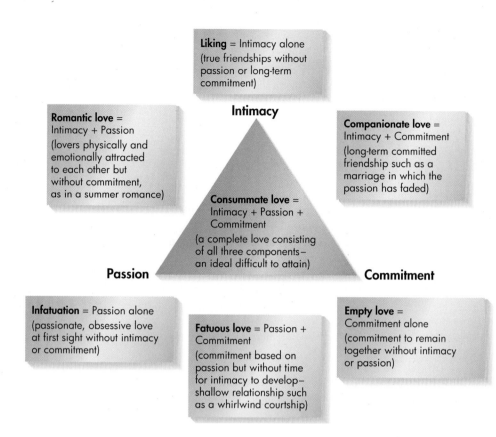

Liking = Intimacy alone (true friendships without passion or long-term commitment)

Romantic love = Intimacy + Passion (lovers physically and emotionally attracted to each other but without commitment, as in a summer romance)

Companionate love = Intimacy + Commitment (long-term committed friendship such as a marriage in which the passion has faded)

Consummate love = Intimacy + Passion + Commitment (a complete love consisting of all three components—an ideal difficult to attain)

Infatuation = Passion alone (passionate, obsessive love at first sight without intimacy or commitment)

Fatuous love = Passion + Commitment (commitment based on passion but without time for intimacy to develop—shallow relationship such as a whirlwind courtship)

Empty love = Commitment alone (commitment to remain together without intimacy or passion)

Figure 14.3 ■ The Triangular Model of Love According to this model, love has three components: intimacy, passion, and commitment. The ideal of consummate love consists of romantic love plus commitment. Check out the Triangular Love Scale on page 482 to see where your loved one might fit in this triangle.

Source: From *The Psychology of Love*, R. J. Sternberg and M. J. Barnes, eds. Copyright © 1988 Yale University Press. Reprinted by permission.

The ideal form of love combines all three: **consummate love.** Consummate love is made up of romantic love plus commitment.

Romantic love is characterized by passion and intimacy. Passion involves fascination (preoccupation with the loved one), sexual craving, and the desire for exclusiveness (a special relationship with the loved one). Intimacy involves closeness and caring—championing the interests of the loved one, even if it entails sacrificing one's own. People are cognitively biased toward evaluating their dating partners positively (Loving & Agnew, 2001). In plain English, we idealize the people we love. People tend to attend to information that confirms their romantic interests. Lovers often magnify each other's positive features and overlook their flaws.

THE AFFECTIVE SHIFT HYPOTHESIS Men are generally more reluctant than women to make commitments in their romantic relationships (Buss, 2009; Confer et al., 2010). The **affective shift hypothesis**, developed by evolutionary psychologist David Buss (2007), offers one possible explanation of men's lesser willingness to commit themselves to relationships. In a study of nearly 200 subjects, Buss found that women tend to experience greater feelings of love and commitment—a positive affective shift—after first-time sex than men do. But not all men are alike. (Really.) As a group, it is true that men are more likely than women to be interested in short-term relationships and multiple sex partners. In fact, it seems accurate to say that men with high numbers of sex partners tend to experience a negative affective shift following first-time sex. The negative shift in feelings motivates them to end the relationship and curbs tendencies toward making a commitment. However, men with fewer sex partners and more of an interest in developing long-term relationships also tend to experience the positive affective shift after first-time sex.

Evolutionary psychologists suggest that men may be naturally more promiscuous than women because they are the genetic heirs of ancestors whose reproductive success was connected with the number of women they could impregnate (Buss, 2007; Confer et al., 2009; Schmitt, 2008). Women, however, can produce relatively few children in their lifetimes. Thus, the theory suggests, women need to be more selective. This controversial theory suggests that a man's "roving eye" and a woman's selectivity are embedded in their genes.

Intimacy Close acquaintance and familiarity; a characteristic of a relationship in which partners share their inmost feelings.

Passion Strong romantic and sexual feelings.

Commitment A pledge or obligation.

Consummate love The ideal form of love within Sternberg's model, which combines passion, intimacy, and commitment.

Romantic love An intense, positive emotion that involves sexual attraction, feelings of caring, and the belief that one is in love.

Affective shift hypothesis The view that men and women tend to experience different shifts in the emotions following initiation of sexual activity, such that women feel more love and commitment, and many men experience less love and commitment.

Which are the strongest components of your love relationship? Intimacy? Passion? Commitment? All three components? Two of them? To complete the following scale, written by Robert Sternberg, fill in the blank spaces with the name of the person you love or care about deeply. Then rate your agreement with each of the items by using a 9-point scale in which 1 = not at all, 5 = moderately, and 9 = extremely. Use points between to indicate intermediate levels of agreement between these values. Then consult the scoring key in Appendix B.

Intimacy Component

_____ 1. I am actively supportive of _____'s well-being.
_____ 2. I have a warm relationship with _____.
_____ 3. I am able to count on _____ in times of need.
_____ 4. _____ is able to count on me in times of need.
_____ 5. I am willing to share myself and my possessions with _____.
_____ 6. I receive considerable emotional support from _____.
_____ 7. I give considerable emotional support to _____.
_____ 8. I communicate well with _____.
_____ 9. I value _____ greatly in my life.
_____ 10. I feel close to _____.
_____ 11. I have a comfortable relationship with _____.
_____ 12. I feel that I really understand _____.
_____ 13. I feel that _____ really understands me.
_____ 14. I feel that I can really trust _____.
_____ 15. I share deeply personal information about myself with _____.

Passion Component

_____ 16. Just seeing _____ excites me.
_____ 17. I find myself thinking about _____ frequently during the day.
_____ 18. My relationship with _____ is very romantic.
_____ 19. I find _____ to be very personally attractive.
_____ 20. I idealize _____.
_____ 21. I cannot imagine another person making me as happy as _____ does.
_____ 22. I would rather be with _____ than with anybody else.

_____ 23. There is nothing more important to me than my relationship with _____.
_____ 24. I especially like physical contact with _____.
_____ 25. There is something almost "magical" about my relationship with _____.
_____ 26. I adore _____.
_____ 27. I cannot imagine life without _____.
_____ 28. My relationship with _____ is passionate.
_____ 29. When I see romantic movies and read romantic books, I think of _____.
_____ 30. I fantasize about _____.

Commitment Component

_____ 31. I know that I care about _____.
_____ 32. I am committed to maintaining my relationship with _____.
_____ 33. Because of my commitment to _____, I would not let other people come between us.
_____ 34. I have confidence in the stability of my relationship with _____.
_____ 35. I could not let anything get in the way of my commitment to _____.
_____ 36. I expect my love for _____ to last for the rest of my life.
_____ 37. I will always feel a strong responsibility for _____.
_____ 38. I view my commitment to _____ as a solid one.
_____ 39. I cannot imagine ending my relationship with _____.
_____ 40. I am certain of my love for _____.
_____ 41. I view my relationship with _____ as permanent.
_____ 42. I view my relationship with _____ as a good decision.
_____ 43. I feel a sense of responsibility toward _____.
_____ 44. I plan to continue my relationship with _____.
_____ 45. Even when _____ is hard to deal with, I remain committed to our relationship.

Source: From *The Psychology of Love* by R. J. Sternberg. Copyright © 1989 Yale University Press. Reprinted by permission of the publisher and author.

LearningConnections • INTERPERSONAL ATTRACTION: ON LIKING AND LOVING

ACTIVE REVIEW (7) Cross-cultural research suggests that in many cultures, men find women with (high or low?) cheekbones more attractive. (8) According to the _____ hypothesis, we tend to date people who are similar to ourselves. (9) According to the triangular model of love, love can include combinations of intimacy, _____, and commitment. (10) _____ love is characterized by a combination of intimacy and passion.

REFLECT AND RELATE Would you be interested in a relationship with a partner whose attitudes toward religion, politics, education, and child rearing differed significantly from your own? Does your answer support the view that "opposites attract" or that "birds of a feather flock together"?

CRITICAL THINKING How might the different features that males and females find attractive provide humans with an evolutionary advantage?

 Go to Psychology CourseMate at **www.cengagebrain.com** for an interactive version of these questions.

An important area of social psychology concerns the ways we perceive other people—for example, the importance of the first impressions they make on us. Next we explore some factors that contribute to **social perception:** the *primacy* and *recency effects* and *attribution theory*.

Primacy and Recency Effects: The Importance of First Impressions

Why do you wear a suit to a job interview? Why do defense attorneys make sure their clients dress neatly and get their hair cut before they are seen by the jury? **Question 11: What are the primacy and recency effects?** Do first impressions really matter? Apparently, they do—a great deal.

Whether we are talking about the business and social worlds, or even the relationship between a therapist and a client, first impressions are important (Bidell et al., 2002; Laungani, 2002). First impressions are an example of the primacy effect. When I was a teenager, a young man was accepted or rejected by his date's parents the first time they were introduced. If he was considerate and made small talk, her parents would allow the couple to stay out past curfew—perhaps even to watch submarine races at the beach during the early morning hours. If he was boorish or uncommunicative, he was seen as a cad forever after. Her parents would object to him no matter how hard he worked to gain their favor.

My experiences demonstrated to me that first impressions often make or break us. This phenomenon is known as the **primacy effect. Truth or Fiction Revisited:** It is apparently not true that you should just "be yourself" in a job interview. Dressing down or cursing may very well cost you the job.

Why are first impressions so important? The answer may be because we infer traits from behavior. If we act considerately at first, we are labeled considerate. The *trait* of consideration is used to explain and predict our future behavior. If, after being labeled considerate, one keeps a date out past curfew, this lapse is likely to be seen as an exception to a rule—excused by circumstances or external causes. If one is first seen as inconsiderate, however, several months of considerate behavior may be perceived as a cynical effort to "make up for it."

Participants in a classic experiment on the primacy effect read different stories about "Jim" (Luchins, 1957). There were four conditions (see Table 14.1 ■). In two conditions, the stories were one paragraph long. In the other two conditions, the stories were two paragraphs long. One of the single-paragraph stories portrayed Jim as friendly; the other single-paragraph story portrayed him as unfriendly. The same paragraphs were used in the two-paragraph stories, but their order was alternated. Some participants read the "friendly" paragraph first, and others read the "unfriendly" paragraph first. As noted in Table 14.1, 95% of participants who read only the "friendly" paragraph rated Jim as friendly compared with 3% of those who read only the "unfriendly" paragraph. Of those who read two-paragraph stories in the "friendly–unfriendly" order, 78% labeled Jim as friendly. When they read the paragraphs in the reverse order, only 18% rated Jim as friendly.

© PhotoAlto Photography/Veer

First Impressions Why is it so important to make a good first impression? What are some ways of doing so?

TABLE 14.1 ■ Luchins's Study of the Primacy Effect—The Story of "Jim"

Number of paragraphs	Nature of Story or Stories	Percent of participants rating Jim as friendly
One	Friendly	95%
One	Unfriendly	3%
Two	Friendly–unfriendly	78%
Two	Unfriendly–friendly	18%

Social perception A subfield of social psychology that studies the ways in which we form and modify impressions of others.

Primacy effect The tendency to evaluate others in terms of first impressions.

How can we encourage people to pay more attention to impressions occurring *after* the first encounter? Abraham Luchins accomplished this by allowing time to elapse between the presentations of the two paragraphs. In this way, fading memories allowed more recent information to take precedence. The tendency to respond to the most freshly presented piece of information is known as the **recency effect**. And Luchins found a second way to counter first impressions: He simply asked participants to avoid making snap judgments and to weigh all the evidence.

There is some interesting research on the role of the handshake in making a first impression. In the United States, a firm handshake is a key to making a good first impression, by women as well as men. Researchers find that a firm handshake is perceived as an indication of being outgoing and open to new experience. A weak handshake was perceived as indicative of shyness and social anxiety (Chaplin et al., 2000).

Attribution Theory: You're Free to Choose, but I'm Caught in the Middle?

When she was 3 years old, one of my daughters believed that a friend's son was a boy because he *wanted* to be a boy. Since she was 3 at the time, this error in my daughter's **attribution** of the boy's gender is understandable. Adults tend to make somewhat similar attribution errors, however. Although they do not believe that people's preferences have much to do with their gender, they do tend to exaggerate the role of choice in their behavior. **Question 12: What is attribution theory?**

An *attribution* is an assumption or belief about why people behave in a certain way. When you assume that one child is mistreating another child because she is "mean," you are making an attribution. The process by which we make inferences about the motives and traits of others through observation of their behavior is the **attribution process**. An English mock-trial study of guilt for rape found that "jurors" were less likely to find a defendant guilty of rape if he claimed that he had been intoxicated at the time the crime was committed (Finch & Munro, 2007). Many members of the jury believed that if the rapist was intoxicated, they could attribute the sexual assault to the alcohol and not to the drinker.

This section focuses on *attribution theory*, or the processes by which people draw conclusions about the factors that influence one another's behavior. Attribution theory is important because attributions lead us to perceive others either as purposeful actors or as victims of circumstances.

DISPOSITIONAL AND SITUATIONAL ATTRIBUTIONS Social psychologists describe two types of attributions. Dispositional attributions ascribe a person's behavior to internal factors such as personality traits and free will. If you assume that one child is mistreating another because she is "mean," you are making a dispositional attribution. **Situational attributions** attribute a person's actions to external factors such as circumstances, pressure from other people, or socialization. If you assume that the child is mistreating the other child because his parents have given him certain attitudes toward the other child, you are making a situational attribution. The jurors in the mock trial of a rapist made a situational attribution when they blamed the alcohol for the rape and not the rapist. (Would *you* let a rapist off the hook because he was drinking at the time of the assault?)

THE FUNDAMENTAL ATTRIBUTION ERROR In cultures that view the self as independent, such as ours, people tend to make dispositional attributions: They tend to attribute other people's behavior primarily to internal factors such as personality, attitudes, and free will (Chiu & Chao, 2009; Reeder, 2009). This bias in the attribution process is known as the **fundamental attribution error**. In such individualistic societies, people tend to focus on the behavior of others rather than on the circumstances surrounding their behavior. For example, if a teenager gets into trouble with the law, individualistic societies are more likely to blame the teenager than the social environment in which she lives. People involved in difficult negotiations have a tendency to attribute the toughness to the personalities of the negotiators on the other side rather than to the nature of the process of negotiation (M. W. Morris et al., 1999). **Truth or Fiction Revisited:** Therefore, we do tend to hold others responsible for their misdeeds but to see ourselves as victims of circumstances when we misbehave.

Recency effect The tendency to evaluate others in terms of the most recent impression.

Attribution A belief concerning why people behave in a certain way.

Attribution process The process by which people draw inferences about the motives and traits of others.

Dispositional attribution An assumption that a person's behavior is determined by internal causes such as personal traits.

Situational attribution An assumption that a person's behavior is determined by external circumstances such as the social pressure found in a situation.

Fundamental attribution error The assumption that others act predominantly on the basis of their dispositions, even when there is evidence suggesting the importance of their circumstances.

Actor–observer effect The tendency to attribute our own behavior to situational factors but to attribute the behavior of others to dispositional factors.

Who Are the Suicide Terrorists? A Case of the Fundamental Attribution Error?

Following the attacks of September 11, 2001, President George W. Bush labeled the suicide terrorists "evil cowards." Senator John Warner declared, "Those who would commit suicide in their assaults on the free world are not rational and are not deterred by rational concepts."

Evil. Cowardly. Irrational. Maniacal. Do these concepts paint a psychological portrait of suicide terrorists? Information about them comes from people who knew them before they committed their acts and from studies of would-be suicide terrorists who were prevented from carrying out their missions.

So, what do we actually know? Those who have studied the nature of evil, such as Stanley Milgram, find that many, perhaps most, perpetrators of evil are "ordinary people" (Zimbardo, 2007). The Consortium of Social Science Associations (COSSA) (2003) testified to Congress that they had to conclude there was no clear profile of the suicide terrorists. They averaged 21 or 22 years of age, but some were younger and many were older. Some were devout Muslims, but most seemed to be no more devout than typical members of their communities. Most had at least some high school education, and some had attended college.

The U.S. Council of Foreign Relations (2002) reported on a study of Palestinian suicide terrorists recruited by Hamas. Whereas suicidal people in general tend to be depressed, even desperate, many suicide bombers had held paying jobs, even in poverty-stricken communities. They harbored hatred of Israel, just as the suicide bombers of 9/11 harbored hatred of the United States. COSSA and the Council speculate that some of the suicide terrorists might have had "masculine self-image problems" and been seeking recognition—but not all of them. Some are dependent types; others are impulsive (Merari et al., 2010).

In seeking a profile, are we making a fundamental attribution error? According to attribution theory, people tend to explain behavior in terms of personal traits and personal choice, even when significant factors are at work in the person's society (L. Miller, 2006). As noted by Scott Altran (2006), who has studied suicide terrorism,

> U.S. government and media characterizations of Middle East suicide bombers as craven homicidal lunatics may suffer from a fundamental attribution error [however] no instances of religious or political suicide terrorism stem from lone actions of cowering or unstable bombers.

If suicide terrorists are responding to group pressure and magnetic leaders, do we absolve them of guilt for their crimes? Not at all. But perhaps there is little if anything that is special or extraordinary about them.

THE ACTOR–OBSERVER EFFECT We already noted that we are biased toward making dispositional attributions when we are explaining other people's behavior. When we see other people doing things that we do not like, we tend to judge them as willful actors (Baron et al., 2009). But when we find *ourselves* doing things that we ordinarily disapprove of, we tend to see ourselves as victims of circumstances (Baron et al., 2009). The combination of the tendency to attribute other people's behavior to dispositional factors and our own behavior to situational influences is called the **actor–observer effect**.

Consider an example. Parents and children often argue about the children's choice of friends or dates. When they do, the parents tend to infer traits from behavior and to see the children as stubborn and resistant. The children also infer traits from behavior. Thus, they may see their parents as bossy and controlling. Parents and children alike attribute the others' behavior to internal causes. That is, both make dispositional attributions about other people's behavior.

How do the parents and children perceive themselves? The parents probably see themselves as being forced into combat by their children's foolishness. If they become insistent, it is in response to the children's stubbornness. The children probably see themselves as responding to peer pressures and, perhaps, to sexual urges that may have come from within but seem like a source of outside pressure. The parents and the children both tend to see their own behavior as motivated by external forces. That is, they make situational attributions for their own behavior.

Try a mini-experiment: The next time you observe friends or family members having an argument, ask one of them afterward why the argument occurred—who had done something wrong and why. If the individual admits to having done something wrong himself, does he make a dispositional or a situational attribution? If he blames the other person, is he making a dispositional or a situational attribution?

The Actor–Observer Effect Who is at fault here? People tend to make dispositional attributions for other people's behavior, but they tend to see their own behavior as motivated by situational factors. Thus, people are aware of the external forces acting on themselves when they behave, but they tend to attribute other people's behavior to choice and will.

© Blend Images Photography/Veer

THE SELF-SERVING BIAS There is also a **self-serving bias** in the attribution process. We are likely to ascribe our successes to internal, dispositional factors but our unacceptable behavior, including our failures, to external, situational influences (Duval & Silvia, 2002; Pronin et al., 2002). When we have done well on a test or impressed a date, we are likely to credit our intelligence and charm. But when we fail, we are more likely to blame bad luck, an unfair test, or our date's bad mood.

We can extend the self-serving bias to sports. A study with 27 college wrestlers found that they tended to attribute their wins to stable and internal conditions such as their abilities. But they believed their losses were due to unstable and external conditions such as an error by a referee (De Michele et al., 1998). Sports fans fall into the same trap. They tend to attribute their team's victories to internal conditions and their losses to external conditions (Rees et al., 2005; Wallace & Hinsz, 2009). However, depressed people are more likely than other people to ascribe their failures to internal factors, even when external forces are mostly to blame (A. T. Beck & Alford, 2009).

Another interesting attribution bias is a gender difference in attributions for friendly behavior. Men are more likely than women to interpret a woman's smile or friendliness toward a man as flirting (Abbey, 1987; Buss, 2000). Perhaps traditional differences in gender roles still lead men to expect that women with whom they have not established relationships should be passive in social settings.

LearningConnections • SOCIAL PERCEPTION: LOOKING OUT, LOOKING WITHIN

ACTIVE REVIEW (11) The tendency to perceive others in terms of first impressions is an example of the _____ effect. (12) The process by which we draw inferences about the motives and traits of others through observation of their behavior is called the _____ process.

REFLECT AND RELATE Did you ever try to "make a good first impression"? What was the occasion? What did you do? Was your effort successful? Explain.

CRITICAL THINKING Why do we tend to hold others accountable for their misdeeds but excuse ourselves for the bad things we do?

 Go to Psychology CourseMate at **www.cengagebrain.com** for an interactive version of these questions.

● SOCIAL INFLUENCE: ARE YOU AN INDIVIDUAL OR ONE OF THE CROWD?

Most people would be reluctant to wear blue jeans to a funeral, walk naked on city streets, or for that matter, wear clothes at a nudist colony. This is because other people and groups can exert enormous pressure on us to behave according to their norms. **Social influence** is the area of social psychology that studies the ways people influence the thoughts, feelings, and behavior of others (Nolan et al., 2008). We already learned how attitudes can be changed through persuasion. In this section, we describe a couple of classic experiments that demonstrate how people influence others to engage in destructive obedience or conform to social norms.

Obedience to Authority: Does Might Make Right?

Throughout history, soldiers have followed orders—even when it comes to slaughtering innocent civilians. The Turkish slaughter of Armenians, the Nazi slaughter of Jews, the slaughter of Tutsis in Rwanda—these are all examples of the tragedies that can arise from simply following orders. We may say we are horrified by such crimes, and we cannot imagine why people engage in them. But how many of us would refuse to follow orders issued by authority figures? **Question 13: Why will so many people commit crimes against humanity if they are ordered to do so?** Why don't they just say no?

THE MILGRAM STUDIES: SHOCKING STUFF AT YALE Yale University psychologist Stanley Milgram wondered how many people would resist immoral requests made by authority figures. To find out, he undertook a series of classic experiments at the university that have become known as the Milgram studies on obedience.

Self-serving bias The tendency to view one's successes as stemming from internal factors and one's failures as stemming from external factors.

Social influence The area of social psychology that studies the ways in which people influence the thoughts, feelings, and behavior of others.

487

SOCIAL INFLUENCE:
ARE YOU AN
INDIVIDUAL OR ONE
OF THE CROWD?

In an early phase of his work, Milgram (1963) placed ads in New Haven (Connecticut) newspapers for people who would be willing to participate in studies on learning and memory. He enlisted 40 people ranging in age from 20 to 50—teachers, engineers, laborers, salespeople, people who had not completed elementary school, people with graduate degrees.

Let's suppose that you have answered the ad. You show up at the university in exchange for a reasonable fee ($4.50, which in the early 1960s might easily fill your gas tank) and to satisfy your own curiosity. You may be impressed. After all, Yale is a venerable institution that dominates the city. You are no less impressed by the elegant labs, where you meet a distinguished behavioral scientist dressed in a white coat and another person who has responded to the ad. The scientist explains that the purpose of the experiment is to study the *effects of punishment on learning*. The experiment requires a "teacher" and a "learner." By chance, you are appointed the teacher, and the other recruit is the learner.

You, the scientist, and the learner enter a laboratory room that contains a threatening chair with dangling straps. The scientist straps the learner in. The learner expresses some concern, but this is, after all, for the sake of science. And this is Yale University, isn't it? What could happen to a person at Yale?

You follow the scientist to an adjacent room, from which you are to do your "teaching." This teaching promises to have an impact. You are to punish the learner's errors by pressing levers marked from 15 to 450 volts on a fearsome-looking console. Labels describe 28 of the 30 levers as running the gamut from "Slight Shock" to "Danger: Severe Shock." The last two levers are simply labeled "000." Just in case you have no idea what electric shock feels like, the scientist gives you a sample 45-volt shock. It stings. You pity the person who might receive more.

Your learner is expected to learn pairs of words, which are to be read from a list. After hearing the list once, the learner is to produce the word that pairs with the stimulus word from a list of four alternatives. This is done by pressing a switch that lights one of four panels in your room. If it is the correct panel, you proceed to the next stimulus word. If not, you are to deliver an electric shock. With each error, you are to increase the voltage of the shock (see Figure 14.4 ■).

You probably have some misgivings. Electrodes have been strapped to the learner's wrists, and the scientist has applied electrode paste "to avoid blisters and burns." You have also been told that the shocks will cause "no permanent tissue damage," although they might be extremely painful. Still, the learner is going along. And after all, this is Yale.

The learner answers some items correctly and then makes some errors. With mild concern, you press the levers up through 45 volts. You've tolerated that much yourself. Then a few more mistakes are made. You press the 60-volt lever, then 75. The learner makes another mistake. You pause and look at the scientist, who is reassuring: "Although the shocks may be painful, there is no permanent tissue damage, so please go on." The learner makes more errors, and soon you are up to a shock of 300 volts. But now the learner is pounding on the other side of the wall! Your chest tightens, and you begin to perspire. "Damn science and the $4.50!" you think. You hesitate and the scientist says, "The experiment requires that you continue." After the delivery of the next stimulus word, the learner chooses no answer at all. What are you to do? "Wait for 5 to 10 seconds," the scientist instructs, "and then treat no answer as a wrong answer." But after the next shock, the pounding on the wall resumes! Now your heart is racing, and you are convinced you are causing extreme pain and discomfort.

> *"A Vietnam veteran, a student in one of my social psychology classes, told of an incident that illustrates [obedience to authority]. He was a member of a unit patrolling the coastline. He saw a boat approaching in the distance. As it got nearer, he realized that it was only a fishing sloop and, therefore, presumably harmless. The officer in charge asked him, 'What are you waiting for? Blow it out of the water.' 'But it's only a fishing sloop,' the soldier replied. 'No,' said the officer, 'it's a gunboat.' The soldier blew it out of the water."*
>
> *Thomas Blass, 2009, p. 41*

Figure 14.4 ■ The Experimental Setup in the Milgram Studies When the "learner" makes an error, the experimenter prods the "teacher" to deliver a painful electric shock.

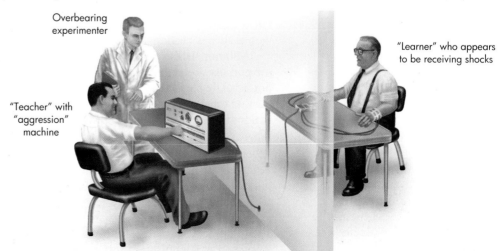

Overbearing experimenter

"Teacher" with "aggression" machine

"Learner" who appears to be receiving shocks

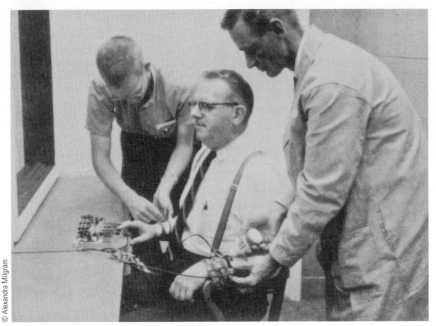

Strapped In In the Milgram experiment, the "learner" was strapped to electrodes while the "teacher"—the actual participant in the study—looked on.

Is it possible that no lasting damage is being done? Is the experiment that important, after all? What to do? You hesitate again, and the scientist says, "It is absolutely essential that you continue." His voice is very convincing. "You have no other choice," he says, "you *must* go on." You can barely think straight, and for some unaccountable reason, you feel laughter rising in your throat. Your finger shakes above the lever. *What are you to do?*

Milgram had foreseen that some "teachers" in his experiment would hesitate. He had therefore conceived standardized statements that his assistants would use when participants balked—for example: "Although the shocks may be painful, there is no permanent tissue damage, so please go on." "The experiment requires that you continue." "It is absolutely essential that you continue." "You have no other choice, you *must* go on."

To repeat: If you are a teacher in the Milgram study, what do you do? Milgram (1963, 1974) found out what most people in his sample would do. The sample was a cross-section of the male population of New Haven. Of the 40 men in this phase of his research, about one third refused to go beyond the 150-volt level, at which point the learner had cried out, "Stop, let me out! I don't want to do this anymore" (Packer, 2008). One in eight refused to go beyond the 300-volt level, the level at which the learner pounded the wall. But nearly two thirds of the participants complied with the scientist throughout the series, believing they were delivering 450-volt, 000-rated shocks. **Truth or Fiction Revisited:** Therefore, it appears to be true that most people will torture an innocent person just because they are ordered to do so.

Were these participants unfeeling? Not at all. Milgram was impressed by their signs of stress. They trembled, they stuttered, they bit their lips. They groaned, they sweated, they dug their fingernails into their flesh. Some had fits of laughter, which was an apparent defense against the brutality of the situation, although laughter was inappropriate. One salesperson's laughter was so convulsive that he could not continue with the experiment.

In various phases of Milgram's research, anywhere from nearly half to the majority of the participants complied throughout the series, believing that they were delivering 450-volt, 000-rated shocks. These findings held for men from the New Haven community, for male students at Yale, and for women.

ON DECEPTION AND TRUTH AT YALE I have said that the "teachers" in the Milgram studies *believed* that they were shocking other people when they pressed the levers on the console. They weren't. The only real shock in this experiment was the 45-volt sample given to the teachers. Its purpose was to make the procedure believable.

The learners in the experiment were actually *confederates* of the experimenter. They had not answered the newspaper ads but were in on the truth from the start. The "teachers" were the only real participants. They were led to believe they had been chosen at random for the teacher role, but the choice was rigged so that newspaper recruits would always become teachers.

Milgram debriefed his participants after the experiment was complete. He explained the purpose and methods of his research in detail. He emphasized the fact that they had not actually harmed anyone. But of course, the participants did believe that they were hurting other people as the experiment was being carried out. As you can imagine, the ethics of the Milgram studies have been debated by psychologists for four decades.

REPLICATION OF THE ORIGINAL EXPERIMENT The Milgram experiments have been replicated many times and in many places (Blass, 2009; Elms, 2009). Milgram's initial research on obedience was limited to a sample of New Haven men. Would college students, who are considered to be independent thinkers, show more defiance? A replication of Milgram's study with a sample of Yale men yielded similar results. What about women, who are supposedly less aggressive than men? In subsequent research, women, too, administered shocks to the learners.

489

SOCIAL INFLUENCE:
ARE YOU AN
INDIVIDUAL OR ONE
OF THE CROWD?

Jerry Burger (2009) recently replicated the experiments in northern California, and there were some differences from Milgram's studies. Burger included women, Latin Americans, and Asian Americans in his sample, whereas Milgram's original experiment was carried out mainly with European Americans and a few African Americans. Burger found that 65% of his sample were willing to go beyond the 150-volt level, just as found by Milgram, but that's where Burger stopped the study, to get the approval of his ethics review committee. He also believed there was little to be gained in seeing whether participants would use the highest-level shock. There were no gender differences in willingness to shock the learner, although women showed more distress than the men. All this took place in a nation that values independence and free will.

WHY DID PEOPLE IN THE MILGRAM STUDIES OBEY THE EXPERI-MENTERS? In any event, many people obey the commands of others even when they are required to perform immoral tasks. But *why?* Why did Germans "just follow orders" during the Holocaust? Why did "teachers" obey the experimenter in Milgram's study? We do not have all the answers, but we can offer a number of hypotheses:

1. *Socialization:* Despite the expressed American ideal of independence, we are socialized from early childhood to obey authority figures such as parents and teachers. Obedience to immoral demands may be the ugly sibling of socially desirable respect for authority figures (Blass, 2009; Twenge, 2009).

2. *Lack of social comparison:* In Milgram's experimental settings, experimenters displayed command of the situation. Teachers (participants), however, were in unfamiliar territory. Moreover, the participants did not have the opportunity to compare their ideas and feelings with those of other people in the same situation. They therefore were less likely to have a clear impression of what to do.

3. *Perception of legitimate authority:* One phase of Milgram's research took place within the hallowed halls of Yale University. Participants might have been overpowered by the reputation and authority of the setting. An experimenter at Yale might have appeared to be a highly legitimate authority figure—as might a government official or a high-ranking officer in the military (Blass, 2009). Yet further research showed that the university setting contributed to compliance but was not fully responsible for it. The percentage of individuals who complied with the experimenter's demands dropped from 65% to 48% when Milgram (1974) replicated the study in a dingy storefront in a nearby town. At first glance, this finding might seem encouraging. But the main point of the Milgram studies is that most people are willing to engage in morally reprehensible acts at the behest of a legitimate-looking authority figure. Hitler and his henchmen were authority figures in Nazi Germany. "Science" and Yale University legitimized the authority of the experimenters in the Milgram studies.

4. *The foot-in-the-door technique:* The foot-in-the-door technique might also have contributed to the obedience of the teachers (Burger, 2009). Once they had begun to deliver shocks to learners, they might have found it progressively more difficult to extricate themselves from the situation. Soldiers, similarly, are first taught to obey orders unquestioningly in unimportant matters such as dress and drill. By the time they are ordered to risk their lives, they have been saluting smartly and following commands without question for quite some time.

5. *Inaccessibility of values:* People are more likely to act in accordance with their attitudes when their attitudes are readily available, or accessible. Most people believe it is wrong to harm innocent people, but strong emotions impair clear thinking. As the teachers in the Milgram experiments became more emotionally involved, their attitudes might thus have become less "accessible." As a result, it might have become progressively more difficult for them to behave according to these attitudes.

6. *Buffers between the perpetrator and the victim:* Several buffers decreased the effect of the learners' pain on the teachers. For example, the "learners" (actually confederates of the experimenter) were in another room. When they were in the same room with the teachers, participant compliance dropped from 65% to 40%. Moreover, when the teacher held the learner's hand on the shock plate, the compliance rate dropped to 30%. In modern warfare, opposing military forces may be separated by great distances. They may be little more than a blip on a radar screen. It is one thing

to press a button to launch a missile or aim a piece of artillery at a distant troop carrier or a faraway mountain ridge. It is another to hold a weapon to a victim's throat.

Psychologists will continue to theorize about the Milgram experiments. As summed up by Jerry Burger, "The haunting images of participants administering electric shocks and the implications of the findings for understanding seemingly inexplicable events such as the Holocaust and Abu Ghraib have kept the research alive for more than four decades" (2009, p. 1).

Conformity In the military, individuals are taught to conform until the group functions in machinelike fashion. What pressures to conform do you experience? Do you surrender to them? Why or why not?

Conformity: Do Many Make Right?

We are said to **conform** when we change our attitudes or behavior to adhere to social norms. **Social norms** are widely accepted expectations concerning social behavior. Explicit social norms are often made into rules and laws such as those that require us to whisper in libraries and to slow down when driving past a school. There are also unspoken or implicit social norms, such as those that cause us to face the front in an elevator or to be "fashionably late" for social gatherings. Can you think of some instances in which you have conformed to social pressure? (Would you wear blue jeans if everyone else wore slacks or skirts?)

The tendency to conform to social norms is often good. Many norms have evolved because they promote comfort and survival. However, group pressure can also promote maladaptive behavior, as when people engage in risky behavior because "everyone is doing it." **Question 14: Why do so many people tend to follow the crowd?**

To answer this question, let's look at a classic experiment on conformity conducted by Solomon Asch in the early 1950s. We then examine factors that promote conformity.

SEVEN LINE JUDGES CAN'T BE WRONG: THE ASCH STUDY Can you believe what you see with your own eyes? Seeing is believing, isn't it? Not if you were a participant in Asch's (1952) study.

You entered a laboratory room with six other participants, supposedly taking part in an experiment on visual discrimination. At the front of the room stood a man holding cards with lines drawn on them.

The seven of you were seated in a series. You were given the sixth seat, a minor fact at the time. The man explained the task. There was a single line on the card on the left. Three lines were drawn on the card at the right (see Figure 14.5 ■). One line was the same length as the line on the other card. You and the other participants were to call out, one at a time, which of the three lines—1, 2, or 3—was the same length as the one on the card on the left. Simple.

The participants to your right spoke out in order: "3," "3," "3," "3," "3." Now it was your turn. Line 3 was clearly the same length as the line on the first card, so you said "3." The fellow after you then chimed in "3." That's all there was to it. Then two other cards were set up at the front of the room. This time line 2 was clearly the same length as the line on the first card. The answers were "2," "2," "2," "2," "2." Again, it was your turn. You said "2," and perhaps your mind began to wander. Your stomach was gurgling a bit. The fellow after you said "2."

> *"Conformity is the jailer of freedom and the enemy of growth."*
>
> JOHN F. KENNEDY

> *"Group conformity scares the pants off me because it's so often a prelude to cruelty towards anyone who doesn't want to—or can't—join the Big Parade."*
>
> BETTE MIDLER

> *"Whenever you find yourself on the side of the majority, it is time to pause and reflect."*
>
> MARK TWAIN

Figure 14.5 ■ Cards Used in the Asch Study on Conformity Which line on card B—1, 2, or 3—is the same length as the line on card A? Line 2, right? But would you say "2" if you were a member of a group, and five people answering ahead of you all said "3"? Are you sure?

A. Standard line

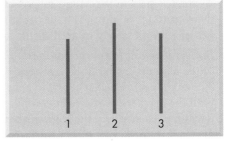

B. Comparison lines

491

SOCIAL INFLUENCE:
ARE YOU AN
INDIVIDUAL OR ONE
OF THE CROWD?

Another pair of cards was held up. Line 3 was clearly the correct answer. The five people on your right spoke in turn: "1," "1 . . ." Wait a second! ". . . 1," "1." You forgot about dinner and studied the lines briefly. No, line 1 was too short by a good half inch. But the next participant said "1," and suddenly, it was your turn. Your hands had become sweaty, and there was a lump in your throat. You wanted to say "3," but was it right? There was really no time, and you had already paused noticeably. You said "1," and so did the last fellow.

Now your attention was riveted on the task. Much of the time you agreed with the other six judges, but sometimes you did not. And for some reason beyond your understanding, they were in perfect agreement even when they were wrong—assuming you could trust your eyes. The experiment was becoming an uncomfortable experience, and you began to doubt your judgment. **Truth or Fiction Revisited:** Therefore, seeing is not always believing—especially when the group sees things differently.

The discomfort in the Asch study was caused by the pressure to conform. Actually, the other six "recruits" were confederates of the experimenter. They prearranged a number of incorrect responses. The sole purpose of the study was to see whether you would conform to the erroneous group judgments.

How many people in Asch's study caved in? How many went along with the crowd rather than give what they thought was the right answer? Seventy-five percent. *Three out of four agreed with the majority's wrong answer at least once.*

Conform To change one's attitudes or overt behavior to adhere to social norms.

Social norms Explicit and implicit rules that reflect social expectations and influence the ways people behave in social situations.

FACTORS THAT INFLUENCE CONFORMITY Several factors increase the tendency to conform. They include the following:

- Belonging to a collectivist rather than an individualistic society (Fukushima et al., 2009).
- The desire to be liked by other members of the group (but valuing being right over being liked *decreases* the tendency to conform).
- Low self-esteem.
- Social shyness (Wagstaff et al., 2009).
- Lack of familiarity with the task.

Other factors in conformity include the group size and social support. The likelihood of conformity, even to incorrect group judgments, increases rapidly as group size grows to five members; it then rises more slowly as the group grows to about eight members. At about that point, the maximum chance of conformity is reached. Yet finding just one other person who supports your minority opinion apparently is enough to encourage you to stick to your guns (Mesoudi, 2009; W. N. Morris et al., 1977).

© Wm Vandivert, courtesy of Susan Vandivert. Asch, S. E. (1951). Effects of group pressure upon the modification and distortion of judgement. In H. Guetzkow (ed.) *Groups, Leadership, and Men.* Pittsburgh, PA: Carnegie Press.

The Quandary of Participant Number 6
Faced with unanimous reporting of the wrong answer, this participant decides whether to go along with the crowd or "stick to his guns." What did most people in the study do?

LearningConnections • SOCIAL INFLUENCE: ARE YOU AN INDIVIDUAL OR ONE OF THE CROWD?

ACTIVE REVIEW (13) Most people (do or do not?) comply with the demands of authority figures when those demands are immoral. (14) The following factors contribute to obedience: socialization, lack of _____ comparison, perception of experimenters as legitimate authority figures, the foot-in-the-door technique, and inaccessibility of values. (15) In Asch's studies of conformity, _____% of the participants agreed with an incorrect majority judgment at least once.

REFLECT AND RELATE Milgram's research has alerted us to a real danger—the tendency of many, if not most, people to obey the orders of an authority figure even when they run counter to moral values. It has happened before. It is happening now. What will you do to stop it?

CRITICAL THINKING Critical thinkers do not overgeneralize. Most people would probably agree that it is good for children to be obedient. But is it always good for children—and for adults—to be obedient? How do you define the limits?

 Go to Psychology CourseMate at **www.cengagebrain.com** for an interactive version of these questions.

● GROUP BEHAVIOR: IS A CAMEL A HORSE MADE BY A COMMITTEE?

To be human is to belong to groups. Groups have much to offer us. They help us satisfy our needs for affection, attention, and belonging. They empower us to do things we could not manage by ourselves. But groups can also pressure us into doing things we might not do if we were acting alone, such as taking great risks or attacking other people.

This section considers ways in which people behave differently as group members than they would as individuals. We begin with social facilitation.

Social Facilitation: Monkey See, Monkey Do Faster?

When you are given a group assignment, do you work harder or less hard than you would alone? Why?

One effect of groups on individual behavior is **social facilitation,** or the process by which performance is enhanced when other members of a group engage in similar behavior. **Question 15: Do we run faster when we are in a group?** Apparently, we do. Runners and bicycle riders tend to move faster when they are members of a group. This effect is not limited to people. Dogs and cats eat more rapidly around others of their kind. Even roaches—yes, roaches—run more rapidly when other roaches are present (Zajonc, 1980). And fruit flies apparently do a better job of retrieving long-term memories—as shown by the display of conditioned responses—in the presence of other fruit flies that have undergone the same conditioning (Chabaud et al., 2009).

Research suggests that the presence of other people increases our levels of arousal, or motivation (Platania & Moran, 2001; Thomas et al., 2002). At high levels of arousal, our performance of simple tasks is facilitated. Our performance of complex responses may be impaired, however. For this reason, a well-rehearsed speech may be delivered more masterfully before a larger audience. An offhand speech or a question-and-answer session may be hampered by a large audience.

Social facilitation may be influenced by **evaluation apprehension** as well as arousal (Rosenberg, 2009; Thomas et al., 2002). Our performance before a group is affected not only by the presence of others but also by concern that they are evaluating us. When giving a speech, we may "lose our thread" if we are distracted by the audience and focus too much on its apparent reaction. If we believe that we have begun to flounder, evaluation apprehension may skyrocket. As a result, our performance may falter even more.

The presence of others can also impair performance not only when we are acting *before* a group but also when we are anonymous members of a group (Guerin, 1999). Workers, for example, may "goof off," or engage in **social loafing,** on humdrum jobs when they believe they will not be found out and held accountable. Under these conditions, there is no evaluation apprehension. There may also be **diffusion of responsibility** in groups. Each person may feel less obligation to help because others are present, especially if the others are perceived as capable of doing the job (Abele & Diehl, 2008; Maiden & Perry, 2010). Group members may also reduce their efforts if an apparently capable member makes no contribution but "rides free" on the efforts of others.

How would you perform in a tug of war? Would the presence of other people pulling motivate you to pull harder? (If so, we might attribute the result to social facilitation, unless you personally enjoy tugging; B. N. Smith et al., 2001.) Or would the fact that no one can tell how hard you are pulling encourage you to "loaf"? (If so, should we attribute the result to diffusion of responsibility?)

Group Decision Making

Organizations use groups such as committees or juries to make decisions in the belief that group decisions are more accurate than individual decisions (Van Swol, 2008). **Question 16: How do groups make decisions?** Social psychologists have discovered a number of "rules," or **social decision**

Social facilitation The process by which a person's performance increases when other members of a group engage in similar behavior.

Evaluation apprehension Concern that others are evaluating our behavior.

Social loafing The process by which a person's performance decreases when other members of a group engage in similar behavior, apparently because the person believes that strenuous effort is unnecessary.

Diffusion of responsibility The spreading or sharing of responsibility for a decision or behavior within a group.

Social Facilitation Runners tend to move faster when they are members of a group. Does the presence of other people raise our level of arousal or produce evaluation apprehension?

schemes, that govern much of group decision making (Stasser, 1999). Here are some examples:

1. *The majority-wins scheme:* In this commonly used scheme, the group arrives at the decision that was initially supported by the majority. This scheme appears to guide decision making most often when there is no single objectively correct decision. An example would be a decision about which car models to build when their popularity has not been tested in the court of public opinion.

2. *The truth-wins scheme:* In this scheme, as more information is provided and opinions are discussed, the group comes to recognize that one approach is objectively correct. For example, a group deciding whether to use SAT scores in admitting students to college would profit from information about whether the scores have successfully predicted college success in the past.

3. *The two-thirds majority scheme:* Juries tend to convict defendants when two-thirds of the jury initially favors conviction.

4. *The first-shift rule:* In this scheme, the group tends to adopt the decision that reflects the first shift in opinion expressed by any group member. If a car-manufacturing group is divided on whether to produce a convertible, it may opt to do so after one member of the group who initially was opposed to the idea changes her mind. Similarly, if a jury is deadlocked, the members may eventually follow the lead of the first juror to switch position.

How Will They Make Their Decision? Will the majority prevail? Will someone point to a significant piece of evidence that sways the day? Will the group follow the lead of the first person to change his or her mind? What other possibilities are there?

Polarization and the "Risky Shift"

We might think that a group decision would be more conservative than an individual decision. After all, shouldn't there be an effort to compromise, to "split the difference"? We might also expect that a few mature individuals would be able to balance the opinions of daredevils. **Question 17: Are group decisions riskier or more conservative than those of individual group members?** Why?

Groups do not always appear to work as we might expect, however. Consider the **polarization** effect. As an individual, you might recommend that your company risk an investment of $500,000 to develop or market a new product. Other company executives, polled individually, might risk similar amounts. If you were gathered together to make a group decision, however, you would probably recommend either an amount well above this figure or nothing at all (Kamalanabhan et al., 2000; Mordock, 1997). This group effect is called *polarization,* or the taking of an extreme position. If you had to gamble on which way the decision would go, however, you would do better to place your money on movement toward the higher sum—that is, to bet on a **risky shift.** Why?

One possibility is that one member of the group may reveal information that the others were not aware of. This information may clearly point in one direction or the other. With doubts removed, the group becomes polarized. It moves decisively in the appropriate direction. It is also possible that social facilitation occurs in the group setting and that the resulting greater motivation prompts more extreme decisions.

Why, however, do groups tend to take *greater* risks than those their members would take as individuals? One answer is diffusion of responsibility (A. S. Brown, 2007; Kamalanabhan et al., 2000). If the venture flops, the blame will not be placed on you alone. Remember the self-serving bias: You can always say (and think) that the failure was the result of a group decision. You thus protect your self-esteem (Fleming, 2008). If the venture pays off, however, you can attribute the outcome to your cool analysis and boast of your influence on the group. Note that all this behavior fits right in with what is known about the self-serving bias.

"Participating in a well-functioning group is really hard. It requires the ability to trust people outside your kinship circle, read intonations and moods, [and] understand how the psychological pieces each person brings to the room can and cannot fit together."

DAVID BROOKS

Social decision schemes Rules for predicting the final outcome of group decision making.

Polarization In social psychology, taking an extreme position or attitude on an issue.

Risky shift The tendency to make riskier decisions as a member of a group than as an individual acting independently.

493

Groupthink: When Smart People Think as One, Bad Decisions May Follow

"I will not wait on events, while dangers gather. I will not stand by, as peril draws closer and closer. The United States of America will not permit the world's most dangerous regimes to threaten us with the world's most destructive weapons."

PRESIDENT GEORGE W. BUSH, FROM STATE OF THE UNION SPEECH, 2002

Groupthink? Did President George W. Bush (center) and his advisers (Secretary of Defense Donald Rumsfeld, left, and Vice President Dick Cheney, right) fall prey to groupthink in making the decision to invade Iraq?

President Bush delivered this speech just 4 months after the events of September 11, 2001. The attackers had been identified. The nation was looking for ways to prevent a repetition. Many wanted revenge. Some intelligence reports suggested that Saddam Hussein, the leader of Iraq, was preparing weapons of mass destruction (WMDs) for use against the United States. In 2003, the United States invaded Iraq, deposed Hussein, and undertook what turned out to be a fruitless search for WMDs. Three years later, the United States was spending blood and treasure to fight an insurgency in Iraq, but a growing majority of Americans believed the invasion should not have occurred. Bob Woodward (2006) published a book titled *State of Denial,* in which he reported that the Bush administration had focused selectively on bad intelligence in arriving at the belief that Iraq possessed WMDs.

How did the invasion occur? Woodward and other observers (e.g., Fitzsimmons, 2008) point to the role of *groupthink,* a concept originated by social psychologist Irving Janis (1982). **Question 18: What is groupthink? Groupthink** is a problem that may arise in group decision making when group members are swayed more by group cohesiveness and a dynamic leader than by the realities of the situation (Esser & Lindoerfer, 2006; Packer, 2009). Groupthink grows more likely when the group senses an external threat (Byrne & Senehi, 2008). Under stress, group members may not carefully weigh all their options, and flawed decisions may be made.

Groupthink has been connected with historic fiascos such as the botched Bay of Pigs invasion of Cuba, the Watergate scandal, in which members of the Nixon administration believed they could cover up a theft, and NASA's decision to launch the *Challenger* space shuttle despite engineers' warnings about the dangers created by unusually cold weather (Brownstein, 2003; Esser & Lindoerfer, 2006). Janis and other researchers (Brownstein, 2003; Packer, 2009) note characteristics of groupthink that contribute to flawed decisions:

1. *Feelings of invulnerability:* In the Watergate Affair, the decision-making group might have believed they were beyond the reach of critics or the law because they were powerful people who were close to the president of the United States.

2. *The group's belief in its rightness:* These groups apparently believed in the rightness of what they were doing. In the case of the *Challenger* launch, NASA had a track record of successful launches. Members of the Bush administration believed they had the evidence of WMDs that they needed.

3. *Discrediting information contrary to the group's decision:* Members of the Bush administration discredited reports that raised doubt, such as a report from Mohamed El-Baradei, the director general of the International Atomic Energy Agency, and some of the United States' own intelligence reports.

4. *Pressures on group members to conform:* Striving for unanimity overrides realistic assessment, and authority can trump expertise. According to Woodward, members of the administration who sought to invade Iraq overrode dissenting voices. After the disastrous invasion of the Bay of Pigs in Cuba, President John F. Kennedy is reported to have said, "How could we have been so stupid?"

5. *Stereotyping members of the out-group:* In the cases of the invasions of the Bay of Pigs and Iraq, proinvasion group members stereotyped members of the out-group as being out of touch with reality.

President John F. Kennedy Kennedy remarked, "How could we have been so stupid?" when the Bay of Pigs invasion of Cuba ended in disaster. Kennedy and his advisors had apparently engaged in groupthink in arriving at the decision to invade.

The goal of the invasion of Iraq was to find and destroy WMDs. The weapons were never found and apparently did not exist. But the United States had been attacked, and the desire to do *something* was riding high in the country. Not only Republicans supported the invasion. Twenty-nine of fifty Democratic senators, including Hillary Clinton of New York and John Kerry of Massachusetts, voted to authorize the use of military force. Given that President Bush had an approval rating of nearly 90%, one may wonder whether many millions of Americans fell prey to the same groupthink that gripped politicians.

Mob Behavior and Deindividuation: The "Beast with Many Heads"

Have you ever done something as a member of a group that you would not have done as an individual? What was it? What motivated you? How do you feel about it?

Frenchman Gustave Le Bon (1895/1960) branded mobs and crowds as irrational, resembling a "beast with many heads." Mob actions such as race riots and lynchings sometimes seem to operate on a psychology of their own. **Question 19: Why do mild-mannered people commit mayhem when they are part of a mob?** Do mobs "bring out the beast in us"?

When people act as individuals, fear of consequences and self-evaluation tend to prevent them from engaging in antisocial behavior. But in a mob, they may experience deindividuation, a state in which they are willing to follow a norm that emerges in a specific situation, even if it means ignoring their own values (Lan & Zuo, 2009; Postmes & Spears, 1998). Many factors lead to deindividuation. These include anonymity, diffusion of responsibility, arousal due to noise and crowding, and a focus on emerging group norms rather than on one's own values (Postmes & Spears, 1998; S. L. Taylor et al., 2006). Under these circumstances, crowd members behave more aggressively than they would as individuals.

Police know that mob actions are best averted early by dispersing small groups that could gather into a crowd. On an individual level, perhaps we can resist deindividuation by instructing ourselves to stop and think whenever we begin to feel highly aroused in a group. If we dissociate ourselves from such groups when they are forming, we are more likely to remain critical and avoid behavior that we might later regret.

Groupthink A process in which group members are influenced by cohesiveness and a dynamic leader to ignore external realities as they make decisions.

Deindividuation The process by which group members may discontinue self-evaluation and adopt group norms and attitudes.

Altruism Unselfish concern for the welfare of others.

Altruism and the Bystander Effect: Some Watch While Others Die

Altruism—selfless concern for the welfare of others—is connected with some heroic and some very strange behavior throughout the animal kingdom (Zahavi, 2003). Humans have been known to sacrifice themselves to ensure the survival of their children or of comrades in battle. Nonhuman primates sometimes suicidally attack a leopard to give others the opportunity to escape.

These behaviors are heroic and apparently selfless, and among humans, self-sacrifice often earns status in the eyes of others (Willer, 2009). But consider the red spider's strange ways (Begley & Check, 2000). After depositing its sperm into a female red spider, the male of the species will do a flip into her mouth and become her dinner! Clearly, the red spider does not make a decision to sacrifice itself. But evolutionary psychologists might argue that the self-sacrificing behavior of the male red spider is actually selfish from an evolutionary point of view. How, you might wonder, can individuals sacrifice themselves and at the same time be acting in their own self-interests? To answer the question, you should also know that female red spiders are promiscuous; they will mate with multiple suitors. However, eating a "lover" slows them down, increasing the probability that *his* sperm will fertilize her eggs and that his genes will survive and be transmitted to the next generation. We could thus say that the male red spider is altruistic in that he puts the welfare of future generations ahead of his own. Fatherhood ain't easy.

Are Mobs Beasts with Angry Heads? French social thinker Gustave Le Bon branded mobs as irrational, like a "beast with many heads." Police are taught that it's useful to confront groups as early as possible and prevent them from becoming so highly aroused emotionally that they forget their values as individuals and focus only on the emerging group norms.

© Ulf Sjostedt/Photographer's Choice/Getty Images

Red spiders, of course, do not think—at least, not in any humanly understandable sense of the concept of thinking. But people do. So how, one might ask, could the murder of 28-year-old Kitty Genovese have happened? It took place in New York City more than a generation ago. **Truth or Fiction Revisited:** Some 40 people stood by and did nothing while she was being stabbed to death. Murder was not unheard of in the Big Apple, but Kitty had screamed for help as her killer stalked her for more than half an hour and stabbed her in three separate attacks (Manning et al., 2007). At least 38 neighbors heard the commotion. Twice the assault was interrupted by their voices and bedroom lights. Each time, the attacker returned. Yet nobody came to the victim's aid. No one even called the police. Why? Some witnesses said matter-of-factly that they did not want to get involved. One said that he was tired. Still others said, "I don't know." As a nation, are we a callous bunch who would rather watch than help when others are in trouble?

THE BYSTANDER EFFECT Question 20: Why do people sometimes sacrifice themselves for others and, at other times, ignore people who are in trouble? Why did 38 bystanders allow Kitty Genovese to die? Why did they—and Kitty!—fell prey to the **bystander effect.** That is, nobody came to Kitty's aid because they saw that other people were present—or, because the murder took place in crowded New York City, they assumed that other people were also available to help.

When Do We Decide to Come to the Aid of Someone Who is in Trouble? It turns out that many factors are involved in helping behavior. The following are among them:

1. Observers are more likely to help when they are in a good mood (Schnall et al., 2010). Perhaps good moods impart a sense of personal power—the feeling that we can handle the situation (Cunningham et al., 1990; Dulin & Hill, 2003).

2. People who are empathic are more likely to help people in need (Batson & Ahmad, 2009). Empathic people feel the distress of others, feel concern for them, and can imagine what it must be like to be in need. Women are more likely than men to be empathic and thus more likely to help people in need (Yamasue et al., 2008).

3. Bystanders may not help unless they believe that an emergency exists (Cocking et al., 2009). Perhaps some people who heard Kitty Genovese's calls for help were not certain what was happening. (But remember that others admitted they did not want to get involved.)

4. Observers must assume the responsibility to act (Piliavin, 2009). It may seem logical that a group of people would be more likely to have come to the aid of Kitty Genovese than a lone person. After all, a group could more effectively have overpowered her attacker. Yet research by Darley and Latané (1968) suggests that a lone person would have been more likely to help her. In their classic experiment, male participants were performing meaningless tasks in cubicles when they heard a (convincing) recording of a person apparently having an epileptic seizure. When the men thought four other persons were immediately available, only 31% tried to help the victim. When they thought no one else was available, however, 85% of them tried to help. As in other areas of group behavior, it seems that *diffusion of responsibility* inhibits helping behavior in groups or crowds. When we are in a group, we are often willing to let George (or Georgette) do it. When George isn't around, we are more willing to help others ourselves. (Perhaps some who heard Kitty Genovese thought, "Why should I get involved? Other people can hear her, too.")

5. Observers must know what to do (Baron et al., 2009). We hear of cases in which people impulsively jump into the water to save a drowning child and then drown themselves. Most of the time, however, people do not try to help unless they know what to do. For example, nurses are more likely than people without medical training to try to help accident victims (Cramer et al., 1988). Observers who are not sure they can take charge of the situation may stay on the sidelines for fear of making a social blunder and being ridiculed. Or they may fear getting hurt themselves. (Perhaps some who heard Kitty Genovese thought, "If I try to intervene, I may get killed or make an idiot of myself.")

6. Observers are more likely to help people they know (Rutkowski et al., 1983). Aren't we also more likely to give to charity when asked directly by a coworker or supervisor in the socially exposed situation of the office compared with a form

Bystander effect The tendency to avoid helping other people in emergencies when other people are also present and apparently capable of helping.

letter received in the privacy of our own homes? Evolutionary psychologists suggest that altruism is a natural aspect of human nature—even if not in the same way as in the case of the red spider! For example, self-sacrifice sometimes helps close relatives (such as our children) or others who are similar to us survive. Self-sacrifice is therefore "selfish" from a genetic or evolutionary point of view (Bruene & Ribbert, 2002; Waring, 2010). It helps us perpetuate a genetic code similar to our own. This view suggests that we are more likely to be altruistic with our relatives than with strangers, however. The Kitty Genoveses of the world may remain out of luck unless they are surrounded by kinfolk or friends.

7. Observers are more likely to help people who are similar to themselves. Being able to identify with the person in need appears to promote helping behavior (Cialdini et al., 1997). Poorly dressed people are more likely to succeed in requests for a dime with _____ poorly dressed strangers. Well-dressed people are more likely to get money from well-dressed strangers (Hensley, 1981).

So, Which One Would You Give a Ride? Social psychologists note that we are more willing to help people who are similar to ourselves. On the other hand, women are more likely to be helped than men. Is it because women appear to pose less of a threat or to be more in need? Is it chivalry? Or is it something else at work?

© Patrick Byrd/Science Factior./Corbis

© Lou Cypher/Corbis

The Victim: Who Is Helped? Although women are more likely than men to help people in need, it is traditional for men to help women, particularly in the South. Women were more likely than men to receive help, especially from men, when they dropped coins in Atlanta (a southern city) than in Seattle or Columbus (northern cities) (Latané & Dabbs, 1975). Why? The researchers suggest that traditional gender roles persist more strongly in the South.

Women are also more likely than men to be helped when their cars have broken down on the highway or they are hitchhiking. Is this gallantry, or are there sexual overtones to some of this "altruism"? There may be sexual overtones, because attractive and unaccompanied women are most likely to be helped by men (Benson et al., 1976).

Research concerning altruism and the bystander effect highlight the fact that we are members of a vast, interdependent social fabric. The next time you see a stranger in need, what will you do? Are you sure?

As you complete this text, I hope that you will have decided to allow psychology to become a key part of your education. A professor of mine once remarked that the true measure of the success of a course is whether the student decides to take additional courses in the field. The choice is yours. *Enjoy.*

LearningConnections • GROUP BEHAVIOR: IS A CAMEL A HORSE MADE BY A COMMITTEE?

ACTIVE REVIEW (16) Social _____ refers to the enhancement of performance that results from the presence of others. (17) Social _____ schemes seem to govern group decision making: the majority-wins scheme, the truth-wins scheme, the two-thirds majority scheme, and the first-shift rule. (18) Groups are (more or less?) likely than individuals to take extreme positions. (19) Groupthink is usually (realistic or unrealistic?). (20) Members of a group may experience _____, which is a state of reduced self-awareness and lowered concern for social evaluation. (21) Self-sacrifice to help others is known as _____. (22) Kitty Genovese's death has been attributed to the _____ effect.

REFLECT AND RELATE Families, classes, religious groups, political parties, nations, circles of friends, bowling teams, sailing clubs, conversation groups, therapy groups—to how many groups do you belong? How do these groups influence your behavior?

CRITICAL THINKING According to evolutionary theory, self-sacrifice can be "selfish." How does the theory explain this view?

Go to Psychology CourseMate at **www.cengagebrain.com** for an interactive version of these questions.

Attitudes: "The Good, the Bad, and the Ugly"

1. What is social psychology?
Social psychology is the field of psychology that studies the nature and causes of behavior and mental processes in social situations.

2. What are attitudes?
Attitudes are behavioral and cognitive tendencies expressed by evaluating particular people, places, or things with favor or disfavor.

3. Do people do as they think?
When we are free to act as we wish, our behavior is often consistent with our beliefs and feelings. But, as indicated by the term *A–B problem*, the links between attitudes (A) and behaviors (B) are often weak to moderate.

4. Where do attitudes come from?
Attitudes can be learned means of conditioning or observation. However, people also appraise and evaluate situations and often form their own judgments.

5. Can you really change people—their attitudes and behavior, that is?
According to the elaboration likelihood model, persuasion occurs through both central and peripheral routes. Repeated messages generally "sell" better than messages delivered only once. People tend to show greater response to fear appeals than to purely factual presentations. Persuasive communicators tend to show expertise, trustworthiness, attractiveness, or similarity to the audience.

6. What is cognitive-dissonance theory?
Cognitive-dissonance theory hypothesizes that people are discomforted by situations in which their attitudes and behavior are inconsistent. Such situations induce cognitive dissonance, which people can reduce by changing their attitudes. People engage in effort justification to explain their participation in boring or fruitless behavior.

Prejudice: A Particularly Troublesome Attitude

7. What are prejudice and discrimination?
Prejudice is a negative attitude toward a group. Discrimination is behavior that is hostile toward groups toward whom one is prejudiced.

8. What are the sources of prejudice?
The sources of prejudice include dissimilarity to groups against whom one is prejudiced, social conflict, social learning, information processing, and social categorization.

Interpersonal Attraction: On Liking and Loving

9. What factors contribute to attraction in our culture?
Men seem to find large eyes and narrow jaws attractive in women. In our culture, slenderness is considered attractive in both men and women, and tallness is valued in men. Similarity in attitudes and sociocultural factors enhance attraction. According to the attraction-similarity hypothesis, we tend to seek dates and mates at our own level of attractiveness.

10. Just what is love?
Sternberg's theory suggests that love has three components: intimacy, passion, and commitment. Romantic love is characterized by passion and intimacy.

Social Perception: Looking Out, Looking Within

11. What are the primacy and recency effects?
First impressions can last because we tend to label or describe people in terms of the behavior we see initially (the primacy effect). The recency effect occurs when the freshest information is recalled.

12. What is attribution theory?
Attribution theory involves the inference of the motives and traits of others through observation of their behavior. Dispositional attributions ascribe people's behavior to internal factors such as their personality traits and decisions. Situational attributions ascribe people's behavior to external forces such as their circumstances. The actor–observer effect suggests we attribute other people's behavior to internal, dispositional factors but our own behavior to external, situational factors. The fundamental attribution error is the tendency to attribute too much of other people's behavior to dispositional factors.

Social Influence: Are You an Individual or One of the Crowd?

13. Why will so many people commit crimes against humanity if they are ordered to do so?
The majority of participants in the Milgram studies complied with the demands of authority figures. Factors contributing to obedience include socialization, lack of social comparison, perception of legitimate authority figures, the foot-in-the-door technique, inaccessibility of values, and buffers between the perpetrator and the victim.

14. Why do so many people tend to follow the crowd?
Asch's research suggests that the majority of people will follow the crowd because of factors such as desire to be liked by group members, low self-esteem, lack of familiarity with the task, and social shyness.

Group Behavior: Is a Camel a Horse Made by a Committee?

15. Do we run faster when we are in a group?
Yes, we run faster when we are in a group—because of social facilitation. Social facilitation refers to the effects on performance that result from the presence of other people, perhaps because of increased arousal and evaluation apprehension. However, anonymous group members may experience diffusion of responsibility, and task performance may fall off, as in social loafing.

16. How do groups make decisions?
Social psychologists have identified several decision-making schemes, including the majority-wins scheme, the truth-wins scheme, the two-thirds majority scheme, and the first-shift rule.

17. Are group decisions riskier or more conservative than those of individual group members?
Group decisions tend to be more polarized and riskier than individual decisions, largely because groups diffuse responsibility.

18. What is groupthink?
Groupthink is an unrealistic kind of decision making that is fueled by the perception of external threats to the group. It is facilitated by a dynamic group leader, feelings of invulnerability, the group's belief in its rightness, discrediting information that contradicts the group's decision, conformity, and stereotyping members of the out-group.

18. Why do mild-mannered people commit mayhem when they are part of a mob?
Highly emotional crowds may induce attitude-discrepant behavior through the process of *deindividuation,* which is a state of reduced self-awareness and lowered concern for social evaluation.

19. Why do people sometimes sacrifice themselves for others and, at other times, ignore people who are in trouble?
Factors contributing to altruism include empathy, being in a good mood, feelings of responsibility, knowledge of how to help, and acquaintance with—and similarity to—the person in need of help. According to the bystander effect, we are less likely to aid people in distress when other people are present.

KEY TERMS

A–B problem (p. 468)
Actor–observer effect (p. 485)
Affective shift hypothesis (p. 481)
Altruism (p. 495)
Attitude (p. 468)
Attitude-discrepant behavior (p. 473)
Attraction (p. 477)
Attraction-similarity hypothesis (p. 478)
Attribution (p. 484)
Attribution process (p. 484)
Bystander effect (p. 496)
Central route (p. 470)
Cognitive-dissonance theory (p. 472)
Commitment (p. 480)
Conform (p. 490)
Consummate love (p. 481)

Deindividuation (p. 495)
Diffusion of responsibility (p. 492)
Discrimination (p. 475)
Dispositional attribution (p. 484)
Effort justification (p. 473)
Elaboration likelihood model (p. 470)
Evaluation apprehension (p. 492)
Fear appeal (p. 471)
Foot-in-the-door technique (p. 473)
Fundamental attribution error (p. 484)
Groupthink (p. 494)
Intimacy (p. 480)
Passion (p. 480)
Peripheral route (p. 470)
Polarization (p. 493)
Prejudice (p. 474)
Primacy effect (p. 483)

Recency effect (p. 484)
Reciprocity (p. 480)
Risky shift (p. 493)
Romantic love (p. 481)
Selective avoidance (p. 471)
Selective exposure (p. 471)
Self-serving bias (p. 486)
Situational attribution (p. 484)
Social decision schemes (p. 493)
Social facilitation (p. 492)
Social influence (p. 486)
Social loafing (p. 492)
Social norms (p. 490)
Social perception (p. 483)
Social psychology (p. 468)
Stereotype (p. 468)
Triangular model of love (p. 480)

ACTIVE LEARNING RESOURCES

Log in to **www.cengagebrain.com** to access the resources your instructor requires. For this book, you can access:

CourseMate brings course concepts to life with interactive learning, study, and exam preparation tools that support the printed textbook. A textbook-specific website, Psychology CourseMate includes an integrated interactive eBook and other interactive learning tools including quizzes, flashcards, videos, and more.

CENGAGENOW Need help studying? This site is your one-stop study shop. Take a Pre-Test and CengageNOW will generate a Personalized Study Plan based on your test results. The Study Plan will identify the topics you need to review and direct you to online resources to help you master those topics. You can then take a Post-Test to determine the concepts you have mastered and what you still need to work on.

Appendix A

Statistics

© Pixand/Jupiterimages/Photospin

MAJOR TOPICS

Descriptive Statistics 502
The Normal Curve 506
Inferential Statistics 507

T F   Professional basketball players are abnormal.

page 502

T F   Being a "10" is not necessarily a good thing.

page 502

T F   You should not assume that you can walk across a river with an average depth of 4 feet.

page 503

T F   Adding people's incomes and then dividing them by the number of people is the best way to show the average income.

page 504

T F   Psychologists express your IQ score in terms of how deviant you are.

page 507

T F   An IQ score of 130 suggests greater academic potential than an SAT score of 500.

page 507

Are these items truth or fiction? We will be revisiting them throughout the appendix.

Imagine that aliens from outer space arrive outside Madison Square Garden in New York City. Their goal this dark and numbing winter evening is to learn all they can about planet Earth. They are drawn inside the Garden by lights, shouts, and warmth. The spotlighting inside rivets their attention to a wood-floored arena where the New York Big Apples are hosting the California Quakes in a briskly contested basketball game.

Our visitors use their sophisticated instruments to take some measurements of the players. Some interesting statistics are sent back to their planet of origin: It appears that (a) 100% of Earthlings are male and (b) the height of Earthlings ranges from 6 feet 1 inch to 7 feet 2 inches.

These measurements are called **statistics**. **Question 1: What is statistics?** Statistics is the science concerned with obtaining and organizing numerical information or measurements. Now let's sort truth from fiction: Our visitors have sent home statistics about the gender and size of human beings that are at once accurate and misleading. Although they accurately measured the basketball players, their small sample of Earth's population was, shall we say, distorted. Fortunately for us Earthlings, about half of the world's population is female. And the *range* of heights observed by the aliens—6 feet 1 inch to 7 feet 2 inches—is both restricted and too high. People vary in height by more than 1 foot and 1 inch. And our **average** height is not between 6 feet 1 inch and 7 feet 2 inches; rather, it is a number of inches lower.

Psychologists, like our aliens, are concerned with measuring human as well as animal characteristics and traits—not only physical characteristics such as height but also psychological traits such as intelligence, sociability, aggressiveness, neatness, anxiety, and depression. By observing the *central tendencies* (averages) and variations in measurement

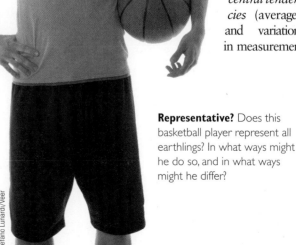

Representative? Does this basketball player represent all earthlings? In what ways might he do so, and in what ways might he differ?

© Stefano Lunardi/Veer

from person to person, psychologists can say that one person is average or above average in intelligence or that someone else is less anxious than, say, 60% of the population.

But psychologists, unlike our aliens, attempt to select a sample that accurately represents the entire population. **Truth or Fiction Revisited:** Professional basketball players can be considered "abnormal"—statistically speaking—in their physical traits. That is, they are taller, stronger, and more agile than most of us. (They also make more sneaker commercials.) Of course, their "abnormalities" are assets to them, not deficits.

In this appendix, we survey some of the statistical methods that psychologists use to draw conclusions about the measurements they take in research. First we discuss *descriptive statistics* and learn what types of statements we can make about height and other human traits. Then we discuss the *normal curve* and learn why basketball players are abnormal—at least in terms of height. We have a look at *inferential statistics,* and we see why we can be bold enough to say that the difference in height between basketball players and other people is not a chance fluctuation or fluke. Basketball players are *statistically significantly* taller than the general population.

> *"Smoking is one of the leading causes of all statistics."*
>
> LIZA MINNELLI

DESCRIPTIVE STATISTICS

Being told that someone is a "10" may sound great; however, it is not very descriptive unless you know something about how the scores on the scale are distributed and how frequently one finds a 10. Fortunately—for 10s, if not for the rest of us—people usually mean that the person is a 10 on a scale from 1 to 10 and that 10 is the highest possible score. If this is not sufficient, one will also be told that 10s are few and far between—rather unusual statistical events. **Truth or Fiction Revisited:** But note that the scale could also vary from 0 to 100, in which case a score of 10 would place an individual near the bottom of the scale and make a score of 50 the center point. With such a scale, being a 10 would not be impressive.

The idea of the scale from 1 to 10 may not be very scientific, but it does suggest something about descriptive statistics. **Question 2: What is descriptive statistics?** Descriptive statistics is the branch of statistics that provides information about a distribution of scores. We can use descriptive statistics to clarify our understanding of a distribution of scores such as heights, test grades, IQs, or even increases or decreases in measures of aggressive behavior following the drinking of alcohol. For example, descriptive statistics can help us determine measures of central tendency (averages) and determine how much fluctuation or variability there is in the scores. Being a 10 loses much of its charm if the average score is an 11. Being a 10 is more remarkable in a distribution whose scores range from 1 to 10 than it is in a distribution whose scores range from 9 to 11.

Statistics Numerical facts assembled in such a manner that they provide useful information about measures or scores (from the Latin *status,* meaning "standing" or "position").

Average The central tendency of a group of measures, expressed either as the mean, median, or mode of a distribution.

Descriptive statistics The branch of statistics concerned with providing descriptive information about a distribution of scores.

© Noel Hendrickson/Photodisc/Getty Images

Good or Bad? Being a 10 may not be such a good thing if the average score is 11.

Let's now consider some of the concerns of descriptive statistics: measures of central tendency (types of averages) and measures of variability.

Measures of Central Tendency

> *"Never try to walk across a river just because it has an average depth of four feet."*
>
> MARTIN FRIEDMAN

Truth or Fiction Revisited: A river with an average depth of 4 feet could be over your head in many places, so, as suggested in the quip by Martin Friedman, a measure of central tendency can sometimes be misleading. **Question 3: What are measures of central tendency?** Measures of central tendency are "averages" that show the center, or balancing points, of a distribution of scores or measurements. There are three commonly used types of measures of central tendency: the *mean, median,* and *mode.* Each attempts to describe something about the scores through the use of a typical, or representative, number.

THE MEAN The **mean** is what most people think of as "the average." We obtain the mean of a distribution by adding up the scores and then dividing the sum by the number of scores. Table A.1 ■ shows the rosters for a recent basketball game between the California Quakes and the New York Big Apples. The players are listed according to the numbers on their uniforms. Let's convert their heights into a single unit, such as inches (6' 1" becomes 73" and so on). If we add all the heights in inches and then divide by the number of players (22), we obtain a mean height of 78.73". If we convert that number back into units of feet and inches, we obtain 6' 6.73".

THE MEDIAN The **median** is the score of the *middle case* in a distribution. It is the score beneath which 50% of the cases fall. In a distribution with an even number of cases, such as the distribution of the heights of the 22 basketball players, we obtain the median by finding the mean of the two middle cases. When we list the 22 cases in ascending order (moving from lowest to highest), the 11th case is 6' 6" and the 12th case is 6' 7". Therefore, the median of the distribution is (6' 6" + 6' 7") / 2, or 6' 6 ½".

TABLE A.1 ■ Rosters of Quakes Versus Big Apples at New York

California Quakes		New York Big Apples	
2 Callahan	6' 7"	3 Roosevelt	6' 1"
5 Daly	6' 11"	12 Chaffee	6' 5"
6 Chico	6' 2"	13 Baldwin	6' 9"
12 Capistrano	6' 3"	25 Delmar	6' 6"
21 Brentwood	6' 5"	27 Merrick	6' 8"
25 Van Nuys	6' 3"	28 Hewlett	6' 6"
31 Clemente	6' 9"	33 Hollis	6' 9"
32 Whittier	6' 8"	42 Bedford	6' 5"
41 Fernando	7' 2"	43 Coram	6' 2"
43 Watts	6' 9"	45 Hampton	6' 10"
53 Huntington	6' 6"	53 Ardsley	6' 10"

A glance at the rosters for a recent basketball game in which the New York Big Apples "entertained" the California Quakes shows that the heights of the team members, combined, ranged from 6 feet 1 inch to 7 feet 2 inches. Do the heights of the team members represent those of the general male population? What do you think?

Measures of central tendency "Averages" that show the center or balancing points of a distribution of scores or measurements.

Mean A type of average that is calculated by adding all the scores in a distribution and then dividing the sum by the number of scores.

Median The central score in a frequency distribution; the score beneath which 50% of the cases fall.

When we analyze the heights of the basketball players, we find that the mean and median are similar. Either one serves as a useful indicator of the central tendency of the data. But suppose we are trying to find the average savings of 30 families living on a suburban block. Let's assume that 29 of the 30 families have savings between $8,000 and $12,000, adding up to $294,000. But the 30th family has savings of $1,400,000! The mean savings for a family on this block would thus be $56,467. The mean can be greatly distorted by one or two extreme scores. An IQ score of 145 would similarly distort the mean of the IQ scores of a class of 20 students, among whom the other 19 IQ scores range from 93 to 112. Then, too, if a few basketball players signed up for one of your classes, the mean of the students' heights would be distorted in an upward direction. **Truth or Fiction Revisited:** Therefore, adding people's incomes and then dividing them by the number of people can be an awful way of showing the average income. A few extremely high incomes or IQ scores or heights can distort the average of a group in an upward direction.

When there are a few extreme scores in a distribution, the median is a better indicator of central tendency. The median savings on our hypothetical block would lie between $8,000 and $12,000 and be more representative of the central tendency of savings.

THE MODE The **mode** is the most frequently occurring score or measure in a distribution. The mode of the data in Table A.1 is 6' 9" because this height occurs most often among the players on the two teams. With this particular distribution, the mode is somewhat higher than the mean or median.

In some cases, the mode is a more appropriate description of the central tendency of a distribution than the mean or the median. Figure A.1 ■ shows a **bimodal** distribution—that is, a distribution with two modes. This is a hypothetical distribution of test scores obtained by a class. The mode at the left indicates the most common class interval (45 to 49) for students who did not study, and the mode at the right shows the most common class interval (65 to 69) for students who did study. The mean and median test scores would probably lie within the 55 to 59 class interval, yet use of that interval as the measure of central tendency would obscure rather than reveal important information about this distribution of scores. It might suggest that the test was too hard, not that several students chose not to study. It is clearly best to visualize this distribution of scores as bimodal.

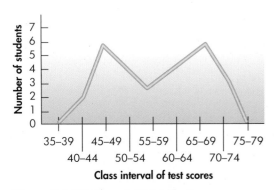

Figure A.1 ■ A Bimodal Distribution
This hypothetical distribution represents students' scores on a test. The mode at the left represents the central tendency of the test scores of students who did not study. The mode at the right represents the mode of the test scores of students who did study.

Measures of Variability

Our hypothetical class obtained test scores ranging from class intervals of 35 to 39 to class intervals of 75 to 79. That is, the scores *varied* from the lower class interval to the higher class interval. Now, if all the students had obtained scores from 55 to 59 or from 65 to 69, the scores would not have varied as much; that is, they would have clustered closer to one another and would have had lower variability.

Question 4: What are measures of variability? The measures of the variability of a distribution inform us about the spread of scores—that is, about the typical distances of scores from the average score. Two commonly used measures of variability are the *range* and the *standard deviation* of scores.

THE RANGE The **range** of scores is the difference between the highest score and the lowest score. It is obtained by subtracting the lowest score from the highest score. The range of heights in Table A.1 is obtained by subtracting 6' 1" from 7' 2", or 1' 1". It is useful to know the range of temperatures when we move to an area with a different climate so that we may anticipate the weather and dress appropriately. A teacher must have some understanding of the range of abilities or skills in a class to teach effectively. An understanding of the range of human heights can be used to design doorways, beds, and headroom in automobiles. Even so, the typical doorway is 6' 8" high; and as we saw with the California Quakes and New York Big Apples, some people will have to duck to get through.

The range is strongly influenced by extreme scores. The range of savings of the 30 families on our suburban block is $1,400,000 minus $8,000, or $1,392,000. This is a large number, and it is certainly true. However, it tells us little about the *typical* variation of savings accounts, which lies within a more restricted range of $8,000 to $12,000.

Mode The most frequently occurring number or score in a distribution.

Bimodal Having two modes.

Range A measure of variability defined as the high score in a distribution minus the low score.

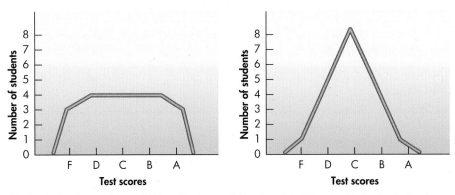

Figure A.2 ■ Hypothetical Distributions of Student Test Scores Each distribution has the same number of scores, the same mean, and even the same range, but the standard deviation (a measure of variability) is greater for the distribution on the left because the scores tend to be farther from the mean.

THE STANDARD DEVIATION The **standard deviation** does a better job of showing how the scores in a distribution are distributed (spread) about the mean. It is usually better than the range because it considers every score in the distribution, not just the highest and lowest scores. Consider Figure A.2 ■. Each distribution in the figure has the same number of scores, the same mean, and the same range of scores. However, the scores in the distribution on the right side cluster more closely about the mean. Therefore, the standard deviation of the distribution on the right is smaller. That is, the typical score deviates less from the mean score.

The standard deviation is usually abbreviated as S.D. It is calculated by the formula

$$\text{S.D.} = \sqrt{\frac{\text{Sum of } d^2}{N}}$$

where d equals the deviation of each score from the mean of the distribution and N equals the number of scores in the distribution.

FINDING THE MEAN AND STANDARD DEVIATION Let's find the mean and standard deviation of the IQ scores listed in column 1 of Table A.2 ■. To obtain the mean, we add all the scores, obtain 1,500, and then divide by the number of scores

"Statistics show that of those who contract the habit of eating, very few survive."

GEORGE BERNARD SHAW

Standard deviation A measure of the variability of a distribution, obtained by the formula

$$\text{S.D.} = \sqrt{\frac{\text{Sum of } d^2}{N}}$$

TABLE A.2 ■ Hypothetical Scores Obtained from an IQ Testing

IQ Score	d (Deviation Score)	d² (Deviation Score Squared)
85	15	225
87	13	169
89	11	121
90	10	100
93	7	49
97	3	9
97	3	9
100	0	0
101	−1	1
104	−4	16
105	−5	25
110	−10	100
112	−12	144
113	−13	169
117	−17	289
Sum of IQ scores = 1,500		Sum of d² scores = 1,426

$$\text{Mean} = \frac{\text{Sum of scores}}{\text{Number of scores}} = \frac{1{,}500}{15} = 100$$

$$\text{Standard Deviation} = \sqrt{\frac{\text{Sum of } d^2}{N}} = \sqrt{\frac{1{,}426}{15}} = \sqrt{95.07} = 9.75$$

TABLE A.3 ■ Computation of Standard Deviations for Test-Score Distributions in Figure A.3

Distribution at Left			Distribution to the Right		
Grade	d	d^2	Grade	d	d^2
A (4)	2	4	A (4)	2	4
A (4)	2	4	B (3)	1	1
A (4)	2	4	B (3)	1	1
B (3)	1	1	B (3)	1	1
B (3)	1	1	B (3)	1	1
B (3)	1	1	C (2)	0	0
B (3)	1	1	C (2)	0	0
C (2)	0	0	C (2)	0	0
C (2)	0	0	C (2)	0	0
C (2)	0	0	C (2)	0	0
C (2)	0	0	C (2)	0	0
D (1)	−1	1	C (2)	0	0
D (1)	−1	1	C (2)	0	0
D (1)	−1	1	D (1)	−1	1
D (1)	−1	1	D (1)	−1	1
F (0)	−2	4	D (1)	−1	1
F (0)	−2	4	D (1)	−1	1
F (0)	−2	4	F (0)	−2	4

Sum of grades = 36	Sum of grades = 36
Mean grade = 36 / 18 = 2	Mean grade = 36 / 18 = 2
Sum of d^2 = 32	Sum of d^2 = 16
S.D. = $\sqrt{\dfrac{32}{18}}$ = 1.33	S.D. = $\sqrt{\dfrac{16}{18}}$ = 0.94

(15) to obtain a mean of 100. We obtain the deviation score (d) for each IQ score by subtracting the score from 100. The d for an IQ score of 85 equals 100 minus 85, or 15, and so on. Then we square each d and add the squares. The S.D. equals the square root of the sum of squares (1,426) divided by the number of scores (15), or 9.75.

As an additional exercise, we can show that the S.D. of the test scores on the left (in Figure A.2) is greater than that for the scores on the right. First, we assign the grades a number according to a 4.0 system. Let A = 4, B = 3, C = 2, D = 1, and F = 0. The S.D. for each distribution is computed in Table A.3 ■. The larger S.D. for the distribution on the left indicates that the scores in that distribution are more variable, or tend to be farther from the mean.

Bell-Shaped A so-called normal curve is shaped like a bell, which is why it is also called a bell-shaped curve.

Normal distribution A symmetrical distribution that is assumed to reflect chance fluctuations, giving rise to a normal curve or bell-shaped curve.

● THE NORMAL CURVE

Many human traits and characteristics, including height and intelligence, seem to be distributed in a pattern known as a normal distribution. **Question 5: What is a normal distribution?** A **normal distribution** is a symmetrical distribution that is assumed to reflect chance fluctuations, giving rise to a bell-shaped curve. The mean, median, and mode all fall at the same score. Scores cluster most heavily about the mean, fall off rapidly in either direction at first (as shown in Figure A.3 ■), and then taper off more gradually.

Figure A.3 shows a normal distribution or bell-shaped curve. This curve is believed to represent the distribution of scores that are determined by chance variation—for example, the differences in the lengths of tosses of hundreds of baseballs by the same

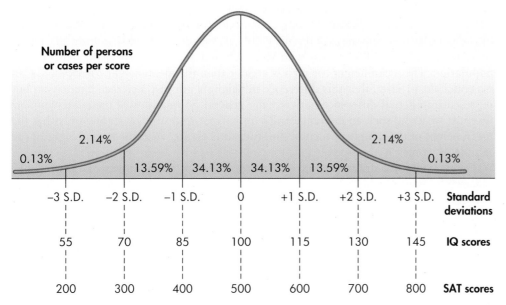

Number of persons or cases per score

| 0.13% | 2.14% | | | | | 2.14% | 0.13% |
| | | 13.59% | 34.13% | 34.13% | 13.59% | | |

	−3 S.D.	−2 S.D.	−1 S.D.	0	+1 S.D.	+2 S.D.	+3 S.D.	**Standard deviations**
IQ scores	55	70	85	100	115	130	145	
SAT scores	200	300	400	500	600	700	800	

Figure A.3 ■ A Bell-Shaped or Normal Curve In a normal curve, approximately two of three cases (68%) lie within a standard deviation (S.D.) from the mean. The mean, median, and mode all lie at the same score. IQ tests and SATs are constructed so that their distributions approximate the normal curve.

person. (We could space out the timing of the tosses so that fatigue didn't enter the picture.) People's heights are thought to be largely determined by chance combinations of genetic material, and it does happen that the distribution of the heights of a random sample of the population approximates normal distributions for men and women. The mean of the distribution for men is higher than the mean for women.

Test developers traditionally assumed that intelligence was also randomly, or normally, distributed among the population. For that reason, they constructed intelligence tests so that scores would be distributed in as close to a normal curve as possible. In actuality, IQ scores are also influenced by environmental factors and chromosomal abnormalities so that the actual curves are not quite bell-shaped. The means, or averages, of most IQ tests, including the Wechsler Intelligence Scales, are defined as scores of 100 points. That is, the average IQ is 100. The Wechsler Intelligence Scales are also constructed to have a standard deviation (S.D.) of 15 points (see Figure A.3). With a standard deviation of 15 points, 50% of the Wechsler scores fall between 90 and 110, which is called the "broad average" range of intelligence. About 68% of scores (two of three) fall between 85 and 115 (within a standard deviation of the mean). More than 95% fall between 70 and 130—that is, within two standard deviations of the mean. **Truth or Fiction Revisited:** Psychologists, therefore, may express your IQ score in terms of how "deviant" you are. Very high and very low IQ scores deviate far from the mean score.

The SAT was constructed so that the mean scores would be 500 points and the S.D. would be 100 points. Thus, a score of 600 would equal to or excel that of some 84% to 85% of the test takers. Because the variables that determine SAT scores—including intelligence, motivation, and education—are not distributed by chance, the distribution of SAT scores is not perfectly bell-shaped either. Moreover, the actual mean, or average, scores vary somewhat from year to year.

Truth or Fiction Revisited: An IQ score of 130 may therefore be more impressive than an SAT score of 500. The IQ score of 130 is two standard deviations above the mean and exceeds that of more than 97% of the population. An SAT score of 500 represents the mean SAT score and equals or excels that of 50% of the population taking the test.

"There are lies, damned lies and statistics."

MARK TWAIN

● INFERENTIAL STATISTICS

Head Start programs have apparently raised children's intellectual functioning, as reflected in their grades and IQ scores. In one such study, children enrolled in a Head Start program obtained a mean IQ score of 99, whereas children similar in background who were not enrolled in Head Start obtained a mean IQ score of 93. Is this difference of six points in IQ *significant*, or does it represent a chance fluctuation in scores?

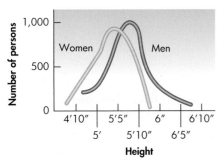

Figure A.4 ■ Distribution of Heights for Random Samples of Men and Women Note that the mean height of the men is greater than that of the women. Is the group mean difference in height statistically significant? Researchers use a tool called inferential statistics to determine the answer.

Inferential statistics The branch of statistics concerned with the confidence with which conclusions drawn about samples can be extended to the populations from which the samples were drawn.

Infer To go to the general from the particular; to draw a conclusion.

Statistically significant difference A difference between groups that is large enough so that it is unlikely to be due to chance fluctuation.

Question 6: What is inferential statistics? Inferential statistics helps us determine whether we can conclude that the differences between such samples can be generalized to the populations that they represent. Figure A.4 ■ shows the distribution of heights of 1,000 men and 1,000 women who were selected at random from the general U.S. population. The mean height for men is greater than the mean height for women. Can we conclude, or **infer**, that this difference in height is not just a chance fluctuation but represents an actual difference between the general populations of men and women? Or must we avoid such an inference and summarize our results by stating only that the mean height of the sample of men in the study was greater than the mean height of the sample of women in the study?

If we could not draw inferences about populations from studies of samples, our research findings would be limited indeed. We could speak only about the specific individuals studied. There would be no point to learning about any study in which you did not participate because it would not apply to you! Fortunately, that is not the case. Inferential statistics enables us to extend findings with samples to the populations from which they were drawn.

Statistically Significant Differences

Researchers tend not to talk about "real differences" or "actual differences" between groups. Instead, they speak of *statistically significant differences*. **Question 7: What are statistically significant differences?** Statistically significant differences are differences that are unlikely to be due to chance fluctuation. Psychologists usually do not accept a difference as statistically significant unless the probability (*p*) that it is due to chance fluctuation is less than 1 in 20 (that is, $p < .05$). They are more comfortable labeling a difference as statistically significant when the probability (*p*) that it is due to chance fluctuation is less than 1 in 100 (that is, $p < .01$).

Psychologists use formulas involving the means (for example, mean IQ scores of 93 versus 99) and the standard deviations of sample groups to determine whether differences in means are statistically significant. As you can see in Figure A.5 ■, the farther apart group means are, the more likely it is that the difference between them is statistically significant. In other words, if the men are on average 5 inches taller than the women, it is more likely that the difference is statistically significant than if men are only 0.25 inch taller on average. *Principle 1:* Everything else being equal, the greater the difference between means, the greater the probability that the difference is statistically significant. This makes common sense. After all, if you were told that your neighbor's car had gotten one-tenth of a mile more per gallon of gas than your car in the past year, you would probably attribute the difference to chance fluctuation. But if the difference were 14 miles per gallon, you would probably assume that the difference reflected an actual difference in driving habits or in the efficiency of the automobile.

As you can see in Figure A.6 ■, the smaller the standard deviations (a measure of variability) of the groups, the more likely it is that the difference between means is statistically significant. Consider the extreme example in which there is *no* variability within each group. That is, imagine that every woman in the randomly selected sample of 1,000 women is exactly 5' 5" tall. Similarly, imagine that every man in the randomly selected sample of 1,000 men is exactly 5' 10" tall. In such a case, the heights of the men and women would not overlap at all, and it would appear that the differences were statistically significant. Consider the other extreme—one with unnaturally large variability. Imagine that the heights of the women vary from 2' to 14' and that the heights of the men vary from 2' 1" to 14' 3". In such a case, we might be more

Figure A.5 ■ Decreasing and Increasing the Mean Group Difference in Heights Everything else being equal, the greater the difference in group means, the greater the probability that the difference is statistically significant. The distribution on the right shows a greater difference in group means; therefore, there is a greater probability that the difference is statistically significant.

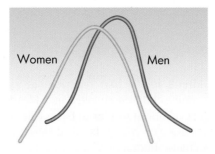

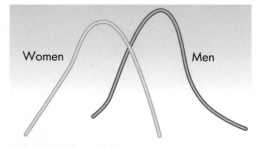

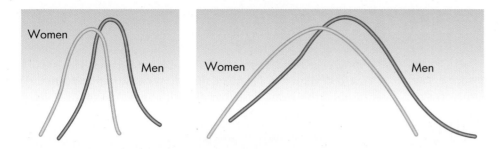

Figure A.6 ■ Decreasing and Increasing the Variability of the Distributions of Scores
Everything else being equal, the smaller the variability in group scores, the greater the probability that the difference in groups means is statistically significant. The distribution on the right shows a greater difference in the variability of the groups; therefore, there is a lower probability that the difference in group means is statistically significant.

likely to assume that the difference in group means of 5" was a chance fluctuation. *Principle 2:* Everything else being equal, the smaller the variability of the distributions of scores, the greater the probability that the difference in group means is statistically significant.

Therefore, we cannot conclude that men are taller than women unless we know the average heights of men and women and how much the heights within each group vary. We must know both the central tendencies (means) and variability of the two distributions of heights to infer that the mean heights are statistically significantly different.

We have been "eyeballing" the data and making assumptions. We have been relying on what one professor of mine called the "Wow!" effect. As noted, psychologists and other researchers actually use mathematical techniques that take group means and standard deviations into account to determine whether group differences are statistically significant. Eyeballing real data may not yield clear results or even good guesses.

1. What is statistics?
Statistics is the science that assembles data in such a way that they provide useful information about measures or scores. Such measures or scores include people's height, weight, and scores on psychological tests such as IQ tests.

2. What is descriptive statistics?
Descriptive statistics is the branch of statistics that provides information about average scores and how much scores differ from one another.

3. What are measures of central tendency?
Measures of central tendency are "averages" that show the center, or balancing points, of a frequency distribution. The mean—which is what most people consider the average—is obtained by adding the scores in a distribution and dividing by the number of scores. The median is the score of the middle, or central, case in a distribution. The mode is the most common score in a distribution.

4. What are measures of variability?
Measures of variability provide information about the spread of scores in a distribution. The range is defined as the difference between the highest and lowest scores. The standard deviation is a statistic that shows how scores cluster around the mean. Distributions with higher standard deviations are more spread out.

5. What is a normal distribution?
The normal, or bell-shaped, curve is hypothesized to occur when the scores in a distribution occur by chance. In a normal curve, approximately two of three scores (68%) are found within one standard deviation of the mean. Fewer than 5% of cases are found beyond two standard deviations from the mean.

6. What is inferential statistics?
Inferential statistics is the branch of statistics that indicates whether researchers can extend their findings with samples to the populations from which they were drawn.

7. What are statistically significant differences?
Statistically significant differences are believed to represent real differences between groups and not chance fluctuation.

KEY TERMS

Average (p. 502)
Bimodal (p. 504)
Descriptive statistics (p. 502)
Infer (p. 508)
Inferential statistics (p. 508)
Mean (p. 503)

Measures of central tendency (p. 503)
Median (p. 503)
Mode (p. 504)
Normal distribution (p. 506)
Range (p. 504)
Standard deviation (p. 505)

Statistically significant difference (p. 508)
Statistics (p. 502)

Answer Keys to Self-Assessments and Active Reviews

Answer Keys to Self-Assessments

Scoring Key for "The Social-Desirability Scale" (Chapter 1, p. 25)

Place a check mark on the appropriate line of the scoring key each time your answer agrees with the one listed. Add the check marks and record the total number of check marks below.

1. T_____	10. F_____	19. F_____	28. F_____
2. T_____	11. F_____	20. T_____	29. T_____
3. F_____	12. F_____	21. T_____	30. F_____
4. T_____	13. T_____	22. F_____	31. T_____
5. F_____	14. F_____	23. F_____	32. F_____
6. F_____	15. F_____	24. T_____	33. T_____
7. T_____	16. T_____	25. T_____	
8. T_____	17. T_____	26. T_____	
9. F_____	18. T_____	27. T_____	

Interpreting Your Score

Low Scorers (0–8). About one respondent in six earns a score between 0 and 8. Such respondents answered in a socially *undesirable* direction much of the time. Perhaps they are more willing than most people to respond to tests truthfully, even when their answers might meet with social disapproval.

Average Scorers (9–19). About two respondents in three earn a score from 9 through 19. They tend to show an average degree of concern for the social desirability of their responses, and possibly, their general behavior represents an average degree of conformity to social rules and conventions.

High Scorers (20–33). About one respondent in six earns a score between 20 and 33. These respondents may be highly concerned about social approval and respond to test items in such as way as to avoid the disapproval of people who may read their responses. Their general behavior may show high conformity to social rules and conventions.

Scoring Key for "Are You Getting Your Z's?" (Chapter 4, p. 128)

Psychologist James Maas, the author of *Power Sleep* (HarperCollins, 1999), writes that an answer of "true" to two or more of the statements in the questionnaire may be a sign of a sleep problem.

Scoring Key for "Do You Have a Problem with Alcohol?" (Chapter 4, p. 140)

As noted in Chapter 4, just one "yes" answer suggests a possible alcohol problem. Two or more "yeses" make it highly likely that a problem exists. In either case, it is advisable to discuss your answers with your doctor or another health-care provider.

Scoring Key for "Five Challenges to Your Memory" (Chapter 6, p. 184)

Answers to these challenges are discussed throughout Chapter 6.

Answer Key for "Puzzles, Problems, and Just Plain Fun" (Chapter 7, p. 223) and to the Duncker Candle Problem

You will find the answers to Problems 1a and 1b as you read along in the text. For Problem 1c, note that each of the letters is the first letter of the numbers one through eight. Therefore, the two missing letters are NT, for nine and ten.

The solutions to Problems 2 and 3 and to the Duncker candle problem are shown in the illustration here. To solve the Duncker candle problem, use the thumbtack to pin the matchbox to the wall. Then set the candle on top of the box. Functional fixedness prevents many people from conceptualizing the matchbox as anything more than a device to hold matches. Commonly given wrong answers include trying to affix the bottom of the candle to the wall with melted wax or trying to tack the candle to the wall.

You will find the answers to Problem 4 as you read along in the text.

Scoring Key for "The Remote Associates Test" (Chapter 7, p. 243)

1. Dog	4. Club	7. Black
2. Cold	5. Boat	8. Pit
3. Glasses	6. Defense	9. Writer

Scoring Key for "The Sensation-Seeking Scale" (Chapter 8, p. 263)

Because this is a shortened version of a questionnaire, no norms are available. However, answers in agreement with the following key point in the direction of sensation-seeking.

1. A	6. B	11. A
2. A	7. A	12. A
3. A	8. A	13. B
4. B	9. B	
5. A	10. A	

Scoring Key for "Eating Disorders Quiz" (Chapter 8, p. 273)

The quiz addresses only some of the signs and symptoms of an eating disorder. If you answered "yes" to any of the questions, there is a possibility that you have an eating disorder, and you may want to seek assistance. If you answered "yes" to five or more items, we strongly advise obtaining professional advice.

Scoring Key for "How Long Will You Live? The Life Expectancy Scale" (Chapter 9, p. 330)

To complete the scale, begin with the age of 72. Then add or subtract years according to the directions for each item, as explained in the text.

Scoring Key for "Will You Be a Hit or a Miss? The Expectancy for Success Scale" (Chapter 10, p. 353)

To calculate your total score for the Expectancy for Success Scale, first reverse the scores for the following items: 1, 2, 4, 6, 7, 8, 14, 15, 17, 18, 24, 27, and 28. That is, change a 1 to a 5; a 2 to a 4; leave a 3 alone; change a 4 to a 2; and a 5 to a 1. Then add the scores.

The range of total scores can vary from 30 to 150. The higher your score, the greater your expectancy for success in the future—and, according to social-cognitive theory, the more motivated you will be to apply yourself in facing difficult challenges.

Fibel and Hale administered their test to undergraduates taking psychology courses and found that women's scores ranged from 65 to 143 and men's from 81 to 138. The average score for each gender was 112 (112.32 for women and 112.15 for men).

Scoring Key for "Do You Strive to Be All That You Can Be?" (Chapter 10, p. 357)

There are no numbers here. No comparison with anyone else. Just be honest with yourself and consider the meanings of your "yes" and "no" answers.

Scoring Key for "Going Through Changes: How Stressful Is Your Life?" (Chapter 11, p. 372)

To evaluate your level of stress, select the items you have experienced during the past year. Calculate your overall stress level by adding up the ratings of the selected items. Compare your total stress rating (total score) with those of a sample of 257 introductory psychology students. The average (mean) score in the sample was 1,247. About two out of three of the students obtained stress-rating scores ranging from 806 to 1,688. Your total stress score can help you gauge how stressful your life has been during the preceding year compared to other students, but it does not reveal how stress may be affecting you and what you are doing about it.

Scoring Key for "Are You Type A or Type B?" (Chapter 11, p. 377)

Type A people are ambitious, hard driving, and chronically discontent with their current achievements. Type A people also have a sense of time urgency. Type B's, by contrast, are more relaxed and more involved with the quality of life.

"Yes" answers are suggestive of the Type A behavior pattern. In appraising your "type," you need not be overly concerned with the precise number of "yes" answers; we have no normative data for you. But as Friedman and Rosenman (1974, p. 85) note, you should have little trouble spotting yourself as "hard core" or "moderately afflicted"—that is, if you are honest with yourself.

Answer Key for "The Locus of Control Scale" (Chapter 11, p. 380)

Place a check mark in the blank space in the following scoring key each time your answer agrees with the answer in the key. The number of check marks is your total score.

Scoring Key

1. Yes ___	11. Yes ___	21. Yes ___	31. Yes ___
2. No ___	12. Yes ___	22. No ___	32. No ___
3. Yes ___	13. No ___	23. Yes ___	33. Yes ___
4. No ___	14. Yes ___	24. Yes ___	34. No ___
5. Yes ___	15. No ___	25. No ___	35. Yes ___
6. No ___	16. Yes ___	26. No ___	36. Yes ___
7. Yes ___	17. Yes ___	27. Yes ___	37. Yes ___
8. Yes ___	18. Yes ___	28. No ___	38. No ___
9. No ___	19. Yes ___	29. Yes ___	39. Yes ___
10. Yes ___	20. No ___	30. No ___	40. No ___

TOTAL SCORE _____

Interpreting Your Score

Low Scorers (0–8). About one respondent in three earns a score from 0 to 8. Such respondents tend to have an internal locus of control. They see themselves as responsible for the reinforcements they attain (and fail to attain) in life.

Average Scorers (9–16). Most respondents earn from 9 to 16 points. Average scorers may see themselves as partially in control of their lives. Perhaps they see themselves as in control at work but not in their social lives—or vice versa.

High Scorers (17–40). About 15 percent of respondents attain scores of 17 or above. High scorers tend largely to see life as a game of chance, and success as a matter of luck or the generosity of others.

Scoring Key for "Are You Depressed?" (Chapter 12, p. 413)

Rating your responses: If you agree with at least five of the statements, including either item 1 or 2, and if you have had these complaints for at least 2 weeks, professional help is strongly recommended. If you answered "yes" to statement 3, seek consultation with a professional immediately. If you don't know whom to turn to, contact your college counseling center, neighborhood mental health center, or health provider.

Scoring Key for "Do You Speak Your Mind or Wimp Out? The Assertiveness Schedule" (Chapter 13, p. 445)

Tabulate your score as follows: For those items followed by an asterisk (*), change the signs (plus to minus; minus to plus). For example, if the response to an asterisked item was 2, place a minus sign (–) before the 2. If the response to an asterisked item was 23, change the minus sign to a plus sign (+). Then add up the scores of the 30 items.

Scores on the assertiveness schedule can vary from −90 to +90. Table B.1 ■ will show you how your score compares to those of 764 college women and 637 men from 35 campuses across the United States. For example, if you are a woman and your score was 26, it exceeded that of 80% of the women in the sample. A score of 15 for a male exceeds that of 55% to 60% of the men in the sample.

TABLE B.1 ■ Percentiles for Scores on the Assertiveness Schedule

Women's Scores	Percentile	Men's Scores
55	99	65
48	97	54
45	95	48
37	90	40
31	85	33
26	80	30
23	75	26
19	70	24
17	65	19
14	60	17
11	55	15
8	50	11
6	45	8
2	40	6
−1	35	3
−4	30	1
−8	25	−3
−13	20	−7
−17	15	−11
−24	10	−15
−34	5	−24
−39	3	−30
−48	1	−41

Source: Nevid, J. S., & Rathus, S. A. (1978). Multivariate and normative data pertaining to the RAS with the college population. *Behavior Therapy, 9,* 675.

Scoring Key for "The Triangular Love Scale" (Chapter 14, p. 482)

First add your scores for the items on each of the three components—intimacy, passion, and decision/commitment—and divide each total by 15. This procedure will yield an average rating for each subscale. An average rating of 5 on a particular subscale indicates a moderate level of the component represented by the subscale. A higher rating indicates a greater level. A lower rating indicates a lower level. Examining your ratings on these components will give you an idea of the degree to which you perceive your love relationship to be characterized by these three components of love. For example, you might find that passion is stronger than decision/commitment, a pattern that is common in the early stages of an intense romantic relationship. You might find it interesting to complete the questionnaire a few months or perhaps a year or so from now to see how your feelings about your relationship change over time. You might also ask your partner to complete the scale so that the two of you can compare your scores.

Answer Keys to Active Reviews

Chapter 1 What Is Psychology?

1. Behavior
2. Predict
3. Theories
4. Pure
5. Psychotherapy
6. School
7. Developmental
8. Social
9. Experimental
10. Aristotle
11. Wilhelm Wundt
12. Functionalism
13. John B. Watson
14. Gestalt
15. Sigmund Freud
16. Evolutionary
17. Cognitive
18. Existential
19. Social
20. Mary Whiton Calkins
21. Clark
22. Skepticism
23. Conclusions
24. Populations
25. Random
26. Case
27. Survey
28. Cause
29. Independent
30. Control
31. Blind
32. Ethical
33. Informed
34. Debriefed

Chapter 2 Biology and Psychology

1. Survival
2. Fitted, adapted, suited
3. Evolutionary
4. Instincts (or fixed action patterns)
5. Genes
6. Chromosomes
7. Down
8. Identical, monozygotic
9. Neurotransmitters
10. Axon
11. Myelin
12. Synapse
13. Hippocampus
14. Schizophrenia
15. Autonomic
16. Resonance
17. Cerebellum
18. Hypothalamus
19. Callosum
20. Frontal, prefrontal
21. Left
22. Hypothalamus
23. Prolactin
24. Thyroxin
25. Medulla

Chapter 3 Sensation and Perception

1. Sensation
2. Perception
3. Absolute
4. Difference
5. Wavelength
6. Cornea
7. Lens
8. Rods, cones
9. Optic
10. Whole
11. Figure
12. Retina
13. Stroboscopic
14. Compress
15. 20,000
16. Pitch
17. Organ of Corti
18. Odor
19. Olfactory
20. Bitter
21. Taste
22. Two-point
23. More
24. Position
25. Upright
26. Semicircular canals
27. Extrasensory perception
28. Telepathy
29. File-drawer

Chapter 4 Consciousness

1. Behavior
2. Awareness
3. Freud
4. Paradoxical
5. Five
6. REM
7. Activation
8. Hypermnesia
9. Response
10. Mantra
11. Heart
12. Abuse
13. Abstinence (or withdrawal)
14. More
15. Attention
16. Cocaine
17. Nicotine
18. Hallucinogenic

Chapter 5 Learning

1. Behavior
2. Represent
3. Stimulus
4. Unconditioned
5. Conditioned
6. Extinguish
7. Spontaneous
8. Discrimination
9. Albert
10. Flooding
11. Effect
12. Reinforcement
13. Positive
14. Secondary
15. Extinction
16. Discriminative
17. Fixed-interval
18. Programmed
19. Cognitive
20. Latent
21. Contingency

Chapter 6 Memory

1. Explicit
2. Episodic (or autobiographical)
3. Semantic
4. Encoding
5. Maintenance
6. Elaborative
7. Sensory, short-term, long-term
8. Eidetic
9. Serial
10. Interference
11. Flashbulb
12. Tip
13. Sharply
14. Retroactive
15. Proactive
16. Hippocampus
17. Synapses
18. Serotonin
19. New
20. Thalamus

Chapter 7 Thinking, Language, and Intelligence

1. Concepts
2. Algorithm
3. Heuristic
4. Mental
5. Insight
6. Have
7. Grammar
8. Linguistic
9. Holophrases
10. Overregularization
11. Acquisition
12. *g*
13. Multiple
14. Practical
15. Intelligence quotient
16. Wechsler

Chapter 8 Motivation and Emotion

1. Motives
2. Deprivation
3. Incentive
4. Evolutionary, ethological
5. Homeostasis
6. Deprivation
7. Self-actualization
8. Stomach
9. Ventromedial
10. Blood
11. Anorexia
12. Bulimia
13. Testosterone
14. Excitement
15. Organizing
16. Orientation
17. Do
18. Hypothalamus
19. Testosterone
20. Appraise, interpret
21. Apperception
22. Performance
23. Universal
24. Do
25. Action
26. Cognitive

Chapter 9 The Voyage Through the Life Span

1. Longitudinal
2. Cross-sectional
3. Cohort
4. Ovulation
5. Placenta
6. Fetal
7. Oxygen
8. Reflexes
9. Concrete (or formal)
10. Zone
11. Initial-preattachment
12. Contact
13. Secondary
14. Formal
15. Imaginary
16. Universal
17. Diffusion
18. Affluent
19. Yes and no
20. More
21. Less
22. Crystallized
23. Fluid
24. Do not
25. Sandwich
26. Programmed
27. Increases
28. Is not
29. Compensate
30. Denial
31. Terminally

Chapter 10 Personality: Theory and Measurement

1. Id
2. Ego
3. Superego
4. Anal
5. Collective
6. Inferiority
7. Horney
8. Traits
9. Stability, instability
10. Conscientiousness
11. Antisocial
12. Social
13. Situational
14. Are
15. Actualization
16. Reference
17. Individualists
18. Collectivists
19. Highest
20. Behavior
21. Objective
22. True
23. Ambiguous
24. Rorschach

Chapter 11 Stress, Health, and Coping

1. Hassles
2. Adjustment, adaptation, coping
3. Conflict
4. Ellis
5. Higher
6. Commitment
7. Decreases
8. Alarm
9. Fight-or-flight
10. Corticosteroids, steroids
11. Befriend
12. Adrenaline, epinephrine
13. Immune
14. Migraine
15. Cholesterol
16. Play

Chapter 12 Psychological Disorders

1. Possession
2. Medical
3. Perception
4. Biopsychosocial
5. Phobia
6. Panic
7. Compulsive
8. Do
9. Amnesia
10. Identity
11. Abuse
12. Somatoform
13. Conversion
14. Major
15. Elation
16. Flight
17. Helplessness
18. Internal
19. Do
20. Serotonin
21. Delusions
22. Catatonic
23. Does
24. Fewer
25. Dopamine
26. Personality
27. Lower

Chapter 13 Methods of Therapy

1. Psychological
2. Decreased
3. Unconscious
4. Catharsis, abreaction
5. Free
6. Dreams
7. Humanistic
8. Nondirective
9. Directive
10. Learning
11. Desensitization
12. Operant
13. Functional
14. Consequences
15. Cognitive, cognitive-behavioral
16. Absolutist
17. Irrational
18. Systems
19. About as
20. Meta
21. Is
22. Minor
23. Dopamine
24. Serotonin
25. Depression
26. Prefrontal

Chapter 14 Social Psychology

1. Attitude
2. Cognitive
3. Cognitive
4. Dissonance
5. Discrimination
6. Categorization
7. High
8. Attraction-similarity
9. Passion
10. Romantic
11. Primacy
12. Attribution
13. Do
14. Social
15. 75
16. Facilitation
17. Decision
18. More
19. Unrealistic
20. Deindividuation
21. Altruism
22. Bystander

References

A

Abbey, A. (1987). Misperceptions of friendly behavior as sexual interest. *Psychology of Women Quarterly, 11*, 173–194.

Abele, S., & Diehl, M. (2008). Finding teammates who are not prone to sucker and free-rider effects: The Protestant work ethic as a moderator of motivation losses in group performance. *Group Processes and Intergroup Relations, 11*(1), 39–54.

Aboa-Éboulé, C., et al. (2007). Job strain and risk of acute recurrent coronary heart disease events. *Journal of the American Medical Association, 298*, 1652–1660.

Abraham, C. (2002). *Possessing genius: The bizarre odyssey of Einstein's brain*. New York: St. Martin's Press.

Acevedo, A., & Loewenstein, D. A. (2007). Nonpharmacological cognitive interventions in aging and dementia. *Journal of Geriatric Psychiatry and Neurology, 20*(4), 239–249.

Ackard, D. M., Fulkerson, J. A., & Neumark-Sztainer, D. (2007). Prevalence and utility of *DSM-IV* eating disorder diagnostic criteria among youth. *International Journal of Eating Disorders, 40*(5), 409–417.

Adams, A. L., Doucette, T. A., James, R., & Ryan, C. L. (2009). Persistent changes in learning and memory in rats following neonatal treatment with domoic acid. *Physiology and Behavior, 96*(4–5), 505–512.

Adams, G. R., Berzonsky, M. D., & Keating, L. (2006). Psychosocial resources in first-year university students: The role of identity processes and social relationships. *Journal of Youth and Adolescence, 35*(1), 81–91.

Adams, H., & Phillips, L. (2006). Experiences of two-spirit and gay Native Americans: An argument for standpoint theory in identity research. *Identity, 6*(3), 273–291.

Adler, A. (2005, May 2). Educator Kenneth Clark and his fight for integration. *National Public Radio*. Retrieved from http://www.npr.org/templates/story/story.php?storyId=4627755

Agras, W. S., Walsh, T., Fairburn, C. G., Wilson, G. T., & Kraemer, H. C. (2000). A multicenter comparison of cognitive-behavioral therapy and interpersonal psychotherapy for bulimia nervosa. *Archives of General Psychiatry, 57*(5), 459–466.

Agrawal, A., Silberg, J. L., Lynskey, M. T., Maes, H. H., & Eaves, L. J. (2010). Mechanisms underlying the lifetime co-occurrence of tobacco and cannabis use in adolescent and young adult twins. *Drug and Alcohol Dependence, 108*(1–2), 49–55.

Ahs, F., et al. (2009). Disentangling the web of fear: Amygdala reactivity and functional connectivity in spider and snake phobia. *Psychiatry Research, 172*(2), 103–108.

Aich, P., Potter, A. A., & Griebel, P. J. (2009). Modern approaches to understanding stress and disease susceptibility: A review with special emphasis on respiratory disease. *International Journal of General Medicine, 2*, 19–32.

Ainsworth, M. D. S., & Bowlby, J. (1991). An ethological approach to personality development. *American Psychologist, 46*, 333–341.

Ainsworth, M. D. S., Blehar, M. C., Waters, E., & Wall, S. (1978). *Patterns of attachment: A psychological study of the strange situation*. Hillsdale, NJ: Erlbaum.

Ajdacic-Gross, V., et al. (2008). Suicide after bereavement. *Psychological Medicine, 38*(5), 673–676.

Akerstedt, T., Kecklund, G., & Hoerte, L. (2001). Night driving, season, and the risk of highway accidents. *Sleep: Journal of Sleep and Sleep Disorders Research, 24*(4), 401–406.

Akman, Y. (2007). Identity status of Turkish university students in relation to their evaluation of family problems. *Social Behavior and Personality, 35*(1), 79–88.

Alarcón, R., et al. (2009). Issues for *DSM-V*: The role of culture in psychiatric diagnosis. *Journal of Nervous and Mental Disease, 197*(8), 559–660.

Alberts, A., Elkind, D., & Ginsberg, S. (2007). The personal fable and risk-taking in early adolescence. *Journal of Youth and Adolescence, 36*(1), 71–76.

Alexander, C. N., et al. (1996). Trial of stress reduction for hypertension in older African Americans: II. Sex and risk subgroup analysis. *Hypertension, 28*, 228–237.

Alexander, G. M., Wilcox, T., & Woods, R. (2009). Sex differences in infants' visual interest in toys. *Archives of Sexual Behavior, 38*(3), 427–433.

Allen, J. P., & Antonishak, J. (2008). Adolescent peer influences: Beyond the dark side. In M. J. Prinstein & K. A. Dodge (Eds.), *Understanding peer influence in children and adolescents* (pp. 141–160). New York: Guilford.

Allport, G. W., & Odbert, H. S. (1936). Traitnames: A psycholexical study. *Psychological Monographs, 47*, 211.

Almeida, D. M., & Horn, M. C. (2004). Is daily life more stressful during middle adulthood? In O. G. Brim, C. D. Ryff, & R. C. Kessler (Eds.), *How healthy are we? A national study of well-being at midlife* (pp. 425–451). *The John D. and Catherine T. MacArthur Foundation series on mental health and development. Studies on successful midlife development*. Chicago: University of Chicago Press.

Altgassen, M., Kliegel, M., & Martin, M. (2008). Event-based prospective memory in depression: The impact of cue focality. *Cognition and Emotion, 23*(6), 1041–1055.

Altman, S. E., & Shankman, S. A. (2009). What is the association between obsessive-compulsive disorder and eating disorders? *Clinical Psychology Review, 29*(7), 638–646.

Altran, S. (2006). Genesis and future of suicide terrorism. http://www.interdisciplines.org/terrorism/papers/1. Accessed May 2006.

Amanatullah, E. T., & Morris, M. W. (2010). Negotiating gender roles: Gender differences in assertive negotiating are mediated by women's fear of backlash and attenuated when negotiating on behalf of others. *Journal of Personality and Social Psychology, 98*(2), 256–267.

Ambach, W., Bursch, S., Stark, R., & Vaitl, D. (2010). A concealed information test with multimodal measurement. *International Journal of Psychophysiology, 75*(3), 258–267.

Ambrosius, U., et al. (2008). Heritability of sleep electroencephalogram. *Biological Psychiatry, 64*(4), 344–348.

America's Children. (2007). Centers for Disease Control and Prevention. National Center for Health Statistics. Childstats.gov. *America's children: Key national indicators of well-being, 2007*. Adolescent births. Indicator Fam6: Birth Rates for Females Ages 15–17 by Race and Hispanic Origin, 1980–2005. Available at http://www.childstats.gov/americaschildren/ famsoc6.asp

American Cancer Society. (2010). http://www.cancer.org/

American Lung Association. (2003). Retrieved from http:/www.lungusa.org

American Lung Association. (2010). *Smoking*. Retrieved from http://www.lungusa.org/stop-smoking/about-smoking/health-effects/smoking.html

American Psychiatric Association. (2000). *Diagnostic and statistical manual of mental disorders* (4th ed., text revision). *DSM–IV–TR*. Washington, DC: Author.

American Psychological Association. (1998, March 16). Sexual harassment: Myths and realities. *APA Public Information Home Page*. Retrieved from http://www.apa.org

American Psychological Association. (2002). Ethical principles of psychologists and code of conduct. *American Psychologist, 57*(12), 1060–1073.

American Psychological Association. (2008). Award for distinguished scientific contributions: Michael S. Gazzaniga. *American Psychologist, 63*(8), 636–638.

American Psychological Association. (2009a). *Doctoral psychology workforce fast facts. Health service provider subfields.* Center for Workforce Studies. Retrieved from http://research.apa.org/fastfacts-09.pdf

American Psychological Association. (2009b). *Model legislation for prescriptive authority. Approved by APA Council of Representatives, 2009.* Washington, DC: Author.

American Psychological Association. (2009c). Stress in America 2009: Executive summary. Retrieved from http://www.apa.org/news/press/releases/stress-exec-summary.pdf

American Psychological Association. (2009d). Award for Distinguished Contributions to Research in Public Policy: Charlotte J. Patterson. *American Psychologist, 64*(8), 725–736.

Amodio, D. M., & Showers, C. J. (2005). "Similarity breeds liking" revisited: The moderating role of commitment. *Journal of Social and Personal Relationships, 22*(6), 817–836.

Amstadter, A. B., Broman-Fulks, J., Zinzow, H., Ruggiero, K. J., & Cercone, J. (2009). Internet-based interventions for traumatic stress-related mental health problems: A review and suggestion for future research. *Clinical Psychology Review, 29*(5), 410–420.

Ances, B. M. (2002). New concerns about thalidomide. *Obstetrics & Gynecology, 99*, 125–128.

Anchin, J. C., & Pincus, A. L. (2010). Evidence-based interpersonal psychotherapy with personality disorders: Theory, components, and strategies. In J. J. Magnavita (Ed.), *Evidence-based treatment of personality dysfunction: Principles, methods, and processes* (pp. 113–166). Washington, DC: American Psychological Association.

Andersen, A. E., & Ryan, G. L. (2009). Eating disorders in the obstetric and gynecologic patient population. *Obstetrics and Gynecology, 114*(6), 1353–1367.

Andersen, B. L. (2002). Biobehavioral outcomes following psychological interventions for cancer patients. *Journal of Consulting and Clinical Psychology, 70*(3), 590–610.

Andersen, B. L., et al. (2008). Psychologic intervention improves survival for breast cancer patients. *Cancer, 113*(12), 3450–3458.

Andersen, B. L., Kiecolt-Glaser, J. K., & Glaser, R. (1994). A biobehavioral model of cancer stress and disease course. *American Psychologist, 49*, 389–404.

Andersen, M. L., & Taylor, H. H. (2009). *Sociology: The essentials* (5th ed.). Belmont, CA: Wadsworth.

Anderson, C. A., et al. (2008). Longitudinal effects of violent video games on aggression in Japan and the United States. *Pediatrics, 122*(5), e1067–e1072.

Anderson, C. A., et al. (2010). Violent video game effects on aggression, empathy, and prosocial behavior in Eastern and Western countries: A meta-analytic review. *Psychological Bulletin, 136*(2), 151–173.

Anderson, P. (2002). Assessment and development of executive function (EF) during childhood. *Child Neuropsychology, 8*(2), 71–82.

Andreano, J. M., & Cahill, L. (2009). Sex influences on the neurobiology of learning and memory. *Learning and Memory, 16*, 248–266.

Andrews, B. (1998). Self-esteem. *Psychologist, 11*(7), 339–342.

Andrews, J. A., Tildesley, E., Hops, H., & Li, F. (2002). The influence of peers on young adult substance use. *Health Psychology, 21*(4), 349–357.

Ansell, E. B., et al. (2010). The prevalence and structure of obsessive-compulsive personality disorder in Hispanic psychiatric outpatients. *Journal of Behavior Therapy and Experimental Psychiatry, 41*(3), 275–281.

Antoni, M. H., & Lutgendorf, S. (2007). Psychosocial factors and disease progression in cancer. *Current Directions in Psychological Science, 16*(1), 42–46.

Antonuccio, D. (1995). Psychotherapy for depression: No stronger medicine. *American Psychologist, 50*, 452–454.

Apovian, C. M. (2010). The causes, prevalence, and treatment of obesity revisited in 2009: What have we learned so far? *American Journal of Clinical Nutrition, 91*(1), 277S–279S.

Aquilino, W. S. (2005). Impact of family structure on parental attitudes toward the economic support of adult children over the transition to adulthood. *Journal of Family Issues, 26*(2), 143–167.

Archer, J. (2000). Sex differences in aggression between heterosexual partners: A meta-analytic review. *Psychological Bulletin, 126*(5), 651–680.

Archer, J. (2009). The nature of human aggression. *International Journal of Law and Psychiatry, 32*(4), 202–208.

Archer, J., & Parker, S. (2006). Social representations of aggression in children. *Aggressive Behavior, 20*(2), 101–114.

Archer, R. P., Buffington-Vollum, J. K., Stredny, R. V., & Handel, R. W. (2006). A survey of psychological test use patterns among forensic psychologists. *Journal of Personality Assessment, 87*(1), 84–94.

Archer, S. L., & Grey, J. A. (2009). The sexual domain of identity. *Identity: An International Journal of Theory and Research, 9*(1), 33–62.

Ardelt, M. (2008). Wisdom, religiosity, purpose in life, and death attitudes of aging adults. In A. Tomer, G. T. Eliason, T. Grafton, & P. T. P. Wong (Eds.), *Existential and spiritual issues in death attitudes* (pp. 139–158). Mahwah, NJ: Erlbaum.

Ardrey, R. (1961). *African genesis: A personal investigation into the animal origins and nature of man.* London: Collins.

Arendt, J. (2000). Melatonin, circadian rhythms, and sleep. *New England Journal of Medicine online, 343*(15).

Arendt, J. (2009). Managing jet lag: Some of the problems and possible new solutions. *Sleep Medicine Reviews, 13*(4), 249–256.

Arias, E., Rostron, B. L., & Tejada-Vera, B. (2010). United States life tables, 2005. *National Vital Statistics Report, 58*(10). Hyattsville, MD: National Center for Health Statistics. Retrieved from http://198.246.98.21/nchs/data/nvsr/nvsr58/nvsr58_10.pdf

Arnett, J. J. (2000). Emerging adulthood. *American Psychologist, 55*(5), 469–480.

Arnett, J. J. (2007). Socialization in emerging adulthood: From the family to the wider world, from socialization to self-socialization. In J. E. Grusec & P. D. Hastings (Eds.), *Handbook of socialization: Theory and research* (pp. 208–231). New York: Guilford.

Arnett, J. J., & Brody, G. H. (2008). A fraught passage: The identity challenges of African American emerging adults. *Human Development, 51*(5–6), 291–293.

Arroyo, J. A., Miller, W. R., & Tonigan, J. S. (2003). The influence of Hispanic ethnicity on long-term outcome in three alcohol-treatment modalities. *Journal of Studies on Alcohol, 64*(1), 98–104.

Arthritis Foundation. (2000, April 6). *Pain in America: Highlights from a Gallup survey.* Retrieved from http://www.arthritis.org/answers/sop_factsheet.asp

Artigas, F. (2008). Serotonin receptors: Role in depression. *Actas Españolas de Psiquiatría, 36*(Suppl. 1), 28–30.

Asch, S. E. (1952). *Social psychology*. Englewood Cliffs, NJ: Prentice Hall.

Ash, D. (2004). Reflective scientific sense-making dialogue in two languages: The science in the dialogue and the dialogue in the science. *Science Education, 88*(6), 855–884.

Ashtari, M., et al. (2009). Diffusion abnormalities in adolescents and young adults with a history of heavy cannabis use. *Journal of Psychiatric Research, 43*(3), 189–204.

Ashton, A. K., et al. (2000). Antidepressant-induced sexual dysfunction and *Ginkgo biloba. American Journal of Psychiatry, 157,* 836–837.

Ashworth, P. C. H., Davidson, K. M., & Espie, C. A. (2010). Cognitive-behavioral factors associated with sleep quality in chronic pain patients. *Behavioral Sleep Medicine, 8*(1), 28–39. Retrieved from http://www.informaworld.com/smpp/title-db=all-content=t775648093-tab=issueslist-branches=8-v8

Atkins, M. S., et al. (2002). Suspensions and detention in an urban, low-income school: Punishment or reward? *Journal of Abnormal Child Psychology, 30*(4), 361–371.

Atkinson, R. C. (1975). Mnemotechnics in second-language learning. *American Psychologist, 30,* 821–828.

Atkinson, R. C., & Shiffrin, R. M. (1968). Human memory: A proposed system and its control processes. In K. Spence (Ed.), *The psychology of learning and motivation* (Vol. 2). New York: Academic Press.

Auyeung, B., et al. (2009). Fetal testosterone predicts behavior in girls and in boys. *Psychological Science, 20*(2), 144–148.

Aviezer, O., & Sagi-Schwartz, A. (2008). Attachment and non-maternal care: Towards contextualizing the quantity versus quality debate. *Attachment and Human Development, 10*(3), 275–285.

Ayllon, T., & Haughton, E. (1962). Control of the behavior of schizophrenic patients by food. *Journal of the Experimental Analysis of Behavior, 5,* 343–352.

Azar, B. (2002). At the frontier of science. *Monitor on Psychology online, 33*(1).

B

Babb, B., Danziger, G., & Moran, J. (2009). Substance abuse and addiction in family courts [Special issue]. *Family Court Review, 204.*

Babyak, M., et al. (2000). Exercise treatment for major depression: Maintenance of therapeutic benefit at 10 months. *Psychosomatic Medicine, 62*(5), 633–638.

Back, S. E., et al. (2008). Early life trauma and sensitivity to current life stressors in individuals with and without cocaine dependence. *American Journal of Drug and Alcohol Abuse, 34*(4), 389–396.

Baddeley, A. (1982). *Your memory: A user's guide.* New York: Macmillan.

Bae, S., Holloway, S. D., Li, J., & Bempechat, J. (2008). Mexican-American students' perceptions of teachers' expectations: Do perceptions differ depending on student achievement levels? *Urban Review, 40*(2), 210–225.

Baer, H., Allen, S., & Braun, L. (2000). Knowledge of human papillomavirus infection among young adult men and women: Implications for health education and research. *Journal of Community Health: Publication for Health Promotion and Disease Prevention, 25*(1), 67–78.

Bagchi, D., & Preuss, H. G. (2007). *Obesity: Epidemiology, pathophysiology, and prevention.* Boca Raton, FL: CRC Press.

Bahrick, H. P., Bahrick, P. O., & Wittlinger, R. P. (1975). Fifty years of memory for names and faces. *Journal of Experimental Psychology: General, 104,* 54–75.

Bahrick, H. P., Hall, L. K., & Da Costa, L. A. (2008). Fifty years of memory of college grades: Accuracy and distortions. *Emotion, 8*(1), 13–22.

Bajor, J. K., & Baltes, P. B. (2003). The relationship between selection optimization with compensation, conscientiousness, motivation, and performance. *Journal of Vocational Behavior, 63*(3), 347–367.

Baker, J. H., et al. (2009). Genetic risk factors for disordered eating in adolescent males and females. *Journal of Abnormal Psychology, 118*(3), 576–586.

Baker, L. A., DeFries, J. C., & Fulker, D. W. (1983). Longitudinal stability of cognitive ability in the Colorado adoption project. *Child Development, 54,* 290–297.

Baker, M. C. (2001). *The atoms of language: The mind's hidden rules of grammar.* New York: Basic Books.

Bakst, S., Rabinowitz, J., & Bromet, E. (2009). Is premorbid functioning a risk factor for suicide attempts in first-admission psychosis? *Schizophrenia Research, 116*(2), 210–216.

Baldwin, S. A., Wampold, B. E., & Imel, Z. E. (2007). Untangling the alliance–outcome correlation: Exploring the relative importance of therapist and patient variability in alliance. *Journal of Consulting and Clinical Psychology, 75,* 842–852.

Balsam, K. F., Huang, B., Fieland, K. C., Simoni, J. M., & Walters, K. L. (2004). *Cultural Diversity and Ethnic Minority Psychology, 10*(3), 287–301.

Balsam, P. D., Fairhurst, S., & Gallistel, C. R. (2006). Pavlovian contingencies and temporal information. *Journal of Experimental Psychology: Animal Behavior Processes, 32,* 284–294.

Balter & C. S. Tamis-LeMonda (Eds.) (2006). Child psychology: *A handbook of contemporary issues* (2nd ed.) (pp. 53–77). New York: Psychology Press.

Baltes, M., & Carstensen, L. L. (2003). The process of successful aging: Selection, optimization and compensation. In U. M. Staudinger, & U. Lindenberger (Eds.), *Understanding human development: Dialogues with lifespan psychology* (pp. 81–104). Dordrecht, Netherlands: Kluwer Academic Publishers.

Baltes, P. B., & Baltes, M. M. (1990). Psychological perspectives on successful aging: The model of selective optimization with compensation. In P. B. Baltes & M. M. Baltes (Eds.), *Successful aging: Perspectives from the behavioral sciences* (pp. 1–34). New York: Cambridge University Press.

Baltes, P. B., & Staudinger, U. M. (2000). Wisdom: A metaheuristic (pragmatic) to orchestrate mind and virtue toward excellence. *American Psychologist, 55,* 122–136.

Banaji, M. R., & Heiphetz, L. (2008). Attitudes. In S. T. Fiske, D. T. Gilbert, & G. Lindzey (Eds.), *Handbook of social psychology* (5th ed., Vol. 1., pp. 353–393). Hoboken, NJ: Wiley.

Bandelow, B., et al. (2000). Salivary cortisol in panic attacks. *American Journal of Psychiatry, 157,* 454–456.

Bandura, A. (1986). *Social foundations of thought and action: A social-cognitive theory.* Englewood Cliffs, NJ: Prentice Hall.

Bandura, A. (1999). Social cognitive theory: An agentic perspective. *Asian Journal of Social Psychology, 2*(1), 21–41.

Bandura, A. (2008). An agentic perspective on positive psychology. In S. J. Lopez (Ed.), *Positive psychology: Discovering human strengths* (pp. 167–214). Santa Barbara, CA: ABC-CLIO.

Bandura, A., & Locke, E. A. (2003). Negative self-efficacy and goal effects revisited. *Journal of Applied Psychology, 88*(1), 87–99.

Bandura, A., Barbaranelli, C., Vittorio Caprara, G., & Pastorelli, C. (2001). Self-efficacy beliefs as shapers of children's aspirations and career trajectories. *Child Development, 72*(1), 187–206.

Bandura, A., Blanchard, E. B., & Ritter, B. (1969). The relative efficacy of desensitization and modeling approaches for inducing behavioral, affective, and cognitive changes. *Journal of Personality and Social Psychology, 13,* 173–199.

Bandura, A., Ross, S. A., & Ross, D. (1963). Imitation of film-mediated aggressive models. *Journal of Abnormal and Social Psychology, 66,* 3–11.

Bandura, A., Taylor, C. B., Williams, S. L., Medford, I. N., & Barchas, J. D. (1985). Catecholamine secretion as a function of perceived coping self-efficacy. *Journal of Consulting and Clinical Psychology, 53,* 406–414.

Barak, A., Boniel-Nissim, M., & Suler, J. (2008). Fostering empowerment in online support groups. *Computers in Human Behavior, 24*(5), 1867–1883.

Barber, J. G. (2001). Relative misery and youth suicide. *Australian and New Zealand Journal of Psychiatry, 35*(1), 49–57.

Barber, T. A., Meyers, R. A., & McGettigan, B. F. (2010). Memantine improves memory for taste-avoidance learning in day-old chicks exposed to isolation stress. *Pharmacology Biochemistry and Behavior, 95*(2), 203–208.

Barber, T. X. (2000). A deeper understanding of hypnosis: Its secrets, its nature, its essence. *American Journal of Clinical Hypnosis, 42*(3–4), 208–272.

Barbey, A. K., & Barsalou, L. W. (2009). Reasoning and problem solving: Models. *Encyclopedia of Neuroscience, 8,* 35–43.

Barbosa, P., Torres, H., Silva, M. A., & Khan, N. (2010). Agapé Christian reconciliation conversations: Exploring the intersections of culture, religiousness, and homosexual identity in Latino and European Americans. *Journal of Homosexuality, 57*(1), 98–116.

Bard, P. (1934). The neurohumoral basis of emotional reactions. In C. A. Murchison (Ed.), *Handbook of general experimental psychology.* Worcester, MA: Clark University Press.

Barelli, C., Heistermann, M., Boesch, C., & Reichard, U. H. (2008). Mating patterns and sexual swellings in pair-living and multiple groups of wild white-handed gibbons, *Hylobates lar. Animal Behaviour, 75*(3), 991–1001.

Barlow, D. H., Gorman, J. M., Shear, M. K., & Woods, S. W. (2000). Cognitive-behavioral therapy, imipramine, or their combination for panic disorder: A randomized controlled trial. *Journal of the American Medical Association, 283,* 2529–2536.

Barnett, J. E., & Dunning, C. (2003). Clinical perspectives on elderly sexuality. *Archives of Sexual Behavior, 32*(3), 295–296.

Baron, R. A., Branscombe, N. R., & Byrne, D. R. (2009). *Social psychology* (12th ed.). Boston: Allyn & Bacon.

Baron-Cohen, S., & Belmonte, M. K. (2005). Autism: A window onto the development of the social and the analytic brain. *Annual Review of Neuroscience, 28,* 109–126.

Barr, R. G., Paterson, J. A., MacMartin, L. M., Lehtonen, L., & Young, S. N. (2005). Prolonged and unsoothable crying bouts in infants with and without colic. *Journal of Developmental & Behavioral Pediatrics, 26*(1), 14–23.

Bartels, M., Rietveld, M. J. H., Van Baal, G. C. M., & Boomsma, D. I. (2002). Genetic and environmental influences on the development of intelligence. *Behavior Genetics, 32*(4), 237–249.

Bartone, P. T., et al. (2008). Psychological hardiness predicts success in U.S. Army special forces candidates. *International Journal of Selection and Assessment, 16*(1), 78–81.

Bartoshuk, L. M. (2000). Psychophysical advances aid the study of genetic variation in taste. *Appetite, 34*(1), 105.

Basch, M. F. (1980). *Doing psychotherapy.* New York: Basic Books.

Batchat, L. (2010). Crying babies. *InnovAiT, 3*(2), 95–101.

Bates, D. D. (2010). Once-married African-American lesbians and bisexual women: Identity development and the coming out process. *Journal of Homosexuality, 57*(2), 197–225.

Batson, C. D., & Ahmad, N. Y. (2009). Empathy-induced altruism: A threat to the collective good. *Advances in Group Processes, 26,* 1–23.

Batson, C. D., Qian, Z., & Lichter, D. T. (2006). Interracial and intraracial patterns of mate selection among America's diverse Black populations. *Journal of Marriage and the Family, 68,* 658–672.

Baucom, D. H., Epstein, N. B., LaTaillade, J. J., & Kirby, J. S. (2002). Cognitive-behavioral couple therapy. In A. S. Gurman (Ed.), *Handbook of couple therapy* (pp. 31–72). New York: Guilford Press.

Baumrind, D. (1989). Rearing competent children. In W. Damon (Ed.), *Child development today and tomorrow.* San Francisco: Jossey-Bass.

Baumrind, D. (2005). Taking a stand in a morally pluralistic society: Constructive obedience and responsible dissent in moral/character education. In L. Nucci (Ed.), *Conflict, contradiction, and contrarian elements in moral development and education* (pp. 21–50). Mahwah, NJ: Erlbaum.

Baumrind, D., Larzelere, R. E., & Cowan, P. A. (2002). Ordinary physical punishment: Is it harmful? Comment on Gershoff (2002). *Psychological Bulletin, 128*(4), 580–589.

Baynes, K., & Gazzaniga, M. S. (2000). Callosal disconnection. In M. J. Farah & T. E. Feinberg (Eds.), *Patient-based approaches to cognitive neuroscience. Issues in clinical and cognitive neuropsychology* (pp. 327–333). Cambridge, MA: MIT Press.

Bear, R. E., Fitzgerald, P., Rosenfeld, J. V., & Bittar, R. G. (2010). Neurosurgery for obsessive–compulsive disorder: Contemporary approaches. *Journal of Clinical Neuroscience, 17*(1), 1–5.

Beck, A. T. (2000). Cited in Chamberlin, J. (2000). An historic meeting of the minds. *Monitor on Psychology, 31*(9), 27.

Beck, A. T., & Alford, B. A. (Eds.). (2009). *Depression: Causes and treatment* (2nd ed.). Philadelphia: University of Pennsylvania Press.

Beck, A. T., et al. (2001). Dysfunctional beliefs discriminate personality disorders. *Behaviour Research and Therapy, 39*(10), 1213–1225.

Beck, D. R. M. (2010). Collecting among the Menomini: Cultural assault in twentieth-century Wisconsin. *American Indian Quarterly, 34*(2). doi:10.1353/aiq.0.0103

Beck, H. P., Levinson, S., & Irons, G. (2009). Finding Little Albert: A journey to John B. Watson's infant laboratory. *American Psychologist, 64*(7), 605–614.

Beesdo, K., et al. (2010). Incidence and risk patterns of anxiety and depressive disorders and categorization of generalized anxiety disorder. *Archives of General Psychiatry, 67*(1), 47–57.

Begley, S., & Check, E. (2000, August 5). Sex and the single fly. *Newsweek,* pp. 44–45.

Behar, E., et al. (2009). Current theoretical models of generalized anxiety disorder (GAD): Conceptual review and treatment implications. *Journal of Anxiety Disorders, 23*(8), 1011–1023.

Bell, M. A., Wolfe, C. D., & Adkins, D. R. (2007). Frontal lobe development during infancy and childhood. In D. Coch et al. (Eds.), *Human behavior, learning, and the developing brain* (pp. 247–276). New York: Guilford.

Bell, S. M., & Ainsworth, M. D. S. (1972). Infant crying and maternal responsiveness. *Child Development, 43*(4), 1171–1190.

Belsky, J. (1990a). Developmental risks associated with infant day care: Attachment insecurity, noncompliance and aggression? In S. Cherazi (Ed.), *Psychosocial issues in day care.* New York: American Psychiatric Press.

Belsky, J. (1990b). The "effects" of infant day care reconsidered. In N. Fox & G. G. Fein (Eds.), *Infant day care: The current debate.* Norwood, NJ: Ablex.

Belsky, J. (2001). Emanuel Miller Lecture: Developmental risks (still) associated with early child care. *Journal of Child Psychology and Psychiatry and Allied Disciplines, 42*(7), 845–859.

Belsky, J. (2006a). Determinants and consequences of infant–parent attachment. In L. Bender et al. (2007). Use of harsh physical discipline and developmental outcomes in adolescence. *Development and Psychopathology, 19*(1) 227–242.

Belsky, J. (2006b). Early child care and early child development: Major findings of the NICHD Study of Early Child Care. *European Journal of Developmental Psychology, 3*(1), 95–110.

Belsky, J. (2009). Classroom composition, childcare history and social development: Are childcare effects disappearing or spreading? *Social Development, 18*(1), 230–238.

Belsky, J., & Pluess, M. (2009). Beyond diathesis stress: Differential susceptibility to environmental influences. *Psychological Bulletin, 135*(6), 885–908.

Belsky, J., Conger, R., & Capaldi, D. M. (2009). The intergenerational transmission of parenting: Introduction to the special section. *Developmental Psychology, 45*(5), 1201–1204.

Belsky, J., et al. (2007). Are there long-term effects of early child care? *Child Development, 78*(2), 681–701.

Belsky, J., Weinraub, M., Owen, M., & Kelly, J. (2001, April). Quantity of child care and problem behavior. In J. Belsky (Chair), *Early childcare and children's development prior to school entry.* Symposium conducted at the 2001 biennial meetings of the Society for Research in Child Development, Minneapolis, MN.

Bem, D. J. (2008). Is there a causal link between childhood gender nonconformity and adult homosexuality? *Journal of Gay and Lesbian Mental Health, 12*(1–2), 61–79.

Bem, D. J. (2011). Feeling the future: Experimental evidence for anomalous retroactive influences on cognition and affect. *Journal of Personality and Social Psychology, 100*(3), 407–425.

Bem, D. J., & Honorton, C. (1994). Does psi exist? Replicable evidence for an anomalous process of information transfer. *Psychological Bulletin, 115*, 4–18.

Bem, S. L. (1993). *The lenses of gender.* New Haven, CT: Yale University Press.

Benda, B. B., & Corwyn, R. F. (2002). The effect of abuse in childhood and in adolescence on violence among adolescents. *Youth and Society, 33*(3), 339–365.

Benke, K., & Fallin, M. (2010). Methods: Genetic epidemiology. *Psychiatric Clinics of North America, 33*(1), 15–34.

Benson, H. (1975). *The relaxation response.* New York: Morrow.

Benson, P. L., Karabenick, S. A., & Lerner, R. M. (1976). Pretty pleases: The effects of physical attractiveness, race, and sex on receiving help. *Journal of Experimental Social Psychology, 12*, 409–415.

Ben-Zur, H. (2002). Associations of Type A behavior with the emotional traits of anger and curiosity. *Anxiety, Stress and Coping: An International Journal, 15*(1), 95–104.

Berke, J. (2009). Deaf culture—Deaf? Disabled? Both? How do deaf people view themselves? http://deafness.about.com/od/deafculture/a/deafdisabled.htm. Accessed January 14, 2011.

Berkowitz, L. (1994). Is something missing? Some observations prompted by the cognitive-neoassociationist view of anger and emotional aggression. In L. R. Huesmann (Ed.), *Aggressive behavior: Current perspectives* (pp. 35–40). New York: Plenum Press.

Berlin, H. A., & Koch, C. (2009, April–May–June). Consciousness redux: Neuroscience meets psychoanalysis. *Scientific American Mind, 20.*

Bermudez, P., Lerch, J. P., Evans, A. C., & Zatorre, R. J. (2009). Neuroanatomical correlates of musicianship as revealed by cortical thickness and voxel-based morphometry. *Cerebral Cortex, 19*(7), 1583–1596.

Bernardin, H. J., Cooke, D. K., & Villanova, P. (2000). Conscientiousness and agreeableness as predictors of rating leniency. *Journal of Applied Psychology, 85*(2) 232–236.

Bernstein, D. M., & Loftus, E. F. (2009). How to tell if a particular memory is true or false. *Perspectives on Psychological Science, 4*(4), 370–374.

Bernstein, I. (1996). Cited in Azar, B. (1996). Research could help patients cope with chemotherapy. *APA Monitor, 27*(8), 33.

Berscheid, E. (2009). Love in the fourth dimension. *Annual Review of Psychology, 61,* 1–25.

Berten, H., & Rossem, R. V. (2009). Doing worse but knowing better: An exploration of the relationship between HIV/AIDS knowledge and sexual behavior among adolescents in Flemish secondary schools. *Journal of Adolescence, 32*(5), 1303–1319.

Berzonsky, M. D. (2005). Ego identity: A personal standpoint in a postmodern world. *Identity, 5*(2), 125–136.

Berzonsky, M. D., & Kuk, L. S. (2005). Identity style, psychosocial maturity, and academic performance. *Personality and Individual Differences, 39*(1), 235–247.

Bevan, W., & Kessel, F. (1994). Plain truths and home cooking. *American Psychologist, 49,* 505–509.

Bexton, W. H., Heron, W., & Scott, T. H. (1954). Effects of decreased variation in the sensory environment. *Canadian Journal of Psychology, 8,* 70–76.

Bidell, M. P., Turner, J. A., & Casas, J. M. (2002). First impressions count: Ethnic/racial and lesbian/gay/bisexual content of professional psychology application materials. *Professional Psychology: Research and Practice, 33*(1), 97–103.

Bienvenu, O. J., Hettema, J. M., Neale, M. C., Prescott, C. A., & Kendler, K. S. (2007). Low extraversion and high neuroticism as indices of genetic and environmental risk for social phobia, agoraphobia, and animal phobia. *American Journal of Psychiatry, 164,* 1714–1721.

Bierman, K. L., Domitrovich, C. E., Nix, R. L., Gest, S. D., & Welsh, J. A. (2008). Promoting academic and social-emotional school readiness: The Head Start REDI program. *Child Development, 79*(6), 1802–1817.

Bigelow, B. J. (2001). Relational scaffolding of school motivation: Developmental continuities in students' and parents' ratings of the importance of school goals. *Journal of Genetic Psychology, 162*(1), 75–92.

Bigger, S. (2009). Review, *The Lucifer effect: How good people turn evil* by Philip Zimbardo. *Journal of Beliefs and Values,* 1–3.

Binder, A., & Baron, R. (2010). Utility of transcutaneous electrical nerve stimulation in neurologic pain disorders. *Neurology, 74,* 1–2.

Binder, E. B., & Nemeroff, C. B. (2009). The CRF system, stress, depression, and anxiety—Insights from human genetic studies. *Molecular Psychiatry, 15*(6), 574–588.

Biran, M. (1988). Cognitive and exposure treatment for agoraphobia: Reexamination of the outcome research. *Journal of Cognitive Psychotherapy, 2*(3), 165–178.

Bishop, D. V. M. (2009). Genes, cognition, and communication. *Annals of the New York Academy of Sciences, 1156,* 1–18.

Bishop, E. G., et al. (2003). Development genetic analysis of general cognitive ability from 1 to 12 years in a sample of adoptees, biological siblings, and twins. *Intelligence, 31*(1), 31–49.

Bjorklund, D. F. (2000). *Children's thinking* (3rd ed.). Pacific Grove, CA: Brooks/Cole.

Blackwell, D. L., & Lichter, D. T. (2004). Homogamy among dating, cohabiting, and married couples. *Sociological Quarterly, 45*(4), 719–737.

Blake, P., Fry, R., & Pesjack, M. (1984). *Self-assessment and behavior change manual.* New York: Random House.

Blass, E. M., & Camp, C. A. (2003). Changing determinants in 6- to 12-week-old human infants. *Developmental Psychobiology, 42*(3), 312–316.

Blass, T. (2009). From New Haven to Santa Clara: A historical perspective on the Milgram obedience experiments. *American Psychologist, 64*(1), 37–45.

Blavatsky, P. R. (2009). Betting on own knowledge: Experimental test of overconfidence. *Journal of Risk and Uncertainty, 38*(1), 39–49.

Blechert, J., et al. (2010). Respiratory, autonomic, and experiential responses to repeated inhalations of 20% CO_2 enriched air in panic disorder, social phobia, and healthy controls. *Biological Psychology, 84*(1), 104–111.

Block, N. (2009). The mind as the software of the brain. In S. Schneider (Ed.), *Science fiction and philosophy: From time travel to superintelligence* (pp. 170–185). Hoboken, NJ: Wiley.

Bloom, L., & Mudd, S. A. (1991). Depth of processing approach to face recognition. *Journal of Experimental Psychology: Learning, Memory, and Cognition, 17*, 556–565.

Blum, K., et al. (2009). Genes and happiness. *Gene Therapy and Molecular Biology, 13*, 91–129.

Bodamer, M. D., & Gardner, R. A. (2002). How cross-fostered chimpanzees *(Pan troglodytes)* initiate and maintain conversations. *Journal of Comparative Psychology, 116*(1), 12–26.

Bogen, J. E. (1969). The other side of the brain II: An appositional mind. *Bulletin of the Los Angeles Neurological Society, 34*, 135–162.

Bogen, J. E. (2000). Split-brain basics: Relevance for the concept of one's other mind. *Journal of the American Academy of Psychoanalysis, 28*(2), 341–369.

Bogle, K. (2008). *Hooking up: Sex, dating, and relationships on campus.* New York: New York University Press.

Bolinskey, K. P., & Gottesman, I. I. (2010). Premorbid personality indicators of schizophrenia-related psychosis in a hypothetically psychosis-prone college sample. *Scandinavian Journal of Psychology, 51*(1), 68–74.

Bonanno, G. A., & Boerner, K. (2007). The stage theory of grief. *Journal of the American Medical Association, 297*, 2693.

Bongar, B. (2002). *The suicidal patient: Clinical and legal standards of care* (2nd ed.). Washington, DC: American Psychological Association.

Bonn-Miller, M. O., Zvolensky, M. J., & Bernstein, A. (2007). Marijuana use motives: Concurrent relations to frequency of past 30-day use and anxiety sensitivity among young adult marijuana smokers. *Addictive Behaviors, 32*(1), 49–62.

Boora, K., Chiappone, K., Dubovsky, S., & Xu, J. (2009). Ziprasidone-induced spontaneous orgasm. *Journal of Psychopharmacology, 24*(6), 947–948.

Born, J., et al. (2002). Sniffing neuropeptides: A transnasal approach to the human brain. *Nature Neuroscience, 5*(6), 514–516.

Bouchard, C. (2010). Defining the genetic architecture of the predisposition to obesity: A challenging but not insurmountable task. *American Journal of Clinical Nutrition, 91*(1), 5–6.

Bouton, M. E. (2010). The multiple forms of "context" in associative learning theory. In B. Mesquita, L. F. Barrett, & E. R. Smith (Eds.), *The mind in context* (pp. 233–258). New York: Guilford Press.

Bower, G. H., Gluck, M. A., Anderson, J. R., & Kosslyn, S. M. (2007). *Memory and mind: A festschrift for Gordon H. Bower.* New York: Erlbaum.

Bowlby, J. (1988). *A secure base.* New York: Basic Books.

Boyatzis, R. E. (1974). The effect of alcohol consumption on the aggressive behavior of men. *Quarterly Journal for the Study of Alcohol, 35*, 959–972.

Boyd-Franklin, N., & Lockwood, T. W. (2009). Spirituality and religion. In F. Walsh (Ed.), *Spiritual resources in family therapy* (2nd ed., pp. 141–155). New York: Guilford Press.

Braarud, H. C., & Stormark, K. M. (2008). EJ814142—Prosodic modification and vocal adjustments in mothers' speech during face-to-face interaction with their two- to four-month-old infants: A double video study. *Social Development, 17*(4), 1074–1084.

Bradley, R. H. (2006). The home environment. In N. F. Watt et al. (Eds.), *The crisis in youth mental health: Critical issues and effective programs, Vol. 4: Early intervention programs and policies: Child psychology and mental health* (pp. 89–120). Westport, CT: Praeger/Greenwood.

Bramlett, M. D., & Mosher, W. D. (2002). Cohabitation, marriage, divorce, and remarriage. National Center for Health Statistics, Vital Health Statistics, 23(22). Available at http://www.cdc.gov/nchs/data/series/sr_23/sr23_022.pdf

Brand, J. (2000). Cited in McFarling, U. L. (2000, August 27). Sniffing out genes' role in our senses of taste and smell. *The Los Angeles Times online.*

Brand, J. S., & van der Schouw, Y. T. (2010). Testosterone, SHBG and cardiovascular health in postmenopausal women. *International Journal of Impotence Research, 22*, 91–104.

Brandtjen, H., & Verny, T. (2001). Short and long term effects on infants and toddlers in full time daycare centers. *Journal of Prenatal & Perinatal Psychology & Health, 15*(4), 239–286.

Bransford, J. D., Nitsch, K. E., & Franks, J. J. (1977). Schooling and the facilitation of knowing. In R. C. Anderson, R. J. Spiro, & W. E. Montague (Eds.), *Schooling and the acquisition of knowledge* (pp. 31–55). Hillsdale, NJ: Erlbaum.

Braun, B. G. (1988). *Treatment of multiple personality disorder.* Washington, DC: American Psychiatric Press.

Bravender, T., et al. (2010). Classification of eating disturbance in children and adolescents: Proposed changes for the *DSM-V. European Eating Disorders Review, 18*(2), 79–89.

Brewer, M. B., & Chen, Y-R. (2007). Where (who) are collectives in collectivism? Toward conceptual clarification of individualism and collectivism. *Psychological Review, 114*(1), 133–151.

Briñol, P., Petty, R., & Barden, J. (2007). Happiness versus sadness as a determinant of thought confidence in persuasion: A self-validation analysis. *Journal of Personality and Social Psychology, 93*(5), 711–727.

Briones, T. L., Klintsova, A. Y., & Greenough, W. T. (2004). Stability of synaptic plasticity in the adult rat visual cortex induced by complex environment exposure. *Brain Research, 1018*(1), 130–135.

Brody, J. E. (2000, April 25). Memories of things that never were. *The New York Times,* p. F8.

Brooks, K. D., Bowleg, L., & Quina, K. (2009). Minority sexual status among minorities. In S. Loue (Ed.), *Sexualities and identities of minority women* (pp. 41–63). New York: Springer.

Brooks, M. V. (2008). Health-related hardiness in individuals with chronic illnesses. *Clinical Nursing Research, 17*(2), 98–117.

Brotto, L. A., & Klein, C. (2010). Psychological factors involved in women's sexual dysfunctions. *Expert Review of Obstetrics and Gynecology, 5*(1), 93–104.

Brown, A. S. (2003). A review of the déjà vu experience. *Psychological Bulletin, 129*(3), 394–413.

Brown, A. S. (2006). Prenatal infection as a risk factor for schizophrenia. *Schizophrenia Bulletin, 32*(2), 200–202.

Brown, A. S. (2007). Identifying risks using a new assessment tool: The missing piece of the jigsaw in medical device risk assessment. *Clinical Risk, 13,* 56–59.

Brown, A. S., & Derkits, E. J. (2010). Prenatal infection and schizophrenia: A review of epidemiologic and translational studies. *American Journal of Psychiatry, 167*, 261–280.

Brown, G. R. (2009). Evolutionary perspectives on sexual coercion in human beings and other primates: The future of the rape debate. *Journal of Evolutionary Psychology, 7*(4), 347–350.

Brown, J., O'Brien, P. M. S., Marjoribanks, J., & Wyatt, K. (2009). Selective serotonin reuptake inhibitors for premenstrual syndrome. *Cochrane Database of Systematic Reviews*, Issue 2. Art. No.: CD001396. doi:10.1002/14651858.CD001396.pub2

Brown, R. J., Schrag, A., Krishnamoorthy, E., & Trimble, M. R. (2007). Are patients with somatization disorder highly suggestible? *Acta Psychiatrica Scandinavica, 117*(3), 232–235.

Brown, R., & McNeill, D. (1966). The tip-of-the-tongue phenomenon. *Journal of Verbal Learning and Verbal Behavior, 5,* 325–337.

Brown, S. L., & Manning, W. D. (2009). Family boundary ambiguity and the measurement of family structure: The significance of cohabitation. *Demography, 46*(1), 85–101.

Brown, S. L., Van Hook, J., & Glick, J. E. (2008). Generational differences in cohabitation and marriage in the U.S. *Population Research and Policy Review, 27*(5), 531–550.

Brown, W. H., et al. (2009). Social and environmental factors associated with preschoolers' nonsedentary physical activity. *Child Development, 80*(1), 45–58.

Brownstein, A. L. (2003). Biased predecision processing. *Psychological Bulletin, 129*(4), 545–568.

Bruce, T. J., & Sanderson, W. C. (2004). Evidence-based psychosocial practices: The past, present, and future. In C. Stout & R. Hayes (Eds.), *Evidence-based practice: Methods, models and tolls for mental health professionals* (pp. 220–243). New York: Wiley.

Bruene, M., & Ribbert, H. (2002). Grundsaetzliches zur Konzeption einer evolutionaeren Psychiatrie. *Schweizer Archiv für Neurologie und Psychiatrie, 153*(1), 4–11.

Brugger, P., et al. (2009). Semantic, perceptual and number space. *Neuroscience Letters, 418*(2), 133–137.

Brun, C. C., et al. (2009). Sex differences in brain structure in auditory and cingulate regions. *NeuroReport: For Rapid Communication of Neuroscience Research, 20*(10), 930.

Bryant, J., & Davies, J. (2006). Selective exposure processes. In J. Bryant & P. Vorderer (Eds.), *Psychology of entertainment* (pp. 19–34). London: Routledge.

Bryant, R. (2006). Acute stress disorder. *Psychiatry, 5*(7), 238–239.

Brydon, L., Walker, C., Wawrzyniak, A. J., Chart, H., & Steptoe, A. (2009). Dispositional optimism and stress-induced changes in immunity and negative mood. *Brain, Behavior, and Immunity, 23*(6), 810–816.

Buchanan, C. M., Eccles, J. S., & Becker, J. B. (1992). Are adolescents the victims of raging hormones? Evidence for activational effects of hormones on moods and behavior at adolescence. *Psychological Bulletin, 111,* 62–107.

Buchanan, T. W., et al. (2010). Medial prefrontal cortex damage affects physiological and psychological stress responses differently in men and women. *Psychoneuroendocrinology, 35*(1), 56–66.

Buckley, P. F., Buchanan, R. W., Tamminga, C. A., & Schulz, S. C. (2000). Schizophrenia research. *Schizophrenia Bulletin, 26*(2), 411–419.

Budney, A. J., Vandrey, R. G., Hughes, J. R., Moore, B. A., & Bahrenburg, B. (2007). Oral delta-9-tetrahydrocannabinol suppresses cannabis withdrawal symptoms. *Drug and Alcohol Dependence, 86*(1), 22–29.

Bull, N. J., Hunter, M., & Finlay, D. C. (2003). Cue gradient and cue density interact in the detection and recognition of objects defined by motion, contrast, or texture. *Perception, 32*(1), 29–39.

Bunting, L., & McAuley, C. (2004). Teenage pregnancy and motherhood: The contribution of support. *Child and Family Social Work, 9*(2), 207–215.

Burger, J. M. (2009). Replicating Milgram: Would people still obey today? *American Psychologist, 64*(1), 1–11.

Burger, J. M., & Cosby, M. (1999). Do women prefer dominant men? The case of the missing control condition. *Journal of Research in Personality, 33*(3), 358–368.

Burghardt, G. M. (2009). Darwin's legacy to comparative psychology and ethology. *American Psychologist, 64*(2), 102–110.

Bushman, B. J. (2002). Does venting anger feed or extinguish the flame? Catharsis, rumination, distraction, anger, and aggressive responding. *Personality and Social Psychology Bulletin, 28*(6), 724–731.

Bushman, B. J., & Anderson, C. A. (2007). Measuring the strength of the effect of violent media on aggression. *American Psychologist, 62*(3), 253–254.

Buss, D. M. (2000). The evolution of happiness. *American Psychologist, 55,* 15–23.

Buss, D. M. (2007). The evolution of human mating. *Acta Psychologica Sinica, 39*(3), 502–512.

Buss, D. M. (2009a). The great struggles of life: Darwin and the emergence of evolutionary psychology. *American Psychologist, 64*(2), 140–148.

Buss, D. M. (2009b) How can evolutionary psychology successfully explain personality and individual differences? *Perspectives on Psychological Science, 4*(4), 359–366.

Buston, K., Williamson, L., & Hart, G. (2007). Young women under 16 years with experience of sexual intercourse: Who becomes pregnant? *Journal of Epidemiology & Community Health, 61*(3), 221–225.

Butler, A. C., Chapman, J. E., Forman, E. M., & Beck, A. T. (2006). The empirical status of cognitive-behavioral therapy: A review of meta-analyses. *Clinical Psychology Review, 26*(1), 17–31.

Buyukyazi, G., et al. (2010). The effects of different intensity walking programs on serum blood lipids, high-sensitive C-reactive protein, and lipoprotein-associated phospholipase A2 in premenopausal women. *Science and Sports, 25*(5), 245–252.

Byrne, S., & Senehi, J. (2008). Conflict analysis and resolution as a multidiscipline. In D. J. D. Sandole & S. Byrne (Eds.), *Handbook of conflict analysis and resolution* (pp. 3–18). Oxford, England: Taylor & Francis.

C

Calcagni, E., & Elenkov, I. (2006). Stress system activity, innate and T helper cytokines, and susceptibility to immune-related diseases. *Annals of the New York Academy of Sciences, 1069,* 62–76.

Caldwell, H. K., Lee, H-J., Macbeth, A. H., & Young, W. S. (2008). Vasopressin: Behavioral roles of an "original" neuropeptide. *Progress in Neurobiology, 84*(1), 1–24.

Callahan, J. J. (2007). Sandwich anyone? *Gerontologist, 47*(4), 569–571.

Callan, D. E., & Schweighofer, N. (2009). Neural correlates of the spacing effect in explicit verbal semantic encoding support the deficient-processing theory. *Human Brain Mapping, 31*(4), 645-659.

Calzo, J. P., & Ward, L. M. (2009). Contributions of parents, peers, and media to attitudes toward homosexuality: Investigating sex and ethnic differences. *Journal of Homosexuality, 56*(8), 1101–1116.

Campbell, R. A., Machlus, K. R., & Wolberg, A. S. (2010). Smoking out the cause of thrombosis. *Arteriosclerosis, Thrombosis, and Vascular Biology, 30*(7), 75–79.

Campbell, T. (2000). First person account: Falling on the pavement. *Schizophrenia Bulletin, 26*(2), 507–509.

Campbell, W. K., Sedikides, C., Reeder, G. D., & Elliott, A. J. (2000). Among friends? An examination of friendship and the self-serving bias. *British Journal of Social Psychology, 39*(2), 229–239.

523

Campolongo, P., et al. (2009). Endocannabinoids in the rat basolateral amygdala enhance memory consolidation and enable glucocorticoid modulation of memory. *Proceedings of the National Academy of Sciences, 106*(12), 4888–4893.

Campos, J. J. (2000). Cited in Azar, B. (2000). What's in a face? *Monitor on Psychology, 31*(1), 44–45.

Campos, J. J., Hiatt, S., Ramsey, D., Henderson, C., & Svejda, M. (1978). The emergence of fear on the visual cliff. In M. Lewis & L. Rosenblum (Eds.), *The origins of affect.* New York: Plenum Press.

Cañal-Bruland, R., van der Kamp, J., & van Kesteren, J. (2010). An examination of motor and perceptual contributions to the recognition of deception from others' actions. *Human Movement Science, 29*(1), 94–102.

Cannon, W. B. (1927). The James–Lange theory of emotions: A critical examination and an alternative theory. *American Journal of Psychology, 39,* 106–124.

Cannon, W. B. (1932). *The wisdom of the body.* New York: Norton.

Cannon, W. B., & Washburn, A. (1912). An explanation of hunger. *American Journal of Physiology, 29,* 441–454.

Cantalupo, C., & Hopkins, W. D. (2001). Asymmetric Broca's area in great apes: A region of the ape brain is uncannily similar to one linked with speech in humans. *Nature, 414*(6863), 505.

Caprara, G. V., et al. (2009). Human optimal functioning: The genetics of positive orientation towards self, life, and the future. *Behavior Genetics, 39*(3), 277–284.

Carey, B. (2007, March 26). Poor behavior is linked to time in day care. *New York Times online.*

Carey, B. (2009, November 27). Psychosurgery for mental ills offers both hope and risk. *The New York Times,* p. A1.

Carlsson, K., et al. (2000). Tickling expectations: Neural processing in anticipation of a sensory stimulus. *Journal of Cognitive Neuroscience, 12,* 691–703.

Carmichael, L. L., Hogan, H. P., & Walter, A. A. (1932). An experimental study of the effect of language on the reproduction of visually perceived form. *Journal of Experimental Psychology, 15,* 73–86.

Carney, C. E., et al. (2010). Examining maladaptive beliefs about sleep across insomnia patient groups. *Journal of Psychosomatic Research, 68*(1), 57–65.

Carpusor, A. G., & Loges, W. E. (2006). Rental discrimination and ethnicity in names. *Journal of Applied Social Psychology, 36*(4), 934–952.

Carré, J. M., & Putnam, S. K. (2010). Watching a previous victory produces an increase in testosterone among elite hockey players. *Psychoneuroendocrinology, 35*(3), 475–479.

Carré, J. M., Putnam, S. K., & McCormick, C. M. (2009). Testosterone responses to competition predict future aggressive behaviour at a cost to reward in men. *Psychoneuroendocrinology, 34*(4), 561–570.

Carroll, D. (2004). *Psychology of language* (4th ed.). Belmont, CA: Wadsworth.

Carroll, J. S., et al. (2007). So close, yet so far away: The impact of varying marital horizons on emerging adulthood. *Journal of Adolescent Research, 22*(3), 219–247.

Cartreine, J. A., Ahern, D. K., & Locke, S. E. (2010). A roadmap to computer-based psychotherapy in the United States. *Harvard Review of Psychiatry, 18*(2), 80–95.

Carver, C. S., & Harmon-Jones, E. (2009). Anger is an approach-related affect: Evidence and implications. *Psychological Bulletin, 135*(2), 183–204.

Carver, L. J., & Cluver, A. (2009). Stress effects on the brain system underlying explicit memory. In J. A. Quas & R. Fivush (Eds.), *Emotion and memory in development: Biological, cognitive, and social considerations* (pp. 278–311). New York: Oxford University Press.

Cassaday, H. J. et al. (2003). Intraventricular 5,7-dihydroxytryptamine lesions disrupt acquisition of working memory task rules but not performance once learned. *Progress in Neuro-Psychopharmacology & Biological Psychiatry, 27*(1), 147–156

Castelli, L., Corazzini, L. L., & Geminiani, G. C. (2008). Spatial navigation in large-scale virtual environments: Gender differences in survey tasks. *Computers in Human Behavior, 24*(4), 1643–1667.

Castelli, L., Zogmaister, C., & Tomelleri, S. (2009). The transmission of racial attitudes within the family. *Developmental Psychology, 45*(2), 586–591.

Castillo-Richmond, A., et al. (2000). Effects of stress reduction on carotid atherosclerosis in hypertensive African Americans. *Stroke, 31,* 568.

Castor, D., et al. (2010). Sexual risk reduction among non-injection drug users: Report of a randomized controlled trial. *AIDS Care, 22*(1), 62–70.

Cathcart, S. (2009). A neural hypothesis for stress-induced headache. *Medical Hypotheses, 73*(6), 1011–1013.

Cattaneo, L., & Rizzolatti, G. (2009). The mirror-neuron system. *Archives of Neurology, 66*(5), 557–560.

Cattaneo, L., Sandrini, M., & Schwarzbach, J. (2010). State-dependent TMS reveals a hierarchical representation of observed acts in the temporal, parietal, and premotor cortices. *Cerebral Cortex, 20*(9), 2252–2258.

Cattell, R. B. (1949). *The culture-free intelligence test.* Champaign, IL: Institute for Personality and Ability Testing.

Catts, V. S., & Catts, S. V. (2009). Psychotomimetic effects of PCP, LSD, and Ecstasy: Pharmacological models of schizophrenia? In P. S. Sachdev & M. S. Keshavan (Eds.), *Secondary schizophrenia* (pp. 141–168). Cambridge, England: Cambridge University Press.

Cavallaro, F. I., et al. (2010). Hypnotizability-related EEG alpha and theta activities during visual and somesthetic imageries. *Neuroscience Letters, 470*(1), 13–18.

Cavelaars, A. E. J. M., et al. (2000). Educational differences in smoking: International comparison. *British Medical Journal, 320,* 1102–1107.

CDC (See Centers for Disease Control and Prevention)

Ceci, S. J., Kulkofsky, S., Klemfuss, J. Z., Sweeney, C. D., & Bruck, M. (2007). Unwarranted assumptions about children's testimonial accuracy. *Annual Review of Clinical Psychology, 3,* 311–328.

Ceci, S. J., Williams, W. M., & Barnett, S. M. (2009). Women's underrepresentation in science: Sociocultural and biological considerations. *Psychological Bulletin, 135*(2), 218–261.

Cellar, D. F., Nelson, Z. C., & Yorke, C. M. (2000). The five-factor model and driving behavior: Personality and involvement in vehicular accidents. *Psychological Reports, 86*(2) 454–456.

Cellard, C., Lefèbvre, A-A., Maziade, M., Roy, M-A., & Tremblay, S. (2010). An examination of the relative contribution of saturation and selective attention to memory deficits in patients with recent-onset schizophrenia and their unaffected parents. *Journal of Abnormal Psychology, 119*(1), 60–70.

Centers for Disease Control and Prevention. (2005). *DES update: For consumers.* Retrieved afrom http://www.cdc.gov/DES/consumers/index.html

Centers for Disease Control and Prevention. (2009). *FastStats: Suicide and self-inflicted injury.* Retrieved from http://www.cdc.gov/nchs/fastats/suicide.htm

Cernoch, J., & Porter, R. (1985). Recognition of maternal axillary odors by infants. *Child Development, 56,* 1593–1598.

Cervilla, J. A., et al. (2000). Long-term predictors of cognitive outcome in a cohort of older people with hypertension. *British Journal of Psychiatry, 177,* 66–71.

Chabaud, M., Isabel, G., Kaiser, L., & Preat, T. (2009). Social facilitation of long-lasting memory retrieval in *Drosophila. Current Biology, 19*(19), 1654–1659.

Chadwick, P. D. J., & Lowe, C. F. (1990). Measurement and modification of delusional beliefs. *Journal of Consulting and Clinical Psychology, 58,* 225–232.

Chafee, M. V., & Goldman-Rakic, P. S. (2000). Inactivation of parietal and prefrontal cortex reveals interdependence of neural activity during memory-guided saccades. *Journal of Neurophysiology, 83*(3), 1550–1566.

Chai, X. J., & Jacobs, L. F. (2009). Sex differences in directional cue use in a virtual landscape. *Behavioral Neuroscience, 123*(2), 276–283.

Chaiyavej, S., & Morash, M. (2009). Reasons for policewomen's assertive and passive reactions to sexual harassment. *Police Quarterly, 12*(1), 63–85.

Champagne, F. A., Curley, J. P., Swaney, W. T., Hasen, N. S., & Keverne, E. B. (2009). Epigenetic mechanisms mediating the long-term effects of maternal care on development. *Behavioral Neuroscience, 123*(3), 469–480.

Chan, R. C. K., & Gottesman, I. I. (2008). Neurological soft signs as candidate endophenotypes for schizophrenia: A shooting star or a northern star? *Neuroscience and Biobehavioral Reviews, 32*(5), 957–971.

Chance, W. T., Xiao, C., Dayal, R., & Sheriff, S. (2007). Alteration of NPY and Y1 receptor in dorsomedial and ventromedial areas of hypothalamus in anorectic tumor-bearing rats. *Peptides, 28*(2), 295–301.

Chao, A., et al. (2007). Pain relief by applying transcutaneous electrical nerve stimulation (TENS) on acupuncture points during the first stage of labor: A randomized double-blind placebo-controlled trial. *Pain, 127*(3), 214–220.

Chapleau, K. M., Oswald, D. L., & Russell, B. L. (2008). Male rape myths: The role of gender, violence, and sexism. *Journal of Interpersonal Violence, 23,* 600.

Chaplin, W. F., Phillips, J. B., Brown, J. D., Clanton, N. R., & Stein, J. L. (2000). Handshaking, gender, personality, and first impressions. *Journal of Personality and Social Psychology, 79*(1), 110–117.

Chard, K. M., et al. (2010). A comparison of OEF and OIF veterans and Vietnam veterans receiving cognitive processing therapy. *Journal of Traumatic Stress, 23*(1), 25–32.

Chen, J., & Rizzo, J. (2010). Racial and ethnic disparities in use of psychotherapy: Evidence from U.S. national survey data. *Psychiatric Services, 61,* 364–372.

Cheng, Y., et al. (2008). Gender differences in the mu rhythm of the human mirror-neuron system. *Public Library of Science, ONE, 3*(5), e2113.

Cheng, Y., et al. (2009). Sex differences in the neuroanatomy of human mirror-neuron system: A voxel-based morphometric investigation. *Neuroscience, 158*(2), 713–720.

Cherniak, C. (2009). Brain wiring optimization and non-genomic nativism. In M. Piatelli-Palmarini, P. Salaburu, & J. Uriagereka (Eds.), *Of minds and language: A dialogue with Noam Chomsky in the Basque country* (pp. 108–122). New York: Oxford University Press.

Cheung, C-K., & Leung, K-K. (2008). Ways by which comparable income affects life satisfaction in Hong Kong. *Social Indicators Research, 87*(1), 169–187.

Chida, Y., & Steptoe, A. (2009). The association of anger and hostility with future coronary heart disease: A meta-analytic review of prospective evidence. *Journal of the American College of Cardiology, 53*(11), 936–946.

ChildStats. (2009). America's children: Key national indicators of well-being. Forum on Child and Family Statistics. www.childstats.gov/americaschildren/famsoc3.asp. Accessed March 12, 2011.

Chisholm, J., & Greene, B. (2008). Women of color: Perspectives on multiple identities in psychological theory, research, and practice.

In F. L. Denmark & M. A. Paludi (Eds.), *Psychology of women* (2nd ed., pp. 40–69). Westport, CT: Greenwood.

Chiu, C., & Chao, M. M. (2009). Society, culture, and the person. In R. S. Wyer, C. Chiu, & Y. Hong (Eds.), *Understanding culture: Theory, research, and application* (pp. 457–468). Boca Raton, FL: CRC Press.

Chivers, M. L., Seto, M. C., & Blanchard, R. (2007). Gender and sexual orientation differences in sexual response to sexual activities versus gender of actors in sexual films. *Journal of Personality and Social Psychology, 93*(6), 1108–1121.

Christ, S. E., et al. (2009). The contributions of the prefrontal cortex and executive control to deception. *Cerebral Cortex, 19*(7), 1557–1566.

Chumlea, W. M. C., et al. (2009). The first seriatim study into old age for weight, stature and BMI: The Fels Longitudinal Study. *Journal of Nutrition, Health and Aging, 13*(1), 3–5.

Cialdini, R. B. (2000). Cited in McKinley, J. C., Jr. (2000, August 11). It isn't just a game: Clues to avid rooting. *The New York Times online.*

Cialdini, R. B., et al. (1997). Reinterpreting the empathy-altruism relationship: When one into one equals oneness. *Journal of Personality and Social Psychology, 73*(3), 481–494.

Cifani, C., et al. (2009). A preclinical model of binge eating elicited by yo-yo dieting and stressful exposure to food: Effect of sibutramine, fluoxetine, topiramate, and midazolam. *Psychopharmacology, 204*(1), 113–225.

Cirelli, C. (2009). The genetic and molecular regulation of sleep: From fruit flies to humans. *Nature Reviews Neuroscience, 10,* 548–560.

Cirincione, C., Steadman, H. J., & McGreevy, M. A. (1995). Rates on insanity acquittals and the factors associated with successful insanity pleas. *Bulletin of the American Academy of Psychiatry and Law, 23*(3), 399-409.

Clancy, S. A. (2008). How do people come to believe they were abducted by aliens? In E. Goode & D. A. Vail (Eds.), *Extreme deviance* (pp. 54–63). Thousand Oaks, CA: Pine Forge Press.

Clancy, S. A., McNally, R. J., Schacter, D. L., Lenzenweger, M. F., & Pitman, R. (2002). Memory distortion in people reporting abduction by aliens. *Journal of Abnormal Psychology, 111*(3), 455–461.

Clark, A., & Misyak, J. B. (2009). Language, innateness, and universals. In *Language universals* (pp. 253–261). *Oxford Scholarship* Online Monographs.

Clark, E. V., & Nikitina, T. V. (2009). One vs. more than one: Antecedents to plural marking in early language acquisition. *Linguistics, 47*(1), 103–140.

Clark, M. D., & Carroll, M. J. (2008). Acquaintance rape scripts of men and women: Similarities and differences. *Sex Roles, 58*(9–10), 616–625.

Clark, S. (2009). Sleep deprivation: Implications for obstetric practice in the United States. *American Journal of Obstetrics and Gynecology, 201*(2), 136.e1–136.e4.

Clark, S. E., & Loftus, E. F. (1996). Space alien memories and scientific scrutiny. *PsycCRITIQUES, 41*(3), 294.

Clark, T. T. (2010). Reviewing the connection between paradigms and theories to understand adolescent drug use. *Journal of Child and Adolescent Substance Abuse, 19*(1), 16–32.

Clarke, P. A. (2009). Australian aboriginal ethnometeorology and seasonal calendars. *History and Anthropology, 20*(2), 79–106.

Clayton, A. (2008). Symptoms related to the menstrual cycle: Diagnosis, prevalence, and treatment. *Journal of Psychiatric Practice, 14*(1), 13–21.

Clayton, E. C., & Williams, C. L. (2000). Adrenergic activation of the nucleus tractus solitarius potentiates amygdala norepinephrine release and enhances retention performance in emotionally arousing and spatial memory tasks. *Behavioural Brain Research, 112*(1–2), 151–158.

Cnattingius, S. (2004). The epidemiology of smoking during pregnancy: Smoking prevalence, maternal characteristics, and pregnancy outcomes. *Nicotine & Tobacco Research, 6*(Suppl. 2), S125–S140.

Cnattingius, S., et al. (2000). Caffeine intake and the risk of first-trimester spontaneous abortion. *New England Journal of Medicine, 343*(25), 1839–1845.

Cobb, C., Ward, K. D., Maziak, W., Shihadeh, A. L. & Eissenberg, T. (2010). Waterpipe tobacco smoking: An emerging health crisis in the United States. *American Journal of Health Behavior, 34*(3), 275–285.

Cobb, K. (2008). Eating disorders in athletes. In S. R. Bakere (Ed.), *Hot topics in sports and athletics* (pp. 17–50). Hauppauge, NY: Nova Science.

Cocking, C., Drury, J., & Reicher, S. (2009). The psychology of crowd behaviour in emergency evacuations. *Irish Journal of Psychology, 30*(1–2), 59–73.

Cohen, A., et al. (2009). Anxiolytic effects of nicotine in a rodent test of approach–avoidance conflict. *Psychopharmacology, 204*(3), 541–549.

Cohen, D., et al. (2000). Absence of cognitive impairment at long-term follow-up in adolescents treated with ECT for severe mood disorder. *American Journal of Psychiatry, 157*, 460–462.

Cohen, L. L. (2002). Reducing infant immunization distress through distraction. *Health Psychology, 21*(2), 207–211.

Cohen, L. S., et al. (2006). Relapse of major depression during pregnancy in women who maintain or discontinue antidepressant treatment. *Journal of the American Medical Association, 295*(5), 499–507.

Cohen, S., & Williamson, G. M. (1991). Stress and infectious disease in humans. *Psychological Bulletin, 109*, 5–24.

Cohen-Bendahan, C. C. C., van de Beek, C., & Berenbaum, S. A. (2005). Prenatal sex hormone effects on child and adult sex-typed behavior: Methods and findings. *Neuroscience and Biobehavioral Reviews, 29*(2), 353–384.

Colas, E. (1999). *Just checking: Scenes from the life of an obsessive–compulsive.* New York: Simon & Schuster.

Collaer, M. L., & Hill, E. M. (2006). Large sex difference in adolescents on a timed line judgment task: Attentional contributors and task relationship to mathematics. *Perception, 35*(4), 561–572.

Collins, R. L., et al. (2010). Off-premise alcohol sales policies, drinking, and sexual risk among people living with HIV. *American Journal of Public Health, 100*(10), 1890–1892.

Collins, W. A., & Laursen, B. (2006). Parent–adolescent relationships. In P. Noller & J. A. Feeney (Eds.), *Close relationships: Functions, forms and processes* (pp. 111–125). Hove, England: Psychology Press/Taylor & Francis.

Colom, R., Flores-Mendoza, C., & Rebollo, I. (2003). Working memory and intelligence. *Personality and Individual Differences, 34*(1), 33–39.

Coltraine, S., & Messineo, M. (2000). The perpetuation of subtle prejudice: Race and gender imagery in 1990s television advertising. *Sex Roles, 42*(5–6), 363–389.

Comas-Diaz, L. (2008). Latino psychospirituality. In K. J. Schneider (Ed.), *Existential-integrative psychotherapy: Guideposts to the core of practice* (pp. 100–109). New York: Routledge/Taylor & Francis Group.

Commons, M. L. (2004). The state of the art on Perry and epistemological development? *Journal of Adult Development, 11*(2), 59–60.

Comtois, K. A., Schiff, M. A., & Grossman, D. C. (2008). Psychiatric risk factors associated with postpartum suicide attempt in Washington State, 1992–2001. *American Journal of Obstetrics and Gynecology, 199*(2), 120.e1–120.e5.

Concar, D. (2002, April 20). Ecstasy on the brain. http://www.NewScientist.com.

Confer, J. C., et al. (2010). Evolutionary psychology: Controversies, questions, prospects, and limitations. *American Psychologist, 65*(2), 110–126.

Conger, R. D., Belsky, J., & Capaldi, D. M. (2009). The intergenerational transmission of parenting: Closing comments for the special section. *Developmental Psychology, 45*(5), 1276–1283.

Conley, C. S., & Rudolph, K. D. (2009). The emerging sex difference in adolescent depression: Interacting contributions of puberty and peer stress. *Development and Psychopathology, 21*, 593–620.

Connor, P. D., Sampson, P. D., Streissguth, A. P., Bookstein, F. L., & Barr, H. M. (2006). Effects of prenatal alcohol exposure on fine motor coordination and balance: A study of two adult samples. *Neuropsychologia, 44*(5), 744–751.

Consortium of Social Science Associations. (2003). McQuery testifies to Homeland Security Science Subcommittee. *Washington Update, 22*(10), 1–7.

Cook, J. M., Biyanova, T., & Coyne, J. C. (2009). Influential psychotherapy figures, authors, and books: An Internet survey of over 2,000 psychotherapists. *Psychotherapy: Theory, Research, Practice, Training, 46*(1), 42–51.

Cooke, B. (2008). The right to be human and human rights: Maslow, McCarthyism and the death of humanist theories of management. *Management and Organizational History, 3*(1), 27–47.

Cooper, M. L. (2002). Alcohol use and risky sexual behavior among college students and youth: Evaluating the evidence. *Journal of Studies on Alcohol* (Suppl. 14), 101–117.

Cooper, M. L. (2006). Does drinking promote risky sexual behavior? A complex answer to a simple question. *Current Directions in Psychological Science, 15*(1), 19–23.

Cooper, M., Galbraith, M., & Drinkwater, J. (2001). Assumptions and beliefs in adolescents with anorexia nervosa and their mothers. *Eating Disorders: Journal of Treatment and Prevention, 9*(3), 217–223.

Cooper, Z., & Shafran, R. (2008). Cognitive behaviour therapy for eating disorders. *Behavioural and Cognitive Psychotherapy, 36*, 713–722.

Coovadia, H. (2004). Antiretroviral agents—How best to protect infants from HIV and save their mothers from AIDS. *New England Journal of Medicine, 351*, 289–292.

Corballis, M. C. (2009). The evolution and genetics of cerebral asymmetry. *Philosophical Transactions of the Royal Society, 364*(1519), 867–879.

Cornoldi, C. (2006). The contribution of cognitive psychology to the study of human intelligence. *European Journal of Cognitive Psychology, 18*(1), 1–17.

Cosgrove, K., Mazure, C., & Staley, J. (2007). Evolving knowledge of sex differences in brain structure, function, and chemistry. *Biological Psychiatry, 62*(8), 847–855.

Coskun, O., et al. (2010). Stress-related Epstein-Barr virus reactivation. *Clinical and Experimental Medicine, 10*(1), 15–20.

Costigan, C. L., Cauce, A. M., & Etchison, K. (2007). Changes in African American mother–daughter relationships during adolescence: Conflict, autonomy, and warmth. In B. J. R. Leadbeater & N. Way (Eds.), *Urban girls revisited: Building strengths* (pp. 177–201). New York: New York University Press.

Costin, C. (1996). *Your dieting daughter.* New York: Psychology Press.

Cotton, S. M., & Richdale, A. L. (2010). Sleep patterns and behaviour in typically developing children and children with autism, Down syndrome, Prader-Willi syndrome and intellectual disability. *Research in Autism Spectrum Disorders, 4*(3), 490–500).

Courtenay, W. H. (2000). Engendering health: A social constructionist examination of men's health beliefs and behaviors. *Psychology of Men & Masculinity, 1*(1), 4–15.

Cousin, E., Perrone, M., & Baciu, M. (2009). Hemispheric specialization for language according to grapho-phonemic transformation and gender. A divided visual field experiment. *Brain and Cognition, 69*(3), 465–471.

Cowen, P. J. (2002). Cortisol, serotonin and depression: All stressed out? *British Journal of Psychiatry, 180*(2), 99–100.

Cox, W. M., & Alm, R. (2005, February 28). Scientists are made, not born. *The New York Times* online.

Craik, F. I. M., & Bialystok, E. (2006). Cognition through the lifespan: Mechanisms of change. *Trends in Cognitive Sciences, 10*(3), 131–138.

Craik, F. I. M., & Lockhart, R. S. (2008). Levels of processing and Zinchenko's approach to memory research. *Journal of Russian and East European Psychology, 46*(6), 52–60.

Cramer, P. (2009). The development of defense mechanisms from pre-adolescence to early adulthood: Do IQ and social class matter? A longitudinal study. *Journal of Research in Personality, 43*(3), 464–471.

Cramer, R. E., McMaster, M. R., Bartell, P. A., & Dragna, M. (1988). Subject competence and minimization of the bystander effect. *Journal of Applied Social Psychology, 18,* 1133–1148.

Crighton, D. A., & Towl, G. J. (Eds.). (2010). *Forensic psychology.* Hoboken, NJ: Wiley.

Crittenden, P. M., & Dallos, R. (2009). All in the family: Integrating attachment and family systems theories. *Clinical Child Psychology and Psychiatry, 14*(3), 389–409.

Crocetti, E., Rubini, M., Berzonsky, M. D., & Meeus, W. (2009). Brief report: The Identity Style Inventory—Validation in Italian adolescents and college students. *Journal of Adolescence, 32*(2), 425–433.

Crofoot, M. C., & Wrangham, R. W. (2010). Intergroup aggression in primates and humans: The case for a unified theory. In P. M. Kappeler & J. B. Silk (Eds.), *Mind the gap: Tracing the origins of human universals* (pp. 171–195). New York: Springer.

Crusco, A. H., & Wetzel, C. G. (1984). The Midas touch: The effects of interpersonal touch on restaurant tipping. *Personality and Social Psychology Bulletin, 10,* 512–517.

Cuijpers, P., van Straten, A., van Oppen, P., & Andersson, G. (2008a). Are psychological and pharmacologic interventions equally effective in the treatment of adult depressive disorders? A meta-analysis of comparative studies. *Journal of Clinical Psychiatry, 69*(11), 1675–1685.

Cuijpers, P., van Straten, A., Andersson, G., & van Oppen, P. (2008b). Psychotherapy for depression in adults: A meta-analysis of comparative outcome studies. *Journal of Consulting and Clinical Psychology, 76*(6), 909–922.

Cuijpers, P., et al. (2009a). Computer-aided psychotherapy for anxiety disorders: A meta-analytic review. *Cognitive Behaviour Therapy, 38*(2), 66–82.

Cuijpers, P., van Straten, A., Warmerdam, L., & Andersson, G. (2009b). Psychotherapy versus the combination of psychotherapy and pharmacotherapy in the treatment of depression: A meta-analysis. *Depression and Anxiety, 26*(3), 279–288.

Cummins, R. A., & Nistico, H. (2002). Maintaining life satisfaction: The role of positive cognitive bias. *Journal of Happiness Studies, 3*(1), 37–69.

Cunningham, G. B. (2008). Importance of friendship potential in reducing the negative effects of dissimilarity. *Journal of Social Psychology, 148*(5), 595–608.

Cunningham, M. G., Connor, C. M., Carlezon, W. A., & Meloni, E. (2009). Amygdalar GABAergic-rich neural grafts attenuate anxiety-like behavior in rats. *Behavioural Brain Research, 205*(1), 146–153.

Cunningham, M. R., Shaffer, D. R., Barbee, A. P., Wolff, P. L., & Kelley, D. J. (1990). Separate processes in the relation of elation and depression to helping. *Journal of Experimental Social Psychology, 26,* 13–33.

Cunningham, W. A., Nezlek, J. B., & Banaji, M. R. (2004). Implicit and explicit ethnocentrism: Revisiting the ideologies of prejudice. *Personality and Social Psychology Bulletin, 30,* 1332.

Cutler, B. L. (2009). *Expert testimony on the psychology of eyewitness identification.* New York: Oxford University Press.

Cutler, B. L., & Kovera, M. B. (2010). *Evaluating eyewitness identification.* New York: Oxford University Press.

Cutler, W. B. (1999). Human sex-attractant hormones: Discovery, research, development, and application in sex therapy. *Psychiatric Annals, 29*(1) 54–59.

Cutler, W. B., Friedmann, E., & McCoy, N. L. (1998). Pheromonal influences on sociosexual behavior in men. *Archives of Sexual Behavior, 27*(1), 1–13.

D

Dabbs, J. M., Jr., Chang, E-L., Strong, R. A., & Milun, R. (1998). Spatial ability, navigation strategy, and geographic knowledge among men and women. *Evolution and Human Behavior, 19*(2), 89–98.

Dabbs, J. M., Jr., Hargrove, M. F., & Heusel, C. (1996). Testosterone differences among college fraternities: Well-behaved vs. rambunctious. *Personality and Individual Differences, 20*(2), 157–161.

Dagyte, G., Den Boer, J. A., & Trentani, A. (2010). The cholinergic system and depression. *Behavioural Brain Research, 221*(2), 574–582.

Dahlquist, L. M., et al. (2009). Effects of videogame distraction using a virtual reality type head-mounted display helmet on cold pressor pain in children. *Journal of Pediatric Psychology, 34*(5), 574–584.

Dai, S. R., Racette, N. M., Laird, J., Kagan, N, & Snidman, D. (2003). Association of a genetic marker at the corticotropin-releasing hormone locus with behavioral inhibition. *Biological Psychiatry, 54*(12), 1376–1381.

Daley, A. (2009). Exercise and premenstrual symptomology: A comprehensive review. *Journal of Women's Health, 18*(6), 895–899.

Damasio, A. R. (2000). A neural basis for sociopathy. *Archives of General Psychiatry online, 57*(2).

Dana, R. H. (2002). Mental health services for African Americans: A cultural/racial perspective. *Cultural Diversity and Ethnic Minority Psychology, 8*(1), 3–18.

Dang-Vu, T. T., Desseilles, M., Peigneux, P., & Maquet, P. (2006). A role for sleep in brain plasticity. *Pediatric Rehabilitation, 19*(2), 98–118.

Danhauer, J. L. (2009). Survey of college students on iPod use and hearing health. *Journal of the American Academy of Audiology, 20*(1), 5–27.

Danner, M. (2005). Taking stock of the forever war. *The New York Times Magazine,* September 11, pp. 44–53, 68, 86–87.

Darley, J. M., & Latané, B. (1968). Bystander intervention in emergencies: Diffusion of responsibility. *Journal of Personality and Social Psychology, 8,* 377–383.

Dart, A. M., et al. (2006). Brachial blood pressure but not carotid arterial waveforms predict cardiovascular events in elderly female hypertensives. *Hypertension, 47,* 785.

Darwin, C. A. (1872). *The expression of the emotions in man and animals.* London: J. Murray.

Darwin, C. A. (1892/1958). The autobiography of Charles Darwin. Edited by Nora Barlow. London: Collins.

Dasgupta, N., & Greenwald, A. G. (2001). On the malleability of automatic attitudes: Combating automatic prejudice with images of admired and disliked individuals. *Journal of Personality and Social Psychology, 81*(5), 800–814.

Daud, M. K., et al. (2010). The effect of mild hearing loss on academic performance in primary school children. *International Journal of Pediatric Otorhinolaryngology, 74*(1), 67–70.

David, D., Lynn, S. J., & Ellis, A. (Eds.). (2010). *Rational and irrational beliefs: Research, theory, and clinical practice.* New York: Oxford University Press.

David, E. J. R., Okazaki, S., & Saw, A. (2009). Bicultural self-efficacy among college students: Initial scale development and mental health correlates. *Journal of Counseling Psychology, 56*(2), 211–226.

Davidoff, J., Fonteneau, E., & Goldstein, J. (2008). Cultural differences in perception: Observations from a remote culture. *Journal of Cognition and Culture, 8*(3–4), 189–209.

Davidson, Z., Simen-Kapeu, A., & Veugelers, P. J. (2010). Neighborhood determinants of self-efficacy, physical activity, and body weights among Canadian children. *Health and Place, 16*(3), 567–572.

Davies, M. F. (2008). Irrational beliefs and unconditional self-acceptance. III: The relative importance of different types of irrational belief. *Journal of Rational-Emotive and Cognitive-Behavior Therapy, 26*(2), 102–118.

Davis, J. I., Senghas, A., & Ochsner, K. N. (2009). How does facial feedback modulate emotional experience? *Journal of Research in Personality, 43*(5), 822–829.

Dawood, K., Bailey, J. M., & Martin, N. G. (2009). Genetic and environmental influences on sexual orientation. In Y-K. Kim (Ed.), *Handbook of behavior genetics* (pp. 269–279). New York: Springer.

Day, E., Wilkes, S., & Copello, A. (2003). Spirituality is not everyone's cup of tea for treating addiction. *British Medical Journal, 326*(7394), 881.

De Berardis, D., et al. (2007). Treatment of premenstrual dysphoric disorder (PMDD) with a novel formulation of drospirenone and ethinyl estradiol. *Therapeutics and Clinical Risk Management, 3*(4), 585–590.

De Guerrero, M. C. M., & Villamil, O. S. (2000). Activating the ZPD: Mutual scaffolding in L2 peer revision. *Modern Language Journal, 84*(1), 51–68.

de Hoog, N., Stroebe, W., & de Wit, J. B. F. (2007). The impact of vulnerability to and severity of a health risk on processing and acceptance of fear-arousing communications: A meta-analysis. *Review of General Psychology, 11*(3), 258–285.

De Houwer, J., Thomas, S., & Baeyens, F. (2001). Associative learning of likes and dislikes: A review of 25 years of research on human evaluative conditioning. *Psychological Bulletin, 127*(6), 853–869.

De Michele, P. E., Gansneder, B., & Solomon, G. B. (1998). Success and failure attributions of wrestlers: Further evidence of the self-serving bias. *Journal of Sport Behavior, 21*(3), 242–255.

De Rooij, S. R., Painter, R. C., Swaab, D. F., & Roseboom, T. J. (2009). Sexual orientation and gender identity after prenatal exposure to the Dutch famine. *Archives of Sexual Behavior, 38*(3), 411–416.

De Schipper, J. C., Tavecchio, L. W. C., & Van IJzendoorn, M. H. (2008). Children's attachment relationships with day care caregivers: Associations with positive caregiving and the child's temperament. *Social Development, 17*(3), 454–470.

De Sousa, A., De Sousa, J., & Kapoor, H. (2008). An open randomized trial comparing disulfiram and topiramate in the treatment of alcohol dependence. *Journal of Substance Abuse Treatment, 34*(4), 460–463.

De Vos, H. M., & Louw, D. A. (2009). Hypnosis-induced mental training programmes as a strategy to improve the self-concept of students. *Higher Education, 57*(2), 141–154.

Deacon, B. J., Sy, J. T., Lickel, J. J., & Nelson, E. A. (2010). Does the judicious use of safety behaviors improve the efficacy and acceptability of exposure therapy for claustrophobic fear? *Journal of Behavior Therapy and Experimental Psychiatry, 41*(1), 71–80.

DeAngelis, T. (1994). Educators reveal keys to success in classroom. *APA Monitor, 25*(1), 39–40.

DeAngelis, T. (2009a). Understanding terrorism. *Monitor on Psychology, 40*(10), 60.

DeAngelis, T. (2009b). Virtual healing. *Monitor on Psychology, 40*(8), 36.

DeAngelis, T. (2010). "Little Albert" regains his identity. *Monitor on Psychology, 41*(1), 10.

DeCasper, A. J., & Prescott, P. A. (1984). Human newborns' perception of male voices. *Developmental Psychobiology, 17*, 481–491.

Deep, A. L., et al. (1999). Sexual abuse in eating disorder subtypes and control women: The role of comorbid substance dependence in bulimia nervosa. *International Journal of Eating Disorders, 25*(1), 1–10.

Dehaene-Lambertz, G., Pena, M., Christophe, A., & Landrieu, P. (2004). Phoneme perception in a neonate with a left sylvian infarct. *Brain and Language, 88*(1), 26–38.

Del Giudice, M. J. (2010). What might this be? Rediscovering the Rorschach as a tool for personnel selection in organizations. *Journal of Personality Assessment, 92*(1), 78–89.

Delaney-Black, V., et al. (2004). Prenatal cocaine: Quantity of exposure and gender influences on school-age behavior. *Developmental and Behavioral Pediatrics, 25*(4), 254–263.

Delgado, J. M. R. (1969). *Physical control of the mind.* New York: Harper & Row.

Dell, P. F. (2010). Involuntariness in hypnotic responding and dissociative symptoms. *Journal of Trauma and Dissociation, 11*(1), 1–18.

DeMarree, K. G., Petty, R. E., & Briñol, P. (2007). Self and attitude strength parallels: Focus on accessibility. *Social and Personality Psychology Compass, 1*(1), 441–468.

Demeyer, M., De Graef, P., Wagemans, J., & Verfaillie, K. (2009). Transsaccadic identification of highly similar artificial shapes. *Journal of Vision, 9*(4), 1–14.

Demir, M., & Weitekamp, L. A. (2007). I am so happy 'cause today I found my friend: Friendship and personality as predictors of happiness. *Journal of Happiness Studies, 8*(2), 181–211.

Denmark, F. L. (1998). Women and psychology: An international perspective. *American Psychologist, 53*(4), 465–473.

Dennis, J., Markey, M., Johnston, K., Vander Wal, J., & Artinian, N. (2008). The role of stress and social support in predicting depression among a hypertensive African American sample. *Heart and Lung: Journal of Acute Critical Care, 37*(2), 105–112.

Depp, C. A., & Jeste, D. V. (2006). Definitions and predictors of successful aging: A comprehensive review of larger quantitative studies. *American Journal of Geriatric Psychiatry, 14*, 6–20.

Depression Research at the National Institute of Mental Health. (2000). NIH Publication No. 00-4501. Retrieved from http://www.nimh.nih.gov/publicat/depresfact.cfm

DeRubeis, R. J., & Crits-Christoph, P. (1998). Empirically supported individual and group psychological treatments for adult mental disorders. *Journal of Consulting and Clinical Psychology, 66*, 37–52.

Devilly, G. J. (2002). Eye movement desensitization and reprocessing: A chronology of its development and scientific standing. *Scientific Review of Mental Health Practice, 1*(2), 113–138.

Devine, P. G., Plant, E. A., Amodio, D. M., Harmon-Jones, E., & Vance, S. L. (2002). The regulation of explicit and implicit race bias: The role of motivations to respond without prejudice. *Journal of Personality and Social Psychology, 82*(5), 835–848.

Dick, D. M., Prescott, C., & McGue, M. (2009). The genetics of substance use and substance use disorders. In Y-K. Kim (Ed.), *Handbook of behavior genetics* (pp. 433–453). New York: Springer.

Dickerson, B. C., & Eichenbaum, H. (2009). The episodic memory system: Neurocircuitry and disorders. *Neuropsychopharmacology Reviews, 35,* 86–104.

Dickerson, F. D., Tenhula, W. N., & Green-Paden, L. (2005). The token economy for schizophrenia: Review of the literature and recommendations for future research. *Schizophrenia Research, 75*(2–3), 405–416.

Dickerson, F., Tenhula, W., & Green-Paden, L. (2005). The token economy for schizophrenia: Review of the literature and recommendations for future research. *Schizophrenia Research, 75*(2), 405–416.

Dienes, Z., et al. (2009). Hypnotic suggestibility, cognitive inhibition, and dissociation. *Consciousness and Cognition, 18*(4), 837–847.

Difede, J. (2005). In Lake, M. (2005, May 2). Virtual reality heals 9/11 wounds. http://www.cnn.com/2005/TECH/04/29/spark.virtual/index.html

Difede, J., et al. (2007). Virtual reality exposure therapy for the treatment of posttraumatic stress disorder following September 11, 2001. *Journal of Clinical Psychiatry, 68*(11), 1639–1647.

DiGiorgio, J. (2007). Emotional variables and deviant sexual fantasies in adolescent sex offenders. *Journal of Psychiatry and Law, 35*(2), 109–124.

DiGiuseppe, R. A. (2009). Rational-emotive behavior therapy. In N. Kazantzis, M. A. Reinecke, F. M. Dattilio, & A. Freeman (Eds.), *Cognitive and behavioral theories in clinical practice* (pp. 115–147). New York: Guilford Press.

Dodge, K. A. (2006). Translational science in action: Hostile attributional style and the development of aggressive behavior problems. *Development and Psychopathology, 18*(3), 791–814.

Dodge, K. A., & McCourt, S. N. (2010). Translating models of antisocial behavioral development into efficacious intervention policy to prevent adolescent violence. *Developmental Psychobiology, 52*(3), 277–285.

Dollard, J., Doob, L. W., Miller, N. E., Mowrer, O. H., & Sears, R. R. (1939). *Frustration and aggression.* New Haven, CT: Yale University Press.

Dominguez, M. H., & Rakic, P. (2009). Language evolution: The importance of being human. *Nature, 462,* 169–170.

Donaldson, Z. R., & Young, L. J. (2008). Oxytocin, vasopressin, and the neurogenetics of sociality. *Science, 322*(5903), 900–904.

Donovan, J. E. (2009). Estimated blood alcohol concentrations for child and adolescent drinking and their implications for screening instruments. *Pediatrics, 123*(6), e975–e981.

Doob, A. N., & Wood, L. (1972). Catharsis and aggression. *Journal of Personality and Social Psychology, 22,* 236–245.

Dorfberger, S., Adi-Japha, E., & Karni, A. (2009). Sex differences in motor performance and motor learning in children and adolescents: An increasing male advantage in motor learning and consolidation phase gains. *Behavioural Brain Research, 198*(1), 165–171.

Dotson, V. M., Kitner-Triolo, M. H., Evans, M. K., & Zonderman, A. B. (2009). Effects of race and socioeconomic status on the relative influence of education and literacy on cognitive functioning. *Journal of the International Neuropsychological Society, 15,* 580–589.

Doucet, E., et al. (2007). Evidence for the existence of adaptive thermogenesis during weight loss. *British Journal of Nutrition, 85,* 715–723.

Dovidio, J. F., Gaertner, S. L., & Saguy, T. (2009). Commonality and the complexity of "we": Social attitudes and social change. *Personality and Social Psychology Review, 13*(1), 3–20.

Downey, J. I. (2009). What women want: Psychodynamics of women's sexuality in 2008. *Journal of the American Academy of Psychoanalysis and Dynamic Psychiatry, 37*(2), 253–268.

Driessen, E., et al. (2010). The efficacy of short-term psychodynamic psychotherapy for depression: A meta-analysis. *Clinical Psychology Review, 30*(1), 25–36.

Driscoll, C. A., Macdonald, D. W., & O'Brien, S. J. (2009). From wild animals to domestic pets, an evolutionary view of domestication. *Proceedings of the National Academy of Sciences, 106*(Suppl. 1), 9971–9978.

Drossel, C., Rummel, C., & Fisher, J. E. (2008). Assessment and cognitive behavior therapy: Functional analysis as key process. In W. T. O'Donohue & J. E. Fisher (Eds.), *General principles and empirically supported techniques of cognitive behavior therapy* (pp. 15–41). Hoboken, NJ: Wiley.

Drury, L. J. (2003). Community care for people who are homeless and mentally ill. *Journal of Health Care for the Poor and Underserved, 14*(2), 194–207.

Dube, S. R., Asman, K., Malarcher, A., & Caraballo, R. (2009). Cigarette smoking among adults and trends in smoking cessation—United States, 2008. *Morbidity and Mortality Weekly Report, 58*(44), 1227–1232.

Dubiela, F. P., et al. (2010). Inverse benzodiazepine agonist [beta]-CCM does not reverse learning deficit induced by sleep deprivation. *Neuroscience Letters, 469*(1), 169–173.

Dubow, E. F., et al. (2010). Exposure to conflict and violence across contexts: Relations to adjustment among Palestinian children. *Journal of Clinical Child and Adolescent Psychology, 39*(1), 103–116.

Duckworth, A. L., & Seligman, M. E. P. (2005) Self-discipline outdoes IQ in predicting academic performance of adolescents. *Psychological Science, 16*(12), 939–944.

Dufresne, A., et al. (2009). Do children undergoing cancer procedures under pharmacological sedation still report pain and anxiety? A preliminary study. *Pain Medicine, 11*(2), 215–223.

Duke, N. N., Pettingell, S. L., McMorris, B. J., & Borowsky, I. W. (2010). Adolescent violence perpetration: Associations with multiple types of adverse childhood experiences. *Pediatrics, 125*(4), e778–e786.

Dulin, P. L., & Hill, R. D. (2003). Relationships between altruistic activity and positive and negative affect among low-income older adult service providers. *Aging and Mental Health, 7*(4), 294–299.

Dummett, N. (2010). Cognitive-behavioural therapy with children, young people and families: From individual to systemic therapy. *Advances in Psychiatric Treatment, 16,* 23–36.

Dunkley, D. M., et al. (2009). Self-criticism versus neuroticism in predicting depression and psychosocial impairment for 4 years in a clinical sample. *Comprehensive Psychiatry, 50*(4), 335–346.

Dunn, J. R. (2008). Effects of housing circumstances on health, quality of life and healthcare use for people with severe mental illness: A review. *Health and Social Care in the Community, 16*(1), 1–15.

Durán, M., Moya, M., Meglas, J. L., & Viki, G. T. (2010). Social perception of rape victims in dating and married relationships. *Sex Roles, 62*(7–8), 505–519.

Durante, K. M., Li, N. P., & Haselton, M. G. (2008). Changes in women's choice of dress across the ovulatory cycle: Naturalistic and laboratory task-based evidence. *Personality and Social Psychology Bulletin, 34*(11), 1451–1460.

Durbin, D. L., Darling, N., Steinberg, L., & Brown, B. B. (1993). Parenting style and peer group membership among European-American adolescents. *Journal of Research on Adolescence, 3*(1), 87–100.

Duval, T. S., & Silvia, P. J. (2002). Self-awareness, probability of improvement, and the self-serving bias. *Journal of Personality and Social Psychology, 82*(1), 49–61.

Dweck, C. S. (2006). *Mindset: The new psychology of success.* New York: Random House.

Dweck, C. S. (2007). Is math a gift? Beliefs that put females at risk. In S. J. Ceci & W. M. Williams (Eds.), *Why aren't more women in science? Top researchers debate the evidence* (pp. 47–55). Washington, DC: American Psychological Association.

Dweck, C. S. (2009). Self-theories and lessons for giftedness: A reflective conversation. In T. Balchin, B. Hymer, & D. J. Matthews (Eds.), *The Routledge international companion to gifted education* (pp. 308–316). New York: Routledge/Taylor & Francis.

Dweck, C. S., & Master, A. (2008). Self-theories motivate self-regulated learning. In D. H. Schunk & B. J. Zimmerman (Eds.), *Motivation and self-regulated learning: Theory, research, and applications* (pp. 31–51). Mahwah, NJ: Erlbaum.

Dwivedi, Y. (2010). Brain-derived neurotrophic factor and suicide pathogenesis. *Annals of Medicine, 42*(2), 87–96.

Dworzynski, K., Happe, F., Bolton, P., & Ronald, A. (2009). Relationship between symptom domains in autism spectrum disorders: A population based twin study. *Journal of Autism and Developmental Disorders, 39*(8), 1197–1210.

Dzieweczynski, T. L., Mack, C. L., & Granquist, R. M. (2009). Lovers and fighters: Male stickleback, *Gasterosteus aculeatus,* differ in their responses to conflicting stimuli. *Animal Behaviour, 78*(2), 399–406.

E

Eagle, M. (2000). Repression, part I of II. *Psychoanalytic Review, 87*(1), 1–38.

Eagly, A. H. (2000). Cited in Goode, E. (2000, May 19). Response to stress found that's particularly female. *The New York Times,* p. A20.

Eagly, A. H. (2009). The his and hers of prosocial behavior: An examination of the social psychology of gender. *American Psychologist, 64*(8), 644–658.

Eagly, A. H., & Chaiken, S. (2007). The advantages of an inclusive definition of attitude. *Social Cognition, 25*(5), 582–602.

Eagly, A. H., Ashmore, R. D., Makhijani, M. G., & Longo, L. C. (1991). What is beautiful is good, but.... *Psychological Bulletin, 110,* 109–128.

Ebben, M. R., & Spielman, A. J. (2009). Non-pharmacological treatments for insomnia. *Journal of Behavioral Medicine, 32*(3), 244–254.

Ebbinghaus, H. (1913). *Memory: A contribution to experimental psychology* (H. A. Roger & C. E. Bussenius, Trans.). New York: Columbia University Press. (Original work published 1885)

Ebeling, M. (2008). Neuronal periodicity detection as a basis for the perception of consonance: A mathematical model of tonal fusion. *Journal of the Acoustical Society of America, 124*(4), 2320–2329.

Eberhart, N. K., & Hammen, C. L. (2010). Interpersonal style, stress, and depression: An examination of transactional and diathesis–stress models. *Journal of Social and Clinical Psychology, 29*(1), 23–38.

Ebstein, R., Israel, S., Chew, S., Zhong, S., & Knafo, A. (2010). Genetics of human social behavior. *Neuron, 65*(6), 831–844.

Edmundson, M. (1999, August 22). Psychoanalysis, American style. *The New York Times online.*

Egawa, T., et al. (2002). Impairment of spatial memory in kaolin-induced hydrocephalic rats is associated with changes in the hippocampal cholinergic and noradrenergic contents. *Behavioural Brain Research, 129*(1–2), 31–39.

Egerton, A., Allison, C., Brett, R. R., & Pratt, J. A. (2006). Cannabinoids and prefrontal cortical function: Insights from preclinical studies. *Neuroscience and Biobehavioral Reviews, 30*(5), 680–695.

Ehrlich, P. R. (2000). Cited in Angier, N. (2000, October 10). A conversation with Dr. Paul R. Ehrlich—On human nature, genetics and the evolution of culture. *The New York Times online.*

Eich, E., Macaulay, D., & Lam, R. W. (1997). Mania, depression, and mood dependent memory. *Cognition & Emotion, 11*(5–6), 607–618.

Eichenbaum, H., & Fortin, N. (2003). Episodic memory and the hippocampus: It's about time. *Current Directions in Psychological Science, 12*(2), 53–57.

Einat, H. (2007). Different behaviors and different strains: Potential new ways to model bipolar disorder. *Neuroscience and Biobehavioral Reviews, 31*(6), 850–857.

Eisend, M. (2007). Understanding two-sided persuasion: An empirical assessment of theoretical approaches. *Psychology and Marketing, 24*(7), 615–640.

Ekman, P. (1980). *The face of man.* New York: Garland Press.

Ekman, P. (1993). Facial expression and emotion. *American Psychologist, 48,* 384–392.

Ekman, P. (2003). Cited in Foreman, J. (2003, August 5). A conversation with Paul Ekman: The 43 facial muscles that reveal even the most fleeting emotions. *The New York Times online.*

Ekman, P., et al. (1987). Universals and cultural differences in the judgments of facial expressions of emotion. *Journal of Personality and Social Psychology, 53,* 712–717.

Elkind, D. (1967). Egocentrism in adolescence. *Child Development, 38,* 1025–1034.

Elkind, D. (1985). Egocentrism redux. *Developmental Review, 5,* 218–226.

Elkind, D., & Bowen, R. (1979). Imaginary audience behavior in children and adolescents. *Developmental Psychology, 15*(1), 38–44.

Elkins, D. N. (2009). Why humanistic psychology lost its power and influence in American psychology. *Journal of Humanistic Psychology, 49*(3), 267–291.

Elklit, A., & Christiansen, D. M. (2010). ASD and PTSD in rape victims. *Journal of Interpersonal Violence, 25*(8), 1470–1488.

Ellickson, P. L., Tucker, J. S., Klein, D. J., & McGuigan, K. A. (2001). Prospective risk factors for alcohol misuse in late adolescence. *Journal of Studies on Alcohol, 62*(6), 773–782.

Elliot, A. J., & Mapes, R. R. (2005). Approach–avoidance motivation and self-concept evaluation. In A. Teaser, J. V. Wood, & D. A. Stapel (Eds.), *On building, defending, and regulating the self: A psychological perspective* (pp. 171–196). New York: Psychology Press.

Elliot, A. J., & Niesta, D. (2008). Romantic red: Red enhances men's attraction to women. *Journal of Personality and Social Psychology, 95*(5), 1150–1164.

Elliot, A. J., et al. (2010). Red, rank, and romance in women viewing men. *Journal of Experimental Psychology: General, 139*(3), 399–417.

Elliot, A. J., Maier, M. A., Moller, A. C., Friedman, R., & Meinhardt, J. (2007). Color and psychological functioning: The effect of red on performance attainment. *Journal of Experimental Psychology: General, 136,* 154–168.

Ellis, A. (2000). Cited in Chamberlin, J. (2000). An historic meeting of the minds. *Monitor on Psychology, 31*(9), 27.

Ellis, A. (2005). *How to stubbornly refuse to make yourself miserable about anything—yes, anything.* New York: Kensington.

Ellis, A., & Dryden, W. (1987). *The practice of rational-emotive therapy (RET).* New York: Springer.

Ellis, M. A., Weiss, B., & Lochman, J. E. (2009). Executive functions in children: Associations with aggressive behavior and appraisal processing. *Journal of Abnormal Child Psychology, 37*(7), 945–956.

Ellison, N. B., Steinfield, C., & Lampe, C. (2007). The benefits of Facebook "friends": Social capital and college students' use of online social network sites. *Journal of Computer-Mediated Communication, 12*(4), 1143–1168.

Ellsworth, P. C., Carlsmith, J. M., & Henson, A. (1972). The stare as a stimulus to flight in human subjects. *Journal of Personality and Social Psychology, 21*, 302–311.

Elms, A. C. (2009). Obedience lite. *American Psychologist, 64*(1), 32–36.

Else-Quest, N. M., Hyde, J. S., Goldsmith, H. H., & Van Hulle, C. A. (2006). Gender differences in temperament: A meta-analysis. *Psychological Bulletin, 132*(1), 33–72.

Else-Quest, N. M., Hyde, J. S., & Linn, M. C. (2010). Cross-national patterns of gender differences in mathematics: A meta-analysis. *Psychological Bulletin, 136*(1), 103–127.

Elzinga, B. M., et al. (2007). Neural correlates of enhanced working-memory performance in dissociative disorder: A functional MRI study. *Psychological Medicine, 37*(2), 235–245.

Embry, D., Hankins, M., Biglan, A., & Boles, S. (2009). Behavioral and social correlates of methamphetamine use in a population-based sample of early and later adolescents. *Addictive Behaviors, 34*, 343–351.

Emmons, R. A., & King, L. A. (1988). Conflict among personal strivings: Immediate and long-term implications for psychological and physical well-being. *Journal of Personality and Social Psychology, 54*(6), 1040–1048.

Engelhard, I. M., van den Hout, M. A., Janssen, W. C., & van der Beek, J. (2010). Eye movements reduce vividness and emotionality of "flashforwards." *Behaviour Research and Therapy, 48*(5), 442–447.

Engelhardt, H., Buber, I., Skirbekk, V., & Prskawetz, A. (2010). Social involvement, behavioural risks and cognitive functioning among the aged. *Ageing and Society, 30*, 779–809.

Epp, J., et al. (2008). Retrograde amnesia for visual memories after hippocampal damage in rats. *Learning and Memory, 15*, 214–221.

Erikson, E. H. (1963). *Childhood and society.* New York: Norton.

Erikson, E. H. (1968). *Identity: Youth and crisis.* New York: Norton.

Eriksson, C. J. P. (2008). Role of alcohol and sex hormones on human aggressive behavior. In D. W. Pfaff, C. Kordon, P. Chanson, & Y. Christen (Eds.), *Hormones and social behavior* (pp. 177–185). Berlin: Springer-Verlag.

Erixon, E., Högstorp, H., Wadin, K., & Rask-Andersen, H. (2009). Variational anatomy of the human cochlea: Implications for cochlear implantation. *Otology and Neurotology, 30*(1), 14–22.

Eron, L. D. (1982). Parent–child interaction, television violence, and aggression of children. *American Psychologist, 37*, 197–211.

Eron, L. D. (1993). Cited in DeAngelis, T. (1993). It's baaack: TV violence, concern for kid viewers. *APA Monitor, 24*(8), 16.

Escorial, S., et al. (2003). Abilities that explain the intelligence decline: Evidence from the WAIS-III. *Psicothema, 15*(1), 19–22.

Esser, J. K., & Lindoerfer, J. S. (2006). Groupthink and the space shuttle *Challenger* accident: Toward a quantitative case analysis. *Journal of Behavioral Decision Making, 2*(3), 167–177.

Etaugh, C. A., & Bridges, J. S. (2006). Midlife transitions. In J. Worell & C. D. Goodheart (Eds.), *Handbook of girls' and women's psychological health: Gender and well-being across the lifespan* (pp. 359–367). *Oxford series in clinical psychology.* New York: Oxford University Press.

Ewedemi, F., & Linn, M. W. (2006). Psychodynamics and psychopathology: Health and hassles in older and younger men. *Journal of Clinical Psychology, 43*(4), 347–353.

Eysenck, H. J. (1952). The effects of psychotherapy: An evaluation. *Journal of Consulting Psychology. 16*, 319–324.

Eysenck, H. J., & Eysenck, M. W. (1985). *Personality and individual differences.* New York: Plenum Press.

Ezzati M., Friedman, A. B., Kulkarni, S. C., & Murray, C. J. L. (2008, April 22). The reversal of fortunes: Trends in county mortality and cross-county mortality disparities in the United States. *PLoS Medicine, 5*(4), e66.

F

Fagan, J. F., & Holland, C. R. (2009). Culture-fair prediction of academic achievement. *Intelligence, 37*(1), 62–67.

Fanti, K. A., Vanman, E., Henrich, C. C., & Avraamides, M. N. (2009). Desensitization to media violence over a short period of time. *Aggressive Behavior, 35*(2), 179–187.

Fantz, R. L. (1961). The origin of form perception. *Scientific American, 204*(5), 66–72.

Farber, B. A., Brink, D. C., & Raskin, P. M. (1996). *The psychotherapy of Carl Rogers: Cases and commentary.* New York: Guilford Press.

Farrer, L. A., et al. (2009). Association of variants in MANEA with cocaine-related behaviors. *Archives of General Psychiatry, 66*(3), 267–274.

Farzan, F., et al. (2010). Evidence for gamma inhibition deficits in the dorsolateral prefrontal cortex of patients with schizophrenia. *Brain, 133*(5), 1505–1514.

Fasmer, O., Akiskal, H., Hugdahl, K., & Oedegaard, K. (2008). Non-right-handedness is associated with migraine and soft polarity in patients with mood disorders. *Journal of Affective Disorders, 108*(3), 217–224.

Fatemi, S. H., & Folsom, T. D. (2009). The neurodevelopmental hypothesis of schizophrenia, revisited. *Schizophrenia Bulletin, 35*(3), 528–548.

Feder, A., Nestler, E. J., Westphal, M., & Charney, D. S. (2010). Psychobiological mechanisms of resilience to stress. In J. W. Reich, A. J. Zautra, & J. S. Hall (Eds.), *Handbook of adult resilience* (pp. 35–54). New York: Guilford Press.

Fehr, B. (2008). Friendship formation. In S. Sprecher, A. Wenzel, & J. H. Harvey (Eds.), *Handbook of relationship initiation* (pp. 29–54). New York: CRC Press.

Feinstein, J. S., Adolphs, R., Damasio, A., & Tranel, D. (2010). The human amygdala and the induction and experience of fear. *Current Biology, 22*(1), 34–38.

Felsted, J. A., et al. (2010). Genetically determined differences in brain response to a primary food reward. *Journal of Neuroscience, 30*(7), 2428–2432.

Fenton, B. W. (2010). Measuring quality of life in chronic pelvic pain syndrome. *Expert Review of Obstetrics and Gynecology, 5*(1), 115–124.

Fernandez-Twinn, D. S., & Ozanne, S. E. (2006). Mechanisms by which poor early growth programs type-2 diabetes, obesity and the metabolic syndrome. *Physiology and Behavior, 88*(3), 234–243.

Ferrer, E., O'Hare, E. D., & Bunge, S. A. (2009). Fluid reasoning and the developing brain. *Frontiers in Neuroscience, 3*(1), 46–51.

Ferry, B., & McGaugh, J. L. (2008). Involvement of basolateral amygdala α2-adrenoceptors in modulating consolidation of inhibitory avoidance memory. *Learning and Memory, 15*, 238–243.

Festinger, L., & Carlsmith, J. M. (1959). Cognitive consequences of forced compliance. *Journal of Abnormal and Social Psychology, 58*, 203–210.

Festinger, L., Riecken, H. W., Jr., & Schachter, S. (1956). *When prophecy fails.* Minneapolis: University of Minnesota Press.

Fetissov, S. O., & Meguid, M. M. (2010). Serotonin delivery into the ventromedial nucleus of the hypothalamus affects differently feeding pattern and body weight in obese and lean Zucker rats. *Appetite, 54*(2), 346–353.

Fibel, B., & Hale, W. D. (1978). The generalized expectancy for success scale—A new measure. *Journal of Consulting and Clinical Psychology, 46,* 924–931.

Fiehler, K., Burke, M., Bien, S., Röder, B., & Rösler, F. (2008). The human dorsal action control system develops in the absence of vision. *Cerebral Cortex, 19*(1), 1–12.

Fields, R. D. (2005, February). Making memories stick. *Scientific American,* 75–81.

Fife, R. S., & Schrager, S. B. (2009). *The ACP handbook of women's health.* Philadelphia: ACP Press.

Filosa, A., et al. (2009). Neuron-glia communication via EphA4/ ephrin-A3 modulates LTP through glial glutamate transport. *Nature Neuroscience, 12*(10), 1285–1292.

Finch, E., & Munro, V. E. (2007). The demon drink and the demonized woman: Socio-sexual stereotypes and responsibility attribution in rape trials involving intoxicants. *Social and Legal Studies, 16*(4), 591–614.

Fineberg, N. A., & Craig, K. J. (2009). Pharmacotherapy for obsessive–compulsive disorder. In D. J. Stein, E. Hollander, & B. O. Rothbaum (Eds.), *Textbook of anxiety disorders* (pp. 311–338). Arlington, VA: American Psychiatric Publishing.

Finkelstein, E. A., Brown, D. S., Wrage, L. A., Allaire, B. T., & Hoerger, T. J. (2010). Individual and aggregate years-of-life-lost associated with overweight and obesity. *Obesity, 18*(2), 333–339.

Fischer, M., Hand, I., & Angenendt, J. (1998). Langzeiteffekte von Kurzzeit-Verhaltenstherapien bei Agoraphobie. *Zeitschrift für Klinische Psychologie. Forschung und Praxis, 17*(3), 225–243.

Fischer, P., Greitemeyer, T., & Frey, D. (2008). Unemployment and aggression: The moderating role of self-awareness on the effect of unemployment on aggression. *Aggressive Behavior, 34*(1), 34–45.

Fisher, B. S., Daigle, L. E., & Cullen, F. T. (2008). Rape against women. *Journal of Contemporary Criminal Justice, 24*(2), 163–177.

Fisher, B. S., Daigle, L. E., Cullen, F. T., & Turner, M. G. (2003). Reporting sexual victimization to the police and others: Results from a national-level study of college women. *Criminal Justice and Behavior, 30*(1), 6–38.

Fisher, C. B. (2009). *Decoding the ethics code: A practical guide for psychologists* (2nd ed.). Thousand Oaks, CA: Sage.

Fiske, S. T., & Borgida, E. (2008). Providing expert knowledge in an adversarial context: Social cognitive science in employment discrimination cases. *Annual Review of Law and Social Science, 4,* 123–148.

Fitzsimmons, D. (2008). Coherence in crisis: Groupthink, the news media, and the Iraq war. *Journal of Military and Strategic Studies, 10*(4), 1–52.

Flack, W. F., Jr., Laird, J. D., & Cavallaro, L. A. (1999). Separate and combined effects of facial expressions and bodily postures on emotional feelings. *European Journal of Social Psychology, 29*(2–3), 203–217.

Flavell, J. H. (2000). Development of children's knowledge about the mental world. *International Journal of Behavioral Development, 24*(1), 15–23.

Flavell, J. H., Miller, P. H., & Miller, S. A. (2002). *Cognitive development* (4th ed.). Upper Saddle River, NJ: Prentice Hall.

Flegal, K. M., Carroll, M. D., Ogden, C. L., & Curtin, L. R. (2010). Prevalence and trends in obesity among U.S. adults, 1999–2008. *Journal of the American Medical Association, 303*(3), 235–241.

Fleming, A. S. (2008). Group decision-making and leadership: An experimental examination in an executive compensation scenario. *Advances in Management Accounting, 17,* 113–149.

Flett, G. L., Besser, A., Hewitt, P. L., & Davis, R. A. (2007). Perfectionism, silencing the self, and depression. *Personality and Individual Differences, 43*(5), 1211–1222.

Fligor, B. J., & Cox, L. C. (2004) Output levels of commercially available portable compact disc players and the potential risk to hearing. *Ear and Hearing, 25,* 513–527.

Flood, M., & Pease, B. (2009). Factors influencing attitudes to violence against women. *Trauma, Violence, and Abuse, 10*(2), 125–142.

Flouri, E., & Buchanan, A. (2003). The role of father involvement and mother involvement in adolescents' psychological well-being. *British Journal of Social Work, 33*(3), 399–406.

Folkman, S., & Moskowitz, J. T. (2000b). The context matters. *Personality and Social Psychology Bulletin, 26*(2), 150–151.

Folkman, S., & Moskowitz, T. (2000a). Positive affect and the other side of coping. *American Psychologist, 55*(6), 647–654.

Follingstad, D., & McCormick, M. (2002). *Law and mental health professionals.* Washington, DC: American Psychological Association.

Fontaine, R. G., Tanha, M., Yang, C., Dodge, K. A., Bates, J. E., & Pettit, G. S. (2010). Does response evaluation and decision (RED) mediate the relation between hostile attributional style and antisocial behavior in adolescence? *Journal of Abnormal Child Psychology, 38*(5), 615–626.

Food and Drug Administration. (2004, July 20). *Decreasing the chance of birth defects.* Retrieved from http://www.fda.gov/ fdac/features/996_bd.html

Foote, B., Smolin, Y., Kaplan, M., Legatt, M. E., & Lipschitz, D. (2006). Prevalence of dissociative disorders in psychiatric outpatients. *American Journal of Psychiatry, 163*(4), 623–629.

Forcehimes, A. A., & Tonigan, J. S. (2008). Self-efficacy as a factor in abstinence from alcohol/other drug abuse: A meta-analysis. *Alcoholism Treatment Quarterly, 26*(4), 480–489.

Ford, K., Wirawan, D. N., Reed, B. D., Muliawan, P., & Sutarga, M. (2000). AIDS and STD knowledge, condom use, and HIV/STD infection among female sex workers in Bali, Indonesia. *AIDS Care, 12*(5), 523–534.

Forhan, G., Martiel, J-L., & Blum, M. G. B. (2008). A deterministic model of admixture and genetic introgression: The case of Neanderthal and Cro-Magnon. *Mathematical Biosciences, 216*(1), 71–76.

Forrest, D. V. (2008). Alien abduction: A medical hypothesis. *Journal of the American Academy of Psychoanalysis and Dynamic Psychiatry, 36*(3), 431–442.

Förster, J. (2009). Cognitive consequences of novelty and familiarity: How mere exposure influences level of construal. *Journal of Experimental Social Psychology, 45*(2), 444–447.

Fortenberry, J. D., Schick, V., Herbenick, D., Sanders, S. A., Dodge, B., & Reece, M. (2010). Sexual behaviors and condom use at last vaginal intercourse: A national sample of adolescents ages 14 to 17 years. *Journal of Sexual Medicine, 7*(Suppl. 5), 305–314.

Foster, J. D. (2008). Beauty is mostly in the eye of the beholder: Olfactory versus visual cues of attractiveness. *Journal of Social Psychology, 148*(6), 765–774.

Fowles, D. C., & Dindo, L. (2009). Temperament and psychopathy: A dual-pathway model. *Current Directions in Psychological Science, 18*(3), 179–183.

Fox, N. A., & Rutter, M. (2010). Introduction to the special section on the effects of early experience on development. *Child Development, 81*(1), 23–27.

Fox, S. E., Levitt, P., & Nelson, C. A., III. (2010). How the timing and quality of early experiences influence the development of brain architecture. *Child Development, 81*(1), 28–40.

Fraknoi, A. (2008). Preparing for the 2009 International Year of Astronomy: A hands-on symposium. In M. G. Gibbs, J. Barnes, J. G. Manning, & B. Partridge (Eds.), *ASP Conference Series, Vol. 400, proceedings of the conference held June 1–5, 2008, in St. Louis* (p. 35). San Francisco: Astronomical Society of the Pacific.

Franceschini, M. A., et al. (2007). Assessment of infant brain development with frequency-domain near-infrared spectroscopy. *Pediatric Research, 61*(5), 546–551.

Franco, K., et al. (2009). The role of perfectionism in eating behaviors among women with eating disorder. *Appetite, 52*(3), 832.

Franklin, T. R., et al. (2009). The GABA B agonist baclofen reduces cigarette consumption in a preliminary double-blind placebo-controlled smoking reduction study. *Drug and Alcohol Dependence, 103*(1–2), 30–36.

Frasure-Smith, N., & Lespérance, F. (2008). Depression and anxiety as predictors of 2-year cardiac events in patients with stable coronary artery disease. *Archives of General Psychiatry, 65*(1), 62–71.

Freedman, J. L., & Fraser, S. C. (1966). Compliance without pressure: The foot-in-the-door technique. *Journal of Personality and Social Psychology, 4*, 195–202.

Freeman, D., Pugh, K, Vorontsova, N., Antley, A., & Slater, M. (2010). Testing the continuum of delusional beliefs: An experimental study using virtual reality. *Journal of Abnormal Psychology, 119*(1), 83–92.

Freeman, M. S., Spence, M. J., & Oliphant, C. M. (1993, June). *Newborns prefer their mothers' low-pass filtered voices over other female filtered voices.* Paper presented at the annual convention of the American Psychological Society, Chicago.

Freese, T. E., Miotto, K., & Reback, C. J. (2002). The effects and consequences of selected club drugs. *Journal of Substance Abuse Treatment, 23*(2), 151–156.

Freitas, A. L., Clark, S. L., Kim, J. Y., & Levy, S. R. (2009). Action-construal levels and perceived conflict among ongoing goals: Implications for positive affect. *Journal of Research in Personality, 43*(5), 938–941.

Freud, S. (1955). Analysis of a phobia in a 5-year-old boy. In J. Strachey (Trans.), *The complete psychological works of Sigmund Freud.* London: Hogarth Press. (Original work published 1909)

Freud, S. (1964). A religious experience. In *Standard edition of the complete psychological works of Sigmund Freud* (Vol. 21). London: Hogarth Press. (Original work published 1927)

Freund, A. M., & Baltes, P. B. (2002). The adaptiveness of selection, optimization, and compensation as strategies of life management. *Journals of Gerontology: Series B: Psychological Sciences & Social Sciences, 57B*(5), 426–434.

Freund, M. (2009). On the notion of concept: II. *Artificial Intelligence, 173*(1), 167–179.

Friedman, L. J. (1999). *Identity's architect: A biography of Erik H. Erikson.* New York: Scribner.

Friedman, M., & Rosenman, R. H. (1974). *Type A behavior and your heart.* New York: Random House.

Friedman, R. A. (2006). The changing face of teenage drug abuse—the trend toward prescription drugs. *New England Journal of Medicine, 354*, 1448–1450.

Friedman, R. C., & Downey, J. I. (2008). Sexual differentiation of behavior. *Journal of the American Psychoanalytic Association, 56*, 147–175.

Friedman, S. R., et al. (2001). Correlates of anal sex with men among young adult women in an inner city minority neighborhood. *AIDS, 15*(15), 2057–2060.

Friedrich, C. K., Schild, U., & Roder, B. (2009). Electrophysiological indices of word fragment priming allow characterizing neural stages of speech recognition. *Biological Psychology, 80*(1), 105–113.

Frisch, R. (1997). Cited in Angier, N. (1997). Chemical tied to fat control could help trigger puberty. *The New York Times,* pp. C1, C3.

Fritsch, G., & Hitzig, E. (1960). On the electrical excitability of the cerebrum. In G. von Bonin (Ed.), *Some papers on the cerebral cortex.* Springfield, IL: Thomas. (Original work published 1870)

Froeliger, B., Gilbert, D. G., & McClernon, F. J. (2009). Effects of nicotine on novelty detection and memory recognition performance: Double-blind, placebo-controlled studies of smokers and nonsmokers. *Psychopharmacology, 205*(4), 625–633.

Fuentes, R., et al. (2009). Spinal cord stimulation restores locomotion in animal models of Parkinson's disease. *Science, 323*(5921), 1578–1582.

Fuji, K. (2002). Field experiments on operant conditioning of wild pigeons (*Columbia livia*). *Japanese Journal of Animal Psychology, 52*(1), 9–14.

Fukushima, M., Sharp, S., & Kobayashi, E. (2009). Born to bond, collectivism, and conformity: A comparative study of Japanese and American college students. *Deviant Behavior, 30*(5), 434–466.

Furnham, A. (2009). Sex differences in mate selection preferences. *Personality and Individual Differences, 47*(4), 262–267.

Fylkesnes, K., et al. (2001). Declining HIV prevalence and risk behaviours in Zambia: Evidence from surveillance and population-based surveys. *AIDS, 15*(7), 907–916.

G

Galdo-Alvarez, S., Lindín, M., & Díaz, F. (2009). Age-related prefrontal over-recruitment in semantic memory retrieval: Evidence from successful face naming and the tip-of-the-tongue state. *Biological Psychology, 82*(1), 89–96.

Gallagher-Thompson, D., Gray, H. L., Dupart, T., Jiminez, D., & Thompson, L. W. (2008). Effectiveness of cognitive/behavioral small group intervention for reduction of depression and stress in non-Hispanic White and Hispanic/Latino women dementia family caregivers: Outcomes and mediators of change. *Journal of Rational-Emotive Cognitive-Behavior Therapy, 26*(4), 286–303.

Gallese, V., Fadiga, L., Fogassi, L., & Rizzolatti, G. (1996). Action recognition in the premotor cortex. *Brain, 119*(2), 593–609.

Gans, D., & Silverstein, M. (2006). Norms of filial responsibility for aging parents across time and generations. *Journal of Marriage and Family, 68*(4), 961–976.

Gao, Y., Raine, A., Venables, P. H., Dawson, M. E., & Mednick, S. A. (2010a). Association of poor childhood fear conditioning and adult crime. *American Journal of Psychiatry, 167*, 56–60.

Gao, Y., Raine, A., Venables, P. H., Dawson, M. E., & Mednick, S. A. (2010b). Reduced electrodermal fear conditioning from ages 3 to 8 years is associated with aggressive behavior at age 8 years. *Journal of Child Psychology and Psychiatry, 51*(5), 550–558.

Garb, H. N., Wood, J. M., Lilienfeld, S. O., & Nezworski, M. T. (2005). Roots of the Rorschach controversy. *Clinical Psychology Review, 25*(1), 97–118.

Garcia, J. (1993). Misrepresentation of my criticism of Skinner. *American Psychologist, 48*, 1158.

Garcia, J., & Koelling, R. A. (1966). Relation of cue to consequences in avoidance learning. *Psychonomic Science 4*, 123–124.

Garcia-Falgueras, A., & Swaab, D. F. (2010). Sex hormones and the brain: An essential alliance for sexual identity and sexual orientation. In S. Loche et al. (Eds.), *Pediatric neuroendocrinology* (Vol. 17, pp. 22–35). Basel, Switzerland: Karger.

Garcia-Moreno, C., & Watts, C. (2000). Violence against women: Its importance for HIV/AIDS. *AIDS, 14*(Suppl. 3), S253–S265.

Gardini, G. G., et al. (2009). Respiratory function in patients with stable anorexia nervosa. *Chest, 136*(5), 1356–1363.

Gardner, H. (1983/1993). *Frames of mind.* New York: Basic Books.

Gardner, H. (2001, April 5). Multiple intelligence. *The New York Times,* p. A20.

Gardner, H. (2009). Birth and the spreading of a "meme." In J-Q. Chen, S. Moran, & H. Gardner (Eds.), *Multiple intelligences around the world* (pp. 3–16). Hoboken, NJ: Wiley.

Garrett, R. K. (2009). Politically motivated reinforcement seeking: Reframing the selective exposure debate. *Journal of Communication, 59*(4), 676–699.

Garza, Y., & Watts, R. E. (2010). Filial therapy and Hispanic values: Common ground for culturally sensitive helping. *Journal of Counseling and Development, 88*(1), 108–113.

Gaser, C., & Schlaug, G. (2003). Brain structures differ between musicians and nonmusicians. *Journal of Neuroscience, 23*(27), 9240–9245.

Gatchel, R. J., & Kishino, N. D. (2010). Managing pain. In J. C. Thomas & M. Hersen (Eds.), *Handbook of clinical psychology competencies* (pp. 1181–1192). New York: Springer.

Gavin, N. I., et al. (2005). Perinatal depression: A systematic review of prevalence and incidence. *Obstetrics & Gynecology, 106*, 1071–1083.

Gazzaniga, M. S. (2008). *Human: The science behind what makes us unique.* New York: HarperCollins.

Gerdes, A. B. M., Uhl, G., & Alpers, G. W. (2009). Spiders are special: Fear and disgust evoked by pictures of arthropods. *Evolution and Human Behavior, 30*(1), 66–73.

Gershoff, E. T. (2002). Corporal punishment by parents and associated child behaviors and experiences: A meta-analytic and theoretical review. *Psychological Bulletin, 128*(4), 539–579.

Gershoff, E. T., & Bitensky, S. H. (2007). The case against corporal punishment of children: Converging evidence from social science research and international human rights law and implications for U.S. public policy. *Psychology, Public Policy, and Law, 13*(4), 231–272.

Getzels, J. W., & Jackson, P. W. (1962). *Creativity and intelligence.* New York: Wiley.

Gibbons, C. J., Fourneir, J. C., Stirman, S. W., DeRubeis, R. J., Crits-Christoph, P., & Beck, A. T. (2010). The clinical effectiveness of cognitive therapy for depression in an outpatient clinic. *Journal of Affective Disorders, 125*(1–3), 169–176.

Giedd, J. N., et al. (2009). Anatomical brain magnetic resonance imaging of typically developing children and adolescents. *Journal of the American Academy of Child and Adolescent Psychiatry, 48*(5), 465–470.

Gigerenzer, G. (2010). Personal reflections on theory and psychology. *Theory & Psychology, 20*(6), 733–743.

Gigerenzer, G., Hoffrage, U., & Goldstein, D. G. (2008). Postscript: Fast and frugal heuristics. *Psychological Review, 115*(1), 238–239.

Gilbert, P. (2009). Biopsychosocial approaches and evolutionary theory as aids to integration in clinical psychology and psychotherapy. *Clinical Psychology and Psychotherapy.* doi:10.1002/cpp.5640020302

Gilbert, S. L., et al. (2008). Atypical recruitment of medial prefrontal cortex in autism spectrum disorders: An fMRI study of two executive function tasks. *Neuropsychologia, 46*(9), 2281–2291.

Gillham, J., et al. (2011). Character strengths predict subjective well-being during adolescence. *The Journal of Positive Psychology, 6*(1), 31–44.

Gilligan, C. (1977). In a different voice: Women's conceptions of self and morality. *Harvard Educational Review, 47*, 481–517.

Gilligan, C. (1982). *In a different voice.* Cambridge, MA: Harvard University Press.

Gilligan, C., & Attanucci, J. (1988). Two moral orientations: Gender differences and similarities. *Merrill-Palmer Quarterly, 34*, 223–237.

Ginsburg, G., & Bronstein, P. (1993). Family factors related to children's intrinsic/extrinsic motivational orientation and academic performance. *Child Development, 64*, 1461–1474.

Giussani, D. A. (2006). Prenatal hypoxia: Relevance to developmental origins of health and disease. In P. Gluckman & M. Hanson (Eds.), *Developmental origins of health and disease* (pp. 178–190). New York: Cambridge University Press.

Glantz, L., et al. (2010). Pro-apoptotic Par-4 and dopamine D2 receptor in temporal cortex in schizophrenia, bipolar disorder and major depression. *Schizophrenia Research, 118*(1–3), 292–299.

Glaser, R., et al. (1993). Stress and the memory T-cell response to the Epstein-Barr virus. *Health Psychology, 12*, 435–442.

Glass, D. C., et al. (2007). Effect of harassment and competition upon cardiovascular and plasma catecholamine responses in Type A and Type B individuals. *Psychophysiology, 17*(5), 453–463.

Glasser, C. L., Robnett, B., & Feliciano, C. (2009). Internet daters' body type preferences: Race–ethnic and gender differences. *Sex Roles, 61*(1–2), 14–33.

Glenn, S. S., Ellis, J., & Greenspoon, J. (1992). On the revolutionary nature of the operant as a unit of behavioral selection. *American Psychologist, 47*, 1326–1329.

Glynn, R. J. (2010). The USPSTF recommendation statement on coronary heart disease risk assessment. *Annals of Internal Medicine, 152*, 403–404.

Godden, D. R., & Baddeley, A. D. (1975). Context-dependent memory in two natural environments: On land and underwater. *British Journal of Psychology, 66*, 325–331.

Goddyn, H., et al. (2008). Deficits in acquisition and extinction of conditioned responses in mGluR7 knockout mice. *Neurobiology of Learning and Memory, 90*(1), 103–111.

Goez, H., & Zelnik, N. (2008). Handedness in patients with developmental coordination disorder. *Journal of Child Neurology, 23*(2), 151–154.

Goghari, V. M., & MacDonald, A. W., III. (2009). The neural basis of cognitive control: Response selection and inhibition. *Brain and Cognition, 71*(2), 72–83.

Goldman, J. S., Adamson, J., Karydas, A., Miller, B. L., & Hutton, M. (2008). New genes, new dilemmas: FTLD genetics and its implications for families. *American Journal of Alzheimer's Disease and Other Dementias, 22*(6), 507–515.

Goldman-Rakic, P. S. (1995). Cited in Goleman, D. (1995, May 2). Biologists find site of working memory. *The New York Times,* pp. C1, C9.

Goldschmidt, L., Day, N. L., & Richardson, G. A. (2000). Effects of prenatal marijuana exposure on child behavior problems at age 10. *Neurotoxicology and Teratology, 22*(3), 325–336.

Goldston, D. B., & Compton, J. S. (2010). Adolescent suicidal and nonsuicidal self-harm behaviors and risk. In E. J. Marsh & R. A. Barkley (Eds.), *Assessment of childhood disorders* (pp. 305–346). New York: Guilford Press.

Goleman, D. (2006). *Social intelligence: The new science of social relationships.* New York: Bantam Books.

Goleman, D. J. (1995). *Emotional intelligence.* New York: Bantam Books.

Golombok, S., et al. (2008). Developmental trajectories of sex-typed behavior in boys and girls: A longitudinal general population study of children aged 2.5–8 years. *Child Development, 79*(5), 1583–1593.

González, H. M., et al. (2010). Depression care in the United States: Too little for too few. *Archives of General Psychiatry, 67*, 37–46.

González, Y. S., Moreno, D. S., & Schneider, B. H. (2004). Friendship expectations of early adolescents in Cuba and Canada. *Journal of Cross-Cultural Psychology, 35*(4), 436–445.

Goodenough, F. (1926). *Measurement of intelligence by drawings.* Yonkers, NY: World Book.

Goodman, W., et al. (2010). Deep brain stimulation for intractable obsessive compulsive disorder: Pilot study using a blinded, staggered onset design. *Biological Psychiatry, 67*(6), 535–542.

Goodwin, P. J., et al. (2001). The effect of group psychosocial support on survival in metastatic breast cancer. *New England Journal of Medicine, 345*(24), 1719–1726.

Gordon, G. R. J., Mulligan, S. J., & MacVicar, B. A. (2009). Astrocyte control of blood flow. In V. Parpura & P. G. Haydon (Eds.), *Astrocytes in (patho)physiology of the nervous system* (pp. 462–486). New York: Springer Science + Business Media.

Gorodetsky, M., & Klavir, R. (2003). What can we learn from how gifted/average pupils describe their processes of problem solving? *Learning and Instruction, 13*(3), 305–325.

Gotlib, I. H., & Joormann, J. (2010). Cognition and depression: Current status and future directions. *Annual Review of Clinical Psychology, 6,* 285–312.

Gottesman, I. I. (1991). *Schizophrenia genesis.* New York: Freeman.

Gottfredson, G. D. (2009). John Holland (1919–2008). *American Psychologist, 64*(6), 561.

Gottfredson, L. S. (1997). Mainstream science on intelligence: An editorial with 52 signatories, history and bibliography. *Intelligence, 24*(1), 13–23.

Gottfredson, L., & Saklofske, D. H. (2009). Intelligence: Foundations and issues in assessment. *Canadian Psychology/Psychologie Canadienne, 50*(3), 183–195.

Gottlieb, B. H., Still, E., & Newby-Clark, I. R. (2007). Types and precipitants of growth and decline in emerging adulthood. *Journal of Adolescent Research, 22*(2), 132–155.

Gottlieb, G. (2007). Developmental neurobehavioral genetics: Development as explanation. In B. C. Jones & P. Mormède (Eds.), *Neurobehavioral genetics: Methods and applications* (2nd ed., pp. 17–27). Boca Raton, FL: CRC Press.

Gottschalk, L. J. (2007). Carol Gilligan—Psychologist, feminist, educator, philosopher. *Behavioral & Social Sciences Librarian, 26*(1), 65–90.

Grabe, S., Hyde, J. S., & Lindberg, S. M. (2007). Body objectification and depression in adolescents: The role of gender, shame, and rumination. *Psychology of Women Quarterly, 31,* 164–175.

Grace, D. M., David, B. J., & Ryan, M. K. (2008). Investigating preschoolers' categorical thinking about gender through imitation, attention, and the use of self-categories. *Child Development, 79*(6), 1928–1941.

Grant, I., Gonzalez, R., Carey, C. L., Natarajan, L., & Wolfson, T. (2003, July). Minimal long-term effects of marijuana use found in central nervous system. *Journal of the International Neuropsychological Society, 9*(5), 679–689.

Gray, S. L., et al. (2008). Antioxidant vitamin supplement use and risk of dementia or Alzheimer's disease in older adults. *Journal of the American Geriatrics Society, 56*(2), 291–295.

Greenberger, E., Chen, C., Tally, S. R., & Dong, Q. (2000). Family, peer, and individual correlates of depressive symptomology among U.S. and Chinese adolescents. *Journal of Consulting and Clinical Psychology, 68,* 209–219.

Greene, B. (2000). African American lesbian and bisexual women. *Journal of Social Issues, 56*(2), 239–249.

Greene, J. (1982). The gambling trap. *Psychology Today, 16*(9), 50–55.

Greenhalgh, J., Dickson, R., & Dundar, Y. (2010). Biofeedback for hypertension: A systematic review. *Journal of Hypertension, 28*(4), 644–652.

Greenwood, P. M., et al. (2009). Both a nicotinic single nucleotide polymorphism (SNP) and a noradrenergic SNP modulate working memory performance when attention is manipulated. *Journal of Cognitive Neuroscience, 21*(11), 2139–2153.

Gregory, V. L., Jr. (2010). Cognitive-behavioral therapy for schizophrenia: Applications to social work practice. *Social Work in Mental Health, 8*(2), 140–159.

Gregory-Roberts, E. M., Naismith, S. L., Cullen, K. M., & Hickie, I. B. (2010). Electroconvulsive therapy-induced persistent retrograde amnesia: Could it be minimised by ketamine or other pharmacological approaches? *Journal of Affective Disorders, 126*(1–2), 39–45.

Greidanus, E., & Everall, R. D (2010). Helper therapy in an online suicide prevention community. *British Journal of Guidance and Counselling, 38*(2), 191–204.

Griffin, A. M., & Langlois, J. H. (2006). Stereotype directionality and attractiveness stereotyping: Is beauty good or is ugly bad? *Social Cognition, 24*(2), 187–206.

Griffin, C. (2001). Imagining new narratives of youth: Youth research, the "new Europe" and global youth culture. *Childhood: Global Journal of Child Research, 8*(2), 147–166.

Grillon, M-L., et al. (2010). Episodic memory and impairment of an early encoding process in schizophrenia. *Neuropsychology, 24*(1), 101–108.

Gronau, N., Ben-Shakhar, G., & Cohen, A. (2005). Behavioral and physiological measures in the detection of concealed information. *Journal of Applied Psychology, 90*(1), 147–158.

Gross, A. L., Gallo, J. J., & Eaton, W. W. (2010). Depression and cancer risk: 24 years of follow-up of the Baltimore Epidemiologic Catchment Area. *Cancer Causes and Control, 21*(2), 191–199.

Grosser, B. I., Monti-Bloch, L., Jennings-White, C., & Berliner, D. L. (2000). Behavioral and electrophysiological effects of androstadienone, a human pheromone. *Psychoneuroendocrinology, 25*(3), 289–300.

Grundy, E., & Henretta, J. C. (2006). Between elderly parents and adult children: A new look at the intergenerational care provided by the "sandwich generation." *Ageing & Society, 26*(5), 707–722.

Grusec, J. E. (2006). The development of moral behavior and conscience from a socialization perspective. In M. Killen & J. G. Smetana (Eds.), *Handbook of moral development* (pp. 243–265). Mahwah, NJ: Erlbaum.

Guadagno, R. E., & Cialdini, R. B. (2010). Preference for consistency and social influence: A review of current research findings. *Social Influence, 5*(3), 152–163.

Guerin, B. (1999). Social behaviors as determined by different arrangements of social consequences: Social loafing, social facilitation, deindividuation, and a modified social loafing. *Psychological Record, 49*(4), 565–578.

Guerrini, I., Thomson, A. D., & Gurling, H. D. (2007). The importance of alcohol misuse, malnutrition and genetic susceptibility on brain growth and plasticity. *Neuroscience and Biobehavioral Reviews, 31*(2), 212–220.

Gulledge, A. T., et al. (2009). M1 receptors mediate cholinergic modulation of excitability in neocortical pyramidal neurons. *Journal of Neuroscience, 29*(31), 9888–9902.

Gump, B. B., & Matthews, K. A. (2000). Are vacations good for your health? The 9-year mortality experience after the Multiple Risk Factor Intervention Trial. *Psychosomatic Medicine, 62*(5), 608–612.

Gunter, C., & Dhand, R. (2002). Human biology by proxy. Introductory article to an entire issue on the mouse genome. *Nature, 420,* 509.

Gurba, E. (2005). On the specific character of adult thought: Controversies over postformal operations. *Polish Psychological Bulletin, 36*(3), 175–185.

Guttmacher Institute. (2009, June 8). Available at http://www.guttmacher.org/

Guzzetti, B. J. (2010). Feminist perspectives on the new literacies. In E. A. Baker & D. J. Leu (Eds.), *The new literacies* (pp. 242–264). New York: Guilford Press.

H

Haaf, R. A., Smith, P. H., & Smitley, S. (1983). Infant response to facelike patterns under fixed trial and infant-control procedures. *Child Development, 54,* 172–177.

Haandrikman, K., Harmsen, C., van Wissen, L. J. G., & Hutter, I. (2008). Geography matters: Patterns of spatial homogamy in the Netherlands. *Population, Space, and Place, 14,* 387–405.

Hadamitzky, M., & Koch, M. (2009). Effects of acute intra-cerebral administration of the 5-HT2A/C receptor ligands DOI and ketanserin on impulse control in rats. *Behavioural Brain Research, 204*(1), 88–92.

Haenen, J. (2001). Outlining the teaching–learning process: Piotr Gal'perin's contribution. *Learning and Instruction, 11*(2), 157–170.

Hafemeister, L., et al. (2010). Perception: Insights from the sensorimotor approach. *European Workshop of Visual Information Processing,* Paris. http://hal.archives-ouvertes.fr/hal-00520433/. Accessed January 14, 2011.

Hagler, D. J., Jr., Riecke, L., & Sereno, M. I. (2007). Parietal and superior frontal visuospatial maps activated by pointing and saccades. *NeuroImage, 35*(4), 1562–1577.

Haier, R. J., Karama, S., Leyba, L., & Jung, R. E. (2009). MRI assessment of cortical thickness and functional activity changes in adolescent girls following three months of practice on a visual-spatial task. *BMC Research Notes, 2*(174), 1–7.

Hale, L., et al. (2009). Does mental health history explain gender disparities in insomnia symptoms among young adults? *Sleep Medicine, 10*(10), 1118–1123.

Hall, G. C. N., Sue, S., Narang, D. S., & Lilly, R. S. (2000). Culture-specific models of men's sexual aggression: Intra- and interpersonal determinants. *Cultural Diversity and Ethnic Minority Psychology, 6*(3), 252–267.

Hall, J. A., Park, N., Song, H., & Cody, M. J. (2010). Strategic misrepresentation in online dating: The effects of gender, self-monitoring, and personality traits. *Journal of Social and Personal Relationships, 27*(1), 117–135.

Halpern, D. F. (2007). The nature and nurture of critical thinking. In R. J. Sternberg, H. L. Roediger, & D. F. Halpern (Eds.), *Critical thinking in psychology* (pp. 1–14). New York: Cambridge University Press.

Halpern, D. F., & LaMay, M. L. (2000). The smarter sex: A critical review of sex differences in intelligence. *Educational Psychology Review, 12*(2), 229–246.

Halpern, D. F., et al. (2007). The science of sex differences in science and mathematics. *Psychological Science in the Public Interest, 8*(1), 1–51.

Halpern, R. (2005). Book review: Examining adolescent leisure time across cultures: New directions for child and adolescent development, No. 99. *Journal of Adolescent Research, 20*(4), 524–525.

Hancock, J. (2007). Digital deception: When, where, and how people lie online. In K. McKenna, T. Postmes, U. Reips, & A. Joinson (Eds.), *Oxford handbook of Internet psychology* (pp. 287–301). Oxford, England: Oxford University Press.

Harker, L., & Keltner, D. (2001). Expressions of positive emotion in women's college yearbook pictures and their relationship to personality and life outcomes across adulthood. *Journal of Personality and Social Psychology, 80*(1), 112–124.

Harkness, K. L., & Stewart, J. G. (2009). Symptom specificity and the prospective generation of life events in adolescence. *Journal of Consulting and Clinical Psychology, 77*(6), 1067–1077.

Harlow, H. F. (1959). Love in infant monkeys. *Scientific American, 200,* 68–86.

Harlow, H. F., & Zimmermann, R. R. (1959). Affectional responses in the infant monkey. *Science, 130,* 421–432.

Harmon-Jones, E., & Harmon-Jones, C. (2008). Cognitive dissonance theory: An update with a focus on the action-based model. In J. Y. Shah & W. L. Gardner (Eds.), *Handbook of motivation science* (pp. 71–83). New York: Guilford Press.

Harmon-Jones, E., Amodio, D. M., & Harom-Jones, C. (2009). Action-based model of dissonance: A review, integration, and expansion of conceptions of cognitive conflict. *Advances in Experimental Social Psychology, 41,* 119–127.

Harper, S., Lynch, J., Burris, S., & Smith, G. D. (2007). Trends in the Black–White life expectancy gap in the United States, 1983–2003. *Journal of the American Medical Association, 297,* 1224–1232.

Harris, J. L., Bargh, J. A., & Brownell, K. D. (2009) Priming effects of television food advertising on eating behavior. *Health Psychology, 28*(4), 404–413.

Hart, A. J., et al. (2000). Differential response in the human amygdala to racial outgroup vs. ingroup face stimuli. *NeuroReport, 11*(11), 2351–2355.

Harter, S. (1990). Self and identity development. In S. S. Feldman & G. R. Elliott (Eds.), *At the threshold: The developing adolescent.* Cambridge, MA: Harvard University Press.

Hartup, W. W. (1993). Adolescents and their friends. In B. Laursen (Ed.), *Close friendships in adolescence* (pp. 3–22). San Francisco: Jossey-Bass.

Hasin, D. S., Goodwin, R. D., Stinson, F. S., & Grant, B. F. (2005). Epidemiology of major depressive disorder. *Archives of General Psychiatry, 62,* 1097–1106.

Hassett, J. M., Siebert, E. R., & Wallen, K. (2008). Sex differences in rhesus monkey toy preferences parallel those of children. *Hormones and Behavior, 54*(3), 359–364.

Hatzimouratidis, K., et al. (2010). Guidelines on male sexual dysfunction: Erectile dysfunction and premature ejaculation. *European Urology, 57*(5), 804–814.

Hauge, A. W., Kirchmann, M., & Olesen, J. (2010). Trigger factors in migraine with aura. *Cephalalgia, 30*(3), 346–353.

Haustein, K-O., & Groneberg, D. (2009). Pharmacology and pharmakinetics of nicotine. In K-O. Haustein & D. Groneberg (Eds.), *Tobacco or health?* (pp. 61–86). New York: Springer.

Haworth, C. M. A., Dale, P. S., & Plomin, R. (2009). Sex differences and science: The etiology of science excellence. *Journal of Child Psychology and Psychiatry, 50*(9), 1113–1120.

Haworth, C. M. A., et al. (2009). A twin study of the genetics of high cognitive ability selected from 11,000 twin pairs in six studies from four countries. *Behavior Genetics, 39*(4), 359–370.

Hayes, B. (2001). *Sleep demons: An insomniac's memoir.* New York: Washington Square Press.

Hearne, K. (2003). Retrieved from http://ourworld.compuserve.com/homepages/keithhearne/Cultural.html

Heath, J., & Goggin, K. (2009). Attitudes towards male homosexuality, bisexuality, and the down low lifestyle: Demographic differences and HIV implications. *Journal of Bisexuality, 9*(1), 17–31.

Heber, D. (2010). An integrative view of obesity. *American Journal of Clinical Nutrition, 91*(1), 280S–283S.

Heindel, J. J., & Lawler, C. (2006). Role of exposure to environmental chemicals in developmental origins of health and disease. In P. Gluckman & M. Hanson (Eds.), *Developmental origins of health and disease* (pp. 82–97). New York: Cambridge University Press.

Heitland, K., & Bohner, G. (2010). Reducing prejudice via cognitive dissonance: Individual differences in preference for consistency moderate the effects of counter-attitudinal advocacy. *Social Influence, 5*(3), 164–181.

Helms, J. E. (2006). Fairness is not validity or cultural bias in racial-group assessment: A quantitative perspective. *American Psychologist, 61*(8), 845–859.

Helton, W. S. (2010). Does perceived trainability of dog (*Canis lupus familiaris*) breeds reflect differences in learning or differences in physical ability? *Behavioural Processes, 83*(3), 315–323.

Henderson, A. S. (2009). Alzheimer's disease in its epidemiological context. *Acta Neurologica Scandinavica, 88*(S149), 1–3.

Henderson, T. L., Roberto, K. A., & Kamo, Y. (2010). Older adults' responses to Hurricane Katrina. *Journal of Applied Gerontology, 29*(1), 48–69.

Hendin, H., Maltsberger, J. T., Lipschitz, A., Pollinger H., & Kyle, J. (2001). Recognizing and responding to a suicide crisis. *Suicide and Life-Threatening Behavior, 31*(2), 115–128.

Hendricks, P. S., Delucchi, K. L., & Hall, S. M. (2010). Mechanisms of change in extended cognitive behavioral treatment for tobacco dependence. *Drug and Alcohol Dependence, 109*(1–3), 114–119.

Heng, M. A. (2000). Scrutinizing common sense: The role of practical intelligence in intellectual giftedness. *Gifted Child Quarterly, 44*(3), 171–182.

Henley, C. L., Nunez, A. A., & Clemens, L. G. (2010). Exogenous androgen during development alters adult partner preference and mating behavior in gonadally intact male rats. *Hormones and Behavior, 57*(4–5), 488–495.

Henry, D. B. (2008). Changing classroom social settings through attention to norms. In M. Shinn & H. Yoshikawa (Eds.), *Toward positive youth development* (pp. 40–57). New York: Oxford University Press.

Henry, J. D., MacLeod, M. S., Phillips, L. H., & Crawford, J. R. (2004). A meta-analytic review of prospective memory and aging. *Psychology and Aging, 19*(1), 27–39.

Henseler, I., Falkai, P., & Gruber, O. (2009). Disturbed functional connectivity within brain networks subserving domain-specific subcomponents of working memory in schizophrenia: Relation to performance and clinical symptoms. *Journal of Psychiatric Research, 44*(6), 364–372.

Hensley, W. E. (1981). The effects of attire, location, and sex on aiding behavior. *Journal of Nonverbal Behavior, 6*, 3–11.

Herbenick, D., Reece, M., Sanders, S. A., Schick, V., Dodge, B., & Fortenberry, J. D. (2010a). Sexual behavior in the United States: Results from a national probability sample of males and females ages 14 to 94. *Journal of Sexual Medicine, 7*(Suppl. 5), 255–265.

Herbenick, D., Reece, M., Schick, V., Sanders, S. A., Dodge, B., & Fortenberry, J. D. (2010b). Sexual behaviors, relationships, and perceived health among adult women in the United States: Results from a national probability sample. *Journal of Sexual Medicine, 7*(Suppl. 5), 277–290.

Herbenick, D., Reece, M., Schick, V., Sanders, S. A., Dodge, B., & Fortenberry, J. D. (2010c). An event-level analysis of the sexual characteristics and composition among adults ages 18 to 59: Results from a national probability sample in the United States. *Journal of Sexual Medicine, 7*(Suppl. 5), 346–361.

Herbert, B. (2005, September 26). A waking nightmare. *The New York Times online.*

Hergenhahn, B. R. (2009). *An introduction to the history of psychology* (6th ed.). Belmont, CA: Cengage.

Heron, M., & Tejada-Vera, B. (2009). Deaths: Leading causes. *National Vital Statistics Reports, 58*(8). Retrieved from http://www.cdc.gov/nchs/data/nvsr/nvsr58/nvsr58_08.pdf

Herr, I., & Büchler, M. W. (2010). Dietary constituents of broccoli and other cruciferous vegetables: Implications for prevention and therapy of cancer. *Cancer Treatment Reviews, 70*(12), 5004–5013.

Herring, M. P., O'Connor, P. J., & Dishman, R. K. (2010). The effect of exercise training on anxiety symptoms among patients. *Archives of Internal Medicine, 170*(4), 321–331.

Herrmann, D. J. (1991). *Super memory.* Emmaus, PA: Rodale.

Hersen, M., Bellack, A. S., Himmelhoch, J. M., & Thase, M. E. (1984). Effects of social skill training, amitriptyline, and psychotherapy in unipolar depressed women. *Behavior Therapy, 15*(1), 21–40.

Hetherington, E. M., et al. (1992). Coping with marital transitions. *Monographs of the Society for Research in Child Development, 57*(2–3, ser. 227).

Hettema, J. M., Prescott, C. A., Myers, J. M., Neale, M. C., & Kendler, K. S. (2005). The structure of genetic and environmental risk factors for anxiety disorders in men and women. *Archives of General Psychiatry, 62*, 182–189.

Higgins, J. A., Hoffman, S., & Dworkin, S. J. (2010). Rethinking gender, heterosexual men, and women's vulnerability to HIV/AIDS. *American Journal of Public Health, 100*(3), 435–445.

Higgs, S., & Woodward, M. (2009). Television watching during lunch increases afternoon snack intake of young women. *Appetite, 52*(1), 39–43.

Hilgard, E. R. (1994). Neodissociation theory. In S. J. Lynn & J. W. Rhue (Eds.), *Dissociation: Clinical, theoretical and research perspectives* (pp. 32–51). New York: Guilford Press.

Hilsenroth, M. J., Baity, M. R., Mooney, M. A., & Meyer, G. J. (2004). DSM-IV major depressive episode criteria: An evaluation of reliability and validity across three different rating methods. *International Journal of Psychiatry in Clinical Practice, 8*(1), 3–10.

Hingson, R., et al. (2002). *A call to action: Changing the culture of drinking at U.S. colleges.* Washington, DC: National Institutes of Health: National Institute of Alcohol Abuse and Alcoholism.

Hirst, W., et al. (2009). Long-term memory for the terrorist attack of September 11: Flashbulb memories, event memories, and the factors that influence their retention. *Journal of Experimental Psychology: General, 138*(2), 161–176.

Ho, M. Y., Cheung, F. M., & Cheung, S. F. (2010). The role of meaning in life and optimism in promoting well-being. *Personality and Individual Differences, 48*(5), 658–663.

Hobson, J. A. (1999). Arrest of firing of aminergic neurones during REM sleep: Implications for dream theory. *Brain Research Bulletin, 50*(5–6), 333–334.

Hobson, J. A. (2003). *Dreaming: An introduction to the science of sleep.* New York: Oxford University Press.

Hockett, J. M., Saucier, D. A., Hoffman, B. H., Smith, S. J., & Craig, A. W. (2009). Oppression through acceptance? *Violence Against Women, 15*(8), 877–897.

Hoff, E. (2005). *Language development* (3rd ed.). Belmont, CA: Wadsworth.

Hoffman, H. G. (2004). Virtual reality therapy. *Scientific American, 291*(2), 58–65.

Hoffman, H. G., et al. (2008). Virtual reality pain control during burn wound debridement in the hydrotank. *Clinical Journal of Pain, 24*(4), 299–304.

Hoffman, W., & Friese, M. (2008). Impulses got the better of me: Alcohol moderates the influence of implicit attitudes toward food cues and eating behavior. *Journal of Abnormal Psychology, 117*(2), 420–427.

Hojnoski, R. L., Morrison, R., Brown, M., & Matthews, W. J. (2006). Projective test use among school psychologists. *Journal of Psychoeducational Assessment, 24*(2), 145–159.

Holden, C. (1980). Identical twins reared apart. *Science, 207*(4437), 1323–1328.

Hollan, D. (2009). The influence of culture on the experience and interpretation of disturbing dreams. *Culture, Medicine, and Psychiatry, 33*(2), 313–322.

Holland, A. C., & Kensinger, E. A. (2010). Emotion and autobiographical memory. *Physics of Life Reviews, 7*(1), 88–131.

537

Holland, J. J. (2000, July 25). Groups link media to child violence. Associated Press online.

Hollinger, L. M., & Buschmann, M. B. (1993). Factors influencing the perception of touch by elderly nursing home residents and their health caregivers. *International Journal of Nursing Studies, 30*, 445–461.

Hollingshead, A. B., & Redlich, F. C. (1958). *Social class and mental illness.* New York: Wiley.

Hollon, S. D., & Shelton, R. C. (2001). Treatment guidelines for major depressive disorder. *Behavior Therapy, 32*(2), 235–258.

Holmes, T. H., & Rahe, R. H. (1967). The social readjustment rating scale. *Journal of Psychosomatic Research, 11*, 213–218.

Holroyd, K. A., Drew, J. B., Cottrell, C. K., Romanek, K. M., & Heh, V. (2007). Impaired functioning and quality of life in severe migraine: The role of catastrophizing and associated symptoms. *Cephalalgia, 27*(10), 1156–1165.

Honorton, C. (1985). Meta-analysis of psi Ganzfeld research. *Journal of Parapsychology, 49*, 51–91.

Honorton, C., et al. (1990). Psi communication in the Ganzfeld. *Journal of Parapsychology, 54*, 99–139.

Honts, C. R., Hodes, R. L., & Raskin, D. C. (1985). Effects of physical countermeasures on the physiological detection of deception. *Journal of Applied Psychology, 70*(1), 177–187.

Hoover, R. N. (2000). Cancer—Nature, nurture, or both? *New England Journal of Medicine online, 343*(2).

Horan, W. P., Wynn, J. K., Kring, A. M., Simons, R. F., & Green, M. F. (2010). Electrophysiological correlates of emotional responding in schizophrenia. *Journal of Abnormal Psychology, 119*(1), 18–30.

Horgan, J. (2009). *Walking away from terrorism.* London: Routledge.

Horn, J. L., & Noll, J. (1997). Human cognitive capabilities: Gf-Gc theory. In D. P. Flanagan, J. L. Genshaft, & P. L. Harrison (Eds.), *Contemporary intellectual assessment: Theories, tests, and issues* (pp. 53–91). New York: Guilford Press.

Horn, J. M. (1983). The Texas adoption project. *Child Development, 54*, 268–275.

Hovey, J. D. (2000). Acculturative stress, depression, and suicidal ideation in Mexican immigrants. *Cultural Diversity and Ethnic Minority Psychology, 6*(2), 134–151.

Howard, G. S., et al. (2009). Do research literatures give correct answers? *Review of General Psychology, 13*(2), 116–121.

Howard, K. J., Ellis, H. B., & Khaleel, M. A. (2010). Psychological factors that may influence outcome after joint replacement surgery. *Current Orthopaedic Practice, 21*(2), 144–148.

Hrabosky, J., et al. (2009). Multidimensional body image comparisons among patients with eating disorders, body dysmorphic disorder, and clinical controls: A multisite study. *Body Image, 6*(3), 155–163.

Hu, F. B., et al. (2000). Physical activity and risk of stroke in women. *Journal of the American Medical Association, 283*, 2961–2967.

Hu, X., Yang, Y., Liu, L., Liu, X., & Tong, Y. (2010). Early psychological intervention following a natural disaster. *Social Behavior and Personality, 38*(1), 71–74.

Hubel, D. H., & Wiesel, T. N. (1979). Brain mechanisms of vision. *Scientific American, 241*, 150–162.

Huchard, E., et al. (2009). Studying shape in sexual signals: The case of primate sexual swellings. *Behavioral Ecology and Sociobiology, 63*(8), 1231–1242.

Huesmann, L. R., Moise-Titus, J., Podolski, C., & Eron, L. D. (2003). Longitudinal relations between children's exposure to TV violence and their aggressive and violent behavior in young adulthood: 1977–1992. *Developmental Psychology, 39*(2), 201–221.

Huestis, M. A., et al. (2002). Drug abuse's smallest victims: In utero drug exposure. *Forensic Science International, 128*(2), 20.

Hugdahl, K., Thomsen, T., & Ersland, L. (2006). Sex differences in visuo-spatial processing: An fMRI study of mental rotation. *Neuropsychologia, 44*(9), 1575–1583.

Hughes, M. E., Alloy, L. B., & Cogswell, A. (2008). Repetitive thought in psychopathology: The relation of rumination and worry to depression and anxiety symptoms. *Journal of Cognitive Psychotherapy, 22*(3), 271–288.

Hughes, T. F., Andel, R., Small, B. J., Borenstein, A. R., & Mortimer, J. A. (2008). The association between social resources and cognitive change in older adults. *Journals of Gerontology Series B: Psychological Sciences and Social Sciences, 63*, P241–P244.

Huizink, A. C., & Mulder, E. J. H. (2006). Maternal smoking, drinking or cannabis use during pregnancy and neurobehavioral and cognitive functioning in human offspring. *Neuroscience & Biobehavioral Reviews, 30*(1), 24–41.

Hunt, M. (1993). *The story of psychology.* New York: Anchor Books.

Hunt, R. R. (2002). How effective are pharmacologic agents for alcoholism? *Journal of Family Practice, 51*(6), 577.

Hunt, R. W. (2010). Psychological responses to cancer: A case for cancer support groups. *Community Health Studies, 14*(1), 35–38.

Hunter, D. J. (2005). Gene–environment interactions in human diseases. *Nature Reviews Genetics, 6*, 287–298.

Huntjens, R. J. C., et al. (2003). Interidentity amnesia for neutral, episodic information in dissociative identity disorder. *Journal of Abnormal Psychology, 112*(2), 290–297.

Hurd, Y. L., et al. (2005). Marijuana impairs growth in mid-gestation fetuses. *Neurotoxicology and Teratology, 27*(2), 221–229.

Hurka, T. (2010). Morality and political violence. *Philosophical Review, 119*(1), 115–117.

Husain, G. (2003). Cited in Elias, M. (2003, August 17). Music affects mood, but it won't make kids smarter. *USA Today.*

Hussain, A. (2002, June 26) It's official. Men really are afraid of commitment. Reuters.

Hustad, J. T. P., Barnett, N. P., Borsari, B., & Jackson, K. M. (2010). Web-based alcohol prevention for incoming college students: A randomized controlled trial. *Addictive Behaviors, 35*(3), 183–189.

Hutchings, J. (2004). Color in folklore and tradition—The principles. *Color Research and Application, 29*, 57–66.

Hutton, H. E. (2008, March 11). *Gender differences in alcohol use and risky sexual behaviors and STDs among STD clinic patients.* Paper presented at the 2008 National STD Prevention Conference, Chicago.

Hwang, C. H., et al. (2010). Role of bone morphogenetic proteins on cochlear hair cell formation. *Developmental Dynamics, 239*(2), 505–513.

Hyde, J. S. (2005). The gender similarities hypothesis. *American Psychologist, 60*, 581–592.

Hyde, J. S., & Mertz, J. E. (2009). Gender, culture, and mathematics performance. *Proceedings of the National Academy of Sciences, 106*(22), 8801–8807.

Hyde, J. S., & Plant, E. A. (1995). Magnitude of psychological gender differences. *American Psychologist, 50*, 159–161.

Hyde, J. S., Fennema, E., & Lamon, S. J. (1990). Gender differences in mathematics performance: A meta-analysis. *Psychological Bulletin, 107*, 139–155.

Hyde, J. S., Lindberg, S. M., Linn, M. C., Ellis, A. B., & Williams, C. C. (2008). Gender similarities characterize math performance. *Science, 321*, 494–495.

Hyman, R. (2011). Cited in B. Carey. (2011, January 5). Journal's paper on ESP expected to prompt outrage. *The New York Times online.*

I

Iacoboni, M. (2009a). Do adolescents simulate? Developmental studies of the human mirror neuron system. In T. Striano & V. Reid (Eds.), *Social cognition: Development, neuroscience and autism* (pp. 39–51). Hoboken, NJ: Wiley-Blackwell.

Iacoboni, M. (2009b). Imitation, empathy, and mirror neurons. *Annual Review of Psychology, 60*, 653–670.

Iacono, W. G. (2008). Accuracy of polygraph techniques: Problems using confessions to determine ground truth. *Physiology and Behavior, 95*(1–2), 24–26.

Imel, Z. E., Wampold, B. E., Miller, S. D., & Fleming, R. R. (2008). Distinctions without a difference: Direct comparison of psychotherapies for alcohol use disorders. *Psychology of Addictive Behaviors, 22*(4), 533–543.

Inaba, M., et al. (2009). Facilitation of low-frequency stimulation-induced long-term potentiation by endogenous noradrenaline and serotonin in developing rat visual cortex. *Neuroscience Research, 64*(2), 191–198.

Indlekofer, F., et al. (2009). Reduced memory and attention performance in a population-based sample of young adults with a moderate lifetime use of cannabis, ecstasy and alcohol. *Journal of Psychopharmacology, 23*(5), 495–509.

Inhelder, B., & Piaget, J. (1958). *The growth of logical thinking.* New York: Basic Books.

International Human Genome Sequencing Consortium. (2004). Finishing the euchromatic sequence of the human genome. *Nature, 431*, 931–945.

Ironson, G. H., O'Cleirigh, C., Schneiderman, N., Weiss, A., & Costa, P. T., Jr. (2008). Personality and HIV disease progression: Role of NEO-PI-R openness, extraversion, and profiles of engagement. *Psychosomatic Medicine, 70*(2), 245–253.

Irwin, H. J. (2009). *The psychology of paranormal belief: A researcher's handbook.* Hertfordshire, England: University of Hertfordshire Press.

Isarida, T., & Isarida, T. K. (2006). Influences of environmental context on the recency effect in free recall. *Memory and Cognition, 34*(4), 787–794.

Isen, J., et al. (2010). Sex-specific association between psychopathic traits and electrodermal reactivity in children. *Journal of Abnormal Psychology, 119*(1), 216–225.

Ismail, S. A., & Mowafi, H. A. (2009). Melatonin provides anxiolysis, enhances analgesia, decreases intraocular pressure, and promotes better operating conditions during cataract surgery under topical anesthesia. *Anesthesia and Analgesia, 108*, 1146–1151.

Itier, R. J., & Batty, M. (2009). Neural bases of eye and gaze processing: The core of social cognition. *Neuroscience and Biobehavioral Reviews, 33*(6), 843–863.

Ito, M. (2008). Cited in T. Lewin (2008, November 19). Study finds teenagers' Internet socializing isn't such a bad thing, *The New York Times online.*

Ito, M., Robinson, L., Horst, H. A., Pascoe, C. J., & Bittanti, M. (2009). *Living and learning with new media: Summary of findings from the Digital Youth Project.* Cambridge, MA: MIT Press.

Iverson, P., et al. (2003). A perceptual interference account of acquisition difficulties for non-native phonemes. *Cognition, 87*(1), B47–B57.

Iwasaki, A., & Medzhitov, R. (2010). Regulation of adaptive immunity by the innate immune system. *Science, 327*(5963), 291–295.

Izard, C. E. (1984). Emotion–cognition relationships and human development. In C. E. Izard, J. Kagan, & R. B. Zajonc (Eds.), *Emotions, cognition, and behavior* (pp. 17–37). New York: Cambridge University Press.

J

Jaaniste, T., Hayes, B., & von Baeyer, C. L. (2007). Effects of preparatory information and distraction on children's cold-pressor pain outcomes: A randomized controlled trial. *Behaviour Research and Therapy, 45*(11), 2789–2799.

Jackson, B., & Beauchamp, M. R. (2010). Self-efficacy as a meta-perception within coach–athlete and athlete–athlete relationships. *Psychology of Sport and Exercise, 11*, 188–196.

Jackson, E. C. (2009). Nocturnal enuresis: Giving the child a "lift." *Journal of Pediatrics, 154*(5), 636–637.

Jackson, H., & Nuttall, R. L. (2001). Risk for preadolescent suicidal behavior: An ecological model. *Child and Adolescent Social Work Journal, 18*(3), 189–203.

Jackson, L. A., et al. (2009). Self-concept, self-esteem, gender, race, and information technology use. *CyberPsychology & Behavior, 12*(4), 437–440.

Jackson, L. C., & Greene, B. (2000). *Psychotherapy with African American women: Innovations in psychodynamic perspectives and practice.* New York: Guilford Press.

Jackson, M. L. (2009). *The effects of sleep deprivation on simulated driving, neurocognitive functioning and brain activity in professional drivers.* Retrieved from http://researchbank. swinburne .edu.au/vital/access/manager/Repository/swin:14257

Jacob, S., & McClintock, M. K. (2000). Psychological state and mood effects of steroidal chemosignals in women and men. *Hormones and Behavior, 37*(1), 57–78.

Jacob, S., McClintock, M. K., Zelano, B., & Ober, C. (2002). Paternally inherited HLA alleles are associated with women's choice of male odor. *Nature Genetics, 30*, 175–179.

Jacobs, S. (1993). *Pathologic grief: Maladaptation to loss.* Washington, DC: American Psychiatric Press.

Jacobsen, J. S., et al. (2006). Early-onset behavioral and synaptic deficits in a mouse model of Alzheimer's disease. *Proceedings of the National Academy of Sciences, 103*, 5161–5166.

James, W. (1890). *The principles of psychology.* New York: Henry Holt.

Jamison, K. R. (2000). Suicide and bipolar disorder. *Journal of Clinical Psychiatry, 61*(Suppl. 9), 47–51.

Janero, D. R., & Makriyannis, A. (2009). Cannabinoid receptor antagonists: Pharmacological opportunities, clinical experience, and translational prognosis. *Expert Opinion on Emerging Drugs, 14*(1), 43–65.

Jang, K. L., Livesley, W. J., Vernon, P. A., & Jackson, D. N. (2007). Heritability of personality disorder traits: A twin study. *Acta Psychiatrica Scandinavica, 94*(6), 438–444.

Janis, I. L. (1982). *Groupthink* (2nd ed.). Boston: Houghton Mifflin.

Janos, P. M. (1987). A fifty-year follow-up of Terman's youngest college students and IQ-matched agemates. *Gifted Child Quarterly, 31*, 55–58.

Janowitz, H. D., & Grossman, M. I. (1949). Effects of variations in nutritive density on intake of food in dogs and cats. *American Journal of Physiology, 158*, 184–193.

Janowsky, J. S., Chavez, B., & Orwoll, E. (2000). Sex steroids modify working memory. *Journal of Cognitive Neuroscience, 12*, 407–414.

Jaušovec, N., & Jaušovec, K. (2009). Gender related differences in visual and auditory processing of verbal and figural tasks. *Brain Research, 1300*, 135–145.

Jemal, A., et al. (2008). Mortality from leading causes by education and race in the United States, 2001. *American Journal of Preventive Medicine, 34*(1), 1–8.

Jemal, A., et al. (2009). Cancer statistics, 2009. *CA: Cancer Journal for Clinicians, 59*, 225–249.

539

Jennings, M., Heitner, K., & Heravi, N. (2009). Identification of factors associated with academic success and persistence to graduation in online learning environments. In *Proceedings of World Conference on Educational Multimedia, Hypermedia and Telecommunications 2009* (pp. 4216–4219). Chesapeake, VA: AACE.

Jensen, M. (2009). Hypnosis for chronic pain management: A new hope. *Pain, 146*(3), 235–237.

Jensen, M., & Patterson, D. R. (2006). Hypnotic treatment of chronic pain. *Journal of Behavioral Medicine, 29*(1), 95–124.

Jensen, M., et al. (2009). Effects of self-hypnosis training and EMG biofeedback relaxation training on chronic pain in persons with spinal-cord injury. *International Journal of Clinical and Experimental Hypnosis, 57*(3), 239–268.

Jester, J. M., et al. (2008). Trajectories of childhood aggression and inattention/hyperactivity. *Journal of the American Academy of Child and Adolescent Psychiatry, 47*(10), 1158–1165.

Jhangiani, R. (2010). Psychological concomitants of the 11 September 2001 terrorist attacks: A review. *Behavioral Sciences of Terrorism and Political Aggression, 2*(1), 38–69.

Joffe, P. (2008). An empirically supported program to prevent suicide in a college student population. *Suicide and Life-Threatening Behavior, 38*(1), 87–103.

Johansen, M., Karterud, S., Pedersen, G., Gude, T., & Falkum, E. (2004). An investigation of the prototype validity of the borderline DSM-IV construct. *Acta Psychiatrica Scandinavica, 109*(4), 289–298.

Johnson, J. L., Eaton, D. K., Pederson, L. L., & Lowry, R. (2009). Associations of trying to lose weight, weight control behaviors, and current cigarette use among U.S. high school students. *Journal of School Health, 79*(8), 355–360.

Johnson, S. B., Sudhinaraset, M., & Blum, R. W. (2010). Neuromaturation and adolescent risk taking: Why development is not determinism. *Journal of Adolescent Research, 25*(1), 4–23.

Johnson, W., & Bouchard, T. J., Jr. (2007). Sex differences in mental abilities: *g* masks the dimensions on which they lie. *Intelligence, 35*(1), 23–39.

Johnson, W., & Bouchard, T. J., Jr. (2009). Linking abilities, interests, and sex via latent class analysis. *Journal of Career Assessment, 17*(1), 3–38.

Johnson, W., & Krueger, R. F. (2006). How money buys happiness: Genetic and environmental processes linking finances and life satisfaction. *Journal of Personality and Social Psychology, 90*(4), 680–691.

Johnson, W., Deary, I. J., & Iacono, W. G. (2009). Genetic and environmental transactions underlying educational attainment. *Intelligence, 37*(5), 466–478.

Johnson, W., Jung, R. E., Colom, R., & Haier, R. J. (2008). Cognitive abilities independent of IQ correlate with regional brain structure. *Intelligence, 36*(1), 18–28.

Johnston, L. D., O'Malley, P. M., Bachman, J. G., & Schulenberg, J. E. (2009). *Monitoring the future national results on adolescent drug use: Overview of key findings, 2008* (NIH Publication No. 09-7401). Bethesda, MD: National Institute on Drug Abuse.

Jones, J. L., & Leary, M. R. (1994). Effects of appearance-based admonitions against sun exposure on tanning intentions in young adults. *Health Psychology, 13*, 86–90.

Jonsdottir, I. H., Hellstrand, K., Thoren, P., & Hoffman, P. (2000). Enhancement of natural immunity seen after voluntary exercise in rats: Role of central opioid receptors. *Life Sciences, 66*(13), 1231–1239.

Jorgensen, G. (2006). Kohlberg and Gilligan: Duet or duel? *Journal of Moral Education, 35*(2), 179–196.

Judd, C. (2011). Cited in B. Carey. (2011, January 5). Journal's paper on ESP expected to prompt outrage. *The New York Times online.*

K

Kagan, J., & Saudino, K. J. (2001). Behavioral inhibition and related temperaments. In R. N. Emde & J. K. Hewitt (Eds.), *Infancy to early childhood: Genetic and environmental influences on developmental change* (pp. 111–122). New York: Oxford University Press.

Kahana, E., Kahana, B., Wykle, M., & Kulle, D. (2009). Marshalling social support: A care-getting model for persons living with cancer. *Journal of Family Social Work, 12*(2), 168–193.

Kaiser, N. C., & Miller-Perrin, C. L. (2009). Examining the relationship between parental psychological aggression, parental neglect, and substance abuse in young adults. *Journal of Integrated Social Sciences, 1*(1), 96–119.

Kakko, J., et al. (2007). A stepped care strategy using buprenorphine and methadone versus conventional methadone maintenance in heroin dependence: A randomized controlled trial. *American Journal of Psychiatry, 164*, 797–803.

Kalavana, T. V., Maes, S., & De Gucht, V. (2010). Interpersonal and self-regulation determinants of healthy and unhealthy eating behavior in adolescents. *Journal of Health Psychology, 15*(1), 44–52.

Kalil, A., Ziol-Guest, K. M., & Coley, R. L. (2005). Perceptions of father involvement patterns in teenage-mother families: Predictors and links to mothers' psychological adjustment. *Family Relations, 54*(2), 197–211.

Kamalanabhan, T. J., Sunder, D. L., & Vasanthi, M. (2000). An evaluation of the Choice Dilemma Questionnaire as a measure of risk-taking propensity. *Social Behavior and Personality, 28*(2), 149–156.

Kamphaus, R. W., Petoskey, M. D., & Rowe, E. W. (2000). Current trends in psychological testing of children. *Professional Psychology: Research and Practice, 31*(2), 155–164.

Kanayama, G., Hudson, J. I., & Pope, H. G. (2009). Features of men with anabolic-androgenic dependence: A comparison with nonindependent AAS users and with AAS users. *Drug and Alcohol Dependence, 102*(1–3), 130–137.

Kandel, E. R. (2006). *In search of memory: The emergence of a new science of mind.* New York: Norton.

Kaplan, K., Talbot, L., & Harvey, A. (2009). Cognitive mechanisms in chronic insomnia: Processes and prospects. *Sleep Medicine Clinics, 4*(4), 541–548.

Kaplan, R. M., & Saccuzzo, D. P. (2008). *Psychological testing: Principles, applications, and issues.* Belmont, CA: Cengage.

Karlberg, L., et al. (1998). Is there a connection between car accidents, near accidents, and Type A drivers? *Behavioral Medicine, 24*(3), 99–106.

Karolewicz, B., et al. (2009). Reduced level of glutamic acid decarboxylase-67 kDa in the prefrontal cortex in major depression. *International Journal of Neuropsychopharmacology. 13*(4), 411–420.

Karremans, J., Stroebe, W., & Claus, J. (2006). Beyond Vicary's fantasies: The impact of subliminal priming and brand choice. *Journal of Experimental Social Psychology, 42*, 792–798.

Karwautz, A., et al. (2001). Individual-specific risk factors for anorexia nervosa: A pilot study using a discordant sister-pair design. *Psychological Medicine, 31*(2), 317–329.

Katigbak, M. S., Church, A. T., Guanzon-Lapeña, M. A., Carlota, A. J., & del Pilar, G. H. (2002). Are indigenous personality dimensions culture specific? Philippine inventories and the five-factor model. *Journal of Personality and Social Psychology, 82*(1), 89–101.

Kawano, Y. (2010). Physio-pathological effects of alcohol on the cardiovascular system: Its role in hypertension and cardiovascular disease. *Hypertension Research, 33*, 181–191.

Kazdin, A. E. (2008). Evidence-based treatment and practice: New opportunities to bridge clinical research and practice, enhance the knowledge base, and improve patient care. *American Psychologist, 63*(3), 146–159.

Kazim, S. F., et al. (2008). Attitudes toward suicide bombing in Pakistan. *Crisis: Journal of Crisis Intervention and Suicide Prevention, 29*(2), 81–85.

Keenan, P. A., & Soleymani, R. M. (2001). Gonadal steroids and cognition. In R. E. Tarter et al. (Eds.), *Medical neuropsychology: Clinical issues in neuropsychology* (2nd ed.) (pp. 181–197). Dordrecht, Netherlands: Kluwer Academic.

Kegeles, L. S., et al. (2010). Increased synaptic dopamine function in associative regions of the striatum in schizophrenia. *Archives of General Psychiatry, 67*(3), 231–239.

Keller, A., et al. (2003). Progressive loss of cerebellar volume in childhood-onset schizophrenia. *American Journal of Psychiatry, 160,* 128–133.

Keller, M. B., et al. (2000). A comparison of nefazodone, the cognitive behavioral-analysis system of psychotherapy, and their combination for the treatment of chronic depression. *New England Journal of Medicine, 342*(20), 1462–1470.

Keller, S. S., Roberts, N., & Hopkins, W. (2009). A comparative magnetic resonance imaging study of the anatomy, variability, and asymmetry of Broca's area in the human and chimpanzee brain. *Journal of Neuroscience, 29*(46), 14607–14616.

Kellerman, J., Lewis, J., & Laird, J. D. (1989). Looking and loving: The effects of mutual gaze on feelings of romantic love. *Journal of Research in Personality, 23,* 145–161.

Kelley, H. H., & Michela, J. L. (1980). Attribution theory and research. *Annual Review of Psychology, 31,* 457–501.

Kellman, P. J., & Arterberry, M. E. (2006). Infant visual perception. In D. Kuhn et al. (Eds.), *Handbook of child psychology,* Vol. 2, *Cognition, perception, and language* (6th ed.) (pp. 109–160). Hoboken, NJ: Wiley.

Kelly, J. F., Stout, R. L., Magill, M., Tonigan, J. S., & Pagano, M. E. (2010). Mechanisms of behavior change in Alcoholics Anonymous: Does AA lead to better alcohol use outcomes by reducing depression symptoms? *Addiction, 105*(4), 626–636.

Kemeny, M. E. (2009). Psychobiological responses to social threat: Evolution of a psychological model in psychoneuroimmunology. *Brain, Behavior, and Immunity, 23*(1), 1–9.

Kendler, K. S., Myers, J., Prescott, C. A., & Neale, M. C. (2001). The genetic epidemiology of irrational fears and phobias in men. *Archives of General Psychiatry, 58*(3), 257–265.

Kerlin, J. R., Shahin, A. J., & Miller, L. M. (2010). Attentional gain control of ongoing cortical speech representations in a "cocktail party." *Journal of Neuroscience, 30*(2), 620–628.

Kessler, R. C. (2003). Epidemiology of women and depression. *Journal of Affective Disorders, 74*(1), 5–13.

Kessler, R. C., et al. (2003). The epidemiology of major depressive disorder: Results from the National Comorbidity Survey Replication (NCS-R). *Journal of the American Medical Association, 289*(23), 3095–3105.

Kessler, R. C., et al. (2005). Lifetime prevalence and age-of-onset distributions of DSM-IV disorders in the National Comorbidity Survey Replication. *Archives of General Psychiatry, 62*(6), 593–602.

Key, W. B. (1973), *Subliminal seduction: Ad media's manipulation of a not so innocent America.* Englewood Cliffs, NJ: Prentice Hall.

Kiecolt-Glaser, J. K., Marucha, P. T., Atkinson, C., & Glaser, R. (2001). Hypnosis as a modulator of cellular immune dysregulation during acute stress. *Journal of Consulting and Clinical Psychology, 69*(4), 674–682.

Kiecolt-Glaser, J. K., McGuire, L., Robles, T. F., & Glaser, R. (2002b). Emotions, morbidity, and mortality: New perspectives from psychoneuroimmunology. *Annual Review of Psychology, 53*(1), 83–107.

Kiene, S. M., et al. (2010). Risky sexual behavior, partner HIV testing, disclosure, and HIV care seeking. *AIDS Patient Care and STDs, 24*(2), 117–126.

Kikuchi, H., et al. (2010). Memory repression: Brain mechanisms underlying dissociative amnesia. *Journal of Cognitive Neuroscience, 22*(3), 602–613.

Kilpatrick, D. G., Amstadter, A. B., Resnick, H. S., & Ruggiero, K. J. (2007). Rape-related PTSD: Issues and interventions. *Psychiatric Times, 24*(7). Retrieved from http://www.psychiatrictimes.com/ptsd/content/article/10168/53921?pageNumber=3

Kim, B. S. K., & Omizo, M. M. (2003). Asian cultural values, attitudes toward seeking professional psychological help, and willingness to see a counselor. *Counseling Psychologist, 31*(3), 343–361.

Kimble, D. P. (1988). *Biological psychology.* New York: Holt, Rinehart and Winston.

King, B. J. (2008). ME...ME...WASHOE: An appreciation. *Sign Language Studies, 8*(3), 315–323.

King, R. (2000). Cited in Frazier, L. (2000, July 16). The new face of HIV is young, Black. *The Washington Post,* p. C01.

King, S. (2005). Virtual reality heals 9/11 wounds. Cited in M. Lake (2005), http://www.cnn.com/2005/TECH/04/29/spark.virtual/index.html

Kinsey, A. C., Pomeroy, W. B., & Martin, C. E. (1948). *Sexual behavior in the human male.* Philadelphia: Saunders.

Kinsey, A. C., Pomeroy, W. B., Martin, C. E., & Gebhard, P. H. (1953). *Sexual behavior in the human female.* Philadelphia: Saunders.

Kirke, D. M. (2009). Gender clustering in friendship networks. *Methodological Innovations Online, 4,* 23–36.

Kiviniemi, M. T., & Rothman, A. J. (2010). Specifying the determinants of people's health beliefs and health behavior. In J. M. Suls, K. W. Davidson, & R. M. Kaplan (Eds.). *Handbook of health psychology and behavioral medicine.* (pp. 64–83). New York: Guilford Press.

Klein, S. B., Robertson, T. E., & Delton, A. W. (2010). Facing the future: Memory as an evolved system for planning future acts. *Memory and Cognition, 38*(1), 13–22.

Kleinke, C. L. (1977). Compliance to requests made by gazing and touching experimenters in field settings. *Journal of Experimental Social Psychology, 13,* 218–223.

Kleinmuntz, B., & Szucko, J. J. (1984). Lie detection in ancient and modern times. *American Psychologist, 39,* 766–776.

Klintsova, A. Y., & Greenough, W. T. (1999). Synaptic plasticity in cortical systems. *Current Opinion in Neurobiology, 9*(2), 203–208.

Klüver, H., & Bucy, P. C. (1939). Preliminary analysis of functions of the temporal lobe in monkeys. *Archives of Neurology and Psychiatry, 42,* 979–1000.

Knapp, L.G., Kelly-Reid, J.E., and Ginder, S.A. (2011). *Enrollment in Postsecondary Institutions, Fall 2009; Graduation Rates, 2003 & 2006 Cohorts; and Financial Statistics, Fiscal Year 2009* (NCES 2011-230). U.S. Department of Education. Washington, DC: National Center for Education Statistics. Retrieved February 16, 2011, from http://nces.ed.gov/pubsearch

Knickmeyer, R., et al. (2005). Gender-typed play and amniotic testosterone. *Developmental Psychology, 41,* 517–528.

Knight, R. G., & Titov, N. (2009). Use of virtual reality tasks to assess prospective memory: Applicability and evidence. *Brain Impairment, 10*(1), 3–13.

Koenig, P., et al. (2008). Medial temporal lobe involvement in an implicit memory task: Evidence of collaborating implicit and explicit memory systems from fMRI and Alzheimer's disease. *Cerebral Cortex, 18*(12), 2831–2843.

Koerber, A., et al. (2006). Covariates of tooth-brushing frequency in low-income African Americans from grades 5 to 8. *Pediatric Dentistry, 28*(6), 524–530.

Kohl, C. (2004). Postpartum psychoses: Closer to schizophrenia or the affective spectrum? *Current Opinion in Psychiatry, 17*(2), 87–90.

Kohlberg, L. (1969). *Stages in the development of moral thought and action.* New York: Holt, Rinehart and Winston.

Kohlberg, L. (1981). *The philosophy of moral development.* San Francisco: Harper & Row.

Kohlberg, L., & Kramer, R. (1969). Continuities and discontinuities in childhood and adult moral development. *Human Development, 12,* 93–120.

Kohn, N., & Smith, S. M. (2009). Partly versus completely out of your mind: Effects of incubation and distraction on resolving fixation. *Journal of Creative Behavior, 43*(2), 102–118.

Kolb, B., Halliwell, C., & Gibb, R. (2009). Factors influencing neocortical development in the normal and injured brain. In M. S. Blumberg, J. H. Freeman, & S. R Robinson (Eds.), *Oxford Handbook of Developmental Behavioral Neuroscience* (pp. 375–387). New York: Oxford University Press.

Kong, L. L., Allen, J. B., & Glisky, E. L. (2008). Interidentity memory transfer in dissociative identity disorder. *Journal of Abnormal Psychology, 117*(3), 686–692.

Kontak, A. C., Wang, Z., Arbique, D., & Victor, R. G. (2009). Central sympatholysis with dexmedetomidine is an effective countermeasure for cocaine-induced sympathetic activation and peripheral vasoconstriction in chronic cocaine abusers. *Circulation, 120,* S1178.

Koo, M., & Oishi, S. (2009). False memory and the associative network of happiness. *Personality and Social Psychology Bulletin, 35*(2), 212–220.

Kooijman, C. M., et al. (2000). Phantom pain and phantom sensations in upper limb amputees: An epidemiological study. *Pain, 87*(1), 33–41.

Koscik, T., O'Leary, D., Moser, D. J., Andreasen, N. C., & Nopoulos, P. (2009). Sex differences in parietal lobe morphology: Relationship to mental rotation performance. *Brain and Cognition, 69*(3), 451–459.

Koss, M. P. (1993). Rape. *American Psychologist, 48,* 1062–1069.

Koss, M. P. (2003). Evolutionary models of why men rape: Acknowledging the complexities. In C. B. Travis (Ed.), *Evolution, gender, and rape* (pp. 191–205). Cambridge, MA: MIT Press.

Koss, M. P., Figueredo, A. J., & Prince, R. J. (2002). Cognitive mediation of rape's mental, physical and social health impact: Tests of four models in cross-sectional data. *Journal of Consulting and Clinical Psychology, 70*(4), 926–941.

Koster, E. H. W., Fox, E., & MacLeod, C. (2009). Introduction to the special section on cognitive bias modification in emotional disorders. *Journal of Abnormal Psychology, 118*(1), 1–4.

Kotagal, S. (2009). Parasomnias in childhood. *Sleep Medicine Reviews, 13*(2), 157–168.

Kovacs, N., et al. (2009). Neuroimaging and cognitive changes during déjà vu. *Epilepsy and Behavior, 14*(1), 190–196.

Kownacki, R. J., & Shadish, W. R. (1999). Does Alcoholics Anonymous work? The results from a meta-analysis of controlled experiments. *Substance Use and Misuse, 34,* 1897–1916.

Krähenbühl, S., Blades, M., & Eiser, C. (2009). The effect of repeated questioning on children's accuracy and consistency in eyewitness testimony. *Legal and Criminological Psychology, 14*(2), 263–278.

Kramer, M. D., Krueger, R. F., & Hicks, B. M. (2008). The role of internalizing and externalizing liability factors in accounting for gender differences in the prevalence of common psychopathological syndromes. *Psychological Medicine, 38,* 51–61.

Kramer, P. D. (2003, June 22). Your Zoloft might prevent a heart attack. *The New York Times,* p. WK3.

Krantz, D. S., Contrada, R. J., Hill, D. R., & Friedler, E. (1988). Environmental stress and biobehavioral antecedents of coronary heart disease. *Journal of Consulting and Clinical Psychology, 56,* 333–341.

Krogh, J., et al. (2010). Growth hormone, prolactin and cortisol response to exercise in patients with depression. *Journal of Affective Disorders, 125*(1), 189–197.

Krueger, F. et al. (2008). Integral calculus problem solving: An fMRI investigation. *Neuroreport, 19*(11), 1095–1099.

Kubinyi, E., Turcsán, B., & Miklósi, A. (2009). Dog and owner demographic characteristics and dog personality trait associations. *Behavioural Processes, 81*(3), 392–401.

Kuczmarski, R. J., et al. (2000, December 4). CDC growth charts: United States. *Advance data from vital and health statistics* (No. 314). Hyattsville, MD: National Center for Health Statistics.

Kübler-Ross, E. (1969). *On death and dying.* New York: Macmillan.

Kuehn, B. M. (2009). Sexually transmitted infections. *Journal of the American Medical Association, 301*(8), 817.

Kumari, V., et al. (2009). Neural and behavioural responses to threat in men with a history of serious violence and schizophrenia or antisocial personality disorder. *Schizophrenia Research, 110*(1), 47–58.

Kuntzman, G. (2007). Stop "iPod oblivion." Retrieved from http://www.brooklynpaper.com/stories/30/6/30_06ipods.html

Kuo, P-H., et al. (2010). Genome-wide linkage scans for major depression in individuals with alcohol dependence. *Journal of Psychiatric Research, 44*(9), 616–619.

Kurth, T., et al. (2006). Healthy lifestyle and the risk of stroke in women. *Archives of Internal Medicine, 166,* 1403–1409.

Kurzban, R., & Weeden, J. (2005). HurryDate: Mate preferences in action. *Evolution and Human Behavior, 26*(3), 227–244.

Kvavilashvili, L., Mirani, J., Schlagman, S., Foley, K., & Kornbrot, D. E. (2009). Consistency of flashbulb memories of September 11 over long delays: Implications for consolidation and wrong time slice hypotheses. *Journal of Memory and Language, 61*(4), 556–572.

Kwok, H-K. (2006). A study of the sandwich generation in Hong Kong. *Current Sociology, 54*(2), 257–272.

Kwok, H-K. (2007). Psychopharmacology in autism spectrum disorders. *Current Opinion in Psychiatry, 16*(5), 529–534.

L

Laaksonen, E., et al. (2008). A randomized, multicentre, open-label, comparative trial of disulfiram, naltrexone and acamprosate in the treatment of alcohol dependence. *Alcohol and Alcoholism, 43*(1), 53–61.

Labouvie-Vief, G. (2006). Emerging structures of adult thought. In J. J. Arnett & J. L. Tanner (Eds.), *Emerging adults in America* (pp. 59–84). Washington, DC: American Psychological Association.

Labouvie-Vief, G., & Gonzalez, M. M. (2004). Dynamic integration: Affect optimization and differentiation in development. In D. Y. Dai & R. J. Sternberg (Eds.), *Motivation, emotion, and cognition* (pp. 237–272). Mahwah, NJ: Erlbaum.

Lachman, M. E. (2004). Development in midlife. *Annual Review of Psychology, 55,* 305–331.

Lai, C. K., et al. (2009). Global variation in the prevalence and severity of asthma symptoms: Phase three of the International Study of Asthma and Allergies in Childhood (ISAAC). *Thorax, 64*(6), 476–483.

Lam, M. P., et al. (2009). Effects of acute ethanol on β-endorphin release in the nucleus accumbens of selectively bred lines of alcohol-preferring AA and alcohol-avoiding ANA rats. *Psychopharmacology, 208*(1), 121–130.

Lamers, C. T. J., Bechara, A., Rizzo, M., & Ramaekers, J. G. (2006). Cognitive function and mood in MDMA/THC users, THC users and non-drug using controls. *Journal of Psychopharmacology, 20*(2), 302–311.

Lan, Y-J., & Zuo, B. (2009). An introduction to social identity model of deindividuation effects. *Advances in Psychological Science, 17*(2), 467–472.

Lander, K., & Pritchett, J. (2009). When to care: The economic rationale of slavery health care provision. *Social Science History, 33*(2), 155–182.

Landy, F. J. (2006). The long, frustrating, and fruitless search for social intelligence: A cautionary tale. In K. R. Murphy (Ed.), *A critique of emotional intelligence: What are the problems and how can they be fixed?* (pp. 81–123). Mahwah, NJ: Erlbaum.

Lane, R. D., et al. (2009). Neural correlates of heart rate variability during emotion. *NeuroImage, 44*(1), 213–222.

Laney, C., & Loftus, E. F. (2009). Eyewitness memory. In R. N. Kocsis (Ed.), *Applied criminal psychology: A guide to forensic behavioral sciences* (pp. 121–145). Springfield, IL: Thomas.

Lang, A. R., Goeckner, D. J., Adesso, V. J., & Marlatt, G. A. (1975). Effects of alcohol on aggression in male social drinkers. *Journal of Abnormal Psychology, 84*, 508–518.

Lang, E. V., et al. (2000). Adjunctive non-pharmacological analgesia for invasive medical procedures: A randomised trial. *Lancet, 355*, 1486–1490.

Lange, R. A., & Hillis, L. D. (2010). Sudden death in cocaine abusers. *European Heart Journal, 31*(3), 271–273.

Langlois, J. H., et al. (2000). Maxims or myths of beauty? A meta-analytic and theoretical review. *Psychological Bulletin, 126*(3), 390–423.

Lappalainen, T., & Dermitzakis, E. T. (2010). Evolutionary history of regulatory variation in human populations. *Human Molecular Genetics, 19*(2), 197–203.

Larsen, J. T., Berntson, G. G., Poehlmann, K. M., Ito, T. A., & Cacioppo, J. T. (2008). The psychophysiology of emotion. In M. Lewis, J. M. Haviland-Jones, & L. F. Barrett (Eds.), *Handbook of emotions* (pp. 180–195). New York: Guilford Press.

Lashley, K. S. (1950). In search of the engram. In *Symposium of the Society for Experimental Biology* (Vol. 4). New York: Cambridge University Press.

Latané, B., & Dabbs, J. M. (1975). Sex, group size, and helping in three cities. *Sociometry, 38*, 180–194.

Lau, A. S., Litrownik, A. J., Newton, R. R., Black, M. M., & Everson, M. D. (2006). Factors affecting the link between physical discipline and child externalizing problems in Black and White families. *Journal of Community Psychology, 34*(1), 89–103.

Laucht, M., et al. (2009). Impact of psychosocial adversity on alcohol intake in young adults: Moderation by the LL genotype of the serotonin transporter polymorphism. *Biological Psychiatry, 66*(2), 102–109.

Laumann, E. O., et al. (2006). Sexual activity, sexual disorders and associated help-seeking behavior among mature adults in five Anglophone countries from the Global Survey of Sexual Attitudes and Behaviors. *Archives of Sexual Behavior, 35*(2), 145–161.

Laumann, E. O., Gagnon, J. H., Michael, R. T., & Michaels, S. (1994). *The social organization of sexuality.* Chicago: University of Chicago Press.

Laungani, P. (2002). The counselling interview: First impressions. *Counselling Psychology Quarterly, 15*(1), 107–113.

Lavee, Y., & Ben-Ari, A. (2003). Daily stress and uplifts during times of political tension: Jews and Arabs in Israel. *American Journal of Orthopsychiatry, 73*(1), 65–73.

Lawless, H. T., & Heymann, H. (2010). Measurement of sensory thresholds. In H. T. Lawless & H. Heymann (Eds.). *Sensory evaluation of food* (2nd ed.) (pp. 125–147). New York: Springer.

Lazarus, R. S., DeLongis, A., Folkman, S., & Gruen, R. (1985). Stress and adaptational outcomes. *American Psychologist, 40*, 770–779.

Le Bon, G. (1960). *The crowd.* New York: Viking Press. (Original work published 1895)

Le, T. N., Lai, M. H., & Wallen, J. (2009). Multiculturalism and subjective happiness as mediated by cultural and relational variables. *Cultural Diversity and Ethnic Minority Psychology, 15*(3), 303–313.

Leach, K. P. (2008). Serotonin transporter and depression: From the emotional to the social brain. *Actas Españñolas de Psiquiatríia, 36*(Suppl. 1), 21–24.

LeDoux, J. E., & Phelps, E. A. (2008). Emotional networks in the brain. In M. Lewis, J. M. Haviland-Jones, & L. F. Barrett (Eds.), *Handbook of emotions* (pp. 159–179). New York: Guilford Press.

Lee, A., & Hankin, B. L. (2009). Insecure attachment, dysfunctional attitudes, and low self-esteem predicting prospective symptoms of depression and anxiety during adolescence. *Journal of Clinical Child and Adolescent Psychology, 38*(2), 219–231.

Lee, D. J., Owen, C. M., Khanifar, E., Kim, R. C., & Binder, D. K. (2009). Isolated amygdala neurocysticercosis in a patient presenting with déjà vu and olfactory auras: Case report. *Journal of Neurosurgery, 3*(6), 538–541.

Lee, I-C., & Crawford, M. (2007). Lesbians and bisexual women in the eyes of scientific psychology. *Feminism and Psychology, 17*(1), 109–127.

Lee, S. A. S., & Davis, B. L. (2010). Segmental distribution patterns of English infant- and adult-directed speech. *Journal of Child Language, 37*, 767–791.

Lee, S. J., Bellamy, J. L., & Guterman, N. B. (2009). Fathers, physical child abuse, and neglect. *Child Maltreatment, 14*(3), 227–231.

Lee, Y. (2006). *Man as the prayer: The origin and nature of humankind.* New York: Trafford.

Leenaars, A. A. (2006). Altruistic suicide: Update. *Archives of Suicide Research, 10*(1), 99.

Lefcourt, H. M. (1997). Cited in Clay, R. A. (1997). Researchers harness the power of humor. *APA Monitor, 28*(9), 1, 18.

Lefcourt, H. M., Miller, R. S., Ware, E. E., & Sherk, D. (1981). Locus of control as a modifier of the relationship between stressors and moods. *Journal of Personality and Social Psychology, 41*, 357–369.

Lehman, B. J., & Crano, W. D. (2002). The pervasive effects of vested interest on attitude-criterion consistency in political judgment. *Journal of Experimental Social Psychology, 38*(2), 101–112.

Leichsenring, F., & Leibing, E. (2003). The effectiveness of psychodynamic therapy and cognitive behavior therapy in the treatment of personality disorders: A meta-analysis. *American Journal of Psychiatry, 160*, 1223–1232.

Lejeune, C., et al. (2006). Prospective multicenter observational study of 260 infants born to 259 opiate-dependent mothers on methadone or high-dose buprenophine substitution. *Drug and Alcohol Dependence, 82*(3), 250–257.

Lengen, C., et al. (2008). Anomalous brain dominance and the immune system: Do left-handers have specific immunological patterns? *Brain and Cognition, 69*(1), 188–193.

Lenroot, R. K., et al. (2007). Sexual dimorphism of brain developmental trajectories during childhood and adolescence. *NeuroImage, 36*(4), 1065–1073.

Lenroot, R. K., et al. (2009). Differences in genetic and environmental influences on the human cerebral cortex associated with development during childhood and adolescence. *Human Brain Mapping, 30*(1), 163–173.

Leonard, B. E. (2008). Current antidepressant drugs. *Actas Españolas de Psiquiatríia, 36*(Suppl. 1), 31–34.

Leonardo, E. D., & Hen, R. (2006). Genetics of affective and anxiety disorders. *Annual Review of Psychology, 57,* 117–137.

Leppel, K. (2002). Similarities and differences in the college persistence of men and women. *Review of Higher Education: Journal of the Association for the Study of Higher Education, 25*(4), 433–450.

Leung, P., Curtis, R. L., Jr., & Mapp, S. C. (2010). Incidences of sexual contacts of children: Impacts of family characteristics and family structure from a national sample. *Children and Youth Services Review, 32*(5), 650–656.

Levine, D. (2000). Virtual attraction: What rocks your boat. *CyberPsychology and Behavior, 3*(4), 565–573.

Levine, E. S., & Schmelkin, L-P. (2006). The move to prescribe: A change in paradigm? *Professional Psychology: Research and Practice, 37*(2), 205–209.

Levinson, D. J. (1996). *The seasons of a woman's life.* New York: Knopf.

Levinson, D. J., Darrow, C. N., Klein, E. B., Levinson, M. H., & McKee, B. (1978). *The seasons of a man's life.* New York: Knopf.

Levis, D. J. (2008). The prolonged CS exposure techniques of implosive (flooding) therapy. In W. O'Donohue & J. E. Fisher (Eds.), *General principles and empirically supported techniques of cognitive behavior therapy* (pp. 370–393). Hoboken, NJ: Wiley.

Levy, D., Strassman, A. M., & Burstein, R. (2009). A critical view on the role of migraine triggers in the genesis of migraine pain. *Headache: Journal of Head and Face Pain, 49*(6), 953–957.

Levy, R. A., & Ablon, J. S. (Eds.). (2009). *Handbook of evidence-based psychodynamic psychotherapy: Bridging the gap between science and practice.* New York: Humana Press.

Ley, J., Bennett, P., & Coleman, G. (2008). Personality dimensions that emerge in companion canines. *Applied Animal Behaviour Science, 110*(3), 305–317.

Ley, J., Bennett, P., & Coleman, G. (2009). A refinement and validation of the Monash Canine Personality Questionnaire (MCPQ). *Applied Animal Behaviour Science, 116*(2), 220–227.

Li, C., Ford, E., Huang, T., Sun, S., & Goodman, E. (2009). Patterns of change in cardiometabolic risk factors associated with the metabolic syndrome among children and adolescents: The Fels Longitudinal Study. *Journal of Pediatrics, 155*(3), S5.e9–S5.e16.

Li, M., & Chapman, G. B. (2009). "100% of anything looks good": The appeal of one hundred percent. *Psychonomic Bulletin and Review, 16,* 156–162.

Li, S., et al. (2009). Validation of a new REM sleep behavior disorder questionnaire (RBDQ-HK). *Sleep Medicine, 11*(1), 43–48.

Li, T. Y., et al. (2006). Obesity as compared with physical activity in predicting risk of coronary heart disease in women. *Circulation, 113,* 499–506.

Lickliter, R., & Logan, C. (2007). Gilbert Gottlieb's legacy: Probabilistic epigenesis and the development of individuals and species [Special issue]. *Developmental Psychobiology, 49*(8), 747–748.

Lieber, C. S. (1990, January 14). Cited in Barroom biology: How alcohol goes to a woman's head. *The New York Times,* p. E24.

Liem, J. H., Cavell, E. C., & Lustig, K. (2010). The influence of authoritative parenting during adolescence on depressive symptoms in young adulthood: Examining the mediating roles of self-development and peer support. *Journal of Genetic Psychology, 171*(1), 73–92.

Lim, M. M., & Young, L. J. (2006). Neuropeptidergic regulation of affiliative behavior and social bonding in animals. *Hormones and Behavior, 50*(4), 506–517.

Lim, R. F. (2009). Prevalence and presentation of psychiatric illnesses in Asian Americans. In W. B. Bateman, N. Abesamis-Mendoza, & H. Ho-Asjoe (Eds.), *Praeger handbook of Asian American health: Taking notice and taking action* (pp. 301–310). Santa Barbara, CA: ABC-CLIO.

Lincoln, T. M., Ziegler, M., Mehl, S., & Rief, W. (2010). The jumping to conclusions bias in delusions: Specificity and changeability. *Journal of Abnormal Psychology, 119*(1), 40–49.

Lindberg, L. D., & Singh, S. (2008). Sexual behavior of single adult American women. *Perspectives on Sexual and Reproductive Health, 40*(1), 27–33.

Lindgren, A. P., Mullins, P. M., Neighbors, C., & Blayney, J. A. (2010). Curiosity killed the cocktail? Curiosity, sensation seeking, and alcohol-related problems in college women. *Addictive Behaviors, 35*(5), 513–516.

Lippa, R. A. (2008). The relationship between childhood gender nonconformity and adult masculinity–femininity and anxiety in heterosexual and homosexual men and women. *Sex Roles, 59*(9–10), 684–693.

Lippa, R. A. (2009). Sex differences in sex drive, sociosexuality, and height across 53 nations: Testing evolutionary and social structural theories. *Archives of Sexual Behavior, 38*(5), 631–651.

Lippa, R. A. (2010). Sex differences in personality traits and gender-related occupational preferences across 53 nations: Testing evolutionary and social-environmental theories. *Archives of Sexual Behavior, 39*(3), 619–636.

Lipsitt, L. P. (2003). Crib death: A biobehavioral phenomenon? *Current Directions in Psychological Science, 12*(5), 164–170.

Liu, A. (2009). Critical race theory, Asian Americans, and higher education: A review of research. *InterActions: UCLA Journal of Education and Information Studies, 5*(2). Retrieved from http://www.escholarship.org/uc/item/98h4n45j

Liu, W. M. (2010). Exploring the lives of Asian American men. In S. R. Harper & F. Harris, III (Eds.), *College men and masculinities* (pp. 425–456). Hoboken, NJ: Wiley.

Livesley, W. J., & Jang, K. L. (2008). The behavioral genetics of personality disorder. *Annual Review of Clinical Psychology, 4,* 247–274.

Lloyd, K. B., & Hornsby, L. B. (2009). Complementary and alternative medications for women's health issues. *Nutrition in Clinical Practice, 24*(5), 589–608.

Lock, J. (2009). Trying to fit square pegs in round holes: Eating disorders in males. *Journal of Adolescent Health, 44*(2), 99–100.

Lockenhoff, C. E., & Carstensen, L. L. (2004). Socioemotional selectivity theory, aging, and health: The increasingly delicate balance between regulating emotions and making tough choices. *Journal of Personality, 72*(6), 1395–1424.

Loftus, E. F. (1979). The malleability of human memory. *American Scientist, 67*(3), 312–320.

Loftus, E. F. (1993). Psychologists in the eyewitness world. *American Psychologist, 48,* 550–552.

Loftus, E. F., & Davis, D. (2006). Recovered memories. *Annual Review of Clinical Psychology, 2,* 469–498.

Loftus, E. F., & Palmer, J. C. (1974). Reconstruction of automobile destruction. *Journal of Verbal Learning and Verbal Behavior, 13,* 585–589.

Lohman, D. F., & Lakin, J. M. (2009). Consistencies in sex differences on the Cognitive Abilities Test across countries, grades, test forms, and cohorts. *British Journal of Educational Psychology, 79*(2), 389–407.

Lonstein, J. S., & Auger, A. P. (2009). Perinatal gonadal hormone influences on neurobehavioral development. In M. S. Blumberg, J. H. Freeman, & S. R. Robinson (Eds.), *Oxford handbook of developmental behavioral neuroscience* (pp. 424–453). New York: Oxford University Press.

Lonsway, K. A., Cortina, L. M., & Magley, V. J. (2008). Sexual harassment mythology: Definition, conceptualization, and measurement. *Sex Roles, 58*(9–10), 599–615.

López, P., Martín, J., & Cuadrado, M. (2002). Pheromone-mediated intrasexual aggression in male lizards, *Podarcis hispanicus*. *Aggressive Behavior, 28,* 154–163.

Lopez, S. R., & Guarnaccia, P. J. J. (2000). Cultural psychopathology: Uncovering the social world of mental illness. *Annual Review of Psychology, 51,* 571–598.

Lorenz, K. Z. (1981). *The foundations of ethology.* New York: Springer-Verlag.

Loving, T. J., & Agnew, C. R. (2001). Socially desirable responding in close relationships: A dual-component approach and measure. *Journal of Social and Personal Relationships, 18*(4), 551–573.

Lu, L. (2001). Understanding happiness: A look into the Chinese folk psychology. *Journal of Happiness Studies, 2*(4), 407–432.

Lubinski, D., & Benbow, C. P. (2006). Study of mathematically precocious youth after 35 years: Uncovering antecedents for the development of math-science expertise. *Perspectives on Psychological Science, 1*(4), 316–345.

Luchins, A. S. (1957). Primacy-recency in impression formation. In C. I. Hovland (Ed.), *The order of presentation in persuasion* (pp. 33–61). New Haven, CT: Yale University Press.

Luchins, A. S., & Luchins, E. H. (1959). *Rigidity of behavior.* Eugene: University of Oregon Press.

Ludwick-Rosenthal, R., & Neufeld, R. W. J. (1993). Preparation for undergoing an invasive medical procedure. *Journal of Consulting and Clinical Psychology, 61,* 156–164.

Lukaszewski, A., & Roney, J. (2009). Kind toward whom? Mate preferences for personality traits are target specific. *Evolution and Human Behavior, 31*(1), 29–38.

Luo, L., & Craik, F. I. M. (2009). Age differences in recollection: Specificity effects at retrieval. *Journal of Memory and Language, 60*(4), 421–436.

Lupien, S. J., McEwen, B. S., Gunnar, M. R., & Heim, C. (2009). Effects of stress throughout the lifespan on the brain, behaviour and cognition. *Nature Reviews Neuroscience, 10,* 434–445.

Lurigio, A. J. (2009). The rotten barrel spoils the apples: How situational factors contribute to detention officer abuse toward inmates. *Prison Journal, 89*(Suppl. 1), 70S–80S.

Luszczynska, A., et al. (2009). Self-efficacy mediates effects of exposure, loss of resources, and life stress on posttraumatic distress among trauma survivors. *Applied Psychology: Health and Well-Being, 1*(1), 73–90.

Lykken, D. T. (2007). A more accurate estimate of heritability. *Twin Research and Human Genetics, 10*(1), 168–173.

Lykken, D. T., & Csikszentmihalyi, M. (2001). Happiness—Stuck with what you've got? *Psychologist, 14*(9), 470–472.

Lykken, D. T., McGue, M., Tellegen, A., & Bouchard, T. J., Jr. (1992). Emergenesis: Genetic traits that may not run in families. *American Psychologist, 47,* 1565–1577.

Lynn, B. M., McCord, J. L., & Halliwell, J. R. (2007). Effects of menstrual cycle and sex on progesterone hemodynamics. *American Journal of Physiology: Regulatory, Integrative, and Comparative Physiology, 292,* R1260–R1270.

Lynn, S. J., Kirsch, I., & Hallquist, M. N. (2008). Social cognitive theories of hypnosis. In M. R. Nash & A. J. Barnier (Eds.), *The Oxford handbook of hypnosis: Theory, research, and practice* (pp. 111–139). New York: Oxford University Press.

Lynn, S. J., Matthews, A., & Barnes, S. (2008). Hypnosis and memory: From Bernheim to the present. In K. D. Markman et al. (Eds.), *Handbook of imagination and mental stimulation* (pp. 103–118). Danvers, MA: CRC Press.

M

Maas, J. B. (1998). *Power sleep: Revolutionary strategies that prepare your mind and body for peak performance.* New York: Villard.

Machery, E. (2009). Three fundamental kinds of concept: Prototypes, exemplars, theories. In E. Machery (Ed.), *Doing Without Concepts* (pp. 76–121). Oxford Scholarship Online Monographs.

Machery, O., & Carlyon, R. P. (2010). Temporal pitch percepts elicited by dual-channel stimulation of a cochlear implant. *Journal of the Acoustical Society of America, 127*(1), 339–349.

Maciejewski, P. K., Zhang, B., Block, S. D., & Prigerson, H. G. (2007). An empirical examination of the stage theory of grief. *Journal of the American Medical Association, 297,* 716–723.

Macrae, C. N., Mitchell, J. P., & Pendry, L. F. (2002). What's in a forename? Cue familiarity and stereotypical thinking. *Journal of Experimental Social Psychology, 38*(2), 186–193.

Maddi, S. R. (2008). The courage and strategies of hardiness as helpful in growing despite major, disruptive stresses. *American Psychologist, 63*(6), 563–564.

Maddi, S. R., Harvey, R. H., Khoshaba, D. M., Fazel, M., & Resurreccion, N. (2009). The personality construct of hardiness, IV. *Journal of Humanistic Psychology, 49*(3), 292–305.

Magno, C. (2010). Looking at Filipino pre-service teachers' values for education through epistemological beliefs about learning and Asian values. *Asia-Pacific Education Researcher, 19*(1), 61–78.

Maiden, B., & Perry, B. (2010). Dealing with free riders in assessed group work: Results from a study at a UK university. *Assessment and Evaluation in Higher Education.* doi:10.1080/02602930903429302

Maier, N. R. F., & Schneirla, T. C. (1935). *Principles of animal psychology.* New York: McGraw-Hill.

Mair, C., Martincova, M., & Shepperd, M. (2009). A literature review of expert problem solving using analogy. *EASE— Evaluation and Assessment in Software Engineering.* Retrieved from http://www.bcs.org/upload/pdf/ewic_ea09_s5paper1.pdf

Major, G. C., et al. (2007). Clinical significance of adaptive thermogenesis. *International Journal of Obesity, 31,* 204–212.

Mamelak, M. (2009). Narcolepsy and depression and the neurobiology of gammahydroxybutyrate. *Progress in Neurobiology, 89*(2), 193–219.

Mandal, M., Marzouk, A. C., Donnelly, R., & Ponzio, N. M. (2010). Maternal immune stimulation during pregnancy affects adaptive immunity in offspring to promote development of TH17 cells. *Brain, Behavior, and Immunity,* doi:10.1016/j. bbi.2010.09.011.

Maniglio, R. (2009). The impact of child sexual abuse on health: A systematic review of reviews. *Clinical Psychology Review, 29*(7), 647–657.

Manning, R., Levine, M., & Collins, A. (2007). The Kitty Genovese murder and the social psychology of helping: The parable of the 38 witnesses. *American Psychologist, 62*(6), 555–562.

Mansouri, F. A., Tanaka, K., & Buckley, M. J. (2009). Conflict-induced behavioural adjustment: A clue to the executive functions of the prefrontal cortex. *Nature Reviews Neuroscience, 10,* 141–152.

Mantovani, A., & Sica, A. (2010). Macrophages, innate immunity and cancer: Balance, tolerance, and diversity. *Current Opinion in Immunology, 22*(2), 231–237.

Manuck, S. B., Craft, S., & Gold, K. J. (2007). Coronary-prone behavior pattern and cardiovascular response. *Psychophysiology, 15*(5), 403–411.

Marcia, J. E. (1991). Identity and self-development. In R. M. Lerner, A. C. Petersen, & J. Brooks-Gunn (Eds.), *Encyclopedia of adolescence.* New York: Garland.

Marcus, D., Hughes, K., & Arnau, R. (2008). Health anxiety, rumination, and negative affect: A meditational analysis. *Journal of Psychosomatic Research, 64*(5), 495–501.

Marian, V., & Neisser, U. (2000). Language-dependent recall of autobiographical memories. *Journal of Experimental Psychology: General, 129*(3), 361–368.

Markham, B. (2006). Older women and security. In J. Worell & C. D. Goodheart (Eds.), *Handbook of girls' and women's psychological health: Gender and well-being across the lifespan* (pp. 388–396). *Oxford series in clinical psychology.* New York: Oxford University Press.

Markon, K. E., Krueger, R. F., Bouchard, T. J., Jr., & Gottesman, I. I. (2002). Normal and abnormal personality traits: Evidence for genetic and environmental relationships in the Minnesota Study of Twins Reared Apart. *Journal of Personality, 70*(5), 661–693.

Marlatt, G. A. (2010). Update on harm-reduction policy and intervention research. *Annual Review of Clinical Psychology, 6,* 591–606.

Marquis, C. (2003, March 16). Living in sin. *The New York Times,* p. WK2.

Martin, C. L., & Ruble, D. (2004). Children's search fof gender cues: Cognitive perspectives on gender development. *Current Directions in Psychological Science, 13*(2), 67–70.

Martin, E., Ressler, K., Binder, E., & Nemeroff, C. (2009). The neurobiology of anxiety disorders: Brain imaging, genetics, and psychoneuroendocrinology. *Psychiatric Clinics of North America, 32*(3), 549–575.

Martin, R. A., & Lefcourt, H. M. (1983). Sense of humor as a moderator of the relation between stressors and moods. *Journal of Personality and Social Psychology, 45,* 1313–1324.

Martin, S. (2002). Easing migraine pain. *Monitor on Psychology, 33*(4), 71.

Martinez, E., et al. (2010). Correlates of smoking cessation self-efficacy in a community sample of smokers. *Addictive Behaviors, 35*(2), 175–178.

Marttunen, M. J., et al. (1998). Completed suicide among adolescents with no diagnosable psychiatric disorder. *Adolescence, 33*(131), 669–681.

Marziali, E., McDonald, L., & Donahue, P. (2008). The role of coping humor in the physical and mental health of older adults. *Aging and Mental Health, 12*(6), 713–718.

Maslow, A. H. (1970). *Motivation and personality* (2nd ed.). New York: Harper & Row.

Mason, V., Andrews, H., & Upton, D. (2010). The psychological impact of exposure to floods. *Psychology, Health and Medicine, 15*(1), 61–73.

Massad, L. S., et al. (2010). Knowledge of cervical cancer prevention and human papillomavirus among women with HIV. *Gynecologic Oncology, 117*(1), 70–76.

Masters, W. H., & Johnson, V. E. (1966). *Human sexual response.* Boston: Little, Brown.

Masters, W. H., & Johnson, V. E. (1970). *Human sexual inadequacy.* Boston: Little, Brown.

Mata, I. et al. (2009). A neuregulin 1 variant is associated with increased lateral ventricle volume in patients with first-episode schizophrenia. *Biological Psychiatry, 65*(6), 535–540.

Mathews, J. R., & Barch, D. M. (2010). Emotion responsivity, social cognition, and functional outcome in schizophrenia. *Journal of Abnormal Psychology, 119*(1), 50–59.

Mathews, T. J., & MacDorman, M. F. (2007). Infant mortality statistics from the 2004 period linked birth/infant death data set. *National Vital Statistics Reports, 55*(14). Hyattsville, MD: National Center for Health Statistics.

Matsumoto, D., Keltner, D., Shiota, M. N., O'Sullivan, M., & Frank, M. (2008). Facial expressions of emotion. In M. Lewis, J. M. Haviland-Jones, & L. F. Barrett (Eds.), *Handbook of emotions* (pp. 211–234). New York: Guilford Press.

Maxwell, J. P., Visek, A. J., & Moores, E. (2009). Anger and perceived legitimacy of aggression in male Hong Kong Chinese athletes: Effects of type of sport and level of competition. *Psychology of Sport and Exercise, 10*(2), 289–296.

May, D. E., & Kratochvil, C. J. (2010). Attention-deficit hyperactivity disorder: Recent advances in paediatric pharmacotherapy. *Drugs, 70*(1), 15–40.

May, R. (2005). How do we know what works? *Journal of College Student Psychotherapy, 19*(3), 69–73.

Mayer, J. D., Salovey, P., & Caruso, D. R. (2008). Emotional intelligence: New ability or eclectic traits? *American Psychologist, 63*(6), 503–517.

Mayers, A. G., et al. (2009). Subjective sleep, depression, and anxiety. *Human Psychopharmacology, 24*(6), 495–501.

Mayes, L. C., & Ward, A. (2003). Principles of neurobehavioral teratology. In D. Cicchetti & E. Walker (Eds.), *Neurodevelopmental mechanisms in psychopathology* (pp. 3–33). New York: Cambridge University Press.

Mazure, C. M., et al. (2000). Adverse life events and cognitive personality characteristics in the prediction of major depression and antidepressant response. *American Journal of Psychiatry, 157,* 896–903.

Mbwana, J., et al. (2008). Limitations to plasticity of language network reorganization in localization-related epilepsy. *Brain, 132*(2), 347–356.

McCall, R. (1997). Cited in Sleek, S. (1997). Can "emotional intelligence" be taught in today's schools? *APA Monitor, 28*(6), 25.

McCardle, P., Colombo, J., & Freud, L. (2009). Measuring language in infancy. In J. Colombo, P. McCardle, & L. Freud (Eds.), *Infant pathways to language: Methods, models, and research disorders* (pp. 1–12). New York: Psychology Press.

McCarley, R. W. (1992). Cited in Blakeslee, S. (1992, January 7). Scientists unraveling chemistry of dreams. *The New York Times,* pp. C1, C10.

McCarthy, M. M., et al. (2009). The epigenetics of sex differences in the brain. *Journal of Neuroscience, 29*(41), 12815–12823.

McCauley, J. L., Ruggiero, K. L., Resnick, H. S., & Kilpatrick, D. G. (2010). Incapacitated, forcible, and drug/alcohol-facilitated rape in relation to binge drinking, marijuana use, and illicit drug use: A national survey. *Journal of Traumatic Stress, 23*(1), 132–140.

McClave, E. Z. (2000). Linguistic functions of head movements in the context of speech. *Journal of Pragmatics, 32*(7), 855–878.

McClelland, D. C. (1958). Methods of measuring human motivation. In J. W. Atkinson (Ed.), *Motives in fantasy, action, and society.* Princeton, NJ: Van Nostrand.

McClelland, D. C. (1965). Achievement and entrepreneurship. *Journal of Personality and Social Psychology, 1,* 389–392.

McCormick, B., et al. (2007). Relationship of sex to symptom severity, psychiatric comorbidity, and health care utilization in 163 subjects with borderline personality disorder. *Comprehensive Psychiatry, 48*(5), 406–412.

McCrae, R. R., & Costa, P. T., Jr. (1997). Personality trait structure as a human universal. *American Psychologist, 52*(5), 509–516.

McCrae, R. R., Costa, P. T., Jr., et al. (2000). Nature over nurture: Temperament, personality, and life span development. *Journal of Personality and Social Psychology, 78*(1), 173–186.

McCrae, R. R., et al. (2005). Universal features of personality traits from the observer's perspective: Data from 50 cultures. *Journal of Personality and Social Psychology, 88*, 547–561.

McDevitt-Murphy, M. E., et al. (2010). PTSD symptoms, hazardous drinking, and health functioning among U.S. OEF and OIF veterans presenting to primary care. *Journal of Traumatic Stress, 23*(1), 108–111.

McDonald, M. G. (2008). The nature of epiphanic experience. *Journal of Humanistic Psychology, 48*(1), 89–115.

McDonald-Miszczak, L., Gould, O. N., & Tychynski, D. (1999). Metamemory predictors of prospective and retrospective memory performance. *Journal of General Psychology, 126*(1), 37–52.

McDougall, W. (1904). The sensations excited by a single momentary stimulation of the eye. *British Journal of Psychology, 1,* 78–113.

McDougall, W. (1908). *An introduction to social psychology.* London: Methuen.

McGaugh, J. L., McIntyre, C. K., & Power, A. E. (2002). Amygdala modulation of memory consolidation: Interaction with other brain systems. *Neurobiology of Learning and Memory, 78*(3), 539–552.

McGreal, C. (2009, July 20). Teen pregnancy and disease rates rose sharply during Bush years, agency finds. *The Guardian online.*

McGue, M., Bouchard, T. J., Jr., Iacono, W. G., & Lykken, D. T. (1993). Behavioral genetics of cognitive ability: A life-span perspective. In R. Plomin & G. E. McClearn (Eds.), *Nature, nurture & psychology* (pp. 59–76). Washington, DC: American Psychological Association.

McGuffin, P. (2008). The genetics of bipolar disorder and its relationship with unipolar depression. *Actas Españolas de Psiquiatría, 36*(Suppl. 1), 48–50.

McKee, P., & Barber, C. E. (2001). Plato's theory of aging. *Journal of Aging and Identity, 6*(2), 93–104.

McKenzie, C. R. M., Lee, S. M., & Chen, K. K. (2002). When negative evidence increases confidence: Changes in belief after hearing two sides of a dispute. *Journal of Behavioral Decision Making, 15*(1), 1–18.

McKimmie, B. M., Terry, D. J., & Hogg, M. A. (2009). Dissonance reduction in the context of group membership: The role of meta-consistency. *Group Dynamics: Theory, Research, and Practice, 13*(2), 103–119.

McLachlan, N., & Wilson, S. (2010). The central role of recognition in auditory perception: A neurobiological model. *Psychological Review, 117*(1), 175–196.

McLaughlin, K. A., Conron, K. J., Koenen, K. C., & Gilman, S. E. (2010). Childhood adversity, adult stressful life events, and risk of past-year psychiatric disorder: A test of the stress sensitization hypothesis in a population-based sample of adults. *Psychological Medicine, 40*, 1647–1658.

Mead, G. E., et al. (2009). Exercise for depression. *Cochrane Database of Systematic Reviews* (3). doi:10.1002/14651858. CD004366.pub4

Mead, M. (1935). *Sex and temperament in three primitive societies.* New York: Dell.

Mechner, F. (2009). Analyzing variable behavioural contingencies. *Behavioural Processes, 81*(2), 316–321.

Medland, S. E., et al. (2008). Genetic influences on handedness: Data from 25,732 Australian and Dutch twin families. *Neuropsychologia, 47*(2), 330–337.

Mehta, J., et al. (2010). Racial disparities in prescriptions for cardioprotective drugs and cardiac outcomes in Veterans Affairs hospitals. *American Journal of Cardiology, 105*(7), 1019–1023.

Mehta, P. H., & Beer, J. (2009). Neural mechanisms of the testosterone-aggression relation: The role of orbito-frontal cortex. *Journal of Cognitive Neuroscience, 21*(11), 1–12.

Mehta, P. H., & Gosling, S. D. (2008). Bridging human and animal research: A comparative approach to studies of personality and health. *Brain, Behavior, and Immunity, 22*(5), 651–661.

Meier, B. P., Robinson, M. D., Carter, M. S., & Hinsz, V. B. (2010). Are sociable people more beautiful? A zero-acquaintance analysis of agreeableness, extraversion, and attractiveness. *Journal of Research in Personality, 44*(2), 293–296.

Meijer, J., & Elshout, J. J. (2001). The predictive and discriminant validity of the zone of proximal development. *British Journal of Educational Psychology, 71*(1), 93–113.

Meijer, W. M., Faber, A., van den Ban, E., & Tobi, H. (2009). Current issues around the pharmacotherapy of ADHD in children and adults. *Pharmacy World and Science, 31*(5), 509–516.

Meinert, C. L., & Breitner, J. C. S. (2008). Chronic disease long-term drug prevention trials: Lessons from the Alzheimer's Disease Anti-Inflammatory Prevention Trial (ADAPT). *Alzheimer's & Dementia, 4*(1, Suppl. 1), S7–S14.

Meltzoff, A. N. (1997). Cited in Azar, B. (1997). New theory on development could usurp Piagetian beliefs. *APA Monitor, 28*(6), 9.

Meltzoff, A. N., & Brooks, R. (2009). Social cognition and language: The role of gaze following in early word learning. In J. Colombo, P. McCardle, & L. Freund (Eds.), *Infant pathways to language: Methods, models, and research disorders.* (pp. 169–194). New York: Psychology Press.

Meltzoff, A. N., & Gopnik, A. (1997). *Words, thoughts, and theories.* Cambridge, MA: MIT Press.

Meltzoff, A. N., & Prinz, W. (2002). *The imitative mind: Development, evolution, and brain bases.* Cambridge, England: Cambridge University Press.

Melzack, R. (2006). Phantom limbs. *Secrets of the senses* [Special editions]. *Scientific American.*

Melzack, R. (2007). 51 Workshop summary: Phantom limb pain—Mechanisms and therapy. *European Journal of Pain, 11*(1), 21.

Melzack, R., & Katz, J. (2006). Pain in the 21st century: The neuromatrix and beyond. In G. Young et al. (Eds.), *Psychological knowledge in court* (pp. 129–148). New York: Springer.

Mendelsohn, F., & Warren, M. (2010). Anorexia, bulimia, and the female athlete triad: Evaluation and management. *Endocrinology and Metabolism Clinics of North America, 39*(1), 155–167.

Merari, A., Diamant, I., Bibi, A., Broshi, Y., & Zakin, G. (2010). Personality characteristics of "self martyrs"/"suicide bombers" and organizers of suicide attacks. *Terrorism and Political Violence, 22*(1), 87–101.

Mercado, E. (2008). Neural and cognitive plasticity: From maps to minds. *Psychological Bulletin, 134*(1), 109–137.

Mesoudi, A. (2009). How cultural evolutionary theory can inform social psychology and vice versa. *Psychological Review, 116*(4), 929–952.

Metcalfe, J. (1986). Premonitions of insight predict impending error. *Journal of Experimental Psychology: Learning, Memory, and Cognition, 12*, 623–634.

Metz, R. (2005, March 10). Think of a number… Come on, think! *The New York Times online.*

Meyer-Lindenberg, A., et al. (2001). Evidence for abnormal cortical functional connectivity during working memory in schizophrenia. *American Journal of Psychiatry, 158*, 1809–1817.

Meyersburg, C. A., Bogdan, R., Gallo, D. A., & McNally, R. J. (2009). False memory propensity in people reporting recovered memories of past lives. *Journal of Abnormal Psychology, 118*(2), 399–404.

Milevsky, A., Schlechter, M., Netter, S., & Keehn, D. (2007). Maternal and paternal parenting styles in adolescents: Associations with self-esteem, depression and life-satisfaction. *Journal of Child and Family Studies, 16*(1), 39–47.

Milgram, R. M., & Livne, N. L. (2006). Research in creativity in Israel: A chronicle of theoretical and empirical development. In J. C. Kaufman, & R. J. Sternberg (Eds.), *The international handbook of creativity* (pp. 307–336). New York: Cambridge University Press.

Milgram, S. (1963). Behavioral study of obedience. *Journal of Abnormal and Social Psychology, 67*, 371–378.

Milgram, S. (1974). *Obedience to authority.* New York: Harper & Row.

Milius, S. (2002). Rescue rat. *Science News, 161*(18), 276.

Miller, A. L., Rathus, J. H., DuBose, A. P., Dexter-Mazza, E. T., & Goldklang, A. R. (2007). Dialectical behavior therapy for adolescents. In L. A. Dimeff & K. Koerner (Eds.), *Dialectical behavior therapy in clinical practice* (pp. 245–297). New York: Guilford Press.

Miller, C. F., Lurye, L. E., Zosuls, K. M., & Ruble, D. N. (2009). Accessibility of gender stereotype domains: Developmental and gender differences in children. *Sex Roles, 60*(11–12), 870–881.

Miller, G. A. (1956). The magical number seven, plus or minus two: Some limits on our capacity for processing information. *Psychological Review, 63*, 81–97.

Miller, G., Tybur, J., & Jordan, B. D. (2007). Ovulatory cycle effects on tip earnings by lap dancers: Economic evidence for human estrus? *Evolution and Human Behavior, 28*(6), 375–381.

Miller, J. L. (1992). Trouble in mind. *Scientific American, 267*(3), 180.

Miller, L. (2006). The terrorist mind: I. A psychological and political analysis. *International Journal of Offender Therapy and Comparative Criminology, 50*(2), 121–138.

Miller, M. A., Weafer, J., & Fillmore, M. T. (2009). Gender differences in alcohol impairment of simulated driving performance and driving-related skills. *Alcohol and Alcoholism, 44*(6), 586–593.

Miller, M. F., Barabasz, A. F., & Barabasz, M. (1991). Effects of active alert and relaxation hypnotic inductions on cold pressor pain. *Journal of Abnormal Psychology, 100*, 223–226.

Miller, N. E. (1944). Experimental studies of conflict. In J. McVicker Hunt (Ed.), *Personality and the behavior disorders* (Vol. 1, pp. 431–465). Oxford, England: Ronald Press.

Miller, N. E. (1969). Learning of visceral and glandular responses. *Science, 163*, 434–445.

Miller, N. E. (1995). Clinical-experimental interactions in the development of neuroscience. *American Psychologist, 50*, 901–911.

Miller, N. E., & Dollard, J. (1941). *Social learning and imitation.* New Haven, CT: Yale University Press.

Miller, S. L., & Maner, J. K. (2010). Scent of a woman: Men's testosterone responses to olfactory ovulation cues. *Psychological Science, 21*(2), 276-283.

Milne, R. D., Syngeniotis, A., Jackson, G., & Corballis, M. C. (2002). Mixed lateralization of phonological assembly in developmental dyslexia. *Neurocase, 8*(3), 205–209.

Milstead, M., Lapsley, D., & Hale, C. (1993, March). *A new look at imaginary audience and personal fable.* Paper presented at the meeting of the Society for Research in Child Development, New Orleans, LA.

Milton, J., & Wiseman, R. (1999). Does psi exist? Lack of replication of an anomalous process of information transfer. *Psychological Bulletin, 125*(4), 387–391.

Mineka, S., & Oehlberg, K. (2008). The relevance of recent developments in classical conditioning to understanding the etiology and maintenance of anxiety disorders. *Acta Psychologica, 127*(3), 567–580.

Mineka, S., & Öhman, A. (2002). Phobias and preparedness: The selective, automatic, and encapsulated nature of fear. *Biological Psychiatry, 52*(10), 927–937.

Miniño A. M. (2010). *Mortality among teenagers aged 12–19 years: United States, 1999–2006* (NCHS Data Brief No. 37). Hyattsville, MD: National Center for Health Statistics.

Miyahira, S. D., Folen, R. A., Hoffman, H. G., Garcia-Palacios, A., & Schaper, K. M. (2010). Effectiveness of a brief VR treatment for PTSD in warfighters. *Annual Review of CyberTherapy and Telemedicine, 8*, 169–172.

Miyake, Y., et al. (2010). Neural processing of negative word stimuli concerning body image in patients with eating disorders: An fMRI study. *NeuroImage, 50*(3), 1333–1339.

Mohr, D. C., et al. (2010). Perceived barriers to psychological treatments and their relationship to depression. *Journal of Clinical Psychology, 66*(4), 394–409.

Molenda-Figueira, H. A., et al. (2006). Nuclear receptor coactivators function in estrogen receptor- and progestin receptor-dependent aspects of sexual behavior in female rats. *Hormones and Behavior, 50*(3), 383–392.

Molfese, V. J., DiLalla, L. F., & Bunce, D. (1997). Prediction of the intelligence test scores of 3- to 8-year-old children by home environment, socioeconomic status, and biomedical risks. *Merrill-Palmer Quarterly, 43*(2), 219–234.

Montero, I., & De Dios, M. J. (2006). Vygotsky was right. An experimental approach to the relationship between private speech and task performance. *Estudios de Psicología, 27*(2), 175–189.

Montgomery, G. H., DuHamel, K. N., & Redd, W. H. (2000). A meta-analysis of hypnotically induced analgesia: How effective is hypnosis? *International Journal of Clinical and Experimental Hypnosis, 48*(2), 138–153.

Montoya, R. M., Horton, R. S., & Kirchner, J. (2008). Is actual similarity necessary for attraction? A meta-analysis of actual and perceived similarity. *Journal of Social and Personal Relationships, 25*(6), 889–922.

Moore, C. C., Romney, A. K., & Hsia, T. (2002). Cultural, gender, and individual differences in perceptual and semantic structures of basic colors in Chinese and English. *Journal of Cognition and Culture, 2*(1), 1–28.

Moos, R. H., & Moos, B. S. (2006). Participation in treatment and Alcoholics Anonymous: A 16-year follow-up of initially untreated individuals. *Journal of Clinical Psychology, 62*(6), 735–750.

Mordock, B. (1997). Skepticism, data, risky shift, polarization, and attitude change: Their role in implementing innovations. *Psychologist-Manager Journal, 1*(1), 41–46.

Morewedge, C. K., & Norton, M. I. (2009). When dreaming is believing: The (motivated) interpretation of dreams. *Journal of Personality and Social Psychology, 96*(2), 249–264.

Mori, N. (2008). Styles of remembering and types of experience: An experimental investigation of reconstructive memory. *Integrative Psychological and Biological Science, 42*(3), 291–314.

Morris, M. W., Larrick, R. P., & Su, S. K. (1999). Misperceiving negotiation counterparts: When situationally determined bargaining behaviors are attributed to personality traits. *Journal of Personality and Social Psychology, 77*(1), 52–67.

Morris, W. N., Miller, R. S., & Spangenberg, S. (1977). The effects of dissenter position and task difficulty on conformity and response conflict. *Journal of Personality, 45*, 251–256.

Morrison, E. S., et al. (1980). *Growing up sexual.* New York: Van Nostrand Reinhold.

Morton, S. M. B. (2006). Maternal nutrition and fetal growth and development. In P. Gluckman & M. Hanson (Eds.), *Developmental origins of health and disease* (pp. 98–129). New York: Cambridge University Press.

Moruzzi, G., & Magoun, H. W. (1949). Brain stem reticular formation and activation of the EEG. *Electroencephalography and Clinical Neurophysiology, 1*, 455–473.

Mosher, W. D., Chandra, A., & Jones, J. (2005). *Sexual behavior and selected health measures: Men and women 15–44 years of age, United States, 2002. Advance data from vital and health statistics* (National Center for Health Statistics No. 362). Washington, DC: Centers for Disease Control and Prevention.

Moshman, D. (2005). *Adolescent psychological development* (2nd ed.). Mahwah, NJ: Erlbaum.

Most, S. B., Sorber, A. V., & Cunningham, J. G. (2007). Auditory Stroop reveals implicit gender association in adults and children. *Journal of Experimental Social Psychology, 43*(2), 287–294.

Mott, M. (2005, January 4). Did animals sense tsunami was coming? *National Geographic News.* Retrieved from http://news.nationalgeographic.com/news/2005/01/0104_050104_tsunami_animals.html

Moyers, B. (1993). *Healing and the mind.* New York: Doubleday.

Mukamal, K. J., & Rimm, E. B. (2008). Alcohol consumption: Risks and benefits. *Current Atherosclerosis Reports, 10*(6), 536–543.

Mullally, W. J., Hall, K., & Goldstein, R. (2009). Efficacy of biofeedback in the treatment of migraine and tension type headache. *Pain Physician, 12*(6), 1005–1011.

Muñoz, R. F., Hollon, S. D., McGrath, E., Rehm, L. P., & VandenBos, G. R. (1994). On the AHCPR *Depression in Primary Care* guidelines: Further considerations for practitioners. *American Psychologist, 49,* 42–61.

Munro, G. D., & Munro, J. E. (2000). Using daily horoscopes to demonstrate expectancy confirmation. *Teaching of Psychology, 27*(2), 114–116.

Muraleedharan, V., et al. (2010). Testosterone replacement may be beneficial in hypogonadal men with cardiovascular disease. *Endocrine Abstracts, 21,* 176.

Murata, A., & Fuson, K. (2006). Teaching as assisting individual constructive paths within an interdependent class learning zone: Japanese first graders learning to add using 10. *Journal for Research in Mathematics Education, 37*(5), 421–456.

Murphy, F. C., Nimmo-Smith, I., & Lawrence, A. D. (2003). Functional neuroanatomy of emotions: A meta-analysis. *Cognitive, Affective, and Behavioral Neuroscience, 3,* 207–233.

Murray, C. J. L., et al. (2006). Eight Americas: Investigating mortality disparities across races, counties, and race-counties in the United States. *PLoS Med 3*(9): e260 doi:10.1371/ journal.pmed.0030260

Murray, L., Creswell, C., & Cooper, P. J. (2009). The development of anxiety disorders in childhood: An integrative review. *Psychological Medicine, 39,* 1413–1423.

Mussweiler, T., & Bodenhausen, G. V. (2002). I know you are, but what am I? Self-evaluative consequences of judging in-group and outgroup members. *Journal of Personality and Social Psychology, 82*(1), 19–32.

Muzzatti, B., & Agnoli, F. (2007). Gender and mathematics: Attitudes and stereotype threat susceptibility in Italian children. *Developmental Psychology, 43*(3), 747–759.

Myers, L. B., & Brewin, C. R. (1994). Recall of early experience and the repressive coping style. *Journal of Abnormal Psychology, 103,* 288–292.

Mystkowski, J. L., & Mineka, S. (2007). Behavior therapy for specific fears and phobias: Context specificity of fear extinction. In T. A. Treat, R. R. Bootzin, & T. B. Baker (Eds.), *Psychological clinical science: Papers in honor of Richard M. McFall* (pp. 197–222). London: Routledge.

N

Nader, K., Schafe, G. E., & Le Doux, J. E. (2000). Fear memories require protein synthesis in the amygdala for reconsolidation after retrieval. *Nature, 406,* 722–726.

Naimi, T., Nelson, D., & Brewer, R. (2010). The intensity of binge alcohol consumption among U.S. adults. *American Journal of Preventive Medicine, 38*(2), 201–207.

Nampiaparampil, D. E. (2008). Prevalence of chronic pain after traumatic brain injury: A systematic review. *Journal of the American Medical Association, 300*(6), 711–719.

Naragon-Gainey, K. (2010). Meta-analysis of the relations of anxiety sensitivity to the depressive and anxiety disorders. *Psychological Bulletin, 136*(1), 128–150.

Narayan, V. M., et al. (2007). Regional cortical thinning in subjects with violent antisocial personality disorder or schizophrenia. *American Journal of Psychiatry, 164,* 1418–1427.

Narlikar, J. V., et al. (2009). A statistical test of astrology. *Current Science, 96*(5), 641–643.

Narusyte, J., et al. (2008). Testing different types of genotype–environment correlation: An extended children-of-twins model. *Developmental Psychology, 44*(6), 1591–1603.

National Center for Health Statistics. (2010). *Health, United States, 2009: With special feature on medical technology.* Hyattsville, MD: Author. Retrieved from http://www.cdc.gov/nchs/data/hus/hus09.pdf#032

National Eating Disorders Association. (2010). Retrieved from http://www.nationaleatingdisorders.org/information-resources/general-information.php

National Institute on Alcohol Abuse and Alcoholism (NIAAA). (2005). *Cage questionnaire.* Retrieved from http://pubs.niaaa.nih.gov/publications/inscage.htm

National Institutes of Health. (2002). Retrieved from http://cerhr.niehs.nih.gov/genpub/topics/ vitamin_a-ccae.html

National Science Foundation. (2002). Cited in Associated Press. (2002, April 30). *Study: Science literacy poor in U.S.* Associated Press.

National Sleep Foundation. (2000b). *2000 Omnibus Sleep in America Poll.* Retrieved from http://www.sleepfoundation.org/publications/2000poll.html#3

National Sleep Foundation. (2001, November 19). *Events of 9-11 took their toll on Americans' sleep, particularly for women, according to new National Sleep Foundation poll.* Retrieved from http://www.sleepfoundation.org/whatsnew/crisis_poll.html

National Sleep Foundation. (2009). *Sleep apnea and sleep.* Retrieved from http://www.sleepfoundation.org/article/sleep-related-problems/obstructive-sleep-apnea-and-sleep

Ndekha, M. (2008). Kwashiorkor and severe acute malnutrition in childhood. *The Lancet, 371*(9626), 1748.

Nduati, R., et al. (2000). Effect of breastfeeding and formula feeding on transmission of HIV-1: A randomized clinical trial. *Journal of the American Medical Association, 283,* 1167–1174.

Neiss, M. B., Stevenson, J., Legrand, L. N., Iacono, W. G., & Sedikides, C. (2009). Self-esteem, negative emotionality, and depression as a common temperamental core: A study of mid-adolescent twin girls. *Journal of Personality, 77*(2), 327–346.

Neisser, U. (1997a). Never a dull moment. *American Psychologist, 52,* 79–81.

Neisser, U. (1997b). Cited in Sleek, S. (1997). Can "emotional intelligence" be taught in today's schools? *APA Monitor, 28*(6), 25.

Neisser, U., et al. (1996). Intelligence: Knowns and unknowns. *American Psychologist, 51,* 77–101.

Nelson, C. A., & Luciana, M. (Eds.). (2001). *Handbook of developmental cognitive neuroscience.* Cambridge, MA: MIT Press.

Nestoriuc, Y., Rief, W., & Martin, A. (2008). Meta-analysis of biofeedback for tension-type headache: Efficacy, specificity, and treatment moderators. *Journal of Consulting and Clinical Psychology, 76*(3), 379–396.

Neve, K. A. (2009). *The dopamine receptors* (2nd ed.). New York: Springer.

Nevid, J. S., Rathus, S. A., & Greene, B. (2012). *Abnormal psychology in a changing world* (8th ed.). Upper Saddle River, NJ: Prentice Hall.

Newman, S. D., Greco, J. A., & Lee, D. (2009). An fMRI study of the Tower of London: A look at problem structure differences. *Brain Research, 1286*, 123–132.

Newport, F., & Strausberg, M. (2001). Americans' belief in psychic and paranormal phenomena is up over last decade. *Gallup Poll News Service*. Retrieved from http://www.gallup.com/poll/content/login.aspx?ci=4483

Nguyen, M., & Hamill-Ruth, R. J. (2009). Pain management: Acute pain. In M. Miller, J. Hart, & J. MacKnight (Eds.), *Essential orthopaedics* (pp. 115–120). Philadelphia: Saunders.

Nidich, S. I., et al. (2009). A randomized controlled trial on effects of the Transcendental Meditation Program on blood pressure, psychological distress, and coping with young adults. *American Journal of Hypertension, 22*(12), 1326–1331.

Nilsson, H., Juslin, P., & Olsson, H. (2008). Exemplars in the mist: The cognitive substrate of the representativeness heuristic. *Scandinavian Journal of Psychology, 49*(3), 201–212.

Nir, Y., & Tononi, G. (2010). Dreaming and the brain: From phenomenology to neurophysiology. *Trends in Cognitive Sciences, 14*(2), 88–100.

Nisbett, R. E. (2009). *Intelligence and how to get it: Why schools and cultures count.* New York: Norton.

Nock, M. K., & Kazdin, A. E. (2002). Examination of affective, cognitive, and behavioral factors and suicide-related outcomes in children and young adolescents. *Journal of Community Psychology, 31*(1), 48–58.

Nokes, T. J., & VanLehn, K. (2008). Bridging principles and examples through analogy and explanation. In *Proceedings of the eighth International Conference for the Learning Sciences* (Vol. 3, pp. 100–102). Utrecht, the Netherlands: International Conference on Learning Sciences.

Nolan, J. M., Schultz, P. W., Cialdini, R. B., Goldstein, N. J., & Griskevicius, V. (2008). Normative social influence is underdetected. *Personality and Social Psychology Bulletin, 34*(7), 913–923.

Nolen-Hoeksema, S. (2001). Gender differences in depression. *Current Directions in Psychological Science, 10*(5), 173–176.

Nolen-Hoeksema, S., & Hilt, L. M. (Eds.). (2008). *Handbook of depression in adolescents.* New York: Routledge/Taylor & Francis Group.

Nolen-Hoeksema, S., Wisco, B. E., & Lyubomirsky, S. (2008). Rethinking rumination. *Perspectives on Psychological Science, 3*(5), 400–424.

Nomura, Y., Marks, D., & Halperin, J. M. (2010). Prenatal exposure to maternal and paternal smoking on attention deficit hyperactivity disorders symptoms and diagnosis in offspring. *Journal of Nervous & Mental Disease, 198*(9), 672–678.

Nonaka, A. M. (2004). The forgotten endangered languages: Lessons on the importance of remembering from Thailand's Ban Khor Sign Language. *Language in Society. 33*(5), 737–767.

Nordgren, L. F., van der Pligt, J., & van Harreveld, F. (2008). The instability of health cognitions: Visceral states influence self-efficacy and related health beliefs. *Health Psychology, 27*(6), 722–727.

Norton, A., & D'Ambrosio, B. S. (2008). ZPC and ZPD: Zones of teaching and learning. *Journal for Research in Mathematics Education, 39*(3), 220–246.

Novick, L. R., & Coté, N. (1992). The nature of expertise in anagram solution. In *Proceedings of the 14th annual conference of the Cognitive Science Society.* Hillsdale, NJ: Erlbaum.

Nowicki, S., & Strickland, B. R. (1973). A locus of control scale. *Journal of Consulting and Clinical Psychology, 40*(1), 148–154.

Numan, M., & Stolzenberg, D. S. (2009). Medial preoptic area interactions with dopamine neural systems in the control of the onset and maintenance of maternal behavior in rats. *Frontiers in Neuroendocrinology, 30*(1), 46–64.

O

O'Dell, C. D., & Hoyert, M. D. (2002). Active and passive touch: A research methodology project. *Teaching of Psychology, 29*(4), 292–294.

O'Driscoll, M. P., & Brough, P. (2010). Work organization and health. In S. Leka & J. Houdmont (Eds.), *Occupational health psychology* (pp. 57–87). Hoboken, NJ: Wiley.

Oertelt-Prigione, S., & Regitz-Zagrosek, V. (2009). Gender aspects in cardiovascular pharmacology. *Journal of Cardiovascular Translational Research, 2*(3), 258–266.

Ohayon, M. M., Guilleminault, C., & Priest, R. G. (1999). Night terrors, sleepwalking, and confusional arousals in the general population: Their frequency and relationship to other sleep and mental disorders. *Journal of Clinical Psychiatry, 60*(4), 268–276.

Ohayon, M., & Schatzberg, A. (2010). Social phobia and depression: Prevalence and comorbidity. *Journal of Psychosomatic Research, 68*(3), 235–243.

Ohlsson, M. G. O. (2005). Relationship between complexity and liking as a function of expertise. *Music Perception, 22*(4), 583–611.

Öhman, A., & Mineka, S. (2001). Fears, phobias, and preparedness: Toward an evolved module of fear and fear learning. *Psychological Review, 108*(3), 483–522.

Öhman, A., & Mineka, S. (2003). The malicious serpent: Snakes as a prototypical stimulus for an evolved module of fear. *Current Directions in Psychological Science, 12*(1), 5–9.

Olanow, W. M. (2000, July). *Clinical and pathological perspective on Parkinsonism.* Paper presented to the World Alzheimer Congress 2000, Washington, DC.

Olatunji, B. O. & Wolitzky-Taylor, K. B. (2009). Anxiety sensitivity and the anxiety disorders: A meta-analytic review and synthesis. *Psychological Bulletin, 135*(6), 974–999.

Old, S. R., & Naveh-Benjamin, M. (2008). Memory for people and their actions: Further evidence for an age-related associative deficit. *Psychology and Aging, 23*(2), 467–472.

Oldenburg, D. (2005, January 9). A sense of doom: Animal instinct for disaster. *The Washington Post online.*

Olds, J. (1969). The central nervous system and the reinforcement of behavior. *American Psychologist, 24*, 114–132.

Olds, J., & Milner, P. (1954). Positive reinforcement produced by electrical stimulation of the septal area and other regions of the rat brain. *Journal of Comparative and Physiological Psychology, 47*, 419–427.

Oliveira, T., Gouveia, M. J., & Oliveira, R. F. (2009). Testosterone responsiveness to winning and losing experiences in female soccer players. *Psychoneuroendocrinology, 34*(7), 1056–1064.

Oliver, B. R., & Plomin, R. (2007). Twins' Early Development Study (TEDS): A multivariate, longitudinal genetic investigation of language, cognition and behavior problems from childhood through adolescence. *Twin Research and Human Genetics, 10*(1), 96–105.

Olson, M. J. (2003). Counselor understanding of Native American spiritual loss. *Counseling and Values, 47*(2), 109–117.

Olthof, A., & Roberts, W. A. (2000). Summation of symbols by pigeons (*Columba livia*): The importance of number and mass of reward items. *Journal of Comparative Psychology, 114*(2), 158–166.

Ong, J. C., Stapenski, E. J., & Gramling, S. E. (2009). Pain coping strategies for tension-type headache. *Journal of Clinical Sleep Medicine, 5*(1), 52–56.

Orsi, J. M., Margellos-Anast, H., & Whitman, S. (2010). Black–White health disparities in the United States and Chicago: A 15-year progress analysis. *American Journal of Public Health, 100*(2), 349–356.

P

Packard, M. G. (2009). Exhumed from thought: Basal ganglia and response learning in the plus-maze. *Behavioural Brain Research, 199*(1), 24–31.

Packer, D. J. (2008). Identifying systematic disobedience in Milgram's obedience experiments: A meta-analytic review. *Perspectives on Psychological Science, 3*(4), 301–304.

Packer, D. J. (2009). Avoiding groupthink. *Psychological Science, 20*(5), 546–548.

Paffenbarger, R. S., Hyde, R. T., Hsieh, C-C., & Wing, A. L. (2009). Physical activity, other life-style patterns, cardiovascular disease, and longevity. *Acta Medica Scandinavica, 220*(S711), 85–91.

Paffenbarger, R. S., Lee, I-M., & Leung, R. (2007). Physical activity and personal characteristics associated with depression and suicide in American college men. *Acta Psychiatrica Scandinavica, 89*(S377), 16–22.

Page, K. (1999, May 16). The graduate. *The Washington Post Magazine*, pp. 152, 18, 20.

Pang, J-J., et al. (2010). Direct rod input to cone BCs and direct cone input to rod BCs challenge the traditional view of mammalian BC circuitry. *Proceedings of the National Academy of Sciences, 107*(1), 395–400.

Pani, P. P., et al. (2009). Delineating the psychic structure of substance abuse and addictions: Should anxiety, mood and impulse-control dysregulation be included? *Journal of Affective Disorders, 122*(3), 185–197.

Pansky, A., Goldsmith, M., Koriat, A., & Pearlman-Avnion, S. (2009). Memory accuracy in old age: Cognitive, metacognitive, and neurocognitive determinants. *European Journal of Cognitive Psychology, 21*(2–3), 303–329.

Panza, F., et al. (2009). Alcohol drinking, cognitive functions in older age, predementia, and dementia syndromes. *Journal of Alzheimer's Disease, 17*(1), 7–31.

Papadatou-Pastou, M., Martin, M., Munafò, M. R., & Jones, G. V. (2008). Sex differences in left-handedness: A meta-analysis of 144 studies. *Psychological Bulletin, 134*(5), 677–699.

Papadopoulos, F. C., Ekbom, A., Brandt, L., & Ekselius, L. (2009). Excess mortality, causes of death and prognostic factors in anorexia nervosa. *British Journal of Psychiatry, 194*, 10–17.

Park, B., & Judd, C. M. (2005). Rethinking the link between categorization and prejudice within the social cognition perspective. *Personality and Social Psychology Review, 9*(2), 108–130.

Park, G., Lubinski, D., & Benbow, C. P. (2008). Ability differences among people who have commensurate degrees matter for scientific creativity. *Psychological Science, 19*(10), 957–961.

Park, J., & Banaji, M. R. (2000). Mood and heuristics: The influence of happy and sad states on sensitivity and bias in stereotyping. *Journal of Personality and Social Psychology, 78*(6), 1005–1023.

Park, N., Peterson, C., & Seligman, M. E. P. (2005). *Character strengths in forty nations and fifty states*. Unpublished manuscript, University of Rhode Island.

Parker, K. J., Kinney, L. F., Phillips, K. M., & Lee, T. M. (2001). Paternal behavior is associated with central neurohormone receptor binding patterns in meadow voles (*Microtus pennsylvanicus*). *Behavioral Neuroscience, 115*(6), 1341–1348.

Parr, L. A., Winslow, J. T., Hopkins, W. D., & de Waal, F. B. M. (2000). Recognizing facial cues: Individual discrimination by chimpanzees (*Pan troglodytes*) and rhesus monkeys (*Macaca mulatta*). *Journal of Comparative Psychology, 114*(1), 47–60.

Parrot, A. (Ed.). (2003). Cognitive deficits and cognitive normality in recreational cannabis and ecstasy/MDMA users. *Human Psychopharmacology: Clinical & Experimental, 18*(2), 89–90.

Pastor, L. H. (2004). Countering the psychological consequences of suicide terrorism. *Psychiatric Annals, 34*(9), 701–704.

Paterson, D. S., et al. (2006). Multiple serotonergic brainstem abnormalities in sudden infant death syndrome. *Journal of the American Medical Association, 296*, 2124–2132.

Patterson, C. J. (2009a). Children of lesbian and gay parents: Psychology, law, and policy. *American Psychologist, 64*(8), 727–736.

Patterson, C. J. (2009b). Lesbian and gay parents and their children: A social science perspective. In D. A. Hope (Ed.), *Nebraska Symposium on Motivation: Vol. 54. Contemporary perspectives on lesbian, gay, and bisexual identities* (pp. 141–182). New York: Springer.

Patterson, G. R., Dishion, T. J., & Yoerger, K. (2000). Adolescent growth in new forms of problem behavior: Macro- and micro-peer dynamics. *Prevention Science, 1*(1), 3–13.

Paulussen-Hoogeboom, M. C., Stams, G. J. J. M., Hermanns, J. M. A., & Peetsma, T. T. D. (2007). Child negative emotionality and parenting from infancy to preschool: A meta-analytic review. *Developmental Psychology, 43*(2), 438–453.

Pavlov, I. (1927). *Conditioned reflexes*. London: Oxford University Press.

Penedo, F. J., et al. (2003). Personality, quality of life and HAART adherence among men and women living with HIV/AIDS. *Journal of Psychosomatic Research, 54*(3), 271–278.

Penfield, W. (1969). Consciousness, memory, and man's conditioned reflexes. In K. H. Pribram (Ed.), *On the biology of learning*. New York: Harcourt Brace Jovanovich.

Penton-Voak, I. S., & Chang, H. Y. (2008). Attractiveness judgments of individuals vary across emotional expression and movement conditions. *Journal of Evolutionary Psychology, 6*(2), 89–100.

Penton-Voak, I. S., & Perrett, D. I. (2000). Female preference for male faces changes cyclically: Further evidence. *Evolution and Human Behavior, 21*(1), 39–48.

Peplau, L. A. (2003). Human sexuality: How do men and women differ? *Current Directions in Psychological Science, 12*(2), 37–40.

Perea, G., Navarrete, M., & Araque, A. (2009). Tripartite synapses: Astrocytes process and control synaptic information. *Trends in Neurosciences, 32*(8), 421–431.

Perls, F. S. (1971). *Gestalt therapy verbatim*. New York: Bantam Books.

Perna, F. M., Antoni, M. H., Baum, A., Gordon, P., & Schneiderman, N. (2003). Cognitive behavioral stress management effects on injury and illness among competitive athletes: A randomized clinical trial. *Annals of Behavioral Medicine, 25*(1), 66–73.

Perrett, D. I., May, K. A., & & Yoshikawa, S. (1994). Facial shape and judgments of female attractiveness, *Nature, 368*, 239–242.

Perry, W. G. (1970/1998). *Forms of intellectual and ethical development in the college years: A scheme*. New York: Holt, Rinehart and Winston.

Perry, W. G. (1981). Cognitive and ethical growth: The making of meaning. In A. W. Chickering & Assoc. (Eds.). *The modern American college* (pp. 76–116). San Francisco: Jossey-Bass.

Peterka, M., Likovsky, Z., & Peterkova, R. (2007). Environmental risk and sex ratio in newborns. *Congenital Diseases and the Environment, 23*, 295–319.

Petersen, J. L., & Hyde, J. S. (2010). A meta-analytic review of research on gender differences in sexuality, 1993–2007. *Psychological Bulletin, 136*(1), 21–38.

Peterson, C., & Seligman, M. E. P. (2004). *Character strengths and virtues: A handbook and classification*. Washington, DC: American Psychological Association.

Peterson, C., Park, N., & Seligman, M. E. P. (2005). Orientations to happiness and life satisfaction: The full life versus the empty life. *Journal of Happiness Studies, 6*(1), 25–41.

Peterson, D. (2006). *Jane Goodall: The woman who redefined man.* Boston: Houghton Mifflin.

Peterson, L. R., & Peterson, M. J. (1959). Short-term retention of individual verbal items. *Journal of Experimental Psychology, 58,* 193–198.

Petrill, S. A., et al. (2010). Genetic and environmental influences on the growth of early reading skills. *Journal of Child Psychology and Psychiatry, 51*(6), 660–667.

Petry, N. M., Martin, B., Cooney, J. L., & Kranzler, H. R. (2000). Give them prizes and they will come: Contingency management for treatment of alcohol dependence. *Journal of Consulting and Clinical Psychology, 68,* 250–257.

Petty, R. E., Briñol, P., & Priester, J. R. (2009a). Mass media attitude change: Implications of the elaboration likelihood model of persuasion. In J. Bryant & M. B. Oliver (Eds.), *Media effects: Advances in theory and research* (pp. 125–164). Oxford, England: Taylor & Francis.

Petty, R. E., Fazio, R. H., & Briñol, P. (Eds.). (2009b). *Attitudes: Insights from the new implicit measures.* New York: Psychology Press.

Phelps, E. A., O'Connor, K. J., Cunningham, W. A., Funayama, E. S., & Banaji, M. R. (2000). Performance on indirect measures of race evaluation predicts amygdala activation. *Journal of Cognitive Neuroscience, 12*(5), 729–738.

Phinney, J. S. (2006). Acculturation is not an independent variable: Approaches to studying acculturation as a complex process. In M. H. Bornstein & L. R. Cote (Eds.), *Acculturation and parent–child relationships: Measurement and development* (pp. 79–96). London: Routledge.

Phinney, J. S., & Alipuria, L. L. (2006). Multiple social categorization and identity among multiracial, multiethnic, and multicultural individuals: Processes and implications. In R. J. Crisp & M. Hewstone (Eds.), *Multiple social categorization: Processes, models and applications* (pp. 211–238). New York: Psychology Press.

Phinney, J. S., & Ong, A. D. (2007). Ethnic identity in immigrant families. In J. E. Lansford, K. Deater-Deckard, & M. H. Bornstein (Eds.), *Immigrant families in contemporary society. Duke series in child development and public policy* (pp. 51–68). New York: Guilford Press.

Phoenix, C. H. (2009). Organizing action of prenatally administered testosterone propionate on the tissues mediating mating behavior in the female guinea pig. *Hormones and Behavior, 55*(5), 566.

Piaget, J. (1932). *The moral judgment of the child.* London: Kegan Paul.

Piaget, J. (1963). *The origins of intelligence in children.* New York: Norton.

Piaget, J., & Smith, L. (Trans.). (2000). Commentary on Vygotsky's criticisms of language and thought of the child and judgment and reasoning in the child. *New Ideas in Psychology, 18*(2–3), 241–259.

Piccinni, A., et al. (2009). Plasma brain-derived neurotrophic factor in treatment-resistant depressed patients receiving electroconvulsive therapy. *European Neuropsychopharmacology, 19*(5), 349–355.

Pietrzak, R., et al. (2010). Psychosocial buffers of traumatic stress, depressive symptoms, and psychosocial difficulties in veterans of Operations Enduring Freedom and Iraqi Freedom: The role of resilience, unit support, and postdeployment social support. *Journal of Affective Disorders, 120*(1), 188–192.

Piffer, R. C., Garcia, P. C., & Pereira, O. C. M. (2009). Adult partner preference and sexual behavior of male rats exposed prenatally to betamethasone. *Physiology and Behavior, 98*(1–2), 163–167.

Pihl, R. O., Peterson, J. B., & Finn, P. (1990). Inherited predisposition to alcoholism. *Journal of Abnormal Psychology, 99,* 291–301.

Piliavin, J. A. (2009). Altruism and helping: The evolution of a field. *Social Psychology Quarterly, 72*(3), 209–225.

Pind, J., Gunnarsdottir, E. K., & Johannesson, H. S. (2003). Raven's Standard Progressive Matrices: New school age norms and a study of the test's validity. *Personality and Individual Differences, 34*(3), 375–386.

Pinker, S. (1994a, June 19). Building a better brain. *The New York Times Book Review,* pp. 13–14.

Pinker, S. (1994b). *The language instinct.* New York: William Morrow.

Pinker, S. (1997). Words and rules in the human brain. *Nature, 387*(6633), 547–548.

Pinker, S. (2007). *The stuff of thought: Language as a window into human nature.* New York: Penguin Books.

Piolino, P., Desgranges, B., & Eustache, F. (2009). Episodic autobiographical memories over the course of time: Cognitive, neuropsychological and neuroimaging findings. *Neuropsychologia, 47*(11), 2314–2329.

Plant, E. A., & Devine, P. G. (2009). The active control of prejudice: Unpacking the intentions guiding control efforts. *Journal of Personality and Social Psychology, 96*(3), 640–652.

Platania, J., & Moran, G. P. (2001). Social facilitation as a function of the mere presence of others. *Journal of Social Psychology, 141*(2), 190–197.

Plomin, R. (2000). Behavioural genetics in the 21st century. *International Journal of Behavioral Development, 24*(1), 30–34.

Plomin, R., & Asbury, K. (2005). Nature and nurture: Genetic and environmental influences on behavior. *The Annals of the American Academy of Political and Social Science, 600*(1), 86–98.

Plomin, R., & Crabbe, J. (2000). DNA. *Psychological Bulletin, 126*(6), 806–828.

Plomin, R., & Daniels, D. (1987). Why are children in the same family so different from one another? *Behavioral and Brain Sciences, 10*(1), 1–16.

Plomin, R., & Haworth, C. M. A. (2009). Genetics of high cognitive abilities. *Behavior Genetics, 39*(4), 347–349.

Plomin, R., & Schalkwyk, L. C. (2007). Microarrays. *Developmental Science, 10*(1), 19–23.

Plomin, R., & Spinath, F. M. (2004). Intelligence: Genetics, genes, and genomics. *Journal of Personality and Social Psychology, 86*(1), 112–129.

Plomin, R., DeFries, J. C., McClearn, G. E., & McGuffin, P. (2008). *Behavioral genetics.* New York: Worth Publishers.

Plomin, R., Owen, M. J., & McGuffin, P. (1994). The genetic basis of complex human behaviors. *Science, 264,* 1733–1739.

Plous, S. (1996). Attitudes toward the use of animals in psychological research and education. *American Psychologist, 51,* 1167–1180.

Pluess, M., Conrad, A., & Wilhelm, F. H. (2009). Muscle tension in generalized anxiety disorder: A critical review of the literature. *Journal of Anxiety Disorders, 23*(1), 1–11.

Pogue-Geile, M. F., & Gottesman, I. I. (2007). Schizophrenia: Study of a genetically complex phenotype. In B. S. Jones & P. Mormède (Eds.), *Neurobehavioral genetics: Methods and applications* (2nd ed., pp. 209–226). Boca Raton, FL: CRC Press.

Polanczyk, G., et al. (2010). Etiological and clinical features of childhood psychotic symptoms. *Archives of General Psychiatry, 67*(4), 328–338.

Polina, E. R., Contini, V., Hutz, M. H., & Bau, C. H. D. (2009). The serotonin 2A receptor gene in alcohol dependence and tobacco smoking. *Drug and Alcohol Dependence, 101*(1–2), 128–131.

Pollatos, O., Schandry, R., Auer, D. P., & Kaufmann, C. (2007). Brain structures mediating cardiovascular arousal and interoceptive awareness. *Brain Research, 1141*, 178–187.

Pope, H. G., Kouri, E. M., & Hudson, J. I. (2000). Effects of supraphysiologic doses of testosterone on mood and aggression in normal men: A randomized controlled trial. *Archives of General Psychiatry, 57*, 133–140.

Popma, A., et al. (2007). Cortisol moderates the relationship between testosterone and aggression in delinquent male adolescents. *Biological Psychiatry, 61*(3), 405–411.

Porsolt, R. D., Moser, P. C., & Castagne, V. (2010). Behavioral indices in antipsychotic drug discovery. *Journal of Pharmacology and Experimental Therapeutics, 333*(3), 632–638.

Porter, R. H., Makin, J. W., Davis, L. B., & Christensen, K. M. (1992). Breast-fed infants respond to olfactory cues from their own mother and unfamiliar lactating females. *Infant Behavior and Development, 15*, 85–93.

Porter, S., & ten Brinke, L. (2008). Reading between the lies: Identifying concealed and falsified emotions in universal facial expressions. *Psychological Science, 19*(5), 508–514.

Posada, G., et al. (2002). Maternal caregiving and infant security in two cultures. *Developmental Psychology, 38*(1), 67–78.

Postmes, T., & Spears, R. (1998). Deindividuation and antinormative behavior: A meta-analysis. *Psychological Bulletin, 123*(3), 238–259.

Potter, W. J. (2008). Adolescents and television violence. In P. E. Jamieson & D. Romer (Eds.), *The changing portrayal of adolescents in the media since 1950* (pp. 221–249). New York: Oxford University Press.

Pradhan, D. S., et al. (2010). Aggressive interactions rapidly increase androgen synthesis in the brain during the non-breeding season. *Hormones and Behavior, 57*(4-5), 381–389.

Prato-Previde, E., Fallani, G., & Valsecchi, P. (2006). Gender differences in owners interacting with pet dogs: An observational study. *Ethology, 112*(1), 64–73.

Pressman, S. D., & Cohen, S. (2005). Does positive affect influence health? *Psychological Bulletin, 131*(6), 925–971.

Preti, A., & Vellante, M. (2007). Creativity and psychopathology: Higher rates of psychosis proneness and nonright-handedness among creative artists compared to same age and gender peers. *Journal of Nervous and Mental Disease, 195*(10), 837–845.

Priner, R., Freeman, S., Perez, R., & Sohmer, H. (2003). The neonate has a temporary conductive hearing loss due to fluid in the middle ear. *Audiology & Neurotology, 8*(2), 100–110.

Prochaska, J. O., & Norcross, J. C. (2010). *Systems of psychotherapy* (7th ed.). Belmont, CA: Wadsworth.

Project MATCH Research Group. (1997). Matching alcoholism treatments to client heterogeneity: Project MATCH post-treatment drinking outcomes. *Journal of Studies on Alcohol, 58*, 7–29.

Pronin, E., Lin, D. Y., & Ross, L. (2002). The bias blind spot: Perceptions of bias in self versus others. *Personality and Social Psychology Bulletin, 28*(3), 369–381.

Proverbio, A. M., Riva, F., & Zani, A. (2010). When neurons do not mirror the agent's intentions: Sex differences in neural coding of goal-directed actions. *Neuropsychologia, 48*(5), 1454–1463.

Pulido, R., & Marco, A. (2000) El efecto Barnum en estudiantes universitarios y profesionales de la psicologia en Mexico [The Barnum effect in university students and psychology professionals in Mexico]. *Revista Intercontinental de Psicologia y Educacion, 2*(2), 59–66.

Pulley, B. (1998, June 16). Those seductive snake eyes: Tales of growing up gambling. *The New York Times*, pp. A1, A28.

Purdie-Vaughns, V., Steele, C. M., Davies, P. G., Ditlmann, R., & Crosby, J. R. (2008). Social identity contingencies: How diversity cues signal threat or safety for African Americans in mainstream institutions. *Journal of Personality and Social Psychology, 94*(4), 615–630.

Puri, B. K. (2010). Progressive structural brain changes in schizophrenia. *Expert Review of Neurotherapeutics, 10*(1), 33–42.

Pusey, A., et al. (2008). Severe aggression among female *Pan troglodytes schweinfurthii* at Gombe National Park, Tanzania. *International Journal of Primatology, 29*(4), 949–973.

Q

Qi, Z., & Gold, P. E. (2009). Intrahippocampal infusions of anisomycin produce amnesia: Contribution of increased release of norepinephrine, dopamine, and acetylcholine. *Learning and Memory, 16*, 308–314.

Qin, W., et al. (2006). Calorie restriction attenuates Alzheimer's disease type brain amyloidosis in squirrel monkeys (*Saimiri sciureus*). *Journal of Alzheimer's Disease, 10*(4), 417–422.

Quinlan, M. B. (2010). Ethnomedicine and ethnobotany of fright, a Caribbean culture-bound psychiatric syndrome. *Journal of Ethnobiology and Ethnomedicine, 6*(9). Retrieved from http://www.biomedcentral.com/content/pdf/1746–4269-6-9.pdf

Quinlivan, J. A., & Condon, J. (2005). Anxiety and depression in fathers in teenage pregnancy. *Australian and New Zealand Journal of Psychiatry, 39*(10), 915–920.

R

Rachman, S. (2009). Psychological treatment of anxiety: The evolution of behavior therapy and cognitive behavior therapy. *Annual Review of Clinical Psychology, 5*, 97–119.

Radcliffe, R. A., et al. (2009). A major QTL for acute alcohol sensitivity in the alcohol tolerant and non-tolerant rat lines. *Genes, Brain, and Behavior, 8*(6), 611–625.

Raine, A. (2008). From genes to brain to antisocial behavior. *Current Directions in Psychological Science, 17*(5), 323–328.

Raine, A., Yang, Y., Narr, K. L., & Toga, A. W. (2011). Sex differences in orbitofrontal gray matter as a partial explanation for sex differences in antisocial personality. *Molecular Psychiatry, 16*, 227–236.

Rajasethupathy, P., et al. (2009). Characterization of small RNAs in *Aplysia* reveals a role for miR-124 in constraining synaptic plasticity through CREB. *Neuron, 63*(6), 803–817.

Ramagopalan, S. V., et al. (2010). A genome-wide scan of male sexual orientation. *Journal of Human Genetics, 55*, 131–132.

Ramasubramanian, S., & Oliver, M. B. (2007). Activating and suppressing hostile and benevolent racism: Evidence for comparative media stereotyping. *Media Psychology, 9*(3), 623–646.

Randel, B., Stevenson, H. W., & Witruk, E. (2000). Attitudes, beliefs, and mathematics achievement of German and Japanese high school students. *International Journal of Behavioral Development, 24*(2), 190–198.

Randolph, M. E., et al. (2009). Alcohol use and sexual risk behavior among college students. *American Journal of Drug and Alcohol Abuse, 35*(2), 80–84.

Rappaport, N. B., McAnulty, D. P., & Brantley, P. J. (1988). Exploration of the Type A behavior pattern in chronic headache sufferers. *Journal of Consulting and Clinical Psychology, 56*, 621–623.

Rathus, J. H., & Sanderson, W. C. (1999). *Marital distress: Cognitive behavioral interventions for couples.* Northvale, NJ: Jason Aronson.

553

Rathus, S. A. (1973). A 30-item schedule for assessing assertive behavior. *Behavior Therapy, 4,* 398–406.

Rathus, S. A., Nevid, J. S., & Fichner-Rathus, L. (2011). *Human sexuality in a world of diversity* (8th ed.). Boston: Allyn & Bacon.

Rattan, S. I. S. (2008). Increased molecular damage and heterogeneity as the basis of aging. *Biological Chemistry, 389*(3), 267–272.

Rawley, J. B., & Constantinidis, C. (2008). Neural correlates of learning and working memory in the primary posterior parietal cortex. *Neurobiology of Learning and Memory, 91*(2), 129–138.

Rayner, L., Kershaw, K., Hanna, D., & Chaplin, R. (2009). The patient perspective of the consent process and side effects of electroconvulsive therapy. *Journal of Mental Health, 18*(5), 379–388.

Read, C. N., & Greenberg, B. D. (2009). Psychiatric neurosurgery 2009: Review and perspective. *Seminars in Neurology, 29*(3), 256–265.

Reaney, P. (2000, February 14). *In matters of the heart, France tops EU neighbors.* Reuters News Agency online.

Redrobe, J. P., & Bourin, M. (2009). The effect of lithium administration in animal models of depression. *Fundamental and Clinical Pharmacology, 13*(3), 293–299.

Reece, M., Herbenick, D., Schick, V., Sanders, S. A., Dodge, B., & Fortenberry, J. D. (2010). Sexual behaviors, relationships, and perceived health among adult men in the United States: Results from a national probability sample. *Journal of Sexual Medicine, 7*(Suppl. 5), 291–304.

Reed, S. C., Levin, F. R., & Evans, S. M. (2008). Changes in mood, cognitive performance and appetite in the late luteal and follicular phases of the menstrual cycle in women with and without PMDD (premenstrual dysphoric disorder). *Hormones and Behavior, 54*(1), 185–193.

Reeder, G. D. (2009). Mindreading: Judgments about intentionality and motives in dispositional inference. *Psychological Inquiry, 20*(1), 1–18.

Rees, T., Ingledew, D. K., & Hardy, L. (2005). Attribution in sports psychology: Seeking congruence between theory, research and practice. *Psychology of Sport and Exercise, 6*(2), 189–204.

Regier, T. (2005). The emergence of words: Attentional learning in form and meaning. *Cognitive Science: A Multidisciplinary Journal, 29*(6), 819–865.

Rehm, L. P. (2008). How far have we come in teletherapy? Comment on "Telephone-administered psychotherapy." *Clinical Psychology: Science and Practice, 15*(3), 259–261.

Reich, M., Lesur, A., & Perdrizet-Chevallier, C. (2008). Depression, quality of life and breast cancer: A review of the literature. *Breast Cancer Research and Treatment, 110*(1), 9–17.

Reid, L. W. (2008). Disaggregating the effects of racial and economic equality on early twentieth-century execution rates. *Sociological Spectrum, 28*(2), 160–174.

Reinders, A., et al. (2006). Psychobiological characteristics of dissociative identity disorder: A symptom provocation study. *Biological Psychiatry, 60*(7), 730–740.

Reinecke, M. A., DuBois, D. L., & Schultz, T. M. (2001). Social problem solving, mood, and suicidality among inpatient adolescents. *Cognitive Therapy and Research, 25*(6), 743–756.

Reis, O., & Youniss, J. (2004). Patterns in identity change and development in relationships with mothers and friends. *Journal of Adolescent Research, 19*(1), 31–44.

Reiser, M. (2001). The dream in contemporary psychiatry. *American Journal of Psychiatry, 158*(3), 351–359.

Rendell, P. G., Castel, A. D., & Craik, F. I. M. (2005). Memory for proper names in old age: A disproportionate impairment? *The Quarterly Journal of Experimental Psychology A: Human Experimental Psychology, 58A*(1), 54–71.

Renninger, K. A., & Wozniak, R. H. (1985). Effect of interest on attentional shift, recognition, and recall in young children. *Developmental Psychology, 21,* 624–632.

Rescorla, R. A. (1967). Inhibition of delay in Pavlovian fear conditioning. *Journal of Comparative and Physiological Psychology, 64*(1), 114–120.

Rescorla, R. A. (1988). Pavlovian conditioning: It's not what you think it is. *American Psychologist, 43,* 151–160.

Rescorla, R. A. (1999). Partial reinforcement reduces the associative change produced by nonreinforcement. *Journal of Experimental Psychology: Animal Behavior Processes, 25*(4), 403–414.

Reynolds, C. A., Barlow, T., & Pedersen, N. L. (2006). Alcohol, tobacco and caffeine use: Spouse similarity processes. *Behavior Genetics, 36*(2), 201–215.

Rhee, S. H., & Waldman, I. D. (2002). Genetic and environmental influences on antisocial behavior: A meta-analysis of twin and adoption studies. *Psychological Bulletin, 128*(3), 490–529.

Ricca, V., et al. (2009). Correlations between binge eating and emotional eating in a sample of overweight subjects. *Appetite, 53*(3), 418–421.

Richardson, J., et al. (2006). Hypnosis for nausea and vomiting in cancer chemotherapy: A systematic review of the research evidence. *European Journal of Cancer Care, 16*(5), 402–412.

Richardson, K. M., & Rothstein, H. R. (2008). Effects of occupational stress management intervention programs: A meta-analysis. *Journal of Occupational Health Psychology, 13*(1), 69–93.

Rimm, E. (2000, May). *Lifestyle may play role in potential for impotence.* Paper presented to the annual meeting of the American Urological Association, Atlanta.

Ringach, D. L., & Jentsch, J. D. (2009). We must face the threats. *Journal of Neuroscience, 29*(37), 11417–11418.

Risch, N., et al. (2009). Interaction between the serotonin transporter gene (*5-HTTLPR*), stressful life events, and risk of depression. *Journal of the American Medical Association, 301*(23), 2462–2471.

Rizzo, A. A., & Schultheis, M. T. (2002). Expanding the boundaries of psychology: The application of virtual reality. *Psychological Inquiry, 13*(2), 134–140.

Rizzo, A., Reger, G., Gahm, G., Difede, J., & Rothbaum, B. O. (2009). Virtual reality exposure therapy for combat-related PTSD. In P. J. Shiromani, T. M. Keane, & J. E LeDoux (Eds.), *Post-traumatic stress disorder* (pp. 375–399). New York: Springer.

Rizzolatti, G., & Craighero, L. (2004). The mirror-neuron system. *Annual Review of Neuroscience, 27,* 169–172.

Robbins, J. (2000, July 4). Virtual reality finds a real place as a medical aid. *The New York Times online.*

Roberson, D., Davidoff, J., & Shapiro, L. (2002). Squaring the circle: The cultural relativity of good shape. *Journal of Cognition and Culture, 2*(1), 29–51.

Roberts, J., Lennings, C. J., & Heard, R. (2009). Nightmares, life stress, and anxiety. *Dreaming, 19*(1), 17–29.

Roberts, S. (2009, November 24). Economy is forcing young adults back home in big numbers, survey finds. *The New York Times online.*

Robins, R. W., Gosling, S. D., & Craik, K. H. (1999). An empirical analysis of trends in psychology. *American Psychologist, 54*(2), 117–128.

Robinson, E. (2011). *Disintegration: The splintering of black America.* New York: Simon & Schuster.

Rocca, W. A., Grossardt, B. R., & Maraganore, D. M. (2008). The long-term effects of oophorectomy on cognitive and motor aging are age dependent. *Neurodegenerative Disease, 5,* 257–260.

Rodin, G., et al. (2009). Pathways to distress: The multiple determinants of depression, hopelessness, and the desire for hastened death in metastatic cancer patients. *Social Science and Medicine, 68*(3), 562–569.

Rodrigues-Galdino, A. M., et al. (2010). Development of the neotropical catfish *Rhamdia quelen* (Siluriformes, Heptapteridae) incubated in different temperature regimes. *Zygote, 18,* 131–144.

Rodriguez, C. J., et al. (2008). Effect of social support on nocturnal blood pressure dipping. *Psychosomatic Medicine, 70,* 7–12.

Roediger, H. L., & McCabe, D. P. (2007). Evaluating experimental research. In R. J. Sternberg, H. L. Roediger, & D. F. Halpern (Eds.), *Critical thinking in psychology* (pp. 15–36). New York: Cambridge University Press.

Roepke, S., et al. (2011). Dialectic behavioural therapy has an impact on self-concept clarity and facets of self-esteem in women with borderline personality disorder. *Clinical Psychology and Psychotherapy, 18*(2), 148–158.

Rogers, C. R. (1951). *Client-centered therapy.* Boston: Houghton Mifflin.

Rogers, D. (2009). The other philosophy club: America's first academic women philosophers. *Hypatia, 24*(2), 164–185.

Rogers, P., & Soule, J. (2009). Cross-cultural differences in the acceptance of Barnum profiles supposedly derived from Western versus Chinese astrology. *Journal of Cross-Cultural Psychology, 40*(3), 381–399.

Rohr, M. K., & Lang, F. R. (2009). Aging well together—A mini-review. *Gerontology, 55,* 333–343.

Roid, G. H., & Tippin, S. M. (2009). Assessment of intellectual strengths and weaknesses with the Stanford–Binet Intelligence Scales—5th edition. In J. A. Naglieri & S. Goldstein (Eds.), *Practitioner's guide to assessing intelligence and achievement* (pp. 127–152). Hoboken, NJ: Wiley.

Roland, D. L., & Incrocci, L. (2008). *Handbook of sexual and gender identity disorders.* Hoboken, NJ: Wiley.

Rolls, E. T. (2009). Functional neuroimaging of *umami* taste: What makes *umami* pleasant? *American Journal of Clinical Nutrition, 90*(3), 804S–813S.

Romero, E., Luengo, M. A., & Sobral, J. (2001). Personality and antisocial behaviour: Study of temperamental dimensions. *Personality and Individual Differences, 31*(3), 329–348.

Rosekind, M. R., et al. (2010). The cost of poor sleep: Workplace productivity loss and associated costs. *Journal of Occupational and Environmental Medicine, 52*(1), 91–98.

Rosenberg, M. J. (2009). The conditions and consequences of evaluation apprehension. In R. Rosenthal & R. L. Rosnow (Eds.), *Artifacts in behavioral research* (pp. 211–263). New York: Oxford University Press.

Rosenstein, D., & Oster, H. (1988). Differential facial responses to four basic tastes. *Child Development, 59,* 1555–1568.

Ross, C. A. (2006). Dissociative identity disorder. *Current Psychosis and Therapeutics Reports, 4*(3), 112–116.

Ross, J. L., Roeltgen, D., Feuillan, P., Kushner, H., & Cutler, W. B. (2000). Use of estrogen in young girls with Turner syndrome: Effects on memory. *Neurology, 54*(1), 164–170.

Ross, L., & Nisbett, R. E. (1991). *The person and the situation.* New York: McGraw-Hill.

Roth, T. L., Lubin, F. D., Sodhi, M., & Kleinman, J. E. (2009). Epigenetic mechanisms in schizophrenia. *Biochimica et Biophysica Acta, 1790*(9), 869–877.

Rotter, J. B. (1990). Internal versus external control of reinforcement. *American Psychologist, 45,* 489–493.

Rouder, J. N., & Morey, R. D. (2009). The nature of psychological thresholds. *Psychological Review, 116*(3), 655–660.

Rowatt, W. C., Cunningham, M. R., & Druen, P. B. (1999). Lying to get a date: The effect of facial physical attractiveness on the willingness to deceive prospective dating partners. *Journal of Social and Personal Relationships, 16*(2), 209–223.

Rozee, P. D., & Koss, M. P. (2001). Rape: A century of resistance. *Psychology of Women Quarterly, 25*(4), 295–311.

Rubella. (2009, March 2). *The New York Times Health Guide.* Retrieved from http://health.nytimes.com/health/guides/disease/rubella/overview.html

Rubia, K. (2009). The neurobiology of meditation and its clinical effectiveness in psychiatric disorders. *Biological Psychology, 82*(1), 1–11.

Ruck, C., et al. (2008). Capsulotomy for obsessive–compulsive disorder. *Archives of General Psychiatry, 65*(8), 914–921.

Rudd, M. D. (2008). Suicide warning signs in clinical practice. *Current Psychiatry Reports, 10*(1), 87–90.

Rudy, D., & Grusec, J. E. (2006). Authoritarian parenting in individualist and collectivist groups: Associations with maternal emotion and cognition and children's self-esteem. *Journal of Family Psychology, 20*(1), 68–78.

Ruiter, R. A. C., Abraham, C., & Kok, G. (2001). Scary warnings and rational precautions: A review of the psychology of fear appeals. *Psychology and Health, 16*(6), 613–630.

Rumbold, A. R., et al. (2006). Vitamins C and E and the risks of preeclampsia and perinatal complications. *New England Journal of Medicine, 354,* 1796–1806.

Runyan, D. K., Dunne, M. D., & Zolotor, A. Z. (2009). Introduction to the development of the ISPCAN child abuse screening tools. *Child Abuse and Neglect, 33*(11), 842–845.

Rupp, H., et al. (2009). Neural activation in women in response to masculinized male faces: Mediation by hormones and psychosexual factors. *Evolution and Human Behavior, 30*(1), 1–10.

Rusconi, A. (2004). Different pathways out of the parental home: A comparison of West Germany and Italy. *Journal of Comparative Family Studies, 35*(4), 627–649.

Rush, A. J., Khatami, M., & Beck, A. T. (1975). Cognitive and behavior therapy in chronic depression. *Behavior Therapy, 6,* 398–404.

Rushton, J. P., Skuy, M., & Fridjhon, P. (2003). Performance on Raven's Advanced Progressive Matrices by African, East Indian, and White engineering students in South Africa. *Intelligence, 31*(2), 123–137.

Rutkowski, G. K., Gruder, C. L., & Romer, D. (1983). Group cohesiveness, social norms, and bystander intervention. *Journal of Personality and Social Psychology, 44,* 545–552.

S

Sabatini, E., et al. (2009). Brain structures activated by overt and covert emotional visual stimuli. *Brain Research Bulletin, 79*(5), 258–264.

Sadalla, E. K., Kenrick, D. T., & Vershure, B. (1987). Dominance and heterosexual attraction. *Journal of Personality and Social Psychology, 52,* 730–738.

Sadker, M., & Sadker, D. (1994). *How America's schools cheat girls.* New York: Scribner.

Safford, S., Alloy, L., Abramson, L., & Crossfield, A. (2007). Negative cognitive style as a predictor of negative life events in depression-prone individuals: A test of the stress-generation hypothesis. *Journal of Affective Disorders, 99*(1), 147–154.

Saffran, J. R. (2009). Acquiring grammatical patterns: Constraints on learning. In J. Colombo, P. McCardle, & L. Freud (Eds.), *Infant pathways to language: Methods, models, and research disorders* (pp. 31–47). New York: Psychology Press.

Saggino, A., Perfetti, B., Spitoni, G., & Galati, G. (2006). Fluid intelligence and executive functions: New perspectives. In L. V. Wesley (Ed.), *Intelligence: New research* (pp. 1–22). Hauppauge, NY: Nova Science.

Salovey, P., Detweiler-Bedell, B. T., Detweiler-Bedell, J. B., & Mayer, J. D. (2008). Emotional intelligence. In M. Lewis, A. M. Haviland-Jones, & L. F. Barrett (Eds.), *Handbook of emotions* (3rd ed., pp. 533–545). New York: Guilford Press.

Salovey, P., Rothman, A. J., Detweiler, J. B., & Steward, W. T. (2000). Emotional states and physical health. *American Psychologist, 55,* 110–121.

Salthouse, T. A. (2001). Structural models of the relations between age and measures of cognitive functioning. *Intelligence, 29*(2), 93–115.

Salthouse, T. A., & Davis, H. P. (2006). Organization of cognitive abilities and neuropsychological variables across the lifespan. *Developmental Review, 26*(1), 31–54.

Salzarulo, P., & Ficca, G. (Eds.). (2002). *Awakening and sleep–wake cycle across development.* Amsterdam: John Benjamins.

Sanchez, D. T., Shih, M., & Garcia, J. A. (2009). Juggling multiple racial identities: Malleable racial identification and psychological well-being. *Cultural Diversity and Ethnic Minority Psychology, 15*(3), 243–254.

Sanders, G. S. (1984). Effects of context cues on eyewitness identification responses. *Journal of Applied Social Psychology, 14,* 386–397.

Sanders, S. A., Reece, M., Herbenick, D., Schick, V., Dodge, B., & Fortenberry, J. D. (2010). Condom use during most recent vaginal intercourse event among a probability sample of adults in the United States. *Journal of Sexual Medicine, 7*(suppl 5), 362–373.

Sandman, C., & Crinella, F. (1995). Cited in Margoshes, P. (1995). For many, old age is the prime of life. *APA Monitor, 26*(5), 36–37.

Sanjuan, P. M., Langenbucher, J. W., & Labouvie, E. (2006). The role of sexual assault and sexual dysfunction in alcohol and other drug use disorders. *Child Abuse and Neglect, 30*(4), 327–339.

Santarius, T., Shipley, J., Brewer, D., Stratton, M. R., & Cooper, C. S. (2010). Epigenetics and genetics: A census of amplified and overexpressed human cancer genes. *Nature Reviews Cancer, 10*(1), 59–64.

Sarbin, T. R., & Coe, W. C. (1972). *Hypnosis.* New York: Holt, Rinehart and Winston.

Saroglou, V., & Galand, P. (2004). Identities, values, and religion: A study among Muslim, other immigrant, and native Belgian young adults after the 9/11 attacks. *Identity, 4*(2), 97–132.

Saul, A. L., Grant, K. E., & Carter, J. S. (2008). Post-traumatic reactions in adolescents: How well do the *DSM-IV* PTSD criteria fit the real life experience of trauma exposed youth? *Journal of Abnormal Child Psychology, 36*(6), 915–925.

Saunders, K. W. (2003). Regulating youth access to violent video games: Three responses to First Amendment concerns. Retrieved from http://www.law.msu.edu/lawrev/2003-1/2-Saunders.pdf

Sava, S., & Yurgelun-Todd, D. A. (2008). Functional magnetic resonance in psychiatry. *Topics in Magnetic Resonance Imaging, 19*(2), 71–79.

Savic, I., & Lindström, P. (2008, June 16). PET and MRI show differences in cerebral asymmetry and functional connectivity between homo- and heterosexual subjects. Published online. *Proceedings of the National Academy of Sciences, 105*(27), 9403–9408.

Savin-Williams, R. C. (2006). Who's gay? Does it matter? *Current Directions in Psychological Science, 15*(1), 40–44.

Savin-Williams, R. C., & Cohen, K. M. (2007). Development of same-sex attracted youth. In I. H. Meyer & M. E. Northridge (Eds.), *The health of sexual minorities: Public health perspectives on lesbian, gay, bisexual, and transgender populations* (pp. 27–47). New York: Springer Science + Business Media.

Sayette, M. A., Reichle, E. D., & Schooler, J. W. (2009). Lost in the sauce: The effects of alcohol on mind wandering? *Psychological Science, 20*(6), 747–752.

Saywitz, K. J., Mannarino, A. P., Berliner, L., & Cohen, J. A. (2000). Treatment for sexually abused children and adolescents. *American Psychologist, 55*(9), 1040–1049.

Scarr, S., & Weinberg, R. A. (1976). IQ test performance of Black children adopted by White families. *American Psychologist, 31,* 726–739.

Scarr, S., & Weinberg, R. A. (1977). Intellectual similarities within families of both adopted and biological children. *Intelligence, 1,* 170–191.

Scarr, S., & Weinberg, R. A. (1983). The Minnesota adoption studies: Genetic differences and malleability. *Child Development, 54,* 260–267.

Schachter, S., & Singer, J. E. (1962). Cognitive, social, and physiological determinants of emotional state. *Psychological Review, 69,* 379–399.

Schacter, D. L. (1992). Understanding implicit memory: A cognitive neuroscience approach. *American Psychologist, 47*(4), 559–569.

Schacter, D. L., Gallo, D. A., & Kensinger, E. A. (2007). The cognitive neuroscience of implicit and false memories: Perspectives on processing specificity. In H. L. Roediger & J. S. Nairne (Eds.), *The foundations of remembering: Essays in honor of Henry L. Roediger III* (pp. 355–379). New York: Psychology Press.

Schaie, K. W. (1994). The course of adult intellectual development. *American Psychologist, 49,* 304–313.

Schaie, K. W., Willis, S. L., & Caskie, G. I. L. (2004). The Seattle longitudinal study: Relationship between personality and cognition. *Aging, Neuropsychology, and Cognition, 11*(2–3), 304–324.

Scheff, T. J. (2007). Catharsis and other heresies: A theory of emotion. *Journal of Social, Evolutionary, and Cultural Psychology, 1*(3), 98–113.

Scherf, K. S., Behrmann, M., Kimchi, R., & Luna, B. (2009). Emergence of global shape processing continues through adolescence. *Child Development, 80*(1), 162–177.

Schick, V. R., Rima, B. N., & Calabrese, S. K. (2011). Evulvalution: The portrayal of women's external genitalia and physique across time and the current Barbie doll ideals. *Journal of Sex Research. 48*(1), 74–81.

Schiffman, S. S. (2000). Taste quality and neural coding: Implications from psychophysics and neurophysiology. *Physiology and Behavior, 69*(1–2), 147–159.

Schmidt, N. B., et al. (2010). Anxiety sensitivity: Prospective prediction of anxiety among early adolescents. *Journal of Anxiety Disorders, 24*(5), 503–508.

Schmitt, D. P. (2008). An evolutionary perspective on mate choice and relationship initiation. In S. Sprecher, A. Wenzel, & J. H. Harvey (Eds.), *Handbook of relationship initiation* (pp. 55–74). New York: CRC Press.

Schmitt, D. P., Realo, A., Voracek, M., & Allik, J. (2008). Why can't a man be more like a woman? Sex differences in Big Five personality traits across 55 cultures. *Journal of Personality and Social Psychology, 94*(1), 168–182.

Schnall, S., Roper, J., & Fessler, D. M. T. (2010). Elevation leads to altruistic behavior. *Psychological Science, 21*(3), 315–320.

Schneider, R. H., et al. (1995). A randomized controlled trial of stress reduction for hypertension in older African Americans. *Hypertension, 26,* 820.

Schneider-Garces, N. J., et al. (2010). Span, CRUNCH, and beyond: Working memory capacity and the aging brain. *Journal of Cognitive Neuroscience, 22*(4), 655–669.

Schonfeld, L., et al. (2010). Screening and brief intervention for substance misuse among older adults: The Florida BRITE Project. *American Journal of Public Health. 100*(1), 108–114.

556

Schubert, S., & Lee, C. W. (2009). Adult PTSD and its treatment with EMDR: A review of controversies, evidence, and theoretical knowledge. *Journal of EMDR Practice and Research, 3*(3), 117–132.

Schuckit, M. A. (1996). Recent developments in the pharmacotherapy of alcohol dependence. *Journal of Consulting and Clinical Psychology, 64,* 669–676.

Schuetze, P., Lawton, D., & Eiden, R. D. (2006). Prenatal cocaine exposure and infant sleep at 7 months of age: The influence of the caregiving environment. *Infant Mental Health Journal, 27*(4), 383–404.

Schulte, M. T., Ramo, D., & Brown, S. A. (2009). Gender differences in factors influencing alcohol use and drinking progression among adolescents. *Clinical Psychology Review, 29*(6), 535–547.

Schuster, M. A., et al. (2001). A national survey of stress reactions after the September 11, 2001, terrorist attacks. *New England Journal of Medicine, 345*(20), 1507–1512.

Schwartz, B. L. (2008). Working memory load differentially affects tip-of-the-tongue states and feeling-of-knowing judgments. *Memory and Cognition, 36*(1), 9–19.

Schwartz, N. (2007) Evaluating surveys and questionnaires. In R. J. Sternberg, H. L. Roediger, & D. F. Halpern (Eds.), *Critical thinking in psychology* (pp. 54–74). New York: Cambridge University Press.

Schwartz, R. M., & Gottman, J. M. (1976). Toward a task analysis of assertive behavior. *Journal of Consulting and Clinical Psychology, 44,* 910–920.

Schwartz, S. J. (2001). The evolution of Eriksonian and neo-Eriksonian identity theory and research: A review and integration. *Identity, 1*(1), 7–58.

Schwartz, S. J., Unger, J. B., Zamboanga, B. L., & Szapocznik, J. (2010). Rethinking the concept of acculturation: Implications for theory and research. *American Psychologist, 65*(4), 237–251.

Schwartz, S. J., Zamboanga, B. L., Weisskirch, R. S., & Rodriguez, L. (2009). The relationships of personal and ethnic identity exploration to indices of adaptive and maladaptive psychosocial functioning. *International Journal of Behavioral Development, 33*(2), 131–144.

Scott, J. (1994, May 9). Multiple personality cases perplex legal system. *The New York Times,* pp. A1, B10, B11.

Scott-Sheldon, L. A. J., Kalichman, S. C., Carey, M. P., & Fielder, R. L. (2008). Stress management interventions for HIV+ adults: A meta-analysis of randomized controlled trials, 1989 to 2006. *Health Psychology, 27*(2), 129–139.

Sebe, N., et al. (2007). Authentic facial expression analysis. *Image and Vision Computing, 25*(12), 1856–1863.

Secker-Walker, R. H., & Vacek, P. M. (2003). Relationships between cigarette smoking during pregnancy, gestational age, maternal weight gain, and infant birthweight. *Addictive Behaviors, 28*(1), 55–66.

Segal, N. L. (2009). Mistaken identity: Results and repercussions/ Twin research reviews: Ovarian transplants; kidney donation; false beliefs and emotion understanding/in the news: Surfing twins; driving twins/Tribute: Daniel G. Freedman [Special section]. *Twin Research and Human Genetics, 12*(2), 201–205.

Segerdahl, P., Fields, W., & Savage-Rumbaugh, S. (2006). *Kanzi's primal language: The cultural initiation of primates into language.* New York: Palgrave Macmillan.

Sekizuka, H., et al. (2010). Relationship between sleep apnea syndrome and sleep blood pressure in patients without hypertension. *Journal of Cardiology, 55*(1), 92–98.

Self, D. R., et al. (2007). Thrill seeking: The Type T personality and extreme sports. *International Journal of Sport Management and Marketing, 2*(1–2), 175–190.

Seligman, M. (1975). *Helplessness: On depression, development, and death.* New York: Freeman.

Seligman, M. E. P. (1996, August). *Predicting and preventing depression.* Master lecture presented to the meeting of the American Psychological Association, Toronto.

Seligman, M. E. P., Steen, T. A., Park, N., & Peterson, C. (2005). Positive psychology progress: Empirical validation of interventions. *American Psychologist, 60*(5), 410–421.

Selye, H. (1976). *The stress of life* (Rev. ed.). New York: McGraw-Hill.

Seren, S., et al. (2008). Lycopene in cancer prevention and treatment. *American Journal of Therapeutics, 15*(1), 66–81.

Shadish, W. R. (2002). Revisiting field experiments: Field notes for the future. *Psychological Methods, 7*(1), 3–18.

Shadish, W. R., Matt, G. E., Navarro, A. M., & Phillips, G. (2000). The effects of psychological therapies under clinically representative conditions: A meta-analysis. *Psychological Bulletin, 126*(4), 512–529.

Shah, C., et al. (2009). Common stressors and coping with stress by medical students. *Journal of Clinical and Diagnostic Research, 3,* 1621–1626.

Shansky, R. M., Bender, G., & Arnsten, A. F. (2009). Estrogen prevents norepinephrine alpha-2a receptor reversal of stress-induced working memory impairment. *Stress, 12*(5), 457–463.

Shapiro, F. (1989). Efficacy of the eye movement desensitization procedure in the treatment of traumatic memories. *Journal of Traumatic Stress, 2,* 199–223.

Shedler, J. (2010). The efficacy of psychodynamic psychotherapy. *American Psychologist, 65*(2), 98–109.

Sheeber, L. B., Davis, B., Leve, C., Hops, H., & Tildesley, E. (2007). Adolescents' relationships with their mothers and fathers: Associations with depressive disorder and subdiagnostic symptomatology. *Journal of Abnormal Psychology, 116*(1), 144–154.

Sheldon, K. M. (2009). Providing the scientific backbone for positive psychology: A multi-level conception of human thriving. *Psychological Topics, 18*(2), 267–284.

Sherman, D. K., Bunyan, D. P., Creswell, J. D., & Jaremka, L. M. (2009). Psychological vulnerability and stress: The effects of self-affirmation on sympathetic nervous system responses to naturalistic stressors. *Health Psychology, 28*(5), 554–562.

Sherrington, J. M., Hawton, K. E., Fagg, J., Andrews, B., & Smith, D. (2001). Outcome of women admitted to hospital for depressive illness: Factors in the prognosis of severe depression. *Psychological Medicine, 31*(1), 115–125.

Sherwood, C. C., Rilling, J. K., Holloway, R. L., & Hof, P. R. (2008). Evolution of the brain: In humans—Specializations in a comparative perspective. In M. D. Binder, N. Hirokawa, U. Windhorst, & M. C. Hirsch (Eds.), *Encyclopedia of neuroscience* (pp. 1–5). New York: Springer-Verlag.

Shirayama, Y., et al. (2010). Specific metabolites in the medial prefrontal cortex are associated with the neurocognitive deficits in schizophrenia: A preliminary study. *NeuroImage, 49*(3), 2783–2790.

Shneidman, E. S. (2001). *Comprehending suicide.* Washington, DC: American Psychological Association.

Short, S., et al. (2010). Maternal influenza infection during pregnancy impacts postnatal brain development in the rhesus monkey. *Biological Psychiatry, 67*(10), 965–973.

Shrager, Y., Kirwan, C., & Squire, L. R. (2008). Activity in both hippocampus and perirhinal cortex predicts the memory strength of subsequently remembered information. *Neuron, 59*(4), 547–553.

Shuper, P. A., et al. (2010). Causal considerations on alcohol and HIV/AIDS—A systematic review. *Alcohol and Alcoholism, 45*(2), 159–166.

557

Shyrack, J., Steger, M. F., Krueger, R. F., & Kallie, C. S. (2010). The structure of virtue: An empirical investigation of the dimensionality of the virtues in action inventory of strengths. *Personality and Individual Differences, 48*(6), 714–719.

Siegel, J. M. (2009). Sleep viewed as a state of adaptive inactivity. *Nature Reviews Neuroscience, 10*, 747–753.

Siegel-Hinson, R. I., & McKeever, W. F. (2002). Hemispheric specialisation, spatial activity experience, and sex differences on tests of mental rotation ability. *Laterality: Asymmetries of Body, Brain and Cognition, 7*(1), 59–74.

Silberman, S. A. (2009). *The insomnia workbook: A comprehensive guide to getting the sleep you need*. Oakland, CA: New Harbinger Publications.

Silver, R. C., & Wortman, C. B. (2007). The stage theory of grief. *Journal of the American Medical Association, 297*, 2692.

Silver, S. M., Rogers, S., Knipe, J, & Colelli, G. (2005). EMDR therapy following the 9/11 terrorist attacks: A community-based intervention project in New York City. *International Journal of Stress Management, 12*(1), 29–42.

Simeon, D., et al. (2007). Hypothalamic-pituitary-adrenal axis function in dissociative disorders, post-traumatic stress disorder, and healthy volunteers. *Biological Psychiatry, 61*(8), 966–973.

Simon, T. R., et al. (2009). The ecological effects of universal and selective violence prevention programs for middle school students: A randomized trial. *Journal of Consulting and Clinical Psychology, 77*(3), 526–542.

Simons, A. D., Gordon, J. S., Monroe, S. M., & Thase, M. E. (1995). Toward an integration of psychologic, social, and biologic factors in depression. *Journal of Consulting and Clinical Psychology, 63*, 369–377.

Simonton, D. K. (2009). *Genius 101*. New York: Springer.

Singareddy, R. K., & Balon, R. (2002). Sleep in posttraumatic stress disorder. *Annals of Clinical Psychiatry, 14*(3), 183–190.

Singh, L., Nestor, S., Parikh, C., & Yull, A. (2009). Influences of infant-directed speech on early word recognition. *Infancy, 14*(6), 654–666.

Sio, U. N., & Ormerod, T. C. (2009). Does incubation enhance problem solving? *Psychological Bulletin, 135*(1), 94–120.

Sixsmith, R., & Furnham, A. (2010). A content analysis of British food advertisements aimed at children and adults. *Health Promotion International, 25*(1), 24–32.

Skinner, B. F. (1938). *The behavior of organisms: An experimental analysis*. New York: Appleton.

Skinner, B. F. (1948). *Walden Two*. New York: Macmillan.

Sleepers suffer WTC nightmares. (2001, November 22). Associated Press.

Slobin, D. I. (1983). *Crosslinguistic evidence for basic child grammar*. Paper presented to the biennial meeting of the Society for Research in Child Development, Detroit, MI.

Sloman, S. A., Harrison, M. C., & Malt, B. C. (2002). Recent exposure affects artifact naming. *Memory and Cognition, 30*(5), 687–695.

Small, E., et al. (2010). Tobacco smoke exposure induces nicotine dependence in rats. *Psychopharmacology, 208*(1), 143–158.

Smillie, L. D., et al. (2009). Variation in DRD2 dopamine gene predicts extraverted personality. *Neuroscience Letters, 468*(3), 234–237.

Smith, B. N., Kerr, N. A., Markus, M. J., & Stasson, M. F. (2001). Individual differences in social loafing: Need for cognition as a motivator in collective performance. *Group Dynamics, 5*(2), 150–158.

Smith, G. F., & Dorfman, D. (1975). The effect of stimulus uncertainty on the relationship between frequency of exposure and liking. *Journal of Personality and Social Psychology, 31*, 150–155.

Smith, K. L. (2009). Humor. In M. Snyder & R. Lindquist (Eds.), *Complementary and alternative therapies in nursing* (pp. 107–122). New York: Springer.

Smith, M. L., & Glass, G. V. (1977). Meta-analysis of psychotherapy outcome studies. *American Psychologist, 32*, 752–760.

Smith, N. A., & Trainor, L. J. (2008). Infant-directed speech is modulated by infant feedback. *Infancy, 13*(4), 410–420.

Smith, S. E. P., Li, J., Krassimira Garbett, K. M., & Patterson, P. H. (2007). Maternal immune activation alters fetal brain development through Interleukin-6. *The Journal of Neuroscience, 27*(40), 10695–10702.

Smith, S. W., Hilsenroth, M. J., & Bornstein, R. F. (2009). Convergent validity of the SWAP-200 dependency scales. *Journal of Nervous and Mental Disease, 197*(8), 613–618.

Snarey, J. R., & Bell, D. (2003). Distinguishing structural and functional models of human development. *Identity, 3*(3), 221–230.

Snarey, J., & Samuelson, P. (2008). Moral education in the cognitive developmental tradition: Lawrence Kohlberg's revolutionary ideas. In L. P. Nucci & D. Narváez (Eds.), *Handbook of moral and character education* (pp. 53–79). London: Routledge.

Snijders, T., et al. (2007). Modeling the coevolution of networks and behavior. In K. van Montfort, J. Oud, & A. Satorra (Eds.), *Longitudinal models in the behavioral and related sciences* (pp. 41–71). London: Routledge.

Snyder, C. R., Lopez, S. J., & Pedrotti, J. T. (2010). *Positive psychology* (2nd. ed.). Newbury Park, CA: Sage Publications.

Snyder, D. J., & Bartoshuk, L. M. (2009). Epidemiological studies of taste function: Discussion and perspectives. *Annals of the New York Academy of Sciences, 1170*, 574–580.

Soares, C. N., & Zitek, B. (2008). Reproductive hormone sensitivity and risk for depression across the female life cycle: A continuum of vulnerability? *Journal of Psychiatry and Neuroscience, 33*(4), 331–343.

Solomon, R. C. (2008). The philosophy of emotions. In M. Lewis, J. M. Haviland-Jones, & L. F. Barrett (Eds.), *Handbook of emotions* (pp. 3–16). New York: Guilford Press.

Somerfield, M. R., & McCrae, R. R. (2000). Stress and coping research: Methodological challenges, theoretical advances, and clinical applications. *American Psychologist, 55*(6), 620–625.

Sommers, M. S. (2008). Age-related changes in spoken word recognition. In D. B. Pisoni & R. E. Remez (Eds.), *The handbook of speech perception. Blackwell handbooks in linguistics* (pp. 469–493). Malden, MA: Blackwell Publishing.

Sorensen, S. B., & Rutter, C. M. (1991). Transgenerational patterns of suicide attempt. *Journal of Consulting and Clinical Psychology, 59*, 861–866.

Souren, N. Y., et al. (2007). Anthropometry, carbohydrate and lipid metabolism in the East Flanders Prospective Twin Survey: Heritabilities. *Diabetologia, 50*(10), 2107–2116.

Soussignan, R. (2002). Duchenne smile, emotional experience, and autonomic reactivity: A test of the facial feedback hypotheses. *Emotion, 2*(1), 52–74.

Southall, D., & Roberts, J. E. (2002). Attributional style and self-esteem in vulnerability to adolescent depressive symptoms following life stress: A 14-week prospective study. *Cognitive Therapy and Research, 26*(5), 563–579.

Spelts, K., & Gaynor, J. (2010). Pain management strategies. In S. Bryant (Ed.), *Anesthesia for veterinary technicians* (pp. 345–356). Hoboken, NJ: Wiley.

Spencer, M. D., et al. (2008). Low birthweight and preterm birth in young people with special educational needs: A magnetic resonance imaging analysis. *BMC Medicine, 6*(1). doi:10.1186/1741-7015-6-1

Spencer, M. S., Chen, J., Gee, G. C., Fabian, C. G., & Takeuchi, D. T. (2010). Discrimination and mental health–related service use in a national study of Asian Americans. *American Journal of Public Health, 100*(12), 2410–2417.

Spencer, N. (2006). Explaining the social gradient in smoking in pregnancy: Early life course accumulation and cross-sectional clustering of social risk exposures in the 1958 British national cohort. *Social Science & Medicine, 62*(5), 1250–1259.

Spencer, T. J., et al. (2009). Object priming and recognition memory: Dissociable effects in left frontal cortex at encoding. *Neuropsychologia, 47*(13), 2942–2947.

Sperling, G. (1960). The information available in brief visual presentations. *Psychological Monographs, 74,* 1–29.

Spieker, S. J., et al. (2003). Joint influence of child care and infant attachment security for cognitive and language outcomes of low-income toddlers. *Infant Behavior and Development, 26*(3), 326–344.

Spinhoven, P., et al. (2010). The specificity of childhood adversities and negative life events across the life span to anxiety and depressive disorders. *Journal of Affective Disorders, 126*(1), 103–112.

Spittle, A. J., et al. (2009). Predicting motor development in very preterm infants at 12 months' corrected age. *Pediatrics, 123*(2), 512–517.

Sporer, S. L., & Goodman-Delahunty, J. (2009). Disparities in sentencing decisions. In M. E. Oswald, S. Bieneck, & J. Hupfeld-Heinemann (Eds.), *Social psychology of punishment of crime* (pp. 379–401). Hoboken, NJ: Wiley.

Sprecher, S., & Felmlee, D. (2008). Insider perspectives on attraction. In S. Sprecher, A. Wenzel, & J. H. Harvey (Eds.), *Handbook of relationship initiation* (pp. 297–314). New York: CRC Press.

Sprecher, S., Sullivan, Q., & Hatfield, E. (1994). Mate selection preferences. *Journal of Personality and Social Psychology, 66*(6), 1074–1080.

Sprecher, S., Wenzel, A., & Harvey, J. H. (Eds.). (2008). *Handbook of relationship initiation.* New York: CRC Press.

Spritzer, M. D., Gill, M., Weinberg, A., & Galea, L. A. M. (2008). Castration differentially affects spatial working and references memory in male rats. *Archives of Sexual Behavior, 37*(1), 19–29.

Squire, L. R. (1993). Memory and the hippocampus. *Psychological Review, 99,* 195–231.

Squire, L. R. (1996, August). *Memory systems of the brain.* Master lecture presented to the meeting of the American Psychological Association, Toronto.

Squire, L. R. (2004). Memory systems of the brain: A brief history and current perspective. *Neurobiology of Learning and Memory, 82*(3), 171–177.

Squire, L. R. (2009). The legacy of patient H. M. for neuroscience. *Neuron, 61*(1), 6.

Squire, L. R., & Kandel, E. R. (2008). *Memory: From mind to molecules.* Greenwood Village, CO: Roberts.

Srnick, J. L. (2007). *Illicit prescription drug use among college undergraduates: A study of prevalence and an application of social learning theory* (Master's thesis, Ohio University). Retrieved from http://etd.ohiolink.edu/send-pdf.cgi/ Srnick%20Jennifer%20L.pdf?acc_num=ohiou1172203693

Sroufe, L. A. (1998). Cited in S. Blakeslee (1998, August 4), Re-evaluating significance of baby's bond with mother, *New York Times,* pp. F1, F2.

Stacy, A. W., Bentler, P. M., & Flay, B. R. (1994). Attitudes and health behavior in diverse populations: Drunk driving, alcohol use, binge eating, marijuana use, and cigarette use. *Health Psychology, 13*(1), 73–85.

Staff, J., Mortimer, J. T., & Uggen, C. (2004). Work and leisure in adolescence. In R. M. Lerner & L. Steinberg (Eds.), *Handbook of adolescent psychology* (2nd ed.) (pp. 429–450). Hoboken, NJ: Wiley.

Stanley, B., & Siever, L. J. (2010). The interpersonal dimension of borderline personality disorder: Toward a neuropeptide model. *American Journal of Psychiatry, 167,* 24–39.

Starratt, V. G., & Shackelford, T. K. (2010). The basic components of the human mind were solidified during the Pleistocene epoch. In F. J. Ayala & R. Arp (Eds.), *Contemporary debates in philosophy of biology* (pp. 243–252). Hoboken, NJ: Wiley.

Stasser, G. (1999). A primer of social decision scheme theory: Models of group influence, competitive model-testing, and prospective modeling. *Organizational Behavior and Human Decision Processes, 80*(1), 3–20.

Steele, C. M., & Aronson, J. (1995). Stereotype threat and the intellectual test performance of African Americans. *Journal of Personality and Social Psychology, 69,* 797–811.

Steele, C. M., & Josephs, R. A. (1990). Alcohol myopia. *American Psychologist, 45,* 921–933.

Steele, H. (2005). Editorial. *Attachment & Human Development, 7*(4), 345.

Stein, A. D., et al. (2009). Maternal exposure to the Dutch famine before conception and during pregnancy. *Epidemiology, 20*(6), 909–915.

Steinmayr, R., & Spinath, B. (2009). The importance of motivation as a predictor of school achievement. *Learning and Individual Differences, 19*(1), 80–90.

Sternberg, R. J. (1988). Triangulating love. In R. J. Sternberg & M. J. Barnes (Eds.), *The psychology of love* (pp. 119–138). New Haven, CT: Yale University Press.

Sternberg, R. J. (2000). In search of the zipperump-a-zoo. *Psychologist, 13*(5), 250–255.

Sternberg, R. J. (2006). Creating a vision of creativity: The first 25 years. *Psychology of Aesthetics, Creativity, and the Arts, S*(1), 2–12.

Sternberg, R. J. (2007a). Critical thinking in psychology: It really is critical. In R. J. Sternberg, H. L. Roediger, & D. F. Halpern (Eds.), *Critical thinking in psychology* (pp. 289–296). New York: Cambridge University Press.

Sternberg, R. J. (2007b). Intelligence and culture. In S. Kitayama & D. Cohen (Eds.), *Handbook of cultural psychology* (pp. 547–568). New York: Guilford Press.

Sternberg, R. J. (2009). *Cognitive psychology* (5th ed.). Belmont, CA: Cengage.

Sternberg, R. J., & The Rainbow Project Collaborators. (2006). The Rainbow Project: Enhancing the SAT through assessments of analytical, practical, and creative skills. *Intelligence, 34*(4), 321–350.

Sternberg, R. J., Grigorenko, E. L., & Kidd, K. K. (2005). Intelligence, race, and genetics. *American Psychologist, 60*(1), 46–59.

Sternberg, R. J., Jarvin, L., & Grigorenko, E. L. (2009). *Teaching for wisdom, intelligence, creativity, and success.* Thousand Oaks, CA: Corwin Press.

Stevens, B., et al. (2005). Consistent management of repeated procedural pain with sucrose in preterm neonates: Is it effective and safe for repeated use over time? *Clinical Journal of Pain, 21*(6), 543–548.

Stewart, A. J., & Ostrove, J. M. (1998). Women's personality in middle age: Gender, history, and midcourse corrections. *American Psychologist, 53*(11), 1185–1194.

Stewart, A. J., Ostrove, J. M., & Helson, R. (2001). Middle aging in women: Patterns of personality change from the 30s to the 50s. *Journal of Adult Development, 8*(1), 23–37.

Stewart, J. Y., & Armet, E. (2000, April 3). Aging in America: Retirees reinvent the concept. *Los Angeles Times online.*

Stewart, R. E., & Chambless, D. L. (2009). Cognitive-behavioral therapy for adult anxiety disorders in clinical practice: A meta-analysis of effectiveness studies. *Journal of Consulting and Clinical Psychology, 77*(4), 595–606.

559

Stewart, S. H., & Watt, M. C. (2008). Introduction to the special issue on interoceptive exposure in the treatment of anxiety and related disorders: Novel applications and mechanisms of action. *Journal of Cognitive Psychotherapy, 22*(4), 291–302.

Stocco, A., & Anderson, J. A. (2008). Endogenous control and task representation: An fMRI study in algebraic problem-solving. *Journal of Cognitive Neuroscience, 20*(7), 1300–1314.

Stone, J., & Fernandez, N. C. (2008). How behavior shapes attitudes: Cognitive dissonance processes. In W. D. Crano & R. Prislin (Eds.), *Attitudes and attitude change* (pp. 313–336). Boca Raton, FL: CRC Press.

Story, P. A., Hart, J. W., Stasson, M. F., & Mahoney, J. M. (2009). Using a two-factor theory of achievement motivation to examine performance-based outcomes on self-regulatory processes. *Personality and Individual Differences, 46*(4), 391–395.

Strack, F., Martin, L. L., & Stepper, S. (1988). Inhibiting and facilitating conditions of the human smile: A nonobtrusive test of the facial feedback hypothesis. *Journal of Personality and Social Psychology, 54*(55), 768–777.

Strathearn, L., Mamun, A. A., Najman, J. M., & O'Callaghan, M. J. (2009). Does breastfeeding protect against substantiated child abuse and neglect? A 15-year cohort study. *Pediatrics, 123*(2), 483–493.

Straus, M. (1995). Cited in Collins, C. (1995, May 11). Spanking is becoming the new don't. *The New York Times*, p. C8.

Strickland, T. (2007). *Assessing enhancing neurobehavioral outcomes among incarcerated youth*. Paper presented to the 115th annual convention of the American Psychological Association, San Francisco.

Striegel-Moore, R. H., & Franko, D. L. (2008). Should binge eating disorder be included in the *DSM-V*? A critical review of the state of the evidence. *Annual Review of Clinical Psychology, 4*, 305–324.

Striegel-Moore, R. H., et al. (2003). Eating disorders in White and Black women. *American Journal of Psychiatry, 160*, 1326–1331.

Stuart, K., & Conduit, R. (2009). Auditory inhibition of rapid eye movements and dream recall from REM sleep. *Sleep, 32*(3), 399–408.

Stunkard, A. J., Harris, J. R., Pedersen, N. L., & McLearn, G. E. (1990). A separated twin study of the body mass index. *New England Journal of Medicine, 322*, 1483–1487.

Su, R., Rounds, J., & Armstrong, P. I. (2009). Men and things, women and people: A meta-analysis of sex differences in interests. *Psychological Bulletin, 135*(6), 859–884.

Suarez, E., & Gadalla, T. M. (2010). Stop blaming the victim: A meta-analysis on rape myths. *Journal of Interpersonal Violence, 25*(11), 2010–2035.

Substance Abuse and Mental Health Services Administration. (2007). *Results from the 2006 National Survey on Drug Use and Health: National findings* (Office of Applied Studies, NSDUH Series H-32, DHHS Publication No. SMA 07-4293). Rockville, MD: Author.

Sue, S., & Zane, N. (2009). The role of culture and cultural techniques in psychotherapy: A critique and reformulation. *Asian American Journal of Psychology, S*(1), 3–14.

Sue, S., Zane, N., Hall, G. C. N., & Berger, L. K. (2009). The case for cultural competency in psychotherapeutic interventions. *Annual Review of Psychology, 60*, 525–548.

Suinn, R. M. (2001). The terrible twos—anger and anxiety: Hazardous to your health. *American Psychologist, 56*(1), 27–36.

Sumter, S. R., Bokhorst, C. L., Steinberg, L., & Westenberg, P. M. (2009). The developmental pattern of resistance to peer influence in adolescence: Will the teenager ever be able to resist? *Journal of Adolescence, 32*(4), 1009–1021.

Suschinsky, K. D., Lalumière, M. L., & Chivers, M. L. (2009). Sex differences in patterns of genital sexual arousal: Measurement artifacts or true phenomena? *Archives of Sexual Behavior, 38*(4), 559–573.

Suslow, T., et al. (2010). Automatic brain response to facial emotion as a function of implicitly and explicitly measured extraversion. *Neuroscience, 167*(1), 111–123.

Susser, E., St. Clair, D., & He, L. (2009). Latent effects of prenatal malnutrition on adult health: The example of schizophrenia. *Annals of the New York Academy of Sciences, 1136*, 185–192.

Sutin, A. R., et al. (2010). Cholesterol triglycerides, and the five-factor model of personality. *Biological Psychology, 84*(2), 186–191.

Swami, V., Furnham, A., Haubner, T., Stieger, S., & Voracek, M. (2009). The truth is out there: The structure of beliefs about extraterrestrial life among Austrian and British respondents. *Journal of Social Psychology, 149*(1), 29–43.

Swan, G. E., et al. (2007). Joint effect of domanimergic genes on likelihood of smoking following treatment with bupropion SR. *Health Psychology, 26*(3), 361–368.

Swartout, K. M., & White, J. W. (2010). The relationship between drug use and sexual aggression in men across time. *Journal of Interpersonal Violence, 25*(9), 1716–1735.

Sweeny, T. D., Grabowecky, M., Suzuki, S., & Paller, K. A. (2009). Long-lasting effects of subliminal affective priming from facial expressions. *Consciousness and Cognition: An International Journal, 18*(4), 929–938.

Szala, M. (2002). Two-level pattern recognition in a class of knowledge-based systems. *Knowledge-Based Systems, 15*(1–2), 95–101.

Szentirmai, E., et al. (2010). Restricted feeding-induced sleep, activity, and body temperature changes in normal and preproghrelin-deficient mice. *American Journal of Physiology—Regulatory, Integrative, and Comparative Physiology, 298*, R467–R477.

T

Taber, C. S., Cann, D., & Kucsova, S. (2009). The motivated processing of political arguments. *Political Behavior, 31*(2), 137–155.

Taffe, M. A., et al. (2002). Cognitive performance of MDMA-treated rhesus monkeys: Sensitivity to serotonergic challenge. *Neuropsychopharmacology, 27*(6), 993–1005.

Tait, M., et al. (2010). Bilateral versus unilateral cochlear implantation in young children. *International Journal of Pediatric Otorhinolaryngology, 74*(2), 206–211.

Takahaski, T., et al. (2009). Progressive gray matter reduction of the superior temporal gyrus during transition to psychosis. *Archives of General Psychiatry, 66*(4), 366–376.

Talboom, J. S., Williams, B. J., Baxley, E. R., West, S. G., & Bimonte-Nelson, H. A. (2008). Higher levels of estradiol replacement correlate with better spatial memory in surgically menopausal young and middle-aged rats. *Neurobiology of Learning and Memory, 90*(1), 155–163.

Talwar, S. K. et al. (2002). Rat navigation guided by remote control. *Nature, 417*, 37–38.

Tamis-LeMonda, C. S., Cristofaro, T. N., Rodriguez, E. T., & Bornstein, M. H. (2006). Early language development: Social influences in the first years of life. In L. Balter & C. S. Tamis-LeMonda (Eds.), *Child psychology: A handbook of contemporary issues* (2nd ed., pp. 79–108). New York: Psychology Press.

Tanji, J., & Hoshi, E. (2008). Role of the lateral prefrontal cortex in executive behavioral control. *Physiological Reviews, 88*, 37–57.

Tanner, J. M. (1989). *Fetus into man: Physical growth from conception to maturity*. Cambridge, MA: Harvard University Press.

Task Force on SIDS (Sudden Infant Death Syndrome). (2005). The changing concept of Sudden Infant Death Syndrome: Diagnostic coding shifts, controversies regarding the sleeping environment, and new variables to consider in reducing risk. *Pediatrics, 116*(5), 1245–1255.

Taylor, A., Goehler, L., Galper, D., Innes, K., & Bourguignon, C. (2010). Top-down and bottom-up mechanisms in mind–body medicine. *EXPLORE: Journal of Science and Healing, 6*(1), 29–41.

Taylor, M. J. (2000). The influence of self-efficacy on alcohol use among American Indians. *Cultural Diversity and Ethnic Minority Psychology, 6*(2), 152–167.

Taylor, S. E. (2000). Cited in Goode, E. (2000). Response to stress found that's particularly female. *The New York Times,* p. A20.

Taylor, S. E. (2006). Tend and befriend: Biobehavioral bases of affiliation under stress. *Current Directions in Psychological Science, 15*(6), 273–277.

Taylor, S. E., et al. (2000b). Biobehavioral responses to stress in females: Tend-and-befriend, not fight-or-flight. *Psychological Review, 107*(3), 411–429.

Taylor, S. E., Kemeny, M. E., Reed, G. M., Bower, J. E., & Gruenewald, T. L. (2000a). Psychological resources, positive illusions, and health. *American Psychologist, 55*(1), 99–109.

Taylor, S. L., O'Neal, E. C., Langley, T., & Butcher, A. H. (2006). Anger arousal, deindividuation, and aggression. *Aggressive Behavior, 17*(4), 193–206.

Taylor, S., et al. (2003). Comparative efficacy, speed, and adverse effects of three PTSD treatments: Exposure therapy, EMDR, and relaxation training. *Journal of Consulting and Clinical Psychology, 71,* 330–338.

Teachout, T. (2000, April 2). For more artists, a fine old age. *The New York Times online.*

Tenenbaum, H. R., et al. (2010). "It's a boy because he's painting a picture." Age differences in children's conventional and unconventional gender schemas. *British Journal of Psychology, 101*(1), 137–154.

Terracciano, A., et al. (2009). Facets of personality linked to underweight and overweight. *Psychosomatic Medicine, 71*(6), 682–689.

Terrace, H. S., & Metcalfe, J. A. (2005). *The missing link in cognition: Origins of self-reflective consciousness.* New York: Oxford University Press.

Terry, D. (2000, July 16). Getting under my skin. *The New York Times online.*

Terry, D. F., Nolan, V. G., Andersen, S. L., Perls, T. T., & Cawthon, R. (2008). Association of longer telomeres with better health in centenarians. *Journals of Gerontology Series A: Biological Sciences and Medical Sciences, 63,* 809–812.

Teti, A., & Zallone, A. (2009). Do osteocytes contribute to bone mineral homeostasis? Osteocytic osteolysis revisited. *Bone, 44*(1), 11–16.

Tetlock, P. E., & McGraw, A. P. (2005). Theoretically framing relational framing. *Journal of Consumer Psychology, 15*(1), 35–37.

Thomas, A. K., & Loftus, E. F. (2002). Creating bizarre false memories through imagination. *Memory and Cognition, 30*(3), 423–431.

Thomas, J. (2010). The past, present, and future of medical marijuana in the United States. *Psychiatric Times, 27*(1), 1–3.

Thomas, K. R. (2008). *An exploratory study of factors that relate to academic success among high-achieving African American males.* College of William and Mary, DAI-A 69/12, 3340955.

Thomas, S. L., Skitka, L. J., Christen, S., & Jurgena, M. (2002). Social facilitation and impression formation. *Basic and Applied Social Psychology, 24*(1), 67–70.

Thompson, L. E., Barnett, J. R., & Pearce, J. R. (2009). Scared straight? Fear-appeal anti-smoking campaigns, risk, self-efficacy and addiction. *Health, Risk, and Society, 11,* 181–196.

Thompson, M. E. (2009). Human rape: Revising evolutionary perspectives. In M. N. Muller & R. W. Wrangham (Eds.), *Sexual coercion in primates and humans* (pp. 346–376). Cambridge, MA: Harvard University Press.

Thompson, R. A. (2008). Measure twice, cut once: Attachment theory and the NICHD Study of Early Child Care and Youth Development. *Attachment and Human Development, 10*(3), 287–297.

Thompson, S. C. (2009). The role of personal control in adaptive functioning. In I. C. R. Snyder & S. J. Lopez (Eds.), *Oxford handbook of positive psychology* (pp. 271–278). New York: Oxford University Press.

Thurstone, L. L. (1938). Primary mental abilities. *Psychometric Monographs, 1.*

Tigner, R. B., & Tigner, S. S. (2000). Triarchic theories of intelligence: Aristotle and Sternberg. *History of Psychology, 3*(2), 168–176.

Timmerman, L. M. (2006). Family care versus day care: Effects on children. In B. M. Gayle et al. (Eds.), *Classroom communication and instructional processes: Advances through meta-analysis* (pp. 245–260). Mahwah, NJ: Erlbaum.

Tohidian, I. (2009). Examining linguistic relativity hypothesis as one of the main views on the relationship between language and thought. *Journal of Psycholinguistic Research, 38*(1), 65–74.

Tolman, E. C., & Honzik, C. H. (1930). Introduction and removal of reward, and maze performance in rats. *University of California Publications in Psychology, 4,* 257–275.

Toma, C. L., Hancock, J. T., & Ellison, N. B. (2008). Separating fact from fiction: An examination of deceptive self-presentation in online dating profiles. *Personality and Social Psychology Bulletin, 34*(8), 1023–1036.

Tomiyama, T., et al. (2008). A new amyloid beta variant favoring oligomerization in Alzheimer's-type dementia. *Annals of Neurology, 63*(3), 377–387.

Tong, H. (2001). Loneliness, depression, anxiety, and the locus of control. *Chinese Journal of Clinical Psychology, 9*(3), 196–197.

Tønnesen, P. (2009). Smoking cessation: How compelling is the evidence? A review. *Health Policy, 91,* S15–S25.

Tormala, Z. L., & Petty, R. E. (2007). Contextual contrast and perceived knowledge: Exploring the implications for persuasion. *Journal of Experimental Social Psychology, 43*(1), 17–30.

Tost, H., Alam, T., & Meyer-Lindenberg, A. (2009). Dopamine and psychosis: Theory, pathomechanisms and intermediate phenotypes. *Neuroscience and Biobehavioral Reviews, 34*(5), 689–700.

Touhara, K., & Vosshall, L. B. (2009). Sensing odorants and pheromones with chemosensory receptors. *Annual Review of Physiology, 71,* 307–332.

Townsend, E., et al. (2001). The efficacy of problem-solving treatments after deliberate self-harm: Meta-analysis of randomized controlled trials with respect to depression, hopelessness and improvement in problems. *Psychological Medicine, 31*(6), 979–988.

Trautman, E., & Kröner-Herwig, B. (2009). A randomized controlled trial of Internet-based self-help training for recurrent headache in childhood and adolescence. *Behaviour Research and Therapy, 49*(1), 28–37.

Travis, S. G., et al. (2010). Hippocampal damage produces retrograde but not anterograde amnesia for a cued location in a spontaneous exploratory task in rats. *Hippocampus, 20*(9), 1095–1104.

Triandis, H. C. (2001). Individualism–collectivism and personality. *Journal of Personality, 69*(6), 907–924.

Triandis, H. C. (2006). Cultural aspects of globalization. *Journal of International Management, 12*(2), 208–217.

Triandis, H. C., & Suh, E. M. (2002). Cultural influences on personality. *Annual Review of Psychology, 53*(1), 133–160.

Tripodi, S. J., Bender, K., Litschge, C., & Vaughn, M. G. (2010). Interventions for reducing adolescent alcohol abuse: A meta-analytic review. *Archives of Pediatric and Adolescent Medicine, 164*(1), 85–91.

Trudel, G. A., Goldfarb, M. R., Preville, M., & Boyer, R. (2007). Relationship between psychological distress and marital functioning in the elderly. American Psychological Association, Conference abstract.

Trull, T. J., Stepp, S. D., & Durrett, C. A. (2003). Research on borderline personality disorder: An update. *Current Opinion in Psychiatry, 16*(1), 77–82.

Tsang, Y. C. (1938). Hunger motivation in gastrectomized rats. *Journal of Comparative Psychology, 26,* 1–17.

Tsui, J. M., & Maziocco, M. M. M. (2007). Effects of math anxiety and perfectionism on timed versus untimed math testing in mathematically gifted sixth graders. *Roeper Review, 29*(2), 132–139.

Tulving, E. (1985). How many memory systems are there? *American Psychologist, 40,* 385–398.

Tulving, E., & Markowitsch, H. J. (1998). Episodic and declarative memory: Role of the hippocampus. *Hippocampus, 8*(3), 198–204.

Turk, D. C., & Okifuji, A. (2002). Psychological factors in chronic pain: Evolution and revolution. *Journal of Consulting and Clinical Psychology, 70*(3), 678–690.

Turnbull, C. M. (1961). Some observations regarding the experiences and behavior of the BaMbuti Pygmies. *American Journal of Psychology, 74,* 304–308.

Turner, E. A., Chandler, M., & Heffer, R. W. (2009). Influence of parenting styles, achievement motivation, and self-efficacy on academic performance in college students. *Journal of College Student Development, 50*(3), 337–346.

Turner, J., & Turk, D. (2008). The significance of clinical significance. *Pain, 137*(3), 467–468.

Tversky, A., & Kahneman, D. (1982). Judgment under uncertainty. In D. Kahneman, P. Slovic, & A. Tversky (Eds.), *Judgment under uncertainty: Heuristics and biases* (pp. 3–22). New York: Cambridge University Press.

Tversky, A., & Kahneman, D. (2003). Emotional versus intuitive reasoning: The conjunction fallacy in probability judgment. In E. Shafir (Ed.), *Amos Tversky: Preference, belief, and similarity: Selected writings* (pp. 221–256). Cambridge, MA: MIT Press.

Twenge, J. M. (2009). Change over time in obedience: The jury's still out, but it might be decreasing. *American Psychologist, 64*(1), 28–31.

Tyagi, H., Brummond, L. M., & Fineberg, N. A. (2010). Treatment for obsessive compulsive disorder. *Current Psychiatry Reviews, 6*(1), 46–55.

U

U.S. Bureau of the Census. (2006). *Statistical abstract of the United States* (126th ed.). Washington, DC: U.S. Government Printing Office.

U.S. Bureau of the Census. (2008). *Statistical abstract of the United States* (128th ed.). Washington, DC: U.S. Government Printing Office.

U.S. Census Bureau. (2011). Families and living arrangements. (Accessed April 19, 2011). http://www.census.gov/population/www/socdemo/hh-fam.html

U.S. Council on Foreign Relations. (2002). *Terrorism.* Retrieved from http://cfrterrorism.org/groups/hamas_print.html

U.S. Department of Housing and Urban Development. (2002). *Housing discriminatory study (HDS2000): Discrimination in metropolitan housing markets. National results from Phase I of HDS2000. 1989–2000 report.* Washington, DC: U.S. Government Printing Office.

Uhlhaas, P. J., et al. (2010). Neural synchrony and the development of cortical networks. *Trends in Cognitive Sciences, 14*(2), 72–80.

Umek, L. M., Podlesek, A., & Fekonja, U. (2005). Assessing the home literacy environment: Relationships to child language comprehension and expression. *European Journal of Psychological Assessment, 21*(4), 271–281.

United Nations Special Session on AIDS. (2001, June 25–27). *Preventing HIV/AIDS among young people.* New York: Author.

Uzakov, S., Frey, J. U., & Korz, V. (2005). Reinforcement of rat hippocampus LTP by holeboard training. *Learning and Memory, 12,* 165–171.

V

Valenzuela, A., et al. (2010). Supplementing female rats with DHA-lysophosphatidylcholine increases docosahexaenoic acid and acetylcholine contents in the brain and improves the memory and learning capabilities of the pups. *Grasas y Aceites, 61*(1), 16–23.

Valkenburg, P. M., Peter, J., & Schouten, A. P. (2006). Friend networking sites and their relationship to adolescents' well-being and social self-esteem. *CyberPsychology & Behavior, 9*(5), 584–590.

van de Beek, C., van Goozen, S. H. M., Buitelaar, J. K., & Cohen-Kettenis, P. T. (2009). Prenatal sex hormones (maternal and amniotic fluid) and gender-related play behavior in 13-month-old infants. *Archives of Sexual Behavior, 38*(1), 6–15.

van de Wetering, S., Bernstein, D. M., & Loftus, E. F. (2002). Public education against false memories: A modest proposal. *International Journal of Cognitive Technology, 7*(2), 4–7.

Van der Kolk, B. A., et al. (2007). A randomized clinical trial of eye movement desensitization and reprocessing (EMDR), fluoxetine, and pill placebo in the treatment of posttraumatic stress disorder. *Journal of Clinical Psychiatry, 68,* 1–10.

Van Guilder, G. P., et al. (2007). Endothelin-1 vasoconstrictor tone increases with age in healthy men but can be reduced by regular aerobic exercise. *Hypertension, 50,* 403.

van Straaten, I., Engels, R. C. M. E., Finkenauer, C., & Holland, R. W. (2009). Meeting your match: How attractiveness similarity affects approach behavior in mixed-sex dyads. *Personality and Social Psychology Bulletin, 35*(6), 685–697.

Van Swol, L. M. (2008). Performance and process in collective and individual memory: The role of social decision schemes and memory bias in collective memory. *Memory, 16*(3), 274–287.

Vanhaudenhuyse, A., et al. (2009). Pain and non-pain processing during hypnosis: A thulium-YAG event-related fMRI study. *NeuroImage, 47,* 1047–1054.

Veenstra-Vanderweele, J., & Cook, E. H. (2003). Genetics of childhood disorders: XLVI. Autism, part 5: Genetics of autism. *Journal of the American Academy of Child and Adolescent Psychiatry, 42*(1), 116–118.

Vellas, B., Gillette-Guyonnet, S., & Andrieu, S. (2008). Memory health clinics—A first step to prevention. *Alzheimer's & Dementia, 4*(1, Suppl 1), S144–S149.

Venneman, M. M., et al. (2009a). Does breastfeeding reduce the risk of sudden infant death syndrome? *Pediatrics, 123*(3), e406–e410.

Venneman, M. M., et al. (2009b). Sleep environment risk factors for sudden infant death syndrome. *Pediatrics, 123*(4), 1162–1170.

Vercelli, D., & Piattelli-Palmarini, M. (2009). Language in an epigenetic framework. In M. Piattelli-Palmarini, J. Uriagereka, & P. Salaburu (Eds.), *Of minds and language: A dialogue with*

Noam Chomsky in the Basque Country (pp. 97–107). New York: Oxford University Press.

Verhagen, A. P., et al. (2009). Behavioral treatments of chronic tension-type headache in adults: Are they beneficial. *CNS Neuroscience and Therapeutics, 15*(2), 183–205.

Verkuyten, M. (2009). Self-esteem and multiculturalism: An examination among ethnic minority and majority groups in the Netherlands. *Journal of Research in Personality, 43*(3), 419–427.

Vermeer, H. J., & van IJzendoorn, M. H. (2006). Children's elevated cortisol levels at daycare: A review and meta-analysis. *Early Childhood Research Quarterly, 21*(3), 390–401.

Vernon, D., et al. (2003). The effect of training distinct neurofeedback protocols on aspects of cognitive performance. *International Journal of Psychophysiology, 47*(1), 75–85.

Verona, E., & Sullivan, E. A. (2008). Emotional catharsis and aggression revisited: Heart rate reduction following aggressive responding. *Emotion, 8*(3), 331–340.

Veselka, L., Schermer, J. A., Petrides, K. V., & Vernon, P. A. (2009). Evidence for a heritable general factor of personality in two studies. *Twin Research and Human Genetics, 12*(3), 254–260.

Viets, V. L., et al. (2009). Reducing health disparities through a culturally centered mentorship program for minority faculty: The Southwest Addictions Research Group (SARG) experience. *Academic Medicine, 84*(8), 1118–1126.

Visintainer, M. A., Volpicelli, J. R., & Seligman, M. E. P. (1982). Tumor rejection in rats after inescapable or escapable shock. *Science, 216*(23), 437–439.

Visscher, W. A., Feder, M., Burns, A. M., Brady, T. M., & Bray, R. M. (2003). The impact of smoking and other substance use by urban women on the birthweight of their infants. *Substance Use and Misuse, 38*(8), 1063–1093.

Viulli, W. F. (2008). On Joseph Banks Rhine. *Monitor on Psychology, 39*(6), 4.

Vodosek, M. (2009). The relationship between relational models and individualism and collectivism: Evidence from culturally diverse work groups. *International Journal of Psychology, 44*(2), 120–128.

Volz, J. (2000). Successful aging: The second 50. *Monitor on Psychology, 30*(1), 24–28.

Von Békésy, G. (1957, August). The ear. *Scientific American*, pp. 66–78.

Voorspoels, W., Vanpaemel, W., & Storms, G. (2008). Exemplars and prototypes in natural language concepts: A typicality-based evaluation. *Psychonomic Bulletin and Review, 15*(3), 630–637.

Voss, J. L. (2009). Long-term associative memory capacity in man. *Psychonomic Bulletin and Review, 16*, 1076–1081.

Voytko, M. L., Murray, R., & Higgs, C. J. (2009). Executive function and attention are preserved in older surgically menopausal monkeys receiving estrogen or estrogen plus progesterone. *Journal of Neuroscience, 29*(33), 10362–10370.

Vukman, K. B. (2005). Developmental differences in metacognition and their connections with cognitive development in adulthood. *Journal of Adult Development, 12*(4), 211–221.

Vygotsky, L. (1978). *Mind in society: The development of higher psychological processes*. Cambridge, MA: Harvard University Press.

W

Wacker, J., Chavanon, M-L., & Stemmler, G. (2009). Resting EEG signatures of agentic extraversion: New results and meta-analytic integration. *Journal of Research in Personality, 44*(2), 167–179.

Wade, N. (1998, January 6). Was Freud wrong? Are dreams the brain's start-up test? *The New York Times online*.

Wade, T. D., Bulik, C. M., Neale, M., & Kendler, K. S. (2000). Anorexia nervosa and major depression: Shared genetic and environmental risk factors. *American Journal of Psychiatry, 157*(3), 469–471.

Wagner, J. J. (2005). A meta-analysis/literature review comparing the effectiveness of SSRI antidepressants, cognitive behavioral therapy, and placebo for the treatment of depression. *Dissertation Abstracts International: Section B: Sciences and Engineering, 66*(4-B), 2319.

Wagstaff, G. S., et al. (2009). Some cognitive and neuropsychological aspects of social inhibition and facilitation. *European Journal of Cognitive Psychology, 20*(4), 828–846.

Wais, P. E., Wixted, J. T., Hopkins, R., & Squire, L. R. (2006). The hippocampus supports both the recollection and the familiarity components of recognition memory. *Neuron, 49*(3), 459–466.

Waite, L. J., Luo, Y., & Lewin, A. C. (2009). Marital happiness and marital stability: Consequences for psychological well-being. *Social Science Research, 38*(1), 201–212.

Waitt, C., Gerald, M. S., Little, A. C., & Krasielburd, E. (2006). Selective attention toward female secondary sexual characteristics. *American Journal of Primatology, 68*, 738–744.

Walk, R. D., & Gibson, E. J. (1961). A comparative and analytical study of visual depth perception. *Psychological Monographs, 75*(15).

Walker, J. S., & Bright, J. A. (2009). Cognitive therapy for violence: Reaching the parts that anger management doesn't reach. *Journal of Forensic Psychiatry and Psychology, 20*(2), 174–201.

Wallace, D. M., & Hinsz, V. B. (2009). Group members as actors and observers in attributions of responsibility for group performance. *Small Group Research, 40*(1), 52–71.

Wallen, K., & Hassett, J. M. (2009). Sexual differentiation of behaviour in monkeys: Role of prenatal hormones. *Journal of Neuroendocrinology, 21*(4), 421–426.

Wanchoo, S. J., Lee, M. J., Swann, A. C., & Dafny, N. (2010). Bilateral six-hydroxydopamine administration to PFC prevents the expression of behavioral sensitization to methylphenidate. *Brain Research, 1312*(2), 89–100.

Wang, L., et al. (2008). Prefrontal mechanisms for executive control over emotional distraction are altered in major depression. *Psychiatry Research: Neuroimaging, 163*(2), 143–155.

Wang, Q. (2008). Emotion knowledge and autobiographical memory across the preschool years: A cross-cultural longitudinal investigation. *Cognition, 108*(1), 117–135.

Wang, X., Dow-Edwards, D., Anderson, V., Minkoff, H., & Hurd, Y. L. (2004). In utero marijuana exposure associated with abnormal amygdala dopamine d-sub-2 gene expression in the human fetus. *Biological Psychiatry, 56*(12), 909–915.

Wang, X., et al. (2000). Longitudinal study of earthquake-related PTSD in a randomly selected community sample in North China. *American Journal of Psychiatry, 157*, 1260–1266.

Wang, Y., & Chiew, V. (2010). On the cognitive process of human problem solving. *Cognitive Systems Research, 11*(1), 81–92.

Wang, Y., et al. (2009). A doctrine of cognitive informics. *Fundamenta Informaticae, 90*(3), 203–228.

Wann, D. L. (2006). The causes and consequences of sport team identification. In A. A. Raney & J. Bryant (Eds.), *Handbook of sports and media* (pp. 331–352). London: Routledge.

Ward, C. P., et al. (2009). Spatial learning and memory deficits following exposure to 24 h of sleep fragmentation or intermittent hypoxia in a rat model of obstructive sleep apnea. *Brain Research, 1294*, 128–137.

Ward, E. (2007). Childhood cancers. In V. Shaw & M. Lawson (Eds.), *Clinical paediatric dietetics* (pp. 461–472). Hoboken, NJ: Wiley-Blackwell.

Wareham, J., Boots, D. P., & Chavez, J. M. (2009). A test of social learning and intergenerational transmission among batterers. *Journal of Criminal Justice, 37*(2), 163–173.

Waring, T. M. (2010). New evolutionary foundations: Theoretical requirements for a science of sustainability. *Ecological Economics, 69*(4), 718–730.

Warman, D. M., & Cohen, R. (2000). Stability of aggressive behaviors and children's peer relationships. *Aggressive Behavior, 26*(4), 277–290.

Wartik, N. (2000, June 25). Depression comes out of hiding. *The New York Times*, pp. MH1, MH4.

Washburn, D. A., Gulledge, J. P., James, F., & Rumbaugh, D. M. (2007). A species difference in visuospatial working memory: Does language link "what" with "where"? *International Journal of Comparative Psychology, 20*, 55–64.

Waters, M. (2000). Psychologists spotlight growing concern of higher suicide rates among adolescents. *Monitor on Psychology, 31*(6), 41.

Watson, H. J., et al. (2011). Mediators between perfectionism and eating disorder psychopathology: Shape and weight overvaluation and conditional goal-setting. *International Journal of Eating Disorders, 44*(2), 142–149.

Watson, J. B. (1913). Psychology as the behaviorist views it. *Psychological Review, 20*, 158–177.

Watson, J. B. (1924). *Behaviorism*. New York: Norton.

Webb, R. T., et al. (2010). Influence of environmental factors in higher risk of sudden infant death syndrome linked with parental mental illness. *Archives of General Psychiatry, 67*(1), 69–77.

Webster, J. D. (2003). An exploratory analysis of a self-assessed wisdom scale. *Journal of Adult Development, 10*(1), 13–22.

Weems, C. F., et al. (2010). Post traumatic stress, context, and the lingering effects of the Hurricane Katrina disaster among ethnic minority youth. *Journal of Abnormal Child Psychology, 38*(1), 49–56.

Wegener, D. T., Petty, R. E., Detweiler-Bedell, B. T., & Jarvis, W. B. G. (2001). Implications of attitude change theories for numerical anchoring: Anchor plausibility and the limits of anchor effectiveness. *Journal of Experimental Social Psychology, 37*(1), 62–69.

Weiner, B. (2006). *Social motivation, justice, and the moral emotions: An attributional approach*. Mahwah, NJ: Erlbaum.

Weiner, B. (2010). The development of an attribution-based theory of motivation: A history of ideas. *Educational Psychologist, 45*(1), 28–36.

Weiner, I. B. (2006). The Rorschach inkblot method. In R. P. Archer (Ed.), *Forensic uses of clinical instruments* (pp. 181–208). London: Routledge.

Weingardt, K., Cucciare, M., Bellotti, C., & Lai, W. (2009). A randomized trial comparing two models of web-based training in cognitive–behavioral therapy for substance abuse counselors. *Journal of Substance Abuse Treatment, 37*(3), 219–227.

Weinmann, M., Bader, J., Endrass, J., & Hell, D. (2001). Sind Kompetenz- und Kontrollueberzeugungen depressionsabhaengig? Eine Verlaufsuntersuchung. *Zeitschrift fuer Klinische Psychologie und Psychotherapie, 30*(3), 153–158.

Weinstein, A. A., et al. (2010). Neurohormonal and inflammatory hyper-responsiveness to acute mental stress in depression. *Biological Psychology, 84*(2), 228–234.

Weiss, R. D., Mirin, S. M., & Bartel, R. (1994). *Cocaine* (2nd ed.). Arlington, VA: American Psychiatric Publishing.

Weisskirch, R. S. (2007). Feelings about language brokering and family relations among Mexican American early adolescents. *Journal of Early Adolescence, 27*(4), 545–561.

Welch, K. A., et al. (2010). The impact of substance use on brain structure in people at high risk of developing schizophrenia. *Schizophrenia Bulletin*. doi:10.1093/schbul/sbq013

Welling, L. L. M., Jones, B. C., & DeBruine, L. M. (2008). Sex drive is positively associated with women's preferences for sexual dimorphism in men's and women's faces. *Personality and Individual Differences, 44*(1), 161–170.

Weng, X., Odouli, R., & Li, D. K. (2008). Maternal caffeine consumption during pregnancy and the risk of miscarriage: A prospective cohort study. *American Journal of Obstetrics & Gynecology, 198*, 279.e1–279.e8.

Werner, L. A., & Bernstein, I. L. (2001). Development of the auditory, gustatory, olfactory, and somatosensory systems. In E. B. Goldstein (Ed.), *Blackwell handbook of perception, Handbook of experimental psychology series* (pp. 669–708). Boston: Blackwell.

Wessel, J., et al. (2007). C-reactive protein, an "intermediate phenotype" for inflammation: Human twin studies reveal heritability, association with blood pressure and the metabolic syndrome, and the influence of common polymorphism at catecholaminergic/[beta]-adrenergic pathway loci. *Journal of Hypertension, 25*(2), 329–343.

Westen, D. I., Stirman, S. W., & DeRubeis, R. J. (2006). Are research patients and clinical trials representative of clinical practice? In J. C. Norcross, L. E. Beutler, & R. F. Levant (Eds.), *Evidence-based practices in mental health: Debate and dialogue on the fundamental questions* (pp. 161–189). Washington, DC: American Psychological Association.

Wetzler, S. E., & Sweeney, J. A. (1986). Childhood amnesia. In D. C. Rubin (Ed.), *Autobiographical memory* (pp. 191–201). New York: Cambridge University Press.

Wheeler, M. A., & McMillan, C. T. (2001). Focal retrograde amnesia and the episodic–semantic distinction. *Cognitive, Affective and Behavioral Neuroscience, 1*(1), 22–36.

Wheeler, M. E., & Treisman, A. M. (2002). Binding in short-term visual memory. *Journal of Experimental Psychology: General, 131*(1), 48–64.

Wheeler, S. C., & Petty, R. E. (2001). The effects of stereotype activation on behavior: A review of possible mechanisms. *Psychological Bulletin, 127*(6), 797–826.

White, M. A., Masheb, R. M., & Grilo, C. M. (2009). Regimented and lifestyle restraint in binge eating disorder. *International Journal of Eating Disorders, 42*(4), 326–331.

Whitehead, B. D., & Popenoe, D. (2006). *The state of our unions: The social health of marriage in America*. New Brunswick, NJ: Rutgers University.

Whorf, B. (1956). *Language, thought, and reality*. New York: Wiley.

Wickwire Jr., E. M., Roland, M. M. S., Elkin, T. D., & Schumacher, J. A. (2008). Sleep disorders. In M. Hersen & D. Michel (Eds.), *Handbook of psychological assessment, case conceptualization, and treatment. Vol 2: Children and adolescents* (pp. 622–651). Hoboken, NJ: Wiley.

Widiger, T. A., & Simonsen, E. (2005). Alternative dimensional models of personality disorder: Finding a common ground. *Journal of Personality Disorders, 19*(2), 110–130.

Wiebe, R. E., & McCabe, S. B. (2002). Relationship perfectionism, dysphoria, and hostile interpersonal behaviors. *Journal of Social and Clinical Psychology, 21*(1), 67–91.

Wienke, C., & Hill, G. J. (2009). Does the "marriage benefit" extend to partners in gay and lesbian relationships? *Journal of Family Issues, 30*(2), 259–289.

Wiens, A. N., & Menustik, C. E. (1983). Treatment outcome and patient characteristics in an aversion therapy program for alcoholism. *American Psychologist, 38*, 1089–1096.

Wijers, S. L. J., Saris, W. H. M., & van Marken Lichtenbelt, W. D. (2009). Recent advances in adaptive thermogenesis: Potential implications for the treatment of obesity. *Obesity Reviews, 10*(2), 218–226.

Wild, R. A. (2007). Introduction to special issue on surgical menopause. *Menopause, 14,* 556–561.

Wilhelm, K., et al. (2010). Predicting mental health and well-being in adulthood. *Journal of Nervous and Mental Disease, 198*(2), 85–90.

Willcutt, E., & McQueen, M. (2010). Genetic and environmental vulnerability to bipolar spectrum disorders. In D. J. Miklowitz & D. Cicchetti (Eds.), *Understanding bipolar disorder: A developmental psychopathology perspective* (pp. 225–258). New York: Guilford Press.

Willer, R. (2009). Groups reward individual sacrifice: The status solution to the collective action problem. *American Sociological Review, 74*(1), 23–43.

Williams, J. E., & Best, D. L. (1994). Cross-cultural views of women and men. In W. J. Lonner & R. Malpass (Eds.), *Psychology and culture*. Boston: Allyn & Bacon.

Williams, J. E., et al. (2000). Anger proneness predicts coronary heart disease risk: Prospective analysis from the Atherosclerosis Risk In Communities (ARIC) study. *Circulation, 101*(17), 2034–2039.

Williams, L. M., et al. (2006). Amygdala–prefrontal dissociation of subliminal and supraliminal fear. *Human Brain Mapping, 27*(8), 652–661.

Willmott, C., Ponsford, J., Hocking, C., & Schönberger, M. (2009). Factors contributing to attentional impairments after traumatic brain injury. *Neuropsychology, 23*(4), 424–432.

Wills, T. A., Sandy, J. M., & Yaeger, A. M. (2002). Moderators of the relation between substance use level and problems: Test of a self-regulation model in middle adolescence. *Journal of Abnormal Psychology, 111*(1), 3–21.

Wilner, P., Bergman, J., & Sanger, D. (2009). Behavioural pharmacology of impulse control. *Behavioural Pharmacology, 20*(5–6), 558–560.

Wilson, A. (2002, November 3). War and remembrance: Controversy is a constant for memory researcher Elizabeth Loftus, newly installed at UCI. *Orange County Register.*

Wilson, C. R. E., Baxter, M. G., Easton, A., & Gaffan, D. (2008). Addition of fornix transection to frontal-temporal disconnection increases the impairment in object-in-place memory in macaque monkeys. *European Journal of Neuroscience, 27*(7), 1814–1822.

Wilson, G. T., Fairburn, C. C., Agras, W. S., Walsh, B. T., & Kraemer, H. (2002). Cognitive–behavioral therapy for bulimia nervosa: Time course and mechanisms of change. *Journal of Consulting and Clinical Psychology, 70*(2), 267–274.

Wilson, G. T., Wilfley, D. E., Agras, W. S., & Bryson, S. W. (2010). Psychological treatments of binge eating disorder. *Archives of General Psychiatry, 67*(1), 94–101.

Wilson, H. W., & Widom, C. S. (2009). A prospective examination of the path from child abuse and neglect to illicit drug use in middle adulthood: The potential mediating role of four risk factors. *Journal of Youth and Adolescence, 38*(3), 340–345.

Wilson, I. B., Carter, A. E., & Berg, K. M. (2009). Improving the self-report of HIV antiretroviral medication adherence: Is the glass half full or half empty? *Current HIV/AIDS Reports, 6*(4), 177–186.

Wilson, K. D., & Farah, M. J. (2003). When does the visual system use viewpoint-invariant representations during recognition? *Cognitive Brain Research, 16*(3), 399–415.

Wilson, R. S. (1983). The Louisville twin study: Developmental synchronies in behavior. *Child Development, 54,* 298–316.

Windich-Biermeier, A., et al. (2007). Effects of distraction on pain, fear, and distress during venous port access and venipuncture in children and adolescents with cancer. *Journal of Pediatric Oncology Nursing, 24*(1), 8–19.

Windischberger, C., et al. (2010). Area-specific modulation of neural activation comparing escitalopram and citalopram revealed by pharmaco-fMRI: A randomized cross-over study. *NeuroImage, 49*(2), 1161–1170.

Wisco, B. E., & Nolen-Hoeksema, S. (2009). The interaction of mood and rumination in depression: Effect on mood maintenance and mood-congruent autobiographical memory. *Journal of Rational-Emotive and Cognitive-Behavior Therapy, 27*(3), 144–159.

Wong, A. K., et al. (2009). A comprehensive linkage map of the dog genome. *Genetics.* doi:10.1534/genetics.109.106831

Wong, C. F., Kipke, M. D., & Weiss, G. (2008). Risk factors for alcohol use, frequent use, and binge drinking among young men who have sex with men. *Addictive Behaviors, 33*(8), 1012–1020.

Wong, M. D., Ettner, S. L., Boscardin, W. J., & Shapiro, M. F. (2009). The contribution of cancer incidence, stage at diagnosis and survival to racial differences in years of life expectancy. *Journal of General Internal Medicine, 24*(4), 475–481.

Wood, R. G., Goesling, B., & Avellar, S. (2007, June 19). *The effects of marriage on health: A synthesis of recent research evidence.* Department of Health and Human Services: Office of the Assistant Secretary for Planning and Evaluation. Retrieved from http://njwedding.org/business/report_marriage_on_health.pdf

Wood, W. (2000). Attitude change: Persuasion and social influence. *Annual Review of Psychology, 51,* 539–570.

Woodward, B. (2006). *State of denial.* New York: Simon & Schuster.

World Health Organization. (2003). *Training in the management of severe malnutrition.* Geneva: World Health Organization Department of Nutrition for Health and Development. Retrieved from http://www.who.int/nut/documents/manage_severe_ malnutrition_training_fly_eng.pdf

World Health Organization. (2004, March 3). *Alleviating protein-energy malnutrition.* Retrieved from http://www.who.int/nut/pem.htm

Wozniak, J. R., & Lim, K. O. (2006). Advances in white matter imaging: A review of in vivo magnetic resonance methodologies and their applicability to the study of development and aging. *Neuroscience & Biobehavioral Reviews, 30*(6), 762–774.

Wright, D. B., & Loftus, E. F. (2008). Eyewitness memory. In G. Cohen & M. A. Conway (Eds.), *Memory in the real world* (3rd ed., pp. 91–105). New York: Psychology Press.

Wu, A. H., et al. (2009). Dietary patterns and breast cancer risk in Asian American women. *American Journal of Clinical Nutrition, 89,* 1145–1154.

Wu, C-P. (2009). *Exploring the relationship between self-regulating intentional Internet search (IIS) and critical thinking skills.* Syracuse University, DAI-A 69/08, pub. #3323093.

Wu, J., et al. (1999). Serotonin and learned helplessness: A regional study of 5-HT1A, 5-HT2A receptors and the serotonin transport site in rat brain. *Journal of Psychiatric Research, 33*(1), 17–22.

Wyatt, T. D. (2009). Fifty years of pheromones. *Nature, 457,* 262–263.

Wykes, T., Steel, C., Everitt, B., & Tarrier, N. (2008). Cognitive behavior therapy for schizophrenia: Effect sizes, clinical models, and methodological rigor. *Schizophrenia Bulletin, 34*(3), 523–537.

Wylie, K., & Manoun, S. (2009). Sexual response models in women. *Maturitas, 63*(2), 112–115.

Wylleman, P., Harwood, C. G., Elbe, A-M., Reints, A., & de Caluwé, D. (2009). A perspective on education and professional development in applied sport psychology. *Psychology of Sport and Exercise, 10*(4), 435–446.

X

Xie, Y., & Goyette, K. (2003). Social mobility and the educational choices of Asian Americans. *Social Science Research, 32*(3), 467–498.

Xu, A. G., et al. (2010). Intergenic and repeat transcription in human, chimpanzee and macaque brains measured by RNA-seq. *PLos Computational Biology, 6*(7): e1000843. doi:10.1371/journal.pcbi.1000843.

Y

Yamada, Y., et al. (2008). Bus drivers' mental conditions and their relation to bus passengers' accidents with a focus on the psychological stress concept. *Journal of Human Ergology, 37,* 1–11.

Yamamoto, S., et al. (2009). Can dietary supplementation of monosodium glutamate improve the health of the elderly? *American Journal of Clinical Nutrition, 90*(3), 844S–849S.

Yamasue, H., et al. (2008). Sex-linked neuroanatomical basis of human altruistic cooperativeness. *Cerebral Cortex, 18*(10), 2331–2340.

Yang, L., et al. (2009). Reported reasons for initiating drug use among drug-dependent adolescents and youths in Yunnan, China. *American Journal of Drug and Alcohol Abuse, 35*(6), 445–453.

Yang, M., Eldridge, S., & Merlo, J. (2009). Multilevel survival analysis of health inequalities in life expectancy.*International Journal for Equity in Health, 8,* 31.

Yap, C., et al. (2008). The impact of support group activity on the relationship between Alzheimer's patients and their caregivers: Reporting of change of misbehavior by caregivers. *Alzheimer's and Dementia, 4*(4), T444–T445.

Yartz, A. R., Zvolensky, M. J., Bernstein, A., Bonn-Miller, M. O., & Lejuez, C. W. (2008). Panic-relevant predictability preferences: A laboratory test. *Journal of Abnormal Psychology, 117*(1), 242–246.

Yazzie, A. (2010). Visual-spatial thinking and academic achievement: A concurrent and predictive validity study. *Dissertation Abstracts International: Section A, Humanities and Social Sciences, 70*(8-A), 2897.

Yeh, C., & Chang, T. (2004). Understanding the multidimensionality and heterogeneity of the Asian-American experience. *PsycCRITIQUES, 49*(5), 583–586.

Yehuda, R. (2002). Post-traumatic stress disorder. *New England Journal of Medicine, 346*(2), 108–114.

Yin, L., Smith, R. G., Sterling, P., & Brainard, D. H. (2009). Physiology and morphology of color-opponent ganglion cells in a retina expressing a dual gradient of S and M opsins. *Journal of Neuroscience, 29*(9), 2706–2724.

Yokota, F., & Thompson, K. M. (2000). Violence in G-rated animated films. *Journal of the American Medical Association, 283,* 2716–2720.

Yuan, N. P., Koss, M. P., & Stone, M. (2006). The psychological consequences of sexual trauma. *VAWnet, or the Pennsylvania Coalition Against Domestic Violence: National Online Resource Center on Violence Against Women, 1–10.*

Yurgelun-Todd, D. A. (2007). Emotional and cognitive changes during adolescence. *Current Opinion in Neurobiology, 17*(2), 251–257.

Z

Zahavi, A. (2003). Indirect selection and individual selection in sociobiology. *Animal Behaviour, 65,* 859–863.

Zaitsoff, S. L., & Grilo, C. M. (2010). Eating disorder psychopathology as a marker of psychosocial distress and suicide risk in female and male adolescent psychiatric patients. *Comprehensive Psychiatry, 51*(2), 142–150.

Zajonc, R. B. (1968). Attitudinal effects of mere exposure. *Journal of Personality and Social Psychology, Monograph Supplement, 2*(9), 1–27.

Zajonc, R. B. (1980). Compresence. In P. Paulus (Ed.), *The psychology of group influence.* Hillsdale, NJ: Erlbaum.

Zanarini, M. C., Frankenburg, F. R., Reich, D. B., & Fitzmaurice, G. (2010). Time to attainment of recovery from borderline personality disorder and stability of recovery: A 10-year prospective follow-up study. *American Journal of Psychiatry, 167,* 663–667.

Zapf, P. A., Zottoli, T. M., & Pirelli, G. (2009). Insanity in the courtroom: Issues of criminal responsibility and competency to stand trial. In J. D. Lieberman & D. A. Krauss, *Psychological expertise in court* (pp. 79–102). Farnham, Surrey, England: Ashgate.

Zayas, L., Gulbas, L. E., Fedoravicius, N., & Cabassa, L. J. (2010). Patterns of distress, precipitating events, and reflections on suicide attempts by young Latinas. *Social Science and Medicine, 70*(11), 1773–1779.

Zeifman, D. M. (2004). Acoustic features of infant crying related to intended caregiving intervention. *Infant and Child Development, 13*(2), 111–122.

Zhang, Q. (2009). A computational account of dreaming: Learning and memory consolidation. *Cognitive Systems Research, 10*(2), 91–101.

Zhang, S. M., et al. (2007). Alcohol consumption and breast cancer risk in the Women's Health Study. *American Journal of Epidemiology, 165*(6), 667–676.

Zhang, Z., et al. (2009). Estimation of heritabilities, genetic correlations, and breeding values of four traits that collectively define hip dysplasia in dogs. *American Journal of Veterinary Research, 70*(4), 483–492.

Zilberman, M. L. (2009). Substance abuse across the lifespan in women. In K. T. Brady, S. E. Back, & S. F. Greenfield (Eds.), *Women and addiction* (pp. 3–13). New York: Guilford Press.

Zimbardo, P. (2007). *The Lucifer effect: How good people turn evil.* New York: Random House.

Zimbardo, P. G. (2004). A situationist perspective on the psychology of evil: Understanding how good people are transformed into perpetrators. In A. G. Miller (Ed.), *The social psychology of good and evil* (pp. 21–50). New York: Guilford Press.

Zimbardo, P. G. (2007). Thoughts on psychologists, ethics, and the use of torture in interrogations: Don't ignore varying roles and complexities. *Analyses of Social Issues and Public Policy, 7*(1), 1–9.

Zimbardo, P. G. (2008). The journey from the Bronx to Stanford to Abu Ghraib. In R. Levine, A. Rodrigues, & L. Zelezny (Eds.), *Journeys in social psychology: Looking back to inspire the future* (pp. 85–104). New York: Psychology Press.

Zimbardo, P. G., LaBerge, S., & Butler, L. D. (1993). Psychophysiological consequences of unexplained arousal. *Journal of Abnormal Psychology, 102,* 466–473.

Zimmer, C. (2002, December–2003, January). Searching for your inner chimp. *Natural History, 112.*

Zohar, J., & Westenberg, H. G. M. (2007). Anxiety disorders: A review of tricyclic antidepressants and selective serotonin reuptake inhibitors. *Acta Psychiatrica Scandinavica, 101*(S403), 39–49.

Zosuls, K. M., et al. (2009). The acquisition of gender labels in infancy: Implications for gender-typed play. *Developmental Psychology, 45*(3), 688–701.

Zucker, A. N., Ostrove, J. M., & Stewart, A. J. (2002). College-educated women's personality development in adulthood: Perceptions and age differences. *Psychology and Aging, 17*(2), 236–244.

Glossary

A

A–B problem The issue of how well we can predict behavior on the basis of attitudes.

Absolute threshold The minimal amount of energy that can produce a sensation.

Abstinence syndrome A characteristic cluster of symptoms that results from a sudden decrease in an addictive drug's level of usage.

Accommodation According to Piaget, the modification of schemas so that information inconsistent with existing schemas can be integrated or understood.

Acculturation The process of adaptation in which immigrants and native groups identify with a new, dominant culture by learning about that culture and making behavioral and attitudinal changes.

Acetylcholine (ACh) A neurotransmitter that controls muscle contractions.

Acoustic code Mental representation of information as a sequence of sounds.

Acquired drives Drives acquired through experience or that are learned.

Acrophobia Fear of high places.

Action potential The electrical impulse that provides the basis for the conduction of a neural impulse along an axon of a neuron.

Activating effect The arousal-producing effects of sex hormones that increase the likelihood of sexual behavior.

Activation–synthesis model The view that dreams reflect activation of cognitive activity by the reticular formation and synthesis of this activity into a pattern.

Actor–observer effect The tendency to attribute our own behavior to situational factors but to attribute the behavior of others to dispositional factors.

Acute stress disorder A disorder, like PTSD, that is characterized by feelings of anxiety and helplessness and caused by a traumatic event. Acute stress disorder occurs within a month of the event and lasts from 2 days to 4 weeks.

Adolescence The period of life bounded by puberty and the assumption of adult responsibilities.

Affective shift hypothesis The view that men and women tend to experience different shifts in the emotions following initiation of sexual activity, such that women feel more love and commitment, and many men experience less love and commitment.

Afferent neurons Neurons that transmit messages from sensory receptors to the spinal cord and brain. Also called *sensory neurons*.

Afterimage The lingering visual impression made by a stimulus that has been removed.

Agoraphobia Fear of open, crowded places.

Alarm reaction The first stage of the GAS, which is triggered by the impact of a stressor and characterized by sympathetic activity.

Algorithm A systematic procedure for solving a problem that works invariably when it is correctly applied.

All-or-none principle The fact that a neuron fires an impulse of the same strength whenever its action potential is triggered.

Alpha waves Rapid low-amplitude brain waves that have been linked to feelings of relaxation.

Altruism Unselfish concern for the welfare of others.

Alzheimer's disease A progressive form of mental deterioration characterized by loss of memory, language, problem solving, and other cognitive functions.

Amniotic sac A sac within the uterus that contains the embryo or fetus.

Amphetamines Stimulants derived from *alpha-methyl-beta-phenyl-ethyl-amine*.

Amygdala An almond-shaped structure in the frontal part of the temporal lobe that is part of the limbic system and involved in processing and expressing emotions, particularly fear.

Analytical psychology Jung's psychodynamic theory, which emphasizes the collective unconscious and archetypes.

Anchoring and adjustment heuristic A decision-making heuristic in which a presumption or first estimate serves as a cognitive anchor. As we receive additional information, we make adjustments but tend to remain in the proximity of the anchor.

Androgens Male sex hormones.

Anorexia nervosa A life-threatening eating disorder characterized by dramatic weight loss and a distorted body image.

Anterograde amnesia Failure to remember events that occurred after physical trauma because of the effects of the trauma.

Antibodies Substances formed by white blood cells that recognize and destroy antigens.

Antidepressant Acting to relieve depression.

Antigen A substance that stimulates the body to mount an immune system response to it. (*Antigen* is the contraction of *anti*body *gen*erator.)

Antisocial personality A personality descriptive of an individual who is in frequent conflict with society yet who is undeterred by punishment and experiences little or no guilt or anxiety.

Antisocial personality disorder The diagnosis given a person who is in frequent conflict with society, yet who is undeterred by punishment and experiences little or no guilt and anxiety.

Anxiety disorders Disorders characterized by excessive worrying, fear of losing control, nervousness, and inability to relax.

Aphagic Characterized by undereating.

Aphasia A disruption in the ability to understand or produce language.

Applied research Research conducted in an effort to find solutions to particular problems.

Approach–approach conflict A type of conflict in which the goals that produce opposing motives are positive and within reach.

Approach–avoidance conflict A type of conflict in which the same goal produces approach and avoidance motives.

Aptitude A natural ability or talent.

Archetypes Basic, primitive images or concepts hypothesized by Jung to reside in the collective unconscious.

Assimilation According to Piaget, the inclusion of a new event into an existing schema.

Asylum An institution for the care of the mentally ill.

Attachment The enduring affectional tie that binds one person to another.

Attention-deficit/hyperactivity disorder A disorder that begins in childhood and is characterized by a persistent pattern of lack of attention with or without hyperactivity and impulsive behavior.

Attitude An enduring mental representation of a person, place, or thing that typically evokes an emotional response and related behavior.

Attitude-discrepant behavior Behavior inconsistent with an attitude that may have the effect of modifying an attitude.

Attraction In social psychology, an attitude of liking or disliking (negative attraction).

Attraction-similarity hypothesis The view that people tend to choose persons similar to themselves in attractiveness and attitudes in the formation of interpersonal relationships.

Attribution A belief concerning why people behave in a certain way.

Attributional style The tendency to attribute one's behavior to internal or external factors, stable or unstable factors, and global or specific factors.

Attribution process The process by which people draw inferences about the motives and traits of others.

Auditory Having to do with hearing.

Auditory nerve The axon bundle that transmits neural impulses from the organ of Corti to the brain.

Autokinetic effect The tendency to perceive a stationary point of light in a dark room as moving.

Autonomic nervous system (ANS) The division of the peripheral nervous system that regulates glands and activities such as heartbeat, respiration, digestion, and dilation of the pupils.

Availability heuristic A decision-making heuristic in which our estimates of frequency or probability of events are based on how easy it is to find examples.

Average The central tendency of a group of measures, expressed either as the mean, median, or mode of a distribution.

Aversive conditioning A behavior-therapy technique in which undesired responses are inhibited by pairing repugnant or offensive stimuli with them.

Avoidance–avoidance conflict A type of conflict in which the goals are negative, but avoidance of one requires approaching the other.

Avoidant personality disorder A personality disorder in which the person is unwilling to enter relationships without assurance of acceptance because of fears of rejection and criticism.

Axon A long, thin part of a neuron that transmits impulses to other neurons, an organ, or muscle from branching structures called *terminal buttons*.

B

Barbiturate An addictive depressant used to relieve anxiety or pain and to treat epilepsy, high blood pressure, and insomnia.

Basilar membrane A membrane that lies coiled within the cochlea.

Behavioral genetics The area of biology and psychology that focuses on the transmission of traits that give rise to behavior.

Behaviorism The school of psychology that defines psychology as the study of observable behavior and studies relationships between stimuli and responses.

Behavior modification Therapy techniques based on principles of learning that teach adaptive behavior and extinguish or discourage maladaptive behavior.

Behavior-rating scale A systematic means for recording the frequency with which target behaviors occur.

Behavior therapy Systematic application of the principles of learning to the direct modification of a client's problem behaviors.

Bimodal Having two modes.

Binocular cues Stimuli suggestive of depth that involve simultaneous perception by both eyes.

Biofeedback training (BFT) The systematic feeding back to an organism information about a bodily function so that the organism can gain control of that function.

Biological perspective The approach to psychology that seeks to understand the nature of the links between biological processes and structures such as the functioning of the brain, the endocrine system, and heredity, on the one hand, and behavior and mental processes, on the other.

Biological preparedness Readiness to acquire a certain kind of conditioned response due to the biological makeup of the organism.

Biopsychosocial model The view that psychological disorders can be explained by a combination of (a) possible biological vulnerabilities; (b) psychological factors such as stress and self-defeating thoughts; and (c) sociocultural factors such as family relationships and cultural beliefs and expectations.

Bipolar cells Neurons that conduct neural impulses from rods and cones to ganglion cells.

Bipolar disorder A disorder in which the mood alternates between two extreme poles (elation and depression); also referred to as *manic–depression*.

Blind In experimental terminology, being unaware of whether one has received a treatment or not.

Blind spot The area of the retina where axons from ganglion cells meet to form the optic nerve.

Borderline personality disorder A personality disorder characterized by instability in relationships, self-image, and mood, plus lack of impulse control.

Bottom-up processing The organization of the parts of a pattern to recognize, or form an image of, the pattern they compose.

Brightness constancy The tendency to perceive an object as being just as bright even though lighting conditions change its intensity.

Broca's aphasia A language disorder characterized by slow, laborious speech.

Bulimia nervosa An eating disorder characterized by repeated cycles of binge eating and purging.

Bystander effect The tendency to avoid helping other people in emergencies when other people are also present and apparently capable of helping.

C

Cannon–Bard theory of emotion The view that emotions *accompany* bodily responses but are not caused by them.

Case study A carefully drawn biography that may be obtained through interviews, questionnaires, and psychological tests.

Catastrophize To interpret negative events as being disastrous; to "blow things out of proportion."

Catatonic schizophrenia A type of schizophrenia characterized by striking motor impairment.

Catharsis In psychoanalysis, the expression of repressed feelings and impulses to allow the release of the psychic energy associated with them.

Center According to Piaget, to focus one's attention.

Central nervous system The brain and spinal cord.

Central route In persuasive arguments, providing substantive information about the issues involved.

Cerebellum A part of the hindbrain involved in muscle coordination and balance.

Cerebral cortex The wrinkled surface area (gray matter) of the cerebrum.

Cerebrum The large mass of the forebrain, which consists of two hemispheres.

Chromosome A microscopic rod-shaped body in the cell nucleus carrying genes that transmit hereditary traits from generation to generation.

Chunk A stimulus or group of stimuli that is perceived as a discrete piece of information.

Circadian rhythm Referring to cycles that are connected with the 24-hour period of the Earth's rotation. (From the Latin *circa,* meaning "about," and *dia,* meaning "day.")

Classical conditioning A simple form of learning in which an organism comes to associate or anticipate events. A neutral stimulus comes to evoke the response usually evoked by another stimulus by being paired repeatedly with the other stimulus. Also referred to as *respondent conditioning* or *Pavlovian conditioning.*

Claustrophobia Fear of tight, small places.

Client-centered therapy Carl Rogers's method of psychotherapy, which emphasizes the creation of a warm, therapeutic atmosphere that frees clients to engage in self-exploration and self-expression.

Closure The tendency to perceive a broken figure as being complete or whole.

Cochlea The inner ear; the bony tube that contains the basilar membrane and the organ of Corti.

Cognition Mental activity involved in understanding, processing, and communicating information.

Cognitive-dissonance theory The view that we are motivated to make our cognitions, or beliefs, consistent with each other and with our behavior.

Cognitive map A mental representation of the layout of one's environment.

Cognitive perspective The approach to psychology that focuses on the nature of consciousness and on mental processes such as sensation and perception, memory, problem solving, decision making, judgment, language, and intelligence.

Cognitive therapy A form of therapy that focuses on how clients' cognitions (expectations, attitudes, beliefs, etc.) lead to distress and may be modified to relieve distress and promote adaptive behavior.

Cohort effect Similarities in behavior that stem from the fact that group members are approximately the same age.

Collective unconscious Jung's hypothesized store of vague racial memories.

Collectivist A person who defines himself or herself in terms of relationships to other people and groups and gives priority to group goals.

Color constancy The tendency to perceive an object as being the same color even though lighting conditions change its appearance.

Commitment A pledge or obligation.

Common fate The tendency to perceive elements that move together as belonging together.

Complementary Descriptive of colors of the spectrum that when combined produce white or nearly white light.

Concept A mental category that is used to class together objects, relations, events, abstractions, ideas, or qualities that have common properties.

Concordance Agreement.

Concrete-operational stage Piaget's third stage, characterized by logical thought concerning tangible objects, conservation, and subjective morality.

Conditional positive regard Judgment of another person's value on the basis of the acceptability of that person's behaviors.

Conditioned reinforcer Another term for a secondary reinforcer.

Conditioned response (CR) A learned response to a conditioned stimulus.

Conditioned stimulus (CS) A previously neutral stimulus that elicits a conditioned response because it has been paired repeatedly with a stimulus that already elicited that response.

Conditions of worth Standards by which the value of a person is judged.

Conductive deafness The forms of deafness in which there is loss of conduction of sound through the middle ear.

Cones Cone-shaped photoreceptors that transmit sensations of color.

Conflict Being torn in different directions by opposing motives. Feelings produced by being in conflict.

Conform To change one's attitudes or overt behavior to adhere to social norms.

Conscious Self-aware.

Consciousness A concept with many meanings, including sensory awareness of the world outside, direct inner awareness of one's thoughts and feelings, personal unity, and the waking state.

Conservation According to Piaget, recognition that basic properties of substances such as weight and mass remain the same when superficial features change.

Consummate love The ideal form of love within Sternberg's model, which combines passion, intimacy, and commitment.

Contact comfort A hypothesized primary drive to seek physical comfort through contact with another.

Context-dependent memory Information that is better retrieved in the context in which it was encoded and stored, or learned.

Continuity The tendency to perceive a series of points or lines as having unity.

Continuous reinforcement A schedule of reinforcement in which every correct response is reinforced.

Control groups In experiments, groups whose members do not obtain the treatment, while other conditions are held constant.

Conventional level According to Kohlberg, a period during which moral judgments largely reflect social conventions; a "law and order" approach to morality.

Convergence A binocular cue for depth based on the inward movement of the eyes as they attempt to focus on an object that is drawing nearer.

Convergent thinking A thought process that narrows in on the single best solution to a problem.

Conversion disorder A disorder in which anxiety or unconscious conflicts are "converted" into physical symptoms that often have the effect of helping the person cope with anxiety or conflict.

Cornea Transparent tissue forming the outer surface of the eyeball.

Corpus callosum A thick fiber bundle that connects the hemispheres of the cortex.

Correlation An association or relationship among variables, as we might find between height and weight or between study habits and school grades.

Correlational method A mathematical method of determining whether one variable increases or decreases as another variable increases or decreases. For example, there is a correlation between intelligence test scores and grades in school.

Correlation coefficient A number between +1.00 and −1.00 that expresses the strength and direction (positive or negative) of the relationship between two variables.

Counterconditioning A fear-reduction technique in which pleasant stimuli are associated with fear-evoking stimuli so that the fear-evoking stimuli lose their aversive qualities.

Couple therapy A form of therapy in which a couple is treated as the client and helped to improve communication skills and manage conflict.

Creative self According to Adler, the self-aware aspect of personality that strives to achieve its full potential.

Creativity The ability to generate novel and useful solutions to problems.

Critical period In prenatal development, a period during which an embryo is particularly vulnerable to a certain teratogen. In infancy, the term is usually used to refer to a period during which infants are most likely to form bonds of attachment with caregivers.

Critical thinking An approach to the examination of arguments based on skepticism, logical analysis, and insistence upon the importance of empirical evidence.

Cross-sectional research The study of developmental processes by taking measures of people of different age groups at the same time.

Crystallized intelligence One's lifetime of intellectual achievement as shown largely through vocabulary and knowledge of world affairs.

Cultural bias A factor that provides an advantage for test takers from certain cultural backgrounds, such as using test items that are based on middle-class culture in the United States.

Culture-bound Determined by the experiences of being reared within a certain cultural setting.

D

Daily hassles Notable daily conditions and experiences that are threatening or harmful to a person's well-being.

Dark adaptation The process of adjusting to conditions of lower lighting by increasing the sensitivity of rods and cones.

Debrief To elicit information about a completed procedure.

Decentration Simultaneous focusing on more than one dimension of a problem so that flexible, reversible thought becomes possible.

Decibel (dB) A unit expressing the loudness of a sound.

Defense mechanism In psychodynamic theory, an unconscious function of the ego that protects it from anxiety-evoking material by preventing accurate recognition of this material.

Deindividuation The process by which group members may discontinue self-evaluation and adopt group norms and attitudes.

Delta waves Strong, slow brain waves usually emitted during stage 3 and 4 sleep.

Delusions False, persistent beliefs that are unsubstantiated by sensory or objective evidence.

Dementia A condition characterized by deterioration of cognitive functioning.

Dendrites Rootlike structures, attached to the cell body of a neuron, that receive impulses from other neurons.

Dependent variable A measure of an assumed effect of an independent variable.

Depolarize To reduce the resting potential of a cell membrane from about −70 millivolts toward zero.

Depressant A drug that lowers the rate of activity of the nervous system.

Descriptive statistics The branch of statistics concerned with providing descriptive information about a distribution of scores.

Desensitization The type of sensory adaptation in which we become less sensitive to constant stimuli; also called negative adaptation.

Diathesis–stress model The view that psychological disorders can be explained in terms of an underlying vulnerability (diathesis) and problems that create pressure or tension (stress).

Dichromat A person who is sensitive to black–white and either red–green or blue–yellow and hence partially color-blind.

Difference threshold The minimal difference in intensity required between two sources of energy so that they will be perceived as different.

Diffusion of responsibility The spreading or sharing of responsibility for a decision or behavior within a group.

Direct inner awareness Knowledge of one's own thoughts, feelings, and memories without the use of sensory organs.

Discrimination Hostile behavior that is directed against groups toward whom one is prejudiced; In conditioning, the tendency for an organism to distinguish between a conditioned stimulus and similar stimuli that do not forecast an unconditioned stimulus.

Discriminative stimulus In operant conditioning, a stimulus that indicates that reinforcement is available.

Disorganized schizophrenia A type of schizophrenia characterized by disorganized delusions and vivid hallucinations.

Displace In memory theory, to cause information to be lost from short-term memory by adding new information.

Displacement The quality of language that permits one to communicate information about objects and events in another time and place.

Dispositional attribution An assumption that a person's behavior is determined by internal causes such as personal traits.

Dissociative amnesia A dissociative disorder marked by loss of memory or self-identity; skills and general knowledge are usually retained; Amnesia thought to stem from psychological conflict or trauma.

Dissociative disorders Disorders in which there are sudden, temporary changes in consciousness or self-identity.

Dissociative fugue A dissociative disorder in which one experiences amnesia and then flees to a new location.

Dissociative identity disorder A disorder in which a person appears to have two or more distinct identities or personalities that may alternately emerge.

Divergent thinking A thought process that attempts to generate multiple solutions to problems.

Dizygotic (DZ) twins Twins that develop from two fertilized ova and who are thus as closely related as brothers and sisters in general. Also called *fraternal twins*.

DNA Abbreviation for deoxyribonucleic acid, the substance that forms the basic material of chromosomes. It takes the form of a double helix and contains the genetic code.

Dopamine A neurotransmitter that is involved in Parkinson's disease and that appears to play a role in schizophrenia.

Double-blind study A study in which neither the participants nor the observers know who has received the treatment.

Down syndrome A condition caused by an extra chromosome on the 21st pair and characterized by mental deficiency, a broad face, and slanting eyes.

Drive A condition of arousal in an organism that is associated with a need.

Drive for superiority Adler's term for the desire to compensate for feelings of inferiority.

Drive-reduction theory The view that organisms learn to engage in behaviors that have the effect of reducing drives.

E

Eardrum A thin membrane that vibrates in response to sound waves, transmitting the waves to the middle and inner ears.

Eating disorders A group of disorders marked by persistent, gross disturbances in eating patterns.

Echo A mental representation of an auditory stimulus (sound) that is held briefly in sensory memory.

Echoic memory The sensory register that briefly holds mental representations of auditory stimuli.

Efferent neurons Neurons that transmit messages from the brain or spinal cord to muscles and glands. Also called *motor neurons*.

Effort justification In cognitive-dissonance theory, the tendency to seek justification (acceptable reasons) for strenuous efforts.

Ego The second psychic structure to develop, characterized by self-awareness, planning, and delay of gratification.

Ego analyst A psychodynamically oriented therapist who focuses on the conscious, coping behavior of the ego instead of the hypothesized, unconscious functioning of the id.

Egocentrism According to Piaget, the assumption that others view the world as one does oneself.

Ego identity A firm sense of who one is and what one stands for.

Eidetic imagery The maintenance of detailed visual memories over several minutes.

Ejaculation The process of propelling seminal fluid (semen) from the penis.

Elaboration likelihood model The view that persuasive messages are evaluated (elaborated) on the basis of central and peripheral cues.

Elaborative rehearsal The kind of coding in which new information is related to information that is already known.

Electra complex A conflict of the phallic stage in which the girl longs for her father and resents her mother.

Electroconvulsive therapy (ECT) Treatment of disorders like major depression by passing an electric current (that causes a convulsion) through the head.

Electromyograph (EMG) An instrument that measures muscle tension.

Embryonic stage The baby from the third through the eighth weeks following conception, during which time the major organ systems undergo rapid differentiation.

Emerging adulthood A theoretical period of development, spanning the ages of about 18 to 25, in which young people in developed nations engage in extended role exploration or preparation.

Emotion A state of feeling that has cognitive, physiological, and behavioral components.

Empathic understanding In client-centered therapy, the ability to perceive a client's feelings from the client's frame of reference.

Empirical science A science that obtains evidence by experience or experimentation.

Empty-nest syndrome A sense of depression and loss of purpose felt by some parents when the youngest child leaves home.

Encoding Modifying information so that it can be placed in memory; the first stage of information processing.

Endocrine system The body's system of ductless glands that secrete hormones and release them directly into the bloodstream.

Endorphins Neurotransmitters that are composed of amino acids and that are functionally similar to morphine.

Engram An assumed electrical circuit in the brain that corresponds to a memory trace.

Epigenesis The fact that children's development reflects continuing bidirectional exchanges between their genetic heritage and the environments in which they find themselves or place themselves.

Epilepsy Temporary disturbances of brain functions that involve sudden neural discharges.

Episodic memory Memories of events that happen to a person or that take place in the person's presence.

Erogenous zone An area of the body that is sensitive to sexual sensations.

Estrus The periodic sexual excitement of many female mammals as governed by levels of sex hormones.

Ethical Moral; referring to one's system of deriving standards for determining what is moral.

Ethnic group A group characterized by common features such as cultural heritage, history, race, and language.

Eustress (YOU-stress). Stress that is healthful.

Evaluation apprehension Concern that others are evaluating our behavior.

Evidence-based practices A method of therapy that has been shown effective in experiments in which participants are assigned at random to the treatment under investigation or to another treatment or placebo, and in which the methods being tested are clearly outlined.

Evolutionary perspective The view that our behavior and mental processes have been shaped, at least in part, by natural selection as our ancestors strived to meet prehistoric and historic challenges.

Evolutionary psychology The branch of psychology that studies the ways adaptation and natural selection are connected with mental processes and behavior.

Excitement phase The first phase of the sexual response cycle, which is characterized by muscle tension, increases in the heart rate, and erection in the male and vaginal lubrication in the female.

Exemplar A specific example.

Exhaustion stage The third stage of the GAS, characterized by weakened resistance and possible deterioration.

Existentialism The view that people are free and responsible for their own behavior.

Experiment A scientific method that seeks to confirm cause-and-effect relationships by introducing independent variables and observing their effects on dependent variables.

Experimental groups In experiments, groups whose members obtain the treatment.

Experimenter bias A condition in which a researcher expects or desires a certain outcome in a research study, possibly affecting the outcome.

Explicit memory Memory that clearly and distinctly expresses (explicates) specific information; also referred to as *declarative memory*.

Externals People who perceive the ability to attain reinforcements as largely outside themselves.

Extinction The process by which stimuli lose their ability to evoke learned responses because the events that had followed the stimuli no longer occur. (The learned responses are said to be *extinguished*.)

Extrasensory perception (ESP) Perception of objects or events through means other than the recognized sensory organs.

Extraversion A trait characterized by tendencies to be socially outgoing and to express feelings and impulses freely.

Extrinsic rewards The rewards associated with performance goals, such as a good salary, health care, and retirement benefits.

F

Facial-feedback hypothesis The view that stereotypical facial expressions can contribute to stereotypical emotions.

Factor analysis A statistical technique that allows researchers to determine the relationships among a large number of items, such as test items.

Family therapy A form of therapy in which the family unit is treated as the client.

Fear appeal A type of persuasive communication that influences behavior on the basis of arousing fear instead of rational analysis of the issues.

Feature detectors Neurons in the sensory cortex that fire in response to specific features of sensory information such as lines or edges of objects.

Feeling-of-knowing experience Same as *tip-of-the-tongue phenomenon*.

Fetal alcohol syndrome (FAS) A cluster of symptoms caused by maternal drinking of alcohol, in which the child shows developmental lags and characteristic facial features such as an underdeveloped upper jaw, flattened nose, and widely spaced eyes.

Fetal stage The baby from the third month following conception through childbirth, during which time there is maturation of organ systems and dramatic gains in length and weight.

Fight-or-flight reaction A possibly innate adaptive response to the perception of danger.

Fixation time The amount of time spent looking at a visual stimulus.

Fixed-interval schedule A schedule in which a fixed amount of time must elapse between the previous and subsequent times that reinforcement is available.

Fixed-ratio schedule A schedule in which reinforcement is provided after a fixed number of correct responses.

Flashbacks Distorted perceptions or hallucinations that occur days or weeks after LSD usage but mimic the LSD experience.

Flashbulb memory A memory that is highly detailed and strongly emotionally elaborated because of its great and unusual significance.

Flavor A complex quality of food and other substances that is based on their odor, texture, and temperature as well as their taste.

Flooding A behavioral fear-reduction technique based on principles of classical conditioning. Fear-evoking stimuli (CSs) are presented continuously in the absence of actual harm so that fear responses (CRs) are extinguished.

Fluid intelligence Mental flexibility as shown in learning rapidly to solve new kinds of problems.

Foot-in-the-door technique A method for inducing compliance in which a small request is followed by a larger request.

Forced-choice format A method of presenting test questions that requires a respondent to select one of a number of possible answers.

Formal-operational stage Piaget's fourth stage, characterized by abstract logical thought; deduction from principles.

Fovea An area near the center of the retina that is dense with cones and where vision is consequently most acute.

Frame of reference In client-centered therapy, one's unique patterning of perceptions and attitudes, according to which one evaluates events.

Framing effect The influence of wording, or the context in which information is presented, on decision making.

Free association In psychoanalysis, the uncensored uttering of all thoughts that come to mind.

Frequency theory The theory that the pitch of a sound is reflected in the frequency of the neural impulses that are generated in response to the sound.

Frontal lobe The lobe of the cerebral cortex that lies in front of the central fissure.

Functional analysis A systematic study of behavior in which one identifies the stimuli that trigger problem behavior and the reinforcers that maintain it.

Functional fixedness The tendency to view an object in terms of its name or familiar usage.

Functionalism The school of psychology that emphasizes the uses or functions of the mind and behavior rather than just the elements of experience.

Fundamental attribution error The assumption that others act predominantly on the basis of their dispositions, even when there is evidence suggesting the importance of their circumstances.

G

Gamma-aminobutyric acid (GABA) An inhibitory neurotransmitter that apparently helps calm anxiety.

Ganglion cells Neurons whose axons form the optic nerve.

Gender The culturally defined concepts of masculinity and femininity.

Gender-schema A concept of the distribution of behavior patterns into feminine and masculine roles that motivate and guide the gender-typing of the child.

Gender-typing The process by which people acquire a sense of being female or male and acquire the traits considered typical of females or males within a cultural setting.

Gene A basic unit of heredity, which is found at a specific point on a chromosome.

General adaptation syndrome (GAS) Selye's term for a hypothesized three-stage response to stress.

Generalization In conditioning, the tendency for a conditioned response to be evoked by stimuli that are similar to the stimulus to which the response was conditioned.

Generalize To extend from the particular to the general; to apply observations based on a sample to a population.

Generalized anxiety disorder Feelings of dread and foreboding and sympathetic arousal of at least 6 months' duration.

Genetics The area of biology that focuses on heredity.

Genotype One's genetic makeup based on the sequencing of the nucleotides we term A, C, G, and T.

Genuineness In client-centered therapy, openness and honesty in responding to the client.

Germinal stage The first stage of prenatal development, during which the dividing mass of cells has not become implanted in the uterine wall.

Gestalt psychology The school of psychology that emphasizes the tendency to organize perceptions into wholes and to integrate separate stimuli into meaningful patterns.

Gestalt therapy Fritz Perls's form of psychotherapy, which attempts to integrate conflicting parts of the personality through directive methods designed to help clients perceive their whole selves.

Gland An organ that secretes one or more chemical substances such as hormones, saliva, or milk.

Glia Cells that nourish neurons, remove waste products from the nervous system, and help synchronize the messages sent by neurons.

Gray matter In the spinal cord, the grayish neurons and neural segments that are involved in spinal reflexes.

Groupthink A process in which group members are influenced by cohesiveness and a dynamic leader to ignore external realities as they make decisions.

g Spearman's symbol for general intelligence, which he believed underlay more specific abilities.

H

Hallucination A perception that occurs in the absence of sensory stimulation and is confused with reality.

Hallucinogenic drugs Substances that give rise to hallucinations.

Health psychology The field of psychology that studies the relationships between psychological factors (e.g., attitudes, beliefs, situational influences, and behavior patterns) and the prevention and treatment of physical illness.

Heredity The transmission of traits from parent to offspring by means of genes.

Heritability The degree to which the variations in a trait from one person to another can be attributed to, or explained by, genetic factors.

Hertz (Hz) A unit expressing the frequency of sound waves. One hertz equals one cycle per second.

Heterosexual Referring to people who are sexually aroused by, and interested in forming romantic relationships with, people of the other sex.

Heuristics Rules of thumb that help us simplify and solve problems.

Hierarchy of needs Maslow's ordering of needs from most basic (physiological needs such as hunger and thirst) to most elaborate and sophisticated (self-actualization).

Higher order conditioning A classical conditioning procedure in which a previously neutral stimulus comes to elicit the response brought forth by a *conditioned* stimulus by being paired repeatedly with that conditioned stimulus.

Hippocampus A structure in the limbic system that plays an important role in the formation of new memories.

Holophrase A single word used to express complex meanings.

Homeostasis The tendency of the body to maintain a steady state.

Homosexual Referring to people who are sexually aroused by, and interested in forming romantic relationships with, people of the same sex. (Derived from the Greek *homos,* meaning "same," not from the Latin *homo,* meaning "man.")

Hormone A substance secreted by an endocrine gland that regulates various body functions.

Hue The color of light as determined by its wavelength.

Humanism The philosophy and school of psychology that asserts that people are conscious, self-aware, and capable of free choice, self-fulfillment, and ethical behavior.

Humanistic therapy A form of psychotherapy that focuses on the client's subjective, conscious experience in the "here and now."

Hydrocarbons Chemical compounds consisting of hydrogen and carbon.

Hyperphagic Characterized by excessive eating.

Hypertension High blood pressure.

Hypnagogic state The drowsy interval between waking and sleeping characterized by brief, hallucinatory, dreamlike experiences.

Hypnosis An altered state of consciousness in which people appear to be highly suggestible and behave as though they are in a trance.

Hypochondriasis Persistent belief that one is ill despite lack of medical findings.

Hypothalamus A bundle of nuclei below the thalamus involved in body temperature, motivation, and emotion.

Hypothesis Within the science of psychology, a specific statement about behavior or mental processes that is testable through research.

I

Icon A mental representation of a visual stimulus that is held briefly in sensory memory.

Iconic memory The sensory register that briefly holds mental representations of visual stimuli.

Ideas of persecution Erroneous beliefs that one is being victimized or persecuted.

Id The psychic structure, present at birth, that represents physiological drives and is fully unconscious.

Illusions Sensations that give rise to misperceptions.

Imaginary audience An aspect of adolescent egocentrism; the belief that other people are as concerned with our thoughts and behaviors as we are.

Immune system The system of the body that recognizes and destroys foreign agents (antigens) that invade the body.

Implicit memory Memory that is suggested (implied) but not plainly expressed, as illustrated in the things that people *do* but do not state clearly; also referred to as *nondeclarative memory.*

Imprinting A process occurring during a critical period in the development of an organism, in which that organism responds to a stimulus in a manner that will afterward be difficult to modify.

Incentive An object, person, or situation perceived as capable of satisfying a need or as desirable for its own sake.

Incubation In problem solving, a process that may sometimes occur when we stand back from a frustrating problem for a while and the solution "suddenly" appears.

Independent variable A condition in a scientific study that is manipulated so that its effects may be observed.

Individualist A person who defines herself or himself in terms of personal traits and gives priority to her or his own goals.

Individual psychology Adler's psychodynamic theory, which emphasizes feelings of inferiority and the creative self.

Infantile amnesia Inability to recall events that occurred prior to the age of 3 or so; also termed *childhood amnesia*.

Infer To go to the general from the particular; to draw a conclusion.

Inferential statistics The branch of statistics concerned with the confidence with which conclusions drawn about samples can be extended to the populations from which the samples were drawn.

Inferiority complex Feelings of inferiority hypothesized by Adler to serve as a central motivating force.

Infinite creativity The capacity to combine words into original sentences.

Inflammation Increased blood flow to an injured area of the body, resulting in redness, warmth, and an increased supply of white blood cells.

Informed consent A participant's agreement to participate in research after receiving information about the purposes of the study and the nature of the treatments.

Insanity A legal term descriptive of a person judged to be incapable of recognizing right from wrong or of conforming his or her behavior to the law.

Insight In Gestalt psychology, a sudden perception of relationships among the mentally represented elements of a problem that permits its solution.

Instinct A stereotyped pattern of behavior triggered by a particular stimulus and nearly identical among members of a species, even when reared in isolation.

Instinctive An inborn pattern of behavior that is triggered by a particular stimulus.

Intelligence A general mental capability that involves the ability to reason, plan, solve problems, think abstractly, comprehend complex ideas, learn quickly, and learn from experience.

Intelligence quotient (IQ) (a) Originally, a ratio obtained by dividing a child's score (or mental age) on an intelligence test by chronological age. (b) Generally, a score on an intelligence test.

Interference theory The view that we might forget stored material because other learning interferes with it.

Internals People who perceive the ability to attain reinforcements as largely within themselves.

Interneuron A neuron that transmits a neural impulse from a sensory neuron to a motor neuron.

Interposition A monocular cue for depth based on the fact that a nearby object obscures a more distant object behind it.

Interpretation In psychoanalysis, an explanation of a client's utterance according to psychoanalytic theory.

Intimacy Close acquaintance and familiarity; a characteristic of a relationship in which partners share their inmost feelings.

Intrinsic rewards The rewards associated with learning goals, such as self-esteem and increased understanding and insight.

Introspection Deliberate looking into one's own cognitive processes to examine one's thoughts and feelings and to gain self-knowledge.

Introversion A trait characterized by tendencies to direct one's interests inward and to inhibit impulses.

Iris A muscular membrane whose dilation regulates the amount of light that enters the eye.

J

James–Lange theory of emotion The view that certain external stimuli instinctively trigger specific patterns of arousal and action, such as fighting or fleeing. This theory says that we experience emotions as a consequence of our physiological and behavioral responses.

Just noticeable difference (jnd) The minimal amount by which a source of energy must be increased or decreased so that a difference in intensity will be perceived.

K

Kinesthesis The sense that informs us about the positions and motion of parts of our bodies.

L

La belle indifférence A French term descriptive of the lack of concern sometimes shown by people with conversion disorder.

Language The communication of information by means of symbols arranged according to rules of grammar.

Language acquisition device (LAD) In psycholinguistic theory, neural "prewiring" that facilitates the child's learning of grammar.

Latent content In psychodynamic theory, the symbolized or underlying content of dreams.

Latent learning Learning that is hidden, or concealed.

Lateral hypothalamus An area at the side of the hypothalamus that appears to function as a start-eating center.

Law of effect Thorndike's view that pleasant events stamp in responses, and unpleasant events stamp them out.

Learned helplessness A model for the acquisition of depressive behavior based on findings that organisms in unchangeable aversive situations may learn to do nothing.

Learning A relatively permanent change in behavior that results from experience.

Lens A transparent body behind the iris that focuses an image on the retina.

Lesion An injury that results in impaired behavior or loss of a function.

Leukocytes White blood cells.

Life expectancy The amount of time a person can be expected to live in a given setting.

Life span The maximum amount of time a person can live under optimal conditions.

Limbic system A group of structures involved in memory, motivation, and emotion that forms a fringe along the inner edge of the cerebrum.

Linguistic-relativity hypothesis The view that language structures the way we view the world.

Locus of control The place (locus) to which an individual attributes control over the receiving of reinforcers—either inside or outside the self.

Longitudinal research The study of developmental processes by taking repeated measures of the same group of people at various stages of development.

Long-term memory The type or stage of memory capable of relatively permanent storage.

Long-term potentiation (LTP) Enhanced efficiency in synaptic transmission that follows brief, rapid stimulation.

LSD Lysergic acid diethylamide. A hallucinogenic drug.

M

Maintenance rehearsal Mental repetition of information to keep it in memory.

Major depressive disorder A serious to severe depressive disorder in which the person may show loss of appetite, psychomotor retardation, and in extreme cases, delusions of worthlessness.

Manic Elated; showing excessive excitement.

Manifest content In psychodynamic theory, the reported content of dreams.

Marijuana The dried vegetable matter of the *Cannabis sativa* plant.

Maturation The process of development as guided by the unfolding of the genetic code.

Mean A type of average that is calculated by adding all the scores in a distribution and then dividing the sum by the number of scores.

Means–end analysis A heuristic device in which we try to solve a problem by evaluating the difference between the current situation and the goal.

Measures of central tendency "Averages" that show the center or balancing points of a distribution of scores or measurements.

Median The central score in a frequency distribution; the score beneath which 50% of the cases fall.

Medulla An oblong area of the hindbrain involved in regulation of heartbeat and respiration.

Memory The processes by which information is encoded, stored, and retrieved.

Memory trace An assumed change in the nervous system that reflects the impression made by a stimulus. Memory traces are said to be "held" in sensory registers.

Menarche The beginning of menstruation.

Menopause The cessation of menstruation.

Mental age (MA) The accumulated months of credit that a person earns on the Stanford–Binet Intelligence Scale.

Mental image An internal image or visual representation that is used in thinking and memory.

Mental set The tendency to respond to a new problem with an approach that was successfully used with similar problems.

Mescaline A hallucinogenic drug derived from the mescal (peyote) cactus.

Meta-analysis A method for combining and averaging the results of individual research studies.

Metamemory Self-awareness of the ways memory functions, allowing the person to encode, store, and retrieve information effectively.

Method of savings A measure of retention in which the difference between the number of repetitions originally required to learn a list and the number of repetitions required to relearn the list after a certain amount of time has elapsed is calculated.

Migraine headaches Throbbing headaches that are connected with changes in the supply of blood to the head.

Misinformation effect The shaping of bogus or slanted memories by providing inaccurate information as, for example, in the form of "leading questions."

Model An organism that engages in a response that is then imitated by another organism.

Modeling A behavior-therapy technique in which a client observes and imitates a person who approaches and copes with feared objects or situations; In social-cognitive theory, exhibiting behaviors that others will imitate or acquire through observational learning.

Mode The most frequently occurring number or score in a distribution.

Monochromat A person who is sensitive to black and white only and hence color-blind.

Monocular cues Stimuli suggestive of depth that can be perceived with only one eye.

Monozygotic (MZ) twins Twins that develop from a single fertilized ovum that divides in two early in prenatal development. MZ twins thus share the same genetic code. Also called *identical twins*.

Mood disorder A disturbance in expressed emotions, generally involving excessive or inappropriate sadness or elation.

Motion parallax A monocular cue for depth based on the perception that nearby objects appear to move more rapidly in relation to our own motion.

Motivation The state in which an organism experiences an inducement or incentive to do something.

Motive A hypothetical state within an organism that propels the organism toward a goal.

Motor cortex The section of cortex that lies in the frontal lobe, just across the central fissure from the sensory cortex. Neural impulses in the motor cortex are linked to muscular responses throughout the body.

Multiple approach–avoidance conflict A type of conflict in which each of a number of goals produces approach and avoidance motives.

Multiple personality disorder The previous term for *dissociative identity disorder*.

Mutation A sudden variation in an inheritable characteristic as distinguished from a variation that results from generations of gradual selection.

Mutism Refusal to talk.

Myelin A fatty substance that encases and insulates axons, facilitating transmission of neural impulses.

Myotonia Muscle tension.

N

Narcolepsy A "sleep attack" in which a person falls asleep suddenly and irresistibly.

Narcotics Drugs used to relieve pain and induce sleep. The term is usually reserved for opiates.

Naturalistic observation A scientific method in which organisms are observed in their natural environments.

Natural selection A core concept of the theory of evolution that holds that adaptive genetic variations among members of a species enable individuals with those variations to survive and reproduce. As a result, such variations tend to be preserved, whereas nonadaptive variations tend to drop out.

Nature The inborn, innate character of an organism.

Need A state of deprivation.

Negative correlation A relationship between two variables in which one variable increases as the other decreases.

Negative reinforcer A reinforcer that when *removed* increases the frequency of an operant.

Negative symptoms Those symptoms of schizophrenia that reflect the absence of appropriate behavior, such as blank faces, monotonic voices, and motionless bodies.

Neonate A newborn child, especially during the first month.

Nerve A bundle of axons from many neurons.

Neural impulse The electro chemical discharge of a nerve cell, or neuron.

Neuron A specialized cell of the nervous system that transmits messages.

Neuroticism A personality trait characterized largely by persistent anxiety; Eysenck's term for emotional instability.

Neurotransmitters Chemical substances involved in the transmission of neural impulses from one neuron to another.

Nonconscious Descriptive of bodily processes, such as growing hair, of which we cannot become conscious. We may "recognize" that our hair is growing but cannot directly experience the biological process.

Non-rapid-eye-movement (NREM) sleep The first four stages of sleep.

Nonsense syllables Meaningless sets of two consonants, with a vowel sandwiched between, that are used in the study of memory.

Norepinephrine A neurotransmitter whose action is similar to that of the hormone epinephrine and that may play a role in depression.

Normal distribution A symmetrical distribution that is assumed to reflect chance fluctuations, giving rise to a normal curve or bell-shaped curve.

Nurture The sum total of the environmental factors that affect an organism from conception onward. (In another usage, *nurture* refers to the act of nourishing and otherwise promoting the development of youngsters.)

O

Objective responsibility According to Piaget, the assignment of blame according to the amount of damage done rather than the motives of the actor.

Objective tests Tests whose items must be answered in a specified, limited manner. Tests whose items have concrete answers that are considered correct.

Object permanence Recognition that objects removed from sight still exist, as demonstrated in young children by continued pursuit.

Observational learning A form of cognitive learning in which we learn by observing others—regardless of whether we perform what we have learned or not.

Obsessive–compulsive disorder (OCD) An anxiety disorder defined by recurrent, anxiety-provoking thoughts or images that seem irrational and beyond control (obsessions) and seemingly irresistible urges to engage in thoughts or behaviors that tend to reduce the anxiety (compulsions).

Occipital lobe The lobe that lies behind and below the parietal lobe and behind the temporal lobe.

Oedipus complex A conflict of the phallic stage in which the boy wishes to possess his mother sexually and perceives his father as a rival in love.

Olfactory nerve The nerve that transmits information concerning odors from olfactory receptors to the brain.

Operant The same as an operant behavior.

Operant behavior Behavior that operates on, or manipulates, the environment.

Operant conditioning A simple form of learning in which an organism learns to engage in certain behavior because it is reinforced.

Opiates A group of narcotics derived from the opium poppy that provide a euphoric rush and depress the nervous system.

Opioids Chemicals that act on opiate receptors but are not derived from the opium poppy.

Opponent-process theory The theory that color vision is made possible by three types of cones, some of which respond to red or green light, some to blue or yellow, and some to the intensity of light.

Optic nerve The nerve that transmits sensory information from the eye to the brain.

Organizing effect The directional effect of sex hormones—for example, along typical male or female patterns of mating.

Organ of Corti The receptor for hearing that lies on the basilar membrane in the cochlea.

Orgasm The height, or climax, of sexual excitement, involving involuntary muscle contractions, release of sexual tensions, and usually, subjective feelings of pleasure.

Orienting response An unlearned response in which an organism attends to a stimulus.

Overregularization The application of regular grammatical rules for forming inflections (e.g., past tense and plurals) to irregular verbs and nouns.

P

Paired associates Nonsense syllables presented in pairs in experiments that measure recall.

Panic disorder The recurrent experiencing of attacks of extreme anxiety in the absence of external stimuli that usually elicit anxiety.

Paranoid personality disorder A personality disorder characterized by persistent suspiciousness but not involving the disorganization of paranoid schizophrenia.

Paranoid schizophrenia A type of schizophrenia characterized primarily by delusions—commonly of persecution—and by vivid hallucinations.

Parasympathetic nervous system The branch of the autonomic nervous system that is most active during processes that restore reserves of energy to the body, such as relaxing and eating. When people relax, the parasympathetic nervous system decelerates the heart rate, normalizes blood pressure, relaxes muscles, and so on. The parasympathetic division also stimulates digestion.

Parasympathetic The branch of the ANS that is most active during processes such as digestion that restore the body's reserves of energy.

Parietal lobe The lobe that lies just behind the central fissure.

Partial reinforcement One of several reinforcement schedules in which not every correct response is reinforced.

Passion Strong romantic and sexual feelings.

Passive smoking Inhaling smoke from the tobacco products and exhalations of other people; also called *secondhand smoking*.

Perception The process by which sensations are organized into an inner representation of the world.

Perceptual organization The tendency to integrate perceptual elements into meaningful patterns.

Peripheral nervous system The part of the nervous system consisting of the somatic nervous system and the autonomic nervous system.

Peripheral route In persuasive arguments, associating viewpoints with tangential issues, such as who endorses a product rather than the qualities of the product itself.

Personal fable Another aspect of adolescent egocentrism; the belief that our feelings and ideas are special and unique and that we are invulnerable.

Personality The reasonably stable patterns of emotions, motives, and behavior that distinguish one person from another.

Personality disorders Enduring patterns of maladaptive behavior that are sources of distress to the individual or others.

Perspective A monocular cue for depth based on the convergence (coming together) of parallel lines as they recede into the distance.

Phallic symbol A sign that represents the penis.

Phencyclidine (PCP) Another hallucinogenic drug whose name is an acronym for its chemical structure.

Phenotype One's actual development and appearance based on one's genotype and environmental influences.

Pheromone A chemical secretion detected by other members of the same species that stimulates a certain kind of behavior.

Phi phenomenon The perception of movement as a result of sequential presentation of visual stimuli.

Photoreceptors Cells that respond to light.

Pitch The highness or lowness of a sound as determined by the frequency of the sound waves.

Pituitary gland The gland that secretes growth hormone, prolactin, antidiuretic hormone, and other hormones.

Placebo A bogus treatment that has the appearance of being genuine.

Placenta A membrane that permits the exchange of nutrients and waste products between the mother and her developing child but does not allow the maternal and fetal bloodstreams to mix.

Place theory The theory that the pitch of a sound is determined by the section of the basilar membrane that vibrates in response to the sound.

Plateau phase The second phase of the sexual response cycle, which is characterized by increases in vasocongestion, muscle tension, heart rate, and blood pressure in preparation for orgasm.

Polarization In social psychology, taking an extreme position or attitude on an issue.

Polarize To ready a neuron for firing by creating an internal negative charge in relation to the body fluid outside the cell membrane.

Polygenic Referring to traits that are influenced by combinations of genes.

Pons A structure of the hindbrain involved in breathing, attention, sleep, and dreams.

Population A complete group of organisms or events.

Positive correlation A relationship between variables in which one variable increases as the other also increases.

Positive psychology The field of psychology that is about personal well-being and satisfaction; joy, sensual pleasure, and happiness; and optimism and hope for the future.

Positive reinforcer A reinforcer that when *presented* increases the frequency of an operant.

Positive symptoms Those symptoms of schizophrenia that indicate the presence of inappropriate behavior, such as hallucinations, delusions, agitation, and inappropriate giggling.

Postconventional level According to Kohlberg, a period during which moral judgments are derived from moral principles and people look to themselves to set moral standards.

Postformal stage A proposed stage of cognitive development in which the individual has achieved knowledge that judgments of people and behavior are made within certain value systems, has begun to narrow infinite possibilities into practical choices, and has overcome the egocentrism of adolescence.

Posttraumatic stress disorder (PTSD) A disorder that follows a distressing event outside the range of normal human experience and that is characterized by features such as intense fear, avoidance of stimuli associated with the event, and reliving of the event.

Preconscious In psychodynamic theory, descriptive of material that is not in awareness but can be brought into awareness by focusing one's attention.

Preconventional level According to Kohlberg, a period during which moral judgments are based largely on expectation of rewards or punishments.

Predictive validity The extent to which a diagnosis permits one to predict the course of a disorder and the type of treatment that may be of help.

Prefrontal lobotomy The severing or destruction of a section of the frontal lobe of the brain.

Prejudice An attitude toward a group that leads people to evaluate members of that group negatively.

Preoperational stage The second of Piaget's stages, characterized by illogical use of words and symbols, spotty logic, and egocentrism.

Presbyopia A condition characterized by brittleness of the lens.

Primacy effect The tendency to evaluate others in terms of first impressions; The tendency to recall the initial items in a series of items.

Primary drives Unlearned, or physiological, drives.

Primary mental abilities According to Thurstone, the basic abilities that make up intelligence.

Primary reinforcer A reinforcer whose effectiveness is based on the biological makeup of the organism and not on learning.

Priming The activation of specific associations in memory, often as a result of repetition and without making a conscious effort to access the memory.

Proactive interference The interference of old learning with the ability to retrieve material learned recently.

Programmed learning A method of teaching that breaks down tasks into small steps, each of which is reinforced and then combined to form the correct behavioral chain.

Projective test A psychological test that presents ambiguous stimuli onto which the test-taker projects his or her own personality in making a response.

Prospective memory Memory to perform an act in the future, as at a certain time or when a certain event occurs.

Prototype A concept of a category of objects or events that serves as a good example of the category.

Proximity Nearness. The perceptual tendency to group together objects that are near one another.

Psychic structure In psychodynamic theory, a hypothesized mental structure that helps explain different aspects of behavior.

Psychoactive substances Drugs that have psychological effects such as stimulation or distortion of perceptions.

Psychoanalysis Freud's method of exploring human personality; The school of psychology that asserts that much of our behavior and mental processes is governed by unconscious ideas and impulses that have their origins in childhood conflicts.

Psychodynamic theory Sigmund Freud's perspective, which emphasizes the importance of unconscious motives and conflicts as forces that determine behavior. *Dynamic* refers to the concept of (psychological) forces in motion.

Psychodynamic therapy A type of psychotherapy that is based on Freud's thinking and that assumes that psychological problems reflect early childhood experiences and internal conflicts.

Psycholinguistic theory The view that language learning involves an interaction between environmental factors and an inborn tendency to acquire language.

Psychological disorders Patterns of behavior or mental processes that are connected with emotional distress or significant impairment in functioning.

Psychological hardiness A cluster of traits that buffer stress and are characterized by commitment, challenge, and control.

Psychology The science that studies behavior and mental processes.

Psychomotor retardation Slowness in motor activity and (apparently) in thought.

Psychoneuroimmunology The field that studies the relationships between psychological factors (e.g., attitudes and overt behavior patterns) and the functioning of the immune system.

Psychosexual development In psychodynamic theory, the process by which libidinal energy is expressed through different erogenous zones during different stages of development.

Psychosocial development Erikson's theory of personality and development, which emphasizes social relationships and eight stages of growth.

Psychosurgery Surgery intended to promote psychological changes or to relieve disordered behavior.

Psychotherapy A systematic interaction between a therapist and a client that brings psychological principles to bear on influencing the client's thoughts, feelings, and/or behavior to help that client overcome psychological disorders, adjust to problems in living, or develop as an individual.

Puberty The period of physical development during which sexual reproduction first becomes possible.

Punishment An unpleasant stimulus that suppresses the behavior it follows.

Pupil The apparently black opening in the center of the iris through which light enters the eye.

Pure research Research conducted without concern for immediate applications.

R

Random sample A sample drawn so that each member of a population has an equal chance of being selected to participate.

Range A measure of variability defined as the high score in a distribution minus the low score.

Rapid-eye-movement (REM) sleep A stage of sleep characterized by rapid eye movements, which have been linked to dreaming.

Rapid flight of ideas Rapid speech and topic changes, characteristic of manic behavior.

Rational-emotive behavior therapy (REBT) Albert Ellis's form of therapy that encourages clients to challenge and correct irrational beliefs and maladaptive behaviors.

Reality testing The capacity to perceive one's environment and oneself according to accurate sensory impressions.

Rebound anxiety Anxiety that can occur when one discontinues use of a tranquilizer.

Recall Retrieval or reconstruction of learned material.

Recency effect The tendency to evaluate others in terms of the most recent impression; The tendency to recall the last items in a series of items.

Receptor site A location on a dendrite of a receiving neuron tailored to receive a neurotransmitter.

Reciprocal determinism Bandura's term for the social-cognitive view that people influence their environment just as their environment influences them.

Reciprocity In interpersonal attraction, the tendency to return feelings and attitudes that are expressed about us.

Recognition In information processing, the easiest memory task, involving identification of objects or events encountered before.

Reflex A simple unlearned response to a stimulus.

Refractory period A phase following firing during which a neuron is less sensitive to messages from other neurons and will not fire; In the sexual response cycle, a period of time following orgasm during which an individual is not responsive to sexual stimulation.

Reinforce To follow a response with a stimulus that increases the frequency of the response.

Reinforcement A stimulus that follows a response and increases the frequency of the response.

Relearning A measure of retention. Material is usually relearned more quickly than it is learned initially.

Reliability The consistency of a method of measurements, as, for example, shown by obtaining similar scores on different testing occasions.

Replicate Repeat, reproduce, copy.

Representativeness heuristic A decision-making heuristic in which people make judgments about samples according to the populations they appear to represent.

Repression In Freud's psychodynamic theory, the ejection of anxiety-evoking ideas, impulses, or images from conscious awareness.

Resistance The tendency to block the free expression of impulses and primitive ideas—a reflection of the defense mechanism of repression.

Resistance stage The second stage of the GAS, characterized by prolonged sympathetic activity in an effort to restore lost energy and repair damage; also called the *adaptation stage*.

Resolution phase The fourth phase of the sexual response cycle, during which the body gradually returns to its prearoused state.

Resting potential The electrical potential across the neural membrane when it is not responding to other neurons.

Reticular formation A part of the brain involved in attention, sleep, and arousal.

Retina The area of the inner surface of the eye that contains rods and cones.

Retinal disparity A binocular cue for depth based on the difference in the image cast by an object on the retinas of the eyes as the object moves closer or farther away.

Retrieval The process of locating stored information and returning it to consciousness; the third stage of information processing.

Retrieval cue A clue or prompt that can be used to enable, or trigger, the recovery of a memory in storage.

Retroactive interference The interference of new learning with the ability to retrieve material learned previously.

Retrograde amnesia Failure to remember events that occurred prior to physical trauma because of the effects of the trauma.

Retrospective memory Memory for past events, activities, and learning experiences, as shown by explicit (episodic and semantic) and implicit memories.

Reversibility According to Piaget, recognition that processes can be undone, and things can be made as they were.

Reward A pleasant stimulus that increases the frequency of the behavior it follows.

Risky shift The tendency to make riskier decisions as a member of a group than as an individual acting independently.

Rods Rod-shaped photoreceptors that are sensitive only to the intensity of light.

Romantic love An intense, positive emotion that involves sexual attraction, feelings of caring, and the belief that one is in love.

Rooting The turning of an infant's head toward a touch, such as by the mother's nipple.

Rote Mechanical associative learning that is based on repetition.

S

s Spearman's symbol for *specific* factors, or *s factors,* which he believed accounted for individual abilities.

Saccadic eye movement The rapid jumps made by a person's eyes as they fixate on different points.

Sample Part of a population.

Sandwich generation People in middle adulthood who are responsible for meeting the needs of their children yet also burdened by the needs of aging parents.

Satiety The state of being satisfied; fullness.

Savings The difference between the number of repetitions originally required to learn a list and the number of repetitions required to relearn the list after a certain amount of time has elapsed.

Scaffolding Vygotsky's term for temporary cognitive structures or methods of solving problems that help the child as he or she learns to function independently.

Schema A way of mentally representing the world, such as a belief or an expectation, that can influence perception of persons, objects, and situations; According to Piaget, a hypothetical mental structure that permits the classification and organization of new information.

Schizoid personality disorder A personality disorder characterized by social withdrawal.

Schizophrenia A psychotic disorder characterized by loss of control of thought processes and inappropriate emotional responses.

Schizotypal personality disorder A personality disorder characterized by oddities of thought and behavior but not involving bizarre psychotic behaviors.

Scientific method An approach to acquiring or confirming knowledge that is based on gathering measurable evidence through observation and experimentation. Evidence is often obtained to test hypotheses.

Secondary reinforcer A stimulus that gains reinforcement value through association with established reinforcers.

Secondary sex characteristics Characteristics that distinguish females and males, such as distribution of body hair and depth of voice, but that are not directly involved in reproduction.

Sedative A drug that relieves nervousness or agitation or puts one to sleep.

Selection factor A source of bias that may occur in research findings when participants are allowed to choose for themselves a certain treatment in a scientific study.

Selective attention The focus of one's consciousness on a particular stimulus.

Selective avoidance Diverting one's attention from information that is inconsistent with one's attitudes.

Selective exposure Deliberately seeking and attending to information that is consistent with one's attitudes.

Selective optimization with compensation Reshaping of one's life to concentrate on what one considers important and meaningful in the face of physical decline and possible cognitive impairment.

Selective serotonin-reuptake inhibitors (SSRIs) Antidepressant drugs that work by blocking the reuptake of serotonin by presynaptic neurons.

Self-actualization According to Maslow and other humanistic psychologists, self-initiated striving to become what one is capable of being. The motive for reaching one's full potential, for expressing one's unique capabilities.

Self-efficacy expectations Our beliefs that we can bring about desired changes through our own efforts.

Self-ideal A mental image of what we believe we ought to be.

Self-serving bias The tendency to view one's successes as stemming from internal factors and one's failures as stemming from external factors.

Semantic Having to do with the meanings of words and symbols.

Semantic code Mental representation of information according to its meaning.

Semanticity Meaning. The quality of language in which words are used as symbols for objects, events, or ideas.

Semantic memory General knowledge, as opposed to episodic memory.

Semicircular canals Structures of the inner ear that monitor body movement and position.

Sensation The stimulation of sensory receptors and the transmission of sensory information to the central nervous system.

Sensitization The type of sensory adaptation in which we become more sensitive to stimuli that are low in magnitude; also called positive adaptation.

Sensorimotor stage The first of Piaget's stages of cognitive development, characterized by coordination of sensory information and motor activity, early exploration of the environment, and lack of language.

Sensorineural deafness The forms of deafness that result from damage to hair cells or the auditory nerve.

Sensory adaptation The processes by which organisms become more sensitive to stimuli that are low in magnitude and less sensitive to stimuli that are constant or ongoing in magnitude.

Sensory memory The type or stage of memory first encountered by a stimulus. Sensory memory holds impressions briefly, but long enough so that series of perceptions are psychologically continuous.

Sensory register A system of memory that holds information briefly, but long enough so that it can be processed further. There may be a sensory register for every sense.

Serial-position effect The tendency to recall more accurately the first and last items in a series.

Serotonin A neurotransmitter, deficiencies of which have been linked to affective disorders, anxiety, and insomnia.

Serum cholesterol Cholesterol in the blood.

Set point A weight range that one's body is programmed to maintain such that the body will increase or decrease its metabolic rate according to the amount of calories one consumes.

Sex chromosomes The 23rd pair of chromosomes, whose genetic material determines the sex of the individual.

Sexual orientation The directionality of one's sexual and romantic interests; that is, whether one is sexually attracted to, and desires to form a romantic relationship with, members of the other sex or of one's own sex.

Sexual response cycle Masters and Johnson's model of sexual response, which consists of four stages or phases: excitement, plateau, orgasm, and resolution.

Shadowing A monocular cue for depth based on the fact that opaque objects block light and produce shadows.

Shape constancy The tendency to perceive an object as being as the same shape although the retinal image varies in shape as it rotates.

Shaping A procedure for teaching complex behaviors that at first reinforces approximations of the target behavior.

Short-term memory The type or stage of memory that can hold information for up to a minute or so after the trace of the stimulus decays; also called *working memory*.

Signal-detection theory The view that the perception of sensory stimuli involves the interaction of physical, biological, and psychological factors.

Similarity The perceptual tendency to group together objects that are similar in appearance.

Situational attribution An assumption that a person's behavior is determined by external circumstances such as the social pressure found in a situation.

Size constancy The tendency to perceive an object as being the same size even as the size of its retinal image changes according to the object's distance.

Sleep apnea Temporary absence or cessation of breathing while asleep. (From Greek and Latin roots meaning "without" and "breathing.")

Sleep terrors Frightening dreamlike experiences that occur during the deepest stage of NREM sleep. Nightmares, in contrast, occur during REM sleep.

Social-cognitive theory A school of psychology in the behaviorist tradition that includes cognitive factors in the explanation and prediction of behavior; formerly termed social-learning theory.

Social decision schemes Rules for predicting the final outcome of group decision making.

Social facilitation The process by which a person's performance increases when other members of a group engage in similar behavior.

Social influence The area of social psychology that studies the ways in which people influence the thoughts, feelings, and behavior of others.

Social loafing The process by which a person's performance decreases when other members of a group engage in similar behavior, apparently because the person believes that strenuous effort is unnecessary.

Social norms Explicit and implicit rules that reflect social expectations and influence the ways people behave in social situations.

Social perception A subfield of social psychology that studies the ways in which we form and modify impressions of others.

Social phobia An irrational, excessive fear of public scrutiny.

Social psychology The field of psychology that studies the nature and causes of behavior and mental processes in social situations.

Social skills training A behavior-therapy method for helping people in their interpersonal relations that uses self-monitoring, behavior rehearsal, and feedback.

Sociocultural perspective The view that focuses on the roles of ethnicity, gender, culture, and socioeconomic status in personality formation, behavior, and mental processes.

Somatic nervous system The division of the peripheral nervous system that connects the central nervous system with sensory receptors, skeletal muscles, and the surface of the body.

Somatoform disorders Disorders in which people complain of physical (somatic) problems even though no physical abnormality can be found.

Somatosensory cortex The section of cortex in which sensory stimulation is projected. It lies just behind the central fissure in the parietal lobe.

Species A category of biological classification consisting of related organisms that are capable of interbreeding. *Homo sapiens*—humans—make up one species.

Specific phobia Persistent fear of a specific object or situation.

Spinal cord A column of nerves within the spine that transmits messages from sensory receptors to the brain and from the brain to muscles and glands.

Spinal reflex A simple, unlearned response to a stimulus that may involve only two neurons.

Spontaneous recovery The recurrence of an extinguished response as a function of the passage of time.

Standard deviation A measure of the variability of a distribution, obtained by the formula

$$\text{S.D.} = \sqrt{\frac{\text{Sum of } d^2}{N}}$$

Standardization In psychological testing, the process by which one obtains and organizes test scores from various population groups, so that the results of a person completing a test can be compared to those of others of his or her sex, in his or her age group, and so on.

State-dependent memory Information that is better retrieved in the physiological or emotional state in which it was encoded and stored, or learned.

Statistically significant difference A difference between groups that is large enough so that it is unlikely to be due to chance fluctuation.

Statistics Numerical facts assembled in such a manner that they provide useful information about measures or scores (from the Latin *status*, meaning "standing" or "position").

Stereotype A fixed, conventional idea about a group.

Stimulant A drug that increases the rate of activity of the nervous system.

Stimulus An environmental condition that elicits a response.

Stimulus motive A state within an organism that propels it toward increasing the amount of stimulation it obtains.

Storage The maintenance of information over time; the second stage of information processing.

Stratified sample A sample drawn so that identified subgroups in the population are represented proportionately in the sample.

Stress The demand that is made on an organism to adapt, cope, or adjust.

Stressor An event that gives rise to feelings of stress.

Stroboscopic motion A visual illusion in which the perception of motion is generated by a series of stationary images that are presented in rapid succession.

Structuralism The school of psychology that argues the mind consists of three basic elements—sensations, feelings, and images—that combine to form experience.

Stupor A condition in which the senses, thought, and movement are dulled.

Subjective moral judgment According to Piaget, moral judgment that is based on the motives of the perpetrator.

Subliminal stimulation Sensory stimulation that is below a person's absolute threshold for conscious perception.

Substance abuse Repeated use of a substance despite the fact that it is causing or compounding social, occupational, psychological, or physical problems.

Substance dependence Loss of control over use of a substance. Biologically speaking, dependence is typified by tolerance, withdrawal symptoms, or both.

Successive approximations In operant conditioning, a series of behaviors that gradually become more similar to a target behavior.

Superego The third psychic structure, which functions as a moral guardian and sets forth high standards for behavior.

Suppression The deliberate, or conscious, placing of certain ideas, impulses, or images out of awareness.

Survey A method of scientific investigation in which a large sample of people answer questions about their attitudes or behavior.

Sympathetic The branch of the ANS that is most active during emotional responses— such as fear and anxiety— that spend the body's reserves of energy.

Sympathetic nervous system The branch of the autonomic nervous system that is most active during processes that spend body energy from stored reserves, such as in a fight-or-flight reaction to a predator or when you are anxious about a big test. When people experience fear, the sympathetic nervous system accelerates the heart rate, raises blood pressure, tenses muscles, and so on.

Synapse A junction between the axon terminals of one neuron and the dendrites or cell body of another neuron.

Syntax The rules for forming grammatical phrases and sentences in a language.

Systematic desensitization Wolpe's method for reducing fears by associating a hierarchy of images of fear-evoking stimuli with deep muscle relaxation.

Systematic random search An algorithm for solving problems in which each possible solution is tested according to a particular set of rules.

T

Taste buds The sensory organs for taste. They contain taste cells and are located on the tongue.

Taste cells Receptor cells that are sensitive to taste.

Temporal lobe The lobe that lies below the lateral fissure, near the temples of the head.

Teratogens Environmental influences or agents that can damage the embryo or fetus.

Texture gradient A monocular cue for depth based on the perception that closer objects appear to have rougher (more detailed) surfaces.

Thalamus An area near the center of the brain involved in the relay of sensory information to the cortex and in the functions of sleep and attention.

Theory A formulation of relationships underlying observed events.

Theory of multiple intelligences Gardner's view that there are several intelligences, not just one.

Theta waves Slow brain waves sometimes accompanied by a hypnagogic state.

Thinking Paying attention to information, mentally representing it, reasoning about it, and making decisions about it.

Time out Removal of an organism from a situation in which reinforcement is available when unwanted behavior is shown.

Tip-of-the-tongue (TOT) phenomenon The feeling that information is stored in memory although it cannot be readily retrieved; also called the *feeling-of-knowing experience*.

Token economy A controlled environment in which people are reinforced for desired behaviors with tokens (such as poker chips) that may be exchanged for privileges.

Tolerance Habituation to a drug, with the result that increasingly higher doses of the drug are needed to achieve similar effects.

Top-down processing The use of contextual information or knowledge of a pattern to organize parts of the pattern.

Trait A relatively stable aspect of personality that is inferred from behavior and assumed to give rise to consistent behavior.

Transcendental meditation (TM) The simplified form of meditation brought to the United States by the Maharishi Mahesh Yogi and used as a method for coping with stress.

Transference Responding to one person (such as a spouse or the psychoanalyst) in a way that is similar to the way one responded to another person (such as a parent) in childhood.

Treatment In experiments, a condition received by participants so that its effects may be observed.

Triangular model of love Sternberg's view that love involves combinations of three components: intimacy, passion, and commitment.

Triarchic theory of intelligence Sternberg's theory that intelligence has three prongs, consisting of analytical, creative, and practical intelligence ("street smarts").

Trichromat A person with normal color vision.

Trichromatic theory The theory that color vision is made possible by three types of cones, some of which respond to red light, some to green, and some to blue.

Two-point threshold The least distance by which two rods touching the skin must be separated before the person will report that there are two rods, not one, on 50% of occasions.

Type A behavior The Type A behavior pattern is characterized by a sense of time urgency, competitiveness, and hostility.

U

Umbilical cord A tube between the mother and her developing child through which nutrients and waste products are conducted.

Unconditional positive regard In client-centered therapy, the acceptance of the value of another person, although not necessarily acceptance of everything the person does.

Unconditioned response (UCR) An unlearned response to an unconditioned stimulus.

Unconditioned stimulus (UCS) A stimulus that elicits a response from an organism prior to conditioning.

Unconscious In psychodynamic theory, descriptive of ideas and feelings that are not available to awareness.

Uplifts Notable pleasant daily conditions and experiences.

V

Validity The extent to which a method of measurement measures what it is supposed to measure, as, for example, shown by the extent to which test scores predict or are related to an external standard. In the case of intelligence tests, the external standard might involve academic performance.

Variable-interval schedule A schedule in which a variable amount of time must elapse between the previous and subsequent times that reinforcement is available.

Variable-ratio schedule A schedule in which reinforcement is provided after a variable number of correct responses.

Vasocongestion Engorgement of blood vessels with blood, which swells the genitals and breasts during sexual arousal.

Ventromedial nucleus (VMN) A central area on the underside of the hypothalamus that appears to function as a stop-eating center.

Vestibular sense The sense of equilibrium that informs us about our bodies' positions relative to gravity.

Visible light The part of the electromagnetic spectrum that stimulates the eye and produces visual sensations.

Visual acuity Sharpness of vision.

Visual code Mental representation of information as a picture.

Volunteer bias A source of bias or error in research reflecting the prospect that people who offer to participate in research studies differ systematically from people who do not.

W

Waxy flexibility A feature of catatonic schizophrenia in which people can be molded into postures that they maintain for quite some time.

Weber's constant The fraction of the intensity by which a source of physical energy must be increased or decreased so that a difference in intensity will be perceived.

Wernicke's aphasia A language disorder characterized by difficulty comprehending the meaning of spoken language.

White matter In the spinal cord, axon bundles that carry messages from and to the brain.

Wish fulfillment In dreams, the acting out of ideas and impulses that are repressed when one is conscious.

Working memory Same as *short-term memory*.

Z

Zone of proximal development (ZPD) Vygotsky's term for the situation in which a child carries out tasks with the help of someone who is more skilled, frequently an adult who represents the culture in which the child develops.

Zygote A fertilized ovum (egg cell).

Name Index

A

Abbey, A., 486
Abele, S., 492
Ablon, J. S., 455
Aboa-Éboulé, C., 391
Abraham, C., 59
Ackard, D. M., 270
Adams, A. L., 213
Adler, Alfred, 12, 344, 439
Agras, W. S., 454
Agrawal, A., 138
Ahmad, N. Y., 496
Ahs, F., 63
Aich, P., 386
Ainsworth, Mary Salter, 18, 312, 312–313, 314
Akerstedt, T., 124
Alberts, A., 319
Albrecht, Karl, 233
Alexander, G. M., 354
Alford, B. A., 486
Ali, Muhammad, 54
Allen, J. P., 321
Allen, Woody, 41, 277, 325, 333
Allport, G. W., 346
Alm, R., 250
Almeida, D. M., 327
Alston, J. Henry, 18
Altgassen, M., 188
Altman, S. E., 272
Altran, Scott, 485
Amanatullah, E. T., 354
Ambrosius, U., 47
Amodio, D. M., 180
Ances, B. M., 300
Anchin, J. C., 454
Andersen, A. E., 270
Andersen, B. L., 394, 395
Andersen, M. L., 328
Andersen, P., 394
Anderson, C. A., 176, 177
Anderson, J. A., 28
Andreano, J. M., 249, 278
Andrews, B., 414
Angelou, Maya, 48, 207, 386
Ansell, E. B., 272
Antoni, M. H., 393
Antonishak, J., 321
Antonuccio, D., 458
Apovian, C. M., 266, 267
Archer, J., 281, 365
Ardrey, Robert, 280
Arendt, J., 71
Aristotle, 8, 220, 240, 241
Arnett, J. J., 323
Arterberry, M. E., 302
Artigas, F., 415

Asbury, K., 43
Asch, S. E., 490–491, 491
Ashtari, M., 148
Ashworth, P. C. H., 129
Atkinson, R. C., 191, 205
Attanucci, J., 320
Auden, W. H., 404
Auger, A. P., 279
Austen, Jane, 185
Auyeung, Bonnie, 354
Aviezer, O., 316
Azar, B., 477

B

Babb, B., 316
Babyak, M., 461
Back, S. E., 370
Baddeley, A. D., 203, 210
Bae, S., 248
Bagchi, D., 394
Bahrick, Harry, 187, 205
Bajor, J. K., 332
Baker, J. H., 272
Baker, L. A., 253
Baker, M. C., 237
Baker, S. L., 370
Bakst, S., 417
Baldwin, S. A., 453
Balsam, P. D., 174
Baltes, Margaret, 332
Baltes, P. B., 332
Banaji, M. R., 470, 471
Bandelow, B., 405
Bandura, A., 176, 351–352, 378, 408, 443
Barak, A., 452
Barber, C. E., 332
Barber, J. G., 416
Barber, T. X., 132
Barbey, A. K., 201
Barch, D. M., 420
Bard, Philip, 290
Bardem, Javier, 7
Barelli, C., 479
Barnett, J. E., 329
Barnett, Susan, 249
Baron, R., 110, 126
Baron, R. A., 476, 485
Baron-Cohen, S., 66
Barry, Dave, 321
Barsalou, L. W., 201
Bartels, M., 252
Bartone, P. T., 379
Bartoshuk, L. M., 105
Basho, 100
Batson, C. D., 480, 496
Baucom, D. H., 454
Baumrind, Diana, 314

Baynes, K., 67
Beck, Aaron, 27, 447–448, 449, 454
Beck, A. T., 454, 486
Beck, D. R. M., 402
Beck, Hall P., 160
Beer, J., 414
Beesdo, K., 409
Begley, S., 495
Behar, E., 406
Behrman, Andy, 413
Bell, M. A., 303
Belmonte, M. K., 66
Belsky, J., 23, 312, 316, 402
Bem, Daryl J., 112, 114
Benbow, C. P., 238
Bender, L., 315
Benke, K., 388
Benoit, Chris/Nancy, 72
Benson, Herbert, 134
Benson, P. L., 497
Ben-Zur, H., 377
Berke, J., 81
Berkowitz, L., 281
Berlin, H. A., 411
Bermardin, H. J., 348
Bermudez, P., 317
Bernal, Martha E., 18
Bernstein, Carl, 494
Bernstein, D. M., 19, 25, 197
Bernstein, I. L., 302
Berra, Yogi, 203
Bexton, W. H., 262
Bhutto, Benazir, 467
Bialystok, E., 201
Bidell, M. P., 483
Bienvenu, O. J., 408
Bierman, K. L., 253
Binder, A., 110
Binder, E. B., 409
Binet, Alfred, 244, 245, 253
Binswanger, Ludwig, 356
Biran, M., 450
Bishop, E. G., 253
Biyanova, T., 27
Bjorklund, D. F., 308, 309
Blass, T., 487, 488, 489
Blavatsky, P. R., 230
Block, N., 59
Blum, K., 43
Bodamer, M. D., 232
Boehner, John, 470
Bogen, Joseph, 68
Bohner, G., 476
Bolinskey, K. P., 422
Bombeck, Erma, 265, 323
Bongar, B., 417
Bonn-Miller, M. O., 147
Boora, K., 415

Borgida, E., 292
Boss, Medard, 356
Bouchard, C., 267
Bourin, M., 457
Bouton, M. E., 156
Bowen, R., 319
Bower, Gordon, 204
Bowlby, John, 313, 314
Boyatzis, R. E., 31, 33
Boyd-Franklin, Nancy, 18
Braarud, H. C., 236
Bradley, R. H., 253
Brand, J. S., 105, 274
Bransford, J. D., 200
Bravender, T., 271
Brewer, Charles L., 210
Brewer, M. B., 360, 361
Brewin, C. R., 340
Bridges, J. S., 327
Bright, J. A., 447
Briñol, P., 471
Briones, T. L., 303
Bronstein, P., 315
Brooks, David, 493
Brooks, M. V., 394, 395
Brooks, R., 236
Brough, P., 373
Brown, A. S., 203, 204, 423, 493
Brown, G. R., 303
Brown, R., 202–203
Brown, R. J., 412
Brown, W. H., 73, 74
Brownstein, A. L., 494
Bruce, T. J., 454
Brucne, M., 497
Bryant, J., 471
Bryant, R., 407
Bryant, William Cullen, 333
Brydon, L., 373
Buchanan, A., 321
Buchanan, T. W., 373
Buckley, P. F., 421
Bucy, Paul, 63
Budney, A. J., 147
Bunting, L., 322
Burger, J. M., 473, 478, 489, 490
Burns, Robert, 480
Bush, George W., 485, 494, 495
Bushman, B. J., 176
Buss, D. M., 42, 280, 354, 477, 481, 486
Buston, K., 322
Butler, A. C., 450, 454
Buyukyazi, G., 387
Byrne, S., 494
Byron, Lord, 80

C

Cahill, L., 249, 278
Calcagni, E., 385
Calkins, Mary Whiton, 17
Callahan, J. J., 327
Callan, D. E., 199, 200
Campbell, T., 420
Campolongo, P., 148
Campos, Joseph, 286
Camus, Albert, 130
Cañal-Bruland, R., 175
Cannon, W. B., 265, 290, 382, 384
Cantalupo, C., 231
Carey, B., 112, 459
Carlsmith, J. M., 473
Carlsson, K., 65
Carlyon, R. P., 103
Carney, C. E., 129
Carré, J. M., 281
Carrey, Jim, 212
Carroll, D., 67
Carroll, J. S., 323
Carroll, Lewis, 230, 231
Carson, Rachel, 185
Carstensen, L. L., 332
Cartwright, Joanne ("Miss Muffet"), 433, 434
Carver, C. S., 284
Carver, L. J., 184
Cassaday, H. J., 146
Castelli, L., 249, 321
Castor, D., 166
Cathcart, S., 389
Cattell, Raymond B., 248
Catts, S. V., 147
Catts, V. S., 147
Cavallaro, F. I., 133
Ceci, S. J., 199, 249
Cellar, D. F., 348
Cellard, C., 419
Cerletti, Ugo, 457
Cervilla, J. A., 140
Chabaud, M., 492
Chadwick, P. D. J., 460
Chafee, M. V., 214
Chai, X. J., 249
Chambless, D. L., 450
Champagne, F. A., 71
Chan, R. C. K., 422
Chance, W. T., 265
Chang, H. Y., 478
Chang, T., 248
Chao, A., 110
Chao, M. M., 484
Chaplin, W. F., 348, 484
Chapman, G. B., 229
Chard, K. M., 407
Charles, Prince, 68
Check, E., 495
Chen, J., 455
Chen, Y-R., 360, 361
Cheney, Dick, 494
Cheng, Y., 66

Cherniak, C., 237
Chiew, V., 225
Chiu, C., 484
Chivers, M. L., 277
Chomsky, Noam, 237
Christ, S. E., 214
Chumlea, W. M. C., 298
Churchill, Sir Winston, 265
Cialdini, R. B., 476, 497
Cifani, C., 271
Cirelli, C., 125
Clancy, S. A., 19
Clark, A., 237
Clark, E. V., 235
Clark, Kenneth Bancroft, 18
Clark, Mamie Phipps, 18
Clark, S., 124
Clark, S. E., 19
Clark, T. T., 138
Clayton, A., 73, 74
Clayton, E. C., 207
Clinton, Hillary, 494–495
Cnattingius, S., 300
Cobb, C., 148
Cocking, C., 496
Coe, W. C., 133
Cohen, A., 144
Cohen, D., 458
Cohen, K. M., 278
Cohen, L. L., 394
Cohen, R., 172, 177
Cohen, S., 381
Colette, 379
Collette, Toni, 410
Collins, R. L., 139
Collins, W. A., 321
Colom, R., 238
Coltraine, S., 476
Comas-Diaz, Lillian, 18
Compton, J. S., 416
Concar, D., 146
Conduit, R., 126
Confer, J. C., 280, 481
Conger, R. D., 316
Connor, P. D., 300
Constantinidis, C., 65
Cook, J. M., 27
Cooke, B., 263
Cooper, M., 263, 271
Cooper, Z., 450
Coovadia, H., 301
Corballis, M. C., 67
Cornoldi, C., 237
Cosby, Bill, 323
Cosby, M., 478
Cosgrove, K., 59
Coskun, O., 386
Costa, Paul T., 347–348
Costigan, C. L., 321
Cotton, S. M., 130
Cowen, P. J., 414
Cox, L. C., 102
Cox, W. M., 250
Coyne, J. C., 27
Crabbe, J., 46

Craighero, Laila, 66
Craig, K. J., 408
Craik, F. I. M., 199, 200, 201
Cramer, P., 345, 496
Crano, W. D., 469, 471
Crawford, M., 16
Crick, Francis, 43
Crits-Christoph, P., 454
Crittenden, P. M., 271
Crofoot, M. C., 281
Crowe, Russell, 420
Csikszentmihalyi, M., 47, 286
Cuijpers, P., 454, 458, 459
Culver, A., 184
Cummins, R. A., 286
Cunningham, M. R., 496
Cutler, B. L., 199
Cutler, Winnifred, 275

D

Dabbs, J. M., 249, 281, 497
Dagyte, G., 457
Dahlquist, L. M., 111
Dai, S. R., 349
Daley, A., 74
Dallos, R., 271
D'Ambrosio, B. S., 309
Dana, R. H., 455
Dangerfield, Rodney, 376
Danhauer, Jeffrey, 102
Danner, Mark, 467
Darley, J. M., 496
Dart, A. M., 16
Dart, Raymond, 280
Darwin, Charles, 9, 14, 39, 40, 41, 42, 163, 285
Dasgupta, Nilanjana, 476
Daud, M. K., 103
David, D., 373, 375, 376, 454
David, E. J. R., 361
Davidoff, J., 221
Davies, J., 471
Davies, M. F., 377
Da Vinci, Leonardo, 68
Davis, D., 207
Davis, H. P., 326
Davis, J. I., 287
Dawood, K., 278, 279
DeAngelis, T., 433
De Berardis, D., 73
DeCasper, A. J., 302
De Dios, M. J., 309
de Hoog, N., 471
De Houwer, J., 469
Delgado, José, 65
Del Giudice, M. J., 365
Dell, P. F., 133
DeMarree, K. G., 469
Demeyer, M., 193
De Michele, P. E., 486
Demir, M., 287
Democritus, 8
Denmark, F. L., 16

Dennis, J., 381
DeRubeis, R. J., 454
Descartes, René, 221
De Sousa, A., 141
Devilly, G. J., 447
Devine, P. G., 475
De Vos, H. M., 132
Dhand, R., 46
Diana, Princess, 201
Dick, D. M., 138
Dickerson, B. C., 184, 185
Dickerson, F. D., 444
Dickinson, Emily, 59, 107, 473
Diehl, M., 492
Dienes, Z., 132
DiGiuseppe, R. A., 376, 377
Dindo, L., 427
Dix, Dorothea, 435
Doctorow, E. L., 80
Dodge, K. A., 281
Dollard, J., 159
Dominguez, M. H., 232
Domino, Fats, 456
Donaldson, Z. R., 71
Donovan, J. E., 139
Dorfman, D., 470
Dougherty, Darin D., 459
Dovidio, J. F., 475
Downey, J. L., 274
Driessen, E., 453
Drossel, C., 446
Drury, L. J., 435
Dube, S. R., 146
Dubiela, F. P., 124, 125
Dubow, E. F., 177
Duckworth, A. L., 29
Dufresne, A., 131
Duke, N. N., 416
Dulin, P. L., 496
Dumas, Alexandre, 24
Dummett, N., 111
Dunning, C., 329
Dunn, J. R., 421
Durante, K. M., 479
Durbin, D. L., 315
Duval, T. S., 486
Dweck, C. S., 283, 284
Dwivedi, Y., 415
Dzieweczynski, T. L., 42

E

Eagle, M., 207
Ebben, M. R., 129
Ebbinghaus, Hermann, 204, 206
Ebeling, M., 103
Eberhart, N. K., 402
Ebstein, R., 43
Egawa, T., 54
Egerton, A., 147
Ehrlich, Paul, 254
Eichenbaum, H., 184, 185, 214

Einat, H., 415
Einstein, Albert, 48, 59, 68, 222, 341, 376
Eisend, M., 471
Ekman, Paul, 285–286, 286, 288, 291
El-Baradei, Mohamed, 494
Elenkov, I., 385
Eliot, George, 332
Elizabeth II, Queen, 68
Elkind, D., 319, 321
Elkins, D. N., 15
Ellickson, P. L., 472
Elliot, A. J., 375, 479
Ellis, A., 375, 375–377, 404, 449, 454
Ellis, M. A., 281
Elms, A. C., 488
Elshout, J. J., 309
Embry, D., 142
Emerson, Ralph Waldo, 9, 311
Emmons, R. A., 375
Engelhard, I. M., 447
Engelhardt, H., 187
Epp, J., 209
Erikson, Erik, 12, 15, 311, 311–312, 321, 325, 326–327, 332, 333, 344–345, 345, 439
Eriksson, C. J. P., 31, 103
Erixon, E., 102
Eron, L. D., 175, 177
Escorial, S., 326
Esser, J. K., 494
Etaugh, C. A., 327
Everall, R. D., 452
Eysenck, Hans, 20, 347, 452–453
Ezzati, M., 328

F

Fallin, M., 388
Fantz, Robert, 303
Farah, M. J., 94
Farber, B. A., 440
Farrer, L. A., 138
Farzan, F., 422
Fasmer, O., 68
Fatemi, S. H., 423
Faye, Cathy, 160
Fechner, Gustav Theodor, 9
Feder, A., 373
Fehr, B., 480
Feinstein, J. S, 63
Felmlee, D., 480
Felsted, J. A., 267
Fenton, B. W., 108
Fernandez, N. C., 474
Fernandez-Twinn, D. S., 301
Ferry, B., 213
Fertissov, S. O., 265
Festinger, L., 259, 260, 473
Fiehler, K., 83

Fields, R. D., 214
Fife, R. S., 73, 74
Filosa, A., 49
Finch, E., 484
Fineberg, N. A., 408
Fischer, P., 281
Fisher, B. S., 381
Fisher, C. B., 34, 35
Fisher, M., 162
Fiske, S. T., 292
Fitzsimmons, D., 494
Flavell, J. H., 309, 318
Flegal, K. M., 266
Fleming, A. S., 493
Flett, G. L., 415
Fligor, B. J., 102
Flouri, E., 321
Folkman, S., 381
Follingstad, D., 34
Folsom, T. D., 423
Foote, B., 411
Forcehimes, A. A., 452
Forhan, G., 46
Forrest, D. V., 19
Förster, J., 470
Fortin, N., 214
Foster, J. D., 106
Foster, Jodie, 400
Fowles, D. C., 427
Fox, Michael J., 54
Fox, N. A., 303
Fox, S. E., 303
Franco, K., 271
Frankl, Viktor, 356
Franklin, Benjamin, 127, 138
Franklin, T. R., 144
Franko, D. L., 403
Fraser, S. C., 473
Frasure,-Smith, N., 388
Freedman, J. L., 473
Freeman, D., 419
Freeman, M. S., 302
Freese, T. E., 146
Freud, Anna, 439
Freud, Sigmund, 11, 13, 120, 126, 133, 143, 196, 207, 261, 280, 281, 305, 340, 340–345, 341, 342, 343, 356, 381, 436–437, 438, 439, 441, 480
Freund, A. M., 332
Freund, M., 221
Friedman, Martin, 503
Friedman, R. A., 141
Friese, M., 139
Fritsch, G., 65
Froeliger, B., 144
Fromm, Erich, 126
Frost, Robert, 60, 124
Fuentes, R., 54
Fuji, Ken'ichi, 165
Fukushima, M., 491
Furnham, A., 267, 478
Fuson, K., 309

G

Gaatchel, R. J., 106
Gage, Phineas, 27, 27–28, 59
Galton, Sir Francis, 40, 250, 346
Galvani, Luigi/wife, 50–51
Gandhi, Mahatma, 68, 127, 221
Gans, D., 327
Gao, Y., 349
Garb, H. N., 365
Garcia, J., 156
Garcia-Falgueras, A., 279
Gardini, G. G., 270
Gardner, Howard, 238–240, 239, 241, 242
Gardner, R. A., 232
Garn, Stanley, 248
Garrett, R. K., 471
Garza, Y., 455
Gatchel, R. J., 111
Gates, Bill, 68, 163
Gavin, N. I., 322
Gaynor, J., 110
Gazzaniga, Michael S., 67, 68, 120, 131
Genovese, Kitty, 496, 497
Gerdes, A. B. M., 161, 409
Gershoff, E. T., 167, 168
Getzels, J. W., 243
Gibbons, C. J., 450
Giedd, Jay, 318
Gigerenzer, G., 82, 228
Gilbert, P., 402
Gillham, J., 348
Gilligan, Carol, 320
Ginsburg, G., 315
Giussani, D. A., 301
Glaser, R., 386
Glass, D. C., 378
Glass, Gene, 453–454
Glasser, C. L., 478
Glenn, S. S., 164
Godden, D. R., 203
Goddyn, H., 213
Goez, H., 68
Goghari, V. M., 14
Gold, P. E., 54
Goldman, J. S., 331
Goldman-Rakic, P. S., 214
Goldston, D. B., 416
Goleman, Daniel, 241
Golombok, S., 355
González, H. M., 455
González, M. M., 324
González, Y. S., 321
Goodall, Jane, 27, 232
Goodenough, Florence, 248–249
Goodman-Delahunty, J., 475
Goodman, W., 459
Goodwin, P. J., 395
Gopnik, A., 308
Gordon, G. R. J., 49

Gorodetsky, M., 226
Gosling, S. D., 35
Gotlieb, G., 370
Gottesman, I. I., 422
Gottfredson, L., 238, 242, 350
Gottlieb, B. H., 48, 323
Gottman, J. M., 472
Gottschalk, L. J., 320
Goyette, K., 248
Grabe, S., 414
Grace, D. M., 355
Graham, Martha, 356
Grant, I., 148
Greenberg, B. D., 459
Greenberger, E., 414
Greene, B., 455
Greene, Brian, 241, 249
Greene, J., 170
Greenhalgh, J., 135
Greenough, W. T., 303
Greenwald, Anthony G., 476
Greenwood, P. M., 144
Greer, Germaine, 436
Gregory-Roberts, E. M., 458
Gregory, V. L., Jr., 459
Greidanus, E., 452
Griffin, A. M., 474
Griffin, C., 320
Grilo, C. M., 415
Gronau, N., 292
Groneburg, D., 143
Gross, A. L., 393
Grosser, B. I., 275
Grossman, M. I., 265
Grundy, E., 327
Grusec, J. E., 315
Guadagno, R. E., 476
Guarnaccia, P. J. J., 401
Guerin, B., 492
Guerrini, I., 300, 301
Gulledge, A. T., 213
Gump, B. B., 373
Gunter, C., 46
Guzzetti, B. J., 354

H

Haaf, R. A., 303
Hadamitzky, M., 142
Haenen, J., 309
Hafemeister, L., 80
Hagler, D. J., Jr., 83
Hale, L., 127
Hall, G. Stanly, 320
Hall, J. A., 292
Halpern, D. F., 20, 321
Hammen, C. L., 402
Hancock, J., 292
Hankin, B. L., 312
Hannity, Sean, 471
Harker, L., 478
Harker, LeeAnne, 288
Harkness, K. L., 373
Harlow, Harry F., 313–314
Harmon-Jones, C., 472–473

Harmon-Jones, E., 284, 472–473
Harper, S., 391
Harris, J. L., 267
Hart, A. J., 63
Hartup, W. W., 321
Hasin, D. S., 412
Hauge, A. W., 390
Haustein, K-O, 142
Haworth, C. M. A., 43, 45, 47, 252
Hawthorne, Nathaniel, 9, 479
Hayes, B., 130
Heber, D., 266, 267, 268
Heidegger, Martin, 356
Heindel, J. J., 300
Heiphetz, L., 470
Heitland, K., 476
Helmholtz, Hermann von, 90, 102
Helms, J. E., 248
Helton, W. S., 350
Hen, R., 43
Henderson, T. L., 370
Hendin, H., 417
Heng, M. A., 241
Henley, C. L., 278
Henretta, J. C., 327
Henry, D. B., 282
Henry, J. D., 186
Henseler, I., 14
Hensley, W. E., 497
Herbernick, D., 278
Hergenhahn, B. R., 26, 345, 401
Hering, Ewald, 90
Heron, M., 415
Herring, M. P., 461
Hettema, J. M., 408
Heymann, H., 83
Higgs, S., 266
Hilgard, E. R., 133
Hill, G. J., 287
Hill, R. D., 496
Hillis, L. D., 143
Hilsenroth, M. J., 403
Hilt, L. M., 18
Hinckley, John, 399, 400, 401, 424
Hingson, R., 139
Hinsz, V. B., 486
Hippocrates, 346, 347, 401
Hirst, W., 201
Hitzig, E., 65
Ho, M. Y., 287
Hobson, J. A., 126
Hoff, E., 232, 235
Hoffman, H. G., 111, 433, 434
Hoffman, W., 139
Hogarth, William, 95, 95–96
Hojnoski, R. L., 365
Holden, Constance, 47
Hollan, D., 126
Holland, A. C., 201

Hollingshead, A. B., 421
Hollon, S. D., 454, 458
Holmes, T. H., 373
Homer, 480
Honts, C. R., 292
Honzik, C. H., 173
Hoover, R. N., 388
Hopkins, W. D., 231
Horan, W. P., 420
Horney, Karen, 12, 15, 344, 345, 414, 439
Horn, J. L., 326
Horn, J. M., 253
Horn, M. C., 327
Hornsby, L. B., 74
Howard, G. S., 114
Howard, K. J., 378
Hoyert, Mark, 107
Hrabosky, J., 270
Hu, F. B., 387
Hu, X., 381
Hubel, David, 82
Huchard, E., 479
Huesmann, L. R., 175, 176, 177
Huestis, M. A., 300
Hughes, M. E., 414
Hughes, T. F., 187
Huizink, A. C., 300
Hull, Clark, 261
Hurd, Y. L., 300
Hurka, T., 281
Hustad, J. T. P., 139
Hutchins, Robin, 407
Hyde, J. S., 249
Hyman, Ray, 112

I

Iacono, W. G., 292
Imel, Z. E., 452
Incrocci, L., 72
Indlekofer, F., 148
Inhelder, B., 233
Innocent VIII, Pope, 401
Irons, Gary, 160
Ironson, G. H., 348
Isarida, T. K., 203
Isen, J., 349
Ismail, S. A., 71
Iwasaki, A., 385
Izard, C. E., 289

J

Jaaniste, T., 111
Jackson, E. C., 130
Jackson, H., 416
Jackson, L. C., 455
Jackson, M. L., 124
Jackson, P. W., 243
Jacob, S., 106, 275
Jacobs, L. F., 249
Jacobsen, J. S., 331
James, Henry, 9

James, LeBron, 471
James, William, 9, 12, 17, 21, 33, 119, 191, 192, 201, 228, 261, 286, 289, 302, 346, 352, 358, 373, 376, 460
James I, King, 143
Janero, D. R., 148
Jang, K. L., 427
Janis, I. L., 494
Janowitz, H. D., 265
Janowsky, J. S., 72
Jemel, A., 393
Jennings, M., 29
Jensen, M., 111, 131
Jentsch, J. D., 35
Jester, J. M., 177
Jhangiani, R., 201
Joffe, P., 418
Johansen, M., 403
Johnson, J. L., 144
Johnson, Samuel, 105, 137, 193, 231, 260, 262, 352
Johnson, S. B., 139
Johnson, Virginia, 274
Johnson, W., 287, 317
Johnston, L. D., 136, 138, 141, 143
Jolie, Angelina, 68
Jones, J. L., 471
Jones, Mary Cover, 161–162
Joorman, J., 370
Jorgensen, G., 320
Judd, Charles, 112
Judd, C. M., 477
Jung, Carl, 343, 344, 347, 439, 441

K

Kagan, J., 349
Kahana, E., 381
Kahneman, Daniel, 229
Kaiser, N. C., 315
Kakko, J., 141
Kalavana, T. V., 378
Kamalanabhan, T. J., 493
Kamphaus, R. W., 363
Kanayama, G., 72
Kandel, E. R., 212, 213, 214
Kaplan, K., 129
Kaplan, R. M., 247
Karolewicz, B., 55
Karremans, Johan, 81
Karwautz, A., 271
Katigbak, M. S., 348
Katz, Joel, 108, 109
Kazdin, A. E., 417, 455
Kazim, S. F., 467
Keech, Marian, 259–260, 473
Kegeles, L. S., 423
Keller, A., 422
Keller, Helen, 84, 104, 106
Keller, S. S., 231
Kellman, P. J., 302

Kelly, J. F., 452
Keltner, Dacher, 288, 478
Kemeny, M. E., 383, 385
Kendler, K. S., 408
Kennedy, John F., 201, 490, 494
Kensinger, E. A., 201
Kerlin, J. R., 120
Kerry, John, 494–495
Kessler, R. C., 403, 405, 412
Kiecolt-Glaser, J. K., 131, 388
Kikuchi, H., 209
Kilpatrick, D. G., 407
Kim, B. S. K., 361, 455
Kimble, D. P., 274
King, B. J., 231
King, L. A., 375
Kinsey, Alfred, 26
Kirke, D. M., 321
Kishino, N. D., 108, 111
Kiviniemi, M. T., 468
Klavir, R., 226
Klein, S. B., 186
Kleinmuntz, B., 292
Klintsova, A. Y., 303
Klüver, Heinrich, 63
Knapp, L. G., 248
Knickmeyer, R., 354
Knight, R. G., 186
Kobasa, Suzanne, 379
Koch, C., 411
Koch, M., 142
Koelling, R. A., 156
Koenig, P., 186
Koerber, A., 26
Koffka, Kurt, 10–11, 12
Kohlberg, Lawrence, 309–311, 310, 319, 320
Köhler, Wolfgang, 10–11, 12
Kohn, N., 227
Kolb, B., 213
Kontak, A. C., 143
Koo, M., 204
Koster, E. H. W., 408
Kotagal, S., 130
Kovacs, N., 203
Kovera, M. B., 199
Kownacki, R. J., 452
Krähenbühl, S., 199
Kramer, M. D., 414
Kramer, R., 320
Krantz, D. S., 391
Kratochvil, C. J., 142
Krogh, J., 461
Krueger, F., 28, 287
Kubinyi, E., 350
Kübler-Ross, Elisabeth, 333
Kuczmarski, R. J., 302
Kumari, V., 426
Kuntzman, G., 102
Kuo, P-H., 138
Kurth, T., 387
Kurzban, R., 478

L

Laaksonen, E., 141
Labouvie-Vief, Gisella, 324
Lachman, M. E., 327
Ladd-Franklin, Christine, 17
Laing, R. D., 419
Lakin, J. M., 249
Lam, M. P., 139
Lamers, C. T. J., 147
Lan, Y-J., 495
Lander, K., 346
Landon, Alf, 23
Landy, F. J., 241
Lang, Alan, 31, 33, 35
Lang, E. V., 131
Lange, A. R., 35
Lange, Karl G., 289
Lange, R. A., 143
Langlois, J. H., 474
Larsen, J. T., 291
Lashley, Karl, 212
Latané, B., 496, 497
Lau, A. S., 315
Laucht, M., 140
Laumann, E. O., 276, 329
Laungani, P., 483
Laursen, B., 321
Lawler, C., 300
Lawless, H. T., 83
Lazarus, R. S., 371
Le, T. N., 16
Leach, K. P., 415
Leary, M. R., 471
Le Bon, Gustave, 495
LeDoux, J. E., 284
Lee, A., 312
Lee, C. W., 447
Lee, D. J., 203
Lee, I-C., 16
Lee, S. J., 236, 316
Lee, Y., 479
Leenaars, A. A., 467
Lefcourt, H. M., 373, 379
Lehman, B. J., 469, 471
Lejeune, C., 300
Lenroot, R. K., 59
Leonardo, E. D., 43
Leppel, K., 360
Lespérance, F., 388
Leung, P., 271
Levenson, Sam, 311
Levine, Deb, 480
Levine, E. S., 402
Levinson, D. J., 325, 327
Levinson, Sharman, 160
Levy, D., 390
Levy, R. A., 455
Lewis, Ted, 286
Ley, J., 350
Li, C., 298
Li, M., 229
Li, T. Y., 387
Lickliter, R, 48
Lieber, C. S., 139

Lief, Harold, 208
Lim, M. M., 71
Lim, R. F., 402
Limbaugh, Rush, 471, 472
Lincoln, Abraham, 40
Lincoln, T. M., 419, 420
Lindegren, A. P., 138
Lindoerfer, J. S., 494
Lindstrom, P., 278
Lippa, R. A., 322, 354
Liu, A., 248
Livesley W. J., 427
Livne, N. L., 243
Lloyd, K. B., 74
Locke, E. A., 352
Löckenhoff, C. E., 332
Lockhart, R. S., 199, 200
Loftus, E. F., 18, 19, 25, 197, 198, 199, 207, 208, 340
Logan, C., 48
Lohman, D. F., 249
Lonstein, J. S., 279
Lopez, Jennifer, 104
Lopez, S. R., 400
Lorenz, Konrad, 314
Louw, D. A., 132
Lowe, C. F., 460
Lu, L., 287
Lubinski, D., 238
Luchins, Abraham, 483, 483–484
Ludwick-Rosenthal, R., 381
Lukaszewski, A., 42
Lupien, S. J., 382
Lurigio, A. J., 34
Luszczynska, A., 378
Lutgendorf, S., 393
Lykken, D. T., 47, 286
Lynn, B. M., 479
Lynn, S. J., 133

M

Ma, Yo Yo, 46
MacDonald, A. W., III, 14
MacDorman, M. F., 322
Machery, E., 221
Machery, O., 103
Maddi, S. R., 378, 379
Magno, C., 360
Magoun, Horace, 62
Mahesh, Maharishi Yogi, 134
Maiden, B., 492
Maier, N. R. F., 227
Mair, C., 225, 226
Makriyannis, A., 148
Maldonado, E., 146
Mamelak, M., 128
Mandal, M., 300
Mandela, Nelson, 46
Maniglio, R., 271
Manning, R., 496
Manoun, 274
Manuck, S. B., 378
Mapes, R. R., 375

Marcus, D., 412
Marian, V., 203
Markham, B., 324
Markon, K. E., 47
Markowitsch, H. J., 185
Marlatt, G., 138
Martin, C. L., 355
Martin, R. A., 379
Martin, S., 355
Martinez, E., 378, 409
Marttunen, M. J., 416
Marziali, E., 379
Maslow, Abraham, 15, 263–264, 264, 356, 357, 358
Mason, V., 369
Masters, William, 274
Mata, I., 28
Mathews, J. R., 420
Mathews, T. J., 322
Matisse, Henri, 87
Matsumoto, D., 286
Matthews, Chris, 471, 472
Matthews, K. A., 373
Maxwell, J. P., 281
May, D. E., 142
May, R., 447
Mayer, J. D., 241
Mayers, A. G., 125
Mayes, L. C., 300
Mazure, C. M., 414
Mbwana, J., 66
McAuley, C., 322
McCabe, D. P., 30
McCabe, S. B., 377
McCall, R., 298
McCardle, P., 234
McCarley, R. W., 126
McCarthy, M. M., 59
McCauley, J. L., 136, 139, 407
McClelland, David, 283
McClintock, M. K., 275
McCormick, M., 34
McCrae, R. R., 47, 345, 347–348, 470
McDevitt-Murphy, M. E., 407
McDonald, M. G., 356
McDonald-Miszczak, L., 188
McDougall, William, 191, 261
McGaugh, J. L., 207, 213
McGraw, A. P., 229
McGreal, C., 322
McGue, M., 250
McHugh, Paul, 208
McKee, P., 332
McKenzie, C. R. M., 471
McKimmie, B. M., 282
McLachlan, N., 120
McLaughlin, K. A., 373
McMillan, C. T., 209
McNeill, D., 202–203
McQueen, M., 415
Meachem, Jon, 20
Mead, G. E., 461

Mead, Margaret, 163, 280, 328, 357, 381
Mechner, F., 213
Medzhitov, R., 385
Meguid, M. M., 265
Mehta, J., 392
Mehta, P. H., 35, 414
Meier, B. P., 478
Meijer, J., 309
Meijer, W. M., 142
Meltzoff, A. N., 175, 236, 308
Melzack, Ronald, 108, 109, 110
Mendelsohn, F., 271
Menustik, C. E., 433
Merari, A., 467, 485
Mercado, E., 66
Merritte, Douglas ("Little Albert"), 10, 160, 161, 163
Mesmer, Franz, 131
Mesoudi, A., 491
Messineo, M., 476
Metcalfe, J. A., 226, 231
Metz, R., 183
Meyer-Lindenberg A., 422
Meyersburg, C. A., 19
Michelangelo, 68
Midler, Bette, 490
Milgram, R. M., 243
Milgram, Stanley, 467, 485, 486–489
Milius, S., 169
Mill, John Stuart, 9
Miller, A. L., 416
Miller, Arthur, 425
Miller, C. F., 193
Miller, George, 195
Miller, Henry, 105
Miller, J. L., 120
Miller, L., 485
Miller, M. A., 139
Miller, N. E., 134–135, 172, 266
Miller-Perrin, C. L., 315
Milne, R. D., 67
Milner, Peter, 62, 134
Mineka, S., 156, 161, 162, 408, 409
Miniño, A. M., 330
Minnelli, Liza, 502
Misyak, J. B., 237
Miyahira, S. D., 433
Miyake, Y., 270
M'Naghten, Daniel, 424
Mohr, D. C., 455
Molfese, Victoria, 253
Monet, Claude, 87
Moniz, Antonio Egas, 458
Monroe, Marilyn, 425
Montero, I., 309
Montoya, R. M., 480
Moore, C. C., 233
Moos, B. S., 452
Moos, R. H., 452

Moran, G. P., 492
Mordock, B., 493
Morewedge, C. K., 125
Morey, R. D., 80, 82
Morgan, Christiana, 365
Morris, M. W., 354, 484
Morris, W. N., 491
Morrison, E. S., 322
Morton, S. M. B., 301
Moruzzi, Guiseppe, 62
Moses, "Grandma", 331
Mosher, W. D., 277
Moskowitz, T., 381
Mott, M., 79
Mowafi, H. A., 71
Mozart, 46
Mukamal, K. J., 140, 141
Mulder, E. J. H., 300
Mullally, W. J., 391
Muñoz, R. F., 458
Munro, V. E., 484
Muraleedharan, V., 274
Murata, A., 309
Murray, C. J. L., 328
Murray, Henry, 283, 365
Murray, L., 315
Myers, L. B., 340
Mystkowski, J. L., 162

N

Nader, K., 211
Naimi, T., 139
Naragon-Gainey, K., 406
Narusyte, J., 48
Nash, John Forbes, 420
Navarro, 146
Naveh-Benjamin, M., 187
Neeson, Liam, 26
Neisser, U., 203, 240, 241, 248, 253
Nemeroff, C. B., 409
Nesbitt, Richard E., 247, 248
Nestoriuc, Y., 391
Neufeld, R. W. J., 381
Nevarez, Carmen, **266**
Neve, K. A., 54
Newman, S. D., 28
Newton, Sir Isaac, 84
Niesta, D., 479
Nikitina, T. V., 235
Nir, Y., 130
Nisbett, R. E., 29, 238, 248, 253
Nistico, H., 286
Nixon, Richard, 494
Nock, M. K., 417
Nokes, T. J., 226
Nolan, J. M., 486
Nolen-Hoeksema, S., 18, 407, 414
Noll, J., 326
Nonaka, A. M., 236
Norcross, J. C., 439, 441, 450, 451

Norton, A., 309
Norton, M. I., 125
Nuttall, R. L., 416

O

Odbert, H. S., 346
O'Dell, Cynthia, 107
O'Driscoll, M. P., 373
Oehlberg, K., 161, 408, 409
Oertelt-Prigione, S., 139
Oh, Sandra, 46
Ohayon, M. M., 130, 405
Ohlsson, M. G. O., 470
Öhman, A., 156, 161
Oishi, S., 204
O'Keeffe, Georgia, 87
Olatunji, B. O., 409
Olbermann, Keith, 471
Old, S. R., 187
Oldenburg, D., 79
Olds, James, 62, 134
Oliver, M. B., 476
Olson, M. J., 455
Olthof, A., 166
Omizo, M. M., 455
Ong, A. D., 16
Ong, J. C., 128
Oressman, S. D., 381
Ormerod, T. C., 227
Orsi, J. M., 394
Osmond, Marie, 414
Ostrave, J. M., 327
Ozanne, S. E., 301

P

Packard, M. G., 54
Packer, D. J., 488, 494
Paffenbarger, R. S., 387
Palmer, J. C., 197, 199
Pang, J-J., 90
Pani, P. P., 136
Pansky, A., 188
Park, B., 477
Park, J., 471
Park, N., 348
Parker, Dorothy, 321
Parker, S., 281
Parr, L. A., 287
Parrott, A., 146
Patrick, Danica, 471
Patterson, D. R., 111
Paulussen-Hoogeboom, M. C., 315
Pavlov, Ivan, 154–155, 155, 157, 158, 159, 160
Peel, Robert, 424
Pelosi, Nancy, 470
Penfield, Wilder, 60, 196–197
Penton-Voak, I. S., 72, 478
Perea, G., 49
Perls, Fritz, 439, 441
Perna, F. M., 373
Perrett, D. I., 72, 477

Perry, B., 492
Perry, William, 324
Peterson, C., 348
Peterson, Lloyd/Margaret, 196
Petrill, S. A., 250
Petry, N. M., 444
Petty, R. E., 468, 469, 470, 471
Phelps, E. A., 284
Phinney, J. S., 16, 360, 361
Piaget, Jean, 199, 233, 304–309, 306, 318
Piattelli-Palmarini, M., 48
Picasso, Pablo, 331
Piccinni, A., 457, 460
Pietrzak, R., 378, 379, 381
Piffer, R. C., 278
Piliavin, J. A., 496
Pincus, A. L., 454
Pind, J., 238
Pinel, Philippe, 401, 435
Pinker, S., 66, 221, 230, 231–232, 234, 236, 237, 346
Piolino, E. R., 208
Plant, E. A., 249, 475
Platania, J., 492
Plato, 100, 106, 331–332
Plomin, R., 43, 45, 46, 47, 250
Pluess, M., 135, 402
Pogue-Geile, M. F., 422
Polanczyk, G., 423
Polina, E. R., 54
Popma, A., 281
Porsolt, R. D., 457
Porter, S., 286, 287
Posada, G., 312
Postmes, T., 495
Potter, W. J., 175, 176, 177
Pradham, D. S., 281
Prato-Previde, E., 236
Prescott, P. A., 302
Preti, A., 68
Preuss, H. G., 394
Prinz, W., 175
Pritchett, J., 346
Prochaska, J. O., 439, 441, 450, 451
Pronin, E;, 486
Proverbio, A. M., 281
Pulley, B., 170
Purdie-Vaughns, V., 18
Puri, B. K., 422
Putnam, S. K., 281

Q

Qi, Z., 54
Quindlen, Anna, 72
Quinlan, M. B., 402

R

Rachman, S., 442, 450
Radcliffe, R. A., 138

Rahe, R. H., 373
Raine, Adrian, 349, 427
Rajasethupathy, P., 213
Rakic, Pasko T., 63, 232
Ramasubramanian, S., 476
Randolph, M. E., 139
Rappaport, N. B., 390
Rathus, J. H., 451
Rathus, Jill, 416
Rathus, S. A., 24, 276, 326
Rawley, J. B., 65
Rayner, L., 458
Rayner, Rosalie, 10, 160
Read, C. N., 459
Reagan, Ronald, 399, 424
Redlich, F. C., 421
Redrobe, J. P., 457
Reece, M., 278
Rees, T., 486
Reeve, Christopher, 286, 287
Regier, T., 233
Regitz-Zagrosek, V., 139
Reid, L. W., 476
Reinecke, M. A., 414
Reis, O., 321
Reiser, M., 126
Reninger, K. A., 193
Rescorla, R. A., 159, 170, 174
Rhee, S. H., 427
Ribbert, H., 497
Richardson, J., 394
Richardson, K. M., 387
Richdale, A. L., 130
Rimm, E. B., 140, 141
Ringach, D. L., 35
Risch, N., 54
Rizzo, A. A., 433
Rizzo, J., 455
Rizzolatti, Giacomo, 66
Roberson, D., 221
Roberts, S., 126
Roberts, W. A., 166
Robinson, Eugene, 248
Robins, R. W., 13
Rocca, W. A., 72
Rodin, G., 352
Rodrigues-Galdino, A. M., 105
Rodriguez, C. J., 381
Roediger, H. L, 30
Roepke, S., 425
Rogers, Carl, 15, 27, 356–358, 439–440, 440
Rogers, Will, 470
Roid, G. H., 247
Roland, D. L., 72
Rolls, E. T., 105
Romero, E., 426
Roney, J., 42
Rooney, Andy, 265
Roosevelt, Eleanor, 359
Roosevelt, Franklin D., 23
Rorschach, Hermann, 365
Rosekind, M. R., 125
Rosenberg, M. J., 492

Ross, C. A., 411
Ross, J. L., 275
Roth, T. L., 54
Rothman, A. J., 468
Rothstein, H. R., 387
Rotter, Julian B., 379
Rouder, J. N., 80, 82
Rubia, K., 134
Ruble, 355
Rudd, M. D., 417
Rudy, D., 315
Ruiter, R. A. C., 471
Rumbold, A. R., 300
Rumsfeld, Donald, 494
Runyan, D. K., 315
Rupp, H., 479
Rush, A. J., 448
Russell, Bertrand, 222
Rutkowski, G. K., 496
Rutter, C. M., 416
Rutter, M., 303
Ryan, G. L., 270

S

Saccuzzo, D. P., 247
Safford, S., 415
Saffran, J. R., 235
Sagan, Carl, 20, 22, 224
Saggino, A., 238
Sagi-Schwartz, A., 316
Saklofske, D. H., 238
Salovey, Peter, 241
Salthouse, T. A., 326
Sanchez, D. T., 16
Sanchez, Jorge, 18
Sanders, G. S., 199
Sanderson, W. C., 451, 454
Santarius, T., 393
Santayana, George, 298
Sarbin, Theodore, 133
Sartre, Jean-Paul, 356
Satir, Virginia, 321
Saudino, K. J., 349
Savage-Rumbaugh, Sue, 231
Sava, S., 317
Savic, I., 278
Savin-Williams, R. C., 278
Sayette, M. A., 30
Saywitz, K. J., 316
Scarr, S., 253
Schachter, Stanley, 290,
    290–291
Schacter, D. L., 185, 186
Schaie, K. W., 251, 326
Schatzberg, A., 405
Scheff, T. J., 382
Schick, V. R., 272
Schiffman, S. S., 105
Schmelkin, L-P., 402
Schmidt, N. B., 406
Schmitt, D. P., 354, 481
Schnall, S., 496
Schneider-Garces, N. J., 201
Schneirla, T. C., 227

Schrager, S. B., 73, 74
Schubert, S., 447
Schuckit, M. A., 140
Schuetze, P., 300
Schulte, M. T., 138
Schultheis, M. T., 433
Schwartz, N., 26
Schwartz, R. M., 472
Schwartz, S. J., 360, 361
Schweighofer, N., 199, 200
Scott-Sheldon, L. A., 386
Segerdahl, P., 231, 232
Sekizuka, H., 128
Self, D. R., 263
Seligman, Martin, 414–415
Seligman, M. E. P., 29, 348
Selye, H., 370, 373, 376,
    379, 382
Senehi, J., 494
Seurat, Georges, 88–89, 89
Shackelford, T. K., 161, 409
Shadish, W. R., 452, 453
Shafran, R., 450
Shah, C., 55
Shakespeare, William, 100,
    125, 419, 436, 447
Shankman, S. A., 272
Shansky, R. M., 213
Shapiro, Francine, 447
Shaw, George Bernard,
    265, 502
Shedler, J., 453
Sheldon, K. M., 348
Shelton, R. C., 454, 458
Sherkits, E. J., 423
Sherman, D. K., 352
Sherrington, J. M., 414
Sherwood, C. C., 231
Shiffrin, Richard, 191
Shneidman, E. S., 418
Short, S., 423
Showers, C. J., 480
Shuper, P. A., 166
Shyrack, J., 348
Siegel, J. M., 127
Siever, L. J., 425
Silver, S. M., 447
Silverstein, M., 327
Silvia, P. J., 486
Simeon, D., 411
Simon, Carly, 375–377, 404
Simon, Theodore, 244, 245
Simon, T. R., 282
Simons, A. D., 454
Simonsen, E., 427
Simonton, D. K., 241, 243
Singareddy, R. K., 126
Singer, J. E., 290, 290–291
Singh, L., 236
Sio, U. N., 227
Sixsmith, R., 267
Sizemore, Chris, 26
Skinner, B. F., 10, 11, 12, 164,
    164–165, 165, 167, 168,
    172, 351

Slobin, D. I., 235
Sloman, S. A., 221
Small, E., 144
Smetana, J. G., 321
Smillie, L. D., 349
Smith, B. N., 492
Smith, G. F., 470
Smith, K. L., 379
Smith, Mary Lee, 453–454
Smith, N. A., 236
Smith, S. E. P., 300
Smith, S. M., 227, 403
Snyder, C. R., 348
Snyder, D. J., 105
Soares, C. N., 414
Socrates, 8–9, 14, 240
Solomon, R. C., 284
Somerfield, M. R., 345
Sommers, M. S., 329
Sorensen, S. B., 416
Souren, N. Y., 46
Soussignan, R., 288
Spanos, Nichola, 133
Spearman, Charles, 238,
    242, 346
Spears, R., 495
Spelts, K., 110
Spencer, M. D., 186, 423
Spencer, M. S., 455
Sperling, George, 191–192
Spieker, S. J., 312
Spielman, A. J., 129
Spinath, B., 248
Spinath, F. M., 250
Spinhoven, P., 415
Spittle, A. J., 303
Sporer, S. L., 475
Sprecher, S., 480
Spritzer, M. D., 213
Squire, L. R., 209,
    213, 214
Srnick, J. L., 141
Sroufe, L. A., 312
Staff, J., 321
Stanley, B., 425
Starratt, V. G., 161, 409
Staudinger, U. M., 332
Steele, Claude, 18
Steele, H., 312
Stein, A. D., 423
Steinem, Gloria, 324
Steinmary, R., 248
Sternberg, R. J., 20, 119, 237,
    240, 240–241, 242, 243,
    248, 332, 480–481, 481
Stewart, A. J., 327
Stewart, J. G., 373
Stewart, R. E., 450
Stewart, S. H., 174
Stinnett, Caskie, 411
Stocco, A., 28
Stone, J., 474
Stormark, K. M., 236
Strack, F., 288
Strathearn, L., 316

Straus, M., 316
Strickland, Tony, 18
Striegel-Moore, R. H.,
    270, 403
Stuart, K., 126
Stunkard, Albert, 266–267
Sue, Stanley, 18, 455
Suh, E. M., 360, 361
Suinn, Richard, 18
Susser, E., 423
Swaab, D. F., 279
Swami, V., 19
Swan, G. E., 26
Swartout, K. M., 139
Sweeney, J. A., 207
Sweeny, T. D., 81
Szala, M., 226
Szasz, Thomas, 419
Szentirmai, E., 262
Szucko, J. J., 292

T

Taber, C. S., 471
Taffe, M. A., 146
Tait, M., 104
Takahashi, T., 422
Talboom, J. S., 72, 73
Talwar, Sanjiv, 169
Tamis-LeMonda, C. S., 234
Tanner, J. M., 303
Taylor, A., 134
Taylor, H. H., 328
Taylor, M. J., 379
Taylor, S., 447
Taylor, Shelley E., 383, 384
Tejada-Vera, B., 415
ten Brinke, L., 286, 287
Tenenbaum, H. R., 355
Tennyson, Alfred Lord, 9
Terman, Louis, 244
Terracciano, A., 348
Terrace, Herbert, 231–232
Terry, D. F., 329
Tetlock, P. E., 229
Thomas, A. K., 207
Thomas, J., 148
Thomas, K. R., 29
Thomas, S. L., 492
Thompson, Helen Bradford,
    18
Thompson, K. M., 175
Thompson, L. E., 471
Thompson, R. A., 316
Thompson, S. C., 381
Thoreau, Henry David,
    9, 460
Thorndike, Edward L., 163
Thurstone, Louis, 238,
    239, 242
Tipin, S. M., 247
Titov, N., 186
Tohidan, I., 233
Tolman, E. C., 173
Tomiyama, T., 331

Tomlin, Lily, 231
Tong, H., 414
Tonigan, J. S., 452
Tononi, G., 130
Tormala, Z. L., 470
Tost, H., 423
Townsend, E., 417
Trainor, L. J., 236
Travis, S. G., 209
Treisman, A. M., 214
Triandis, H. C., 360, 361
Trudel, G. A., 329
Trull, T. J., 454
Tsang, Y. C., 265
Tuke, William, 435
Tulving, E., 185
Turk, D., 110
Turnbull, Colin, 98
Turner, E. A., 283
Turner, J., 110
Tversky, Amos, 229
Twain, Mark, 11, 143, 163,
    173, 341, 379, 388, 470,
    490, 502
Twenge, J. M., 489

U

Uhlhaas, P. J., 125
Umek, L. M., 309
Uzakov, S., 213

V

Valenzuela, A., 213
Van der Kolk, B. A., 447
van der Schouw, Y. T., 274
van de Wetering, S., 207
Van Guilder, G. P., 387
VanLehn, K., 226
van Straaten, I., 480
Van Swol, L. M., 492
Vellante, M., 68
Vercelli, D., 48
Verhagen, A. P., 454
Vernon, D., 172
Veselka, L., 47
Viets, V. L., 455
Visintainer, M. A., 394
Visscher, W. A., 300
Viulli, W. F., 112
Vodosek, M., 16
Von Békésy, Georg, 102
Voorspoels, W., 221
Voss, J. L., 198

Voytko, M. L., 72, 73
Vukman, K. B., 324
Vygotsky, Lev, 304, 309

W

Wacker, J., 349
Wade, N., 127
Wade, T. D., 271
Wagner, J. J., 458
Wagstaff, G. S., 491
Waite, L. J., 287
Waldman, I. D., 427
Walker, J. S., 447
Wall, Patrick, 110
Wallace, Alfred Russel, 40
Wallace, D. M., 486
Wanchoo, S. J., 142
Wang, Q., 208
Wang, X., 381
Wang, Y., 198, 225
Ward, A., 300
Ward, C. P., 124, 125
Ward, E., 395
Wareham, J., 177
Waring, T. M., 497
Warman, D. M., 172, 177
Warner, John, 485
Warren, M., 271
Wartik, N., 414
Washburn, A. L., 265
Washburn, D. A., 231
Washburn, Margaret Floy,
    17–18
Waters, M., 416
Watson, H. J., 271
Watson, James D., 43
Watson, John B., 10, 11, 12,
    15, 119, 160, 161, 305, 351
Watt, M. C., 174
Watts, R. E., 455
Weber, Ernst, 81
Webster, J. D., 331
Wechsler, David, 240,
    245–247, 247
Weeden, J., 478
Weems, C. F., 369
Wegener, D. T., 470
Weinberg, R. A., 253
Weiner, B., 379
Weiner, I. B., 173, 365
Weinmann, M., 414
Weisskirch, R. S., 361
Weitekamp, L. A., 287
Weng, X., 300

Werner, L. A., 302
Wertheimer, Max, 10–11,
    12, 92
Wessel, J., 47
Westen, D. I., 455
Westenberg, H. G. M., 457
Wetzler, S. E., 207
Wheeler, M. A., 209
Wheeler, M. E., 214
Wheeler, S. C., 468
White, J. W., 139
White, M. A., 271
Whorf, Benjamin Lee, 233
Widiger, T. A., 427
Widom, C. S., 315
Wiebe, R. E., 377
Wienke, C., 287
Wiens, A. N., 443
Wiesel, Torsten, 82
Wijers, S. L. J., 267
Wild, R. A., 72
Wilde, Oscar, 142, 260, 283,
    315, 470, 471, 480
Wilhelm, K., 287
Willcutt, E., 415
William, Prince, 68
Williams, C. L., 207
Williams, J. E., 391
Williams, Wendy, 249
Williamson, G. M., 381
Willmott, C., 201
Wilner, P., 142
Wilson, H. W., 315
Wilson, I. B., 26
Wilson, K. D., 94
Wilson, R. E., 214
Wilson, R. S., 253
Wilson, S., 120
Windich-Biermeier, A., 394
Winfrey, Oprah, 46, 68
Winslet, Kate, 212
Wisco, B. E., 414
Wittgenstein, Ludwig, 410
Wolfe, W. Bertram, 340
Wolitzky-Taylor, K. B., 409
Wolpe, Joseph, 443
Wong, A. K., 330, 349
Wood, R. G., 373
Wood, W., 469
Woodward, Bob, 494
Woodward, M., 266
Woolf, Virginia, 20
Wozniak, R. H., 193
Wrangham, R. W., 281
Wright, D. B., 199

Wright, Frank Lloyd, 331
Wu, A. H., 21, 388
Wu, J., 415
Wundt, Wilhelm, 9, 12
Wyatt, T., 275
Wykes, T., 459
Wylie, K., 274

X

Xie, Y., 248

Y

Yamada, Y., 377
Yamamoto, S., 105
Yamasue, H., 281, 496
Yang, L., 138, 330
Yartz, A. R., 381
Yazzie, A., 249
Yeh, C., 248
Yehuda, R., 393
Yin, L., 90
Yokota, F., 175
Young, L. J., 71
Young, Thomas, 88, 89–90
Younis, J., 321
Yurgelun-Todd, D. A., 317,
    318

Z

Zagrosek, 136
Zahavi, A., 495
Zaitsoff, S. L., 415
Zajonc, R. B., 470, 492
Zanarini, M. C., 426
Zapf, P. A., 424
Zayas, L., 416
Zelnik, N., 68
Zeta-Jones, Catherine, 413
Zhang, Q., 127
Zhang, S. M., 141
Zhang, Z., 349
Zilberman, M. L., 138
Zimbardo, P. G., 34, 291, 467,
    468, 485
Zimmer, C., 231
Zimmerman, R. R., 313–314
Zitek, B., 414
Zohar, J., 457
Zosuls, K. M., 355
Zuckerman, Marvin, 263
Zuo, B., 495

Subject Index

Note: Italic page numbers material in tables or figures. Bold page numbers indicate definitions.

A

A-B problem, 468–469, **468**, *469*

Absolute threshold
definition/description, 80–81, **80**
by different senses, 80

Abstinence syndrome, **137**

Abu Ghraib prison, Iraq, 34

Accommodation, 304, **305**

Acculturation, **361**

Acetylcholine (ACh), 54, **54**, *55*, 213

Achievement motivation, 283–284, *283*

Acoustic code, **189**

Acquired drives, 261–262, **262**

Acrophobia, 405, **405**

ACTH (adrenocorticotrophic hormone), 70, 382, *383*

Action potential, *52*, **52**

Activating effects, **274**, 277

Activation-synthesis model, 126–127, **126**

Actor-observer effect, **484**, 485, *485*

Acupuncture, *110*

Acute stress disorder, 407, **407**

Adaptive thermogenesis, 267

Adipose tissue, 267

Adolescence
brain development, 317–318, *317*
defined, **317**
identity vs. role diffusion, *311*, 321–322
overview, 317–322
pregnancy, 322
puberty, 317, **317**
relationships with parents/peers, 321, *321*
risky behavior, 319, 320–321
sexuality, 322, *322*
social/emotional development, 320–322, *321, 322*

Adolescence cognitive development
egocentrism, 318–319, *319*
formal-operational stage, 318, **318**
overview, 318–320, *319*
postconventional level (moral reasoning), *310*, 311, 319–320, *319*

Adoptee studies, 47–48, 252–253

Adrenal cortex, 70

Adrenal glands
anatomy, 71
hormones/functions, *70*, 71–72, 274

Adrenalin (epinephrine), *70*, 71–72, 213, 378, 409

Adrenocorticotrophic hormone (ACTH), 70, 382, *383*

Affective shift hypothesis, 481, **481**

Afferent neurons, 50, **51**

African Americans
adolescent sexuality and, 322
anorexia nervosa and, 270, *270*
bulimia nervosa and, 270, *270*
doll experiment and, 18, *18*
early pioneers in psychology, 18, *18*
intelligent tests and, 248–249
life expectancy and, 330
psychotherapy and, 455
stereotype threat, 18
weight and, 266, *267*
See also specific individuals

Afterimages, 88, 89, **89**, 90, *90*

Agequake, 328, *328*

Aggression
biology/chemistry and, 280–281
learning and, 282
overview, 280
primate distant past, 280, *280*
psychological aspects of, 281–282
situational factors and, 282
testosterone and, 281

Aging
melatonin and, 71
theories on, 329
See also specific life stages

Agoraphobia, 405, **405**, 406, 449–450

Alarm reaction, 382–383, *382*, **382**, *383*

Alcohol
aldehyde dehydrogenase and, 139, 140

benefits, 140
prenatal development and, 300, *300*
preventable deaths and, 390
weight and, 140

Alcohol abuse
binge drinking, 139
cultural differences, 140
effects overview, 139–140
ethnicity and, 140
gender and, 139, *140*
self-assessment, *140*
summary, *149*
treatment, 141
uses/use statistics, 138–139, *139*

Alcoholics Anonymous (AA), 141, 452

Aldehyde dehydrogenase and alcohol, 139, 140

Algorithms, 224–225, **224**

Alien kidnappings, 19–20

All-or-none principle, **53**

Alpha waves, **123**

Altruism, 495–496, **495**

Alzheimer's disease, 54, 140, 331, **331**

American Heart Association diet recommendations, 269

American Psychology Association, 17, 35, 375

Ames Room, 97

Amniocentesis, 301

Amniotic sac, **299**

Amphetamines
defined, **142**
neurotransmitters and, 54
overview, 142, *149*

Amplitudes of sound waves, 100, *100*

Amygdala
anatomy, *63, 285*
definition/functions, 63, *63*, **63**, 284, 285, **285**
fear and, *285*, 284
PET scans of, **279**

Anagrams, 224–225, 226

Anal-expulsive traits, 343

Anal fixations, 343

Anal-retentive traits, 343

Anal stage, 342–343

Analytical intelligence, 240, *240*

Analytical psychology, 344, **344**

Anchoring and adjustment heuristic, 229, *229*, **229**

Androgens, 274, **299**

Androstadienone, *275*

Angular gyrus, 67

Animal Mind, The (Washburn), 17–18

Animal senses
compared to humans, 79, *79*
tsunami (2004), 79, *79*

Animism, 306, *308*

Anorexia nervosa, 269, 270–271, *270*, **270**

ANS. *See* Autonomic nervous system (ANS)

Anterograde amnesia, 209, **209**

Antianxiety drugs, 456–457

Antibodies, **385**

Antidepressants, 457, **457**

Antidiuretic hormone (ADH), 70, 71

Antigen, **385**

Antipsychotic drugs, 457

Antisocial personality/disorder, 349, *349*, **349**, 426, *426*, **426**

Anxiety disorders
definition/description, 404, **404**
origins of, 408–409
summary, *428*
types overview, 404–407
See also specific disorders

"Anxiety dreams," 125

Anxiety sensitivity, 406

Aphagic, **266**

Aphasia, **67**

Applied research, **5**

Approach-approach conflict, 374, *374*, **374**

Approach-avoidance conflict, 374–375, *374*, **374**

Aptitude, **364**

Archetypes, **344**

Artificial ears, 104

Artificialism, 306, *308*

Asian Americans
early pioneers in psychology, 18
intelligent tests and, 248–249, *248*
psychotherapy and, 455
See also specific individuals

Assertiveness self-assessment, *445*

Assimilation, 304, **304**
Asylums, 435, **435**
Attachment
 defined, **312**
 overview, 312–314,
  313, 314
 strange situation method,
  312
 theoretical views of,
  313–314
 types/stages of, 312–313
Attention-deficit/hyperactivity
  disorder
 defined, **142**
 stimulants and, 142
Attitude-discrepant behavior,
  473
Attitudes
 A-B problem, 468–469,
  468, *469*
 changing through cognitive
  dissonance, 472–474,
  473
 changing through persua-
  sion, 470–472, *471, 472*
 definition/description, 468,
  468
 origins, 469–470
Attraction
 definition/description,
  477, **477**
 love and, 480–481, *481*
 physical appearance
  importance, 477–478,
  477, 478
 proximity and, 480
 reciprocity and, 480, **480**
 red color and, *479*
Attraction-similarity hypothesis, 478, **478**, 480, *480*
Attribution, 484, **484**
Attributional style, 415, **415**
Attribution process, **484**
Attribution theory
 definition/description,
  484–486, **484**, *485*
 self-serving bias and,
  486, **486**
 suicide terrorists and, *485*
Auditory, **101**
Auditory nerve, **102**, *103*
Authoritarian parents, 314,
  315, *315*
Authoritative parents, 314,
  315, *315*
Autistic disorders, *66*
Autobiographical memory,
  185
 See also Episodic memory
Autokinetic effect, **94**
Automatic prejudice, 475
Autonomic nervous system
  (ANS)
 anxiety disorders and, 409
 branches of, 57–58, *57*

definition/description,
  56–57, **56**, *284*
Autonomy vs. shame/doubt,
  311, 312
Availability heuristic,
  229, **229**
Average, 501, **501**, *503*
Aversive conditioning, 443,
  443, **443**
Avoidance-avoidance conflict,
  374, *374*, **374**
Avoidant personality disorder,
  426, **426**
Axons
 changes with development,
  50
 definition/description,
  49, **49**, *51*
 synapse and, *51*

B

Babinski reflex, 302
Barbiturates, 141–142,
  141, *149*
Basilar membrane, 101,
  102, *103*
Bay of Pigs invasion of Cuba,
  494, *494*
Beautiful Mind, A, 420, *420*
"Bedlam," 435
Bed-wetting, 127, 130
Behavioral genetics, **43**
Behaviorism
 defined, **11**
 description, 10
 overview, 351, *351*
 summary, *12*
Behavior modification,
  172, **172**
 See also Behavior therapies
*Behavior of Organism,
  The* (Skinner), 164
Behavior-rating scales,
  363–364, **363**
Behavior therapies
 aversive conditioning, 443,
  443, **443**
 definition/description, 442,
  442
 fear-reduction methods,
  442–443, *442*
 operant-conditioning procedures, 443–446, *444*
 self-control methods, 446
 summary, *462*
Bell-shaped curve, 506–507,
  506, **506**, *507*
BFT. *See* Biofeedback training
  (BFT)
"Big Five" (Five-Factor) model,
  347–348, *347, 362*
Bimodal distribution, 504,
  504, **504**
Binet, Alfred, 253

Binge drinking, 139
Binocular cues, 96, **96**
Biofeedback training (BFT)
 definition/description,
  134–135, **134**, *135*, **445**
 headaches and, 391
 operant conditioning/
  therapy and, 172,
  445–446, **445**
Biological perspective, **14**
Biological preparedness, 156,
  160–161, **160**, *161*
Biological rhythms, 121–122
Biological therapies
 description, 456
 drug therapy, 456–457, *456*
 electroconvulsive therapy
  (ECT), 457–458,
  457, *458*
 evaluation of, 458–460,
  458
 psychosurgery, 458, *459*
 summary, *463*
Biopsychosocial approach and
  health, 388
Biopsychosocial model
 definition/description, 402,
  402, **402**
 of schizophrenia,
  423–424, *423*
Bipolar cells, 85, 86
Bipolar disorder, 413, *413*,
  413, 457
Bismarck (rat), 227, *227*
Blind men and elephant
  (fable), 339
Blind spot, 85, 86, *87*
Blind studies, 31, **31**
BMI (body mass index), 266,
  272, *272*
Body-kinesthetic talents (intelligence)a, 239, *239*
Body mass index (BMI), 266,
  272, *272*
Bone density and aging, 329
Borderline personality disorder, **424**, 425–426, *425*
Bottom-up processing, **94**
Botulism, 54
Brain imaging
 Gage/Gage's accident,
  27–28, *27*
 meditation and, 134
 overview, 28, *28, 32*, 60
 See also specific methods
Brains
 damage effects, 59–60
 experimenting with, 60
 gender and, 59
 humans compared to other
  animals, 49, *50*
 left-/right-handed people,
  68, *68*
 left-brained/right-brained,
  67

parts overview, 60–63, *61*
 "pleasure center," 62, 134
 split-brain experiments,
  68–69, *69*
 See also specific parts
Brain waves, 60
Brightness constancy, 98,
  98, **100**
Broca's aphasia, 67, *67*
Broca's area (cerebral cortex),
  66–67, *67*
Bulimia nervosa, 269, 271,
  271, **271**
Bystander effect
 definition/description,
  496–497, **496**
 Kitty Genovese murder and,
  496, 497
 who is helped, 497, *497*

C

Caffeine and prenatal
  development, 300
Cancer
 definition/description, 393
 factors in, *389*
 preventing/coping with, 395
 psychological factors in
  treatment, 394–395, *394*
 risk factors, 393–394
Cannon-Bard theory of
  emotion, *289*, 290, **290**
Capsulotomy, *459*
Case study
 defined, **24**
 example/description, 25,
  26, 32
 inaccuracy sources, 24–25
 social desirability and, 24
CAT (computerized axial
  tomography) scans, 14,
  28, *28*, 60
Catastrophize, 376, **376**
Catatonic schizophrenia,
  420–421, *420, 421*
Catharsis, **437**
Cell-phone memory loss story,
  183, 184
Cells, *44*
Cellular damage theories of
  aging, 329
Center, **307**
Centers for Disease Control
  and Prevention,
  320–321, 322
Central nervous system
 defined, **56**
 See also Brain; Spinal cord
Central route in persuasion,
  470, **470**
Cerebellum
 alcohol effects on, 61, *62*
 definition/description,
  61, *61*, **61**

Cerebral cortex
    anatomy, 64–65, *64*
    association areas, 65
    defined, **63**
    functions, 63, *64*, 65–67
    language functions and,
        66–67
    right/left hemispheres and,
        65
Cerebrum, *61*, 63, **63**
CFIT (Culture-Fair Intel-
    ligence Test), 248–249,
    249
Challenger launch, 494
Chemical senses
    description, 104
    See also Smell; Taste
Child abuse, 315–316
Childhood cognitive
    development
    Kohlberg's theory of moral
        development, 309–311,
        310
    Piaget's cognitive-
        developmental theory,
        304–309
    Vygotsky's sociocultural
        theory, 309, *309*
Childhood development
    attachment, 312–314,
        312, *313*, *314*
    brain development, 303,
        303
    as continuous/discontinuous,
        305, 309
    day care and, 316
    motor development, 303,
        304
    nature/nurture in brain
        development, 303
    neonates, 302, *302*
    overview, 301–316
    parenting and, 314–316,
        315
    perceptual development,
        303–304
    physical development (first
        2 years), 302–304
    social/emotional develop-
        ment, 311–312, *311*,
        344–345, *345*
Childhood (infantile) amnesia,
    207–209, **207**
Child sexual abuse, 316
Chorionic villus sampling
    (CVS), 301
Chromosomes
    defined, **43**, *44*
    human numbers of,
        44–45, *45*
Chunk/chunking, 195–196,
    195, *196*, 199–200
Cigarette smoking, 145–146,
    145, *146*, 166, *166*, 390
Cinderella (film), 126

Cingulotomy, *459*
Circadian rhythm, **122**
Clairvoyance, 112, 114
Classical conditioning
    applications, 161–162
    biological preparedness
        and, 160–161, **160**, *161*
    defined, **154**
    discrimination, 159, **159**
    example with infant, 155
    extinction, 157–158,
        157, *158*
    extinction curves, *158*
    fear of reptiles, 161, *161*
    generalization, 159,
        159, **159**
    higher order conditioning,
        159–160, *160*, **160**
    "Little Albert," 10, 160,
        160, 161, 163
    Pavlov's work, 154–155,
        155, *156*, 157, 158, *158*,
        159, 160
    spontaneous recovery, 157,
        158, *158*, **158**
    summary, *156*, *178*
    See also Taste aversions
Claustrophobia, 405, **405**
Clearness and depth
    perception, 97
Client-centered therapy, 358,
    439–440, *440*, **440**
Clinical psychologists, 6
Closure, *91*, **92**
Cocaine
    denial and, *144*
    Freud and, 143
    neurotransmitters and,
        54, *143*
    overview, 142–143, *142*,
        143, 149
    use statistics, 139, 143
Coca leaves, 142, 143
Cochlea, 101, **101**, *103*
Cochlear implants, 104
Cognition, **16**, 220
Cognitive appraisal and
    attitudes, 469–470
Cognitive development
    adolescence, 318–320, *319*
    early adulthood, 324–325
    late adulthood, 329,
        329, 331
    middle adulthood,
        326, *327*
    See also Childhood
        cognitive development
Cognitive-dissonance/theory
    changing attitudes and,
        472–474, *473*
    definition/description,
        259–260, 472–473, **472**
Cognitive map, **173**
Cognitive perspective,
    14–15, **14**

Cognitive psychology and
    aggression, 281–282
Cognitive therapies
    correcting cognitive errors,
        447–4489, *448*
    definition/description,
        447, **447**, 449–450
    rational-emotive behavior
        therapy (REBT),
        449, **449**
    summary, *463*
Cohort effect, *298*, **298**
Coke, 142
Collective unconscious, **344**
Collectivists, 360–361,
    360, *361*
College Life Stress Inventory,
    372
Color blindness, 91
Color constancy, 98, **100**
Color vision
    about, 87–88
    color wheel, *88*
    mixture of lights/pigments,
        88–89, *88*
    perception of color, *90*
    perceptual dimensions
        of, 88
    theories on, 89–90, *90*
    warm/cool colors, 88, *88*
Commitment, 480–481,
    481, **481**
Common fate, *93*, **94**
Community mental health
    movement, 435
Complementary colors, **88**
Compulsions, 407
Computerized axial tomogra-
    phy (CAT) scans, 14, 28,
    28, 60
Concepts
    definition/description,
        220–221, **220**
    organizing into hierarchies,
        221, *221*, *222*
Concordance, **408**
Concrete-operational stage,
    307–308, **307**
Conditional positive regard,
    358, **358**
Conditioned reinforcer, **166**
Conditioned response (CR),
    154, **155**
Conditioned stimulus (CS),
    155
Conditioning and attitudes,
    469
Conditions of worth, 358, **358**
Conductive deafness,
    103–104, **103**
Cones, 85, 86, *86*, **86**
Conflict
    definition/description,
        374–375, **374**
    models of, 374–375, *374*

Conform, **491**
Conformity
    Asch's study on, 490–491,
        490, *491*
    factors influencing, 491
    overview, 490–491, *490*,
        491
Conscious, 340, **340**, *341*
Consciousness
    defined, **120**
    description, 119–120
    as sense of self,
        121, *121*
    as waking state, 121
Consciousness altering
    about, 131
    biofeedback/biofeedback
        training, 134–135, **134**,
        135
    meditation, 134, *134*
    See also Hypnosis
Conservation, 306–307,
    306, *308*
Consortium of Social Science
    Associations (COSSA),
    485
Consumer psychologists, 7
Consumer Reports, 469
Consummate love, **481**
Contact comfort, 313–314,
    313, **313**, *314*
Context-dependent memory,
    203–204, **203**, *204*
Contingency theory, 174
Continuity, *93*, **93**
Continuous positive airway
    pressure (CPAP), 128
Continuous reinforcement,
    170
Control groups, 30–31, **31**
Conventional level, *310*,
    311, **311**
Convergence, **96**
Convergent thinking,
    243, **243**
Conversion disorder,
    411–412, **411**
Cornea, 84, *85*
Coronary heart disease
    death statistics on, *392*
    factors in, 389
    job-strain model, *392*
    risk factors, 390–393, *390*
Coronary-prone behavior pat-
    tern, 378
Corpus callosum, *61*, **63**
Correlation, **23**
Correlational method
    cause/effect and, 29, *30*
    definition/description,
        29, *32*
    positive/negative correla-
        tion, 29, *29*
Correlation coefficient, **29**
Corticosteroids, 70, 71

Corticotrophin releasing hormone, 70, 382, *383*, 409
Cortisol, *110*
Cosmic rays, 84, *84*
Cosmopolitan, 26–27, 271–272
Council of Foreign Relations (U.S.), *485*
Counseling psychologists, 6–7
Counterconditioning, 161–162, **161**
Couple therapy, 451, **451**
CPAP (continuous positive airway pressure), 128
Creative intelligence, *240*, 241, 243
Creative self, **345**
Creativity
    definition, **243**
    intelligence, and, 242–244, *243*
    self-assessment, *243*
Critical period
    attachment, 314
    prenatal development, **300**
Critical thinking
    alien kidnappings and, 19–20
    defined, **20**
    Internet psychological advice and, 21
    principles of, 20–21
    tabloid stories and, 19–20, *19*
Cross-sectional research, 298, **298**
Crystallized intelligence, 326, **326**
Cuddlehormone.com, 71
Cultural bias
    defined, **249**
    measuring intelligence and, 18, 248–249
Culture-bound, 402, **402**
Culture-Fair Intelligence Test (CFIT), 248–249, *249*
Curare, 54
CVS (Chorionic villus sampling), 301
CyberPsychology and Behavior, 480

D

Daily hassles
    health and, 373, *373*
    stress and, 370–371, *371*, **371**
Dani people, New Guinea, 233
Dark adaptation, 87, **87**
Day care, 316
Deafness

conductive deafness, 103–104, **103**
    Hunter's notch, 104
    sensorineural deafness, 103, 104, **104**
    statistics on, 103
Death/dying, 332–333
Debrief, **35**
Debriefing, 35
Decentration, **308**
Decibel (dB)
    definition/description, 100, **101**
    sound ratings, 100, *101*
Decision making/judgment
    about, 228, *228*
    framing effect and, 229, **229**
    heuristics and, 228–229, *229*
    overconfidence and, 230
Declarative memory, 185
    See also Explicit memory
Defense mechanism, **341**
Deindividuation, 282, **495**
Déjà vu experience, 203–204
Delta waves, **124**
Delusions, **419**
Dementia, 329, 331, **331**
Demonological model (psychological disorders), 401, *401*
Dendrites, **49**
Denial, *342*
Dependent variable, **30**
Depolarize, **52**
Depressants
    definition/description, **136**, 138
    overview, 138–142
    See also Alcohol; *specific depressants*
Depression
    alleviating, 460–461
    examples, 288–289, *415*
    exercise and, *461*
    gender and, 414
    irrational thoughts and, *461*
    neurotransmitters and, 54, 55
    psychosurgery, *459*
    responses by treatments, *458*
    self-assessment, *413*
    See also specific types
Depth perception, 95–96, *95*, *97*
Descent of Man, The (Darwin), 39, 40, *41*
Descriptive statistics
    definition/description, 502–503, *502*, **502**
    measures of central tendency, 503–504, *503*, **503**, *504*

measures of variability, 504–506, *505*, *506*
Desensitization, **83**
Developmental psychologists, 7, *7*
Dexter (dog), *407*
Diagnostic and Statistical Manual (DSM), 403
Diathesis-stress model, 402, **402**
Dichromats, *91*, **91**
Difference threshold
    defined, **81**
    Weber's constant and, 81–82
Diffusion of responsibility, 282, 293, 492, **492**, *495*, 496
Dinosaurs, *41*, *161*
Direct inner awareness, **120**
Disaster survivors and "robo" rats, *169*
Discrimination, 475, *475*, **475**
Discrimination, conditioning, 159, **159**
Discriminative stimulus, 168–169, *168*, **169**
Diseases of adaptation, 385
Disinhibition, 176
Disorganized schizophrenia, 420, **420**
Displace, **196**
Displacement, **233**, *342*, 343
Dispositional attribution, 484, **484**
Dissociative amnesia, **207**, 410, **410**
Dissociative disorders
    definition/description, *410*, **410**
    origins, 410–411
    summary, *428*
    types, 410
Dissociative fugue, **410**, 411
Dissociative identity disorder (DID), 399, 410, *410*, **411**
Divergent thinking, 243, **243**
Dizygotic (DZ) twins
    defined, **45**
    twin studies, 45, 46, 47, 252, *252*
DNA, **43**, *44*
Dogs
    behavior with chewing bones, 3–4
    domestication/breeding, 4, 349–350
    personalities research, 350
    PTSD cases and, *407*
    sense of smell, 104, *105*
    sense of taste, 105
    skills development, 4
    wolves and, 4, 349, *349*, 350

Dopamine, 54, **54**, 55–56, *55*, 415, 423
Double-blind studies, 31, **31**, 33
Down syndrome, 45, *45*, **45**
Draw-A-Person test, 248
Dream analysis, 438
Dreams
    about, 125
    activation-synthesis model, 126–127, **126**
    "anxiety dreams," 125
    consolidating memories, 127
    Freud and, 126
    nightmares, 125
    NREM sleep and, 125
    as protecting sleep, 126
    REM sleep and, 125
    "residue of the day" and, 125–126, *126*
    "unconscious desires" and, 126
Drive, **260**
Drive for superiority, **345**
Drive-reduction theory, 261–262, **261**
Drugs
    drug therapy, 456–457, *456*
    See also Psychoactive substances
DSM (Diagnostic and Statistical Manual), 403
Duncker candle problem, 227, *227*
Dyslexia, 67, 68

E

Eardrum, 101, **101**, *103*
Early adulthood, 324–325
Ears
    anatomy, 101, *103*
    locating sound, 101–102
Eating disorders
    anorexia nervosa, 269, 270–271, *270*, **270**
    bulimia nervosa, 269, 271, *271*, **271**
    defined, **269**
    ethnicity and, 270, *270*
    origins of, 271–272
    report on, 268–269
    self-assessment, *273*
    sociocultural factors and, 271–272, *272*
Echo, **193**
Echoic memory, 193, *193*, **193**
Ecstasy (MDMA), *146*
ECT (electroconvulsive therapy), 457–458, **457**, *458*, 460
Educational psychologists, 7
EEG. *See* Electroencephalograph (EEG)

Efferent neurons, 50, **51**
Effort justification, 473–474, **473**
Ego, 341, *341*, **341**
Ego analyst, **439**
Egocentrism
  adolescence, 318–319, *319*
  childhood, 306, 308, *308*
  defined, **306**
Ego identity, 345, **345**
Eidetic imagery, **193**
Ejaculation, **275**
Elaboration likelihood model, **470**
Elaborative rehearsal, **190**, 200
Electra complex, 343, **343**, 345
Electroboy (Behrman), 413
Electroconvulsive therapy (ECT), 457–458, *457*, *458*, 460
Electroencephalograph (EEG)
  biofeedback and, 446
  defined, **60**
  hypnosis and, 132
  sleep and, 122–123, *123*
Electromagnetic spectrum, 84, *84*
Electromyograph (EMG), 135, **135**, 446
Elements of Psychophysics (Fechner), 9
Elle, 26–27
Embryonic stage, **299**
EMDR (eye-movement desensitization and reprocessing), 447
Emerging adulthood, 323, **323**, *324*
EMG (electromyograph), 135, **135**, 446
Emotional intelligence, *241*
Emotions
  definition/description, 284–285, **284**
  Ekman's photographs, 285–286, *286*
  expression/communication and, 285–286, *286*
  facial-feedback hypothesis, 287–288, *287*, *288*
  See also Social/emotional development; *specific emotions*
Emotions/theories
  Cannon-Bard theory, *289*, 290, **290**
  cognitive appraisal, *289*, 290–291, *290*
  "commonsense theory," 289
  evaluation of, 291
  "how do you feel," 288–289

James-Lange theory, 289–290, *289*, **289**
  Schachter-Singer study, 290–291, *290*
Empathic understanding, 440, **440**
Empirical science, **22**
Empty-nest syndrome, 327, **327**
Encoding, **189**
Endocrine system
  anxiety disorders and, 409
  defined, **70**
  hormones and, 70
  negative feedback loop, 70
  parts/functions summary, 70
  See also specific glands; specific hormones
Endorphins, *55*, **55**, 110
Engram, **212**
Environmental psychologists, 7
Epigenesis, **49**
Epigenetic framework, 48
Epilepsy
  defined, **68**
  split-brain operations and, 68
Epinephrine (adrenalin), 70, 71–72, 213, 378, 409
Episodic memory, 184, 185, **185**, *188*
Erikson's stages of psycho-social development, 311–312, *311*, 344–345, **345**
Erogenous zone, 341–342, **342**
Eros, 341
ESP (extrasensory perception), 112, **112**, 114
Estratetraenol, 275
Estrogen, 70, 72, 213, 275, *384*, 414
Estrus, 274, **274**
Eternal Sunshine of the Spotless Mind (film), 212, *212*, 214
Ethical, **33**
Ethical research
  with animals, 35, *35*
  debriefing and, 35
  deception of participants and, 34–35
  with humans, 33–35, *34*
Ethics review committees, 33
Ethnic group, **16**
Ethnicity
  adolescent sexuality and, 322, *322*
  alcohol abuse and, 140
  cancer and, 394
  discrimination and, 475
  doll experiment, 18, *18*

eating disorders and, 270, *270*
  heart disease and, 392–393
  intellectual functioning and, 247–248, *248*
  psychoactive drugs' effects and, 18
  psychology and, 16, 18–19
  psychotherapy and, 455–456, *455*
  sexual behavior and, 277, *277*
  suicide and, 416
  See also Sociocultural perspective
European Americans
  adolescent sexuality and, 322
  anorexia nervosa and, 270, *270*
  bulimia nervosa and, 270, *270*
  intelligent tests and, 248–249, *248*
  life expectancy and, 330
  psychotherapy and, 455
Eustress, **370**
Evaluation apprehension, 492, **492**
Event-based prospective memory, 187
Evidence-based practices, 454–455, *454*, **454**
Evolution
  Darwin and, 9, 14, 39, 40, *41*
  functionalism and, 9
  of humans, 39, 40, *41*, 46
  natural selection and, 40
  red spiders' mating behavior, 495
  sleep time, *122*
  spontaneous recovery and, 158, *158*
  struggle for survival, 39–40, *41*
Evolutionary perspective, **14**
Evolutionary psychology, **42**
Excitement phase, **274**
Exemplar, **221**
Exercise
  coping with PMS, 74, *74*
  depression and, *461*
  health benefits, 387, 390, *461*
  stress and, 387
Exhaustion stage, 385, **385**
Existential intelligence, 239, *239*
Existentialism, **15**, 356, **356**
Exorcism, *401*
Experiment
  defined, **30**
  in scientific method, 22

Experimental groups, 30–31, **30**
Experimental method
  alcohol effects example, 30, *30*, 31, *31*, 33, 35
  blinds/double blinds, 31, *31*, **31**, 33
  experimental/control groups, 30–31
  overview, 29–30, *29–31*, *32*, 33
Experimental psychologists, 7
Experimenter bias, **31**
Expertise, 226
Explicit memory, 185, **185**, *188*
Exposure therapy, 447
Externals, **381**
Extinction
  classical conditioning, 157–158, **157**, *158*
  operant conditioning, 168
Extrasensory perception (ESP), 112, **112**, 114
Extraversion, 347, *347*, **347**
Extrinsic rewards, **283**
Eye-movement desensitization and reprocessing (EMDR), 447
Eyes
  anatomy, *85*
  light and, 84–86, *85*
Eyewitness testimony, *199*
Eysenck's trait theory, 347, *347*

F

Facial analysis, *23*
Facial-feedback hypothesis, 287–288, **287**, *288*
Factor analysis, 238, **238**, 346
Factor theories, 238, 239, 242
False memory syndrome, *208*
Family therapy, 451, **451**
Fear appeal, 470, **471**
Fear Factor, 404
Fear-reduction methods (behavior therapies), 442–443, *442*
Feature detectors, **82**
Feeling-of-knowing experience, 202–203, **202**
Fels Longitudinal Study, 298
Fetal alcohol syndrome (FAS), 300, *300*, **300**
Fetal stage, **299**
Fight-or-flight response, 57, 382–383, **382**, *384*
Fissures of cerebral cortex, 63
Five-Factor ("Big Five") model, 347–348, *347*, 362
Fixation time, 303, **303**
Fixed-action patterns (FAPs), 261, *261*
  See also Instinct

Fixed-interval schedule, *170*, **170**
Fixed-ratio schedule, **170**, 171
Flashbacks, *54–55*, **147**
Flashbulb memories, 201, *201*, **201**
Flavor, **104**, 105, *107*
Flooding, 162, *162*, **162**, 442
Fluid intelligence, 326, **326**
fMRI (functional magnetic resonance imaging), 14, 28, *28*, 60
Follicle-stimulating hormone, 70
Food and Drug Administration, 31
Foot-in-the-door technique, **473**, *473*, 489
Forced-choice format, 364, **364**
Forensic psychologists, 7, 8
Forgetting
    Ebbinghaus's classic curve of, 206, *206*
    interference and, 206–207, *206*
    nonsense syllables, 204–205
    tasks used to measure, 205–206, *205*
Formal-operational stage, 318, **318**
Fossil record, *41*
Fovea, **85**, **86**
Frame of reference, 357, **357**, 440
Framing effect, 229, **229**
Free association, **437**, 438
Frequencies of sound waves, 100, *100*
Frequency theory, 102–103, **102**
Frontal lobe, **64**
Frustration and Aggression (behavioral psychologists), 159
Functional analysis, 446, **446**
Functional fixedness, 227, *227*, **227**
Functionalism
    defined, **9**
    habits and, 9–10
    summary, *12*
Functional magnetic resonance imaging (fMRI), 14, 28, *28*, 60
Fundamental attribution error, 484, **484**, *485*

G

G (general intelligence symbol), 238, **238**
Gambling and reinforcement schedules, 170, *171*

Gamma-aminobutyric acid (GABA), **54**, 55, *55*, 409
Gamma knife surgery, *459*
Ganglion cells, 85–86, *85*, **85**
Ganzfeld procedure, 114
GAS. *See* General adaptation syndrome (GAS)
Gate theory of pain, *110*
Gay males, 278
Gender
    alcohol abuse and, 139, *140*
    brain size and, *59*
    cigarette smoking and, 146, *146*
    defined, **16**
    depression and, 414
    fight-or-flight response and, *384*
    intellectual functioning and, 249–250, *250*
    life expectancy and, 330
    moral development and, *320*
    pain and, 107–108, *108*
    psychology and, 16
    sexual behavior and, 277, *277*
    sleep disorders and, *127*
    suicide and, 416, *416*
Gender-schema, 355, **355**
Gender-typing
    biology and, 354
    definition/description, 354, **355**
    gender-schema theory of, 355, **355**
    social cognition and, 355, *355*
    stereotypical masculine/feminine traits, 354, *354*
General adaptation syndrome (GAS)
    alarm reaction, 382–383, *382*, **382**, *383*
    defined, **382**
    hormones and, 382, *383*, *384*
    overview, 382–385, *382*, *383*
    stages, 384–385
Generalization, conditioning, 159, *159*, **159**
Generalize
    defined, **23**
    problems with, 23–24
Generalized anxiety disorder, 406, **406**
Generativity vs. stagnation, *311*, 326–327
Genes
    definition/description, **43**, *44*
    human-human overlap, *46*, 46

human-other species overlap, 46
Genetic code
    definition/description, 43, *44*
    human-human overlap, *46*, 46
    human-other species overlap, 46
Genetic-environmental correlation, 48, *48*
Genetics
    anxiety disorders and, 408–409
    defined, **43**
    personality disorders and, 427
    relatives genes in common, 45
    schizophrenia and, 422–423, *423*
    See also Heredity; Kinship studies
Genital stage, 343
Genotype, **44**
Genuineness, 440, **440**
Germinal stage, **299**
Gestalt psychology
    about, 11, 13
    closure and, 92, *92*
    context and, *11*
    defined, **11**
    history/contributors, 10–11
    summary, *12*
Gestalt therapy, 439, 441, *441*, **441**
Gland, **70**
Glial cells, 49, *50*
Glutamate, 213
Grand Theft Auto (video game), 175
Gray matter, **58**, *422*
Great Depression, 23
Group behavior
    altruism and, 495–496, **495**
    bystander effect, 496–497, **496**, *497*
    group decision making, 492–495, *493*, *494*
    groupthink, 494–495, *494*, **495**
    mob behavior, 282, 495, *495*
    social facilitation, 492, *492*
Group decision making
    groupthink, 494–495, *494*, **495**
    polarization/"risky shift," 493
    "rules" on, 492–493, *493*
Group therapies
    couple therapy, 451, **451**
    description, 450–451, *451*
    family therapy, 451, **451**

self-help/support groups, 452
Groupthink, 494–495, *494*, **495**
Growth hormone, 70, 71
Growth-hormone-releasing factor (hGRF), *70*, 71

H

Habits and functionalism, 9–10
Habituation, 177
Hallucinations, 19, *400*, **400**
Hallucinogenic drugs, **146**
    See also specific drugs
Hallucinogen persisting perception disorder (HPPD), 147
Hamlet (Shakespeare), 447
Hammer of Witches, 401
Hanunoo people, Philippines, 233
Happiness
    Ekman's photographs, *286*
    example, 286, *287*
    facial-feedback hypothesis and, 287–288, **287**, *288*
    factors contributing to, 286–287
    positive psychology and, 286, **286**, 348
    research lessons, *287*
    virtuous traits and, 348
Headaches
    about, 388, *390*
    coping with/preventing, 391
    migraine headaches, 389–390, **389**
    muscle-tension headaches, 389
    stress and, 388
Head Start programs, 29, 253, 507
Health problems
    genetics and, 388
    preventable deaths in US., 390
    psychology and (overview), 388
    See also specific problems; Stress; Stress and health
Health psychologists, 7
Health psychology
    cancer patients and, 394–395, *394*
    definition/description., 370, **370**
Hearing
    absolute threshold, 80
    summary, *113*
    See also Deafness; Ears; Sound
Hearing damage

decibel level and, 100, *101*, *102*
iPods, *102*
Heart disease. *See* Coronary heart disease
Heredity
building blocks of, 43–45, *44*
defined, **43**
examples, 43
left-/right-handedness and, 68
See also Genetics; Kinship studies
Hering-Helmholtz illusion, *99*, *99*
Heritability, **252**
Heroin, 139, 141
Hertz (Hz), 100, **101**
Heterosexual, **278**
Heuristics
decision making and, 228–229, *229*
definition/description, 225, **225**
hGRF (growth-hormone-releasing factor), *70*, 71
Hibernation of animals, 122
Hierarchical structure, 201–202, *202*
Hierarchy of needs, 263–264, **263**, *264*
Higher order conditioning, 159–160, *160*, **160**
Himba of Namibia, *220*, 221
Hindbrain, 61, *62*
Hippocampus, 54, 63, *63*, **208**, *209*
HIV/AIDS, 301, 331
H.M.S. *Beagle*, 39, 40, *40*
Holophrase, **234**
Homeostasis, **262**
Homosexuals, **278**, *475*, *475*
Hopi Indians, 233
Hormones
definition/description, 70, 73–74
general adaptation syndrome and, 382, *383*, *384*
See also Endocrine system; *specific hormones*
HPPD (hallucinogen persisting perception disorder), 147
Hue, **84**
Human development
adolescence, 317–322, **317**
childhood, 301–316
death/dying, 332–333
early adulthood, 324–325
emerging adulthood, 323, **323**, *324*
late adulthood, 328–332

middle adulthood, 325–327, *326*, *327*
prenatal development, 299–301
studying, 297–298
See also specific stages
Human factors psychologists, 7
Human Genome Project, 44
Humanism, **15**, *356*, **356**
Humanistic-existential perspective
description, 15
evaluation of, 359
overview, 356–359, *356*
self-actualization and, 356
self-theory (Rogers), 356–357
summary, *363*
Humanistic theory, 263–264, *264*
Humanistic therapies
client-centered therapy, 358, 439–440, *440*, **440**
definition/description, **439**
gestalt therapy, 439, 441, *441*, **441**
summary, *462*
Humor, 379
Hunger
biological influences on, 265–266
food as symbol, 265
psychological influences on, *265*, 266
Hunger pangs, 265
Hunter's notch, 104
Hydrocarbons, **145**
Hyperphagic, **265**, *266*
Hypersomnia, 122
Hypertension, **391**
Hyperthyroidism, 71
Hypnagogic state, **123**
Hypnosis
consciousness changes with, *132*
definition/description, 131, **131**
EEG recordings and, 132
Freud and, 133
induction, *133*
pain and, *111*, 131
theoretical views of, 133
uses, *111*, 131–132
Hypnotic suggestibility, 132
Hypnotic trance, 132
Hypochondriasis, 412, *412*, **412**
Hypothalamus
definition/description, *61*, **62**
functions, 62, 70, 71
lateral hypothalamus, 266, *266*
lesions and, 60

Hypothesis, *22*, **22**, **23**
Hypothyroidism, 71

I

Icon, **193**
Iconic memory, 193, **193**
Id, 341, *341*, **341**
Ideas of persecution, **400**
Identification, 341
Illusions, **94**
Imaginary audience, 318, 319, *319*
Immune system
definition/description, 385, **385**, *388*
stress and, 385–386
Immunizations for infectious diseases, 390
Implanted memories
examples, *198*, 199
misinformation effect and, 199, *208*
Implicit memory, 185–186, **185**, *188*
Imprinting, 314, *314*, **314**
Incentive, **260**
Incest taboo, 343
Incubation, 227, **227**
Independent variable, **30**
Individualists, 360–361, **360**, *361*
Individual psychology, **345**
Industrial psychologists, 7
Industry vs. inferiority, *311*, 312
Infant-directed speech (IDS), *236*
Infantile (childhood) amnesia, 207–209, **207**
Infer, *508*, **508**
Inferential statistics
definition/description, 507–508, **507**, *508*
overview, 507–509
statistically significant differences, 508–509, *508*, **508**, *509*
Inferiority complex, 344, **344**
Infinite creativity, **232**
Inflammation, 385, *385*
Informed consent, **34**
Initiative vs. guilt, *311*, 312
Insanity, **400**
Insanity plea, *424*
Insight
Bismarck (rat) and, 227, *227*
chimpanzee/bananas example, *13*
definition/description, **11**, **226**, 227–228
Insomnia
after September 11 attacks, *408*

coping with, *129*
description, 122, 127–128, *127*
sleep fears and, *129*
Instinct
definition/description, **42**, **261**
fixed-action patterns (FAPs), 261, *261*
Instinctive behavior
about, 154
examples, 42, *42*, 154, *154*
fixed-action patterns (FAPs), 261, *261*
Instinctive perspective, **14**
Insulin, *70*
Integrity vs. despair, *311*, 332
Intellectual functioning
changes with age, 326
education and, 253, *254*
ethnicity and, 247–248, *248*
factors affecting (summary), *254*
gender and, 249–250, *250*
genetics and, 250, *251*, 252–253, *254*
Head Start programs and, 29, 253, *507*
home environment and, *251*, 253, *254*
nurture and, *251*, 253–254
socioeconomic differences, 247–248, *251*
Intelligence
adaptation to varying environments and, 219, *219*
concept of, 237–238
creativity and, 242–244, *243*
defined, **237**, *242*
See also Measuring intelligence; Thinking
Intelligence quotient (IQ), **244**
Intelligence tests. *See* Measuring intelligence
Intelligence theories
factor theories, 238, *239*, *242*
summary, *242*
theory of emotional intelligence, *241*
theory of multiple intelligences, 238–240, **238**, *239*, *242*
theory of social intelligence, *241*
triarchic theory of intelligence, 240–241, *240*, **240**, *242*, *243*
Interference theory, **206**
Internals, 381
Internet surveys, 26–27
Interneuron, 58
Interpersonal skills (intelligence), 239, *239*

Interposition, *96*, **96**
Interpretation, **437**
Intimacy, 480–481, *481*, **481**
Intimacy versus isolation, *311*, 325, *325*
Intrapersonal skills (intelligence), 239, *239*
Intrinsic rewards, **283**
Introspection, 8
Introversion, 347, *347*, **347**
Inuit (Eskimos), 233
iPod oblivion, *102*
iPods, *102*
Iraq invasion and groupthink, 494–495, *494*
Iris, **84**, *85*
Irrational beliefs
  controlling, 386, *386*, *461*
  examples, *376*, *461*
  stress and, 375–377, *376*

J

Jackson (dog), 3–4, *4*
James-Lange theory of emotion, 289–290, *289*, **289**
Japan tsunami/nuclear power plant damage, 369
Jet lag, 71
Jigsaw puzzles, 94, *94*
Journal of Personality and Social Psychology, 112, 114
Just noticeable difference (jnd), **81**

K

Kanzi (chimpanzee), 231
Kinesthesis, **110**, *113*
Kinsey (film), *26*
Kinsey reports, 276, *276*
Kinship studies
  adoptee studies, 47–48, 252–253
  description, 45
  twin studies, 45–47, *47*, 250, 252, *252*
Kohlberg's theory of moral development
  levels/stages summary, *310*
  overview, 309–311, *310*
Kübler-Ross stages of dying, 333

L

La belle indifference, **411**
LAD (language acquisition device), 237, **237**
Language
  apes/chimps and, 231–232, *231*, *232*

brain Broca's area and, 231, *231*, *232*
  cerebral cortex and, 66–67
  culture and, 233–234, *233*
  definition/description, 232, **232**
  properties of, 232
  thinking relationship, 232–233
Language acquisition device (LAD), 237, **237**
Language development
  baby talk/"motherese," *236*
  children (overview), 234–235, *236*
  first word age range, 234
  grammar and, 234–235
  infants, 234, *234*
  nature/nurture and, 235–237
  theories, 235–237
Language intelligence, 239, *239*
Late adulthood
  cognitive development, 329, *329*, 331
  overview, 328–332
  physical development, 328–329, *329*, *331*
  sexuality changes, 329
  social/emotional development, 331
  successful aging, 332
Latent content, **438**
Latent learning, **173**
Lateral hypothalamus, 266, **266**
Latin Americans
  adolescent sexuality and, 322
  early pioneers in psychology, 18
  life expectancy and, 330
  psychotherapy and, 455
  weight and, 266
  See also specific individuals
Law of effect, **163**
Learned helplessness, 414–415, **414**
Learning
  cognitive factors in, 173
  cognitive psychologists definition of, 153–154
  contingency theory, 174
  definition/description, 153–154, **154**
  dog/fetch example, 153
  repetition and, 5, 10
  types summary, *178*
  See also Classical conditioning; Observational learning; Operant conditioning
Learning-theory perspectives
  behaviorism overview, 351, *351*

evaluation of, 352–353
  humanistic-existential perspective, 356–359, *356*
  overview, 350–353
  social-cognitive theory, 351–352, *352*, *353*
  summary, *363*
Left-handed people, 68, *68*
Lens, **85**, *85*
Lesbians, 278
Lesion, **60**
Leukocytes, 385, **385**, *388*
Libido/libidinal energy, 341–342
Lie detectors (polygraphs), 292
Life changes
  health and, 373, *373*
  stress and, 371, 373
Life expectancy, 328, **328**
Life expectancy scale, *330*
Life span, 328, **328**
Light
  visible light spectrum, *84*
  Weber's constant for, 81–82
Limbic system, 62–63, **62**, *63*
Linguistic-relativity hypothesis, 233–234, *233*, **233**
Linnean Society, 40
Literary Digest, 23
Lithium, 457
"Little Albert" (Douglas Merritte), *10*, 160, *160*, 161, 163
Locus of control
  defined, **379**
  self-assessment, *380*
  stress and, 379, 381, *381*
Logical-mathematical intelligence, 239, *239*
London suicide bomber attacks, 467, *467*
Long-term memory
  accuracy of, 197–198
  amount of information stored, 198
  definition/description, *192*, 196–197, **196**
  feeling-of-knowing experience, 202–203, **202**
  flashbulb memories, 201, *201*, **201**
  levels of processing information, 200–201
  organization in, 201–202, *202*
  schemas and, 197–198, *197*, *198*
  tip-of-the-tongue (TOT) phenomenon, 202–203, **202**
  transferring short-term memory to, 198–200

Long-term potentiation (LPT), **213**
Longitudinal studies/research, 298, **298**
Los Angeles Times poll, 332
Loulis (chimpanzee), 231
LSD, 54–55, *147*, **147**, *149*
Lucifer effect, 468
Luteinizing hormone, *70*
Lying, 292

M

MacArthur Longitudinal Twin Study, 252
MacBeth (Shakespeare), 419, 436
Maintenance rehearsal, *190*, **190**, 198–199
Major depressive disorder, 412–413, **412**
Malnutrition and prenatal development, 301
Manic, **413**
Manifest content, **438**
Marijuana
  defined, **146**
  as medicine, *148*
  overview, 146–147, *147*, *149*
Maslow's hierarchy of needs, 263–264, *264*
Masturbation, 276, 322, 345
Maturation, **299**
McEnroe, John, 68
MDMA (ecstasy), *146*
Mean, 503, **503**, *505*
Means-end analysis, 225, **225**
Measures of central tendency, 503–504, *503*, **503**, *504*
Measures of variability, 504–506, *505*, *506*
Measuring intelligence
  cultural bias and, 18, 248–249
  Culture-Fair Intelligence Test (CFIT), 248–249, *249*
  Draw-A-Person test, 248
  group tests, 247
  reliability/validity, 247
  Stanford-Binet Intelligence Scale (SBIS), 244–245, *245*, 247
  Wechsler Scales, 245–247, *246*, 247
Measuring personality
  behavior-rating scales, 363–364, **363**
  objective tests, 364, *364*, **364**
  overview, 362–365
  projective tests, 365, **365**
  uses, 364

Media violence/aggression
  about, 175–177, *176*, *177*
  Bandura's experiment on, 176, *176*
  observational learning and, 175–177, *176*, *177*
  teaching against imitating, 177
Median, –504503, **503**
Medical model (psychological disorders), 401–402, *401*
Meditation, 134, *134*, 387
Medulla, 61, *61*, **61**
Melatonin
  functions, 70, 71, 134
  meditation and, 134
Memory
  biology of, 212–214, *213*
  brain structures and, 209, *209*, 214
  defined, **190**
  hippocampus and, 209, *209*, 214
  improving, *210–211*
  neurotransmitters and, 54
  processes of, 189–190
  reconstruction of inaccurate memory, 185, *197*, 198, *199*, *200*
  relationships between types of, *188*
  self-assessment of, *184*
  stages of, 191–193, *192*
  study on retention, *187*
  See also Forgetting; *specific types*
Memory trace, **191**
Menarche, 317, **317**
Menopause, 326, **326**
Menstrual cycle
  hormones and, 72
  male attractiveness and, 72–73, *73*
  See also Premenstrual syndrome (PMS)
Mental age (MA), 244, *244*
Mental hospitals, 435
Mental image, **226**
Mental set, 226, **226**
Mental Traits of Sex, The (Thompson), 18
Mescaline, **148**, *149*
Meta-analysis, 453, **453**, 458–459
Metamemory, **190**
Metastasize, 393
Methadone, 141
Method of loci, 210
Method of savings, **206**
Middle adulthood, 325–327, *326*, *327*
  cognitive development, 326, *327*
  physical development, 326

as sandwich generation, 327, **327**
social/emotional development, 326–327, *327*
Middle ear, 101, *103*
Midlife crisis, 327
Migraine headaches, 389–390, **389**
Migration of animals, 121–122
Milgram studies
  description/results, 486–488, *487*, *488*
  obedience reasons, 489–490
  replications of, 488–489
Minnesota Multiphasic Personality Inventory (MMPI), 364, *364*
Minnesota Study of Twins Reared Apart, 47, 253
Mirror neurons
  defined, 66
  imitation in infants, *175*
  observational learning and, 174–175, *175*
Misinformation effect, **199**
Miss America, 172
M'Naghten rule, *424*
Mnemonic devices, *211*
Mob behavior, 282, 495, *495*
Mode, 504, **504**
Model, **174**
Modeling, 353, 443, **443**
Monochromat, **91**
Monocular cues, 95–96, *95*, *95*, *97*
Monozygotic (MZ) twins
  defined, 45
  twin studies, 45–46, 47, *47*, 252, *252*
Mood disorders
  definition/description, 412, **412**
  origins of, 414–415
  summary, *429*
  types, 412–413
  See also Suicide
Moral development
  gender and, *320*
  See also Kohlberg's theory of moral development
Moral principle, 341
Moro reflex, 302
Morphine, 141
Motion parallax, **96**
Motion perception, 94–95, *95*
Motivation
  achievement and, 282–284, *283*
  defined, **260**
  psychology of (overview), 260
  sensation-seeking scale, *263*
  See also Sexual motivation

Motivation theories
  drive-reduction theory, 261–262, **261**
  evolutionary perspective, 261, *261*
  humanistic theory, 263–264, *264*
  Maslow's hierarchy of needs, 263–264, *264*
  stimulation search, 262, *262*, *263*
Motive, **260**
Motor cortex, **65**
Müller-Lyer illusion, 99, *99*
Multifactorial theory, hypnosis, 133
Multiple approach-avoidance conflict, 374, 375, **375**
Multiple intelligences theory, 238–240, **238**, *239*, *242*
Multiple personality disorder, 399, **411**
Muscle-tension headaches, 389
Musical intelligence, 239, *239*
Mutation, **41**
Mutism, **419**
"My Blue Heaven" (song/drug), 456
Myelin, 50, *51*
Myelination, 50
Myotonia, **274**

N

Nadine (dog), 3–4, *4*
Narcolepsy, 128, **128**, *130*
Narcotics, **141**
National Eating Disorders Association, 268–269
National Health and Social Life Survey (NHSLS), 276–277, *277*
National Sleep Foundation, 121, 127
National Survey of Family Growth, 277
Native Americans
  Hopi Indians, 233
  intelligence tests and, 248
  life expectancy and, 330
  psychotherapy and, 455–456
  self-efficacy expectations and, 379
Nativist theory of language development, 237
Naturalistic observation, 27, *27*, *32*
Naturalist intelligence, 239, *239*
Natural selection, 40, 409, *409*
Nature, **44**
Neanderthals, 46
Nearsightedness, 86

Necker cube, 93, *93*
Need, **260**
Negative adaptation (sensitization), 83
Negative correlation, 29, *29*
Negative feedback loop, 70
Negative punishment, 167, *167*, 168
Negative reinforcer, *165*, **165**
Negative symptoms, **419**
Neoanalysts, 439
Neodissociation theory, 133
Neonate, **299**, 302
Nerve, **56**
Nervous system
  components summary, 56
  divisions of, *56*
  See also specific components
Neural impulse
  definition, **51**
  description/electrical changes, 51–53, *52*
  early experiment on, 50–51
  recovery, 53
  threshold for firing, 53
Neurons
  anatomy, 49, *51*
  defined, **49**
  description, 49
  nucleus of, 49, *51*
  synapse and, 53
  transmission between, 53
  See also specific components
Neuroticism, 347, 415, **415**
Neurotransmitters
  amphetamines and, 54
  cocaine and, 54, *143*
  definition/functions, 51, 53–55, *53*, *55*
  examples, 54–55
  opiates and, 141
  reuptake of, 53
  summary/functions, *55*
Niche-picking, 48
Nicotine
  cigarette smoking, 145–146, *146*, 166, *166*, 390
  effects, 143–144, *145*, 149
  heart disease and, *390*
  prenatal development and, 300, *300*
  preventable deaths and, 390
  summary, *149*
Nociceptors, 108
No Country for Old Men (film), 7
Nonconscious, 120, **121**
Nondeclarative memory, 185
  See also Implicit memory
Non-rapid-eye-movement (NREM), 123, *123*, **123**, *124–125*
Nonsense syllables, 204–205, **204**

Norepinephrine (noradrenalin), 54, *54*, **55**, *70*, 71, 213, 378, 409
Normal curve/distribution, 506–507, *506*, **506**, *507*
Normal distribution, **506**
NREM (non-rapid-eye-movement), 123, *123*, **123**, *124–125*
Nucleotides, 43, 44
Nucleus of cell, *44*
Nurture, **44**

O

Obedience to authority
  crimes against humanity and, 486, 487, 489, 490
  overview, 486–490
  See also Milgram studies
Obesity, 266
Obesogenic environment, 267–268
Objective responsibility, 307, **307**
Objective tests, **364**
Object permanence, 305, *307*
Observational conditioning summary, *178*
Observational learning
  attitudes and, 469
  definition/description, 174, **174**
  media violence/aggression and, 175–177, *176*, *177*
  mirror neurons and, 174–175, *175*
Observation methods
  overview, 24–28
  See also specific methods
Obsessions, 407
Obsessive-compulsive disorder (OCD), 406–407, *406*, **406**, *459*
Occipital lobe, **64**
Oedipus complex, 343, **343**, 345, 426–427
Olfactory nerve, **105**
On the Origin of Species (Darwin), 40
Operant, **164**
Operant behavior, **164**
Operant conditioning
  applications, 172
  definition/description, 163, **164**
  disaster survivors and "robo" rats, *169*
  discriminative stimulus, 168–169, *168*, **169**
  extinction, 168
  "Little Albert" and, 163
  methods of, 164–165, *165*
  Project Pigeon, 163–164, *164*

reinforcement, 163–164
reinforcement schedules, 170–171
reinforcer types, 165–166, *165*, *166*
reinforcers vs. rewards/punishment, 167–168, *167*
rewards/punishment, 167–168, *167*
shaping, 170, 171–172, *171*
Skinner box, 164–165, *165*, 168
Skinner's work, 163–165, *164*, *165*, 167, 168, 172
spontaneous recovery, 166
summary, *178*
Thorndike's work, 163
Operant-conditioning procedures (behavior therapies)
  biofeedback training (BFT), 445–446, **445**
  overview, 443–446, *446*
  social skills training, 444–445, *444*, **444**
  successive approximations, 444, **444**
  token economies and, 444, **444**
Opiates, 141, *141*, *149*
Opioids, **141**
Opium poppy, 141
Opponent-process theory, 89, *90*, **90**
Optic nerve, *86*, **86**
Oral fixation, 342
Oral stage, 342, *343*
Organizational psychologists, 7
Organizing effect, **277**
Organ of Corti, 101, **102**, *103*
Orgasm, 275, **275**
Orienting response, **155**
Ovaries, *70*, 72, 274
Overlapping (depth perception), 97
Overregularization, 235, **235**
Overweight condition
  ethnic differences, 266, *267*
  factors influencing, 266–268, *267*
  statistics, 266
  weight control tips, *268–269*
  years of life lost comparisons, *267*
Ovulation, 72
Oxytocin, *70*, 71, *384*

P

Pain
  coping with, *110–111*
  gender and, 107–108, *108*
  hypnosis and, *111*, 131
  opiates and, 141

perception of, 108, *109*
phantom limb pain, 109
psychological methods for coping with, *110–111*
statistics on, 107
Pain relief, *110–111*, 131
Paired associates, *205*, **207**
Palmar reflex, 302
Pancreas, *70*
Panic disorder, 405–406, **405**
Panic disorder with agoraphobia, 406
Paradoxical sleep, 124
  See also Rapid-eye-movement (REM) sleep
Parallel processing, 226
Paranoid personality disorder, 425, **425**
Paranoid schizophrenia, 420, **420**
Parapsychological (psi) phenomena, 112
Parasympathetic nervous system, *57*, **57**, *57*, 285
Parenting styles, 314–315, *315*
Parietal lobe, **64**
Parkinson's disease, 54, *54*
Partial reinforcement, **170**
Passion, 480–481, *481*, **481**
Passive (secondhand) smoking, **145**, *390*
PCP (phencyclidine), **148**, *149*
Penis envy, 344
Perception, **80**
  See also Sensation/perception
Perceptual constancies, 97–98, *98*
Perceptual organization, 92
Peripheral nervous system, **56**
Peripheral route in persuasion, 470, **470**
Peri Psyches (Aristotle), 8
Permissive parents, 314, 315, *315*
Personal fable, **319**
Personality
  defined, **340**
  learning-theory perspectives, 350–353
  perspectives summary, *362–363*
  psychodynamic perspective of, **15**, 340–345, *340*
  sociocultural perspective, 360–361
  trait perspective, 346–350
  See also Measuring personality; *specific perspectives/theories*
Personality disorders
  brain impairment and, *426*
  definition/description, 425, **425**

origins of, 426–427
summary, *429*
types, 425–426
Personality psychologists, 7
"Person-in-the-situation" phenomenon, *348*
Person variables, 352, *352*
Perspective, **95**, *97*
PET (positron emission tomography) scans, 28, *28*, 60
Phallic stage, 343
Phallic symbol, **438**
Phantom limb pain, 109
Phencyclidine (PCP), **148**, *149*
Phenotype, **44**
Pheromones, 274, *275*, **275**
Phi phenomenon, **95**
Phobic disorders, 405, *405*
Phoebe (dog), 153, *153*
Photoreceptors, **85**
Piaget's cognitive-developmental theory
  assimilation/accommodation, 304, **304**
  concrete-operational stage, 307–308, **307**
  evaluation of, 308–309
  object permanence, *307*
  overview, 304–309
  preoperational stage, 306–307, *306*, **306**, *308*
  sensorimotor stage, 304–305, **305**, *306*, *307*
  stages summary, **306**
Pineal gland functions, *70*, 71
Pitch
  definition/description, **81**, 100
  Weber's constant for, 81–82
Pituitary gland
  definition/description, *61*, *70*, **71**
  hormones/functions, *70*, 71
  as master gland, 71
Placebo, **31**
Placenta, **299**
Place theory, 102, **102**
Plateau phase, 275
"Pleasure center" of brain, 62, 134
PMS. *See* Premenstrual syndrome (PMS)
Polarization, 493, *493*
Polarize, **52**
Polygenic, **44**
Polygraphs (lie detectors), 292
Pons, 61, *61*, **61**
Ponzo illusion, 99, *99*
Population, **23**
Population growth (U.S.), *328*
Positive adaptation (sensitization), 83
Positive correlation, 29, **29**

Positive psychology, 286, **286**, 348
Positive punishment, 167–168, *167*
Positive reinforcer, *165*, **165**
Positive symptoms, **419**
Positron emission tomography (PET) scans, 28, *28*, 60
Postconventional level (moral reasoning), *310*, 311, 319–320, **319**
Postformal stage, **325**
Posttraumatic stress disorder (PTSD), 369, 407, *407*, **407**
Practical (street smarts) intelligence, *240*, 241
Practicing psychologists overview, 5
Precognition, 112
Preconscious, **120**, 340, 341, *341*
Preconventional level, *310*, 311, **311**
Predictability and stress, 379, 381
Predictive validity, 403, **403**
Predispositions to health problems, 388
Preeclampsia, 300
Prefrontal cortex
  description, 60
  functions, 28, *60*, 214
Prefrontal lobotomy, 458, **458**
Pregnancy and adolescents, 322
Prejudice
  combating, *476–477*
  definition/description, 474–475, **474**
  discrimination and, *475*, **475**
  sources of, 475–478
  stereotyping and, 474–475, *475*
Premenstrual syndrome (PMS)
  about, 73
  coping with, 73, 74, *74*
Prenatal development
  environmental influences on, 300–301, *301*
  genetic counseling/prenatal testing, 301
  overview, 299–301
Preoperational stage, 306–307, *306*, **306**, *308*
Presbyopia, 86–87, *86*, 329
Prescription drugs and prenatal development, 300
Primacy effect, **195**, 483–484, *483*, **483**
Primary drives, **261**, 262
Primary mental abilities, 238, **238**, *239*, 242

Primary reinforcer, **166**
Primary sex characteristics, *70*, 72
Priming, **186**
Prince and the Pauper, The (Twain), 11
Prism, 84, *84*
Proactive interference, 207, **207**
Problem solving
  algorithms and, 224–225, **224**
  analogies and, 225
  factors effecting, 225–227
  heuristics, 225, **225**
  self-assessment, *223*
  tools and, 222
  understanding the problem, 222, 224, *224*
Progesterone, 72
Programmed learning, 172, **172**
Programmed theories of aging, 329
Projection, *342*
Projective test, **365**
Prolactin, *70*, 71
Prospective memory, 184, 186–188, **186**, *188*
Prototype, **221**
Proximity, *93*, **93**
Psi (parapsychological) phenomena, 112
Psychic structures, **341**, 345
Psychoactive substances
  12th graders, 136, *137*
  19 to 30 year olds, 136, *137*
  abuse/dependence, 136–138
  causal factors of abuse/dependence, 138, *138*
  defined, **135**
  overview, 135–136
  prenatal development and, 300
  summary/effects, *149*
  use statistics, 136, *137*
  See also specific substances
Psychoanalysis
  definition/description, 11, 13, **13**, *341*, 436, 436–439, **436**
  Freud and, 436–437, *437*, 438, 439
  summary, *12*
Psychodynamic perspective/theory
  aggression and, 281
  defense mechanisms, 341, **341**, *342*
  definition/description, 15, **340**
  evaluation of, 345

Freud's theory of psychosexual development, 340–343, *341*, *342*, *343*
  neo-Freudians, 343–345, *344*, *345*
  overview, 340–345
  summary, *362*
Psychodynamic therapies
  definition/description, **436**
  modern approaches, 439
  summary, *462*
  See also Psychoanalysis
Psychokinesis, 112
Psycholinguistic theory, **237**
Psychological disorders
  classifying, 402–403
  definition/description, 399–400, **400**
  perspectives on, 401–402, *401*, *402*
  prevalence of, 403, *404*
  summary, *428–429*
  See also specific disorders; specific types
Psychological hardiness, 379, **379**
Psychologists work
  research overview, 5
  types, 6–8, *8*
Psychology
  defined, **4**
  goals, 4–5
  statistics on doctorates, 6
Psychology history
  early contributors, 8–9
  schools of, 9–11, *12*, 13
Psychology/today's perspectives
  about, 13–14, *15*
  biological perspective, **14**
  cognitive perspective, 14–15, **14**
  evolutionary perspective, **14**
  humanistic-existential perspective, **15**
  instinctive perspective, **14**
  psychodynamic perspective, **15**
Psychomotor retardation, **413**
Psychoneuroimmunology, **385**
Psychosexual development
  defined, **342**
  overview, 340–343, *341*, *342*, *343*
  stages of, 341–343, *343*
Psychosocial development (Erikson), 311–312, *311*, 344–345, **345**
Psychosurgery, 458, **458**, *459*
Psychotherapy
  definition/description, 434, **434**
  ethnicity and, 455–456, *455*
  "recovered memories" and, *208*

See also specific types
Psychotherapy evaluation
  analyses of effectiveness, 453–454, *454*
  evidence-based practices, 454–455, *454*, **454**
  Eysenck's review on, 452–453
  problems in research, 453, *453*
Psychotherapy Networker (PN), 27
PTSD (posttraumatic stress disorder), 369, 407, *407*, **407**
Puberty, 317, **317**
Punishment
  defined, **163**
  disapproval of, 168
  negative reinforces vs., *167*
  positive vs. negative, 167–168, *167*
Pupil, *85*, **85**, 86
Pure research, 5

R

Radio rays, 84, *84*
Rainbows, 84
Random controlled experiments (RCEs), 454
Random sample, **24**
Range, 504, **504**, 505–506, *505*
Rapid-eye-movement (REM) sleep, 123, *123*, **123**, 124, *124–125*, 125
Rapid flight of ideas, **413**
Rational-emotive behavior therapy (REBT), 449, **449**
Rationalization, *342*
Reaction formation, *342*
Reality testing, 365, **365**
Rebound anxiety, **457**
REBT (rational-emotive behavior therapy), 449, **449**
Recall, 205, *205*, 207
Recency effect, **195**, 484
Receptor site, 53
Reciprocal determinism, **353**
Reciprocity, 480, **480**
Recognition, 205, *205*, 207
Recovered memories, *208*
Red color and sexual attraction, *479*
Red spiders' mating behavior, 495
Reflex arc, *58*
Reflexes
  defined, 154, 302
  of neonates, 302
  sexual response and, 59
Refractory period, 53, 276

Regression, *342*
Reinforce, **163**
Reinforcement
  defined, **11**
  examples, 10, *10*
  immediate vs. delayed,
    166, *166*
  operant conditioning,
    163–164
  types, 165–166, *165*, *166*
Relative size and depth
  perception, *97*
Relaxation response,
  meditation, 134
Relaxation training,
  111, 447
Relearning, 205–206, **207**
Reliability, 247, **362**, **403**
REM (rapid-eye-movement)
  sleep, *123*, *123*, **123**, 124,
    124–125, 125
REM rebound, 125
Remote Associates Test, *243*
Replicate, **23**
Representative heuristic, **229**
Repression, **121**, **196**, 207,
  340, *342*
Research methods overview
  case studies, 24–25, *24*,
    26, *32*
  correlation method, 29, *29*,
    29, *30*, *32*
  correlational method, 29,
    29, *30*, *32*
  experimental method,
    29–30, *32*, *33*
  observation, 24–28, *32*
  scientific method, 22–23,
    22, **22**
  summary, *32*
  surveys, 26–27, **26**, *32*
  See also specific methods
Resistance, **437**
Resistance stage (GAS),
  384, **384**
Resolution phase, 276, **276**
Response set theory, hypnosis,
  133
Resting potential, **52**
Reticular formation, *61*,
  62, **62**
Retina, *85*, **85**
Retinal disparity, **96**
Retrieval, **190**, 205
Retrieval cue, **190**
Retroactive interference, 206,
  206, **206**
Retroactive theory, **206**
Retrograde amnesia,
  209–211, **209**
Retrospective memory,
  186, *188*
Reversibility, 308, **308**
Reward, **163**
Rh incompatibility, 300

Rhine, Joseph Bans, 112,
  114, *114*
Right-handed people, 68
Risky shift, 493, **493**
"Robo" rats, *169*
Rods, 85, 86, *86*, **86**
"Roid rage," 72, *72*
Role theory, hypnosis, 133
Romantic love, 481, **481**
Rooting, 302, *302*, **302**
Rorschach inkblot test,
  365, *365*
Rote, **195**, 200
Rubin vase, 93, *93*
"Runner's high," 55, *55*

S

S (specific factors symbol),
  238, **238**
Saccadic eye movement,
  191, 193
Sample, **23**
Sampling
  problems with, 23–24
  types, 24
  See also specific types
Sandwich generation,
  327, **327**
Satiety, **265**
Savings, **206**
SBIS (Stanford-Binet Intelligence Scale), 244–245,
  245, 247
Scaffolding, 309, *309*, **309**
Scarlet Letter, The
  (Hawthorne), *479*
Schachter-Singer study,
  290–291, *290*
Schemas
  defined, **197**, **304**
  memory accuracy and,
    197–198, *197*, *198*
Schizoid personality disorder,
  425, **425**
Schizophrenia
  biopsychosocial model of,
    423–424, *423*
  brain deficits and, 422, *422*
  definition/description,
    418–419, **419**
  dopamine/dopamine theory,
    54, *55*, 423
  drug treatment, 54, 457,
    458
  examples, 418–419, 420
  "loose associations" with,
    422
  origins, 421–424, *422*, *423*
  summary, *429*
  symptoms, 54, 419–420
  types, 420–421, *421*
Schizotypal personality disorder, 425, **425**
School psychologists, 7

Scientific American, 433
Scientific method, 22–23,
  22, **22**
  *See also specific compo-
    nents*
Sclera, 84
Secondary reinforcer, **166**
Secondary sex characteristics
  definition/description,
    317, **317**
  hormones and, *70*, 72
Secondhand (passive)
  smoking, **145**, *390*
Sedative, **457**
"Seekers," 259–260, *259*
Seep brain stimulation, *459*
Selection factor, **23**
Selective attention,
  119–120, **120**
Selective avoidance, **470**
Selective exposure, **470**
Selective optimization with
  compensation, **332**
Selective permeability, 51
Selective serotonin-reuptake
  inhibitors (SSRIs), 73, 74,
  457, *458*, *458*
Self-actualization, **263**, *264*,
  356, *357*, **357**
  See also Client-centered
    therapy
Self-assessment
  alcohol abuse, *140*
  assertiveness, *445*
  creativity, *243*
  depression, *413*
  eating disorders, *273*
  life expectancy scale, *330*
  locus of control, *380*
  memory, *184*
  problem solving, *223*
  self-actualization, *357*
  self-efficacy expectations,
    353
  sensation-seeking scale, *263*
  sleep, *128*
  stress, *372*
  triangular love scale, *482*
  Type A/Type B, *377*
Self-awareness, *241*
Self-concept, 357
Self-control methods
  (behavior therapies),
  446
Self-efficacy expectations
  building, *359*
  definition/description,
    353, *379*
  self-assessment, *353*
  stress moderation and,
    378–379
Self-esteem
  acculturation/assimilation
    and, 361
  description, 357–358

enhancing, 358–359,
  358–359
Self-help/support groups, 452
Self-ideal, **358**, *359*
Self-serving bias, 386, **486**
Self-theory (Rogers), 356–357
Semantic, **231**
Semantic code, **189**
Semanticity, **232**
Semantic memory, 185,
  185, *188*
Semicircular canals, *103*,
  111–112, **112**
Sensation, **80**
Sensation/perception,
  overview, 80
Sense of humor, 379
Senses
  overview, *113*
  *See also specific organs;
    specific senses*
Sensitization, **83**
Sensorimotor stage, 304–305,
  305, *306*
Sensorineural deafness, 103,
  104, **104**
Sensory adaptation, **83**
Sensory memory, 191–193,
  191, *192*
Sensory register, **191**
September 11, 2001 attacks,
  8, *169*, 201, *201*, 407,
  408, 467, 485, 494
Serial-position effect,
  194–195, **195**
Serotonin, 54, **54**, *55*, 213
Serum cholesterol, **391**
Sesame Street, 175
Set point, **267**
Sex chromosomes, 44–45, **44**
*Sexual Behavior in the
  Human Female* (Kinsey
  and colleagues), 26
*Sexual Behavior in the
  Human Male* (Kinsey and
  colleagues), 26
Sexual behavior surveys,
  276–277, *277*
Sexually transmitted
  infections (STIs),
  319, 390
Sexual motivation
  hormones and, 273–274
  pheromones and, 274,
    275, **275**
Sexual orientation
  brain shape and, 278, *279*
  definition/description,
    277–278, **277**, *278*
  origins of (humans), 278,
    279, *279*
  studies with nonhumans,
    278–279
Sexual response cycle,
  274–276, **274**

Shadowing, **96**, *97*
Sham feeding, *265*
Shape constancy, *98*, *98*, **101**
Shaping, **170**, 171–172, *171*
Shortsightedness, *86*
Short-term memory
  chunking and, 195–196,
    195, *195*, *196*, 199–200
  definition/description, *192*,
    193–194, **194**
  interference in, *196*, *196*
  serial-position effect,
    194–195, **195**
  transferring to long-term
    memory, 198–200
Siamese fighting fish, *261*, *261*
Signal detection/theory, *82*,
  82, *196*
Similarity, *93*, **93**
Situational attribution,
  484, **484**
Situational variables, *352*, *352*
Size constancy, *96*, 97–98, *98*
Skin senses
  pressure, *80*, *107*
  summary, *113*
  temperature, *107*
  touch, *80*, 106–107
  See also Pain
Skinner box, 164–165,
  165, *168*
Sleep
  amount needed and, *125*
  brain waves during,
    122–123, *123*
  functions, 124–125
  inability to move during,
    19, *128*
  learning/memory and, *125*
  "night owls," *122*, *122*
  non-rapid-eye-movement
    (NREM) sleep, 123, *123*,
    123, *124–125*
  rapid-eye-movement (REM)
    sleep, 123, *123*, **123**, *124*,
    124–125, *125*
  self-assessment on, *128*
  stages of, 122–124, *123*
  statistics on adults (U.S.),
    121
  time for mammals, *122*
  See also Dreams
Sleep apnea, *128*, **128**
Sleep cycles, *124–125*
Sleep deprivation
  combating, *124*
  traffic accidents and, *124*
Sleep disorders
  gender and, *127*
  overview, 127–130
  See also specific disorders
Sleeping pills, *129*
Sleep paralysis, *19*, *128*
Sleep spindles, 123, *123*
Sleep talking, *130*

Sleep terrors, *127*,
  129–130, **129**
Sleepwalking, *127*, *130*
Smell
  absolute threshold, *80*
  dogs sense of smell,
    104, *105*
  mate selection and, *106*
  process of, 104–105
  summary, *113*
  T-shirt study, *106*
  taste and, 104, *105*
Social awareness, *241*
Social-cognitive theory
  defined, **16**
  gender-typing and, *355*, *355*
  overview, 351–352, *352*
  self-efficacy expectations
    and, *353*, **353**
Social decision schemes, **493**
Social desirability, *24*
Social desirability scale, *25*
Social/emotional development
  adolescence, 320–322,
    321, *322*
  early adulthood, *325*, *325*
  late adulthood, *331*
  middle adulthood,
    326–327, *327*
Social facilitation, *492*,
  492, **492**
Social influence
  conformity, 490–491,
    490, *491*
  definition/description,
    486, **486**
  obedience to authority
    (overview), 486–490
Social Intelligence (Goleman),
  241
Social intelligence theory, *241*
Social loafing, *492*, **492**
Social norms, *490*, **491**
Social perception
  attribution theory and,
    484–486, *485*
  definition/description,
    483, **483**
  first impressions,
    483–484, *483*
  primacy effect/study,
    483–484, *483*
  See also Social influence
Social phobias, *405*, **405**
Social psychologists, *7*
Social psychology
  definition/description,
    468, **468**
  See also specific
    components
Social skills training,
  444–445, *444*, **444**
Social support and stress
  coping, *381*
Sociocultural perspective

definition/description, **16**,
  360, **360**
  evaluation of, *361*
  individualism vs. collectiv-
    ism, 360–361, *361*
  overview, 360–361
  summary, *363*
  See also Ethnicity; Gender
Sociocultural theory, *309*, **309**
Socioeconomic differences,
  247–248, *251*
Sodium-potassium pump, *52*
Somatic nervous system,
  56, **56**
Somatoform disorders,
  411–412, **411**, *428*
Somatosensory cortex, **64**
Sonogram, *301*
Sound
  decibel ratings, *100*, *101*
  description, *1*
  frequency theory,
    102–103, **102**
  locating, 101–102
  loudness, *100*
  place theory, 102, **102**
  volley principle,
    102, *103*
  See also Hearing; Pitch
Sound waves
  creation, 100, *100*
  frequencies/amplitudes,
    100, *100*
Spatial-relations skills
  (intelligence), 239, *239*
Species, **42**
Species-specific behavior.
  See Instinctive behavior
Specific phobias, *405*, **405**
Spinal cord
  definition/description,
    58, **58**
  gray/white matter and, *58*
  reflexes and, 58, *58*
Spinal reflex, *58*
Split-brain experiments,
  68–69, *69*
Spontaneous recovery, 157,
  158, *158*, **158**, *166*
Sport psychologists, *8*
Sri Lanka's Yala National
  Park, *79*
SSRIs (selective serotonin-
  reuptake inhibitors), *73*,
  74, *457*, *458*, *458*
Standard deviation, *505*, *505*,
  505, *506*, *506*
Standardization (tests),
  363, **363**
Stanford-Binet Intelligence
  Scale (SBIS), 244–245,
  245, *247*
Stanford Prison Experiment,
  34, *34*
Startle reflex, *302*

State-dependent memory,
  204, **204**
State of Denial (Woodward),
  494
Statistically significant
  differences, 508–509,
    508, **508**, *509*
Statistics
  definition/description,
    501–502, *501*, **501**
  descriptive statistics
    overview, 502–506
  inferential statistics over-
    view, 507–509
  normal curve, 506–507,
    506, **506**, *507*
Stereotypes
  definition/description, **468**
  groupthink and, *494*
  living up to, *468*
  prejudice, 474–475, *475*
Stereotype threat, *18*
Steroid effects, *72*, *72*
Stimulants
  defined, **136**
  overview, 142–146
  See also specific stimulants
Stimulus, **154**
Stimulus motive, **262**
STIs (sexually transmitted
  infections), *319*, *390*
Storage, **190**
Stranger anxiety, *313*
Strange situation method, *312*
Stratified sample, **24**
Stress
  coping with, 386–387, *386*
  defined, **370**
  endocrine system and, *383*,
    383, *384*, *384*
  psychological moderators
    of, 378–379, *381*
  reducing arousal and, *387*
  self-assessment, *372*
  sources overview, 370–371,
    373–378, *375*
  survey on (U.S.), *375*
  UCLA study, *370*, *370*
  See also specific sources
Stress and health
  diseases of adaptation, *385*
  general adaptation syn-
    drome (GAS), 382–385,
    382, **382**, *383*
  immune system/illness and,
    385–386
Stress disorders, *407*
Stressors, *370*, **370**
Stroboscopic motion, *95*, **95**
Structuralism
  defined, *8*, *9*
  summary, *12*
Stupor, **420**
Subjective moral judgment,
  308, **308**

Sublimation, *342*
Subliminal stimulation, 81, *81*, **81**
Substance abuse, *136*, **136**
  See also Alcohol abuse; Psychoactive substances
Substance dependence, 136–138, **136**
Successive approximations, **170**, 171, 444, **444**
Suicide
  about/statistics, 415–416
  gender and, 416, *416*
  myths on, 416–417
  preventing, 418
  sociocultural factors in, 416
  warning signs, 417
Suicide terrorists, 467, *468*, *485*
Sunday Afternoon on the Island of La Grande Jatte (Seurat), 88–89, *89*
Superego, 341, *341*, **341**
Suppression, **121**
Surveys
  about, 26
  defined, **26**
  Internet surveys, 26–27
  summary, *32*
Sympathetic nervous system, 57–58, *57*, **57**, **285**
Synapses, *51*, *53*, 213, 214
Synaptic cleft, *51*, *53*
Synaptic vesicles, 53
Syntax, 236, **237**
Systematic desensitization, **162**, 442–443, *442*, **443**
Systematic random search, **224**

T

Tabloid stories, 19–20, *19*
Taste
  absolute threshold, 80
  flavors of food, **104**, 105, *107*
  humans vs. other animals, 105
  process, 105
  smell and, 104, 105
  summary, *113*
Taste aversions
  description, 156, *157*
  evolution of, 156–157, *157*
  popcorn incident, 156
Taste buds, 105, **105**
Taste cells, **105**
TAT (Thematic Apperception Test), 283, *283*, 365
Telegraphic speech, 235
Telepathy, 112, 114
Tempest, The (Shakespeare), 125

Temporal lobe, **64**
TENS (transcutaneous electrical nerve stimulation), *110*
Teratogens, 300, **300**
Terminals/terminal buttons (of neurons), 49, *51*
Test-retest reliability, 247
Testes functions, 70, 72
Testosterone, 70, 72, 213, 274, 281, 354, *384*, 414
Texture gradient, **96**, *97*
Thalamus, **62**, 214
"Thanatopsis" (Bryant), 333
Thematic Apperception Test (TAT), 283, *283*, 365
Theory, **5**
Theory of cognitive appraisal, 289, 290–291, *290*
Theory of multiple intelligence, **238**
Therapy history, 435, *435*
Therapy methods
  summary, *462–463*
  See also specific types
Theta waves, **123**
Thinking
  decision making/judgment, 228–239
  defined, **220**
  language and, 232–233
  See also Concepts; Critical thinking; Problem solving
Three Faces of Eve, The (film), 25, *26*
Thyroid gland functions, 70, 71
Thyrotrophin, 70
Thyroxin, 70, 71
Time-based prospective memory, 187
Time out, 168, *169*, *172*
Tip-of-the-tongue (TOT) phenomenon, 202–203, **202**
TM (transcendental meditation), 134, **134**
Token economy, 444, **444**
Tolerance, **137**
Top-down processing, **94**
Touch
  absolute threshold, 80
  skin's sense of, 106–107
Toxemia, 300
Trait perspective (personality)
  "Big Five"/Five-Factor model, 347–348, *347*, *362*
  biology and, 349–350, *349*
  dogs and, 349–350, *349*
  evaluation of, 350
  Eysenck's trait theory, 347, *347*

Hippocrates' "humors" and, 346, 347, *347*
  overview, 346–350
  positive psychology and, 348
  summary, *362*
Traits, **346**
Transcendental meditation (TM), 134, **134**
Transcutaneous electrical nerve stimulation (TENS), *110*
Transference, 437–438, **437**
Treatment, **30**
Triangular model of love, 480–481, **480**, *481*, *482*
Triarchic theory of intelligence, 240–241, *240*, **240**, *242*, 243
Trichromatic theory, 89–90, **89**, *90*, 102
Trichromats, 91, **91**
Trust vs. mistrust, *311*, 312, 344–345
Tsunami
  animals sensing (2004), 79, *79*
  description (2011), 369
Twin studies, 45–47, *47*, 250, 252, *252*
Two-point threshold, **107**
2001 (film), *280*
Type A behavior/people, 377–378, *377*, **377**, *389*, 390
Type B behavior/people, 378

U

Ultrasound, 301
Umbilical cord, **299**
Unconditional positive regard, 358, **358**, 440, **440**
Unconditioned response (UCR), **155**
Unconditioned stimulus (UCS), **155**
Unconscious, **120**, 340–341, **340**, *341*
Uninvolved parents, 314, 315, *315*
United States of Tara, 410
Uplifts, 371, **371**

V

Validity, **247**, 362, 403
Variable-interval schedule, 170–171, **170**
Variable-ratio schedule, 170, 171, *171*
Vasocongestion, 274–275, **274**
Vasopressin, 213

Ventromedial nucleus (VMN), **265**, *265*
Vestibular sense, **110**, 111–112, *113*
Virtual reality therapy
  description, 433, *434*, 447
  examples, 433, *434*
Visible light, **84**
Visible light spectrum, *84*
Vision
  absolute threshold, 80
  significance of, 83
  summary, *113*
  See also Color vision; Eyes; Light
Visual acuity, **86**
Visual cliff, 304, *305*
Visual code, **189**
Visual illusions, 98–99, *99*
Visual perception
  about, 91–92
  figure-ground perception, 92–93, *93*, *94*
  Gestalt organization rules, 92–94, *92*, *93*, *94*
VNO (vomeronasal organ), *275*
Volley principle, 102, 103
Volunteer bias, **24**
Vomeronasal organ (VNO), *275*
Vygotsky's sociocultural theory, 309, *309*

W

Walden Two (Skinner), 351
Washoe (chimpanzee), 231
Watergate scandal, 494
Waxy flexibility, 421, *421*, **421**
Weber's constant, 81–82, *81*
Weight (humans)
  American Heart Association diet recommendations, 269
  control tips, *268–269*
  genetics and, 267, *267*
  obesity, 266
  obesogenic environment and, 267–268
  See also Eating disorders; Overweight condition
Weight lifting, 81–82
Wernicke-Korsakoff syndrome, 140–141
Wernicke's aphasia, 67, **67**
Wernicke's area (cerebral cortex), 66–67, *67*
When Prophecy Fails (Festinger and colleagues), 260
White matter, **58**
Wills, T. A., 139

Wish fulfillment, 438, **438**
Withdrawal reflex, 302
Wolves (*Canis lupus*), 4, 349,
   349, 350
Women
   pioneers in psychology,
     17–18, *17*

STEM fields and,
   249–250, *251*
See also Gender
Working memory, 194,
   194, 326
See also Short-term memory

World Health Organization
   (WHO), 272

Y

Young-Helmholtz theory,
   90, 102

Z

Zener cards, 114, *114*
Zone of proximal
   development (ZPD),
   309, *309*, **309**
Zygote, **299**

Credits

This page constitutes an extension of the copyright page. We have made every effort to trace the ownership of all copyrighted material and to secure permission from copyright holders. In the event of any question arising as to the use of any material, we will be pleased to make the necessary corrections in future printings. Thanks are due to the following authors, publishers, and agents for permission to use the material indicated.

Text Credits

Assessment, 25: D. P. Crowne and D. A. Marlowe, "A New Scale of Social Desirability Independent of Pathology," *Journal of Consulting Psychology*, 24 (1960): 351. Copyright © 1960 by the American Psychological Association. Reproduced by permission. **Figure 1.8, 31:** From Rathus. *PSYCH (with Review Cards and Printed Access Card) 1/e.* Copyright © 2009 Wadsworth, a part of Cengage Learning, Inc. Reproduced by permission. www.cengage.com/permissions. **Figure 2.4, 49:** From Kalat. *Biological Psychology, 10/e.* Copyright © 2009 Wadsworth, a part of Cengage Learning, Inc. Reproduced by permission. www.cengage.com/permissions. **Figure 2.6, 52:** From Weiten. *Psychology, 8/e.* Copyright © 2010 Wadsworth, a part of Cengage Learning, Inc. Reproduced by permission. www.cengage.com/permissions. **Figure 2.8, 57:** From Weiten. *Psychology, 8/e.* Copyright © 2010 Wadsworth, a part of Cengage Learning, Inc. Reproduced by permission. www.cengage.com/permissions. **Figure 3.23, 55:** Ponzo illusion illustration from *Mind Sights* by Roger N. Shepard, © 1990 by Roger N. Shepard. Reprinted by permission of Henry Holt and Company, LLC. **Self Assessment, 127:** From *Power Sleep* by James B. Maas, copyright © 1998 by James B. Maas, Ph.D. Used by permission of Villard Books, a division of Random House, Inc. **Figure UN 5.2, 169:** From Sanjiv K. Talwar et al., "Behavioral Neuroscience: Rat Navigation Guided by Remote Control"." *Nature* 417(2002), fig. 1, p. 37. Reprinted by permission of Nature Publishing Group. **Figure 7.10, 249:** Sample Items from Cattell's Culture-Fair Intelligence Test-Copyright © 1949, 1960. Reproduced with permission from the publishers, Hogrefe Ltd, from Culture Fair Scale 2, Test A by R. B. Cattell and A. K. S. Cattell. The UK version of this test is soon to be updated and restandardized. **Figure 7.11, 252:** From Weiten. *Psychology, 8/e.* Copyright © 2010 Wadsworth, a part of Cengage Learning, Inc. Reproduced by permission. www.cengage.com/permissions. **Sensation, 263:** From M. Zuckerman, "Sensation Seeking" in *Dimensions of Personality*, H. London and J. Exner, eds., © 1980 John Wiley & Sons. Reprinted by permission. **Figure 8.5, 285:** From Kalat. *Biological Psychology 10/e.* Copyright © 2009 Wadsworth, a part of Cengage Learning, Inc. Reproduced by permission. www.cengage.com/permissions. **Figure 9.1, 303:** from *The Postnatal Development Of The Human Cerebral Cortex, Vols. I-VIII* by Jesse LeRoy Conel, Cambridge, Mass: Harvard University Press, Copyright © 1939, 1941, 1947, 1951, 1955, 1959, 1963, 1967 by the President and Fellows of Harvard College. Copyright © renewed 1967, 1969, 1975, 1979, 1983, 1987, 1991. **Figure 9.10, 326:** K. Warner Schaie. "The Course of Adult Intellectual Development." *American Psychologist*, 49, 304–313, Figure 6. Copyright © 1994 American Psychological Association. Reprinted by permission. **Self-Assessment, 353:** From Fibel, B. & Hale, D. W. "The Generalized Expectancy for Success Scale: A New Measure" *Journal*

of Consulting and Clinical Psychology, vol. 46 (5), pp. 924-931. Copyright © 1978 by APA. Reprinted by permission. **Self Assessment, 372:** From Renner, M.J., and Mackin, R. S. "A Life Stress Instrument for Classroom Use". *Teaching of Psychology*, 25. copyright © 1998 Taylor and Francis. Reprinted by Permissions. **Figure 11.4, 375:** From American Psychological Association, "Stress in America 2011: Executive Summary". Copyright © 2011 by American Psychological Association. Reprinted by permission. **Beliefs, 376:** From *Self-Assessment and Behavioral Change Manual* by Peggy Blake, Robert Fry, and Michael Pesjack, pp. 43–47. Copyright © 1984 by Peggy Blake. Reprinted by permission of McGraw-Hill Companies. **Figure 11.6, 383:** From Rathus. *PSYCH (with Review Cards and Printed Access Card) 1/e.* Copyright © 2009 Wadsworth, a part of Cengage Learning, Inc. Reproduced by permission. www.cengage.com/permissions. **Figure 13.1, 459:** From Benedict Carey, "Surgery for Mental Ills Offers Both Hope and Risk," *The New York Times*, 11/26/09. Copyright © 2006 by The New York Times. Reprinted by permission. **Figure 14.3, 481:** From *The Psychology of Love* by R. J. Sternberg. Copyright © 1988 Yale University Press. Reprinted by permission of the publisher. **Love Scale, 482:** From *The Psychology of Love* by R. J. Sternberg. Copyright © 1988 Yale University Press. Reprinted by permission of the publisher.

Photo Credits

Chapter 1. 2: © age fotostock/SuperStock **4:** right, © Andrew Adolphus **4:** left, © Spencer A. Rathus **6:** © Royalty-Free/Corbis **7:** top, © Bill Aron/PhotoEdit Inc. **7:** bottom, © Miramax/Courtesy Everett Collection **8:** © SuperStock/Getty Images **9:** bottom, top © Archives of the History of American Psychology, The Center for the History of Psychology—The University of Akron **10:** bottom right, © Bob and Marian Breland-Bailey, Hot Springs, AR **10:** bottom left, © Tom McHugh/Photo Researchers **10:** top, © Archives of the History of American Psychology, The Center for the History of Psychology—The University of Akron **12:** bottom right, © UPI/Bettmann/Corbis **12:** top, center left, center, © Archives of the History of American Psychology, The Center for the History of Psychology—The University of Akron **12:** bottom center, bottom left, © Bettmann/Corbis **12:** center right, © Christopher Johnson/Stock Boston, Inc. **16:** © David Buffington/Getty Images **17:** © Archives of the History of American Psychology, The Center for the History of Psychology—The University of Akron **18:** top, © Ken Heyman/Woodfin Camp **18:** bottom, © Eudora Welty/Corbis **19:** © Tim Boyle/Bloomberg via Getty Images **21:** © Getty Images/Inspirestock RF/Jupiterimages **26:** bottom, © Photos 12/Alamy **26:** top, TM & Copyright 20th Century Fox Film Corp./courtesy Everett Collection **27:** bottom right, © Collection of Jack and Beverly Wilgus **27:** bottom left, Reprinted with permission from Damasio H., Grabowski T., Frank R., Galaburda A. M., Damasio A. R.: The return of Phineas Gage: Clues about the brain from a famous patient. *Science*, 264: 1102–1105, © 1994. Department of Neurology and Image Analysis Facility, Univeristy of Iowa. **27:** top, © Bruce Coleman Inc./Alamy **28:** bottom right, © CNRI/SPL/Photo Researchers, Inc. **28:** top right, © Ohio Nuclear Corporation/SPL/Photo Researchers, Inc. **28:** center right, © Spencer Grant/Stock Boston, Inc. **30:** © Purestock/Getty Images **32:** bottom, © Nina Leen/Time & Life Pictures/Getty Images **32:** center,